THE
GARDENS
of BRITAIN
& IRELAND

THE
GARDENS
of BRITAIN
& IRELAND

PATRICK TAYLOR

LONDON, NEW YORK, MUNICH, MELBOURNE AND DELHI

For Caroline, with all love

Managing Editor	Anna Kruger
Managing Art Editor	Lee Griffiths
Art Editor	Murdo Culver
Project Editor	Helen Fewster
Designer	James Culver
DTP Designer	Louise Waller
Production Controller	Heather Hughes
Map illustration	John Woodcock
Author photograph	Peter Anderson

Gardens illustrated: *p.1* Rousham House;
p.2 Iford Manor; *p.3* Grizedale;
p.4 Sheffield Park Garden

First American Edition, 2003
03 04 05 06 10 9 8 7 6 5 4 3 2 1

Published in the United States by
DK Publishing, Inc.
375 Hudson Street
New York, New York 10014

A catalog record for this book is available
from the Library of Congress

ISBN 0-7894-9645-3

Color reproduction by Colourscan, Singapore
Printed and bound in Slovakia by Neografia

Discover more at
www.dk.com

CONTENTS

INTRODUCTION

Britain and Ireland have a greater number and range of notable surviving gardens than any region of comparable size in the world. The reasons for this are complex but the rare continuity of our culture, and a love of tradition, are at its heart. Gardens occupy a special place in our affections and the desire to have one's own plot remains important. Well into the 20th century, terraced houses with their own gardens remained the norm for urban housing, even in cities like London where land values rose so high. In Europe, by contrast, blocks of flats had by the 19th century become the universal solution to the problem of accommodating the growing urban population. The historian Sir Keith Thomas suggested that one of the explanations of our distaste for revolution is that the working man, in full control of the microcosm of his own garden, had no desire to overthrow the world outside.

The purpose of this book is to describe as wide a range, and as large a number, of notable British and Irish gardens of every kind. I have interpreted the word "garden" very broadly to include, as well as gardens of flowers, arboreta, botanic gardens, cemeteries, hospitals, landscape parks, public gardens and indeed almost any form of designed landscape that enlivens the scene. The book is divided into two parts – the Guide and the Gazetteer. The Guide describes only gardens that are regularly open to the public. It includes the great and famous gardens like Chatsworth or Stourhead, as well as smaller private gardens like Bury Court or Herterton House. It also

The Mussenden Temple at Downhill Castle

includes most of the gardens generally considered masterpieces of their kind, such as Crathes Castle, Powerscourt, Powis Castle and Rousham. These gardens are, for the most part, fine and complete examples of their type, and well maintained, but I have also included some which, although fragmentary, retain potent atmosphere. Reversals of fortune, or genteel decay, can sometimes bring magic to a landscape. The poignant remains of Lyveden New Bield are, to my taste, one of the most movingly beautiful sights of any garden. The long deserted Hackfall Wood in its wild and lovely Yorkshire setting, now choked with undergrowth and with only ruinous buildings surviving, touches the heart and fires the imagination in a way that immaculate borders and pristine lawns can sometimes fail to do. The windswept coastal site of Downhill Castle, with its suavely classical temple/library teetering among crying gulls on a cliff high above the Atlantic, is both dramatic and mysterious. In some other cases I describe places where almost nothing at all remains except their history and the glories of the past.

These were all once private gardens. We also have an unusually long history of gardens that are accessible to the public. The former royal deer park of Green Park in London was open to the public as early as 1662. In Preston in Lancashire a public promenade, the Avenham Walk, was laid out in 1697 to provide a place to take the air and to relish a fine view. Exactly the same purpose

▷ **The Maze** at Chatsworth

was fulfilled in around 1700 by Richmond Terrace Walk with its Arcadian views of the winding Thames. Towards the end of the 18th century, when both population and urban expansion increased so dramatically at the height of the industrial revolution, the need for public green space was widely recognised. The municipal public parks of the 19th century were much loved, often superbly laid out and finely maintained – a source of civic pride and popular enjoyment. They suffered grievously in the 20th century from lack of funding and from increasing vandalism. Under the Heritage Lottery Fund Urban Parks programme, £178,000,000 has been allocated to their restoration, and by 2003 the effects were being seen in places like Battersea Park in London, Lister Park in Bradford, Norfolk Park in Sheffield and Sefton Park in Liverpool. Unfortunately, however, many others of these once glorious places still present a scene of depressing neglect. I have included descriptions of a few of the parks in the Guide, and a wider selection, in both good and bad repair, in the Gazetteer.

The Gazetteer allows me to cast the net much wider. The places included here are usually described more briefly than those in the Guide. They include many distinguished gardens that are open, or open occasionally; many that are not open to the public; some (like Nonsuch Palace or Oatlands) that no longer exist but were in their day of major importance and influence; and others that survive only as archaeological sites with fragmentary but often eloquent remains. The rare 16th-century garden terraces at St Donat's Castle, the mysterious early 17th-century water gardens at Tackley and the enigmatic lumps and bumps of the great Elizabethan garden of Raglan Castle have much to tell us about gardens and add new dimensions to our pleasure and understanding. Some of the places, although of only minor historic importance, nevertheless form handsome ingredients in the landscape today. Who has not had the pleasurable experience, while driving in unfamiliar country, of glimpsing a fine cedar of

The Flower Garden at Herterton House

Lebanon rising enticingly over an old brick wall, or a piece of decorative yew topiary standing guard over a cottage garden path?

In the Gazetteer I explore some of the kinds of landscape that are inappropriate for the Guide, such as allotments, cemeteries and the grounds of hospitals. Also included are various almost unique oddities, such as the churchyard of St Mary's Painswick, packed with an extraordinary collection of 18th-century yew topiary; the Mellor's Garden which traces the obstacles in *Pilgrim's Progress*; the 17th-century maze on the village green at Hilton; and the dapper officers' gardens laid out at Chatham Naval Dockyard in the early 18th century. The Marquess of Hertford founded Stoney Road allotments in 1819, on a site going back to the middle ages. Hill Close Gardens, dating from the 19th century, are a series of hedged gardens for letting, in which flowers and vegetables could be cultivated and where the tenants could sit peacefully in their summerhouses. Both these groups survive, the latter with some of their original charming summerhouses.

Cemeteries were a kind of designed landscape held in high esteem in the past. The magnificent Necropolis in Glasgow, a very early cemetery, of 1828, is filled with the tombs of the Glaswegian great and the good – their posthumous monuments almost as prominent as they were themselves in their lives. Dean Cemetery, on the banks of the Water of Leith in Georgian Edinburgh, was finely planted and takes every advantage of its picturesque setting. The City of London Cemetery, laid out on what had been farmland on the fringe of Epping Forest, retains its Victorian character, with the evergreens and weeping trees thought suitable for such gardens of their time. It is still finely cared for today (by no means frequently the

The Temple of Flora at Stourhead

case), with some good modern planting, and must surely be a source of consolation.

Another aspect of an enlightened attitude towards the social value of gardens was the 19th-century belief that gardens had a therapeutic value, in particular for psychiatric patients. When Cheadle Royal Hospital was founded in 1849, its original remit specified "spacious ground for husbandry, and gardening, and exercise". The gardens at Fairmile Hospital were laid out in 1871 by Robert Marnock, one of the most distinguished landscape designers of the day. A tuberculosis sanatorium, the King Edward VII Hospital, had planting schemes designed by Gertrude Jekyll. Even Broadmoor Hospital, for the criminally insane, had planned views of the countryside, lawns for croquet and bowls, and a kitchen garden in which inmates were allowed to work, when it opened in 1863. The idea of the hospital, whether as a place of healing or of shelter, but either way as a place of high quality in a finely designed setting, has origins much earlier than the 19th century. The Royal Hospital in Chelsea was, after all, designed by Sir Christopher Wren with grounds laid out by George London and Henry Wise, easily the grandest designers of their day. In which early 21st-century hospital would the aesthetic quality of the building and the beauty of the setting be regarded as of importance?

The one type of garden which is not thoroughly covered in this book is the

The Gnome Reserve

commonest of all – the kind of garden that most people have behind their houses. These vernacular gardens, as often as not governed by a passion for plants, are a key indicator of horticultural health – just as, in those countries with high standards of food, it is the quality of ordinary, everyday fare that is far more significant than the kind of food served in the temples of gastronomy. The thousands of gardens that are open to the public and described in the National Gardens Scheme's Yellow Book (*Gardens of England and Wales Open for Charity*), and in that of the Scotland Gardens Scheme (*Gardens of Scotland*), cover the whole range of vernacular gardens (and some that are much grander). Whereas the Guide section of this book includes only those gardens that

are regularly open to the public, in the Gazetteer I have included many Yellow Book gardens of historic importance that open only occasionally. Some are quite small and several are outstanding, such as the magnificent Badminton House in Gloucestershire with its great 17th-century and 18th-century landscape and charming 20th-century gardens, or the exquisite Inkpen House in Berkshire, with its rare early 18th-century formal gardens.

This is not a book about garden history; it is about the pleasures of gardens and the fascinating ways in which gardens and landscapes have been designed. But these pleasures are immensely increased by an understanding of the influences that made them as they are. Much of the historical information in this book comes from the books listed in the Reading List and, most importantly, from a series of priceless sources: the English Heritage *Register of Parks and Gardens of Special Historic Interest*; the Scottish *Inventory of Gardens and Designed Landscapes* (produced jointly by Scottish Natural Heritage and Historic Scotland); and the Cadw/ICOMOS *Register of Landscapes, Parks and Gardens of Special Historic Interest in Wales*. If a garden is included in any of these, I indicate it. The very detailed descriptions in the Registers and the Inventory are of huge value as a first source of information about historic landscapes or gardens. Furthermore, the English and Welsh Registers grade gardens according to their importance, in exactly the same way as historic buildings are listed (Grades I, II★ and II), and I include these grades – though it should be emphasised that the grading is an indication of historical importance rather than of horticultural excellence. A garden may be listed Grade I, for example, simply because it has some very rare feature, such as a medieval garden wall. Tudor terraces, the traces of 17th-century avenues in a deer park, splendid surviving 18th-century parkland trees or a temple on a wooded eminence are all thrilling ingredients of the landscape, but they are more than that, for they are also part of the long, complicated and fascinating story of the way in which people have laid out gardens.

USING THIS BOOK

The Guide is divided into regions and the gardens are listed alphabetically within each group. Opening times are given, but please note that these are subject to change, so it is essential to phone if you are planning a long journey. It is also possible that some of the gardens shown as not opening will start to do so. Gardens in the Gazetteer are listed in alphabetical order and include page references to those in the Guide. The Gazetteer thus serves as an index for all the gardens included in the book. In addition, all the gardens mentioned are grouped by counties in the Index by County at the end of the book.

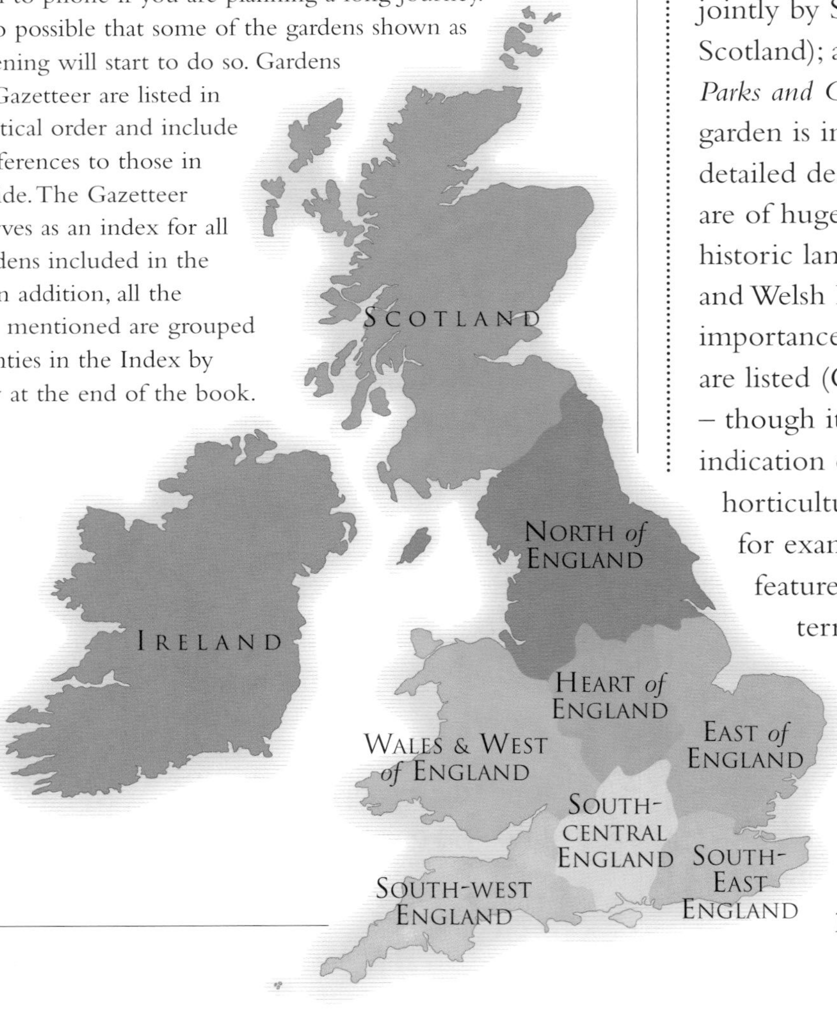

SCOTLAND

NORTH *of* ENGLAND

IRELAND

HEART *of* ENGLAND

WALES & WEST *of* ENGLAND

EAST *of* ENGLAND

SOUTH-CENTRAL ENGLAND

SOUTH-EAST ENGLAND

SOUTH-WEST ENGLAND

Piet Oudolf's garden at Bury Court

It is a matter of some puzzlement, and regret, that so few gardens in Britain and Ireland are inspired by innovative ideas about design. The work of the late Maggie Keswick and Charles Jencks in their own remarkable modernist garden at Portrack is described in the Gazetteer, but the garden is not open to the public. Charles Jencks, however, has designed a marvellous new feature for the Scottish National Gallery of Modern Art in Edinburgh, which is open to the public. I know of only one garden by the designer Christopher Bradley-Hole that is accessible to the public: Bury Court. It is curious that the National Trust, the guardian of so many exceptional gardens, should never, until 2003, have commissioned a new garden – the first departure is to be one designed by Arne Maynard for Dyrham Park. Easily one of the most interesting, attractive and important living designers is Ian Hamilton Finlay, but there have been more commissions for his work abroad than in his native Scotland. At Alnwick Castle we now have a fine example of the work of the Belgian family firm of Wirtz International, and there are two examples of the work of the splendid Piet Oudolf (at Wisley and, again, at Bury Court).

In the past British gardeners were pioneers of new styles. The 18th-century landscape park and 19th-century herbaceous borders were the *avant garde* of their day. In the 20th century we have been too strongly in thrall to the past – may we recover a spirit of originality in the 21st century.

PATRICK TAYLOR

SOUTH-WEST
ENGLAND

ABBOTSBURY SUBTROPICAL GARDENS

A GREAT JUNGLE OF RARE PLANTS
THAT TAKES ADVANTAGE OF AN UNUSUAL
MICROCLIMATE

Few gardens display such an extraordinary collection of exotic plants in such thrilling surroundings as Abbotsbury. The gardens here are of historic importance but they wear their history lightly. The impression they give is of a benign jungle in which species from many of the world's subtropical climates flourish in splendid harmony. The microclimate here is unusual. The climate on the Dorset coast is generally mild here, right by the Chesil bank, there is seldom any frost and good protection from the wind from old tree plantations. The vital ingredient, however, is the proximity of the sea: it is very deep close to the shore, plummeting sharply to a depth of 50ft/15m, and acts as a permanent storage heater, warding off the coldest temperatures. The sea also adds to the air humidity, giving the moisture that is needed for such plants as tree ferns. The rainfall is around 30in/75cm per

The water garden at Abbotsbury

annum, a happy medium, providing enough for the many Asiatic shrubs but not drowning plants from drier regions.

The land here came to the Strangways family after the dissolution of the monastic estates in 1541. In the 18th century a walled kitchen garden was built, to which was added a woodland garden in the early 19th century. William Fox-Strangways (1795–1865), the 4th Earl of Ilchester and a distinguished gentleman botanist, started the plant collection for which the gardens became famous. By the end of the 19th century well over 4,000 species were cultivated here. The gardens remain in the ownership of the Ilchester Estate which maintains them to high standards and continues the tradition of new plant introductions.

The gardens, disposed on the gently undulating slopes of a valley, are irrigated by a stream which is dammed to form ornamental pools. There is little formality here; plants are arranged in naturalistic style – but in a lavishly heterogenous profusion never found in nature. Skilful use is made of different microclimates within the garden: a south-facing steeply

pitched bank is filled with tender plants from the Mediterranean or from subtropical regions – cistuses, lavenders and myrtles from the Mediterranean; succulents from Mexico; gleaming leucadendrons and stately watsonias from South Africa. Down by the stream, in wooded shade, is a long walk of hydrangeas, one of the best groups of the giant *Gunnera manicata* in England, and beautifully grown tree ferns. The high canopy of countless mature trees and the larger shrubs also gives protection to other plants. New, and often threatened, plants are constantly being added. In 1999 the lovely Caranday palm (*Trithrinax campestris*), under threat in its native Argentina, found a home here; its grey, stiff fan-shaped fronds had never been seen in England before. Abbotsbury pulls off the difficult trick of being a botanic garden of importance as well as a landscape of rare enchantment.

Location Abbotsbury, nr Weymouth DT3 4LA, Dorset **OS** SY5685 ½m W of Abbotsbury, 9m NW of Weymouth by B3157 **Tel** 01305 871412/871344 **Fax** 01305 871092 **English Heritage Register** Grade I **Owner** Ilchester Estates **Open** daily 10–5 (dusk in winter); closed 25 Dec **Area** 20 acres/8 hectares

ANTONY HOUSE

GRAND FORMAL GARDENS, A HUMPHRY
REPTON LANDSCAPE AND A BEAUTIFUL
SETTING ON PLYMOUTH SOUND

Once seen, the ensemble of breathtakingly beautiful house – early 18th-century, built of silver Pentewan stone – and serene landscape is unlikely to be forgotten. A drawing by Edmund Prideaux dated 1727 shows an elaborate formal garden here of topiary and avenues. Under Reginald Pole Carew in the late 18th century many changes took place, with much planting of new trees. Most important of all, Humphry Repton was consulted. He produced a Red Book for Antony in 1792 and although not all his recommendations were adopted, his advice to remove the walled garden that lay directly in front of the north façade of the house and plant trees to form vistas running through woods led to the creation of the most memorable views at Antony today. Below the north terrace of the house a giant lawn is embellished with a single tree, a beautiful American black walnut (*Juglans nigra*) with a dramatically spreading crown. It is known that Reginald Pole Carew had seeds of trees from North America and this could have been planted by him. Far beyond the walnut, parkland slopes gently down to the Tamar estuary with openings in Repton's woodland revealing delicious glimpses of the shimmering water of the estuary and, to the east, the arches of the Tamar bridge. The views radiate from the house like a *patte d'oie*, centred on the window of the Saloon, but instead of the

Antony House from the woodland

close-clipped alignments of a French *patte d'oie* these are lined with bushy burgeoning trees, many of them holm oaks (*Quercus ilex*).

IN THE FORMAL GARDENS

The gardens to the west of the house match the stately formality of the house. A conical fountain by William Pye echoes a gigantic cone of yew nearby, whose interior has been partly hollowed out to form a summerhouse. A broad turf walk is enclosed in castellated yew hedges, ending in a bench and two 18th-century statues in niches cut into the yew. To the south is a wonderful cork oak (*Quercus suber*) with deeply fissured bark and a magnificent crown – Cornwall is a great county for these beautiful trees and this is one of the best. A finely contrived knot garden of box and germander (*Teucrium × lucidrys*) and a formal flower garden are enclosed in yew hedges. Scattered about the garden is a very large collection of daylilies – a National Collection of around 600 cultivars.

There is plenty to admire in the garden at Antony but the things that stick in the mind are the beautifully tailored yew hedges close to the house and the sight of the shimmering water of the Tamar at the end of the long tree-lined walks.

Location Torpoint PL11 2QA, Cornwall **OS** SX4156 5m W of Plymouth by Torpoint car ferry and A374 **Tel** 01752 812191 **English Heritage Register** Grade II **Owner** The National Trust **Open** Apr to Oct, Tue to Thur and Bank Hol Mon (Jun to Aug, also Sun) 1.30–5.30 **Area** 25 acres/10 hectares

ANTONY WOODLAND GARDEN AND WOODS

A SECRET GARDEN OF TREES AND SHRUBS ENRICHED WITH MODERN SCULPTURES AND FINE VIEWS

The woodland garden immediately adjacent to Antony House gardens was established in separate ownership by the Carew Pole family. The entrance from the National Trust garden is low-key and charming – an inconspicuous gate with an honesty box opens onto a path fringed in summer with cow parsley and buttercups. This was the special preserve of Sir John Carew Pole who died in 1993 and started the woodland garden just before World War II, although his father, Sir Reginald, had already begun planting hybrid rhododendrons in this area.

It is a woodland garden of great atmosphere in which exotics – especially camellias, outstanding magnolias and large numbers of rhododendrons – look marvellously at home, with waves of bluebells, wild garlic and wood anemones lapping at their feet. Old oaks (both the English oak and the holm oak *Quercus ilex*) and Scots pines form much of the background planting in the woodland garden but with many young plantings of, for example, sweet chestnut and flowering shrubs. *Michelia doltsopa*, a close relation of the magnolia, gives off its sweetly exotic scent in May. Everywhere there are good trees – Japanese maples, *Gingko biloba*, Himalayan birches, a cut-leafed walnut (*Juglans regia* 'Laciniata') and much else. The gardens are set in a shallow combe protected by windbreaks to the west. Walks lead through the woods to the banks of the river Lynher giving are idyllic glimpses across the water to the castellated silhouette of Ince Castle. A curiosity here, in the western part of the garden, is an 18th-century bath house, partly open to the sky and filled with salt water from the river Lynher.

Sir John's son, Richard, has continued to cherish the garden, and add to it. A rocky mount on Jupiter Point is now crowned with an upright slab of stone designed and lettered by Tom Perkins with the words "and still a garden by the water blows" on one side and "Remember John and Cynthia Carew Pole

Wildflowers and exotics in Antony Woodland Garden

who loved the garden" on the other. From this point there are splendid views back towards the house. Below the mount, in a circle mown into the long grass, a mossy boulder is cut neatly into two, its inside faces carved with a maze-like pattern – the work of Peter Randall Page. A little further round the coast is a graceful sweep of curved bronze by Eilis O'Connell. The charm of this woodland garden lies in its essentially wild character, while the occasional sculpture, distant views of the great house and walks along the very edge of the water make it an altogether delightful place.

Location Torpoint PL11 2QA, Cornwall **OS** SX4156 5m W of Plymouth by Torpoint car ferry and A374 **English Heritage Register** Grade II **Owner** Carew Pole Garden Trust **Open** Mar to Oct, daily 11–5.30 **Area** 100 acres/40 hectares

ARLINGTON COURT

A VICTORIAN FLOWER GARDEN AND GREENHOUSE, AND A WOODLAND WALK TO A MYSTERIOUS LAKE

Arlington Court is not a place for horticultural hijinks but it does possess the memorably harmonious character of a well-run and delightful estate. The house, its wooded surroundings and pleasure grounds give the impression of having been made to please the family rather than to dazzle the cognoscenti. The estate is still intact, with over 2,000 acres/810 hectares of largely tenanted farms. The house was built between 1820 and 1823, to the designs of Thomas Lee, for Colonel John Palmer Chichester whose family had lived here since the 16th century. The grounds had been landscaped by the middle of the 19th century and there is no evidence of earlier gardens here. The Victorian garden with its terraced lawns to the east of the house preserves the character of its period. A splendid pair of cast-iron herons with worms wriggling in their beaks – the crest of the Chichester family – flank the steps, and the roof of a decoratively gabled glasshouse is again crowned with the Chichester heron. Double borders on each side of the glasshouse include vigorous

thickets of the unusual *Cautleya spicata* 'Robusta', a member of the ginger family, with maroon and yellow flowers in late summer. Below the glasshouse a pool with a fountain is flanked by arbours garlanded with roses and honeysuckle; young monkey puzzles – that archetypal mid-Victorian tree – stand on either side; beds are enclosed in metalwork edging (Hardenberg baskets) and planted with bedding schemes of annuals.

The parish church of St James lies within the grounds of Arlington Park and is worth visiting for the Chichester memorials – especially a charming plaque to Miss Rosalie Chichester (who died in 1949) decorated with ferns and shells and designed by John Piper. It was she who was

The Victorian Garden at Arlington

responsible for the quirky collections of ships, shells, pewter and so forth still preserved in the house. That has nothing to do with gardening but it does bring to mind the continuity of ownership and careful stewardship which enabled places like Arlington Court to flourish and survive.

In the wooded valley at some distance to the west of the house a lake was created in 1850 by damming the river Yeo. At this time, too, there was a plan to create a new entrance drive which would have swept across the lake on a great bridge. Only the stone piers were completed and they remain, gaunt and

forlorn, by the banks of the lake. Nearby is a handsome neo-classical urn, with an inscription by Reynolds Stone, erected in memory of Rosalie Chichester – an atmospheric Arcadian scene.

Location Arlington, nr Barnstaple EX31 4LP, Devon **OS** SS6140 7m NE of Barnstaple by A39 **Tel** 01271 850296 **Fax** 01271 850711 **English Heritage Register** Grade II* **Owner** The National Trust **Open** Apr to Oct, daily except Sat (open Bank Hol Sat) 11–5.30 (closes 4 mid Sept to end Oct) **Area** 25 acres/10 hectares

ATHELHAMPTON HOUSE GARDENS

A MASTERPIECE OF ARTS AND CRAFTS DESIGN – ARCHITECTURAL ENCLOSURES, MAGNIFICENT TOPIARY AND SUPERB STONEWORK

The garden at Athelhampton is one of the most beautiful examples of the English architectural garden. The house, dating from the late middle ages, was substantially rebuilt in the 16th and 17th centuries, although it still has enough of its original charm for Pevsner to describe it as "the *beau idéal* of the late medieval manor house". Nothing is known about earlier gardens on the site but Alfred Cart de Lafontaine commissioned the architect Francis Inigo Thomas to lay out new gardens between 1891 and 1893. Inigo Thomas created a beguiling sequence of enclosed spaces in which architectural ornament made the use of plants almost superfluous.

WALLED ENCLOSURES
At the heart of the garden is the Corona, a circular walled enclosure with a parapet of gracefully sweeping curves separated by slender obelisks, a pool at its centre and openings leading to other parts of the garden, flanked with decorative stone piers. The Great Court with its twelve unforgettable pyramids of clipped yew, rising over 35ft/10m high, is overlooked by a raised walk with stone balustrades and dashing summerhouses – the effect is simultaneously serene and dramatic. The restraint of a slender lily pool running arrow straight from the east façade of the house is spectacularly enlivened by a

The Corona at Athelhampton House

superlative old cedar of Lebanon spreading over the garden walls. In Inigo Thomas's last enclosure, east of the Corona, a fountain and pool are embraced by a moss-nibbled Gothic niche. Here there was originally a chaste parterre but it now overflows with boisterous modern plantings of tender exotics. Further gardens have since been added to Inigo Thomas's masterly design but, alas, they seem incoherent and clumsy by comparison; in any other context their merits might have shone.

Athelhampton is a model of its kind, one of those gardens which cause visiting gardeners to resolve to create light and order in their own muddled plots at home.

Location Athelhampton DT2 7LG, Dorset **OS** SY7794
5m NE of Dorchester on A35 **Tel** 01305 848363
Fax 01305 848135 **English Heritage Register** Grade I
Owner Patrick Cooke **Open** Mar to Oct, daily except
Sat 10.30–5; Nov to Feb, Sun 10.30–5 **Area** 15 acres/6
hectares

BARRINGTON COURT

A GRAND TUDOR HOUSE WITH
DECORATIVE EARLY 20TH-CENTURY
GARDENS INFLUENCED BY GERTRUDE JEKYLL

The great house at Barrington and its splendid outhouses are a handsome mixture of Tudor, 17th-century and early 20th-century Arts and Crafts architecture. The estate seems to have been bought from the Daubeney family in 1552 by William Clifton who built the splendid house we can see today. But the garden is almost entirely 20th-century, made after Colonel Lyle took a tenancy of the ruinous house from the National Trust in 1920. He recruited the architect J.E. Forbes to restore the house and its fine outhouses and it is his work that has had the greatest influence on the character of the garden. Gertrude Jekyll was asked to advise on the planting but did not visit the site and worked only from Forbes's plans. Traces of her style of planting survive (such as the use of bergenias as emphatic structural plants) but, it must be said, not much of her spirit. In the walled Lily Garden she had specified banks of hydrangeas in raised beds flanking the long sides of the scalloped lily pond – azaleas have taken their place. For the corners she chose a favourite plant of emphatic architectural form, *Yucca gloriosa* – these now have clumps of pink *Crinum × powellii*. The scarlet *Dahlia* 'Bishop of Llandaff' is planted *en masse* in the two short beds at each end of the pool, while deep beds that surround the garden have a vigorous colour scheme of yellow and red – it is all very jolly, but is it Jekyll?

Barrington's 17th-century sundial

Alongside the walled garden a formal rose garden with modern bedding varieties is partly enclosed by a spectacular humped hedge of box and nearby, spreading its branches expansively over the old calf-pens, is the most beautiful plant in the garden, a majestic old ash. Another beauty of the garden is the pattern of virtuoso paths of narrow bricks laid in endlessly inventive patterns, now basket-weave, now herringbone, and always beautifully cambered to shed water. The most intricate one runs south of the house, with intermingled patterns of wonderful virtuosity. Here, an open expanse of lawn, with a scattering of old oaks, gives one of the best views at Barrington, back to the great house, with its gables, barley-sugar chimney stacks and finials, looking serenely outwards over lovely parkland. In the setting of the great house, and fine architectural detail, the detailed planting at Barrington Court does not quite pull its weight.

Location Barrington, nr Ilminster TA19 0NQ, Somerset **OS** ST3918 5m NE of Ilminster off A303 **Tel** 01460 241938 **Email** barringtoncourt@ntrust.org.uk **English Heritage Register** Grade II* **Owner** The National Trust **Open** Mar and Oct, Fri, Sat and Sun 11–4.30; Apr to Jun and Sept, daily except Fri 11–5.30; Jul to Aug, daily 11–5.30 **Area** 9 acres/3.6 hectares

Barrington Court from the park

BATH BOTANICAL GARDENS

IN THE CENTRE OF GEORGIAN BATH, AN EXCELLENT COLLECTION OF PLANTS WELL MAINTAINED IN A FINE SETTING

As soon as you enter the Bath Botanical Gardens from the south-western gate you see splendid trees – a huge pendent silver lime (*Tilia* 'Petiolaris'), an elegant *Cornus controversa* 'Variegata' and a wide-spreading golden catalpa (*Catalpa bignonioides* 'Aurea'). They give an immediate foretaste of the

A 19th-century urn in Bath Botanical Gardens

character of these exceptionally attractive public gardens which were first laid out in 1840 but completely replanned in 1887 by John Milburn who came from Kew as Superintendent. The Botanical Gardens form an extension to the Royal Victoria Park (*see page 59*), laid out between 1830 and 1831 for "the enjoyment of the free burgesses inhabiting the city". Already, with the rapid expansion of the city in the Georgian period, the need was felt for public open space, and the gardens were at first named The Royal Victoria Horticultural and Botanical Gardens. However, the botanical element took on a new lease of life when a local amateur botanist, Christopher Broome, left his collection of 2,000 plants to the gardens in 1886, and later in the century the distinguished gardening cleric, Canon Ellacombe of nearby Bitton Vicarage, also donated plants. Today it admirably combines the functions of a public garden (with suitably brilliant bedding schemes here and there) and a finely gardened collection of good plants.

The site slopes gently southwards and is enlivened by a serpentine pool and stream. There are many fine trees, some of them rare (such as the Chinese *Catalpa fargesii* f. *duclouxii* with spectacular pink flowers) and some of them especially fine specimens of less rare plants – among them several beautiful, and venerable, magnolias and an outstanding

Cornus kousa var. *chinensis*. Much of the planting is attractively informal, of which an exceptional example is the meadow planting beneath old Japanese maples by the rock garden. Here in spring is an enchanting sight – wood anemones, bluebells, scillas and snake's head fritillaries growing in marvellous profusion. Although there are polite, and more or less conventional borders, much use is made of species roses which also give a touch of wildness.

On the northern side of the garden, separated by the Royal Victoria Park carriage drive and on the site of a former quarry, is a garden of different character: the Dell garden, shaded by lugubrious conifers. In an atmospheric clearing a memorial to Shakespeare, placed here in 1864 to celebrate the tercentenary of his birth, is in the shape of a Roman votive altar. Hidden away – or as well hidden as such a huge thing can be – is a monument of an altogether more extravagant kind: John Osborne's statue of Jupiter (1839), a fierce and boldly modelled head mounted on an immensely tall plinth, rivalling the trees for height.

The gardens are one of the few public parks still maintained by the municipality, rather than by the cheapest available contractor, and look all the better for it. They perfectly fulfil their two functions of providing an agreeable

place in which to do nothing at all and displaying a wonderful collection of often unfamiliar plants for the delectation and education of gardeners. Until I came here I had never seen the beautiful slender *Malus trilobata* with its distinguished grey three-lobed leaves, white flowers and shapely but compact presence; it would make the perfect ornamental tree for a garden of modest size.

Location Royal Victoria Park, Upper Bristol Road, Bath BA1 2NQ, Somerset **OS** ST7365 W of city centre by Upper Bristol Road **English Heritage Register** Grade II **Owner** City of Bath **Open** daily 9–sunset **Area** 3 acres/1.2 hectares

BICTON COLLEGE OF AGRICULTURE

OUTSTANDING TREES, TENDER SHRUBS AND SUPERB COLLECTIONS OF AGAPANTHUS AND PITTOSPORUMS

This is the other surviving part of Bicton Park. (For a brief history of the whole estate see the entry on Bicton Park Gardens *page 20*.) Bicton College is a college of agriculture and horticulture and although there is little garden design to be seen there are many memorable plants and occasional good planting. The entrance to the park starts off with a splendid Victorian trumpet-blast, not to everyone's taste: an avenue of monkey puzzles which lines the upper part of the drive. This was planted in 1843–44 under

the supervision of the famous Exeter nurseryman James Veitch and of no less a figure than J.C. Loudon, the greatest garden writer and expert of his day. Parkland on either side, with grazing cattle or sheep, has many exceptional trees – among several evergreen oaks are superb examples of a local tree, *Quercus × hispanica* 'Lucombeana', named after the man who started the nursery of Lucombe & Plince in Exeter in 1720, and who spotted a chance seedling of a hybrid of the Turkey oak (*Q. cerris*) and the cork oak (*Q. suber*). There are immense tulip trees (*Liriodendron tulipifera*) with giant gnarled stems, and some beautiful common limes (*Tilia × europaea*).

WALLED GARDENS AND GLASSHOUSES At the head of the drive the house, built in 1800 by James Wyatt but rebuilt in dapper Edwardian style by Sir Walter Tapper in 1908 and 1909, faces south over land that slopes gently down across the tree-studded park to a lake fringed with fine trees, and the old pinetum on the far bank. To one side of the house are the college's walled gardens, glasshouses and a small nursery with some good plants. A large garden spread out in front of a glasshouse has island beds with humdrum planting of bedding roses and annual bedding schemes. But it also has an astonishing thicket of agapanthus with occasional tufts of *Eucomis comosa* thrusting through. Bicton College keeps National Collections of agapanthus (90 species and cultivars) and pittosporum (70 species and cultivars). Two beds of ornamental grasses also have attractive combinations of plants. The richly planted walled Yard Garden is lined with deep mixed borders of tender plants such as *Michelia doltsopa* and dozens of species of salvias, few of which would survive a winter in most English gardens.

In the car park you will see a magnificent Lucombe oak, and as you leave you will inevitably stop to admire the majestic trees in the fields on either side of the drive.

Location East Budleigh, Budleigh Salterton EX9 7DP, Devon **OS** SY0786 6m NE of Exmouth by A376 **Tel** 01395 562300 **English Heritage Register** Grade I **Owner** Bicton College **Open** daily 11–4.30 **Area** 19 acres/7.7 hectares

◁ **Agapanthus and grasses** at Bicton College

BICTON PARK GARDENS

18TH-CENTURY FORMAL GARDENS, VICTORIAN EXUBERANCE AND A WONDERFUL EARLY GLASSHOUSE

Great gardens survive by different means. In the case of the ancient Bicton Park estate it has meant that the two major parts of the garden have gone their separate ways (*see* Bicton College *page 19*). This was the estate of the ancient Rolle family who came by it in the early 17th century by marriage to a Dennys heiress. Two Rolles played a vital role in the evolution of the gardens here: Henry, the 1st Lord Rolle, who laid out the Italian Gardens in about 1735, and his nephew, John, who was responsible for the great garden works, especially tree planting, that took place in the first half of the 19th century. The family died out and in 1935 Bicton Park became a girls' school. In 1957 the estate was dismembered and the chief part of the garden now belongs to Simon Lister and is run very much as a tourist attraction, with a miniature railway running through the woods. If this is the only means by which a great garden may survive in some form, then who can complain?

THE ITALIAN GARDEN
The Italian Garden at the heart of Bicton is partly walled on three sides and slopes gently downhill, with a pedimented stone conservatory, flanked by glasshouses, following the curve of the wall at the top. It is a jolly Victorian scene – two fountain pools surrounded by many small beds cut into a lawn and filled with silver *Senecio cineraria*, scarlet pelargoniums, mop-headed marigolds and rich purple verbenas. At the foot of the hill are the remains of the 1st Lord Rolle's formal gardens. Rumour, but no more than that, has attached the name of André Le Nôtre to this scheme – but he died in 1700. Here, a handsome rectangular pool has a great tiered fountain spouting a plume of three jets high into the air, and a curious amphitheatre-like shape cut into the turf banks with, aligned on it, a distant obelisk revealed in a gap between trees. Empty plinths surround the pool where in the recent past there had been fine statues.

There are other exceptionally attractive and unusual features in the garden. To the east is the Shell House and American garden. The Shell House, dating from about 1840, is a hermitage-like stubby tower fashioned of rough lumps of flinty stone; stones line the paths and the interior has a display of exotic shells arranged on shelves lining the wall. The American Garden was made in about 1832 when Robert Glendinning was head gardener and is one of the very few surviving examples of a type of garden which was fashionable in the second half of the 18th century when new North American plants were coming to England in increasing numbers. A few American trees can still be seen: *Catalpa bignonioides*, tulip tree (*Liriodendron tulipifera*), tupelo (*Nyssa sylvatica*) and Wellingtonia.

THE GREAT PALM HOUSE
Above the Italian Garden is a garden building so beautiful that it alone would have made Bicton famous: the Palm House is one of the earliest surviving glasshouses in the country, dating from around 1820. Built against a wall and three-lobed in shape, it has a framework of cast-iron with very thin glazing bars and overlapping fish-scale glass panes. After restoration in 1985 it is in marvellous condition and houses a collection of palms with a shapely date palm (*Phoenix dactylifera*) occupying the central area.

The Pinetum was started in around 1839 under Robert Glendinning's surpervision, with the help of J.C. Loudon, and although the storm of 1990 destroyed many trees what remains is remarkable – a huge

The Palm House at Bicton

collection of conifers, one of the most atmospheric in the country, with countless fine specimens. Beyond is the Hermitage, an octagonal rustic summerhouse dating from 1839 with, as Barbara Jones records in her *Follies & Grottoes* (1974), "a knucklebone floor and an uncommon basketwork lining nicely free of the spiders and earwigs that usually attend the rustic style". There is much to relish at Bicton, with or without miniature railways.

Location East Budleigh, Budleigh Salterton EX9 7DP, Devon **OS** SY0785 6m NE of Exmouth by A376 **Tel** 01395 568465 **Fax** 01935 568889 **English Heritage Register** Grade I **Owner** Simon Lister **Open** Mar to Oct, daily 11–5 **Area** 50 acres/20 hectares

BLAISE CASTLE AND BLAISE VILLAGE

AN 18TH-CENTURY PICTURESQUE LANDSCAPE WITH A ROMANTIC SHAM CASTLE AND EXQUISITE REGENCY ESTATE VILLAGE

The Blaise estate, with its dramatic topography of hill and gorge, is an eloquent reminder of Bristol's astonishing garden history. The site goes back at least to the middle ages but the first notable garden here was that of Sir Samuel Astry who rebuilt Henbury Manor in 1688. He also made ambitious formal gardens, with a double avenue soaring to the top of Blaise Hill which was crowned with a summerhouse and winding paths. From 1762 onwards a new owner, Thomas Farr, laid out a romantic landscape park with walks to take advantage of the beauties of the place and its distant views, and a Gothic Sham Castle, designed by Robert Mylne, rising on the heights. Jane Austen's Isabella Thorpe enthused about it in *Northanger Abbey*: "The finest place in England; worth going fifty miles to see", and it remains today on its lofty wooded eminence.

Farr went bankrupt and the estate was bought by John Scandrett Harford who consulted Humphry Repton about the landscape – a Red Book was produced in 1796. Repton made a new driveway to bypass the village of

The sham castle at Blaise

Henbury, built a new lodge and added a "woodman's cottage" to enliven the gloom of the woods. A little later Repton's son George collaborated with John Nash to build Blaise Hamlet, between 1810 and 1811. This – a group of nine picturesque cottages originally designed for retired estate staff – still survives and is impeccably cared for by the National Trust. Grouped about a village green, they are designed in full-blown fantasy rural vernacular with leaded lights, thatched roofs, Gothic detailing and ornate chimney stacks.

The picturesque lie of the land, the Sham Castle on the wooded hill and the decorative hamlet on the other side of the road make a wonderful scene. Blaise Castle House, now a

A cottage *orné* at Blaise

museum owned by the City of Bristol, contains Repton's original Red Book for Blaise, providing a rare opportunity to see one of these fascinating documents.

Location Henbury, Bristol BS10 7QS **OS** ST5578 5m NW of Bristol by A4108 **Tel** 0117 950789 **English Heritage Register** Grade II* **Owner** Bristol City Council/The National Trust **Open** daily dawn–dusk **Area** 50 acres/20 hectares

BOSVIGO HOUSE

MASTERLY AND VARIED PLANTING IN WELL DESIGNED ENCLOSURES AS THE SETTING FOR AN 18TH-CENTURY HOUSE

Virtually all the famous Cornish gardens are informal woodland gardens, at their best in spring when the camellias, magnolias and rhododendrons are in full flower. Bosvigo is a rarity in Cornwall in that it is a formal garden which, though interesting to see at any time of the year, hits its peak of floriferousness in high summer.

Michael and Wendy Perry bought the handsome 18th-century house in 1980, and its wooded grounds preserve a remarkably rural air even though they lie within the city of Truro. The formality of the house is reflected in the enclosures which constitute the heart of the garden. A Victorian conservatory overlooks a walled garden with fastidiously composed mixed borders of rich purples, magentas, soft pinks and wine-reds. The Vean (Cornish for a dower house) Garden has a four-part parterre, each bed having at its centre a clipped cone of golden privet (*Ligustrum ovalifolium* 'Aureum') surrounded by plants with gold and yellow flowers or foliage spiked with the occasional striking blue or violet of *Delphinium* 'Alice Artindale' or the sea-holly *Eryngium × zabellii*. At a higher level a hidden garden is overlooked by a William Kent-ish arbour of white painted wood where pink and silver dominate the cottage-garden mixed planting. To one side of the house is a Cornish woodland garden with a radical twist – a fine spring garden filled with bulbs, ferns, the smaller

◁ **The walled garden** at Bosvigo

rhododendrons and Japanese maples erupts in
late summer with exotic colour: veils of
orange lilies and golden alstroemerias, blood-
red roses and the scarlet nasturtium *Tropaeolum
majus* 'Hermine Grasshof' spreading across the
path. Hidden in the woods, this explosive
surprise produces its pyrotechnics of colour
deep into the autumn.

AN INSPIRATION FOR GARDENERS

The Perrys' chief interest is plants but they
have had the sense to plan their garden with a
strong framework thoroughly at ease with
their house, and their plantings, despite their
exuberance, are controlled by thoughtful
colour harmonies. The garden is most
beautifully maintained; the Perrys do all the
work themselves and even have time to run
an admirable small nursery of choice plants, all
propagated from those in the garden. Private
gardens such as this one are an inspiration to
gardeners as well as a source of unusual plants.

Location Bosvigo Lane, Truro TR1 3NH, Cornwall
OS SW8145 In the W suburbs of Truro by A390; at
Highertown take Dobbs Lane (nr Sainsbury roundabout);
Bosvigo House is 500 yards down on the left **Tel** and **Fax**
01872 275774 **Owner** Michael and Wendy Perry **Open**
Mar to Sept, Thur to Sat 11–6 **Area** 3 acres/1.2 hectares

CAERHAYS CASTLE

EXTRAVAGANTLY PICTURESQUE CASTLE IN A
MARVELLOUS POSITION, WITH ONE OF THE
FINEST PLANT COLLECTIONS IN CORNWALL

The castle at Caerhays is the work of John
Nash and was built between 1805 and
1807. It fits into its already dramatic landscape
to perfection – a low-lying castellated
mansion with splendid trees crowding all
about except on the slopes below it where
there are unimpeded views southwards down
the wide valley to Porthluney Bay. Humphry
Repton, who sometimes worked with Nash, is
rumoured to have had a hand in the shaping
of the landscape here, but there is no record
of it. He would certainly have loved it – but
could he have added to its beauties?

The estate was bought in 1854 by Michael

Wild garlic and azaleas at Caerhays

Williams II, a Cornish mine-owner, whose grandson, John Charles Williams, established Caerhays as an outstanding plantsman's garden. He was a subscriber to several plant-hunting expeditions in their greatest period, in particular those of George Forrest, Reginald Farrer, Frank Kingdon Ward and E.H. Wilson. Through them, vast numbers of camellias, magnolias and rhododendrons made their way to Caerhays. By 1917, for example, there were 264 species and wild varieties of rhododendron in cultivation here. J.C. Williams's name is commemorated in the beautiful *Rhododendron williamsianum* and also in hybrid camellias, *C. × williamsii*.

THE SPIRIT OF THE PLACE

For the plant lover the great attraction of Caerhays is the very large number of Asiatic flowering shrubs, often venerable and beautiful specimens of the earliest introductions to European gardens, but for those who just enjoy beautiful landscape the pleasures are no less intense. There is, in truth, little design at Caerhays, and nothing as obvious as the contrived plant associations, least of all the studious colour combinations, of tamer gardens. One of the charms of the place is the intermingling of native plants — among them some exceptional old beeches and great waves of bluebells and wild garlic — with rare exotics.

The lie of the land is marvellous too, and when a milky-white sea mist rolls in off the bay you could easily imagine yourself with Frank Kingdon Ward in the Himalayan foothills.

Location nr Gorran FA1 7DE, Cornwall **OS** SW9741 SE of Caerhays village, 10m S of St Austell by minor roads **Tel** 01872 501319 **Fax** 01872 501870 **English Heritage Register** Grade II* **Owner** F.J. Williams **Open** mid Mar to mid May, Mon to Fri 11–4 **Area** 100 acres/40 hectares

CASTLE DROGO

DRAMATIC EARLY 20TH-CENTURY CASTLE BY EDWIN LUTYENS, ADORNED WITH A FINE FLOWER GARDEN

No 20th-century country house in England has such striking presence in its landscape as Castle Drogo. Sir Edwin Lutyens designed it for Julius Drewe and it was built between 1910 and 1930. The great granite house dominates a bluff overlooking the Teign valley on the edge of Dartmoor — only a building of strong character would be at ease in such dramatic scenery. The exterior has the bold simplicity of some early medieval fortress but made more cheerful with high, intricate stone-mullioned windows. Drewe wanted to keep the approach to his castle informal and unfussy. The winding drive passes between ramparts of clipped yew and a grove of holm oaks (*Quercus ilex*) and Gertrude Jekyll advised on a naturalistic planting scheme of birch, blackthorn, holly, Scots pine and wild roses here. (It is often forgotten that Gertrude Jekyll, like her friend and associate, William Robinson, had an acute eye for appropriately wild planting of this sort.)

Changing levels at Castle Drogo

The garden is quite detached from the castle, much against the wishes of Lutyens who had wanted an axial string of enclosures firmly related to the house. In the 1920s a garden of formal character with a strong Lutyens flavour but unrelated to the castle was eventually made by George Dillistone of Tunbridge Wells, who had worked on other Drewe houses. Hidden behind walls of yew north-east of the house, it is an admirable design with two sharply contrasting enclosures.

THE SUNKEN GARDEN

The first is a vast sunken garden of subtly contrived changes of level. In each corner *Parrotia persica* is trained over a metal framework to form a spacious leafy arbour – especially beautiful in early spring with the extraordinary scarlet stamens of its flowers and in autumn the crimson and gold of its foliage. In the shade of the parrotias beds of ferns are edged with the gleaming foliage of *Asarum europaeum*. Two central lawns are surrounded by terraces with mixed borders on each side,

between which scalloped paths of Mughal influence thread their way and beds of modern roses run round the edges of the lawns. In late spring a vast beautifully trained wisteria snakes along the crest of a retaining wall and a little formal herb garden above it has lollipops of clipped bay and is clasped by curving hedges of yew enlivened with niches and benches.

A path between a flowery walk with azaleas, enkianthus, magnolias and Japanese maples leads to the second enclosure, one of Lutyens's most marvellous garden conceits. A high yew hedge encloses a circular lawn, 150ft/45m in diameter, originally a tennis court but now used for croquet. The deep green drum of yew surrounding the pale green of fine turf has an aura of mystery and splendour, like the temple of some forgotten religion.

Location Drewsteignton EX6 6PB, Devon **OS** SX7290 21m W of Exeter by A30 **Tel** 01647 433306 **Fax** 01647 433186 **English Heritage Register** Grade II* **Owner** The National Trust **Open** daily dawn–dusk **Area** 12 acres/4.8 hectares

CHIFFCHAFFS

THE ESSENTIAL COTTAGE GARDEN, WITH BEAUTIFULLY KEPT FLOWER GARDEN AND WOODLAND GARDEN OF CHARACTER

The idea of the cottage garden may be interpreted in many different ways; its commonest use is as a licence for more or less amiable chaos. The Potts came here in 1977 and although their charming thatched house is undeniably a cottage their garden is as unchaotic as could be. Everything is bursting with vigour and the garden is impeccably maintained – wherever you look you will search in vain for a weed.

In the month of April you will be greeted by the exhilarating fanfare of an avenue of Japanese cherries in full flower – the lovely white *Prunus* 'Shirotae' and a single rogue pink-flowered *P. sargentii*. The gardens about the house fill a gently south-west facing slope with an irrepressible array of plants and carefully made enclosures. The slope is terraced, with stone retaining walls and a network of paved or gravel paths. A crescent of lawn is embraced by mixed borders in which the smaller conifers jostle with azaleas (and other small rhododendrons), roses and viburnums – all lavishly underplanted for spring and summer. A stepped pool in a shady corner is planted about with snake's head fritillaries and bloodroot (*Sanguinaria canadensis*). There are elaborately clipped yew hedges, and at the top of the garden a pergola of clematis and roses leads to a little kitchen garden tucked away in a corner.

At a little distance from the house is a woodland garden where paths running along the upper contours look down on magnolias and rhododendrons underplanted with drifts of narcissi, primulas and shuttlecock ferns. The slopes are punctuated with ornamental trees and shrubs – camellias, cherries, pieris and many maples – while beautiful old oaks, a great ornament of the landscape in these parts, rise imperturbably above. Kenneth Potts's nursery, Abbey Plants, sells a wide range of high-quality plants almost entirely propagated on the premises.

◁ **The cherry avenue** at Chiffchaffs

Location Chaffeymoor, Bourton, nr Gillingham SP8 5BY, Dorset **OS** ST7630 At W end of Bourton village, 3m E of Wincanton off A303 **Tel** 01747 840841
Owner Mr and Mrs K.R. Potts **Open** Apr to Oct, Wed and Thur and on other days for the NGS 2–5
Area 11 acres/4.5 hectares

CLAVERTON MANOR

A RARE GARDEN OF AMERICAN FLAVOUR
FOR A GEORGIAN MANSION WHICH HOUSES
THE AMERICAN MUSEUM IN BRITAIN

The old manor at Claverton was built in about 1580 at the centre of an elaborate terraced garden and close to the church. The terraces remain, still with some of the garden walls, intricate stone balustrades and old gate piers capped with openwork obelisks, but in 1820 the house was demolished and an entirely new Bath stone mansion was built for John Vivian to Sir Jeffry Wyatville's design. It occupies a fine position on raised ground with broad views across the Avon valley.

There had been 19th-century pleasure grounds about the house, and good trees along the drive survive from this time, but the gardens took on an entirely new life in 1961 when the estate was acquired as the American Museum in Britain. The new garden was given a pronounced American flavour, and an arboretum of North American trees and shrubs is a vivid reminder to British gardeners of the debt owed to America. Close to the house is a collection of medicinal, culinary and dying herbs used

The Dutch summerhouse at Claverton

The Mount Vernon Garden at Claverton

in colonial times, with a straw-covered bee skep at the centre. The walls of the house are garlanded with excellent roses, among them 'Climbing Mrs Herbert Stevens', 'Zéphirine Drouhin' and the exquisite pale apricot 'Climbing Lady Hillingdon', all seen to perfection against a background of honey-coloured Bath stone. A fine mixed border, against high terrace walls, was designed by the American garden designer Lanning Roper. Here, tall clipped Irish yews trained hard against the walls rise like pilasters to the parapet high above, whose stone urns seem to crown them. Beyond the house a curious little 19th-century Dutch summerhouse looks across the valley. At a lower level, a copy of part of George Washington's garden at Mount Vernon has a parterre-like arrangement of box- or brick-edged beds. Shrub roses fill some of the beds and herbaceous plants, many of them American, fill the others, with domes of clipped *Prunus glandulosa* soaring above. A facsimile of a Washingtonian octagonal pavilion with pepper-pot roof mounts guard in a corner, and a pretty white-painted paling fence encloses two sides of the garden.

Location Claverton, nr Bath BA2 7BD, Somerset
OS ST7864 4m SE of Bath by A36 **Tel** 01225 460503
Fax 01225 480726 **English Heritage Register** Grade II
Owner The American Museum in Britain **Open** end Mar to beginning Nov, daily except Mon 1–6 (Sat and Sun 12–6; Bank Hol Sun and Mon 11–6)
Area 10 acres/4 hectares

COLETON FISHACRE GARDEN

REMOTE AND IRRESISTIBLE, A VALLEY
GARDEN IN A HIDDEN CORNER OF DEVON,
WITH EXCELLENT PLANTS

Coleton Fishacre has a remote feel to it, isolated at the tip of a promontory with the river Dart to the west and the sea to the south and east. It sits in a shallow valley which runs down to the sea at Pudcombe Cove, and a stream flowing through it is dammed from time to time to form pools. The soil is acid, the rainfall around 40in/100cm per annum and the coastal position creates a very mild microclimate. The handsome stone Arts and Crafts house, built in 1926 for Rupert D'Oyly Carte to the designs of Oswald Milne, faces down the valley. Terracing on the south side of the house makes an especially protected site for such tender shrubs as *Beschorneria yuccoides*, the autumn-flowering *Camellia sasanqua*, the rare banana-scented Chinese *Michelia figo*, and other exotic things that need cosseting. The house itself on this side

is shrouded in tender exotics, and the little walled Rill Garden also provides special shelter for tender plants.

A PLANT-FILLED WALK

Paths run down the valley on either side of the stream, edged with notable and often rare plants. Here are excellent trees – a noble tulip tree (*Liriodendron tulipifera*), *Metasequioa glyptostroboides*, *Ailanthus altissima* and many Japanese maples. Appropriate planting continues along the banks of the stream – bamboos, ferns, *Gunnera manicata*, hostas and rheum. If you love plants – and it would be madness to come here if you do not – you will want to walk slowly along each path, with the National Trust plant list in hand. Spring is the overwhelming season, with rhododendrons filling the air with scent and providing shamelessly glamorous blossom, but any season has its beauties of one kind or another. At the foot of the valley a gate leads into wild woodland which gives out onto a narrow coastal path with a vertiginous view of Pudcome Cove, the definitive smuggler's hideaway. When you have had your fill of the garden you may walk up the hill to the Gazebo, from which there are lovely views to the sea and the sinister Eastern Black Rock.

Location Coleton, Kingswear, Dartmouth TQ6 0EQ, Devon **OS** SX9050 4m S of Brixham off B3205
Tel 01803 752466 **Email** coletonfishacre@ntrust.org.uk
English Heritage Register Grade II* **Owner** The National Trust **Open** Mar, Sun 11–5; Apr to Oct, daily except Mon and Tue (open Bank Hol Mon) 10.30–5.30
Area 20 acres/8 hectares

The Rill Garden at Coleton Fishacre

COMPTON ACRES

A CLIFFTOP COLLECTION OF THEMED
GARDENS CARRIED OUT WITH PANACHE

A dizzying anthology of garden styles clinging to the cliffs on the Dorset coast sounds an alarming prospect. The experience of visiting Compton Acres is, however, simultaneously soothing, exhilarating and, just occasionally, wince-making. Thomas William Simpson came here just after World War I, built a new house and started a garden in which ingredients of very different periods and types would be linked together with a walk that ambled along the contours of the slopes. When he started work the coast was much less built up than it is now and the site offered marvellous gardening possibilities. It has a very mild microclimate, allowing the cultivation of a wide range of plants that enjoy acid soil, and has beautiful views of sea and coast with a splendid distant panorama of the Purbeck hills. Working the ground on such a site was an expensive and labour-intensive business, especially as Simpson had to bring in much of the soil.

THE JAPANESE GARDEN

During World War II the garden fell into neglect but after several changes of ownership it is now well cared for and has for many years been opened as a self-contained tourist attraction (Simpson's house was demolished in 1986 and replaced by a block of flats). Not all the features that may be seen today date from Simpson's time; others have been added, some of them in keeping with the spirit of the place and others (a deer sanctuary?) rather less so.

The features also vary in their authenticity: for example, the Roman Garden dazzles the eye with wildly inauthentic bedding plants while the charming Japanese Garden – one of the best in the country – has a more convincing air and provides perhaps the most memorably attractive part of the garden. Built by Japanese craftsmen in 1920, its setting is a rocky valley with a cascade and tall stone pagoda at its head and a

The Japanese Garden at Compton Acres

backdrop of largely coniferous planting. Clumps of bamboos, flowering cherries, Japanese maples and clipped azaleas clothe the slopes. A scarlet teahouse, clasped by wisterias, stands at the side of a pool ornamented with bronze cranes and snow lanterns. The Italian Garden, inspired by renaissance designs, has a long, narrow lily pool and fountain with a little domed temple, mounds of clipped golden yew, statues and ornaments, gravel walks and summer bedding schemes of more than Tuscan splendour cut into the turf. On a summer's evening, though, when the light is low and the fountains are playing, it has a decidedly agreeable effect.

PLACES FOR PLANTS

Parts of the garden – the Heather Dell and the Rock and Water Gardens, for example – are devoted to types of plants, but distinguished plants, especially trees and shrubs, are scattered liberally throughout. Many of these are of a woodland type – *Hydrangea quercifolia* or *Rhododendron sinogrande* for example – but others, such as the several species of eucalyptus, relish the sun-baked slopes and open exposure.

The spirit evoked by Compton Acres seems to me to be that of the lively public-minded municipal park of Victorian times. There is plenty to see, you can sit on a bench at a viewpoint and eat an ice-cream; or, notebook and occasionally binoculars in hand, you can get down to some serious plant-spotting.

Location Canford Cliffs Road, Poole BH13 7ES, Dorset **OS** SZ0589 1½m W of Bournemouth by A35 and B3065 **Tel** 01202 700778 **Fax** 01202 707537 **English Heritage Register** Grade II* **Owner** Mr I. Green **Open** Mar to Oct, daily 10–5.30 (closes 4.30 in early Mar and late Oct) **Area** 10 acres/4 hectares

COTEHELE

THE ANCIENT ESTATE OF THE EDGCUMBES IN LOVELY CORNISH COUNTRYSIDE WITH RICHLY ATMOSPHERIC GARDENS

The wooded country of the upper reaches of the river Tamar is one of the most beautiful parts of Cornwall and Devon. This is the setting for the marvellously romantic Cotehele House which passed to the Edgcumbe family in 1353 when William Edgcumbe married the de Cotehele heiress. The Edgcumbes' grander estate at Mount Edgcumbe (*see page 54*) later on commanded most of the family's attention and they moved there permanently in 1553. So Cotehele was left to potter on as very much a secondary

residence, which it remained until the 6th Earl of Mount Edgcumbe handed over the estate to the National Trust in lieu of death duties in 1947.

It seems that there was never much ornamental gardening at Cotehele though it was famous for its ancient trees – in the early 19th century J.C. Loudon noted on the slopes between the house and the river "some of the most magnificent oaks and chestnuts in England". When the National Trust took over, these fine old trees were the chief ornament of the estate and most of the interesting planting has been made since 1947. The grey granite walls of the house, in particular those of the entrance courtyard, give protection for several fine climbing plants – among them the beautiful Macartney rose (*Rosa bracteata*) and the tender pale yellow *Jasminum mesnyi*. In the upper garden, on the slopes above the house, are beautifully detailed high yew hedges, with topiary lollipops at corners and above entrances. A square pool is overhung with the unusual ash *Fraxinus excelsior* 'Jaspidea' whose foliage in early spring and in autumn is butter yellow. Here, too, is a handsome tulip tree (*Liriodendron tulipifera*), grass bright in spring with daffodils, and a mixed border running along the boundary wall.

On the far side of the house the sloping ground has been terraced and is embellished with beautiful magnolias. At the foot of the terraced garden a hidden passage leads under

Spring in the woodland garden at Cotehele

the road to a surprise – a woodland garden studded with fine trees and shrubs (camellias, enkianthus, hoherias, hydrangeas and maples) which runs down to the banks of the Tamar. A rare domed dovecote with a stone-tiled roof and inhabited by a flock of white doves looms above a pool with azaleas, flowering cherries and rich red tree rhododendrons (*R. arboreum*). At the bottom of the garden a path leads to the 15th-century family chapel of Saints George and Thomas à Becket above the river Tamar.

The garden at Cotehele, with its lovely ancient setting, is one of intermittent but very definite pleasures rather than a blindingly revelatory horticultural experience. But who wants blinding revelations every day?

Location St Dominick, nr Saltash PL12 6TA, Cornwall **OS** SX4268 8m SW of Tavistock off A390 **Tel** 01579 351346 **Infoline** 01579 352739 **Fax** 01579 351222 **Email** cotehele@ntrust.org.uk **English Heritage Register** Grade II **Owner** The National Trust **Open** daily 11–dusk **Area** 11 acres/4.4 hectares

COTHAY MANOR

BEAUTIFUL MEDIEVAL HOUSE WITH
20TH-CENTURY GARDEN OF COMPARTMENTS
RESTORED WITH EXCELLENT PLANTING

The manor at Cothay is a rare house, remarkably complete and unchanged from the late 15th century, and well cared for. Its rural setting is exceedingly beautiful – a countryside of high hedgerows, narrow lanes and rolling pasture land. The estate was owned between 1925 and 1937 by Colonel Reginald Cooper, an inspired lover of old houses whose hobby was buying places in need of affection, restoring them and moving on. He was a brilliant garden designer, a friend and confidant of Lawrence Johnston at Hidcote and of Harold Nicolson at Sissinghurst Castle. At Cothay he laid out a long yew walk running parallel to the western façade of the house and linking various hedged enclosures, one of which is an unusual and striking box parterre.

The west terrace at Cothay Manor

When the present owners came here in 1993 the garden needed much revitalisation; this they have provided with great energy and, above all, a real feeling for the horticultural spirit of the place. They have restored Cooper's magnificent yew hedges and filled the garden with planting of beauty and distinction. Mary-Anne Robb is a knowledgeable plantswoman and she and her husband, Alastair, are most accomplished practical gardeners. One of the most striking qualities of the planting is the way in which it is sensitively deployed in different contexts. The gatehouse, for example, a bold, castellated building like the entrance to an Oxford or Cambridge college, is swathed in *Vitis coignetiae* whose huge heart-shaped leaves tumble down to intermingle with *Magnolia grandiflora*, and is flanked with *Ampelopsis glandulosa* var. *brevipedunculata* whose jewel-like fruit in autumn are as brilliant as medieval stained glass. Within the entrance courtyard the planting is restricted to apricot, red and yellow, with *Campsis radicans* garlanding the wall. Below the western windows of the house a self-sown sea of plants such as *Erigeron karvinskianus*, *Geranium palmatum* and *Sisyrinchium californicum* on a paved terrace gives an air of abundant informality.

The Robbs have also added new areas to the garden, among them a bog garden by the banks of the river Tone, which flows through the grounds, and a long formal avenue of mop-headed acacias (*Robinia pseudoacacia* 'Umbraculifera') underplanted with thousands of 'White Triumphator' tulips and clouds of catmint. Cothay was fortunate to find new owners who respected its special character and yet were bold enough to put their own sympathetic stamp on it.

Location Greenham, nr Wellington TA21 0JR, Somerset
OS ST7221 5m W of Wellington by A38 and minor roads (follow signs to Thorne St Margaret)
Tel 01823 672283 **Owner** Mr and Mrs A.H.B. Robb
Open May to Sept, Wed, Thur, Sun and Bank Hol Mon 2–6 **Area** 5 acres/2 hectares

CRANBORNE MANOR GARDENS

THE ANCIENT HOUSE OF THE CECILS, WITH ROMANTIC LATE 20TH-CENTURY GARDENS

First built as a royal hunting lodge in the early 13th century, Cranborne Manor is one of the most beguiling houses imaginable. It was rebuilt by Robert Cecil (later Earl of Salisbury) between 1608 and 1611 when he was also building the great house at Hatfield in Hertfordshire (*see page 306*). Cranborne Manor is built on a more modest, domestic scale than the princely magnificence of Hatfield but as at Hatfield Robert Cecil embarked on a new garden while building works on the house were still going on. John Tradescant the Elder was at work on the garden, planting trees, in 1610 and 1611, by which time 100,000 bricks had already been made for garden walls.

Of Tradescant's time the only garden survival is the mount to the west of the house; the design of the garden today is largely the work of the present Marchioness of Salisbury who as Viscountess Cranborne came to live here in 1954. The mount, crowned with a sundial, is now at the centre of a formal garden of box-edged beds of lavishly underplanted shrub roses, with tall Irish yews marking the outer edges. A wrought-iron gate in the enclosing yew hedges gives views west over the rural landscape. An informal area of simple but memorable character has fine old beeches and long grass, enlivened by a majestic giant bronze head by Elizabeth Frink on a tall plinth, and a stone figure of a crouching wild boar in the grass. Beyond the brick entrance lodges an enfilade of formal gardens is enclosed in hedges of beech or yew. An intricate four-part knot of box surrounds an octagonal pool, its compartments filled with herbs; a broad grass path now leads between mixed borders given structure by towers of

Elizabeth Frink's bronze head at Cranborne

Clematis tangutica or hop (*Humulus lupulus*) and the occasional substantial tree (such as a *Cercis siliquastrum*) or shrub (*Osmanthus × burkwoodii*), generously underplanted. The southern border is backed by a yew hedge clipped into swooping shapes, and "windows" cut into each upward sweep give views of pasture and woodland. A gate leads to a further garden quartered with grass paths, a sundial at its centre, with eight beds edged in santolina and filled with shrub roses underplanted with culinary herbs.

Cranborne Manor lies on the edge of the village of Cranborne, where the square tower of the parish church of St Mary and St Bartholomew can be seen rising above the garden enclosures. The garden reflects the orderliness of the village while allowing views of rural landscape, with the house doing a perfect balancing act between the two.

Location nr Wimborne BH21 5PP, Dorset **OS** SU0513 In Cranborne village, 16½m SW of Salisbury by A354 and B3081 **Tel** and **Fax** 01725 517248 **English Heritage Register** Grade II* **Owner** Viscount and Viscountess Cranborne **Open** Mar to Sept, Wed 9–5 **Area** 10 acres/4 hectares

DARTINGTON HALL

NOBLE GARDENS WITH EXCELLENT TREES AND SHRUBS FOR A MAGNIFICENT MEDIEVAL HOUSE

Dartington Hall is a beautiful 14th-century house at the heart of an estate which was bought in 1925 by Leonard and Dorothy Elmhirst who were filled with idealistic plans for the regeneration of the rural economy and for education. They restored the medieval house, created distinguished new gardens while preserving the earlier landscape, and commissioned new architecture in the very latest International Modern style in the grounds. All this makes Dartington a most exciting place to visit.

The garden, to the west of the house, lies in a beautiful undulating site; at its centre are the curious and dramatic grassy terraces of the Tournament Ground with its row of twelve apostles – tall clipped yews. The origins of the Tournament Ground are obscure; it has been

described as a medieval "tilting yard" but is much more likely to date from the early 18th century and is probably related to similar turf terraces at Bicton Park (*see page 20*) and the amphitheatre at Claremont Park (*see page 129*).

In refashioning the gardens the Elmhirsts had the advice of three people: H. Avray Tipping, Percy Cane and Beatrix Farrand. The work they did is not only harmonious but also makes the best of the existing landscape. Tipping's work was chiefly to do with preserving and enhancing the existing fine features, like the Tournament Ground, for which Percy Cane devised two breathtaking stone staircases. Both have shallow steps of York stone which follow the descending slopes of the turf terraces and are generously broad – anything narrower would have looked mean in this setting. Cane's planting is skilfully chosen – one flight of steps is edged with waves of epimediums with cream, pink and yellow azaleas rising above; the other is overshadowed by huge old specimens of *Magnolia × soulangeana* and its dark-purple flowered cultivar 'Lennei'. On the sloping land above the Tournament Ground the planting is informal, of a woodland kind, and here

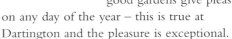

Henry Moore's Reclining Woman

Grass terraces at Dartington Hall

Beatrix Farrand made long walks that follow the contours of the land, and lined them with camellias or rhododendrons.

Everywhere there are memorable plantings: fine specimens of Chinese dogwoods (especially *Cornus kousa*), *Davidia involucrata* and *Cercidiphyllum japonicum*; beautiful groups of Chinese crab-apples (*Malus hupehensis*), an exuberant froth of white blossom in spring; an aristocratic procession of venerable sweet chestnuts with, at their end, a Henry Moore bronze of a reclining woman gazing back into the woodland. There is nothing ungenerous or fiddly at Dartington; everything is of the right scale and character, taking its cue from the noble house and powerful landscape. All good gardens give pleasure on any day of the year – this is true at Dartington and the pleasure is exceptional.

Location Dartington, Totnes TQ9 6EL, Devon **OS** SX7962 2m NW of Totnes by A384 **Tel** and **Fax** 01803 862367 **English Heritage Register** Grade II* **Owner** Dartington Hall Trust **Open** daily dawn–dusk **Area** 30 acres/12 hectares

DUNSTER CASTLE

HIGH ON A WOODED HILL ON THE
SOMERSET COAST, TENDER PLANTS
FLOURISH ON THE CASTLE SLOPES

If you approach Dunster from the east along the coastal road, the A39, you will have a spectacular view of the castle rising on its wooded knoll across pastures. It is an ancient place, associated with one of the oldest Somerset families, the Luttrells, who still live in these parts. A castle was built here by the Norman Mohun family which sold the estate to Lady Elizabeth Luttrell in the 14th century. The present building dates from the 13th century but with many subsequent changes culminating in a comprehensive remodelling by the Victorian specialist in such things, Anthony Salvin. There was a medieval deer park here to the north-east of the castle but a new one was made south of the castle in the mid 18th century by Henry Fownes Luttrell, an area of pastures today but still marked "Deer Park" on the Ordnance Survey map. There was also a certain amount of picturesque landscaping done at this time, and north of the castle and no longer part of the estate there is a fine prospect tower, the castellated Conygar Tower, built in 1775 and commanding superb views east over the sea and the Bristol Channel.

The climate is very mild, the nearby coast well warmed by the Gulf Stream Drift, and the south and west slopes of the castle tor have an especially benign microclimate. The western terraces date back to at least the 18th century when they were planted as vineyards and since at least the mid 19th century a lemon trees has been cultivated here, planted out against the south wall of the castle and protected when necessary by movable lights.

Conygar Tower from the Castle

The slopes below the castle walls are today densely planted with shrubs, with much self-sown laurustinus, and with paths ambling along the contours. The drainage is sharp and the south terrace provides the perfect site for many other tender plants – the common mimosa (*Acacia dealbata*), the Mexican *Beschorneria yuccoides*, the shrimp bush (*Justicia brandegeeana*), olive trees and many others. The south-facing wall of the castle is clothed in such climbers as *Clianthus puniceus* (white and red), *Rosa banksiae* 'Lutea', *Solanum laxum* and thickets of such tender shrubs as *Salvia elegans* 'Scarlet Pineapple'. A National Collection of strawberry trees (*Arbutus*) is kept here, with 9 species and 6 cultivars. The Keep Garden to the west of the castle – a bowling green in the 18th century – is overlooked by an octagonal gazebo. There are good shrubs here too: the tender *Acca sellowiana*, *Drimys winteri*, several magnolias, myrtles, pittosporums and the beautiful pink rose of wild Himalayan parentage, *Rosa* 'Anemone'. Not the least charm of this part of the garden is the delicious panoramic view that is to be had – of the castle park, the village and magnificent sea views opening out.

At the southern foot of the tor, along the banks of the river Avill, is a garden of quite different character. The Mill Walk, at the foot of vertiginous paths zigzagging down the castle ramparts, is a woodland garden which takes advantage of the lime-free soil to grow magnificent camellias, dogwoods, eucryphias, hydrangeas, pieris and rhododendrons, with much herbaceous underplanting of acanthus, comfrey, ferns, gunneras and hostas. The river is crossed by a picturesque 18th-century rustic bridge above a cascade.

Location Dunster, nr Minehead TA24 6SL, Somerset **OS** SS9943 3m SE of Minehead by A396 **Tel** 01643 821314 **Infoline** 01643 823004 **Fax** 01643 823000 **Email** dunstercastle@ntrust.org.uk **English Heritage Register** Grade I **Owner** The National Trust **Open** Jan to Mar, Oct to Dec, daily 11–4 (closed 25–29 Dec); Apr to Sept, daily 10–5 **Area** 17 acres/7 hectares

EAST LAMBROOK MANOR

MARGERY FISH'S VILLAGE GARDEN,
WELL RESTORED AND FULL OF THE
PLANTS SHE MADE FAMOUS

For anyone seeking to understand what is meant by a cottage garden East Lambrook Manor is an excellent starting place. Not, of course, that it is a cottage – it is a pretty, late Tudor manor house of modest size. But the style of gardening practised here, uninfluenced by any grand theories and enriched by an unpretentious love of plants, encapsulates the

The Mill Walk garden at Dunster

essential cottage garden ideal.

The garden history of the place starts in 1938 when Margery Fish came to live here with her redoubtable husband, Walter. They found "a poor battered old house…and a wilderness instead of a garden". She described their first steps in gardening in a most attractive book, *We Made a Garden* (1956), in which she explains that they wanted to make a garden that was "as much part of the house as possible".

A PRIVATE WORLD OF PLANTS

Today, more than thirty years after her death, the house is shrouded in plants and the garden seems keen to embrace it. The site undulates and there are virtually no straight lines – any path that sets off to follow a direct route finds its edges blurred with plants. There is no attempt at contrived formality; one of the few firm structural shapes is an irregular line of pollarded willows that rises in the ditch garden – home to a lovely profusion of essential Margery Fish plants. Here are hellebores (forms of *Helleborus* × *hybridus*), swathes of snowdrops (of which she had over 50 varieties in her day) and her beloved primroses, of which she rescued odd forms spotted in

Somerset hedgerows. Throughout the garden Margery Fish grew a bewildering range of plants, with the emphasis, no doubt through lack of space, on herbaceous perennials, paying great attention to siting them so that they had the best conditions in which to flourish. Although the garden is not an enormous one it gives the impression of much greater size because of the maze-like network of paths, many half-concealed nooks and crannies and no distant views. This is an inward-looking garden, concentrating the attention on the abundant planting and creating a microcosm isolated from the surrounding world. The present owners, the third since Margery Fish's death, maintain the garden as closely as possible to the tradition she established. They also have a valuable nursery attached to the garden with a good stock of Fish plants.

Location East Lambrook, South Petherton TA13 5HL, Somerset **OS** ST4318 2m N of South Petherton, signed from A303 **Tel** 01460 240328 **Fax** 01460 242344 **Email** enquiries@eastlambrook.com **Website** www.eastlambrook.com **English Heritage Register** Grade I **Owner** Mr and Mrs R. Williams **Open** Feb to Oct, daily 10–5 **Area** 1½ acres/0.6 hectares

The ditch garden at East Lambrook

THE EDEN PROJECT

A 21ST-CENTURY PHENOMENON – MAGNIFICENT GREENHOUSES AND A COLLECTION OF PLANTS WITH A MESSAGE

The Eden Project opened to the public in 2000 while it was still being built and opened fully, with planting in place, the following spring. At its heart are two immense greenhouses – "biomes" designed by Nicholas Grimshaw and Partners as mounded organic shapes – built of a pattern of hexagonal frames covered in a double film of ETFE (ethyltetrafluoroethylene). The larger of the two is 790ft/240m long, 180ft/55m high and 370ft/110m wide. Two climates are housed – a humid tropical climate and a warm temperate climate, each containing characteristic plants from appropriate regions. It was announced in 2003 that a third dome is to be built.

The biomes nestle against the south-facing wall of a former china clay pit whose slopes are landscaped, to the designs of Land Use Consultants, with sweeping shapes of planting, partly ornamental and partly educational. Many useful plants (hemp, indigo, tea, hops and so forth) are grown, together with plants

The Eden Project biomes

have been fairly successful. Does the Project, as he hopes, tell "the story of mankind's dependency on the plant world"? Yes, it does. Will it (as the landscape architect Dominic Cole hopes) convince us that ideas such as conservation and sustainability are obvious needs "rather than heavyweight political or academic relics". Who knows?

Location Bodelva, St Austell PL24 2SG, Cornwall **OS** SX0555 1½m NE of St Austell, signed off A390 **Tel** 01726 811911 **Fax** 01726 811912 **Website** www.edenproject.com **Owner** The Eden Trust **Open** Mar to Oct, daily 10–6; Nov to Feb, daily 10–4.30 (closed 24 and 25 Dec) **Area** 37 acres/15 hectares

EDMONDSHAM HOUSE

AN ORGANIC KITCHEN GARDEN WITH SPLENDID BORDERS FOR A FINE GEORGIAN HOUSE

House, garden and outhouses at Edmondsham seem to share a similar spirit and belong to the same world. Far removed from the business-like heritage industry, Edmondsham House is simply a house where someone lives and follows a certain way of life.

The house is enchanting, with two façades of quite different character. A crisp, pedimented Georgian façade faces you as you enter, and round the corner, at right angles to this, is a gabled Tudor or Jacobean façade with ornate gables and projecting bays. The stable block, no less delightful, is late Victorian, built in 1894 of pale pink, grey or cream brick and roofed in small clay tiles. It is embellished with a clock and crowned with a bellcote and weather vane. Modest but attractive outhouses behind the house have space for storing logs, and a pretty hexagonal dairy with patterns of differently shaped roof tiles has louvred windows and several milking stools inside. This is a very domestic world of which the kitchen garden – quite close to the house – is at the heart. One acre/0.4 hectares in area, it is enclosed in fine brick and cob walls, and although restored kitchen gardens have become fashionable in recent times this well-kept garden has none of the rather self-conscious character of so many born-again kitchen gardens.

typical of different regions (Cornwall; the steppes; prairies and so on). The purpose of the Eden Project goes well beyond the usual motives for making a garden. It was the intention here "to provide a living theatre of plants and people"; in the words of Tim Smit, whose idea the Eden Project was and who masterminded its astonishing fruition, "Eden isn't so much a destination as a place in the heart." Its purpose is to divert, instruct and inspire. These are rare aspirations for a garden and indeed it is rare enough that any garden maker has such an explicit programme.

THE BIOMES REVEALED

The biomes are sunk into the china pit so as to be invisible from afar. Their revelation, clustered and gleaming below, is a thrilling sight. The curved visitor centre (also designed by Nicholas Grimshaw and Partners), clad in cedar shingles, sweeps along a contour facing across the pit towards the biomes. Between the two, curved patterns of plantings and paths firmly relate the buildings to their site,

making agreeable spaces in which to wander, to scrutinise the plants and admire the shifting views of the remarkable buildings and their dramatic setting.

The interiors of the biomes are very different in character: the humid tropical zone has a naturalistic jungle air, with a waterfall plummeting through exotic foliage from a great height, a stream and a pool, all shrouded in dense vegetation; the warm temperate zone offers rather a series of vignettes – a group of different grapevines, for example, is disposed on a slope with a sculpture of Dionysus cavorting with his maenads (by Tim Shaw). Many other works of art embellish the biomes. Most plants are well labelled and placards explain their significance.

Anyone with the slightest interest in plants, or in remarkable environments, should not think twice about visiting the Eden Project. Tim Smit does not want it to be taken for "an upmarket theme park" and in this he seems to

Kitchen garden borders at Edmondsham

As you enter, you look down a west-facing double flower border which runs the whole length of the kitchen garden. There are very few fashionable plants here, certainly nothing trendy – cranesbills of several kinds, daylilies, delphiniums, foxtail lilies (*Eremurus* cultivars), lady's mantle, many herbaceous peonies, poppies and scabious. The occasional substantial woody plant – the statuesque *Rosa* 'Geranium' or a buddleia – gives authority, and the remains of a few ancient espaliered apple trees also add character. The rest of the walled garden, divided by a range of potting sheds and a gardener's bothy, is almost entirely devoted to produce – and the whole is gardened organically. There is a fruit-cage, asparagus bed, a range of greenhouses, a compost-making area and a bed for growing comfrey – a precious source of potash for the organic gardener.

There are other attractions at Edmondsham, among them a beautiful American black walnut (*Juglans nigra*) growing close to the kitchen garden wall, and good shrubs and trees about the main lawn in front of the house. But it is the unostentatious and charming kitchen garden, the sense of domestic productivity that surrounds the beautiful house and outhouses, that make Edmondsham so memorable.

Location Edmondsham, nr Wimborne Minster BH21 5RE, Dorset **OS** SU0612 9m N of Wimborne Minster by B3078 and minor roads **Tel** 01725 517207 **Owner** Mrs Julia E. Smith **Open** Apr to Oct, Wed, Sun and Bank Hol Mon 2–5 **Area** 6 acres/2.4 hectares

ENDSLEIGH HOUSE

IN THE LOVELY TAMAR VALLEY,
HUMPHRY REPTON'S MASTERLY
LANDSCAPE WITH MAGNIFICENT TREES

It would be worth travelling a long way to see anything as beautiful as Endsleigh. The upper Tamar valley, on the borders of Devon and Cornwall, is dramatically lovely country. It is famous among anglers, for this stretch of the river has some of the finest salmon fishing in England. The estate here had belonged in the middle ages to Tavistock Abbey and passed to the Russell family (later Dukes of Bedford) in the early 16th century, at the time of the dissolution of the monastic estates. The Russells never lived here, merely farming the land, until the early 19th century when the 6th Duke decided to build a cottage *orné* to the designs of Jeffry Wyatt (or Wyattville as he later became). Wyatt designed a dazzlingly picturesque house with gables, frilly bargeboards, rustic verandahs and stone mullioned windows. It is long, low and of irregular plan, hugging the contours of the land and taking every advantage of the exquisite southerly views down to the wooded river. William White described it in 1850 as "a beautiful occasional seat…delightfully situated in the picturesque valley of the Tamar, in the midst of sylvan pleasure grounds". Wyatt also designed a series of enchanting estate buildings of picturesque character.

REPTON'S PICTURESQUE MAGIC
The house was completed in 1810 and a little later Humphry Repton was asked to advise. In 1814 he produced a Red Book for Endsleigh, the last of the surviving examples. In it he emphasised the beauties of "that line of River which constitutes the leading feature of the Place by an interrupted continuity of glitter". He devised terraces to the south-east of the house and laid out a pattern of paths from which beautiful views are exposed across the valley. In the woods on the far bank of the river a cottage was placed as an eyecatcher. It is said that Repton, to complete the effect of picturesque domesticity, desired a perpetual plume of smoke from its chimney, so a fire was kept continually burning well into the 20th century. The visitor today may follow his paths and saunter along his terraces and the views are, without exaggeration, breathtakingly

Endsleigh House in the Tamar valley

lovely. Repton recognised the unique beauty of the place and displayed it with the humility that only great designers possess. In recent years the terraced garden with a herbaceous border, tunnel-arbour of clematis and roses and yew walk have all been restored. At its eastern end, also restored, is a hexagonal gazebo-like early 19th-century grotto with an elaborate vaulted interior of exotic shells, coral quartz and other minerals, niches with benches and stained-glass windows. Outside it is a viewing platform commanding one of the best views of the valley.

Endsleigh also has a remarkable collection of trees, planted later in the 19th century. These are for the most part in a sheltered subsidiary valley, running north of Wyatt's delicious Dairy Cottage and protected from the strongest winds. Others, in particular notable conifers, are planted on the valley slopes south-east of the house. Fourteen of the trees are "champion" specimens, the largest examples of their species in the country; among these are the tallest katsura (*Cercidiphyllum japonicum*) at 80ft/25m and the tallest tiger tail spruce (*Picea torano*) at 95ft/29m.

Location Milton Abbot, Tavistock PL19 0PQ, Devon **OS** SX3978 4m NW of Tavistock on B3362 **Tel** 01822 870248 **Fax** 01822 870502 **English Heritage Register** Grade I **Owner** Endsleigh Charitable Trust **Open** Apr to Sept, Fri to Tue, 11–5; also by appointment **Area** 196 acres/79 hectares

UNIVERSITY OF EXETER

A HISTORICAL SETTING FOR A 20TH-CENTURY UNIVERSITY, WITH FINE PLANTING AND SCULPTURES

The University of Exeter has its origins in a group of colleges which became the University College of South-West England in 1922 and a fully independent university in 1955. It acquired land and buildings in a piecemeal fashion, one of which is a fine Italianate mansion, Reed Hall (originally called Streatham Hall), which had been built for Richard Thornton West, an East India merchant, around 1860. West employed Robert Veitch of the Exeter firm of nurserymen to

Barbara Hepworth's Figure for Landscape

design and plant his garden – the cost was £70,000 [£3,010,000 today]. This house, the fine remains of its garden and many superlative trees, lie at the heart of the Streatham Campus, the main campus of the university. The oldest building on the site, however, at its extreme north-western corner, is Thomas Hall, formerly known as Great Duryard, built in the late 17th century. Here are some specimens of the Lucombe oak (*Quercus* × *hispanica* 'Lucombeana'), the beautiful form of evergreen oak discovered by the Exeter nurseryman William Lucombe in the 1760s; these trees are said to survive from his original grafts. Such old features give depth and character to the landscape and these, together with imaginative newer planting by the university, make this one of the most attractive of all 20th-century university campuses.

FINE PLANTS AND SCULPTURES

The undulating site is high and airy and the climate mild with fairly low rainfall. Many of the more recent plantings have taken advantage of this – tender trees and shrubs include acacias, *Albizia julibrissin*, callistemons, eucalyptus and much else. At the centre of the campus some notable plant catches the eye at every turn. On Streatham Drive, for example, close to an ornamental pool, is a splendid trio of trees – an oriental plane, an English oak and

a holm oak – none rare but all magnificent, while immediately south of Reed Hall excellent trees, in particular conifers, survive from Richard Thornton West's arboretum planted in the 1860s – fine specimens of sometimes rare trees, such as the Turkish black pine (*Pinus nigra* var. *caramanica*) with branches dividing low down and a striking scaly bark. In the more open area to the south, overlooked by Queen's Building, Barbara Hepworth's Figure for Landscape (1960) is seen to great advantage among the trees – one of several sculptures adorning buildings and landscape by such artists as Michael Ayrton, Richard Kindersley and Henry Moore. Other parts of the campus have a more intimate character. Immediately behind Queen's Building is a densely planted area with an *Arbutus menziesii*, two fine *Zelkova carpinifolia* and a *Sophora microphylla*. If only other 20th-century universities took such an interest in their landscape setting!

Location Northcote House, The Queen's Drive, Exeter EX4 4QJ, Devon **OS** SX9194 1m NW of the centre of Exeter by A377, close to St David's railway station **Tel** 01392 263146 **Fax** 01392 263060 **Email** s.d.franklin@exeter.ac.uk **Owner** The University of Exeter **Open** daily dawn–dusk **Area** 400 acres/162 hectares

FORDE ABBEY

WONDERFULLY ROMANTIC HOUSE WITH THE COMPLETE GARDEN – BORDERS, TREES, WATER GARDEN AND SUPERB KITCHEN GARDEN

Forde is an unforgettable place – the remains of a Cistercian abbey started in the 12th century, onto which were grafted in the mid 17th century an elaborate castellated mansion with a dashing Italianate loggia. Built of golden Ham stone, it lies low in the valley of the river Axe, pinned down by avenues which follow lines already established in the early 18th century. Although the garden today is almost entirely of the 20th century, largely created by Geoffrey Roper, the present owner's father, it is given depth and richness by features from the past. South-west of the house a canal on an east-west axis, the Long Pond, dates from the early 18th century.

The Long Pond at Forde Abbey

Mixed borders along its north side, punctuated by a procession of clipped yew columns, are filled in late summer with an explosion of dahlias. A grassy walk rises among trees to a statue of Diana the Huntress silhouetted against the sky. A modern neo-classical domed rotunda above a cascade marks the head of the Long Pond, whose south bank in February is a tapestry of crocuses and wild daffodils (*Narcissus pseudonarcissus*) which still grow in Dorset meadows.

An avenue of limes and American black walnuts (*Juglans nigra*), following the early 18th-century axis, marches south across the garden into the fields that rise gently above it. A former 18th-century Wilderness has a series of pools with much good planting, culminating in the Great Pond which is overlooked by a rare and enchanting pavilion of pleached beech (making a perfect hide for bird watchers). A bog garden is rich in Asiatic primulas, *Gunnera manicata*, ferns and the

skunk cabbage (*Lysichiton americanus*).

Below the north walls of the abbey lies one of the great glories of Forde – the walled kitchen garden. This is kept up to old country-house standards, nothing flashy and a far cry from the fashionable *potager*. Great quantities of varied fruit and vegetables are skilfully cultivated and standards of maintenance are impeccable – a thrilling sight. A pair of borders, filled with late summer flowers, perennials and annuals, runs down the central path, and the beautiful old walls of the 13th-century monks' dormitory protect the east side. The garden has a further attraction – a high class nursery of well-chosen plants.

Location nr Chard TA20 4LU, Somerset **OS** ST3505 3m SE of Chard by B3162 and minor roads **English Heritage Register** Grade II* **Owner** Mark Roper **Open** daily 10–4.30 **Area** 30 acres/12 hectares

THE GARDEN HOUSE

REMARKABLE PLANTSMAN'S GARDEN IN AN IDYLLIC DARTMOOR SETTING WITH EXCELLENT PLANTING

The garden was the creation of an intrepid retired schoolmaster, Lionel Fortescue, who came here in 1945. The charm of the place comes from its fine setting on the edge of Dartmoor, with its distant prospect of the tower of St Andrew's church rising above blowsy trees, and an atmospheric old walled enclosure built on a slope with terracing. Here are the ruins of an early 16th-century house built for the abbot of Buckland Abbey, a square tower with stone mullioned windows. At 400ft/120m above sea level the climate can be harsh here – the temperature fell to −15°C/5°F in the winter of 1979/80, killing anything slightly tender in the garden, including every ceanothus. However, the walls

do provide protection, and this was enhanced by planting windbreaks.

Fortescue's ambition was to unite a sense of design with discerning plantsmanship and his success in doing this may be seen today. Just before his death in 1981 he wrote, "Owing to

limited space available, the qualifying test for plants has to be severe. We search for the best forms and pay great attention to our grouping for colour, form and foliage." Before his death he had already recruited as his gardener Keith Wiley, who remains here and has maintained the tradition of the garden and expanded it with new interests. The walled garden still forms the garden's heart and here the essential layout has scarcely been altered. A grass path makes a strong axis in the lower part of the garden, linking gates in the walls. Here, and on the slopes above, is a vast range of plants taking advantage of microclimates and the fluctuation in the acidity of the soil – alkaline at the bottom and acid at the top. Substantial shrubs provide shapely structure in the profusion – a pair of *Eucryphia × nymansensis* 'Nymansay', magnolias, the beautiful *Hoheria* 'Glory of Amlwch'.

◁ **The Garden House** walled garden

To the west of the walled garden Keith Wiley has made a new garden – now far larger than Lionel Fortescue's original creation – with a raised bed of creeping thyme, sedums and white and purple-flowered rhodohypoxis, a "ruined" cottage garden with a spectacular spread of appropriate plants, and a 300ft/90m long sweeping glade of Japanese maples. More than 7,000 different species and cultivars are grown here, some of which are available in the nursery attached to the garden. Plantsmanship remains the paramount interest, together with high standards of horticulture. It remains, as it was in Fortescue's day, strongly idiosyncratic.

Location Buckland Monachorum, Yelverton
PL20 7LQ, Devon **OS** SX4968 5m S of Tavistock
by A386 **Tel** 01822 854769 **Fax** 01822 855358
Email office@thegardenhouse.org.uk **Website**
www.thegardenhouse.org.uk **Owner** The Fortescue
Garden Trust **Open** Mar to Oct, daily 10.30–5
Area 8 acres/3.2 hectares

THE GEORGIAN GARDEN

CHARMING RECONSTRUCTED 18TH-
CENTURY GARDEN WITH PERIOD
PLANTING FOR A GEORGIAN HOUSE

The garden lies behind 4 The Circus, designed by John Wood the Elder and built between 1754 and 1758, but is approached by the Gravel Walk which runs behind the south-west side of the Circus. It is a typical Bath town garden, a sliver of ground enclosed in stone walls immediately behind the house. The Bath Archaeological Trust excavated the site in 1990 and laid bare the original layout of a garden dating back to between 1761 and 1770. With the advice of Dr John Harvey a garden was reinstated to follow the historic layout, using only plants known to have been available at the time.

A RARE TOWN GARDEN

It is a beautiful and rare sight, quite unlike any other 18th-century garden that we may see today. Most reconstructed historical gardens belong to grand houses, usually in the country, but here is something quite unfamiliar: a small town garden of the sort that must have been common in its day but which scarcely survives. Borders run down each side of the garden, filled with hibiscus, irises, laurustinus, peonies, rosemary and thalictrum. Apples and figs are trained against the walls and strips of paving run along the edges of the borders. The centre of the garden is a rectangle of hoggin with three beds (two circles and one oval), edged with box and planted with such old roses as *Rosa gallica* 'Versicolor' and *R.* 'Maiden's Blush'. An

An **18th-century seat** in the Georgian Garden

intricately wrought 18th-century style wooden bench is partly bowered in roses.

In the 18th century the garden was thought of chiefly as an ornament to be viewed from the windows of the house rather than as an extension of the living quarters. Today, close to the busy shopping streets of Bath, this is a delightful retreat which adds a new dimension to our understanding of how people lived and gardened in the 18th century.

Location Gravel Walk, Bath BA1 2EW, Somerset
OS ST7465 In the centre of Bath close to The Circus
Tel 01225 477752 **Email**
costume_enquiries@bathnes.gov.uk **Owner** Bath
Museum Services **Open** May to Oct, Mon to Fri except
Bank Hol Mon 9–4.30 **Area** ¼ acre/0.1 hectare

GLENDURGAN GARDEN

EARLY 19TH-CENTURY WOODLAND
GARDEN WITH SUPERB TREES AND
SHRUBS AND A FINE MAZE

The great gardening family of Fox made the garden at Glendurgan, taking every advantage of the wonderful site – a ravine irrigated by streams that plunges southwards to the fishing village of Durgan. Alfred Fox came here in the 1820s and gradually cleared the ground and planted windbreaks, especially of the maritime pine, *Pinus pinaster*. Alfred Fox used part of the gardens as an orchard but gradually he, and his son George who inherited in 1891, began to introduce the ornamental exotics, especially camellias and rhododendrons, for which the garden became famous. An early surviving feature from Alfred's time, supposedly planted in 1833, is the irregular maze of cherry laurel with its winding walks and thick rounded hedges. It looms up dramatically, spread out on its slope, the only piece of topiary in the whole garden.

Glendurgan was given to the National Trust in 1962 and the Fox family continues to live in the house.

PLANTS RELISH THE BENIGN CLIMATE

Streams feed many pools that run along the bottom of the valley, crossed from time to time by decorative bridges. Here, enough space is given to plants for their character to

The ravine at Glendurgan

be displayed; on the slopes above, the planting is far more dense though frequently enlivened by the brilliant colour of some flowering shrub. The camellia walk at the head of the valley contains specimens going back to the 19th century; old cultivars such as *C. japonica* 'Preston Rose' and 'Ville de Nantes' were probably planted by George Fox. The climate is remarkably benign and many tender plants grow superbly – *Michelia doltsopa*, with its waxy cream flowers; a conifer, *Cupressus cashmeriana*, with wonderfully graceful tumbling cascades of ferny foliage, and the myrtle *Luma apiculata* with its cream and coffee bark.

Like most old gardens in the south-west,

Glendurgan lost many trees in the storm of 1990. There is little sign of that today, with much replanting among the surviving older specimens which give the place its rare character. It is rich in the characteristic Cornish flowering shrubs but it has much else, including a stupendous old tulip tree (*Liriodendron tulipifera*) with gnarled and mossy bark and widespread branches.

Location Helford River, Mawnan Smith, nr Falmouth TR11 5JZ, Cornwall **OS** SW7727 4m SW of Falmouth on road to Helford Passage **Tel** 01326 250906 (opening hours only) or 01872 862090 **Fax** 01872 865808 **Email** glendurgan@ntrust.org.uk **English Heritage Register** Grade II **Owner** The National Trust **Open** end Feb to end Oct, Tue to Sat (open Bank Hol Mon; closed Good Fri) 10.30–5.30 **Area** 25 acres/10 hectares

GNOME RESERVE

THE PRIVATE RETREAT OF A COMMUNITY OF GNOMES IN A WOODLAND SETTING

I realise that gnomes are treated with the greatest contempt by most right-thinking gardeners. Indeed, it is said that the Royal Horticultural Society refuses them admission to the Chelsea Flower Show. However, there is another, pretty numerous, body of gardeners who treasure them, and anyone driving about the country will spy them (gnomes I mean) occupying positions of greater or lesser importance in many a front garden. Here at the Gnome Reserve – the very name of which suggests a threatened race – they find a happy home where they are not merely tolerated but given pride of place. A community numbering over 1,000 live in bosky comfort here in North Devon, doing their gnomely thing, cushioned in moss or masked by ivy in the shade of handsome old beeches. Gravel paths wind through the woods and the visitor may find it easy to succumb to the enchanted atmosphere. Pointed felt hats are issued to make humans seem more congenial to the natives. A gnome museum traces their long history and new gnomes are produced in large quantities on the premises and may be watched as they are given their gleaming sets of clothes. To one side the 2-acre/0.8-hectare Pixies' Wildflower Garden displays over 250 native plants arranged in naturalistic habitats.

I have never been able to make up my mind how seriously the owner takes her subject. The best approach for the visitor is to keep an open mind and enjoy whatever it is that seems enjoyable. For better or for worse gnomes are part of garden history and it is hard to imagine them being more sympathetically displayed than they are here.

The head gardener at the Gnome Reserve

Location West Putford, nr Bradworthy EX22 7XE, Devon **OS** SS3616 7½m N of Holsworthy by A388 and minor roads (follow rose sign) **Tel** and **Fax** 01409 241435 **Email** gnomereserve@enterprise.net **Open** late Mar to Oct, daily 10–6 **Area** 4 acres/1.6 hectares

GREENCOMBE

AN EXCEPTIONAL GARDENER'S WORLD IN AN EXQUISITE SETTING OVERLOOKING PORLOCK BAY

In the end all the best gardens are made by a single person. That person may build on what others have done in the past but it is the individual inspiration, and the intimate understanding of the site, that creates the distinctive sense of place that makes an exceptional garden. The garden at Greencombe was started in 1946 by Horace Stroud who terraced the ground about the house and made the lawn that lies at the heart of the formal gardens. He also acquired the ancient woodland west of the garden, which was threatened with destruction, and began to plant distinguished trees and shrubs. In 1966 house and garden were acquired by Joan Loraine, an outstanding gardener who has made it a most remarkable place.

A DRAMATIC SITE

The garden has a curious site on north-facing slopes in a notably balmy part of the country, close to the sea at Porlock. This is the point at which Exmoor plummets dramatically into the Bristol Channel, across which there are marvellous views of the hills of Wales. Rainfall is around 40in/100cm per annum, the soil is acid and hard frosts are rare. Although the house is 20th-century the site is ancient, with woodland of great antiquity to the west of the house, with old holly trees, English oaks and coppiced sweet chestnut. Between the woods and the 13th-century former Porlock deer park below, the deer leap, or "gut", is still visible.

Miss Loraine is deeply knowledgeable about plants and gardening. There is an

Greencombe is a whole world and Miss Loraine gardens in accordance with firmly held beliefs about the environment. She rid the garden of honey fungus by digging up and disposing of every affected plant and burning on sight every trace of spore. She makes tons of compost every year, taking its temperature periodically to make sure it achieves sufficient heat to destroy weed seeds. (I have never seen such compost – it is as rich and friable as the finest chocolate cake.) Few gardens are as well gardened as Greencombe and few take advantage of the site to such marvellous effect.

For the millennium Miss Loraine commissioned a new building, the Chapel of our Lady of the Secret, which stands at the western extremity of the wood. Circular in shape, it is beautifully built of sweet chestnut wood taken from a tree at Greencombe. Inside is a fine carving of a mother and child, also in sweet chestnut, by Tom Preater.

Location Porlock TA24 8NU, Somerset   **OS** SS8747 ½m W of Porlock by road to Porlock Weir   **Tel** 01643 862363   **Owner** Miss Joan Loraine   **Open** Apr to Jul, Oct to Nov, Sat to Wed 2–6   **Area** 3½ acres/1.4 hectares

HADSPEN GARDENS

AN 18TH-CENTURY WALLED KITCHEN GARDEN WITH LIVELY PLANTING IN COLOUR-THEMED BORDERS

Hadspen is a fine late 18th-century house looking south over pastures and protected to the north by old woodland. The old garden was essentially of Victorian and Edwardian character when Penelope Hobhouse took it in hand in the 1960s. She sharpened the structure of the garden and immensely increased the range and quality of plants grown, helped by the plantsman Eric Smith – noted for his hellebores and hostas – who started a nursery here.

The part of the garden accessible to visitors today is the walled former kitchen garden at a little distance from the house, and an adjacent area with a large water tank backed by a high wall. All this was replanned by Penelope Hobhouse and remodelled after Nori and Sandra Pope came to garden here in 1987.

The Popes have kept up high standards of

easy flow of movement within the garden but this is, supremely, a place for plants, and everywhere one has the impression of plants flourishing – in the right sites and well cared for. Joan Loraine benefited from having as her neighbour Norman Hadden, a great connoisseur of plants, from whom she received many cuttings and seeds. She greatly developed the terraced garden close to the house before turning her attention westwards into the woods where the gardens become increasingly wild.

Sweeping lawns and terraces frame the house and here the planting is intricate – mossy stones edge beds of shrubs and trees which are densely underplanted with ferns, hellebores, hostas, primulas and violas. Camellias, of which there is an admirable range, are finely used not like exhibits in a beauty show but as the lovely garden plants they are. There are also skilful contrasts of shape among larger plants – for example, a

The woodland garden at Greencombe

columnar Lawson cypress challenging a sprawling hummock of a Japanese maple.

THE WOODLAND GARDEN

The woodland parts of the garden have marvellous acers, magnolias and rhododendrons. A National Collection of erythroniums (22 species and 24 cultivars), whose native habitats include California, southern Europe, China and Japan, finds a magnificent home here. Another National Collection held here is that of polystichum ferns (24 species, 100 cultivars). More specialised are the National Collections of gaultherias (including pernettyas – 45 species and 7 cultivars) and of vacciniums (44 species, 7 cultivars). All these exotics consort well with the native wood anemones, bluebells, celandines and scillas that ornament the mossy woods with their natural beauty.

A hot border at Hadspen

plantsmanship and in the borders in the kitchen garden have introduced fastidious colour combinations using shrubs, climbers, herbaceous perennials and annuals deployed with great skill. The kitchen garden is unusual in shape, roughly like a horseshoe, with the higher curved part facing south to trap the sun. An axial path, partly lined with beech

hedges, is planted with creams and yellows with much contrast of foliage – waves of hostas lap the path, with the strong shapes of achillea, eryngium, fennel and hollyhock rising above. Parts of the garden are given over to the growing of fruit and vegetables which are disposed in formal patterns. In the water tank garden borders are rich in campanulas, penstemons and salvias, and tender climbers clothe the walls. From the top of the garden there are views down onto lavish plantings on the far side of the tank – of *Gunnera manicata*, ornamental grasses, bold-leafed hostas and rodgersias, of which Hadspen holds a National Collection. A nursery with good plants is still maintained, some of them cultivars bearing the Hadspen name. The one sorrow at Hadspen is that the garden visitor sees no connection with the house. Close to the house Penelope Hobhouse, in conjunction with her son Niall, has introduced some bold formal planting of trees and shrubs, and fashioned a splendid turf terrace to its east.

Location nr Castle Cary BA7 7NG, Somerset
OS ST6531 2m SE of Castle Cary by A371 **Tel** and **Fax** 01749 813707 **Owner** Niall Hobhouse **Open** Mar to Oct, Thur to Sun and Bank Hol Mon 10–5
Area 5 acres/2 hectares

HEADLAND

WINDY CLIFF-TOP GARDEN ON THE FOWEY ESTUARY, OF RARE CHARM AND CHARACTER

When all is said and done, it is the site that determines the possibilities of a garden, and Headland demonstrates this more vividly than any garden I know. The garden clings to the top of a rocky cliff high on the eastern headland above the estuary of the river Fowey. The views westwards across the estuary to the village of Fowey and along the coast beyond it to Gribbin Head are lovely. Good views frequently mean exposure to the elements but seldom so dramatically as at Headland, where violent winds from the west or south-west will hurl salt water spray against the very windows of the house high up above the sea. Although cold weather is rare here, when it is cold the wind chill factor can be devastating to plants. *Euonymus japonicus*, for example, that evergreen plant impervious to

The cliff-edge garden at Headland

salt and universally used for hedging in coastal gardens, may lose its leaves here in an icy winter blast. Other stalwarts of coastal gardens such as the Monterey pine (*Pinus radiata*) and Monterey cypress (*Cupressus macrocarpa*) also suffer grievously in the wind. From Headland you can see, a little way up the estuary, a more protected garden where finer specimens of these trees have grown to twice the height. Given these fearsome limitations, what kind of garden can be made in such a place?

PLANTS FOR A COASTAL SETTING

Jagged stone outcrops mottled or bearded with lichen form a beautiful backdrop to the garden. Terraces with stone walls are linked by precipitous steps and paths of gravel or paving stones. Some shrubs do seem impervious to salt and wind, among them arbutus, cistus, hebes, the prostrate form of rosemary which tumbles decoratively over rocks, the sweetly scented *Pittosporum tobira*, santolina and

olearias. Among herbaceous plants, for the most part low-growing and more easily protected, are hardy aeoniums, erigerons, geraniums, lampranthus and periwinkles. Indeed, any protection from the wind transforms the possibilities for plant life. In the lee of the battered Monterey pines are surprisingly healthy shrubs of camellia and rhododendron which would stand no chance if fully exposed to the wind.

Any coastal gardener who wants to learn more will relish Headland. Others, except those with the slightest susceptibility to vertigo, will enjoy the unusual charm of the place and its sublime views.

Location Battery Lane, Polruan-by-Fowey PL23 1PW, Cornwall **OS** SW1351 In the centre of Polruan. Park in the main car park and walk down St Saviour's Hill, turning left at T junction **Tel** 01726 870243 **Email** hilljap@aol.com **Owner** Mrs Jean Hill **Open** May to mid Sept, Thur 2–6 **Area** ¾ acre /0.3 hectare

HELIGAN

NOTABLE 19TH-CENTURY CORNISH PLANTSMAN'S GARDEN BROUGHT BACK TO LIFE IN AN EPIC FEAT OF RESTORATION

When the restoration of this garden started, and it opened to the public, it was called the Lost Gardens of Heligan. However, since its immense success as a star of TV and books, and with its huge number of visitors (more than any other garden in Cornwall until the opening of the Eden Project), it is perhaps time to revert to its plainer name – few gardens look less lost. Yet only a cynic would criticise Heligan's success. The plain fact is that it is a fine and interesting garden, and the publicity that Tim Smit generated for it has done the cause of garden conservation a great deal of good and

The jungle garden at Heligan

is an extraordinary, and attractive, example of the possibilities of private initiative.

The estate belongs to the ancient Tremayne family which had lived at St Martin in Meneage on the Helford River since the 15th century. Sampson Tremayne bought Heligan in 1569 and the first signs of garden activity appeared a hundred years later when a walled garden was built in front of the house. Here, according to a surviving plan, John Tremayne laid out in 1735 an elaborate garden of parterres, distinctly old-fashioned and delightful. All this was removed when the grounds were landscaped in the 1770s. In the early 19th century John Hearle Tremayne started the tradition of plant collecting which earned Heligan its reputation. In 1825 he received seed of the tender Himalayan dogwood *Cornus capitata* which had been discovered by Nathaniel Wallich in Nepal in 1821. Some of the trees he raised survive to this day. John's son and grandson continued the plant collecting throughout the 19th century, receiving seeds from J.D. Hooker's Himalayan expedition of 1847–50. One of the grandest of all rhododendrons, *R. sinogrande*, discovered by George Forrest in 1912, first flowered in Cornwall at Heligan in 1919. Later in the 20th century things stood still at Heligan until, after World War II, they dramatically declined, and eventually gardening ceased altogether. In 1991 the restoration of the by now completely overgrown garden began, supervised by Tim Smit and his colleagues.

THE EXCEPTIONAL JUNGLE GARDEN

Smit's great genius is as a motivator of people and as a marketeer of epic stature. Heligan is an attractive garden, not in the first division horticulturally but with plenty to admire. There is no evidence, historical or visual, that it was ever the work of a great designer. The jungle garden, however, with its watery ravine filled with bamboos, tall tree ferns and gigantic specimens of unusual trees — *Toona sinensis*, *Pinus thunbergii* and *Podocarpus totara* — has exceptional character and beauty. The rest of the site is flat — very flat as Cornish gardens go — with some good trees and very large clumps of cultivars of *Rhododendron arboreum*. Here, the most memorable features are the

beautiful kitchen garden and ancillary garden buildings — the wall of bee-skeps, the potting shed, the fully restored and fully working pineapple pit and melon house.

Location nr Megavissey, St Austell OL26 6EN, Cornwall **OS** SW9946 4m S of St Austell by B3273 **Tel** 01726 845100 **Fax** 01726 845101 **Email** info@heligan.com **Website** www.heligan.com **English Heritage Register** Grade II **Owner** Heligan Gardens Ltd **Open** daily 10–6 **Area** 57 acres/23 hectares

BARBARA HEPWORTH MUSEUM AND SCULPTURE GARDEN

THE PRIVATE AND IDIOSYNCRATIC GARDEN OF A GREAT ARTIST

Gardens made by artists often have a special atmosphere. Although not necessarily of any particular horticultural interest they are, nonetheless, the products of exceptional visual sensitivity and take on a special interest in relation to the artist's work. The Trewyn Studio in the heart of St Ives was bought by the sculptor Barbara Hepworth in 1949. On her death in 1975 she asked her executors to explore the possibility "of establishing a permanent exhibition of some of [my] works in Trewyn Studio and its garden". This they have done and the place, diminutive and packed with plants and sculptures, has an extraordinarily powerful character. Much of the planting is bold and brassy with special emphasis on foliage — bamboos, cordylines, spires of *Echium pininana* and giant blades of New Zealand flax. Hepworth's sculptures, especially those of organic character, look splendid in this setting, far more beautiful than in the frigid featureless rooms of museums or dealers' galleries. The studio in which she worked has been left more or less as it was when she died, with her overalls hanging on a peg, chippings of white marble scattered on the floor, and tools ready to hand. I should find it hard to believe that anyone could visit this place and come away unmoved.

Location Trewyn Studio, Barnoon Hill, St Ives TR26 1TG, Cornwall **OS** SW5140 In the centre of St Ives **Tel** 01736 796226 **Fax** 01736 794480 **English Heritage**

A bronze in the Barbara Hepworth Garden

Register Grade II **Owner** The Tate Gallery **Open** Tue to Sun 10.30–5.30 (Jul and Aug, also open Mon) **Area** ¼ acre/0.1 hectare

HESTERCOMBE

A MASTERPIECE BY EDWIN LUTYENS AND GERTRUDE JEKYLL, AND A DELIGHTFUL 18TH-CENTURY LANDSCAPE GARDEN

The special interest of Hestercombe is that it offers two exceptionally attractive gardens, of completely different kinds yet subtly linked, for the price of one. To start with the more recent and more famous garden: in 1903 Edwin Lutyens was commissioned by the Hon. E.W.B. Portman to lay out a new garden. The site is a very beautiful one, commanding Elysian views of rural calm over the Vale of Taunton towards the Blackdown hills. Lutyens disapproved of the house, an awkward Victorian mansion that had replaced a pretty Queen Anne house. He therefore laid out the garden to make the best advantage of the rural views and distract the eye as far as possible from the house, creating a dazzlingly inventive pattern of garden spaces and subtle changes of level, with walls of Ham stone and paving of Morte slate, and delightful architectural detail.

At the heart of Lutyens's garden is the sunken Great Plat in the form of a giant square parterre overlooked by raised terraces. It is flanked by a pair of terraces with narrow rills cut into the paving. These run from beautifully fashioned niches and curved lily pools towards a rose-enshrouded pergola which gently frames views of the countryside. Above the Great Plat is a characteristic piece of Lutyens legerdemain: to make a harmonious link between two awkward axes he designed a circular enclosure with a circular pool – the Rotunda – clasped by high stone walls lined with winter-sweet (*Chimonanthus praecox*) and climbing roses. In winter the encircling walls trap any sun and intensify the delicious scent of the winter-sweet. Beyond lies the Dutch Garden, a deft parterre of lavender, roses, yuccas and lamb's ears and, like a triumphant trumpet blast, a dashing orangery in Lutyens's full blown "Wrenaissance" style.

All these architectural spaces are enriched by Gertrude Jekyll's bold and simple planting. Her favourite bergenias outline the divisions of the Great Plat; bushes of myrtle guard gateways; the sharply drained terraces are

Hestercombe's 18th-century Mausoleum

studded with cistus, rosemary, santolina and, everywhere, swags of Mexican daisy (*Erigeron karvinskianus*); a delightful arbour is fashioned of tightly clipped wych elm. This is no plantsman's garden – Miss Jekyll's original plans allowed for fewer than 300 different plants – but it is a brilliant display of what lay at the heart of her gardening: of using, as she recommended, "the best plants in the best places". Architecture and planting work together and make what is by Edwardian standards a modest space – only 1½ acres/0.6 hectares – seem wonderfully rich and varied. This masterpiece had been almost

irretrievably lost when the Somerset County Council took it on in 1973 and carried out a pioneer feat of faithful garden restoration, putting all garden lovers in its debt.

THE LOST GARDEN

The other garden at Hestercombe, an astonishing piece of rediscovery, is a miniature 18th-century landscape garden. It is glimpsed from Lutyens's Dutch Garden, framed in a gateway piercing a wall. Here a wooded combe cradling a lake rises to the north, with temples gleaming among the trees. Long known to more intrepid garden explorers, this was by 1995 a jungle of saplings and undergrowth when Philip White first saw it and, mesmerised by its beauty, resolved to launch a campaign to bring it back to life. The garden was created by Coplestone Warre Bampfylde who inherited the Hestercombe estate in 1750. With Henry Hoare II of Stourhead in Wiltshire (*see page 106*) and Sir Charles Kemeys Tynte of Halswell (*see page 484*) in Somerset, he was one of a trio of friends who were landowners and ardent gentleman landscapers. Bampfylde was a gifted amateur artist and his paintings of the garden at Stourhead and of his own park at Hestercombe give a vivid flavour of the great days of the landscape park. At Hestercombe he created a charming landscape, with a majestic cascade erupting from rocky crags, ornamental buildings on the slopes of the valley, and a serene pear-shaped lake at its foot. Today, once again, it resembles the views depicted in Bampfylde's own watercolours.

The 18th-century landscape garden presents an instructive and pleasurable contrast to the Lutyens and Jekyll garden of a hundred and fifty years later, and together they represent two of the most thrilling moments in English garden design – the serenely romantic landscape park and the harmonious, irrepressibly ingenious architectural garden enlivened with perfect planting.

Location Cheddon Fitzpaine, nr Taunton TA2 8LQ, Somerset **OS** ST2428 2m NE of Taunton off A361 **Tel** 01823 413923 **Website** www.hestercombegardens.com **English Heritage Register** Grade I **Owner** Somerset County Council/Hestercombe Garden Project Ltd **Open** daily 10–6 **Area** 50 acres/20 hectares

The Great Plat at Hestercombe

KILLERTON

SUPERB TREES AND SHRUBS ADORN A
NOBLE 18TH-CENTURY LANDSCAPE, WITH
A FINE FLOWER GARDEN

Fine trees are magnificently displayed at Killerton, rising from improbably perfect close-mown turf on the slopes about a late 18th-century mansion. The site is a splendid one for a garden, lying below the volcanic mound of Killerton Clump, with rich, fertile soil and rainfall that averages 36in/90cm per annum. The Acland family had lived in these parts for centuries and the gardens at Killerton were started by Sir Thomas Acland in the 1770s, shortly before he started work on rebuilding the 17th-century family house. In his garden making he was helped by John Veitch, the founding father of the great dynasty of nurserymen, who started his business at Budlake, quite close to Killerton, and later moved it to Exeter. The connection between the Aclands and the Veitches continued well into the 20th century. The Veitch nursery was one of the first to invest in plant-hunting expeditions, travelling themselves or financing others like William Lobb and E.H. Wilson to hunt on their behalf. Many of their discoveries made their way to Killerton and thus there are large numbers of early specimens of new

Spring at Killerton

introductions or uncontaminated species propagated from seed gathered in the wild. Such trees as the cork oak (*Quercus suber*) perform magnificently here, but everywhere you look you will see marvellous trees finely displayed: a lovely American horse chestnut (*Aesculus californica*), which first flowered in Veitch's Exeter nursery in 1858; the Japanese *Zelkova serrata*, another Veitch introduction; another exceptional tree from Japan, the walnut *Juglans ailanthifolia*; and, a tree of special local significance, the Lucombe oak (*Quercus × hispanica* 'Lucombeana') – Lucombe was a nurseryman in Exeter. These, many other rare, beautiful and venerable species and dozens of distinguished flowering shrubs, are seen here at their best – given plenty of breathing space and disposed on lawns as green as you will ever see.

ORNAMENTAL INTERLUDES

Trees and shrubs in a parkland setting are what make Killerton special, but there are also good ornamental interludes on a smaller scale. Close to the house decorative mixed borders with fine Coade stone urns are all that remains of a garden designed by William Robinson in about 1900. At a distance from the house an admirable rock garden is rich in camellias, Japanese maples, ferns, primulas and,

in late spring, the delicious scent of sheets of *Cyclamen repandum*. The Bear's Hut nearby is a rustic summerhouse out of Grimm's fairy tales, with a lavishly decorated interior of wickerwork, rattan and patterns of pine cones.

Location Broadclyst, Exeter EX5 3LE, Devon **OS** SY9700 5m NE of Exeter by B3181 and B3185; Jnct 28 of M5 **Tel** 01392 881345 **Fax** 01392 883112 **Email** killerton@ntrust.org.uk **English Heritage Register** Grade II* **Owner** The National Trust **Open** daily dawn–dusk **Area** 22 acres/9 hectares

KINGSTON LACY

FINE TREES AND MAGNIFICENT ORNAMENTS
FOR A GREAT HOUSE, WITH A PRETTY
19TH-CENTURY FERNERY

The house at Kingston Lacy was built in the 1660s for Sir Ralph Bankes and twice altered, most unhappily in the 1830s by Sir Charles Barry who seemed intent on making it look like a St James's club. In this he was not entirely successful and much of the beautiful Restoration house is still visible – especially if you do not raise your eyes to the attic floor. In 1982 the Bankeses gave the estate to the National Trust, which has restored both house and garden.

The garden is not a flowery place – it is best seen as a magnificent landscape setting for the house. South of the house a terrace and deep gravel walk are ornamented with pink stone urns supported on bronze tortoises, superb Venetian wellheads (planted with clipped bay) and a pair of bronze lions tussling with snakes. The only flowers visible are *Campsis radicans* neatly trained along the retaining wall of the terrace, underplanted with eyestopping scarlet pelargoniums. Southwards from here a great sweep of lawn opens out. On each side trees press in and, in the distance, an obelisk is centred on the house. The lawn, with its trees and ornaments, is essentially the work of William John Bankes. It was he who placed the obelisk here in 1827; dating from *c.*150 BC, it is dedicated to King Ptolemy who authorised its original erection "as a perpetual memorial of exemption from taxation". It is flanked, at a discreet distance, by two beautiful trees – a fern-leafed beech (*Fagus sylvatica* var.

heterophylla 'Aspleniifolia') and a holm oak (*Quercus ilex*). Beyond the obelisk a ha–ha forms the boundary of the garden, with field and woodland beyond, and a row of small cannons point out to the countryside. Two further obelisks are visible: one to the south-east commemorates Queen Victoria's diamond jubilee of 1887, and the other, to the south-west, probably dates from the 18th century.

From the lawn there is just enough ornament to be easy on the eye and not to detract from the beauty of the trees and the orchestrated view of the rural landscape; equally, looking back towards the house, the trees on either side concentrate the attention on the house, giving it a frame of noble simplicity. The grandly simple setting of grass, trees and a few superlative ornaments is all that is needed – not minimalist, but exactly enough on exactly the right scale.

Immediately below the east façade of the house, in a sunken space overlooked by grassy terraces, is a dapper parterre of L-shaped beds filled with pink begonias and egg-shaped topiaries of clipped golden yew, designed by C.E. Ponting and put in place in 1899. Beyond it, running eastwards, is a majestic procession of venerable cedars of Lebanon – a symphonic blast after the piccolo parterre. These were planted in 1835 by William John Bankes. Dating from the same period is a rare and charming fernery, with groups of ferns on raised beds supported on dry-stone walls.

The Edwardian garden at Kingston Maurward

Beyond is a lime avenue, with only the narrowest of passages when the trees are in leaf – the atmospheric remains of the 17th-century formal planting put in place when the house was built. There are agreeable walks in this part of the garden, with groups of flowering shrubs and ornamental trees, but they lack the drama and consequence of the great south lawn.

Location nr Wimborne Minster BH21 4EA, Dorset **OS** ST9701 1½m W of Wimborne by B3082 **Tel** 01202 883402 (Mon to Fri 9–5) and 01202 842913 (Sat and Sun 11–5) **Infoline** 01202 880413 **Fax** 01202 882402 **Email** kingstonlacy@ntrust.org.uk **English Heritage Register** Grade II **Owner** The National Trust **Open** Feb to Mar, Sat and Sun 11–4; Apr to Oct, daily 11–6; Nov to 23 Dec, Fri to Sun 11–4 **Area** 20 acres/8 hectares

The parterre at Kingston Lacy

KINGSTON MAURWARD GARDENS

EDWARDIAN GARDEN OF COMPARTMENTS WITH EXCELLENT PLANTS FOR AN 18TH-CENTURY HOUSE

Kingston Maurward House is a cool 18th-century mansion built for the Pitt family on a fine site that slopes down towards the river Frome. The estate was bought just before World War I by Cecil Hanbury whose father, Sir Thomas, had made the remarkable plantsman's garden of La Mortola on the Italian riviera near Ventimiglia. During World War II the house was requisitioned and the garden went rapidly downhill. In 1947 the estate was bought by the County Council as the campus for the Dorset College of Agriculture and Horticulture. Since then the gardens, at a quickening pace, have been restored and embellished, opening to the public from 1995.

The garden made by the Hanburys – the Edwardian garden west of the house – is a series of formal enclosures which retains much of its original character, enlivened by new planting. A sunken scalloped pool is surrounded by paving, with clipped shapes of yew, box and *Pittosporum tobira*, and the whole is surrounded by mixed borders backed by balustraded walls. A Lutyens bench stands on a raised platform in the shade of a shapely *Catalpa bignonioides*.

Here, and elsewhere in the garden, much use is made of the tender and often flamboyant plants that became so fashionable in the last decade of the 20th century: the dramatic foliage of bananas, brilliantly coloured cannas and dahlias, and the bold shapes of the castor-oil plant (*Ricinus communis*). The microclimate is benign, with south-facing slopes of free-draining soil and the sea not far away. Tender plants such as the South American *Salvia guaranitica* with its rich blue flowers are hardy here, and the garden contains a National Collection of over 100 species and cultivars of tender salvias. A croquet lawn is edged in dry-stone walls lavishly scattered with valerian (*Centranthus ruber*) and Mexican daisy (*Erigeron karvinskianus*). On a grassy slope a rotunda stands in the shade of trees, and a terrace above the lawn has beds filled with penstemons – a National Collection of 95 species and cultivars.

A circular parterre of box, with statues in niches cut into the surrounding yew hedging, leads to a terraced walk punctuated by pairs of yew obelisks. Hidden away is the Crown Garden, an expansive circle of yew hedging with clipped triangular finials about the top and bold hemispheres marking the entrance. The planting in the beds that run round the enclosure is less assured – a cottage-garden miscellany of aquilegias, foxgloves and sweet williams where something much grander is needed. On the slopes below the house is a slightly sketchy Japanese garden and a lake with many good trees (including an exceptional old London plane).

It seems a specially happy outcome that such an estate should become the training ground of gardeners who seem to relish the opportunity to show their paces in such a distinguished setting.

Location Dorchester DT2 8PY, Dorset **OS** SY7191
On the E edge of Dorchester by A35 bypass
Tel 01305 215003 **Fax** 01305 215001 **Email** administration@kmc.ac.uk **English Heritage**
Register Grade II* **Owner** Kingston Maurward College **Open** Easter to Oct, daily 10–5
Area 35 acres/14 hectares

KNIGHTSHAYES COURT

BEAUTIFUL 20TH-CENTURY WOODLAND GARDEN AND A STATELY VICTORIAN SETTING FOR A 19TH-CENTURY HOUSE

Knightshayes has two faces, formal and wild, both exceptionally attractive. The house was designed by William Burges for Sir John Heathcoat Amory and built from 1867 onwards. Alas, although the fine house was completed, the economic collapse of the 1870s meant that Burges's elaborate interiors were never carried out (in the words of Burges's biographer, John Mordaunt Crook, "those magical interiors remained a half-formed dream"). In the garden, however, we have a completed, fully formed dream of an altogether different kind, and today the formal gardens close to the house merge seamlessly with the exquisite woodland garden to its east.

Immediately south of the house the garden designer Edward Kemp had laid out formal

The woodland garden at Knightshayes

grass terraces when the house was built. These, with gravel walks, monumental yew topiary and central steps leading down to a fountain pool flanked by stone urns, survive, commanding splendid views over parkland beyond to a distant prospect of the town of Tiverton (and indeed of the Heathcoat lace-making works from which the family's fortune came). However, the most important period in the garden's development took place after World War II under Sir John and Lady Heathcoat Amory. They replanted the upper terrace beds, which in Kemp's time had been devoted to bedding schemes, with distinguished mixed plantings of shrubs and herbaceous perennials and, most important of all, extended the garden eastwards – adding to the existing formal garden and creating a woodland garden of exceptional beauty immediately beyond it. They continued the axis of the upper terrace with a path passing through a corridor of yew hedges, and leading off it created a brilliantly dramatic enclosure – a square of fine lawn surrounded by castellated yew hedges with, at its centre, a circular pool edged with stone. Apart from a scattering of water plants the only other plant in the garden is a silver weeping pear (*Pyrus salicifolia* 'Pendula') at the edge of the pool. It is a masterly example of beauty achieved by the simplest of means.

"A GARDEN IN A WOOD"

The path continues, up further gentle steps, to the woodland garden or what Lady Heathcoat Amory insisted was "a garden in a wood". Underneath high old beeches, Scots pines, larches and oaks are countless distinguished ornamental trees and shrubs – dogwoods, hydrangeas, magnolias, maples, nothofagus, rhododendrons and the beautiful spring-flowering *Stachyurus praecox* with tassels of pale yellow flowers. These are underplanted with immense numbers of naturalised plants – exotics such as cyclamen, erythroniums, ferns, fritillaries, gentians, leucojums, narcissi and ranunculus intermingling happily with native anemones, bluebells, foxgloves, scillas, violets and wild garlic. The effect is completely unlike that of the woodland gardens of the Cornish coast, for the microclimate here is not especially mild and the exotics that may

be grown at Knightshayes are much less exotic in appearance than those found in Cornish gardens. It is as if a piece of wild native English woodland had been gently transformed into an extraordinary cornucopia of plants, disposed in the most natural fashion. Of its kind there is nothing to beat it anywhere in the country – in April one of the loveliest of woodland gardens.

Location Bolham, Tiverton EX16 7RQ, Devon **OS** SS9615 2m N of Tiverton by A396 **Tel** 01884 254665 **Fax** 01884 243050 **Email** knightshayes@ntrust.org.uk **English Heritage Register** Grade II* **Owner** The National Trust **Open** Apr to Oct, daily 11–5.30 **Area** 40 acres/16 hectares

KNOLL GARDENS AND NURSERY

EXCELLENT COLLECTION OF PLANTS SKILFULLY ARRANGED AND FULL OF LESSONS FOR GARDENERS

The owners disarmingly say of the garden that they like to think of visitors meandering back and forth and enjoying the plants. Indeed, although there is the occasional designed set piece, this is a garden that is

The dragon fountain at the Knoll Gardens

primarily about plants – a piece of woodland with beech and oak, the occasional whopping eucalyptus, many excellent smaller ornamental trees and shrubs with lavish underplantings. The site is gently undulating and paths wind hither and yon. What is most admirable about the garden is the presence of sometimes unfamiliar and frequently well-grown plants often skilfully placed. A beautiful *Metasequoia glyptostroboides* rises up in a suitably jungly setting; the altogether more dainty, and unusual, *Broussonetia papyrifera*, with its soft, shapely leaves, spreads out in an open glade and is cleverly underplanted with a circle of that fashionable golden grass *Hakonechloa macra* 'Alboaurea'; one of the better yellow-leafed trees, *Gleditsia triacanthos* 'Sunburst', rises from a neat thicket of the statuesque scarlet *Crocosmia* 'Lucifer'. The climate is mild here and plants grow quickly, sometimes presenting an awful warning for gardeners. A New Zealand flax (*Phormium tenax*) is 10ft/3m high and as much across; it is not a plant that grows old gracefully and if it gets too big for its boots it is incredibly hard work digging up its tangled fibrous roots.

GOOD PLANTS FINELY GROWN

A formal water garden with a stream, pool and waterfalls presents an opportunity for deploying moisture-loving plants but it has a slightly forlorn air. The Dragon Garden, with boisterous herbaceous borders, has a central pool and an attractive and intriguing sculpture by Susan Ford showing St Dunstan and the Dragon curiously entwined to form the shape of a harp whose strings are evoked by thin vertical water jets. There are nods at horticultural fashion – a gravel garden; much use of tender and brilliantly coloured exotics; and a garden of grasses, for example. But I guess what will draw people to the garden is the eternal truth – that good plants finely grown are lovely things.

Location Hampreston, nr Wimborne Minster BH21 7ND, Dorset **OS** SU0600 2m E of Wimborne Minster by A31 and minor roads **Tel** 01202 873931 **Fax** 01202 870842 **Email** enquiries@knollgardens.co.uk **Website** www.knollgardens.co.uk **Owner** Neil Lucas **Open** Apr to Sept, daily 10–5; Oct, Nov and Mar, daily 10–4.30 **Area** 4 acres/1.6 hectares

mossy rocks, ferns, and in April drifts of rich purple Himalayan primulas. The wooded slopes above are studded with fine trees and shrubs – camellias, cherries, dogwoods, hydrangeas, magnolias, rhododendrons and Himalayan rowans. At the top a delicious view awaits you. Look back eastwards over the house, formal gardens and avenue to distant glimpses of Bodmin Moor – a lovely mixture of domestic order in a wild setting.

Location Bodmin PL30 5AD, Cornwall **OS** SX0863 2½m SE of Bodmin by A38 or B3268 **Tel** 01208 73320 **Fax** 01208 74084 **Email** lanhydrock@ntrust.org.uk **English Heritage Register** Grade II* **Owner** The National Trust **Open** Apr to Sept, daily 11–5.30; Oct, daily 11–5; Nov to Feb, daily during daylight hours **Area** 25 acres/10 hectares

LANHYDROCK

SUPERB PARKLAND SETTING FOR A
HOUSE WITH A VICTORIAN FORMAL
GARDEN AND EXCELLENT SHRUBS

The Robartes family from Truro came to live here in 1620 and the estate continued in family ownership until it was given to the National Trust in 1953. The house and garden at Lanhydrock, set in romantic ancient parkland, form a rare and beautiful ensemble, successfully yoking together elements of very different periods and giving the place great character. Linking landscape and house is a long double avenue of beech, originally planted in the 17th century with sycamore, of which a few original trees survive. The castellated stone house, U-shaped about a courtyard, is a mixture of the 17th and 19th centuries. A 17th-century granite gatehouse with battlements, its parapet rising in a fanfare of finials, guards the entrance to the house. In 1857 George Gilbert Scott built walls to enclose the court between gatehouse and house, cleverly embellishing their coping with battlements and finials resembling those on the gatehouse. At the same time new formal gardens were laid out within the walls: six lawns, on gently terraced slopes, are each marked with four Irish yews enclosing a shaped bed planted with a block of a single variety of bedding roses – 'The Fairy' and 'Else

The courtyard garden at Lanhydrock

Poulsen' (both pink), 'Bright Smile' (yellow) and 'Escapade' (pink). The beautiful bronze urns that decorate the garden are copies of those made for Louis XIV's Versailles by the goldsmith Claude Ballin, of which Lawrence Weaver wrote: "…it is doubtful if any sculptor has ever produced a series of garden ornaments more exquisite in modelling and craftsmanship." (These copies were commissioned in the 1860s by the 4th Marquis of Hertford for his garden at the Château de Bagatelle in the Bois de Boulogne. He was a friend of the Emperor Napoleon III who allowed Lord Hertford to make the copies – the first ever made.) On the north side of the house a parterre in an intricate pattern of shaped beds is cut out of grass and edged with box, and planted with spring and summer bedding schemes.

Behind the house informality reigns except for the herbaceous circle, a pattern of four quadrants encircled with yew hedges and filled with herbaceous perennials – in particular crocosmias, of which Lanhydrock has a National Collection (about 60 cultivars). Paths wind through woodland, animated from time to time by some special planting. At Borlase's Stream is a wonderful collection of magnolias, started in the 1930s and continued in more recent times. The stream itself, tumbling down a cascade, is fringed with

LYTES CARY MANOR

DELIGHTFUL MEDIEVAL HOUSE WITH
TOPIARY, BORDERS, ORCHARD AND A
CHARMING ATMOSPHERE

The house is a late medieval hall-house, and despite a certain amount of subsequent fiddling preserves its essential delightful character. The Lyte family lived in these parts from the 13th to the 18th century. In the 16th century the lord of the manor was Sir Henry Lyte who translated into English a famous Flemish book about herbs, Rembert Dodoens's *Cruÿdeboeck*, which appeared in English in 1578 as *Nievve Herball*. Lyte added his own observations on plants, recording, for example, that bluebells grew "not far from my poore house at Lytescarie". Nothing is known of gardens at Lytes Cary until the estate was bought in 1907 by Sir Walter Jenner, the son of Sir Edward Jenner the inventor of vaccination. It was Jenner who was responsible for making the delightful formal gardens close to the house.

The entrance forecourt has an avenue of yew topiary – curious dumpy pudding shapes surmounted by a flattened cone, vaguely echoing the shape of an old dovecote seen across a field, on which the avenue is precisely aligned. To the side of the house a flagged path runs between a mixed border and a yew hedge that breaks out from time to time in buttresses capped with finely wrought topknots. A raised grass walk with a row of Irish yews overlooks a formal orchard planted with rows of crab-apples, medlars, pears, quinces and walnuts with, at each corner, an arbour formed of a weeping ash. In spring the grass in the orchard is brilliant with cowslips, snake's head fritillaries and narcissi. Running along the southern boundary of the garden a long broad path of turf is flanked by noble hedges of yew. There is no ornament save for a curvaceous bench at one end and topknots of yew topiary at the other end. Here, screens of yew partly conceal a circular pool with a fine fountain in the form of a lead statue of Triton spouting water. An enticing tunnel of hornbeam leads through to an enclosed glade lightened by walls of *Weigela* 'Florida Variegata', creating a mysterious effect. The unostentatiously attractive gardens at Lytes Cary, with occasional idiosyncrasies, precisely suit the character of the house.

Location Charlton Mackrell, Somerton TA11 7HU, Somerset **OS** ST5326 4m SE of Somerton off B3151 **Tel** 01985 843600 **Fax** 01985 843624 **Email** lytescarymanor@ntrust.org.uk **English Heritage Register** Grade II **Owner** The National Trust **Open** Apr to Oct, Mon, Wed and Sat (Jun–Aug, also Fri) 2–6 or dusk if earlier **Area** 3 acres/1.2 hectares

The forecourt garden at Lytes Cary

MAPPERTON HOUSE GARDENS

LOVELY AND MYSTERIOUS FORMAL GARDENS FOR A BEAUTIFUL HOUSE IN A SECRET VALLEY

Mapperton is a memorable place – a completely unspoilt rural setting, a beautiful house of the 16th and 17th centuries, equally attractive outhouses, and an astonishing garden that suddenly reveals itself, like a burst of sunshine, in the valley behind the house. There had been formal gardens here in the 17th century, of which traces survive today, but the formal valley garden dates almost entirely from the late 1920s when the house was owned by Mrs Labouchère. Parts of the valley garden look much older – the crisply shaped grass terraces on the western side have an early 18th-century look. But what Mrs Labouchère made, almost certainly with the help of a local architect, Charles William Pike, was an Italianate pastiche – a feast of decorative exuberance executed with panache. None of this is visible as you first enter the garden.

The entrance courtyard has shapes of clipped bay, a majestic *Magnolia*

delavayi, and other decorative plants. This is followed by a large empty lawned space enclosed by the house, walls and a yew hedge. Camellias are planted between the windows of the house and a *Garrya elliptica* and *Magnolia grandiflora* against a wall. Walk through an opening in the yew hedge and the valley garden is suddenly displayed below – a splendid revelation. The upper part of the garden, the Fountain Court, is arranged in a series of paved terraces following the line of the valley, with a pool at the centre and, at each end of a cross axis, facing grotto-like summerhouses built into the valley slope. Lavish ornament animates the scene – composition stone or lead figures; benches and urns interspersed with processions of monumental yew topiary. Such is the unexpected and delightful ebullience of the formal garden that plants seem almost superfluous. Christopher Lloyd described it as "the best unplanty garden I know".

At the southern end of the Fountain Court a slightly muddled pergola leads to a high-roofed 17th-century summerhouse, and at a lower level a long canal is edged with tall, rounded cones of clipped yew. But the garden does not stop here, for the valley is planted with good trees and shrubs as it falls away towards the sea.

The canal garden at Mapperton House

Location nr Beaminster DT8 3NR, Dorset **OS** SY5099
2m SE of Beaminster by B3163 **Tel** 01308 862645 **Fax**
01308 863348 **Email** office@mapperton.com **Website**
www.mapperton.com **English Heritage Register**
Grade II* **Owner** The Earl and Countess of Sandwich
Open Mar to Oct, daily 2–6 **Area** 12 acres/5 hectares

MARWOOD HILL GARDENS

PLANTSMAN'S GARDEN FILLED WITH RARE AND LOVELY THINGS IN A CHARMING SETTING

Dr Jimmy Smart who made this garden thought of gardening as "a disease, at times infectious, and certainly, as far as I am concerned, quite incurable". Dr Smart himself became infected when he bought Marwood Hill in 1949. With land sloping down to a stream it was an admirable site for a garden but he got off to a bad start – the only plant of much note in the garden was a very fine *Rhododendron* Nobleanum Group which died of honey fungus the year after he arrived. His aim, however, was to "make trees and shrubs grow happily" and in this he was very successful, clothing both sides of the valley with birches, cherries, dogwoods, firs, magnolias, maples, oaks, pines and the occasional jolt of eucalyptus, while well-drained south-facing positions in the valley provide good conditions for many of the less hardy shrubs – abutilons, *Acca sellowiana*, cistus, olearias and phygelius. The far bank (which has acid soil) has a memorable grove of camellias.

WET AND DRY PLANTING

The banks of the stream are planted with relatively chaste astilbes, hostas, lysichitons and primulas, but in late summer there is an explosion of the showiest crocosmias and lobelias. At the head of the stream a life-size bronze statue of Jimmy Smart, erected by his family to celebrate the millennium, gazes quizzically down the valley as if itching to do a spot of planting. A National Collection of *Iris ensata* cultivars is kept here, over 200 of them, many of them gathered about a pool in the valley – a flamboyant sight in the Devon countryside. A quite different National Collection also finds a home here – of

▷ **The valley garden** at Marwood

tulbaghias (15 species), those elegant South African bulbs with a savoury scent of onions and daintily nodding flowers, which are planted high up in well-drained soil in a sunny position.

In a walled garden a good nursery sells all sorts of plants, many of them hard to come by elsewhere, propagated from those in the garden. The walls provide protection for some

of the more tender plants – callistemons, ceanothus, *Carpenteria californica* and leptospermums – while a large camellia house has those too delicate to flourish out-of-doors. Marwood Hill is an excellent example of the garden of an ardent collector who does not give a fig for fashion. Dr Smart knew what he liked and you may well like it too.

Location nr Barnstaple EX31 4EB, Devon **OS** SS5437 4m NW of Barnstaple, signed off A361 **Tel** 01271 342528 **Owner** Mrs J.A. Smart **Open** daily dawn–dusk **Area** 20 acres/8 hectares

MILTON LODGE

AN EARLY 20TH-CENTURY GARDEN OF COMPARTMENTS, WITH PRETTY PLANTING AND SUPERB VIEWS

Spectacular views are not necessarily advantageous to a garden; there is always the anxiety that nothing in the garden can compete with nature's master landscaping. The view from Milton Lodge, with its lofty position in the wooded foothills of the Mendips, is lovely. It looks southwards over the city of Wells, with the grand square crossing tower of the cathedral looming among trees, and beyond the city the Vale of Avalon with a distant prospect of Glastonbury Tor.

The garden which clusters about the slopes below the house has an intimate, richly planted character, with much to lure the eye from the splendours of the view. It dates from the period just before World War I when the present owner's grandfather, Charles Tudway, came to live here. He was a partner in the firm of garden designers Parsons & Partridge, whose chief designer, Alfred Parsons, practised in a refined Arts and Crafts style. The new garden here, laid out before World War I, is an excellent example of that tradition.

The terraces that lie to the south of the house, with their sunny exposure and sharp drainage, provide perfect conditions for the tender shrubs that flourish here – abelias, *Acca selloviana*, abutilons, a beautiful old *Clerodendrum trichotomum*, *Teucrium fruticans* – while swathes of *Erigeron karvinskianus* colonise the steps. Jasmine and lemon verbena are trained against the house. Yew hedges,

Wells Cathedral from the terrace at Milton Lodge

planted when the garden was first laid out, now give seclusion, wind protection and crisp structure amidst the profusion of mixed plantings. A very large cedar of Lebanon stands near the end of the top terrace, and a lawn with a row of cannons acts as a viewing platform over the gardens below to fields full of grazing sheep and the city of Wells beyond. A long pretty border of yellows and blues ornaments the swimming pool garden at a lower level and a magnificent old English oak stands in grass nearby. At this lower level is an excellent collection of trees – *Acer griseum*, a fern-leafed beech (*Fagus sylvatica* var. *heterophylla* 'Aspleniifolia'), a silver lime (*Tilia* 'Petiolaris'), and a Lucombe oak (*Quercus* × *hispanica* 'Lucombeana').

A RARE ARBORETUM

At a little distance from the garden, on the other side of the road, is the Coombe, a miniature late 18th-century arboretum of rare charm – originally part of the garden of a mid-Georgian Tudway house in the centre of Wells, The Cedars, which is now part of the Cathedral School. The Coombe, a wooded shallow valley, has some fine native trees – particularly beeches, limes and English oaks – which form a backdrop to a delightful collection of exotics – acers, birches, a beautiful old cedar of Lebanon, flowering cherries, *Davidia involucrata*, *Paulownia*

tomentosa, sorbus and much else. The Coombe, so close to the city centre and open all the time throughout the year, is a rare amenity for the people of Wells, a sylvan retreat hard by the busy road to Bristol.

Location nr Wells BA5 3AQ, Somerset **OS** ST5446 ½m N of Wells off A39 **Tel** 01749 672168 **English Heritage Register** Grade II **Owner** D.C. Tudway Quilter **Open** Good Fri to Oct, daily except Sat 2–6 **Area** 12 acres/4.8 hectares

MINTERNE

A WOODLAND AND WATER GARDEN OF 18TH-CENTURY ORIGINS WITH BEAUTIFUL 20TH-CENTURY PLANTINGS OF TREES AND SHRUBS

The house at Minterne was an Edwardian replacement, designed by Leonard Stokes, for a 17th-century house. Pevsner finds "verve and freshness" in its design; others may be struck by its blockish disconnection from its site. At all events, although you pass the house to enter the garden, it scarcely impinges on the character of the garden whose chief part lies in the densely wooded valley below.

The Digby family came here in the mid 18th century when Admiral the Hon. Robert Digby bought the estate from the Churchill

The woodland garden at Minterne

family. Digby took much interest in the garden and embarked on an immense programme of tree planting on what was then bare downland. He also saw the picturesque possibilities of the river Cerne in the valley below, where he built bridges and created several dams and cascades. An entry in his diary in 1768 reads, "Spent the day at my favourite ploy, cascading."

Early in the 20th century the west side of the valley, below the house, was enriched with many new exotics introduced by Reginald Farrer, Frank Kingdon Ward and E.H. Wilson. Some of these are now substantial trees, such as a *Davidia involucrata* (one of several in the garden) planted in 1909; Wilson had introduced the tree to Europe only six years previously, sending seed to Veitch's nursery. Superlative Japanese maples and beautiful specimens of *Cercidiphyllum japonicum* also decorate the slopes. In April and May the wooded valley and the banks of the pools at the valley bottom glow with rhododendrons and waves of candelabra primulas brilliantly colonise the moist ground. The walks along the wooded banks of the river, crossed by bridges from time to time and fringed with ferns and irises, are delightful.

Location Minterne Magna, nr Dorchester DT2 7AU, Dorset **OS** ST6604 9m N of Dorchester by A352 **Tel** 01300 341370 **Fax** 01300 341747 **English Heritage Register** Grade II **Owner** Lord Digby **Open** end Mar to early Nov, daily 10–7 **Area** 21 acres/8.5 hectares

MONTACUTE HOUSE

A GREAT TUDOR HOUSE WITH MAGNIFICENT GARDENS REPLANTED IN THE 20TH CENTURY

When the great golden house at Montacute rose majestically from the ground in the late 16th century it must have astonished the villagers, few of whom could ever have seen a building of such size and splendour. It was built for a prosperous lawyer and Member of Parliament, Sir Edward Phelips, who had become an influential courtier to Queen Elizabeth. A suitably splendid garden was made – as early as 1630 a visitor described "large and spacious Courtes, gardens, orchards, a parke". The "courtes" were walled enclosures, several of which survive today. The essential garden layout survived the 18th-century craze for landscaping and remains, albeit with later

The East Court garden at Montacute House

additions and modern planting, one of the best preserved and most attractive surviving formal gardens of its period.

The East Court, formerly the entrance courtyard to the house, is enclosed in balustraded walls with coping decorated with narrow obelisks and openwork stone lanterns. The outer corners of the court are triumphantly closed by enchanting ogee-roofed gazebos. In the 19th century exuberant borders were made to line the walls here (G.S. Elgood's watercolour of 1886 shows veils of pale colours fizzing from time to time with eruptions of scarlet zinnias or sunflowers). In the 1950s these borders were redesigned by Phyllis Reiss who lived nearby at Tintinhull House (*see page 63*) and a version of her scheme, tweaked by the National Trust, survives today. The North Garden is at a lower level, with terrace walks. Rows of Irish yews, clipped into rounded cones, and thorns (*Crataegus × lavalleei*) frame the garden, which has a galleried pool at its centre. An excellent border of species and shrub roses runs along the south wall, laid out in the late 1940s by Vita Sackville-West and Graham Thomas –

pioneers in the rediscovery of old roses. The Cedar Lawn, enclosed on two sides by huge and memorably baggy ancient yew hedges, has two spectacular trees of *Cupressus arizonica* var. *arizonica* – the largest specimens in England – and a beautiful sweet chestnut. Throughout the garden there is planting and architecture to be relished, but at its heart, dominating the atmosphere, is the great house, a garden ornament of irresistible splendour.

Location Montacute, nr Yeovil TA15 6XP, Somerset **OS** ST4917 4m W of Yeovil by A3088 **Tel** and **Fax** 01935 823289 **Email** montacute@ntrust.org.uk **English Heritage Register** Grade I **Owner** The National Trust **Open** end Mar to Oct, daily except Tue 11–5.30 or dusk if earlier; Nov to Mar, Wed to Sun 11.30–4 **Area** 12 acres/4.8 hectares

MOUNT EDGCUMBE

GREAT CORNISH GARDEN WITH CLIFFTOP WALKS, FINE FORMAL GARDENS AND EXCELLENT PLANTING

Celia Fiennes came here in 1698 and wrote, "its scituation makes it esteemed by me the finest seat I have seen." She was by no means the first to be bowled over by the site of Mount Edgcumbe – a dramatic sloping headland, bursting out into cliffs, overlooking Plymouth Sound. If it is not true that Admiral Medina Sidonia had already earmarked the estate for himself when his Armada had conquered England, it would be easy to understand his covetousness. Sir Piers Edgcumbe (of Cotehele, *see page 27*) had a royal licence to make a deer park here in 1539; the house was built a little later. When Celia Fiennes visited the garden she saw "a hill all bedeck'd with woods which are divided into severall rowes of trees in walks". Badeslade's engraving of 1737 shows the house with a double avenue and formal walks, straight or winding, cut through woods. A grand triple avenue of oaks and limes, of 20th-century planting, gives a similar effect today, sweeping down the hill in front of the house.

In the 18th century the Edgcumbes embarked on improvements to the landscape: a series of zigzag walks leading along the edge of the cliffs south-east of the house; a ruinous

ivy-clad folly placed on grassy slopes leading down to the sea; Milton's Temple, with a dome and pillars, below an amphitheatre close to the sea; and Thomson's Seat, an open Doric Pavilion in a grove of holm oaks with a quotation from Thomson's "The Seasons" reading, "On either hand/Like a long wintry forest, groves of masts/Shot up their spires; the bellying sheets between/Possessed the breezy wind." More surprisingly, at the end of the 18th and beginning of the 19th centuries, the Lords Mount Edgcumbe laid out a new series of formal gardens. The Italian Garden has a conservatory, a grand double staircase with a statue of Apollo, a bust of Ariosto and other figures, a fountain supported by a double-tailed mermaid standing in a twelve-sided pool and surrounded by citrus plants in pots, and box topiary clipped into spirals. The French Garden has an elaborate box parterre filled with bedding plants and a shell fountain in an octagonal pool at its centre, the whole overlooked by an orangery. In the English Garden an early 18th-century pedimented garden house overlooks a flower garden and some magnificent old cork oaks (*Quercus suber*).

CAMELLIAS AND SPLENDID WALKS

A more recent development, some considerable distance away, is the remarkable National Collection of camellias – 20 species

The French Garden at Mount Edgcumbe

and 500 cultivars – arranged in a combe well south of the house near Picklecombe Point. The climate is mild here and the camellias burst into flower very early, making one of the most magnificent winter flowering sights you could imagine. Another modern development is the Earl's Garden immediately alongside the house which was completely rebuilt after being destroyed in World War II. Pleasant enough, it is of only modest interest compared to the multi-layered splendours of the park. If you are energetic the best way to enjoy this is to take a long walk, starting in the Kingsand car park and walking all round the coast until you come to the formal gardens north of the house. Best of all, take a picnic and make a day of it. The wooded walks along the cliffs, with views of the sea and occasional ornamental buildings, are marvellous. For the less energetic there is a car park at Cremyll Lodge, at the northern tip of the park, immediately alongside the formal gardens.

Location Cremyll, Torpoint PL10 1HZ, Cornwall **OS** SX4552 2½m SE of Torpoint **Tel** 01752 822236 **Fax** 01752 822199 **English Heritage Register** Grade I **Owner** Plymouth City Council and Cornwall County Council **Open** daily 8–dusk; Earl's Garden (entrance by house) Apr to mid Oct, Wed to Sun and Bank Hol Mon 11–4.30 **Area** 865 acres/350 hectares

OVERBECKS GARDEN

A SEA-SIDE GARDEN OF CHARACTER FILLED
WITH TENDER EXOTIC PLANTS

Otto Overbeck was a scientist who lived here from 1928 to 1937 and left both house and garden to the National Trust. Part of his house is now a youth hostel and part a museum of antique artefacts connected with ships, early photographs of the area, shells, stuffed animals and other magpie glories of a miscellaneous kind. The site, with dreamy views over the Salcombe estuary, has a strong flavour of the *corniche* of the Côte d'Azur. The garden is terraced, 200ft/60m above the water, and is well protected to the north and east. With around 40in/100cm of rain a year, plenty of sun, neutral gravelly soil and sharp drainage, the site is the closest on the British mainland to that of Tresco Abbey. All sorts of tender plants flourish here, some of them becoming naturalised, such as the brilliant yellow *Calceolaria mexicana*. The very tender camphor tree (*Cinnamomum camphora*), groves

of self-sown *Echium pininana*, March-flowering mimosa (*Acacia dealbata*), marvellous ramparts of *Drimys winteri* jostle together in exotic profusion. Bulbous plants, many of them from South Africa, sparkle like jewels among the shrubby foliage. In truth there is not much design in the garden at Overbecks apart from a pretty box parterre with gravels of different colours and the Statue Garden with its pattern of symmetrical herbaceous beds and a bronze statue, First Flight, by Albert Bruce-Joy. The pleasures of the garden come from the atmosphere of leafy, tropical abundance, the brilliant colours and curious shapes of exotic flowers and, from the top of the garden, the view on a fine day of an improbably blue sea with a jungle of Chusan palms and other exotics in the foreground.

Location Sharpitor, Salcombe TQ8 8LW, Devon
OS SX7237 1½m SW of Salcombe by minor roads
Tel 01548 842893 **Fax** 01548 844038 **Email** overbecks@ntrust.org.uk **English Heritage Register** Grade II **Owner** The National Trust **Open** daily 10–8 or sunset if earlier **Area** 6 acres/2.4 hectares

Soaring echiums in the borders at Overbecks

PENCARROW HOUSE

GRAND VICTORIAN FORMAL GARDEN,
ROMANTIC WOODLAND WALKS AND
SPLENDID TREES AND SHRUBS

Molesworths have lived at Pencarrow since the 16th century. The house was rebuilt in the 1760s and thoroughly Georgianised with the addition of a smart pediment on the east façade. It faces south along a broad valley, with open pastures flanked by woodland. Before you arrive at the house you have already followed the main drive which passes through the earthworks of an Iron Age hill fort with mossy rocks and beech woods. Closer to the house the drive is lined with camellias and rhododendrons and in spring the grass verges are spangled with primroses. The estate was inherited in 1831 by Sir William Molesworth who made many changes in the garden. He laid out an elaborate sunken Italian Garden south of the house, with sweeping grass terraces and a fountain-pool modelled on Bernini's 17th-century pool in the Piazza Navona in Rome. In its heyday the fountain was surrounded by bedding schemes, gravelled walks, balustrades and plantings of shrubs. Today the fountain survives but stands on lawns at the centre of a much simplified arrangement in which the bold shapes of the turf terraces have striking presence. To the east, marked by a billowing phalanx of old Irish yews, is an overgrown rockery with rhododendrons and a superlative Japanese maple standing out among rocks swathed in rich green moss.

"THAT WOULD PUZZLE A MONKEY"
Sir William was a great plant collector and it was he who gave the garden the interest that we may admire today. He built up a fine collection of conifers at the very moment when new species were being introduced in great quantities, especially from the American continent. Many of these came from Veitch's nursery in Exeter, among them monkey puzzles, of which an avenue was planted; parts of it survive. The tree is said to have acquired its common name here when a visitor, seeing it for the first time, said, "That would puzzle a monkey." Some of the original conifers may

A **woodland walk** at Pencarrow

still be seen in the rockery to one side of the Italian garden. Others, including an astonishing old Monterey pine (*Pinus radiata*) with a formidable trunk, are in the American Garden in the woods to the south of the house. Here a stream with occasional pools and cascades follows the path and the underplanting ranges from Himalayan primulas and *Gunnera manicata* to kingcups, foxgloves and flag irises. The walk through the woods is delightful, running past a lake and then curving up through the woods to return at an upper level from which you may look down through giant thickets of cherry laurel and many exotics to the waters of the lake below. The return walk takes you through a kissing gate into a field with a huge old *Cryptomeria japonica*, battered but noble, and views down to the house. A gate leads to a path through waves of wild garlic to a mound of rich red *Rhododendron arboreum* and back to the Italian Garden. The ancient landscape of the hill fort, the mixture of native plants and exotics, and the gentle unfolding of memorable scenes untouched by fashionable

gimmickry make Pencarrow an exceptional place to visit.

Location Washaway, Bodmin PL30 3AG, Cornwall
OS SX0471 3½m NW of Bodmin by A389 and B3266
Tel and **Fax** 01208 841369 **Email** pencarrow@aol.com
English Heritage Register Grade II **Owner** Molesworth-St Aubyn family **Open** Apr to mid Oct, daily dawn–dusk **Area** 50 acres/20 hectares

PENJERRICK

UNSPOILT JUNGLE-LIKE WOODLAND GARDEN,
FILLED WITH RARE TREASURES

Cornish woodland gardens all draw on a similar repertory of plants but they vary strongly in character. Penjerrick is unusual in preserving a powerful atmosphere of wildness – paths are narrow and vistas vague, giving a strong feeling of penetrating some thrilling Himalayan forest. Robert Were Fox made the garden at Penjerrick in the 1840s while his

brothers Alfred (at Glendurgan, *see page 38*) and Charles (at Trebah, *see page 64*) were making their gardens. Taking advantage of the mild climate and protected position, he introduced immense numbers of appropriate plants. His elder daughter, Anna Maria, also took an interest in the garden, creating the Wilderness, a sort of idealised jungle in which cockatoos and monkeys played in a grove of tree ferns (*Dicksonia antarctica*), some of which survive today. They have become naturalised here and now form one of the best old groups of these plants in the country.

A SECRETIVE CHARACTER
Later in the 19th century, when Samuel Smith was head gardener, there was much hybridising of rhododendrons – the famous Cornish crosses between *R. griffithianum* and *R. thomsonii*. In 1874 *The Gardener's Chronicle*, comparing Penjerrick with other gardens, wrote, "I doubt if there is [anywhere] which can compete with Penjerrick in a certain indescribable effect – the effect of landscape gardening carried out with the most

exquisitely cultivated taste." Today the great charm of Penjerrick is that it preserves a secretive, densely planted character. Marvellous examples of common trees (like copper beeches) provide a background for splendid specimens of rarities such as *Eucryphia moorei*, *Laurelia sempervirens*, *Amomyrtus luma* and many others. Some plants are exceptional specimens, such as a magnificent *Davidia involucrata* and a gigantic *Podocarpus salignus* well over 50ft/15m high. Everything grows exceptionally vigorously here, partly because of the wet warm climate but also because of the springs that irrigate the garden. Early in the season a walk among the densely planted groves, suffused with heady whiffs of the scented rhododendron 'Lady Alice Fitzwilliam', is one of the finest pleasures that Cornish gardens can offer. Visitors should be warned that paths can be muddy and precipitous, and although the garden is not huge, it is remarkably easy to lose one's way.

Deep in the jungle at Penjerrick

Location Budock, nr Falmouth TR11 5ED, Cornwall
OS SW7730 3m SW of Falmouth by minor roads
Tel 01872 870105 **English Heritage Register** Grade II
Owner Mrs R. Morin **Open** Mar to Sept, Wed, Fri and Sun 1.30–4.30 **Area** 15 acres/6 hectares

PINE LODGE GARDENS

LATE 20TH-CENTURY GARDENS WITH A REMARKABLE COLLECTION OF BEAUTIFULLY GROWN PLANTS

As you walk from the car park at Pine Lodge you pass a delightful Cornish dry-stone wall capped with turf and planted with ferns and navelwort; there is also a very urban street lamp of the slightly old-fashioned kind often seen in suburban gardens. The garden too reflects a certain clash of styles, but the plants, and the standards of practical horticulture, are superb. Much of the detailing is marvellous, too. Granite slabs of lovely quality are used for paving paths or for making steps; the steps which lead down to

Fine planting at Pine Lodge Gardens

the arboretum, for example, becoming deeper as they descend, are magnificent. Occasionally there are attractive but simple ornaments – a fine terracotta pot-bellied pot placed alongside *Viburnum plicatum* f. *tomentosum* 'Mariesii', for example – but elsewhere in the garden poor quality statues or fiddly interludes of paving are unworthy of the quality of the plants. Having said that, anyone who loves plants and prefers to see them bursting with vigour, will have a marvellous time here.

The Clemos have been building up their garden since 1976, starting with 2 acres/0.8 hectares and expanding to 30 acres/12 hectares. Much of the garden consists of intricate planting and winding paths surrounding the house, but west of the house are handsome open areas with an arboretum, a lake and a pinetum (planted in 1993; who else has planted a private pinetum in the last fifty years?). Everything is impeccably labelled and over 6,000 different species and cultivars are grown – an astonishing collection for a private garden. A National Collection of the Australian genus *Grevillea* (15 species and cultivars) is kept here. It is a place that is most pleasurable to visit, where one may also learn about unfamiliar plants.

Location Cuddra, Holmbush, St Austell PL25 3RQ, Cornwall **OS** SX0452 On the E edge of St Austell, signed on the A390 **Tel** and **Fax** 01726 73500 **Email** sclemo@talk21.com **Website** www.pine-lodge.co.uk **Owner** Shirley and Ray Clemo **Open** Apr to Sept, Wed to Sun and Bank Hol Mon 2–5 **Area** 30 acres/12 hectares

PRIOR PARK LANDSCAPE GARDEN

EXQUISITE 18TH-CENTURY LANDSCAPE
GARDEN IN A MEMORABLE POSITION
WITH VIEWS OVER BATH

By comparison with other 18th-century landscape parks Prior Park is delightful chamber music rather than formidable symphony. The site is very beautiful – a shallow wooded valley scooping down to the north, with Elysian views of Bath. The Palladian mansion (now a school) was built between 1735 and 1748 to the designs of John Wood the Elder for Ralph Allen, an entrepreneur and quarry owner who supplied stone for the building of Georgian Bath. The park was laid out from 1734 onwards, probably by Allen himself, with help from Richard Jones and the poet Alexander Pope who corresponded with Allen and made several visits. Jones, Allen's clerk of works, also acted as an architect, and it was he who, in 1756, designed the key garden building here – the lovely Palladian bridge which spans the neck of an ornamental lake at the foot of the valley. Capability Brown was consulted about Prior Park in about 1764 and although there is no evidence that he worked here, the garden certainly changed from the intricate semi-formality of

Pope's ideas to the Arcadian landscape of shorn turf, placid water, brisk descents and distant prospects which the visitor sees today.

Location Bath, Somerset **OS** ST7662 On Combe Down, 1m S of the centre of Bath **Tel** 01225 833422 **Infoline** 09001 335242 **Email** priorpark@ntrust.org.uk **English Heritage Register** Grade I **Owner** The National Trust **Open** daily except Tue 12–5.30 or dusk if earlier (closed 25 and 26 Dec and 1 Jan) **NB** No parking at the garden; phone for details of access **Area** 28 acres/11 hectares

ROSEMOOR GARDEN

THE PRIVATE GARDEN OF A NOTED
PLANTSWOMAN TRANSFORMED BY
THE RHS INTO A FINE DISPLAY GARDEN

The fame of the garden at Rosemoor dates back to the 1960s when Lady Anne Palmer, a skilful gardener and consummate plantswoman, started opening the garden for the National Gardens Scheme. Its description in the Yellow Book ended with the words, irresistibly seductive to all gardeners, "Plants for Sale", and for many years this was an admirable source of quirky, rare or merely desirable plants of the sort not often found in garden centres.

Colonel J.E. and Lady Anne Palmer had come here in 1959 and started to make a garden on a west-facing slope running southwards from the house. The garden was essentially informal, with a large range of trees and shrubs of the kind that flourish in acid soil. Lady Anne became a friend of "Cherry" Ingram, from whom many distinguished flowering trees and shrubs found their way to Rosemoor. The garden had, in addition, notable collections of primulas and of the smaller decorative bulbous plants.

A NEW DISPLAY GARDEN

In 1988 Lady Anne Berry (as she had become) gave the estate to the Royal Horticultural Society. The garden has since been greatly extended to form a display garden, and has a visitor centre built at a discreet distance from the house. Lady Anne's garden survives, with some of its original character, and the new garden, separated by the A3124, does not impinge on it but is craftily connected by a tunnel under the road. The two gardens, one busy with plants and information, the other serenely reticent, serve very different purposes. The chief part of the new garden, spread out below the visitor centre, is packed with compartments showing different garden styles and containing a very wide range of plants. These

The Palladian Bridge at Prior Park

The Foliage Garden at Rosemoor

gardens are either thematic (*Potager*, Herb and Cottage Gardens), devoted to particular groups of plants (Modern Roses and Shrub Roses) or are model gardens for particular sites or seasons (a Shade Garden, a Winter Garden, a Terrace Garden). It would be unlikely that even the most experienced gardener could fail to find something of interest here. The Plantsman's Garden, for example, has the attractive idea of gathering together many of the exotics which were introduced by the great local firm of Veitch & Son of Exeter. A Foliage Garden skilfully deploys ornamental grasses, shapely plants like euphorbias and New Zealand flax (*Phormium* cultivars), trees and shrubs with decorative foliage (*Eucalyptus* and *Pittosporum*) and a curious screen of clipped *Sorbus* aff. *thibetica* 'John Mitchell' with very large rounded leaves, underplanted with ferns. At a little distance from this is a lake and bog garden and an outstanding decorative kitchen garden enclosed in split chestnut paling. Although prettily ornamental, with swags of runner beans, espaliered fruit and edgings of Welsh onion, this is an efficient working garden seen in full productive action. Throughout Rosemoor emphasis is placed on plants which are suitable for the relatively wet, relatively warm climate of the south-west, making it an admirable resource for local gardeners.

Location Great Torrington EX38 8PH, Devon
OS SS5018 1m SE of Great Torrington by A3124
Tel 01805 624067 **Fax** 01805 624717 **Website** www.rhs.org.uk **Owner** The Royal Horticultural Society
Open Apr to Sept, daily 10–6; Oct to Mar, daily 10–5
Area 40 acres/16 hectares

ROYAL VICTORIA PARK

BEAUTIFUL 19TH-CENTURY PUBLIC PARK
IN AN OUTSTANDING 18TH-CENTURY
URBAN SETTING

Royal Victoria Park was designed by Bath's city architect, Edward Davis, and opened in 1830 by Princess Victoria – the only park in Britain designated "royal" throughout her very long reign. It remains today, still finely maintained by the City of Bath Parks Department, one of the most attractive of public parks. The Royal Avenue entrance, which leads off Queen's Parade in the heart of the city close to Queen's Square, has gates ornamented with a pair of Coade stone lions – copies of the Michelangelo lions with one forepaw resting on a ball. Soon, the splendid sight of the Royal Crescent (1767–74 by John Wood the Younger) is revealed, partly shrouded in trees, the curve of golden Bath stone performing the same role in the landscape here as an 18th-century country house would in a landscape park. In front of the crescent, forming the southern boundary of its private lawn, is an 18th-century ha-ha, and until Crescent Lawn was incorporated into the Royal Victoria Park in 1846, sheep used to graze here.

URNS OF SPLENDOUR

An avenue of horse chestnuts runs along the Royal Avenue and south of it is a delightful bandstand, delicately Rococo rather than jolly Victorian, designed in about 1880 by C.E. Davis; on old maps it is called the Orchestra which gives a notion of its dignified purpose. On each side is an urn of unexpected splendour. Sculpted by Antonio Canova, these were commissioned in 1805 by Napoleon as a present for the Empress Josephine; the inscription says that they "were bought from France after the Peninsula War, by Col Page and bequeathed by the will of Joseph Fuller Esq of 19 Lansdown Cresent (1874)". A beautiful grove of beeches partly veils the scene and many other good trees are planted in the close-mown turf. West of Marlborough Lane, where there is an entrance colonnade crowned with crouching sphinxes, a triumphant obelisk commemorates the first year of Queen Victoria's reign (1837). Across

A Canova urn for Napoleon

the grass is the delightful sight of Park Dairy, farm buildings rebuilt by Edward Davis in the style of a cottage *orné*, with an old sprawling cedar of Lebanon. The carriage drive now embarks on its circuit of the park, passing soon in front of an intricate lake, or Fish Pond, whose waters come from the hills above Bath. The north-western corner of the park is occupied by the Bath Botanical Gardens (*see page 18*).

Memorial in Royal Victoria Park

Location Bath, Somerset **OS** ST7465 In the centre of Bath, W and S of Royal Crescent **English Heritage Register** Grade II **Owner** The City of Bath **Open** daily, unlimited access **Area** 49 acres/20 hectares

SALTRAM HOUSE

AN 18TH-CENTURY HOUSE IN HANDSOME PARKLAND WITH A CONTEMPORARY ORANGERY AND GOOD TREES AND SHRUBS

There has been a house at Saltram since at least the 16th century but the present house is 18th-century, of various periods, with grand interiors designed by Robert Adam for the Parker family between 1768 and 1772. It is set in beautiful parkland but uncomfortably close to busy roads. The garden spreads west from the house with a lawn overlooked by an 18th-century pedimented orangery with giant sash windows; it is agreeable, and rare, to see an orangery still used for oranges. Nearby is a magnificent old sweet chestnut. Walks among trees and shrubs beyond the orangery show many fine plants – a huge bush of *Euphorbia mellifera*, *Albizzia julibrissin* and *Cornus* 'Norman Hadden'. Hidden away is an octagonal Gothic summerhouse with a pretty blue and white interior and a fireplace in the style of William Kent. An avenue of limes leads back towards the house, underplanted in spring with pale narcissi and beautiful later in the season with immense drifts of cow parsley. The avenue runs along the garden's boundary with lovely views southwards over old parkland. There are no horticultural fireworks at Saltram – it is a gentlemanly setting for a gentlemanly house, and perfect in its understated way.

Location Plympton, Plymouth PL7 3UH, Devon **OS** SX5255 3m E of Plymouth by A38 **Tel** 01752 333500 **Fax** 01752 336474 **Email** saltram@ntrust.org.uk **English Heritage Register** Grade II* **Owner** The National Trust **Open** end Mar to beginning Nov, daily except Fri (open Good Fri) 11–5; Nov to mid Dec, Jan to Mar, daily except Fri 11–4 **Area** 21 acres/8.5 hectares

The lime avenue at Saltram Park

SHUTE HOUSE

A MAGICAL 20TH-CENTURY GARDEN – SIR GEOFFREY JELLICOE'S MASTERPIECE OF WATER, TREES AND TURF

The eastern face of Shute House is early 18th-century, with a pretty pedimented façade, but much of the house is far older, straggling decoratively along the road. There was no known garden here before Michael and Lady Anne Tree bought the estate in 1968 and asked Sir Geoffrey Jellicoe to design a new garden for them. The garden that eventually emerged was made over many years – the result of a happy collaboration between Jellicoe and his clients. Jellicoe regarded his work at Shute as "a laboratory of ideas" yet the impression that visitors have of the garden as it exists today is one of complete inevitability. Set comfortably within its rural surroundings and providing a perfect setting for the house, garden and landscape have become a seamless garment.

The most important ingredient at Shute is water, and this dominated Jellicoe's ideas. South of the house, beyond a ha-ha, beautiful views over the valley to downs beyond are enlivened by a sequence of naturalistic ponds. West of the house, the same water, which originates from a mysterious and beautiful pool hidden in woodland on the western boundary of the garden, is used in more formal ways. The site at Shute is irregular, with slopes and bumps, but where the land falls away no attempt is made to regularise it into terraces and crisp changes of level as a garden of the Italian Renaissance would certainly have done.

MAGICAL WATER

The centrepiece of Jellicoe's design is a long stepped formal rill in a gentle slope, its upper part masked by dense and informal planting. Each of the three steps of the rill is traversed by a stone slab where the water cascades over varying numbers of copper V shapes, designed by Jellicoe to interrupt the flow and so produce a "harmonic water chord". (In fact, the sound is simply that of falling water.) From a romantic viewing point at the head of the rill, paths on each side lead down through

arbours of wisteria with lavish plantings of honeysuckle, Japanese anemones and shrub roses. The banks are planted with bold foliage plants such as goatsbeard (*Aruncus dioicus*), hostas, ligularia and lysichiton. The lower part of the cascade, now a narrower rill, flows across an uneven open lawn, dropping into pools that are octagonal, hexagonal or square, with a bubbling jet at the centre of each. Finally, the water falls into a fern-lined rill and is carried away to other watery parts of the garden. From here, standing in an ivy-shrouded niche, a statue of Flora gazes back up the rill.

From the head of the rill a secretive passage leads between hedges of yew and beech to show water used in an entirely different way. Here, splendid 17th-century busts of Diana, Neptune and Zeus, standing in niches cut into a beech hedge, look over a low amphitheatre of box down a long, still, rectangular pool. (In Jellicoe's time the busts were herms of Roman poets.) Clumps of arum lilies are planted regularly down one side of the pool, and on the other side are viewing platforms set in a grove of ilexes. From the far end a mown path leads down into the woods where the source of Shute's water, a pool with bubbling springs, gleams in the shade. Nearby, a bench is placed

to encompass two views: one, the classical view, of the formal pool with its busts; the other, the romantic view, of a larger informal pool at right angles to the first, its irregular outlines shrouded in trees and shrubs, like a miniature lake in a landscape park.

On the south side of the ilex grove are six large square beds hedged in box, with a path through the middle. A beautiful *Catalpa bignonioides* stands nearly at the centre of one. In Lady Anne Tree's time four of these beds were filled with herbaceous ornamental planting and two with fruit and vegetables. A similar arrangement, with formal plantings of flowers or vegetables, is soon to be reinstated.

INTREPID ECLECTICISM

The Lewises came to Shute in 1993 and have finely restored the existing garden, adding excellent ideas of their own, especially around the house. With Jellicoe's advice, just before he died, they moved the ha-ha to make a deeper lawn south of the house, and planted a long and flowery terrace to provide sitting places under the south façade of the house. In front of the pedimented east façade they have completed the enclosure of a forecourt with high yew hedges, put in place a magnificent

The rill at Shute House

pair of wrought-iron gates, and added clematis and climbing roses to the walls of the house. In the hidden lower part of the garden, near Jellicoe's rustic temple of ivy (made "under the influence of Ovid") they have continued the theme, with a sinister planting of dark and poisonous plants round a bust of Pan.

The garden at Shute is an important one, and the atmosphere of Jellicoe's original design remains remarkably intact. It is probably the best and most attractive place in which to understand his ideas. A work of intrepid eclecticism, it welds together the sacred groves of classical culture, the austere geometry of Mughal gardens, the exuberant formality of elements of the Italian Renaissance and the romantic yearnings of the 18th-century landscape park. Beyond all that, it is a most delightful place in which to be.

Location Donhead St Mary, Shaftesbury SP7 9DG, Dorset **OS** ST9124 In Donhead St Mary village, 3m E of Shaftesbury by A30 and minor roads **Tel** 01747 828866 **Owner** Mr and Mrs John Lewis **Open** only to groups of between 20 and 40 by written appointment **Area** 7 acres/2.8 hectares

STICKY WICKET

A LATE 20TH-CENTURY GARDEN WHERE
THE ENVIRONMENT IS AS IMPORTANT AS THE
DELIGHTFUL COLOUR HARMONIES

The Lewises came to live here in 1987, inheriting the name of the house (which may refer to the heavy underlying clay of their garden soil or it may be a less explicit reference to cricket). The garden they made, in double quick time, opened for the National Gardens Scheme for the first time in 1989. It was described as "designed to show different planting styles and colour themes" with the additional aim of "attracting bees, butterflies and birds". Over the years, although the ornamental qualities of the garden remain, the ecological and wildlife principles have come to the fore.

The formal parts of the garden, although there is nothing so formal as a straight line, are gathered together about the house. The Frog Garden behind the house has swerving mixed borders about a lawn and a pool. Blue and yellow dominate the colour scheme, with shrubs such as *Cytisus battandieri*, *Euphorbia mellifera* and *Rosa* 'Maigold' underplanted with crocosmias, daylilies and geraniums, and grasses such as *Milium effusum* 'Aureum'. A pergola and terrace continue the theme with *Coreopsis verticillata* and *Lonicera periclymenum*

The Round Garden at Sticky Wicket

'Graham Thomas'. The Bird Garden, below the east windows of the house so that the many visiting birds are easily visible, has a more sprightly colour scheme of deep reds, purples and pinks. A circular gravel bed has a spreading sea of the white and pink Mexican daisy (*Erigeron karvinskianus*), trailing silver-pink *Convolvulus althaeoides* and the native sea thrift, *Armeria maritima*.

CIRCLES AND MEADOWS

On ground sloping up from the house to the south is the Round Garden, a series of concentric circles in which the planting ebbs and flows from pastels to rich red, magenta or purple. Grasses, especially festuca, pennisetums and the delicate little *Agrostis nebulosa*, are repeatedly used, providing crisp structure or blurred texture. The site is open and receives any sun, making it attractive to bees and butterflies. Further away from the house the White Garden, largely of trees and shrubs, extends the theme to white doves in a dovecote and the geese in an adjacent poultry run. A hay meadow has been recreated by removing the excessively fertile topsoil and sowing the subsoil with seed gathered from another meadow. It is now a splendid sight, with bird's-foot trefoil, corky-fruited dropwort, orchids, ragged robin, yellow rattle

and much else. A smaller garden version of the principle includes non-native plants such as campanulas and geraniums and also makes use of bulbs such as narcissi and snowdrops. A little copse of birch has been planted to provide habitats – as many as 229 fauna will thrive among birch; piles of logs or dry-stone walls give habitats for many other creatures. The planting, much of which is beautiful, displays the occasional surprise juxtaposition – the grand *Cornus controversa* 'Variegata' soars above groves of rosebay willow herb.

Many beautiful gardens pay little attention to the demands of nature's fauna. A garden such as Sticky Wicket where provision for such creatures is a guiding principle may arrive at a different kind of beauty, not a visual aesthetic but a moral one. Even so, it is only a version of nature, for foxes are excluded by an electric wire and rabbits are kept at bay with netting. Are the natural rights of rabbits and foxes less worthy than those of bees, butterflies and birds?

Location Buckland Newton DT2 7BY, Dorset **OS** ST6905
In Buckland Newton village, between the church, the school and the Gaggle of Geese pub, 10m N of Dorchester by B3143 **Tel** 01300 345476 **Owner** Peter and Pam Lewis **Open** Jun to Sept, Thurs 10.30–8
Area 2 acres/0.8 hectares

STONE LANE GARDENS

A RARE WILD DARTMOOR GARDEN WITH
A COLLECTION OF ALDERS AND BIRCHES
ANIMATED WITH MODERN SCULPTURES

Unless you have a consuming interest in plants, collections of plants can be tedious places. The Ashburners have chosen a relatively austere subject for their collection – alders and birches – but have made of it a garden of rare charm.

Kenneth's plants, which constitute National Collections of their genera, are propagated from seed gathered in the wild. (Seed gathered in gardens is almost certain not to come true – birches in particular hybridise very easily.) Furthermore, since there are characteristic differences between specimens of a particular species found in different sites in the wild, all the trees at Stone Lane have been planted in groups of a single species raised from seed from a single site in the wild. Carefully manicured naturalistic groves, like miniature samples of wild woodland, enable the subtle differences between groups to be more easily observed. Variations of the beautiful Himalayan birch, *Betula utilis*, are especially striking, with the colour of their distinctively peeling bark varying from very pale silver-pink to a rich tawny caramel.

The site for the garden is suitably wild, 600ft/180m up on the very edge of Dartmoor where rainfall is high and winters are frequently harsh. The site slopes gently downwards and is well watered with pools created by damming a stream. The Ashburners have added other plantings of an appropriately naturalistic character: thickets of *Rubus cockburnianus* and *R. odoratus*; wild North American roses like *Rosa virginiana* and *R. nitida*; the native English bilberry *Vaccinium myrtillus*, grown alongside its North American cousin, *V. uliginosum* (the bog bilberry), and several other species of vaccinium (all of which relish the damp acid soil); and the Japanese holly, *Ilex crenata* is used to form billowing informal hedges along paths. In all this the Ashburners have reconciled the demands of a botanical collection with the nature of the site and made something that is horticulturally delightful. It serves as an admirable model for a naturalistic planting style that could be used to similar effect in a much smaller garden.

The Ashburners

also mount an annual exhibition of modern sculpture, all of which is for sale, handsomely displayed in appropriate settings among the trees. The garden at Stone Lane shows great originality of an unostentatious kind, resulting in a place of quite special charm.

Location Stone Farm, Chagford TQ13 8JU, Devon **OS** SX6988 Off A382, 14m W of Exeter by A30 and Whiddon Down exit **Tel** and **Fax** 01647 23111 **Owner** Kenneth and June Ashburner **Open** end May to mid Sept, daily 2–6 **Area** 5½ acres/2.2 hectares

TAPELEY PARK

MAGNIFICENT EDWARDIAN TERRACED GARDEN FOR AN 18TH-CENTURY HOUSE IN A BEAUTIFUL POSITION

The house at Tapeley occupies a wonderful position high up on wooded slopes above the Torridge estuary with broad views south-west. Commodore William Clevland, who built the house in about 1700, was a naval officer, so this was an appropriate place to live. Between 1898 and 1916 the exterior of the house was completely rebuilt under the supervision of John Belcher for Augustus and Lady Rosamond Christie; they also asked him to make a new garden. On the slopes below the southern façade of the

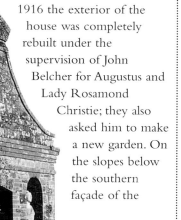

Tapeley Park's summerhouse

Statue at Stone Lane Gardens

house Belcher made three Italianate terraces linked by brick steps and decorated with statues. To descend the terraces you squeeze between a pair of old Irish yews, with thickets of lavender and fuchsia on either side. Many distinguished tender plants flourish in the protection of the terraces – the showiest of all buddleias, *Buddleja colvilei*, *Callistemon cirtrinus*, *Crinodendron hookerianum* and *Drimys winteri*. A sundial sits at the centre of the middle terrace and a row of Irish yews guards the lowest terrace to the west. On the other side a long flight of steps watched over by a pair of putti climbs a slope, and nearby is a pretty brick summerhouse, a former tool house, with statues in niches and a sweeping gable of Dutch character. At the top of the hill are a so-called grotto, in fact a shellhouse, and an icehouse – these must both date from the 18th century. In recent years new planting schemes have been commissioned from Mary Keen and Carol Klein but sadly these have not been well cared for. It is the breathtaking position of the house, the noble terraces and the older garden buildings which give Tapeley Park its distinction.

Location Instow EX39 4NT, Devon **OS** SS4729 2m N of Bideford by A39 **Tel** 01271 342558 **Fax** 01271 342371 **English Heritage Register** Grade II* **Owner** Tapeley Park Trust **Open** Good Fri to Oct, daily except Sat 10–5 **Area** 10 acres/4 hectares

TINTINHULL HOUSE

A MASTERLY GARDEN OF COMPARTMENTS WITH DISTINGUISHED PLANTING AND WONDERFUL CHARACTER

Tintinhull is among the most rewarding of English gardens. It is in essence like a miniature Hidcote or Sissinghurst in the way in which a harmonious sequence of spaces, often with strong architectural features, is embellished with carefully thought-out planting. The house is a very pretty 17th-century Ham stone village house, with a fine early 18th-century façade facing west over the garden. The garden is chiefly the creation of a remarkable woman, Phyllis Reiss, who came here in 1933, though she inherited some strong formal features made by her predecessor, Dr Price.

An exact rectangle, almost entirely walled in stone, spreads out west and north of the house. The garden's great beauty comes from the easy and logical flow of events leading from enclosure to enclosure. From the garden door in the west façade of the house a long axial vista is marked by a paved path which

facing east intermingles strong reds, an occasional splash of yellow, the soothing grey of artemisias and brachyglottis, while the pale border facing it is dominated by white and pink and grey with notes of purple and blue. Lastly, the Cedar Court has magnolias planted in a lawn with a fortissimo purple and gold border backed by a yew hedge.

In 1980 Penelope Hobhouse came to live at Tintinhull with her husband, Professor John Malins. They both worked in the garden, much improving standards of maintenance,

erupted at regular, widely spaced intervals from the grass – precisely wrong for this setting. Despite such misjudgements of planting, however, Tintinhull remains one of the best designed and most attractive gardens in the country – approachable because of its modest size and an inexhaustible model for all gardeners.

Location Tintinhull, nr Yeovil BA22 8PZ, Somerset **OS** ST5019 5m S of Yeovil, signed from A303 **Tel** 01935 822545 **Email** tintinhull@ntrust.org.uk **English Heritage Register** Grade II **Owner** The National Trust **Open** Apr to Sept, Wed to Sun 12–6 **Area** ¾ acre/0.3 hectares

TREBAH

EXCEPTIONAL CORNISH PLANTSMAN'S GARDEN IN A RAVINE SITE OF OUTSTANDING BEAUTY

In 1904, when the garden was in its maturity, S.W. Fitzherbert wrote: "For the natural beauty of its grounds…none can excel Trebah". A house had existed here from the mid 18th century and the estate was later acquired by Robert Were Fox I, of the great dynasty of Cornish garden makers. His son, Charles, took over in 1842 and embarked on a new garden. In the valley immediately adjacent his brother, Alfred Fox, had already been hard at work on his garden at Glendurgan since 1821 (*see page 38*). On Charles's death in 1868 the Trebah estate was left to his son-in-law, Edmund Backhouse, but throughout the 20th century it changed hands repeatedly and the garden became increasingly neglected, seemingly doomed.

runs between rows of clipped box mounds. The first enclosure, the walled Eagle Court, has stone eagles rising on piers and mixed borders under the walls. In the Middle Garden the box mounds continue but the planting on either side of the lawns is more free-flowing, with a woodland character. Finally, the Fountain Garden, hidden away behind walls of yew, has a more intimate atmosphere, with a circular lily pool and corner beds rich in white-flowered and variegated foliage plants. This sequence of gardens runs parallel to three others, all intercommunicating. The formal (but highly productive) kitchen garden has much ornamental flower planting. The Pool Garden has a slender rectangular pool running across a lawn to a pillared south-facing summerhouse. Mixed borders on either side of the lawn have controlled colour schemes: the hot border

The Eagle Court at Tintinhull House

but they also transformed the quality of detailed planting. In this Penelope Hobhouse fully recognised the brilliant skills of Phyllis Reiss – whom she describes as "one of the great gardeners of the 20th century" – but she sensitively revitalised the garden, adding much of her own but always respecting the essential qualities of Phyllis Reiss's work. Penelope Hobhouse left Tintinhull in 1993 and the garden has lost much of its magic. Some of this must be attributed to the reduction in labour required for such an intricate and subtly planted garden. When last visited, in spring 2002, exceptionally inappropriate red and yellow tulips, of municipal beefiness, had been planted in the east-facing border. In the orchard, across which visitors walk from the car park, very large and coarse daffodils

REMARKABLE RESTORATION

In 1981 Trebah was bought by Major Tony Hibbert and his wife, Eira, who have together carried out a remarkable feat of privately funded restoration. The site is one of the best, with a vertiginous ravine plunging southwards towards Polgwiddon Cove on the Helford estuary. The view from the top of the ravine, with distant glimpses of water, is very beautiful. The upper slopes of each side of the valley are clothed with dark trees, giving the ravine a greater sense of drama than any other Cornish

The ravine garden at Trebah

garden. The upper banks of the valley are threaded with paths offering wide views across a jungle of astonishing vegetation. It is best to walk down the valley on one side, zigzagging up and down when something draws the eye, and then return in the same way on the other side. The tallest specimens of Chusan palm (*Trachycarpus fortunei*) in England rise from the valley floor and a group of giant tree rhododendrons with blood-red flowers, *R.* 'Trebah Gem', erupts from the side of the ravine. At the foot of the valley a stream links pools whose banks are planted with a grove of *Gunnera manicata* and immense thickets of hydrangea. There are admirable specimens of camellias, tender *Cornus capitata*, magnolias, *Podocarpus totara*, a superlative wide-spreading *Davidia involucrata* var. *vilmoriniana* over a path, rhododendrons and tree ferns which are thoroughly naturalised here. It is the profusion of exotic flower and foliage, cultivated in naturalistic informality in a dramatic and lovely site, that gives Trebah such beauty.

Location Mawnan Smith, nr Falmouth TR11 5JZ, Cornwall **OS** SW7627 4m SW of Falmouth, signed from A394 and A39 approaches to Falmouth **Tel** 01326 250448 **Fax** 01326 250781 **Email** mail@trebah-garden.co.uk **Website** www.trebah-garden.co.uk **English Heritage Register** Grade II **Owner** The Trebah Garden Trust **Open** daily 10.30–5 **Area** 25 acres/10 hectares

TRELISSICK

IN A HIDDEN SITE ON THE WOODED BANKS OF THE RIVER FAL, A FINE COLLECTION OF PLANTS

Trelissick is one of the grandest of the Cornish estates, with a smart grandee's mansion rebuilt in 1825 with a columned portico. The estate had been bought in 1800 by a mine owner, Ralph Allen Daniell (known as Guinea-a-minute Daniell after his income from just one of his mines). Daniell's son Thomas became High Sheriff and a great power in the county, wildly overspending so that he was forced to sell the estate in 1832. It changed hands many times before passing into the ownership of the Copeland family (of china fame) which gave the estate to the National Trust in 1955. Although there is fine old parkland here, and good plantings of woodland to the east, the garden is quite recent as Cornish gardens go – most of the distinguished planting was carried out by the Copeland family after World War II.

As you enter the garden, past outhouses, you walk between two small enclosures – a garden of figs (8 different cultivars of *Ficus carica*), and opposite it, against a south-facing wall, the Parsley Garden. This was originally for the cultivation of early vegetables (what the French call *primeurs*) and is now given over to choice and tender flowering plants. The garden proper lies among woodland to

Cryptomeria japonica at Trelissick

the north and east. On the Main Lawn is a remarkable truncated *Cryptomeria japonica* of dinosaurian splendour. Below it, Carcadden is a large-scale shrub garden, with camellias, magnolias and rhododendrons and brilliant spreads of daffodils in spring. The jungly dell is one of the most protected parts of the garden and here are echiums, marvellous tree ferns (*Dicksonia antarctica*) and beautiful specimens of the late-flowering *Rhododendron maddenii* whose rose-flushed white flowers in high summer are deliciously scented. The boggier parts of the dell are lavishly planted with the Chilean fern *Blechnum chilense*, *Gunnera manicata*, lysichiton, Asiatic primulas and rodgersias. The best, and most memorable, pleasure of Trelissick is, however, the surrounding landscape, of which there are several carefully orchestrated views. The garden runs along the banks of the Fal whose wooded slopes and protected coves remain perfectly unspoilt, with the odd sailing boat drifting peacefully past. Various viewing points direct the gaze to fine views, and south-east of the house on the edge of pasture land, is a pavilion roofed with wooden shingles and decorated with patterns of pine cones and an inlaid pebble floor.

Location Feock, nr Truro TR3 6QL, Cornwall **OS** SW8339 4m S of Truro by B3289 **Tel** 01872 862090 **Fax** 01872 865808 **Email** trelissick@ntrust.org.uk **English Heritage Register** Grade II **Owner** The National Trust **Open** mid Feb to Oct, Mon to Sat 10.30–5.30, Sun 12.30–5.30 (closes 5 in Feb, Mar and Oct) **Area** 25 acres/10 hectares

TRENGWAINTON GARDEN

TENDER PLANTS, OUTSTANDING OLD
FLOWERING SHRUBS, AND WONDERFUL
VIEWS OF ST MICHAEL'S MOUNT

The estate of Trengwainton is an ancient one but its garden fame belongs to the 20th century. It was bought in 1867 by a banker from an old Cornish family, Thomas Simon Bolitho, and was inherited in 1925 by his great-nephew, Lieutenant-Colonel Sir Edward Bolitho, who gave the garden its present distinction. The site is an especially favoured one, close to the tip of the Cornish peninsula on slopes that face south-east, and to the north and west the garden is protected by old woodland. This, together with a fairly high rainfall and the benign effect of the North Atlantic Drift, makes it a wonderful place to grow plants.

The most protected part of the garden is on the northern edge of the drive close to the visitors' entrance and it is here that there is the greatest concentration of plant excitement. A series of walled gardens has exceptional magnolias, many of which date back to Colonel Bolitho's first plantings. Everywhere there are excellent specimens of shrubs and ornamental trees, while tender herbaceous plants such as *Echium pininana* and *Geranium palmatum* seed themselves profusely. Beside the far side of the drive the margins of a stream are densely planted with *Darmera peltata*, Himalayan primulas, ligularia, lysichiton and meconopsis, and woods

An old magnolia at Trengwainton

flanking the drive are rich in camellias and rhododendrons. In front of the house a lawn opens out and reveals the first views of the open countryside – with the breathtaking distant prospect of St Michael's Mount. Trengwainton has a wonderful collection of plants but it also possesses a bewitching atmosphere, enfolded in its exotic woodland with a secretive air.

Location Madron, nr Penzance TR20 8RZ, Cornwall
OS SW4431 2m NW of Penzance by B3312 **Tel** 01736
362297 (opening times only) **Fax** 01736 362297 **Email**
trengwainton@ntrust.org.uk **English Heritage Register**
Grade II **Owner** The National Trust **Open** late Feb to
Oct, Sun to Thur (open Good Fri) 10–5.30 (closes 5 in
Mar and Oct) **Area** 15 acres/6 hectares

TRESCO ABBEY GARDENS

A DAZZLING TERRACED JUNGLE OF
RARE AND TENDER PLANTS IN A
CLIMATE UNIQUE IN BRITAIN

In gardens where plants reign supreme the climate is the key to the spirit of the place. Tresco has much sunshine, little frost, and moderate rainfall of 30in/75cm per annum; violent, salt-laden winds and poor soil are usually the only enemies to gardening here. The garden was started in 1834 by Augustus Smith who built a new house above the ruins of a Benedictine priory on a south-facing slope. He chose Tresco for his house and garden because it had a good water supply and was protected by the other islands. Around the ruins of the priory he built new walls and made a small garden which is still one of the most atmospheric parts of the garden. He greatly extended the scope of the garden by terracing the steep south-facing slopes above the priory and by planting windbreaks of Monterey pine (*Pinus radiata*) and Monterey cypress (*Cupressus macrocarpa*). As he began to collect plants, many specimens came from Lord Ilchester's garden at Abbotsbury and from Kew, where Smith made contact with Sir William Hooker. Tender species from the southern hemisphere flourish here and Augustus Smith and his descendants eventually built up one of the greatest

The subtropical jungle of Tresco

collections of subtropical plants in Europe.

However, although the climate here is usually remarkably benign, in 1987 and 1990 nature showed her claws as never before in these parts and devastated the gardens. In January 1987 heavy snow fell, breaking the branches of many trees and shrubs. The snow was immediately followed by frost, with the temperature falling to −8°C /17°F for two weeks. This was made even worse by a fierce easterly wind, and huge numbers of plants were destroyed. A rescue operation was mounted and plants brought back to Tresco from countless different sources. Then, in January 1990, a hurricane tore through the old windbreaks, destroying 90% of the trees planted by Augustus Smith (800 mature trees) and many of the newly planted replacements of those lost in the great frost. The work of clearing the debris and restoring the planting is a remarkable saga, eloquently described in the book written by the garden curator, Mike Nelhams: *Tresco Abbey Garden* (2000).

An astonishing recovery has been made from these setbacks, and the gardens once again present a scene of extraordinarily exotic abundance. Agaves from the Mexican desert, proteas and silver-leafed leucadendrons from South Africa, banksias from Australia, olearias from New Zealand and spectacular echiums from the Canary Islands now clothe the slopes. Many exotics seed themselves here – clouds of purple-flowered *Geranium maderense*, *Euphorbia mellifera* giving off its honey-scented perfume – while *Agapanthus praecox* subsp. *orientalis* has escaped out of the gardens to scatter its rich blue flowers in the countryside.

The paths that run along the terraces give marvellous views over the gardens, and exhilarating cross vistas are opened by paths or steps that cut vertically up the slopes. There are subtle differences in the microclimates between the upper terraces and the lowest point of the garden. Plants that like it hot and dry flourish at the highest point and those like tree ferns that need shade and humidity enjoy air humidified by the close proximity of the sea at the foot of the slopes. The range of plants grown at Tresco makes it unique in the British Isles – but distinguished collections of plants do not necessarily make satisfying landscapes. Quite early in the history of the

garden Augustus Smith contrived a design which made the best of the site and created a wonderful setting for these subtropical exotics.

Location Tresco, Isles of Scilly TR24 0QQ, Cornwall **OS** SV8914 31m off the SW coast of Cornwall. Access by helicopter or ferry from Penzance **Tel** 01720 424105 **Fax** 01720 422868 **Email** mikenelhams@tresco.co.net **English Heritage Register** Grade I **Owner** R. Dorrien Smith **Open** daily 10–4 **Area** 16 acres/6 hectares

TREWITHEN

AN 18TH-CENTURY GARDEN TRANSFORMED IN THE 20TH CENTURY INTO A WOODLAND GARDEN OF EXCEPTIONAL BEAUTY

Trewithen is a Cornish woodland garden that is strikingly different from others. The name Trewithen means "house in a spinney" – the essence of its character today. Unlike the coastal gardens, it is not set in a precipitous ravine but is nevertheless beautifully laid out to create drama and beauty. The house is especially beautiful, rebuilt in silver Pentewan stone between 1738 and 1740 for Thomas Hawkins to the design of a London architect, Thomas Edwards. A garden was made in the 18th century "with all sorts of English and foreign plants" as a contemporary record says. It was Thomas Hawkins who created the open apron of lawn on the south side of the house, originally framed in formal beech hedges and still a spectacular feature. In the early 20th century

The woodland garden at Trewithen

the estate was inherited by George Johnstone who added huge numbers of new plants to the old woodland around the house. He was a friend of both J.C. Williams of Caerhays (*see page 22*) and of Lord Aberconway at Bodnant (*see page 192*), from both of whom he acquired countless good plants. Spectacular flowering shrubs, especially rhododendrons, were planted about the perimeter of the great lawn, and the woodland on either side was opened out and enriched with many new species. Today, paths snake among the trees and shrubs and at every turn there is something remarkable to admire. Here are the aristocrats of Cornish gardens – camellias, magnolias, Japanese maples, rhododendrons and stewartias.

The woodland garden is the great attraction at Trewithen but the delightful formal walled garden should not be overlooked. Here a pergola is garlanded with wisteria, and fine borders run along the walls which are draped with the curious lobster-claw plant (*Clianthus puniceus*). Here too is the splendidly vigorous ceanothus cultivar discovered in the garden, *C. arboreus* 'Trewithen Blue'.

Location Grampound Road, nr Truro TR2 4DD, Cornwall **OS** SW9147 7m W of St Austell by A390 **Tel** 01726 883647 **Fax** 01726 882301 **English Heritage Register** Grade II* **Owner** A.M.J. Galsworthy **Open** Mar to Sept, Mon to Sat 10–4.30 (Apr and May, also open Sun); walled garden open Apr to Jul, Mon, Tue and Bank Hol Mon 2–4 **Area** 25 acres/10 hectares

SOUTH-CENTRAL ENGLAND

ASCOTT

A ROTHSCHILD GARDEN WITH
SUMPTUOUS TOPIARY AND ORNAMENT,
GRAND BORDERS AND DELICIOUS VIEWS OF
THE VALE OF AYLESBURY

The house, originally a farmhouse built in
the early 17th century, was acquired by
Baron Mayer de Rothschild in 1873 as part of
the neighbouring Mentmore estate. Shortly
afterwards it was transferred to his nephew
Leopold de Rothschild who, in a succession
of alterations, transformed it into the "palace-
like cottage" it is today. The estate was given
to the National Trust by Anthony de
Rothschild in 1949.

The site is a splendid one, on the edge of
the Vale of Aylesbury over which it has fine
views. Much of the architectural work on the
house was done by George Devey who also
made a design for the gardens in collaboration
with Leopold de Rothschild. For the planting
they had the help of Sir Harry Veitch and his
nursery, Veitch & Son. The garden, with its
exuberant sense of decoration, still keeps
much of its original high Victorian character.

The Victorian garden is at a little distance
from the house, separated from it by
magnificent trees disposed in turf to provide a
park-like setting. Grand steps lead down,
passing under old weeping beeches. On the

The Venus fountain at Ascott

slope below is a rare topiary sundial fashioned
of box and yew; the now rather lumpy
gnomon is of yew, the figures of box, and a
motto is made of clipped golden box – "Light
and shade by turn but love always." In the
shade of trees to one side, the Sunken Garden
is a parterre of box with a central pool, its
basin supported by dolphins. Swirling shapes
of clipped box or mounds of ivy decorate the
compartments. This, thoroughly in keeping
with the Victorian character but not slavishly
so, is the work of Arabella Lennox-Boyd who
has done much work on the garden – often in
parts inaccessible to the public.

At the heart of the Victorian garden is the
Madeira Walk, a gravel path running between
mixed borders which are backed by a hedge
of golden yew on one side and a terrace wall
on the other, capped with a hedge of gold
variegated holly. The colour scheme is
restricted to purple, lilac and pink, with much
repeated planting of alliums, bergenias,
caryopteris, delphiniums, lavender and
penstemons. The beds are punctuated by the
bold foliage of artichokes and by stone urns
brimming with pink pelargoniums. Spring
and summer bedding plants are put into place
to maintain the momentum and to fill gaps.
In an enclosure of yew hedges leading off the
walk is a sumptuous bronze statue of Venus by

Thomas Waldo Story, of around 1890, at the
centre of a circular pool enclosed in hedges of
golden yew. Venus stands on the back of a
turtle in a marble cockleshell pulled by
frolicking seahorses. Narrow beds line the yew
hedges, planted with annuals in spring and
summer. Openings on each side lead to lawns
with giant topiary pieces of gold and
common yew, or of variegated holly, and fine
specimen trees; the ground slopes away to the
south giving beautiful views.

To the west is a further surprise. Concealed
behind a sweeping yew hedge the Dutch
Garden is entered by rustic stone steps which
sweep round a tufa grotto fringed with ferns.
A figure of Eros, again by Thomas Waldo
Story, rises at the summit of a multi-tiered
fountain about which is a geometric
arrangement of beds filled with patterns of
different colours of coleus, of which a
National Collection is held here.

The garden at Ascott is an unusual one,
deftly combining Victorian decorative
exuberance, stately parkland, excellent trees
and a refined sense of place while making the
most of fine views over the Vale of Aylesbury.

Location Wing, nr Leighton Buzzard LU7 0PS,
Buckinghamshire **OS** SP8922 2m SW of Leighton
Buzzard by A418 **Tel** 01296 688242 **Fax** 01296 681904
Email info@ascottestate.co.uk **English Heritage
Register** Grade II* **Owner** The National Trust **Open**
Apr, and end Aug to beginning of Oct, daily except Mon
2–6; May to end Aug, Wed and last Sun in each month
Area 39 acres/16 hectares

ASHDOWN HOUSE

THE REMOTE AND BEAUTIFUL LANDSCAPE
OF A 17TH-CENTURY HUNTING LODGE,
WITH RIDES THROUGH WOODLAND, HIGH
UP ON THE BERKSHIRE DOWNS

The Berkshire Downs (as they are still
known, despite the county boundary
change of 1974) are surprisingly wild and
unspoilt. This is an ancient site, already settled
in Iron Age times and with a pattern of
Roman fields. Owned by the Abbey of
Glastonbury in the middle ages, there was a
deer park here, and a herd of wild fallow deer
has been reintroduced. Fields are scattered

with sarsens among which shaggy highland cattle graze. It is the kind of memorable landscape which makes gardening seem almost superfluous.

Ashdown House is on high, intermittently wooded land and presents an appearance that is at once mysterious and dramatic, sharpened by the ghostly pale "clunch" (in effect, chalk) of which it is built. Built as a hunting lodge in the 1660s for the 1st Earl of Craven, it was possibly designed by William Winde who had worked on other houses for Lord Craven. A Kip engraving of 1707 shows it standing at the centre of a square courtyard with four rides shooting out through dense woods enclosing the house, and in the heathland beyond, huntsmen, a pack of hounds and a fox. There is a romantic story that Lord Craven also proposed the house as a refuge from the plague for King Charles I's sister, Elizabeth of Bohemia, The "Winter Queen", who died in 1662 before the house was complete. The estate now belongs to the National Trust which has planted avenues of limes following some of the original rides and laid out a double parterre of box scrolls.

The parterre
at Ashdown House

The knot garden at Basing House

The house is crowned with a lantern and gallery from which there are magnificent views over Ashdown Forest and the downs, and surrounding woodland makes a marvellous place for walks, punctuated from time to time by sudden revelations of the immensely elegant house. With minimal but splendid means Ashdown possesses a powerful sense of place.

Location Lambourn, nr Newbury RG16 7RE, Oxfordshire **OS** SU2882 **Tel** 01488 72584 **Email** ashdownhouse@ntrust.org.uk **English Heritage Register** Grade II* **Owner** The National Trust **Open** (House and grounds) Apr to Oct, Wed and Sat (guided tours of house only at 2.15, 3.15 and 4.15); (Woodland) daily except Fri dawn–dusk **Area** 346 acres/140 hectares

BASING HOUSE

A RECONSTRUCTED PARTERRE GARDEN SET IN THE POIGNANT REMAINS OF AN ELIZABETHAN PALACE DESTROYED IN THE CIVIL WAR

A castle was built here in the middle ages, probably by Hugh de Port, which was inherited by the Paulet family in 1428. Sir William Paulet, 1st Marquess of Winchester, Comptroller to Henry VIII and Treasurer to Elizabeth I, built a great palace of suitable splendour for such a powerful royal servant. Not only was it splendid but it was also in the latest style, showing the renaissance influence seen at Hampton Court. Under the Commonwealth the palace was stormed and virtually demolished. The citizens of Basing were told "whoever will come for brick and stone shall freely have the same for his pains", and old houses survive in Basing built from materials taken in this way. The Paulets retrieved their land at the Restoration and a grand new house was built, only to be demolished in 1740.

The walled Elizabethan garden

The Italian Garden at Blenheim

survived, being used for much of the time as a kitchen garden. The fact that it was more or less continuously cultivated meant that when an archaeological dig was made in 1987 it yielded no detailed information about the kind of garden that originally existed here. However, Hampshire County Council commissioned an elaborate knot garden which was designed by Elizabeth Banks using plants that an Elizabethan garden might have contained, among them box, cotton lavender, germander, hyssop, rue and sage. The motto of the Paulet family is picked out in planting – "Aymez Loyaulte"; it was the 5th Marquess's loyalty to his monarch that had occasioned the destruction of his palace. The knot stands in a corner of the walled garden which is partly terraced and has in two corners decorative octagonal Elizabethan dovecotes.

The knot, somewhat forlorn, certainly evokes the lively ornament of a 16th-century garden but it occupies only a very small part of a large space which is otherwise bereft of planting or decoration. Much more

memorable are the atmospheric earthworks of the medieval castle and the fragmentary ruins of the Tudor house. The County Council has made an excellent museum tracing the fortunes of the Paulet family and their great house. To study this and understand the splendour of the old house, and walk among its ruins, is a poignant experience. Poignant in a different way is the view to the west where you will see the towering office blocks of brave new Basingstoke.

Location Redbridge Lane, Basing, Basingstoke RG24 7HB, Hampshire **OS** SU6652 2m E of Basingstoke, signed from the centre **Tel** 01256 467294 **English Heritage Register** Grade II **Owner** Hampshire County Council **Open** Apr to Sept, Wed to Sun (open Bank Hol Mon) 2–6 **Area** 10 acres/4 hectares

BLENHEIM PALACE

AN EARLY 18TH-CENTURY PALACE BUILT TO CELEBRATE A GREAT SOLDIER, WITH MAGNIFICENT FORMAL GARDENS AND A LANDSCAPE PARK BY CAPABILITY BROWN

There is nothing cosy about Blenheim. The monumental palace was built in the early 18th century to honour the victor of a great battle, and the surrounding landscape is in scale with it. But long before all this, in the 12th century, Henry II made a garden at Woodstock Palace, quite close to modern Blenheim, which sticks insistently in the mind. Here King Henry created the enclosed pleasance of Everswell, "consisting", in the words of the garden historian John Harvey, "of an orchard with a series of pools fed by a natural spring". Here, too, the

The Italian Garden fountain

king is supposed to have installed his mistress, Rosamund de Clifford. The garden, fictitious or not, certainly gave rise to a fashion for enclosed pleasure gardens which may have been intended to evoke a scene (in which the lovers meet in an orchard with a spring) from the romance of *Tristan and Isolde*, one version of which was possibly written for Henry II himself.

Woodstock Palace survived in a more or less ruinous state until Sir John Vanbrugh arrived in 1704 to build the new palace, in collaboration with Nicholas Hawksmoor, for the Duke of Marlborough. Vanbrugh loved the ruins and urged the duchess to preserve them as a picturesque adornment of the landscape – "one of the most agreeable objects that the best of landscape-painters can invent", as he wrote. She refused and the building was finally demolished in 1723. However, the spring of Rosamund's Bower survives and may still be seen north-west of the present palace on the north bank of the lake.

In 1705 a new garden for Blenheim was started as the palace was being built. To the south of the palace Vanbrugh and the royal gardener, Henry Wise, devised a formal garden of formidable elaboration, guarded by eight 150ft/45m bastions of suitably military aspect. This vast garden was short-lived for Capability Brown came in 1764 to introduce a new kind of landscape. The traveller Colonel John Byng wrote after his visit in 1782, "Here Lancelot Brown (the great planner of land) will be immortalised in his management of the ground about the house and the formation of the superb water; at which, when finish'd, he exclaimed with his usual pompous drollery, 'Thames, Thames, you will never forgive me.'"

Brown is often accused of destroying earlier formal landscapes with ruthless insensitivity. However, at Blenheim there is much evidence of his appreciation of the existing genius of the place. He preserved Vanbrugh's splendid bridge over the river Glyme and above all he maintained the northern vista from the palace, over the bridge, to the giant Column of Victory and beyond, up the hill to Vanbrugh and Wise's Grand Avenue (originally of elms but now of limes). Brown's great coup was to dam the river and created a wasp-waisted lake spanned by Vanbrugh's bridge. The view of all this from the Triumphal Gate in Woodstock village is one of the most unforgettable of any English landscape.

The last great episode in the story of the garden at Blenheim is the creation by Achille Duchêne of the Italian Garden and the Water Terraces flanking the palace, which have a sprightly, festive character that contrasts admirably with the more solemn Baroque spirit of the palace. Duchêne was a French garden designer whose speciality, usually in collaboration with his father, Henri, was reinstating the great 17th-century gardens of France, in particular those of André Le Nôtre. The Italian Garden (completed in 1910) is a parterre with hedges of golden yew, swooping arabesques of box and a fountain by Thomas Waldo Story of a naked nymph holding a ducal coronet aloft while standing in a pool supported by mermaids and dolphins. The Water Terraces, completed in 1930, are in two parts. The upper level has elaborately scalloped pools, each with a fountain, and with *parterres de broderie* of box. The lower level is much calmer, with two rectangular pools, one of which has a small-scale version of Bernini's superb river gods fountain of 1651 in the Piazza Navona in Rome. The Water Terraces, magnificently enlivened with splendid statuary, have skilfully orchestrated changes of level which multiply the viewpoints and add to the decorative exuberance. From the lower terrace an Arcadian view of the wooded lake and its tree-shrouded banks opens out.

The route by which visitors leave runs across parkland with superlative old oaks. The great 8-acre/3.2-hectare kitchen garden, completed in about 1712, with high walls and rounded bastions, houses various modern amusements – a herb garden, butterfly house, adventure playground and maze. Blenheim is run as a tourist attraction but it is skilfully managed so that the beauties of the palace, park and gardens remain intact.

Location Woodstock OX20 1PX, Oxfordshire
OS SP4416 In Woodstock, 8m N of Oxford by A44
Tel 01993 811325 **Fax** 01993 813527 **English Heritage Register** Grade I **Owner** The Duke of Marlborough **Open** (Formal gardens) mid Mar to Oct, daily 10.30–4.45; (Park) daily 9–4.45 **Area** 2,000 acres/810 hectares

BOWOOD

A ROBERT ADAM HOUSE WITH DECORATIVE VICTORIAN GARDENS, A FINE 19TH-CENTURY PINETUM, A RHODODENDRON WOOD AND AN ARCADIAN LANDSCAPE BY CAPABILITY BROWN

Few places are better than Bowood for displaying the peculiar genius of Capability Brown, though the garden has other memorable attractions besides. The kind of landscape that Brown devised, an idealised view of rural scenery, is so unostentatious and so widely influential on the English countryside that it is easy to start thinking of it as the norm from which other kinds of landscapes are an unfortunate aberration. At Bowood the scenery he devised is a distillation of his vision. He was consulted by the Earl of Shelburne in 1757 and work started on the new park in 1761. A stream was dammed – which required the demolition of a hamlet – and a long serpentine lake formed which, when a wind ruffles its surface, resembles from certain viewpoints a flowing river. That single feature is the essence of Brown's work at Bowood although he was also much involved with boundary planting and the design of drives.

The lake and its surroundings have, however, been gently titivated in ways that enhance the bold simplicity of the initial work. At the north end of the lake is a spectacular naturalistic cascade, designed in about 1785 by the Hon. Charles

The cascade at Bowood

Hamilton of Painshill. As you walk through the woods you hear the noise of the tumbling water before the cascade is revealed, gushing down among huge rocks in three tiers and flowing into a peacefully winding stream fringed with ferns. In the cliff to one side are grottoes made by Josiah Lane of Tisbury, the ensemble forming, in Geoffrey Grigson's words, "a masterpiece…of romantic naturalism". On the bank of the lake Josiah Lane also made a hermit's cave decorated with tufa, its ceiling studded with ammonites and stalactites. Nearby, a grassy isthmus projects from densely planted woodland, ornamented with an early 19th-century Doric temple which has moved to the site from elsewhere in the garden in 1864.

RHODODENDRONS AND A PINETUM

Brown was also involved in the woodland planting that now forms the Rhododendron Walks at some distance from the house – a design that was associated with the great mausoleum built by Robert Adam in 1761 to celebrate the life of the 1st Earl of Shelburne. The domed building rises on a slight eminence, with a gap in the woods revealing distant views of the house and its larger setting. In the 19th century a rhododendron collection was started in the woods, and this has been much enriched by the present Marquess of Lansdowne.

These are the best parts of the garden at Bowood but tree-lovers will also relish the remains of a good pinetum which dates back to the mid 19th century. Two ornamental terraces, of 1818 and 1851, immediately south of the house have rows of clipped Irish yews and rose beds. A particularly coarse figure of a sprawling nude woman is an exceptionally unhappy late 20th-century addition. The terraces, decorative as they are for the most part, are minor pleasures compared with the uncontrived grandeur and simplicity of Capability Brown's work.

Location Calne SN11 0LZ, Wiltshire **OS** ST9769 ½m W of Calne by A4 **Tel** 01249 812102 **English Heritage Register** Grade I **Owner** The Marquess of Lansdowne **Open** Apr to Oct, daily 11–6; Rhododendron Walks Apr to early Jun depending on flowering (phone for times) **Area** 100 acres/40 hectares

BROADLEAS GARDENS

A 20TH-CENTURY WOODLAND GARDEN OF MESMERISING CHARM CREATED BY AN ACCOMPLISHED PLANTSWOMAN

The approach to Broadleas Gardens is as unexpected as could be. To arrive at the head of the drive you have to pass through a large modern housing estate. All the more unexpected in this suburban setting, therefore, is the intensely rural scene that confronts you, with its garden of Arcadian charm. Lady Anne Cowdray came here in 1946 and, having exhausted the delights of hunting and shooting, began to make a garden. In this otherwise rather flat part of the country the site at Broadleas is unusually hilly. The terrace of the early 19th-century house looks over a fine tennis lawn to a meadow and trees set in a strongly sculpted landscape. In addition to the charms of the land the place is especially attractive to a gardener for the soil here is excellent greensand.

When Lady Anne came the only ornamental plants were thickets of *Rhododendron ponticum* but there was the protection of some good old trees, in particular beeches, oaks and Scots pines. She seized upon this to make an intimate woodland garden, the Dell, in an occasionally precipitous valley now planted with an outstanding collection of trees and shrubs. The lower part of the Dell is protected from the south-westerly winds by a tall serpentine hedge of Leyland cypress. In this protected setting plants have grown astonishingly well. A southern beech (*Nothofagus × alpina*), with a dramatically gnarled trunk, shoots up to a great height, far taller than would be expected of a tree that is less than fifty years old. The tree connoisseur Alan Mitchell described this as "the fastest thing on roots" but it is nonetheless surprising. The acid soil has allowed the cultivation of admirable ericaceous plants. The rhododendrons are almost entirely species ones, and there are beautiful camellias, enkianthus and stewartias. A fine collection of magnolias, several grown to great size, is one of the greatest beauties. Throughout the Dell herbaceous underplanting adds to the attractions of the place – erythroniums, ferns, hostas and primulas – and occasionally more unusual plants like the giant lily *Cardiocrinum giganteum*, the beautiful *Tulipa sprengeri* and, a rare sight in Wiltshire, Himalayan poppies.

The Dell at Broadleas

Such exotic planting gives way from time to time to pretty groups of wild flowers such as bluebells, buttercups, red campion and stitchwort. The planting is for the most part naturalistic with an occasional touch of something more contrived: a *Catalpa × erubescens* 'Purpurea' standing at the centre of a close-mown glade; or a crescent of clipped beech hedging embracing a terracotta urn on a plinth. Paths run along each side of the glade, sometimes striking out in a stiff zig-zag up the slope. The same plants are often to be seen from different viewpoints and groups are juggled with kaleidoscopic variety.

Formal gardens cluster about the house. A sunken garden has old roses, a secret garden is veiled by a beautiful spreading Japanese maple, and a grey border running along a wall is full of cistus, elaeagnus, olearias and rosemaries. These are pretty, but it is the Dell that really catches the heart.

Location Devizes SN10 5JQ, Wiltshire **OS** SU0060 1m S of Devizes W of A360, signed from centre of Devizes **Tel** 01380 722035 **Owner** Broadleas Gardens Charitable Trust **Open** Apr to Oct, Sun, Wed and Thur 2–6 **Area** 9 acres/3.6 hectares

BROOK COTTAGE

A 17TH-CENTURY VILLAGE HOUSE IN
A FINE VALLEY SETTING, ADORNED WITH A
GARDEN RICH IN UNUSUAL PLANTS

Many gardens start as a gradual response to the setting of a house. A distinctive English way of doing it, with no preconceived ideas of layout, is to clothe the landscape in appropriate plants. The Hodges came to Brook Cottage, an attractive 17th-century house, in 1964 when there was no garden to speak of. The site slopes, sometimes precipitously, to the south-west of the house and the surroundings are thoroughly rural. Close to the house are passages of formality – an enclosed courtyard behind it is carpeted with hostas, and has a large datura in a pot and *Cobaea scandens* festooning the wall. A terrace with a grand Venetian wellhead and steps provides the entrance to the garden at the front of the house. The steps leading down from the terrace, well protected and facing

The terrace at Brook Cottage

south-west, display tender plants in pots; a beautiful Australian shrub, *Alyogyne huegelii*, with silky purple flowers was the star of the display when I visited in the summer of 2002.

From here, a long lawn, with a single tree of purple-leaved Norway maple (*Acer platanoides* 'Crimson King'), points the way into the garden proper. Red arrows show the way and you immediately find yourself squeezing between a huge variegated holly and a bush of yellow potentilla. In an atmosphere of jungly profusion you pass a grove of glaucous conifers to where a hedge of copper beech turns into a tunnel. The path winds uphill beside a shady damp spot leafy with arum lilies, cimicifuga, ferns, lysichiton and rodgersias. You soon find you are skirting a stream, the boundary of the garden, and passing a grand *Parrotia persica* you arrive at a grove of shrub and species roses. These are much used throughout the garden, and this is certainly the way to use them – completely at home in a wild setting instead of being cooped up primly in a border. A collection of different species of rowans is lovely in early autumn, flaunting pale orange, bright orange, deep red or pink berries. On your right is a beautiful spreading Caucasian wingnut (*Pterocarya fraxinifolia*) with, of sharply contrasting habit, an unusual fastigiate beech, *Fagus sylvatica* 'Rohanii' with fretted oak-like leaves of a curious brownish-purple. A stiffish ascent now takes you past a thicket of *Parrotia persica* to a cascading bank of species roses from

where a path leads back towards the house. Venus stands above a white bench and a pool. From here the red arrows take you under flowering cherries on steep sloping banks north of the house where a swooping border is filled with alstroemeria, daylilies, echinops, penstemons and persicaria. A little vegetable garden seems threatened with ornamental encroachment. The slope leads down past the house and a white border to a sinuous pool on a lawn to the west of the house. On its banks are good trees: a very pretty cut-leafed alder (*Alnus glutinosa* 'Laciniata'), a variegated sweet chestnut (*Castanea sativa* 'Albomarginata') and a young tulip tree (*Liriodendron tulipifera*).

The walls of the house, and any other suitable supports, are shrouded in climbing plants, in particular clematis of which there are well over 50 varieties, and in climbing roses, for the most part the older varieties. It is a love of plants that dominates the garden at Brook Cottage. They are well used so that, individually or in groups, they brilliantly enliven the jungly walk that constitutes the garden's chief pleasure.

Location Well Lane, Alkerton, nr Banbury OX15 6NL, Oxfordshire **OS** SP3742 In the village of Alkerton 6m NW of Banbury by A422 **Tel** 01295 670303 **Owner** Mrs David Hodges **Open** Apr to Oct Mon to Fri 9–6; also by appointment **Area** 4 acres/1.6 hectares

BROUGHTON CASTLE

A MOATED LATE MEDIEVAL FORTIFIED
MANOR HOUSE WITH A DELIGHTFUL
VICTORIAN FORMAL GARDEN AND
OUTSTANDING 20TH-CENTURY BORDERS
PARTLY DESIGNED BY LANNING ROPER

Broughton Castle is a marvellous house in
an exceptional setting. Friendlier than
most castles, more a fortified manor house, it
is built of toffee-coloured stone and dates
from the 14th century but with much
rebuilding in the 16th century. Close to the
edge of the village, it overlooks a moat and is
set in serene parkland. Nothing is known of
the garden before the late 19th century when
the estate was let to Lord Algernon Gordon
Lennox who did much work on the garden. A
Country Life article in 1898 describes the
result as having "the all-pervading influence of
dainty and cultivated taste". Accompanying
photographs show a rather busy garden of
which a single, delightful feature survives
today: My Lady's Garden.

Since the 1960s the garden has been raised
to a standard of high excellence. Lanning
Roper was consulted in 1969 and he designed
a virtuoso mixed border, 200 yards long,
following a west-facing wall between the
castle and the moat. In his notes on the
garden he wrote: "Treat area simply and play
up the beauty of the buildings, walls and
landscape" – the admirable response of an
unusually sensitive and subtle designer. The
border is given harmony and balance by a
carefully arranged colour scheme, with
predominantly reds and blues at the north end
and pink, purple, white and silver at the
south, spiked with the occasional note of blue
to make a connection with the other half.

My Lady's Garden is a walled enclosure
lying immediately below the castle walls. It
retains its 19th-century design, laid out as a
kind of parterre, with a pattern of box-edged
beds in shapes of *fleurs-de-lys*. In the middle of
the garden a circular bed is edged in stone
with an inscription of lines from "The
Rubáiyát of Omar Khayyám": "I sometimes
think that never blows so red/The rose as
where some buried Caesar bled." The
ornamental planting in the box-edged beds is

My Lady's Garden at Broughton

entirely modern, with pink roses ('Gruss an
Aachen' and 'Heritage') and rich purple roses
('De Rescht') underplanted with annuals
varying from year to year. Mixed borders line
the walls, with shrub roses underplanted with
lavish waves of herbaceous perennials in pink,
purple, blue or white – alliums, aquilegias,
foxgloves, penstemons, poppies, sages and
verbascums. The area is small but the crisply
shaped *fleur-de-lys* shapes give clarity at the
centre and the borders, exuberant as they are,

have a deftly harmonious colour scheme. This
garden, and Lanning Roper's border, strike
exactly the right note of celebratory gaiety but
allow the rare character of the castle and its
ancient setting the prominence they deserve.

Location Broughton, nr Banbury OX15 5EB, Oxfordshire
OS SP4138 2m SW of Banbury by B4035 **Tel** 01295
262624 **Fax** 01295 272694 **English Heritage
Register** Grade II **Owner** Lord Saye and Sele **Open**
mid May to mid Sept, Wed, Sun and Bank Hol Mon 2–5
(Jul and Aug, also open Thur 2–5). **Area** 3 acres/1.2
hectares

BURY COURT

OLD FARM BUILDINGS AS THE BACKGROUND
TO TWO OUTSTANDING MODERN GARDENS –
ONE LATE 20TH-CENTURY BY PIET OUDOLF
AND ONE EARLY 21ST-CENTURY BY
CHRISTOPHER BRADLEY-HOLE

John Coke came to the attention of
gardeners when he opened his nursery,
Green Farm Plants, on the other side of
Bentley. He did not carry a large stock;
everything was handpicked and you
immediately wanted to buy it. He has now
almost entirely retreated from the nursery
business and become a full-time gardener. The
fastidious care he brought to the nursery now
finds expression in a garden that bristles with
excitement.

The setting is very attractive – high, airy,
surrounded by a rural landscape. An old

Piet Oudolf's garden at Bury Court

farmhouse of brick and stone, with walled enclosures and fine outhouses, provides a beautiful framework for the garden. In fact, there are two gardens, quite different and quite unlike any other gardens accessible to the public that I know. The first, behind the house, was started in 1995 and designed in collaboration with the Dutch garden designer and nurseryman Piet Oudolf. The space is divided by paths of paving stone or cobbles, straight or curved, but there are no overwhelming axes. A gravel bed is planted with plants such as eryngiums, euphorbias, sages, santolina and sedums. They are given plenty of space so that their whole character is visible, like precious exhibits in a jeweller's window. A circular arbour of dogwood has a millstone at its centre and a wheel pattern of bricks and cobbles. The shape of the arbour echoes the towers of two old oast houses attached to the house. Grasses are repeatedly used both as structural thickets or as ingredients in borders to contrast with, say, the striking foliage of acanthus or macleaya.

The planting is generally fluid and the division of space is free and flowing but there are interludes of formality. Below the stone wall of a noble old barn a raised pool is edged with brick and stone and has at its centre an explosive sculpture – baulks of timber of varying lengths erupt from the centre of the pool like a starburst. Two corners of the pool are emphatically marked by the unusual fastigiate form of *Koelreuteria paniculata*, with a frothy hedge of ornamental grass between them. A parterre of box with criss-cross patterns of hedging has compartments filled with yew. A curved screen of yew and a burgeoning mound of clipped box lend firm shape amid profuse planting. Most of the planting is herbaceous and when a woody plant is used it is given emphasis – *Catalpa bignonioides*, dogwoods (*Cornus* species) and Judas tree (*Cercis siliquastrum*). There is not a single rose in the garden; John Coke thought "they would add nothing". A path between densely planted borders is so narrow that in late summer soft grasses brush your face as you walk along. The garden is dominated by the contrasts of hard and soft – of sharp edges and the cloudy insubstantial form of grasses.

At the entrance to the house a new garden

designed by Christopher Bradley-Hole was laid out in 2001. The ground, rising very slightly as it extends from the house, is subtly terraced and disposed in a grid of metal-edged squares. Most of these are beds but some are occupied by a pool or a plain expanse of the coffee-coloured gravel which is used for the paths that flow between the squares. Each bed is slightly raised and given a narrow border, varying in width, of paler gravel than that of the paths. This subtle variation gives movement to the rigidity of the grid. The squares that are planted have, for the most part, herbaceous perennials, and frequent use is made of grasses, spiked with the occasional brilliant kniphofia or lobelia. No blues or yellows are used and the outer beds tend towards monochrome. It is an immensely successful minimalist design.

The two gardens at Bury Court, quite different in style, suit the vernacular farm buildings equally well. They show very vividly how successful a modern design can be in an old setting.

Location nr Bentley GU10 5LZ, Hampshire **OS** SU7845 1m N of Bentley off the Crondall road **Tel** 01420 520351 **Fax** 01420 22382 **Owner** John Coke **Open** May to Oct, Thur 10–6; groups by appointment **Area** 2 acres/0.8 hectares

BUSCOT PARK

A MASTERLY EARLY 20TH-CENTURY GARDEN BY HAROLD PETO WITH A DAZZLING WATER GARDEN AND DECORATIVE NEW PLANTING IN AN OLD WALLED GARDEN

The house at Faringdon, by an unknown architect, was built in the late 18th century and there are indications of contemporary landscaping east of the house of which the surviving lake must have formed part. Apart from this the gardens are entirely of the 20th century, dominated by a mesmerising water garden that links house and lake, designed by Harold Peto in 1904 for Alexander Henderson, later the 1st Lord Faringdon.

On ground that slopes gently downhill through woods, Peto created a stepped canal which opens out from time to time – now a scalloped circular pool with a dolphin fountain, now a plain rectangle – and is traversed by bridges of different kinds. The water channel itself narrows and widens, with water cascading down at changes in level. It is edged in mown grass and enclosed in box hedges which follow the shape of the canal,

Peto's water garden at Buscot Park

with statues ornamenting the larger compartments and occasional exclamation marks of Irish yews or fastigiate juniper (*Juniperus communis* 'Fastigiata'). When you make the leisurely descent you find yourself crossing back and forth, the scene varying with your viewpoint. As you descend you see on the far side of the lake a domed and pillared temple exactly aligned with the canal. Retracing your steps, new permutations of views present themselves on the uphill walk. The woods press in all about and the filtered light and flickering shade add to the charm.

There are other pretty things at Buscot. There is a pattern of avenues of different trees (one of Lombardy poplars opens with a pair of Egyptian figures), and some of the trees are unusual avenue species (for example, the fastigiate English oak, *Quercus robur* f. 'Fastigiata'). These are ingeniously planned, with two long avenues radiating out from the house to form a three-part *patte d'oie* with the water garden. Cross vistas link subsidiary avenues with the water garden, and urns and other ornaments decorate junctions.

Swashbuckling borders

The walled kitchen garden is now partly turned over to beautifully maintained ornamental gardens. Here are swashbuckling borders by Peter Coats in blue and yellow, which almost redeem that overplanted and bilious tree *Robinia pseudoacacia* 'Frisia'. The very attractive formal plantings in the garden are designed by Tim Rees, with an alley of pleached hop hornbeam (*Ostrya carpinifolia*) underplanted with daylilies and a tunnel of Judas trees (*Cercis siliquastrum*). A virtuoso flight of steps negotiates the steep slope which swoops down from the house to the kitchen garden. Stone steps link brief stretches of grass terracing, while powerful bastions of yew flank each flight of steps and lower hedges of yew the grass terracing. The steps are aligned with a grand entrance gate piercing the kitchen garden wall, and with the axial path that lies beyond. This refined and subtle scheme could also be the work of Peto. In its way it is as memorable as Peto's water garden – one of the grandest and most richly atmospheric pieces of 20th-century garden design in the country.

Location Faringdon SN7 8BU, Oxfordshire **OS** SU2496 3m NW of Faringdon on A417 **Tel** 01367 240786 **Fax** 01367 241794 **Email** estbuscot@aol.com **Website** www.buscot-park.com **English Heritage Register** Grade II* **Owner** The National Trust **Open** Apr to Sept, Mon to Fri (closed Bank Hol Mon) and every 2nd and 4th Sat and Sun (including Easter) 2–6 **Area** 20 acres/8 hectares

CHASTLETON HOUSE

A POETIC, ANCIENT GARDEN AS THE SETTING FOR AN UNALTERED JACOBEAN HOUSE IN AN IDYLLIC COUNTRYSIDE

The phrase "time capsule" has been done to death by the heritage industry but, whatever you call it, the quality possessed by those rare houses and gardens which preserve their ancient character untouched by later fashions is wonderfully attractive. The last important event at Chastleton seems to have

The Best Garden at Chastleton House

been the publication in 1868 of *Croquet Tactics* by the then squire, Walter Jones Whitmore, who did more than any other person to codify the rules of that splendid game.

BAGGY BOX

The estate at Chastleton had been bought by Walter Jones, a wool merchant, in 1602 and he started to build his house very shortly afterwards. Of pale coffee-coloured limestone with tall mullioned windows and gabled bays, it remains exactly as built: the perfect Jacobean house of gentlemanly demeanour. The Best Garden, north-east of the house and enclosed in 17th-century stone walls, presents a blurred sketch of venerable formality. A disc of grass edged in yew is enlivened with a series of marvellous shapes of clipped box – lumpy, dumpy, billowing and baggy; none of the shapes is precisely indentifiable, all are vaguely organic. Metal archways garlanded in roses rise above the entrances. There is always a tendency to exaggerate the age of apparently ageless gardens and a photograph taken in the 1920s of this part of the garden shows the topiary in its apparent youth, rising higher than the encircling yew hedge and part of a much more elaborate scheme of concentric paths and triangular beds. All this makes it seem much more likely to be a piece of Victorian neo-formality. In the east wall an iron *claire-voie* gives views of parkland and the Boscobel Oak, supposedly grown from an acorn taken from the Royal Oak of Boscobel (*see page 448*) in 1842. The Great Garden is a delightful sight in a subdued sort of way – scarcely a full meal as gardens go but a very tasty *hors d'oeuvre*. It also suits the house to perfection. Visitors park on the slopes above the house and the walk down, skirting a field, gives a lovely and unforgettable view of the house cradled in its ancient wooded setting.

Location Chastleton, Moreton-in-Marsh GL56 0SU, Oxfordshire **OS** SP2429 ENE of Stow-on-the-Wold, signposted off A436 **Tel** 01608 674355 **Bookings** 01494 755572 **Infoline** 01494 755560 **Fax** 01608 674355 **Email** chastleton@ntrust.org.uk **English Heritage Register** Grade II* **Owner** The National Trust **Open** Apr to Oct, Wed to Sat 1–5 (NOTE: Visits must be pre-booked using the number given above) **Area** 37 acres/15 hectares

CHENIES MANOR

A MEDIEVAL AND TUDOR MANOR
HOUSE WITH AN ARTS AND CRAFTS
GARDEN ENLIVENED BY BRILLIANT
MODERN FLOWER PLANTING

The manor house at Chenies was built in
the 15th and 16th centuries by the
Cheyne family and later belonged to the
Russells who became Dukes of Bedford. Built
of beautiful slender bricks and bristling with
ornament – crow-stepped gables, barley-sugar
twisted chimneys and battlemented bay
windows – it has a dashingly decorative air. In
front of the house a sunken garden has
possible Tudor origins but today has more of
the character of the Arts and Crafts
movement. Behind a screen of clipped ivy and
a row of lollipops of clipped yew, it is divided
into four with paths of stone flags: a circular
pool in the middle is surrounded by domed
drums of clipped box; the entrance and exit
are flanked by dumpy rounded cones of
clipped box; lawns fill each of the four
quarters; and narrow beds run round the
retaining brick walls. These beds are in May
the scene of a rare and wonderful sight. Every
year Elizabeth MacLeod Matthews beds out
thousands of tulips from the bulb specialist
Walter Blom & Son, planting them in groups
of a single kind and accompanying them with
forget-me-nots and pansies in different
colours. It is rare to see tulips used with such
prodigal abandon in a private garden, and here
their lavish use brilliantly decorates the
splendid historic setting. The celebratory
cheerfulness of this classic combination of
plants seems appropriate to the Tudor setting.
In late May the tulips are whipped out and
replaced with a summer scheme dominated
by yellow – argyranthemums, Wisley
primroses, variegated hostas and golden
origanum forming ribbons of gold about the
sunken garden.

There is much else to admire at Chenies – a
white garden (which also makes use of tulips);
a physic garden of both medicinal and useful
plants evoking the Tudor past; a walk of
clipped yew and Lawson cypress; a turf maze
(replacing in a different site one that had been
at Chenies in the 17th century). The whole

The sunken garden at Chenies Manor

garden is finely maintained and always a
pleasure to see. But at tulip time at the
beginning of May the pleasure takes on an
altogether more thrilling quality.

Location Chenies, Rickmansworth WD3 6ER,
Buckinghamshire **OS** TQ0198 4m E of Amersham on
A404 **Tel** and **Fax** 01494 762888 **Owner** Lt Col and
Mrs MacLeod Matthews **Open** Apr to Oct, Wed, Thur
and Bank Hol Mon 2–5 **Area** 3 acres/1.2 hectares

CLIVEDEN

A GREAT THAMES-SIDE HOUSE, WITH
RICHLY VARIED GARDENS RANGING FROM
THE 17TH CENTURY TO THE 20TH CENTURY,
SET IN EXQUISITE SCENERY

Cliveden is one of the most attractive, and
varied, gardens in the country. The house
– now a very grand hotel with delicious food
– was built in the 17th century to the designs
of William Winde for the Duke of
Buckingham but completely refashioned for

the 2nd Duke of Sutherland by Sir Charles
Barry, in an unusually subdued mood,
between 1849 and 1851. That is an immense
simplification of a much more complicated
story which, among other things, involves the
house being destroyed by fire on two
occasions. It is easy to understand why anyone
should want to live and garden in such a place
for the position is one of breathtaking beauty
on the brow of wooded slopes high above the
Thames whose waters curve gently away to
the west.

The garden history of Cliveden is even
busier than that of the house, for it continues
well into the 20th century. Many of the more
recent changes occurred after the estate was
bought in 1893 by William Waldorf Astor
(later the 1st Viscount Astor) whose
descendants lived here until 1966, although
the family had given the estate to the
National Trust in 1942.

A view of the garden must start with the
terraces south of the house, where William
Winde built a long retaining wall with blind
arches. The lower terrace has a beautiful 17th-
century balustrade made for the Villa Borghese

in Rome, which, like so many of the wonderful architectural fragments and classical antiquities in the garden, was brought to Cliveden by William Waldorf Astor. These terraces overlook a long apron of lawn pointing away from the house where the Duke of Buckingham had laid out a noble parterre. The present arrangement is a simplified version of a design by the Duke of Sutherland's head gardener, John Fleming, laid out between 1851 and 1853. Fleming's scheme had spring and summer bedding requiring vast quantities of plants – 10,000 tulips and 20,000 other plants for a spring arrangement. (William Robinson saw it in 1872 and hated it: "one of the most repulsive examples of the extra formal school, thrusting itself in a rather awkward manner into the great landscape".) Today the pattern of narrowly triangular beds is edged in box, and each compartment filled with blocks of santolina or *Senecio* 'Sunshine' (now correctly *Brachyglottis* Dunedin Group 'Sunshine'), while rows of slender pyramids of clipped yew give vertical emphasis. At the far end of the parterre in a circle of hedging is a bronze statue of the Rape of Proserpine by Vincenzo de Rossi.

To the west of the parterre the wooded ground slopes onwards to the Thames. The woods on this side of the garden are full of interest, including an early 18th-century turf amphitheatre by Charles Bridgeman, and both woods and banks of the river are enlivened by buildings such as the pretty Octagon Temple, designed by Giacomo Leoni in 1735. From here a walk of yews, some dating back to the early 18th century, descends to the river and a palatial half-timbered boathouse built for Lord Astor.

In the forecourt north of the house is the finest 20th-century addition to the garden: a pair of virtuoso herbaceous borders – warm colours on one side, cooler on the other – laid out in 1969 by Graham Stuart Thomas when he was Gardens Adviser to the National Trust. Here, too, are more of Lord Astor's collection of antiquities – some beautiful marble sarcophagi.

The lake at Cliveden

Anyone with a taste for a varied visual diet will study these lovely things and contrast them with the hideous clock tower looming nearby (by Henry Clutton, 1861, inspired, if that is the word, by a Sir Charles Barry design for Trentham Park). An avenue of limes leads to Thomas Waldo Story's late 19th-century Fountain of Love with cavorting nymphs and a giant cockleshell. Close by is the enigmatic and attractive Long Garden with snaking hedges of box, whimsical yew topiary and Lord Astor's wonderful 18th-century Venetian characters from the Commedia dell'Arte. At this northern end of the garden a water garden has an irregular lake overlooked by a ravishing little Chinese pavilion, made originally for the Exposition Universelle of 1867, and acquired from Bagatelle in the Bois de Boulogne in Paris. There is much attractive planting of trees and shrubs – azaleas, flowering cherries, dogwoods, magnolias and Japanese maples.

Closer to the house, past a fine grove of holm oaks, is the Secret Garden. Formerly known as the Rose Garden, this was originally designed in 1959 by Sir Geoffrey Jellicoe as "a glade garden", a place of retreat for the Astor family. In 2001 it was replanted to the designs

The Rape of Proserpine

of Isabelle van Groeningen "in the spirit of Jellicoe's vision". A sinuous path winds about curved beds whose herbaceous planting is disposed in serpentine sweeps. Arches of clematis and honeysuckle span the paths and classical statuary is dotted about in a slightly miscellaneous fashion. A petulant Apollo seems surprised to find himself standing in clumps of achilleas and poppies.

The garden at Cliveden is a series of episodes, rather disparate but often delightful, occurring in a generally haphazard fashion. The notable garden features, ranging in date from the 17th to the late 20th centuries, seem more like a beguiling anthology of garden taste than a unified and harmonious layout. The only strong unifying shape is the house itself, with its entrance avenue on one side axially extended by the parterre on the far side. This variousness may possibly irritate the more purist garden designer but it provides rich entertainment for visitors.

Location Taplow, Maidenhead SL6 0JA, Buckinghamshire **OS** SU9185 2m N of Taplow on B476; Jnct 7 of M4 and Jnct 4 of M40 **Tel** 01628 605069 **Infoline** 01494 755562 **Fax** 01628 669461 **Email** cliveden@ntrust.org.uk **English Heritage Register** Grade I **Owner** The National Trust **Open** mid Mar to Dec, daily 11–6 (closes at 4 in Nov and Dec) **Area** 375 acres/152 hectares

CORSHAM COURT

An Elizabethan house with pleasure grounds by Capability Brown and distinguished 20th-century planting

Corsham Court was built in 1582 for Thomas Smythe but much altered after Paul Methuen bought the estate in 1745. It occupies an unusually attractive position on the edge of the town, overlooking the church square. Nothing is known of the early garden history until Capability Brown was asked by Paul Methuen in 1761 to alter the house and grounds. Brown was responsible for some of the most attractive surviving parts of the garden.

Behind the house he designed a richly decorative Bath House with a sunken plunge pool behind a three-arched opening in the ground floor – this was further Gothicised by John Nash c.1800. It has an upper changing room with Gothic windows and the whole is capped with a castellated parapet and finials bristling with crockets. It is connected to the adjacent walled garden by a tunnel, originally prettily decorated with patterns of pine cones set into lime putty, of which only traces remain. The tunnel opens out today into a building put up in 1967 and incorporating 15th-century vaulting brought here from a house in Bradford-on-Avon.

Brown's walk of fine trees

The Bath House stands close to the southern end of the North Walk which Brown laid out between the pleasure grounds and the park, separated by a ha-ha immediately to the east. At the start of the walk there is a remarkable group of trees. A venerable yew walk leads to a lovely and startlingly expansive oriental plane (*Platanus orientalis*), some of whose limbs sprawl dramatically sideways giving it the appearance of a grove of trees rather than one only. Now well over 90ft/28m high, it is one of the two or three tallest in the country and could date from Brown's time. Brown planted other fine trees along the walk, of which a very handsome cedar of Lebanon and two Turkey oaks (*Quercus cerris*) are other possible survivors. The walk leads, as Brown planned, all the way to what is now the A4, where it

culminated in a grand gateway indicating to those passing on the main road the existence of an important estate. Brown's estimate for this work, dated 6th December 1760, lists "Making the great Walks and sunke Fence between the House and the Chippenham Road". Today the A4, with its relentless traffic, is a less attractive destination for a garden walk. Brown also planted shelter belts to the north and east, where he proposed a lake which was not executed until Humphry Repton came to work here in 1797. From a deep lawn below the eastern façade of the house it now ornaments the middle distance, backed by trees and revealing, on its far bank, Lake Cottage designed by John Nash.

Formal gardens close to the house present a largely 19th-century air. The flower garden has long narrow beds edged in box and animated by topiary of box and yew. The planting here, chiefly roses in the past, is rather scrappy but is to be restored. To the north, a walk of hornbeam runs along the side of the walled garden where a central path is flanked by trees of *Catalpa bignonioides* which curve round at

the head of the garden to embrace a circular pool ringed with ironwork adorned with climbing roses. In a border on one side is a superlative large *Paeonia rockii*, one of several examples in the garden of this most beautiful of flowering shrubs.

Lastly, though this is what visitors see first, there is the splendid entrance court. It is flanked by perfunctory mixed borders and lawns in which two fine trees stand: a sadly truncated but grand cedar of Lebanon and a perfect *Gingko biloba*. Corsham, happily untouched by any recent passing fashions, is not as well known as it deserves. With some exceptional plants, finely designed landscape and all the atmosphere of an old estate, it has memorable character.

Location Corsham SN13 0BZ, Wiltshire **OS** ST8770 In Corsham town, 4m W of Chippenham by A4 **Tel** and **Fax** 01249 701610 **English Heritage Register** Grade II* **Owner** James Methuen-Campbell **Open** End Mar to Sept, daily except Mon (open Bank Hol Mon) 2–5.30; Oct to end Mar, Sat and Sun 2–4.30 **Area** 360 acres/146 hectares

The Bath House at Corsham Court

THE COURTS

A GEORGIAN VILLAGE HOUSE WITH A
GARDEN OF DAZZLING INVENTIVENESS —
TOPIARY, MAGNIFICENT HEDGES, WATER
AND EXCELLENT PLANTING

The early 18th-century house ("wildly overdone in all its details" says Pevsner) stands behind a stone wall in the centre of the village. It originally served as a court of law to which weavers came to settle disputes. The garden is wholly 20th-century, made when Sir George Hastings lived here between 1900 and 1910. In 1943 it was given to the National Trust which opens it in an agreeably low-key way – no shop, no tea room, no lavatory and no access to the house. It is an exceptionally attractive garden which retains much of its original Arts and Crafts atmosphere. Like the house, it teeters on the verge of decorative excess but never tumbles over. Topiary, in many different forms, is a running theme. You are immediately confronted, below the entrance façade of the house, with four clipped shapes of box, 6ft/1.8m high, resembling moulded blancmanges starting to melt in a hot sun. To one side is a beautifully wrought yew hedge that directs the eye down a vista to a dapper little summerhouse in the form of a pillared temple. This hedge, breaking out from time to time into high clipped ramparts and bursting into occasional additional ornamentation, encloses the chief part of the formal gardens; south-east of the house it opens out into a sweeping curve with stone piers and wrought-iron gates at its centre, festooned in spring with *Clematis alpina* 'Frances Rivis'.

Beyond the gates the garden changes gear. Here an arboretum with a fine collection of trees and many spring bulbs curves about the formal garden on the far side of the yew hedge. There is topiary here, too, in the form of a wriggling hedge of holly shaped into a series of giant cottage loaves.

In the south-western part of the formal garden a feast of cunningly deployed topiary is partly hidden behind a procession of clipped Irish yews rising above a border of euphorbias, fritillaries, geraniums, lamb's lugs, *Thalictrum aquilegiifolium* and white tulips. Here a gentle step in a lawn forms a stage-like

The water garden at The Courts

area, backed by the curving boundary hedge of yew, with piers of clipped yew on each side. The opening of the stage is flanked by elaborately tiered shapes of box and mushrooms of silver pear (*Pyrus salicifolia*) underplanted with irises. This splendid set piece by no means exhausts the use of topiary, which crops up throughout the garden, appearing to delight in its own virtuosity.

Behind castellations of yew close to the house, a water garden forms the eastern boundary of the garden. A long stepped runnel, breaking out at its far end in a fit of curves, opens into a sweeping pool shaded by a swamp cypress (*Taxodium distichum*) and a wide-spreading yew, with drifts of shuttlecock ferns on its shady bank. A rectangular lily pool is associated with excellent ornamental trees and mixed borders run along on each side. The Courts, with much good planting and an irrepressible decorative character, has been gently restored in recent years and is beautifully cared for.

Location Holt, nr Trowbridge BA14 6RR, Wiltshire **OS** ST8661 In Holt village, 3m SW of Melksham by B3107 **Tel** and **Fax** 01225 782340 **Email** courtsgarden@ntrust.org.uk **English Heritage Register** Grade II **Owner** The National Trust **Open** end Mar to mid Oct, daily except Sat 12–5.30; out of season by appointment **Area** 7 acres/2.8 hectares

EXBURY GARDENS

ONE OF THE FINEST RHODODENDRON
GARDENS IN THE COUNTRY — A SUPERB
COLLECTION AGAINST A BACKGROUND
OF MAGNIFICENT TREES

The estate at Exbury was bought in 1918 by Lionel de Rothschild whom someone described as "a banker by hobby but a gardener by profession". The site is a beautiful one, on the east bank of the estuary of the river Beaulieu, looking south across the Solent. The acid soil and the benign climate make it a wonderful place for growing rhododendrons and other ericaceous plants.

Lionel de Rothschild embarked on the garden with meticulous fervour. From 1919 a hundred and fifty men were set to double dig the whole area, enriching it with huge quantities of leafmould – it took them ten years. There was insufficient water and this was remedied by drilling boreholes, building a water tower and reservoirs and laying twenty-two miles of pipes which could deliver 250,000 gallons a day. It was Rothschild's intention to plant every woody plant that could be cultivated in such a site. His particular interests were rhododendrons, of which he bred countless successful hybrids, and orchids, for which he built an enormous glasshouse. Lionel de Rothschild died in 1942 and after the war his son, Edmund, took over, having inherited whatever genes determine a passion for gardening. New plants continue to be added and the garden, now regularly open to the public, is magnificently cared for.

The site at Exbury is mostly flat, with occasional gentle hollows and hillocks. Native Scots pines and oaks, with some superb cedars of Lebanon which must have been planted when the house was built in the 18th century, make a fine background to the exotics which now fill the garden. There is little running water but two streams, at the northern and southern ends of the garden, provide water for pools in which rhododendrons are at times magnificently reflected. The landscape intermingles open spaces of grass, frequently ornamented with specimen trees of every kind, and intimate woodland laced with paths and opening out from time to time into airy glades. One of the largest open spaces, shaded by scattered oaks, is provided as a picnic space for visitors. The paths are more often than not densely lined with rhododendrons, of which Exbury probably has the largest collection in the British Isles. Also lavishly represented are the other two major groups of Asiatic flowering shrubs: camellias and magnolias.

Lionel de Rothschild made a great rock garden, completed in 1930 and covering an area of 2 acres/0.8 hectares – probably the largest in Europe. The rocks are treated ornamentally rather than as a monotonous background, rising up among plantings of conifers (many of them fastigiate), azaleas (many of them blue) and heathers.

As a place to learn about trees and shrubs in the most agreeable of circumstances, Exbury is a precious garden. To do it thoroughly you need several hours and a copious notebook. You may relish, too, the miniature railway train from which to view at your leisure some of the best features, including the rock garden,

The ponds at Exbury

as you glide gently past.

Location Exbury, nr Southampton SO45 1AZ, Hampshire **OS** SU4200 In Exbury village, 11m from Totton (W of Southampton) by A326 and B3054 **Tel** 023 8089 1203 **Fax** 023 8089 9940 **Website** www.exbury.co.uk **English Heritage Register** Grade II* **Owner** E.L. de Rothschild **Open** Mar to Oct, daily 10–5.30 or sunset if earlier **Area** 200 acres/81 hectares

FOLLY FARM

A MASTERPIECE BY SIR EDWIN LUTYENS WHO DESIGNED THE HOUSE AND GAVE IT A DAZZLING GARDEN OF BORDERS, HEDGES, CANAL, TERRACES AND FINELY LAID PATHS

There are three houses at Folly Farm, woven together by Sir Edwin Lutyens at his most ingenious. In 1905–6, for H.H. Cochrane, he added an elegant small William and Mary house to a 17th-century farmhouse. In 1912 the house was bought by Zachary Merton who needed something larger and Lutyens made a completely different addition

– a new wing in his most vernacular manner. Lutyens also made gardens for these houses, relating them to each house but giving the whole ensemble perfect harmony.

The William and Mary garden is dominated by a canal, surprisingly grand for what is an ungrand house. Planted with waterlilies, it is edged with mown grass, paving stones and yew hedges. The planting about it is recent; there were originally beds on each side. Nearest the house is a mushroom of *Salix caprea* var. 'Pendula' on each corner of the canal, and the far end has a curved balustrade above it entwined with wisteria.

The Arts and Crafts house has a remarkable cloistered pool enclosed in the L-shape of the house. Beyond is a flower garden in the form of a parterre, enclosed in yew hedges, with plantings of shrub roses, delphiniums, geraniums, irises, peonies and phlox. At the meeting point of exquisitely fine brick paths is a monumental block of Purbeck stone with a slight indentation in the centre – a heroic bird bath. An axial walk, aligned with a bedroom window, leads through the yew

hedges, along a walk of crab-apples, towards the entrance to a higher walled kitchen garden with generous semicircular steps.

A third garden lies to the west of the flower parterre – a dramatic square sunken rose garden. At its centre is an octagonal lily pool with a scalloped island planted with lavender and roses. The pool is edged in a circle of turf and a circular path of herringbone-laid bricks edges the whole. In each corner of the garden is a raised platform linked to the lower level by monumental sweeping steps. Curved rose beds follow the outer edge of the brick path at the level of the pool and the inside wall of the yew hedge is curved to accommodate them. The planting is entirely modern but the strength and originality of Lutyens's design makes the planting almost superfluous. Running parallel to the north side of the rose garden, and linked to it by an inconspicuous entrance, is a long narrow corridor of yew ending in a simple fountain pool and aligned with a west-facing window of the house.

The three main gardens, at slightly different levels, descending in the order in which I have described them, are linked by a walk that runs parallel to the garden side of the house. The original slope must have made the site awkward but Lutyens has obliterated the difficulty. The gardens are interconnected but they also lead harmoniously to the lawns and trees that lie between them and the great kitchen garden. The detailing of paths, hedges and paving throughout the garden is of the highest quality and the brick walls of the kitchen garden are also worth scrutinising – the coping is formed of sloping tiles, like a little roof, and shallow brick pilasters flank sunken panels of brick. Such details, so often neglected in modern gardens, contribute so much to the atmosphere of the place. The whole garden, despite its sometimes unhappy planting, is a delight.

Location Sulhamstead, nr Reading RG7 4DF, Berkshire **OS** SU6368 In Sulhampstead village, 7m SW of Reading, Jnct 12 of M4 **Tel** 01635 841541 **English Heritage Register** Grade II* **Open** occasionally for the NGS and by appointment for groups of 15 to 20 **Area** 7½ acres/3 hectares

The moon gate at Greys Court

GREYS COURT

AN OLD HOUSE IN AN EXCEPTIONAL CHILTERNS SETTING WITH WALLED GARDENS OF GREAT CHARM AND IDIOSYNCRATIC ORNAMENTS

The house at Greys Court is delightful – built of brick, silver flint and ashlar in different periods from the 16th to the 19th century. It is garnished by atmospheric outhouses, the remains of an earlier house, a medieval tower and a dower house, all grouped about a courtyard and forming a heterogenous ensemble (if that is not a contradiction) of the greatest charm. The site also is lovely, looking southwards over the park in its valley, with wooded land sweeping upwards on the far side.

There is no record of any early garden here but it is known that there was a park in the 18th century. The present gardens are essentially the work of the Brunner family which came to live here in 1937 and gave the estate to the National Trust in 1968. The Brunners did have advice – from the garden designer Humphry Waterfield and from the rose authority Hilda Murrell – but this is not a designed garden; it has gradually gathered itself about the house and outhouses in a delightfully unconstrained way. On the eastern side of the courtyard a series of brick and flint walls, and some of the outhouses themselves, form spaces which have been planted in a sometimes dramatically original way. From one enclosure, with mixed borders rich in shrub roses on each side, a tunnel of wisteria, underplanted with ghostly pale irises, leads to an irregular enclosure entirely roofed in wisteria, below whose twisted branches in spring are waves of bluebells and intense blue lithodora. A door leads through to the old kitchen garden where a paved walk has a border of peonies on one side and old espaliered fruit trees on the other. Here are also a tunnel of roses and honeysuckle, an orchard, arbours, yew hedges and raised beds of fruit and vegetables.

There are also idiosyncratic ornaments. A tree trunk is splendidly carved (by J.D. Geldart in 1987) into a niche of foliage in which a gently smiling gardener stands, spade at the ready. The back of the trunk is finely lettered with a poem by Walter de la Mare: "Very old are the woods/And the buds that break/Out of the briars' boughs/When March winds wake." An octagonal raised pool with a fountain, approached by an avenue of morello cherries, bears an inscription from Horace about the fertility of mother earth. In a

Folly Farm

courtyard formed by the Cromwellian stables a screen of pleached laburnum gently veils the scene: divided into four by a path of brick and cobbles, the courtyard has the character of a knot garden, with box-edged compartments of columbines, cranesbills, herbs and pinks, above which rise tall old mushrooms of clipped box. This miniature garden is a perfect example of the virtues of laid-back formality.

North-west of the house, spanning a ha-ha and leading to parkland, is a red-painted Japanese bridge and moon gate. It stands in the shade of trees, an exotic interloper in a thoroughly English scene. In a Japanese garden such an object would be used in strict accordance with ancient rules of garden design; here it epitomises the carefree charm that gives the garden its lovely character.

Location Rotherfield Greys, Henley-on-Thames RG9 4PG, Oxfordshire **OS** SU7582 3m W of Henley-on-Thames by A423 **Tel** 01491 628529 **Infoline** 01494 755564 **Email** greyscourt@ntrust.org.uk **English Heritage Register** Grade II **Owner** The National Trust **Open** Apr to Sept, Tue to Sat (closed Good Fri) 2–6 **Area** 9 acres/4 hectares

HARCOURT ARBORETUM

THE WOODLAND GARDEN AND ARBORETUM OF THE OXFORD BOTANIC GARDEN INCLUDES A SUPERLATIVE 10-ACRE BLUEBELL WOOD

Originally part of the Nuneham Courtenay estate (*see page 518*), the arboretum has been in the care of the University of Oxford Botanic Garden since 1962. It dates from 1835 when W.S. Gilpin, who was a protégé of the 3rd Earl Harcourt, was asked to lay out a picturesque pinetum on land newly acquired, running along the Oxford road. A chief ingredient of Gilpin's design was a pattern of serpentine walks and the Main Ride, a broad grassy walk lined with ramparts of *Rhododendron ponticum* and backed by trees, in particular conifers. This survives today, with some magnificent old specimens of such trees as Corsican pines (*Pinus nigra* subsp. *laricio*), of which a dramatic trio confronts you as you enter the garden. There are also fine specimens of Wellingtonias and several of the incense cedar (*Calocedrus*

The bluebell wood at Harcourt Arboretum

decurrens) whose emphatic upright form punctuates the arboretum.

From the Oxford Botanic Garden's point of view the Harcourt Arboretum formed the perfect country department for its activities. Apart from providing much more room and a fine existing collection it has, unlike the Botanic Garden, acid soil which greatly extends the range of plants that they can grow. With the precious backdrop of old conifers and native silver birch and oaks, many trees and shrubs have been added – among them azaleas, Japanese maples, such beautiful flowering shrubs as witch hazels (*Hamamelis* species), the exquisite *Halesia monticola* (including its rarely seen pink form) and rhododendrons. A superb 10-acre/4-hectare bluebell wood and a 37-acre/15-hectare meadow of wild flowers add to its decorative charms. The garden also has a National Collection of bamboos.

The arboretum has a strongly educational remit. When I visited in the spring of 2002 there was an excellent timber trail with placards spelling out the precise uses of the wood of 15 different trees grown in the arboretum, with an admirable accompanying leaflet. For many visitors it will be the beauty of the plants, triumphantly animating an otherwise featureless site, that will be the chief attraction.

Location Nuneham Courtenay OX44 9PX, Oxfordshire **OS** SU5598 6m S of Oxford by A4074 **Tel** 01865 343501 **Fax** 01865 341828 **Email** postmaster@botanic-garden.ox.ac.uk **Website** www.botanic-garden.ashmol.co.ac.uk **English Heritage Register** Grade I **Owner** University of Oxford **Open** May to Oct, daily 10–5; Nov to Apr, Mon to Fri 10–4.30 (closed 22 Dec to 3 Jan) **Area** 55 acres/22 hectares

HEALE GARDEN

A 17TH-CENTURY HOUSE IN WATER MEADOWS BY THE RIVER AVON, WITH A FORMAL GARDEN BY HAROLD PETO, A RAVISHING KITCHEN GARDEN AND EXCELLENT PLANTING

Some exceptionally attractive gardens seem more or less oblivious to passing fashion, ruled by the passion for gardening rather than by the rise and fall of horticultural hemlines. Heale is the perfect country house garden, memorable for the beauty of the setting, the excellence of the design, fine plants and irresistible charm. On low-lying ground by the river Avon the house, built in rosy pink bricks with stone dressings, is 17th century with thoroughly convincing late 19th-century additions designed by Detmar Blow.

The architect and garden designer Harold Peto came here in 1906 to advise the new owner, the Hon. Louis Greville. With the lightest of hands Peto made new formal gardens which take their cue from the house. A terrace below the western façade has scalloped lily pools from which a central flagstoned path leads up a gentle terraced slope, with stone balustrades marking the changes in level, and lawns on either side. The planting of the deep mixed borders at the top was done by Lady Anne Rasch who lived and gardened at Heale from 1959 until 1998. She simplified the elaborate herbaceous borders of Peto's time and introduced mixed plantings, with many shrub roses and repeated structural

shrubs like *Cotinus coggygria* 'Royal Purple' and *Philadelphus coronarius* 'Aureus' all richly underplanted with herbaceous perennials.

It was Lady Anne, too, who was responsible for the exceptional ornamental kitchen garden south of the house. Enclosed on three sides with 18th-century walls of brick and cob, its long south side is marked by an open pergola garlanded with the purple-leafed grapevine *Vitis vinifera* 'Purpurea', and such swashbuckling roses as 'Easlea's Golden Rambler', 'Maigold' and 'White Cockade'. The garden is divided into four, as all old kitchen gardens used to be, its centre marked by a rectangular lily pool surrounded by eight giant domes of clipped box. A wide tunnel of espaliered fruit trees – apples and pears – runs down the length of the garden, interrupted by the pool at its centre, its grass path flanked with narrow borders sparkling with self-sown *Alchemilla mollis*, aquilegias, foxgloves and poppies. Three of the four divisions of the garden are given over to fruit and vegetables. The fourth is a lawn with a gazebo beautifully fashioned of tightly clipped pears. Mixed borders line the walls and within the garden

The kitchen garden at Heale

there is a delightful mixture of productive orderliness and unpretentious ornament.

Immediately south of the kitchen garden the land slopes gently down towards the river. Here is a Japanese garden, made in 1901, with a graceful orange-red bridge spanning a stream, a teahouse (with the stream flowing under it) and stone snow lanterns among ferns and Japanese maples. This startling piece of orientalism seems remarkably at home. This, and Harold Peto's formal gardens by the house, are vital ingredients in the character of Heale, but it is Lady Anne Rasch's detailed planting throughout the garden, and the exquisite kitchen garden, that make Heale exceptional. Visitors may take some of it home by buying plants in the excellent nursery.

Location Middle Woodford, nr Salisbury SP4 6NT, Wiltshire **OS** SU1236 In the Woodford valley, 4m NW of Salisbury by minor roads, signed from A345 and A360 **Tel** 01722 782504 **English Heritage Register** Grade II* **Owner** Guy Rasch **Open** daily 10–5 **Area** 8 acres/3.2 hectares

THE SIR HAROLD HILLIER GARDENS AND ARBORETUM

ONE OF THE BEST COLLECTIONS OF
TREES AND SHRUBS IN THE COUNTRY –
A MEMORIAL TO A NURSERYMAN AND
COLLECTOR OF GENIUS

The Hillier dynasty of nurserymen who took over the Farthing Nursery in Winchester in 1864 made it in the 20th century one of the finest nurseries for trees and shrubs in the world. It reached its zenith under Sir Harold Hillier (1905–85) who himself collected many seeds in the wild to propagate for the nursery. In his day the firm's catalogue, *Hillier's Manual of Trees and Shrubs*, offered 7,000 species of woody plants for sale. This catalogue was for many gardeners far more than merely a commercial list; it was a detailed guide to woody plants worth growing in the garden, and provided much valuable information about their cultivation.

Sir Harold lived at Jermyn's House and his garden and private arboretum now form a large part of the Sir Harold Hillier Gardens and Arboretum which is owned by Hampshire County Council. With 12,500 different woody plants, it is one of the finest collections of hardy trees and shrubs in the world. The soil is acid, the rainfall around 30in/75cm and the climate fairly mild. Several National Collections of plants are held, of which some are of major interest to gardeners, in particular those of cotoneaster, dogwoods, oaks, pines and witch hazels, though there are also more specialist collections of hazels, hornbeam, lithocarpus, photinia and privet. But every genus of woody plants hardy in the British Isles is well represented. The nursery, with various branches, including one on the premises here, still exists and still sells excellent plants but not in the range that was available in the 1960s and 1970s.

The arboretum is primarily a collection of plants and this overrides any notion of the aesthetics of the landscape. However, close to the house there are areas that are attractively designed. The magnolia avenue which runs up to the front door is, with its attractive underplanting, a dazzling sight. The heather garden nearby and the long Centenary Border west of the house also have their charms. But it is the plant collections that are the overwhelming attraction. These are arranged by genus (such as Acer Valley or Oak Field) or by habitat (such as Peat Garden or Bog Garden). A resource like this, apart from the delight of seeing so many fine plants displaying their beauties in different seasons, is of precious value to gardeners.

Location Jermyns Lane, Ampfield, nr Romsey SO51 0QA, Hampshire **OS** SU3723 3m NE of Romsey by A31 **Tel** 01794 368787 **Fax** 01794 368027 **English Heritage Register** Grade II **Owner** Hampshire County Council **Open** Apr to Oct, daily 10.30–6; Nov to Mar, daily 10.30–5 **Area** 180 acres/73 hectares

The magnolia avenue at the Sir Harold Hillier Gardens

HINTON AMPNER GARDEN

AN EXCEPTIONAL 20TH-CENTURY GARDEN
OF TERRACES, TOPIARY, BORDERS AND TREES,
WITH GLIMPSES OF ARCADIAN LANDSCAPE

Ralph Dutton, the 8th and last Lord Sherborne, inherited the estate at Hinton Ampner in 1935. His ancestors had lived here for many generations but the gloomy house he inherited had been heavily Victorianised and was not at all to his taste. In his youth, as he wrote, he had passed there "some light and many heavy hours". He rebuilt the house, revealing its late Georgian core, and created something more to his taste – a gentlemanly neo-Georgian house of brick in the style of many 18th-century houses in this part of Hampshire. The garden he created takes the house as its cue.

TERRACES OF BEAUTY

From the wooded entrance drive the house has a secretive air but beyond it, on its southern side, the land falls away and there are long, open prospects of fields and parkland. Dutton terraced the slopes below the southern façade of the house. Each terrace extends well beyond the width of the house, running to the very boundaries of the garden at either end, and to each level he gave a distinctive character. A paved terrace below the windows of the house has a lily pool at its eastern end. At the next level a simple, very large lawn is hedged on its far side in yew; at its west end a statue of a nymph is framed by the branches of a horse chestnut, with a ha-ha and long views of parkland beyond; its eastern end leads down to a little formal garden with hexagonal raised beds filled in spring with tulips and in summer with bedding schemes or single bold plantings of dahlias. The axis of this terrace is continued to the east by a walk of Irish yews leading to an elaborate wrought-iron gate and views of the rural landscape framed by a pair of lime trees. The lowest terrace is a dramatic flourish of splendid panache. A long walk starts at the west with a sundial ("The silent hours steal on") and an avenue of yews clipped into solemn rounded cones backed with boisterous thickets of shrub roses. The central part, in front of the house, has a series of yews clipped into the shapes of giant staddle stones at the end of long narrow beds with tulips in spring and pale pink dahlias ('Park Princess') in summer. Below the supporting wall of the upper terrace, taking advantage of a protected south-facing exposure, are beds on each side of linking steps; these are filled with *Convolvulus althaeoides*, penstemons, tender salvias, scabious and such ornamental woody plants as indigofera and a Judas tree. The walk continues to the east with a change of atmosphere – the grass path passes between beds densely planted with shrubs, among which is suddenly revealed a pedimented summerhouse. Facing south, it looks down a path through a formal wilderness of shrubs and is aligned with an avenue of limes in parkland well beyond the garden boundary, focussing on a distant obelisk. The far, eastern, end of the walk culminates in a stone statue of Diana.

On the north side of the house the drive skirts a walled former kitchen garden where a deep border planned for late summer effect runs along the outer wall. Opposite is a formal orchard, made on the site of the house that existed here in Tudor times. Divided into four by box hedges, and embellished by tall cones of clipped yew, the grassy compartments are planted with apples, cherries, crab-apples and quinces underplanted with bulbs – anemones and narcissi in spring; autumn-flowering crocus (*C. speciosus*) in September and October.

With its strong sense of design, unfussy sense of ornament and excellent planting, the garden at Hinton Ampner is exceptionally attractive. Ralph Dutton said that in his garden designing he was particularly anxious to obey Alexander Pope's advice to "conceal the bounds". He does this with great success – either by the use of planting or by carrying the eye beyond the boundary, often through carefully framed views as the culminating point of a vista. For reasons inexplicable to me, Hinton Ampner is not a well-known garden. Yet it is one of the finest English gardens of its period and worthy of comparison with both Hidcote and Sissinghurst – two other 20th-century gardens made by amateurs of genius.

Location Bramdean, nr Alresford SO24 0LA, Hampshire **OS** SU5927 1m W of Bramdean village by A272 **Tel** 01962 771305 **Fax** 01962 793101 **Email** hintonampner@ntrust.org.uk **Website** www.nationaltrust.org.uk/southern **Owner** The National Trust **Open** Apr to Sept, Sat, Sun, Tue, Wed and Bank Hol Mon 1.30–5.30 **Area** 8 acres/3.2 hectares

The lowest terrace at Hinton Ampner

IFORD MANOR

HAROLD PETO'S OWN GARDEN – BRILLIANT ITALIANATE TERRACES LAID OUT IN THE HEART OF THE WILTSHIRE COUNTRYSIDE

The architect and garden designer Harold Peto came to live here in 1899 and made a marvellous garden, the most eloquent expression of the English love affair with Italy. The site is very beautiful, on wooded slopes facing south-west over the valley of the river Frome. The house is Elizabethan but was rebuilt in the 1720s with a fine classical front of Bath stone. Quite close to the river, it overlooks a beautiful double-arched 15th-century bridge on whose parapet Peto placed an 18th-century figure of Britannia.

The garden to one side and behind the house had been terraced at some time in the past and Peto seized upon this as the essential ingredient of his garden. The entrance to it is charmingly inconspicuous – a fine wrought-iron gate in a stone wall leads through to a paved enclosure where an Italianate loggia juts out from the house, garlanded with grapevines and wisteria, and facing on the other side a semicircular pool. A mound of clipped *Choisya ternata* glistens in the sunshine. From here a flight of stone steps rises steeply to the terraces to the north, quite narrow with tall stone piers capped with splendid lead urns or stone figures. Tufts of *Campanula poscharskyana* and *Erigeron karvinskianus* have established themselves in the steps. The first terrace is quite small, leading up to a conservatory built against the wall of the house. The steps pass under the spreading limbs of an old yew into which a *Vitis coignetiae* has grown, soaring to the top and in autumn splashing the dark green with its brilliant red leaves. The next terrace, of mown grass, has at its centre a fountain and an oval pool fringed with wisterias. Trees ornament the lawn, among them, to the west, a perfect old specimen of *Cercidiphyllum japonicum*, surely planted by Peto himself. Beyond the pool double steps, flanked with bold clumps of bergenia, pass under a peristyle to the top, and grandest, terrace. Surfaced with immaculately raked gravel

▷ **The terrace steps** at Iford

(sometimes twice a day), the terrace is broad and calm. Italian cypresses (*Cupressus sempervirens*) run along on either side, with wonderful statuary – stone dogs, sarcophagi, a Byzantine wellhead, stone seats and columns. One end of the terrace is marked by an early 18th-century octagonal pavilion with pilasters and crisply ornamented cornice below the steeply pitched roof of stone tiles. The other end has a semicircular seat jutting out beyond the perimeter of the formal garden, with views westwards over a simple orchard. This end of the terrace is embellished by colonnades on either side. Past a bronze figure of Romulus and Remus, a path leads up to yew topiaries of the Chigi arms – six money-bags surmounted by a star – in memory of Mrs Cartwright Hignett's Chigi grandmother. North of the terrace the colonnade screens a little hidden garden (a true *giardino segreto*), with superb tightly clipped shapes of *Phillyrea latifolia*, a loggia, parterres of box and magnificent Tuscan pots of clipped box.

ALI BABA AND A JAPANESE GARDEN

The slopes above the top terrace are densely wooded but the uphill axis, established by the first flights of steps, continues deep into the woods. From a semicircular paved area flanked by giant Ali Baba terracotta pots and flowering cherries, with a majestic London plane on one side, rustic steps climb upwards, flanked from time to time by old staddle stones clothed in ivy. Almost immediately on your left, in the shade, is an unusually convincing Japanese garden overlooked by a rustic summerhouse. An irregular pool fringed with mossy rocks and ferns is overarched by a Japanese maple with a thicket of bamboo rearing up on one side; snow lanterns and an airy stone pagoda stand among tall old box trees with pale stems. More steps continue up the wooded hill. At the summit is a tall column of stone inscribed "To King Edward VII the peacemaker Harold Peto dedicated this column in the midst of the great war in 1916".

As you make your way down the hill again you look past the columns of the peristyle, out over the formal garden, and across the river to the rural landscape. In Tuscany the renaissance maker of a garden of this sort would have taken delight in drawing the eye beyond the confines of the garden to olive groves and vineyards spread out on the slopes. Here in Wiltshire, Peto evoked exactly the same spirit, revealing views of cattle grazing in pastures edged with hedgerows thick as bolsters.

Location Iford, nr Bradford-on-Avon BA15 2BA, Wiltshire **OS** ST8058 7m SE of Bath by A36, 2m SW of Bradford-on-Avon by B3109 and Westwood **Tel** 01225 863146 **Fax** 01225 862364 **English Heritage Register** Grade I **Owner** Mrs Cartwright Hignett **Open** Apr to Oct, Sun 2–5; May to Sept, daily except Mon and Fri 2–5 **Area** 2½ acres/1 hectare

KELMSCOTT MANOR

A SHRINE TO WILLIAM MORRIS – A 16TH-CENTURY COTSWOLD HOUSE WITH A FLOWERY GARDEN OF LOVELY SIMPLICITY

The great designer and craftsman William Morris came to the gabled Elizabethan house of Kelmscott Manor in 1871 and stayed here intermittently until his death in 1896. He rarely spent more than a few days here at a time but was devoted to the place – "the only house in England worth inhabiting!". He loved the setting with its meadow running down to the Thames (where he delighted to fish) and saw the garden as the perfect frame for the house: "The garden, divided by old clipped yew hedges, is quite unaffected and very pleasant, and looks in fact as if it were part of the house, yet at least the clothes of it: which I think ought to be the aim of the layer-out of a garden." Although little is known of the detailed appearance of the garden at Kelmscott in Morris's time, much is known of his garden philosophy and of his taste in plants. He believed that the garden should be as vernacular as the house: he despised bedding schemes ("I blush with shame at the thought"); he loved hedgerow plants, which inspired many of his textile designs, considering the wild English roses far more beautiful than garden cultivars; and it was essential that the garden should be productive and provide an agreeable setting for family life.

After Morris's death his daughter May lived at Kelmscott until she died in 1938 when it passed to the University of Oxford and, in 1962, to the Society of Antiquaries which restored the house in 1967. Nothing much, however, was done to the garden until in recent years it too was restored, under the direction of Hal Moggridge. This is no purist

The flower garden at Kelmscott Manor

restoration but an attempt to make a garden true to Morris's ideas, based on data available from paintings, photographs and Morris's own writings.

A TOPIARY DRAGON

The garden is entirely enclosed by stone walls. The entrance forecourt closely resembles the drawing by C.M. Gere used as a frontispiece to William Morris's *News from Nowhere* (1892). A flagstone path edged with standard roses runs across a lawn to the front door and the walls of the house are decorated with climbing plants. The roses are 20th-century cultivars and the front porch is flanked with borders of acanthus, bergenias, catmint, ferns and irises. A weeping beech and substantial bushes of cotinus and philadelphus are planted in the grass. A curiously shaped yew hedge, separating the forecourt from the rest of the garden, was clipped by Morris into the shape of a dragon (which he called "Fafnir" after the dragon of Sigurd the Volsung in the Icelandic saga) and a great ritual was made of its annual clipping. In the large lawn area beyond is a rustic pergola fashioned of coppiced chestnut, draped with grapevine and roses and underplanted with aquilegias, campanulas, feverfew, forget-me-not, geraniums and lilies. There are borders of unpretentious cottage character, one of which is backed with a rustic fence of ash and hazel on which roses are trained. Under a fine old mulberry dating from Morris's time the grass is jewelled in the spring with snakeshead fritillaries and *Tulipa sylvestris* which May Morris said used to run "riot over all the beds". An orchard contains 19th-century cultivars of apple and plum underplanted with bulbs. Visitors, remembering that for Morris house and garden were an entity, should also visit the house which has wonderful vernacular furniture and many exquisite Morris textiles. Views of the garden from these interiors are enchanting.

Location Kelmscott GL7 3HJ, Oxfordshire **OS** SU2599 In Kelmscott village, 6½ m NW of Faringdon by A417, B4449 and minor road **Tel** 01367 252486 **Fax** 01367 253754 **English Heritage Register** Grade II **Owner** The Society of Antiquaries **Open** Apr to Sept, Wed 11–1, 2–5 **Area** 1½ acres/0.6 hectares

LACOCK ABBEY

AN 18TH-CENTURY GOTHIC HOUSE IN A SETTING OF OLD WOODED PLEASURE GROUNDS, WINDING WALKS AND WAVES OF NATURALISED BULBS

The village of Lacock in the hands of the National Trust is now thoroughly given over to the heritage industry – one expects at any corner to bump into a period-clad serving wench proffering a plate of freshly-baked lardy cake. However, Lacock Abbey and its immediate setting remain a charming place. Founded in the 13th century for Augustinian nuns, it was acquired by Sir William Sharington in 1540 after the dissolution of the monasteries. His niece married a Mr Talbot whose descendants lived at Lacock Abbey until 1958, having given the estate, which included the village of Lacock, to the National Trust in 1944. The great pioneer of photography

▷ **Tuscan columns** at Lacock

The meadows at Lacock Abbey

William Henry Fox Talbot (1800–77) lived here from 1833 and Lacock Abbey is the first building in England to have been photographed. An excellent museum of photography has been installed in a fine barn here. The abbey was Gothicised by Sanderson Miller in the 1750s, giving the building its distinctive external appearance.

The abbey has a beautiful setting among water meadows on the edge of the village; the river Avon flows through the eastern part of the grounds. Nothing is known of the garden until the 18th century when plans for it were drawn up in 1714 and 1764; but the present garden bears little resemblance to them. Features that do survive from this time are the beautifully built ha-ha separating the pleasure grounds from parkland and a splendid monument of a sphinx (carved by Benjamin Carter), rising high on a pair of Tuscan columns, which stands among trees beside the entrance drive. The wooded pleasure grounds with winding walks which form the chief part of the garden were planted by W.H. Fox Talbot and some of the distinguished surviving trees date from his time – tulip tree (*Liriodendron tulipifera*), *Pterocarya fraxinifolia*, swamp cypress (*Taxodium distichum*), American black walnut (*Juglans nigra*) and many others. The grounds are spectacular in winter and spring with splendid aconites, naturalised *Crocus vernus* subsp. *albiflorus*, dog's tooth violets (*Erythronium dens-canis*), narcissi, snakeshead fritillaries and snowdrops.

Location Lacock, near Chippenham SN15 2LG, Wiltshire **OS** ST9268 3m S of Chippenham by A350 **Tel** and **Fax** 01249 730227 **English Heritage Register** Grade II **Owner** The National Trust **Open** Mid Mar to Oct, daily 11–5.30 (closed Good Fri) **Area** 9 acres/3.6 hectares

LARMER TREE GARDENS

RARE ORNAMENTAL GROUNDS LAID OUT IN THE LATE 19TH CENTURY AS A PUBLIC PLEASURE GARDEN WITH EXOTIC BUILDINGS AND WOODED WALKS

Augustus Henry Lane Fox Pitt Rivers (1827–1900), a lieutenant-general in the Grenadier Guards, was a remarkable person in a remarkable age. Apart from his career as a soldier he was also a pioneer collector of ethnographic objects and a great believer in public education. The Larmer Tree Gardens were founded (as the Larmer Grounds) shortly after Pitt Rivers inherited the estate in 1880. With 28,000 acres/11,336 hectares it was the largest estate in the country owned by a

The Lower Indian Room

commoner. Pitt Rivers created the garden as a place of recreation for the public who were allowed – at no charge – to picnic here, admire the gardens and on Sundays to listen to music from a bandstand.

The gardens are animated by a series of heterogeneous buildings. The Singing Theatre, a triumphant proscenium-like arch flanked by classical pilasters with a painted backdrop of a landscape in the style of Poussin, overlooks the General's Lawn with other buildings round it. The Lower Indian Room and the General's Room are made in part from antique Indian carved woodwork and resemble the kind of decorative buildings one might have found in an Indian hill station under the Raj. The General's Room has a finely panelled interior, with antique Turkish tiles set in arches in the Mughal style. It also contains a fragment of ancient wood – a piece of the original larmer tree (a local word for the wych elm, *Ulmus glabra*), a venerable specimen of which used to grow here. The Roman Temple is a domed octagonal building of stone with an inscription which reads "Augustus Pitt Rivers erexit MDCCCXXX". The interior has a white marble fireplace, a classical frieze

The Roman Temple at Larmer Tree Gardens

and a bust of the general. Beyond it is a surprise view – from the level lawn the land plummets down a wooded slope to a leafy water garden with bronze cranes on an island. Buildings of rustic character also decorate the garden. The Vista, a thatched pavilion with steeply overhanging eaves and an interior of prettily patterned rustic woodwork, stands at the head of a laurel walk with an oak acting as an eyecatcher on the far side of the lawn.

These heterogeneous buildings combine to create a sprightly atmosphere of jollification, and in their heyday before World War I the gardens received many thousands of visitors each year – 44,417 of them in 1899. The anticipation of a delicious picnic, some rousing music from the bandstand or an operetta from the Singing Theatre, followed by a walk about the gardens, must have been an enchanting prospect.

Location Rushmore Estate, Tollard Royal, nr Salisbury SP5 5PT, Wiltshire **OS** ST9416 2m S of Tollard Royal by minor roads **Tel** 01725 516228 **Fax** 01725 516449 **English Heritage Register** Grade II* **Owner** Pitt-Rivers Trustees **Open** Apr to Jun, Aug to Oct, daily except Sat 11–6 **Area** 11 acres/4.5 hectares

LONGLEAT

A MAGNIFICENT ELIZABETHAN HOUSE
IN A PARK BY CAPABILITY BROWN, WITH
LIVELY FORMAL GARDENS OF THE 19TH
AND 20TH CENTURIES

Sir John Thynne bought the estate here, formerly an Augustinian priory, in 1541 after the dissolution of the monasteries. He built a palatial mansion, probably starting in the 1560s, and it is one of the most complete surviving great houses of the Elizabethan period – and one of the most beautiful.

A garden was made in the 16th century and its remains are depicted in a painting by Jan Siberechts of 1675, which can be seen at Longleat. It shows an entrance forecourt with two pools south of the house and a much simplified four-part walled formal garden to the east. The radical alteration of this garden by George London from 1682 is illustrated in two Kip engravings in *Britannia Illustrata* (1707): the entrance forecourt is little changed, but to the east a giant new garden of parterres, pools, fountains and pavilions runs up into the distant woods which are divided by a pattern of rides. These gardens lasted only briefly for Capability Brown came in 1757 and by 1760 Mrs Delany wrote: "the gardens are no more". Altogether £4,500 (£324,000 today) was spent removing the formal gardens, making an informal lake, creating a new serpentine drive and planting many trees in the park. Humphry Repton was consulted and produced a Red Book in 1804, and as a result further minor changes were made.

THE PARK AND FORMAL GARDENS

The visitor to Longleat today passes through a lively sequence of views before arriving at the house. The first part of the drive is a splendid high Victorian set piece laid out for the 4th Marquess of Bath in the 1870s and finely restored by Russell Page in the 1930s. Mature monkey puzzles and Wellingtonias rise up among beautiful old beeches and other deciduous trees and, in front of them on either side, a procession of azaleas and rhododendrons. This gives way to views down the slopes to part of the Safari Park, with dromedaries and exotic African Ankole cattle. Finally Brown's park unfolds, with rolling grassland and belts and clumps of trees, and the pale golden stone of Longleat House gleaming by the banks of a lake. The lake, immediately to the east of the house, was in the 17th century a formal canal. Fed by the water of a stream, the Long Leat, it was converted by Brown into a string of pools which now forms one of the most striking features of the landscape close to the house. A picturesque cascade tumbles into a pool close to the drive.

The formal gardens are chiefly hidden away behind the house. A pleached lime walk leads to a noble passage of yew hedges culminating in a large white marble urn. To one side is a garden of formal rose beds, each decorated with very large topiary birds and the whole shaded by crab-apples. Beyond it is the Maze of Love instated by the present Marquess of Bath in 1993. A pattern of low box hedges and roses has heart-shaped rose arbours rising above the paths. A sign says that "you are expected to kiss your partner each time you pass under a heart-shaped arch." Overlooking the maze is a magnificent neo-Elizabethan orangery, exactly matching the architecture of the house, built here in the early 19th century. An inconspicuous door leads to a secret garden with several beautiful trees of *Davidia involucrata* and blowsy beds of shrub roses. Standing on a lawn is a mysterious 17th-century lead statue of Sir Jeffery Hudson, "a dwarf presented in a pie to King Charles 1st". A separate enclosure is laid out as a pets' cemetery, one of the most charming versions

The pets' cemetery at Longleat

of this distinctively English garden feature: in the turf miniature headstones, going back to the 19th century, are arranged in neat lines with a noble 18th-century urn on a plinth on each side. The whole is guarded by a pair of Chinese statues of crouching dogs and backed by a high wall planted with climbing roses and a central plaque commemorating Pansy a Pekinese: "No one can fill your special place/ My pansy with a sooty face."

There are other fine garden features at Longleat, among them a most remarkable yew hedge maze designed by Greg Bright and laid out in 1975. Its horribly convoluted path is said to be the longest in the world (1.69 miles). It forms part of the group of family amusements built for the delectation of the immense numbers of visitors who come here. These things, tactfully tucked away behind the car park north-west of the house, scarcely impinge on the beauties of the old landscape. Brown's park, a newly planted avenue of horse chestnuts streaking towards the southern horizon and the lovely beech hangers on the encircling hills provide a remarkably unspoilt background for the great house.

Location nr Warminster BA12 7NW, Wiltshire
OS ST8143 4m SW of Warminster by A36 and A362
Tel 01985 844400 **Fax** 01985 844885 **Email**
enquiries@longleat.co.uk **English Heritage Register**
Grade I **Owner** The Marquess of Bath **Open** daily
10–5.30 (closed 25 Dec; closes 4 in winter) **Area**
900 acres/364 hectares

LONGSTOCK WATER GARDENS

A LOVELY LABYRINTH OF POOLS AND STREAMS SUPERBLY LAID OUT TO FORM A MESMERISING AND RICHLY PLANTED NATURALISTIC GARDEN

The gardens at Longstock are maintained for the delectation of the staff (or "partners" as they are called) of the John Lewis Partnership. Nothing could be less institutional than this rare water garden. Close to the river Test, with its famously gin-clear water, the garden is a miniature archipelago of grassy islands about which flows a bewildering network of streams which from time to time

Naturalistic planting at Longstock

open out into pools. The islands, linked by simple board bridges, are meticulously mown and their banks are lavishly planted with bold, naturalistic clumps of appropriate herbaceous plants – geraniums, hostas, irises, ligularias, lysichitons and primulas. Ornamental grasses are often skilfully deployed, running in long swathes along the island banks and curving over towards the water. A rustic thatched pavilion sits in the middle of one of the islands, embellished in early summer with clumps of yellow flag irises. Fine trees and substantial shrubs provide a backdrop to the maze of planted islands: a beautiful cut-leaf alder (*Alnus glutinosa* 'Laciniata'), a swamp cypress (*Taxodium distichum*) relishing a notably swampy position, Himalayan birches and *Liquidambar styraciflua*. The occasional brilliantly flowered rhododendron provides a surprise among the sombre woodland planting.

In many gardens water is an ingredient of greater or less importance. At Longstock it is the essence of the garden, both providing the essential moist conditions for many plants but also a reflective surface in which the shapes and colours of herbaceous plants and distant foliage of trees are mirrored. Although some of the ingredients, and the setting, are those appropriate to a Robinsonian wild garden there is nothing wild about it. The garden is exceptionally well cared for, with wonderfully pampered herbaceous plants, and there is a perfection about it that creates an atmosphere of dream-like intensity. In spring the racemes of a white wisteria hang in veils over the water and ribbons of crimson Asiatic primulas or piercing blue-purple irises along the banks are reflected in the crystalline water.

Reflections at Longstock

Location Longstock, Stockbridge SO20 6EH, Hampshire **OS** SU3738 1½ m NE of Longstock village **Tel** 01264 810894 **Fax** 01264 810439 **Owner** The John Lewis Partnership **Open** Apr to Sept, 1st and 3rd Sun in each month 2–5 **Area** 8 acres/3 hectares

THE MANOR HOUSE

AN ARTS AND CRAFTS VILLAGE HOUSE SET IN GERTRUDE JEKYLL GARDENS BRILLIANTLY, AND AUTHENTICALLY, BROUGHT BACK TO LIFE BY PRIVATE OWNERS

The idea of restoring a historic garden is a surprisingly new one – no-one really thought of it before the 20th century – and private restorations, carried out with meticulous accuracy, are exceedingly rare. What Rosamund and John Wallinger did at Upton Grey, bringing back to life a beautiful Gertrude Jekyll garden, is an altogether exceptional feat. When they came here in 1984 they knew that the house had been built about the shell of a Tudor building to the designs of Ernest Newton for Charles Holme, the founder of *The Studio* and a central figure in the Arts and Crafts movement but they did not know that the garden had been designed by Gertrude Jekyll. Her original designs

survived in the Reef Point Gardens Collection at the University of California at Berkeley and the Wallingers bought copies of these and immersed themselves in a study of a house and garden. Their restoration of the garden is excellently described in Rosamund Wallinger's *Gertrude Jekyll's Lost Garden: The Restoration of an Edwardian Masterpiece* (2000) – one of the most valuable, and attractive, books to describe the restoration of a garden. In the restoration the Wallingers had much advice from organisations such as the Hampshire Gardens Trust and individuals such as Jane Brown and Penelope Hobhouse. But it is the Wallingers' perseverance, dedication to the finest points of detail and sheer hard slog which have made the restoration so successful.

The garden, spreading out to the south-east and north-west of the house, presents two completely different aspects and vividly show the range and character of Gertrude Jekyll's skills. Below the southern façade of the house the garden is terraced, with a central axis strongly linking the parts. Dry-stone walls of typical Jekyll style support the terraces and are

lavishly planted with the aubrieta, cerastium, fumitory, phlox, poppies and sedums which Gertrude Jekyll loved to use. The top terrace is divided by a pergola of roses and *Aristolochia macrophylla*, making an emphatic start to the descending axis. Immediately below, the rose lawn has a pattern of formal beds lavishly planted with double pink peonies (*Paeonia lactiflora* 'Sarah Bernhardt'), *Lilium regale*, the rare shrub form of the sumptuous pink rose 'Madame Caroline Testout' and other roses, irises and edgings of lambs' lugs. The geometry of the beds is all but blurred by the boisterous planting. Steps leading down to the next terrace, a rectangular bowling green, are flanked with billowing hummocks of rosemary – a characteristic Jekyll emphasis. The final terrace, a flawless grass tennis court, is enclosed on three sides by impeccably tailored yew hedges with niches and subtle openings, and overlooked by an arbour of roses. The upper terraces are flanked by terraced walks edged by herbaceous borders whose planting moves from cool blues through warmer colours to blazing reds. The sequence of events in the formal garden resembles the contrasts of a well planned meal. Lavishly detailed planting is held in check by the crisp pattern of spaces. Sumptuous effects are contrasted with cool open lawns.

The far side of the house displays a Jekyll garden of a much more unfamiliar sort but

The wild garden at the Manor House

one that was especially dear to her heart. The wild garden on gently sloping ground is divided by close mown paths which sweep across meadows of long grass planted with buttercups, daffodils, meadowsweet, oxslips, speedwell or wood anemones. There are thickets of roses of wild character (some of them English natives like *Rosa arvensis*) as well as trees – crab-apples, a grove of walnuts, silver birch and weeping ash (*Fraxinus excelsior* 'Pendula'). A stream tumbles down a cascade to feed a pool whose margins are clothed in campanulas, ferns, geraniums, irises and willows. To the west the village church stands behind clumps of roses, completing a perfect scene of an informal English kind.

The Manor House at Upton Grey is the perfect garden in which to learn about Gertrude Jekyll's genius. It displays the full repertory of her art and is maintained to the same high standards which she would have demanded. But it does more than provide a horticultural history lesson; it is an exceptionally enjoyable garden, delightful to be in, with pleasures at every turn.

Location Upton Grey, nr Basingstoke RG25 2RD, Hampshire **OS** SU6948 In the centre of Upton Grey village, 6m SE of Basingstoke by minor roads; Jnct 5 of M3 **Tel** 01256 862827 **Fax** 01256 861035 **Email** wallmoll@lineone.net **Website** www.gertrudejekyllgarden.co.uk **English Heritage Register** Grade II* **Owner** Mr and Mrs John Wallinger **Open** Apr to Oct, Mon to Fri by appointment only **Area** 5 acres/2 hectares

MOTTISFONT ABBEY GARDEN

MEDIEVAL MONASTIC BUILDINGS SET IN ATMOSPHERIC WOODED GROUNDS, WITH 20TH-CENTURY FORMAL GARDENS AND A FAMOUS COLLECTION OF OLD ROSES

The abbey at Mottisfont was an Augustinian foundation, some of whose 13th-century buildings survive, with a suave brick house of the 1740s grafted onto them. As early as 1833 the garden was famous for its trees, one of which, a London plane (*Platanus × hispanica*), survives today, one of the largest in the country, and a tree of exceptional beauty. In 1930 Sir Geoffrey Jellicoe designed a fine pleached lime walk underplanted with sheets of blue chionodoxa. At about the same time Norah Lindsay laid out a box parterre which follows the pattern of the fanlight of a garden door and whose compartments are planted with spring and summer bedding schemes. These formal features are well done and associate harmoniously with the character of the house.

However, for most visitors the immense attraction of the garden lies elsewhere. To rose lovers, and gardeners in general, Mottisfont is famous for its great collection of pre-1900 shrub roses (over 300 species and cultivars, a National Collection), to which has been added many climbing roses and 20th-century cultivars of distinction. Disposed in the former walled kitchen garden, they celebrate a remarkable man, Graham Stuart Thomas, who rediscovered many old roses and was a pioneer

Plant associations at Mottisfont

in their revaluation as the marvellous garden plants we cherish today. As gardens adviser to the National Trust from 1955 to 1974, Thomas took an altogether special interest in the making of this garden.

The roses were planted in the winter of 1972/3 and the charm of the garden lies in the way in which they are deployed, not merely presented as exhibits in a museum. The walled garden is divided, as all old kitchen gardens were, into four parts, with four clipped Irish yews making emphatic shapes about a circular pool at its centre. Each quarter has a lawn which is surrounded by beds of roses. Box-edged beds run about the walls on which climbing roses are trained. The occasional old apple tree was preserved with, as often as not, some appropriate rose scrambling through its branches. Furthermore, excellent use was made of companion plants – an important consideration, for most old shrub roses flower once only and need a supporting cast to enliven other seasons. The range of companion planting is wide but many perfectly ordinary plants are used with panache. Thickets of ferns, aquilegias in many colours, white foxgloves or Jacob's ladder, spreading cushions of scented pinks and veils of artemisia or meadow sage are effective yet unpretentious. In late June the exuberance of flower, colour and scent provides one of the most memorable experiences of any garden in the country.

Location Mottisfont, nr Romsey SO51 0LJ, Hampshire **OS** SU3227 4½m N of Romsey signed off A3057 **Tel** 01794 340757 **Fax** 01794 341492 **Email**

The rose garden at Mottisfont

mottisfontabbey@ntrust.org.uk **English Heritage Register** Grade II **Owner** The National Trust **Open** mid Mar to Oct, Sat to Wed (open Good Fri) 12–6 or dusk if earlier (in the second half of June, at rose time, the gardens close at 8.30; phone for details) **Area** 21 acres/8.5 hectares

THE OLD RECTORY

A PRIVATE GARDEN MADE BY A PLANTSWOMAN OF GREAT ORIGINALITY, WITH OUTSTANDING BORDERS, MANY UNUSUAL PLANTS AND IDIOSYNCRATIC ORNAMENT

Ralph and Esther Merton came here in 1950 and started a garden shortly after. Esther Merton, who died in 1995, was of a distinctive breed of English gardeners – independent-minded, strong-willed, enterprising and intrepid. Although she had an original and highly developed taste in plants, the layout of her garden follows classical principles. The house is a handsome pedimented rectory and the gardens take their cue from it. Immediately behind the house a large lawn is ornamented with a splendid old cedar of Lebanon and a free-standing *Magnolia grandiflora* 'Exmouth'. Leading the eye away from the house is a pair of herbaceous borders backed by yew hedges. Pure herbaceous borders, with no help from woody plants, are a rare thing these days. Here there is much repetition of plants and the use of bold foliage

– acanthus, cardoon, fennel, geraniums, iris, thalictrum and tradescantia. The path between the borders points towards a statue of Antinous standing in a pond whose banks are densely planted with ferns, irises, Japanese maples, rhododendrons and rodgersias. To one side, lurking inconspicuously in woodland, is a stone carving of a rhinoceros which in winter stands hoof-deep in snowdrops and in summer seems to graze peacefully among martagon lilies. A former kitchen garden, enclosed in yew hedges on three sides, is now an ornamental swimming pool garden. A pedimented pavilion stands with its back to a wall, overlooking the pool. Climbing plants clothe the wall – *Actinidia kolomikta*, clematis, roses and wisteria. Borders on each side of the pavilion are planted with *Aralia elata* 'Variegata', cistus, hoheria, shrub roses and yucca.

MRS MERTON'S TOUCH

The garden has a powerful and simple layout enlivened everywhere by the unusual plants gathered by Mrs Merton, often in her travels to exotic places, planted in troughs by the house or tucked away in countless appropriate corners of the garden. Such well-judged idiosyncrasies as the stone rhinoceros, and additional statues of a great bull in the swimming pool garden and a grand elephant close to the house, add strongly to the exotic flavour of the place.

Location Burghfield, nr Reading RG3 3TH, Berkshire **OS** SU6768 In Burghfield village, 5m SW of Reading **Tel** 01189 833200 **Owner** Mr A.R. Merton **Open** on several days for the NGS and to groups by appointment **Area** 4½ acres/1.8 hectares

Antinous in the pond at the Old Rectory

OSBORNE HOUSE

MID 19TH-CENTURY GARDENS OF THE
HOLIDAY PALACE OF QUEEN VICTORIA AND
HER FAMILY NOW BRILLIANTLY BROUGHT
BACK TO LIFE BY ENGLISH HERITAGE

On the 3rd April 1845 Queen Victoria wrote to Lord Melbourne of the newly acquired Osborne: "it is impossible to imagine a prettier spot – valley and woods which would be beautiful anywhere; but all this near the sea (the woods grow into the sea) is quite perfection; we have a charming beach quite to ourselves. The sea was so blue and calm that the Prince said it was like Naples. And then we can walk out anywhere by ourselves without fear of being followed and mobbed." Queen Victoria and Prince Albert built a

The terraced gardens at Osborne

new house, made a new garden and contrived a life as private as was possible. In recent years house and grounds have been magnificently restored by English Heritage. The garden is probably the best surviving example of a formal early Victorian layout in the country and the house gives a brilliant and delightful glimpse of Victoria and Albert, and their family, at home.

The estate at Osborne has a long history; parts of it were mentioned in the Domesday Book. When it was bought by Queen Victoria it was essentially of the late 18th century, with a house, walled kitchen garden and pleasure grounds of that date. Starting in 1845, a new house was built, designed jointly by Prince Albert and Thomas Cubitt. By the 1850s new terraced gardens were underway to the north of the house, from which there are splendid views

Topiary deer at Osborne

across the Solent. Designed by Prince Albert with his artistic adviser, Professor Ludwig Gruner of Dresden, these gardens bristle with ornament: a gravel terrace under the walls of the house has a pattern of shaped lawns with stags of clipped *Lonicera nitida* prancing in beds of blue *Felicia amelloides*, tufts of *Festuca glauca* and red pelargoniums; a grand triple tiered fountain pool surmounted by a kneeling figure of Venus has a pink marble basin supported on dolphins' tails, while old topiary mushrooms of gold variegated holly stand on either side. To one side, a balustraded terrace with an ornate pattern of shaped beds filled with bedding plants and decorated with gold or green juniper clipped into lollipops or spirals has four statues of women holding flaming torches. At its centre winged sphinxes support a giant basin planted with an agave and the encircling balustrade is decorated with urns and spheres.

At a lower level a paved and balustraded terrace has a figure of Venus at the centre of a circular sunken pool. Four flights of steps lead down to the pool, each guarded by a pair of seahorses mounted on plinths. Shaped beds filled with bedding plants are cut into turf and a wall is covered in neatly clipped *Magnolia grandiflora* with an arched alcove at the centre. Opposite is a very grand pergola of square stone pillars covered in grapevines and roses and beyond this are beds with clipped tracery of cotton lavender and tall Chusan palms.

AN 18TH-CENTURY WALLED GARDEN
To the south of the house, across lawns of beautiful evergreen trees, cedars and holm oaks, is the 18th-century walled garden. This has been redesigned by the garden designer Rupert Golby to present a dazzling scene of ornament and productivity. Central walks of

lavender and a tunnel of roses have borders on each side backed by espaliered fruit. An octagonal raised lily pool stands at the centre. Against a south-facing wall is a lean-to glasshouse with fine metal glazing bars, filled with a superb display of tender ornamental plants. Nearby you can peer into a flawless double potting shed. In the garden you will see handsome pots with the Victoria and Albert cipher.

THE SWISS COTTAGE AND A MUSEUM

About a mile from the house – there is an excellent minibus service – is an enchanting pair of buildings. In 1850 a Swiss Cottage was brought from Switzerland for the children. In front of it is a pretty pattern of rectangular beds in which Prince Albert encouraged his children to cultivate vegetables which he would buy from them at the current market rate. A thatched summerhouse displays the small garden tools and wheelbarrows used by the children. The interior of the Swiss Cottage houses all sorts of treasures. Among them is a most elegant little spade with a mahogany handle "used by The Queen when Her Majesty planted a Brahea Roezli [a kind of palm] in the Garden of the Villa Victoria, Grasse. April 11th 1891". (The Villa Victoria belonged to Baronne Alice de Rothschild.) A separate Swiss-style building houses the children's museum, filled with stuffed birds, eggs, geological specimens and all sorts of ethnographic curiosities displayed in beautiful cabinets. Also displayed nearby, of no horticultural interest but a most intriguing sight, is Queen Victoria's bathing machine.

On the way back there is a splendid view of the house – its pantiled towers rising, among cedars and holm oaks, giving it a decidedly Mediterranean air. Disraeli perfectly summed up the character of Osborne: "A Sicilian palazzo with gardens, terraces, statues and vases shining in the sun, than which nothing can be conceived more captivating".

Location East Cowes PO32 6JY, Isle of Wight
OS SZ5194 1½m SE of East Cowes by A3021
Tel 01893 200022 **Fax** 01983 281380 **Website** www.englishheritage.org.uk **English Heritage Register** Grade II* **Owner** English Heritage **Open** Apr to Sept, daily 10–6; Oct, daily 10–5 **Area** 247 acres/100 hectares

OXFORD BOTANIC GARDEN

FOUNDED IN THE EARLY 17TH CENTURY IN A BEAUTIFUL ARCHITECTURAL SETTING OF THE PERIOD, THE GARDENS ARE MARVELLOUSLY PLANTED FOR BOTH BOTANISTS AND GARDENERS

The splendid entrance gates, designed by Nicholas Stone and built 1632–33, are like a fanfare greeting visitors. This is the first botanic garden in Britain, founded in 1621 as a "phiseck garden", and its chief purpose remains to provide plants for the teaching of botany and biology. In recent years, however, it has gone out of its way to make the garden attractive to gardening members of the public. The chief part of the garden corresponds exactly to the print by Loggan published in *Oxonia Illustrata* (1675), which shows it contained within the same handsome 17th-century stone walls with their ornamental carved door-surrounds to the gateways. It also shows the four-part division which survives today, although in 1675 there was a series of fanciful maze-like beds alongside the traditional strips of botanical order beds. A major difference, however, is that today the gardens have spilled out beyond the walls to colonise the banks of the Cherwell.

Most of the walled garden is still given over to the order beds. These, devoted to essentially botanical purposes, nevertheless contain some

The old bog garden at Oxford Botanic Garden

groups (of *Paeoniaceae*, for example) that are dazzlingly ornamental. A group of "economic beds" contain plants used for culinary purposes, for dyeing, for medicine and for their fibres. The walled garden also contains collections of ornamental garden plants, among them a National Collection of euphorbias (well over 100 species and around 30 cultivars), a collection of old cultivars of bearded irises, and collections of ferns and bamboos. Several excellent trees provide striking ornament – a magnificent Austrian pine (*Pinus nigra* subsp. *nigra*) planted in 1800, a yew planted in 1645 by Jacob Bobart, the first director the garden, and an especially fine collection of rowans. Among the latter is a splendid *Sorbus domestica* f. *pomifera* planted in 1790, one of the oldest and best specimens. A particularly attractive part of the garden is given over to "geographical borders", where plants from a particular region take advantage of the protection of the south- or west-facing walls. The South African collection, for example, is rich in agapanthus, amaryllis, kniphofias and phygelius, and there is a collection of species pelargoniums (many delightful and unfamiliar to gardeners) which are given winter protection in the conservatory. There are also collections of plants from South America, the Mediterranean countries and Australasia.

South-west of the walled garden an

admirable deep herbaceous border runs along the outside wall; a rock garden has many alpine plants and bulbs; there is a collection of winter-flowering plants; and flowing borders of cardoons, *Melianthus major*, *Elaeagnus* 'Quicksilver' underplanted with carmint, Californian poppies and ornamental grasses. The former bog garden has recently been replanted with moisture-loving plants and given a small pool. On the banks of the Cherwell, against the east-facing outside wall, a range of glasshouses has alpine plants, tender ferns and lilies, orchids, palms and succulents.

The botanic garden is exceptional for its historic setting, the charm of its layout and the rare interest of its plant collection.

Location High Street, Oxford OX1 4AX, Oxfordshire **OS** SP5026 In the centre of Oxford, near Magdalen bridge **Tel** 01865 276920 **English Heritage Register** Grade I **Owner** Oxford University **Open** Apr to Sept, daily 9–5; Oct to Mar, daily 9–4.30 (closed 25 Dec and Good Fri); greenhouses open 2–4 when the garden is open **Area** 4½ acres/1.8 hectares

OXFORD COLLEGE GARDENS

RARE COLLEGIATE GARDENS SHOWING FEATURES FROM THE MIDDLE AGES TO THE 20TH CENTURY AMONG WONDERFULLY BEAUTIFUL BUILDINGS

Henry James in his *A Passionate Pilgrim* (1875) was deeply smitten with Oxford. He particularly loved the college gardens: "locked in their antique verdure…they seem places in which to lie down on the grass in for ever, in the happy faith that life is all a vast old English garden, and time an endless summer afternoon." All Oxford Colleges have some kind of garden even if it is only a lawn in a quadrangle or a few climbing plants on the walls. A walk round the city is always enlivened by enticing views of green space or brilliant colours glimpsed through an arch or iron gate. It is remarkable how much college land in central Oxford is still given over to the delights of gardening, or at least of green space, when it could have provided so many no doubt much needed building sites. The colleges have a fascinating garden history, well

Terraced garden at Christ Church

documented and vividly described in Mavis Batey's invaluable *Oxford Gardens* (1982). The following is a selection only of those which either have notable garden histories or possess an existing garden of particular merit. Some are both historical *and* beautiful, and all are delightful places to see. Opening times are subject to change and it is essential to telephone beforehand if you intend to make a long journey to visit a college garden.

CHRIST CHURCH

The college was founded by Thomas Wolsey (as Cardinal College) in 1525 and after his fall refounded by Henry VIII in 1546. Visitors enter the college through the War Memorial Gardens south of the college, with pretty cottage-like borders and splendid views over Christ Church meadow which is still grazed. The Broad Walk, beyond the War Memorial Gardens, was laid out in 1668. The 17th-century globe and serpent fountain now in a rose garden was originally at the centre of Tom Quad. Tom Quad (properly known as the Great Quadrangle), the grandest and most public quadrangle in Oxford, is partly early Tudor and partly late 17th-century – the famous Tom Tower has a Tudor base capped with a Gothic top designed by Sir Christopher Wren, reluctantly in the Gothic style. The centre of the quadrangle is sunken, with grand steps leading down to a four-part lawn, and at its centre a circular lily pool with a lead copy of Giambologna's Mercury in the middle. Peckwater Quad is remarkably early Palladianism, built between 1705 and 1714 and designed by Henry Aldrich, Dean of Christ Church. An engraving by William Williams of

1732 in *Oxonia Depicta* shows a pattern of Baroque shapes, probably turf and paths, in the quadrangle. These had probably never been executed but in 1978 when work had to be done on the surfacing they were put into place. In the cathedral cloisters a medieval garden, with lattice-work fencing entwined with a grapevine, has some of the plants, ornamental or herbal, found in medieval gardens – columbines, lavender, rosemary, roses and rue. It lacks sun and is rather tatty, unlike the rest of the college which is impeccably cared for. In Pococke's Garden, not normally open but opened occasionally for the National Gardens Scheme, is an oriental plane planted in 1636 by Dr Pococke. The Dean's Garden was the inspiration for the garden of the Alice books whose author Lewis Carroll (real name Charles Dodgson) was a maths tutor at Christ Church and a friend of Dean Liddell whose daughter Alice inspired the books.

Location St Aldates OX1 1DP **OS** SP5105 **Tel** 01865 276150 **Website** www.chch.ox.ac.uk **English Heritage Register** Grade I **Open** Mon to Sat 9.30–5.30, Sun 11.30–5.30

MAGDALEN COLLEGE

Magdalen College was founded in 1458. In front of the New Building (1733) is a noble arrangement of rectangular plats of grass. At the western end of the New Building is a magnificent London plane planted in 1801 to celebrate the Peace of Amiens, and at the east end of the building, running along a boundary wall, a lively mixed border. But the greatest excitement, and one of the most enchanting features of the Oxford landscape, lies beyond the wall. Here are walks along the river, already established in the 16th century and marked on Loggan's plan in *Oxonia Illustrata* (1675) as "Magdalen College Water Walkes". In the 19th century they were renamed Addison's Walk after the garden theorist Joseph Addison (1672–1719), whose rooms in Cloister Quadrangle at Magdalen overlooked the Cherwell and the water meadow beyond. It was Addison's relish for the walks that fired his enthusiasm for the "beautiful wildness of Nature" in preference to the "nicer elegancies of Art" and whose writings on such themes in

▷ **Tom Quad** at Christ Church

The Spectator made him a prophet of the 18th-century landscape park. The "Water Walkes" remain much as Addison had known them: a path shaded with beech, horse chestnut, English oak and yew curves round between the Cherwell and the boundary of the meadow. There was a particular spot which Addison especially loved where the square tower of the chapel and the old buildings of the college were seen far across the meadow. The stone seat on which he used to sit is still there and the view, apart from the presence of New Building which was built after Addison's death, is much as he would have known it. In 1801 Humphry Repton advised the college to float a lake in the meadow, but the advice was rejected. Magdalen meadow is today famous for its snake's head fritillaries; it is one of the few places in England, where these beautiful flowers may seen flowering so lavishly. In July, after the fritillaries have seeded, the Magdalen herd of deer is moved from the Grove, immediately beneath the New Building, to graze here until the end of the year. In the early part of the year the herd, established since at least 1705, gives the New Building the appearance of a venerable country house standing in its ancestral park. **Location** High Street OX1 4AU **OS** SP5206 **Tel** 01865 276000 **Website** www.magd.ox.ac.uk **English Heritage Register** Grade I **Open** daily 2–6

NEW COLLEGE

New College was founded in 1379 hard by the old city walls. In the Garden Quad are splendid railings and wrought-iron gates

Addison's Walk at Magdalen College

erected in 1711 by Thomas Robinson, a pupil of the great Huguenot craftsman Jean Tijou who made the wrought-iron at Hampton Court. Beyond the gates are the remains of the mount which Celia Fiennes had seen when she came here before 1691. She described "Myrtle Oringe and Lemons and Lorrestine [Laurustinus] growing in potts of

earth…gravell and grass, some shady, and a great mount in the middle which is ascended by degrees…and on the top is a Summer House". All this is seen in an engraving of 1732 by William Williams showing four elaborate parterres with much topiary and a pyramid-like mount. By the early 19th century the formal gardens had gone and the mount had become overgrown and picturesque. Today, where Williams's 18th-century picture showed neat rows of crisply clipped topiary running along the city wall there is a boisterous mixed border by the garden writer Robin Lane-Fox who is Garden Fellow of the college. **Location** Holywell St OX1 3BN **OS** SP5106 **Tel** 01865 279555 **Website** www.new.ox.ac.uk **English Heritage Register** Grade I **Open** Apr to Oct, daily 11–5; Nov to Mar, daily 2–4

ST CATHERINE'S COLLEGE

St Catherine's College was founded in 1962 and designed by the Danish architect Arne Jacobsen, one of his last works. This was, to put it mildly, a dim period for English architecture and a very bright one for Danish. As well as the building and the furnishings, Jacobsen also designed the garden, making it unique among Oxford colleges – buildings and landscape conceived as an entity. The site, on the eastern edge of collegiate Oxford, runs along the river Cherwell. Although the river is not visible from the college (it is hidden behind a beech hedge), Jacobsen made a watery reference to it by laying out a long thin canal along the western side of the college, giving strong visual unity. The entrance to the college is across a bridge with a Barbara Hepworth abstract bronze to one side. The buildings, of brick, concrete and occasional metal facings, are long and low. The only part that could be thought of as a quadrangle is a large open space as soon as you enter. At its centre is a huge circular lawn with a large pendulous Atlantic cedar (*Cedrus atlantica* 'Glauca Pendula') on its edge, a *Cercidiphyllum japonicum* to one side and a sprawling mulberry (*Morus nigra*) on the other. The tall end wall of a building is masked in ivy with a narrow bed of irises at its foot. All sorts of nooks and crannies break up the space, often hedged in yew or – a favourite device – separated by rows of short brick walls with alternate short yew hedges between them. Irregular patterns of rectilinear beds in concrete paving slabs are planted with peonies and irises, with a beautiful tall eucryphia erupting among them. Yew hedges are sometimes planted with waves of glistening *Asarum europaeum* at their base. Excellent trees – not architect's clichés – are frequently planted, such as a noble *Parrotia persica* emerging from billowing mounds of heather. At the end of the Bernard Sunley Building an amphitheatre of concrete slabs is enclosed in a sweep of yew hedging. "Big statements and intimate corners" is what I wrote in my notebook, and that seems about right.

Location Manor Road OX1 3UT **OS** SP5206 **Tel** 01865 271700 **English Heritage Register** Grade II **Open** daily 9–5

ST JOHN'S COLLEGE

St John's College was founded in 1555. An engraving by William Williams in *Oxonia Depicta* (1732) shows three enclosures, each containing formal rows of trees and topiary, the President's garden full of evergreen obelisks. By the late 18th century a much more informal layout of flowering shrubs in beds was in place. A late 19th-century rock garden was laid out by the college bursar, Dr H.J. Bidder, which survives. In the garden today you pass through Front Quad and Canterbury Quad, from whose beautiful 17th-century garden gateway there is a view of a large lawn edged on three sides with trees and shrubs with a perimeter walk. There is no interesting detailed planting but some good trees – an old holm oak, a fine fern-leafed

beech and a huge weeping beech.

Location St Giles OX1 3JP **OS** SP5106 **Tel** 01865 277300 **English Heritage Register** Grade II **Open** daily 1–5

TRINITY COLLEGE

The college was founded in 1555 – in fact a refoundation based on the 13th-century Durham College, a Benedictine Foundation which was suppressed in 1544. A fragment only survives of the earlier college, the 15th-century Old Library on the east side of Durham Quad, with buildings of the 17th and 18th centuries grafted onto it. Williams's *Oxonia Depicta* (1732) shows a spectacular formal garden between Durham Quad and Parks Road with topiary, two mounts crowned with columns and an intricate wilderness with maze-like passages cut into groves of trees. A central walk culminates in a set of grand wrought-iron gates with splendid Baroque stone piers. These gardens survived for an exceptionally long time – they were still essentially in place when Robert Southey returned to Oxford in 1809; even the formal wilderness remained. The walk and the gateway still survive to this day and, miraculously, some ancient and baggy yews which must be remnants of the early 18th-century topiary. The walk is today flanked by superb lawns with a very well-kept border running the whole length against the north wall. The gardens are generally especially

well maintained – even the window boxes are of high quality.

Location Broad Street OX1 3BN **OS** SP5106 **Tel** 01865 279900 **English Heritage Register** Grade II **Open** daily 10.30–12, 2–5

WADHAM COLLEGE

Wadham was founded in 1610 and the college buildings, which remain substantially unchanged, were finished by 1613. John Evelyn visited the garden in 1654 and found all sorts of curiosities including "Transparent Apiaries…built like Castles and Palaces… adorn'd in variety of Dials, little Statues, Vanes etc" and "an Hollow statue which gave a Voice and utterid Words". Mavis Batey also records that there was a machine for producing rainbows. Loggan's *Oxonia Illustrata* (1675) shows the garden with a mount with an elaborate staircase and crowned with a statue of Atlas at the centre of a four-part arrangement of formal beds. By 1755 the statue had blown down and the mount was demolished. This started the process of informality which has led to the present garden with its herbaceous borders, lawn and good trees, among them a magnificent magnolia and a grove of fastigiate oaks (*Quercus robur* f. 'Fastigiata').

Location Parks Road OX1 3PN **OS** SP5106 **Tel** 01865 277900 **English Heritage Register** Grade II **Open** daily (Term) 1–4.15; (Vacation) 10.30–11.45; 1–4.15

The canal at St Catherine's College

POUND HILL GARDEN

A LATE 20TH-CENTURY GARDEN FOR
AN OLD FARMHOUSE WITH SKILFULLY
DESIGNED ENCLOSURES FILLED WITH
DECORATIVE PLANTING

The garden at Pound Hill gathers itself about the house like a well-fitted garment. The old stone farmhouse overlooks a paved courtyard with cistus, *Dierama pulcherrimum*, wild strawberries and thymes growing in the cracks. A lawn at a higher level is edged with criss-cross patterns of box hedges, with tall cones of yew marking the ends and tall pots of white begonias or the rose 'The Fairy' filling the compartments. The lawn continues, flowing through an opening in a stone wall, to be surrounded on three sides by mixed borders backed by walls or yew hedges. Spheres or columns of clipped yew punctuate the borders and there is much repetition of such bold plants as cardoon

(*Cynara cardunculus*), the biennial clary (*Salvia sclarea*) and the great thistle *Onopordum acanthium*. A gap in the borders leads through a yew hedge to a hidden water garden with a pool edged with alders, bulrushes, *Gunnera manicata*, primulas and *Rheum palmatum*. Behind a tennis court a wavy path leads along a walk of Himalayan birches (*Betula utilis* var. *jacquemontii*) underplanted with pulmonaria to a grove of clipped sweet chestnuts with shrub roses planted in the grass among them. Beyond it an old-fashioned orchard is crossed by a pergola of the rose 'Paul's Himalyan Musk' and wisteria.

Immediately west of the house a long narrow formal rose garden has a central paved path and hedges and domes of clipped box. Repeated standard plants of the roses 'Little White Pet' and 'The Fairy' are planted along the centre of each side and underplanted with more roses and geraniums, lavender, *Lilium regale* and pulmonaria. Steps lead up to a formal miniature kitchen garden where four

beds edged in box have tall box cones at the corners and an arbour of roses where the paths meet.

About the house there are many sitting places. Pots and troughs are arranged with impeccable collections of gentians or saxifrages, all neatly labelled. The planting in the garden is of a generally old-fashioned kind but there are passages of originality such as the Himalayan birch walk and the garden of chestnuts and roses. All these fit together with perfect harmony. The Stockitts also have a nursery attached to the garden, selling herbaceous perennials, roses, topiary and good garden pots.

Location West Kington, nr Chippenham SN14 7JG, Wiltshire **OS** ST8177 8m NW of Chippenham by A420 and B4039 and minor roads; Jnct 18 of M4 **Tel** 01249 783880 **Fax** 01249 782953 **Email** poundhillplants@westkingtonnurseries.co.uk **Website** www.poundhillplants.co.uk **Owner** Mr and Mrs Philip Stockitt **Open** Mar to Oct, daily 2–5 **Area** 2 acres/0.8 hectares

The courtyard at Pound Hill

ROUSHAM HOUSE

WILLIAM KENT'S MASTERPIECE, AN
ENCHANTING EARLY 18TH-CENTURY
ARCADIA, STILL PRIVATELY OWNED AND
STILL WONDERFULLY BEAUTIFUL

Gardens that interest garden historians by no means invariably please garden visitors. Rousham, however, though universally regarded as a garden of great historical importance, is an altogether lovable place. This is partly because of its intrinsic beauties and partly because, still in private hands, it has no whiff of the heritage industry about it. There is no tea room, no gift shop and no ticket kiosk. You put your money in a machine and the garden is yours.

The beauty of Rousham depends on the way in which views of the surrounding rural landscape are drawn into the garden and made part of it. Many 18th-century landscape parks – Stourhead, for example – are self-contained worlds of their own, isolated and inward-looking. At Rousham the visitor's eye moves from intimate detail within the garden to wide, carefully orchestrated views of the

surrounding rural landscape. This is a garden for wandering in; different routes will yield different pleasures and the same building, ornament or view will be revealed in a different guise.

The garden that we see at Rousham was made by William Kent between 1737 and 1741 for General James Dormer, a veteran of the battle of Blenheim, who intended the place for his "philosophical retirement". Kent used the bones of the royal garden designer Charles Bridgeman's earlier garden, made between 1725 and 1734 (which Alexander Pope saw in 1728 and thought "the prettiest place for waterfalls, jets, ponds, inclosed with beautiful scenes of green and hanging wood, that I ever saw"). Parts of Bridgeman's garden survive, of which a fine bowling green extending north from the house is one. At the far edge of the lawn, beyond a statue by Scheemakers of a lion attacking a horse, the ground falls away, swooping down to the banks of the river Cherwell with peaceful, long views of the countryside beyond. To the left and the right of the statue are alcove seats

designed by Kent and impassive marble herms standing out against the dark foliage of yews. An inconspicuous path through woodland leads to a figure of a dying gladiator (also by Scheemakers), sprawling with his back to a stone balustrade, beyond which the river is seen once again. What you cannot see at this point is that the balustrade runs along the top of Praeneste, a lovely arcaded building by Kent whose arched openings frame views. On a broad open grassy slope, Venus's Vale, the goddess teeters on the apex of a rustic cascade, looking over an octagonal pool, below which is a second cascade. She is flanked by cupids riding on swans, and lead figures of fauns lurk among the trees. A winding rill now lures you on, gleaming in the woodland shade and opening into a pool overlooked by a simple grotto. The rill continues until you see a fine cedar of Lebanon with the Temple of Echo (William Kent, c.1740) standing at the head of a grassy slope with the river at its foot. A distant view is revealed of the 13th-century Heyford Bridge, a pretty piece of borrowed landscape,

The dying gladiator at Rousham

and, closer at hand, a statue of Apollo with his back to a ride through the woods – the Long Walk, part of Bridgeman's original scheme. Walks follow the curving river bank with many fine oaks and beautiful old horse chestnuts. Soon Venus's Vale is displayed from a new angle, now enlivened by an optical illusion: the pool separating the two cascades is invisible from below and the upper cascade appears to flow directly into the lower. From this point there is also a splendid view of Praeneste on the wooded slopes to one side. Continuing along the river you come to the shadowy remains of Bridgeman's turf amphitheatre – now a semicircular glade – with lead figures by John van Nost of Ceres, Mercury and Bacchus. Passing the foot of the slope below the bowling green you come to a pyramid-roofed pavilion by William Kent facing out over the river.

Throughout the garden the ingredients seem only lightly sketched in, forming painterly scenes which shift as the visitor

◁ **The lake** and Pantheon at Stourhead

progresses. On the grassy slopes above the river, statues turn their backs on the garden and gaze out over the river towards the fields and farms of the countryside. Framed views across the river are directed, too, by the arched openings of the Praeneste. Within the building were finely made seats, designed by Kent, so that visitors could sit and relish these views. Horace Walpole thought that Rousham was "the most engaging of all Kent's works. It is Kentissimo." The miracle is that the garden, still owned by a descendant of General Dormer, has survived so marvellously to shed brilliant light on the pioneer days of the English landscape movement and to entrance any 21st-century visitor.

Rousham owes its fame to the William Kent garden, but it also possesses a delightful 17th-century walled former kitchen garden. A box parterre of roses is overlooked by a 17th-century dovecote, old espaliered fruit trees follow paths and a long, finely kept mixed border runs along a wall. This forms a flowery but no less enjoyable pendant to the more serious pleasures of Kent's magical landscape garden.

Location Steeple Aston OX5 3QX, Oxfordshire
OS SP4724 12m N of Oxford by A4260 and B4030
Tel 01869 347110 **English Heritage Register** Grade I
Owner C. Cottrell-Dormer **Open** daily 10–4.30
Area 30 acres/12 hectares

STOURHEAD

AN ICON OF GARDEN TASTE – A MID 18TH-
CENTURY LANDSCAPE GARDEN ENRICHED
WITH SUPERB ORNAMENTAL BUILDINGS AND
WOODLAND PLANTING ABOUT A LAKE

Many famous gardens take on a life independent of their true nature, assuming the character of an icon and making it difficult to see their essence. Stourhead is probably the most famous 18th-century landscape garden but it has the power of instant enchantment to which visitors succumb as soon as they enter. It is, in any weather in any season, a wonderful place to visit. Quite big enough to conceal even large numbers of visitors, even in high summer it is easy to find parts of the garden where you may experience those feelings of solitary melancholy so attractive to 18th-century landscapers.

The house is a cool Palladian villa designed by Colen Campbell and built *c.*1720–24 for the banker Henry Hoare. Although the house and garden as seen by visitors today seem quite unconnected, there was originally a visual connection between the two. To appreciate this I recommend visitors to park in the car park and make their way towards the house so as to approach the garden from that direction, winding down the wooded

slopes until the garden gradually reveals itself. This gentle unveiling is much more satisfactory than the abrupt revelation experienced by the direct route to the garden.

The garden is the work of Henry Hoare II who shortly after inheriting the estate in 1741 transformed the valley of the river Stour into a landscape that was a pioneer of romantic taste. He first dammed the stream to form a lake of irregular shape, remarkably resembling a map of England. About the lake he planted trees and placed ornamental buildings – largely the work of the architect Henry Flitcroft – in carefully chosen positions. These buildings are for the most part of classical inspiration, of the sort that an English gentleman would have admired on the Grand Tour. The pillared and pedimented Temple of Flora (1744) on the eastern bank of the lake has an inscription from Virgil's *Aeneid*: "*Procul, o procul este, profani*" ("Be gone, be gone you who are uninitiated") – the warning that Aeneas encountered as he was about to enter the underworld. However, the visitor today needs no special qualifications to submit to the spirit of the magical landscape that surrounds him.

TEMPLES AND A SHIVERY GROTTO
The lake is girdled by a path which winds about its banks, with offshoots making occasional deviations to lead the steps to such buildings as the Temple of Apollo which stands high among trees on the southern edge of the lake. As one walks, the garden composes itself into different views in which the ingredients of water, shorn turf, ornamental buildings and trees and shrubs play varied roles. Different atmospheres evoke different emotions – the Temple of Apollo rising triumphantly on its lofty crag on the sunny side of the garden fills the heart with elation. On the western bank, where the path leads down into a shivery grotto in which lurk a river god and a sleeping nymph, the mood of gloomy introspection is broken by an exhilarating view through a hole pierced in the grotto wall – the lake is revealed with distant prospects of the Temple of Flora on the eastern bank. The Pantheon standing on a grassy promontory is visible from many parts

of the garden. Near it, veiled by trees, is Watch Cottage, a little Gothic building of striking contrast; the Gothic style was regarded by 18th-century landscapers as a reminder of ancient freedom.

Stourhead also possesses a remarkable collection of trees. Planting had been started by Henry Hoare II but it was his son, Richard Colt Hoare, who began recording all tree plantings from 1791. Many survive from his time, and some are the largest examples of their species in the country, such as a Japanese white pine (*Pinus parviflora*) and a tulip tree (*Liriodendron tulipifera*). Subsequent generations of the Hoare family have added to the planting and in 1946 Sir Henry Hoare gave the estate to the National Trust. "One of the most picturesque scenes in the world" was Horace Walpole's description of Stourhead in 1762, and who could disagree?

Location Stourton, Warminster BAS 12 6QH, Wiltshire **OS** ST7734 In Stourton village, 3m NW of Mere by A303 and B3092 **Tel** 01747 841152 **Fax** 01747 842005 **Email** stourhead@.ntrust.org.uk **English Heritage Register** Grade I **Owner** The National Trust **Open** daily 9–7 or sunset if earlier **Area** 40 acres/16 hectares

STOWE GARDEN

SUPERB LANDSCAPE GARDEN ON THE GRANDEST SCALE DESIGNED BY THE BEST ARCHITECTS AND GARDEN DESIGNERS OF THE 18TH CENTURY

Like other gardens great in size and historical importance, Stowe may be approached in different ways. But the first thing to emphasise about it is that it is an immensely enjoyable place. As a garden for a long walk punctuated by beautiful trees, marvellous works of architecture and thrilling vistas, it is enchanting. As a piece of landscape design enriched with buildings and ornaments of the finest quality it is certainly among the most absorbing in the country. For anyone interested in garden history, and in particular the early development of the English landscape park, it is a living document. Having said all that, I had better admit that I find the garden lacks unity – it presents a sequence of often marvellous and occasionally disparate delights that never seem quite to coalesce. The fact that it has a golf course in its midst is unfortunate – brilliantly coloured

anoraks do not suit well with the spirit of the 18th-century landscape park. Furthermore, the house (now a school) has a slightly semi-detached relationship with its setting, when, historically, it had been at its heart.

Charles Bridgeman, William Kent and the youthful Capability Brown, who became head gardener here at the age of twenty-five, each wove their magic at Stowe in different periods. Among the architects who worked on garden buildings and the house in the 18th century were Sir John Vanbrugh, James Gibbs and Robert Adam. Perhaps the only other garden in Europe that employed the talents of so many exceptional artists to such resounding effect was the Versailles of Louis XIV.

The Temple family, later Viscounts Cobham, had owned the estate in the 17th century. It was Sir Richard Temple who recruited Charles Bridgeman in 1713 and set in motion the creation of the new garden. Bridgeman's work – a long axial vista south of the house, with a mixture of formal allées and winding walks to its west – has largely disappeared, though the ha-ha he built remains as the garden boundary.

Stowe's Temple of British Worthies

lie of the land. It is this, the large-scale animation of the landscape, that is the most thrilling and memorable quality of Stowe. Some very large gardens, often designed to proclaim the importance of the owner, can crush the spirit. Stowe has the opposite effect; it induces a feeling of delighted exhilaration.

Location Buckingham MK18 5EH, Buckinghamshire **OS** SP6636 3m NW of Buckingham on A422 **Tel** 01280 822850 **Infoline** 01494 7555568 **Fax** 01280 822437 **Email** stowegarden@ntrust.org.uk **English Heritage Register** Grade I **Owner** The National Trust **Open** Apr to Jun, Wed to Sun 10–5.30; Jul to mid Sept, Tue to Sun, 10–5.30; Dec, Wed to Sun 10–4 **Area** 250 acres/101 hectares

TUDOR HOUSE GARDEN

A PRETTY 16TH-CENTURY HOUSE WITH
A RECREATED GARDEN IN THE TUDOR
STYLE SHOWING THE CHARACTERISTIC
DECORATIVENESS OF THE PERIOD

The Temple of Ancient Virtue at Stowe

William Kent came here in the 1720s and by 1735 he had created the Elysian Fields in a hollow to the east of Bridgeman's vista. This was a famous moment in English garden history when, in Horace Walpole's words, "Kent first leapt the fence and saw that all nature was a garden". Here, often masked by trees, a winding stream separates Kent's Temple of British Worthies (1735) and his Temple of Ancient Virtue (1736). The first is a curiously decorative curved screen of golden stone with niches containing busts of Lord Cobham's special heroes – among them Bacon, Milton, Shakespeare and Pope. The second, domed and pillared and rising on an eminence on the far side of the stream, originally contained statues by Peter Scheemakers of the greatest poet (Homer), philosopher (Socrates), general (Epaminondas) and lawyer (Lycurgus) of the ancient world. These figures, along with many other precious garden ornaments, were sold at auction in 1921.

North-east of the Elysian Fields is Brown's unemphatic Grecian Valley, decorated with no buildings or ornaments but already deploying his characteristic vocabulary of subtly undulating belts of trees and shorn turf as smooth as a fitted carpet. The stream that flows through the Elysian Fields emerges in the Octagon Lake with the Eleven-acre Lake to one side. The first is the site of Bridgeman's formal octagonal pool which formed a

punctuation mark at the end of his long vista. Its easterly neck is spanned by the Palladian Bridge (1738) attributed to James Gibbs. With cattle grazing in the meadows on either side, it has the treasured English atmosphere of rural life coupled with classical harmony. On the far side of the bridge, tucked away in a glade, is the painted Chinese House (1738), possibly by Kent. This is one of the earliest Chinoiserie buildings in the country, removed from the garden in 1751, and after a long exile in other gardens in England and Ireland, restored and returned to Stowe in 1991.

There are many other buildings and ornaments at Stowe – all have their charms and all play their part in the atmosphere of the place. But too great a concentration on the individual buildings, marvellous as they are, detracts from one of the essential beauties of the park. The buildings are reference points in the landscape, deftly fitted into glades, eminences and walks. They form part of an elaborate network of vistas, spanning great distances and rising and falling with the

Heraldic stag at Tudor House

Bugle Street in the centre of the old walled city of Southampton is a surprising, and delightful, survival. With its domestic and commercial buildings ranging from the middle ages to the 20th century it presents exactly the lively jumble of architecture that planners seem to hate but everyone else finds so enjoyable. The Tudor House is part of this cityscape, a charming merchant's house of the early 16th century which has been made into a museum. The house was at one time the home of Sir Richard Lyster, Lord Chief Justice to Henry VIII.

Southampton City Council had the clever idea of creating a little garden of appropriate character in the small space behind the house, and the garden historian Dr Sylvia Landsberg designed a knot garden of characteristically Tudor style. No garden survives in England from this period, and small gardens are even more ephemeral than those attached to great houses. However, enough is known about hem to make it possible to make an authentic, and charming, reconstruction.

The square central knot framed in low edges of santolina has an interlaced tracery pattern of box, winter savory (*Satureja montana*) and wall germander (*Teucrium × lucidrys*) round a cone of clipped box. Surrounding it is a gravel path with small beds of plants known to have been used in gardens of the period – irises, lavender, *Lychnis coronaria*, roses, sage and thyme. The whole is enclosed by a low wooden fence, painted a cheerful red/brown, with decoratively turned uprights. This part of the garden is overlooked by a bower of grapevines and roses, and is flanked by wooden columns of a distinctive Tudor style, painted in chevron patterns of green and white (the Tudor royal colours) and crowned with heraldic beasts – a stag and a unicorn (the emblems of the first two owners of the house). A tunnel arbour of grapevines and summer jasmine runs along one side of the knot, with beds planted with *Rosa gallica*, stinking iris and wild strawberries. To the far side of the bower a tiered stone fountain, supported by griffons, stands in a circular pool hedged in hyssop and rosemary. Despite the limited space the garden

The knot garden
at Tudor House

also contains a handsome sprawling mulberry and an old yew tree. In a corner are bee skeps, an essential part of the garden environment in early days. The Tudor House garden gives a vivid impression of a modest garden of its period and makes admirable use of its rare urban setting.

Location Bugle Street, Southampton SO14 2AD, Hampshire **OS** SU4111 In the centre of Southampton; follow signs to Old Town and docks **Tel** 023 8063 5904 **Fax** 023 8033 9601 **Owner** Southampton City Council **Open** Tue to Fri 10–12, 1–5, Sat 10–12, 1–4, Sun 2–5 **Area** ¼ acre/0.1 hectare

TYLNEY HALL HOTEL

GRAND 19TH-CENTURY FORMAL GARDENS
IN A WOODED SETTING FOR AN OPULENT
NEO-JACOBEAN MANSION

There has been a house here since at least the 16th century but the present house, a grand brick neo-Jacobean mansion, was built in the 1870s for Charles Harris to the designs of Edward Birchett. Very shortly after, between 1899 and 1904, it was altered for Sir Lionel Philips by Seldon Wornum and Robert Weir Schultz. It was at this stage that the garden was made, although it was influenced by the

remains of an early 18th-century garden. Since 1984 the estate has been owned by a hotel which has done much restoration to the house and garden. A separate part of the estate, to the north-east of the house, is a golf course – the original 18th-century entrance avenue may still be seen striding across the fairway.

AN EXCITING ITALIAN GARDEN
The new entrance drive curves through the well-wooded grounds which have a strong 19th-century flavour, with many Wellingtonias. The most exciting part of the garden is the Italian Garden spreading out below the north-west façade of the house. This was designed by Seldon Wornum and Robert Weir Schultz, with planting plans by Gertrude Jekyll who supplied plants from her own nursery in 1906. A deep paved terrace has stone balustrades decorated with repeated obelisks. A grand double staircase leads to a lawn with rows of yew topiary and a central pool and tiered fountain. A herbaceous border runs along the far edge of the terrace, backed with a yew hedge clipped into castellations. At each end of the border is a splendid open arched gazebo with a sweeping ogee roof. At each end of the terrace stately flights of steps lead up to the pleasure grounds which surround the house

The Italian Garden at Tylney Hall

WADDESDON MANOR

THE EPITOME OF ROTHSCHILD TASTE – A
LOIRE CHÂTEAU IN WOODED GROUNDS WITH
SUPERB 19TH-CENTURY FORMAL BEDS AND
MAGNIFICENT ORNAMENTS

on this side. Beyond the lower terrace the ground falls away, with trees pressing in on either side, to a boating lake.

West of the house there had been a Dutch Garden – this in late Victorian or Edwardian times would have been a pattern of formal beds with bedding schemes and topiary. It is now a swimming pool but a pair of magnificent wrought-iron gates by Robert Weir Schultz survives. These, made in about 1903, have entwined roses, strongly modelled and forming marvellous patterns.

The Dutch Garden was originally laid out to form a passage between the house and the kitchen garden, which survives, now with further hotel rooms attractively arranged in cottage-like buildings, some of them converted from old outhouses. Robert Weir Schulz's fine glasshouse, with the thinnest of glazing bars and prettily decorated ridges, are used for raising bedding plants for the garden. A pergola of oak beams and brick pillars planted with roses forms a cross axis leading to a gateway which originally led down through a terraced garden where the upper walk had clipped topiaries of golden yew; these remain. Part of the kitchen garden has been replanted as an orchard and more fruit trees are espaliered about the walls.

Robert Weir Schultz laid out a rare picturesque water garden to the south-east of the kitchen garden, and this has been substantially restored. Two large pools are

linked by a bewildering sequence of curving streams, rustic bridges, cascades, stepping stones, eruptions of rockwork. *Gunnera manicata*, irises, petasites, primulas and rheums are lavishly spread on the banks, and there are many good trees. The upper pool, now with waterlilies and an irregular shape, had in the 18th century been a formal canal.

To convert a capacious and attractive country house into a hotel seems an admirable idea. That it should also lead to the restoration, and preservation, of a notable garden (which adds of course to the allure of the hotel) is a splendid bonus.

Location Rotherwick, Hook RG27 9AZ, Hampshire **OS** SU7055 5½m NE of Basingstoke by A3010 and minor roads; 1½m from Jnct 5 of M3 via Newnham

Tel 01256 764881 **Fax** 01256 768141 **Email** sales@tylneyhall.com **Website** www.tylneyhall.com **English Heritage Register** Grade II* **Owner** Tylney Hall Hotel Ltd **Open** to guests of the hotel or restaurant **Area** 67 acres/27 hectares

The house at Waddesdon, a dazzling pastiche of a renaissance Loire château, was completed in 1889 for Baron Ferdinand de Rothschild to the designs of Hippolyte Destailleur. It sits on the top of a knoll with beautiful views across well-wooded grounds to the Vale of Aylesbury.

The site was landscaped between 1874 and 1881 by Elie Lainé who clothed the slopes in mature trees and devised an ingenious pattern of looping drives and walks which girdle the hill. Lainé was responsible only for the broad scheme of things and it was Ferdinand de Rothschild himself who looked after the detail. He recorded in his privately published *Red Book* (1897): "the pleasure grounds and gardens were laid out by my bailiff and gardener according to my notions and under my superintendence." The result is a beguiling mixture of formality and informality enriched with a lively decorative sense.

FOUNTAINS AND A GREAT PARTERRE
From the *rondpoint* of the North Fountain – an 18th-century sculpture of Triton and frolicking nereids by Giuliano Mozani – an avenue of oaks (the English oak and turkey oak (*Quercus cerris*) intermingled) runs straight up to the north façade of the house. On the south side of the house the terrace and its parterre is the scene of spectacular high Victorian decorative exuberance. Here tens of thousands of bedding plants are deployed in patterns known as raised ribbon bedding, which creates a padded effect like a well-filled eiderdown. At the centre of the parterre is a fountain with Pluto and Proserpine, also by

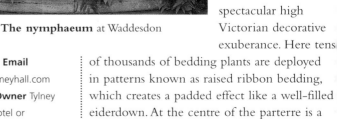

The nymphaeum at Waddesdon

Mozani. A splendid new initiative has been launched in the parterre – every year part of the garden is devoted to a bedding scheme designed by an artist. The first, to John Hubbard's design, was planted in 2000 to celebrate the new millennium and in the following year a design by Oscar de la Renta.

To the north-west of the house is another piece of ornamental formality: the aviary garden. A splendid Rococo ironwork aviary with sweeping wings houses a collection of exotic birds. It overlooks a garden designed by Lanning Roper in the 1960s – hedges of hornbeam and box, clipped lollipops of bay, two slender beds of 'Iceberg' roses and charming 18th-century marble lions are the ingredients of a satisfying exercise in restrained simplicity. Further from the house, with a backdrop of trees and hedges, many fine statues are skilfully placed to enliven

The terrace parterre at Waddesdon

the scene, lurking in groves or acting as eyecatchers.

No visitor to the gardens at Waddesdon should fail also to visit the house, which has beautiful interiors filled with the finest furniture, pictures and china. House and garden are all of a piece, springing from the same desire to make something of the highest quality.

Location nr Aylesbury HP18 0JH, Buckinghamshire
OS SP7416 6m NW of Aylesbury by A41
Tel 01296 653211 **Fax** 01296 653212 **Email** waddesdonmanor@.ntrust.org.uk **Website** www.waddesdon.org.uk **English Heritage Register** Grade I **Owner** The National Trust **Open** Mar to 24 Dec, Wed to Sun (open Bank Hol Mon) 10–5
Area 160 acres/65 hectares

WATERPERRY GARDENS

EXCELLENT PLANTS, AN INVENTIVE
WALLED GARDEN AND THE SPLENDID STOCK
BEDS OF A BUSY NURSERY

Waterperry was founded in 1932 by a remarkable woman, Beatrix Havergal, to educate women in all branches of horticulture. It still has that purpose, in the form of a multitude of garden courses, but it also has a large nursery and garden centre and an attractive and diverse garden.

The flat site, with many good trees, lies by the river Thame and benefits from rich loam soil that is slightly alkaline. The entrance to the garden leads along a deep herbaceous border, past a fine statue (Meditation by Nathan David) standing in a thicket of *Macleaya* × *kewensis*. Other sculptures adorn

The Formal Garden at Waterperry

the garden and temporary exhibitions are mounted (in the summer of 2002 it was an interesting collection of works by the Shona people of Zimbabwe). Apart from the Long Walk which links various of the garden's ingredients, there is no strong layout to the garden; it is a place for ambling in. The most strongly designed part is the Formal Garden, designed by Bernard Saunders and Mary Spiller. Enclosed in yew hedges and bristling with decorative ideas skilfully executed, it has a swirling knot garden of box and purple berberis compartments filled with summer bedding. There are lavish herbaceous borders, a tunnel of white wisteria, columns of clipped hornbeam, a vine arbour and shady sitting places. At its centre is a slightly sugary statue of a young girl, The Lamp of Wisdom.

One of the most alluring sights, at the garden's heart, is the very large array of nursery beds of herbaceous perennials to provide propagation material for the nursery. A rose garden nearby is enclosed in yew hedges and decorated with a charmingly wonky arbour of oak. It contains a wide-ranging collection – from shrub and species roses to modern bedding varieties. A long south-facing herbaceous border runs along the outer wall (18th-century, of very pretty silvery brick) of the area which now houses the garden centre. Honeysuckle, *Solanum laxum* 'Album', *Vitis coignetiae* and wisteria clothe the wall and the bed is planted with bold groups of delphiniums, *Eupatorium purpureum*, geraniums,

Michaelmas daisies, mulleins and phlox. A collection of dwarf conifers and of heathers shows what varieties can be cultivated in alkaline soil. A charming riverside walk is planted with aconites, snake's head fritillaries, narcissi and snowdrops. Of special interest to alpinists is the National Collection of Kabschia and Engleria saxifrages – a staggering range of over 300 species and cultivars.

Location Waterperry, nr Wheatley OX33 1JZ, Oxfordshire **OS** SP6306 9m E of Oxford by A40, signed Jnct 8 of M40 **Tel** 01844 339254 **Fax** 01844 339883 **Email** office@waterperrygardens.fsnet.co.uk **Website** www.waterperrygardens.co.uk **Owner** The School of Economic Science **Open** Apr to Oct, daily 9–5.30; Nov to Mar, daily 9–5 **Area** 83 acres/34 hectares

WEST GREEN HOUSE GARDEN

A LOVELY 18TH-CENTURY HOUSE WITH WALLED GARDENS SUPERBLY PLANTED BY A MODERN PLANTSWOMAN AND ARCHITECTURAL EMBELLISHMENTS BY QUINLAN TERRY

West Green House is an exceptionally decorative early 18th-century house built for "Hangman" Hawley, a cavalry general at the Battle of Culloden. Of its early garden history nothing is known; indeed it scarcely

comes into focus until 1975 when Alistair McAlpine (later Lord McAlpine) took a tenancy on the estate which had been owned by the National Trust since 1957. McAlpine, a voracious collector, was deeply bitten by the gardening bug and was determined, as he wrote in his autobiography, to make "a place that was once beautiful, not just beautiful again, but yet more beautiful than ever before". Apart from much restoration of the garden, including the wholesale replanting of hedges, his major contribution was to commission a series of monuments from the architect Quinlan Terry. Among them is a handsome rusticated column at the head of a lime avenue, which bears an inscription in Latin explaining that it was paid for with "a large sum of money that would otherwise have fallen into the hands of the tax-gatherers". An ornate Baroque nymphaeum with trick perspective, copied from the fountain of Santa Maria della Scala in Rome, forms an eyecatcher at the end of a vista from the kitchen garden. Perhaps most memorable among the monuments from this time is that erected to McAlpine's gardener, Thomas Mann, who died in 1986. An obelisk soars up from the bank of a pool with a splendid sculpture of Mr Mann, elbow cocked on the obelisk's plinth, a jaunty grin on his face and a spade at the ready in his hand. McAlpine's gardening idyll came to an unhappy end in 1990 when an IRA bomb severely damaged the house. The second stage in the garden's development started in 1993 when Marylyn Abbott restored house and garden and introduced refined new flower plantings.

A BRILLIANT EYE FOR COLOUR In classical fashion the formal gardens are clustered about the house. To its west the theatre lawn is a brilliant exercise in creating drama out of restraint. A long rectangle of lawn, enclosed in tall yew hedges and gently terraced in steps, extends away from the house. It is devoid of ornament except for a pair of urns and one or two benches. The walled former kitchen garden is the scene of Marylyn Abbott's most detailed attentions. Part of it has been retained as a true kitchen garden with ornamental fruit-cages, with Chinoiserie roofs designed by Oliver Ford.

Flawlessly precise rows of vegetables, with lively associated flower plantings, radiate outwards from the fruit-cages and paths are decorated with lollipops of standard *Weigela florida* and *Viburnum × burkwoodii*. The other half of the walled garden is divided into four lawns planted with fruit trees. Running along its south-facing wall, borders are filled with shrub roses, peonies, philadelphus and lilacs underplanted with geraniums, irises and violas. Marylyn Abbott has a brilliant eye for colour and texture and is constantly experimenting with new plantings. All this is finely kept and gives a vivid impression of ornament and productivity. The Quinlan Terry and other monuments are skilfully integrated into the pattern of the garden. The house overlooks no flower garden and the explosion of floriferousness that meets the eye in the walled garden is all the more effective for being hidden away. It is all most craftily done,

The nymphaeum at West Green House

providing both pleasure and inspiration.

Location Thackhams Lane, West Green, nr Hartley Wintney RG27 8JB, Hampshire **OS** SU7456 2½m NE of Jnct 5 of M3 **Tel** and **Fax** 01252 844611 **Owner** Marylyn Abbott/The National Trust **Open** May to Aug, Wed to Fri and Bank Hol Mon 11–4 **Area** 6 acres/2.4 hectares

WEST WYCOMBE PARK

A MYSTERIOUS BUT CHARMING
18TH-CENTURY LANDSCAPE PARK WITH A
LAKE, FINE ORNAMENTAL BUILDINGS AND
ASSOCIATIONS WITH THE HELLFIRE CLUB

West Wycombe house was built for Sir Francis Dashwood shortly after 1707. His son, another Sir Francis, was the chief maker of the garden, but is probably more famous as the instigator of the so-called Hellfire Club which had its meetings at Medmenham Abbey where hanky-panky of various kinds took place. This has little relevance to the garden today, although in the past the Temple of Venus contained, in the chaste words of Pevsner, an "embracing circle of lead statues of erotic meaning".

A painting of the lake at West Wycombe Park in 1752 by William Hannan shows a charming, light-hearted scene. Ornamental miniature naval ships, with the white ensign fluttering, cruise the water. On an island in the lake elegant periwigged figures disport themselves by a swagged and caparisoned tent. In the middle ground a group of elaborately dressed women look across to a cascade surmounted by a river god pouring water from an urn and framed in picturesque rock work. In the foreground gardeners shave the turf with scythes and in the distance a Chinoiserie bridge spans a stream. On the slopes above the lake the house looks down a long formal ride through woodland. All this has the distinctive atmosphere of a certain kind of playful 18th-century landscape garden

with a Rococo flavour. However, a painting of 1781 by William Daniell shows a very different setting for the house, which is now engulfed in a picturesque clutter of trees, and in 1794–95 Humphry Repton worked on the landscape and removed "some useless and unmeaning gardens".

SEDUCTIVE VIEWS

The landscape today presents a delightful scene. The house faces north-east down a long grassy slope towards the lake with the river Wye flowing into it. A wooded island is embellished with a beautiful Music Temple designed by Nicholas Revett between 1778 and 1780. The lake itself, part of the landscape possibly designed by Maurice-Louis Jolivet, is supposed to represent a swan, and the stream to the west does resemble a slender serpentine neck. A cascade, guarded by two recumbent nymphs, links the river to the lake and below it is a new bridge designed by Quinlan Terry (1985). The Gothic boathouse on an isthmus jutting out from the southern bank of the lake is also a modern recreation, by Patrick Crawford in 1983, based on an 18th-century design. West of the lake the Broad Walk has a tall column surmounted with a figure of Britannia, put up in 1987 to celebrate the Queen's sixtieth birthday. Nearby is Quinlan Terry's domed Temple of Venus (1982) above an 18th-century mound and cavern. The stream winds peacefully across meadowland and the pillared house to the south is partly veiled in trees which continue in belts and clumps on the land that rises above it. All the ingredients of the park are harmoniously related and form a series of shifting and seductive views. In the distance, on the far side of the A40, are the wooded slopes of West Wycombe Hill which also formed part of the Dashwoods' 18th-century landscape. The medieval church of St Lawrence, which stands at the top of the hill, was remodelled in the 1750s when a new tower was built, surmounted by a giant golden sphere, making a striking eyecatcher from the park. More extraordinary than this is an immense mausoleum which Pevsner suggests may be the largest mausoleum built in Europe since

◁ **The Music Temple** at West Wycombe

Antiquity. A hexagonal, roofless enclosure of soaring flint walls whose parapet is busy with urns, it houses several Dashwood memorials. The side of the mausoleum facing the house has monumental stone columns and an elaborate frieze at the parapet. It is precisely aligned with the West Wycome to London road which is seen running straight as an arrow below. At a slightly lower level than the church, it is less visible from the house because of the growth of the encircling woodland. Half way up the hill are the Hellfire Caves, built of flint in the 1750s in the Gothic style and containing the various rooms in which the Hellfire Club had its meetings. Now attached to a tea room, they can be visited.

Location West Wycombe HP14 3AJ, Buckinghamshire **OS** SU8294 At the W end of West Wycombe, S of the A40 **Tel** 01494 513569 **English Heritage Register** Grade I **Owner** The National Trust **Open** Apr to May, Sun, Wed and Bank Hol 2–6; Jun to Aug, Sun to Thur 2–6 **Area** 46 acres/19 hectares

GILBERT WHITE'S HOUSE

THE CHARMING AND IDIOSYNCRATIC GARDEN OF A GREAT NATURALIST MAKES THE BEST OF ITS FINE NATURAL SETTING

Gilbert White's house, properly known as The Wakes, straggles charmingly along the high street of Selborne, built in several different periods from the 16th century onwards. White was born in Selborne and came back to live here at the age of thirty-five. Apart from his passion for natural history, he was also an assiduous gardener with a decidedly original turn of mind. One of the great charms of the place is that you enter the house, pass through its rooms, and find that the garden is continuous with the remarkably unspoilt countryside behind it, which rises to the beech wood, the Hanger, beyond fields. White was very conscious of the beauty of this setting, and with his brother John he created a "zig-zag" walk leading up to the Hanger, for the delectation of the village. So that the views from his garden should be unbroken, he also created a ha-ha, most unusually supported with a wooden palissade

which has recently been restored. White was knowledgeable about current ideas in gardening and had visited Stowe twice in 1752 but it is unusual to see avant-garde ideas about opening up views of the landscape put into practice in a garden of such modest size.

If, as you come out into the garden, you turn left and walk up a gentle hill, past a clapboarded barn and a beautiful oak, you will find yourself in the perfect position from which to admire the garden in its setting. Across a meadow the house is seen fringed with flowery beds, and on your left the land rises to the dark and mysterious Hanger.

White was interested in all aspects of gardening. Although his *Garden Kalendar* is precoccupied with his epic struggle to grow melons ("This bed by means of the great rains lost its heat, so that the cucumbers, melons and squashes never came up") he also loved flowers, and many of the plants that he knew have been reintroduced into the garden. Some of these are English natives – corncockle (*Agrostemma githago*), feverfew (*Tanacetum parthenium*), meadow cranesbill (*Geranium pratense*), yellow fumitory (*Corydalis lutea*) and many others. But there are also many old garden exotics – evening primrose (*Oenothera biennis*; White called it "Tree Primerose"), sweet

peas (*Lathyrus odoratus*; White grew the old pink and white cultivar 'Painted Lady'), the ancient Damask rose 'Quatre Saisons' and so on. Several attractive features have also been created in the garden. The Orchard Walk, with 18th-century cultivars of apples, cherries, pears and plums, leads to a quincunx of Italian cypresses (*Cupressus sempervirens*), with an old terracotta pot on a mound at its centre. White's Alcove is a simple pavilion made of oak boards. A Naturalist's Garden, not part of White's original scheme, would surely have delighted him. An informal pond, with a base of puddled clay, is surrounded by native plants, and nearby is a miniature herb and vegetable garden containing many varieties mentioned in White's writings.

The garden preserves its 18th-century landscape views with remarkable fidelity and is filled with those plants which gave White so much pleasure. Unlike many shrines, it will evoke for most gardeners precisely the pleasures that its creator enjoyed.

Location Selborne, nr Alton GU34 3JH, Hampshire **OS** SU7433 In Selborne village, 5m SE of Alton by B3006 **Tel** 01420 511275 **English Heritage Register** Grade II* **Owner** Oates Memorial Trust **Open** Jan to 24 Dec, daily 11–5 **Area** 5 acres/2 hectares

The garden front at Gilbert White's House

SOUTH-EAST ENGLAND

ALBURY PARK

REMARKABLE 17TH-CENTURY
GARDEN WITH EXCELLENT
19TH-CENTURY TREES

The battlemented brick and flint house dates from the 16th century but it was remodelled in the 17th century and, most dramatically, in the mid 19th century by A.W.N. Pugin for Henry Drummond. The chief interest of the garden is that it was laid out for Henry Howard (later 6th Duke of Norfolk) by John Evelyn – the most complete surviving design by one of the key garden figures of the 17th century. In Evelyn's diary for March 1655 he notes, "I went to Alburie to visit Mr. Howard, who had begun to build and alter the gardens much."

The approach to the house takes you across old parkland with many good trees and beautiful views of the rolling landscape of the Tillingbourne valley. The house looks north across its own valley, with turf terraces, and a croquet lawn, descending towards a stream. On the other side of the valley is the dramatic garden designed by John Evelyn. He laid out two giant terraces with grass walks – each 1,400ft/400m long. The lower terrace is edged with a long line of yews and at its centre two flights of steps lead to the upper terrace. Between the stairs is the entrance to a vaulted underground chamber with the date 1676 inscribed on the keystones above the windows. On the upper terrace a large semicircular pool is backed by a curved wall with deep niches with, at its centre, the opening to a tunnel which runs 480ft/146m through the hill behind to emerge on its far side. The opening is barred by an iron gate but you may peer in; as your eyes become accustomed to the dark, the stone walls of the tunnel are revealed and seem to go on for

ever. Evelyn referred to this as his *crypta*; it was inspired by the tunnel with Virgil's tomb at Posilippo near Naples, which he had seen in 1645. This must be one of the first gardens in England designed under the inspiration of the classical past. If you stand with your back to the opening of Evelyn's great tunnel and look back across the valley, you see that the opening is exactly aligned on the house – precisely the kind of thing a renaissance garden designer would tend to do. Evelyn also laid out canals but these do not survive; no doubt they would have been at the bottom of the valley where a sluggish stream now flows among thickets of *Gunnera manicata*.

SPLENDID 19TH-CENTURY TREES

On either side of the stream is an arboretum, with some trees going back to Henry Drummond's ownership in the mid 19th century. A curving lime walk – the trees planted so close together as to form a tunnel – was planted in 1862. Among the notable trees are maples, nothofagus, swamp cypresses (*Taxodium distichum*) and tall Wellingtonias. Among several oaks are fine specimens of the uncommon North American black oak (*Quercus velutina*) and the Algerian oak (*Q. canariensis*). There has been much recent tree planting,

John Evelyn's terrace at Albury

with the oak tradition continued with another American species, a young plant of the very attractive willow oak (*Q. phellos*). Immediately east of the house is a magnificent tree, also a great rarity, which had its origin at Albury: a form of black walnut, *Juglans nigra* 'Alburyensis', whose fruit are lavishly borne in bunches of four or five instead of the usual one or two.

Albury Park now belongs to the Country Houses Association and has been divided into flats for active retired people. Only 6 acres/2.4 hectares of grounds belong to the house; the remainder, including the Evelyn terraces,

are part of a 12,000-acre/4,858-hectare estate owned by the Duke of Northumberland. The Country Houses Association looks after its grounds well and gives access to the terraces. The place has a potent atmosphere that is unlike that of any other garden that I know. The terraces seen from the house across the valley have monumental presence. The view across the wooded valley from the terraces is very fine.

Location Albury, Guildford GU5 9BB, Surrey **OS** TL0647 1½m E of Albury off A248 **Tel** 01483 202964 **Fax** 01483 205023 **Website** www.cha.org.uk **English Heritage Register** Grade I **Owner** Country Houses Association **Open** May to Sept, Wed and Thur 2–5 **Area** 321 acres/130 hectares

ALFRISTON CLERGY HOUSE

A MEDIEVAL HOUSE WITH A CHARMING
SMALL GARDEN FULL OF IDEAS

Alfriston Clergy House was the first house to be acquired by the National Trust – in 1896. It is an enchanting place: a 14th-century house which deploys an amazing repertory of vernacular ingredients – half-timbering, daub, brick, flint, hung tiles and a roof that is partly thatched and partly tiled. The garden, designed in the 1920s by Robert Witt, is exceptionally attractive and full of lessons for garden owners – showing great inventiveness in a small space and achieving variety without clutter. The site slopes and the garden has made the best use of this with clever changes of levels, using terraces and paths laid with brick.

INTRICATE SMALL GARDENS

Immediately west of the house is a court enclosed in yew hedges. Divided into four parts by a cross-shaped brick path, it has a sundial at the centre and four great umbrellas of clipped box, each underplanted with a mass of pinks. A little bed against the wall of the house is filled with brilliant blue *Convolvulus sabatius*, feverfew, geraniums, *Perovskia atriplicifolia* and lamb's lugs.

From here, a narrow passage leads through a corridor of yew hedges to a kitchen garden where a pattern of raised beds is neatly edged n woven hazel branches and hedged in lavender. This is a proper working kitchen garden – pretty and extremely productive – fitting seamlessly into the fabric of the place.

Running along the south side of the house a sequence of small gardens at different levels are hedged in yew or with low walls of brick and flint, enlivened with fine pots and a magnificent lead cistern dated 1788. Below all this a long grass walk forms the southern boundary of the garden, with a border of geraniums, irises, michaelmas daisies, persicaria and shrub roses. At the east end of the house, past a superb sprawling Judas tree, is an orchard of apples and a medlar.

There are few startling plants at Alfriston but the strongly designed framework, breaking out into informality, provides an admirable setting for the house. It presents a scene of domestic harmony and completeness – an Arts and Crafts garden in a pocket handkerchief. Of all National Trust gardens this is one of the most lovable and one from which any gardener can learn.

Location The Tye, Alfriston, Polegate BN26 5TL, East Sussex **OS** TQ5202 11m E of Lewes by A27 and B2108 **Tel** 01323 870001 **Fax** 01323 871318

The south garden at Alfriston

Email alfriston@ntrust.org.uk **Owner** The National Trust **Open** Mar, Sat and Sun 11–4; Apr to Oct, daily except Tue and Fri (open Good Fri) 10–5 **Area** ½ acre/0.2 hectares

BATEMAN'S

RUDYARD KIPLING'S DELIGHTFUL
GARDEN, REDOLENT OF THE
EDWARDIAN AGE

Rudyard Kipling lived at Bateman's from 1902 until his death in 1936. The house – an early 17th-century stone ironmaster's house which bears the date 1634 carved on the entrance porch – contains much Kiplingiana: his study remains as it was when he died, and his Rolls Royce is preserved in the garage – a 1928 Phantom I Limousine with special fittings (total cost £1,880 – the equivalent of £54,294 today). As a literary shrine Bateman's is by no means overdone but Kipling is nevertheless the powerful presiding spirit. The attractive garden, in which he took much interest and delight, has been kept largely as it was in his time; a painting by Sir Edward Poynter of the house and garden, painted before 1919 and still hanging in the hall at Bateman's, shows it much as it is today. Kipling loved the house and revelled in the

The lily pool at Bateman's

surrounding countryside – the hill which inspired *Puck of Pook's Hill* (1906) may be seen from the house.

The garden, to the south and west of the house, has an Arts and Crafts formality, with screens of pleached lime and a rectangular lily pool. The north side of the pool is marked by a yew hedge which embraces a curved bench and has clipped piers rising high on either side. At the end of the pool there is a rose garden with flagged paths, and to one side of the house Kipling made a tunnel of late-season pears ('Conference', 'Doyenné de Comice' and 'Winter Nelis'); trained over a broad metal framework, the ripening fruit makes a splendid sight in autumn. A brick path runs along the tunnel, with beds on each side filled with herbaceous perennials suitable for the shady position – bergenias, comfrey, hardy geraniums, Corsican hellebores and pulmonaria. Down the side of the house a yew hedge has occasional windows cut in it, framing views of the rural scenery beyond. Bateman's has a strongly nostalgic air, redolent of the Edwardian period – the kind of garden dreamed of by homesick men in Poona.

Location Burwash, Etchingham TN19 7DS, East Sussex **OS** TQ6723 ½m S of Burwash by A265 **Tel** 01435 882302 **Fax** 01435 882811 **Email** batemans@ntrust.org.uk **English Heritage Register** Grade II **Owner** The National Trust **Open** Apr to Oct, Sat to Wed (open Good Fri) 11–5.30 **Area** 10 acres/4 hectares

BATTERSEA PARK

A GREAT 19TH-CENTURY PUBLIC
PARK WITH LIVELY
20TH-CENTURY ADDITIONS

Battersea Park was laid out by James Pennethorne and John Gibson between 1854 and 1857 as part of the wholesale development of this part of London. It was opened by Queen Victoria in 1858. The original design, largely intact, is simple and very effective. The site is encircled by a winding carriage drive which links the four main entrances with a broad central avenue overlooking an irregular boating lake with islands. The site is naturally as flat as a pancake but the design allowed for the mounding of earth into

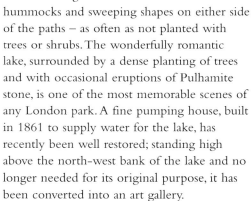

Moore's Three Standing Figures

hummocks and sweeping shapes on either side of the paths – as often as not planted with trees or shrubs. The wonderfully romantic lake, surrounded by a dense planting of trees and with occasional eruptions of Pulhamite stone, is one of the most memorable scenes of any London park. A fine pumping house, built in 1861 to supply water for the lake, has recently been well restored; standing high above the north-west bank of the lake and no longer needed for its original purpose, it has been converted into an art gallery.

Two fine sculptures enliven the banks of the lake – Barbara Hepworth's Single Form (1961–62) and Henry Moore's Three Standing Figures (1955–56). Towards the eastern boundary of the park is an exceptional stone memorial to World War I carved by Eric Kennington (1924): a group of three soldiers trampling a snake entwined in their legs. Throughout the park are excellent trees, many of which go back to the original plantings – several fine London planes, a magnificent strawberry tree (*Arbutus unedo*) close to the lake, a lovely but leaning tree of heaven (*Ailanthus altissima*), and a walk of honey locust (*Gleditisa triacanthos*). In 1985 a delightful Buddhist Peace Pagoda was built

overlooking the river, a cheering sight for those stuck in traffic jams on Chelsea Embankment. The horticultural therapy organization THRIVE has set up a cottage garden in the park as a base for its activities.

In association with the Festival of Britain in 1951, a large part of the park was turned over to the Festival Pleasure Gardens where lighthearted and amusing temporary attractions were intended to provide a contrast to the more serious cultural fare of the rest of the festival. Artists such as Osbert Lancaster and John Piper were involved in their design. However, some of the features were of more lasting substance, such as a flower garden designed by Russell Page, and this is to be reinstated following his original planting plans. The original Victorian riverside walk, now incorporating the Pagoda, was under restoration in 2002 and in July of that year, when I last visited, the park was in the throes of a major restoration as a result of an award of £6.9m from the Heritage Lottery Fund, to which Wandsworth Borough Council is adding £3.4m of its own. No London park merits such a restoration more than Battersea.

Location Battersea, London SW11 4NJ **OS** TQ27777 SW of central London on the south bank of the Thames between Albert and Chelsea bridges
Tel 020 8871 7530 **English Heritage Register** Grade II* **Owner** Wandsworth Borough Council
Open daily 7–dusk **Area** 200 acres/81 hectares

BEDGEBURY NATIONAL PINETUM AND FOREST GARDENS

A FOREST OF MAGNIFICENT CONIFERS
FORMS A BEGUILING LANDSCAPE

Bedgebury Manor was built in the 1830s, a remodelling of a 17th-century house for Marshall Viscount Beresford. In 1919 the estate was divided, the house becoming a school and most of the land acquired by the Crown. In 1924 the chief part of Bedgebury Forest became the property of the Forestry Commission which, addingto the existing 19th-century plantings, immensely enlarged the scope of the collection, in particular of conifers. Here is the fashionable pinetum of

Bedgebury National Pinetum

Victorian estates but on a heroic scale.

The site is a hilly one with two valleys and lakes. This in itself makes an attractive piece of landscape but the planting is not obviously dominated by aesthetic considerations; its chief aim is to build up a reference collection of conifers that will grow in a temperate climate. It now contains 61 per cent of such conifers, with 488 species and over 1,600 cultivars. These are grouped largely according to genus, with a few arranged regionally – the Japanese Glade, American Glade and Chinese Glade. Several of the groups – of junipers, Lawson cypresses, Leyland cypresses, thujas and yews – constitute National Collections of their genera. It is the intention to increase the collection so that it contains every conifer hardy in the south of England. All this is obviously of great scientific value and irresistible to conifer enthusiasts, but is it of interest to the rest of us?

THE PLEASURES OF CONIFERS

The problem about conifers is that they seem at first so obvious. They stay green (or, much worse, glaucous or yellow) all the year round; many of them grow with bewildering speed, forming huge cones like perpetual Christmas trees; they produce no pretty flowers. However, an open-minded visit to Bedgebury, and a close look at the trees, shows how wrong these assumptions are. Many conifers change colour with beguiling subtlety; they are immensely varied in habit, some of them (like the podocarps) producing long leaves which sway gracefully in the wind; others, like the startlingly prostrate forms, being merely curious, an affront to the vertical ambitions of many of their tribe; they do not, indeed, have pretty flowers but they do sometimes have the most beautiful cones, intricately shaped and at times startling in colour, ranging from crimson (*Picea orientalis*) to a sumptuous blue (*Abies koreana*).

Even if you do not feel like studying the conifers with any care, to walk among them on a hot summer's day is a delicious pleasure. Their scent is strangely invigorating, their shade seems far denser than that of deciduous trees, and their sheer size is a thrilling sight. No deciduous tree is anywhere near as tall as

the biggest conifer, and whereas the dwarf conifer can be seen as a ghastly error of nature or a blatant vulgarity of the nurseryman, real conifers are something else. Bedgebury is one of the finest collections in the world of these astonishing trees. It has recently been raising funds for a dramatic increase in its scope and the facilities it offers to visitors. By the time this book appears in print I hope this will have been achieved but even if it has not Bedgebury is still a place worthy of the interest of anyone who likes trees.

Location nr Goudhurst, Cranbrook TN17 2SL, Kent **OS** TQ7233 4½m S of Goudhurst by B2079 **Tel** 01580 211044 **Fax** 01580 212423 **Email** bedgebury@forest.gov.uk **English Heritage Register** Grade II* **Owner** Forestry Commission **Open** Mar to 25 Dec, daily 10–7 or dusk if earlier; Jan and Feb, Sat and Sun 10–dusk **Area** 300 acres/121 hectares

BELMONT PARK

AN 18TH-CENTURY PARK AND GARDEN WITH SPRIGHTLY MODERN PLANTING

Belmont Park is a remodelling of an earlier house by Samuel Wyatt in 1787–92 for General Lord Harris – the victor of the battle of Seringapatam and defeater of Tippoo Sahib. The setting is very beautiful, on one side of a wooded valley which was finely landscaped in the 18th century. A grand orangery

The belvedere at Belmont Park

attached to the south façade of the house was built in 1790. One of the most attractive features of Belmont is the Coronation Walk, a long grass path running north-west away from the house. It is flanked with yew hedges behind which are sweet chestnuts. At its northern end is a splendid eyecatcher – a flint and stone belvedere like a miniature castle. Of irregular shape, it has a round tower with a pointed roof, Gothic arch windows and a battlemented parapet. It is owned by the Landmark Trust and may be rented as a holiday house. If the coronation referred to is that of George IV, it suggests that 1820 is the date of the belvedere.

A NEW WALLED GARDEN

Behind the house a walled pleasure garden has mixed borders about a lawn, two venerable cottage-loaves of yew topiary, old trees of gold variegated holly and a lily pond. A pinetum is laid out on a lawn behind, with a splendid grotto/alcove shrouded in ivy and ferns and built of a wonderful mixture of flint, tufa, fossils and bones.

An 18th-century walled kitchen garden was given a completely new layout by Arabella Lennox-Boyd in 2001. Its shape is irregular but a strongly formal layout has given it an illusion of symmetry. Paths run through tunnels of pears, apples or grapevines towards a central square lily pond surrounded with L-shaped herbaceous borders planted in white and pink. Beds of herbs and vegetables surround the borders on three sides. Mixed borders flank a central walk and other narrow beds filled with roses or with different varieties of lavender are criss-crossed with low espaliered pears. The northern part of the garden, where the walls form an awkward point, has a pleached semicircle of the pear *Pyrus calleryana* 'Chanticleer' with an 18th-century sundial at the centre. Gravel paths radiate out from the curve, with a pattern of cross paths, all enclosing shapes of lawn. Each meeting place of paths is shaded by a lofty arbour of golden hop (*Humulus lupulus* 'Aureus'). A long border

for cutting flowers runs along a south-facing wall against which are apricots, cherries, pears and plums. A large range of glasshouses have been restored and filled with cucumbers, grapevines and tomatoes, and collections of tender ornamentals. Outside the kitchen garden Arabella Lennox-Boyd

The grotto at Belmont Park

has laid out a new garden: a circular box parterre as a mandala – the Hindhu and Buddhist symbol of the universe – celebrating the 1st Baron Harris's Indian connection.

Much of the Belmont estate has been sold, including the site of a discreetly placed golf course, but the immediate surroundings of the house, with its fine views over parkland, are unimpaired. The old features of the garden are well cared for and it is splendid to see new ventures under way.

Location Throwley, Faversham ME13 0HH, Kent **OS** TQ9856 4½m SSW of Faversham by A251 and minor roads **Tel** 01795 890202 **Fax** 01795 890042 **Email** belmontadmin@brconnect.com **Website** www.belmont-house.org **English Heritage Register** Grade II **Owner** Harris (Belmont) Charity **Open** Apr to Sept, Sat, Sun and Bank Hol Mon 2–5; groups by appointment at other times **Area** 13 acres/5 hectares

BORDE HILL GARDEN

A GREAT COLLECTION OF FLOWERING SHRUBS AND TREES IN A SPLENDID SETTING

Borde Hill is in the heart of a part of Sussex famous for woodland gardens, especially those associated with the Loder family. All benefit from the acidic loam of the Hastings Beds which is shown on the Ordnance Survey geological map as an alluring expanse of tawny gold running from Horsham in the west to Dungeness in the east, and from Tonbridge in the north to Bexhill in the south. The distinction of the garden at Borde Hill is due to Colonel Stephenson Clarke who bought the estate in 1892 and became a sponsor of some of the great plant-collecting expeditions of the 20th century. He built up a very large collection of trees and shrubs, with a particular interest in camellias, magnolias and rhododendrons. Colonel Clarke was also a gifted hybridiser and among his most successful crosses was *Camellia × williamsii* 'Donation'.

The charm of Borde Hill comes from the beauty of the groups and individual specimens of these plants, many of which are very large, set in a fine gently undulating landscape. With 300 acres/81 hectares and a vast range of plants, there is much to explore and marvel at. Many of the best plants are close to the house, but to do the place justice you should walk to Warren Wood, spectacular in May with brilliant rhododendrons in the native woodland. There are also excellent conifers here, with some very large specimens such as the Formosan cypress (*Chamaecyparis formosensis*) propagated from the first seed brought to England in 1910. A little further on is Little Bentley Wood with particularly good, and often rare, deciduous trees such as *Carya cordiformis*, which will give even knowledgeable tree-

▷ **The formal garden** at Borde Hill

spotters some delightful headaches.

Close to the house new formal gardens are attractively done. These give much flowery pleasure in the summer when the woodland gardens with their remarkable collections are not at their best. However, it is certainly the great trees and shrubs that gives Borde Hill its distinction.

Location Haywards Heath RH16 1XP, West Sussex **OS** TQ3226 1½m N of Haywards Heath by minor roads **Tel** 01444 450326 **Fax** 01444 440427 **Email** info@bordehill.co.uk **English Heritage Register** Grade II* **Owner** Borde Hill Gardens Ltd **Open** daily 10–6 **Area** 200 acres/81 hectares

BROGDALE HORTICULTURAL TRUST

A GIANT ORCHARD OF HISTORIC FRUIT VARIETIES IN THE GARDEN OF ENGLAND

Brogdale is the home of the National Fruit Collection, one of the greatest collections of its kind in the world. Its chief aim is conservation – to preserve from extinction the vast range of fruit varieties and their genes. The site is superficially as unpropitious as you could imagine: flat and windswept, horribly close to the permanent roar of the M2. The contents, however, are absolutely wonderful. This corner of England is a sacred spot for fruit growing. Kent is, of course, the orchard of England, and one of the first large-scale orchards was planted at Teynham, quite near Brogdale, by Henry VIII's

The plum 'Agen Early' at Brogdale

fruiterer, Richard Harris.

The collection at Brogdale has over 2,300 varieties of apple, 550 of pears, 350 of plums, 220 of cherries, 320 of bush fruit (gooseberries, black currants, etc) and many varieties of nut (over 40 hazelnuts) and grapevines. The National Collection consists of rows of plants grouped by varieties and is not open to unsupervised visits. Tours of the collection are organised from March to November four times a day and are extraordinarily interesting. Your guide will be deeply knowledgeable and what he or she has to tell of the history of these fruit is gripping. Many of the fruit you will see will be unfamiliar and often beautiful. Many of the fields are protected by high hedges which are themselves frequently ornamental. One of the plants most used for hedges is the native alder (*Alnus glutinosa*) whose glossy leaves shimmer attractively in the wind. Another beautiful hedge is planted of alternate hazelnut and dog rose which scrambles high up through the trees.

BROGDALE EVENTS

Other parts of the garden at Brogdale are open to unsupervised visits: the collection of cider apples, a fine orchard of quinces and an orchard of cherries among them. In addition there is a plant centre with many ornamentals as well as hundreds of different fruit plants sold containerised or, between November and March, bare rooted. Several special events celebrate different aspects of fruit growing – among them a Plum Weekend in July, a Cider Festival in September and an Apple Festival in October. Day courses, workshops and demonstrations cover practical fruit growing, pruning and grafting, preserving and planning an orchard. Advisory services on plant identification and designing orchards are also available.

The explosion of spring blossom and the dazzling profusion of autumn fruits are the most exciting events at Brogdale. A walk through the collection at these times is one of the finest pleasures – but it is more than that. The work of the Trust is important, and there is no other organisation undertaking it. Supporting it is vital.

'**Early Strawberry' apples** at Brogdale

Location Brogdale Road, Faversham ME13 8XZ, Kent **OS** TQ9958 1m SW of Faversham; Jnct 6 of M2 **Tel** 01795 535286/535462 **Fax** 01795 531710 **Email** info@brogdale.org.uk **Website** www.brogdale.org.uk **Owner** Brogdale Horticultural Trust **Open** daily 10–5 (9.30–4.30 in winter) **Area** 150 acres/61 hectares

CABBAGES AND KINGS

FINE PLANTING AND AN INVENTIVE
LAYOUT IN A GARDEN
DESIGNER'S SHOWCASE

Once you have overcome a moment of anxiety over the slightly twee name of this garden you will find it easy to succumb to its charms. The garden designer Ryl Nowell had the idea of making a display garden in which a dazzling array of garden possibilities is shown in a small area. From 1989 she converted a group of pretty but derelict farm buildings (a stable, an L-shaped cart shed and walls), and laid out a series of gardens in the space they enclosed. As soon as you enter you appreciate what she is aiming to do with plants, hard surfaces and ornaments.

The planting is immediately seen to be both ornamental and structural. Steps leading down from a deep terrace surfaced with bricks, cobbles and gravel are flanked by a pair of spiral clipped gold Leyland cypresses (× *Cupressocyparis leylandii* 'Castlewellan') and throughout the garden the entrance to a path or the beginning of a flight of steps is marked by mounds of box, thickets of purple-leafed ligularia or waves of the sinister black *Ophiopogon planiscapus* 'Nigrescens'. The site is gently sloping and changes of level, and of direction, are skilfully manipulated. The horizontal emphasis is frequently challenged by some dramatic plant: an explosion of cardoon (*Cynara cardunculus*), a noble pine tree (*Pinus monticola*) or an exuberant froth of *Euphorbia wulfenii*. All the plants, of which well over 300 are used, are identified by numbers unobtrusively and ornamentally worked in wire. These refer to a master list of plant names, with Ryl Nowell's pithy notes on the plants' virtues.

CLEVER COLOUR, IDYLLIC VIEWS
Much attention is paid to the colour of painted surfaces: window frames and doors are painted a chalky blue and a swimming pool is overlooked by a pedimented pavilion

(glittering with mirrors arranged at different angles in the pediment) painted an intense blue. There are sitting places, pools and fountains, containers and sculptures. A metal openwork sphere stands at the centre of a starburst of edge-on tiles of exactly the sort that Lutyens made.

The place is busy with ideas but views of the surrounding countryside are not excluded: a glimpse of the idyllic wooded valley south of the stable is visible from the garden proper but is fully displayed – a splendid panorama – from a lawn behind the stable, like an 18th-century viewing platform. Through large glazed windows in the blue walls flanking the swimming pool pavilion can be seen an Arcadian view of rolling close-mown turf and a pool – a landscape park in a pocket handkerchief.

The garden serves two purposes: it gives excellent practical ideas for planting and design but, much more important, encourages consideration of a garden's ingredients and the relationship with its surroundings.

Location Wilderness Farm, Hadlow Down TN22 4HU, East Sussex **OS** TQ5322 5½m NE of Uckfield by A26 and A272, signed in the village of Hadlow Down **Tel** 01825 830552 **Fax** 01825 830736 **Website** www.ckings.co.uk **Owner** Ryl Nowell **Open** Easter to Sept, Thur to Mon 10.30–5.30 **Area** 1 acre/0.4 hectare

Glass sculpture at Cabbages and Kings

CAPEL MANOR

THE GARDEN OF A HORTICULTURAL
COLLEGE, BRISTLING WITH IDEAS
AND GOOD PLANTS

Although very busy and built-up, Enfield still preserves corners which show its original character as one of London's desirable outlying rural villages. Capel Manor is an 18th-century brick house, with the outhouses and walled garden which would be expected of a country house of its time. It is now a

Miracle-Gro garden at Capel Manor

college of horticulture, garden design, floristry and other subjects (such as animal care) associated with country life. Its interest to gardeners is multifarious. The National Gardening Centre is a collection of display gardens planned to provide a shop window for suppliers of horticultural products and plants, each sponsored by an individual company. For the most part these do their job admirably but few are examples of good design (though there are exceptions). The heart sinks a little at the thought of something called the Miracle-Gro Garden but Nuala Hancock's and Matthew Bell's design, which won a Gold Medal at the 1994 Chelsea Flower Show, is a delightful little garden. With a striking screen of stained glass, pools, fountains, paving and pebble inlays, it has a simple but stylish planting of shrub roses and herbs. In an entirely different mood is Lucy Huntingdon's Low Allergen Garden designed for asthma sufferers, containing no lawn, no hedges and no wind-pollenated plants.

Gardening Which? has a large presence here with 12 theme gardens covering a dizzying range of such subjects as container gardening, wildlife gardening and woodland gardening. In addition it sponsors 32 trial gardens covering individual genera, for example of achilleas of which this is a National Collection; of types of plants – such as

climbers, heathers and herbaceous perennials; and of garden features – fruit gardens, pergolas, vegetable gardens or water gardens. All this provides a useful resource for gardeners seeking a product or an idea.

Of gardens which simply provide an attractively designed space, the best examples are those designed by the college and close to Capel Manor itself. A series of yew-hedged enclosures with a central basket-weave brick path is a strong and simple design with plants of striking foliage – *Aralia elata*, *Fatsia japonica*, *Phormium tenax* and several with variegated leaves, all finely disposed. A water garden and rock garden has cascades and is shaded by good trees, among them some old Japanese maples. A maze of holly hedges was reconstructed from W.A. Nesfield's design for the 1851 Great Exhibition. The original 18th-century walled kitchen garden has paths radiating from a handsome central sundial, mixed borders, bedding schemes, pergolas, and glasshouses with a large display of tropical plants.

Some may find Capel Manor rather daunting, like a restaurant with an overwhelming choice of dishes. But if you wander through, sampling this and that, indigestion is easily kept at bay. At weekends the place buzzes with activity and shows vividly how thrilling gardening can be.

Location Bullsmoor Lane, Enfield EN1 4RQ, Greater London **OS** TQ3499 14m N of central London by A10; Jnct 25 of M25 **Tel** 020 8366 4442 **Fax** 01992 717544 **Email** enquiries@capel.ac.uk **Website** www.capel.ac.uk **Owner** Capel Manor Charitable Organization **Open** Mar to Oct, daily 10–6; Nov to Feb, Mon to Fri 10–6 **Area** 30 acres/12 hectares

CHARLESTON

THE IDIOSYNCRATIC AND
CHARMING COUNTRY GARDEN OF
THE BLOOMSBURY SET

On a visit to Charleston in August 1929, Frances Partridge wrote, vividly evoking the character of the place, "The garden here is a rampant jungle of sunflowers and holly-hocks, and the apple-trees are bowed down with scarlet apples; pears hanging bobbing at one's head." The garden of the rural retreat of

Levitating Lady at Charleston

the Bloomsbury Group is no great work of horticultural art but it is nonetheless delightful and imbued with a most distinctive atmosphere.

The 17th-century farmhouse was discovered by Virginia and Leonard Woolf in 1916 when Virginia's sister, Vanessa Bell, was looking for a house. Vanessa Bell came to live here with the painter Duncan Grant and the writer David Garnett and over the years Charleston established itself as a great meeting place for the Bloomsbury Group. The interior of the house, and its furniture, was decorated with abandon – swirling patterns on the walls, frescoed fireplaces, tumbling acrobats or vases of flowers on the panels of doors, and eruptions of angels in unexpected places. The house was full of books and of capacious and squashy armchairs with reading lights close to hand.

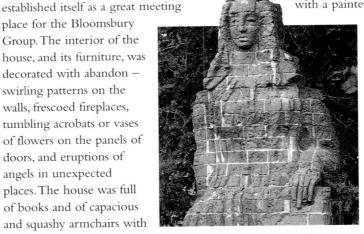
Quentin Bell's Spink

The atmospheric character of the house spills over into the garden, walled in brick and flint, which lies behind the north façade of the house. It was laid out in the 1920s by Roger Fry whose garden at Guildford (Durbins), had been designed by Gertrude Jekyll. At Charleston he laid down a firm pattern of paths and lawn, making a simple framework to which the detailed planting could be added. Here are gravel paths, sitting places, old apple trees and borders abundantly filled with flowers, and here the Bloomsbury *furor decorandi* is given full rein. The garden seems more like a series

of decorative explosions than anything more sedate. A truncated pottery torso (female) filled with roses, flanked by troughs of nasturtiums, sits on concrete slabs (not entirely horizontal) mounted on brick piers. Below her is a charming row of zonal pelargoniums in terracotta flower pots. A patio is surfaced in sprightly patterns of broken flower pots and shards of pottery or porcelain (much of it of fine quality, some of it rubbish). A pottery mask peers over a pool between the upright leaves of an iris. Box hedges are clipped into rolling curvaceous mounds, as plump as a fine South Down sheep before shearing, and among the curves a copy of Giovanni da Bologna's Venus adds her own distinction. Behind a little hedge of santolina a spreading forest of sweet peas nudges thickets of statuesque plants – pink hollyhocks, sweetly scented tobacco plants, yellow mulleins and great grey veils of thistles. Miscellaneous busts crown the top of a garden wall on which a plaque of pottery tiles, prettily decorated with a painted trellis of vines with purple grapes, reads, "Two of the above heads were given by friends to celebrate Quentin Bell's 80th birthday and commemorate others that are gone. August 1980".

The east-facing entrance front of the house overlooks a pool with overarching willow trees. The banks of the pool are decorated with sculptures by Quentin Bell – a figure of Pomona, made of concrete with a basket of prettily glazed apples on her head, a truncated Venus, a bust of a woman (named Spink) made of finely carved brick, and a mysterious horizontal figure, Levitating Lady, rising in the grass.

One of the great attractions of the Bloomsbury attitude to life was that much was taken seriously but much was not; they were never afraid of what Henry James called "intellectual larking". High art coexisted with junk and profound ideas with frivolity – juxtapositions designed to sharpen the judgement. Charleston – both house and garden – most vividly evokes the Bloomsbury world and epitomises the paradoxes within it. Even the austere J.M. Keynes was known to work in the garden; Vanessa Bell wrote to Roger Fry, "One would often find Maynard on the gravel path at the front of the house kneeling like a muslim on his prayer mat and, with enormous thoroughness, weeding a small patch of pathways with a penknife."

A visit to the house is essential to understanding the garden: views from the windows show house and garden to be all of a piece – the decorative exuberance forming a continuum. Few gardens possess such a strong flavour of the people who made them and such a strong sense of place.

Location nr Firle, Lewes BN8 6LL, East Sussex **OS** TQ4906 6m E of Lewes by A27 **Tel** 01323 811265 (visitor information) 01323 811626 (administration) **Fax** 01323 811626 **Email** charles@solutions-inc.co.uk **Owner** The Charleston Trust **Open** Apr to Oct, Wed to Sun (open Bank Hol Mon) 2–6 (Jul and Aug, Wed to Sat 11.30–6, Sun and Bank Hol Mon 2–6) **Area** 1 acre/0.4 hectare

CHELSEA PHYSIC GARDEN

A 17TH-CENTURY WALLED PHYSIC
GARDEN; AN URBAN OASIS FILLED
WITH FINE PLANTS

John Evelyn visited the Chelsea Physic Garden in August 1685: "I went to see Mr Wats, keeper of the Apothecaries Garden of Simples at Chelsea, where there is a collection of innumerable rarities of that sort particularly." He also noted "the tree bearing jesuits bark, which had don such wonders in quartan agues". This, the Peruvian *Cinchona officinalis* whose bark was the source of quinine which had dramatically transformed the treatment of malaria ("quartan ague"), was grown at Chelsea in a conservatory with an ingenious source of "subterranean heate" which Evelyn much admired.

The garden had been founded in 1673, making it the second botanic garden to have been founded in England; only Oxford is older. It entered its period of greatest fame with the appointment as curator in 1722 of the remarkable Philip Miller whose *Gardeners Dictionary* (1731) was one of the best and most successful gardening books published in the 18th century. In 1764 Miller's contemporary, Peter Collinson, wrote of him, "He has raised the reputation of the Chelsea Garden so much that it excels all the gardens of Europe for its amazing variety of plants." The garden continued to flourish after Miller's death in 1770 but in the later 19th century entered a period of decline, to recover splendidly in the 20th century. A delightful place of great character, the finely kept garden is today a lively centre of botany and horticulture.

The Physic Garden presents an alluring aspect to those outside: hidden behind brick walls, its fine trees flaunt their crowns enticingly above. The 4 acres/1.6 hectares of gardens do not disappoint. A grand central walk runs down the centre of the garden, with a pause in the middle marked by Rysbrack's splendid marble statue of Sir Hans Sloane, a great benefactor of the garden. Around a third of the whole area is given over to traditional order beds in which plants are grouped under genera disposed in correct scientific order, and everywhere the garden is animated by old trees – among them a beautiful olive which in a good year produces a fine crop. There are also collections of South African plants (especially agapanthus and kniphofia), of Australasian plants, and of culinary and medicinal herbs. The garden holds a National Collection of cistus (with over 80 species and cultivars), a study collection of hypericums and a beautiful collection of snowdrops for which there are special visits in February. As botanic gardens go, Chelsea is very small but it is unusually packed with interest and charm.

Location 66 Royal Hospital Road, London SW3 4HS **OS** TQ2777 In central London **Tube** Sloane Square **Tel** 020 7352 5646 **Fax** 020 7376 3910 **English Heritage Register** Grade I **Owner** Chelsea Physic Garden Company **Open** Apr to Oct, Wed 12–5 and Sun 2–6; also open Feb for snowdrops and winter festival (phone for details) **Area** 4 acres/1.6 hectares

CHISWICK HOUSE

A PALLADIAN PLEASURE DOME IN A
NOTABLE EARLY 18TH-CENTURY GARDEN

In 1732, Alexander Pope wrote, "I assure you Chiswick has been to me the finest thing this glorious sun has shined on." Richard Boyle, the 3rd Earl of Burlington had built his Palladian pleasure dome in 1725 and laid out, with the help of William Kent in the 1730s, a garden of extraordinary enchantment.

Statue of Sir Hans Sloane in the Chelsea Physic Garden

At first this had been formal but under Kent's influence the straight lines were softened and such romantic features as a grotto cascade at the head of a lake were added. The complicated evolution of the gardens is one of the best documented of its time, most valuably in paintings by Peter Andreas Rysbrack and drawings by Jacques Rigaud – all executed between 1728 and 1734.

Much of this survives: the house superbly restored and the garden preserving many of its original features, among them marvellous statuary and garden buildings. As a monument to the taste of a great and influential connoisseur Chiswick is wonderful. However, there is today a scruffiness about much of the grounds which is quite alien to the spirit of such a place. Even the recently restored cascade has a squalid appearance, partly fenced off with clumsy stakes and pig-wire. A visit to Chiswick is essential to anyone who wants to know about one of the most attractive ensembles of house and garden in the country, but in the present condition of the garden, delight can swiftly turn to deepest gloom.

Lord Burlington died in 1753, leaving

The Italian Garden at Chiswick House

as his heiress his daughter Charlotte who had married the Marquess of Hartington, heir to the dukedom of Devonshire. When he inherited, the 6th Duke bought the neighbouring estate of Moreton Hall in 1812 and linked the two estates. To the north-east of Chiswick House the Duke built a magnificent conservatory, designed by Samuel Ware, which he filled with camellias. In front of the conservatory a semicircular parterre, the Italian Garden, was laid out by

The garden front at Chiswick

Lewis Kennedy. This today is finely kept, with Coadestone urns and mop-headed acacias rising among brilliant bedding schemes.

Location Burlington Lane, Chiswick, London W4 2RP
OS TQ210 775 4m SW of central London by A4 and A316 **Tel** 020 8742 1978 **Owner** English Heritage; gardens in the management of the London Borough of Hounslow **English Heritage Register** Grade I
Open daily 8.30–dusk **Area** 62 acres/25 hectares

CLANDON PARK

FORMAL GARDENS, AN 18TH-CENTURY
GROTTO AND AN EDWARDIAN
SUNKEN GARDEN

Clandon Park, a splendid Palladian house designed by Giacomo Leoni, was built for Thomas, 2nd Baron Onslow c.1730–33. The site is much older for there had been a deer park here in the early 16th century and a Jacobean house before the present one.

Capability Brown worked here and his plan, signed by him and dated 1781, survived at the house until 1927 but has not been seen since. He laid out a park, turned a formal canal into a lake and built new stables, which do not survive, and two lodges, which do. The house and garden were given to the National Trust by the Countess of Iveagh in 1956. The rest of the estate, in particular the Brown park, remains the property of Lord Onslow.

The garden consists of a series of agreeable but disparate incidents on the lawns to the east and south of the house. The south façade overlooks a 20th-century parterre neatly laid out to exactly the width of the house. Cones of clipped box rise above bedding schemes of begonias, busy lizzies and cherry pie disposed about a grand wellhead, and the whole is flanked by palissades of hornbeam. Facing it on the far side of the lawn is as sharp a contrast as you could wish: built into a slope and shaded by old yews is a ruinous brick and flint grotto shrouded in ivy, whose interior has niches, a pool and fringes of harts' tongue ferns. Statues of the three graces used to inhabit the grotto, which was possibly designed by Brown. To one side, sitting on the turf, is a parade of swaggy Corinthian capitals under a grove of beeches and nearby is something never seen before in an English garden – a Maori meeting house. Thatched and ornamented with intricately carved panels and the occasional gleam of shellwork, it was acquired in 1892 by the 4th Earl of Onslow who was Governor of New Zealand. The village to which it belonged had been destroyed by a volcano in 1886. A terrace under the east façade of the house has a touch of Versailles – a parade of Portugal laurels clipped into mushrooms are apparently planted in Versailles boxes but in fact are merely enclosed; the lower trunks are firmly planted in the ground. Lastly, across a lawn of rough grass is a beautifully kept sunken garden of Edwardian flavour, well hidden behind yew hedges – the only garden I know to be supported by the British Airways Cabin Crew Fund. Its two levels are hedged in variegated euonymus or in lavender and decorated with

spirals or mounds of box. A circular lily pond stands at the centre of four lawns, each with a column of roses in the middle.

The most poignant view at Clandon Park is to be had from the entrance to the house. If

The parterre at Clandon Park

you look to the north-west you will see a little domed temple with just the gleam of a lake in the woods below it. Here is Brown's park, tantalisingly out of bounds.

Location West Clandon, Guildford GU4 7RQ, Surrey **OS** TQ0451 3m E of Guildford off A25 **Tel** 01483 222482 **Infoline** 01483 225971 **Fax** 01483 223479 **Email** clandonpark@ntrust.org.uk **English Heritage Register** Grade II **Owner** The National Trust **Open** Apr to Oct, Tue to Thur, and Sun (open Good Fri, Easter Sat and Bank Hol Mon) 11–5 **Area** 8 acres/3 hectares

CLAREMONT LANDSCAPE GARDEN

AN ENCHANTING 18TH-CENTURY
ARCADIAN LANDSCAPE RESTORED
BY THE NATIONAL TRUST

The architect Sir John Vanbrugh bought the estate at Claremont, then called Chargate, for his own use in about 1709, "the situation being singularly Romantick", as the architect Colen Campbell observed. Vanbrugh lived here for a very short time, selling house and garden in 1714 to Sir Thomas Pelham-Holles, later Earl of Clare and Duke of Newcastle, who renamed the estate

Claremont. Vanbrugh, Charles Bridgeman, William Kent and Capability Brown all worked on the garden in the 18th century, sometimes undoing their predecessor's work. In 1816 Princess Charlotte, the daughter of King George IV, came to live here with her husband, Prince Leopold, and it remained a royal estate throughout the century. In the 20th century the estate was broken up, the house became a school and in 1949 the pleasure grounds, by then an uncontrolled sea of *Rhododendron ponticum* and cherry laurel, were acquired by the National Trust. One of the few things of beauty still visible was Sir John Vanbrugh's belvedere. As the historian Dorothy Stroud wrote at the time, "High on the wooded hill, the belvedere, ravaged by time and vandals, stands as a defiant reminder of Vanbrugh's affection for 'something of the Castle Air'."

RESTORED ARCADIA

The National Trust embarked on a great programme of restoration in 1975, much helped by the numerous 18th-century pictures and descriptions of the garden. Today, although divorced from its house, it gives as pretty an idea of an 18th-century landscape park, with features of very different styles, as anywhere in England. Charles Bridgeman's noble turf amphitheatre is spread out on a hillside – in its heyday it was furnished with elaborate carved wood benches on which to sit and imbibe the view, and these have been reinstated here and elsewhere in the garden.

Rustic statuary at Claremont

The amphitheatre looks down on a lake with a wooded island on which William Kent's temple of *c*.1738 is partly veiled by trees. The pool had originally been designed by Bridgeman as a crisply formal circle with an obelisk in the centre, but Kent made the banks irregular and added an informal island. On the south bank of the lake a rustic grotto frames views of the landscape. The grotto is probably the work of the famous mid 18th-century grotto makers Joseph and Josiah Lane, who had made an elaborate grotto for the Hon. Charles Hamilton at Painshill nearby. High on the hill above, and at the end of an *allée* of beech, Vanbrugh's belvedere rises sternly among the trees.

In his *Observations on Modern Gardening* (1770) Thomas Whately gave a verdict on Claremont with which many modern visitors will find it easy to agree: "The whole is a place wherein to tarry with secure delight, or saunter with perpetual amusement." The pleasure given by this Arcadian survival is all the more appreciated because it is engulfed by suburbia.

Location Portsmouth Road, Esher KT10 9JG, Surrey
OS TQ1363 14m SW of central London by A3
Tel 01372 467806 **Fax** 01372 464394 **Email** claremont@ntrust.org.uk **Website**

William Kent's Temple at Claremont

www.nationaltrust.org.uk/southern **English Heritage Register** Grade I **Owner** The National Trust **Open** Jan to Mar, daily except Mon 10–5 or dusk if earlier; Apr to Oct, Mon to Fri 10–6, Sat, Sun and Bank Hol Mon 10–7; Nov to Dec, daily except Mon 10–5 or dusk if earlier (closed 25 Dec) **Area** 49 acres/20 hectares

DENMANS

THE PRIVATE GARDEN OF THE GARDEN DESIGNER JOHN BROOKES, ALIVE WITH INSPIRATION

It is always fascinating to see what professional garden designers get up to in the privacy of their own gardens. The garden at Denmans was started in 1946 by Joyce Robinson who said of her gardening principles, "the emphasis is on the shape, colour and texture of the whole growing picture, rather than on the plants." Mrs Robinson was a pioneer in the use of gravel as a practical and ornamental background to planting and John Brookes has continued in this tradition, adding much else that is emphatically his own.

Although the garden is close to the very busy A27 it is remarkably secluded; if you raise your eyes to the skyline you will see an encircling panorama of trees of all kinds. The atmosphere is unconstrained – in the garden there are no dictatorial routes, scarcely a straight line, and different approaches to its various parts encourage wandering and contemplation.

The entrance through a large glasshouse filled with tender plants leads first to a garden walled in brick and flint where a gravel path meanders, its outline blurred by plants. In summer the boundaries of this large rectangular space are almost invisible, such is the density and luxuriance of the planting, but the profusion is tempered both by skilful grouping and repetition of plants. Very large mounds of clipped box, rising over 6ft/2m high, make shapely reference points or form essential elements of carefully arranged groups of plants which act as interludes punctuating the garden walks. One such group includes a box mound next to a clump of spiky New Zealand flax (*Phormium tenax*), with, at their

The walled garden at Denmans

feet and sprawling over the gravel, waves of sedums, catmint, curry plant (*Helichrysum italicum* subsp. *serotinum*), lamb's lugs and, on the shady side of the group, hostas. There is also much contrast of foliage and plant shape: the feathery fronds of a sumach (*Rhus typhina*) spread alongside a weeping beech and the stately toothed foliage of *Melianthus major* rises among double white dahlias and the bronze stems and explosive scarlet flowers of *Lobelia* 'Queen Victoria'. The walled garden provides an especially privileged microclimate in what is in any case a balmy part of the world – only five miles from the sea and with much sunshine – and bushes of bay, myrtle and rosemary add Mediterranean scents. The only man-made ornaments are a brilliant blue bench and a well placed terracotta pot in a circle of bricks which forms part of the path. The chief part of the garden lies beyond the

walled garden. Here, the strength of the design comes from the sweeping shapes of turf and gravel and the decisively effective but unostentatious grouping of plants. The grass is cut at two levels: close clipped along its periphery where it follows a bed and slightly longer towards the centre where a single specimen tree, or a group of trees, make emphatic statements. Gravel beds flow like a river through the garden, ending up at one point in a pool – fringed with bulrushes and irises, its surface decorated with waterlilies. Beyond the pool, where the garden ends, a dense hedgerow and tall trees form a naturalistic boundary.

Denmans runs counter to the mainstream of English 20th-century garden fashion: its effects are painterly and organic; there are no tyrannical vistas, no contrived borders and no exquisitely artificial colour harmonies; it is full of good plants deployed without fuss; and underlying the design is a rhythmic shapeliness

that is deeply satisfying – "the whole growing picture", as Mrs Robinson called it.

Location Fontwell, nr Arundel BN18 0SU, West Sussex **OS** SU9506 6m E of Chichester by A27 **Tel** 01243 542808 **Fax** 01243 544064 **Owner** John Brookes **Open** Mar to Oct, daily 9–5 **Area** 3½ acres/1.4 hectares

DOWN HOUSE

CHARLES DARWIN'S GARDEN AND EXPERIMENTAL GREENHOUSE, BEAUTIFULLY RESTORED BY ENGLISH HERITAGE

Down House was built in the early 19th century, an unassuming Regency villa with a pretty garden. It owes its fame to the fact that it was the home of Charles Darwin from 1842 until his death in 1882. Houses and gardens of great men vary in their power to evoke their owners. Darwin's study, with many of his possessions still visible, and his garden, with its glasshouse and laboratory, seem to give a powerful notion of the sort of man he was.

Darwin loved this garden, less for its purely horticultural attractions than for the opportunities it afforded to study plants in action. It was his wife, Emma, who was the true gardener of the family. Their daughter, another Emma, remembered "verbenas and the row of lime trees humming with bees, my father lying under them; children trotting about, with probably a kitten and a dog, and my mother dressed in lilac muslin". Many of Darwin's biological observations were based on what he observed in daily life; in his garden he was able to study the intricate connections between creatures and their environment. Noticing, for example, that violas, and some clovers, are pollinated only by bumblebees, and knowing that the bumblebees' greatest enemy are mice which eat the eggs and destroy the combs, he observed that violas and clovers flourished particularly in places where there were cats to kill the mice.

EXPERIMENTING WITH DARWIN

English Heritage has restored much of the garden, aiming as far as possible to recreate its appearance of Darwin's day. To one side of the house is a newly planted orchard and some good old trees – a holm oak (*Quercus ilex*) and a splendid hornbeam. South-west of the house a series of little rectangular beds with rounded corners are edged in bergenias and filled with annuals. Round beds cut into the lawn have bushes of fuchsia or clumps of New Zealand flax (*Phormium tenax*). All this is overlooked by a verandah, leafy with Virginia creeper and furnished with comfortable wicker armchairs. A walk between borders and under an arbour of roses leads to the kitchen garden. Here, Darwin's lean-to glasshouse has been reinstated and is stocked with the kinds of plants in which he had a particular interest – carnivorous plants, climbers and orchids. It looks like a meticulously kept working greenhouse rather than a museum. Neat piles of pots and watering cans stand under the staging and a little folding chair awaits the great man in a corner. By contrast, Darwin's rebuilt laboratory on the other side of the

Kitchen garden borders at Down House

wall, which contains an exhibition about his work, has little atmosphere.

Here, the house is an essential part of the visit. It contains many of Darwin's possessions and gives a vivid notion of his family life. His study, with books and furniture, including the chair in which he wrote *On the Origin of Species*, is a moving sight. Above the fireplace is a portrait of Sir Joseph Hooker, as there had been in Darwin's day. It was from Hooker, the director of Kew and a close friend, that Darwin acquired many of the orchids he tended in his greenhouse.

Darwin's gardener, Mr Lettington, described Darwin in old age: "He moons about in the garden, and I have seen him standing doing nothing before a flower for ten minutes at a time. If he only had something to do,

Darwin's greenhouse

I really believe he would be better." Who knows what absorbing thoughts were occupying Darwin's mind as he gazed for so long at those flowers? There are many surviving gardens associated with great men and women. Few were greater than Darwin and it is wonderful to think of his ideas fostered by this domestic setting.

Location Luxted Road, Downe BE6 7JT, Kent **OS** TQ4361 In the village of Downe, 15m SE of central London by A2 and A21 **Tel** 01689 859119 **English Heritage Register** Grade II **Owner** English Heritage **Open** Apr to Sept, Wed to Sun and Bank Hol Mon 10–6; Oct, Wed to Sun 10–5; Nov to Mar, Wed to Sun 10–4 (closed 23 Dec to early Feb) **Area** 17 acres/7 hectares

ELTHAM PALACE

A RARE MEDIEVAL ROYAL PALACE WITH SPRIGHTLY 20TH-CENTURY GARDENS

Few places have as long and as remarkable a history as Eltham Palace. In the 11th century the estate belonged to the Bishop of Bayeux, half-brother of William I. In the 14th century it passed to Edward II and became one of the most used of the royal palaces. By the beginning of the 17th century the palace was gigantic – 1,000ft/305m at its widest point by 500ft/152m – far larger than Hampton Court. Later in the 17th century the palace began to decay and Charles I was the last king to use it. By the 18th century it had become a picturesque ruin and by the 20th century only the medieval great hall still survived – and that by the skin of its teeth. In the 1930s the hall was restored and a spectacular new house grafted onto it by Seely & Paget for Sir Stephen Courtauld. In 1995 English Heritage took over the estate and has restored what remains of both palace d gardens to resounding effect.

The early garden history of Eltham is etchy. There was a park and a herb garden ere by the 14th century. In Henry VIII's time ere were a privy garden, alleys, arbours and bowling green. By the time the Courtaulds me here there was nothing except the lendour of the site and the now mainly aterless moat spanned by its splendid edieval stone bridge. The garden they laid ut, essentially a thoroughly traditional Arts nd Crafts garden of compartments, is in riking contrast to the extraordinary *avant-arde* Art Deco interiors they commissioned r the new house. Parts of the moat were xcavated and once again filled with water; sunken rose garden was made, edged with vender and mounds of clipped box; a shady hrub garden has tall columns of holly and lantings of Japanese anemones, ferns, ydrangeas and pulmonaria. Beyond it the eflooded part of the moat curves round the alace ramparts, turning into a grass walk nder the medieval bridge. On the far side f the moat, a great rock garden also dates om the Courtaulds' time. Japanese maples

The rock garden at Eltham Palace

and a sprawling old juniper are underplanted with *Alchemilla mollis*, ferns, geraniums, hostas and rheums.

On the south side of the palace, where the moat remains dry, there are sprightly new borders by Isabelle van Groeningen in fashionably explosive style, rich in brilliant yellows and reds. On the grass terrace above them, flamboyant bedding schemes of apricot and scarlet dahlias, cannas and tobacco plants lie below the windows of the medieval hall. On the north-east corner of the palace, in an awkward triangular site, English Heritage has laid out a brilliant little parterre of diamond-shaped beds filled with purple sage, creeping thyme or autumn-flowering kniphofia.

A PATCHWORK OF PLEASURES
Eltham Palace presents an extraordinary mixture of ingredients. The palace ramparts are a patchwork of criss-cross patterns of early Tudor brick and medieval stone. The palace itself lurches from romantically medieval to crisply neo-Georgian. The gardens, newly restored, and very finely kept, show similar diversity with appropriately bold effects and much good detail.

Location Eltham SE9 5QE, Greater London **OS** TQ4273 11m SE of central London by A20, signed from Eltham High St **Tel** 020 8294 2577 **English Heritage Register** Grade II* **Owner** English Heritage **Open** Apr to Sept, Wed to Fri, Sun 10–6; Oct, Wed to Fri, Sun 10–5; Nov to Mar, Wed to Fri, Sun 10–4 (open Bank Hol Mon) **Area** 10 acres/2.4 hectares

New borders at Eltham Palace

EMMETTS GARDEN

A WILD GARDEN OF TREES AND SHRUBS
ON A FINE HILLY SITE

High, wild and windy are the words that spring to mind at Emmetts. The occasional touch of formality – for example, a formal rose garden hedged in thuja – seems like a domestic pussy cat that has wandered into a cage of lions. The garden is 600ft/180m above sea level (reputedly the highest point in the whole of Kent), and is exposed to winds and frequently marvellously shrouded in mist. Frederick Lubbock, a friend of William Robinson, bought the estate in 1893 and made his garden which, in the pointedly accurate words of Graham Stuart Thomas, "owes nothing to design and little to forethought". A rock garden was made under the influence of Robinson, who illustrated it in his *Alpine Flowers for the Garden* (1903). The soil is sufficiently acid to support camellias, eucryphias, *Kalmia latifolia*, rhododendrons and splendid stewartias. All these grow among thickets of distinguished trees – acers, beech, *Davidia involucrata*, dogwoods (*Cornus* species) and tulip trees (*Liriodendron tulipifera*).

Spring at Emmetts

Emmetts gives its greatest pleasure in spring and autumn. In April the lower slopes are thick with bluebells; camellias and azaleas are in flower; and the pale foliage of deciduous trees gives freshness to the scene. In autumn there are the beautiful colours of *Berberis wilsoniae* (red leaves and red fruit), *Cercidiphyllum japonicum* (whose autumn leaves smell of candy floss) and many acers. As you follow the paths winding down the hill the exotic trees and shrubs give way, almost imperceptibly, to the natural wild scrub.

I would not make a long journey in order to visit Emmetts, but it is a wonderful thing to have on one's doorstep – an attractive example of the Robinsonian naturalistic style of gardening wholly appropriate to its site. On a blowy day, with the aromatic whiff of azalea on the air, a brisk walk among the trees and shrubs about the hill can seem exactly what is needed.

Location Ide Hill, Sevenoaks TH14 6AY, Kent **OS** TQ4752 1½m N of Ide Hill by B2042 **Tel** 01732 750367 **Fax** 01732 750490 **Email** emmetts@ntrust.org.uk **English Heritage Register** Grade II **Owner** The National Trust **Open** Apr to May, Wed to Sun, Tue (open Bank Hol Mon) 11–5.30; Jun to Oct, Sat, Sun, Wed and Bank Hol Mon 11–5.30 **Area** 6 acres/2.4 hectares

FENTON HOUSE

A BEAUTIFULLY DESIGNED GARDEN
FOR A HANDSOME LATE 17TH-CENTURY
HAMPSTEAD HOUSE

Fenton House was built in 1693 – the date is scratched on one of the chimneys. In 1703 it was bought by a silk merchant, Joshua Gee, and in 1793 by another merchant Philip Fenton. It is one of the prettiest and least spoilt houses of its date surviving in Hampstead and, together with its garden, gives a delightful idea of the sort of

The walled garden at Fenton

gentlemanly life led in the past in one of London's outlying villages. The house was given to the National Trust in 1952.

CHEERFUL FORMALITY

The approach to the house has a village feel, through narrow streets to a beautiful set of wrought-iron gates which date from Joshua Gee's time and bear the initials J.A.G. A short drive, with an avenue of *Robinia pseudoacacia*, leads to the front door. The garden lies almost entirely to the north of the house and its layout is a model for a garden of this sort. Of rectangular plan, enclosed in old brick walls, it is edged on its eastern and northern boundaries by a raised gravel terrace. This, in all likelihood, would have been the garden's original layout: a raised walk to give views over a neatly formal garden spread out below. Box-edged beds line the walls which are clothed in clematis, grapevine, passion flower and roses. Large tubs of blue agapanthus and clipped Portugal laurel follow the edge of the terrace. At the lower level is a sequence of small gardens enclosed in yew hedges occasionally embellished with topiary. Immediately below the north wall of the house a lawn has rows of lollipops of holly and cones of variegated holly; a sunken garden has rose borders; and the smallest of the enclosures has miniature herbaceous borders. The largest area is given to a splendid orchard, lovely in spring with anemones, narcissi and snake's head fritillaries in the grass. At its far end is a vegetable garden. Containing all the ingredients one could wish for in a garden, everything is on exactly the right scale and the garden's cheerful formality precisely echoes that of the house. Village gardens of this sort are rare pleasures in great cities. The garden at Fenton House brings a delicious air of rural life to the heart of residential London.

Location Windmill Hill, Hampstead, London NW3 6RT **OS** TQ2686 5m NW of central London in Hampstead Village **Tube** Hampstead **Tel** and **Fax** 020 7435 3471 **Infoline** 01494 755563 **Email** fentonhouse@ntrust.org.uk **Owner** The National Trust **Open** Mar, Sat, Sun 2–5; Apr to Nov, Wed to Sun (open Bank Hol Mon) 2–5 (weekends and Bank Hol Mon 11–5) **Area** 1 acre/0.4 hectares

Grapevine pergola at Fishbourne

FISHBOURNE ROMAN PALACE GARDEN

THE EXCAVATED SITE OF A GRAND ROMAN VILLA SHOWING HOW THE ROMANS GARDENED

Near the sea at the foot of the south downs must have been just about as close to a Roman climate as could be found in England. Between AD 75 and 100 a palatial villa was built at Fishbourne, hard by one of the inland creeks of Chichester harbour. Roman remains were discovered in 1960 and excavation over a long period revealed evidence of one of the grandest Roman villas ever found in England, with beautiful mosaics and the remains of delightful ornamental stucco work. It was plain that this was the house of a cultivated grandee and it is possible that it belonged to a man called Tiberius Claudius Cogidubnus. He was a local man of great influence who had helped the Romans at the time of the invasion and who acquired status with the Roman administration. His increasing importance may be reflected in the archaeological evidence of the palace's growing size and magnificence.

All such Roman houses had gardens, and evidence of a courtyard garden was found at Fishbourne, with planting trenches plainly visible. Little is known about the design of Roman gardens in Britain but a simple garden has been reconstructed, with a central gravel path flanked by box hedges shaped into alternating curves and half squares. Ornamental features in the garden – a pool, garden pots, a pergola covered in grapevines, trellis work and an outdoor dining area (or *triclinium*) – are based on what is known from gardens at Pompeii and Herculaneum. More recently a display garden has been added, whose chief purpose is to show the range of plants known to have been used in gardens during the Roman occupation of Britain. These are for the most part medicinal, culinary or useful plants (including madder, soapwort, valerian and woad) but there are also some ornamentals, among them acanthus, myrtle, pinks, roses, sweet rocket and violets. It gives a vivid idea of the repertory of plants which could be drawn on. An orchard is planted with apples, bitter and sweet cherries, olives and pears. A Roman potting shed, perhaps not totally authentic, has a full size model gardener who starts to speak as you enter, complaining of the interruption.

Location Fishbourne PO19 3QR, West Sussex **OS** SU8405 1½m W of Chichester by A259 **Tel** 01243 785859 **Fax** 01243 539266 **Email** adminfish@sussexpast.co.uk **English Heritage Register** Grade II* **Owner** Sussex Archaeological Society **Open** Mar to Jul, Sept to Oct, daily 10–5; Aug, daily 10–6; early to end Feb, Nov to mid Dec, daily 10–4; remainder of year, Sun 10–4 **Area** 2 acres/0.8 hectares

GODINTON HOUSE

OUTSTANDING FORMAL GARDENS AND
ANCIENT PARKLAND FOR AN ENCHANTING
17TH-CENTURY HOUSE

Leaving the suburban busyness of Ashford and turning into the drive at Godinton, you find yourself in a different world: marvellous old parkland studded with ancient Spanish chestnuts and English oaks. This sort of approach to a country house is one of the great attractions of English country estates but at Godinton it is exceptional for its antiquity, going back to Norman or even Saxon times. Parts of the estate south-west of the house were later landscaped by Samuel Driver, probably in the 1770s. The brick house, of a lovely silver-russet colour, is essentially early 17th century, built for Nicholas Toke, but it incorporates a medieval house. The façade breaks out into bays which are crowned by sweeping curved gables.

The garden is a surprise – a sequence of architectural hedges and other enclosures designed by Sir Reginald Blomfield for G. Ashley-Dod in 1898, one of his grandest surviving gardens. East and south of the house

The Italian Garden at Godinton

high yew hedges are topped with curved gables echoing those of the house. Behind the yew hedges further divisions are marked by substantial hedges of box, and they too are often decorated with architectural features. This architecture of greenery makes a strong visual connection with the house and also screens the formal pleasure grounds from the noble parkland, of which there are frequent lovely glimpses. Within the hedges is a sequence of gardens of different moods. Pan's Garden is a maze-like parterre of monumental shapes of box whose tops are clipped into sturdy pyramids; a statue of a pensive Pan rises among them. A sunken garden has a long narrow pool

with a scalloped end overlooked by a statue of Venus, with willow fronds falling to the water. Below the south wall of the house, where Blomfield had laid out a formal rose garden, a new rose garden with mixed plantings and good statues has recently been put into place.

At Godinton Blomfield brilliantly linked the garden's various ingredients in a flowing progression. From the mysterious drama of Pan's Garden an unadorned rectangular lawn leads towards a pair of weeping silver pears and a figure of Ceres. Behind her a pair of 'Taihaku' cherries stand at the head of excellent herbaceous borders. The path between them leads down to the sunken pool garden. At the far end of the pool garden, to one side of it, a viewing bastion with a curved balustrade juts out beyond the garden boundary, centred on a delicious view across parkland of the parish church of St Mary at Great Chart (which has 16th- and 17th-century memorials of the Toke family).

South-west of the house is a little walled garden half-concealed behind a colonnade

New borders and parkland at Godinton

◁ **The walled garden** at Goodnestone

entwined with wisteria. This, the Italian Garden, was designed by Blomfield but not put into place until between the wars. Fine statues of the four continents stand between the columns. Putti frolic with a dolphin at the centre of a lily pool with an Italian cypress at each corner. Raised borders on each side are filled with repeated plantings of eryngiums, lavender, *Perovskia atriplicifolia* and sweetly scented *Pittosporum tobira*. The whole is overlooked at the far end by a semicircular terrace shaded by a pergola of grapevines and roses. A summerhouse built into the wall on one side of the garden leads through to a very large walled kitchen garden.

In recent years the gardens at Godinton have been excellently restored, with advice from Hal Moggridge. They show what a subtle and ingenious garden designer Blomfield was. The formal framework he devised can be adapted in various ways but always maintains a harmonious relationship between the house and its larger setting. In a county that contains many outstanding gardens, Godinton is easily one of the finest.

Location Ashford TN23 3BW, Kent **OS** TQ9843 1½m W of Ashford at Potter's Corner on A20 **Tel** 01233 620773 **Fax** 01233 632652 **English Heritage Register** Grade I **Owner** Godinton House Preservation Trust **Open** mid Apr to mid Oct, Fri to Sun 2–5.30 **Area** 12 acres/5 hectares

GOODNESTONE PARK

A GRAND HOUSE AND GARDEN
CLOSE TO THE VILLAGE,
WITH JANE AUSTEN ASSOCIATIONS

Goodnestone is unusual and full of interest. It is rare to find a grand house and old park of this kind so close to the village. As it is, the village church lies alongside its walled garden, and the church tower forms an eyecatcher at the end of the central axis of the walled former kitchen garden. Thus, despite the splendours of the house and its parkland setting, Goodnestone has a domestic charm, drawn into the life of the village.

The house was built in the very early 18th century – the date 1704 is scratched into one of the bricks. John Harris, in his *History of Kent* (1719), writes, "Brook Bridges hath Built here a very handsome house upon the ruins of the old one, and very much improved the Avenues and Gardens belonging to it." An accompanying engraving by Badeslade shows the house at the centre of an immensely elaborate formal garden. Most of this disappeared later in the 18th century when the garden was landscaped by Samuel Driver. However, traces of it survive, as well as ingredients from other periods, giving the garden much of its beauty.

Below the serenely classical façade of the house the garden has recently been simplified. Fussy borders have been replaced by a boldly simple terraced parterre designed by Charlotte Molesworth to celebrate the millennium. Low box hedges divide the compartments which are filled either with gravel or with blocks of a single variety of lavender. A central sundial is encircled with the tender and very attractive *Lavandula canariensis* with fern-like foliage and slender flowering stems.

On the far side of the house the axis of the early 18th-century formal garden is marked by an avenue of limes rising gently up a slope, with a stone urn as an eyecatcher. Nearby, paths lead among some remarkable trees, including the spectacular remains of an ancient cedar of Lebanon and a superlative sweet chestnut. A youthful arboretum is rich in dogwoods (*Cornus* species), eucryphias, magnolias and *Parrotia persica*. Hidden away in the only part of the garden with acid soil is a rockery garden with a pool and rhododendrons – made in the 1920s by Lady Emily FitzWalter.

DEFT COLOUR, GENTLE FORMALITY
Overhanging the inconspicuous entrance to the walled garden is a huge old specimen of the unusual *Abelia triflora* whose modest pink flowers have a heady tropical scent – a perfumed fanfare in July. The garden, a eries of three long compartments, is walled in 18th-century brick with openings forming a vista that is aligned on the tower of the village church. Here, formality is lightly sketched in and there are frequent deft colour combinations but nothing too showily calculating: rusty orange *Helenium* 'Moerheim Beauty' is seen through a veil of the powdery violet-blue flowers of *Perovskia atriplicifolia*; dahlias (rich red 'Bishop of Llandaff' and deepest blood red 'Arabian Night') jostle with inky purple aconitum; and pale pink-apricot kniphofias erupt from a thicket of crimson fuchsia. A path leads through arbours of roses where swaying *Dierama pulcherrimum* arches over many different penstemons and repeated columns of clematis or of Irish yew draw the eye upwards.

Large parts of the walled garden are given over to vegetables and fruit and, in addition to the irresistible attraction of the neatly tended rows, there are ornamental episodes here too – a rampart of sweet peas and a Coalbrookdale cast-iron bench flanked by buttresses of *Clematis* 'Etoile Violette'. It gives the impression of a skilful gardener having a good time in an emphatically untrendy way.

Jane Austen was a visitor at Goodnestone; her brother Edward had married a Bridges daughter. Goodnestone has an air of old-fashioned permanence, with no trace of ossification but a healthy wariness of fleeting fashion. Such survivals, invariably privately owned, are delightful places.

Location nr Wingham, Canterbury CT3 1PL, Kent
OS TR2554 7m E of Canterbury by A257 and minor roads, or A2 and B2046; signed from Wingham
Tel 01304 840107 **English Heritage Register**
Grade II* **Owner** Lord and Lady FitzWalter
Open Apr to Oct, Mon, Wed to Fri 11–5, Sun 12–6
Area 6 acres/2.4 hectares

GRAVETYE MANOR

THE SPLENDID GARDEN OF WILLIAM ROBINSON, THE PROPHET OF WILD GARDENING

Gravetye is a holy place in garden history: the home of William Robinson, the most influential garden writer of his time, who lived here from 1885 until his death in 1935. Dame Sylvia Crowe described Gravetye in 1987 as "an historic milestone in the evolution of gardens…the epitome of the English garden as it evolved in the last century". Gravetye was both Robinson's home and a kind of horticultural laboratory where he could experiment with his gardening ideas.

When the present owner, Peter Herbert, bought Gravetye Manor in 1957 the garden had long been neglected. He converted the house into a hotel and restaurant of the greatest comfort and luxury and restored the gardens in keeping with Robinson's ideas. Visitors may get a good idea of the spirit of the

Spring at Gravetye Manor

place by following the perimeter walk which shows Robinson's taste for naturalistic planting on the grand scale. Woodland to the north of the gabled 16th-century manor house includes Corsican pines (*Pinus nigra* subsp. *laricio*) (200 of which were destroyed in the great storm of 1987), Scots pines and silver birches. To the south the house looks down over a steeply sloping south-facing meadow which is spangled in spring with anemones, wild daffodils, fritillaries and scillas. A lake lies at the bottom of the meadow and on its far bank the land rises in a patchwork of woodland and fields. The meadow grass is left uncut until the late summer to allow plants to seed – a commonplace in gardening today (at least in theory), but a style of gardening unknown in Robinson's time except at Gravetye.

Robinson is best known for his devotion to naturalistic arrangements of self-supporting communities of hardy plants, but it is a myth that he disapproved of formal gardening.

Certainly he despised the high Victorian fashion for municipal carpet bedding – "pastry cook's gardening" he called it – but he considered a formal pattern of beds close to the house entirely appropriate; believing, in common with many other garden theorists, such a passage of flowery formality to be the best way of linking the architecture of the house with wilder surrounding landscape. At Gravetye he laid out an elaborate scheme of beds of this sort, which Peter Herbert has restored. You may inspect these only as a customer of the hotel or restaurant (lucky the keen gardener, or gourmet, who is). They lie to the south and west of the house and are filled with plants that Robinson loved, although the planting is not restricted to historically correct plants.

ROBINSONIAN PLANTING

The Flower Garden to the west has a symmetrical pattern of beds with mixed plantings in which such shrub roses as 'Belle de Crécy', 'Honorine de Brabant' and 'Ferdinand Pichard' are underplanted with pinks, sedums, violas and, a Robinson favourite, *Silybum marianum* – "bright glistening green with broad white veins", as he wrote. The little walled South Garden retains its original pattern of small beds and paved paths. This too is full of plants about which Robinson wrote, such as *Carpenteria californica*, *Cynara cardunculus* (cardoon), *Melianthus major* and *Perovskia atriplicifolia*, whose popularity Robinson stimulated. Robinson had an extraordinarily perceptive eye for good garden plants and the plant directory section of his *English Flower Garden* (1883) constitutes in effect a list of the essential English garden plants of the 20th century. Gravetye honours a great man, but it is far from being a solemn place of worship – it still palpitates with the excitement of plants and gardening.

Location nr East Grinstead RH19 4LJ, West Sussex **OS** TQ3634 4m SW of East Grinstead by B2110 **Tel** 01342 810567 **Fax** 01342 810080 **English Heritage Register** Grade II* **Owner** Peter Herbert **Open** (Perimeter walk only) Tue and Fri 10–5; entry to Robinson's flower gardens is restricted to hotel and restaurant customers **Area** 30 acres/12 hectares

GREAT COMP

SWEEPING LAWNS, GOOD TREES, FLOWERING SHRUBS, SHAM RUINS AND EXUBERANT BORDERS

Great Comp is an enigmatic place. Sometimes it seems the epitome of Surrey cast adrift in Kent – rolling eiderdowns of heathers, lofty fastigiate conifers and relentlessly sweeping lawns curving out of sight. In complete contrast to this conventional garden style is an appealing individuality, even eccentricity. Roderick Cameron who was, with his wife, Joyce, the chief maker of the garden from 1957, is also an amateur builder of great skill. The garden is dotted with the fruits of his labour which vary from picturesque sham ruins to a dapper Italian Garden. The ruins pop up in a slightly accidental fashion but the Italian Garden, close to the house and of elegant formality, seems to associate with the house and with its surroundings in a more purposeful way. This, an extension of an 1840 walled garden to which Mr Cameron has added brick arcades, has an entrance guarded by a pair of stone figures of child warriors, and a splendid Corinthian column capped with a bold urn rises high above the walls. A tiered fountain stands at the centre of a pool which runs through an arch to disappear under a wall decorated with pilasters and reliefs of Roman emperors. The planting within the Italian Garden is a lavish mixture of trees, shrubs and herbaceous underplanting.

The rotunda at Great Comp

A square lawn to one side of the Italian Garden and under the south façade of the house has on the far side of the lawn a fashionably colourful border – sharp yellow achilleas, the deepest crimson or most brilliant scarlet dahlias, sombre purple eupatoriums, kniphofias and smouldering sedums.

The chief parts of the garden are of a more informal character, with paths winding through trees and shrubs. Azaleas (especially Exbury hybrids), camellias, dogwoods, heathers, magnolias, maples, rhododendrons are often underplanted with quantities of campanulas, geraniums, hostas, lilies and violas. Many of the trees are conifers, of which too many, to my eye, have golden foliage. Why do I hate these plants? It is not for reasons of subjective taste but because they appear to have something wrong with them: photosynthesis seems not to be working properly and they look starved of some arboreal essence. They are invalids – the proper reaction is one of pity rather than dislike. Nature, quite brutal in such matters, does not allow such plants to survive in the wild – did you ever see one in a hedgerow?

WILDER AND LONELIER

The garden becomes wilder as it extends away from the views that open out by the house. Along the southern boundary a long walk leads through woodland – it starts well with an immense sea of Lenten roses (*Helleborus × hybridus*, formerly *H. orientalis*) spreading below the canopy of a blue Atlantic cedar. The path, brilliant with spring colour, leads to the loneliest and best part of the garden, marked by a temple in the form of a rotunda (Chilstone but it has weathered very convincingly). Rearing up behind it is a magnificent English oak.

Throughout the garden are good plants well grown. Mr Cameron's achievement must be saluted, but to run up ruinous towers and elegant arcades is an altogether rarer feat.

Location Comp Lane, Platt, nr Borough Green TN15 8QS, Kent **OS** 6356 2m E of Borough Green by A20 and B2016; Jnct 2a of M26 **Tel** 01732 886154 **Owner** The Great Comp Charitable Trust **Open** Apr to Oct, daily 11–6 **Area** 7 acres/2.8 hectares

GREAT DIXTER

CHRISTOPHER LLOYD'S ICONIC GARDEN
DISPLAYS HIS DELIGHT IN GARDENING

In recent times Great Dixter has been made famous by one man: its present owner and presiding garden spirit, Christopher Lloyd. Christopher Lloyd was brought up here, and there was already a good garden at Great Dixter before he was born. In 1910 his father, Nathaniel Lloyd, bought Great Dixter and extended the house with the help of the architect Sir Edwin Lutyens. With Lutyens he laid out a new garden in the Arts and Crafts spirit, with carefully contrived enclosures of yew hedges and decorative deployment of topiary. They also made clever use of outhouses – for example in Nathaniel Lloyd's design for a sunken garden partly enclosed by outhouse walls. It was a marvellous framework to inherit, embellished with planting devised by Christopher Lloyd's mother, Daisy, an assiduous and knowledgeable gardener.

After training and subsequently lecturing in horticulture at Wye College, Christopher Lloyd returned to Great Dixter in 1954 and, at the age of thirty-three, began to assert himself in the garden. When quite young he had had the novel idea of a mixed border in which woody and herbaceous plants are intermingled, with the judicious addition of bedding plants here and there. Over the last fifty years the Long Border at Great Dixter has been a perpetually evolving testbed for new plants and new arrangements. It is a single-sided south-west facing border, 15ft/4.5m deep by 200ft/60m long, edged with a stone flagged path. Garden design purists might criticise it for starting and ending arbitrarily (which it does) but plant lovers relish it for its exuberant and constantly changing use of plants, including those with distinguished foliage of different kinds, and for its very long season of interest, at least from April to October.

IMPATIENCE WITH CLICHÉS

One of the great charms of Great Dixter is the mixture of formality and informality. There are several meadow-like areas – including those that flank the garden's entrance path – in which countless plants have been naturalised. Here are appropriate species of crocuses, erythroniums, snake's head fritillaries (*Fritillaria meleagris*), narcissus, orchids, primroses, quamash (*Camassia quamash*) and much else. This style of planting, new in its day, was begun by Christopher Lloyd's mother and he has continued it with relish.

Lloyd respects good ideas from the past but likes to look to the future and is ruthlessly impatient with clichés. Growing bored with the enclosed formal rose garden designed by Lutyens, he replaced it with an explosive "tropical" mixture of cannas, brilliant dahlias, tender hedychiums and bananas, and New Zealand flax (*Phormium tenax*), all revealed through diaphanous veils of tall *Verbena*

▷ **The 'tropical' garden** at Great Dixter

bonariensis. This dazzling departure of the 1990s pioneered a "new" taste for the dramatic and brilliant instead of the soporific pastels and greys of genteel "good-taste" gardening. In fact, there was nothing new in it at all; it was a timely resuscitation of William Robinson's "sub-tropical" planting, using exactly the plants he recommended. It is not Lloyd's fault that it has become so imitated as to become a cliché of modern gardening.

At Great Dixter it soon becomes apparent that Christopher Lloyd's great love is plants rather than design, and visitors have learned always to expect the unexpected. Through his writings and his garden he has been one of the strongest influences on gardening life in the second half of the 20th century, and his influence goes beyond matters of taste. He has taught the most precious lessons for all gardeners: to study plants and the way they grow; to be your own master; and to be wary of conventional notions of garden taste. One may learn an enormous amount from Christopher Lloyd without necessarily sharing his taste.

Location Northiam, Rye TN31 6PH, East Sussex
OS TQ8125 11m N of Hastings off A28 **Tel** 01797 252878 **Fax** 01797 252879 **English Heritage Register** Grade I **Owner** Christopher Lloyd
Open Apr to mid Oct, daily except Mon (open Bank Hol Mon) 2–5 **Area** 5 acres/2 hectares

In the Long Border at Great Dixter

GREAT FOSTERS

AN EDWARDIAN GARDEN OF TOPIARY
MAKES A SPLENDID SETTING FOR A
TUDOR HOUSE

The late 16th-century house, a hotel since 1927, was refurbished from 1918 by W.H. Romaine-Walker who also developed the gardens in collaboration with G.H. Jenkins "in such a way as to recreate the old-world charm of the place". Two courtyards lead to the house entrance: the outer yard with tall rounded cones of yew and clipped trees of gold variegated holly and the inner yard with a procession of free-standing *Magnolia grandiflora* and two especially large trees

flanking the entrance.

Behind the house a paved terrace, with a brick loggia at each end, overlooks a splendid array of knot gardens enclosed on three sides by a moat, possibly of ancient origin. Four knots are hedged in yew and arranged about a central mound planted with lavender and ornamented with a multi-faceted 16th-century sundial. Each knot has a pattern of box-edged beds, and each bed is filled with blocks of a single plant – catmint, *Convolvulus cneorum*, geraniums or sage – with a topiary shape and a lead figure standing on a plinth in the centre.

Beyond the knot garden a double lime avenue extends the east–west axis beyond the stream which forms the garden's eastern boundary but the avenue has been truncated by the M25 – made invisible, but alas not inaudible, by an earth bank.

A path leads south from the knot garden to a splendid hump-backed oak bridge built like a pergola and swathed in roses and wisteria, which crosses the moat. Here a sunken rose garden hedged in yew has a circular pool and fountain girdled by curved rose beds, and eight sets of steps radiating up from the lower level. Beyond is a lawn with yew topiary, a long tunnel of apples and a most attractive garden of undulating yew hedges and a grove of cherry trees.

The knot garden at Great Fosters

Great Fosters was a pioneer in turning a fine country house into a hotel, and its garden, an especially attractive one, is finely cared for. As a busy hotel it probably has an atmosphere closer to that of a well-staffed country house than it might if still owned privately and run on slender means.

Location Stroude Road, Egham TW20 9UR, Surrey **OS** TQ0169 1m S of Egham; Jnct 13 of M25 **Tel** 01784 433822 **Fax** 01784 472455 **Email** enquiries@greatfosters.co.uk **Website** www.greatfosters.co.uk **English Heritage Register** Grade II* **Owner** Great Fosters (1931) Ltd **Open** daily 9–5 **Area** 22 acres/9 hectares

GREENWICH PARK

AN ANCIENT PARK IN WHICH HISTORY, LOVELY BUILDINGS AND MAGNIFICENT VIEWS ARE COMBINED

Greenwich, perhaps not the best known of the royal parks, is historically one of the most interesting and certainly one of the most diversely attractive. The site has been occupied since prehistoric times, there are the remains of Roman buildings, and it was the first of London's royal parks to be enclosed. It was inherited in 1427 by Henry V's brother, Humphrey, Duke of Gloucester, who was granted a licence in 1433 to "empark 200 acres of land, pasture, weed, heath and furze at Estgrenewich". His palace, or "Manor of Pleasaunce" was finally demolished when the Queen's House, designed by Inigo Jones, was built for James I's queen, Anne, between 1616 and 1635. In 1664 a new palace was started: the first part of the buildings that became the Royal Naval Hospital – in the end it took over 100 years to complete and involved Nicholas Hawksmoor, John Webb and Sir Christopher Wren. In 1675 Charles II appointed John Flamsteed the first Astronomer Royal; the Royal Observatory (now Flamsteed House), designed by Sir Christopher Wren and Robert Hooke, was finished the following year.

17TH-CENTURY AVENUES

An engraving by Kip of 1699 shows Greenwich Park when much of this work had been completed. Charles II had asked André Le Nôtre to make designs for the landscape, and a drawing of 1662 survives but it is not known if this was ever executed. In the 1660s parts of the park were laid out by Sir William Boreham, Keeper of the palace and park, and some of the sweet chestnuts planted in avenues at this time survive at the eastern end of Great

Cross Avenue. The Kip engraving shows the buildings handsomely united about a single axis which is continued southwards along a double avenue, with Observatory Hill and Flamsteed House clearly shown on one side. The view today, complete with a replanted double avenue of horse chestnuts (now known as Blackheath Avenue) is remarkably similar. In the 18th century Greenwich became a public park. In 1891 a splendid bandstand east of Blackheath Avenue was erected, where summer concerts are still performed.

FLOWERY PLEASURES, AMAZING VIEWS

A walk around Greenwich Park is full of history for those interested in such things (Greenwich was Henry VIII's favourite residence) but it is also an immensely pleasurable experience. The site is an undulating one, with Observatory Hill roughly in the centre at its highest point. From here the views northwards, over the Queen's House and the former Royal Naval Hospital, with the massed buildings of the City beyond, is breathtaking. The park is still threaded with avenues (there was much 20th-century replanting of beech, English oak and horse chestnut) and there are intermittent flowery pleasures. In the southern corner of the park, the Dell in spring is dazzling with

azaleas and rhododendrons. There are also a Flower Garden on the banks of a lake (where anti-aircraft guns stood in World War II), a Rose Garden, a deer park (the red and fallow deer are said to be directly descended from those of Tudor times) and ornaments ranging from a Henry Moore and a statue of General Wolfe to a monumental figure of William IV standing guard at St Mary's Gate in the north-west corner of the park. Apart from the beauties of the landscape, there is something intriguing, too, in standing precisely on the line of the meridian and remembering that the Royal Observatory was an astonishing scientific centre where, among many other things, the speed of light was first calculated.

It is easy to get to Greenwich Park from central London by train or bus but the most beautiful route is by river. If you make the journey by night the view of the Naval Hospital, Queen's House and Observatory shimmering floodlit before you is unforgettable.

Location Greenwich SE10 8QY, Greater London
OS TQ3877 7½m E of central London by A200
Station Greenwich or Maze Hill **Tel** 0802 858 2608
English Heritage Register Grade I **Owner** The Royal Parks **Open** daily 7–dusk (closes 6 in winter)
Area 183 acres/73 hectares

From Observatory Hill at Greenwich

GROOMBRIDGE PLACE

THE ATMOSPHERIC WALLED GARDENS OF 17TH-CENTURY MOATED HOUSE

The moated house was built, to replace an older house, for Philip Packer between 1652 and 1674. Packer was a friend of John Evelyn who visited Groombridge in 1652 and described it in his diary as "A pretty melancholy seate, well wooded and water'd". When I first visited Groombridge, long before reading Evelyn's opinion, I too found the place melancholy. Much later I discovered that Sir Arthur Conan-Doyle, who lived nearby at

The terraced garden at Groombridge

Crowborough, had also known the house; he had used it as the setting of his story "The Valley of Fear" (1895) in which Dr Watson describes what is plainly Groombridge: "a Jacobean house of dingy liver-coloured brick…an old-fashioned garden of cut yews…beautiful broad moat, as still and luminous as quicksilver".

The old-fashioned garden is still there and is by far the most attractive feature of Groombridge. It was supposedly designed with the advice of John Evelyn and it certainly has the character of his period. To the north, land slopes down south towards the house and is terraced, and enclosed in walls and hedges, to form three rectangular compartments with a central axial walk linking them. "Cut yews" are still to be seen here, in particular a splendid procession of drum shapes that run along either side of the axial walk in the central garden. These, and some shapes of golden yew to one side, could have been here in Conan-Doyle's time. Indeed, the planting has a pronounced 19th-century flavour which

◁ **Heraldic topiary** at Hall Place

marries well with the 17th-century setting. In the upper garden the walk is flanked by mixed borders and old hedges of Kentish cobs. To one side is a curious garden of misshapened juniper topiary seemingly bent over by a great wind. Modern mixed borders line the walls in the upper and central gardens. On a lawn in the central garden is a venerable *Cotinus coggygria*, said to be 300 years old. Without documentary evidence estimations of the great age of garden plants should be taken with a pinch of salt, but in this case it is interesting that the plant in question was introduced to England, probably from eastern Europe, in the 1650s. The lowest garden is almost entirely modern, with a box parterre, a large outdoor chess set and a fine row of yew pudding shapes.

THE ENCHANTED FOREST

The garden has been transformed in recent years with a view to opening it to the public. When I first heard about plans for an entirely new creation, the Enchanted Forest, it sounded promising. It has turned out to be a children's fun park with, among much else, a Dark Walk, Jurassic Valley, Dinosaur's Eggs, Action Trail and Pig Racing – involving two New Zealand pigs, of a breed called kune-kune, named Strutt and Parker after their estate agent donors. All good fun for children, and possibly for adults of a jokey disposition, but not resulting in a landscape of beauty.

Location Groombridge, Tunbridge Wells TN3 9QG, Kent **OS** TQ5337 4m SW of Tunbridge Wells by A264 and B2110 **Tel** 01892 863999 **Fax** 01892 863996 **Email** office@groombridge.co.uk **English Heritage Register** Grade II* **Owner** Groombridge Asset Management **Open** end Mar to Oct, daily 9–6 **Area** 164 acres/66 hectares

HALL PLACE

A PUBLIC PARK WITH A TOPIARY GARDEN, ROSE GARDEN AND LIVELY MODERN PLANTING

The house is partly Tudor, of grey and white chequered stone, and partly 17th-century brick. The house, of medieval origins, was bought in 1537 by Sir John Champeneis who had been Lord Mayor of London. Nothing is known of an early garden here but there are 18th-century garden walls and some superb wrought-iron gates of the early 18th century, attributed to Thomas Robinson. The house is now used as the headquarters of the London Borough of Bexley Libraries and Museums Service and since 1969 its garden has been used as a public park.

The first thing to notice is that the garden is flawlessly well kept, well up to the old standards of municipal parks' departments before they were destroyed by the imposition

of competitive tendering. The site is generally level and the river Cray forms an ornamental boundary to the formal part of the garden: dammed at this point, it resembles a canal, and beyond it there is open grass planted with scattered trees, giving the impression of parkland. Here too is a mixed flower meadow and a spring garden.

In the formal gardens the most striking feature is a magnificent parade of yew topiary. A series of beautifully fashioned heraldic figures – the White Horse of Hanover, the Unicorn of Scotland, the Greyhound of Richmond and so on – forms the boundary to a lawn. To one side, beneath the Tudor part of the house, is a huddle of various topiary shapes – birds, dumb waiters, mounds and columns clustered together. All this, very Tudor in spirit, must date from the early 20th century. On the same lawn are a splendid London plane and a grand old holm oak (*Quercus ilex*). Below the heraldic topiary, at a slightly lower level, a large garden of modern roses is laid out in crisply shaped beds cut out of impeccable turf. There is much bedding, all superbly executed, sometimes flamboyant in eyestopping colours – salmon perlargoniums, chalky purple verbenas and electric blue lobelia – but sometimes in gentler and more harmonious colours, so that all, or should I say both, tastes are catered for. A quite different atmosphere reigns in an adjacent garden where, below the branches of a London plane, is a beautiful turf maze whose path is marked by close mowing in a slightly coarser background.

MODEL GARDENS

Quite separate from the main part of the garden by the house is a series of model gardens – a suburban garden, a terraced house garden, and so on. Model allotments show how to manage a kitchen garden with cutting beds. Here too is the London Borough of Bexley's Nursery Garden where plants are propagated for the Borough and some are sold to the public.

The garden at Hall Place is very busy and plainly loved by all sorts of people. It has the sort of atmosphere that the great 19th-century municipal parks must have had in their glory years. The horribly crowded A2 thunders past nearby but in the garden all is peace and contentment.

Location Bourne Road, Bexley DA5 1PQ, Greater London **OS** TQ5074 On the A2 15m SE of central London; Jnct 2 of M25 (northbound) **Tel** 01322 526574 **Fax** 01322 522921 **Email** martin@hallplaceandgardens.com **English Heritage Register** Grade II **Owner** London Borough of Bexley **Open** daily 10–5 (Sun opens 11) (closed Sun from Nov to Feb) **Area** 62 acres/25 hectares

HAM HOUSE

LIVELY RECREATED PERIOD GARDENS ADORN THIS GRAND THAMES-SIDE 17TH-CENTURY VILLA

The banks of the river at Richmond, and the wooded slopes above them, were in the 17th and 18th centuries favourite places on which to build great houses and gardens. Ham House is one of the finest, and best preserved, of these grand riverside villas. Built of brick with stone dressings, it was started in 1610 for Sir Thomas Vavasour, but much altered in 1672–74 for the Duke of Lauderdale and his wife (formerly the Countess of Dysart). John Evelyn visited the house at its most splendid: "After dinner I walked to Ham to see the House and Gardens of the Duke of Lauderdale, which is indeed inferior to few of the best Villas of Italy itself; the House furnished like a great Prince's; the Parterres, Flower gardens, Orangeries, Groves, Avenues, Courts, Statues, Prespectives, Fountains, Aviaries & all this at the banks of the Sweetest River in the World, must needs be surprising."

By 1948, when the National Trust acquired Ham, the house had survived remarkably unchanged but the garden seen by Evelyn had long disappeared. Since 1976 that garden has been painstakingly and most attractively

reinstated, so that once again, house and garden form a harmonious ensemble of 17th-century splendour. The garden is well documented: a drawing by Robert Smythson of *c.*1610 shows, as Sir Roy Strong pointed out, the earliest known example in England of a garden disposed about the central axis of the house; a painting of *c.*1675 by Henry Danckerts shows the Wilderness to the south of the house; and further drawings of the 1670s show other details.

Visitors today approach the house from the river side, welcomed in the entrance forecourt by a grand Coade stone figure of a river god. Drums of clipped bay line the enclosing walls which are decorated with lead busts set into ovals let into the walls. The East Court to one side of the house is now an immense parterre with a lozenge pattern of low hedges of dwarf box and each compartment filled with alternate blocks of santolina and Dutch lavender, both clipped to the same height

The parterre at Ham House

as the box. It is flanked by tunnels of pleached hornbeam and at its centre is a statue of Bacchus.

Behind the house a deep gravel terrace is decorated with pots filled with juniper, laurustinus, myrtle and yellow broom. This overlooks squares of turf arranged in rows and separated by gravel paths with obelisks of clipped yew in Versailles boxes. Beyond it is the Wilderness with hedges of hornbeam above whose tops rise unclipped field maples. Here, a central walk opens out into a circle from which six hedged paths radiate outwards. Within the enclosed areas are elegant little white pavilions, painted blue inside and topped with a gleaming golden finial, and in the long grass of some of the compartments wild plants are naturalised – anemones, campions, cowslips, ox-eye daisies and primroses. At the centre are white-painted shell-backed chairs and copies of the lead statues which are to be seen in Danckerts's painting. It is an attractive mixture of rather austere formality and a lively ornamental sense, with the pavilions and long grass like a scene from some rural midsummer festival.

To the west of all this, where a kitchen garden had been in the 17th century, is a very early orangery, dating from before 1677. It is seen in an engraving in *Vitruvius Britannicus* (1739) looking down over an immense array of neat beds of fruit and vegetables. The walls of the kitchen garden survive, the orangery is now a tea room and some vegetable beds have been reinstated. It is attractive, but more Beatrix Potter than Countess of Lauderdale.

Location Ham, Richmond, Greater London TW10 7RS **OS** TQ1773 9m SW of central London off A307 at Petersham **Tel** 020 8940 1950 **Fax** 020 8332 6903 **Email** hamhouse@ntrust.org.uk **Website** www.nationaltrust.org.uk/southern **English Heritage Register** Grade II* **Owner** The National Trust **Open** Sat to Wed 10.30–6 or dusk if earlier **Area** 18 acres/7 hectares

HAMPTON COURT PALACE

GREAT TUDOR AND 17TH-CENTURY PALACE
WITH RESTORED PRIVY GARDEN AND
LOVELY TRACES OF THE PAST

The most famous picture of Hampton Court Palace in its heyday is Leonard Knyff's giant bird's eye view painted in 1702 and hanging at the palace – one of the grandest of all garden paintings. It is a scene of breathtaking splendour, showing the huge palace with its labyrinthine Tudor and late 17th-century buildings, and gardens spreading out on three sides. In the foreground, east of the palace, three double avenues and a central canal radiate outwards from a semicircle of trees which encloses a brilliant pattern of ornate parterres with pools and water jets. The avenues were the work of André Mollet for King Charles II in 1661–62 and the parterres were designed a little later by the Huguenot Daniel Marot. On the left of the painting, below the south windows of Sir Christopher Wren's new buildings, is the Privy Garden, with four embroidered parterres and circular

The Privy Garden at Hampton Court

pools designed by Henry Wise c.1689. At the southern tip of the garden, by the banks of the Thames, is a curved screen of intricately worked wrought iron by another Huguenot, Jean Tijou. Beyond the Privy Garden a group of small enclosures, the Pond Garden and the Knot Garden are overlooked by Sir Christopher Wren's banqueting house, where Henry VIII had first made a garden after 1525. To the right of the painting, north of the palace, is the astonishing sight of the Wilderness: a maze of clipped hedges designed by George London and Henry Wise in the late 17th century.

SPLENDOUR AND OPPORTUNITY?

In its day Hampton Court was one of the greatest gardens in Europe and even today visitors can see enough of its splendour to appreciate what an overwhelming spectacle it must have been. In 1995 the Privy Garden was superbly restored and now precisely resembles what is seen in the Knyff painting. Henry VIII's gardens below the banqueting house are brilliant with bedding schemes but no water flows in Marot's water parterre and the embroidered patterns have been replaced with bedding schemes. Mollet's avenues, and the central canal, are still in place, but of the

Wilderness there remains only a trace. The palace has been much restored and is one of the most attractive and interesting of all the royal palaces. If only the gardens could, like the Privy Garden, once again match the splendour of the buildings.

Location East Molesey KT8 9AU, Greater London **OS** TQ1568 6m SW of central London at Hampton Wick **Tel** 020 8781 9500 **Fax** 020 8781 9509 **Website** www.hrp.org.uk **English Heritage Register** Grade I **Owner** Historic Royal Palaces **Open** mid Mar to mid Oct, daily 9.30–6 (opens 10.15 Mon); mid Oct to mid Mar, daily 9.30–4.30 (opens 10.15 Mon) **Area** 60 acres/24 hectares

HATCHLANDS PARK

A GERTRUDE JEKYLL FLOWER PARTERRE,
GOOD TREES AND A DREAM-LIKE PARK

Hatchlands Park was built between 1756 and 1757 for Admiral Boscawen, with interiors by Robert Adam. In 1800 Humphry Repton produced a Red Book in which he recommended moving the London road further away from the house and making a raised bank planted with trees to conceal the house from the main road and so

transforming it "from a large red house by the side of a high road to a Gentleman-like residence in the midst of a Park". Repton in any case disliked red brick houses, which reminded him of poorhouses, and he recommended that Hatchlands be painted white. In 1914 Gertrude Jekyll submitted two alternative schemes for a parterre below the south façade of the house. One was a sunburst of bedding plants and the other a parterre of peonies and roses which was put into place. In 1945 the estate was given to the National Trust by H.S. Goodhart-Rendel. The house was let as a finishing school between 1959 and 1980 and is today divided among different tenants. The garden and park have a romantic air, slightly forlorn and shabby about the edges, but still with potent atmosphere.

GOOD TREES AND JEKYLL PLANTING

The entrance drive curves away from the main road – the sort of arrangement Repton liked, for it made the estate seem larger. A grand flight of steps leads towards beautiful brick walls and rusticated gate piers – the former kitchen garden, now neglected. A little further on, standing out among trees, is a temple with a copper cupola brought here in 1953 from Busbridge Hall. Now dangerously decrepit, weeds grow in the steps and entrance is forbidden by chestnut paling. A spectacular oriental plane (*Platanus orientalis*), the most beautiful tree on the estate, stands by the house with a handsome white marble statue of Paris freckled with lichen. Between the plane and the house is Gertrude Jekyll's parterre, restored by the National Trust in 1990. Gravel paths flow between a pattern of box-edged beds filled with irises, red or white *Lychnis coronaria*, peonies, penstemons and roses. In the middle a group of putti hold a vase aloft and pots of yuccas stand among the beds. More good trees – a cedar of Lebanon, a huge holm oak and a Monterey pine (*Pinus radiata*) draw the eye towards woods where a precipitous wooded dell, a former chalk pit, is overlooked by the arched opening of an icehouse.

It is the walks in the park to the north and west of the house that are the most memorable pleasure at Hatchlands. The site is flat and is ornamented with a small lake and

Statue of Paris at Hatchlands

good parkland trees, in particular English oaks. The exterior of the house is seen at its best across the meadows, sometimes shrouded in trees and sometimes seen against woodland with the dapper temple beside it.

Location East Clandon, Guildford GU4 7RT, Surrey **OS** TQ0752 4½m E of Guildford by A246 **Tel** 01483 222482 **Infoline** 01483 225971 **Fax** 01483 223176 **Email** hatchlands@ntrust.org.uk **Owner** The National Trust **Open** (gardens) Apr to Oct, Tue to Thur, Sun 2–5.30; (park) Apr to Oct, daily 11–6 **Area** (garden) 12 acres/4.8 hectares; (park) 430 acres/170 hectares.

HEVER CASTLE

A 14TH-CENTURY MOATED CASTLE
WITH WALLED GARDENS FILLED WITH
ORNAMENT, AND A SERENE LAKE

The moated castle is 14th-century, built for Sir John Cobham and sold to Sir Geoffrey Bullen or Boleyn (Henry VIII's Queen Anne was a descendant) in the 15th century. The garden, however, is all of the 20th century, created from 1903 onwards after the estate was bought by William Waldorf Astor (later 1st Viscount Astor) in 1903. He engaged the architect Frank Pearson and the nurserymen Joseph Cheal & Son to lay out

elaborate formal gardens in keeping with the castle spirit. Astor had built up a large and distinguished collection of classical antiquities and other fine objects which, as in his other garden at Cliveden in Buckinghamshire, he proposed to display in the garden. Themes and atmospheres are juggled here with dexterity, occasionally teetering on the verge of excess.

On the edge of the moat east of the castle is a conscious evocation of "an old English garden" with whimsical yew topiary and a yew maze. Anne Boleyn's garden has a herb garden, beds of modern roses and a set of chess pieces of clipped yew. Lord Astor's treasures are already to be seen, among them a grand early 18th-century astrolabe on a carved plinth and a Roman wellhead with a frieze of frolicking Maenads. To the east an avenue of horse chestnuts marches away from the castle, following the bank of a lake.

LORD ASTOR'S ITALIAN GARDEN

The real excitement of the garden starts, however, with the Italian Garden on the mainland south-east of the maze. This walled enclosure opens with a flourish – a vast semicircular pool backed by a sweep of yew hedging against which a Roman figure of Venus is poised. Within the enclosure the Pompeian Wall runs along the long north wall, divided into bays by stone buttresses housing busts, carved capitals, urns and sarcophagi against a background of shrubs and herbaceous perennials enlivened with spring and summer bedding. On the opposite side, and facing north, is a pergola with stone columns planted with honeysuckle, roses, vines and wisteria.

Spring planting at Hever Castle

Camellias are trained against the wall, flowering well before the deciduous climbers are in leaf and relishing their shade for the rest of the year. Here, too, is series of mossy grotto-like niches with the occasional cascade, planted with ferns, hostas, polygonums, primulas and Welsh poppies. The far end of the Italian Garden, where it overlooks a lake, is the scene of Astor's most grandiose notion. Running the whole width of the garden is an Italianate stone screen with rounded arches and columns. A double flight of steps sweeps down to the water, curving about a scalloped pool with a cascading fountain and a pair of white marble nymphs – perhaps more appropriate for a shady and very grand Roman piazza than for the wooded bank of a lake in the Kentish countryside. If, however, you now walk as far as you can along the south bank of the lake and turn round, the stone screen has a more Arcadian character, seen against trees and reflected in the placid water.

Location nr Edenbridge TN8 7NG, Kent
OS TQ4745 3m SE of Edenbridge by minor roads
Infoline 01732 865224 **Fax** 01732 866796 **Email** mail@hevercastle.co.uk **English Heritage Register** Grade I **Owner** Broadland Properties Ltd **Open** Mar to Nov, daily 11–6 (Mar and Nov, closes 4) **Area** 50 acres/20 hectares

The lake at Hever Castle

THE HIGH BEECHES

A PRIVATE WOODLAND GARDEN OF ENCHANTMENT; MARVELLOUS SHRUBS AND TREES IN A LANDSCAPE TO SUIT

The High Beeches is a kind of minimalist wild garden whose charms are subtle and insidious but once you have succumbed to them impossible to forget. It was formerly a property of the gardening Loders and now belongs to a member of another gardening dynasty, Edward Boscawen. I call the garden minimalist because, although there are great exotics here, the landscape has such a natural air, and so much care has been taken to preserve the character of the place, that it is hard to tell where artifice ends and nature starts. In the woodland garden, for example, the grass is cut only when the enormous range of wildflowers has had a chance to seed, and to see it in any season is marvellous. Some parts of the garden have probably never been cultivated: Front Meadow, for example, with its 15 species of grasses and lavish spread of the orchid *Dactylorhiza fuchsii* in high summer (not a rare plant but seldom seen in such a beautiful circumstances).

In many parts of the garden bulbous plants or perennials have become naturalised to resounding effect – *Cyclamen hederifolium*, the English native daffodil (*Narcissus pseudonarcissus*) and its Mediterranean cousin *N. bulbocodium*, and astonishing drifts of willow gentian (*Gentiana asclepiadea*) in early autumn pouring like rich blue water over the land. The site slopes in a south-westerly direction, breaking out from time to time into small valleys, or "gills" as they are called in these parts, forming secluded spaces.

ROOM TO ADMIRE

The triumph of the High Beeches is that, unlike many woodland gardens, most of the trees and shrubs have plenty of space so that their whole beauty may be admired. At rhododendron time, in late April or early May, when the new foliage of the Japanese maples is at its best, the many old English oaks, not yet fully in leaf, present a bold pattern of shapes. Although many trees were lost in the 1987 storm there are some wonderful survivors, including a handkerchief tree (*Davidia involucrata*) propagated from seed gathered in China by E.H. Wilson in 1904. The soil is acid and the garden is rich in rhododendrons planted by Colonel Loder in the early part of the 20th century, some of them hybrids of his own devising. He was a

The valley garden at the High Beeches

friend of Arthur Soames of nearby Sheffield Park (*see page 176*) from whom he had many good plants, especially American species from wild sources.

The garden has many unfamiliar trees (such as the exceedingly rare Indian oak, *Quercus oxyodon*) and shrubs but it is their arrangement, with each other and within their landscape, that is exciting, rather than the mere flaunting of rarities. After all, anyone can plant something rare, but who could make another High Beeches?

Location Handcross RH17 6HQ, West Sussex
OS TQ2731 1m E of Handcross off B2110
Tel 01444 400589 **Fax** 01444 401543 **English Heritage Register** Grade II* **Owner** High Beeches Gardens Conservation Trust **Open** Apr to Jun, Sept to Oct, daily except Wed 1–5; Jul to Aug, Mon and Tue 1–5 **Area** 20 acres/8 hectares

HIGHDOWN

THE ULTIMATE CHALK GARDEN – WONDERFUL PLANTS FINELY GROWN IN AN IMPOSSIBLE SITE

For anyone gardening on chalk, Highdown is an inspiration. Sir Frederick Stern started gardening here in 1909 on a site that is pure chalk; indeed part of it had been excavated for chalk. He found that "no-one was able to advise us on what would grow on this nearly virgin chalk, and many discouraged us from trying anything. One eminent nurseryman, when asked what to plant on the chalk cliffs…said nothing would grow there." So Sir Frederick studied a geological map of the world and noted which parts of the world seemed have alkaline soil: Japan and North America have very little; the countries round the Mediterranean have a lot. By trial and error he discovered that while many Chinese species would thrive in chalk (including some of the great treasures introduced by E.H. Wilson), American or Japanese species of the same genus would not. Thus the beautiful Chinese maples like *Acer griseum* and *A. davidii* are to be seen, whereas *A. japonicum* is not. Slowly he learned which plants would do, and also how best to enrich the garden with the humus which was almost entirely lacking. The garden slopes steeply to the south, adding to the already sharp drainage, and although some bulbs, and Mediterranean plants such as cistus, relish such conditions, most of the more distinguished trees and shrubs require humus.

The planting is informal; the closest it gets to formality is an avenue of *Prunus serrula*, a Chinese cherry with gleaming mahogany bark. Among shrubs the garden is rich in berberis, buddleias, cistus, cotoneasters, daphnes, junipers, myrtles, roses and viburnums. There is also an immense range of herbaceous and bulbous underplanting

– anemones, crocuses, cyclamens, eremurus, irises, narcissi, peonies, snowdrops and tulips are all to be seen in profusion.

Although the site is a handsome one, no-one would come to Highdown for the beauty of its design. The charm of the place comes from the range of plants that Sir Frederick, through research and experiment, found he could grow. It provides a vivid example of how the need to study the genius of the place extends to the physical as well as the spiritual components of a garden. It is also an object

lesson in what can be achieved by an intelligent gardener of independent mind, navigating without charts, who is prepared to strike out on his own.

Location Littlehampton Road, Goring-by-Sea BN12 6NY, West Sussex **OS** TQ0904 3m W of Worthing by A259 **Tel** 01903 501054 **English Heritage Register** Grade II* **Owner** Worthing Borough Council **Open** Apr to Sept, daily 10–6; Oct to Mar, Mon to Fri 10–4 **Area** 9½ acres/4 hectares

Waterside planting at Highdown

HOLLAND PARK

A 17TH-CENTURY ESTATE TRANSFORMED INTO A SPLENDID PUBLIC PARK WITH GOOD PLANTING AND ORNAMENTS

The Jacobean mansion of Holland House passed to the Fox family (Barons Holland) and in the late 18th century, under the 3rd Baron, became the centre of Whig politics and literature. Lord Fox and his wife met Napoleon in 1802 and, despite the subsequent war, remained staunch supporters, even sending the exiled emperor quantities of plum jam. The 4th Baron and his wife took an interest in the garden at Holland House and, in particular, made the surviving formal iris and Dutch gardens near the house. The house was badly bombed in World War II and the estate was bought in 1952 by the Royal Borough of Kensington and Chelsea which made the remains of the house into a youth hostel and the gardens into a public park.

WILD WOODS AND ACTIVE FRIENDS
The site is especially attractive, undulating and densely planted with trees, often with a wild undergrowth of Guelder rose (*Viburnum opulus*), hawthorn, holly and yew. No other central London park gives such a feeling of a walk in a wood.

A lively and well-organised Friends of Holland Park makes a great contribution to its well-being and in 1999 contributed, among other things "5,000 snowdrops, 14 hedgehogs, 15 peacocks, £10,000 worth of trees and a fountain by William Pye". There is an especially good collection of oaks, and a 19th-century avenue of limes, destroyed in the 1987 storm, was replanted in 2000 with American red oaks (*Quercus rubra*). The Dutch Garden is a geometric pattern of box-edged beds filled with such bedding plants as begonias, busy lizzies and fuchsias. The Iris Garden has a circular pool at its centre, with the fountain by William Pye. It is overlooked by an arcaded loggia with attractive mural paintings by Mao Wen Biao (1994–95) showing a garden party in the grounds of Holland House in the 1870s – a splendid evocation of the period.

In 1991 a Japanese garden, the Kyoto Garden, was deftly infiltrated into the woodland. Especially well done, it was created by Japanese gardeners, and is wonderfully ornamental. A thundering cascade tumbles down among massive rocks to feed a calm pool spanned by an austerely modern bridge of pale paving stones. Birches, Japanese maples and willows fringe the banks, underplanted with ferns and azaleas, and shapely junipers and pines erupt from rocks. A placard explains that the purpose of such gardens was to evoke in "condensed form the grandeur of the natural landscape", which it most effectively does. With its depth of historical interest, good plants and lively modern ingredients, Holland Park is a model of its kind.

Location London W8 **OS** TQ2479 W of central London **Tube** Holland Park **English Heritage Register** Grade II **Owner** The Royal Borough of Kensington and Chelsea **Open** daily 8–sunset **Area** 53 acres/21 hectares

The **Kyoto Garden** in Holland Park

The Serpentine in Hyde Park

HYDE PARK

A FORMER ROYAL HUNTING FOREST
WHICH BECAME A FAMOUS PUBLIC PARK
WITH OUTSTANDING TREES

Hyde Park is an ancient place and has some of the wildest and most naturalistic scenery of any of the central London parks. The Roman roads of Watling Street (now the Edgware Road) and Via Trinobantina (now Oxford Street and Bayswater Road) met at its north-east corner. It became a monastic property, belonging to the Benedictines of St Peter, Westminster, and passed to King Henry VIII in 1536 at the time of the dissolution of the monasteries, when it became a royal hunting forest. The park was opened permanently to the public in the reign of King Charles II in the 17th century. Rotten Row, along Hyde Park's southern boundary, is what remains of a road made by William III to link Kensington Palace with St James's Palace; it was the first artificially illuminated road in the country, lit by 300 oil lamps hanging from the branches of trees. The park was nevertheless plagued with highwaymen and thoughout the 18th century was a favourite duelling ground. The Serpentine lake was made in 1730 and a bridge across it, separating the northern part (now the Long Water) was built a little later. This in turn was replaced in 1825–28 with a new bridge by George and John Rennie.

Hyde Park has a varied and distinguished collection of trees. Some sweet chestnuts, near the Old Police House, go back to 18th-century plantings, and there are many superb London planes. The planes are used both for avenues (in the Broad Walk, for example) and as single splendid specimens (there is a beauty standing alone in a meadow near Cumberland Gate). Among the horse chestnuts, limes, English oaks and sycamores there are also less common species: specimens of both *Zelkova serrata* and *Z. carpinifolia* near the bandstand (and the frightful Queen Elizabeth Gate), as well as the Kentucky yellow wood (*Cladrastis kentukea*), the American hybrid wingnut *Pterocarya × rehderiana* and a lovely Lucombe oak (*Quercus × hispanica* 'Lucombeana'). Densely planted areas are interspersed with meadows and distant prospects are often revealed. One of the most memorable sights is that of riders on horseback cantering along Dorchester Ride (the park is ringed with rides) with the palaces of Park Lane rising among the trees – a quintessential London view.

Location London W2 **OS** TQ2780 In central London immediately W of Park Lane **Tubes** Lancaster Gate (NW corner), Marble Arch (NE corner), Hyde Park Corner (SE corner) and Knightsbridge (S side) **English Heritage Register** Grade I **Owner** The Royal Parks **Open** daily 5–midnight **Area** 312 acres/126 hectares

IGHTHAM MOTE

MEDIEVAL MOATED HOUSE SET IN A
GREEN AND LEAFY VALLEY GARDEN OF
RARE ATMOSPHERE

One of the most dazzlingly attractive houses in the country (do not fail to go inside), Ightham Mote dates from the 14th century, with alterations, always harmonious, of every subsequent century (including work on the interior by Norman Shaw in 1872). Moated, it is built of pale coffee-coloured ragstone with eruptions of timbering round a central courtyard. The estate had many owners before being given to the National Trust by an American, Henry Robinson. The National Trust has carried out a long programme of restoration, still underway in 2002, which has had the happy outcome of leaving the house's charming appearance unaltered.

The setting is immediately attractive – a low-lying watery site and embosomed in greenery. Our earliest detailed knowledge of the garden comes from a map of 1769 showing two pools in front of the house, with formal gardens on either side. The Ordnance Survey map of 1869 shows the lower pool transformed into a lawn, part of the formal gardens turned into a kitchen garden, and a new pool, probably for fish, to the south of the house.

The present layout of the garden follows the pattern of the past. Immediately to the north of the house a large sunken lawn, now called the Bowling Green, has a cascade flowing into two pools at its northern end. The water comes from an upper pool separated by a box hedge and a grass walk. Irregular in shape, its banks are planted with a mixture of natives such as bulrushes and yellow flag irises and with exotics such as *Darmera peltata*, *Kirengeshoma palmata* and rodgersias. The pool is fed by a stream flowing through a wooded valley with walks winding up each side. Here are some very old yews and a remarkable old sweet chestnut, and there are shrubs such as hydrangeas, philadelphus and rhododendrons among ash, cherry laurel, English oaks and rowans. Wooden bridges in a style you might call estate carpenter's Chinese Chippendale cross the stream, and the view of the half-timbered house, gradually revealed as you walk back down the valley, is enchanting.

Close to the house is a sketchy little parterre, with mounds of box and beds of *Salvia officinalis* 'Icterina' and lavender about a circular pool with a water jet emerging from mossy stones. Next to it, behind yew hedges, a jumbly kitchen garden has a tunnel of bent hazel wands on which are trained morning glory, runner beans and sweetpeas, with narrow beds

of herbs running along underneath. One side of the garden is a sea of ornamental herbaceous planting and the other has rows of vegetables. I is a charming but slightly idealised version of a cottage garden of the past.

To the west of the house lawns are enclosed by walls and by the Cottages, a range of decorative 15th-century timbered buildings. An unexpectedly grand stone urn on a plinth stands at the centre, with a herbaceous border along a south-facing wall. Concealed behind the south wall is a paved rectangular garden with a pool and a fountain of the boy with a dolphin. An urn stands on a raised platform backed by a screen of clipped yew, hydrangeas are underplanted with irises, and a mixed border runs along a wall.

The gardens at Ightham Mote are unpretentious and decorative but what is truly memorable about the place is the atmosphere of the setting of the ancient manor deeply concealed in its wooded valley.

Location Ivy Hatch, Sevenoaks TN15 0NT, Kent
OS TQ5853 6m E of Sevenoaks by A25 and minor roads
Tel 01732 810378 **Infoline** 01732 811145 **Fax** 01732 811029 **Email** ighthammote@ntrust.org.uk **Owner** The National Trust **Open** end Mar to Oct, daily except Tue and Sat 10–5.30 **Area** 14 acres/6 hectares

KENSINGTON GARDENS

THE GARDENS OF A 17TH-CENTURY
ROYAL PALACE, NOW A PUBLIC PARK WITH
AVENUES, POOLS AND MONUMENTS

Kensington Gardens is a large, delightful and historically complicated place, one of the most rewarding of all public parks to visit. William III bought Nottingham House here in 1689, had it rebuilt by the Office of Works under Sir Christopher Wren, and commissioned a grand garden designed by the royal gardeners, George London and Henry Wise. It was not until the 18th century that the house was known as Kensington Palace. As early as the reign of King George II (1727–60), under the influence of his queen, Caroline, parts of the gardens were open to the public and it became a fashionable place in which to be seen. From the reign of William

Kitchen garden borders at Ightham Mote

IV (1830–37) the gardens were open to the public all the year round and began to assume the character of a public amenity, with celebratory monuments of various kinds, sitting places, places of refreshment and so on. These developments continue but much of the historical framework remains clearly visible.

The best starting point for a tour of Kensington Gardens is the palace itself. It is handsomely bourgeois rather than royally palatial and the prettiest view of its brick façade with its parapet crowned with a fanfare of white urns is from the south, through fine 17th-century gilt and black wrought-iron gates. It was here, where there are now unadorned lawns, that London and Wise's garden lay below the south windows of the palace.

A FINE ORANGERY, ARCADIAN VIEWS
The best surviving garden building is the 1704 orangery just north of the palace, probably designed by Nicholas Hawksmoor in collaboration with Sir John Vanbrugh. Facing south, it is beautifully executed in two kinds of brick, one orangey-brown and the other pale London stock. Now a restaurant, it is worth visiting if only to admire the interior. A procession of giant dumpy columns of clipped bay or holly marches away from it and behind these are lawns and mop-headed thorns. Hidden away to the south, veiled by screens of pleached lime, is a sunken garden of 1909. You cannot enter it but through one of the several "windows" in the lime you can see a rectangular pool surrounded by terraced beds filled with bedding plants – cherry pie, cosmos, nicotiana and verbena. A curious sight, it is like a Hollywood set for some blurred vision of English garden history.

If you now walk east towards the Round Pond you will find yourself in part of the gardens which were laid out between 1726 and 1734 and which preserve to an astonishing degree their original layout. The Round Pond was part of that design and from it three avenues radiated to the east. The site is flat and it resembles parkland in some ancient estate, were it not that the trees are planted closer together and are more various, and the grass is mown rather than cropped by ancestral deer. It is a wonderful place for tree-spotting, especially as none is labelled. Here are fine specimens of

common and less common trees: beeches, horse chestnuts, limes, nothofagus, oaks, sweet chestnuts and, above all, London planes, of which there are several beautiful examples. The central walk eastwards from the Round Pond leads to G.F. Watts's huge bronze equestrian statue, Physical Energy, of 1907, which stands at the meeting place of six radiating vistas. The southernmost of these has one of the most beautiful eyecatchers in London: Sir George Gilbert Scott's Albert Memorial (1863–72), now magnificently restored. East of Physical Energy is one of those Arcadian views with which the London parks occasionally surprise. The land falls gently towards the glittering surface of the Long Water, on whose far bank a meadow rises slightly to a belt of trees (which also conceals a busy road, West Carriage Drive). It is an effect worthy of Capability Brown. Overlooking The Long Water on its western bank is one of the most delightful buildings – the Queen's Temple, with three arched openings crowned with pediments facing the water. This was built in 1734 and was possibly designed by William Kent.

The Long Water turns into the Serpentine after it passes to the south under the handsome Serpentine Bridge (1825–28 by George and John Rennie). This stretch of water, effectively dividing Kensington Gardens from Hyde Park to the east, was made as early as 1730 when several pools formed by the Westbourne Brook were linked to form a

The sunken garden in Kensington Gardens

single piece of water. To its north, alongside the Bayswater Road at Lancaster Gate, is an irresistibly entertaining piece of Victorian exuberance: the Italian Fountains. A water parterre with four pools and fountains is overlooked by an elegant arcaded *casino* with a tall central chimney – built as a pumping house to the design of Banks & Barry in 1861. The whole is decorated with urns and tubs of summer annuals and overlooked by William Calder-Marshall's posthumous bronze figure (1858) of a pensive Edward Jenner, the discoverer of vaccination. In 2002 a competition to design a memorial water feature to Diana, Princess of Wales, was won by Kathryn Gustafson – but the project was still uncertain in the autumn of 2002.

The landscape of Kensington Gardens is on the grand scale and is marked out by bold features – the Round Pond, the Long Water, radiating avenues and bold monuments such as Physical Energy and the Albert Memorial. Yet it is also rich in detail and in those agreeable nooks and crannies which give visitors such pleasure in public parks.

Location London W8 **OS** TQ2580 In central London between Bayswater Road (to the N) and Kensington Gore (to the S) **Tube** Queensway **English Heritage Register** Grade I **Owner** The Royal Parks **Open** daily dawn–dusk **Area** 275 acres/111 hectares

KENWOOD HOUSE

THE SERENE LANDSCAPE PARK OF AN
18TH-CENTURY HOUSE, ADORNED WITH
SCULPTURES BY BARBARA HEPWORTH
AND HENRY MOORE

The first house built at Kenwood dates from the early 17th century. It was rebuilt in around 1700 and subsequently acquired by John, 3rd Earl of Bute. Rocque's map of 1745 shows formal gardens south of the house, and the terrace formed here at this time has remained an important feature of the landscape. In 1754 the estate was sold to the 2nd Earl of Mansfield and remodelled between 1766 and 1774 for him by Robert and James Adam. The landscape was refashioned in a more informal style at this time, but although it is often claimed that Capability Brown had a hand in it there is no evidence to support this.

As part of the landscaping a sham bridge was built at the east end of the lake; a more recent version may still be seen today, painted white and standing out against the dark trees, crisply reflected in the water. In 1793 the 3rd Earl of Mansfield, having just inherited, called in Humphry Repton who produced a Red Book the same year. Repton recommended doing away with the sham bridge – "an object beneath the dignity of Kenwood". He wanted to open up views to the south so that a splendid panorama of London would be revealed, dominated by the dome of St Paul's. Not many of Repton's suggestions were adopted and even the grand view of London had been concealed by new

The sham bridge at Kenwood

growth when J.C. Loudon saw it in 1838.

The character of the landscape at Kenwood today is very much that of an 18th-century landscape park. The view from the south terrace shows lawns with groups and scattered individual trees sweeping down to the lake whose far banks are densely planted. On the far side of the lake is an open-air auditorium much used for summer musical events. A brick bridge crosses the water and paths lead through the woods – ash, beech, holly, beautiful English oaks and rowans – to emerge eventually on Hampstead Heath. Immediately west of the house is a large open lawn (an extension of the terrace) with a lime walk running along its south side. A border with shrubs forms the lawn's north boundary and paths lead through shrubberies with many rhododendrons to the west. This, in simplified form, is the sort of arrangement that Repton might have done. He, though, cannot be accused of placing Barbara Hepworth's sculpture, Monolith–Empyrean (1953), so that it is all but concealed by two rhododendrons. In the north-west corner of the park is a Henry Moore bronze, Two Piece Reclining Figure (1963–64), finely placed facing down the slopes but disfigured by ugly railings, presumably to protect it from vandalism.

Kenwood House and grounds are open free and thus immensely popular. The atmosphere, especially at weekends, is very lively and the park, peopled with visitors having a good time, seems to come into its own. The house has some of the finest 18th-century interiors in London and a superlative collection of paintings. The view of the park from any of the rooms on the south side of the house is delightful.

Location Hampstead Lane, London NW3 7JR **OS** TQ2787 5m NW of central London between Hampstead and Highgate **Tel** 020 8348 1286 **English Heritage Register** Grade II* **Owner** English Heritage **Open** Apr to Sept, daily 10–6 (Wed and Fri opens 10.30); Oct, daily 10–5 (Wed and Fri opens 10.30); Nov to Mar, daily 10–4 (Wed and Fri opens 10.30) **Area** 112 acres/45 hectares

Kenwood House from the lake

LEEDS CASTLE

A BEAUTIFUL LANDSCAPE, WITH A GARDEN
BY RUSSELL PAGE, SURROUNDS THIS
MEDIEVAL MOATED CASTLE

The view of Leeds Castle from the M20 is very beautiful – the pale stone battlemented buildings safely ringed in their moat and lying in a wooded hollow. The castle was started in the early middle ages and much altered, especially in the 19th century. Its medieval deer park, now with splendid sweet chestnuts and English oaks, still provides a marvellous setting for the castle.

Although Capability Brown did work at Leeds Priory nearby, which does not survive, there is nothing to suggest that he worked on the castle estate. An estate map of 1748 shows field boundaries and the deer park, with avenues of trees to the north and south of the castle of which no traces remain. The gardens that may be seen today date entirely from the 20th century.

In 1926 the estate was bought by Lady Baillie who called in Russell Page to advise on the landscape. He devised the Duckery at the entrance to the garden and flooded the valley

The Culpeper Garden at Leeds Castle

of the river Len to form a new lake south-east of the castle. On the slopes overlooking the lake to the north he designed the Culpeper Garden on the rather awkward site of the old kitchen garden, an irregular shape enclosed by brick walls on three sides but open to the south. This, designed in 1980 and thus one of Russell Page's last works, is pretty and appropriate but not, perhaps, representative of his best work. The area, shaped like a lopsided triangle, is divided into box-edged beds separated by paths of brick, stone or gravel. The beds are filled with substantial shrubs, in particular shrub roses, including such giants as *Rosa moyesii*, and underplanted with the full panoply of cottage-garden herbaceous perennials – day-lilies, delphiniums, geraniums, lupins, poppies and red-hot pokers. The garden also has two National Collections, of *Monarda* (44 species and cultivars) and of *Nepeta* (34 species and cultivars). Much of the planting has changed since Page's time; it is unlikely he would have liked a rose called 'Just Joey'. On the slope below the Culpeper Garden a new terraced garden on two levels has been made, to give views of the lake. This has bold mixed borders, arbours of vines and wisteria, viewing platforms and seats in alcoves. It is the sort of layout you would find only in a garden designed to be open to the public – for jolly

socialising rather than lonely communing with the landscape. But the landscape is worth noticing here – a splendidly Arcadian scene – 20th century but with 18th-century aplomb. Page's lake is sinuous in outline, with gently undulating land on the far bank and groups and copses of parkland trees.

A MAZE AND A GROTTO

At a little distance from the Culpeper Garden is a rare modern maze designed by Vernon Gibberd and Minotaur Designs. A horribly complicated pattern of yew hedges, with castle-like bastions in its outer walls, has at its centre, and goal, a magnificent grotto embellished with rocaille work by Diana Reynell and sculptures by Simon Verity. In the tradition of renaissance grottoes, the interior walls swarm with masks, curious animals, exotic stones and tropical shells. The cave-like gloom is pierced from time to time by light from skylights that glitter with shells. It is an enchanting tour-de-force.

Location nr Maidstone ME17 1PL, Kent **OS** TQ8353 5m E of Maidstone by A20 and B2163; Jnct 8 of M20 **Tel** 01622 765400 **Fax** 01622 735616 **English Heritage Register** Grade II* **Owner** Leeds Castle Foundation **Open** Mar to Oct, daily 10–5; Nov to Feb, daily 10–3 **Area** 500 acres/202 hectares

LEONARDSLEE GARDENS

IN A WOODED VALLEY, ONE OF THE
FINEST RHODODENDRON GARDENS,
CREATED BY THE LODER FAMILY

The woodland garden at Leonardslee was started by Sir Edmund Loder in 1889. The site is not only beautiful – a wooded valley of acid loam which descends to a sequence of lakes – but also perfect for the kind of gardening he wanted to do. Sir Edmund was a rhododendron enthusiast whose hybridising activities produced the highly scented and glamorous Loderi cultivars which became favourites for country house gardens during the rhododendron craze that lasted until World War II. The slopes of the valley are densely planted, opening out into occasional glades, with paths snaking along the contours. There is a vast collection of shrubs – with the great trio of camellias, magnolias and rhododendrons leading the way. Although most of the rhododendrons are cultivars the species are also well represented: *R. arboreum*, *R. campylocarpum*, *R. williamsianum* (an admirable plant for small gardens) and *R. thomsonii* among them. In addition there are many other shrubs: enkianthus, fothergilla, gaultheria, pieris, and the unusual *Symplocos paniculata* (with dazzling turquoise fruit). Excellent deciduous trees are to be seen everywhere – many maples (especially *Acer japonicum* and its cultivars), oaks, including the lovely Hungarian oak (*Quercus frainetto*), Chinese tulip trees (*Liriodendron chinense*), hickories such as the American pignut (*Carya glabra*), liquidambars and so on. Leonardslee was grievously hit by the 1987 storm but one of its effects was to clear congested old plantings of large trees, permitting light through to shrubs previously in the shade of the tree canopy; as a result old shrubs flower as never before.

For the visitor, Leonardslee is a fascinating place for a long garden walk. In May you will be one of thousands when the toothsome colours of the gaudier rhododendrons are doing their stuff. The enclosed rock garden, laid out *c*.1900 by Pulham & Company, has a large collection of the most brilliantly coloured Kurume azaleas intermingled with many dwarf conifers. Some garden lovers (myself included) find such displays too raucous for complete comfort, but there are so many outstanding plants elsewhere, and the lie of the land is so exceptionally attractive, that the garden always has plenty of other pleasures to offer. To my eye it is at least as beautiful in seasons when the rhododendrons are less visible.

Sir Edmund Loder also ornamented his estate with exotic animals; of these only charming wallabies remain, hopping agreeabl about and looking completely at home.

Location Lower Beeding, nr Horsham RH13 6PP, West Sussex **OS** TQ2226 4m SW of Handcross; bottom of M23 by B2110 (signed Cowfold) **Tel** 01403 891212 **Fax** 01403 891305 **English Heritage Register** Grade I **Owner** The Loder Family **Open** Apr to Oct, 9.30–6 (May, 9.30–8) **Area** 200 acres/81 hectares

View to the ponds at Leonardslee

LOSELEY PARK

FINELY REPLANTED GREAT WALLED
FLOWER GARDEN FOR A GRAND
ELIZABETHAN HOUSE

The house at Loseley is a grand mansion built in 1562 for Sir William More. It overlooks handsome parkland, with a small lake in the distance giving it an 18th-century air. Nothing is known of the early garden history at Loseley except that Gertrude Jekyll supplied plants early in the 20th century; the garden that is in place today, laid out in the walled former kitchen garden, was started as recently as 1993.

The walled garden, although it has a corner of vegetables and a large herb garden, is almost entirely ornamental. A long axial path links enclosures of different kinds. Bushes of *Viburnum plicatum* f. *tomentosum* 'Mariesii' mark the entrance to the Fountain Garden which is partly concealed behind clipped columns of yew. At its centre is a rectangular pool with a burbling fountain, surrounded by gravel paths and L-shaped beds with almost symmetrical plantings of plants with white flowers – arum lilies (*Zantedeschia aethiopica*), mounds of *Hebe pinguifolia*, bold clumps of *Hosta sieboldiana*, *Hydrangea arborescens* 'Annabelle' and white rugosa roses. Overlooking the pool is a white bench in a sea of white or cream chrysanthemums, white hydrangeas, plumes of *Macleaya cordata* and white verbascum. All this, without following any precisely Jekyllian scheme (she disapproved of totally monochrome planting), has a strongly Edwardian flavour.

On the other side of the central path a double palissade of crab-apples encloses a symmetrical pattern of beds edged in rope terracotta tiles. In high summer orange and yellow planting fills the beds – crocosmias, dahlias, daylilies, heleniums, potentillas – intermingled with sheaves of ornamental grass. At the centre a *Catalpa bignonioides* is underplanted with annuals, also in orange and yellow. On the other side of the central path is a giant herb parterre with gravel paths and a pattern of triangular beds filled with culinary, dyeing, medicinal or ornamental herbs. Tall bushes of bay, spheres of box and

The walled garden at Loseley Park

trees of mopheaded acacia (*Robinia pseudoacacia* 'Umbraculifera') punctuate the meeting places of paths.

OLD ROSES, A MYSTERIOUS TUNNEL
In a formal garden of old roses beds are edged in box and decorated with occasional monumental cubes or hemispheres of clipped box, mounds of santolina or columns of holly. At the centre is a metal rose arbour on a raised brick plinth with a huge Tuscan terracotta swagged pot. Running along the wall nearby is a tunnel of clematis and purple grapevines, where each metal upright emerges from a pillow of *Hebe pinguifolia*. Between the tunnel and the wall is a bed filled with shrub roses – on a hot summer's day the shady tunnel is suffused with their scent. The wall, at right angles to the main entrance to the garden, is almost entirely covered in an immense old wisteria underplanted with hundreds of irises.

On the south side of the walled garden is a steep bank pierced by a mysterious tunnel. This leads, on the far side of the wall, to a moat running the whole length of the garden, with simple herbaceous borders and grass paths on either side.

The walled garden at Loseley is not of startling originality but it is skilfully planted and excellently maintained. Who knows

what sort of ornamental garden, if any, was here in Tudor times? But this decorative, flowery garden with strong underlying formality is not far from the spirit of 16th-century English gardening.

Location nr Guildford GU3 1HS, Surrey **OS** SU9747 3m SW of Guildford by A3 and B3000 **Tel** 01483 304440 **Fax** 01483 302036 **Email** enquiries@loseley-park.com **Owner** Mr Michael More-Molyneux **Open** May to Sept, Wed to Sun and Bank Hol Mon 11–5 **Area** 6½ acres/2.6 hectares

MUSEUM OF GARDEN HISTORY

A RARE MUSEUM, HOUSED IN A
REDUNDANT CHURCH, WITH A PRETTY,
FORMAL GARDEN

The Museum of Garden history is housed in the parish church of Lambeth. St Mary's became redundant in 1972 and was taken over by the Tradescant Trust in 1979. The churchyard has a special horticultural connection for it contains the sarcophagus of John Tradescant the elder (c.1570–1638) and his son, John the younger (1608–62). Both Tradescants were learned plantsmen and both became royal gardeners under Charles I. John the elder worked for the Cecil family, in particular at Hatfield. Both Tradescants introduced new plants and John the younger made three visits to Virginia which resulted in many plant introductions. The Tradescants lived on the east side of what is now South Lambeth Road and their tomb, behind the church, is magnificently carved with shells, a crocodile, trees, a skull, a many-headed dragon, ruins, obelisks and classical buildings on distant shores – reflecting the wide breadth of their interests. Between them, they built up an extraordinary collection of curiosities of all kinds, which after their death formed the basis of the Ashmolean Museum in Oxford. Another tomb of slightly more remote garden interest is that of John Sealy, close to the porch of the church. Sealy was in partnership with Eleanor Coade whose Coade stone garden ornaments, made in Lambeth from the second half of the 18th century, were found in countless notable gardens.

The Tradescant Trust laid out a garden about the Tradescant tomb. A box knot is filled with plants they would have known – betony (*Stachys officinalis*), campanulas, foxgloves, fritillaries, hellebores, violas and, naturally, *Tradescantia virginiana* from the new world. Not all the plants are old – the rose 'De Rescht', for example, is almost certainly 20th century. About the walls are shrub roses, a bower of jasmine, box topiary and substantial trees

Knot garden at the Museum of Garden History

– among them a medlar and a strawberry tree (*Arbutus unedo*). The small area is packed with plants and provides an agreeably leafy retreat.

The museum is housed in the church and displays a fine permanent collection of cloches, edging tiles, gnomes, horticultural society medals, pots, seed packets, tools, watering cans and other gardening artefacts. Temporary exhibitions illuminate many

aspects of garden history and design, and there is a programme of lectures and day courses. Understanding something of garden history adds immensely to the pleasure of visiting gardens and the museum does valuable work in stimulating an interest in this.

Location Lambeth Palace Road, London SE1 7LB **OS** TQ3079 In central London on the south bank of the Thames close to Lambeth Bridge **Tel** 020 7401 8865 **Fax** 020 7401 8869 **Email** info@museumgardenhistory.org **Website** www.museumgardenhistory.org **Owner** The Tradescant Trust **Open** Feb to mid Dec, daily 10.30–5 **Area** 1 acre/0.4 hectares

MYDDELTON HOUSE GARDENS

THE ESTATE OF A NOTABLE GARDENER AND WRITER, E.A. BOWLES, UNDERGOING SPLENDID RESTORATION

Edwin Augustus Bowles (1865–1954), one of the most attractive of plantsmen, gardeners and authors, lived at Myddelton House. He was descended, via his paternal grandmother, from a Huguenot family called Garnault. The Garnaults were majority shareholders in the New River Company, founded in 1613 to bring water to London and first managed by Sir Hugh Myddelton. Michael Garnault bought Myddelton House, then called Bowling Green House, in 1724.

The terrace garden at Myddleton House

The house was Elizabethan but was rebuilt as a smart late Georgian villa in 1818. When Henry Carrington Bowles inherited the estate in 1861, not wanting to be "Mr Bowles of Bowling Green House", he changed the name to Myddelton House.

BOWLES'S REMARKABLE PLANTS
E.A. Bowles started to garden at Myddelton House as a child and continued until his death. He introduced many new features in the garden and built up a remarkable collection of plants, several of them new cultivars bearing his name and still much-loved today – plants such as *Erysimum* 'Bowles' Mauve' (and 'Purple' and 'Yellow'), and *Viola* 'Bowles' Black'. After his death the estate was bought jointly by the Royal Free Hospital School of Medicine and the School of Pharmacy which used the kitchen garden to grow medicinal plants. In 1969 the Lee Valley Regional Park Authority bought the estate and in 1984 a programme of restoration was started.

Bowles's presence is strongly felt in the garden today. The house overlooks a terrace on the edge of a small lake and tender plants stand on the terrace steps as they did in the past. In Bowles's day a channel of the New River flowed through the garden forming a curved boundary to the south, but this was filled in in 1969 and is now lawned over. Many plants, however, survive from his time. A group of *Viburnum farreri* still fills the garden with winter scent – it was propagated from seed brought from China by Bowles's great friend, Reginald Farrer. An extraordinary old yew, said to survive from the Elizabethan garden, remains – but only because Bowles opposed the rerouting of the New River which would have meant its destruction. Bowles planted the gigantic wisteria which grows through it. A small formal rose garden – "pretty to look at and useful to cut from but nothing to boast of", as Bowles wrote – has a pattern of box-edged beds with shrub roses and at its centre a splendid ornament: the old Enfield market cross, made in 1826 and busily Gothic. The beautiful *Rosa bracteata*, exactly the kind of plant Bowles loved, is trained against it. The rock garden Bowles made, although almost submerged in overgrowth, is still full of bulbs, especially snowdrops, in which he took such delight. Naturalised communities of other bulbs – aconites, colchicums, crocus, cyclamen and daffodils – also flourish. A National Collection of award-winning bearded irises is kept here.

What has been achieved in restoring the garden at Myddelton House is wholly admirable but much remains to be done and it is a noble task. Bowles was an excellent gardener, rare plantsman and delightful writer. His books still delight and inform gardeners and the plant cultivars named after him continue to give pleasure. To restore the whole garden, and grow every plant that he cultivated would be more than an act of piety; it would inspire new generations of gardeners.

Location Bulls Cross, Enfield EN2 9HG, Greater London **OS** TQ3399 Off the A10 14m N of central London; Jnct 25 of M5 **Tel** 01992 702200 **Fax** 01992 702230 **Email** info@leevalleypark.org.uk **Website** www.leevalleypark.com **English Heritage Register** Grade II **Owner** Lee Valley Regional Park Authority **Open** Apr to Sept, Mon to Fri 10–4.30, Sun and Bank Hol Mon 12–4; Oct to Mar, Mon to Fri 10–3, Sun and Bank Hol Mon 12–4 **Area** 6 acres/2.5 hectares

NYMANS GARDEN

AN OUTSTANDING PLANT COLLECTION, WITH DAZZLING SUMMER BORDERS IN A WALLED GARDEN

The garden at Nymans was started in 1890 by Ludwig Messel who saw the potential of the acid loam and the protected site, but it was his son, Lieutenant-Colonel Leonard Messel, and his great head gardener, James Comber, who made the decisive contribution to Nymans. Colonel Messel's daughter Anne (who became Countess of Rosse) was also a notable gardener, at Birr Castle in Ireland (*see page 402*). Under Colonel Messel (he died in 1953) Nymans saw an immense influx of new plants, many of them coming from the plant-hunting expeditions of the 1930s. There was also much hybridising of plants and selections of cultivars, many of which proved outstandingly good – *Magnolia* × *loebneri* 'Leonard Messel', *Eucryphia* × *nymansensis*

Spring in the Wall garden at Nymans

'Nymansay', *Rhododendron* 'Anne Messel' and several others won the RHS Award of Merit.

The garden has a fine collection of plants but its greatest attraction is the subtle but effortless intermingling of formal and informal ingredients. The Wall Garden always seems to me to be the place that expresses most clearly the essence of the garden. This former orchard encloses a large area of irregular shape, roughly that of a stirrup. Two paths meet at right angles in the middle, and subsidiary paths amble away from them. Where the two main paths meet there is a fine pink marble Italian fountain and pool and four monumental yew topiaries: drums topped with open globes and intricately fashioned crowns, a masterpiece of the topiarist's art. The central path that runs roughly south-east–north-west is flanked by the Summer Borders, an introduction of Ludwig Messel's, by tradition influenced

Italian fountain at Nymans

by William Robinson. The borders are relatively narrow, with the plants graded from the smallest at the front to the largest at the back, forming precipitous slopes of flowers. The path, too, is relatively narrow (room for two abreast), so that you have the sensation of walking through a flowery ravine. The planting is almost entirely herbaceous – both perennials and tender bedding – with the occasional large shrub, such as *Buddleja davidii*, at the back. Substantial veils of such herbaceous perennials as *Eupatorium purpureum*, *Echinops ritro* or *Veronicastrum virginicum* form a backdrop to dazzling crimson or yellow dahlias, blushing cannas and a froth of pink cleomes, with a scattering of bedding pelargoniums, petunias and antirrhinums running along the front.

The rest of the Wall Garden has a much more sober but no less delightful planting of ornamental shrubs and small trees grown in grass filled with daffodils, wood anemones and lady's smock. Here eucryphias, several magnolias, the lovely *Styrax hemsleyanus*, the richly scented late summer-flowering *Clerodendrum trichotomum* and the Asiatic *Cornus kousa* form a miniature woodland garden.

The 1987 storm destroyed the Pinetum here, and throughout the garden eighty percent of the trees were lost, including 20 out of the 28 champion specimens. But the National Trust acted quickly to replant and many vigorous adolescent trees have taken their place. A spectacular pergola was another casualty but this too has been reinstated and is once again entwined with wisteria.

A rose garden to the north of the Wall Garden was started by Colonel Messel's wife, with contributions from the famous rosarian Ellen Willmott. Here is a fine collection of mostly old roses, in beds and trained over arches.

Location Handcross, nr Haywards Heath RH17 6EB, West Sussex **OS** TQ2629 7m NW of Haywards Heath by A272 and B2114 **Tel** 01444 400321/400777 **Fax** 01444 400253 **Email** nymans@ntrust.org.uk **Website** www.nationaltrust.org.uk/southern **English Heritage Register** Grade II* **Owner** The National Trust **Open** Mar to Oct, Wed to Sun (open Bank Hol Mon) 11–6 or sunset if earlier; Nov to Mar, Sat and Sun 11–4 **Area** 30 acres/12 hectares

PAINSHILL LANDSCAPE GARDEN

A GREAT 18TH-CENTURY LANDSCAPE PARK BROUGHT BRILLIANTLY BACK TO LIFE

One of the most welcome effects of the growing interest in garden history in the last thirty years of the 20th century has been the will, and public support, that allowed the restoration of places like Painshill. Few gardens were more deserving of salvation than this Elysian park in the heart of Surrey commuter land. The garden was made by the Hon. Charles Hamilton from 1738 until 1773 when he was forced to sell the estate for lack of money. Gardens of this sort decay quickly but the estate was well maintained, as early photographs show, until after World War II when it swiftly declined. Given the immense increase in population of this corner of Surrey, it is remarkable that it survived at all,

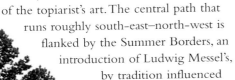

The ruined abbey at Painshill

but it did and a substantial part of Hamilton's park was acquired by the local authority in 1980. In 1981 the Painshill Park Trust embarked on a – triumphantly successful – quest to restore it to its 18th-century state.

At the heart of the park is the river Mole winding through a valley and, running parallel to the river, a long narrow serpentine lake studded with islands. The slopes and the banks of both river and lake are animated with ornamental buildings. Like other 18th-century landscape parks Painshill was conceived as a sequence of visual incidents, the buildings both ornamenting the landscape and marking vantage points from which to admire the scene. The buildings, while being generally romantic in character rather than severely classical, vary strongly in style. The Gothic Temple commands a special vantage point, on the slopes above the lake, but also looks west along the valley. This airy open "umbrello" (as such things were called in the 18th century) has Gothic openings and is crowned with battlements and soaring finials. Horace Walpole criticised it: "The Goths never built summerhouses or temples in a garden." On the bank of the lake the Ruined Abbey (c.1770) is built of brick but rendered to resemble stone and to have the appearance of a crumbling ecclesiastical ruin. An elegant Chinese bridge of white-painted wood links Grotto Island to the shore. Hamilton encrusted the island with limestone outcrops giving it the appearance of some volcanic excrescence, and created a labyrinthine grotto with openings onto water and gleaming crystalline walls which were kept wet by concealed pipes. It is cheerful and lighthearted with none of the stygian gloom of many grottoes. Rising on the grassy slopes far above it, with wonderful views back towards the lake and the Gothic Temple, is the Turkish Tent – blue and white, with golden plumes on its domed roof, folds drawn back to show the inviting interior, an enchanting sight. Much further, to the south-west, the Gothic Tower rises high among trees giving huge views across the land. Hamilton's Hermitage really was inhabited by a hermit, "But," as T. Smith wrote in 1845, "as the hermit had all the hardship, and Hamilton all the sentiment, the arrangement broke down."

The Turkish Tent

Hamilton, unusually among 18th-century landscapers, was a knowledgeable connoisseur of plants, taking a special interest in exotics from North America, which he obtained through Peter Collinson. Many of these have been replanted. Other gardens have been restored with impeccable historical accuracy but the miraculous charm of Painshill is that the result should so bristle with excitement.

Location Portsmouth Road, Cobham KT11 1JE, Surrey **OS** TQ0960 1m W of Cobham by A245 **Tel** 01932 868113 **Fax** 01932 868001 **English Heritage Register** Grade I **Owner** Painshill Park Trust **Open** Apr to Oct, daily except Mon (open Bank Hol Mon) 10.30–6; Nov to Mar, daily except Mon and Fri 11–4 or dusk if earlier **Area** 158 acres/64 hectares

PARHAM HOUSE

DELIGHTFUL WALLED GARDENS FILLED WITH FLOWERS IN A HISTORIC SETTING

Parham House was built in 1577 on the site of a fortified manor house. A park surrounding the house was enclosed from common land by 1643 and fallow deer still graze here. The entrance drive necessarily crosses the park and many beautiful old oaks are to be seen. Few early parts of the garden survive; of these the 18th-century lake, called the Pleasure Pond, north-west of the house and the old kitchen garden are the most prominent. The garden we see today was made almost entirely in the 20th century, after the estate was bought by the Hon. Clive Pearson in 1922.

The decorative heart of the garden is a very large walled garden north of the house, enclosed in brick and stone before 1778. Formerly a kitchen garden, it is now largely given over to ornamental purposes. Lanning Roper designed a white border along the west wall and in 1982 Peter Coats worked on borders that form the east-west central division of the garden – predominantly blue at one end and gold at the other, where a pretty dovecote, visible beyond the garden wall, acts as an eyecatcher. The north-south central walk of the walled garden starts at its southern end with a grand pair of wrought-iron gates flanked by stone lions and draped with *Vitis coignetiae*; to the north, built against the garden wall, is a pedimented summerhouse. Smaller enclosed gardens lead off the southern part: a herb garden behind yew hedges with a pool and a fountain of a boy with a dolphin; a rectangular garden with mixed borders and many roses, the beds edged in small-leafed myrtle (*Myrtus communis* subsp. *tarentina*); and a mysterious space in which a white marble figure of a naked man sprawls on a lawn in the shade of a cherry tree. One of the most attractive parts of the walled garden is the north-west quarter in which a series of large rectilinear beds are edged in sturdy box hedges. These are filled with delightful planting – one is brimming with pumpkins, another has only asparagus, another has wigwams of runner beans underplanted with rows of French beans, another has red Swiss chard, sweet corn, parsnips and a scattering of brilliant dwarf phlox, and another has only rhubarb underplanted with strawberries.

In the walled garden at Parham

Outside the west wall of the kitchen garden is part of the 18th-century pleasure grounds. A mixed border runs the whole length of the wall, with substantial bushes of buddleia and shrub roses underplanted with ferns, geraniums, hellebores, hostas, Solomon's seal and thalictrums. Against the centre of the wall is a magnificent lead figure of a river god reclining on a grand rusticated plinth fringed with ferns, hostas and superb clumps of *Actaea simplex* 'Prichard's Giant', a plant much used in the garden. Nearby is a maze of brick paths set into a lawn with an elaborately interlocking pattern designed by Minotaur Designs in 1991. (The pattern was taken from a piece of 17th-century embroidery in the house.) The lawn, with good beeches, English oaks and a large London plane, sweeps down towards a balustrade at the head of the Pleasure Pond. On the bank is Cannock House, an elegant stone 18th-century summerhouse from whose

Colour-themed borders at Parham

windows are views across the water to a cricket pitch and its pavilion.

The gabled house at Parham is imposing and its setting is on a generous scale. In its detail, however, it gives an attractive feeling of domestic intimacy. The charming little Wendy House built into the north-west corner of the walled garden by Clive Pearson for his three daughters in 1928 is typical of the friendliness of the place.

Location Pulborough RH20 4HS, West Sussex
OS TQ0514 4m S of Pulborough by A283
Tel 01903 744888   **Fax** 01903 746557
Email enquiries@parhaminsussex.co.uk   **Website** www.parhaminsussex.co.uk   **English Heritage Register** Grade II*   **Owner** Parham Park Trust   **Open** Apr to Oct, Wed, Thur, Sun and Bank Hol Mon 12–6   **Area** 11 acres/4 hectares

PASHLEY MANOR

LIVELY MODERN GARDENS WITH GOOD
PLANTING SURROUND A FINE OLD HOUSE

The house has two façades, completely different but both equally attractive: the entrance front, to the north, is early 17th-century with timbering and gables, whereas the garden front is urbane early Georgian brick with a parapet crowned with urns. The house takes its name from the Passele or Passelewe family, prominent in these parts from the middle ages. Nothing is known of a garden here before the Sellicks bought the estate and, with the help of the garden designer Anthony du Gard Pasley, gave the garden its present form.

South of the house the ground slopes down and has been formed into a series of terraces and enclosures. A swimming pool has been deftly introduced into the first enclosure, with lavish Mediterranean planting of cistus, ceanothus, rosemary and *Teucrium fruticans*. From here a pair of handsome gate piers crowned with urns lead down to a large area enclosed in brick walls, which must once have been the kitchen garden. A grass walk with box hedges and espaliered fruit on each side now divides the space into two compartments, and narrow beds below the espaliers are brilliant with tulips in spring and roses in summer. On one side is a kitchen garden and glasshouse; on the other,

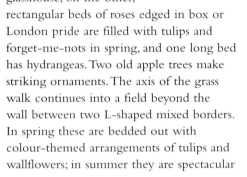

The island rotunda at Pashley

rectangular beds of roses edged in box or London pride are filled with tulips and forget-me-nots in spring, and one long bed has hydrangeas. Two old apple trees make striking ornaments. The axis of the grass walk continues into a field beyond the wall between two L-shaped mixed borders. In spring these are bedded out with colour-themed arrangements of tulips and wallflowers; in summer they are spectacular

with exotic plantings of cannas, dahlias and other "subtropical" delights. Beyond the borders are beautiful views southwards over a ha-ha and across a field to distant woodland. South-west of the house, below the Georgian façade, is a garden of different character. The house itself is draped with huge swags of Banksian rose and wisteria, and smooth-shaven lawns flow down to a curving miniature lake with a wooded island and pillared rotunda. A high-arched metal bridge with pretty wrought-iron railings connects the island to the land. A cascade flows into a spacious lower pool with a water jet, and trees and shrubs crowd about the lawn.

Location nr Ticehurst TN5 7HE, East Sussex **OS** TQ7029 1½m SE of Ticehurst by B2099 **Tel** 01580 200888 **Fax** 01580 200102 **Email** pashleymanor@email.msn.com **Owner** Mr and Mrs James S. Sellick **Open** Apr to Sept, Tue to Thur, Sat and Bank Hol Mon 11–5; Oct, Mon to Fri 10–4 **Area** 8 acres/3 hectares

Spring at Pashley Manor

PENSHURST PLACE

SUPERB WALLED FORMAL GARDENS WITH GOOD 20TH-CENTURY PLANTING FOR A GREAT MEDIEVAL HOUSE

House, garden and parkland setting at Penshurst form a rare group – the battlemented medieval stone house overlooking one of the largest walled gardens in the country. The essential layout of the gardens has not changed since Kip's engraving in John Harris's *History of Kent* (1719) and was in all likelihood established well before that. The parkland, to the north of the walled garden, is even more ancient, having its origins in a medieval deer park. The Sidney Oak, close to a lake in the park, is thought to date from the middle ages.

During the 18th century the walled garden was neglected and was thoroughly restored by the architect George Devey in the 1850s. Although two late 20th-century garden designers, Lanning Roper and John Codrington, executed planting plans for the firm old structure of paths and enclosures, the garden's atmosphere is resolutely untouched by any hint of modishness. In fact, in this area of 10 acres/4 hectares, an astonishing range of garden styles is happily linked together. This includes a vast parterre of the union jack, picked out in brilliantly coloured roses and lavender – not a scheme for the unconfident.

A GRAND PARTERRE AND BORDERS Immediately south of the house is the Italian Garden, a grand parterre of regal simplicity. Enclosed in yew hedges with rounded castellations, the area is sunken and divided into four parts about a central pool with a statue and water jets. Shapes of lawn, box-edged beds of pink roses and blocks of clipped box surround it. The whole is overlooked on two sides by a raised terrace. To the east double mixed borders, designed by Lanning Roper with easy charm, include purple-leafed *Cotinus coggygria* and roses underplanted with *Alchemilla mollis* and lamb's lugs. Another pair of borders forms a cross axis and beyond it John Codrington designed an enclosure of magnolias. Then comes a change of mood and one of the best parts of the garden: an orchard

Rose borders at Penshurst Place

of apples, planted in long grass in neat rows and with close-mown paths through the grass, and a nut garden of different varieties of Kentish cobs. The east-west axis starts beside the nut garden – a path of shaven grass between regularly spaced mounds of clipped golden yew against hedges of plain yew.

The site of the walled garden is as flat as a pancake so that the great house or the spire of the village church repeatedly appear at the end of a vista or are visible over a hedge. Apart from that, the garden is entirely inward-looking, but its richly patterned enclosures and deft switches of atmosphere entirely make up for any lack of distant views.

Location Penshurst, nr Tonbridge TN11 8DG, Kent **OS** TQ5344 In Penshurst village, 5m W of Tonbridge by B2176 **Tel** 01892 870307 **Fax** 01892 870866 **Email** penshurst@pavilion.co.uk **English Heritage Register** Grade I **Owner** Viscount De L'Isle **Open** Mar, Sat and Sun 11–6; Apr to Oct, daily 11–6 **Area** 10 acres/4 hectares

PETWORTH HOUSE

CAPABILITY BROWN'S MOST BEAUTIFUL PARK, WITH EXCEPTIONAL TREES

The estate of Petworth is very ancient – there has been a house here since at least 1309 when the Percy family was granted a licence to crenellate an existing manor house. The present house was built after a Percy heiress married the 6th Duke of Somerset in 1682. The pale stone house is long, low and extremely distinguished, with a decidedly French flavour to it. No-one knows who the architect was but the west façade, looking over the park, manages simultaneously to be very simple and immensely grand.

The park is the work of Capability Brown and is the first Brown park I ever noticed for its beauty. I still remember looking out of a window of the Marble Hall and seeing three women in hats (this was in the 1960s) sitting on a bench just outside the window, chatting earnestly. Beyond them was the vast panorama of Brown's park with its suave undulations and scatterings of groups of trees. The land dips down to a lake, shaped like an enormous swollen foot, and beyond it the deer park continues, with distant prospects of the downs sweeping away.

Although the pleasure grounds close to the house are attractive, and also partly designed by Brown, it is the park with the house that is the truly exceptional thing at Petworth. To enjoy this fully, go to the car park on the edge of the town, which gives direct access to the park. You are now at some distance from the house and from here you must walk down among trees towards the Lower Pond, a secondary lake close to the boundary of the park. As the ground slopes upwards you pause from time to time to marvel at some stupendous old sweet chestnut or English oak. At the top of the slope a hillock is crowned with ancient sweet chestnuts and below you is one of the loveliest landscape views you will ever see: the house to your left with an immense lawn running down to Brown's great lake, the Upper Pond, whose far banks are veiled in trees. You should then walk round the lake to see the endlessly varied prospects conjured out of simple ingredients: trees, grass, the lie of the land, water and the shifting horizon.

Brown worked at Petworth in the 1750s when he was in his thirties, still a relative novice. Earlier in the century George London had laid out a formal garden enclosed in walls and railings under the western windows of the house, and had provided the existing Elizabethan pleasure grounds north of the house, with formal groves and walks. Brown removed the garden to the west and made the pleasure grounds less formal. He left many of the straight walks, built a ha-ha on the western edge where it overlooked the park, and planted a wide range of ornamental shrubs. A bill dated 1753 from the nurseryman John Williamson lists cherries, jasmines, Portugal laurels, roses ('Rosa Mundi', 'Maiden's Blush', 'York and Lancaster') and tamarisks. Historically, Brown's work here is of great interest for it explodes two of the most cherished myths: that he always destroyed formal gardens that interfered with his grand plans and that he had no interest in flowering plants.

The pleasure grounds survive today in much reduced form but they still have the Doric and Ionic temples that Brown placed here in the 1750s. If you have come to visit the pleasure grounds you must also enter the house – which is very beautiful and full of treasures. Turner came to paint at Petworth and there is a room of his paintings, including two views of the lake bathed in the fiery light of sunset. And you, too, may study the beautiful park from the windows of the Marble Hall, as I did some forty years ago.

Location Petworth GU28 0AE, West Sussex **OS** SU9721 In Petworth village 16m E of Petersfield by A272 **Tel** 01798 342207 **Infoline** 01798 343929 **Fax** 01798 342963 **Email** petworth@ntrust.org.uk **Website** www.nationaltrust.org.uk/southern **English Heritage Register** Grade I **Owner** The National Trust **Open** (pleasure grounds) Apr to Oct, daily Sat to Wed (open Good Fri and Fri in Jul and Aug) 12–6 (Jul, Aug and Bank Hol 11–6); (park) daily 8–sunset **Area** 700 acres/283 hectares

POLESDEN LACEY

SMART REGENCY HOUSE IN AN EXQUISITE POSITION WITH DELIGHTFUL WALLED GARDENS

The owner of Polesden Lacey in its Edwardian heyday was a noted political hostess, Mrs Ronald Greville. You may still see displayed in the house, which has a delightful interior, her notes on guests (their taste in food and drink, who disliked whom, and so forth) and plans showing their placing at the dinner table. The garden seems all of a piece with this world, for its decorative appearance and soothing atmosphere would divert and defuse while providing plenty of nooks and crannies where intrigues might be pursued.

The estate occupies a fine hilly position, with a stately avenue of limes leading up towards the house. There had been a garden here in the 18th century but the gardens today were almost entirely created for Mrs Greville after she came here in 1906. She turned part of the walled former kitchen garden west of the house into a rose garden, quartered by paths which meet at a splendid Venetian wellhead in the centre. The roses today are almost entirely Hybrid Teas, Hybrid Musks and Floribundas, disposed in box-edged beds or trained on a wooden pergola and filling the garden with delicious scent throughout the summer. Some of the roses ('Hugh Dickson', 'Dorothy Perkins', 'Excelsa') are varieties which Mrs Greville could have known, and impart an authentic Edwardian luxuriance. The borders lining the walls are filled with bergenias, hardy geraniums, many fuchsias and some fine species lilies.

MRS GREVILLE'S FLOWER GARDEN
Beyond the rose garden is a series of yew-hedged enclosures with a parterre containing an especially attractive collections of irises. Mrs Greville was keen on irises and the National Trust inherited her collection of old cultivars of bearded irises which they have propagated and added to, making a splendid display. Here, too, is an arrangement of beds containing different cultivars of lavender, one with an astrolabe at its centre, and another with three bronze mice mysteriously poking their noses above the foliage. The south wall here is especially attractive, its brick and flint richly encrusted with lichen and moss, and the occasional circular window giving views out.

On the south side of the walls that enclose the former kitchen garden is an admirable herbaceous border which runs its whole length – over 400ft/120m long. Punctuated by statuesque clumps of *Yucca gloriosa*, it is full of border favourites – asters, echinops, geraniums, helianthemums, rudbeckia, sages, sidalcea and verbascums. These are enlivened by less common plants such as the tender *Hedychium densiflorum*,

Capability Brown's lake at Petworth

The walled garden at Polesden Lacey

Amsonia orientalis (with star-shaped pale violet flowers), the lovely ghostly *Galtonia candicans*, and several excellent cultivars of crocosmia and penstemon.

South of the house a terrace with a griffon and urns is edged by a vast lawn which swoops downwards to a low yew hedge. Beyond it the ground falls away precipitously with, on the far side of the valley, pasture, parkland trees and dense woodland – a panorama of wonderful beauty. The rose garden is pretty but this grand view is breathtaking.

The valley view at Polesden Lacey

Location nr Dorking RH5 6BD, Surrey **OS** TQ1352
5m NW of Dorking by A246 **Tel** 01372 452048
Infoline 01372 458203 **Fax** 01372 452023
Email polesdenlacey@ntrust.org.uk **Website**
www.nationaltrust.org.uk/southern **English Heritage**
Register Grade II* **Owner** The National Trust **Open**
Apr to Oct, daily 11–6 **Area** 30 acres/12 hectares

PORT LYMPNE GARDENS

AVANT-GARDE TERRACED GARDENS AND FINE ORNAMENTS FOR AN EDWARDIAN MANSION

Port Lympne is probably most famous for John Aspinall's great collection of animals whose strange barks, cries, whoops, yelps and growls form an essential part of the atmosphere of the place, even if all your attention is on the garden. It is the animals that certainly draw the greatest number of visitors to Port Lympne but the garden is both unusual and outstandingly attractive. The house, on a magnificent site looking over Romney Marsh, was built for Sir Philip Sassoon to the designs of Sir Herbert Baker and Ernest Willmott, in what they called Cape Dutch style, just before World War I. When John Aspinall bought the estate in 1973 he

restored the gardens with the help of Russell Page and founded his zoo here.

The entrance to the house is by a vertiginous flight of steps flanked by stone terraces and hedges of yew. It leads down to a courtyard with a square pool and yew hedges embellished with statues bought in the Stowe sale of 1921. A long lime walk runs west on an axis from the front door, ending in a splendid statue (also originally at Stowe) of George II by John Michael Rysbrack. Parallel to the lime walk, at a lower level, an avenue of *Magnolia grandiflora* starts at the head of a pair of mixed borders designed in 1974 by Russell Page.

To the south of the house the ground slopes down sharply, and here the architect Philip Tilden laid out terraced gardens for Sir Philip Sassoon – Russell Page in his *The Education of a Gardener* (1962) called them "a cataract of gardens". The top terrace, paved in stone and decorated with lead urns, is flanked by stone gazebos with wrought-iron balustrades, shady with clematis, hydrangea and wisteria. At the centre of the top terrace a grand triple flight of steps embraces a goldfish pool and is shrouded with callistemons, *Campsis radicans* and wisteria. On the terrace below, a plain large square pool with a water jet stands at the centre of a lawn. The lawn is hedged in castellated yew and behind this on each side is a remarkable piece of Art Deco garden design,

visible only from the gazebos above: one side has stripes of orange or yellow marigolds edged in electrifying blue lobelia, and the other has a chequerboard of alternate squares of turf and red or white begonias.

VINES, FIGS AND ORNAMENT

From the centre of the pool lawn steps lead down between terraced gardens of completely different character – a vineyard on one side and a garden of figs on the other. A final double flight of steps is made of beautifully laid bricks, with steps and paths in herringbone or basket weave, and wrought-iron balustrading with roses, thistles and fleur-de-lis, designed by Philip Tilden and made by Bembridge Reynolds of Chelsea. The steps sweep round to embrace at the lower level a shady summerhouse, exactly like the *sala terrena* of a renaissance garden, with magnificently vaulted interior and a domed niche wonderfully worked in brick – a virtuoso performance. On this final terrace is a slightly perfunctory rose garden; further gardens which lay on either side have been turfed over.

To understand Port Lympne it is essential also to see the interior of the house. Apart from the exquisitely worked hall floor of dizzying patterns of black and white marble and the more recent jungly murals commissioned by John Aspinall, there is also a "Moorish patio" designed by Philip Tilden. The patio, of the palest pink stucco, has a pool, arcades, rills and glazed green roof tiles – another slice of exoticism to add to this most eclectic of gardens.

Art Deco chequerboard at Port Lympne

Location Lympne, Hythe CR21 4PD, Kent **OS** TR1034 3m W of Hythe by A20 **Tel** 01303 264647 **Infoline** 0891 800 605 **Fax** 01303 264944 **Email** hpl.estates@dial.pipex.com **English Heritage Register** Grade II* **Owner** The Aspinall Family **Open** daily 10–5 **Area** 15 acres/6 hectares

REGENT'S PARK

EARLY 19TH-CENTURY PARK WITH A LAKE, EXUBERANT ROSE GARDENS, FINE TREES AND A SPLENDID VICTORIAN ORNAMENTAL WALK

The great beauty of The Regent's Park (to give it its correct name) is the harmonious blending of an outstanding public park with enlightened town planning. The ensemble is one of the finest, and most delightful, of its kind. The Regent in question was George Prince of Wales who acted as Prince Regent during his father King George III's descent into madness in the last years of his reign (1811–20), and then succeeded him as George IV.

The land here had become part of the royal estate under King Henry VIII, when it was known as Marylebone Park. Under the Prince Regent the architect John Nash was asked to draw up a new plan for the area, which he did in 1811. The essential idea was to build 50 secluded rural villas in the park and terraces about its perimeter. The park would be linked with the north-south development of Portland Place so that it would be on the same axis as Broad Walk which runs right across the park to its northern boundary. It had been the Prince Regent's hope that this axis could begin with a grand avenue starting at his residence, Carlton House, on the northern edge of St James's Park, but this proved impossible. The original density of building in Nash's plan was later reduced – what is now Queen Mary's Garden in the centre of the Inner Circle was to have been a central circus of terraced houses; instead, it became the Royal Botanic Society's garden in 1839. To the west of this a boating lake, with an island, was laid out, giving this part of the park the air of a miniature 18th-century landscape garden, and from 1845 the public was admitted to the park on two days each week. The most important later developments were that of the Avenue Gardens at the southern end of Broad Walk, which were designed by W.A. Nesfield and his son Markham in 1863 "at the wish of the Prince Consort", and in the 1930s Queen Mary's Garden (named after King George V's queen).

NESFIELD'S AVENUE GARDENS

To gain the best impression of Nash's grand idea visitors should approach Regent's Park from the south. From Regent's Park tube you emerge on Nash's Park Crescent (rebuilt 1963–65) from where you cross Marylebone Road and the Outer Circle and enter the gardens. Nesfield's Avenue Gardens were splendidly restored in 1994 and give a dazzling impression of Victorian ornamental gardens at their most exuberant: a lime avenue separates two parallel walks filled with a feast of ornament – scalloped box hedges swerving round columns of clipped holm oak (*Quercus ilex*), ribbons of pale grey santolina enclosing blocks of glowing orange begonias, elaborate stone fountains and pools, vast stone urns brimming with bedding plants – all executed with brio.

Queen Mary's Garden practises a style of rose gardening rarely seen today. Large beds are devoted to a single cultivar (usually of perpetual flowering Hybrid Teas) and climbers are trained on swagged ropes linked by trellis-work towers. Frequent dead-heading and even more frequent spraying keep the roses in full

◁ **The Triton Fountain** in Regent's Park

Central Mosque (1972–78 by Sir Frederick Gibberd).

Regent's Park has fine trees in Queen Mary's Garden and on the banks of the Boating Lake as well as elsewhere; some of these go back to the original 19th-century plantings. Dedicated tree-spotters will track down *Tetradium daniellii*, an elegant, tender and very rare tree from China, close to the Rose Garden café. Lastly, a non-horticultural but important part of the park is the London Zoological Gardens at the northern end of Broad Walk, part of the original design for the park and laid out in 1824 by Decimus Burton. The exotic snorts and roars and the mysterious harrumphs that come from the zoo are a distinctive part of the atmosphere of this corner of the park.

Location London NW1 **OS** TQ2882 N of central London **Tubes** Baker Street (S side), Regent's Park (SE side) and Camden Town (N side) **English Heritage Register** Grade I **Owner** The Royal Parks **Open** daily 7–midnight **Area** 487 acres/197 hectares

THE ROOF GARDENS

RARE 1930s FORMAL ROOF GARDENS FILLED WITH PLANTS, FLAMINGOS AND INVENTIVE ORNAMENT

Nos 101–11 Kensington High Street were built in 1929–31 for the department store Derry & Toms in refined Beaux-Arts style by Bernard George. A little later, in 1937–78, an astonishing roof garden was added. Designed by Ralph Hancock, it covered an area of 1½ acres/0.6 hectares and embraced a wide range of horticultural styles. A garden of Moorish influence has an arcade with barley-sugar columns, an olive tree and a shady cobbled patio overhung with flowering cherries. A tall *campanile* is roofed with thick Roman tiles, and a narrow rill opens out into little circular pools with a bubbling fountain a the centre of each. Another patio has low wall faced with glazed tiles and a feast of foliage rising above – Chusan palms, fatsia, cordyline and New Zealand flax. An enfilade of outdoor rooms, linked with decorative stone arches, is paved with squares of stone, cobbles or finely

flower deep into the autumn. A duck pond is shrouded in weeping willows and a wisteria-clad arched bridge leads to an island ("Access may be restricted during the waterfowl nesting season") with a rock garden showing touches of Japanesery. Even more waterfowl are found on Nash's Boating Lake to the west of Queen Mary's Garden. The lake is ingeniously planned, with long fingers of

water spanned by bridges.

Great private houses like The Holme on the east bank (designed in 1816–18 by Nash's collaborator, Decimus Burton) and Winfield House to the west (the residence of the US Ambassador) preserve the character of country seats. To the south, on the edge of the park, is the unexpected and delightful prospect of the golden dome and minaret of the London

laid brick in herringbone pattern. A "Tudor" garden of Gothic elaboration has dividing walls inset with stone tracery and hung about with thick curtains of climbers – *Ampelopsis glandulosa* var. *brevipedunculata*, grapevines, summer jasmine, *Trachelospermum jasminoides* and wisteria. A narrow path runs past a pool of pink flamingos, shaded by *Ailanthus altissima*, weeping willow and bamboos. The flamingos seem always to be there when I visit and immediately start posing. Best of all they often stand on one leg, head tucked under one wing, looking for all the world like fancy 17th-century tulips.

Pink flamingos in the Roof Garden

On the south side a woodland garden with a winding stream is planted with surprisingly large trees – horse chestnuts, English oaks, a fine *Koelreuteria paniculata* and maples. Most of the roof garden is given over to a restaurant and club and in summer it is busy with parasols and tables and chairs. But it is still an extraordinary example of an ambitious and successful roof garden – a rare place to visit.

Location 99 Kensington High Street, London W8 5ED **OS** TQ2579 W of central London **Tube** High Street Kensington **Tel** 020 7937 7994 **Fax** 020 7938 5197 **English Heritage Register** Grade II **Owner** The Virgin Group **Open** daily 9–5 (but telephone first as sometimes closed for private functions) **Area** 1½ acres /0.6 hectares

ROYAL BOTANIC GARDENS KEW

A GREAT BOTANIC GARDEN AND ONE OF THE MOST ATTRACTIVE GARDENS IN THE WORLD

Some botanic gardens are bigger than Kew, several older, but none combines such beauty of landscape, such a fascinating history and such a profound influence on the world of plants. Its setting on the Thames is the single fact that starts its history, for it began as part of the string of distinguished houses and gardens that took advantage of the setting on the banks of the river. Alexander Pope, who lived nearby at Twickenham, believed that "No scenes of paradise, no happy bowers, are equal to those on the banks of the Thames."

The history of the development of the landscape at Kew is complicated, but essential to an understanding of what it is today. In the early 17th century James I had taken a house as a hunting lodge close to the river in what is now the Old Deer Park (with a golf course) south of Kew Gardens. His son-in-law William III embellished this house with a garden by George London. In 1707 it was leased to the Duke of Ormonde (who named it Ormonde Lodge) but he, as a Jacobite, was forced to sell after the unsuccessful rebellion of 1715. In 1718 it was taken by the Prince and Princess of Wales, later George II and Queen Caroline, renamed Richmond Lodge and rebuilt by William Kent. The Princess, born Caroline Brandenberg–Anspach, had been brought up at the Charlottenburg Palace near Berlin with its great Le Nôtre-style Baroque garden. She took a great interest in gardens and commissioned Charles Bridgeman to lay out a new garden for Richmond Lodge, which was being made by 1725. By 1729 she had expanded her estate at Kew to 400 acres/162 hectares; it ran north along the Thames, to include the Dutch House (now Kew Palace) and houses on Kew Green – a much larger area than that which the Royal Botanic Gardens occupy today.

In 1678 John Evelyn had visited his friend Sir Henry Capel at Kew, where "his garden has the choicest fruit of any plantation in England." Capel's house, later called the White House, was leased in 1731 to George II's son

Frederick Prince of Wales who added to the garden "many curious & forain trees and exotics". White House, which was demolished in 1802, stood on a site close to Kew Palace. With both the King and Queen and the Prince of Wales now owning houses at Kew, it became a favourite haunt of the entire royal family. The Prince married another passionate gardener, Princess Augusta of Saxe-Gotha, but died young, in 1751, of pleurisy caught when soaked in a sudden rainstorm while supervising his gardeners. The Princess continued her garden-making activities, introducing plants and commissioning a series of beautiful garden buildings from William Chambers. Five buildings remain of the twenty-five that Chambers built for the Dowager Princess between 1757 and 1763 – an orangery (1757), the Temple of Arethusa (1758), the Temple of Bellona (1760), the memorably atmospheric Ruined Arch (1759–60) and, most spectacularly, the ravishing Chinoiserie Pagoda (1761), 163ft/49m high, finely built of London brick and embellished with Chippendale-style railings on each storey. Nothing remains, alas, of the formal flower garden which Chambers also designed.

THE MAKERS OF KEW

In the 1760s Capability Brown, now the royal gardener at Hampton Court, was called in to landscape the grounds of Richmond Lodge, which he ruthlessly did, destroying all traces of the formal garden and its ornamental buildings (including William Kent's Merlin's Cave). All that remains of Brown's work today is what is known as the Rhododendron Dell close to the river and the lake which lies north of the Temperate House.

When Princess Augusta died in 1772, George III took over her house as a rural retreat, living here with his family, in the words of Fanny Burney, "as the simplest country gentlefolk". Soon there came onto the scene one of the greatest figures associated with Kew: Sir Joseph Banks. He became an intimate of the king and from 1773 started to transform Princess Augusta's magpie collection of plants into one of consequence. In 1769 *Hortus Kewensis* lists 3,400 species in cultivation, and in the single year of 1773 nearly 800 species of trees were planted in the grounds. Banks became, in effect, the first director of Kew, and was responsible for an astonishing series of plant-collecting expeditions – to Australasia, the Azores, the Canary Islands, China, north Africa, South Africa, India and the West Indies.

In 1802 the boundary between the Kew and Richmond Lodge gardens was removed, uniting the estate. By 1826 Prince Pückler-Muskau was able to write, "Kew… unquestionably possesses the most complete collection of exotic plants in Europe." In 1841 the gardens were transferred from royal ownership to that of the state and Sir William Hooker was appointed director. Under Sir William and his son Joseph, who succeeded him as director in 1865 (retiring in 1885), the gardens expanded immensely. Kew's role in the dissemination of plants throughout the world was of great economic importance – rubber plants from Brazil, for example, were brought to Kew and shipped to Malaya, and tea plants taken from China to India. Between 1844 and 1848 the Palm House was built, designed by Richard Turner and Decimus Burton. W.A. Nesfield was responsible for designing the landscape about it – both the ornate parterres and the brilliant *patte d'oie* of three vistas radiating out from the Palm House, of which two – south-west to Chambers's Pagoda and north-west to Syon View – are still powerful ingredients of the landscape. Decimus Burton, starting in 1859, also built the

The Pagoda at Kew

striking but much less elegant Temperate House. In the 20th century many new buildings were added. The Princess of Wales conservatory, with its several different environments, was designed by Gordon Wilson and opened in 1987; it is built close to the site of Princess Augusta's "Great Stove" where she cultivated tender exotics.

A POWERFUL SENSE OF PLACE

The Royal Botanic Gardens at Kew have grown in size in the 20th century, especially with the tenancy in 1965 of Wakehurst Place in Surrey as its country outpost. Kew's role in plant conservation has become central to its activities but it is also now, in the early 21st century, the most diversely attractive

botanic garden in the world, as well as one of the most popular, attracting nearly 1,000,000 annual visitors – far more, until the advent of the Eden Project, than any other paid-access garden in the British Isles.

What are the reasons for visiting Kew? First, it is an exceptionally beautiful landscape. For the most part boringly flat, the site had no especial natural beauties apart from its riverine setting. The great buildings – Chambers's enchanting Pagoda and his suave Conservatory, Decimus Burton's sublime Palm House, and the smaller ornamental buildings – animate clearings, make alluring eyecatchers or simply create a powerful sense of place. Some are quite odd, like the temple-like pavilion dedicated to the worship of Marianne North, filled – and filled is the word – with almost 900 of her claustrophobic botanical paintings. Second, as a place to enjoy plants Kew is immensely satisfying. You can wander in a trance, making the occasional pilgrimage to some superlative tree – the mighty chestnut-leafed oak (*Quercus castaneifolia*) near the Waterlily House, for example. Planted in 1846, it is now over 100ft/30m high, with a trunk well over 6ft/1.8m in diameter – far bigger than any other example of this species in the British Isles and marvellously beautiful. Or, you can make a beeline for one of the glasshouses. The alpine house is the best in Britain, with small plants, often bulbous and frequently rare,

The Palm House at Kew

displayed like precious jewels with all the care of a window display in Bond Street. At the height of alpine activity, in March, say, the display is cosseted daily so that a constant state of flawless perfection is maintained, with new plants wheeled in to replace laggards as soon as they begin to droop. The other glasshouses, sheltering a vast range of non-hardy plants, are also a never-ending source of pleasure and instruction, while passages of woodland, rich in trees and shrubs, are often underplanted with the loveliest herbaceous plants – erythroniums, lilies and trilliums. The order beds, too, are rich in plants that will both excite and instruct gardeners – a wonderful range of species peonies, for example. But pleasing visitors, which it does superbly, is not the chief purpose of Kew; it remains one of the busiest and most productive institutes of botanical research in the world.

Location Kew, Richmond TW9 3AB, Greater London **OS** TQ1876 7m SW of central London **Tube** Kew Gardens **Tel** 020 8940 1171 **Fax** 020 8332 5197 **English Heritage Register** Grade I **Owner** Trustees of the Royal Botanic Gardens **Open** daily 9.30–4 (summer weekdays 9.30–6.30, Sun and Bank Hol Mon in midsummer 9.30–7.30) **Area** 300 acres/121 hectares

THE ROYAL PAVILION

IRRESISTIBLE REGENCY PLEASURE DOME WITH A RESTORED PERIOD GARDEN

The garden front at Brighton Pavilion

Love drew the Prince of Wales to Brighton, not for the town itself but rather for the charms of Mrs Fitzherbert whom he secretly married in 1785 and wanted to establish in a *nid d'amour*. He had a farmhouse rebuilt by Henry Holland and in 1805 asked Humphry Repton to advise on laying out the gardens. The Prince was so taken with Repton's ideas that he also asked him to transform Holland's neatly classical house into an exotic pavilion. In 1806 Repton produced a Red Book of suggestions for both pavilion – an extravagant Indianist fantasy – and gardens, but his proposals were not adopted by the Prince who proved to be the most elusive of clients. Instead, Repton's former partner, John Nash, was asked to do the job. Between 1815 and 1822 Nash devised and built the present bizarre and delightful confection of onion domes, minarets and verandahs tricked out in styles ranging from Islamic and Indian to Gothic, with a glittering Chinoiserie interior. Nash also laid out the gardens, which are shown in paintings made in 1822 by Augustus Pugin and were illustrated in Nash's *Views of the Royal Pavilion* published in 1826.

In 1982 a programme of complete restoration of the Royal Pavilion started. By then nothing was left of Nash's garden but this has now been reinstated following his plans and other contemporary illustrations and using plants which were available in the early 19th century. Nash's design was very much of its period: an informal flowery style of planting, with winding walks, sinuous shrubberies, and specimen trees planted in lawns in the "gardenesque" style made popular by J.C. Loudon. The perimeter walk east of the Pavilion shows this in action – a curving walk of such shrubs as bay laurel, box, *Cotinus coggygria*, Guelder rose (*Viburnum opulus*) holly, myrtle and yew is underplanted with asarum, foxgloves and geraniums, while north of the Pavilion an open lawn has specimen trees and, to the west, underneath what had been the Prince's private appartment, four curving shrubberies have a similar style of planting but with more seasonal flowers – annuals, bulbs, perennials and biennials such as hollyhocks. The paths are edged with green painted iron hoop fencing, and copies of Regency street-lights have been installed. The grass of the lawns is cut long to imitate the effect of the verges of woodland. I'm not certain whether the clouds of rosebay willowherb are also part of authentic Regency garden style.

The Royal Pavilion garden, which is open all the time without charge, is very popular and thronged with young (or would-be young) people sprawling on the grass, reading on benches, eating sandwiches, busking and generally hanging out. This causes much wear and tear and it is scene more in keeping with a public park than with the garden of a royal house. But passages of the garden, with the irresistible Royal Pavilion rising behind, do evoke its authentic past.

Location Brighton BN1 1EE, East Sussex **OS** TQ3104 In the centre of Brighton **Tel** 01273 290900 **Fax** 01273 292871 **Website** www.royalpavilion.brighton.co.uk **English Heritage Register** Grade II **Owner** Brighton and Hove Council **Open** daily dawn–dusk **Area** 8 acres/3.3 hectares

ST JAMES'S PARK

ONE OF THE MOST ATTRACTIVE OF LONDON PARKS, WITH LOVELY LAKESIDE VIEWS

Of all the London parks, St James's is one of the most alluring. It is on a relatively small scale yet it achieves remarkably big effects without sacrificing its delicious air of intimacy. Perhaps this last is the explanation for the belief that certain benches in the park serve as places of assignation for recruiting spies for delicate jobs with MI5. It is certainly full of civil servants at lunchtime but they seem to be doing nothing more nefarious than peacefully nibbling their sandwiches or reading their newspapers.

St James's is packed with history, with three royal palaces or their remains on its periphery: St James's Palace, Whitehall Palace (of which Inigo Jones's Banqueting House alone survives) and Buckingham Palace. King Henry VIII drained the site in about 1530 to create a deer park for the newly built St James's Palace. After the Restoration, King Charles II had grandiose plans for a new palace in Whitehall looking westwards over a redesigned St James's Park. During his exile in France the King had developed a taste for the new style of formal French garden, and after the Restoration a spectacular layout for the park was designed, probably by André Mollet, in which three

avenues radiated from a semicircle of trees, th central one with a long canal, while to the north was the Mall, a quadruple avenue to whose shade *paille maille* (a primitive form of croquet) was transferred from Pall Mall. The palace was never built but the garden was, an it became an immediate fashionable success. I 1665 John Evelyn admired the collection of rare animals and birds, especially the pelicans ("a fowle between a Storke and a Swan; a melancholy waterfowl brought from Astracan by the Russian ambassador") and in July of the following year Samuel Pepys "lay down upon the grass by the canalle and slept awhile". Most of this formality disappeared in John Nash's romantic reworking of the park i 1828–29, in which the crisp canal was turned into a fine naturalistic lake with wooded islands – a delightful piece of landscaping in the new taste.

COMPOSED VIEWS OF EXOTIC TOWER For the full St James's Park experience I recommend the approach from St James's Street. At its southern end you cross Pall Mall and walk between Marlborough House and St James's Palace with the Mall ahead of you and the wrought-iron entrance gates of St James's Park on the far side. Once in the park, a path leads straight ahead, with the

The lake in St James's Park

possibility of brass-band music from the bandstand on your left, and you soon find yourself on a bridge spanning the lake. To the east and west are wonderfully composed landscape views: to the west, across the water, with weeping willows bending their branches to the surface, lie Buckingham Palace and the Victoria Memorial, framed in trees – a grand country-house scene in the middle of London; to the east is the more urban but no less memorable sight of William Kent's Horse Guards, with immediately behind it the curiously exotic towers, domes and pinnacles of Whitehall Court. At the eastern end of the lake a plume of water erupts from the surface and by Duck Island is the rustic Birdkeeper's Cottage with its own tidy garden of herbaceous perennials. The lake is still rich in waterfowl, and pelicans thrive. The park is densely planted with trees, providing many secret enclosures which make the occasional long views over the lake all the more exhilarating. Nothing ugly can be seen except, looming over the trees to the south, the concrete Home Office building. You need not be an illegal immigrant for it to chill the heart.

Location London SW1 **OS** TQ2979 In central London W of Whitehall, S of the Mall and E of Buckingham Palace **Tubes** St James's Park and Green Park **English Heritage Register** Grade I **Owner** The Royal Parks **Open** daily dawn–dusk **Area** 89 acres/36 hectares

SAVILL AND VALLEY GARDENS

MAGNIFICENT WOODLAND GARDENS WITH SUPERB TREES AND FLOWERING SHRUBS

This wild and beautiful place is adjacent to the populous areas of suburban Surrey and forms a wonderful ornament to it. The gardens lie at the southern end of Windsor Great Park, immediately north of the mid 18th-century man-made lake of Virginia Water, in its day the largest artificial lake in the country. The whole landscape here, which seems so venerable, was fashioned in the 18th century under the supervision of the Duke of Cumberland, reclaimed from bog and heath. Several lakes were formed to drain the land and countless trees were planted, in particular beech, elm, English oaks and sweet chestnut.

Autumn in the Savill Garden

The Savill Garden was started in 1932 when E.H. (later Sir Eric) Savill, who was then Deputy Surveyor at Windsor, began to develop what had been a small estate nursery of ¼ acre/0.1 hectares into a garden. It is rare that any garden is named after its creator. When George V and Queen Mary came to see it in 1934 the Queen said, "It's very nice, Mr Savill, but isn't it rather small?" Granted more land for the garden, Savill began to build up a collection of trees and shrubs in the protection of old beeches and oaks. Between the wars many great estates gave plants, especially rhododendrons – Sir John Ramsden at Bulstrode, the Earl of Stair at Castle Kennedy, Lionel de Rothschild at Exbury, and so on. Savill had an admirable eye for the arrangement of his treasures, which he disposed in glades and used to create long open vistas. He also loved the wilder parts and knew "when to leave well alone", which Gertrude Jekyll identified as the most important skill in woodland gardening.

I vividly remember the first time I went there in the late 1960s when there was a superb old stand of beeches, the ground underneath carpeted with moss. These trees, and many others, were destroyed in the 1987 storm. After World War II, Savill began to extend the garden into the very much larger Valley Garden (400 acres/162 hectares) to the south, running along the northern bank of Virginia Water. The site is very attractive, slightly undulating and sloping southwards towards the lake. Much clearing had to be done to form glades and rides, and drainage carried out. From the start it was decided to form large collections of particular groups of plants. Some of these have grown into National Collections, among them species rhododendrons (an astonishing collection of over 600 species), magnolias (over 30 species and an unbelievable number of over 320 cultivars), mahonias (27 species and 51 cultivars) and ferns (over 130 species and over 150 cultivars) – all of great interest to gardeners. Throughout the two gardens there is much underplanting – wood anemones and bluebells but also colchicums, epimediums, ferns, lilies, meconopsis and narcissi and, in moist places, astilbes, gunnera, lysichiton, Asiatic primulas and rheums. In the Savill Garden there are herbaceous borders and a rose garden but it is the great woodland gardens, with their astonishing collections of plants and subtly beautiful sites, that give the Savill and Valley Gardens their distinction.

Location Wick Lane, Englefield Green, nr Egham TW20 0HH, Surrey **OS** SU9770 3m W of Egham by A30 **Tel** 01753 847518 **Fax** 01753 847536 **English Heritage Register** Grade I **Owner** Crown Property **Open** Savill Garden, daily 10–6 (winter 10–4); Valley Garden, daily sunrise–sunset **Area** 435 acres/176 hectares

SCOTNEY CASTLE GARDEN

EARLY 19TH-CENTURY PICTURESQUE VALLEY GARDEN WITH EXCELLENT PLANTS

There are two castles at Scotney: Anthony Salvin's Jacobethan pile built between 1837 and 1844 for Edward Hussey, and in the valley below the wildly picturesque remains of the original moated medieval and Tudor fortified manor house. Picturesque is the right

word, for the landscape that links the two buildings is a last delightful fling of the picturesque landscape tradition. Fashionable gardens in Salvin's time were turning to elaborate formal arrangements, but at Scotney something much more original and surprising was made: the garden looked back to the late 18th century but simultaneously anticipated the wild gardening of William Robinson.

With the advice of William Sawrey Gilpin, Hussey positioned his new house on an eminence, with the quarried ground below forming a percipitous slope tumbling down towards the old castle. Parts of the 17th-

The quarry garden at Scotney

century addition to the old castle were pulled down to enhance its medieval appearance, making it an enchanting eyecatcher, rising splendidly above the boskage. The rocky slopes between the two castles were planted with exotic shrubs and ornamental trees among native beeches, English oaks, Scots pines and yews. Cedars of Lebanon, incense cedars (the upright American *Calocedrus decurrens*) and other exotic conifers provide evergreen presence among the deciduous trees, while magnolias, Japanese maples, rhododendrons especially azaleas) and *Kalmia latifolia* form xotic mounds among them. Brilliant with owers and new foliage in spring, the autumn olouring from maples, *Nyssa sylvatica, Parrotia ersica* and rhododendrons is a marvellous sight. ll this was severely damaged in the 1987 orm but much replanting has been done and e landscape remains dazzlingly attractive.

Close to the old castle are plantings of a ifferent kind. Here is a herb garden laid out y Lanning Roper, and the banks of the moat rovide a home for moisture-loving plants, mong them spectacular clumps of the fern *Osmunda regalis.* Tucked away on a little isthmus hich juts out into the lake-like extension of e moat is a bronze figure by Henry Moore, ooking quite at home in this wild setting.

ocation Lamberhurst, Tunbridge Wells TN3 8JN,
ent **OS** TQ6835 1m S of Lamberhurst by A21
el 01892 891081 **Fax** 01892 890110 **Email**
otneycastle@ntrust.org.uk **English Heritage Register**
rade I **Owner** The National Trust **Open** Mar, Sat and
un 12–4 (open Bank Hol Mon 12–6); Apr to Oct, Wed
o Fri 11–6, Sat and Sun 12–6 (open Bank Hol Mon
2–6) **Area** 19 acres/8 hectares

SCULPTURE AT GOODWOOD

OUTSTANDING WOODED SCULPTURE
PARK WITH MARVELLOUS WORKS BY
CONTEMPORARY ARTISTS

There has been a spectacular renaissance over the last ten years in the use of sculptures to ornament the landscape. Sculpture at Goodwood, founded in 1992 by Wilfred Cass, was one of the pioneers and has set the highest standards. It is in effect an outdoor dealer's gallery – virtually everything is for sale although some pieces remain in place for years (by no means necessarily the least attractive). Many of the best living British sculptors show their work here – among them, Anthony Caro, Tony Cragg, Andy Goldsworthy, Antony Gormley, Eduardo Paolozzi, William Pye and Bill Woodrow. Many of the pieces are made for a specific site in the garden and all are most skilfully placed – in glades, at the end of rides, under the trees or at the edge of woodland. The sculptures, especially the very large ones, are seen at their best in this setting – with plenty of room. In museums, or the usual dealer's galleries, there is often simply not enough space for their qualities to be revealed. Furthermore, a green background of plants, with occasional glimpses of the surrounding rural landscape, provide far more sympathetic surroundings than the sterile hard-edged buildings in which they are usually seen.

The setting of Sculpture at Goodwood is a youthful piece of woodland criss-crossed with rides and punctutated with clearings. The trees are mostly ash, beech, hawthorn, hazelnut and sycamore – planted sufficiently far apart to allow tantalising glimpses of distant sculptures. Furthermore, the long rides allow really large works to be displayed as dramatic eyecatchers in the landscape. In September 2002, for example, a ride behind the office of Sculpture at Goodwood ended in a gigantic female figure by Allen Jones: Temple (1998). Standing on a very tall plinth, 28ft/8m high, made of steel and partly surfaced in mosaic, she glowed in the leafy penumbra.

Sculpture by Almuth Tebbenhoff at Goodwood

The long southern boundary of the garden looks over open countryside of farms and pasture. Here, clearings in the wood provide beautiful spaces in which to display often huge exhibits, which make a piquant contrast to the domestic scenes of fields, hedgerows and grazing sheep. Sometimes the display areas are themselves beautiful. A sculpture by Almuth Tebbenhoff, In the Beginning (2002) – a stainless steel filgree sphere like a giant dandelion seedhead – was placed on the edge of such a clearing; next to it, a finely conceived great sunken turf circle was overlooked by a group of silver birches echoing the silvery sheen of the sculpture.

Utilitarian woodland is the chief background planting but there are other passages where attractive use is made of shrubs, trees and ground-cover planting. In 2002, Alex Hartley's Pavilion (2000) (a most mysterious building of modernist design through whose frosted windows you only glimpse a vague perspectival interior) stood at the centre of a clearing at the top of the garden edged with sweeping thickets of roughly shaped bushes of box, *Pittosporum tobira* and *Arbutus unedo* underplanted with sprawling *Rubus tricolor* or *R.* 'Betty Ashburner', *Cotoneaster horizontalis* or *C. dammeri*. Sheaves of pale green bamboos stand out against the dark ivy-clad beeches of the woodland. On the edge of the garden Stephen Cox's huge arrangement of granite shapes, Catamarans on a Granite Wave (1994), stands near a fine beech lavishly underplanted with butcher's broom, euphorbia, ferns, geraniums, periwinkle, pulmonaria, wild strawberries and wood grass. In the interior of the garden, beside a beautiful flint estate wall, John Davies's monumental Head (1997) is flanked by a grove of Judas trees (*Cercis siliquastrum*) on one side and rows of apple trees on the other.

Sculpture at Goodwood started with the purpose of displaying works of art, not making a

garden. In the event, as the sculptures elbowed their way in, the setting has been fashioned to create an extraordinary and attractive landscape. The strong sense of place is not derived merely from the exciting presence of the sculptures – their setting has become an exhibit too.

Location Goodwood, Chichester PO18 0QP, West Sussex **OS** SU8908 ½m NE of Chichester by A27 and minor roads; E of Goodwood House **Tel** 01243 771114 (recorded directions) 01243 538449 (enquiries) **Fax** 01243 531853 **Website** www.sculpture.org.uk **Owner** Wilfred and Jeanette Cass **Open** Mar to Nov, Thur to Sat 10.30–4.30 **Area** 20 acres/8 hectares

SHEFFIELD PARK GARDEN

DREAMLIKE LAKESIDE PLANTINGS – TREES, SHRUBS AND SPLENDID HERBACEOUS PERENNIALS

Water is such an important ingredient in the garden at Sheffield Park that it becomes an object of hypnotic fascination. This is in essence a woodland garden with 18th-century landscape antecedents. Both Capability Brown and Humphry Repton worked here for the Holroyd family, who became Earls of Sheffield. John Baker Holroyd bought the estate from Earl de la Warr in 1769 and commissioned James Wyatt to build him a spanking new mansion in the Gothic taste. Brown produced a plan in 1776 for "the alteration of the place particularly…the water and the ground about it". The water in question was the series of lakes in the valley below the house. Nothing is known in detail of what he did but a painting of 1787 by Samuel Grimm shows the banks of the First Lake free of planting and with turf running down to the water in Brownian fashion. Repton's work is even vaguer and it seems that he did not get on well with Lord

Sculpture by Eilis O'Connell at Goodwood

Sheffield. The appearance of the garden today is due to Arthur Gilstrap Soames who bought the estate in 1910 and embarked on a great programme of planting, especially of rhododendrons.

It is the planting crowding about the banks of the lakes, and the occasional clearings, that provide the most memorable scenes at Sheffield. Virginia Woolf, not generally interested in gardens, wrote in 1937 of the "rhododendrons…massed upon the banks and when the wind passes over the real flowers the water flowers shake and break into each other." Native silver birches, English oaks and Scots pines are intermingled with exotics – *Liquidambar styraciflua*, swamp cypresses (*Taxodium distichum*), Wellingtonias, maidenhair trees (*Gingko biloba*) and many others. They show striking contrasts of habit and foliage, often making dramatic companions for the array of smaller trees and shrubs for which they form a dazzling backdrop. A soaring swamp cypress, for example, is seen apparently

emerging from a billowing rounded clump of rhododendrons or the gracefully sprawling shape of a Japanese maple. In spring and early summer the splashes of colour from rhododendrons glow against sombre coniferous foliage. In autumn the explosion of leaf colour from azaleas, tupelos (*Nyssa sylvatica*), maples and scarlet oaks (*Quercus coccinea*) is a famous sight.

Leading away from the banks of the lakes into the richly planted hinterland are paths often fringed with lovely herbaceous planting - ferns, gentians, lilies, primulas and trilliums among the trees and shrubs. Here the mood is more intimate and the detail finer than in the broad brushstrokes and irrepressible flamboyance of the lakeside plantings. Here you can wander for a long time and wallow in the astonishing wealth of plants.

Location Uckfield TN22 3QX, East Sussex **OS** TQ4124 Midway between East Grinstead and Lewes off A275 **Tel** 01825 790231 **Fax** 01825 791264

The middle lake at Sheffield Park

Email sheffieldpark@ntrust.org.uk **English Heritage Register** Grade I **Owner** The National Trust **Open** Jan to Feb, Sat and Sun 10.30–4; Mar to Oct, daily except Mon (open Bank Hol Mon) 10.30–6 or dusk if earlier; Nov to 22 Dec, daily except Mon 10.30–4 **Area** 100 acres/40 hectares

SISSINGHURST CASTLE GARDEN

A FAMOUS 20TH-CENTURY GARDEN, STILL BEAUTIFULLY GARDENED AND LOVELY TO SEE

The garden at Sissinghurst, famous as it is, has become for many people more an idea, a myth, than reality. Yet a visit to the garden (especially when it is not overrun with visitors) remains a thrilling pleasure. The strength of the design, the beauty of the planting and the standards of practical gardening are all marvellous. It is true and regrettable that the unconventional life of the garden's makers, Harold Nicolson and Vita Sackville-West, is of more allure to some visitors than the beauty of the place. But none of this should draw attention from the Nicolsons' most remarkable achievement – the creation of a great garden.

BIRTH OF A GARDEN

They bought Sissinghurst in 1930 when it was a decaying if romantic ruin – "big, broken down and sodden", as Harold Nicolson recorded in his diary. One of the earliest photographs of Sissinghurst, taken in March 1931, shows Vita Sackville-West digging a new border by the castle tower – long before they were able to live in the crumbling buildings. They were not novices, for they had already made (with the help of Sir Edwin Lutyens) an excellent garden at their previous house, Long Barn, also in Kent, and were admirers of such gardeners as Lawrence Johnston at Hidcote Manor, Heather Muir at Kiftsgate Court and William Robinson at Gravetye Manor. At Sissinghurst they used the scattered buildings and old walls as the atmospheric framework for a garden of compartments embellished with an ever-growing collection of plants. Vita Sackville-West was an eternal experimenter – rediscovering the beauties of old shrub roses, for example, but also willing to experiment with a cheap packet of mixed annual seeds from Woolworths (a failure, as she candidly confessed in her journal). Her lively and discerning quest was recorded in the series of articles, "In Your Garden", which she wrote for the *Observer*. They remain among the most attractive and valuable garden journalism ever written.

The excitement of the garden comes from the contrasting identity of the planted enclosures separated by hedges or high walls and linked by paths, vistas or passages. In their harmonious progression the eye is often drawn by an eyecatcher, a distant gate or a fine plant; the strong framework is often blurred by planting and brilliant colour schemes soothed by an intervening cool corridor or mesmerising rondel of yew. The beauty of the famous White Garden comes

not from its colour scheme (best at night when public visitors cannot see it) but from the serene pattern of the box hedge parterre which has all the austere and harmonious simplicity of some Islamic patio. The Cottage Garden, below the building where Harold Nicolson and Vita Sackville-West had their bedrooms, is only a cottage garden by name for it deploys flamboyant reds, oranges and yellows chosen with aristocratic panache. Here, as almost everywhere in the garden, the planting has been altered since their time, but the spirit of the place is honoured. Newly fashionable grasses are to be seen but it is interesting to note that dahlias, a favourite of Harold Nicolson's, were used in the original scheme at a time when smart taste generally thought them vulgar. He and Vita Sackville-west are often thought of as snobs. In some ways, they were, but not in gardening. There is an independence of mind in what they did where a snob would be looking over his shoulder.

ZESTFUL SPIRIT

Much has been written of Sissinghurst and its owners but nothing can quite prepare the visitor for the impact of the garden itself. Although Vita Sackville-West died in 1962 and Harold Nicolson in 1968, their garden remains fresh and original. It is this that is perhaps the greatest testimonial to their gardening skills: they devised a style of gardening which allows change while preserving its essence. The admirable team of National Trust gardeners who now care for it so meticulously have added all sorts of plants unknown to Vita Sackville-West but have maintained her irrepressibly zestful spirit. Gardens can become famous for all sorts of reasons, not all of them worthy. In the end, it is hard to imagine any visitor to Sissinghurst failing to be moved by the beauty of the place.

Location Sissinghurst, nr Cranbook TN17 2AB, Kent **OS** TQ8038 2m NE of Cranbrook off A262 **Tel** 01580 710700 **Infoline** 01580 710701 **Fax** 01580 710702 **Email** sissinghurst@ntrust.org.uk **English Heritage Register** Grade I **Owner** The National Trust **Open** Apr to mid Oct, Tue to Fri 1–6.30, Sat, Sun and Good Fri 10–5.30 **Area** 10 acres/4 hectares

◁ **The cottage garden** at Sissinghurst

WAKEHURST PLACE

THE COUNTRY DEPARTMENT OF THE
ROYAL BOTANIC GARDEN AT KEW –
MAGNIFICENT TREES AND SHRUBS

The house at Wakehurst Place is the remains of a slightly truncated late Tudor mansion built for Sir Edward Culpeper. Nothing is known of an early garden and most of its horticultural interest dates from the acquisition of the estate by Gerald Loder (later Lord Wakehurst) in 1903 and its later incarnation, from 1965, as the country department of the Royal Botanic Gardens, Kew.

The site is beautiful, on the High Weald of Sussex, with a lively rise and fall of land. The interest lies in the very large collection of trees and shrubs displayed in an attractive and varied landscape. In this regard it owes most of its charm to nature; as a piece of landscape design it is not particularly interesting. The plants have been arranged, in the garden's own words, "into geographical areas with the concept of a walk through the temperate woodlands of the world". Plants are grouped in different ways – by genus (for example the collection of birch (*Betula*) species) or by broader classification (conifers); by region (a collection of trees from the American North Pacific Coast); by topography (the Himalayan Glade); by habitat (wetlands); or by season (the Winter Garden). The garden holds four comprehensive National Collections of woody plants – birches, hypericums, nothofagus and skimmias. Throughout the garden, apart from the trees, there is much smaller ornamental planting – huge numbers of bulbs, meconopsis, orchids, witch hazels, viburnums and much else. Close to the house a walled garden contains "cottage garden" plantings. But the main meal at Wakehurst, and the overwhelming reason for visiting it, is the tree collection. A long walk, on any day of the year, is a pleasure and is also the best possible way to learn about trees.

A recent development at Wakehurst is that of the Millennium Seed Bank, housed in a distinguished vaulted building, the Wellcome Trust Millennium Building, designed by the architects Stanton Williams. Raised beds in front of the building contain groups of plants from different British habitats and the slopes round about have been planted with trees and shrubs of the High Weald and with traditional meadow plants. A sculpture by Peter Randall-Page shows three seed-like stone spheres whose surfaces are intricately incised with swirling patterns.

Inside the building an exhibition explains how the seed bank operates and visitors may look through glass partitions into the laboratories with white-coated scientists going about their work. The seeds are prepared for

Mansion Pond at Wakehurst

freezing and stored in underground vaults – by 2010 it is expected that 24,000 different species will be stored here. All this reflects a fundamental change in the purpose of botanic gardens. In the past they were seen, to use a Victorian phrase, as "repositories of nature's marvels" and sources of information about plants; today they have the much more urgent task of conservation.

Location nr Ardingly, Haywards Heath RH17 6TN, West Sussex **OS** TQ3331 1½m NW of Ardingly on B2028 **Tel** 01444 894066 **Fax** 01444 894069 **Email** wakehurst@kew.org **Website** www.kew.org **English Heritage Register** Grade II* **Owner** The National Trust **Open** Feb and Oct, daily 10–5; Mar, 10–6; Apr to Sept, 10–7; Nov to Jan, 10–4 (closed 25 Dec and 1 Jan) **Area** 170 acres/69 hectares

WALMER CASTLE

TUDOR FORT WITH ENCHANTING
FLOWER GARDENS, KITCHEN GARDEN
AND WOODLAND WALK

Walmer Castle was built by Henry VIII in 1539 as a fort, one of a line of such buildings to protect the coast. The traveller Celia Fiennes came to see it in 1697 and noted that the "little fort…holds a few guns but I should think they would be of little effect and give the enemy no trouble." It became the official residence of the Lords Warden of the Cinque Ports and parts of the castle were converted to provide living accommodation in about 1730. It is only in the 18th century that any garden-making is recorded, when the castle governor had a small garden to the west of the moat. The former Prime Minister William Pitt became Lord Warden in 1792 and when William Wilberforce visited him in 1798 he noted that Pitt was "beautifying his place with great taste".

YEW HEDGES IN THE BROAD WALK
In the 1860s a local nurseryman, William Masters, carried out much work when Lord Granville was Lord Warden. He planted many trees, and most importantly for the present appearance of the garden, the splendid long Broad Walk west of the castle, with magnificent blowsy yew hedges backing a

The Queen Mother's Garden at Walmer

pair of deep herbaceous borders. He also planted a partly surviving avenue of holm oaks (*Quercus ilex*) running north-west of the castle, and much flower planting was done at this time, some of it in the characteristic formal style of the period such as "Ribbon Flower Borders and Standard Roses".

A photograph of the Broad Walk taken in 1919 shows the yew hedges in their crisply edged prime. Behind them today is an impeccable working kitchen garden of the old-fashioned kind, and terraces at the head of the walk have, first, a croquet lawn and then a semicircular rose garden (with beds of the rose 'The Queen Elizabeth'), bedding schemes and a curving beech hedge. A long woodland walk continues the axis of the borders, interrupted by a statue of Mercury, and runs across the Paddock with good trees – beech, flowering cherries, hawthorn, lime and English oak – in grass which in spring is dazzling with bulbs. At the top of the walk you may glimpse, but not visit, the Glen, a former chalk quarry made in around 1803 into a picturesque garden by Lady Hester Stanhope.

Most unusually in a historic, gently evolving garden of this kind, one of the most attractive

parts of it is an entirely new garden, commissioned in 1995 from Penelope Hobhouse to celebrate the 95th birthday of Queen Elizabeth the Queen Mother who was then the Lord Warden. In a walled garden south of the castle, previously turned over to tennis courts, Penelope Hobhouse made a formal garden of great simplicity and striking character. A rectangular central pool (95ft/30m long) finely edged in Caithness stone (from near the Queen Mother's Castle of Mey), is planted with waterlilies and flanked by rows of yew pyramids. A loggia-like pavilion designed by Sir Anthony Denny faces south down the pool, and at the other end of the pool is a splendid mount carpeted with ivy and topped with a castle of clipped yew; a ramp leads up to it so that you may admire the garden from its arcade. Below the mount a little box parterre is fashioned out of the letter E (for Elizabeth). Limes have been planted behind the mount to conceal the awkwardly angled end wall of the garden and an ugly house behind. Borders under the walls of the garden have repeated plantings of the round-headed thorn *Crataegus × lavallee* 'Carrierei', underplanted with *Lilium regale* and carpets of periwinkle. Along the paths on each side of the garden are rows of noble benches clasped in bowers of scented *Choisya ternata*, and rows of pots of *Cordyline australis* are underplanted with *Convolvulus sabatius*. More borders flank the pavilion and the ramp that leads to the mount, with much repetition of plants, the use of bold clumps of simple but effective herbaceous perennials (such as catmint), and skilful combinations such as the tall violet flowers of *Verbena bonariensis* intermingled with the fragile white flowers of the Californian poppy (*Romneya coulteri*). Penelope Hobhouse shows her skill in deftly weaving together a strong classical layout, irrepressibly ornamental planting, and historic and personal references.

Location Walmer, Deal CT14 7LJ, Kent **OS** TR3750 On the S edge of Walmer by A258; Jnct 13 of M20 **Tel** 01304 364288 **English Heritage Register** Grade II **Owner** English Heritage **Open** Mar, Wed to Sun 10–4; Apr to Sept, daily 10–6; Oct, daily 10–5; Nov to Dec, Wed to Sun 10–4 (closed 24–26 Dec) **Area** 38 acres/15 hectares

WEALD AND DOWNLAND OPEN AIR MUSEUM

AN OPEN AIR MUSEUM WHERE MANY
OF THE VERNACULAR HOUSES HAVE
CHARMING PERIOD GARDENS TO SUIT

It is usually only relatively grand gardens that survive from the past. In this enchanting open air museum a collection of historic vernacular buildings has been assembled in the fine setting of a wooded valley. Of different periods, they all come from the Weald and Downland area of Hampshire, Kent, Surrey and Sussex and have been painstakingly transported and reassembled to form a scattered rural village of great charm. Some of them are embellished with vernacular gardens of convincing authenticity. Little documentation and few pictures survive of these simple gardens of cottager or yeoman and this museum gives a vivid impression of what they must have been like.

The 15th-century Bayleaf Farmhouse is set in an elaborate and productive landscape. Protecting it is a distinctive Wealden feature, a "shaw", or broad strip of managed woodland used as a field boundary and planted with ash, field maple, oak, hawthorn and hazel — some of which are coppiced or pollarded. These shaws, common before the 18th century, are believed to be the remains of primeval woodland cleared for fields. In the protection of the shaw is an orchard, and in front of the house is a kitchen garden enclosed in a wattle fence. Here the beans, brassicas, herbs, leeks, onions, peas and salads of a medieval household are arranged in separate rectangular beds to allow a three-fold rotation of crops. All the plants are taken from the Fromond list of "Herbys necessary for a gardyn" of about 1525. A bed of such ornamental herbs as hyssop, lavender and sage is raised up and neatly edged with wattle.

Walderton Cottage was built from the 15th to the 17th century and has a garden of fruit, vegetables and herbs which would have been found in a garden of the early 17th century. It shows a greater variety than the earlier Bayleaf garden — including cardoons, endives, turnips, parsnips and winter greens. An area of orchard would have had bee skeps, a ram and possibly geese. It shows the kinds of ornamental plants of the time alongside the vegetables, among them lilies, marigolds, pinks, primroses and roses.

Poplar Cottage dates from the mid 17th century and shows a kitchen garden worked on the three-field rotation system, with one field being left uncultivated for part of the year and enriched with "nightsoil" from the privy. It is gardened as it would have been in the past: no pesticides are used, seed is preserved from year to year, and manure is added to the surface without cultivation.

A clapboard Toll Cottage dating from around 1807 has a narrow brick path, picket fence and beds dotted with hollyhocks, bachelor's buttons, lavender and roses in artless and charming profusion. A vegetable patch, a few herbs, a chicken house and a privy complete the domestic scene. Whittaker's Cottages are a pair of 1860 terraced houses with a communal outside water pump. A little front garden is a jumble of borage, geraniums and hollyhocks with a small vegetable plot.

The oldest house, Hangleton Cottage, is a 13th-century flint cottage of two rooms which scarcely has a garden at all, merely a tangle of herbs in a rough wattle enclosure. But it has the most beautiful view — looking across the valley of pastures, woodland and arable fields.

Location Singleton, Chichester PO18 0EU, West Sussex **OS** SU8712 6½ m N of Chichester by A286 **Tel** 01243 811348 **Fax** 01243 811475 **Owner** Weald and Downland Open Air Museum **Open** Mar to Oct, daily 10.30–4; Nov to Feb, Sat, Sun and Wed 10.30–4 **Area** 60 acres/24 hectares

Bayleaf Farmhouse garden

WEST DEAN GARDENS

A GREAT EDWARDIAN ESTATE WITH SUPERB
RESTORED KITCHEN GARDENS AND A GIANT
PERGOLA BY HAROLD PETO

The setting of West Dean, with the South Downs rising serenely north of the house, is marvellously beautiful. There are plenty of fine trees here to enrich the park-like setting. The flint-faced house, designed by James Wyatt and built in 1804 ("limp" says Pevsner), was greatly extended by George & Peto in 1893 (rather less limp according to Pevsner) for the American William James, a cousin of the novelist Henry James, who had bought the estate in 1891. Mrs James was a Dodge and the house and estate were run on the most opulent scale. The gardens are something of a jumble and no-one seems ever to have taken them in hand in order to introduce some sense of coherence and order. It is surprising that Harold Peto, who worked on both house and garden, should not have had more to say in the overall planning of the garden, and his own contribution to it is odd in

The apple store

The vegetable garden at West Dean

every way. He designed a giant pergola cutting across a lawn to the north of the house – interesting and certainly dramatic in itself but dissociated both in mood and position from the rest of the garden. At one end is a little pavilion, with a floor paved in flint and horse's teeth, and at the other end, at a slightly lower level, a pool and small formal garden. The pergola, which is 300ft/90m long, has been well restored in recent times and is handsomely garlanded with clematis, honeysuckle and roses, while borders running along it are filled with agapanthus, campanulas, daylilies, geraniums and lamiums.

Another distinguished garden designer who worked at West Dean was Gertrude Jekyll who was commissioned to make a wild water garden to the west of the house. Here she found a perfect site in the shallow valley of the river Lavant. This area was very badly damaged in both the 1987 and 1990 storms and has been restored in the tradition of William Robinson.

However, by far the most attractive, and noteworthy,

part of the garden today is the fully restored kitchen garden close to the entrance. In the great establishments of the Victorian and Edwardian periods a large kitchen garden was the engine room of the household, producing fruit, vegetables and cut flowers. There was also much competition to produce out-of-season or exotic fruit, as well as the earliest crops of fairly ephemeral crops, such as peas. The management of such a garden was complex and required great horticultural skills. At West Dean such a garden has been reinstated and is a wonderful sight. The 2½-acre/1-hectare space is divided into two chief enclosures with an area of glasshouses, cold frames, gardeners' bothy and potting sheds between them. The lower enclosure is devoted to fruit trees, planted in grass or espaliered about the walls. A splendid double herbaceous border runs across the garden with a decorative flint and brick Gothic apple store as an eyecatcher on one side. The glasshouses grow a prodigious range – aubergines, capsicums (including many hot chillies), cucumbers, figs, grapevines, melons and tomatoes. Tender ornamentals are also grown in profusion.

A BLAZE OF BORDERS

The upper part of the kitchen garden is largely given over to vegetables which are beautifully cared for; even the handwritten labels are things of beauty. Here, too, is a magnificent double border, planned to be at its peak at the garden's most productive period – a blaze of yellows and oranges in late summer, with crocosmias, dahlias and kniphofias.

It has become fashionable to restore old kitchen gardens in recent years. The standard established by West Dean is the one to emulate – the garden is lovely to look at, business-like and plainly immensely productive. Jim Buckland and Sarah Wain, and the other gardeners who work here, have created something that is worth going a long way to see.

Location West Dean, Chichester PO18 0QZ, West Sussex **OS** SU8612 6m N of Chichester by A286 **Tel** 01243 818210 **Fax** 01243 811342 **Email** westdean@pavilion.co.uk **English Heritage Register** Grade II* **Owner** The Edward James Foundation **Open** Mar to Oct, daily 11–5 **Area** 90 acres/36 hectares

WINKWORTH ARBORETUM

A NOTABLE TREE COLLECTION IN AN EXQUISITE WOODED VALLEY WITH LAKES

It is remarkable how much unspoilt and very beautiful countryside survives in the populous county of Surrey. Dr Wilfred Fox (1875–1962) who lived nearby at Winkworth Farm bought land here in 1937. What drew him to this place, as he said, was the existence of "a valley quite unspoiled, of pastoral and wooded character, patterned with hedgerows and abounding with wild flowers". The soil is rather thin but lime-free and suitable for growing a wide range of the trees and shrubs that Fox loved. The site is exceptionally handsome, with two lakes, Phillimore Lake and Rowe's Flash Lake, running north and south along the bottom of the valley. On the whole there is a minimal amount of design at Winkworth, with the exception of one or two set pieces such as Azalea Steps with great spreads of Kurume azaleas tumbling down a steep slope on either side of wooden steps. This, made in 1939, was originally called "The Adolf Hitler Glade" because it was constructed with the fortuitous help of evacuees.

One of the chief attractions of Winkworth is that it is a garden to explore for yourself. There is a map which indicates notable plant collections, or visual highpoints, but the chief pleasure is to be gained by walking in the woods and discovering all sorts of delights for yourself – such as the beautiful glade of Japanese maples among oaks half way along the west bank of Phillimore Lake. The view from a path along the top of the steep slope above Rowe's Flash Lake distils the essence of the place. You look down over a cascade of exotic trees and shrubs, with the water glittering below, and on the far side of the valley are panoramic views of unspoilt North Downs countryside – copses, rolling pasture and lavish hedgerows.

The background woodland planting is chiefly of ash, beech, holly, oak and sweet chestnut, with prodigious waves of bracken. The entrance to the garden is from its highest point and you soon find yourself gazing down into a chasm full of trees. Most of the planting is on the often steep slopes which run down to the west banks of the lakes, while meadows cover the slopes on the far side. Paths loop along the contours, with the occasional descent cutting straight across them. The banks of Rowe's Flash Lake are relatively unencumbered with planting, giving it more presence in the landscape. At one end is a rustic boathouse; normally open and equipped with tables and chairs, it looks like the setting for a rather highminded Victorian reading party. A derelict bathing hut nearby is equally austere. The banks of Phillimore Lake are much more densely planted, so that water is merely glimpsed gleaming among trunks and foliage, and a walk along the path which closely follows the banks will be enlivened by the squawks, scrambles and splashes of water fowl.

Dr Fox was especially interested in rowans, and a National Collection is held here, which includes the large-leafed hybrid *Sorbus* 'Wilfrid Fox'. Azaleas, eucryphias, hollies, magnolias, maples, rhododendrons and stewartias are also well represented. Dr Fox hoped to strike a balance between merely collecting, and ornamenting the landscape. He chose many plants for their autumn colour and made plantings for specific colour associations – for example, the pale bark of Himalayan birches

The valley at Winkworth in Autumn

rising among bluebells. An attractive oddity at the entrance to the garden is a plantation of sweet chestnuts, coppiced every three years and used for making walking sticks.

Location Hascombe Road, Godalming GU8 4AD, Surrey **OS** SU9941 2m SE of Godalming by B2130 **Tel** 01483 208477 **Fax** 01483 208252 **Email** winkwortharboretum@ntrust.org.uk **Owner** The National Trust **Open** end Mar to mid Nov, Wed to Sun (daily in bluebell season and for autumn colour); mid Nov to mid Dec and mid Jan to end Mar, Sat and Sun 11–5 or dusk if earlier **Area** 113 acres/46 hectares

WISLEY GARDEN

CONSTANTLY IMPROVING SHOW GARDEN, WHERE THE ROYAL HORTICULTURAL SOCIETY SHOWS THE PUBLIC HOW TO DO IT

The garden at Wisley was originally an experimental wild garden laid out from 1878 by G.F. Wilson, a friend of Gertrude Jekyll. It was given to the Royal Horticultural Society by Sir Thomas Hanbury in 1903 as "an Experimental Garden" for "the Encouragement and the Improvement of Scientific and Practical Horticulture in all its branches". Now, with around 750,000 visitors a year, it has become one of the most popular gardens in the country and a precious resource for gardeners as a place to learn about plants and to study the highest standards of practical horticulture. Sir Thomas Hanbury made no mention of aesthetics but gradually that has become important too.

A huge number of different activities goes on at Wisley, and the garden has to accommodate them all in as harmonious a manner as possible. There has never been an overall plan for the garden, which is stylistically heterogenous with entirely different styles of planting scattered hither and yon. There are, nonetheless, various strong axes which allow an easy flow of events.

The chief building is the Laboratory, a picturesque Arts and Crafts design of 1914 by Imrie and Angell. The formal gardens here were laid out by Sir Geoffrey Jellicoe and Lanning Roper in the 1960s. The Laboratory overlooks a fine large rectangular pool with a collection of waterlilies and, at its far end, a

handsome Arts and Crafts open loggia with two walled gardens behind it. One is used for sprightly bedding schemes and the other, with a central pool, intermingles hardy and less hardy plants. A second chief axis starts beyond the conifer lawn to the south. Here is a double mixed border hedged in hornbeam – one of the splendours of Wisley, a masterclass in one of the commonest garden features but perhaps the hardest to do really well. The borders gently climb a hill and on the far side of this is Portsmouth Field where a series of trial beds test different plants – ornamental and edible (sometimes both) – its rows of impeccable beds, packed with plants, a delightful sight.

NEW PLANTING

West of the double borders is one of the busiest and most rewarding parts of the garden. A "Country Garden", laid out in 1999 to Penelope Hobhouse's design, displays her hallmarks: the virtuoso use of plants allied to a crisply classical design. It covers an area of half an acre (0.2 hectares) and for anyone planning a small garden it makes an instructive model. Here too is a rose garden of Edwardian flavour – swagged ropes between pillars garlanded with roses and many standard roses. A collection of model gardens has a forlorn and jumbly air. A pair of monocot borders, filled with agapanthus, daylilies, kniphofias,

The Country Garden at Wisley

phormiums and yuccas, imparts a little botany and also looks splendid in high summer. Near it are two alpine houses – one with cliffs of tufa and one with plants neatly disposed in pots; both are wonderful, especially so in spring. A little distance from all this, rather arbitrarily placed and a trifle lost among the fruit fields, is a pair of borders designed in 2000 by Piet Oudolf, the doyen of ornamental naturalistic design. Very deep and curving, they are filled with alliums, echinaceas, eryngiums, liatris, monarda and sedums, with occasional airy puffs of ornamental grasses that lighten the glowing colours. Large swathes of many of the plants are used, there is much repetition, and the whole is, most unusually for borders, of a fairly uniform height.

A great rock garden lies behind the Jellicoe formal gardens. It was designed by Edward White in 1911 and built by James Pulham & Son, the great specialist in rock work. Now desperately unfashionable, rock gardens may still give much pleasure as an ingenious way of cultivating and displaying alpines – often tricky plants to please. Nearby is the Wild Garden, the oldest part of Wisley, going back to G.F. Wilson's Robinsonian plantings of the late 19th century. With trees and shrubs, and much lovely naturalistic planting, especially of bulbs, it is one of the most attractive parts of the garden. I still remember vividly an immense spread in March of the lovely hoop petticoat daffodil (*Narcissus bulbocodium*). North of all this, past the library and restaurant, is the Pinetum; started in 1909, it now boasts several champion trees. Beyond it, in Howard's Field, is a National Collection of heathers, over 1,000 species and cultivars. Wisley also holds National Collections of crocus, epimedium and snowdrops, and, most delightfully, of rhubarb, of which there are no less than 95 species and cultivars.

Quite apart from what the visitor sees, much else goes on at Wisley. There is a strong educational aspect: full-time professional courses in horticulture; amateur courses; an advisory service; practical demonstrations and an excellent library which all visitors may use. A plant centre sells a very wide range of high quality plants and the shop carries, among other things, the largest range of gardening books of any shop in Britain.

Location nr Ripley, Woking GU23 6QB, Surrey **OS** TQ0658 6m NE of Guildford by A3; Jnct 10 of M25 **Tel** 01483 224234 **Website** www.rhs.org.uk **English Heritage Register** Grade II* **Owner** The Royal Horticultural Society **Open** Mon to Fri 10–sunset; Sat 9–4.30 (Sun 9–4.30 for RHS members and their guests only) **Area** 240 acres/97 hectares

YALDING ORGANIC GARDENS

THE PRINCIPLES AND PRACTICE OF ORGANIC GARDENING DISPLAYED IN A LIVELY GARDEN

Yalding is the Kentish outpost of the Henry Doubleday Research Association which promotes organic gardening. The site is as flat as a pancake and whatever charms it possesses come from the design of the garden. At the centre of the garden, like a mandala, is a circular lawn surrounded by segmental beds; surrounded in turn by a circular pergola clothed in clematis, roses and wisteria and edged with hedges of golden euonymus. The rest of the garden is disposed harmoniously about this strong shape at the heart of the layout.

HISTORIC GARDENS

The underlying theme is, of course, organic gardening. but in addition there is a sequence of historical set pieces ranging from a 13th-century apothecary's garden to an allotment of the kind encouraged by the Ministry of Agriculture's "Dig for Victory" campaign in World War II. These give some notion of the periods they represent but vary considerably in quality. An Edwardian border "based on designs by Gertrude Jekyll", for example, requires much more detailed attention than is evident here. No doubt Gertrude Jekyll was sympathetic to the principles of organic

gardening (there was really no alternative in her day), but her style of gardening was labour intensive and depended on highly skilled labour at that. She also had an artist's eye for every detail of gardening and would certainly not have tolerated motor-car tyres as an aid to cultivating courgettes.

The most rewarding part of the garden is the range of displays showing organic gardening in action, which are excellently done. The control of pests and diseases, the making of compost, the cultivation of the soil and the management of the kitchen garden are all displayed informatively. Apart from the vigour of the plants grown, especially the vegetables, the most beautiful sight when I visited in the summer of 2002 was a field of spelt (a primitive form of wheat) with all the wildflowers associated with arable crops – corncockles, cornflowers, corn chamomile, corn marigold and field poppies – a delightful thing to see.

All gardeners, I suspect, would prefer to garden organically. Places like Yalding are valuable because they not only vividly impart the knowledge but also display the results.

Location Benover Road, Yalding, nr Maidstone ME18 6EX, Kent **OS** TQ6949 S of the village of Yalding, 5m SW of Maidstone on B2162 **Tel** and **Fax** 01622 814650 **Owner** Henry Doubleday Research Association **Open** May to Sept, Wed to Sun 10–5; Apr and Oct, Sat and Sun 10–5 (open Bank Hol Mon 10–5) **Area** 10 acres/4 hectares

The circular lawn at Yalding

WALES & WEST of ENGLAND

ABBEY DORE GARDEN

A PLANTSWOMAN'S RIVERSIDE GARDEN
PACKED WITH GOOD PLANTS

Some gardens build up their own momentum and may be satisfactorily maintained by an anonymous gardener, or even a committee, more or less for ever. Charis Ward's garden is emphatically not of that kind – her garden is a very personal expression of her own tastes and inclinations. She recently moved out of her previous house, Abbey Dore Court, built a new house in the grounds, kept some of her former garden and expanded vigorously into a field.

The shady banks of the river are colonised by ferns, hellebores, ligularias, persicaria and pulmonarias, with occasional substantial shrubs such as hydrangeas and mahonias among the alders and ashes. A humpbacked bridge crosses the river to an aboretum in a meadow, with such ornamental trees as *Acer griseum*, a Judas tree (*Cercis siliquastrum*), a medlar, a *Parrotia persica* and rowans.

The old walled garden, with brick walls and stone piers, is still, as it always was, divided into four. Two of the spaces now contain lawn and the other two seas of herbaceous planting

The herbaceous border at Abbey Dore

(with the occasional small shrub): one with neat herringbone brick paths and the other a sinuous path of paving stones. The paths are essential to bring you closer to the swathes of alstroemerias, crocosmias, *Gaura lindheimeri*, penstemons, poppies, salvias, sedums, verbenas and verbascums. Ornamental grasses are tactfully used (for example the pale glaucous *Elymus magellanicus*), with the occasional ornamental tree – a *Clerodendrum trichotomum* or a snakebark maple – rising above. Running along the south-facing outside wall of the walled garden is more herbaceous planting in a sparkling border.

There is still a nursery here – a valuable place to spot and acquire unfamiliar plants. At a stage in gardening life when some gardeners are trying to do less, Charis Ward seems determined to do more. Her new garden in the field, with a gazebo, borders, bamboos and trees, was too youthful in 2002 to have a clear idea of how it is going to turn out. But her knowledge of plants and how to please them has always brought a spice of excitement to her gardening, and I am sure it will do so here too.

Location Abbey Dore HR2 0AD, Herefordshire
OS SO3830 11m SW of Hereford by A465 and B4347
Tel and **Fax** 01981 240419   **Owner** Mrs C.L. Ward
Open Apr to Sept, daily except Mon and Wed 11–5.30
Area 6 acres/2.4 hectares

ABERGLASNEY GARDENS

DELIGHTFUL AND MYSTERIOUS HISTORIC
GARDEN RESTORED TO BRILLIANT LIFE

Aberglasney has been skilfully promoted with a catchy slogan ("A garden lost in time"), a BBC television series and an excellent history of the garden published to coincide with the garden's opening in the summer of 1999. It is a delightful and remarkable place, set in some of the most beautiful countryside of Wales.

The garden has ancient origins – Aberglasney's "nine green gardens" were celebrated in the 15th century by the bard Lewis Glyn Cothi. In the mid 17th century a new house was built here by the Rudd family who also made a new garden. It later passed to the Dyer family, one of whom was the 18th-century poet John Dyer. (Dyer's poem celebrating the beauties of Grongar Hill – which is visible from Aberglasney – was scorned by Dr Johnson but loved by William Wordsworth who wrote a sonnet to the poet.) The estate changed hands several times until 1955 when it was divided and the house left uninhabited. The Aberglasney Restoration Trust bought the house and the remains of the estate in 1995, and embarked on its restoration.

THE CLOISTER GARDEN

The gardens at Aberglasney present a sequence of beautiful formal enclosures to the west and south of the house; to the east, informal planting in woodland gives exquisite views of the countryside – including the famous Grongar Hill. Immediately below the house is the remarkable Cloister Garden – a series of arched openings round three sides of a courtyard, with a terrace walk above. There has been much debate about the origins and purpose of this enclosure. The archaeological evidence shows that it dates from the very early 17th century and it seems certain that it was indeed a garden. In 2002, after my last visit, it was laid out as a parterre with shaped beds cut into grass planted as a flowery meadow. The terrace walk provides splendid views of this, and of the other formal gardens which have been restored and planted.

A large rectangular pool beyond the Cloister Garden is also probably of Jacobean origin. In each corner and in the middle of each side is a stone-edged rill fed by an underground watercourse. The high stone wall at its northern end, where once there was a lean-to glasshouse, today provides protection for a boisterous mixed border.

Immediately south of the Cloister Garden, and best seen from above, is a slightly irregular walled garden, planted to a design by Penelope Hobhouse in which concentric box-edged curved beds frame a central oval of lawn. The beds contain mainly herbaceous perennials and there is much repeat planting – in particular of achillea, Japanese anemones, bergamot, catmint, geraniums and *Lysimachia ciliata* 'Firecracker'. At the end of each bed, emphasising the curves, are substantial bushes of laurustinus (*Viburnum tinus*). It is a simple, old scheme which maintains its decorative impact throughout the year.

An opening in the wall leads to a walled kitchen and nursery garden with lollipops of clipped bay and a west-facing mixed border. Bishop Rudd's Walk leads east from the house, following a shallow valley and a stream (the Glasney) which flows through woods. In the shade of ash, holly and yew are lovely woodland plants of the kind that flourish in a moist climate in acid soil – cypripediums, ferns, meconopsis, primulas and trilliums.

The walled garden at Aberglasney

Gardens cannot live for long on hype alone and the future of Aberglasney depends on the much more tangible realities of the beauty of the garden and its setting. After an epic feat of restoration, achieved with the help of diverse funding from private and public sources, these now seem triumphantly established.

Location Llangathen SA32 8QH, Carmarthenshire **OS** SN5822 2m W of Llandeilo by A40 **Tel** and **Fax** 01558 668998 **Email** info@aberglasney.org.uk **Website** www.aberglasney.org.uk **CADW/ICOMOS Register** Grade II* **Owner** Aberglasney Restoration Trust **Open** Apr to Oct, daily 10–6; Nov to Mar, Mon to Fri and 1st Sun in month 10.30–3 **Area** 10 acres/4 hectares

ARLEY HALL

SUPERB 19TH-CENTURY BORDERS AND FINE WALLED GARDENS FOR AN ANCIENT ESTATE

The estate at Arley belonged to the Warburton family in the 12th century and has passed by descent ever since. Sir Piers Warburton built a house here in the mid 15th century, which was Georgianised in the 18th century and survived until the 1830s when the present house was built in neo-Jacobean style.

Starting in 1763, William Emes landscaped the park to the south of the house, building a ha-ha to separate it from the pleasure grounds. Later in the 18th century he extended the park, giving it the form it has today. Kitchen gardens were also built in the late 18th century, with flower gardens alongside, and the enclosures built at this time form the framework of the gardens today.

In her book *Some English Gardens* (1904) Gertrude Jekyll described what she admired about the garden at Arley Hall: "How happily mated are formality and freedom; the former in the garden's comfortable walls of living greenery, with their own appropriate ornaments, and the latter in the grandly grown borders and hardy flowers." Backed on one side by yew hedges ornamented with architectural topiary and on the other by a brick wall, the beautiful borders to which she refers still survive in marvellous condition today. They were planted between 1851 and 1852 and are probably the first known borders to use exclusively herbaceous perennials.

LAVISH PLANTING

At the head of the borders stands the surviving 18th-century summerhouse, the Alcove, built in 1791. Each end of the broad grass walk between the borders is marked by a scalloped yew hedge finished with a topiary "dumb waiter" of yew, while buttresses of yew in the borders provide strongly defined shapes among the luxuriant planting and divide what could be an uncomfortably long expanse of border. The planting has, of course, changed over the years but 19th-century watercolours – and Arley was a much painted garden – show the borders displaying exactly the effect that Gertrude Jekyll admired, and this what we see today: a lavish freedom of planting contrasted with the formality of the hedges of "living greenery". The brilliant colours of modern planting are kept well under control by the yew, and there is much repetition, especially of strong shapes of foliage. Bold and big plants such as *Macleaya* × *kewensis*, the giant thistle *Onopordum acanthium* and *Cephalaria gigantea* are used, as well as smaller plants which also have strong shapes – globe-shaped flowers of *Echinops ritro*, bladelike foliage of crocosmias and crisp spires of *Lysimachia ephemerum*. Against this framework is a striking display of orange crocosmias and

The great borders at Arley Hall

alstroemerias, brilliant red phlox, magenta *Lychnis coronaria* and yellow anthemis, cephalaria and helenium.

To one side of the borders, forming a cross axis, is a mysterious avenue of ornamental drums of clipped holm oak. They lead across a lawn to a pair of urns and a small sunken garden from which there are views of the park. A large part of the old kitchen garden has been turned over to decorative purposes, with a scalloped pool surrounded by heraldic figures, tall columns of clipped beech and mixed borders lining the walls. Fruit and vegetables are still grown in one enclosure but even here there is ornamental planting. A walk of rugosa roses is underplanted with *Cyclamen hederifolium*, a seat stands in an arbour of crab-apples, and borders of artichokes and mounds of hebe lead to a lovely domed metal arbour.

Location Arley, nr Northwich CW9 6NA, Cheshire
OS SJ6780 5m W of Knutsford by minor roads; Jnct 19 or 20 of M6; Jnct 9 or 10 of M56 **Tel** 01565 777353
Fax 01565 777465 **Email** arley@info-guest.com
English Heritage Register Grade II* **Owner** Viscount Ashbrook **Open** Apr to Sept, daily except Mon (open Bank Hol Mon) 12–5 **Area** 12 acres/4.8 hectares

BARNSLEY HOUSE

ROSEMARY VEREY'S MUCH-LOVED GARDEN, WITH LIVELY DESIGN AND MARVELLOUS PLANTS

Barnsley House was Rosemary Verey's garden. Mrs Verey's influence on garden taste derived partly from her many books and partly from visitors seeing her ideas in action here in her own garden. She and her husband, the architectural historian David Verey, came to the handsome 17th-century village house in 1951. Mrs Verey became fascinated by garden history and the garden she made was strongly influenced by ideas from the past. However, although the spirit of the garden is essentially formal, and there are strong axial views, this is no lifeless reconstruction: the planting is so rich and the garden so filled with features that the impression is one of bustling energy.

A little knot garden at the end of the house, made in 1970, was inspired by a 17th-century pattern and pioneered the taste for such historical revivals. It has an intertwining ribbon pattern of small-leafed box (*Buxus sempervirens* 'Suffruticosa'), a gold-leafed cultivar (*B. s.* 'Marginata') and wall-germander (*Teucrium × lucidrys*) and each corner is marked by a cheerful double pom-pom of clipped gold variegated holly. A double row of Irish yews (cut down to dumpy rounded shapes in later years) marches away from the garden door of the house, underplanted with swathes of different coloured helianthemums which all but conceal the flagged path. From here a grass path forms a long cross axis linking many of the garden's ingredients.

The pleached laburnum walk (possibly the most photographed view of any late 20th-century English garden) has a path paved in flints and cobbles with, as an eyecatcher, a stone pillar and bench at the end. In spring, before the laburnum is fully in leaf, waves of warm red 'Apeldoorn' tulips line the path; in June purple drumsticks of *Allium hollandicum* rise up below the laburnum's golden tassels. Parallel to this, a long deep mixed border presents a blowsier character, with substantial trees and shrubs, some of them evergreen, lavishly underplanted with herbaceous perennials. At the other end of the axial walk an 18th-century pillared temple adds a crisply classical note, but the effect is contrasted with lavish planting: trees and shrubs, many of which are underplanted with cyclamen, snowdrops and oriental hellebores, crowd around a lily pool surrounded by stone paving.

MRS VEREY'S *POTAGER*

The formal *potager*, or kitchen garden, was also inspired by 17th-century gardens. A book that particularly influenced Rosemary Verey at Barnsley House was William Lawson's early 17th-century gardening manual *A New Orchard and Garden*. He encouraged gardeners to blur the distinction between the flower and vegetable gardens. A flower garden could have herbs arranged in "squares and knots" and the vegetable garden could flaunt a "comely border". An intricate pattern of beds is separated by narrow brick paths lined with box, and strongly formal shapes are provided by clipped apples and pears, and by mounds and pyramids of clipped box. Roses, tulips and scatterings of self-sown Welsh poppies (*Meconopsis cambrica*) enliven the beds. Vegetables are planted with parade ground discipline in finely combined patterns, but beauty and productivity go hand in hand – this is very much a working kitchen garden.

The character of the garden at Barnsley House is delightful. It is also potently instructive: the choice and range of plants, brightly formality here and there, the dazzling standards of practical gardening, and the different moods evoked in the various parts of the garden all combine to make it a feast of inspiration. Barnsley is an icon of the garden taste of its time and a cribber's paradise that few gardens can equal.

Rosemary Verey died in 2001 but her fertile influence will continue to be felt in gardening. In 2002 the house was sold for use as a hotel and restaurant.

Location Barnsley, nr Cirencester GL7 5EE, Gloucestershire OS SP0704 In Barnsley village, 4m N of Cirencester by B4425 Tel 01285 740561 Fax 01285 740628 Owner Tim Haigh and Rupert Pendered Open to those staying at the hotel or taking meals at the restaurant; also open occasionally for charity Area 4 acres/1.6 hectares

BATSFORD ARBORETUM

MAGNIFICENT TREES AND FLOWERING SHRUBS, AND A CHARMING JAPANESE GARDEN

There was a house here by the 17th century and a Kip engraving of 1712, when the estate belonged to Richard Freeman, shows it surrounded by quite elaborate formal gardens on three sides – but none of this survives. The present house, a handsome neo-Elizabethan mansion, was built between 1887 and 1893 by Sir Ernest George & Harold Peto for A.B. Freeman Mitford (later 1st Earl Redesdale of the second creation). As a diplomat in Japan, Freeman Mitford was bitten deeply by the oriental bug and this strongly influenced his gardening activities. He became an expert on bamboos, of which there is a good collection here, wrote *The Bamboo Garden* in 1896, and laid out a Japanese garden

here from 1890. The estate was sold in 1920 to the 1st Lord Dulverton whose son, after 1956, built up a very large collection of trees, adding to existing old plantings, some of which go back to the 18th century.

The site, with undulating ground sloping to the south and a winding stream, is an attractive one. But we are almost 800ft/240m here and winters can be very cold: beautiful specimens of Mexican pines were eventually killed by an especially severe winter. The arboretum, west and north of the house, contains examples of a very wide range of hardy genera of tree, both deciduous and coniferous, though deciduous trees form the bulk of the collection There are especially good acers (180 species and cultivars), birches, cherries (especially Japanese flowering cherries), magnolias (40 species), oaks (over 60 species) and rowans. There are also good

The garden front at Barnsley House

BODNANT GARDEN

AN OUTSTANDING GARDEN OF FORMAL WELL-PLANTED TERRACES AND A GRAND RAVINE OF FLOWERING SHRUBS

Bodnant is a garden of many flavours, most of them delicious, and the prevailing atmosphere is one of plutocratic splendour. The estate was bought in 1874 by a Salford chemical manufacturer, Henry David Pochin, who rebuilt the existing 18th-century house, producing a result that was (in the forthright opinion of Edward Hubbard in his book *Clwyd* in "The Buildings of Wales" series) "Elephantine…like a hotel in some staid Victorian spa". Attached to the house is a superb conservatory of the same date, to which, alas, visitors have no access.

The setting is extraordinarily beautiful, overlooking the Conwy valley with mesmerising views of Snowdonia. Henry Pochin saw the gardening possibilities at Bodnant from early on and began planting trees in the precipitous valley of the river Hiraethlyn which flows through the grounds. He commissioned the landscape architect Edward Milner to make sweeping lawns west of the house, high above the valley, and in around 1882 built the famous laburnum tunnel — an astonishing sight in May with its cascades of flowers and pink azaleas glimpsed below on either side.

THE 2ND LORD ABERCONWAY

However, it was Henry Pochin's grandson, the 2nd Lord Aberconway, who introduced the lively variety of garden styles that flow harmoniously one after the other and who gave the garden most of the character and charm that it possesses today. Formal terraces now descend the west-facing slope below the house where Milner's lawns had been, and each of these reveals something remarkable or beautiful (often both): the battered and sprawling *Arbutus* × *andrachnoides* on the top terrace was planted in 1906 and is a tree of rare character; on the Lily Terrace below is a piquant contrast between the formal and the wild — a scalloped lily pool flanked by two

▷ **The Pin Mill** at Bodnant

---

collections of cedars, junipers, pines and spruce. Three champion trees can be seen at Batsford – the white ash (*Fraxinus americana*), the Syrian juniper (*Juniperus drupacea*) and the California nutmeg (*Torreya californica*). All the trees are impeccably labelled and are disposed about winding walks.

A JAPANESE GARDEN

The only area of even slightly formal gardening is Lord Redesdale's Japanese garden west of the house. Here a Japanese resthouse is crowned with a dragon to ward off evil spirits and has an inscription round the door extolling the merits of bamboo: "It is not good to live in a house without bamboo." The resthouse is shaded by a splendid tree of heaven (*Ailanthus altissima*) and a bronze Buddha under an English oak overlooks a clearing among bamboos, magnolias and Japanese maples. An old Japanese maple (*Acer palmatum*) spreads over a rocky pool overlooked by a Foo Dog – a fierce bronze dog with its front paws resting on a multicoloured *cloisonné* sphere – which stands

Batsford Arboretum

in the shade of a beautiful sugar maple (*Acer saccharinum*). All this, as Barbara Jones pungently observed in her *Follies & Grottoes* (1974), "is very different in scale and sweep from the usual miniature horrors." A more recent addition, quite close to the Japanese garden, is the late 20th-century carved stone statue by Simon Verity of Daphne with flying robes and hair turning into wild branches.

Batsford, now particularly well cared for, is a delightful place to explore in any season and for the ardent tree lover it is a place of quite particular interest.

Location Moreton-in-Marsh GL56 9QF, Gloucestershire **OS** SP1832 1m NW of Moreton-in-Marsh by A44 **Tel** 01386 701441 **Fax** 01386 701829 **Email** batsarb@batsfond.freeserve.co.uk **Website** www.batsford-arboretum.co.uk **English Heritage Register** Grade I **Owner** The Batsford Foundation **Open** beginning of Feb to mid Nov, daily 10–5; mid Nov to beginning Feb, Sat and Sun 10–4 **Area** 55 acres/22 hectares

veteran trees (both planted by Henry Pochin), a blue Atlantic cedar and a cedar of Lebanon; the steps down are enclosed in a superb trelliswork pergola with ceanothus, roses and *Solanum crispum*; and the lowest terrace has a long narrow canal with a scattering of waterlilies at either end. At one end the canal is overlooked by an elegant arcaded building, the Pin Mill – an early 18th-century garden pavilion moved here from a garden in Gloucestershire. At the other end is the Stage – a platform of turf backed by sweeping yew hedges like the flies and backdrop of a theatre; at its centre is a wooden dais with a bench designed by William Kent and, rising magnificently behind it all, a splendid Monterey pine (*Pinus radiata*) with a nobly rounded crown.

THE DAZZLING DELL

An inconspicuous path to one side of the Pin Mill descends a steep slope to the enchanting valley of the Hiraethlyn where the Dell is rich in exotic conifers – many of them planted by Henry Pochin among native Scots pines, English oaks and sycamores. The conifers constitute an anthology of fashionable Victorian trees, with grand specimens of Douglas fir (*Pseudotsuga menziesii*), Grecian fir (*Abies cephalonica*) and Wellingtonia. Their textured trunks and dark foliage make a fine background to the frequently toothsome colours of the shrubs. Early in the year the Dell explodes with camellias, magnolias and rhododendrons, to be followed later by the calmer presence of hydrangeas and drifts of astilbes. Paths high up above the stream give delicious views through the planted profusion.

The gardens at Bodnant are finely maintained – the head gardener, Martin Puddle, is the third generation of his family to occupy the post. The Bodnant style, remote as it is from all but the richest gardener's daily experience, still exemplifies principles that underlie all good gardens – respect for the site, a love of plants and a passion for gardening.

Location Tal-y-Cafn, Colwyn Bay LL28 5RE, Conwy **OS** SH8072 8m S of Llandudno by A470; signed from A55 **Tel** 01492 650460 **Fax** 01492 650448 **Website** www.oxalis.co.uk/bodnant.htm **CADW/ICOMOS Register** Grade I **Owner** The National Trust **Open** mid Mar to Oct, daily 10–5 **Area** 80 acres/32 hectares

BOURTON HOUSE GARDEN

A NEW GARDEN FOR AN OLD VILLAGE HOUSE, WITH BRILLIANT DESIGN AT EVERY TURN

Bourton House is a beautiful 17th-century house rebuilt in the early 18th century. The garden was made by the present owners and presents a dazzling array of formal episodes in keeping with the decorative but sober architecture of the house. Behind the house, to the south, an enormous lawn has borders on each side and a terraced border at its far edge; from a walk along the top there are views over fields, old village houses and woodland. To the west, hidden behind a yew hedge, a knot of box (common and gold variegated) is intricately patterned and studded with pointed topiary pyramids, and has at its centre a very large raised oval basket-weave stone pool. Arbours of clipped ivy enclose stone benches and are flanked with giant balls of box. Against the western end of the house is a beautifully trained pyracantha, its branches horizontal, perfectly spaced, a masterpiece of the plant trainer's art. Below it, a pool in a parterre filled with cherry pie has water trickling over an urn in the middle.

On the eastern side of the lawn a miniature formal kitchen garden is laid out like a parterre. A jigsaw puzzle of box-edged shapes is filled with herbs and vegetables, trelliswork is garlanded with runner beans and sweet peas, and hanging baskets drip with nasturtiums and cherry tomatoes. To one side a path leads between borders to a white and silver garden – roses underplanted with alliums, Japanese anemones, artemisias, *Convolvulus cneorum*, penstemons and *Viola cornuta*. A sliver of a secret garden lies behind hornbeam hedges, with a swagger urn framed by an arch of clipped holm oaks and flanked by weeping mulberries. A gravel walk runs along a wall ornamented with buttresses of clipped box interspersed with tall pots of marguerites. The outer edge of the path is lined with mounds, spheres and spirals of clipped box like a topiarist's shop window. Behind the wall is a border of subtropical flavour – the striking foliage of bananas, cordylines, cannas, New Zealand flax and such exotics as rich blue *Salvia guaranitica*, silver-leafed *Plectranthus argentatus* and *Leonotis leonurus* with its whorls of orange flowers. This ripe flourish of exoticism faces an area of quite different character – a big sloping lawn hedged in hawthorn or beech, with simple country trees such as a weeping ash, flowering cherries, hazels and mulberries, all overlooked by an exquisite 16th-century barn.

This is a busy garden but it is not relentlessly so. There is always the soothing sight of a lawn, an uncluttered vista or a

The knot garden at Bourton House

Burford House from the south lawn

glimpse of the rural landscape to ward off visual overload. It is also flawlessly kept and bristling with good ideas.

Location Bourton-on-the-Hill GL56 9AE, Gloucestershire **OS** SP1832 2m W of Moreton-in-Marsh by A44 **Tel** 01386 700754 **Fax** 01386 701081 **Email** ...@bourtonhouse.com **Owner** Mr and Mrs R. Paice **Open** end May to Aug, Wed to Fri 10–5; Oct, Thur and Fri 10–5 **Area** 3 acres/1.2 hectares

BURFORD HOUSE GARDENS

FINE MIXED BORDERS AND A SUPERB
COLLECTION OF CLEMATIS ON THE
BANKS OF A RIVER

Burford House is a gentlemanly brick house built in 1726 for William Bowles on an ancient site by the river Teme. It was bought in 1954 by John Treasure and his brother and they founded a nursery alongside the house – Treasures of Tenbury – which specialises in clematis. There was no garden to speak of when the Treasures came but John Treasure quickly made up his mind about its possibilities: "The land was flat except on the south and west fronts…I knew what I wanted: formality on these two fronts, and for formality to quickly break down to the informal." This is exactly what he achieved.

To the south and west of the house, where the ground is gently terraced, there are all sorts of ornamental planting. A flight of semicircular steps bristles with *Erigeron karvinskianus*, a pair of fig trees flanks an entrance, and about the front door is an airy colour scheme of nerines, penstemons and roses, blue salvias and grey artemisias. Immediately west of the house, across a path and behind a yew hedge, are mixed borders.

The great set piece at Burford House is the long wide lawn which runs south of the house along the banks of the river. Beds swoop in and out on each side, often with a specimen tree – *Betula ermanii*, *Eucalyptus parviflora*, or a Japanese maple – rising above mixed planting. Specimen trees are also planted in the lawn, sometimes enlivening the space between beds: for example, a fine California nutmeg (*Torreya californica*), *Nyssa sylvatica* and, forming a focal point by the river bank, an old Monterey pine (*Pinus radiata*). Part of the river bank is planted with a splendid jungle of exotic grasses, some of them very large.

East of the house are some large trees, among them a beautiful old yew (one of the few plants already here when John Treasure came) and an *Acer saccharinum*. A group of silver birches and a Monterey pine give shade for a water garden. The banks of a stream are lavishly planted with astilbes, ferns, *Pontederia cordata*, Asiatic primulas and willows.

After John Treasure's death the garden went through an uncertain period but the present owner has taken it energetically in hand. Its original character has been preserved and it is now beautifully looked after. The swooping island beds and repeated use of fastigiate, spreading or glaucous-leafed conifers have a distinct period flavour which you may or may not enjoy. Although the site is undeniably attractive and there are countless excellent plants, it nevertheless always seems to me to lack magic.

Location Tenbury Wells WR15 8HQ, Worcestershire **OS** SO5868 1m W of Tenbury Wells by A456 **Tel** 01584 810777 **Fax** 01584 810673 **Email** enquiries@burford.co.uk **Website** www.burford.co.uk **Owner** Charles Chesshire **Open** daily 10–5 **Area** 4 acres/1.6 hectares

CENTRE FOR ALTERNATIVE TECHNOLOGY

ECOLOGICALLY FRIENDLY
GARDENING SPLENDIDLY DISPLAYED
IN A DRAMATIC SETTING

The Centre for Alternative Technology (CAT for convenience) first opened to visitors in 1975. Its chief concerns are sustainability and man's relationship with the environment. Horticulture plainly has much to do with this and the Centre gardens in accordance with its principles and mounts useful displays demonstrating the techniques

Nature-friendly planting at CAT

of environmentally friendly horticulture.

The site, a former slate quarry, is splendidly dramatic and the ascent, by railway or on foot up the winding wooded lane, full of excitement. In the garden practicalities and aesthetics are intimately interwoven – here, although the results may be decorative, everything arises from function; in this way, the practical and the ornamental become indistinguishable. By conventional standards the garden at CAT is crammed hugger-mugger with plants; even the margins of paths fade away in planting. Buildings too are embraced by the plant world; not merely do climbing plants scale the walls but in one case turf spangled with flowers forms a decorative, sustainable roof-cover that also provides excellent insulation. A little space for plants (I hesitate to call it a garden, which sounds segregationist) outside the building is brilliant with campanulas, chives, crocosmia, lupins, mulleins and poppies, and a dry-stone wall is festooned with strawberries. Some of this is plainly the work of a gardener, but some of it is due to nature claiming her own. Parts of the garden are given over to food plants but ornamentals also find a home here, not self-consciously as in an ornamental *potager* but simply because there is no theoretical division between the edible and the decorative.

COMPOST AND MULCHES

Practical displays demonstrate the techniques of gardening in collaboration with nature. An excellent display of composting shows the results of different techniques and explains the theory of different bins (CAT makes its own, out of recycled plastic). The CAT preferred technique results in a high-fibre cool compost which consumes a very wide range of household rubbish (including cardboard boxes). Different mulches are also compared and the use of green manure explained. Weeds are subdued by planting ground-cover and slugs kept more or less at bay by encouraging the right beetles.

When I visited CAT in August 2001 the garden was full of flowers, vegetables bursting with vigour, and the buzz of bees – like many another garden in that season, organic or otherwise. But any gardener would be wise to take seriously the principles embraced by CAT.

Topiary hedges at Chirk Castle

Alexander Pope emphasised the importance, when making a garden, of consulting the genius of the place. Peter Harper at CAT takes the same view: "The existing site is not abolished, but asked for its opinion."

Location Machynlleth SY20 9AZ, Powys **OS** SH7604 2½m N of Machynlleth by A487 **Tel** 01654 705950 **Fax** 01654 702782 **Email** help@catinfo.demon.co.uk **Website** www.cat.org.uk **Owner** Centre for Alternative Technology **Open** daily 10–5 (closes 4 in winter; closed for a few days at Christmas and New Year). **NB** The car park is at the foot of a steep hill (limited parking for disabled and elderly people at the top); a railway taking visitors to the Centre operates only from Easter to the end of Oct but those who are mobile and fit can walk. **Area** 5 acres/2 hectares

CHIRK CASTLE

SUPERB OLD TOPIARY AND HEDGES, GOOD PLANTS AND A GRAND 18TH-CENTURY PARK

The medieval castle at Chirk was bought in 1595 by Sir Thomas Myddelton whose son, another Thomas, made grandiose formal gardens here in the middle of the 17th century. A Badeslade engraving of 1735 of the "West prospect of Chirk Castle" shows a gigantic layout still disposed about a central axis north of the castle with, over to one side, an extraordinary conical mount with formal walks and plantings. Almost nothing of this survives

for William Emes carried out a comprehensive refashioning of the landscape from 1764 onwards. One survival, however, is Robert Davies's superlative wrought-iron gates made in 1712 for the entrance forecourt. They are shown in another Badeslade engraving and in 1784 elicited from the frequently grumpy John Byng the opinion that they were "one of the most superb iron gates ever seen". They have since been moved to the main entrance of the park and you pass them, painted ghostly white, as you approach the visitors' entrance. Emes's park provides a beautiful setting for the castle and some of his original plantings survive.

The formal gardens by the castle are largely 19th-century and their most memorable feature is the sequence of yew hedges and topiary planted by Richard Myddelton Biddulph after 1872. A gravel walk below the castle ramparts is lined with tall topiary shapes, originally resembling pointed witch's hats but now rounded and wambly with wonderful character. A yew hedge separating the castle forecourt from the flower garden is clipped at regular intervals into piers, thicker and taller than the hedge, but both hedge and topiary have now lost their definition and their wayward but monumental shapes easily hold their own alongside the architecture of the castle. Under the castle ramparts, tucked away behind more yew hedges, is a rose garden of

dwardian flavour, with a sundial, made for
Chirk in the 17th century, at the centre.
From the castle forecourt an opening in
he yew hedge is guarded by a pair of curious
ronze nymphs – both naked, one blindfolded,
he other bound with her hands behind her
ack and an anxious expression on her face.
The effect is slightly unsettling. Beyond them
he ground slopes down and an exhilarating
ista opens out along a broad grassy walk
dged with trees and shrubs. At its head is
weeping silver lime (*Tilia* 'Petiolaris') and
eyond it are repeated groups of flowering
herries and fine conifers. Halfway down
a large thatched summerhouse festooned
vith roses and vines.

On this windy site woodland provides
rotection for magnolias, rhododendrons and
uch unusual plants as the Chilean firebush
Embothrium coccineum) and the beautiful
Eucryphia glutinosa. All this is agreeable in a
ightly minor way. The best things about
Chirk, however, are the Emes park and the
equence of yew shapes and hedges that lie
elow the castle walls.

Location Chirk, nr Wrexham LL14 5AF, Clwyd **OS**
SJ2638 2m W edge of Chirk village, 7m S of Wrexham
off A483 **Tel** 01691 777701 **Fax** 01691 774706
Email chirkcastle@ntrust.org.uk **CADW/ICOMOS**
Register Grade I **Owner** The National Trust **Open**
end Mar to end Oct, Wed to Sun (open Bank Hol Mon)
11–6 (closes 5 in Oct) **Area** 5 acres/2 hectares

CIRENCESTER PARK

MAGNIFICENT EARLY 18TH-CENTURY
LANDSCAPE PARK WITH THE LONGEST
AVENUE IN ENGLAND

The house was built in the early 18th
century for the 1st Earl Bathurst, a
reworking of a late Tudor house which had
belonged to Sir John Danvers. The front of the
house, where it faces the town, was planted
with a yew hedge shortly after it was built, and
survives today – a giant curved bolster of
green along the road, a well-loved landmark to
anyone who has passed through Cirencester.

The enormous park, one of the most

astonishing designed landscapes in the
country, was the result of an extended
collaboration between Lord Bathurst and his
friend Alexander Pope. It is one of the very
few large-scale schemes of this character to
survive from the early 18th century. In 1714
Stephen Switzer coined the term "extensive
or forest gardening" for this style of garden
layout: still retaining formal ingredients such
as avenues and rides, it was a precursor of the
informal landscape park which developed later
in the century. Bathurst, who had also bought
the neighbouring estate of Sapperton, clothed
the land behind his house with trees,
combining forestry and landscaping on a
heroic scale. (Kips's engraving in Atkyns's *The
Ancient and Present State of Glostershire* (1712)
shows the Tudor house with a formal garden
set in an almost naked landscape.) The forestry
produced timber so that commerce and
aesthetics were combined – as they still are at
Cirencester Park to this day.

Bold rides and avenues running through

The Broad Avenue at Cirencester Park

woodland form the structure of the park. The Broad Avenue, of horse chestnuts and beech, is aligned with the church tower of St John the Baptist in Cirencester and runs westwards all the way to Sapperton village 5 miles away. Ornamental buildings punctuate the avenue – a hexagon with cupola (c.1736), stone piers, Pope's Seat (c.1736, a rusticated building with niches and facing seats inside), and the Horse Guards (a pair of arched Ionic alcoves, c.1800) flanking the avenue. Just beyond them the avenue joins a *rond-point* linking ten rides. In Oakley Wood is Alfred's Hall, a very early Gothick castellated building, started in 1721 as a ruin but undergoing changes and certainly completed by 1732 when Dean Swift stayed here. At the centre of Home Park is the Doric Queen Anne's Column (1741).

Lord Bathurst died at the age of ninety-one in 1775, having lived through one of the most turbulent periods in garden history. His park was a pioneer when he started work on it and, gently embracing informality and naturalism, remained an idiosyncratic achievement, beyond fashion, as it is today. The entrance gates bear the following attractive legend: "You are welcome on foot or on horseback by permission of the Lord Bathurst." I know of no other garden in England that offers such a friendly welcome.

Location Cirencester GL7 2BU, Gloucestershire
OS SP0101 In the centre of the town of Cirencester
Tel 01285 653135 **English Heritage Register** Grade I
Owner Lord Bathurst **Open** daily 8–5 **Area** 2,400 acres/971 hectares

The hexagon cupola at Cirencester Park

THE DOROTHY CLIVE GARDEN

A WOODED DELL ALIVE WITH EXCELLENT PLANTING AND INVENTIVE MIXED BORDERS

Some of the best gardens succeed by exploiting to the full some oddity of the landscape. At Willoughbridge Colonel Harry Clive saw the attractions and planting possibilities of an old gravel quarry and started to make a garden here in 1940. The quarry had, in the first part of the 19th century, been part of the Maer Hall estate (*see page 507*) which belonged to Josiah Wedgwood and to which his son-in-law, Charles Darwin, was a frequent visitor. Colonel Clive made the garden as a place of recreation for his wife, Dorothy, whose failing health restricted her activities.

The quarry is on a slope that faces south. It has acid soil, is well watered and benefits from old oaks and beech which give protection to the rhododendrons that Colonel Clive wanted to plant. He built up an excellent collection, not merely of the familiar brilliantly coloured hybrid azaleas but also of the beautiful species. In 1990, to celebrate the half centenary of the garden, a multi-tiered waterfall was made, whose edges today are planted with astilbes,

The cascade in the Quarry Garden

ferns, hostas, irises, ligularias and rodgersias. Distinguished trees and shrubs crowd in on either side of the waterfall – *Embothrium coccineum*, magnolias, Japanese maples, pieris and rhododendrons. The high canopy of oaks gives protection but also filters the light which illuminates the brilliant flowers of the shrubs below. If you continue to the top of the hill, above the quarry, there are splendid views from a gazebo.

At the entrance to the garden, where John Codrington advised on borders and other features in the 1960s, is a completely different style of gardening. Here is an example of that desperately unfashionable garden feature, the scree garden. The best reason for making a scree garden is to provide particular conditions for, say, alpine plants; here, plants from very different environments are unhappily jumbled together: a sea of gravel flows down a gentle slope about dwarf conifers (some with golden foliage), cistus, daphnes, hebes and mounded Japanese maples, while an informal lily pool is edged with bulrushes, *Gunnera manicata*, hostas pampas grass and persicaria. Some of the planting, however, is more effective. A trio of slender Himalayan birches (*Betula utilis* var. *jacquemontii*) stand against the horizontal, tiered shape of *Viburnum plicatum* f. *tomentosum* 'Mariesii', and the pale silvery foliage of *Cornus alternifolia* 'Argentea' froths among thickets of *Crocosmia* 'Lucifer'.

On the slopes above the scree garden are swooping lawns, mixed borders and specimen trees. Some of the trees are planted in grass, some rise among the lavishly planted borders – an Iris yew, a clipped pillar of holly or the sprawling shape of *Parrotia persica*. There are plenty of good plants here and the borders are beautifully cared for. However, to my taste, it is the Quarry Garden that is the overwhelmingly distinguished attraction in the Dorothy Clive Garden.

Location Willoughbridge, nr Market Drayton TF9 4EU, Shropshire **OS** SJ7540 9m SE of Nantwich by A51 **Tel** 01630 647237 **Fax** 01630 647902 **Owner** Willoughbridge Garden Trust **Open** Apr to Oct, daily 10–5.30 **Area** 8 acres/3.2 hectares

CLYNE GARDENS

A WOODLAND GARDEN WITH
BEAUTIFUL FLOWERING SHRUBS ON
A SITE OVERLOOKING SWANSEA BAY

The first house on the site of Clyne Castle, originally called Woodlands, was built for Richard Phillips in 1791. The house changed hands more than once, and was Gothicised in the early 19th century; when William Graham Vivian bought it in 1860 he greatly extended it but did not change its essential character of castellated splendour. The site is marvellous, close to the sea and taking advantage of beautiful views over both the wooded Clyne valley and Swansea Bay. The garden dates largely from Vivian's time, with additions by his descendants – the last of whom, Admiral A. Walker-Heneage Vivian, sold the estate to Swansea Town Council in 1952 when much of the land became a public park and the castle a hall of residence for the University of Swansea.

The gardens spread out on south-facing slopes below the castle. They fall into two chief parts: the upper part with wide expanses of lawn and clumps and groups of trees; and the more intimate and intensively planted area in Brock Hole valley with its winding stream. In the upper part beeches, oaks and Scots pines provide a backdrop for exotics, in particular conifers – *Cunninghamia lanceolata*, Monterey pines (*Pinus radiata*) and Wellingtonias. Among other ornamental plantings are a large bed of heathers, a wildflower meadow and a wood of Turkey oaks (*Quercus cerris*) with lovely spreads of bluebells. The path runs over a grand monumental bridge – but there is no water below it. Close to the house a pretty pavilion was built by Admiral Vivian to give views eastwards to the ships in Swansea Bay.

Walking on the airy upper slopes the eye is constantly drawn to the densely planted area below. At the western end of the valley a scarlet Japanese bridge with crisp white finials crosses the stream and a rocky cascade in the shade of a fine *Davidia involucrata* var. *vilmoriniana*. The banks of the stream flowing through the wooded valley and wriggling between mossy islands are sometimes impenetrably wild and sometimes lavishly planted with *Gunnera manicata, Iris sibirica*, Himalayan primulas, lysichiton, rodgersias and, more unexpectedly, drifts of crocosmia which seem to relish the shade and moisture. At the eastern end of the valley, in a grove of old Loderi rhododendrons, Admiral Vivian built a stone lookout tower from which to view the plants, many of which today rise far higher than it. Rhododendrons flourish here and the garden maintains two National Collections: of subsection Falconera and subsection Triflora.

The hydrangea walk at Clyne Gardens

There are many other kinds of rhododendrons to be seen, some of them bred by Admiral Vivian – in all over 800 species and cultivars. Two other collections of ericaceous plants, enkianthus and pieris, are also kept, and many of these are to be seen along the banks of the stream – their blossom in spring and early summer a spectacular sight. In the early autumn the garden is notable for a quieter but no less impressive display – of billowing hydrangeas – along the path at the eastern end of the stream.

The transfer of the richly planted grounds of Clyne Castle into a beautifully kept public amenity is a great success. They are much used, and relished, by the local community.

Location Mill Lane, Blackpill, Swansea SA3 5BD, Glamorgan **OS** SS6190 3m SW of Swansea by A4067 **Tel** 01792 401737 **CADW/ICOMOS Register** Grade I **Owner** City and County of Glamorgan **Open** daily dawn–dusk **Area** 50 acres/20 hectares

DUNHAM MASSEY

ANCIENT PARKLAND WITH FINE OLD
TREES AND A GARDEN WITH LIVELY
MODERN PLANTING

The Booth family came to Dunham Massey in the 15th century when the site had already been inhabited for a long time – there had been a Norman castle here, of which earthworks still survive. In around the mid 17th century Sir George Booth rebuilt an older house and a Kip engraving of 1697 shows a decorative courtyard house with gables and towers. Between 1732 and 1740 George Booth, 2nd Earl of Warrington, rebuilt the house to the designs of John Norris – plain and rather dull but retaining the ornamental moat to the north and west of the house. In the 18th century the heiress Lady Mary Booth married into the Grey family (Earls of Stamford). The 10th, and last, Earl of Stamford left the estate to the National Trust in 1976.

The landscape at Dunham Massey has a similarly ancient history. The deer park south of the house was in place in the 14th century and still contains some oaks of medieval origin – and there is still a herd of fallow deer. In the 17th century Kip's engraving shows modest formal gardens about the house (the "old but good gardens walled in" seen in 1698 by Celia Fiennes who also noted "a very fine parcke"). Great changes took place from the end of the 17th century under the 2nd Earl of Warrington who planted 100,000 trees. The results of his activities can be seen in four splendid paintings, done by John Harris in 1751 and still at Dunham Massey, which show a great *patte d'oie* of avenues radiating from the south front of the house, an avenue aligned with the north front and expanses of formal and informal water ornamenting the landscape. There are rumours that Capability Brown worked here in the 18th century but there is no evidence, either on the ground or in documents.

SPLENDOURS OF THE PAST

Much of the old landscape at Dunham Massey remains intact and the National Trust has replanted trees to follow this layout. The Old Park, to the south, retains the old alignments of avenues, and some of the original trees, especially magnificent oaks, survive. The island pool to the east of the central avenue, shown in John Harris's

painting, can still be seen, as can an obelisk erected in 1714 in the south-west avenue. The fallow deer graze here, coming right up to the house, disdainfully oblivious of visitors.

One of the most prominent ornaments in Harris's paintings is a great mount north-west of the house. This was the site of the Norman castle and the mount was used in the 16th century as a vantage point from which to view the garden. It may still be seen on a semicircle of ground extending into the moat. The north façade of the house overlooks a formal garden laid out in 1905. A lawn, enclosed on two sides by golden yew (with scarlet tropaeolum) has clipped mounds of *Quercus phillyreoides* – a very attractive and unusual Chinese evergreen oak. L-shaped beds cut into the turf are bedded with lobelia, zonal pelargoniums and sage, and a centrepiece erupts with golden juniper, yucca and verbena. More subtle, and more beautiful, is the view over the moat through a *claire-voie* on the northern edge of the lawn to an avenue piercing through woodland – exactly as it did in the early 18th century.

To the east of the house, in pleasure grounds first laid out in the late 18th century, is a fine 18th-century orangery whose tubs of citrus plants and pomegranates are moved out onto a terrace for the summer. Inside, *Abutilon* 'Ashford Red' is neatly espaliered against the

wall, which is also decorated with the beautiful *Lapageria rosea*. In late summer waves of pink *Crinum × powellii* flow against the orangery's outside walls. Across the lawn, with its good specimen trees, is the Garden Wood which the National Trust has finely replanted with flowering shrubs, a walk of hydrangeas, and many rhododendrons. Drifts (often very big drifts) of cimicifuga, gentians, hostas, ligularias, meconopsis and rodgersias ornament the bank of a stream. In clearings in the wood are newly established groups of ornamental trees, especially of Japanese maples.

The entrance to Dunham Massey takes visitors past gloomy outhouses built of depressingly dark brick. There is also something melancholy about the house itself. The landscape, however, is exhilarating. The noble old avenues, the lively and colourful planting of the Garden Wood and the serene lawns and trees of the pleasure grounds are thoroughly enlivening.

Location Altrincham WA14 4SJ, Cheshire **OS** SJ7387 3m W of Altrincham by A56; Jnct 19 of M6 **Tel** 0161 941 1025 **Infoline** 0161 928 4351 **Fax** 0161 929 7508 **Email** dunhammassey@ntrust.org.uk **Owner** The National Trust **Open** late Mar to Oct, daily 11–5.30 **Area** 250 acres/101 hectares

Fallow deer at Dunham Massey

DYFFRYN GARDENS

A GREAT EDWARDIAN GARDEN OF
FORMAL DESIGN FINELY RESTORED,
WITH GOOD PLANTS

The mansion at Dyffryn was designed by a
Newport architect, E.A. Lansdowne, and
built between 1893 and 1894 for a coal and
shipping tycoon, Sir John Cory. Cory started
to lay out a garden shortly after the house was
built and in 1906 employed the garden
designer Thomas H. Mawson to make a formal
garden as an appropriate setting for the house.
John Cory's son, Reginald, was already a
distinguished plantsman and development of
the garden was essentially a collaboration
between Mawson and Reginald Cory. Mawson
described Reginald Cory as "an amateur
landscape gardener and horticulturist of insight
and ability" and says, " The credit of the success
achieved in these gardens largely belongs to
him." After much excellent restoration in
recent years, with finance from the Heritage
Lottery Fund, the garden is in fine state and is
probably the best surviving example of a
Mawson garden designed for a private client.

Mawson's garden starts with bold axes close
to the house but becomes more intimate and
more attractively jumbly to the west of the
chief vista. Running along the south façade of
the house is a bold balustraded terrace
bristling with urns and vases filled with tender
plants. Immediately below, a croquet lawn

The statue of Lao-tse at Dyffryn

(designed by Mawson for that purpose) is
edged with Irish yews, many of which lean
away from the west wind. A long narrow
cross-shaped lily pool runs south across
another lawn with, at its centre, a later
addition – a great bronze vase with a dragon
entwined about it. This is one of various
Chinese objects presented to the garden in
the 1950s; among them is a fine figure of the
philosopher Lao-tse which is placed on a
grassy eminence close to the house. The
dragon vase is aligned with a sketchy
westwards axis which leads into a sequence of
garden enclosures, most of which are formed
by beautifully fashioned yew hedges. An
informal area of sweeping lawns and trees and
shrubs is outstandingly attractive, containing a
very large Chinese wingnut (*Pterocarya
stenoptera*) and many fine Japanese maples
planted by Reginald Cory.

In the enclosed areas, as Mawson wrote, "we
felt at liberty to indulge in every phase of
garden design which the site and my client's
catholic views suggested." Here are deep
herbaceous borders, a Mediterranean Garden,
a Pompeian Garden (largely built out of
concrete), a Rose Garden, a Bathing Pool
Garden (now containing a very beautiful *Acer
griseum*) and much else. The Theatre Garden,
with a raised stage and curved wings of
clipped yew, was used to display Reginald
Cory's collection of bonsai. At Dyffryn the

beautiful yew hedging, the maze-like
sequence of rooms and the frequently
distinguished planting give great pleasure.

Location St Nicholas, Cardiff CF5 6SU, Glamorgan **OS**
ST0972 7m SW of Cardiff; Jnct 33 of M4, A4232, A48
and minor roads **Tel** 01222 593328 **Fax** 01222 591966
CADW/ICOMOS Register Grade I **Owner** The Vale of
Glamorgan Council **Open** Apr to Oct, daily 10–dusk;
Nov to Mar, daily 10–5 **Area** 55 acres/22 hectares

DYRHAM PARK

TRACES OF A GRAND FORMAL
GARDEN IN LOVELY PARKLAND, AND
A SPLENDID ORANGERY

Dyrham scarcely has a garden to speak of
today but it does have an astonishing
garden past, traces of which still enliven the
scene. Furthermore, the natural lie of the land
and the position of the house within ancient
parkland are memorably beautiful.
The estate here belonged to the Wynter
family in the 16th century. In the following
century Mary Wynter married William
Blathwayt, secretary at war and secretary of
state to William III. Between 1692 and 1701
he transformed the Tudor house into a
grandee's mansion, partly designed by the
Huguenot Samuel Hauduroy and partly by
William Talman. The house was grand enough
but the garden designed by the king's
gardener, George London, was stupendous. A
Kip engraving shows an opulent pattern of
formal gardens spreading out magnificently
both east and west of the house.

The forecourt at Dyrham Park

On this hilly site much work was needed to achieve the level areas the formal garden demanded – in 1698 William Blathwayt moaned, "When will this levelling be at an end?" Among the most remarkable features of London's garden was a giant formal cascade, with 224 falls, whose water was then channelled below the house's stable block to emerge in the formal pools of the west garden. The Kip engraving shows a formal wilderness sweeping down the south-facing slopes on the east side, while ornate parterres extend on the newly levelled ground in front of and behind the house.

THE SURVIVAL OF NEPTUNE

However, by 1779 the grand waterworks were already in a state of neglect and by 1791 the great formal gardens had gone – "reconciled to modern taste". In 1800 the William Blathwayt of the day consulted Humphry Repton who may have advised on tree planting and naturalising the ground. Today, the levelled ground of London's gardens can still be seen, and, most poignantly, the statue of Neptune (1704, by Claude David) which had formed the starting point of the cascade. Correct garden taste insisted that Neptune was always associated with water – but the water gardens have not been here for over 200 years and the statue now stands splendidly redundant amidst trees and parkland. West of the house lie the remains of two formal pools, now shrouded in informal plantings of trees and shrubs.

Today, visitors arrive at the east façade of the house, approaching the house from the back. (The National Trust has had the excellent idea of building a car park on the Bath road and organising a shuttle-bus down to the house, whose setting in the past was marred by parked cars.) The original entrance, however, was from the west, where Samuel Hauduroy's raised entrance courtyard makes a pretty introduction to the house – Talman's east façade is grander but less friendly. Talman also designed an orangery with huge sash windows to form part of the east façade, and this is now finely planted with agaves, lemon trees, myrtles and oleanders. In the west garden the (presumably) 17th-century high retaining wall, with grand arched niches, makes a good background to some bold planting – the evergreen *Magnolia delavayi* with huge leathery leaves, loquat (*Eriobotrya japonica*) and *Garrya elliptica*. In 2003 it was announced that a new formal garden, designed by Arne Maynard, was to be made west of the house.

Location nr Chippenham SN14 8ER, Gloucestershire **OS** ST7475 8m N of Bath by A46; 2m S of Jnct 18 of M4 **Tel** and **Fax** 01779 372501 **Email** dyrhampark@ntrust.org.uk **English Heritage Register** Grade II* **Owner** The National Trust **Open** end Mar to Oct, Fri to Tue 11–5.30; park open daily (closed 25 Dec) 12–5.30 (opens 11 when garden open) **Area** (garden) 6 acres/2.4 hectares; (park) 259 acres/105 hectares

Parkland at Dyrham Park

EASTGROVE COTTAGE GARDEN

THE DEFINITIVE AND IRRESISTIBLE COTTAGE GARDEN, A CHARMING PLACE FILLED WITH GOOD PLANTS

Eastgrove Cottage is a half-timbered 17th-century house in a rural setting. Carol and Malcolm Skinner came to live here in 1975 and set about making a garden to suit the house. The result corresponds closely to many people's ideas of the archetypal cottage garden. As cottage gardens go it is nevertheless in one respect completely atypical, for the Skinners are very knowledgeable about plants and although the true repertory of cottage garden plants – *Alchemilla mollis*, aquilegias, Japanese anemones, astrantias, feverfew, geraniums, irises, lavender, pulmonarias, rue, sage and perennial wallflowers – are all to be found, many of the plants in the garden, (especially such tender plants as *Isoplexis canariensis*) are scarcely part of the average cottager's repertory.

EASTNOR CASTLE

AN OUTSTANDING AND ATMOSPHERIC
COLLECTION OF TREES FOR A ROMANTIC
LAKESIDE CASTLE

The Cocks family came to live at Eastnor in around 1600. Between 1812 and *c*.1820 John Somers Cocks, 1st Earl Somers, built a new house to the designs of Sir Robert Smirke. Facing east on an elevated position and looking across a large irregular lake, it is a wonderfully romantic confection of castellated towers and Norman arches, all built of beautiful pale stone.

The deer park, which is north of the Ledbury to Tewkesbury road, dates from the late middle ages. Its highest point is ornamented with an obelisk, the Monument, designed by Sir Robert Smirke and erected in 1813 to commemorate the 1st Earl Somers's son who fell in the battle of Burgos in 1812. The obelisk rises high above trees and is a notable reference point in the landscape.

Before the present castle was built the lake which it overlooks was merely a fishpond and it acquired its present size, and naturalistic shape, as part of the landscaping for the new

Eastnor Castle reflected in its lake

building. The pleasure grounds were also planted up from around 1813 with the trees for which Eastnor is now notable. Planting continued throughout the 19th century, and especially after the appointment of William Coleman as head gardener in 1860. Many new introductions of trees were taking place at about this time and many of them, from Veitch's nursery or direct from plant-collecting expeditions, came to Eastnor.

What, then, is a cottage garden? The most important characteristic is the vernacular style of the place, in which a general irregularity prevails. Paths amble in the most convenient way, straight lines are a rarity, plants jostle each other in abundant profusion. It is a garden devised for the pleasure of the owners and their friends rather than to impress the neighbours and keep up with the Joneses. There are touches of formality – a flawless waist-high hedge of *Lonicera nitida* with a voluptuously pillowed top zigzags amidst the profusion and suddenly metamorphoses into a beech hedge. Some of the formality seems to be the result of extempore invention – a bush of *Rhamnus alaternus* 'Argenteovariegata' was getting out of hand so it has been tightly clipped to form an emphatic sculptural exclamation mark.

EXOTIC TREES IN THE GLADE

The Skinners have also fashioned a mini-arboretum (not that they would call it that; it is referred to as the Glade and serves the purpose of mediating gently between the garden and the surrounding rural landscape). The trees in the glade are exotic, even aristocratic – *Acer griseum*, *Betula utilis* var. *jacquemontii* and *Prunus serrula* among them – but there is also a business-like compost-

Eastgrove Cottage Garden

making area in one corner.

The cottage garden was not merely an aesthetic choice; it originally implied a way of life, and the Skinners have largely embraced this too. The garden is thoroughly productive, with an orchard and a chicken house, and a pair of brick privies – the cottage was once divided in two – rise up with all the aplomb of elegant gazebos. Nevertheless, plants loom large in their lives. A clump of the distinguished *Melianthus major* consorts with hollyhocks, and a little bed of grit provides a home for a beautiful celmisia. The Skinners also run a nursery of plants propagated on the premises, which are available only to visitors; they are mostly herbaceous perennials and many are rare. Such private nurseries, often associated with an attractive garden, have become one of the most important sources of less common plants.

Location Sankyns Green, Little Witley WR6 6LQ, Worcestershire **OS** SO7965 8m NW of Worcester on road between Shrawley (B4196) and Great Witley (A443) **Tel** 01299 896389 **Website** www.eastgrove.co.uk **Owner** Malcolm and Carol Skinner **Open** Apr to Jul, Thur to Mon 2–5; Sept to mid Oct, Thur to Sat 2–5 **Area** 1 acre/0.4 hectares

The arboretum at Eastnor Castle

As soon as you turn into the drive splendid trees catch the eye, starting with a magnificent wide-spreading blue Atlas cedar (*Cedrus atlantica* Glauca Group). This specimen, grown from seed collected in North Africa in 1859 by the 3rd Earl, has the greatest girth of any in the British Isles. Other distinguished trees line the drive, and countless good specimens in the hinterland include the champion dragon spruce (*Picea asperata*), a grove of *Metasequoia glyptostroboides*, an exceptional coastal redwood (*Sequoia sempervirens*) over 100ft/30m high, and a Lucombe oak (*Quercus × hispanica* 'Lucombeana').

A terraced garden separates the castle from the lake. The terrace wall shrouded is shrouded in *Vitis coignetiae* and honeysuckle and the most striking ornament is a grand stone wall fountain, built in 1885, on which the arms of Lady Henry Somerset in a laurel tree flanked by lions are carved in relief. Walks about the lake have splendid views back towards the castle.

South and south-west of the castle, past groups of ash and oak (one of which has a fine tree house), the arboretum continues.

Here the terrain is agreeably undulating and the planting not too crowded, allowing long views of good specimens and groups – among them a spectacular grove of Wellingtonias and, quite close to the castle, a lovely group of soaring incense cedars (*Calocedrus decurrens*). The trees are largely coniferous but occasional deciduous ones can be seen – southern beeches (*Nothofagus* species), oaks and a handsome group of fern-leafed beech. Some of the trees, not particularly rare, are characterful specimens, such as a noble western red cedar (*Thuja plicata*) whose low-spreading limbs have rooted themselves all about.

Location Ledbury HR8 1RL, Herefordshire **OS** SO7336 2m SE of Ledbury by A438 **Tel** 01531 633160 **Fax** 01531 631776 **Email** enquiries@eastnorcastle.com **Website** www.eastnorcastle.com **English Heritage Register** Grade II* **Owner** Mr J. and the Hon. Mrs Hervey-Bathurst **Open** Apr to Jun, and Sept, Sun (open Bank Hol Mon) 11–5; Jul to Aug, daily except Sat 11–5 **Area** 76 acres/31 hectares

ERDDIG

DELIGHTFUL 18TH-CENTURY WALLED GARDENS WITH VICTORIAN AND EDWARDIAN TOUCHES

Erddig is a gawky house, rather pompous on the entrance front and too relentlessly long and low on the garden side. For all that, the place has devastating charm, chiefly because of the house's wonderful interiors and contents, its working outbuildings, and the delightful old-fashioned – very old-fashioned - garden which the National Trust has put back since 1973. The house dates from the 1680s but was substantially altered twice: widened in the 1720s, and given a new entrance front, encased in stone, by James Wyatt in the 1770s. The estate was bought in a bankruptcy sale in 1716 by John Meller who left it on his death in 1733 to his nephew, Simon Yorke. The Yorkes remained here until 1973 when the last of the line, Philip Yorke, gave the estate to the National Trust.

John Meller made what was even then an old-fashioned formal garden east of the house and the essential shape of this garden remains in place today. From the 1760s onwards the landscape designer William Emes made repeated visits to Erddig and did much planting in the park on the west side of the house, but the Yorkes, in defiance of fashion, preserved the formal garden. The estate decayed, the park was scarred by mining and the house threatened by subsidence. When the National Trust's representative, Merlin Waterson, saw it in 1971, he reported a desolate sight: "Inside the park the road disintegrated into a ridge of mud flanked by almost continuous potholes…Most of the shutters were closed, many of the windows broken and whole sashes were missing. It was the death mask of a house which faced two huge slag heaps in the park."

The formal gardens today present as pretty a picture as you may see. A central walk, lined with tubs of clipped Portugal laurel (*Prunus lusitanica*), leads to a canal flanked by double avenues of limes (*Tilia × europaea*) surviving from the 18th century. The vista is triumphantly closed by a pair of beautiful wrought-iron gates made for Erddig in the 1720s by the local blacksmith, Robert Davies. This strong axis unites the various parts of the formal garden. It starts, immediately below the windows of the saloon of the house, with an anachronistic surprise – a light-hearted Edwardian parterre with domes of clipped box and L-shaped beds filled with tulips and forget-me-nots in spring and with snapdragons, plumbago and verbena in summer. Ornamental walls with eccentrically bulgy Dutch gables made to resemble the façades of pavilions flank the parterre. On either side of the Portugal laurel walk, behind screens of pleached lime (*Tilia × euchlora*), are formal orchards. Here the National Trust has established a large collection of 18th- and 19th-century apple cultivars; they are planted in long grass with close-mown paths running between the rows – a delightful effect. On the long brick walls (made of beautiful 1740s bricks) on each side of the garden are espaliered fruit trees underplanted in many cases with rare cultivars of daffodils. The walls are also used for the huge collection of ivies – a National Collection of 170 species and cultivars. Running along the south wall is the

The Edwardian parterre at Erddig

curious Dutch garden where an avenue of clipped Irish yews, flanked with a low box hedge arranged in a key pattern, leads to a little formal garden of Edwardian flavour with shaped pools and beds of roses and clematis. Beyond it the vista continues into woods where a Moss Walk, a sombre place full of holly, laurel and yew, provides a suitably melancholy place for an introspective saunter.

Location nr Wrexham LL13 0YT, Clwyd **OS** SJ3248 2m S of Wrexham by A525 **Tel** 01978 355314 **Infoline** 01938 557019 **Fax** 01978 313333 **Email** erddig@smtp.ntrust.org.uk **CADW/ICOMOS Register** Grade I **Owner** The National Trust **Open** Apr to Oct, Sat to Wed (open Good Fri) 11–6 (opens 10 in Jul and Aug; closes 5 in Oct) **Area** 13 acres/5 hectares

THE GNOLL ESTATE

A WOODLAND GARDEN WITH A LAKE, STREAMS AND MAGNIFICENT CASCADES

The history of the town of Neath is dominated by its position. The river Neath which snakes about the western side of the modern town flows into the sea close to Port Talbot. In the 17th century Neath became a pioneer city in the industrial revolution chiefly because of water-power from the river, the discovery of coalfields close to the coast, and easy transport by sea.

Sir Humphry Mackworth, an Englishman who married a Welsh heiress, came here and started copper and lead smelting in the 1690s. He also built a great house, Gnoll, on a prominent hill overlooking the town and close to his industrial premises. The house was destroyed in 1957 but garden features survived and since the 1980s have been triumphantly reinstated, revealing an early 18th-century layout of rare character. The gardening activities here were remarkable, for the Mackworths used the same water from the hills both as an essential part of their industrial activities and as the chief ingredient of their landscaping.

Between 1724 and 1727 Thomas Greening laid out formal gardens for Sir Humphry, the chief feature of which was a formal cascade and pool to the east of the house. The pool was subsequently made informal and it now has the appearance of a naturalistic lake, but the cascade, whose stonework had survived though choked by undergrowth, has been restored – and an astonishing sight it is. It descends a stately slope, now planted with fine beeches on either side, in a series of pools and shallow falls. In some places the flow of water is concentrated in a narrow passage, with an upright flat stone below it creating a plume of water. Apart from that detail, it is remarkably similar to the slightly earlier cascade at Chatsworth (*see page 255*), completed in 1696. Chatsworth's cascade has a hidden reservoir as its source but the cascade at Gnoll is fed from an open reservoir which originally provided some of the power for Mackworth's factory.

The great cascade at The Gnoll

At the highest point of the Gnoll estate is a cascade of a very different character. The walk, uphill all the way, is a stiff one but delightful. The grounds are thickly wooded with beeches, larch, oaks and pines, and streams lace the land – often vertiginously far below the paths. On the way you pass Half House, a battlemented 18th-century stone alcove with a seat at the top of a flight of steps, and eventually arrive at a large stretch of water – Mosshouse Wood Reservoir – with an inlet and a dramatic cascade erupting from rocks. But this is not your final goal: for you must now cross a narrow slab of stone over the inlet and follow a path through Mosshouse Woods (named for a long lost ornamental house of moss) to a swampy clearing. Before you, descending the steeply wooded slopes, is yet another astonishing cascade, this time an informal one. It falls from a height of 180ft/55m but owes its beauty to the fact that it is broken into a long series of falls as it curves through the woods. It dates from the 1740s and is therefore among the earliest naturalistic man-made cascades in Britain. (The dramatic but nothing like so extensive example at Bowood (*see page 73*) was made only in 1785.) At the head of the cascade is the remains of a grotto sadly shorn of its tumbling stalactites.

Half House at The Gnoll

Loudon's *Encyclopaedia of Gardening* (1822) describes Gnoll: "The house rises with baronial pomp and grandeur, on the point of a hill, overlooking the town and adjacent country. The grounds most judiciously laid out by the late Sir H. Mackworth." The house has gone but the grandeur remains, and the vestiges of the garden, sketchy as they may be, are memorably impressive.

Location Neath, Glamorgan **OS** SS7697 On the eastern edge of Neath off Gnoll Park Road, B4434 **Tel** 01639 635808 **CADW/ICOMOS Register** Grade II* **Owner** Neath Port Talbot County Borough Council **Open** daily 8–5 **Area** 200 acres/81 hectares

HAMPTON COURT

BRILLIANTLY DESIGNED, FLOWER-FILLED
NEW GARDENS FOR AN OLD ESTATE

The house at Hampton Court has a complicated history. A 15th-century castle owned by the Lenthall family was completely rebuilt towards the end of the 17th century for Lord Coningsby, and in the early 19th century the estate was bought by R. Arkwright (of the "spinning jenny" family) who called in Sir Jeffry Wyattville to restore more of its original castle appearance and add 19th-century comforts.

In the late 17th century Hampton Court had a garden of spectacular magnificence. The Kip engraving shows a house with a pretty blend of medieval and classical features set at the heart of formal gardens – parterres, pools and fountains giving way to avenues which radiate across the land. This garden, in which the royal gardener George London had a hand, was described as it was in the 1730s by William Stukeley in his *Itinerarium curiosum* (1776): "The gardens are very pleasant (the finest greens I ever saw), terminated by vast woods covering all the side of the hill…Here is a great command of water on all sides of the house for fountains, basons, canals…There are lawns, groves, canals, hills, plains…a pool three-qarters of a mile long." By Arkwright's time all this had disappeared. Humphry Repton had been consulted by the previous owner, Lord Malden, in 1794 and it is likely that he had a hand in the removal of the formal gardens which Stukeley had seen.

THE NEW GARDENS

In 1994 the estate was bought by an American, Robert Van Kampen, who restored the house and, in 1996, embarked on the garden, for which Simon Dorrell was commissioned to make an appropriate new layout. This he has splendidly done, chiefly within the walled enclosures of an early 19th-century kitchen garden to one side of the house. The first part of the garden is an ornamental kitchen garden with ranges of glasshouses. The flower garden beyond it is a *tour de force* which makes references to the past but has a sprightly modern feel. Here are walks of pleached lime and two canals, each fed with a stepped cascade. At the centre of each canal, sitting on an island, a beautifully made octagonal gazebo of brick and wood has a pronounced Arts and Crafts character. The pools are flanked by large beds of lavender and weeping silver pears (*Pyrus salicifolia* 'Pendula'). Borders run along the walls with much bold planting – thickets of *Stipa gigantea* and *Eupatorium purpureum* – and much repeat planting, including veils of self-sown *Verbena bonariensis*. In one corner a formal rose garden has box-edged beds of chiefly David Austin English Roses.

The adjacent Dutch Garden comes as a surprise. A long narrow canal is edged in fine

The flower garden at Hampton Court

one paving and rows of pots on each side
rimming with tufts of the ornamental grass
Hakonechloa macra 'Aureola'. Behind these,
unning the whole length of the canal, are
eds of alternate standard Portugal laurels
Prunus lusitanica) alternating with Irish yews,
l underplanted with giant swathes of *Verbena
bonariensis* – a mesmerising sight.

To one side of the walled gardens is a new
edge maze of yew with, as its goal, a fine
othic tower built to match the house. Once
is goal is reached you may descend through
tunnel to emerge in a very different kind of
arden: the Sunken Garden. This is not the
upper flower garden of Edwardian times but
romantic pool garden overlooked by a rustic
atched hermitage and fed by a tumbling
ascade. The surrounding banks are planted
vishly with shade-loving plants – bergenias,
pimediums, ferns, hostas and the lovely
Hydrangea quercifolia. Already there is much
 admire at Hampton Court and further
ans are underway.

Location Hope-under-Dinmore, Leominster
HR6 0PN, Herefordshire **OS** SO5252 5m S of
Leominster by A49; close to junction with A417
Tel 01568 797777 **Fax** 01568 797472 **Email**
vankampengardens@hamptoncourt.org.uk **Owner**
Sola scriptura **Open** Apr to Oct, Wed to Sun (open
Bank Hol Mon) 11–5; Nov to Mar, daily 11– 4 (closed
24 Dec to 4 Jan) **Area** 20 acres/8 hectares

HANBURY HALL

STATELY PERIOD GARDENS OF FLOWERY FORMALITY FOR A GRAND EARLY 18TH-CENTURY HOUSE

James Lees-Milne wrote of his visit in 1938,
"When I got to Hanbury, the park looked
like a battlefield, overgrown with nettles…the
front drive…was fairly choked with weeds."
After delicate and protracted negotiations
with the reclusive Sir George Vernon and his
adopted daughter, the house passed to the
National Trust in 1953, thanks to a last minute
anonymous gift.

Hanbury is a splendid house, built in 1701
for a lawyer, Thomas Vernon, possibly to the
designs of William Talman. Of fine brick, with
stone dressings, it is crowned with an airy
central cupola – the view of it as you cross
the fields that lie on your way is enchanting.
A Victorian entrance court is decorated with a
pair of gauche but charming pavilions whose
roofs start off soberly straight but suddenly
wriggle into ogee shapes. Mixed borders line
the walls and a pair of tall stone vases are
planted with variegated agaves.

South-west of the house the National Trust,
starting in 1993, has recreated the formal
garden which was designed, possibly by the
royal gardener George London, when the
house was built. The original formal garden
had been removed in the late 18th century
when landscaping became the universal fashion
but a plan and bird's eye view made in 1732
by Joseph Doughtery shows the complex.

A sunken parterre surrounded by a gravel
walk is divided into four intricately patterned
beds outlined with box, and has a central
compartment outlined in golden box with a

box topiary shape in the middle. The beds are filled with herbaceous plants – white alyssum, London pride, marigolds, pasque flowers, snapdragons and thrift – and the planting is open, with rows of plants and much bare earth visible, as it would have been in an early 18th-century flower garden. The effect is like a riotously coloured Persian rug but it retains an air of gentlemanly formality.

Alongside it a formal fruit garden, with yew topiary and clipped fruit trees, is decorated with trelliswork pavilions. Rows of apples and pears are planted in grass edged with narrow borders in which shapes of bay or laurustinus are underplanted with the same range of flowers as the parterre. A formal Wilderness nearby has rows of bay, hibiscus, variegated holly, phillyrea, *Rosa gallica* 'Versicolor' and sloes enclosing specimen trees in grass – a Judas tree, flowering cherries or laburnum. The adjoining Grove consists of a pattern of compartments hedged in hornbeam and radiating from a central oval; each compartment is filled with dogwood, guelder rose, hazels and rowans. A bowling green is overlooked by two very pretty ogee-shaped

The sunken parterre at Hanbury Hall

pavilions topped with gilt knobs but the wood of which they are made is starting to split and they will not last long. To one side is an 18th-century orangery with agaves and citrus plants in Versailles boxes, and behind it, against the north wall, is a mushroom house in full action (a rare garden sight), with wonderful truffly smells in its dark moist interior.

A walk north from the garden leads past a splendid old cedar of Lebanon, along a row of newly planted cedars with views of parkland, to an 18th-century icehouse. Its exterior (a grassy knoll) is unprepossessing but the interior is exceedingly impressive: a deep vaulted oubliette of beautifully laid bricks – not for those who suffer from claustrophobia.

The reinstated formal garden, including its idiosyncrasies, seems to me to a great success – attractive in itself and providing an elegant but lively setting for the house.

Location Hanbury, Droitwich WR9 7EA, Worcestershire **OS** SO9463 4½m E of Droitwich by B4090 and minor roads; Jnct 5 of M5 **Tel** 01527 821214 **Fax** 01527 821251 **Email** hanbury@smtp.ntrust.org.uk **Website** www.ntrustsevern.org.uk **English Heritage Register** Grade II **Owner** The National Trust **Open** Apr to Oct, Wed to Sun 12.30–6 **Area** 15 acres/6 hectares

HAWKSTONE PARK

DRAMATIC 18TH-CENTURY LANDSCAPE PARK WITH GROTTOES, ROCKY RAVINES AND REMARKABLE MONUMENTS

This was the ancient estate of the Hill family, whose 13th-century castle was destroyed by Cromwell. In the latter part of the 18th century two generations of Hills (Sir Rowland and Sir Richard) fashioned an extraordinary landscape park which was strongly influenced by their near neighbour, Richard Payne Knight of Downton Castle (*see page 469*). Knight hated the "dull, vapid, smooth and tranquil scene" of the landscapes of Capability Brown and his disciples (those geniuses "of the bare and bald"); he wanted something to set the pulse racing – a sublime landscape of precipitous rocks, tumbling water and a ruined castle "Imbosom'd high upon the mountain's brow/Or nodding o'er the stream that glides below". This is precisely the kind of scene fashioned by the Hills at Hawkstone.

The Hills took every advantage of the gigantic natural craggy outcrops of red sandstone fringed with trees that erupt from the landscape here. They devised walks which

Cliffs at Hawkstone Park

...ed the visitor on a circuitous and frequently ...errifying tour of the park. Paths skirt the ...rags or cross precipitous bridges, from time ...o time suddenly revealing vertiginous ...escents below. A long dark tunnel penetrates ...he cliffs and emerges in a narrow ravine, ...lmost too narrow to walk along, fringed with ...erns and cushioned in moss. Another, almost ...evoid of light, opens out into an astonishing ...ulti-chambered labyrinthine grotto (the ...argest room is 80ft/25m across), with ...indows penetrating the rock sides and an ...pening leading out onto a cliff – not ...ecommended for visitors with vertigo.

"TERRIFICK GRANDEUR"

...here is also a remarkable 100ft/30m column ...n a grove of monkey puzzles. Climbing the ...piral staircase, you emerge on a viewing ...latform to find yourself standing alongside ...he giant legs and under the doublet of a 16th-...entury Sir Rowland Hill, the first Protestant ...ord Mayor of London. He scans the horizon, ...nd you do too, for a gigantic panorama of the ...ncircling landscape is revealed.

In the 18th century the park was even ...igger and was enriched with more ...rnamental buildings than survive today; even ...o it provides one of the least forgettable of all ...arden visiting experiences. Most historic

gardens are impossible to see correctly through 21st-century eyes but here at Hawkstone the power of the landscape elicits from the visitor all the feelings of awe and terror – "the sublime" – that Richard Payne Knight and his followers sought. Dr Johnson, a usually sceptical garden visitor who dismissed landscape gardens as "innocent amusement", visited Hawkstone in 1774 and was moved by the "striking scenes and terrifick grandeur", responding deeply to the atmosphere of the place: "the awfulness of its shades, the horrors of its precipices, the verdure of its hollows and the loftiness of its rocks. The Ideas which it forces upon the mind are the sublime, the dreadful and the vast." Hawkstone is one of the few places where the abstractions of garden history become vivdly real.

Location Weston-under-Redcastle, Shrewsbury SY4 5UY, Shropshire **OS** SJ5729 14m NE of Shrewsbury by A49 or A53 and minor roads **Tel** 01939 200611 **Fax** 01939 200311 **English Heritage Register** Grade I **Owner** Hawkstone Estate **Open** Apr to Oct, daily 10–4; Nov to Feb, Sat and Sun (closed 25 Dec) 10–4 **Area** 300 acres/121 hectares

HERGEST CROFT GARDENS

IDYLLIC PRIVATE WOODLAND GARDENS
IN A LOVELY LANDSCAPE, WITH
SUPERB TREES AND SHRUBS

For those who love trees and shrubs an enthusiast's private aboretum is a special pleasure. Hergest Croft, in a particularly attractive part of one of the most attractive counties, welcomes visitors yet has an agreeably private air.

William Hartland Banks started to build an Arts and Crafts house here in 1896 and began his garden. He was acquiring plants, in particular from Veitch's nursery, at a time when marvellous new introductions were being made, especially by E.H. Wilson in China. Two subsequent generations of the family have built on those foundations, not only forming an exceptional collection but also creating a most seductive landscape. It would be futile to begin to list the plants to be seen here except

Wrought-iron gates at Hergest Croft

in the most general terms, but there are three National Collections – maples (excluding *Acer japonicum* and *A. palmatum* cultivars, 129 species and cultivars), birches (59 species and cultivars) and, more recondite but thrilling, zelkova (6 species and cultivars).

The garden falls into two parts: those areas that lie close to the house and those that are arrived at by walking across the Park and Haywood Common to Park Wood. Close to the house are a few passages of relative formality. A croquet lawn is enclosed in yew hedges with clipped spheres along the top, niches and indentations, and its entrance has a canopy of golden yew and Gothic benches from which to survey the scene. A fine wrought-iron gate and screen, in lively Arts and Crafts style, leads through to the Azalea Garden where in spring the shrubs glow under a canopy of forest trees. Here, the strong axis of an avenue of conifers plunges away, with a cross axis going gently uphill to a beautiful beech. There are good trees all around, including Japanese maples. On the other side of the house, beyond an orchard, is a simple old-fashioned kitchen garden – certainly not the chief reason for coming here but very attractive. Fruit and vegetables are still grown and there are herbaceous borders, a formal rose garden and, prettiest of all, aquilegias, hellebores, peonies, pulmonaria and spring bulbs under espaliered apple trees.

MARVELS OF PARK WOOD

The walk across the Park to Park Wood is very beautiful, with excellent parkland trees and wonderful distant views of the rural landscape. As you enter Park Wood there is little immediate excitement – you are walking under a canopy of native beech and oak, carpeted with bluebells and wood anemones in spring. It is all perfectly agreeable although you begin to wonder if you have taken the right path. But excitement mounts as you come to Pen Pool where a cascade splashes between ferns and rushes into a wooded ravine below. Here, the woodland is more dense, and more exotic, with cypresses, firs, larches, southern beeches (*Nothofagus* species), pines, rowans and spruces. This, and the additional shelter of the hilly terrain, provides exactly the right conditions

for wonderful rhododendrons. Many of them were among the earliest plantings in the garden and have reached great size. Their glowing colours are, to my eye, always best when seen in a densely planted context such as this where they seem as at home as they would in the Himalayas.

The great tree connoisseur Alan Mitchell described Hergest Croft as a "huge collection, especially of conifers, maples and oaks, many very rare". That is certainly true, but it is also, simply as a piece of landscape natural and man-made, exceptionally beautiful.

Location Kington HR5 3EG, Herefordshire **OS** SO2856 ½m W of Kington off A44 **Tel** and **Fax** 01544 230160 **Email** banks@hergest.kc3ltd.co.uk **English Heritage Register** Grade II* **Owner** W.L. Banks **Open** Apr to Oct, daily 1.30–6 **Area** 50 acres/20 hectares

HIDCOTE MANOR GARDEN

THE MOST INFLUENTIAL ENGLISH GARDEN OF THE 20TH CENTURY – A FEAST OF PLANTS AND DESIGN

Hidcote is the work of an expatriate American, Major Lawrence Johnston, who came here in 1907 and made one of the most influential English gardens of the 20th century. It is, overwhelmingly, a garden of plants, but it is also designed with an artist's eye for changes in mood and the brilliant use of enclosed space. Vita Sackville-West caught its essence when she described it as "a cottage garden on the most glorified scale". It is a cottage garden in the sense that it is abundantly planted and has many corners of

The box parterre and circular pool garden at Hidcote

beguiling intimacy, but its glory comes from the occasional dazzlingly long vista, a sudden surprise, the easy intermingling of ingredients, while always preserving a sense of harmony.

At the heart of the garden is one of Johnston's earliest schemes: the Red Borders – a pair of deep mixed borders flanking a broad grass path. Rich and brilliant reds of dahlias, fuchsias, lobelias, poppies and roses are soothed down by the sombre foliage of *Cotinus coggygria* 'Royal Purple' and purple-leafed filbert (*Corylus maxima* 'Purpurea'). Rising up in the profusion are gracefully arching fronds of the Chinese grass *Miscanthus sinensis* 'Gracillimus', sharp blades of *Cordyline australis* and the umbrella-like foliage of *Rheum palmatum*. The borders end with a pair of dapper garden pavilions, at a slightly higher level, flanking a wide flight of steps. Straight ahead is a walk between clipped hornbeam "hedges on stilts", culminating in grand wrought-iron gates and views over the country. This, after the fireworks of the Red Borders, has a calmly soothing effect.

AN EXHILARATING VIEW

The borders and hornbeam walk, though strikingly different in mood, are similar in scale. But a new and startling view is displayed through the open door of the southern pavilion – on its far side an immensely long grass path, flanked by high walls of hornbeam, swoops down and away towards a distant gate on the garden's boundary. The effect is exhilarating, providing a vast expanse of calm, grand simplicity after the enveloping pyrotechnics of the Red Borders.

Closer to the house are several linked compartments – among them a miniature white garden with yew topiary birds, a box parterre of scillas and fuchsias, the Old Garden with lavish mixed borders (and *far* too many bamboos supporting plants), and a circular pool garden of surrealistic proportions, whose pool leaves almost no room for visitors. Quite close to this bustle of gardens is the Theatre Lawn, a huge expanse hedged in yew with a lone old beech tree raised on a circular platform at its far end. This dramatic and beautiful space fulfils exactly the same function as the Long Walk of hornbeam hedges.

Harold Nicolson called the ten acres of Hidcote "the loveliest small garden in England". Few people today would think of it as small and it was certainly never small in effect. For visitors today it is not only enthralling to see as fresh and exciting a garden as you can see anywhere, but also a garden that is so instructive: on making the best use of the site; on plants (exotic or common) deployed to their best effect; on subtle or explosive changes of atmosphere – and all infused with an irrepressible delight in the pleasures of gardening.

Location Hidcote Bartrim, nr Chipping Camden GL55 6LR, Gloucestershire **OS** SP1742 4m NE of Chipping Camden by B4632 **Tel** 01386 438333 **Infoline** 01684 855370 **Fax** 01386 438817 **Email** hidcote@ntrust.org.uk **English Heritage Register** Grade I **Owner** The National Trust **Open** Apr to Oct, daily except Tue and Fri (open Good Fri) 11–7 (Jun and Jul also open Tue 11–7; closes 6 in Oct) **Area** 10 acres/4 hectares

HODGES BARN

EXCELLENT PLANTS IN A HARMONIOUS AND VARIED SETTING FOR A DELIGHTFUL HOUSE

Private gardens of this kind, made for the delight of the owners and not paying too much attention to what is fleetingly fashionable, often give great pleasure. The late Charles Hornby inherited Hodges Barn from his grandmother in 1972. She had converted this beautiful former dovecote, with two square towers and domed roofs, into a house of the greatest character. She had also laid out a firm structure to the garden, with paths, walls and yew hedges, and, in this rather exposed site, had established windbreaks to the west.

The garden surrounds the house and is divided into logical compartments related to it. A long vista starts from the front door, on the north side of the house, with an opening in a yew hedge framed by yew topiaries. A first enclosure has a rectangle of lawn with a pair of *Magnolia × soulangeana* at each end, and the vista is continued in the following enclosure by an avenue of Irish yews running across a croquet lawn and ending in a stone bench which looks back towards the house. The boundary hedge of yew is clipped from

Yew topiary at Hodges Barn

time to time into bold buttresses and a west-facing border is filled with old shrub roses – a running theme of the garden. A little formal garden on the south side of the house is enclosed in stone walls and filled with roses underplanted with artemisia, geraniums, regale lilies, sages and violets. At the southern end an opening allows views over an orchard, out across meadows beyond. Next to this enclosure is a lawn planted with flowering cherries and again hedged in yew.

On the other side of the house the garden becomes wilder. A pool is overhung with a weeping willow and lavishly edged with moisture-loving plants, and an opening leads into a simple woodland garden. Here, acers, magnolias and rowans are underplanted with swathes of spring bulbs and much use is made of species roses – *R. rubrifolia*, *R. sweginzowii* and *R. villosa* proving their worth in this informal setting. There is nothing forced or fussy in the garden at Hodges Barn. Good plants are deployed with relish in a setting that fits house and countryside like a glove.

Location Shipton Moyne, Tetbury GL8 8PR, Gloucestershire **OS** SO8989 On the E edge of Shipton Moyne village, 2½m S of Tetbury by A433 and minor road **Tel** 01666 880202 **Fax** 01666 880373 **Owner** Mrs Charles Hornby **Open** Apr to mid Aug, Mon, Tue and Fri 2–5 **Area** 8 acres/3.2 hectares

HODNET HALL

DREAMY WATERSIDE GARDENS WITH FINE TREES AND FLOWERING SHRUBS

The house at Hodnet, built to the designs of Anthony Salvin in 1870, commands splendid views of all the essential ingredients of what is largely a 20th-century garden, chiefly made between the wars by Brigadier A.G.W. Heber-Percy who dammed a stream to form pools and did immense amounts of planting.

The house looks south over a large pool in the valley below. On the slopes above the far side is a dovecote that makes a distant eyecatcher, with the Shropshire hills rising on the horizon beyond it. A visually echoing eyecatcher on the north side of the house, at the end of an avenue crossing the road, is formed by a stone portico and columns brought here from Apley Castle when it was demolished in 1956.

Immediately below the house the ground is terraced, with a flight of steps running down the middle. These are flanked with artemisia, heathers and lavender, behind which are more substantial shrubs and trees – *Choisya ternata*, Japanese maples and witch hazels. At the bottom of the steps mixed borders open out on each side. South-east of the house is a circular bed with concentric rings of roses, peonies, lavender and hydrangeas and a statue in the middle. Close to it is a large collection of camellias and, to one side, a distinguished walk of magnolias. West of the house a swimming pool is skilfully concealed behind monumental hedges of yew. That, in essence, is the extent of the formal gardens at Hodnet Hall – charming rather than enthralling.

POOLS IN THE WOODED VALLEY

The greatest plant excitement, and the most imaginative use of the landscape, lies to the south-west where a chain of pools snakes along the wooded valley. The banks of the pools are lavishly planted with astilbes, ferns, *Gunnera manicata* (surprisingly hardy in this cold part of the country), lysichiton, primulas and trilliums. Against a background of old beeches and oaks are many exotic trees and

◁ **The water garden** at Hodnet Hall

shrubs – azaleas, birches, cercidiphyllum, hydrangeas, maples and viburnums. Grassy walks between the pools open out vistas along the water – a gleaming passage between the chasms of planting.

The garden, still in private hands, is finely kept and a delightful place to visit.

Location Hodnet, nr Market Drayton TF9 3NN, Shropshire **OS** SJ6128 In the village of Hodnet 5½m SW of Market Drayton by A53; 12m NE of Shrewsbury by A53 **Tel** 01630 685202 **Fax** 01630 685853 **English Heritage Register** Grade II **Owner** Mr and the Hon. Mrs A. Heber-Percy **Open** Apr to Sept, daily except Mon (open Bank Hol Mon) 12–5 **Area** 70 acres/28 hectares

KIFTSGATE COURT

OUTSTANDING 20TH-CENTURY GARDEN, MAGNIFICENT ROSES AND SPRIGHTLY MODERN IDEAS

The great impression of Kiftsgate is one of profusion in which deft areas of formality, and enclosures, give a strong sense of purpose amidst the abundance. The garden was made by Heather Muir from 1920 onwards, with help from her immediate neighbour and friend, Lawrence Johnston of Hidcote (*see page 210*). The two gardens have in common a refined taste in plants and the division into compartments of different character.

Kiftsgate has a far more dramatic setting than Hidcote with its flat and windy site, and a further striking difference is that the garden at Kiftsgate firmly takes its cue from the house whereas that at Hidcote strikes out on its own. Kiftsgate Court rears up on the edge of the Cotswold escarpment with spectacular open views westwards over the Vale of Evesham towards the Malvern hills. The steep stone steps which lead to the path that winds down the wooded hill are guarded by a grove of Scots pines, sweeps of bergenias and martagon lilies, while such plants as abutilons, cistus, *Convolvulus sabatius*, euphorbias and *Teucrium fruticans* adorn the banks above the path as you descend. In the lower garden, with its classical temple and pool, a semicircular viewing platform of turf gives giant views to the west of remarkably unspoilt landscape.

The formal parts of the garden largely

cluster about the house. Four Squares is divided by paved paths, with a sundial at the centre, and has mixed plantings in each of the four beds, with a pronounced colour scheme of pinks, mauves and purples. A paved sunken garden on the far side of the house has an octagonal pool and fountain at the centre. Gentle terracing surrounds the pool, with dense plantings of alliums, alstroemerias, eryngiums, geraniums, penstemons and peonies and the occasional clipped dome of box or vertical Irish juniper. Against the shady north-facing wall are waves of ferns, hostas and trilliums. Metal chairs and tables are painted a startling shade of blue.

Heather Muir, like Lawrence Johnston, was a pioneer devotee of old shrub roses. In her

The new pool at Kiftsgate

rose garden a grass path runs between hedges of *Rosa gallica* 'Versicolor', behind which are high ramparts of shrub roses. At the end an arch of clipped whitebeam frames a stone seat carved in the shape of an odalisque. In one corner a beech tree is shrouded in the famous 'Kiftsgate' rose (*Rosa filipes* 'Kiftsgate'), a staggering sight in June. (This was an accidental discovery of Heather Muir in 1938, who bought from E.A. Bunyard what she thought was *R. moschata*.)

Beyond the rose garden a former tennis court, handsomely hedged in yew, was made in 1999 into a striking minimalist garden. It was commissioned by Heather Muir's granddaughter and her husband, who now look after the garden. A black-lined pool is edged in fine Portland stone paving and has a dazzling fountain by Simon Allison – a row of gently swaying metal stems emerging from the water, each crowned with a bronze cast of the flower head of the aroid *Philodendron mamei* from which water pours back down the stem. Stepping stones of Portland stone, which seem to float on the surface of the inky black water, lead to a rectangular island of turf.

Kiftsgate, now in the third generation of the family that made it, preserves the atmosphere of a family garden – but a family of passionate and discerning gardeners who are not irretrievably buried in the past.

Location Chipping Camden GL55 6LW, Gloucestershire **OS** SP1743 3m NE of Chipping Camden by B4632 **Tel** and **Fax** 01386 438777   **Owner** Mr and Mrs J.G. Chambers   **Open** Apr to May, Wed, Thur and Sun 2–6; Jun to Jul, Wed, Thur, Sat and Sun 12–6; Aug to Sept, Wed, Thur and Sun 2–6 (open Bank Hol Mon 2–6) **Area** 6 acres/2.4 hectares

Kyre Park from the shrubberies

KYRE PARK GARDENS

ATMOSPHERIC 18TH-CENTURY WOODLAND
WALKS WITH STREAMS, POOLS, CASCADES
AND ORNAMENTAL BUILDINGS

Kyre is an ancient place, going back at least to the middle ages – in 1275 a deer park was made and the oaks grown in it were famous in the 16th century. The estate was bought in 1575 by Edward Pytts and passed by descent into the 20th century. The house, which retains a medieval wing and parts dating from the 16th and 17th centuries, was rebuilt with a smart pedimented brick façade in the middle of the 18th century for Sir Edmund Pytts.

The deer park at Kyre survives on high ground north-east of the house, although its herd of fallow deer succumbed in the 19th century. In the second half of the 18th century Sir Edmund Pytts removed formal gardens and laid out a very large lawn west of the house, with a serpentine lake on

Pavilion and lily pool at Kyre Park

its western boundary. A Chinese bridge was made at this time, probably to span the lake. It is rumoured (as it often is) that Capability Brown had a hand in this but there is no evidence; however, it is known that a Shropshire nurseryman and designer, John Davenport, worked here – a letter of his dated 1784 says, "I am now Imployed at Mr Pytts at Kyre and have been for many years." The lawn, or Meadow, was edged with shrubberies and woodland, within which were winding walks which led past several pools and streams with cascades. This layout, restored in recent years, is what is seen today.

Immediately west of the house is a formal rose garden on a terrace with panoramic views of the Meadow. A walk leads north into the woods, past a very beautiful old fern-leafed beech (*Fagus sylvatica* var. *heterophylla* 'Aspleniifolia'). Here a pool, the Fishpond, is crossed by an 18th-century cast-iron bridge and a path leads into a tunnel which plunges into the ground. This, built in the 18th century, had collapsed but has now been restored and opens out into a splendid brick pavilion, crowned by a viewing platform, which

rises over a cascade feeding a huge lily pool. The path continues past other pools and cascades edged in mossy rustic stonework, where the most notable planting consists of old yews, some of which must date back to the original 18th-century plantings. The walk soon arrives at the serpentine lake (or River as it is now called) where it curves round west of the Meadow, giving splendid views back towards the house framed by trees. On the banks of the River are the remains of an 18th-century Gothic Hermitage.

The most memorable feature of the garden at Kyre is the watery walk through the shrubberies and woodland that curve round on three sides of the Meadow. The restoration since 1994 of this most unusual 18th-century garden is a great achievement. More remains to be done but already a landscape of tremendous character has been revealed.

Also housed at Kyre Park is an admirable nursery, Rickard's Hardy Ferns. As you leave, do not miss the magnificent early medieval dovecote marooned on the eastern edge of the car park.

Location Kyre Park, Tenbury Wells WR15 8RP, Worcestershire   **OS** SO6263 4m SE of Tenbury Wells by B4214   **Tel** 01885 410247   **Fax** 01884 410398 **Owner** Mr and Mrs J. Sellers   **Open** Feb to 23 Dec, daily 10–6   **Area** 29 acres/12 hectares

ITTLE MORETON HALL

BRILLIANT LITTLE RECONSTRUCTED
PERIOD GARDEN FOR A WONDERFUL
TIMBERED TUDOR HOUSE

heshire is rich in half-timbered houses
and Little Moreton Hall, built in the late
5th and 16th centuries, is one of the best.
amously lopsided, it is described by Pevsner
his Cheshire volume of "The Buildings of
ngland" (in one of his very rare excursions
to humour) as "happily reeling, disorderly,
it no offence meant – it seems at first
abelievable and then a huge joke". I find the
ouse delightful, with its exquisite timber
ork (best seen in the wonderful internal roof
rpentry), lavishly decorated façades and
andsome internal courtyard.

No-one knows in any detail what the
rdens of houses of this kind, owned by
ovincial gentry, were like in the 16th
ntury. The house is moated and on either
de of the moat two mounds are conceivably
e remains of 16th-century garden mounds.
he house was given to the National Trust in
937 and the garden that exists today, based on
hat we do know about gardens of the
riod, was started in 1975. The design for the
ot garden was taken from Leonard Meager's

The English Gardener, and although this book
was published in 1670 the design chosen
probably dates from around a hundred years
earlier. Enclosed in yew hedges, it has an
intricate pattern of low hedges of small-leafed
box (*Buxus sempervirens* 'Suffruticosa')
enclosing compartments of gravel or of mown
grass, with obelisks of clipped yew rising at the
centre of the four chief compartments. On
either side is a strip of small box-edged beds
with rows of standard gooseberries shaped into
lollipops, each underplanted with some
herbaceous plant known to have been used in
16th-century gardens – London pride,
strawberries, wall germander, white thrift,
woodruff and so on. The garden lies below the
northern façade of the house, not far from one
of the mounds. In the 16th century, mounds of
this kind, sometimes topped with a little
pavilion, were used as vantage points from
which to admire knot gardens such as this.

Between the garden's hedge and the moat is
a narrow walk. This is animated by plenty of
duck life and has plantings of *Darmera peltata*,
ferns, geraniums, hostas and periwinkles on
the water's edge, and against the hedges small
beds of herbs and vegetables. This, and the
reconstructed period garden, are entirely in

The knot garden at Little Moreton Hall

keeping with the decorative vernacular of the
place – what James Lees-Milne called "its
absolutely unpretentious happy-go-luckiness".

Location Congleton CW12 4SD, Cheshire **OS** SJ8459
4m SW of Congleton by A34 **Tel** 01260 272018
Email mimsca@smtp.ntrust.org.uk **Owner** The National
Trust **Open** late Mar to Oct, Wed to Sun (open Bank Hol
Mon) 11.30–5 or dusk if earlier; mid Nov to 23 Dec, Sat
and Sun 11.30–4 **Area** 1 acre/0.4 hectares

LYME PARK

SUPERB ANCIENT PARKLAND AND GRAND
19TH-CENTURY GARDENS FOR A SUPERB
18TH-CENTURY HOUSE

he Legh family acquired the Lyme Park
estate in 1398 and gave it to the National
Trust in 1946. The present house is a radical
remodelling by Giacomo Leoni in the 1720s
and 1730s of a house that goes back to the
16th century. The combination of a very grand
Palladian house (its south front is fifteen bays
wide) with the wild moorland setting on the
edge of the Peak District is memorably strange.

Visitors to Lyme Park leave the A6 and are
plunged immediately into parkland, with the
house on low-lying ground at its centre. The
park has an ancient feel, and rightly so, for it
was established in 1359, originally part of the
royal hunting ground of Macclesfield Forest.
The herd of red deer which still lives here is
thought to be descended from native forest
deer; an additional herd of fallow deer was
introduced in the 1990s. The park was
originally enclosed in a wooden palissade, 9
miles long, but this was replaced between
1598 and 1620 by a dry-stone wall. Visible
from the drive, rising high on an escarpment
to the east, is the Cage, built in the 16th
century and rebuilt by Leoni in the early 18th
century. Originally a hunting lodge, it was
recast by Leoni as an eyecatcher.

Before 1676 Richard Legh laid out avenues
of lime and sycamore – an axial avenue
running north and south from the house
forming the central spoke of a *patte d'oie*
radiating from the southern façade of the
house. A painting of *c.*1720 by an unidentified
artist, illustrated in John Harris's *The Artist and
the Country House* (1979), shows the southern

avenue aligned on an eyecatcher, Stag House, of which only the foundations remain. The southern avenue was replanted, again with limes, in the 1840s.

The gardens, on the south side of the house, are chiefly the work of the architect Lewis Wyatt between 1813 and 1820. He laid out a long terrace against the south façade, overlooking an irregular miniature lake which he had created from a formal stretch of water established in the 17th century. Wyatt also removed a formal garden, the Dutch Garden, put into place in around 1700, but that was reinstated on a different site in 1860. It is a charming piece of kitsch, arranged so that you may look down on it from the high terrace walk. In the middle is a pool with a water jet surrounded by statues of cherubs symbolising the four elements. An elaborate pattern of beds edged in tightly clipped ivy or box spreads all around, filled with bedding schemes for spring and summer.

To the east of the house Wyatt designed an orangery. It has at its centre a grand tiered fountain, with ferns and moss lavishly decorating the stonework, and the floor has prettily patterned tiles. Bananas, tender ferns and figs are grown, but most remarkable is an old camellia beautifully trained against the wall, said to have been planted when the orangery was completed (in 1862, long after Wyatt's time here).

The Dutch Garden at Lyme Park

In front of the orangery are lawns, Irish yews and two sunken gardens with beds cut out of the turf, which are planted with seasonal bedding schemes. In the summer of 2002 they consisted of scarlet lobelias erupting from purple sage, with a centrepiece of purple-leafed cordylines and massed pale blue cherry pie. To one side, concealed behind yew hedges, is an Edwardian rose garden with a secretive air overlooked at one end by a summerhouse flanked by beds of ferns and hostas and, at each side, a big old lime tree.

On the far side of the lake a rhododendron walk leads to a wooded valley with a stream and plantings of astilbes, ferns, *Gunnera manicata* and lysichiton. At the head of the ravine is a great stone bridge and a pool. From here you may now cross the stream and descend through woods, with wonderful atmospheric views, to emerge on stately lawn east of the house. The 1720 painting shows that there were once terraced formal gardens here, and tantalising traces of them remain.

John Byng visited Lyme Park in 1790 and was, as usual, critical of what he saw. He

The orangery and terraces at Lyme Park

thought the house was "in the horrid taste and manner of Chatsworth, all windows; with surrounding parterres and a drizzling cascade; some red deer were the greatest ornament about it. Most of the park is a dreary waste, abandon'd to rabbits." Most of what Byng saw may still be seen, but visitors may react differently to it today. The drive across the bleak park surrounded by great expanses of moorland, with the house gradually coming into view, is memorable. The eclectic gardens seem to provide exactly the right note of decorative jollity to make a foil for the sombre grandeur of the house.

Location Disley, Stockport SK12 2NX, Cheshire **OS** SJ9682 6½ m SE of Stockport by A6 **Tel** 01663 762023/766492 **Fax** 01633 765035 **Email** lymepark@ntrust.org.uk **English Heritage Register** Grade II* **Owner** The National Trust **Open** Apr to Oct, daily 11–5 (Wed and Thur 1–5); Nov to mid Dec, Sat and Sun 12–3 **Area** (garden) 17 acres/6.8 hectares; (park) 1,400 acres/566 hectares

MARGAM PARK

THE GRANDEST ORANGERY IN BRITAIN, AND WILD AND BEAUTIFUL PARKLAND

Margam, so close to the motorway and to unlovely industrial development, is an enthralling place. The site is splendid, facing south with wooded hills sweeping above to the north. As early as the 9th century there was a Christian settlement here, and a Cistercian abbey was founded in the 12th century – its nave survives in the grounds and is now the parish church. At the dissolution of the monasteries the estate passed to the Mansel family which married into the Talbots. In the 18th century Thomas Mansel Talbot went to live at Penrice Castle on Gower, keeping the Margam estate as pleasure grounds for occasional use. His son, however, built a new house from 1830 onwards on rising land east of the garden. Designed by Thomas Hopper in cheerful Elizabethan-Gothic style and crowned with an airy prospect tower, it commands grand views out to sea.

The most striking feature of Margam Park is the astonishing orangery built from 1787 for Thomas Mansel Talbot to the design of

The orangery at Margam Park

Anthony Keck – 327 feet/97 metres long, it has a row of 29 windows on its south façade. Loudon's *Encyclopaedia of Gardening* (1822) describes it "with 110 orange-trees, several of which are 18 feet in height, and remarkably handsome". The source of the orange trees is the subject of various fanciful stories involving a sea voyage, a gift to some European monarch, and the accidental arrival of the plants – piracy?, shipwreck? – on the south Wales coast. At all events, they were here before the orangery was built, for substantial specimens were described as early as 1727 when the gardener, James Kirkman, listed "10 Larg Chaney [China] Oranges, som 8 som 10 som 12 feet Diameter". The orangery is perfectly preserved, with Victorian parterres and bedding schemes running along the front, stone *putti* on a balustrade and a row of swagged urns. A collection of modern sculpture, including a fine bronze head by Elizabeth Frink, is arranged about it. Nearby is the Temple of the Four Seasons – the grandly classical remains of a 17th-century banqueting house with classical figures in niches. Against a wall on one side is the Old Citrus House, a lean-to glasshouse containing a fascinating collection of tender species of fuchsia from Central American and the Andes. The greater landscape setting of Margam Park is also accessible to visitors, including the site of the Mansels' 16th-century deer park. The views are poignant – wild and beautiful scenery contrasting with the M4 and the desolate industrial landscape.

Location Port Talbot SA13 2TJ, Glamorgan **OS** SS8086 4m SE of Port Talbot; Jnct 38 of M4 **Tel** 01639 881635 **Fax** 01639 895897 **CADW/ICOMOS Register** Grade I **Owner** Neathport Talbot County Borough Council **Open** summer, daily 10–5; winter, Wed to Sun 10–5 **Area** 850 acres/344 hectares

MISARDEN PARK

GRAND MIXED BORDERS AND FINE PLANTING FOR A CHARMING GARDEN OF EDWARDIAN CHARACTER

The house at Misarden was built in about 1620 and much rebuilt in the 19th century. Between 1920 and 1921 Sir Edwin Lutyens added a new east wing, joined to the rest of the house by a pillared and arcaded loggia. The original house was embellished with grand formal gardens in the 17th century, which are shown in a Kip engraving in Robert Atkyns's *The Ancient and Present State of Glostershire* (1712).

House and garden have a beautiful position on rising land looking across the valley of the river Frome. The present garden is very much of the 19th and 20th centuries. Lutyens is not known to have done any work on the garden but the monumental yew shapes on the south terrace and the splendid long passage of yew hedges with rounded battlements in the formal gardens to the west of the house would be very much to his taste.

The yew passage divides the kitchen garden from a broad axial walk flanked by deep herbaceous borders which are filled with *Aruncus dioicus*, campanulas, catmint, geraniums, irises, peonies, *Thalictrum aquilegiifolium* and violas. Nothing very unusual here, but the planting is well done, with bold masses and repeated use of such architectural plants as the thistle *Onopordum acanthium* and *Cephalaria gigantea* with its yellow pincushion flowers swaying on very tall stems. Further structure is given by towers on which sweet peas are trained.

The yew passage, running the whole length of the borders, has a turf path and its only ornament is a white marble urn at the top and a wrought-iron gate on stone piers at the bottom. A cross path in the centre connects the borders to the kitchen garden by a path which runs under arches of apples and

between box hedges. There is much ornamental planting here, with a bed of shrub roses and a formal garden in which a spring planting of tulips and alliums is followed by roses and violas.

The deep south terrace of the house is partly protected by massive yew shapes – broad-based pyramids but with the tops cut off, surely designed by Lutyens. Borders running along the terrace walls are filled with acanthus, delphiniums, the darkest purple poppies and white musk roses. At the eastern end of the terrace steps lead down to an ethereal planting of waves of white willow herb flowing under two rows of *Gleditsia triacanthos* 'Sunburst'. This strong mixture of architectural shapes of yew and decorative planting, here and elsewhere in the garden, makes a perfect transition between the house and its surrounding landscape.

Location Miserden, Stroud GL6 7JA, Gloucestershire **OS** SO9409 7m SE of Gloucester by minor roads **Tel** 01285 821303 **Fax** 01285 821530 **English Heritage Register** Grade II* **Owner** Major M.T.N.H. Wills **Open** Apr to Sept, Tue to Thur 10–5 **Area** 12½ acres/5 hectares

The south terrace at Misarden Park

NATIONAL BOTANIC GARDEN OF WALES

IN EXQUISITE 18TH-CENTURY PARKLAND, A SUPERB NEW BOTANIC GARDEN WITH A MAGNIFICENT GLASSHOUSE BY NORMAN FOSTER

The Middleton Hall estate dates back to the early 17th century when Henry Middleton built a house here. In the 18th century it was owned by William Paxton who had made a fortune in India and commissioned a grand new house, built between 1793 and 1795, from Samuel Pepys Cockerell, a favourite architect of the East India Company nabobs. Middleton also had a landscape park laid out to the designs of Samuel Lapidge.

SUSTAINABILITY

The setting, to this day remarkably unspoilt, is exceptionally beautiful – rolling hills, woodland and small fields enclosed by ancient hedgerows. After Paxton's death in 1824 the estate changed hands more than once and the house was gutted by fire in 1931. In the 1990s the importance of the Middleton landscape was recognised and it became the site for a proposed National Botanic Garden which opened to the public in the spring of 2000. In such a setting it would be hard to have no thought for the environment, and from the start the garden embraced notions of sustainability and organic estate management.

The entrance – designed by Norman Foster & Partners – leads past a William Pye water sculpture to the Broad Walk which provides the chief axis of the garden. This runs gently uphill for much of its way, and has on one side a deep mixed border and on the other collections of rocks showing the geology of Wales, arranged in historical order from the youngest to the oldest. At the heart of the garden, and at the head of the Broad Walk, is the beautiful Great Glasshouse, also designed by Norman Foster & Partners. This long low pod-shaped building seems to emerge from the ground like some organic growth, echoing the characteristic gentle curves of the landscape. A ravine 18ft/5.5m deep and terraced on each side dominates the interior which has been most attractively landscaped by Kathryn Gustavson of Gustavson Porter. Covering an area of just under 1 acre/0.4 hectares, the glasshouse displays a collection of plants from Mediterranean climates (from several different zones) arranged in long curving beds. An interactive exhibition displays the whole life cycle of a plant from germination to reproduction.

A determined visitor to the garden could learn an enormous amount about plants and also about sustainability. All the heating for offices, restaurants and glasshouse is provided by a wood-burning furnace using recycled timber and, increasingly, coppiced timber grown in earth enriched by waste from the waste-recycling unit. Nor is the wider landscape ignored. In Paxton's time a series of lakes formed a vital part of the park but these were drained in the 1930s. One has already been reinstated and others will follow – apart from their beauty they will provide habitats for many different flora and fauna. The garden has an atmosphere of lively purpose. There is much to be learned here but there is also much simply to be enjoyed, not least the exquisite surrounding landscape.

Location Middleton Hall, Llanarthne SA32 8HG, Carmarthenshire **OS** SN5117 8m E of Carmarthen by A48, B4310 and minor roads **Tel** 01558 667148/9 **Fax** 01558 667138 **Email** info@gardenofwales.org.uk **Website** www.gardenofwales.org.uk **CADW/ICOMOS Register** Grade II (grounds of Middleton Hall) **Owner** The National Botanic Garden of Wales **Open** May to Aug, daily 10–6; Sept to Oct, daily 10–5.30; Nov to Apr, daily 10–4.30 **Area** 586 acres/237 hectares

The Great Glasshouse

NESS BOTANIC GARDENS

THE GARDENS OF A GREAT PRIVATE PLANT COLLECTOR TRANSFORMED INTO AN OUTSTANDING BOTANIC GARDEN

This exceptionally attractive botanic garden started life as the private garden of A.K. Bulley, a prosperous cotton broker who was also a passionate and learned plantsman. The site, on the Wirral and the estuary of the river Dee, is windswept, with strong winds whipping in from the Irish Sea. When Bulley came here in 1898 he soon saw the need for windbreaks and planted evergreen oaks (*Quercus ilex*) and Scots pines (*Pinus sylvestris*) which today form a distinguished background to the garden. Bulley subscribed to the plant-hunting expeditions of George Forrest and Frank Kingdon Ward and built up a fine collection of their introductions from China, some of which are named after him (such as *Primula bulleyana*). He also developed part of the garden as a commercial nursery which became the well-known firm of Bees & Co. After his death the garden was given to the University of Liverpool in 1948 by Bulley's daughter, who made it a condition of the gift that there should be public access.

Ness is delightful to all visitors and instructive to gardeners. There are many

The rock garden at Ness

collections, especially of such smaller ornamental trees as rowans (*Sorbus* species) and birches (*Betula*) that are of particular interest. The large rock garden is a period piece, with many conifers (including examples of those "dwarf" cultivars that sometimes turn out to have giant ambitions). Here is an enchanting collection of plants of an alpine kind, including many of the species Himalayan primulas in which Bulley took such delight. Here, too, is an exceptional collection of bulbs, springing into life at the beginning of the year with crocuses, irises, scillas and snowdrops in lovely profusion. Later in the season the rock garden displays plants that set the pulse of the true alpinist racing – alpine campanulas, gentians, miniature phlox, roscoeas and saxifrages. A collection of heathers is displayed on a rising slope, and an extended flowering season is ensured by large numbers of all the species and cultivars, laid out in huge swathes to form a giant abstract painting – Brobdingnagian carpet-bedding.

One of the most attractive and unusual parts of the garden is provided by the collection of native British plants on the banks of a lake. Many of these are very rare, some confined to only a few sites in the wild (such as the delightful native primrose, *Primula scotica*, with its deep purple flowers). Apart from opening our eyes to the charms of our own flora, this collection performs a valuable environmental service: all the plants are propagated from seed collected in the wild and in some cases seed from Ness is redistributed to help reestablish dwindling wild communities of the rarer plants.

The garden also displays a very large collection of shrubs – magnolias, mahonias, pieris, a huge range of rhododendrons (species and cultivars) and witch hazels. Anywhere in the garden you are likely to be stopped in your tracks by the sight of something unfamiliar and beautiful – the vast, languishing flowers of *Magnolia campbellii* subsp. *mollicomata*, thickets of the lovely *Lilium monadelphum* or the ghostly silver stems of *Betula utilis* var. *jacquemontii*.

Location Ness, Neston, South Wirral L64 4AY, Cheshire **OS** SJ3076 11m NW of Chester off A540 **Tel** 01513 530123 **Fax** 01513 531004 **English Heritage Register** Grade II **Owner** The University of Liverpool **Open** Mar to Oct, daily 9.30–dusk; Nov to Feb, daily 9.30–4 **Area** 63 acres/25 hectares

PAINSWICK ROCOCO GARDEN

RARE AND CHARMING 18TH-CENTURY
LANDSCAPE GARDEN EXQUISITELY RESTORED

There is a dreamlike quality about the garden at Painswick – entirely pleasurable but slightly unreal and wholly distinctive. Until 1984, when restoration started, the garden was invisible, the site choked with saplings and brambles. Its rediscovery is a tribute to the enterprise of its owner and of the garden historians whose advice he sought.

A delightful painting (1748) by Thomas Robins of the garden at Painswick had survived, hanging in Painswick House itself. But no-one knew if this painting was pure fantasy, a possible proposal for a garden never made, or a portrait of the garden as it had been. It was known that there had been some kind of garden here, for Bishop Pococke described it in 1757: "The garden is on an hanging ground from the house in a vale, and on rising ground on the other side and at the end; all are cut into walks through woods and adorn'd with water and buildings." In 1982

two architectural historians, Roger White and Timothy Mowl, pushed their way through the vegetation and discovered traces of the layout of Robins's garden and even, miraculously, surviving buildings exactly as shown in the paintings – a dazzling revelation. In 1984 the owner, Lord Dickinson, embarked on a restoration based on Robins's painting, during which many of the painting's details were confirmed by archaeological evidence.

One of the charms of the garden is that it is quite concealed from the house – a secret world of its own. It is indeed in a wooded valley, with an open area at its lowest point. There are touches of formality – an avenue of beeches, a walk of clipped yew hedges running up to the Gothic Red House (so called because of the colour of its stucco) – but the overall character is that of an intimate landscape garden enlivened by decorative buildings. Paths run through the woods overlooking the garden but there seems to be no deliberately planned walk linking the various beauties of the garden, as there is, for example, at Stourhead (*see page 106*). The elegant Gothic Eagle House, rising on a slope, the ethereal filigree Exedra in the valley below, overlooking a formal kitchen garden,

The Red House at Painswick

and the rusticated temple-like Doric seat are isolated, delightful, episodes. They are like props for some light-hearted opera whose plot remains a mystery.

The whole garden now corresponds exactly to the Robins painting and this is one of the most enterprising and successful garden restorations, entirely privately funded, of its time. It is also historically important, for Painswick is the only example in Britain of a garden made in Rococo style – which had all but escaped the garden historians.

A further delight at Painswick (nothing to do with Thomas Robins) is the lovely snowdrop grove close to the Gothic alcove on the eastern edge of the garden. Many of the plants here are the large, glaucous-leafed *Galanthus* 'Atkinsii' named after James Atkins, a famous 19th-century snowdrop grower who lived here in Painswick at Rose Cottage. To see them in full flower in February is a wonderful sight.

Location Painswick, nr Stroud GL6 6TH, Gloucestershire **OS** SO8610 ½m N of Painswick by B4073 **Tel** 01452 813204 **Email** Painsgard@aol.com **English Heritage Register** Grade II* **Owner** Painswick Rococo Garden Trust **Open** 2nd Wed in Jan to Nov, Wed to Sun and Bank Hol Mon 11–5 (Jul and Aug, also open Mon and Tue) **Area** 10 acres/4 hectares

The parterres at Penrhyn Castle

PENRHYN CASTLE

DRAMATIC AND LOVELY SCENERY, EXCELLENT
PLANTS AND A PRETTY WALLED GARDEN

Penrhyn Castle is an amazing apparition in grey pink stone. From its dramatic position on a bluff there are immense views all the way from Anglesey to Snowdonia. It was built between 1820 and 1845 for George Pennant whose family made a great fortune out of sugar from the West Indies and slate quarries in Carnarfonshire. The architect, Thomas Hopper, contrived a pared-down neo-Norman style of arched windows and tall square or rounded machicolated towers all swarming with battlements – certainly powerful enough to hold its own in the remarkable natural landscape. The garden respects both the character of the castle and its setting: anything fiddly or small-scale close to the house would look absurd, and instead there are sweeps of turf, shrubs and bold trees – among them a Wellingtonia which Queen Victoria planted here in 1859.

At a little distance from the castle a walled garden, isolated from its surroundings, slopes downhill, becoming increasingly informal in style as it descends. A terrace at the entrance, with thickets of *Trachycarpus fortunei* at each end, is laid out with two parterres in which box-edged beds are filled with blocks of red penstemons or fuchsias, with a scalloped lily pool at the centre of each. Between the two parterres a giant lobed circular pool has a mossy rock at its centre, bubbling with water and edged with Bowles's golden grass (*Milium effusum* 'Aureum'). The terrace is overlooked by a pillared loggia and the walls on either side are swathed in roses, purple grapevine (*Vitis vinifera* 'Purpurea'), tender *Mutisia decurrens*, *Fremontodendron californicum* and *Eccremocarpus scaber*. The beds at the foot of these walls contain *Cordyline indivisa*, the beautiful *Drimys lanceolata*, *Lomatia ferruginea* and other tender exotics.

On the slopes below the terrace a completely different mood reigns. Here are shrubs and flowering trees planted individually in turf in a gardenesque style that emphasises the individual qualities of each. Azaleas, clerodendrons, magnificent eucryphias, hydrangeas, magnolias and the curious Japanese umbrella pine (*Sciadopitys verticillata*) are all displayed in this way. At the foot of the slope a long tunnel of clematis, *Actinidia kolomikta* and fuchsias trained on a metal framework cuts across, with waves of ferns on either side. Beyond this a giant swamp of *Gunnera manicata*, backed by sprawling old Japanese maples, is overlooked by a thatched rustic summerhouse.

Location Bangor LL57, Gwynedd **OS** SH6072 1m E of Bangor by A5122 **Tel** 01248 353084 **Infoline** 01248 371337 **Fax** 01248 371281 **CADW/ICOMOS Register** Grade II* **Owner** The National Trust **Open** Apr to Oct, daily except Tue 11–5 (opens 10 in Jul and Aug) **Area** 47 acres/19 hectares

PIERCEFIELD PARK

GHOSTLY REMAINS OF A NOTABLE 18TH-
CENTURY PICTURESQUE LANDSCAPE GARDEN
BY THE CLIFFS OF THE RIVER WYE

Piercefield Park, now a public park, was a product of the late 18th-century taste for dramatic natural landscape and sublime views. Valentine Morris came to live here in about 1752, shortly after his marriage. With the help of a friend, Richard Owen Cambridge, he animated the landscape in order to make the best of the spectacular views. Paths along (and sometimes through) the cliffs above the river were punctuated from time to time with seats, a grotto, viewing platforms and a miniature stonehenge of which a few stones remain, and Piercefield became a much visited beauty spot. However, overwhelmed by debt, Morris was forced to leave Piercefield in 1785 and retire to his father's plantation estate on Antigua. The park continued to be visited but was closed in the mid 19th century and sold

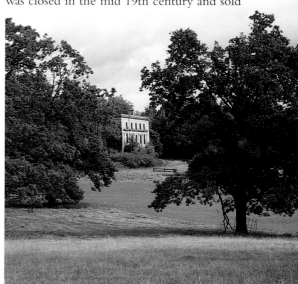

The shell of Piercefield House in its parkland

in 1923 to the Chepstow Race Company; part of it, to the south-west, is still the site of the racecourse today.

Piercefield Park remains a rare and beautiful place. Near the racecourse, the roofless shell of the house faces south-east across parkland with handsome old oaks. The land here slopes gently down to where the river runs through a precipitous wooded gorge, with rocky cliffs rising among the trees on the far bank and long views to the Severn estuary. Many walkers will know the path along the river here, for it lies at the southern end of the Wye Valley Walk.

When Morris first made his walk, his intention was to display the natural charms of the Wye and its valley at an especially beautiful point where the river loops about a headland. He opened his walk to the public and Piercefield, like Tintern Abbey nearby, quickly became an essential stop for those coming in search of the picturesque. Arthur Young wrote in 1768 after a visit here that Piercefield "exceeds any thing of the kind I have seen." He noted that the paths were "an assistance to view the beauties of nature…without a strong design of decoration or ornament." Morris had no wish to add ornamental buildings to the already dramatically beautiful scenery and this reticent approach to the landscape makes Piercefield one of the earliest minimalist gardens – in which what you leave out is more important than what you add.

Location Chepstow, Gwent **OS** ST5295 1m N of Chepstow **CADW/ICOMOS Register** Grade I
Open at all times

PLAS BRONDANW GARDENS

A DELIGHTFUL MASTERPIECE OF FORMAL GARDEN DESIGN IN AN EXCEPTIONAL SNOWDONIA SETTING

Plas Brondanw was bequeathed to the architect Sir Clough Williams-Ellis in 1902 when he was nineteen. The 17th-century house had long been abandoned by his family and he gradually embarked on its restoration and the making of a garden. He was able to finance it only in dribs and drabs: "A cheque for ten pounds would come in and I would order yew hedging to that extent, a cheque for twenty and I would pave a further bit of terrace." The old stone house is sombrely attractive, but the greatest beauty of the place is its site in Snowdonia

Turquoise and gold at Plas Brondanw

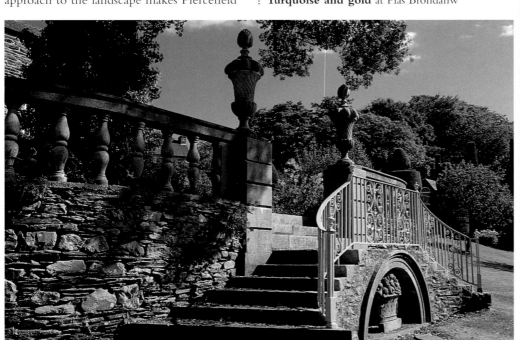

surrounded by some of the grandest scenery in the British Isles.

A garden in such a setting needs bold strokes – this is no place for pretty little borders and tinkling effects. Williams-Ellis made a formal garden, firmly marked out with yew hedges and enlivened by architectural conceits that link house and garden. A broad paved terrace runs along the entire west front of the house, and on a grassy slope below, a fine old holm oak rises from a balustraded platform which commands immense westerly views of the mountains, dominated by the peaks of Moel Hebog and Moel Lefn. The terrace continues far beyond the end of the house to a belvedere from which there are views to the north over pastures and valleys to Mount Snowdon itself.

FORMALITY AND MOUNTAINS

The other end of the terrace, closer to the house, leads to a series of formal enclosures. In order to focus on the peak of Cnicht to the north-east, Williams-Ellis established a new axis here, not quite parallel to the terrace whose orientation is determined by the façade of the house. He lined this axis with tall yew hedges which break out from time to time in piers or finials, and in this enclosed area felt free to indulge his relish for ornamental architecture and statuary – an orangery with rounded windows and high-pitched roof, stone piers capped with swagger urns, and a wrought-iron balustrade painted in his distinctive colours of gold and turquoise. A cross axis has at one end stone niches with statues of Roman emperors and a figure of Apollo, and at the other end a screen of clipped yew framing a view of Moel Hebog. At the far end of the yew walk steps lead to a circular sitting place with a bench facing back over the garden. From this slightly elevated position there are views through the formal garden and its architectural embellishments, past the holm oak in front of the house to, in the dead centre of the view, the sharp outline of Cnicht.

Outside the formal gardens, beyond the entrance drive, Williams-Ellis animated a garden of quite a different kind. Here an avenue of chestnuts leads into picturesque woods with ferns and mossy rocks. On the way you will pass a pavilion of painted

corrugated iron – turquoise and gold on the outside, rich purple inside. You then suddenly come upon an abrupt ravine (the quarry from which the stone for the house was originally taken) plummeting down to a black pool veiled with trees – dramatic and very sinister. A walk continues uphill through woods which give way to pasture and grazing sheep. From Castel Brondanw, a mock fortress and outlook tower at the top of the hill, there is a view over the trees, past the house far below, to a giant and lovely panorama of mountains.

Williams-Ellis had the sensitivity to realise that the surrounding natural landscape was his trump card and he contrived ways of displaying it to its greatest effect, drawing the grand views into the heart of his garden. No garden is such an eloquent practical example of the virtues of consulting the genius of the place as Plas Brondanw.

Location Llanfrothen, Penrhyndeudraeth LL48 6SW, Gwynedd OS SH6142 3m N of Penrhyndeudraeth by A4085 Tel 01766 770228 CADW/ICOMOS Register Grade I Owner The Trustees of the Second Portmeirion Foundation Open daily 9–5 Area 4 acres/1.6 hectares

PLAS NEWYDD

SERENE WOODLAND GARDENS WITH
FINE RHODODENDRONS OVERLOOKING
THE MENAI STRAIT

Plas Newydd has a lovely site overlooking the Menai Strait to the mountains of Snowdonia. The house is a Gothic remodelling of an earlier house, carried out for the 1st Earl of Uxbridge from 1795 onwards by James Wyatt and subsequently by Joseph Potter who completed the work in 1820s. It was during this time that Humphry Repton was called in to rework the landscape. He made a new entrance drive and carried out much tree planting, especially to the south of the house. Today the chief attractions of the garden are a delightful formal garden of the 1930s and the woodland garden which runs along the strait.

North of the house, overlooking the water, is a trelliswork pavilion covered in *Vitis coignetiae* and summer jasmine, with a pool with rustic rockwork covered in ferns, pots of arum lilies and hostas and a floor inlaid with

West Indies at Plas Newydd

pebbles. It stands at the top of a sequence of terraces, the first of which is gravelled; *Cordyline australis* in pots and magnificent clumps of *Itea ilicifolia* stand in each corner. Stone steps lead down to a long strip of grass and box-edged beds filled with acanthus, *Choisya ternata*, cistus, mahonia and myrtle, and repeated Irish yews. Along the retaining wall tall earthernware pots brim with sempervivums, and waves of *Cotoneaster horizontalis* flank steps which lead down to the bottom terrace. At the centre of a lawn a scalloped lily pond is fed by a rill and a lion's mask spouting water. Borders on each side of steps against the retaining wall have what you might call a Christopher Lloyd border – planted with castor oil plants (*Ricinus communis*), crocosmias, *Dahlia* 'Bishop of Llandaff', *Helenium* 'Moerheim Beauty' and *Lysimachia ciliata* 'Firecracker'. On the far side of the lawn are borders of a quite different atmosphere: giant sweeps of blue agapanthus with regular clumps of *Alchemilla mollis*. The final flight of steps is decorated with four

noble stone urns of Grecian character. Gravel paths run below, leading northwards to walks in the woods along the seashore. Here is a splendid collection of rhododendrons, rich in tender species, including *R*. 'Fragrantissimum' whose delicious scent suffuses the woods in spring. This part of the garden is open only during rhododendron time.

South of the house is the area called West Indies, with lawns, shrubs and trees. The distinction of this part of the garden is immediately announced by a splendid and unusual tree – a compact cedar of Lebanon with upward-growing branches and its numerous branches dividing low down (*Cedrus libani* subsp. *libani* 'Stricta'). An old sycamore has the remains of a treehouse and a carpet of the finest turf unrolls into the distance, winding among trees and shrubs.

Location Llanfairpwll, Anglesey LL61 6DQ **OS** SH5269 1m S of Llanfairpwll by A5 **Tel** 01248 714795 **Fax** 01248 713673 **Email** plasnewydd@ntrust.org.uk **CADW/ICOMOS Register** Grade I **Owner** The National Trust **Open** Apr to Oct, Sat to Wed (open Good Fri; rhododendron garden open Apr to beginning Jun) 11–5.30 **Area** 31 acres/12 hectares

PLAS-YN-RHIW

EXQUISITE LITTLE CLIFF-TOP GARDEN CRAMMED WITH PLANTS AND FULL OF CHARACTER

There are few gardens that have less self-importance and more uncontrived charm than Plas-yn-Rhiw. The estate was given to the National Trust by the Keating sisters whose father had been architect to Boots the chemist in Nottingham. Martin Drury, a former director-general of the National Trust, particularly loved the place, and in a memoir describes going to meet Honor and Leonora Keating in 1973, who served him "A memorable lunch…of sardines on toast and individual pink blancmanges, a speciality of Leonora's".

As children the Keatings had spent summer holidays on the lovely Lleyn peninsula which is how they came to buy Plas yn Rhiw – a medieval stone farmhouse with an 18th-century verandah tacked on. Its position is one of the most extraordinary of any house I have seen: protected by folds of land and clinging onto a hillside (*rhiw* is Welsh for

The front garden at Plas-yn-Rhiw

slope) with old woods, it faces south with stupendous views of the Atlantic waves crashing against the coast of Hell's Mouth Bay. The little garden lies on the slope in front of the house, with cobbled paths tumbling down, and beds filled with plants and enclosed in blowsy box hedges that occasionally break out into cheerful fits of topiary. The pillars of a verandah are swathed in roses and fuchsias, and immediately below it a curve of flawless lawn is hedged in small-leafed box. A cottage garden parterre (to admire only, not to be entered) is enclosed in blurred box hedges and filled with agapanthus, azaleas, echinops, lilies, and roses, with occasional weedy but lovely interlopers such as teazels.

TENDER PLANTS

Although blasted by coastal winds, the site is well protected and the climate is mild – bay, fig and myrtle give an unexpectedly Mediterranean air and such tender plants as the sweet-smelling *Euphorbia mellifera*, *Drimys winteri* and the flamboyant pink climber *Lapageria rosea* and *Rhododendron* 'Fragrantissimum' flourish here. There is nothing obviously calculated about the planting but there are memorable effects – sharply purple aconitums or scarlet *Phygelius capensis* rising from clouds of soft pink *Geranium endressii*, for example. Some gardens work hard to achieve their beauty, others, like Plas-yn-Rhiw, seem to weave their magic effortlessly, as though by some horticultural sleight of hand.

Plas-yn-Rhiw is a remote place; there is not much to do in these parts except admire the exceptional beauties of the countryside. The remoteness protects the garden, which is so small and of such intimate character that half a small busload of visitors would ruin its atmosphere.

Location Rhiw, Pwllheli LL53 8AB, Gwynedd **OS** SH2328 12m from Pwllheli on S coast road to Aberdaron, signed from B4413 **CADW/ICOMOS Register** Grade II **Owner** The National Trust **Open** end Mar to mid May, Thur to Mon 12–5; mid May to Oct, Wed to Mon 12–5; Oct, Sat and Sun 12–5 **Area** 1 acre/0.4 hectares

PORTMEIRION

HOLIDAY VILLAGE OF FANTASTICAL ARCHITECTURE WITH A SUPERB OLD WOODLAND GARDEN BY THE SEA

Portmeirion is an extraordinary fantasy village created by the architect Clough Williams-Ellis between 1925 and 1972. He started with a hotel whose profits were to be used to finance the growth of the village. Gradually, further buildings were added, some of them original and some of them recycling all manner of architectural remnants, many of them of high quality. The architectural style is heterogenous – Gothico-Moorish, neo-Classical and Baroque (closest to Williams-Ellis's heart, one feels). Here are domes, towers, minarets, gazebos; no peak is without its finial, golden orb or weather vane. Most buildings are faced with stucco washed in different colours – pink, cream, ochre and white. Williams-Ellis's trademark pale turquoise blue is much in evidence on balconies, benches,

The fantasy roofscape of Portmeirion

railings and gates. The planting is heterogeneous, too: Chusan palms, topiary of bay, tall narrow Irish yews resembling Italian cypresses, ramparts of hydrangeas, lapping waves of bedding pelargoniums.

This is probably the best-known face of Portmeirion but in addition, much less known, is a great woodland garden which provides a soothing contrast after the slightly overheated hijinks of the village. Clough Williams-Ellis bought the Gwyllt Woodlands in 1941. Here, in natural woodland of birch, sessile oak and rowans, Henry Seymour Westmacott had from the 1850s planted many exotics. Some of the conifers still survive – among them deodars (*Cedrus deodara*), Douglas firs (*Pseudotsuga menziesii*), Monterey pines (*Pinus radiata*) and Wellingtonias. Two later owners, Sir William Fothergill Cooke and Caton Haig, added all sorts of exotic trees and shrubs.

The site is beautiful – south-west of the village on a headland overlooking Tremadog Bay. Although there are a few ornamental buildings – a bridge and pavilion of Chinese character and a domed temple – the character of the woodland is essentially wild (*gwyllt* is

the Welsh for wild). The climate is affected by the North Atlantic Drift so many tender plants flourish: such evergreen rhododendrons as the large-leafed *R. sinogrande* and the sweetly-scented *R. maddenii* do well, as do many southern hemisphere plants such as the distinguished Argentine *Lomatia ferruginea*, the rare New Zealand *Plagianthus regius* and over 40 species of eucalyptus. Because the area is so large and so densely planted, like a piece of old native woodland, it is not immediately obvious how astonishingly rich the garden is in exotics. Around 7,000 different species and cultivars are grown here, many of them rarely seen in gardens. Thus the charming village provides an appetising but lighthearted *hors d'oeuvre* for the much weightier meal of a remarkable woodland plant collection.

Location Penrhyndeudraeth LL48 6ET, Gwynedd
OS SH5937 2m SE of Porthmadog by A487
Tel 01766 770000 **Fax** 01766 771331
Email enquiries@portmeirion-village.com **Website** www.portmeirion.com **CADW/ICOMOS Register** Grade II* **Owner** The Second Portmeirion Foundation
Open daily 9.30–5.30 **Area** 110 acres/44 hectares

POWIS CASTLE

DRAMATIC 17TH-CENTURY TERRACES
WITH EXCELLENT MODERN BORDERS AND
A PRETTY WOODLAND GARDEN

Powis Castle dates back to at least the 12th century but the present building is largely of the 13th century with much additional 17th-century work. It had belonged to a dynasty of Welsh princes, the last of whom, Owain ap Gruffydd ap Gwenwynwyn, renounced his title in 1286 and took the name Baron de la Pole. The estate was bought in 1587 by Sir Edward Herbert whose descendant George Herbert (4th Earl of Powis of the second creation) bequeathed the estate to the National Trust in 1952.

The rare historic setting of Powis Castle has been turned into one of the best of modern gardens, but the splendidly cosseted state of house and garden was not always thus. When it was visited by John Byng in 1793 he was appalled by its condition: "There are three curiosities about Powis Castle: first, upon the terraces you cannot walk as the balustrades are fallen down…; secondly, you cannot move upon the floors of the house as they are made like ice from being waxed…; thirdly, you must cautiously look out of the windows as there

Powis Castle terraces from the Wilderness

are no guards before them. It is one of the most neglected, sorrowful places I ever saw."

The terraces are the dazzling feature of Powis – of a distinctly Italianate character, they are not the only example in Wales of such influence: Llanerch in Clwyd (*see page 503*) had Italianate terraces of exactly the same date. Facing south-east and descending in stately progression, each 600ft/180m long, the terraces at Powis were built in the 1660s, probably to the designs of the architect William Winde. They bristle with lively architectural ornament: with stone balustrades and fine urns, and many charming lead statues from the workshop of John Van Nost. Vast and baggy shapes of clipped yew rise above the topmost terrace hard against the ramparts of the castle, and at the extreme eastern end are the extraordinary remains of an ancient yew hedge rising over 50ft/15m high and deformed with age.

All this creates a setting of theatrical splendour which, since the 1980s, has been the scene of much enterprising planting by the National Trust. In the terrace beds colour schemes are skilfully chosen, ranging from the pale and mysterious – veils of *Chamerion angustifolium* 'Album' spiked with pale yellow *Kniphofia* 'Sunningdale Yellow' and Miss Willmott's ghost (*Eryngium giganteum*) – to the explosive – orange-red *Crocosmia* 'Lucifer', tawny *Alstroemeria aurea* and rich scarlet *Dahlia* 'Bishop of Llandaff. Bedding is cleverly used: either hardy annuals such as sweetpeas (the beautiful blue *Lathyrus* 'Lord Nelson') or tender plants such as the silver-leafed *Plectranthus argentatus* and the intense blue *Salvia cacaliifolia*. The effect is flowery and irrepressibly lighthearted.

At the foot of the terraces, where in the 17th century there was a Baroque water garden, there is now the Great Lawn (with wild daffodils in spring). On its far side the Wilderness, first planted in the 1770s when the landscape designer William Emes worked on the estate, is now a miniature woodland garden with such excellent ornamental trees as *Koelreuteria paniculata*, *Quercus* × *hispanica* 'Lucombeana' and *Davidia involucrata*. These are underplanted with shrubs (including several species rhododendrons; in spring the delicious scent of *Rhododendron luteum* fills the air). Views back towards the tawny stone castle, rising high above the terraces and framed in leafy branches, are extraordinarily beautiful. Such a scene, much to 18th-century taste, must have been in William Emes's mind when he first planted the Wilderness.

The terraced garden

Location Welshpool SY21 8RF, Powys **OS** SJ2106 1m S of Welshpool by A483 **Tel** 01938 551920 **Infoline** 01938 551944 **Fax** 01938 554336 **Email** powiscastle@ntrust.org.uk **CADW/ICOMOS Register** Grade **Owner** The National Trust **Open** Apr to Oct, Wed to Sun (Jul and Aug also open Mon) 11–6 **Area** 24 acres/10 hectares

THE PRIORY GARDENS

COLOUR-THEMED BORDERS BY A
PIONEER 20TH-CENTURY GARDENER
IN A FINELY PLANTED GARDEN

The Healings came here in 1939 and it was only gradually after World War II that the garden at Kemerton got going. Peter Healing describes planning the planting in the garden while he was still a prisoner-of-war: "By the end of the war I found myself in Germany with only one book, William Robinson's *English Flower Garden*, perhaps one of the best garden books ever written, and it was through him that I pictured the form that the borders must take". The lack of fuss and the delight, even vicariously, in gardening seem to me peculiarly and attractively English. It is a fine place to garden, with a beautiful position on the southern slopes of Bredon Hill and a handsome 18th-century house. There are good trees, especially acers, a decorative pergola of roses and vines, a secret garden of packed borders in pale colours, and much else that is pretty. But what is exceptional is the Top Border which was started in the late 1950s. This is a colour-themed mixed border of the sort that became increasingly fashionable in the late 20th century – to such an extent that it was sometimes taken to be an acceptable substitute for good design.

The Healings' border faces the house on the far side of a lawn which links different parts of the garden. It thus simultaneously provides a splendid panorama from the house and part of a colourful passage when moving from one part of the garden to another. The border is 100ft/30m long and 16ft/5m deep, and backed by a yew hedge (conventional perhaps but still the best background for mixed plantings). The flower colours are skilfully disposed, starting at the north with fresh cool whites, pinks and silvers, shifting to yellow and gold. The central part erupts into an explosion of reds, rich purples, oranges and the occasional flash of yellow – using achilleas, crocosmias, dahlias, heleniums, kniphofias, penstemons, phlox and roses. A changing dose of annuals adds spice – antirrhinums, castor oil plants, ruby chard, red orach (*Atriplex hortensis* var. *rubra*) and bedding pelargoniums. In its day this kind of planting was innovative; in smart gardening circles brilliant colours were despised and "good taste" dictated pastel colours and grey foliage. But the Healings knew what they wanted and showed themselves to be forerunners of what later became a craze. Their colour-themed border is still delightful and gains additional meaning from the way it is worked skilfully into the structure of a garden.

In making the border the Healings took their time; Peter Healing described this as "one of the great pleasures of gardening… progress is slow, sometimes imperceptible, until one day – maybe years later – the vision seems to become a reality." So much for the joys of instant gardening.

Location Kemerton GL20 7JN, Gloucestershire **OS** SO9537 In Kemerton village, 6m S of Pershore by B4080 **Tel** 01386 725258 **Owner** The Hon. Mrs Peter Healing **Open** Jun to Sept, Thur 2–6 **Area** 4 acres/1.6 hectares

RODMARTON MANOR

OUTSTANDING ARTS AND CRAFTS GARDEN –
HEDGES, TOPIARY, STONE PATHS AND
BRIMMING BORDERS

Rodmarton is a shrine of Cotswolds Arts and Crafts taste. The house was designed by Ernest Barnsley and built for the Hon. Claud Biddulph between 1909 and 1926. The architect C.R. Ashbee saw it, half finished, in 1914 and wrote: "I've seen no modern work to equal it, nothing I know of Lutyens or Baker comes up to it…The English Arts and Crafts movement at its best is here – so are the vanishing traditions of the Cotswolds."

House and garden were conceived as a single entity and the house was to be built in the vernacular style, down to the last detail. The village community was involved in its making – the stone was quarried locally and cut by local masons, the timber was felled on the estate, and only local craftsmen were used for the joinery and carpentry. The furniture was also made locally specially for the house.

The house is of irregular plan – a central block with two ranges, one short and one long, jutting out at an angle at each end to form an eccentric curve; David Ottewill in *The Edwardian Garden* (1989) calls it "long, rambling and accretive". On the north side, where the entrance is, it partly embraces a circular drive and lawn. This, on its far side, is enclosed by a curved double lime walk, giving a very grand and stately effect, as though the

The hot border at the Priory Gardens

circle and lime walk were challenging the higgledy-piggledy nature of the house. This is a running theme throughout the garden, which never settles down into a harmonious and logical flow of events.

ERNEST BARNSLEY'S GARDEN

The gardens, which were planned at the same time as the house and designed by Ernest Barnsley in collaboration with the head gardener, William Scrubey, are on the south side of the house, arranged in a sequence of walled or hedged compartments. They are not linked by any strong axis but give the appearance of having sprung up about the house like some spontaneous organic growth. On a paved terrace immediately behind the house are yew hedges and splendid topiary birds and other shapes. Two enclosures of yew have tubs of agapanthus or abutilons, or urns on plinths planted with annuals, and scattered chairs and benches – two out-of-doors sitting rooms conveniently close to the house. At each end of the terrace is a walk of Portugal laurels and steps lead down from the outer edge of the terrace to borders running along a ha-ha with views of fields. The Leisure Garden at the west end of the house was originally an area of grass; today it is paved and punctuated with beds containing shrubs – Guelder rose, parsley-leafed elder (*Sambucus nigra* f. *laciniata*), shrub roses and *Viburnum plicatum* f. *tomentosum* 'Mariesii' underplanted with smaller herbaceous plants,

The Long Garden at Rodmarton

Kniphofias and gladioli at St Fagans

while substantial conifers and yews lurk in the background.

The most memorable set piece in the garden is the Long Garden, quite hidden behind a wall and yew hedges. A path of flagstones runs between herbaceous borders filled with asters, astrantia, eryngiums, heleniums, hollyhocks, *Macleaya × kewensis*, shrub roses and sedums. Halfway down, the path is interrupted by a circular pool surrounded by monumental shapes of yew, and at the end of the path is a summerhouse with a steeply pitched roof, the whole veiled by roses.

Rodmarton was started just before World War I, and completed after it. C.R. Ashbee was right to refer to the "vanishing traditions" of the Cotswolds – houses and gardens such as these belonged to the end of a tradition. In its heyday Rodmarton had ten gardeners; today it has one. It still possesses marvellous charm but it is overlaid with a pervasive melancholy.

Location Rodmarton, nr Cirencester GL7 6PF, Gloucestershire **OS** ST9498 In Rodmarton village 6m SW of Cirencester **Tel** 01285 841253 **Fax** 01285 841298 **Email** simon.biddulph@farming.co.uk **English Heritage Register** Grade II* **Owner** Mr and Mrs Simon Biddulph **Open** May to Aug, Wed, Sat and Bank Hol Mon 2–5; groups by appointment **Area** 8 acres/3 hectares

ST FAGANS CASTLE

ANCIENT GARDENS WITH A CHARMING MIXTURE OF INGREDIENTS: A KNOT GARDEN, BORDERS AND A VICTORIAN ROSE GARDEN

Somewhat confusingly, St Fagans and its fascinating gardens are hidden away in the bosom of the grounds of the Museum of Welsh Life. The St Fagans estate dates from the 12th century but, by the early 16th century, the old castle had become ruinous. The present house is Elizabethan, built between 1586 and 1596, probably for Nicholas Herbert. The Lewis family bought the estate in 1616 and in 1730 the Lewis heiress, Elizabeth, married the 3rd Earl of Plymouth whose family name was Windsor (later Windsor-Clive). The family repeatedly failed to provide an heir, titles fell into abeyance and were resuscitated, heiresses married into other families, but the estate continued to pass by descent. In 1946 the 3rd Earl of Plymouth (of the second creation) gave the estate to the nation as a site for the celebration of Welsh craft and culture.

ANCIENT FEATURES

The gabled 16th-century house, with its symmetrical entrance front, overlooks walled gardens. This pattern of enclosures follows the Tudor arrangement and the garden is a multiyered accretion of features going back to the middle ages. Although ancient features survive the fishponds are thought to date from the middle ages – much of the existing garden was made in the 19th century. An avenue of pleached limes runs up to the entrance forecourt with a splendid circular lead cistern the centre, raised on a stone plinth and surrounded by clipped box. To one side the house overlooks a box parterre with shapes of clipped golden yew. The compartments are either bedded out with antirrhinums, pelargoniums and silver *Senecio cineraria* or filled with lavender or santolina. A tunnel of hornbeam leads between other formal gardens – a knot garden of box, and a garden of segmental beds set in paving which encircles a large clipped yew and circular bench. At the top a cross walk has borders of roses or herbaceous perennials, and a fine wrought-iron gate leads to a restored Victorian rose garden. A section of the herbaceous border is planted with red hot pokers and white, pink,

purple and yellow gladioli – as jolly a piece of Victorian exuberance as you could want.

West of the house, overlooking a shallow valley and the ancient fishponds, the Windsor-Clives built a viewing platform and a series of terraces running down to the water, with lead figures on the parapets. Is this an evocation of the much grander and more venerable terraces at Powis Castle (*see page 226*) – another Clive house. Walks lead along the banks of the pools towards a dovecote and a 16th-century thatched barn overlooking an orchard. The gardens are still being restored and such features as a rock and water garden made by Pulham & Son and a formal Italian garden will add to the Victorian charms of the place.

Location St Fagans, Cardiff CF5 6XB, Glamorgan
OS ST1277 4m W of Cardiff; Jnct 33 of M4 and A4232
(follow signs to Museum of Welsh Life) **Tel** 029 2057
3500 **Fax** 029 2057 3490 **CADW/ICOMOS Register**
Grade I **Owner** National Museums and Galleries of
Wales **Open** daily 10–5 **Area** 18 acres/7 hectares

SNOWSHILL MANOR

ARCHETYPAL COTSWOLD MANOR HOUSE
GARDEN WITH PROFUSE PLANTING, PRETTY
ORNAMENTS AND OLD WALLS

Snowshill is a charming village – and no doubt realises it – and Snowshill Manor is marvellously attractive. The house is the epitome of Cotswold cosiness, built of that distinctive pale stone, roofed in richly textured stone tiles and given a gentlemanly classical façade in the 18th century. Its entrance looks towards the village street but its garden tumbles, in a thoroughly orderly way, down the slopes west of the house.

Charles Paget Wade, an architect filled with a love of vernacular architecture, bought the estate in 1919 after fighting in World War I. His friend, the Arts and Crafts architect and garden designer M.H. Baillie Scott, designed a

The lower terrace at Snowshill

Mask and pool at Snowshill

garden for him in 1920, which Wade adapted in his own way. The site, and Wade's architectural notions, demanded a terraced garden and a sequence of enclosed walled spaces firmly related to the house. Wade linked the spaces with stone steps and emphasised a bold descending axis with an avenue of Irish yews. Handsome architectural ornaments – an armillary sphere on a tall stone column, a gilt figure of St George and the dragon and various sundials – decorate the enclosures.

The final ornamental enclosure at the foot of the slope epitomises the style. A beautiful Venetian wellhead stands in the middle, shrouded with roses; an elaborate astrological sundial is fixed to the wall above a bench in a ferny niche; ivy and roses garland the walls above borders of acanthus, echinops, Japanese anemones, geraniums and phlox; clipped balls of box echo the stone spheres on gate piers; benches and other joinery are painted "Wade blue" (a greeny-blue of Wade's own devising); inscriptions above gateways take sentimental whimsy to painful extremes: "Hours fly/ Flowers die/New Days/New Ways/Pass by/ Love stays"; and finally an opening in the wall leads through an arbour of honeysuckle to a kitchen garden with marigolds and nasturtiums among the lettuces and hazels lining the path.

Wade recruited a gardener in his own idiosyncratic way: "I liked his name, which was Hodge, his hat, which was mauve, and having asked him, I was satisfied that he knew nothing about gardening beyond cabbages and cauliflowers." Hodge was, however, a skilful mason and the walls at Snowshill were ultimately more important than the flowers. Although Snowshill is swoony with roses

and other flowers in summer, they are in fact inessential; it is the brio of ornamentation, the flow of enclosures, the changing levels, the intimate nooks and crannies and sudden longer vistas that make Snowshill so enchanting.

Charles Wade once wrote: "Few indeed are the botanists that can make a garden; they have instead a 'Nurseryman's Catalogue' come to life." His own "catalogue", on which most of his energies were devoted, consisted of the astonishing heterogenous collections of things that took his fancy and now fill the house and spill over into outhouses. Here are Buddhas, fragments of lace, penny-farthing bicycles, models of villages, Japanese armour, model ships, weapons, prams and much, much more. It is less a collection than an accumulation. Something, probably the influence of M.H. Baillie Scott, prevented Wade's relentless acquisitiveness from colonising the garden which, by comparison, is a model of harmony and discipline.

Location Snowshill, nr Broadway WR12 7JU, Gloucestershire **OS** SP0933 In Snowshill village, 3m S of Broadway by A44 and minor road **Tel** and **Fax** 01386 852410 **Infoline** 01684 855376 **Email** snowshill@smtp.ntrust.org.uk **English Heritage Register** Grade II **Owner** The National Trust **Open** Apr to Oct, Wed to Sun 11–5.30 **Area** 2 acres/0.8 hectares

SPETCHLEY PARK

DREAMLIKE WALLED GARDENS FILLED WITH NOTABLE PLANTS, AND PARKLAND WITH FINE TREES

Spetchley Park was bought in 1606 by Rowland Berkeley, of the family that still owns Berkeley Castle (*see page 445*). Sir Robert Berkeley was given a licence to impark in 1625 but he was also a gardener and a friend of John Evelyn who described him as "most ingenious, virtuous and religious…and very curious in gardening". It is not known what form the garden took at this time and it is not until the 19th century that a clear picture emerges.

A new house was built between 1811 and 1818 to the designs of John Tasker – a slightly inscrutable but suave Georgian mansion. At the same time walled kitchen gardens were built to the east of the house. In 1891 the then Robert Berkeley married Rose Willmott, the sister of the great gardener Ellen Willmott of Warley Place (*see page 555*) who influenced some of the planting here.

In spite of its size Spetchley Park preserves, by some alchemy that I do not quite

A mixed border at Spetchley Park

understand, an attractive secret garden character. Parts are concealed behind enclosures of labyrinthine complexity – few gardens are easier to get lost in – and other parts offer serene open views of parkland, house and water. You enter in a way that most garden designers would disapprove of, through a slightly scruffy yard and some outhouses. Even here, however, you are instantly plunged into the world of plants for in this very protected place are many tender climbers such as *Campsis × tagliabuana* 'Madame Galen' with outrageous scarlet flowers, the handsome evergreen *Pileostegia viburnoides* and the southern Californian *Ribes viburnifolium*, and shrubs such as *Mahonia lomariifolia*, the double-flowered pomegranate (*Punica granatum* f. *plena*) and white *Abutilon vitifolium*.

Beyond the yard is a sequence of enclosed gardens, the first of which is a very handsome brick-walled former kitchen garden, an irregular square whose side walls widen as they extend to the south. Deep mixed borders run along the outside walls, with often substantial shrubs or trees, such as magnolias, and climbing plants clothe the walls. The western part of the kitchen garden is enclosed in yew hedges, and a new garden was designed by Veronica Cross to celebrate the millennium; its most unusual feature is a pergola covered in *Cercis canadensis* 'Forest Pansy' with blood-red foliage. A Victorian tiered fountain stands at the centre of the new garden, surrounded by Italian cypresses, cistuses, dahlias, clumps of *Melianthus major*, ornamental grasses and the occasional slightly dubious rose (*Rosa* 'Oranges and Lemons' seems to me everything that a rose should not be). To one side a sunken garden has an arbour of roses and wisteria and a terraced bed with tender plants – species agapanthus, penstemons and tulbaghias.

THE FOUNTAIN GARDEN

The Fountain Garden to the south of the kitchen garden was probably inspired by Ellen Willmott. Overlooked by a pillared summerhouse and a pair of 18th-century lead statues (Adam and Eve, apparently, but fully clad), the area is divided into four, with a fountain pool at the centre and yew hedges enclosing the major divisions. *Campanula lactiflora* flowers throughout the summer in front of the yew hedges along the central path, and narrow openings lead into hedged compartments divided into regular rows of long narrow beds, like order beds in a botanical garden. Some noble ornamental tree or shrub (a maple, lespedeza, magnolia, sophora or viburnum) in each bed is is underplanted with treasures. Here are alliums (*A. unifolium* or *A. rosenbachianum*; not the corny *A. hollandicum*), colchicums, epimediums, hepaticas, species peonies and pulmonarias.

South of the Fountain Garden is the Rose Lawn with a formal rose garden over which I shall draw a veil (in her *Follies & Grottoes* (1974), Barbara Jones, who otherwise loves Spetchley, calls it a "tragic mistake"). The rose lawn itself has fine trees – a Lucombe oak (*Quercus × hispanica* 'Lucombeana'), 18th-century cedars of Lebanon and a *Picea breweriana* with its decorative pendulous fronds. Nearby is a delightful 18th-century roothouse with a tall thatched roof, slender ogee windows, and an interior of gnarled trunks and delicate geometric patterns of hazel rods.

PARKLAND AND WOODS

A bridge crosses the remains of a Tudor moat, leading to the lake-like "garden pool" (whose banks are lavishly planted with daffodils in spring, including *Narcissus* 'Spetchley'), and from here a path runs among trees, with parkland stretching to the west and south beyond the pool. A statue of the Apollo Belvedere stands out against the woods, where there are marvellous drifts of white and purple *Lilium martagon* in summer. There are countless excellent trees here: among them, several acers, the beautiful *Carpinus japonica* with decorative hanging fruit, *Cornus* 'Ascona', and a thorn with finely cut foliage (*Crataegus tanacetifolia*). Here, with the house seen across fine lawns, framed with splendid trees, the garden at Spetchley has a more patrician air.

Location nr Worcester WR5 1RS, Worcestershire
OS SO8953 3m E of Worcester by A422 **Tel** 01905 345213/345224 **Fax** 01435 511915 **English Heritage Register** Grade II* **Owner** Spetchley Garden Charitable Trust **Open** Apr to Sept, Tue to Fri and Bank Hol Mon 11–5, Sun 2–5 **Area** 25 acres/10 hectares

STANWAY HOUSE

EXTRAORDINARY 18TH-CENTURY CASCADE AND PYRAMID PAVILION FOR A LOVELY OLD HOUSE

Stanway belonged to Tewkesbury Abbey from the 8th century. Sir Richard Tracy, of an ancient Gloucestershire family, leased the estate in 1533 and bought it after the dissolution of the monasteries. The present house was built in the late 16th century; a new south front was added between 1630 and 1640 and, in the same period, a wonderful gatehouse with swooping gables. In the late 18th century the Tracy heiress married into the Charteris family (Earls of Wemyss) to whom the estate has belonged ever since.

The abbey estate had a deer park at Stanway in the middle ages but nothing is known of the garden until a Kip engraving of Stanway was published in Robert Atkyns's *The Ancient and Present State of Glostershire* (1712). It shows the house from the south, with a walled garden and a simple four-part parterre surrounded on three sides by a raised walk.

The Pyramid at Stanway

Two more parterres, and espaliered trees against a wall, are seen in an irregularly shaped enclosure alongside it and, behind the house, a walled kitchen garden. A painting of 1748 by Wiliam Taylor, still at Stanway, shows a new feature – a canal with a long cascade on the slopes east and north-east of the house. The painting is just too early to show the most beautiful and intriguing garden feature at Stanway – the Pyramid.

UNFORGETTABLE PYRAMID

The Pyramid was built in 1750 by Robert Tracy as a memorial to his father. Rising among trees on the top of the slope east of the house, it is square in plan, with rounded openings and urns on its parapet, and is crowned with a soaring pyramid (in fact a cross between a pyramid and an obelisk – too slender to be the former and too plump to be the latter). In front of it is a pool which flows into a long wide cascade of rough stone. All this has been recently restored. The cascade originally flowed into a cross canal (as seen in Taylor's painting) but this was filled in in the 19th century. The interior of the Pyramid has shell-head niches and it used, according to Barbara Jones's *Follies & Grottoes* (1974), to have "a fine plaster ceiling with shells and cupids [which] fell in the Second World War". Behind the Pyramid is a round pool, acting as a reservoir for the cascade, and some beautiful trees – a lovely grove of cedars of Lebanon and a splendid old sweet chestnut. More fine old trees can be seen on either side of the cascade – a huge lime, sweet chestnuts (including a whopper with widespread limbs), old yews and Scots pines.

Nothing remains of the parterres seen in the Kip engraving but the beautiful walls remain; they now enclose a lawn with a tall tulip tree (*Liriodendron tulipifera*) planted in 1905. As you enter and leave (by a yard with a magnificent tithe barn) you will see two superb oriental planes (*Platanus orientalis*). The Pyramid is the unforgettable garden sight at Stanway and the house itself, in its exceptional rural setting, is very beautiful.

Location Stanway, Cheltenham GL54 5PQ, Gloucestershire **OS** SP0632 In Stanway hamlet, 11m SE of Cheltenham by B4632 **Tel** 01386 584469

Fax 01386 584688 **Email** stanwayhouse@btinternet.com **English Heritage Register** Grade I **Owner** Lord Neidpath **Open** Jul to Aug, Tue and Thur 2–5; at other times by appointment **Area** 23 acres/9 hectares

STONE HOUSE COTTAGE

DAZZLING SEQUENCE OF HEDGED AND RICHLY PLANTED GARDENS OVERLOOKED BY SPLENDID GAZEBOS

I can never make up my mind whether this is a garden with a nursery attached or the other way round. At all events, this attractive place is a late 20th-century phenomenon – an excellent specialist nursery together with an admirable garden. The arrangement has the great advantage that the visitor can see many of the nursery's plants in action in the garden.

The site is a brick-walled former kitchen garden which James Arbuthnott, a virtuoso bricklayer, has embellished with a series of gazebos, towers, minarets and other

A gazebo at Stone House Cottage

architectural *jeux d'esprit*. These also serve to display many of the climbing plants which form one of the the specialities of the nursery. The shape of the enclosure is irregular, like a truncated triangle, and strong shapes are needed to impose some feeling of harmony. A brick path runs as straight as an arrow from the entrance in one corner of the walled garden to the house on its far side. The path is edged with tall yew hedges from which openings lead to other parts of the garden. An archway of clipped yew serves as the starting point to a pair of mixed borders backed by a hedge of box on one side and of *Prunus cerasifera* 'Nigra' on the other. A broad turf path runs between the borders, and a sundial on a barley sugar twisted column forms an eyecatcher at the end. The borders are about 12ft/3.6m wide, deep enough to accommodate large shrub roses like *Rosa moyesii* or substantial herbaceous perennials such as *Kitaibela vitifolia* and *Strobilanthes attenuata*. The prunus hedge forms an excellent background to the rich reds and purples of such plants as *Eupatorium purpureum* and *Cirsium rivulare* 'Atropurpureum' which dominate this side of the borders.

LIVING DANGEROUSLY

The walls are garlanded with climbers and tender shrubs – many roses, the twining *Araujia sericifera*, cestrums, jasmines and species honeysuckles. They sell these, and many others, some of which are rare – such as berberidopsis, billardiera, bomarea, campsis, muehlenbeckia, the Australian sollya and the charming sounding wattakaka (now, alas, correctly known as dregea). The Arbuthnotts live dangerously: many of the plants they grow in this cold and landlocked place should not survive at all, but many of them do, exemplifying one of the great rules of gardening – that you do not really know what will thrive in your garden until you have tried it.

Location Stone, nr Kidderminster DY10 4BG, Worcestershire **OS** SO8775 2m SE of Kidderminster by A448 **Tel** 01562 69902 **Fax** 01562 69960 **Email** louisa@shcn.co.uk **Owner** J.F. and L.N. Arbuthnott **Open** Mar to Sept, Wed to Sat 10–5.30 (also some Sun for National Gardens Scheme) **Area** ¾ acre/0.3 hectares

SUDELEY CASTLE

OLD GARDENS OF A HISTORIC
ESTATE BRILLIANTLY REVITALISED: ROSE
GARDEN, TERRACED WALK, SECRET GARDEN
AND KNOT GARDEN

Sudeley Castle rising among woods and fields as you approach is one of the most beautiful country house views you could hope to see. There has been a house at Sudeley since Saxon times but this one, of beautiful golden stone, was built largely in the 15th and 16th centuries; Katherine Parr lived here as Sir Thomas Seymour's wife after King Henry VIII died in 1547. However, much of the castle was destroyed in the Civil War and remained uninhabitable until the Dent (later Dent-Brocklehurst) family came here in 1837. Although there are traces of an ancient deer park, including remains of the walls, nothing is known certainly of early gardens here, and the gardens as they are today are late 20th-century with a strong 19th-century background. The Queen's Garden south-east of the house was laid out in the form of a parterre in 1859 with advice from W.A. Nesfield. At its centre is an octagonal pool

Balustraded pool at Sudeley

edged with a stone balustrade, in the middle of which a triumphant fountain spouts a grand plume of water. Wonderful tunnels of yew planted in the 1850s, with openings cut into the sides, line the long sides of the garden. The whole slightly sunken area is enclosed in stone balustrades and terrace walks from where there are wonderful views over serene parkland. The lawns that encircle it are studded with high domes of clipped yew, both common and golden.

In 1988 the divisions of the parterre were replanted by Jane Fearnley-Whittingstall with old shrub roses – 'Albéric Barbier', 'Laure Davoust', 'New Dawn' and 'François Juranville'

– grown as standards in the Victorian fashion and underplanted with smaller roses like *R. gallica* 'Versicolor', and with *Allium cristophii*, irises, geraniums, lavender and penstemons. It is said that there had been an Elizabethan knot garden on this site and the present arrangement has all the decorative sparkle and stately formality of Tudor times. Jane Fearnley-Whittingstall made a more explicit reference to the past in the very attractive Elizabethan knot garden she designed for the inner courtyard of the castle in 1995.

The 15th-century St Mary's Chapel stands to the north of the Queen's Garden and the Chapel Garden alongside it was redesigned by Rosemary Verey in 1979. This secret garden is long and narrow, with raised beds flanking a strip of grass. The borders have mixed plantings of agapanthus, alliums, clematis, *Kolkwitzia amabilis*, penstemons, philadelphus and roses intermingled with tender bedding plants – arctotis, cherry pie (*Heliotropium arborescens*) and *Plectranthus argentatus*.

The rose parterre at Sudeley

On the far side of the castle the ruins of a tithe barn, overlooking a lily pond, are festooned with clematis, roses and wisteria, and substantial shrubs such as *Mahonia lomariifolia* and *Hydrangea aspera* Villosa Group stand out against the old stone.

It is the castle itself and its ancillary buildings that form the chief ornament at Sudeley, but the cleverly revived Victorian garden with its superb walk and parkland views is memorable too.

Location Winchcombe, nr Cheltenham GL54 5JD, Gloucestershire **OS** SP0327 8m NE of Cheltenham by A46 **Tel** 01242 602308 **Fax** 01242 602959 **Email** marketing @sudeley.ndirect.co.uk **English Heritage Register** Grade II* **Owner** Lady Ashcombe **Open** Mar to Oct, daily 10.30–5.30 **Area** 10 acres/4 hectares

TATTON PARK

GRAND PARKLAND, WALLED GARDENS, SUPERB GLASSHOUSES, BORDERS, VICTORIAN PARTERRES AND A JAPANESE GARDEN

Tatton Park is one of the most diverse, interesting and attractive gardens in the country. When the Egerton family came here in the 16th century it was already an old estate. The house they lived in, now Tatton Old Hall, is a late medieval timber-framed building. The present house, on a different site, was built from 1788 to designs by Samuel Wyatt, with additions by Lewis Wyatt who also designed a splendid orangery in 1818. The Egertons stayed at Tatton until 1958 when they gave the estate to the National Trust.

Of the early gardens here nothing is known until the 18th century when William Emes and John Webb were called in to work on the parkland. Humphry Repton was consulted shortly afterwards to advise on the landscape. He produced a Red Book for the estate in 1791, which opens with his usual studiously deferential enthusiasm: "The situation of Tatton may be justly described, as too splendid to be called interesting, and too vast to be deemed picturesque." What Repton did at Tatton is uncertain, though it is plain that some of his major proposals were never

◁ **The Japanese garden** at Tatton

carried out: one of his rejected plans was to make a grand entrance lodge in Knutsford, itself then a busy industrialised weaving town, which would have involved destroying "a few miserable cottages".

The various parts of the garden today are given a vague link by the Broad Walk which runs, lined with beautiful old beeches, from a point west of the house to the south-east boundary which is marked by the columned Choragic Monument of Lysicrates (the Athenian storyteller) – a columned temple-like monument built in 1820 for Wilbraham Egerton. The formal gardens cluster about the house, dominated by the Italian Garden, designed by Sir Joseph Paxton, and two exceptional glasshouses. Paxton's design, made in 1859, has little to do with Italy and much to do with exuberant Victorian decoration. Finely restored in recent times, the Italian Garden has a pair of flamboyant parterres with elaborately shaped compartments outlined in box or thrift (*Armeria maritima*) and with topiary shapes of Irish juniper (*Juniperus communis* 'Hibernica') and of cypress (*Chamaecyparis pisifera* 'Squarrosa'). Seasonal bedding schemes are laid out in blocks of simple planting: in summer, for example, massed pink *Dahlia* 'Princess Marie José' and strips of powder-blue *Ageratum* 'Blue Mink'.

Lewis Wyatt's orangery has a jungle-like

The Fernery at Tatton

interior, densely packed with tender plants. Close to it, with a much less glamorous exterior, is the Fernery designed by Paxton and his son-in-law, G.H. Stokes, in around 1859. It houses a collection of tender ferns, including magnificent tree ferns (*Dicksonia antarctica*), disposed in a naturalistic setting of rocky ramparts, with drifts of *Agapanthus africanus* among smaller ferns on either side of a winding walk.

A cluster of formal gardens spreads out west of the Fernery – mixed borders, an Edwardian sunken rose garden and the Tower Garden with remarkable old yew topiary. Lady Charlotte's Bower is a ravishing trelliswork alcove seat flanked with filigree wire columns topped with openwork urns and festooned with the roses 'Paul's Lemon Pillar' and 'New Dawn'. This was part of a flower garden designed by Lewis Wyatt in 1814 and enough of it remains – sweeping paths and specimen trees in lawns – to evoke the kind of "gardenesque" layout that J.C. Loudon vaunted. Paths curve across the lawn, which is planted with a group of *Malus hupehensis*, magnolias, *Acer rubrum* and *Cornus controversa* interspersed with the occasional decorative interlude – a tiered fountain or mounded bedding schemes.

The Broad Walk leads across sloping land with excellent trees and attractive glimpses of pools gleaming among the woods to the west. The pools, called the Golden Brook, were formed in the early 19th century from former clay pits. In 1910 a Japanese garden was made, now excellently restored, enclosed in a beautifully made bamboo fence; it has a pool edged with irises and shrouded with azaleas and Japanese maples, a teahouse and snow lantern. Is it like anything in Japan? Probably not, but it is an exceptionally pretty sight.

In 2002 the walled gardens to the west of the house, formerly leased to the Tatton Garden Society, had been taken back and were being restored to their original role of vegetable garden and walled orchard; they include some handsome old glasshouses, among them a vinery and pinery.

Location Knutsford WA16 6QN, Cheshire **OS** SJ7481 3½m N of Knutsford, signed from the centre of the town **Tel** 01625 534400 **Infoline** 01625 534435 **Fax** 01625 534403 **Email** tatton@cheshire.gov.uk **Website** www.tattonpark.org.uk **English Heritage Register** Grade II* **Owner** The National Trust **Open** Apr to Oct, daily except Mon (open Bank Hol Mon) 10.30–6; Oct to Mar, daily except Mon 11–4 **Area** (garden) 60 acres/24 hectares; (park) 2,000 acres/810 hectares

TREDEGAR HOUSE

IMPECCABLE EARLY 18TH-CENTURY
FORMAL GARDENS RECONSTRUCTED
FOR A MAGNIFICENT HOUSE

Tredegar is an irresistibly attractive house built between *c*.1664 and 1672 for the Morgan family which had lived here since the beginning of the 15th century. It is long and low, built of pale brick, with beautiful carved stone ornament to the window and door surrounds – pediments with crouching lions and griffins above the ground-floor windows and swags of fruit below the first-floor windows. The Morgans remained in the house until 1951 when they were forced out by death duties. It subsequently became a school but was then bought by Newport Borough Council which started to restore it in 1976. The restoration of the gardens came a little later and they provide one of the most attractive examples of a restoration of a formal garden of the early 18th century.

South-west of the house a large orangery was built in the first years of the 18th century, together with brick walls enclosing a garden.

The orangery garden at Tredegar

Using the evidence of an archaeological survey, this garden has now been reinstated to its original appearance. The entrance to the orangery is flanked by a pair of *Magnolia grandiflora* (an early 18th-century introduction to Europe but would it have been in the original garden at Tredegar so soon after its introduction?) and in the beds on each side are tender shrubs such as figs, myrtle and oleander. Spread out below the orangery is a parterre fashioned of finely mown turf and intricate strips of raked sand (in two colours: red-brown and milky coffee coloured), crushed white seashells and glistening fragments of coal – all materials identified in the archaeological survey. Fruit trees are espaliered against the walls and the beds below contain alternate cones of box and lollipops of privet, with lavender, roses and sage. A second parterre, on the far side of a path, has a more elaborate scheme. A central scalloped lawn is set within corner-pieces of blade-like shapes of white seashells against red-brown sand and stripes of pale raked sand. Lollipops of holly or bay are planted either in white-painted Versailles tubs or in the ground in the middle of a circle of seashells. In an adjacent walled enclosure a grand cedar of Lebanon rises in a lawn. Nearby, enclosed in shapes of clipped yew, a white marble obelisk commemorates the Hon. Godfrey Morgan's "favourite charger", Sir Briggs, which he rode in the battles of Alma, Balaclava and Inkerman. East of the house is an open lawn with a lovely old sweet chestnut, a sunken rose garden of Edwardian flavour and a lake which was created when Adam Mickle landscaped the grounds in the 1790s.

A POIGNANT SIGHT

From the courtyard that lies close to the orangery can be seen a poigant sight. The yard is enclosed in brick walls with beautiful railings and has a magnificent set of wrought-iron gates, made between 1714 and 1718 by William and Simon Edney of Bristol. These gates form a *claire-voie* aligned on the remains of a lime avenue running up a slope into the distance, but the view is now intersected by the M4 and lorries not limes are the most visible feature of the landscape. When Adam Mickle was landscaping the grounds in the

1790s he concealed the old turnpike road (which became the A48) with a high wall behind a grass bank. This was removed when the M4 was built, leaving the new road visible in all its splendour and, in the words of the garden archaeologist Christopher Taylor in his *Parks and Gardens of Britain* (1998), "with Junction 28 carefully placed across the last remaining early eighteenth-century avenue".

Location Newport NP1 9YW, Gwent **OS** ST2985 2m SW of Newport by A48; Jnct 28 of M4 **Tel** 01633 815880 **Fax** 01633 815895 **Email** tredegar.house@newport.gov.uk **CADW/ICOMOS Register** Grade II* **Owner** Newport County Borough Council **Open** Easter to Sept, Wed to Sun and Bank Hol Mon 11.30–4; Nov to Mar, groups only by appointment **Area** 90 acres/36 hectares

TRETOWER COURT AND CASTLE

ENCHANTING MEDIEVAL GARDEN WITH PERIOD PLANTING FOR A BEAUTIFUL 15TH-CENTURY HOUSE

This is an ancient and richly atmospheric place in the splendid setting of the Usk valley. Here are the remains of a Norman castle which Richard Haslam in his Powys volume in "The Buildings of Wales" describes as "among the best Romanesque domestic work left in Wales". The first house here was built in around 1300, to be succeeded by the present Court (now a well-preserved shell) which was built in the late 15th century for Sir Roger Vaughan. Sir Roger was a Yorkist, a courtier to Edward IV, who moved in cultivated circles. Nothing whatever is known of any garden here but CADW had the idea of creating a garden of the kind that Sir Roger might have known. "Its layout and planting are," as Elizabeth Whittle of CADW writes, "as authentic as is practically possible for a garden of a wealthy commoner in the mid fifteenth century."

PERIOD PLANTING

A chequerboard layout of beds, enclosed in wooden fencing, has a stone fountain at its centre. Only plants known to have been in cultivation in the 15th century are grown

The medieval garden at Tretower

here – cowslips and primroses, irises, species peonies such as *Paeonia officinalis* and *P. mascula*, sweet rocket, the wild field rose (*Rosa arvensis*) and violets. A finely made oak tunnel is smothered with the sweetly scented white *Rosa × alba* 'Alba Semiplena' and grapevines, underplanted with periwinkle, Solomon's seal, violets and wild strawberries. A turf seat overlooks a herber enclosed in a rose-covered trellis, with a raised bed of culinary and medicinal herbs. Old cultivars of fruit trees have splendid names – apples called 'Court Pendu Plat', 'Gennet Moyle' and 'Catshead' and a pear called 'Jargonelle'. A flowery mead is spangled in season with buttercups, celandines, pansies, scarlet pimpernel, selfheal and speedwell. This is charmingly done and the view of it from the first-floor windows of the south side of the Court in high summer, with the scent of roses wafting up, is enchanting. It is the most convincing evocation of a medieval garden that I know.

Location Tretower, nr Crickhowell NP8 2RF, Powys **OS** SO1821 In Tretower village, 3m NW of Crickhowell by A479 **Tel** 01874 730279 **Open** Mar, daily 10–4; Apr to May, daily 10–5; Jun to Sept, daily 10–6; Oct, daily 10–5 **Area** 1 acre/0.4 hectares

WESTBURY COURT

HISTORIC AND DELIGHTFUL LATE 17TH-CENTURY WATER GARDEN BEAUTIFULLY RESTORED BY THE NATIONAL TRUST

When *Country Life* described the garden at Westbury Court in 1908 it recorded "no lack of effective variety and changing scene in this garden of pure formality, perfect flatness and simple design. It is at once dignified and enjoyable, satisfying and alluring." This is an excellent description of the garden that we may see today almost a hundred years later, but between the two dates this rare garden was almost irretrievably lost. When the National Trust took it over in 1967 it was in a state of catastrophic neglect and the house for which it had been made had long since disappeared.

The garden had been created, starting in 1696, by Maynard Colchester whose account book survives in the Gloucestershire Record Office. His meticulous entries ("£21 9s. 8d. Pd. Tho. Wintle in full for laying 120,800 bricks"), an engraving by Kip and 19th-century photographs enabled the National Trust to carry out an impeccable restoration. It is an unusual type of garden which seems to have flourished in this part of the country – a formal water garden of modest size. It lies, enclosed in walls of finely laid bricks, quite close to the main road between Gloucester and Chepstow. A *claire-voie*, an elegant railed gap in the wall flanked by piers and stone urns, permitted passers-by a tantalising glimpse of the garden as they bowled along the road.

Two canals run in parallel down the garden, one with a tall, narrow, very Dutch-looking gazebo at its head, looking straight down the water to the *claire-voie*. Yew hedges line the canal, their tops decorated with lollipops of holly and obelisks of yew. In the other canal an 18th-century stone figure of Neptune defies the water. Alongside it is a knot garden ("paid Thos. Hall towards the knots in the garden £4-14-6") which the National Trust recreated from the Kip engraving. A pattern of box-edged compartments, punctuated by cones and lollipops of box, is filled with plants that Colchester could have used – love-in-the-mist, candytuft (*Iberis sempervirens*), pot marigold (*Calendula officinalis*) and so on. On either side of the knot is a quincunx of clipped mop-headed Portugal laurel (*Prunus lusitanica*). Concealed behind walls in a corner, and overlooked by a brick summerhouse, is a secret garden. Here beds are filled with herbaceous plants of Colchester's time, and under one of

The secret garden at Westbury

the secret garden's outside walls is a charming collection of early cultivars of pinks – a fashionable plant at the end of the 17th century. At Westbury the visitor is taken delightfully back in time to a provincial gentleman's garden of formal character where cheerfulness keeps breaking in.

In 2002 it became apparent that the yew hedges were suffering from waterlogging as a result of the rising water table in this low-lying area. It remains to be seen what can be done to save them.

Location Westbury-on-Severn GL14 1PD, Gloucestershire **OS** SO7114 9m SW of Gloucester by A48 **Tel** 01452 760461 **Infoline** 01684 855377 **Email** westburycourt@ntrust.org.uk **English Heritage Register** Grade II* **Owner** The National Trust **Open** Apr to Oct, Wed to Sun (open Bank Hol Mon) 11–6; at other times by appointment **Area** 4 acres/1.6 hectares

WESTON PARK

WONDERFUL WOODED GROUNDS, FINE
BUILDINGS AND SUPERB FLOWERY
TERRACES FOR A GREAT HOUSE

The estate at Weston Park belonged to the Mytton family in the 15th century and passed by descent, sometimes through the female line, to the Bridgemans (later Earls of Bradford) who gave it to the Weston Park Foundation in 1986. The brick and stone house, with its rounded gables, was rebuilt in 1671 and, with one or two later alterations, remains much as it was at that time.

There was a deer park here by 1346, on the eastern edge of the modern park, to the south-east of the present house; a moated site here may have had a medieval hunting lodge. In 1765 Sir Henry Bridgeman (later 1st Earl of Bradford) commissioned Capability Brown to work on the landscape. This included building a ha-ha to the south of the house to keep out the deer, and laying out new pleasure grounds east of the house in what is now called Temple Wood, with a series of pools of which the largest is Temple Pool. By the end of 1766 Brown had been paid £1,725 (£112,987 today).

In 1770 the architect James Paine designed a beautiful pavilion, the Temple of Diana, on

The parterre at Weston Park

the southern edge of the pleasure grounds. This rare and delightful building serves different purposes as its eclectic style suggests. The south front is an orangery with a magnificent vaulted interior, elaborate plasterwork and tall arched windows from which there are wonderful views over the ha ha and parkland to a wooded escarpment with an eyecatcher, Knoll Tower, built in 188 and formerly part of the Tong Castle estate (*see page 549*). The north part of the temple, in dashing Palladian style with a dome rising over superimposed pediments, had a tea room and a music room and provided "the habitation of the dairy woman". Close to the Temple is an aligment of marvellous old swee chestnuts which may have been planted by Brown (it was a favourite tree of his) but elsewhere in the wood are specimens that must predate him. Some of the paths are edged with rhododendrons and throughout the woods are splendid beeches and oaks wit the occasional exotic such as a fern-leafed beech (*Fagus sylvatica* var. *heterophylla* 'Aspleniifolia'), a swamp cypress (*Taxodium distichum*), southern beeches (*Nothofagus* species) and a weeping spruce (*Picea smithiana*). Across the eastern neck of Temple Pool Paine also designed a noble bridge which originally carried the main drive (the Lichfield Drive) to the house. At each end of the bridge is a grand stone urn on a high plinth, also probably designed by Paine.

Below the southern façade of the house a terraced garden was laid out, partly by the garden designer Edward Kemp, in 1877. On the top terrace a gravel walk overlooks a wn with shaped beds planted with summer edding schemes – gold, silver and white for he Jubilee year of 2002. A lower terrace has long herbaceous border and a sunken rose arden with box-edged compartments, and the centre an oval stone basket filled with ypsophila and irises. The final terrace, eyond a yew hedge, is a giant semicircle f lawn edged with a balustrade, from which there are views over parkland with glimmer of water from Park Pool to the outh-west. Immediately west of the house n orangery overlooks an elegant parterre esigned by Elizabeth Banks, where a calloped fountain pool stands at the centre f a pattern of curving box-edged beds filled rith red begonias, variegated euonymus and urple sage.

Capability Brown also laid out the pleasure rounds to the west of the house – a long ravel walk, Shrewsbury Walk, has specimen trees in lawns, which include cedars of Lebanon and sweet chestnuts. On the edge of the walk, shaded by old yews, is an 18th-century hermitage, Pendrill's Cave.

Weston Park is not as well known as it deserves. Paine's Temple of Diana, one of the finest of garden buildings, alone makes it worth a visit. In addition, the parkland, Brown's pleasure grounds and the flowery formal gardens by the house are all outstandingly attractive.

Location Weston-under-Lizard, nr Shifnal TF11 8LE, Shropshire **OS** SJ8010 8m E of Telford by A5; Jnct 3 of M54 **Tel** 01952 852100 **Fax** 01952 850430 **Email** enquiries@weston-park.com **English Heritage Register** Grade II* **Owner** The Weston Park Foundation **Open** Easter weekend 11–7; Apr to Jun, Sat and Sun 11–7; Jul to Aug, daily 11–7; early Sept, Sat and Sun 11–7 **Area** 1,000 acres/404 hectares

The terraced garden at Weston Park

WESTONBIRT ARBORETUM

ONE OF THE WORLD'S GREATEST COLLECTIONS OF TREES AND SHRUBS – A NATIONAL TREASURE

This is one of the best, and most agreeable, places to see trees and shrubs in the British Isles, with over 3,000 species and cultivars of woody plants arranged in an exhilarating landscape. One of the great attractions of Westonbirt is the result of the passion for trees and shrubs of one man, Robert Holford. His family had owned estates in this part of southern Gloucestershire since the 16th century and in 1829, ten years before inheriting, he started planting trees, choosing the site with care. The soil is rich, fertile greensand which varies from the fairly acid to the slightly alkaline, providing ideal conditions for a very wide range of plants. The rainfall is high here and furthermore the terrain is well irrigated with springs.

BOLD AVENUES

There were no existing trees when Holford started work and his first priority was to plant windbreaks on this exposed site. When he embarked on ornamental planting he planted in bold avenues which radiated out north-west from his house (now separately owned; *see* Westonbirt School *page 240*). This layout formed a fine framework for subsequent planting. Robert, and later on his son, Sir George, planted for the long term, grouping trees with skill and placing enticing specimens to draw the eye. The greatest of their avenues, Holford's Ride, is a wide walk lined with trees and shrubs: on one side a group of soaring slender incense cedars (*Calocedrus decurrens*) is planted alongside a grove of strongly horizontal *Parrotia persica* whose graceful downward-sweeping branches contrast with the vertical emphasis of the cedars; on the other side are spectacular Sierra redwoods (*Sequoiadendron giganteum*), echoing the cedars but far taller. These, and many other great trees at Westonbirt, are given generous space in which to reveal their true character and play their part in the landscape.

The Holfords also paid attention to colour

and atmosphere. Their Colour Circle is a glade of trees chosen for the brilliance of their autumn colouring – acers, *Cercidiphyllum japonicum*, *Liquidambar styraciflua*, *Nyssa sylvatica* and *Parrotia persica*. The greatest number of visitors to Westonbirt come in the autumn, and it is indeed a magnificent sight in that season. However, the collection at Westonbirt is so large, the area so vast, that any day of the year will yield pleasures. Most visitors scarcely stray from the "old" arboretum north of the car park, but south and west, across a field, is Silk Wood, a wilder area where you will often find yourself quite alone surrounded by superb collections of hickories, limes, maples, oaks, pines, poplars and walnuts.

Apart from the notable trees, there is a huge range of shrubs throughout the arboretum –

The Colour Circle at Westonbirt Arboretum

berberis, enkianthus, eucryphias, fothergilla, rhododendrons (many unfamiliar, many gardenworthy, like the charming small Japanese *R. quinquefolium*), stewartias and magnificent witch hazels. In all there are 18,000 specimens of trees and shrubs here – one of the greatest collections in the world, beautifully displayed, and one of the most delightful to explore.

Location Westonbirt, nr Tetbury GL8 8QS, Gloucestershire **OS** SO8590 3m SW of Tetbury by A433 **Tel** 01666 880220 **Fax** 01666 880559 **English Heritage Register** Grade I **Owner** The Forestry Commission **Open** daily 10–8 (or dusk if earlier) **Area** 600 acres/243 hectares

WESTONBIRT SCHOOL GARDENS

MAGNIFICENT 19TH-CENTURY FORMAL GARDENS AND SPLENDID TREES.

The Holford family acquired the 16th-century manor house at Westonbirt in 1665. A new house was built in 1823 which was in turn superseded by the spectacular neo-Elizabethan mansion we see today – built between 1863 and 1870 for Robert Stayner Holford to the designs of Lewis Vulliamy.

Even before Robert Holford inherited the Westonbirt estate in 1839 he had started making new gardens, including the great layout of Westonbirt Arboretum (*see page 239*). With the new house, Lewis Vulliamy also laid

ut architectural terraces below its south
açade and, to the east, the enclosed Italian
Garden. Some trees survived in the pleasure
rounds from the earlier period and there was
much tree-planting in the 19th century,
specially of the new conifers that were being
ntroduced in the middle of the century.

Holfords remained at Westonbirt, the estate
assing to a nephew, the 4th Earl of Morley,
n 1926. Morley already owned the Saltram
state in Devon (*see page 60*) so the Westonbirt
state was put on the market. In 1928 the
ouse became a school, which has cared for
he gardens exceptionally well, enriching
hem with much new planting of trees.

From the south façade of the house a long
xial walk descends a slope, cutting across a
eries of terraces and ending in a circular
ountain pool and an ornate carved stone
ench, with a ha-ha and the park beyond. At
he level of the lowest terrace a long walk
uns from St Catherine's Church (now the
chool chapel) in the west to the Mercury
Garden in the east. The Broad Walk has many
eautiful trees and shrubs – among them

acers, a big old cedar of Lebanon, a splendid
old *Cercidiphyllum japonicum*, *Liquidambar
styraciflua*, magnolias and *Parrotia persica*. Large
bushes of box, cotinus or golden yew are
interspersed among the trees.

The Mercury Garden is full of atmosphere.
A sunken circular lawn has a circular pool with
a statue of Mercury (after Giambologna) in the
middle, and the dense planting of Scots pines,
monkey puzzles and American walnut (*Juglans
nigra*) about the lawn gives a secretive air.

The Italian Garden, close to the Mercury
Garden and enclosed in yew hedges and walls,
is overlooked by two grand brick and stone
pavilions built into its upper corners. The
garden is laid out with a series of shaped beds,
with stone curbing, filled with summer
bedding schemes. In the middle is a
spectacular circular pool with grotesque masks
spouting water. Each pavilion stands at the
head of a path leading at its other end to a
splendidly ornate gateway whose arched
openings are crowned with a great shell,

The Italian Garden at Westonbirt School

obelisks and pine cones. Between the two
gateways a yew hedge is interrupted in the
centre by an elaborate scalloped pool flanked
by richly carved dolphin's masks.

To the south-west of the house is a garden
of quite different, informal character. Here are
winding walks among specimen trees planted
in grass, a rustic rockery and grotto with a
pool, and a lake (formed from what had been
the village pond). Does any other school
possess such a fine garden?

Location nr Tetbury GL8 8QG, Gloucestershire
OS SO8590 **Tel** 01666 880333 **Fax** 01666 880364
Website www.westonbirt.gloucse.sch.uk **English
Heritage Register** Grade I **Owner** Westonbirt School
Open Easter and summer holidays and half-term
holidays in the summer and autumn terms (phone or
consult website for dates and times) **Area** (gardens) 25
acres/10 hectares; (park) 225 acres/91hectares

E.H. WILSON
MEMORIAL GARDEN

A LITTLE WALLED GARDEN
COMMEMORATING A GREAT PLANT
COLLECTOR, FILLED WITH HIS PLANTS

E.H. Wilson (1876–1930), probably the
greatest of all plant hunters, was born in
Chipping Campden and this charming little
garden, entered by a Gothic arch in a stone
wall, reminds gardeners of how much we owe
him. The Wilsons were an old family in these
parts; records in the parish go back to the
early 17th century. When part of the former
vicarage garden (with splendid views of the
tower of the parish church of St James),
became available, the town decided to buy it.
This garden, designed by Sir Peter Shepheard
and with plants chosen by Roy Lancaster
from the 1,200 odd plants introduced by
Wilson, was completed in 1984. Here are
many marvellous aristocrats: trees such as *Acer
griseum* and *Davidia involucrata*; shrubs such as
Ceratostigma willmottianum, *Kolkwitzia amabilis*,
Magnolia delavayi, *Viburnum davidii*, and the
superb *Rosa moyesii*; climbers such as *Actinidia
deliciosa*, the late-flowering *Clematis serratifolia*
and *Lonicera tragophylla* (one of the best
honeysuckles). In June the air is filled with the
tropical scents of *Lilium regale* – this exquisite

The entrance to the E.H. Wilson Garden

stalwart of herbaceous borders was introduced only in 1905. Some of the smaller plants would be an ornament in any garden, yet are rarely seen. *Corydalis cheilanthifolia*, for example, a Chinese cousin of the English native fumitory, forms a burgeoning mound of beautiful, intricately disected fern-like foliage with graceful spikes of lemon-yellow flowers.

This is the only garden I know dedicated to the introductions of a single plant hunter. No other plant collector's work is so worthy of celebration and none resulted in such a feast

of notable garden plants. This tiny plot will help you understand something of the thrill of the chase that inspired men like Wilson in the great age of plant collecting.

Location Leysbourne, Chipping Campden, Gloucestershire **OS** SP1539 In the centre of Chipping Campden on the E side of Leysbourne, a northerly extension of the High Street; the garden is on the E side **Open** daily dawn–dusk **Area** ¼ acre/0.1 hectares

WITLEY COURT

THE BURNT-OUT SHELL OF A PALATIAL
HOUSE AND THE SPECTACULAR REMAINS
OF ITS GREAT GARDENS

Ruins have special appeal. It is partly the romance and partly what you might call the Ozymandias effect: "Look on my works, ye Mighty, and despair!" Witley Court is a stupendous sight – the shell of a great house and, in the grounds, scattered grandiose garden ornaments. It was the creation of William Humble Ward, 1st

Earl of Dudley, a Black Country mining and industrial tycoon whose trustees bought the estate in 1837. From 1854 onwards he employed Samuel Whitfield Daukes to transform the old mansion – partly Jacobean, partly early Georgian, with additions by John Nash in 1806 – into an astonishing Italianate palace, incorporating parts of the earlier house.

W.A. Nesfield was called in to design a garden in keeping with the new house – he called it his "monster work". South and east of the house he laid out terraces, steps, parterres, pavilions and pools. But in 1937 the house was gutted by fire – the ruins were so and the estate dismembered. Proposals to make a caravan park or a motor-racing circu here were rejected and since 1972, now in the care of English Heritage, the buildings have been stabilised and the grounds tidied up. Tw of Nesfield's grandest ornaments survive: the heroic Perseus and Andromeda fountain in a giant scalloped pool, and a pool to the east where Flora disports herself surrounded by spouting Tritons. (By 2002 neither of these yet had its water supply but work was under way.) A pair of curiously oriental

The Perseus and Andromeda Fountain

summerhouses also survive, designed by Daukes and with domes of Moghul character. There are no borders here, nor any plants of note, but the shell of the house has melancholy character and Nesfield's fountains form a powerful presence in the landscape.

The grounds to the north and north-east of the house are well wooded, with a large lake and cascade. This area, rich in trees and shrubs, has now become home to a permanent exhibition of sculptures – the Jerwood Sculpture Park – with works by such artists as Kenneth Armitage, Michael Ayrton, Elizabeth Frink and Antony Gormley, and it is proposed to add others. Some are cleverly placed but most are randomly sited, and in any event seem irrelevant to the place.

SUMPTUOUS RUINS

The overwhelmingly distinctive things about Witley Court are the remains of Nesfield's garden and the ruins of the house, yet this garden, designed for one of the richest men in the world, was once sumptuous and packed with incident. Stripping it down and tidying it up has removed its essence. Perhaps it would have been preferable to shore up the buildings and allow nature to take over the garden – as at Hackfall Wood (*see page 339*) where ruinous monuments loom suddenly through a jungle of seedling sycamores, brambles and nettles.

Location Great Witley, nr Worcester WR6 6JT, Worcestershire **OS** SO7664 10m NW of Worcester by A443 **Tel** 01299 896636 **English Heritage Register Grade II* Owner** English Heritage **Open** Apr to Sept, daily 10–6; Oct, daily 10–5; Nov to Mar, Wed to Sun 10–4 (closed 24–26 Dec and 1 Jan) **Area** 55 acres/22 hectares

WOLLERTON OLD HALL

MASTERLY MODERN GARDENS, FULL OF DISTINGUISHED PLANTING, FOR AN OLD HOUSE

The tradition of Hidcote and Sissinghurst – carefully contrived formal spaces abundantly filled with plants – remains a potent garden style. John and Lesley Jenkins started in 1984 to make a garden as intricate and attractive as their half-timbered Tudor

house. The entrance to the garden sets the dominant tone – a formal procession of clipped yew cones lavishly underplanted with David Austin's English Roses. The sunken rill garden leading off it forms one of the key axes in the garden. Screened behind yew hedges and a latticework fence with turned finials crowning each upright, it has a strong flavour of Arts and Crafts gardens, with a little pool fringed with epimediums, ferns and violas whose water flows into a narrow rill in a finely laid York stone terrace. The axis of the rill is continued, up a flight of stone steps to the north, with a rose-shrouded gazebo. From here a new axis at right-angles has a long, deep, richly floriferous herbaceous border running along the northern boundary wall. At its end an opening leads into a cool white and yellow garden, beyond which a path is overarched with roses and, leading off it, a "hot" garden smouldering with crocosmias, purple-leafed ligularias, *Lobelia cardinalis* and salvias.

Interconnections are subtly contrived, new

The hot garden at Wollerton Old Hall

views are opened at every turn, and everywhere there are planting schemes to be admired. Some of these are very simple – waves of purple-leafed viola flow about the stems of a lime alley. In the Croft Garden, an informal area beyond the easternmost garden wall, is a remarkable collection of trees and shrubs with a winding walk. In the early 21st century a garden such as this already seems old-fashioned. Nonetheless, Wollerton Old Hall shows the continuing potency of the traditions from which it freely draws. It is brilliantly gardened and the Jenkinses are constantly experimenting with new plants and new arrangements.

Location Wollerton, Market Drayton TF9 3NA, Shropshire **OS** SJ6229 14m NE of Shrewsbury, off A53 between Hodnet and Market Drayton **Tel** 01630 685760 **Fax** 01630 685583 **Owner** John and Lesley Jenkins **Open** May to Aug, Fri, Sun and Bank Hol Mon 12–5 **Area** 3 acres/1.2 hectares

HEART *of* ENGLAND

ALTON TOWERS

BEAUTIFUL GARDEN BUILDINGS REMAIN IN
THIS EXTRAVAGANT EARLY 19TH-CENTURY
GARDEN WITH ITS ROCKY WOODED DELL

Alton Towers was the creation of the 15th Earl of Shrewsbury who from 1837 onwards built a gigantic neo-medieval castle, largely to the designs of A.W.N. Pugin, and laid out a prodigious jumble sale of a garden in a rocky wooded dell north of the house. Pugin's house, originally called Alton Abbey, was an extraordinary extravaganza and even as a gutted shell today it is an awesome sight. Pugin wrote to his client describing his plans for the great hall: "I have nailed my colours to the mast – a bay window, high open roof, two good fireplaces, a great sideboard, screen, minstrel gallery – all or none. I will not sell myself to do a wretched thing."

The gardens were laid out chiefly in the period 1814 to 1827. Lord Shrewsbury formed the habit of asking for advice from many of the leading garden designers of the day without commissioning them to do the work. Among them was J.C. Loudon who visited the new garden in 1831 and recorded, sourly, "Though he consulted almost every artist, ourselves among the rest, he seems only to have done so for the purpose of avoiding

The dell garden at Alton Towers

whatever an artist might recommend." Loudon proceeds to list "a labyrinth of terraces, curious architectural walls, trellis-work, arbours, vases, statues, stairs, pavements, gravel and grass walks" and so on, and on – all a tribute to the Earl who had "much more fancy than sound judgement".

Alton Towers owes its survival today to the fact that it has become a family fun park. (The house's pinnacled and gabled silhouette, more like a medieval village than a house, does have a definite touch of Disneyland to it.) Garden visitors of a fastidious disposition may find this regrettable but the Tussauds Group has done a fine job of restoring and maintaining those parts of the garden that survived. The dell garden, shrouded in conifers and Japanese maples, is relatively untouched by fun park amusements and preserves much of its authentic early 19th-century character. Robert Abraham's superb conservatory (c.1820), running along a terrace on its upper slopes, is crowned with a series of ravishing domes with a delicate tracery of cast-iron glazing bars. The vast central dome is surmounted with a gilt Earl's coronet, and three slightly smaller ones on each side by pineapple finials. Abraham also designed a superlative Chinese pagoda (1827) on the lake

at the foot of the dell. Its three storeys of fretwork tracery with pointed Gothic entrances, painted white and scarlet, are each topped with a sweeping roof edged with dangling bells and the whole is finished with a soaring golden finial. It is extraordinary that a garden inspired by vulgar excess should have ended up with these beautiful buildings.

Location Alton ST10 4DB, Staffordshire **OS** SK0743 18m E of Stoke-on-Trent **Tel** 01538 7104015 **Fax** 01538 704097 **English Heritage Register** Grade I **Owner** The Tussauds Group **Open** mid Mar to early Nov, daily 9–6 (9–8 on some summer evenings; check by phone) **Area** 500 acres/202 hectares

DAVID AUSTIN ROSES

IN A CHARMING SETTING, LEARN HOW
SOME 700 SPECIES AND VARIETIES OF ROSES
PERFORM THROUGHOUT THE YEAR

David Austin is the rose breeder who created "English Roses", which aim to combine the beautiful flower shapes and scent of old roses with the perpetual flowering of modern varieties. He is also a rose nurseryman, stocking an immense range of the best modern roses, old shrub and climbing roses, and species. I include his nursery in this book because of the display gardens.

The gardens lay no claim to the heights of garden art but, with their fine sandy or herringbone brick paths, box-edged beds, lawns, arbours and pergolas, display the roses to great and pleasurable effect. Here are around 700 species and varieties which demonstrate vividly why roses, despite their

David Austin's rose 'Gertrude Jekyll'

difficulties, have continued to be such treasured plants of British gardens. At the end of June they make a spectacular and instructive sight; few flowering displays combine such unfettered exuberance with such irresistible beauty of flower and scent.

In other seasons the pleasures are different. You can study the performance of the English Roses and of those old varieties, either early flowering or remontant, which show their charms at other times of the year. For, where most rose specialists tend to concentrate on cultivars of certain periods, David Austin casts his net wider and shows us the great range of this most seductive of genera. The species roses, for example – unequalled in beauty and completely free from the diseases that plague so many of the cultivars – are hard to find. Here, they show their beauty of habit, handsome thorns, and in late summer and autumn the brilliant colouring of often strikingly shaped hips. Their flowering, fleeting though it may be, can take the breath away.

The purpose of coming here is not to study design but to learn about roses, and it is one of the most attractive places in which to do it.

Location Bowling Green Lane, Albrighton, Wolverhampton WV7 3HB, West Midlands **OS** SJ8104 7m NW of Wolverhampton by A41 and A464; Jnct 3 of M54 **Tel** 01902 376300 **Fax** 01902 372142 **Email** retail@davidaustinroses.com **Website** www.davidaustinroses.com **Open** Mon to Fri 9–5, Sat, Sun and Bank Hol Mon 10–6 (or dusk in winter) **Area** 2 acres/0.8 hectares

BADDESLEY CLINTON

PRETTY 19TH- AND 20TH-CENTURY
GARDENS AS THE SETTING FOR A ROMANTIC
MEDIEVAL HOUSE BRILLIANT WITH HERALDRY

Baddesley Clinton sounds almost like a fictitious name, perhaps from a P.G. Wodehouse story. It is a thoroughly romantic place with a house of tremendous character, largely 15th-century with later alterations, standing serenely surrounded by its moat and sheltered by its wooded grounds. It was built for John Brome (murdered in 1468) and passed to the Ferrers family when his granddaughter Constance married Sir Edward Ferrers. The house passed by descent until

The dahlia walk at Baddesley Clinton

1940 when Cecil Ferrers sold the estate (to a Ferrers cousin), which came to the National Trust in 1980.

To the north of the house, fishponds were made in the middle of the 15th century; these, now shrouded in trees, still ornament the landscape. From here is the best view of the house – where it and the tall trees to one side lie reflected in the dark waters of the moat with no distraction of flowers. In the

Reflections at Baddesley Clinton

19th century a woodland walk was laid out about the banks of the largest pond. Also from the 19th century is a little formal garden in the quadrangle of the house itself. Yews clipped into the shape of acorns surround bedding schemes, one of which traces the chief part of the Ferrers arms, a pattern of seven "mascles" (outline lozenge shapes) planted up in their correct heraldic colours. This was probably made in the time of Marmion Edward Ferrers who, in 1867, married an artist, Rebecca Dulcibella Orpen; she came from an even more ancient lineage than her husband, tracing her descent from Charlemagne. She and her husband revelled in their genealogy and in the romance of the past, smothering the house in heraldry.

THE FLOWER GARDEN

South of the house is a garden, enclosed in silver-pink brick walls, with 20th-century planting. Curved rosebeds surround a sundial at the centre of a lawn edged in lines of apple trees. On the eastern side the path is flanked with borders punctuated by neatly clipped cubes of yew on top of larger cubes, which rise rhythmically among agapanthus, artemisias, catmint, crinums, geraniums, peonies and salvias; the wall behind is veiled with clematis and wisteria. Along the southern side a bed of dahlias runs the whole width of the garden in colours of white, yellow and pale pink – pale and ethereal – very different from the fiery reds and smouldering oranges that have become so fashionable in recent times. A little raised terrace at one end of the dahlia bed gives views over the wall to parkland and woods. All this is pretty and unassuming, with no possibility of the garden stealing the thunder from the lovely house that overlooks it across the moat.

Location Rising Lane, Baddesley Clinton, Knowle, Solihull B93 0DQ, Warwickshire **OS** SP1971 In Baddesley Clinton village, 7½ m NW of Warwick by A4177, A4141 and minor road; Jnct 5 of M42 **Tel** 01564 783294 **Fax** 01564 782706 **Email** baddesleyclinton@ntrust.org.uk **English Heritage Register** Grade II **Owner** The National Trust **Open** Mar to mid Dec, Wed to Sun (open Bank Hol Mon) 12–5 (closes 4.30 Nov and Dec; 5 in Apr and Oct) **Area** 123 acres/50 hectares

BIDDULPH GRANGE GARDEN

RESTORED TO DAZZLING EFFECT, THIS UNIQUE EXOTIC GARDEN EVOKES THE PASSIONS AND IMAGINATION OF ITS VICTORIAN CREATORS

At Biddulph many different interests – plantsmanship, landscaping and a taste for the exotic – have been drawn together to create a dream-like garden of startling originality. It is the creation of James Bateman and his friend Edward Cooke from 1842 onwards, at a time when there was intense interest in garden design of other periods and other cultures, and new plant introductions were flooding into the country in great quantities. Bateman was an orchid lover and his wife, Maria, an assiduous plantswoman; Cooke was an artist and garden designer who had married Jane, the daughter of George Loddiges of Hackney, the greatest nurseryman of the day. The garden they made is, to put it mildly, eclectic. Bateman spent a great deal of money on the garden, and the estate was burdened with a mortgage of £35,000 (about

The Chinese pavilion at Biddulph

£1.5m today) when he passed it on to his son who was forced to sell in 1871. The sale catalogue described the garden as containing "The Pinetum", "The Glen", "The Stumpery", "The Parterres", "The Arboretum", "The Rose Garden", "The Dahlia Walk" and so on, and on. After the sale the house became a hospital and the grounds were cared for but increasingly vandalised. In 1988, after a great campaign of fund raising, the estate was taken over by the National Trust which has restored the garden to dazzling effect. What may be seen today is not merely a fascinating glimpse into the byways of Victorian garden taste but also an exceptionally agreeable place to visit.

More remarkable even than the varied contents of the garden at Biddulph is the ingenious way the different parts were linked together, with formality and picturesque informality intermingled with a deft hand. South of the house the land slopes down sharply and the layout of the garden makes inventive use of the changing levels and character. In front of the house the Italian Garden, with terraces and a stepped walk, leads down to a curved lake whose banks are densely planted with rhododendrons – an adroit passage from crisp formality to naturalism. The decorative building which forms an eyecatcher at the end of the Dahlia Walk also leads sideways to the Stumpery and China. (A similar effect is achieved behind Egypt whose rear entrance suddenly becomes a cottage looking southwards along a woodland walk.)

TREES AND STUMPS

East of the house a long, dead-straight axis passes through formal enclosures close to the house, plunges through woodland and follows a long avenue of deodars (*Cedrus deodara*) and Wellingtonias, culminating in a giant stone vase enclosed in hedges of yew. Winding walks lead through to the most exotic parts of the garden. In China a dark tunnel, lit by flickering candles, suddenly opens out into the gold, scarlet and white of a Chinese pavilion overlooking a pool fringed with Japanese maples and overarched by a scarlet bridge. An alternative route to China follows a shaded path through the Stumpery, a phantasmagorical collection of tree stumps. Egypt is a temple of clipped yew guarded by sphinxes, while immediately behind, forming an extraordinarily contrasting rear entrance, is the Cheshire Cottage, half-timbered and picturesque, with the date 1856 picked out on its façade.

Everywhere there are fine plants to admire, some of which (for example in the Pinetum) survive from the original plantings, and the National Trust has scrupulously replaced countless plants of the period. Few gardens so vividly evoke the passions and excitement of Victorian gardening in its heyday.

Location Biddulph, nr Stoke-on-Trent ST8 7SD, Staffordshire **OS** SJ8959 5m SE of Congleton by A527 **Tel** 01782 517999 **Fax** 01782 510624 **Email** biddulphgrange@ntrust.org.uk **English Heritage Register** Grade I **Owner** The National Trust **Open** end Apr to Oct, Wed to Sun (open Bank Hol Mon; closed Good Fri) 12–6 (opens 11 on Sat, Sun and Bank Hol Mon); Nov to mid Dec, Sat and Sun 12–4 (or dusk if earlier) **Area** 15 acres/6 hectares

BIRMINGHAM BOTANIC GARDENS

MODEL GARDENS, GLASSHOUSES, A FINE ROCKERY, A BANDSTAND AND COLLECTIONS OF PLANTS REFLECT THE BUSTLING HORTICULTURAL ACTIVITY OF THIS EARLY 19TH-CENTURY PUBLIC PARK AND BOTANIC GARDEN

The first part of the 19th century was the great period for such societies as the Birmingham Botanical and Horticultural Society which was founded in 1829 and in 1931 leased land on the edge of the city to lay out its gardens. John Claudius Loudon was called in and on the south-facing slopes he designed a layout of curving paths, which took their cue from the design for an extraordinary circular glasshouse which had at its centre a giant curving spiral ramp. However, this visionary masterpiece of *avant-garde* architecture was thought too expensive and never built, and in the course of time more conventional glasshouses were put up. But much of Loudon's layout was adopted and its pattern of paths is still clearly visible – although his long straight walk up to the glasshouse, deprived of its mesmerising eyecatcher, was never made.

From the start the gardens embarked on an ambitious programme of plant acquisition,

The bandstand at Birmingham Botanic Gardens

with 9,000 species of plants listed in the catalogue by 1834. At first owned by a private society, the gardens were initially open only to subscribers; from 1844 they were opened to the paying public and assumed the character of a public park – with a splendid bandstand added in 1873.

GARDENS PLANNED TO PLEASE

For visitors today Birmingham Botanic Gardens are among the most attractive gardens of their kind in the country. The glasshouses contain good collections of tropical plants, tender palms, succulents and citrus plants, and alongside is the National Bonsai Collection housed in Japonaiserie cages. Parts of the gardens have been designed to be of specific interest to gardeners and to those with an interest in particular groups of plants.

A rock garden, built in 1895 by James Backhouse & Son of York, sparkles with alpine plants against a background of magnolias, Japanese maples, rhododendrons and such unusual conifers as the beautiful Chinese lace-bark pine (*Pinus bungeana*). Another garden is devoted to the discoveries of one of the greatest of plant-hunters, E.H. Wilson, who worked here at the age of sixteen. It contains such plants as *Berberis wilsoniae*, *Hamamelis mollis* and *Lilium regale*. A splendid domed aviary, opened in 1996, overlooks a formal rose garden ornamented with statues, topiary and urns. A series of "domestic gardens" shows models of different styles – a children's garden; a low-labour garden; a plantsman's garden and so on. Other gardens are devoted to such groups of plants as conifers, herbs, rhododendrons and roses.

There is an attractive atmosphere here of bustling horticultural activity, and a strong flavour of Victorian exuberance may still be seen in the swashbuckling tender bedding schemes close to the bandstand.

Location Westbourne Road, Edgbaston B15 3TR, Birmingham **OS** SP0485 2m SW of the city centre **Tel** 0121 454 1860 **Fax** 0121 454 7835 **Email** admin@bham-bot-dns.demon.co.uk **English Heritage Register** Grade II* **Owner** Birmingham Botanical and Horticultural Society Ltd **Open** daily 9–dusk (opens 10 on Sun; closed 25 Dec) **Area** 15 acres/6 hectares

BOUGHTON HOUSE PARK

A GREAT 17TH- AND 18TH-CENTURY
FORMAL GARDEN IN A STATE OF
BEAUTIFUL DISHEVELMENT

The estate at Boughton goes back at least to the 15th century when a park of 100 acres/40 hectares was enclosed. In 1528 it was bought by a prosperous lawyer, Edward Montagu, whose descendants have lived here ever since. The present house, incorporating the remains of a medieval house, was started in the 1680s and was built for Ralph Montagu (who became an earl in 1689 and a duke in 1705) who had been Ambassador to Louis XIV from 1669 to 1672 and from 1676 to 1678. In this posting he acquired a taste for French architecture and Boughton House has a decidedly Gallic air – Pevsner describes its north façade as "perhaps the most French-looking C17 building in England".

A formal garden was made to suit the house to the designs of Leonard van Meulen. John Morton's *The Natural History of Northamptonshire* (1712) gives a vivid picture of it: "Below the Western front of the house…three more remarkable Parterres: the Parterre of Statues, the Parterre of Basins, and the Water Parterre…On the North side of the Parterre Garden is a small wilderness which is called the "Wilderness of Apartments", an exceedingly delightful place and nobly adorned with basins, jets d'eaux, statues, with platanus, lime trees, beech, bays, etc., all in exquisite form." These gardens were completed by 1706. Only traces survive but enough to allow the garden archaeologist Dr Christopher Taylor to describe the remains as "the best of their date on England".

What does, spectacularly, survive is the noble pattern of avenues laid out by the 2nd Duke – known as Duke John the Planter – in the 1720s and 30s. From 1726 to 1731 Charles Bridgeman was employed at Boughton but although elaborate bird's eye views of immensely elaborate formal gardens survive it seems probable that his role was advisory. It is said that the 2nd Duke had ambitions to plant an avenue all the way to London – 70 miles/116km as the crow flies. The remains of what he did plant at Boughton, alignments of common lime (*Tilia × europaea*) to the west and south-west of the house, superbly animate the flat landscape. Here too are the great pools made in the 17th century by diverting the course of the river Ise. By the time he died, the 2nd Duke had planted 21m/36km of avenues spread over eight parishes. After his death the estate passed to the Dukes of Buccleuch who had other estates to occupy their attentions. Boughton thus escaped the landscaping fashion in the second part of the 18th century so that the gently disheveled remains of the great formal garden of the earlier period survived to enchant us today.

The west front of Boughton House

Location nr Kettering NN14 1BJ, Northamptonshire **OS** SP9081 3m NE of Kettering on A43 **Tel** 01536 515731 **Fax** 01536 417255 **Email** llt@boughtonhouse.org.uk **English Heritage Register** Grade I **Owner** The Duke and Duchess of Buccleuch and Queensberry **Open** May to Aug, daily except Fri 1–5 (also open Fri in Aug) **Area** 350 acres/141 hectares

CALKE ABBEY

A COMPLETE, WORKING KITCHEN GARDEN – BOTHIES, GLASSHOUSES AND FLOWER GARDEN – FOR A GREAT 18TH-CENTURY HOUSE SET IN FINE PARKLAND

The most unforgettable thing about Calke is the setting of the house in its park. It was built in the first years of the 18th century for Sir John Harpur; Pevsner's description, "very ambitious in scale if somewhat coarse in detail", seems fair. Visitors approach the house by following a long avenue of limes, with delicious views of rolling parkland on either side. The grey stone house is folded in a hollow, with clusters of outhouses about it. Sir John Harpur had commissioned a great formal garden from London and Wise, for which Robert Bakewell made ornamental ironwork in 1720. No traces of this survive, for later in the 18th century it was replaced by a landscape park probably designed by William Emes.

The former kitchen gardens at a little distance from the house form the main garden interest of Calke today. The walk from the house is delightful – up a grassy slope with great views of the park opening out on each side. From here a path winds through a shrubbery to the kitchen garden which was built in 1772–74 and covers an area of 7 acres/2.8 hectares. An enclosure with a curved wall greets you in summer with a fortissimo whiff of cherry pie (*Heliotropium arborescens*) and shaped beds in a lawn of velvety perfection brim with yellow,

The kitchen garden door at Calke

scarlet and rich purple bedding plants. In a corner is that rare piece of garden furnishing, an auricula theatre: a proscenium-like arch frames shelving which in spring is arranged with a collection of *Primula auricula* cultivars like highly wrought jewels in a Bond St window; in summer the staging is also put to good use, displaying rows of potted pelargoniums of a suitably delicate kind.

A further enclosure is dominated by a handsome domed orangery flanked by peach houses built into the south-facing wall (all the paraphernalia of their heating arrangements are visible in adjacent stove houses). Also visible, a rare pleasure, is the gardener's office with its high clerical desk and miniature chest of drawers to hold packets of seeds. The walls are dotted with fading prize tickets (1st or 2nd prizes only) from the Ticknall village flower show. The walls are distempered in glowing chalky blue and piles of terracotta pots lie among old glass

Bedding schemes at Calke Abbey

lights with metal frames. The effect may well be studiously contrived but the impression that nothing much has happened in the gardener's bothy for the last forty years or so is wholly convincing.

The chief part of the garden is a proper working kitchen garden – nothing modish, nothing faintly like a formal *potager*. Generous beds, edged in box, are filled with fruit and vegetables (many of which are old varieties) and, at the far end where the land slopes down, is a meadow-like orchard. The whole garden is protected to the north by old trees. The brick walls are handsome, capped either with stone or, more beautifully, with finely fashioned curved coping bricks. All great country houses had kitchen gardens along these lines but few survive that are so unostentatiously alluring as this.

Location Ticknall DE7 1LE, Derbyshire **OS** SK3722 9m S of Derby by A514 **Tel** 01332 863822 **Fax** 01332 865272 **Email** calkeabbey@ntrust.org.uk **English Heritage Register** Grade II* **Owner** The National Trust **Open** (garden) Apr to Oct, Sat to Wed 11–5.30; (park) most days until 9 or dusk if earlier **Area** 10 acres/4 hectares

CANONS ASHBY HOUSE

FORMAL GARDENS OF GENTLEMANLY DECORATIVENESS MADE FOR THE 18TH-CENTURY DRYDENS

The Dryden family lived at Canons Ashby from the 16th century until the estate was given to the National Trust in 1981. The wonderful house, romantic but mysterious, was built in the mid 16th century, of brick with stone dressings, to which Edward Dryden, a cousin of the poet John Dryden, added in the early 18th century a fine new south façade of stone.

The garden was refashioned at this time in a style of gentlemanly formality which it preserves today. South of the house the sloping land has been shaped into a series of grassy terraces, with a central path on the axis of the house descending to a splendid pair of gates with carved lions on the piers. When Harry Inigo Triggs drew a plan of the garden in 1901 for his book *Formal Gardens in England and Scotland* the lower terraces were planted with fruit gardens on either side of the path and four cedars of Lebanon towered above the steps leading from the first to the second terrace. Beyond the lion gates there had been an avenue of elms which extended the formality beyond the garden walls into the countryside. The National Trust has replanted all of this, using limes for the avenue. The top terrace is marked by four youthful cedars of Lebanon and the descending terraces are ornamented with elaborate shapes of yew topiary, mounds of clipped Portugal laurel and apple trees in long grass; at the foot, the path passes through a wildflower meadow and is edged with billowing bushes of different varieties of *Rosa × alba*.

A simpler formal walled garden, the Green Court, lies below the west façade of the house. Here is a plain lawn with rows of topiary shapes of yew, like partly licked ice lollipops, with a lead figure of a piping shepherd and his dog. Old varieties of pear trees are espaliered against the walls, and through a gate supported on stone piers capped with obelisks on scrolls of stone are views of open fields to the west. The gate is flanked by clumps of phillyrea and in each

The Green Court at Canons Ashby

corner of the court are clipped bushes of bay. This is the best part of the garden at Canons Ashby, a perfect example of atmosphere achieved by small means. Formality rules the garden but it does not turn its back to the rural landscape beyond; the garden at Canons Ashby is a seamless extension of the house and a harmonious link to its larger setting, to which the eye is artfully drawn. If the 18th-century Drydens came back to the house tomorrow they would feel entirely at home.

Location Canons Ashby, Daventry NN11 3SD, Northamptonshire **OS** SP5750 11m NE of Daventry by A361, A422 and B4525 **Tel** 01327 860044 **Fax** 01327 860168 **Email** canonsashby@ntrust.org.uk **English Heritage Register** Grade II* **Owner** The National Trust **Open** Apr to Oct, Sat to Wed 12–5.30 **Area** 3 acres/1.2 hectares

CASTLE ASHBY GARDENS

FROM THE 19TH-CENTURY ITALIAN GARDEN WITH ITS FINE ORANGERY AND GOOD TREES, PATHS LEAD TO CAPABILITY BROWN'S LANDSCAPE PARK

The great house at Castle Ashby was started in the 1570s for Henry Compton and by the Civil War had acquired essentially the appearance it has today. A park already existed at Castle Ashby by 1565, before the house was built. When John Evelyn came in

1688 he thought there was "nothing remarkable" in the garden except for an iron gate into the park "which indeede was very good work, wrought in flowers painted blue and gilded". To celebrate a visit made by William III in 1695, avenues were planted, radiating from the house to the four points of the compass. In 1761 Capability Brown signed an agreement to landscape the grounds and by 1763 £1,816 (£131,133 today) had already been spent. Avenues were removed, a ha-ha built and small pools were formed into two lakes, with much planting about their banks. A temple on the edge of Menagerie Pond, designed by Brown, presents a classical façade towards the water; in the 18th century it concealed a menagerie behind.

VICTORIAN FORMAL GARDENS

Changes in the 19th century give the pleasure grounds at Castle Ashby their distinctive atmosphere today. East of the house formal gardens were designed in 1862 by Joseph Newton, W.B. Thomas and Sir Matthew Digby Wyatt for the 3rd Marquess of Northampton. These, subsequently grassed over, have been beautifully reinstated in recent times, with tiered fountains rising from scalloped pools, ribbon carpet bedding and elaborate arabesques of gravel cut into turf. The whole is surrounded by terracotta balustrading and urns. The balustrading is decorated with biblical quotations worked in large letters, each carrying a message with an allusion to plants, such as: "The grass withereth and the flowers fadeth but the word of God endureth forever." This part of the garden is private but from the path that skirts it you can catch alluring glimpses and also enjoy beautiful views eastwards over Brown's park, still with much of its original planting.

The chief visitable parts of the garden are south-east of the house. The Italian Garden consists of a sequence of enclosed spaces laid out in the 1860s on the site of the former kitchen garden. At the head of the first enclosure is a magnificent orangery designed by Sir Matthew Digby Wyatt and built 1871–72 with a lily pool designed by William Burges. The interior is lavishly planted with abutilons, clivias, figs (including some of the more tender species of the *Ficus* genus), leanders and palms. The orangery overlooks lawns with a central walk of rounded cones of clipped yew and terracotta urns on plinths, and a cross walk lined with Irish yews and lollipops of clipped sweet bay in Versailles boxes. At the back of the lawns good trees make a handsome backdrop – a very large copper beech and a weeping beech, a *Gingko biloba*, a holm oak and enormous billowing mounds of unclipped golden yews. A noble stone archway leads the way to a further garden to the south, where there are more glasshouses and mixed borders backed by yew hedges. From here a path leads through a wall into woodland, beyond which is a ha–ha and the park. A stream which feeds Warren Pond, one of the lakes made by Capability Brown, is

crossed by a balustraded bridge. The banks are planted with good trees – Himalayan birches, oriental planes, *Prunus serrula* and rowans. In the hinterland to the north is a grove of conifers with some huge Monterey pines (*Pinus radiata*) and Wellingtonias.

Visitors are excluded from much of the landscape at Castle Ashby but what they can see is full of interest, with fine ornamental planting and excellent design. The house and garden may be rented for private functions, so you could have the whole place to yourself.

Location Castle Ashby NN7 1LQ, Northamptonshire **OS** SP8659 5m E of Northampton by A428 **Tel** and **Fax** 01604 696187 **English Heritage Register** Grade I **Owner** The Marquess of Northampton **Open** all year, daily 10–dusk **Area** 25 acres/10 hectares

The Italian Garden at Castle Ashby

CASTLE BROMWICH HALL GARDENS

THE RESTORATION OF AN 18TH-CENTURY WALLED GARDEN BY A DEDICATED LOCAL TRUST – SAVED FROM URBAN SPRAWL IN THE NICK OF TIME

The house at Castle Bromwich was built in 1599 for Sir Edward Devereux. In 1657 the estate was bought by Sir John Bridgeman who made changes to the house and garden with the advice of his cousin, Captain William Winde. Winde was a friend of George London whom he introduced to his cousin as "ye beste gardinar in Endgland". Contemporary drawings for elaborate parterres, attributed to Winde and London, survive. Another friend of Winde's was Charles Hatton, the brother of Sir Christopher Hatton of Kirby Hall (*see page 266*), whom he called "a greatt vertueso in gardening". It was Charles Hatton's connections in the world of plantsmen that made Kirby one of the great gardens of its day, and this well-informed knot of garden virtuosi gave Sir John Bridgeman all the advice he needed to make a garden of distinction at Castle Bromwich. An engraving by Henry Beighton shows parts of the garden close to the house as they appeared in 1726: a series of walled or hedged compartments with parterres of various kinds and other formal ingredients, firmly related to the architecture of the house. This pattern survived in essence until the death of Lady Ida Bridgeman in 1936, after which the gardens decayed, with much vandalisation in the 1970s. In 1985 a trust was formed, which has gradually restored the garden, and although the house and parts of the garden immediately surrounding it are today in separate ownership, it is still possible to see how closely house and garden were originally intertwined.

"GILDED EVER GREENS"
The garden is enclosed by beautiful old brick walls with noble piers on the north-west and south-west corners. A walk of variegated hollies, the "gilded ever greens" recommended by Charles Hatton, marches across the garden from north to south, with at one end a very pretty brick pedimented orangery (or "Green

for the Lucy family in the mid 16th century but was rebuilt in the mid 19th century by John Gibson from around 1847 to 1867. Only parts of the Tudor design survive – in particular a charming gatehouse with tall turrets and a fretwork parapet – yet, despite the disastrous Victorianising of the house, its silhouette still preserves an Elizabethan character.

CHANGING LANDSCAPE

A late 17th-century painting at the house shows a delightful scene. The house, pinned down in its landscape by avenues, is embraced by formal gardens with a splendid double canal pointing to the north. Sketchy traces of the alignments of these avenues survive; some of the ancient limes may still be seen along the approach to the gatehouse, and the National Trust has recently been replanting some of the avenues. In 1760 Capability Brown was called in to widen the Avon and to remodel the river banks to impart a "natural and easy level", and he created a cascade where the Hele flows in. He also, in the words of Dorothy Stroud, filled in "the old ponds to the north of the house" – these would have been the remains of the formal canals. It is said that Brown was specifically forbidden to alter the existing avenues. (In fact, with no coercion, he often left such formal features, working them skilfully into his new landscapes.) He also planted trees, among them Scots pines and cedars of Lebanon near the house. In the 19th century new formal gardens were made – a pair of elaborate parterres in the entrance forecourt and another on the terrace overlooking the Avon. These survived until after World War II but were suppressed in the 1950s shortly after the National Trust acquired the estate in 1946.

In recent years the National Trust has revitalised the gardens. Mixed borders enliven the entrance forecourt; there is a collection of plants mentioned by Shakespeare, who is supposed to have poached on Lucy land as a boy; and trees have been replanted. Close to the Shakespeare border is a decorative Victorian tea pavilion built of brick and rustic wood, shrouded in ivy, and thatched, its door panelled in bark and its leaded windows with stained glass insets. The panelled interior is

---

House") and at the other a similar building which was the music room. The holly (*Ilex aquifolium* 'Argentea Marginata') was propagated from a surviving early 18th-century plant. A wilderness of shrubberies and winding walks runs along the holly walk and this is interrupted by a cross axis which allows views westwards from the house, aligned with an avenue beyond the garden walls.

A holly maze (based on George London's original design) and kitchen garden taken from a Batty Langley pattern book have also been reinstated. Hidden behind a yew hedge is an orchard with old varieties of fruit trees. My Lady's Border displays the kind of ornamental plants available to gardeners in the first half of the 18th century; they are arranged like a modern border, with trellis-work obelisks supporting clematises. Lady Bridgeman's Kitchen Garden enclosed in hornbeam hedges displays the kinds of "rare and choice plants" that were collected in the 18th century – auriculas, pinks, primulas and tulips – arranged in narrow strips of beds with lollipops of variegated holly and clipped cones of *Phillyrea latifolia*.

The survival and restoration of the garden at Castle Bromwich Hall is miraculous. The site, with urban development all about and the roar of the M6 always audible, is a beleaguered one. The project is, to put in mildly, not lavishly funded and its success comes from very hard and enterprising work by all sorts of people associated with the Castle Bromwich Hall

---

The orangery at Castle Bromwich

Trust. The ultimate goal must be to unite house, garden and the surrounding surviving parkland. As it is, the old atmosphere of formality and productiveness has crept back into the garden and it has assumed a new and special role – that of an orderly rural retreat all but engulfed by the city.

Location Chester Road, Castle Bromwich B36 9BT, Birmingham **OS** SP1489 6m E of city centre by A47; Jnct 5 of M6 (exit northbound only; entrance southbound only) **Tel** and **Fax** 0121 749 4100 **Email** enq@cbhgt.swinternet.co.uk **Website** www.cbhgt.swinternet.co.uk **English Heritage Register** Grade II* **Owner** Castle Bromwich Hall Trust **Open** Apr to Oct, Tue to Thur 1.30–4.30; Sat, Sun and Bank Hol Mon 2–6 **Area** 10 acres/4 hectares

CHARLECOTE PARK

THE ELIZABETHAN ESTATE OF THE LUCY FAMILY WITH BEAUTIFUL PARKLAND AND FLOWERY INTERLUDES

The most beautiful thing about Charlecote is the setting of the house in its parkland. The gardens by the house, pretty as they may be, scarcely stick in the mind. The site is flat but it has the priceless advantage of the river Avon (and its tributary the Hele, or Wellesbourne brook) curving magnificently across the land close by. The house was built

harming, with spindly chairs and a table laid
or afternoon tea.

A very recent development, in 2000, is the
econstruction of the Victorian parterres
verlooking the Avon. These were designed in
853, also by John Gibson. There had been
arterres here in the late 17th century – they
an be seen in the painting of that date in
he house. The Victorian scheme, with dwarf
ox-edged patterns of beds and jolly
edding schemes, certainly suits the Victorian
rchitectural setting with its ponderous
alustrade, but it does not make a happy
relude to the idyllic views across the river of
arkland and avenues. A much more restrained,
nd magical, way of doing something similar
ay be seen north of the house. If you follow
he wooded walk past the orangery you will
ome, at the edge of the pleasure grounds, to a
arved viewing platform, unadorned except
or turf and handsome old mulberries, with
iews over the park to the church of St
Nicholas in the distance.

Seen from afar, the house and its
etting are still very beautiful and
he best way of enjoying this and

arkland at Charlecote

the ravishing views is to follow the mile-long
circuit walk girdling the estate and along the
banks of the river.

Location Wellesbourne, Warwick CV35 9ER,
Warwickshire **OS** SP2656 5m E of Stratford-upon-Avon
by B4086 **Tel** 01789 470277 **Fax** 01789 470544
Email charlecotepark@ntrust.org.uk **Website**
www.ntrustsevern.org.uk **English Heritage Register**
Grade II* **Owner** The National Trust **Open** late Apr to
early Nov, Fri to Tue 11–6 **Area** 30 acres/12 hectares

CHATSWORTH

ON A VAST SCALE, THIS SPECTACULAR GARDEN
ILLUSTRATES GARDEN STYLES FROM THE
EARLY 18TH CENTURY TO THE 21ST CENTURY

The present Duchess of Devonshire wrote,
"Our garden is an inhibiting place to go
out in with a trowel. It covers 105 acres…" To
the visitor, with no need to do any trowel-
work, the garden is positively alluring. There
are two ways of arranging the visit, each with
much to recommend it. The first is simply to
wander about, from splendour to splendour,
jaw dropping from time to time in
amazement or delight. The
second is to learn a little about
the history of the place, for the
garden is a splendid repository
of garden styles, layer upon layer, going back
to the 17th century.

The Cavendish family has lived at
Chatsworth since the 16th century but it was
in the late 17th century that William
Cavendish, who became the 1st Duke of
Devonshire in 1694, transformed it into a
place of princely splendour. His architect,
from 1687 to 1696, was the splendid if
shadowy William Talman, who was sacked and
succeeded by Thomas Archer who designed
the north front in about 1704. Together, they
converted Chatsworth into a Baroque palace
of suave magnificence. The gardens were
designed at about the same time by George
London and Henry Wise, with splendid
waterworks designed by the Frenchman
Grillet who had worked with Talman on
another Derbyshire house, Bretby Hall (*see
page 449*). Kip's engraving of the house and
garden, published in 1707, shows the house
surrounded by elaborate formal gardens of the
greatest splendour, with avenues quartering
the land. In the 1760s the park was landscaped
by Capability Brown, and a handsome bridge
taking the drive over the river Derwent was
designed by James Paine in about 1760.

In the 19th century the gardens were in
the charge of one of the great horticultural
figures of the time, Sir Joseph Paxton, who
was appointed head gardener in 1826 at the

age of twenty-three. Under Paxton, glasshouses were built – among them the spectacular Great Conservatory (1836–41), the largest glasshouse in England, "a mountain of glass" as it was described at the time. Charles Darwin visited it in 1843: "I was, like a child, transported with delight…more wonderfully like tropical nature, than I could have conceived possible – Art beats nature altogether there." The only glasshouses to survive from Paxton's time are the Vinery (near the potting shed) and, most spectacularly, the Conservative Wall running along the north boundary of the garden and facing southwards over it. It still contains two plants of *Camellia reticulata* 'Captain Dawes' that were here in Paxton's time. Paxton also added a rock garden, an arboretum and a pinetum – the essential ingredients of every respectable grand Victorian garden. Much more surprising, he also

Angela Conner's Revelation

created a garden of non-flowering plants, of lichens, liverworts and mosses. Probably the most interesting changes to the garden since Paxton's time have occurred under the present, the 11th, Duke and his wife.

Although much historic detail has been lost, much of the essential old pattern of the garden survives, forming a strong framework which holds together later additions. Grillet's spectacular formal cascade, with Thomas Archer's cascade house of 1703 at its head, tumbles down the slope to the east of the house. A remarkably early glasshouse, the 1st Duke's conservatory of 1698, overlooks a rose garden enlivened with rows of Irish yews. The Ring Pond, visible in Kip's engraving, is now the starting point of an innovation of the present Duke and Duchess. They enclosed it with tall hedges of beech and from it a long walk between crinkle-crankle beech hedges runs

Spring at Chatsworth

south, ending in an eyecatcher – a bust of the 6th Duke rising above the top of the hedge on a tall column. On the slopes nearby, hidden away behind trees, they also laid out a superb new yew maze with a vertiginous flight of steps leading to Paxton's pinetum. They also simplified the south lawn, where London and Wise had laid out a dazzling embroidered parterre and the 6th Duke had made a fussy Victorian formal rose garden. It now forms an austerely simple preamble to the splendours of the house's south front: a velvety sunken lawn flanked by rows of pleached limes leading up to the sea-horse fountain – all that remains of the London and Wise scheme. The present Duchess has made an entirely new kitchen garden of almost 3 acres/1.2 hectares, with flowery borders and 17th-century sculptures among the rows of vegetables and fruit. She also made a little cottage garden with its own parterre of flowers, miniature kitchen garden, four-poster bed of clipped ivy and forsythia chaise-longue. A very recent innovation, close to the kitchen garden, is Angela Conner's Revelation, an astonishing water sculpture in the shape of a giant metal flower whose petals unfold with dramatic jets of water.

Chatsworth was one of the first great private gardens to welcome the public – after the Midland Railway opened from Derby in 1849, around 80,000 visitors came each year – and visitors today are a vital part of the economics of the estate. Both house and garden are as beautifully maintained as any in the country.

The garden is rich in all kinds of pleasures but perhaps the most beautiful view is that from high up on the slopes rising eastwards from the house. From Thomas Archer's cascade house you may look down on the garden and past the great house, with James Paine's bridge spanning the river, to where the land rises on the other side – a lovely rural landscape with cattle or sheep grazing in the pastures.

Location Bakewell DE4 1PP, Derbyshire **OS** SK2670
4m E of Bakewell by A6 or A619 and minor roads
Tel 01246 582204/565300 **Fax** 01246 583536
English Heritage Register Grade I **Owner** Trustees of
the Chatsworth Settlement **Open** (garden) mid Mar to
Oct, daily 11–4.30; (park) daily throughout the year
Area 105 acres/42 hectares

CLUMBER PARK

AT THE HEART OF A GREAT WOODED PARK –
A SPLENDID GLASSHOUSE AND RESTORED
GARDEN SHEDS CONTAIN PLANTS AND
GARDEN PARAPHERNALIA FROM THE HEYDAY
OF VICTORIAN KITCHEN GARDENING

The Clumber Park estate was part of Sherwood Forest until 1707 when the Duke of Newcastle was granted a licence to impark. A great house was built between 1768 and 1778 to the designs of Stephen Wright and subsequently was much altered. Wright, who had been a protégé of William Kent, also designed buildings in the landscape – most notably the grand balustraded bridge across the narrow Clumber lake (formed by damming the river Poulter in the late 18th century) and a primitive Doric Temple on the east bank of the lake, visible from the house. It is not known who laid out the park in the 18th century; possibly it was Wright himself. When Horace Walpole saw it in 1772 he was unimpressed: "a black heath, full of rabbits

having a narrow river running through it with a small boggy close or two". There was a great programme of tree planting in the late 18th and early 19th centuries. In 1830 a double avenue of limes was planted, 3 miles long, leading from Apleyhead Lodge in the north-east to Carburton Lodge in the south-west. Parts of it survive and many gaps have been filled in.

Clumber House was demolished in 1938. It stood on the west bank of the lake, with elaborate terraced gardens, designed by W.S. Gilpin, running down to the water. Part of a stable block and other outhouses survive and, most spectacularly, a remarkable chapel designed by G.F. Bodley and built between 1886 and 1889 for the 7th Duke of Newcastle. It has an immense central spire and is of a size and style that you would think appropriate for the parish church of some dynamic 19th-century industrial city. It makes a notable ornament in the landscape, rising in the well-treed pleasure grounds which Gilpin laid out east of the house. Some beautiful old trees are still to be seen – a fine Lucombe oak, sweet chestnuts, cedars of Lebanon and old hollies and yews.

To the north of the chapel, at the end of a walk of cedars of Lebanon, the 19th-century brick-walled kitchen gardens survive. In the past these have been used as a camping and

caravanning site and parts still are; but a magnificent glasshouse, the Long Range, 450ft/137m long, has recently been restored. It runs the whole width of the south-facing wall of the garden, breaking out at its centre into a projecting canopied conservatory filled with abutilons, bananas, begonias, palms and other tender exotics. In the main spaces of the glasshouse, of which there are twelve, figs, grapevines, nectarines and peaches are trained on the wall or against the sloping glass, and exotic vegetables like aubergines and chillies are grown in the ground. The rooms behind the glasshouse, formerly potting sheds and a potato store, house a collection of old garden tools, watering cans, plant labels, cucumber jars and all the irresistible paraphernalia of gardening in its great days. A double herbaceous border runs down the centre of the garden, with fruit and vegetables, including many pre-1910 cultivars, growing on either side.

Clumber Park, which is crossed by a public highway, is one of the most visited of National Trust properties. It is used in many different ways – you may hire a bike, walk in the woods, play a game of cricket (the pitch is overlooked by a pretty rustic pavilion), admire birds (including great crested grebes and 129

The kitchen garden at Clumber

other species about the lake), study trees or merely potter. Apart from the intermittent beauties of the designed landscape, Clumber Park has become a nature reserve – a huge area which was spared the intense industrialisation that has afflicted this part of England.

Location The Estate Office, Clumber Park, Worksop S80 3AZ, Nottinghamshire **OS** SK6175 4½m SE of Worksop by A57 and A614 **Tel** 01909 544917 **Fax** 01909 500721 **English Heritage Register** Grade I **Owner** The National Trust **Open** daily dawn–dusk (walled garden Apr to Oct, Wed to Sun and Bank Hol Mon 10.30–5.30) **Area** 4,000 acres/1,619 hectares

COTON MANOR GARDENS

FLOWERY TERRACES, A ROSE GARDEN, A WOODLAND GARDEN, A WILDFLOWER MEADOW AND A WONDERFUL BLUEBELL WOOD IN AN EXCEPTIONAL SETTING

Large private gardens run by owners who are mad on plants and have high standards of maintenance are often the most attractive of places; there is no need to satisfy the demands of a committee. The garden at Coton has evolved gradually, spreading out south and south-west of the 17th-century stone house. Ian Pasley-Tyler's grandparents established much of the garden's bones and his parents continued the development. Since 1990, when Ian and Susie Pasley-Tyler inherited the estate, the quality of the garden has leapt ahead. When they took over, one of the most striking features was a large collection of ornamental birds. These (and especially their various sleeping quarters) have been largely disposed of, though some remain. On my last visit, in the autumn of 2002, I saw a neat circle of elegant ducks relishing the shade of an amelanchier and, most memorably, a group of lurid flamingoes posing beside the gleaming silver trunks of Himalayan birches. But the pleasures of the garden today are essentially horticultural.

There is no strong overall plan to the garden; the foot, or eye, is led gently from enclosure to enclosure. Terraces by the house are rich in ornamental plants and walls

festooned with climbing plants – clematis, *Fremontodendron californicum*, the unusual 'Seven Sisters' climbing rose (correctly known as *Rosa multiflora* 'Grevillei') by the door, scented *Trachelospermum jasminoides* and wisteria. Hedges of yew and holly protect a circular rose garden divided into four by brick paths. Roses, some of them David Austin's English Roses, form the main planting in each bed but along the paths are geraniums, peonies, pinks and violas. On the far side of the holly hedge double herbaceous borders are raised above the edge of a large pool with black swans.

PLANTS IN A WOODLAND GLADE

From the sunny and flower-filled area of terrace and rose garden a passage leads through the yew hedge to a woodland glade where cyclamen, epimediums, erythroniums, ferns, hellebores and trilliums flourish in the shade of a tulip tree (*Liriodendron tulipifera*) and a copper beech. A stream descends in gently splashing falls between ferns, hostas, ligularia, pulmonaria and rodgersias, and at the bottom an orchard of apples and pears is decorated with a central stepped rill – a touch of something Islamic. A gap in a hedge leads to an open area of grass with specimen trees – *Arbutus unedo*, *Cercidiphyllum japonicum*, a fern-leafed beech (*Fagus sylvatica* var. *heterophylla* 'Aspleniifolia') and

mulberries (both black and white). Beyond a meadow of wildflowers and many different grasses is a 5-acre/2-hectare beech wood which in April has an astonishing display of bluebells.

Retracing your steps and taking the most direct route back up the slope towards the house, you pass between borders (including a Mediterranean border taking advantage of a southern exposure and sharp drainage) and a formal herb garden with box-edged beds, espaliered apples and a tunnel of clematis and roses. At the top of the slope you come to a yard shaded by an American black walnut (*Juglans nigra*) and a plant sales area.

Taking advantage of the varied sites that the garden has to offer, a very wide range of plants is grown at Coton, but the garden's pleasures are displayed with no sense of rush, and contrasting themes – busy borders, open lawns, shady water, woodland glades, enclosing hedges and views over meadows – unfold gently as you make your way about it.

Location nr Guilsborough NN6 8RQ, Northamptonshire **OS** SP6771 10m NW of Northampton by A5199 and A428 **Tel** 01604 740219 **Fax** 01604 740838 **Email** pasleytyler@cotonmanor.fsnet.co.uk **Owner** Mr and Mr Ian Pasley-Tyler **Open** Apr to Sept, Tue to Sat and Bank Hol Mon (also Sun Apr to May) 12–5.30 **Area** 10 acres/4 hectares

Terraced gardens at Coton Manor

COTTESBROOKE HALL

AN ELEGANT 18TH-CENTURY HOUSE
COMPLEMENTED BY DECORATIVE 20TH-
CENTURY GARDENS BY ROBERT WEIR
SCHULTZ, DAME SYLVIA CROWE AND
SIR GEOFFREY JELLICOE

The estate at Cottesbrooke was acquired in
the 17th century by Sir John Langham, a
member of the East India Company and an
MP whose grandson, John, built the present
Cottesbrooke Hall from 1702. A beautiful
house of brick and Ketton stone, it was
probably designed by William, the brother of
Francis Smith of Warwick. It is one of the
candidates for the inspiration of Jane Austen's
Mansfield Park and the house certainly
possesses the kind of lively elegance which
she might have enjoyed.

The gardens, almost entirely of the 20th
century, are of an elegance to match the
house. Varied in atmosphere, but always finely
related to the house, they are very well
maintained. An open lawn with the occasional
beech or English oak is the simple setting for
the entrance front. A very old cedar of
Lebanon marks the start of a broad paved path
leading between deep mixed borders planted
with campanulas, catmint, geraniums,
kniphofias, lupins, phlomis, poppies and
repeated clumps of yuccas. Through an
opening in a wall is a noble white marble urn
and, to the south of it, a sombre yew walk
enlivened by statues. These stone figures by
Peter Scheemakers, representing Socrates,
Homer, Lycurgus and Epaminondas, were
originally in the Temple of Ancient Virtue at
Stowe (*see page 107*), and were sold in the
great sale of 1931. The pool garden is the
work of the Arts and Crafts architect Robert
Weir Schultz and contains an elegant little
pavilion designed by Dame Sylvia Crowe. The
entrance to the Monkey Pond Garden, also
designed by Schulz, is marked by piers
crowned with stone eagles garlanded with
white wisteria and flanked with shrubs of
Phlomis fruticosa. Roses decorate the walls and
rectangular pool animates the centre.

The original entrance to the house was on
the south-east side. If there was once a great
formal garden at Cottesbrooke, made when

Mixed borders at Cottesbrooke Hall

the house was built, this, with its forecourt
railings and grand gates, would be the place
for it. As it is, in 1937 Sir Geoffrey Jellicoe
laid out a pretty arrangement of tall cones of
clipped yew, fine statues of Diana, Eros,
Hermes and Venus and beds of creamy white
'Pascali' roses enclosed in L-shapes of yew.
With its lead statues and tubs of brilliant blue
agapanthus, all this has an appropriate
character of decorative formality in keeping
with the façade of the house.

Cottesbrooke Hall stands surrounded by
parkland. In the early 18th century there were
avenues radiating from the north and south
sides of the house. Later in the century the
landscape was made less formal but the identity
of the landscaper is not known. On the south-
east side of the house the view makes much of
the distant prospect of the spire of All Saints,
Brixworth, 3 miles away and exactly centred
on the old entrance to the house. The garden
is otherwise inward-looking and this open
vista provides an exhilarating contrast.

Location nr Northampton NN6 8PF, Northamptonshire
OS SP7173 9m NW of Northampton by A50 **Tel**
01604 505508 **Fax** 01604 505619 **English Heritage
Register** Grade II **Owner** Captain John Macdonald-
Buchanan **Open** Easter to Sept, Tue to Fri and Bank
Hol Mon (also Sat and Sun in Sept) 2–5 **Area** 12
acres/5 hectares

COUGHTON COURT

THE ANCIENT HOME OF THE
THROCKMORTONS EMBELLISHED WITH RICHLY
PLANTED FLOWER GARDENS OF THE LATE 20TH
CENTURY DESIGNED BY CHRISTINA BIRCH

Coughton is the ancient home of the
Throckmorton family who have lived
here since the 15th century. The house is a
romantic one, with a swagger gatehouse at the
front, with sprightly Gothic detailing, and fine
Tudor brick at the back. It is surprising that
such a house seems never to have had a
notable garden in the past. The present
garden, designed by Christina Birch, has been

made since 1991 and is well planned both to fit in harmoniously with its surroundings and to provide beauty and interest in itself.

A NEW FORMAL GARDEN

At the back of the house a courtyard has formal box-edged beds filled with tulips in the spring, followed by penstemons. On the same axis a lime walk leads away from the house towards a sunken garden planted with roses. To one side, beyond the village church, elaborate new formal gardens have been laid out in the walled enclosures of what must have been a kitchen garden. A maze of old shrub roses has a statue of Rosamond Clifford, a Throckmorton relation and mistress of Henry II who created the famous bower in her honour at Woodstock Manor (*see page 560*). Borders of colour harmonies are characteristic of the renewed interest in colour which became such a fashion in the last twenty years of the 20th century. Here are a red garden with cannas, dahlias, lobelias and sages; a white garden with geraniums, lilies, philadelphus and roses; and a "hot" border of crocosmias, daylilies, kniphofias and lobelias. A

The courtyard at Coughton Court

formal orchard contains old varieties of apples and pears – some of them such local varieties such as 'Lord Hindlip' and 'Madresfield Court' – with plums and cherries fan-trained against the wall. The eastern part of the garden is well watered, with a lake and a winding river, and a wooded walk follows the river, with wood anemones, wild garlic and bluebells, more exotic plantings of Asiatic primulas, and ferns, pulmonarias and hellebores.

The garden at Coughton Court makes the best of a flat site whose only intrinsic attractions are the beautiful house and the river. Although a very recent garden, it is already a period piece, reflecting the eclecticism of its time. With its burgeoning borders and crisply marshalled formality, it is the quintessence of the "good taste" garden.

Location Alcester B49 5JA, Warwickshire **OS** SP0860 2m N of Alcester on A435 **Tel** 01789 400777 **Infoline** 01789 762435 **Fax** 01789 765544 **Website** www.coughtoncourt.co.uk **Owner** Mrs C.Throckmorton/The National Trust **Open** mid to end Mar, Sat and Sun 11–5.30; Apr to Jun, Wed to Sun (open Bank Hol Mon and following Tue but closed Good Fri) 11–5.30; Jul and Aug, daily except Mon (open Bank Hol Mon) 11–5.30 **Area** 20 acres/8 hectares

ELVASTON CASTLE COUNTRY PARK

A FEAST OF TOPIARY, PICTURESQUE ROCKWORK AND GOOD TREES REMAIN FROM THIS 19TH-CENTURY EXTRAVAGANZA INSPIRED BY THE THEME OF ROMANTIC LOVE

The estate at Elvaston goes back to the 15th century and it passed in the 16th century to the Stanhope family (created Earls of Harrington in 1742). The present house is of 17th-century origin but was lavishly Gothicised to the designs of James Wyatt in around 1817, after the architect's death. In 1831, the 4th Earl, "a renowned eccentric and dandy", married an actress, Maria Foote, and as a result felt obliged to cut himself off from polite society. Burying himself at Elvaston, he created an extraordinary garden which in part celebrated his intrepid love match.

In the 18th century Capability Brown had been consulted about laying out the grounds but had declined to take on the work "Because the place is so flat, and there is a want of capability in it". Lord Harrington's head gardener, however, William Barron, who had been appointed in 1830 and charged with making an entirely new garden, had a more inventive notion of the capabilities of the place. Barron also developed a new technique for moving large old trees – excavating a large root-ball and so disrupting the plant as little as possible – and at Elvaston was able to create an apparently mature garden in a very short space of time.

THE WORSHIP OF LOVE

As Mark Girouard explains in his *The Return to Camelot* (1981), the garden at Elvaston was conceived as a shrine to the worship of love, the scene of a knight's successful wooing of his lady love. The Alhambra Garden, a parterre of curved shapes of clipped hedging, topiary and statuary, had as its climax in the woods behind it a Moorish Temple which contained a painting of Lord Harrington kneeling before his wife. Mon Plaisir was based on a 17th-century design by Daniel Marot, with a winding *berceau*, or tunnel of greenery with windows cut in it, topiary arbours and a star-shaped bed with a central monkey puzzle.

The **parterre** at Elvaston

According to Barbara Jones in her *Follies & Grottoes* (1974), this part of the garden "had a unique folly, a sham ruin in topiary". Barron also planted great avenues and made a serpentine lake north of the house with much rockwork. Very few outsiders were permitted to see this extravaganza, but J.C. Loudon came here in 1839 and wrote, "the grounds of Elvaston Castle abound with objects of great singularity, rarity, and value."

In the 1930s the Stanhope family left Elvaston and went to live in Ireland. The estate was acquired by Derbyshire County Council and the grounds turned into a country park. When Elvaston was photographed for *Country Life* in 1905, Barron's topiary garden was still largely intact; only parts of it survive today but they are of striking character. To the east, Barron's avenue of mixed conifers and deciduous trees, among them mature cedars already 30ft/9m high when transported by him, makes a grand approach to the castle. Immediately south of the house the banks of a sunken parterre of box hedges and topiary of golden box have billowing mounds and columns of both common and golden yew. (Barron was a great populariser of golden yew – by 1849 there were over 1,000 plants of it at Elvaston.) This was the site of the former Alhambra Garden, and the Moorish Temple, slightly battered, survives. With a sweeping roof of Chinese character, it has monumental oval windows with a criss-cross pattern of stone and a balcony of delicate wrought iron like a spider's web. Nearby is a second garden of topiary with bumpy castellations, mounds of golden yew and dumpy columns of common yew. Steps rise at the end to a frenzy of topiary, with a plump pigeon sitting on a top of a column and in a hidden lawn hedged in yew a single topiary shape like a giant melting witch's hat.

The lake to the north of the house preserves extraordinary rockwork. At its head is a circular archway of tufa; on the far bank, among alders, ash, Scots pines, silver birch and old yews, are monumental ruins. An elaborate rockwork grotto has multiple niches and arches.

Apart from municipal gardens, few gardens of pure 19th-century taste survive – for long they were thought inferior to the suave Arcadian landscapes of the 18th century. The garden at Elvaston, incomplete as it is but with its feast of topiary, is thus a rare pleasure.

Location Elvaston, Derby DE72 3EP, Derbyshire **OS** SK4032 6m SE of Derby by A6 and B5010 **Tel** 01332 571342 **Fax** 01332 758751 **English Heritage Register** Grade II* **Owner** Derbyshire County Council **Open** daily 9–sunset **Area** 200 acres/81 hectares

FARNBOROUGH HALL

AT THE HEART OF THIS MINIATURE ARCADIAN LANDSCAPE A GRASS TERRACE IS ADORNED WITH A RANGE OF BEAUTIFUL 18TH-CENTURY GARDEN BUILDINGS

The ingenious ways in which the landscape may be embellished are always a source of wonder. Farnborough, a generally irresistible place, has one rare feature that makes it of exceptional garden interest: the terrace with its ornamental buildings.

The estate was bought in 1684 by Ambrose Holbech (whose descendants still live here), who rebuilt the elegant house of honey-coloured Hornton sandstone. His grandson, William, inherited in 1717 and shortly afterwards went gallivanting on the Grand Tour, where he bought paintings by Canaletto and Pannini which hung in the dining room but have since been sold and replaced by copies. William extended the house and in the 1750s built a handsome new façade on the north side. A little before that, certainly by 1742 when it was first described, he laid out a miniature landscape park in the new taste with the help of the mysterious but influential Sanderson Miller. The heart of this is a gently curving uphill terrace, about half-a-mile long, which, like similar terraces in Yorkshire at Duncombe Park and Rievaulx (*see pages 337 and 350*), took advantage of the lie of the land to focus attention on the beauties of the landscape. Here, however, the scene is much less dramatic than that of the Yorkshire gardens. Despite the horrifying proximity of the M40 it remains quietly pastoral, with Arcadian views of the Warmington valley and of Edge Hill, with cattle grazing in pastures and water meadows spreading out on the river banks.

Such is the view from an Ionic temple built into the terrace on the right-hand side as you walk. A little further on, on the left among trees, is an unusual oval and domed pavilion with an open loggia on the ground floor and a surprisingly lavish room, with sumptuous Rococo plasterwork, on the first floor. Hidden in the woods that line the terrace to the left is a beautifully fashioned octagonal game larder with elegantly contrived louvred ventilation. It has seats in a loggia framed with Tuscan columns on the side that looks towards the village, to take advantage of the view over a lake and the church of St Botolph to wooded hills beyond.

"HER SPACIOUS TERRACE"

The right-hand side of the terrace is hedged with laurel, and regular semicircular niches are cut into it, each containing a lime tree, while on the left-hand side dense woods press in, with ash, oak, sweet chestnuts and several superb beeches. In his poem *Edge-hill*, which praises the beauty of his native county, the 18th-century Warwickshire poet Richard Jago

described the terrace at Farnborough: "Her spacious terrace, and surrounding lawns/ Deck'd with no sparing cost of planted tufts,/ Or ornamental building."

The end of the terrace is marked by an obelisk of 1751, from which point the land falls sharply away. The noise of the motorway is scarcely muffled by the sound of wind in the trees. Perhaps for those who live in such Arcadian surroundings the sound and sight of 21st-century reality is salutary. But perhaps not.

The oval pavilion at Farnborough

A visit to the house forms an essential part of the pleasure of a visit to Farnborough. In its elegant rooms, with their Rococo plasterwork, remember William Holbech surrounded by his Italian paintings and Roman statuary. In the garden, too, he sought to bring back Italian memories. His classical temples and Elysian views are a Warwickshire version of what he loved in the Roman *campagna*. The terrace here is a distillation of the spirit that created the English 18th-century landscape park. With the greatest of ease Farnborough transports the visitor into a gentlemanly past.

Location nr Banbury OX17 1DU, Warwickshire
OS SP4349 6m N of Banbury off A423 **Tel** 01295 690002 **Email** farnboroughhall@ntrust.org.uk **English Heritage Register** Grade I **Owner** The National Trust **Open** Apr to Sept, Wed and Sat 2–6; terrace walk also open by prior appointment **Area** 16 acres/6 hectares

HADDON HALL

AN IRRESISTIBLY ROMANTIC AND ANCIENT HOUSE, AN EXQUISITE SETTING, AND TERRACED GARDENS OF DEVASTATING CHARM

Visitors to Haddon Hall have often found it difficult to explain exactly what it is that they love about the place. The house is incoherent and the garden a jumble of spaces tumbling down a slope. Yet it seems effortlessly to exert its spell on everyone who goes there. The usually austere Pevsner almost swoons with pleasure, referring to the "lovable house of knights and their ladies, the unreasonable dream-castle of those who think of the Middle Ages as a time of chivalry and valour and noble feelings". Celia Fiennes, who wanted above all to see the latest fashions in houses and gardens, could not resist praising Haddon Hall on her visit in 1697, despite its old-fashioned character. She found it "a good old house…good gardens but nothing very curious as the mode now is". Perhaps it is exactly this lack of modishness that people find so irresistible. Harry Inigo Triggs in 1901 found Haddon Hall "so surrounded with romance that it is difficult to consider it in any but a romantic spirit".

THE WINDING RIVER WYE

The house was built from the 12th century onwards, with scarcely anything added after the 17th century. It was built for the Vernons and passed to the Manners family (later Duke of Rutland) after the romantic elopement of Dorothy Vernon with Sir John Manners in 1563. The approach to Haddon Hall is marvellous, with the grey limestone house rising on wooded heights above the winding river Wye. Despite its castellations and defensive position it is not in the least aggressive, but has a cosily domestic air.

As you walk up the hill you pass a cottage whose garden you may not visit (it is the home of the head gardener) but the dry-stone garden walls fringed with climbing roses are low, to give a delicious glimpse of what it contains – a dazzling array of yew topiary: tall

imb waiters, a plump nesting chicken and
her shapes parade before the cottage walls.
bove you the castle seems to grow out of the
ound rather than to be superimposed on it.
The castle gardens are below the south and
stern ramparts, which face the river. If you
in summer you will find the walls
rouded in roses, while borders beneath the
one-mullioned windows are filled with
lphiniums – purple, pink, white and blue –
ith drifts of white *Viola cornuta* at their feet.
ter in the season, Japanese anemones and
lvias flourish in these borders, with yellow
paeolum (*T. peregrinum*) and nasturtiums
rambling up through the clematis and roses
the walls. In the Fountain Garden a square
ol is ornamented with tufts of lavender and
e lawn is punctuated with flowering
erries and crab-apples; bushes of rosemary
ark the ends of beds of roses which are
anted in sometimes rather garish blocks of a
ngle colour – yellow, pink or scarlet. A noble
th-century flight of stone steps, flanked
ith swathes of richly scented 'Albertine' rose,
ads to a terrace with clipped rounded cones

he Fountain Garden at Haddon Hall

of yew, mixed borders and borders of roses.
Above it, not accessible to visitors, is Dorothy
Vernon's walk, a kind of spacious gallery
overlooking the gardens – the supposed route
of Dorothy's elopement.

From the terraces you look down over the
gardens, across the river (spanned by a fine
old stone bridge) to pastures and woods. As
far as I know, no noted garden designer ever
had anything to do with Haddon Hall. The
garden is bereft of unusual plants – most of
those you see are of the sort any gardener
might have in his or her garden. Here are no
crafty colour schemes or calculated vistas, yet
how easy it is to surrender to its devastating
charm and how difficult it would be for a
garden designer to weave similar magic. It is
the ensemble of house, garden and exquisite
setting that is the secret.

Location nr Bakewell DE4 1LA, Derbyshire **OS** SK2366
2m SE of Bakewell by A6; Jnct 30 of M1 **Tel**
01629 812855 **Fax** 01629 814379 **English**
Heritage Register Grade I **Owner** Lord
Edward Manners **Open** Apr to Sept, daily
10.30–5.45; Oct, Mon to Thur 10.30–4.30
Area 6 acres/2.4 hectares

HARDWICK HALL

THE WALLED GARDENS OF BESS OF
HARDWICK'S TUDOR MANSION REVITALISED
WITH LATE 20TH-CENTURY PLANTINGS
OF RICH COLOUR SCHEMES AND
DECORATIVE PATTERNS

The house, rising splendidly on its bluff,
dominates the garden and the landscape
at Hardwick. It stands slightly higher than the
adjacent shell of Hardwick Old Hall where
Bess of Hardwick had been born in 1520. If
some 21st-century billionairess built a great
house and set her initials in giant letters in the
parapet, she might be thought to be a touch
vulgar. But this is what Bess of Hardwick did
in the 1590s after the death of her fourth
husband, the 6th Earl of Shrewsbury, left
her one of the richest women in England
and well able to afford a
last, unforgettable,
architectural

flourish. The house has an *avant-garde* quality, its austere stone façade rising through four storeys, each pierced with large unornamented windows and crowned triumphantly with the initials ES (Elizabeth Shrewsbury) worked in stone. After Bess of Hardwick's death in 1608 the estate passed to William Cavendish, the second son of her second marriage. The Cavendishes' chief house was Chatsworth (*see page 255*) so Hardwick became a secondary residence which, though well maintained, was never the subject of any later extravagant expenditure. The house is one of the most complete and original houses of its date in the country; just as nothing was lavished on architectural change, so the garden pottered along in its own quiet way.

There is no record of work by any notable garden designer at Hardwick, nor is there any early description of the garden. Nevertheless, one of the great beauties of the place is the surviving Elizabethan courts adjacent to the house. The West Court is the most decorative of these enclosures, with its lively gatehouse, two attractive pavilions flanking it and the parapet decorated with dashing finials. Nothing is known of the original appearance of the gardens in the West Court and the earliest detailed knowledge dates from the 19th century. Loudon's *Encyclopaedia of Gardening* (1822) has little to say about Hardwick except that "The park abounds in fine old oaks" but we know that in 1832 two cedars of Lebanon were planted in the West Court, of which one remains, and by the middle of the 19th century a parterre in the West Court was tricked out in bedding schemes with the initials ES – a scheme that offended Gertrude Jekyll who described it as "not pretty gardening, nor particularly dignified". The gardens were painted by George Elgood in 1897 and show boisterous borders along the walls in the West Court, with standard red roses among lavish herbaceous planting. In the South Court a new garden was made in the 1870s by Lady Louisa Egerton, daughter of the 7th Duke of Devonshire. Elgood's painting shows walks of boldly sculpted yew hedges with statues in niches, much as they are today.

The estate was given to the National Trust in 1959 and the gardens were revitalised in the last twenty years of the 20th century. In the 1980s the West Court borders were replanted under the supervision of Tony Lord in a thoroughly modern style that also shows a Jekyllian influence, with repeated plantings of arching *Cortaderia fulvida* and the handsome foliage plant *Aralia elata* 'Aureovariegata'. The colour scheme modulates from hot colours close to the house to cooler ones, with plenty of blue and yellow, further away. The hot colours include *Crocosmia* 'Lucifer', dahlias, dazzling red penstemons, *Rosa moyesii* and salvias. In the yellow and blue sections are agapanthus, buddleia, ceanothus, *Hosta ventricosa* 'Aureomarginata', *Kniphofia* 'Wrexham Buttercup' and St John's wort. Throughout the borders the vibrant colours are soothed down by occasional sombre notes of purple-leafed cotinus and *Rheum palmatum* 'Atrosanguineum'. The richness and variety of the colour schemes and the lively pattern of leaf shapes suits the Elizabethan architecture admirably.

THE SOUTH COURT

In the South Court the hedges of yew or hornbeam, the four-part division with grass paths, and fine 18th-century statues remain. In one quarter a boldly conceived herb garden was planted in the 1970s with rows of hops (common and gold-leafed) trained into wigwams and underplanted with waves of culinary herbs and beds of vegetables intermingled with ornamental planting. Other quarters contains specimen trees and magnolias, and two orchards: one with old varieties of fruit trees and the other with a walk of the ornamental *Malus hupehensis* and fruit trees.

The East Court is the plainest enclosure, with a scalloped central pool, yew topiary and a border of shrub roses. The eastern boundary has a low yew hedge beyond which is a ha-ha and pasture with, on its far side, an avenue of limes aligned on the house stretching away into the distance.

The garden at Hardwick Hall makes the best of the existing structures without being excessively, and possibly boringly, purist. The planting is sprightly and the whole effect is of a patterned decorativeness of the sort that Bess of Hardwick, with her love of ornamental embroidery, might well have enjoyed.

Location Doe Lea, Chesterfield S44 5QJ, Derbyshire **OS** SK4663 6½m NW of Mansfield by A617 and minor roads Jnct 29 of M1 **Tel** 01246 850430 **Fax** 01246 854200 **Email** hardwickhall@ntrust.org.uk **English Heritage Register** Grade I **Owner** The National Trust **Open** Apr to Oct, daily 12–5.30 **Area** 7 acres/2.8 hectares

The West Court at Hardwick Hall

are now poignantly marooned in pastures, leading nowhere, but the landscape preserves a most powerful character of a much greater significance than the merely archaeological.

Also worthy of note is a little garden designed by Rosemary Verey in 1980 – one of the very few examples of her work to be seen in a garden open to the public. In this hidden garden of Elizabethan character, tucked away behind high yew hedges, only those plants known to have been used in gardens of the late 16th century are grown. A series of formal beds are laid out about a stone sundial encircled by thyme. Each bed has mounds of santolina, clipped shapes of box and billowing clouds of rosemary with, at the centre, plantings of flowering annuals or biennials – cornflower, love-in-the-mist, viper's bugloss (*Echium vulgare*) and wallflowers. The garden is overlooked by an arbour of clipped yew where you may sit on a sunny summer's day with the scent of herbs wafting in.

Location Holdenby, nr Northampton NN8 8DJ, Northamptonshire **OS** SP6968 6½m NW of Northampton by A428 and minor roads; signed off A428 and A50 **Tel** 01604 770074 **Fax** 01604 770962 **English Heritage Register** Grade I **Owner** James Lowther **Open** Apr to Sept, daily except Sat 1–5 **Area** 10 acres/4 hectares

HOLDENBY HOUSE GARDENS

THE GHOSTLY REMAINS OF A GREAT 16TH-CENTURY GARDEN COMPLEMENTED BY A GARDEN OF ELIZABETHAN CHARACTER DESIGNED BY ROSEMARY VEREY

In its day, Holdenby was one of the great gardens of England. The estate belonged to Sir Christopher Hatton, Elizabeth I's courtier who became Lord Chancellor in 1587 and between 1570 and 1589 built a house of palatial splendour, laying out a garden to suit. A rare surviving plan, dated 1587, shows the garden nearing completion: a giant platform of earth jutting out from the centre of the house, ornamented with extravagant parterres and with terraced gardens on either side. William Camden saw it shortly after it was completed and wrote: "Above all is especially to be noted with what industry and toyle of

The hidden garden at Holdenby

man the garden hath been raised, levelled and formed out of a most craggye and unprofitable piece of ground, now framed a most pleasant, sweete, and princely place." To make his garden, Hatton destroyed two existing villages, rebuilding one of them in true renaissance style on the axis of his new garden. This kind of horticultural ethnic cleansing was a regular occurrence in the creation of 18th-century landscape parks but no other example is recorded as early as this.

The estate was bought by James I in 1607 and in 1651, under a new owner, the buildings were almost entirely demolished, apart from some outhouses. Late in the 18th century a new but far smaller house of vaguely renaissance character was built. Only the ghostly shape of the 16th-century survives today, with the bold shaping of the land plainly visible. Two spectacular Elizabethan archways

KEDLESTON HALL

ROBERT ADAM'S GREAT HOUSE AND PARK WITH ITS BEAUTIFUL BUILDINGS FORM A MEMORABLE LANDSCAPE

Dr Johnson visited Kedleston in 1777 and was not impressed by the great house ("It would do excellently for a town hall") but James Boswell "was struck with the magnificence of the building; and the extensive park, with the finest verdure…[the] old oaks filled me with a sort of respectful admiration." The house, built for Nathaniel Curzon, 1st Baron Scarsdale, was started by Matthew Brettingham, continued by James Paine but given its final, splendid form by Robert Adam from 1760 onwards. A little earlier Adam had been delighted to be able to write to his brother James that he had been charged with "the intire Manadgement of

[Curzon's] grounds…with full powers as to Temples, Bridges, Seats and Cascades". So it was that Adam was able to design the landscape setting for his great house. Charles Bridgeman had designed a formal garden in the 1720s and William Emes had been consulted about the park in the 1750s but it seems that he produced no design for it.

Adam's work on the park, in particular some beautiful buildings, are the chief attractions of the landscape today, and the view from the north façade of the house is one of the most satisfying of any 18th-century scheme. The house rises on a slight eminence and a stream, dammed to form two sinuous lakes, snakes across the former deer park below. On the far side of the lakes the land rises gently, with woodland becoming increasingly dense towards the horizon. Adam designed a grand three-arched bridge to span the stream, with a cascade to restrict the flow of water and form a lake. Visitors still approach the house – as was originally intended – over the bridge, with the splendid house suddenly revealed. On the banks of the upper lake Adam built one of his prettiest buildings – a Palladian fishing room. It is in three parts, with the centre rising higher and the side-pieces accommodating boathouses with rusticated arches opening out onto the

Robert Adam's bridge at Kedleston

water. A grand room in the central part, with a Palladian window overlooking the lake, is decorated with fine plasterwork and a fishing scene painted by Francesco Zuccarelli.

THE PLEASURE GROUND

South-west of the house is the Pleasure Ground, a pretty enough garden but relatively minor compared to Adam's subtle but magnificent landscape. A sculpture of the Medicean Lion and an urn in memory of the poet Michael Drayton both date from the 1st Baron Scarsdale's time and were in place by 1766. From the same period, but now in a slightly different position, is the hexagonal summerhouse, designed by George Richardson, which overlooks a modern rose garden. Adam himself had designed pleasure grounds on this side of the house, which included an informal and flower bedecked Long Walk, but nothing remains of them.

The most memorable experience of the landscape at Kedleston may be gained by walking along the drive towards the house, with Adam's lakes snaking across the land, the unforgettable house sitting serenely on a grassy slope above the water, and Adam's

bridge and fishing house animating a scene of restrained splendour.

All visitors should also go round the house – the Adam interiors are remarkably beautiful. From the windows of the saloon on the south side you can look over a lawn which slopes upwards towards woodland whose straight edge is broken by a curved indentation of turf – no doubt planned as a viewing platform from which to savour the grand south façade of the house.

Location nr Derby DE6 4JN, Derbyshire **OS** SK3140 3m NW of Derby by A52 and minor roads **Tel** 01332 842191 **Fax** 01332 841972 **Email** kedlestonhall@ntrust.org.uk **English Heritage Register** Grade I **Owner** The National Trust **Open** Apr to Oct, Sat to Wed 11–6 (park also open Nov to mid Dec, Sat and Sun 12–4) **Area** 864 acres/350 hectares

KIRBY HALL

THE EXQUISITE REMAINS OF A GREAT TUDOR PALACE WITH A RE-CREATION OF SIR CHRISTOPHER HATTON'S GREAT GARDEN OF THE 1690s

In 1654, John Evelyn wrote, "I went to see Kirby, a very noble house of my Lord Hatton's in Northamptonshire, built *à la moderne*; the garden and stables agreeable." The great house at Kirby had been built for Sir Humphrey Stafford in 1570 under the supervision of the mason Thomas Thorpe. Before it was complete, in 1575, the estate was bought by Sir Christopher Hatton, Queen Elizabeth I's Lord Chancellor. The Hattons made a palace of the house which, in the 1690s, under the fourth Sir Christopher Hatton, was embellished with a new Great Garden. This Christopher Hatton's brother, Charles, was a knowledgeable plantsman, and surviving correspondence between the brothers gives evidence of the kinds of plants and seeds which came to Kirby at this time: almond trees, apricot trees, carob seeds, "three score and ten white lilacs", pomegranates, and other "such things as are rare and may be picked up among the sea men". It is probable that George London advised Lady Hatton on the design of the new garden which it is known he visited in 1693.

In the 18th century the house declined and a hundred years later was in a ruinous state. The Revd Canon James described "the very action of decomposition going on, the crumbling stucco of the ceiling feeding the vampire ivy, the tattered tapestry yet hanging on the wall, the picture flapping in its broken frame". Only the shell of the house, now in the care of English Heritage, survives but is, with its enclosed courts and finely carved renaissance masonry, one of the most poignantly beautiful places of its date in England.

THE GREAT GARDEN

In the 1930s the Office of Works carried out an archaeological dig to see what traces of the garden layout survived. In doing so they destroyed 17th-century evidence in pursuit of earlier strata. However, an early 18th-century plan shows some details of Sir Christopher's Great Garden, including a grand four-part parterre west of the house, and in 1994 English Heritage laid out a new parterre, based on a George London design for Longleat House (see page 93), with swirling shapes of cut turf (or *gazon coupé* as it was called) against a background of gravel. The garden is edged with raised walks on two sides and in the centre of

1630s gateway at Kirby Hall

the south-facing retaining wall is a beautiful rusticated stone gateway carved by the sculptor and master-mason Nicholas Stone in the 1630s. Fruit trees are espaliered against the wall and box-edged beds are planted with herbs and repeated shapes of holly and yew. Tubs of topiary, cones of yew and lollipops of holm oak or holly are distributed about the garden.

The simple and distinguished design of the parterre gives a vivid impression of the spirit of the late 17th century but the Hattons, one feels, would certainly have liked to see a bit more plant excitement. Also, such designs

depend upon impeccable maintenance; in September 2002 the topiary was poorly clipped, in some cases misshapen and lurching sideways, and some of the yews were plainly gasping for water. Furthermore, the wooden gate into the garden was lacking some of its planks and looked as though it was leading to a neglected allotment rather than to the remains of a great garden. It must be wondered if English Heritage's heart is truly in this enterprise.

Nevertheless, whatever the superficial deficiencies of upkeep, Kirby Hall remains a bewitching place to visit. Although close to the industrial estate of Corby, it has a remote and desolate air (Kirby village has long since disappeared), rising unexpectedly in the distance above cornfields. On several visits I have usually been entirely alone, surrounded by some of the grandest architecture in the country.

Location Corby, Northamptonshire **OS** SP9292 4m NE of Corby by minor roads; follow signs to the village of Deene from which it is signed **Tel** 01536 203230
English Heritage Register Grade II* **Owner** English Heritage **Open** Apr to Oct, daily 10–6 (closes 5 in Oct); Nov to Mar, Sat and Sun 10–4 (closed 24–26 Dec, 1 Jan)
Area 5 acres/2 hectares

West front and parterre at Kirby

LORD LEYCESTER'S HOSPITAL

AMONG BUILDINGS RANGING FROM THE 14TH TO THE 19TH CENTURY ARE TWO GARDENS: A DECORATIVE LAYOUT TO CELEBRATE THE MILLENNIUM AND THE OLDER, MORE COMPLEX MASTER'S GARDEN OF DIFFERENT PERIODS

The delightful group of buildings that comprise Lord Leycester's Hospital range from the 14th to the 19th century. The hospital, for aged or disabled soldiers and their wives, was founded in 1571 by Robert Dudley, Earl of Leicester, in buildings that had housed two medieval guilds. Today the hospital is still the home of retired servicemen, who help with its administration.

There are two gardens here: one entirely new, made to celebrate the Millennium, and the other, the garden of the hospital's Master, much older. The Millennium Garden was designed by Susan Rhodes and Geoffrey Smith and forms, in effect, an entrance courtyard for visitors to the hospital. A carpenter's work tunnel made of green oak leads into the garden which, in its design and symbolism, is firmly rooted in the hospital itself. A statue immediately presents itself, based on the Dudley arms – a bear with a ragged staff fashioned of sheet metal and skilfully worked by Rachel Higgins. It is mounted on a circular plinth of cobbles backed by a curved bed of golden box and a curved yew hedge, with tall clipped shapes of gold variegated holly between them. The bear faces down a brick path flanked by a pair of knots of Tudor inspiration, which, tricked out in dwarf box, echo the shapes of the half-timbering of the hospital's wall. Compartments are filled with lavender or gravel; lollipops of clipped *Rhamnus alaternus* 'Argenteovariegata' rise out of bushes of lavender; and eight cones of clipped box symbolise the eight hospitallers. A bench has the date 2000 worked into its back. The garden is lighthearted, decorative and thoroughly welcoming.

The Master's Garden lies below the Master's House, built in the middle ages but today of largely Victorian appearance. It overlooks an open lawn with curvaceous edges and cast-iron urns filled with summer bedding plants.

The Master's Garden at the Hospital

A Norman archway under the canopy of two huge magnolias frames a giant stone urn. This was placed here in 1838, with cannon balls from the battlefield of Edge Hill at its base, but is of much earlier origin – possibly Egyptian. Beyond it a herringbone-patterned path runs between borders of *Alchemilla mollis*, bergenias, campanulas, geraniums, phlox and valerian backed by garlands of roses and overlooked by a summerhouse. Behind the roses are a kitchen garden on one side and an open lawn on the other. The edge of the garden has a hidden walk of ancient origin, running along the top of the town walls, giving remarkable views over the rooftops of Warwick. In one corner is an Elizabethan gazebo and an early 18th-century pineapple pit. There is much packed into the Master's Garden but cross-vistas and eyecatchers – a bench, an urn in a niche of yew, a sundial – prevent claustrophia. It is a rare example of an urban garden with a long and interesting history and much charm.

Location High Street, Warwick CV34 4BH, Warwickshire **OS** SP2866 In the centre of Warwick **Tel** 01926 491422 **Owner** The Board of Governors of Lord Leycester Hospital **Open** end Mar to Sept, daily except Mon (open Bank Hol Mon) **Area** 1 acre/0.4 hectare

LYVEDEN NEW BIELD

THE POIGNANT REMAINS OF AN ELABORATE ELIZABETHAN GARDEN ABOUT THE SHELL OF AN EXTRAORDINARY UNFINISHED HOUSE

The estate at Lyveden was acquired by Thomas Tresham of Rushton in the middle of the 15th century and a licence to enclose a park was given in 1540. In 1560 his grandson, another Thomas (who was knighted in 1575), inherited. The family had become Protestant but Sir Thomas went back to the old faith in 1580 at the height of the Elizabethan persecution of Catholicism. He proclaimed his reconversion by building at Rushton Hall (quite near Lyveden) between 1593 and 1597 an extraordinary triangular lodge which may still be seen. Its plan symbolises the Trinity and the building is busy with trefoils – the family crest of the Treshams, whose very name it echoes.

At Lyveden, from 1596, he built a far more spectacular testimony to his religion. The New Bield (which means new building, as opposed to the Old Bield which was the manor house) was built as a "garden lodge", or banqueting house, on the grandest scale. It was built to a cruciform plan and the seven emblems of the Passion were beautifully carved on a frieze on the exterior. While the building was proceeding, Tresham was under constant persecution – under surveillance, house arrest or actually in prison until his death in 1608. Lyveden New Bield was never completed, the Tresham family fortunes were destroyed by Sir Thomas's persecution, and the family died out in the 17th century. The estate changed hands but the New Bield nevertheless survived, its beautiful masonry largely intact, until the National Trust acquired the building and some of its surrounding land in 1922.

Between the Old Bield and the New Bield there had been an elaborate formal garden. Much of the site became arable land, destroying archaeological evidence of the garden, but some land was not ploughed, and surviving earthworks and canals give an idea of the splendour of the place. A moat surrounding the New Bield is now dry but immediately to its north, in an area known as the Middle Garden, a level square space has a moat (with water) on two sides, which curves round grassy mounds on two corners. On its far side a raised grass walk, now planted with hawthorns, overlooks the site of Sir

The banqueting house

The grass walk and moat at Lyveden

Thomas Tresham's orchard which he planted in 1597 with apples, cherries, pears, plums and walnuts. This has been replanted very recently with "walkes" of cherries and walnuts underplanted with wildflowers of the region.

Lyveden New Bield stands on an open, windy site with long views. Crows wheel through the rooms of the beautiful pale stone roofless shell. It is a moving experience to walk along the banks of the canal and stand on the raised walk, thinking of the fate of the Treshams, but even without this the place still possesses a most powerful character.

Location nr Oundle, Peterborough PE8 5AT, Northamptonshire **OS** SP9885 4m SW of Oundle off A427 **Tel** 01832 205358 **Email** lyvedennewbield@ntrust.org.uk **English Heritage Register** Grade II* **Owner** The National Trust **Open** end Mar to beginning Nov, Wed to Sun (open Bank Hol Mon) 10.30–5; beginning Nov to end Mar, Sat and Sun 10.30–4 **Area** 27 acres/11 hectares

garden at Melbourne is an introspective place with no glimpse of a horizon, giving it a romantically melancholy atmosphere. Versailles was emphatically for impressing your neighbours; Melbourne is for getting lost in. The garden historian and Blenheim archivist David Green described Melbourne as "a mild and tranquil garden, a Wilderness of Sweets…It is in fact the perfect compromise, the formal garden grown informal and English: the bob-tailed sheep-dog that was at first taken to be a poodle."

Location Melbourne DE73 1EN, Derbyshire   **OS** SK3825 9m S of Derby by A453; Jnct 24 of the M1   **Tel** 01332 862502   **Fax** 01332 862263   **English Heritage Register** Grade I   **Owner** Lord Ralph Kerr   **Open** Apr to Sept, Wed, Sat, Sun and Bank Hol Mon 2–6   **Area** 16 acres/6.5 hectares

MELBOURNE HALL

THIS ENCHANTING FORMAL GARDEN – A HAPHAZARD, INWARD-LOOKING VERSION OF VERSAILLES – SURVIVES FROM THE EARLY 18TH CENTURY, ALONG WITH ROBERT BAKEWELL'S BEAUTIFUL BIRDCAGE

The garden at Melbourne is an enchanting survival – a formal garden of the early 18th century, untouched by the later fashion for landscaping. The house is an ancient one, substantially rebuilt for Thomas Coke, Vice-Chamberlain to Queen Anne and King George I, by Francis Smith of Warwick in the 1720s. The formal gardens, the work of George London and Henry Wise, were laid out from 1699 – Coke commissioned them to produce a garden "to suit with Versailles". Melbourne is not, remotely, on the scale of the Sun King's gardens but it is craftily designed to seem larger than it really is.

Below the pedimented east façade of the house great stepped terraces of turf descend a stately slope, past beautiful lead statues by John Van Nost, to a grand shaped pool – the Great Basin. On its far side is one of the loveliest garden buildings in England – Robert Bakewell's wrought iron "birdcage". This airy arbour was made in 1706 and cost £120 – the equivalent of about £8,800 today.

The "birdcage" at Melbourne Hall

Running along each side of the turf descent are magnificently blowsy ancient hedges of yew which must date from the garden's making. These curve about to sweep round the back of the birdcage and the hedges are interrupted from time to time by niches to enclose more lead figures by Van Nost. South of the Grand Basin is an intricate pattern of radiating lime alleys, rising and falling with the lie of the land and animated by pools, fountains and eyecatchers. At its heart is a vast lead urn, the Four Seasons, made by John Van Nost and presented to Coke by Queen Anne.

Unlike a French garden of this period (never mind Versailles), the lime walks are asymmetrical, shooting off at odd angles in a haphazard fashion. This absence of any rigidly schematic plan creates diversity and surprise – vistas are multiplied in a kaleidoscopic fashion. Another crucial difference from a garden such as Versailles is that the

THE MENAGERIE

A RESTORED 18TH-CENTURY BANQUETING HOUSE WITH AN ELABORATE AND CHARMING GARDEN MADE IN THE LATE 20TH CENTURY BY THE ARCHITECTURAL HISTORIAN GERVASE JACKSON-STOPS

The Menagerie is a delightful building, designed by Thomas Wright, the architect and garden designer. It was built for the 2nd Earl of Halifax in the late 1750s as a banqueting house and landscape ornament in the park at Horton Hall (*see page 493*). It also concealed a collection of exotic animals which were probably kept in a moated enclosure south of the Menagerie. Horace Walpole wrote about it in 1763, describing "a little wood, prettily disposed with many basons of gold fish".

The Menagerie was bought in a state of advanced dereliction by the architectural historian Gervase Jackson-Stops

Classical pavilion at the Menagerie

in 1975. He restored it, made it habitable and embarked on a garden in keeping with the spirit of the place. South of the house a deep mixed border is lavishly planted with bold foliage and sweet scents – acanthus, artichokes, ceanothus, fennel, *Lychnis coronaria*, *Macleaya* × *kewensis*, *Rhamnus alaternus* 'Argenteovariegata' and roses. A semicircular lawn opens out, edged in yew hedging and with three walks, each hedged in hornbeam, radiating out in the form of a *patte d'oie*. The central walk, broader than the others, has an avenue of limes and, half way along, a mound topped with a stone obelisk and planted with a spiral of the ground-hugging *Acaena microphylla*. The flanking walks each end in a circular restored 18th-century pool, presumably the "basons" seen by Walpole. At this point they open out in a generous circle and from each a path leads to a delightful thatched pavilion. Designed by Charles Morris, one pavilion is circular in plan, with a neatly classical portico with pediment and pillars facing the pool and another portico at the back. This, where it faces wild planting, is suitably rustic, with pillars of unbarked wood. The other pavilion is triangular in plan, with a Gothic portico of pointed arches and tall finials. The heterogenous style of these pavilions is true to the mood of 18th-century gardens which intermingled the Gothic and the Classical with abandon. The spaces between the central walk and those flanking it are densely planted, with serpentine walks leading through to the back of the pavilions. Here are acanthus, aconitums, billowing mounds of box (common and gold-variegated), euphorbias, geraniums, shrub roses and viburnums. Behind the pavilions are a bog garden and water garden.

A FORMAL ROSE GARDEN

To the east of the house is a formal rose garden with box hedges designed by Vernon Russell-Smith. A path leads to a walled garden with beds of fruit, vegetables and ornamental plantings and a central tiered fountain in a pool. Gervase Jackson-Stops had intended a walled garden but he died in 1995 and this was made in 2002. It is not in keeping with the light-hearted but scholarly atmosphere of the rest of the garden.

Location Horton, Northampton NN7 2BX, Northamptonshire **OS** SP8384 5m SE of Northampton off B526; entrance across a field just S of Horton village **Tel** 01604 870957 **English Heritage Register** Grade II **Owner** A. Myers **Open** Apr to Sept, Mon, Thur and last Sun of each month 2–5 **Area** 3 acres/1.2 hectares

MOSELEY OLD HALL

THE DECORATIVE RECONSTRUCTION OF A 17TH-CENTURY GARDEN BY THE NATIONAL TRUST INCLUDES AN ELABORATE KNOT GARDEN, TOPIARY AND PERIOD PLANTS

Moseley Old Hall is a late Elizabethan house, altered in the 17th century and enclosed in brick in the 19th century. It had its moment of glory in 1651 when Charles II took refuge here (disguised as a woodcutter) after the battle of Worcester. It was Thomas Whitgreave who was the King's protector and the house remained in the Whitgreave family until 1925. In 1962 it was acquired by the National Trust "although not of great architectural merit" – it was the connection with Charles II and the Restoration that "justified its acquisition". The interior of the house, which is delightful, is the least altered of any in which the King is known to have taken refuge.

Nothing is known of any early garden at Moseley Old Hall. The National Trust decided to make a garden of the sort that might have been here in the first half of the 17th century. Below the south-facing windows of the house they laid out a knot garden copied from a design by the Revd Walter Stonehouse in 1640 – a sprightly pattern of lollipops of clipped box at the centre of circles of box hedging. Intricately scalloped compartments fill the spaces between the circles and the whole forms a rectangle. Gravel of different colours forms the background – sandy gravel is used for the paths and background; the scalloped beds have small pebbles and the circular beds have larger pale grey pebbles. This is a kind of garden not to walk in but to be seen from above so that the pattern may be admired. To one side of the knot is a tunnel of arcaded "carpenter's work" taken from an illustration in *The Gardeners Labyrinth* by Didymus Mountain (a pseudonym for Thomas Hill), published in 1577. It is planted with Virgin's Bower clematis (*C. flammula*), *C. viticella* and purple-leafed grapevine (*Vitis vinifera* 'Purpurea'), with aquilegias, geraniums and lavender planted below the climbers. The

The knot at Moseley Old Hall

tunnel leads to a walk of hazels underplanted with spring bulbs and, on the far side of the knot, a path flanked by medlars, mulberries and quinces.

The front garden of the house, where the entrance courtyard used to be, has a cobbled path, lawns and box topiary in the form of cones and spirals. The style of planting here is modern but the plants themselves could all have been found in a 17th-century garden. Here are such old rose cultivars and forms as the Jacobite rose (*Rosa* × *alba* 'Alba Maxima') and *R. gallica* var. *officinalis*; "useful" plants like *Saponaria officinalis*; natives like the stinking iris (*I. foetidissima*) and Solomon's seal (*Polygonatum multiflorum*).

The garden at Moseley Old Hall was started in 1963 when faithful reconstructions of old gardens were much less common than they are now. Apart from being delightfully decorative, it gives a vivid idea of the styles of design and the range of plants that were found in 17th-century gardens.

Location Moseley Old Hall Lane, Fordhouses, Wolverhampton WV10 7HY, Staffordshire **OS** SJ9304 3½ m N of Wolverhampton between A460 and A449, S of M54 **Tel** 01902 782808 **Email** moseleyoldhall@ntrust.org.uk **Owner** The National Trust **Open** end Mar to beginning Nov, Sat and Sun,

Bank Hol Mon and following Tue 1.30–5.30 (Bank Hol Mon 11–5) (Jun to Oct, also Wed 1.30–5.30; Jul to Aug, also Tue 1.30–5.30); Nov to Dec, Sun 1–4 **Area** 1 acre/0.4 hectare

NEWSTEAD ABBEY

ENJOYABLE AND FINELY MAINTAINED GARDENS FROM THE 16TH TO THE 20TH CENTURY ORNAMENT LORD BYRON'S FAMILY HOME

An Augustinian priory was founded at Newstead in the 12th century, and this passed to Sir John Byron at the dissolution of the monasteries. The 13th-century west front of the priory church and other monastic remains give the house, with its jumble of later period styles, a wonderfully romantic character. The poet George Gordon, 6th Lord Byron, inherited Newstead from his great-uncle in 1798. He described Newstead in *Don Juan*: "An old, old Monastery once, and now/Still older mansion – of a rich and rare/Mixed Gothic". He celebrated his inheritance by planting an oak whose dead stump still stands on the lawn south of the abbey, entwined with ivy as Byron had hoped.

The garden is a fascinating mixture of ingredients and was, at least in part, possibly

The Japanese garden at Newstead Abbey

laid out in the 16th century; the Eagle Pond, at the centre of the walled garden east of the house, may even have been the monks' stew pond.

From the end of the 17th century the 4th Lord Byron made many improvements to the grounds, and a painting of Newstead Abbey in the late 1720s by Peter Tillemans, reproduced in John Harris's *The Artist and the Country House* (1979), shows a formal canal south of the house, where the irregular Garden Lake stands today. Quite close to the lake a small canal, atmospherically shaded with venerable yews, is known now as the Stew Pond; however, it, too, is much more likely to date from the early 18th century. From 1749, the 5th Lord enlivened the banks of the Upper Lake, west of the abbey, with castellated forts (Horace Walpole called them "silly forts"), which remain, but a Gothic sham castle has gone. In the 18th century mock battles were fought here and the 5th Lord, who had served in the navy in his youth, kept a 20-gun ship on the lake.

The large walled garden east of the abbey preserves much of its 18th-century character. With its turf terraces, raised walks running under the walls, and sunken pool, it has the

pansive air of a formal garden of that period.
pair of beautiful lead statues (of male and
male satyrs), almost certainly by John Van
ost, date from the 4th Lord's time but were
ly placed here in the late 18th century. The
wns are decorated with splendid pieces of
w topiary, among them some virtuoso
rals, and old walnuts planted in formal rows
out the Eagle Pond are being replaced by
unger trees. In recent times a mixed border
s been laid out under the north wall. A
onument to the poet Byron's dog, Boatswain,
ich died in 1808, is an elegant classical urn
a plinth which celebrates his "Strength
thout Insolence, Courage without Ferocity,
d all the Virtues of Man without his Vices".
Immediately below the east wall of the
bey is the 20th-century Spanish Garden — a
ot of box partitions planted with seasonal
dding, and south of the formal walled
rden are two further walled enclosures —
rts of the 18th-century kitchen garden. One
a very large formal rose garden of Edwardian
vour, with L-shaped beds cut into turf and
nes of clipped yew. The other, much smaller,
as a fruit garden and preserves decorative
old espaliers. It now has box-edged beds,

bedding schemes, and a collection of irises.

On the east and south banks of the Garden Lake are gardens of very different character. To the east, a rock and heather garden has wooden bridges spanning rocky ravines, fine old beeches and oaks and such smaller ornamental trees as magnolias and maples which provide shade for ferns, hellebores and hostas. Immediately to the south, laid out in the early 20th century, is a Japanese garden with pools, stepping stones, cascades and snow lanterns of fine quality. *Cercidiphyllum japonicum*, euonymus, Japanese maples and a mulberry ornament the banks of the pools.

Newstead Abbey houses mementoes of the poet Byron, and the wooded grounds of the estate form a popular public park. The gardens, for the most part finely maintained, are exceptionally varied and have a most memorable atmosphere.

Location Linstead NG15 8GE, Nottinghamshire
OS SK5453 10m N of Nottingham by A60 **Tel** 01623 455900 **Fax** 01623 455904 **English Heritage Register** Grade II* **Owner** Nottingham City Council
Open Apr to Sept, daily 9–7.30; Oct to Mar, daily 9–5 (closed Fri in Nov) **Area** 300 acres/121 hectares

PACKWOOD HOUSE

A CHARMING WALLED FLOWER GARDEN
PROVIDES A CONTRAST TO PACKWOOD'S
FAMOUS YEW TOPIARY OF THE SERMON ON
THE MOUNT AND THE MULTITUDE

The garden at Packwood is famous for a single, astonishing feature but it has other attractions besides. The truly jaw-dropping spectacle is the garden of crowding yew topiary beyond the walled garden south of the house. It falls into two parts. The Sermon on the Mount is built on a rounded hillock with a winding path edged in box. On its summit is the tallest yew — symbolising Christ — and on the lower slopes are the twelve apostles and the four evangelists. No-one knows when this explanation was first proposed, but Christian symbolism is very rare in English gardens of any period and it seems probable that these venerable shapes were put into place in the early 18th century. Bustling about below them is the Multitude — truncated conical shapes of various sizes, with a straight

The Multitude at Packwood House

path running across the grass between them to the mount, and dating, in all likelihood, to the 19th century. Whatever their date, or their purpose, they form one of the most mysteriously dramatic garden scenes you will ever clap eyes on. This part of the garden is enclosed on each side by a rolling, lumpy, bumpy box hedge, with fine parkland and notable old oaks beyond.

THE WALLED GARDEN

The house at Packwood is described by Pevsner as "Quite a stately timber-framed house of about the third quarter of the C16". A mid 18th-century drawing shows the gabled house overlooking a walled garden with a gazebo built into one corner, a handsome entrance with semicircular steps, and a series of arched recesses in the outer wall to house beehives. The area of the topiary garden, just beyond the outer wall, is not included. Yet had the yews been in place for thirty years or so they would certainly have formed striking shapes by that time – so it is odd that the artist did not include them.

The walled garden today closely resembles the drawing and it is finely embellished with 20th-century planting. A series of yew "stalls" run along one wall, with each enclosure planted with a single block of yellow or red floribunda roses – a potentially garish scheme soothed down by the sombre deep green of the yew. A sunken garden with a pool is enclosed by low yew hedges lined with frothy miniature borders pricked out with appropriate annuals. Similar planting runs along a raised walk, with a gazebo at each end, against the southern wall. This wall is pierced by an opening with beautiful brick piers, curving steps and wrought-iron gates that are both lively and delicate. The walled garden, flowery and lighthearted, makes an admirable prelude to the solemn enigma of the yew garden. The entrance courtyard, to the west, has impeccable yew hedges enclosing a grand octagonal lawn with a vertical four-faced sundial on a column at its centre. Views to the west, of a lake and parkland, are idyllic and simple.

Location Lapworth, Solihull B94 6AT, Warwickshire
OS SP1772 11m SE of Birmingham by A34

Tel 01564 783294 **Email** packwood@ntrust.org.uk
English Heritage Register Grade II* **Owner** The National Trust **Open** Mar to Oct, Wed to Sun (open Bank Hol Mon) 10–5.30 (closes 4.30 in Mar, Apr and Oct) **Area** 5 acres/2 hectares

RENISHAW HALL

EXQUISITE PLANTING IN SIR GEORGE SITWELL'S REFINED "ITALIAN RENAISSANCE" GARDEN OF THE 1900S MAKES THIS ONE OF THE MOST BEAUTIFUL GARDENS IN ENGLAND

The garden at Renishaw was made by Sir George Sitwell who went to Italy repeatedly for about ten years from the early 1890s to study the gardens of the Renaissance. He visited around 200 of them and wrote a short, beautifully written and perceptive book, *On the Making of Gardens* (1909), describing what he saw. Inspired by these renaissance gardens, he decided to create a garden at Renishaw and put into practice the principles he had observed. The result, impeccably cared for by his grandson, is one of the most beautiful gardens in England and worth going a great distance to see. Rebelling against the 18th-century English park and its claims to imitate nature, Sitwell believed the essential purpose of the garden was to provide a setting for the house and to honour the genius of the place.

At Renishaw he made a gently terraced garden south of the house, hedged in yew and ornamented with fine urns, statues and fountains. The lowermost terrace, in accordance with renaissance ideas, commands great views of the countryside – not here the olive groves and vineyards of Tuscany but the scarred industrial landscape of Sheffield, but that can't be helped. Cross vistas, with openings in the yew hedges marked by tall piers of clipped yew, reveal views of the woodland on either side, like some Tuscan *bosco*. The garden is exactly the width of the house; it is entirely in harmony with it and at the same time firmly related to its larger setting. (This is, of course, what all gardens should be.)

Sir George did not regard flowers as an essential ingredient of a garden ("such flower

The terraces at Renishaw Hall

A cross vista at Renishaw

as might be permitted…should not call attention to themselves by hue or scent") but gradually, over the years, Sir George's finely made enclosures have been sympathetically embellished with flowers, especially shrub roses. The yew hedges provide the best possible background and the plantings now look as though they were an essential part of the designer's plan. The lowermost terrace has spectacular mixed borders which in late June explode with the delicious mixed scent of *Buddleja alternifolia*, philadelphus and roses.

There are other things of a garden kind to admire at Renishaw (including a lovely bluebell wood and spectacular tender plants trained on the south façade of the house) but it is Sir George's sublime renaissance vision that is unforgettable. And Sir George knew when to stop. There is precisely the right degree of austerity in his garden, unadulterated by the later floriferous additions. Sir George's son Osbert, describing his father's garden-making activities, wrote in 1949: "His head throbbed with ideas, the majority of them never put into practice. Glass fountains, aqueducts in rubble, gigantic figures, cascades through the woods, stone boats and dragons in the water of lake or pool, blue-stencilled white cows 'to give distinction to the landscape'."

Location Renishaw, Sheffield S21 3WB, Derbyshire **OS** SK4378 Between the villages of Renishaw and Eckington, 2m WNW of Jnct 30 of M1 **Tel** 01246 432310 **Fax** 01246 430706 **English Heritage Register** Grade II* **Owner** Sir Reresby Sitwell **Open** Good Fri to Sept, Fri to Sun and Bank Hol Mon 10.30–4.30 **Area** 5 acres/2hectares

RYTON ORGANIC GARDENS

EVERY GARDENER CAN LEARN FROM
THE TECHNIQUES AND THE AESTHETICS
OF ORGANIC GARDENING
AT RYTON

Ryton is the best, and most diverse, place in the country to learn about organic gardening. The Henry Doubleday Research Association moved from Essex to Ryton in 1985 and the garden seems to increase in appeal and value to gardeners all the time. The chief purpose is to instruct visitors in the techniques and merits of organic gardening, but there is more emphasis today on aesthetics – in the past the magic came from the muck alone. A border of herbaceous perennials and small shrubs, designed by Brita von Schoenaich and Tim Rees, shows that beauty and organic gardening can live very happily together. Plants are chosen that need no staking and no deadheading (the seedheads are things of beauty) – bold groups of hardy geraniums, lavender, persicaria and *Phlomis russeliana*, enriched with sheaves of ornamental grasses. This is part of a display demonstrating diversity in the landscape, with plants chosen for low maintenance – a far wider range than that found in such low maintenance (and usually very dull) sites as supermarket car parks.

INSPIRATIONAL DISPLAYS

Organic pest, disease and weed control, and compost making, are the techniques which lie at the heart of organic gardening, and Ryton has eloquent practical demonstrations of all these. Among more specialist displays is a garden planned to thrive on little water – partly a matter of choosing drought-resistant plants but also of conserving water. Some of the displays are inspirational, of which one of the best is the Cook's Garden which, in a small space, provides fruit, vegetables and herbs for the kitchen but is also ornamental. A path curves between beds, a small octagonal glasshouse protects tender crops and in summer an arbour of the rose 'Madame Alfred Carrière' suffuses the garden with scent.

The flat site at Ryton makes little contribution to the beauty of the place and exposes the garden to sweeping winds. Trees and shrubs have now grown sufficiently to offer much protection, and within the garden hedged enclosures create pockets of balmy seclusion. Visitors may come to study organic gardening techniques but are frequently ambushed by beautiful sights – a little avenue of fastigiate hornbeams, good borders, handsome individual trees (such as the outstanding thorn *Crataegus pinnatifida* var. *major*) and several attractive display gardens (such as the enclosed garden of unusual vegetables prettily laid out in L-shaped beds).

One of the most valuable initiatives of the HDRA is the Heritage Seed Library which conserves the seed of 800 different vegetable varieties. In 2002 a new building, the Vegetable Kingdom, was being built as a seed conservation and visitor centre. It will also house an ambitious display describing the history of vegetable cultivation in the UK. In the same year it was announced that a new airport for the Midlands was to be built, one of the preferred sites being one mile from Ryton.

Location nr Coventry CV8 3LG, Warwickshire **OS** SP4074 5m SE of Coventry by A45 and minor road **Tel** 024 7630 3517 **Fax** 024 7663 9229 **Email** enquiry@hdra.org.uk **Website** www.hdra.org.uk **Owner** HDRA – The Organic Organisation **Open** daily 9–5 except Christmas week **Area** 20 acres/8 hectares

The perennial garden at Ryton

SHUGBOROUGH

A FEAST OF GARDEN BUILDINGS,
INCLUDING A PIONEER CHINESE HOUSE,
ADORN THIS 18TH-CENTURY PARK

The Anson family has lived here since the early 17th century and the house, originally of the same date, now has the smoothly classical appearance of its final remodelling by Samuel Wyatt between 1790 and 1806. Thomas Anson was the man who made the greatest contribution to the garden. As you approach the house you will see across parkland two monuments commissioned by him in the 1760s from the architect James "Athenian" Stuart: the Tower of the Winds is a tall octagonal temple with two pedimented porticos framed in a group of trees; the Arch of Hadrian rises on an eminence further away, erected to commemorate the circumnavigation of the world by Thomas Anson's younger brother, George, who became 1st Lord of the Admiralty in 1747.

A few years previously, on a voyage to China, George Anson had taken an interest in Chinese architecture; it is said that his second-in-command, Sir Piercy Brett, sketched a Chinese house in Canton for him. As a result, by 1748 the garden at Shugborough had one of the first, and supposedly most authentic, Chinese buildings in England – only a handful antedate it. It may still be seen, in splendid condition, on the bank of a stream which is spanned by a handsome iron bridge painted ox-blood red (of much later date). Philip Yorke on his travels had admired the scene in 1748: "…nearest the River is placed a Chinese Summer house, with a bridge on each side, which makes a very pretty Object."

"THE WIZARD OF DURHAM"

Close to the Chinese house is the enigmatic Cat Monument, a charming urn surmounted by a crouching cat, designed by the equally enigmatic "Wizard of Durham", Thomas Wright, who worked here from 1748 to 1749. Wright also designed the Shepherd's Monument with the inscription *Et in Arcadia Ego*, enclosed in rustic stonework. His most effective garden building in terms of its role in the landscape is the Ruin on the bank of the

The Chinese house at Shugborough

river Sow, commanding a central position in views from the western windows of the house. This ornament, much reduced in size, has become that great paradox, a ruin of a ruin, gently veiled in trees. Much later, formal gardens were made close to the house – a bold and brassy Victorian scheme laid out by W.A. Nesfield in the 1850s with an avenue of clipped golden yews and a fountain pool, and a gentler rose garden of arbours and walks.

The gardens at Shugborough are like a meal consisting of canapés. The canapés are very appetising, of excellent quality and of many different flavours, but they do not quite have the satisfying effect of a solid plateful of meat and two veg.

Location Milford, nr Stafford ST17 0XB, Staffordshire **OS** SJ9922 6m E of Stafford by A513 **Tel** 01889 881388 **Fax** 01889 881323 **Email** shugborough.promotions@staffordshire.gov.uk **English Heritage Register** Grade I **Owner** The National Trust **Open** Apr to Sept, daily except Mon (open Bank Hol Mon) 11–5 **Area** 18 acres/7 hectares

STRATFORD-UPON-AVON GARDENS

A GROUP OF ATTRACTIVE GARDENS WITH
SHAKESPEARIAN CONNECTIONS

The Shakespeare Birthplace Trust owns a group of houses which have, or were thought to have, Shakespearean connections. These houses all have great architectural charm and all possess attractive gardens, although, rather surprisingly, only one attempts to reproduce the appearance of a late Tudor garden. Shakespeare's Birthplace is a source for all information about the gardens described.

SHAKESPEARE'S BIRTHPLACE

The house in which Shakespeare was born in 1564 (originally two houses) was bought in 1847 to serve as a national memorial to the poet. The house was restored and a garden was laid out whose chief purpose was to include as many as possible of those ornamental plants mentioned by Shakespeare. However, many plants which Shakespeare certainly never knew are also included. A broad paved path runs between mixed borders of achilleas, alliums, hollyhocks, kniphofias, lavender, lychnis, penstemons and verbascums. Standard roses, old fruit trees and tall clipped shapes of holly rise among the chiefly herbaceous planting. In little beds close to the house there is more regimented planting with a municipal flavour. At the back of the garden a bust of Rabindranath Tagor stands in the shade of an oak tree.

Location Henley Street, Stratford-upon-Avon CV37 6QW, Warwickshire **OS** SP2054 In the centre of

Borders at Shakespeare's Birthplace

Stratford-upon-Avon **Tel** 01789 204016 **Fax** 01789 296083 **Email** info@shakespeare.org.uk **Website** www.shakespeare.org.uk **Open** mid Mar to mid Oct, daily 9–5.30 (opens 10.30 Sun); mid Oct to mid Mar, daily 9.30–4 (opens 10.30 Sun)

NEW PLACE AND NASH'S HOUSE

New Place was the house Shakespeare bought in 1587 and lived in permanently from 1610 until his death in 1616. His granddaughter, Elizabeth, married Joseph Nash who lived next door and thus united the two properties. They were acquired by the city of Stratford-upon-Avon in 1861 and by the Shakespeare Birthplace Trust in 1884. Only the foundations of New Place survive and here in the bumpy ground, are lawns, a mulberry, a sweetbriar and a garden of herbs. (The garden may be sketchy, but the site is sacred ground.)

In 1918 Ernest Law, a barrister with an interest in historic gardens, designed a new knot garden based on a plan in Didymus Mountain's *The Gardeners Labyrinth* (1577), and this survives, lying behind the site of New Place, concealed behind a fence. Here, sunken at a lower level, is an intricate pattern of compartments of dwarf box, strips of camomile, santolina or thyme, planted in a brilliant bedding scheme of begonias, cherry pie (*Heliotropium arborescens*), marigolds, pelargoniums, petunias and sedums. Such a planting could not have existed in a 16th-century garden but the effect is dazzling; the colours burst upon you as it comes into sight and it may, I suspect, be truer in spirit to Tudor exuberance than some polite good-taste scheme might have been; my guess is that Shakespeare would have loved it. It is surrounded by a terrace with, on the garden side, a low wooden railing draped with honeysuckle and roses, and running along the outer edge of the terrace a hedge of apples, woven with perennial sweet peas and underplanted with irises.

Behind the knot garden is the Great Garden – the original garden of New Place where, it is thought, Shakespeare had his kitchen garden and orchard. Here is a lawn, some fine chestnuts and a mulberry supposedly propagated from one, felled in 1756, that Shakespeare himself had planted (but the age of mulberries is often wildly exaggerated). An

The parterre at New Place

18th-century monument to Shakespeare, originally erected in London but moved here in 1871, stands against the eastern wall. The greatest charm of this garden is the series of borders running along the outside, western, wall. A deep border against the wall is backed by a superb old yew hedge, splendidly topiaried, with occasional outbreaks of golden yew. Yew buttresses, billowing with age, from time to time divide the border which is filled with achilleas, delphiniums, echinops, poppies, thalictrum, verbascums and white willow herb. Parallel to it, on the other side of a path, is a series of borders enclosed in "stalls" of box with a few flourishes of topiary and filled

with summer bedding. It is a delightful design – was it also the work of Ernest Law?
Location Chapel Street, Stratford-upon-Avon, Warwickshire **OS** SP2054 **English Heritage Register** Grade II **Open** mid Mar to mid Oct, daily 9–5.30 (opens 10.30 Sun); mid Oct to mid Mar, daily 9.30–4 (opens 10.30 Sun)

HALL'S CROFT

Hall's Croft, timber framed and built in the late 16th century, was the home of Shakespeare's daughter Susanna after she married Dr John Hall in 1607. It is close to the parish church of the Holy Trinity where Shakespeare was buried in 1616. (The Shakespeare scholar John Dover Wilson says that his stone portrait memorial, by Gerard

Borders at Hall's Croft

Johnson, makes him look like "a self-satisfied pork-butcher".) Behind the house a stone flagged path runs between chiefly herbaceous borders. Drifts of alliums, alstroemerias, campanulas, hollyhocks, lupins, *Macleaya × kewensis* and verbascums are punctuated by standard roses, mostly old-fashioned shrub varieties. A stone sundial marks the far end of the borders from which there is a pretty view back to the gabled house with its intricate timbering. To one side of the borders there are lawns, an old mulberry propped up by brick piers, and a knot of herbs of the kind that Dr Hall might have used.

Location Old Town, Warwick, Warwickshire
OS SP2054 **Open** mid Mar to mid Oct, daily 9–5.30 (opens 10.30 Sun); mid Oct to mid Mar, daily 9.30–4 (opens 10.30 Sun)

ANNE HATHAWAY'S COTTAGE

Anne Hathaway was Shakespeare's wife and this was her parents' house. Parts of the house date back to at least the 15th century and it is a most delightful place. The house overlooks a sea of herbaceous planting – doronicum, foxgloves, geraniums, irises, *Lychnis chalcedonica*, Michaelmas daisies and pinks, with the occasional wambly box hedge and jelly-mould topiary. A rich red rose grows by the front door and nearby a bed is filled with scarlet pelargoniums and edged with white and blue

lobelia. To one side is a little kitchen garden with a rustic wooden fence. Beds of vegetables are protected by Tudor bird scarers – corks with feathers that cause them to spin on a string like propellers. Beyond the kitchen garden is an orchard with old fruit trees and finely mown turf on an undulating site. This unpretentious arrangement, showing a delight in plants but untouched by modish fashion, is what defines a cottage garden. The herbaceous garden was in fact designed by Ellen Willmott who submitted plans to the Shakespeare Birthplace Trust between 1924 and 1925 when the house was being restored. She suggested old-fashioned plants, roses, flowering shrubs and simple topiary. It is a tribute to her skill that she arrived at a scheme so apparently artless yet so appropriate.

Location Shottery, nr Stratford-upon-Avon, Warwickshire
OS SP1854 1 mile west of Stratford-upon-Avon by A422
English Heritage Register Grade II **Open** mid Mar to

Front garden at Anne Hathaway's Cottage

mid Oct, daily 9–5 (opens 9.30 Sun); mid Oct to mid Mar, daily 9.30–4 (opens 10 Sun)

MARY ARDEN'S HOUSE

This was thought to be the house of Shakespeare's mother, Mary Arden. Its identification, however, underwent a dramatic change in 2000 when it was discovered that the *real* Mary Arden's house was Glebe Farm immediately behind what was previously known as Mary Arden's House. Both now belong to the Shakespeare Birthplace Trust, but to avoid confusion I shall refer to them under their old names.

Mary Arden's House, the quintessence of the cottage idea, was built in the early 16th century, with elaborate timber work lavishly displayed, leaded windows and pointed gables rising above a wavy roof of small clay tiles. A narrow front garden separates the house from the road. Originally this must have been a dapper knot but today the box hedges have expanded into billowing cushions, the flagged path is all but obscured and there is little room left for other plants. There nevertheless remain pelargoniums, roses, red and white valerian and, against the wall of the house, regiments of yellow mulleins standing to attention among wisps of perennial sweet peas. The effect – lavishly overgrown and crowded, leaving almost no room for visitors – is enchanting.

Glebe Farm is an early Tudor house with a yard and fine outhouses and a little garden outside the front door. A path of crazy paving runs between shrubs – holly, lilac, shrub roses and variegated weigela – underplanted with bergenias, blue and white *Campanula persicifolia*, linaria and lupins, among which are clipped box spheres. Round the corner a vegetable garden follows a curved stone wall. Sweet williams and variegated sage decorate the neat rows of vegetables, blackberries are espaliered against the wall, and ribbons of chives and lavender line the path.

Location Wilmcote, nr Stratford-upon-Avon, Warwickshire **OS** SP1658 In the village of Wilmcote 3½m NW of Stratford-upon-Avon by A422 and minor roads **Open** mid Mar to mid Oct, daily 9.30–5 (opens 10 Sun); mid Oct to mid Mar, daily 10–4 (opens 10.30 Sun)

▷ **Knot garden** at Mary Arden's House

SULGRAVE MANOR

CHARMING AND BEAUTIFULLY DESIGNED FORMAL GARDEN LAID OUT IN 1921 BY SIR REGINALD BLOMFIELD FOR THE HOME OF GEORGE WASHINGTON'S FOREBEARS

This is the only garden in England owned by the Colonial Dames of America and the only English country house I know to fly the Stars and Stripes. The American connection is an important one for Sulgrave Manor was the home of George Washington's ancestors – Lawrence Washington came to live here in 1540.

Under the supervision of Sir Reginald Blomfield, the house was comprehensively restored and opened to the public in 1921. Sir Reginald, who made good parts of the original house that had been removed, took the limestone house back to its original 16th-century appearance. He also added a charmingly unpretentious formal garden in the tradition of the architectural gardens which he so lovingly described in his book, *The Formal Garden in England* (1892). It is one of the most complete gardens by him to survive. The garden takes its cue, as all gardens of this sort must, from the house. To the south, running up to the front door with its gabled porch, a gravel path forms the central axis of the garden, uniting spaces of different character. Yew hedges and low stone walls enclose a wide rectangle in front of the house, and plump birds of yew topiary guard the front door. An upper lawn has an old walnut tree and a box knot garden filled with herbs. To the side of the house a box parterre, almost certainly a Blomfield original, is planted with summer bedding. At its centre a circular stepped plinth edged with lavender has a 16th-century sundial. Behind the parterre a south-facing border is planted with *Berberis thunbergii*, pale orange kniphofias, *Rosa glauca*, hollyhocks, potentillas and *Lychnis chalcedonica*. In one corner a stone gardener's bothy, swathed in climbing roses, has a collection of old garden tools. From the forecourt the gravel path leads into a formal orchard whose rows of trees are underplanted with daffodils and scillas. Shrub roses are planted along one side and beehives sit among the trees. This, too, is enclosed in yew hedges, which curve round in a semicircle at its southern extremity. This circular shape is repeated on the far side of the house where Blomfield devised a most elegant car entrance and turnaround. The pattern of yew hedges and stone walls, often ornamented with stone cannon balls, is very attractive and suits the house perfectly. The planting, while intermittently pretty, does not rise to this level of architectural distinction; this could be the framework for an outstanding garden.

Location Sulgrave, nr Banbury OX17 2SD, Northamptonshire **OS** SP5645 7m NE of Banbury by B4525; Jnct 11 of M40 **Tel** 01295 760205 **Fax** 01295 768056 **English Heritage Register** Grade II **Owner** Colonial Dames of America **Open** Apr to Oct, daily except Wed 2–5.30 (Sat and Sun 10.30–1 and 2–5.30); Nov, Dec and Mar, Sat and Sun 10.30–1 and 2–4.30 **Area** 2 acres/0.8 hectares

UPTON HOUSE

BEYOND THE GREAT LAWN OF THE LATE 17TH-CENTURY HOUSE A DAZZLING PATCHWORK OF EDWARDIAN GARDENS AND MORE RECENT PLANTING PLUMMETS DOWN THE SLOPE BELOW

The flavour of Upton House and its landscape is vividly given in a painting of 1803 by Anthony Devis, which may still be seen at the house. It is a charming winter scene, with skaters on a frozen lake, a dapper columned temple on its bank, rows of trees on either side, and the house commanding an eminence behind. The house, dating from 1695, was built for Sir Rushout Cullen, possibly to the designs of Francis Smith of Warwick. It was remodelled by Percy Morley Horder in neo-Georgian style, and greatly increased in size, when the estate was bought by Walter Samuel, 2nd Viscount Bearsted, in 1927. Lord Bearsted gave the estate to the National Trust on his death in 1948.

A DAZZLING PATCHWORK
Morley Horder designed the broad paved terraces which run along the south façade of the house, overlooking a great lawn. The terrace is bright with flowers, in particular roses, with underplantings of artemisia, nepeta and pinks. Stately cedars of Lebanon, some going back to the 18th century, fringe the lawn. All this gives the impression of a set piece, with no particular encouragement to explore. In fact, beyond the edge of the lawn

The forecourt at Sulgrave Manor

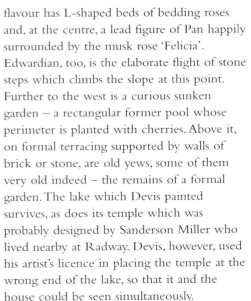

flavour has L-shaped beds of bedding roses and, at the centre, a lead figure of Pan happily surrounded by the musk rose 'Felicia'. Edwardian, too, is the elaborate flight of stone steps which climbs the slope at this point. Further to the west is a curious sunken garden – a rectangular former pool whose perimeter is planted with cherries. Above it, on formal terracing supported by walls of brick or stone, are old yews, some of them very old indeed – the remains of a formal garden. The lake which Devis painted survives, as does its temple which was probably designed by Sanderson Miller who lived nearby at Radway. Devis, however, used his artist's licence in placing the temple at the wrong end of the lake, so that it and the house could be seen simultaneously.

Location Banbury OX15 6HT, Warwickshire **OS** SP3746 7m NW of Banbury by A422 **Tel** 01295 670266 **Email** uptonhouse@ntrust.org.uk **English Heritage Register** Grade II* **Owner** The National Trust **Open** Apr to Oct, Sat to Wed 2–6 (open Good Fri) **Area** 19 acres/8 hectares

WARWICK CASTLE

A CASTLE DATING BACK TO THE 11TH CENTURY (WITH A NORMAN MOUND), AN EXQUISITE CAPABILITY BROWN LANDSCAPE (PAINTED BY CANALETTO), A MAGNIFICENT ORANGERY AND PARTERRE, AND A MAGICAL VICTORIAN ROSE GARDEN

The irrepressible Horace Walpole, writing to his friend George Montague, when he visited Warwick Castle in 1751, describes the scene: "The castle is enchanting; the view pleased me more than I can express; the river Avon tumbles down a cascade at the foot of it. It is well laid out by one Brown…One sees what the prevalence of taste does." The castle – "the most perfect piece of castellated antiquity in the kingdom", as John Byng called it in 1785 – goes back to William the Conqueror. Although most of the surviving building dates from the 14th century, features of the 11th century, such as the mound, may still be seen. Much has been added subsequently but its medieval character remains pervasive. Plainly this was a full-blooded fortified castle,

The borders at Upton

the land falls away into a valley and it is here, on the south-facing slopes, that the true garden excitement of Upton begins. Formal steps and a balustrade entwined with wisteria lead down to a dazzling patchwork of gardens. The protected slope had in the past been devoted to kitchen gardening, which is still practised with exemplary skill, but much of the area has now been given over to ornamental purposes. A pair of herbaceous borders, designed by Kitty Lloyd Jones, plummet down the slope. The borders are filled with achilleas, campanulas, *Echinops ritro*, geraniums, kniphofias and repeated plants of *Kolkwitzia amabilis* and of cardoons. At the bottom is a copper beech and views over a pool

dappled with waterlilies. The slopes to one side are terraced, with many tender plants thriving in the shelter of the walls – such as *Drimys winteri*, *Campsis radicans*, *Carpenteria californica* and *Hoheria lyallii*. This is not a warm part of the country, the garden is 600ft up and winters are cold.

At the foot of the slope, close to the water, is the kitchen garden, a business-like affair growing many different vegetables and soft fruits. At its west end a border contains a National Collection of Michaelmas daisies (*Aster amellus*, *A. cordifolius* and *A. ericoides* cultivars). Nearby, enclosed in a yew hedge, a paved rose garden of Edwardian

An exotic bench

occupying as it does a position of strength, with long views, above the river banks.

There were gardens at Warwick Castle certainly by the 16th century and a map of 1711 by James Fish and Charles Bridgeman shows an elaborate pattern of formal gardens running along the river to the west of the castle. It was this area that was the scene of some of Capability Brown's work that was carried out in the late 1740s. Canaletto's painting of 1753 shows this area masked by picturesque clumps of trees, with further groups of trees following the path that winds up the Norman mound. Visitors today may stand on the top of the mound and see evidence of Brown's later work: the river winding among belts of trees, with fine individual trees in pastures on its far bank, and in the distance more belts of trees and the Cotswold hills. It is one of the grandest views from any city in the country.

Later in the 18th century a superlative orangery was built to the design of the Warwick architect William Eboral. The Earl of Warwick wrote in 1788: "I built a noble green house, and…placed in it a vase considered as the finest remains of Grecian art extant for its size and beauty." This was the Warwick Vase – the huge Roman (as it turned out) vase which had been found at Hadrian's Villa; a facsimile is displayed in the conservatory but the original is now

The rose garden at Warwick Castle

in the Burrell Collection in Glasgow. With its magnificent Gothic tracery windows, now beautifully restored, the conservatory houses a collection of tender plants, some of them very unusual. Here are bananas, Arabian jasmine (*Jasminum sambac*), Jamaican cherry (*Ficus citrifolia*) and the giant fronds of *Strelitzia nicolai* – big plants for a big space. It overlooks a deep paved terrace giving views of a magnificent parterre designed by Robert Marnock in 1868. At its centre a round lily

The orangery parterre

pool and fountain are surrounded by parterre-like segmental beds of clipped yew. In the upper part the hedges are waist high with swathes of floribunda roses filling the compartments. The tops of the hedges are crowned from time to time with a triumphan topiary bird. Real birds play their part, too, for languid peacocks pose here and there, sometimes sprawling on the top of a hedge with tail spread expansively behind. The lower part of the parterre has lower hedges forming compartments that are filled sometimes with a single variety of rose or sometimes with white roses in the middle and scarlet pelargoniums in minor outlying compartments. All this is a tasty prelude to the view to the south that has been opened out so that Pageant Field, an interrupted slope of grass, leads between clumps of trees down to a curve of the river with glimpses of the Castle Park on its far side. *The Gardener's Chronicle* in 1882 described this scene as "one that is not easily surpassed in loveliness".

A HIDDEN ROSE GARDEN

In the 1980s a distinguished feature of the garden was recreated after the discovery in Warwickshire County Record Office of designs made in 1868 by Robert Marnock for a formal rose garden, which had been removed in the 1930s. This, hidden away in woods to the north of the castle, has now been triumphantly reinstated under the supervision of Paul Edwards. It is arranged like a parterre, with a pattern of beds cut into turf, gravel walks, and roses in box-edged beds, soaring on pillars or tumbling from arbours. Many old roses are used, such as 'Adélaïde d'Orléans' and 'The Garland' but also David Austin's English Roses, among them the richly scented pink 'Warwick Castle'. The crisp geometry of the rose garden's layout contrasted with the lavish abundance of the roses make it a dazzling success. To one side, of a slightly later date, is a fine rock garden and pool, the work of James Backhouse & Co of York in about 1900.

Warwick Castle and its immediate surroundings were sold by the 7th Earl of Warwick to the Tussauds Group in 1979. Its condition today, in particular that of the gardens, which have been finely restored and are impeccably maintained, shows that its transformation into a commercial tourist attraction has had a most happy outcome.

Location Warwick CV34 4QU, Warwickshire **OS** SP2864 In the centre of Warwick; Jnct 15 of M40 **Tel** 01926 495421 **Fax** 01926 401692 **English Heritage Register** Grade I **Owner** The Tussauds Group **Open** Apr to Oct, daily 10–6; Nov to Mar, daily 10–5 (closed 25 Dec) **Area** 60 acres/24 hectares

WIGHTWICK MANOR

House and garden, created by an admirer of John Ruskin and William Morris, the epitome of high Victorian decorative taste

Wightwick Manor, with its garden, is a feast of high-minded Victorian taste. It is rare in England to find a house and garden – made together in a relatively short burst of activity – that so vividly and so enjoyably evoke the spirit of their time. Theodore Mander made a fortune out of paint and was filled with excitement by the ideas of John Ruskin and William Morris. He bought the land at Wightwick in 1887 and commissioned a house from Edward Ould, whose firm,

Grayson & Ould of Chester and Liverpool, was a leading designer in the renaissance of half-timbered "old English" houses. The style of architecture at Wightwick is extravagantly vernacular, with lavish use of half-timbering, hung tiles, leaded lights, tall decorated brick chimneys, elaborate barge-boards and pinnacled gables. The interior, with its stained glass by C.E. Kempe and its fabrics and furniture from the Morris workshop, is the epitome of high Victorian decorative taste.

Gardens to match the house

The gardens are of the same date as the house, with Alfred Parsons, a founder member of the Art Workers Guild, starting work on the formal gardens west of the house in 1887. He laid out a rose garden hidden behind zigzag yew hedging – a central circular rose arbour edged with rose beds with columnar yews. An inconspicuous passage leads through to a yew and holly walk – the holly, clipped into majestic haystack shapes, is the golden variegated *Ilex aquifolium* 'Golden Queen', sparkling and sumptuous against the sombre yew. At the end of the walk is the curious rustic Grigg House, whose roof is thatched in heather ("grig" is an old English word meaning heather). Here is a wild garden of streams and pools with many good trees, an

orchard underplanted with daffodils and a curious crescent of "ice-age boulders". A later addition to the garden was made in 1910 by Thomas Mawson who laid out the paved and turfed south terrace. In the beds below the terrace, between buttresses of yew, are plants that came from writers' gardens – from, among others, Dickens's garden at Rochester, William Morris's Kelmscott and Tennyson's garden at Farringford House. On the lawn below, Mawson pulled off a theatrical flourish – a procession of drums of clipped yew marching away from the house; they are now grown so close together as to be almost touching.

Anyone contemplating a visit to Wightwick should under no circumstances miss a visit to the house – a wonderful shrine to the taste of its time – and there are memorably atmospheric views of the garden glimpsed through the leaded lights.

Location Wightwick Bank, Wolverhampton WV6 8EE, West Midlands **OS** SO8698 3m W of Wolverhampton by A454 **Tel** 01902 761108 **Infoline** 01902 761108 **Fax** 01902 764663 **Email** wightwickmanor@ntrust.org.uk **English Heritage Register** Grade II **Owner** The National Trust **Open** Mar to Dec, Wed and Thur 11–6, Sat and Bank Hol Mon 1–6 **Area** 10 acres/4 hectares

The south garden at Wightwick Manor

EAST of ENGLAND

ANGLESEY ABBEY

MAGNIFICENT AVENUES, LIVELY BORDERS
AND A BEAUTIFUL WINTER GARDEN

The garden at Anglesey Abbey, like many distinguished British gardens, was made by an amateur. The ancient estate, with its medieval and 17th-century buildings, was bought in 1926 by Huttleston Broughton, later 1st Lord Fairhaven. Lord Fairhaven laid out a thoroughly original garden on the scale of a great 18th-century landscape park but using the crisply formal language of an earlier period. It is one of the largest, most ambitious and most original private gardens made in the 20th century.

This part of the Cambridgeshire fens is as flat as a pancake, offering no advantages of site to the large-scale landscaper, and the problem of animating such a large area of featureless, windswept land is not one that many gardeners have to confront. Lord Fairhaven sensed that the best solution was to make bold avenues to divide the land and create vistas, adding distinguished statuary to act as eyecatchers and as decorative interludes. Two great avenues of horse chestnuts form the main axes of the garden: the Coronation Avenue running east and west for half a mile was planted to celebrate King George VI's coronation in 1937, and has the Cross Avenue cutting across it. Smaller avenues, of limes

The Winter Walk at Anglesey Abbey

(*Tilia × europaea* 'Pallida'), hornbeam or holm oak, make lighter brush-strokes in the scene. Sculptures and architectural fragments are skilfully woven into this framework – marking the meeting place of two avenues, forming a punctuation mark where they end, or flanking an opening. These, of fine quality, have a superb presence when used in conjunction with the trees. More intimate enclosures are also often enlivened by ornaments – a circle of pale columns on Temple Lawn, a row of white marble urns against a yew hedge on the Rose Garden lawn, and a solemn procession of twelve busts of caesars in the Emperors' Walk.

One of the great pleasures of Anglesey is the generous use of bulbous plants – chionodoxas, cyclamens, fritillaries, leucojums, narcissi, scillas and snowdrops planted in huge swathes among the trees. Close to the house there are formal flower gardens, among them a notable curved herbaceous border behind a horseshoe of beech hedging. To one side another curved beech hedge runs behind a bed filled with different cultivars of dahlia. Beautifully clipped and shaped yew hedges enclose a parterre-like arrangement of shaped beds in turf, which are planted in spring with blue and white hyacinths followed by a summer planting of yellow and red dahlias. The beautiful bronze urns here are copies of the 17th-century Versailles originals made for

the Bagatelle gardens in the Bois de Boulogne in the 19th century.

An admirable new garden has been made by the National Trust since 1998. The Winter Walk is a winding path that runs along the eastern boundary of the garden. The planting, in bold groups, of winter-flowering bulbs, herbaceous perennials and shrubs, and of trees and shrubs with beautiful bark or fine berries, is beautifully done. There is much skilful association. One of the most memorable groups has a grove of silver-stemmed Himalayan birch (*Betula utilis* var. *jacquemontii*), thickets of *Cornus alba* 'Kesselringii', with blackish purple shoots, all underplanted with the purple foliage of *Bergenia purpurascens*.

However, the formal gardens and the Winter Walk, though very attractive, have none of the drama of the great garden of avenues. The most exhilarating pleasures at Anglesey come from the spectacle of these avenues quartering the land, their trees challenging the broad horizons; from their attendant ornaments; and in spring from the prodigal scattering of bulbs. It recalls the great days of garden-making – will any private individual ever again make a garden on this heroic scale?

Location Lode, nr Cambridge CB5 9EJ, Cambridgeshire **OS** TL5262 In Lode village, 6m NE of Cambridge by B1102 **Tel** and **Fax** 01223 811200 **Email** angleseyabbey@ntrust.org.uk **English Heritage Register** Grade II* **Owner** The National Trust **Open** early Jan to late Mar, late Oct to late Dec, Thur to Sun 10.30–dusk; late Mar to early Jul, late Sept to late Oct, Wed to Sun (open Bank Hol Mon) 10.30–5.30; early Jul to mid Sept, daily 10.30–5.30 **Area** 100 acres/40 hectares

AUDLEY END HOUSE

A CAPABILITY BROWN PARK,
DAZZLING FLOWER PARTERRE AND
ELYSIAN WATER GARDEN

Audley End has seen as many changes as any estate in England. There were settlements here in the Iron Age and during the Roman occupation. In the 12th century a Benedictine priory was founded (later elevated to the status of Walden Abbey), which passed to the Audley family, one of whose daughters married a Howard. The present house is essentially Jacobean, built between 1605 and 1614 by Thomas Howard, 1st Earl of Suffolk and Lord Treasurer to James I. (When King James came to see the house he is said to have remarked that it was too big for a king but about right for a Lord Treasurer.) What survives today is only a modest part, the central court, of the 17th-century house.

A contemporary drawing shows a suitably grand formal garden disposed about the axis of the house in renaissance style. In the early 18th century a new formal garden was laid out, possibly to the designs of Charles Bridgeman – a visitor referred to it in 1731 as "prettily improved and a very genteel spot". Later in the 18th century major changes were made by Sir John Griffin Griffin (later 4th Lord Howard de Walden and 1st Baron Braybrooke). From 1763 he employed Capability Brown to remove the formal gardens and it is his work that dominates the landscape today. Brown, most unusually, had an acrimonious disagreement with his client and later withdrew from the contract, but his original schemes were implemented and, as Dorothy Stroud wrote in her *Capability Brown* (1975), "the calm scene in which the house

The parterre at Audley End

stands today gives no hint of the recriminations which attended its creation." A painting by Edmund Garvey, made in 1782, shows the Brown landscape in its heyday, with the river Cam, whose course Brown had serpentined, spanned by the bridge which Robert Adam designed in 1764, and long belts and bushy clumps of trees. Another beautiful building by Robert Adam survives – the domed and pillared Temple of Victory (built in 1772 to celebrate the end of the Seven Years' War in 1763).

Sometime after Brown's work, in the 1780s, the intriguing Elysian Garden was designed by Richard Woods and Placido Columbani on the banks of the river north-west of the house. Originally a tunnel of evergreens led to winding walks wandering among beds of sweet smelling flowers, with a statue of Flora, a Turkish tent and a Coade stone altar (which survives elsewhere in the garden). Although much of the detail is missing, the layout of the Elysian Garden is substantially intact. Water erupts from a rustic cascade (designed by Woods) on the Cam and the pool below is crossed by a delightful covered bridge – the Palladian Teahouse Bridge, designed by Robert Adam in 1782. Superb London planes stand on either side of the river – the one on

the west bank exceptional, with immense spreading branches.

East of the house a new parterre was laid out in around 1831, based on a design from an 18th-century pattern book and with advice from William Sawrey Gilpin. This was reinstated from 1989 after an archaeological dig revealed the original pattern of the parterre. Shaped beds are cut into the turf, some planted with brilliant annuals and some with herbaceous perennials and roses. From here the ground to the east slopes up to a long gravel walk above a ha-ha. In the East Park the Temple of Concord was built in 1790 to Robert Brettingham's design to celebrate George III's return to sanity, and in the old deer park to the north is Lady Portsmouth's Column, designed by Robert Adam in 1774 for Sir John Griffin Griffin who wished to honour his aunt who had bequeathed the Audley End estate to him. A curiosity in the woods to one side of the parterre is a very rare oak – *Quercus × audleyensis*, a hybrid between the holm oak (*Quercus ilex*) and the sessile oak (*Q. petraea*).

THE ORGANIC GARDEN

Behind the stable block, the kitchen gardens are enclosed in beautiful brick walls dating from the 18th and 19th centuries. They are now cultivated by the HDRA organic gardening organisation which has restored a superb lean-to vinery, dating from 1802, in which late and early peaches and table grapes are cultivated, and a "show house" containing pot-grown tender ornamentals. Behind the vinery, against the north-facing wall, are the "back sheds" – the gardeners' bothy, potting shed, boiler room, mushroom cellar, tool shed and head gardener's office.

Since 1948 Audley End has belonged to the state, latterly under the management of English Heritage. The gardens are now excellently cared for and are among the most diversely attractive of any estate in the country.

Location Audley End, nr Saffron Walden CB11 4JF, Essex **OS** TL5238 1m W of Saffron Walden by B1383 **English Heritage Register** Grade I **Tel** 01799 522842 **Infoline** 01799 522399 **Fax** 01799 521276 **Owner** English Heritage **Open** Apr to Sept, Wed to Sun (open Bank Hol Mon) 11–6 **Area** 50 acres/20 hectares

AYSCOUGHFEE HALL

A CHARMING PUBLIC GARDEN WITH ANCIENT
YEW HEDGES, FORMAL ROSE GARDENS AND A
FINE LUTYENS WAR MEMORIAL

The first house on the site was built in the
1430s by a wool merchant, Richard
Alwyn, but the estate changed hands many
times and many alterations were made to the
house. In the 17th century it was acquired by
Maurice Johnson, a barrister and antiquary,
who had married the heiress to the estate and
came to live here in 1685. Johnson took great
interest in the garden and a map of 1732
shows it occupying the same area as it does
today, with a lake, square flower beds, a
kitchen garden and an orchard. The design of
the garden is attributed to a Spalding
architect, William Sands, and it was about this
time that the extraordinary yew walks were
planted (ring-dating suggests a date of around
1725). John Byng saw them on his visit to
Spalding in 1790: "As I enter'd the town, I
had observ'd a very ancient house of bay
windows, surrounded by yew hedge gardens."
In 1898 Isabella Johnson sold the estate to a
group of local citizens and it was transferred
to the Spalding Urban District Council in
1902. The gardens were immediately opened
to the public and the house became a
museum and art gallery.

With its brilliant bedding schemes, the

⊲ **The war memorial** at Ayscoughfee Hall

garden has a municipal flavour – but
unexpected pleasures are in store. The old yew
hedges, now wide and tall and billowing out
into bulges and lumps, remain a lovely feature.
A long sunken canal with a three-tiered
fountain has at its head a noble war memorial
designed by Sir Edwin Lutyens in around
1925: the loggia-like pavilion, with Doric
columns and arches, pantiled roof and grandly
vaulted interior has a decidedly Italian flavour,
while the floor is paved with stone and strips
of herringbone brick in typical Lutyens
fashion. Nearby is a garden celebrating fifty
years of peace (1945–1995), with a pretty
pattern of box-edged beds filled with roses
and bedding schemes and an obelisk at its
centre. To one side of the garden is a tall 19th-
century stone drinking fountain.

The garden now has the role of a public
park and its attractions include an aviary of
exotic birds, tennis courts, a putting green and
a superb bowling green below the east façade
of the house. The museum is largely devoted
to local history and natural history and has a
fascinating exhibit devoted to the draining of
the fens in South Holland – which began in
the 7th century when it was realised that
arable farming and grazing were far more

lucrative than wildfowling and which, much
later, permitted the establishment of bulb
nurseries (especially for tulips).

Location Churchgate, Spalding PE11 2RA, Lincolnshire
OS TF2522 In the centre of Spalding **Tel** 01775 725468
Fax 01775 762715 **Website** www.sholland.gov.uk
English Heritage Register Grade II **Owner** South
Holland District Council **Open** daily dawn–dusk
Area 7 acres/3 hectares

BELTON HOUSE

18TH-CENTURY LANDSCAPE PARK AND
EXUBERANT VICTORIAN GARDENS FOR A
GRAND HOUSE

The house at Belton is very beautiful –
late 17th-century, built of pale honey-
coloured Ancaster stone for Sir John
Brownlow and possibly designed by William
Winde. There were once grand formal gardens
here of a similar date to the house but these
were removed in the landscaping carried out
by William Emes after 1778. Occasional but
attractive garden features survive, however,
from before this date. On a rise in the distance,
for example, at the end of what remains of

The orangery garden at Belton House

Belmount Avenue east of the house, is the eyecatcher once known as Lord Brownlow's Breeches (properly Belmount Tower) — an ungainly arch surmounted by an upper room with a Venetian window, built in 1759 by the mason William Grey; north of the avenue, at the head of a narrow canal, is a charming mid 18th-century stone temple with a rusticated arch and flanking wings with blind arches, very much in the style of William Kent; and, to the west of the house, in the Wilderness by the river Witham, a rustic cascade and sham ruin of advanced picturesque taste dates from 1742.

THE VICTORIAN GARDENS

The gardens round the house are today mainly of the 19th century. Between the house and the church, overlooking a walled garden, is a fine conservatory — originally either an orangery or a camellia house — by Jeffry Wyatville (1820). He also laid out the formal garden here, with a sunken circular pool and fountain — a single high jet of water. Beds edging the pool are planted with *Dahlia* 'Bishop of Llandaff' and a rich purple sage, and the gravel path encircling the pool has a low wall planted with Bowles' golden grass (*Carex elata* 'Aurea') and a hedge of *Prunus cerasifera* 'Nigra'. Gold variegated ivy is clipped close to the wall and stone urns on its top are filled with annuals. The surrounding lawns are adorned with mounds of clipped box and dumpy columns of yew and the southern side of the conservatory garden is enlivened by a curved stone screen with arched niches containing pots filled with *Bidens ferulifolia*, pelargoniums or small-leafed ivy.

A garden of similarly boisterous Victorian character forms a vista north of the house. This, the so-called Dutch Garden, is a late 19th-century arrangement with a broad gravel walk running along an avenue of columns of clipped yew interspersed with mounds of golden yew. Handsome statues and stone urns rise on plinths, and behind them broad bands of lavender surround beds of yellow argyranthemums, from which rise stone troughs filled with cherry-pie (*Heliotropium arborescens*) and standard white roses emerging from drifts of catmint. All this is backed by crisp yew hedges and the atmosphere smacks somewhat of a public garden. But then, a

great house like Belton would have been geared to the entertainment of its guests, especially in the late 19th century, and the gardens would be planned to receive, and impress, large numbers of visitors. Which is exactly what they do today.

Location nr Grantham NG32 2LS, Lincolnshire
OS SK9339 3m NE of Grantham by A607 **Tel** and **Fax** 01476 566116 **Email** belton@ntrust.org.uk **English Heritage Register** Grade I **Owner** The National Trust **Open** Apr to Oct, Wed to Sun (open Bank Hol Mon) 11–5.30; early Nov to late Dec, Sat and Sun 12–4 **Area** 100 acres/40 hectares

BENINGTON LORDSHIP

FORMAL FLOWER GARDENS, A ROSE GARDEN AND LIVELY HERBACEOUS BORDERS

This is a delightful, unassuming place whose subtle charms have a cumulative effect. The house is very good-looking — early 18th-century with a neo-Georgian wing added in 1906 to take advantage of the beautiful views facing west over the valley — and the site interesting, with the remains of a Norman castle. Built onto the 11th-century keep of the castle is a startling flight of fancy: a neo-Norman sham ruin of flint and Pulhamite (indeed James Pulham himself

The rose garden at Benington Lordship

seems to have been the clerk-of-works for the building when it was put up in 1832) in the form of a truncated gatehouse. The entrance is enclosed by a Norman arch, there is a statue of Buddha within, and an ancient tombstone with a Greek inscription.

The garden as it is today takes every advantage of its picturesque setting, but it has been made almost entirely since Harry and Sarah Bott came here in 1971. The former moat of the castle ("cleared with the help of a goat") is densely planted with snowdrops — for which there are special openings in February or March. These are followed by an astonishing spread of the pale blue east European squill (*Scilla bithynica*), flowering among drifts of daffodils. The south façade of the house overlooks a rose garden with a central sundial surrounded by beds of pale pink roses underplanted with irises and edged in lavender. The plinth of the sundial is edged with bergenias (a very Gertrude Jekyll effect) and in summer pots of agapanthus. The land begins to fall away below the rose garden, with views over pools and thickets of alders and willows to long views of the rural landscape. At the top of the slope a path leads purposefully eastwards past a curious early 18th-century figure of Pantalon by John

Cheere surrounded by 'Iceberg' roses and Madonna lilies and a hedge of germander (*Teucrium × lucidrys*). Beyond it, before you arrive at the entrance to the walled kitchen garden, you are ambushed by a surprise – the path cuts across a pair of lavish herbaceous borders running along the outside wall of the kitchen garden. These existed before the Botts came but had been horribly neglected; now comprehensively replanted, they present a cataract of colour tumbling down the slope. The walled garden is still partly given over to fruit and vegetables but is also used for nursery purposes, and there are a few plants for sale.

The rare setting, the delight in good plants and the unassuming charm of the place give Benington great character.

Location Benington, nr Stevenage SG2 7BS, Hertfordshire **OS** TL2923 4m E of Stevenage by minor roads; signed from Watton-at-Stone **Tel** 01438 869668 **Fax** 01438 869622 **Email** rhbott@beningtonlordship.co.uk **Website** www.beningtonlordship.co.uk **English Heritage Register** Grade II **Owner** Mr and Mrs C.H.A. Bott **Open** Apr to Aug, Wed and Bank Hol Mon 12–5, Sun 2–5; Sept, Wed 12–5 (Phone for snowdrop openings in Feb or Mar) **Area** 7 acres/2.8 hectares

BLICKLING HALL

EXQUISITE JACOBEAN HOUSE WITH A SPLENDID FLOWER PARTERRE AND WOODLAND WALKS

Blickling is marvellously beautiful; however often you see it, its sudden revelation from the road will make you catch your breath. The house, bristling with gables, turrets and chimneys, is framed in ancient, immensely wide yew hedges which were already in place in 1745. The house was built between 1618 and 1629 for Sir Henry Hobart to the designs of Robert Lyminge, the architect of another great house of the period – Hatfield (*see page 306*). With its pink-brown brick and pale stone dressings, Blickling combines decorative exuberance with a peacefully rural air; it has devastating charm.

This was not the first house on the site and there has been parkland here since the 12th century, but nothing is known in detail about the landscape before the 17th century when most of the garden activity was on the east side of the house – as it is today. There are signs of 18th-century landscaping, including a curious formal scheme dating from early in the century, and in the early 19th century John Adey Repton advised on some decorative schemes – a picturesque trelliswork pergola and Hardenberg baskets –

drawings of which survive at the house today.

In 1856 the Marquess of Lothian, who had inherited the estate, came to live at Blickling and started a long process of renovation. In the 1860s he introduced formal rides, in the form of *pattes d'oie*, in the woodland to the east of the house, harking back to the 18th-century garden. In the 1870s the east garden was redesigned by Matthew Digby Wyatt and Markham Nesfield with terracing, steps and a parterre, much as it is today, and the planting was devised by Lady Lothian herself. The parterre itself, in true renaissance style, is exactly the width of the house and lies handsomely spread out below the long façade of the house. Lady Lothian's scheme, on the other hand, bore no relation to the character of its setting. It presented a riot of ornament – an immensely fussy pattern of flower beds and topiary spreading around the splendid central 17th-century fountain (bought in the Oxnead Hall sale of 1732). Christopher Hussey, writing in *Country Life* in 1930, referred despairingly to the "multiplicity of dotted beds". In 1932 Norah Lindsay was asked to simplify the parterre, which she did with great success, and it is her design that survives today. She retained the bold shapes of yew topiary – "grand-pianos" and rounded cones – and divided the area into four square beds with a yew cone at

The parterre at Blickling

ach corner. The beds are edged in strips of
oses and catmint and richly planted with
nixed woody and herbaceous plants graded in
ze so that in high summer they form a
oriferous brilliantly coloured pyramid. The
eds close to the house are chiefly planted in
ink, mauve and blue, and those further away
n yellow and orange. The strong design and
isciplined but luxuriantly decorative planting
orm a perfect accompaniment to the house.

The parterre shares an axis with the Temple
Valk which Norah Lindsay also advised on.
teps lead up to the walk which pierces
voodland and ends in a pedimented temple
f *c.*1730. Mrs Lindsay removed the rows of
onifers that lined the walk to reveal the
andsome woodland trees behind. She also
ntroduced azaleas about the temple and along
he subsidiary walks (reinstated in the 19th
entury) that thread the woods on either side.
ll this presents a scene of great variety and
armony, in which the formality of the past is
ombined with lively 20th-century planting.
bove all, it holds its own alongside the
plendour of the house.

ocation Blickling, Norwich NR11 6NF, Norfolk
S TG1728 15m N of Norwich Tel 01263 738030
ax 01263 731660 Email blickling@ntrust.org.uk
nglish Heritage Register Grade II* Owner The
National Trust Open (garden) Apr to Oct, Wed to Sun
(open Bank Hol Mon and Tue in Aug); (park and woods)
daily dawn–dusk Area 46 acres/19 hectares

BRADENHAM HALL

OUTSTANDING TREE COLLECTION AND
EXCELLENT FORMAL GARDENS, BEAUTIFULLY
KEPT BY PRIVATE OWNERS

The distinguished 1740s house is
embowered in trees and serenely faces
south, past a majestic cedar of Lebanon, over a
giant lawn with flanking trees towards the
rural landscape beyond a ha-ha. Such a view is
to many people the *beau idéal* of the English
country house. What is remarkable about the
garden, however, is what has been introduced
by Lieutentant Colonel and Mrs Allhusen
since they came here in 1951 – both the
outstanding collection of trees and the well-
judged formal gardens by the house. Not
many people were planting new arboreta just
after World War II but the Allhusens got to
work quickly, as the garden's tree catalogue
shows. In the 1950s they planted, among
much else, cherries, crataegus, several cultivars
of Lawson cypress, firs, hornbeams, junipers,
limes, maples, oaks and rowans. With many of

The great lawn at Bradenham Hall

these now grown to fine size, and with
countless subsequent additions, the garden
boasts one of the most attractive private tree
collections in the country. Some genera are
particularly well represented – 40 species and
cultivars of oak, over 50 prunus (with a
splendid range of Japanese flowering cherries),
40 spruce, well over 30 beeches (most of
which are cultivars of *Fagus sylvatica*) and over
80 acers. They are for the most part grouped
either side of the lawn in front of the house
and along the entrance drive, and although
impeccably but unobtrusively labelled, do not
give the impression of a purely botanical
collection. Arranged in naturalistic groves,
they play their part in the character of the
landscape and, in particular, the setting of
the 18th-century house.

To the east of the house are formal gardens
of a quite different character. A broad grass
path forms the chief axis here, and on one
side a long mixed border, with a passage in its
centre, has a background of such bold shrubs
as *Abutilon vitifolium*, *Escallonia* 'Iveyi', *Cotinus
coggygria* Rubrifolius Group and *Staphylea
colchica*. Achilleas, agapanthus, *Crocosmia*
'Lucifer', daylilies, delphiniums, *Geranium
psilostemon* and *Helenium* 'Moerheim Beauty'

are among the herbaceous plants that create high summer drama. On the other side of the grass walk are yew hedges, and at the far end of the walk, where the hedge curves in a semicircle, a statue of Apollo rises on a plinth.

Leading off the walk is a sequence of hidden enclosures all hedged in yew. Rows of apples and crab-apples make a delightful background for a large collection of roses – mostly old-fashioned shrub roses. A walk of pleached limes, underplanted with spring bulbs, runs up to a classical statue. A paved garden is divided into four with mop-headed *Prunus fruticosa* 'Globosa', and tender plants in pots are arranged on the paving stones – lemon verbena, *Melianthus major* and *Solanum rantonnetii*. A private swimming pool and tennis court are also concealed behind hedges. Bradenham Hall is still very much a private garden and this is the source of much of its charm.

Location West Bradenham, Thetford IP25 7PQ, Norfolk **OS** TF9308 18m N of Thetford, 6m E of Swaffham by A47 **Tel** 01362 687279 **Fax** 01362 687669 **Owner** C. Allhusen **Open** Apr to Sept, 2nd, 4th and 5th Sun in each month 2–5.30 **Area** 27 acres/11 hectares

BURGHLEY HOUSE

SUPERB ANCIENT PARKLAND FOR A TUDOR PALACE, WITH A CAPABILITY BROWN PARK AND MODERN SCULPTURE GARDEN

In his *Tour Through England and Wales* (1724–27) Daniel Defoe described Burghley as "More like a town than a house…the towers and pinnacles so high, and placed at such a distance from one another…Like so many distant parish churches". The great house was built from the 1550s for William Cecil (later 1st Lord Burghley) and although altered in the late 17th century and in the 1750s by Capability Brown, it has kept its essentially Tudor character. Celia Fiennes visited Burghley in 1697 and was

▷ **The Burghley boathouse**

Sculpture in the lake at Burghley

full of admiration: "the Gardens very fine within one another with lower and higher walls deck'd with all sorts of trees and greens, very fine Gravel walks and Grass squaires with statues…very fine fountaines". Nothing remains of these gardens and nothing is known about any garden activity until 1754 when Capability Brown was consulted by the 9th Earl of Exeter (as this branch of the Cecils had become) about both house and landscape. This was one of the earliest commissions of Brown's career (he was thirty-eight at the time) and one of the longest lasting. Horace Walpole visited in 1763 and wrote, "A noble Pile! Brown is ornamenting the Park and has built a gothic greenhouse." The greenhouse, or orangery, with crenellations and turrets, survives east of the house. Brown also designed a summerhouse with a parapet of fretted stone and high pinnacles overlooking the lake to the south-east of the house and set among old cedars of Lebanon. The serpentine lake was Brown's work, as was the bridge which crosses it at the western end. In all, Brown worked for Lord Exeter for thirty years; it was one of the happiest associations of his career and Nathaniel Dance's portrait of Brown, commissioned by Lord Exeter, still hangs at Burghley.

The park is today one of the most beautiful in England, preserving ingredients from the 16th century, including a deer park of fallow deer and magnificent trees – cedars of Lebanon, limes, oaks, oriental planes and sweet chestnuts, some of which are the remains of old avenues. The site is relatively flat but there is just enough rise and fall to present varying prospects of the two great ornaments in the landscape: the house itself and Brown's serpentine lake.

The gardens close to the house are of relatively modest size. The north forecourt, laid out by Brown, has an oval lawn enclosed in a curve of wrought-iron railings; this is lined by a narrow box-edged rose bed filled with perpetual-flowering roses in blocks of a single colour. Behind the house a garden of 19th-century character, the South Garden, runs down to Brown's lake. Here, lawns, yew hedges, circular rose beds and Coade stone urns are disposed about an avenue of rounded shapes of clipped yew centred on the house. This part of the garden is open to the public in the month of April to take advantage of the large number of bulbs flowering at this time.

A new venture is a Sculpture Park on the north bank of the lake towards its eastern end. The sculptures, some for sale and some part of the garden's permanent collection, are arranged around a lakeside walk and in the woodland nearby. They are uneven in quality and their placing is often arbitrary. Perhaps the most memorable is Giles Kent's series of spiky shapes of oak half submerged in a stream flowing into the lake. Peter Randall-Page's turf maze, with no beginning and no end, forms a fine entrance to the garden. Views of the lake itself at this point are very beautiful, with clumps and belts of trees on the rising ground on its far side, and at the lake's eastern end is a rare, very ornate pedimented boathouse built of pale terracotta by Blackfield & Co of Stamford in 1871 and beautifully restored in 1999.

Although Burghley is rich in the past, it is exciting to see new initiatives in the landscape. The estate, too, is finely cared for.

Location nr Stamford PE9 3JY, Lincolnshire **OS** TF0406 1 mile E of Stamford on the B1443 **Tel** 01780 752451 **Fax** 01780 480125 **Email** burghley@burghley.co.uk **Website** www.burghley.co.uk **English Heritage Register** Grade II* **Owner** Burghley House Preservation Trust Ltd **Open** (park) daily 8–6; (sculpture garden) daily 10–4 (closes 5 in summer); (south garden) Apr, daily 10–5 **Area** 1,400 acres/567 hectares

CAMBRIDGE COLLEGE GARDENS

HIDDEN GARDENS, BOLD VIEWS AND BRILLIANT COLOUR-THEMED BORDERS AMONG WONDERFUL BUILDINGS

Cambridge is not as rich as Oxford in surviving college gardens and to look through old pictures of Cambridge colleges is a depressing experience – so many of the colleges had delightful gardens in the past, of which almost nothing remains today. Trinity College, for example, one of the richest and most distinguished colleges, once had interesting gardens (*see page 551*) but today, apart from river views and the splendid fountain in Great Court, there is little that is noteworthy. However, several of the colleges do have fine gardens with fascinating histories, and Cambridge can also boast that unique and most memorable feature – the Backs. The Backs and a few of the best college gardens are described below. In addition, the following college gardens are described in the Gazetteer that forms the

King's College from the Backs

second part of this book: Christ's College, King's College, Newnham College, Queens' College, Trinity College and Trinity Hall.

THE BACKS

The Backs is a sequence of gardens and green spaces that run along the winding river Cam behind college buildings, starting with St John's College to the north and ending with Queen's College to the south. They occupy a space of about 25 acres/10 hectares. Along their western boundary is Queen's Road, now choked with cars, but something of the Arcadian atmosphere survives, with groves of horse chestnuts, limes, London planes and willows framing remarkably beautiful views of college buildings across the river. The essential flavour of the Backs can be seen from here, but the college gardens along the Backs retain their individuality and all have their own entrances along Queen's Road, although these may be for college members only. (Entrance for visitors is normally by the main entrance to the college on the town side.) An engraving by Samuel and Nathaniel Buck of the Backs in 1743 shows the character which they preserve to this day, although at this time Queen's Road was a rural lane, with fields and trees to its west.

In 1779 Capability Brown was asked to prepare a scheme for landscaping the Backs. Brown's plan shows the whole area between the river and modern Queen's Road laid out like a landscape park, with the river standing in as a lake and with clumps of trees breaking up the greensward and occasionally coming right down to the river banks. The route of Queen's Road was to be planted on either side with regular lines of trees, as were the lanes to the west (modern West Road and Madingley Road), but individual college gardens on this side of the river were to go. Brown's unifying scheme was not attractive to the colleges involved, which saw their identity in jeopardy. Furthermore, some regarded a landscape like that of a gentleman's rural seat to be an unsuitable environment for the serious world of scholarship. So Brown's plan was rejected, although the university made him a present of £50 (£2,988 in today's money). The view today of King's College across the Backs shows something of the effect that Brown sought – the college buildings are seen across pasture, with the occasional tree, like a country house in its park.

CLARE COLLEGE

The college was founded in 1326 but the earliest surviving buildings are of the 17th century. The college buildings are arranged on a single axis running from the entrance in Trinity Lane, over the noble bridge (1639–40 the earliest Cambridge bridge built in the classical style), across the Backs, to the 20th-century New Court west of Queen's Road. Celia Fiennes saw Clare Hall (as it then was) in 1697: "it is very little but most exactly neate; in all parts they have walks with rows of trees and bridges over the river and fine painted gates into the fields." There are still splendid wrought-iron gates and grilles at the entrance on Queen's Road but these were made in 1713–15. This axial walk was established in the 17th century but virtually all the detailed gardening dates from the 20th century. From the bridge there is a view of the garden of the Master's Lodge – a lawn and borders glimpsed through iron railings above the river. The Fellow's Garden lies off the axial walk on the west side of the river. Here, in an enclosure that dates from the late 17th century, is a garden that was designed by Professor Nevill Willmer from 1947. Willmer was interested in the effect of colour on the perception of distance – bright colours appearing closer and muted colours receding. He put these ideas into practice in the planting of borders and planned walks and

The Master's Lodge gardens at Clare College

vantage points so that composed views of the college were revealed. This, although still delightful, has become blurred with the passage of time and a ten-year plan to restore the garden is now underway, supervised by Elizabeth Banks Associates.

Location Trinity Lane CB2 1TL **OS** TL4458 **English Heritage Register** Grade II **Tel** 01223 333200 **Email** webmaster@clare.cam.ac.uk **Website** www.clare.cam.ac.uk **Open** Apr to Sept, daily 10–4.30

EMMANUEL COLLEGE

Emmanuel College was founded in 1584 and built on the site of a Dominican friary. The earliest surviving college buildings are of the 16th century but traces of the monastic site remain. Close to the college entrance Chapman's Garden has a curved pool, waterside planting and a backdrop of fine trees among which is a pair of beautiful tulip trees. In New Court, adjacent to Chapman's Garden, is an ingenious garden in the form of a modern knot designed in 1960 by John Codrington with slender triangular compartments of box hedging filled with culinary herbs – it is conveniently close to the college kitchen. This was an attractive idea to commemorate the founding of an Elizabethan college with a new version of the most striking garden features of that period. North-east of the college the Paddock is an immense lawn with flowering shrubs and trees. The pool, shown in Loggan's *Cantabrigia Illustrata*, was probably originally a monastic fishpond. It survives today, having been given its present shape in 1964 and planted with waterlilies and edged with moisture-loving plants. The walls that enclose the Paddock are at least in part of the middle ages – in the north-west corner they provide the handsome background to a splendid herbaceous border. Close to the college chapel (designed by Sir Christopher Wren in 1666) is another fine herbaceous border. Most of the horticultural charms of Emmanuel College are of the 20th century and they provide an excellent example of how to use spaces enclosed by beautiful architecture.

Location St Andrew's Street CB2 3AP **OS** TL4458 **English Heritage Register** Grade II* **Tel** 01223 334200 **Email** webmaster@emma.cam.ac.uk **Website** www.emma.cam.ac.uk **Open** daily 9–5

ST JOHN'S COLLEGE

The college, which has buildings on either side of the Cam, was founded in 1511 and the earliest buildings date from this period. An engraving in Loggan's *Cantabrigia Illustrata* shows the 17th-century appearance of the gardens, with a bowling green, a meadow running down to the river and walks of regularly planted trees. The bowling green and the walks on each side of it provided the site for a new scheme planned by Capability Brown in 1772. His Wilderness, a lawn surrounded by trees, survives today, much as originally designed, and is now officially known as the Fellows' Garden. After the loss of many trees, especially of elms, the college in recent times has skilfully managed the planting of the Wilderness, replacing moribund trees and replanting to maintain the essential atmosphere. The approach to the gardens is magnificent – through 16th-century courts to the early 18th-century bridge across the river (planned by Sir Christopher Wren but built by Robert Grumbold) from which there is a splendid view of the Gothic Bridge of Sighs (1831). On the west side of the river deep and colourful herbaceous borders run along the Gothic screen of the New Court, which also dates from the early 19th century. A long walk leads towards Queen's Road, ending in an avenue of limes. Off it is the Scholars' Garden with lawns, yew hedges and herbaceous borders.

New Court borders at St John's College

Location St John's Street CB2 1TP **OS** TL4458 **English Heritage Register** Grade II* **Tel** 01223 338600 **Email** enquiries@joh.cam.ac.uk **Website** www.joh.cam.ac.uk **Open** Easter to early Nov, Mon to Fri 10–5; Sat and Sun 9.30–7

CAMBRIDGE UNIVERSITY BOTANIC GARDEN

AN OUTSTANDING COLLECTION OF PLANTS FINELY DISPLAYED, A BEAUTIFUL WINTER GARDEN AND A DRY GARDEN

The botanic garden at Cambridge was founded in 1760 but opened on its present site in 1846. The site is an attractive one, with a handsome curved lake and water garden near the Trumpington Road entrance, and it is animated by many fine mature trees, some of which were planted at the time of their first introduction – including *Sequoiadendron giganteum* (introduced in 1853, planted in 1855) and *Metasequoia glyptostroboides* (introduced in 1947, planted in 1949). The only part of the garden that presents anything like a contrived vista is the main walk which leads straight from the Trumpington Road entrance to a circular pool with a fountain – and from that point you are on your own.

It is the plants, and collections of plants, that are very definitely the chief attraction here – and there is much to delight the gardener. There are several National Collections, of which the most attractive is that of species tulips (56 of them) and their primary hybrids (17). All of these are beautiful and many make admirable garden plants, in some cases naturalising with abandon – unlike the plump and glamorous modern cultivars which peter out quickly. A National Collection of hardy geraniums (over 100 species and over 40 primary hybrids) is also of great interest to gardeners. An astonishing collection of over 70 species of European fritillaries, several of them garden-worthy, will be an eye-opener to most gardeners, as will the collection of over 90 honeysuckles (*Lonicera* species). The collections of alchemilla, bergenias, ribes, ruscus and European saxifrages are of chiefly botanical interest.

The Winter Garden has an admirable display of what may be achieved in that season. The gleaming yellow stems of the dogwood *Cornus sericea* 'Flaviramea' and the Chinese lacquer red of the willow *Salix alba* subsp. *vitellina*

'Britzensis' enliven the gloomiest day. A large collection of heathers forms a glowing eiderdown and the silver-white stems of *Rubus biflorus* sparkle among dwarf conifers. There are spring bedding schemes and herbaceous borders which are perfectly nice in a municipal park sort of way but the overriding interest of the garden lies in the quality of the rare plants and the opportunity gardeners have to see large and fascinating collections of particular plants. A very attractively designed little formal garden uses plants especially suitable for the dry Cambridge climate which has half the national average rainfall. Here euphorbias, fennel, grasses, lavenders and sedums are deployed to good effect. It is so well laid out that it could be the model for many a small private garden.

Location Cambridge CB2 1JF, Cambridgeshire **OS** TL4557 ½m S of the city centre by Trumpington Road (A10) **Tel** 01223 336265 **Fax** 01223 336278 **Email** gardens@hermes.cam.ac.uk **English Heritage Register** Grade II* **Owner** University of Cambridge **Open** daily 10–6 (closes 5 in spring and autumn, 4 in winter; closed 25 and 26 Dec) **Area** 40 acres/16 hectares

Cambridge Botanic Garden

BETH CHATTO GARDENS

THE SUPERB GARDENS OF A BRILLIANT PLANTSWOMAN, WITH A WONDERFUL NURSERY ATTACHED

Many interests of our time converge in Beth Chatto's gardens – respect for the environment, a desire to plant in a naturalistic way and an informed interest in the ecology of plants. These things, worthy as they are, do not by themselves make good gardens, but Beth Chatto, apart from being a deeply knowledgeable practical gardener, is also an artist in the use of plants.

Beth Chatto and her late husband, Andrew, started gardening here in 1960 and opened a nursery in 1967. In the 1970s and 80s she exhibited regularly at Royal Horticultural Society shows, winning ten gold medals in a row at Chelsea. Almost any gardener who saw her displays can remember them to this day – with plants beautifully arranged in naturalistic groups (not so rare today but a great novelty then) and grouped according to the conditions they needed (dry,

Beth Chatto's dry garden

moist, shady and so on). She provided gardeners with wonderfully painless, indeed enjoyable, lessons in that most important thing of all – choosing the right site for the right plant. At the nursery her plants, chiefly herbaceous perennials, are still grouped according to site, and in the garden that she developed alongside she displays her principles in palpitating horticultural action. She started with a garden based on moist conditions along a spring-fed ditch whose banks are fringed with astilbes, ferns, gunneras (*G. tinctoria*), lysichitons and marsh marigold (*Caltha palustris*). Nature never intended such a combination, for these plants come from all over the world, but the fact that they all need the same conditions not only allows them to flourish but also to look *right* together. (Anyone who has planted a cistus alongside a lysichiton must sense that something is wrong.)

In 1991 Beth Chatto embarked on a radical new venture. Throughout the 1980s England enjoyed a sequence of especially dry summers which, together with fears of long-term climate change, turned gardeners' minds to the challenge of dealing with drought. Essex is the driest county in England, averaging around

20in/50cm of rain a year but often getting far less. Beth Chatto made a new garden to capitalise on such conditions, choosing plants that would flourish with no artificial irrigation. She dug up a ¾-acre/0.3-hectare car park, added a couple of feet of compost on top of 20ft/6m of sand and gravel, and started to plant, applying a deep mulch of gravel to conserve moisture. "I had in mind a dried-up river bed as I made a gently sinuous walkway," she wrote, and about this curving walk she disposed a huge number of plants. Many of these are from the Mediterranean area – the cistus, lavender, santolina, spurges and so on which anyone holidaying in the south of Spain has seen. At the edge of the path and weaving their way through low shrubs are many bulbous plants – alliums, alstroemerias, lilies and tulbaghias. Substantial grasses such as *Stipa gigantea*, shrubs like *Atriplex halimus*, or soaring herbaceous plants such as verbascums, give height and drama. There is artistry in their arrangement, with repetition of plants and occasional happy juxtapositions of form or colour, but the triumph of the garden comes

from its abundantly natural appearance and the fact that the plants seem to be relishing the same extreme conditions. Of all the gardens made in Britain in the late 20th century, this was the one that was both deeply in touch with the spirit of the time and managed to make something beautiful of it.

Location Elmstead Market, Colchester CO7 7DB, Essex
OS TM0624 ½m E of Elmstead Market by A133
Tel 01206 822007 **Fax** 01206 825933 **Owner** Mrs Beth Chatto **Open** Mar to Oct, Mon to Sat 9–5; Nov to Feb, Mon to Fri 9–4 **Area** 5 acres/2 hectares

CROSSING HOUSE

A DAZZLING GARDEN FILLED WITH PLANTS
IN A DIMINUTIVE SPACE

Much is made of the fact that the Crossing House garden is, as one might guess, immediately adjacent to the railway line. But if you are a passionate gardener, and your husband is in charge of the railway crossing, where else can you make a garden? In any case, that minor oddity is one of the less remarkable things about the place. Margaret Fuller loves plants, understands how to please them and has created a diminutive garden on a problematical site which gives the greatest pleasure to visitors. Although plants are the essential thing, Mrs Fuller has also

Crossing House topiary

ingeniously designed enticing walks with touches of formality which firmly prevent her garden from being a mere charming jumble. Her plant interests range widely, from alpines, for which she fashioned a mini-Himalaya winding along a path, to noble shrubs – she possesses a fine collection of witch hazel cultivars. In her early gardening days she learned much about plants from knowledgeable garden neighbours at Docwra's Manor (see below), Faith and John Raven.

The Crossing House garden is a garden which is easy to enjoy but it also has great depth of interest. Visitors will find many unfamiliar plants tucked away inconspicuously, and if they come to be amused they will stay to marvel.

Location 78 Meldreth Road, Shepreth, nr Royston SG8 6PS, Cambridgeshire **OS** TL3947 In Shepreth village, 8m S of Cambridge off A10 **Tel** 01763 261071 **Owner** Mr and Mrs Douglas Fuller and Mr John Marlar **Open** daily dawn–dusk (no coaches) **Area** ¼ acre/0.10 hectares

DOCWRA'S MANOR

A LIVELY GARDEN MADE BY TWO EXPERT AMATEUR PLANT-COLLECTORS, FULL OF THEIR FINDS

The house is a very pretty one – 17th-century but with a gentlemanly early 18th-century façade facing the village. John and Faith Raven came here when they married in 1954, and started to remake the garden. Both keen botanists, they preferred the wild species to cultivars, and many plants were introduced into the garden as a result of their own collecting, especially in the eastern Mediterranean. John Raven wrote an admirable book, *A Botanist's Garden* (1971), which describes the garden at Docwra's Manor and their other, very different garden, at Ardtornish on the beautiful coast of Morvern in Argyllshire (see page 438). At Docwra's they found very low rainfall, alkaline soil, excellent drainage and a certain amount of protection from old brick walls and outhouses – an important consideration in this flat country with its bitter and dessicating winds. Although a cold part of the world, the sharp drainage and sunshine allowed the cultivation of many

plants from the Mediterranean (a region which can itself suffer very low temperatures).

The Ravens created a garden of compartments, adding hedges to the existing enclosures of outhouses and, although the garden is chiefly a home for plants, fashioning spaces of very different mood.

To the east and north of the house is a large uncluttered lawn edged with a winding walk and good trees (among them a monumental Irish yew and a big weeping beech), leading to a wilder area where there are some extraordinary shapes of old box and a hidden garden of shrub roses, Japanese maples and *Koelreuteria paniculata*.

A PROFUSION OF PLANTS

West and north-west of the house is a labyrinth of enclosures – yet not so labyrinthine as to prevent longer views from repeatedly opening out and leading the way. To enter the garden west of the house you cross a lawn and squeeze through a slit in a curved beech hedge. Here, where the profusion of plants all but engulfs paths, there are nevertheless touches of formality – L-shapes of clipped yew and cones of gold variegated box. The Ravens had a special interest in certain genera (in several cases long before they became fashionable) and here you will find many flourishing examples of

Touches of formality at Docwra's Manor

artemisias, cistuses, clematis, eryngiums, euphorbias, hellebores, peonies and roses (species or those of wild character). Passing a glasshouse and a paved area with flowering cherries and *Cornus controversa* 'Variegata', you come to a walk of espaliered apples, and dahlias in the autumn. From here a narrow passage through a yew hedge leads to a series of arches of pears and clematis flanked with asparagus and pampas grass (*Cortaderia selloana*). An especially protected enclosed space has *Carpenteria californica*, pelargoniums, salvias and cones of clipped rosemary.

The garden at Docwra's Manor is both very delightful to be in and absorbing. One of the great advantages of a botanical approach to gardening (provided it is not over absorbed in mere rarity) is that it allows one to study groups of plants, uninfluenced by horticultural fashion. Nature proposes a much wider range than even the largest garden centre, and has no interest in notions of shelf-life and ease of mass propagation.

Location Shepreth, nr Royston SG8 6PS, Cambridgeshire **OS** TL3947 In Shepreth village, 8m S of Cambridge off A10 **Tel** 01763 261473/260235 **Owner** Mrs John Raven **Open** Wed and Fri 10–4.30 (Apr to Oct, also 1st Sun in month 2–5) **Area** 2½ acres/1 hectare

DODDINGTON HALL

NOBLE ELIZABETHAN GARDENS
WITH MODERN PLANTING, FINE TREES
AND LOVELY SPRING BULBS

Doddington is a wonderful house – late Elizabethan, almost certainly designed by Robert Smythson and miraculously unchanged in outward appearance since it was built. A Kip engraving in *Britannia Illustrata* (1707) shows the house at the centre of a garden which is for the most part quite simple, with alignments of trees and square lawns, and behind the house a pair of grand parterres with topiary. The parterres have gone but the enclosures of the garden today correspond exactly to Kip's engraving, with courts to the east and west linked by a central axis which starts at the entrance drive and, beyond the west court on the far side of the house, is extended into the landscape by an avenue.

The entrance forecourt, with its dashing gabled gatehouse on one side and the dazzlingly ornamental house on the other, needs little ornament of a horticultural kind. Here today are plain lawns, low box hedges and gravel paths with cones of clipped yew about the perimeter, and a pair of free-standing *Magnolia grandiflora* flanking the entrance. Mounds of pink hydrangea billow against the walls of the house, with plumes of *Aruncus dioicus*, and close to the front door are topiary box unicorns holding shields. The upper part of the west court behind the house has a knot garden of box, with its hedges clipped at subtly different heights. The compartments are filled with plantings of a single colour – irises, catmint and white or yellow roses. At the lower level of the court (the site of the early 18th-century parterres) two octagonal pools with water jets are surrounded by beds of purple irises. In summer the outer beds are filled with silver *Senecio cineraria* and with bedding lobelias – deep purple and pale blue in alternative beds, a pretty effect. Borders run round the walls of the court, filled with alliums, campanulas, daylilies, echinops, peonies, phlox and sedums, with much repetition. Clematis, honeysuckle and roses are trained on the beautiful Tudor brick walls. In spring these beds are filled with red and yellow crown imperials, thoroughly naturalised here.

An 18th-century Italian wrought-iron gate leads to an avenue of Irish yews underplanted in spring with sheets of *Crocus tommasinianus* and *C. sieberi*. The wild garden opens out to the north, with many flowering cherries, a group of ancient yews, a walk of rowans and a handsome *Catalpa bignonoides*. A turf maze is a modern version of this ancient oddity. Close to the edge of the garden an open Tuscan rotunda, a Temple of the Winds, has fine views over countryside and back towards the house. A huge cedar of Lebanon, planted in 1845, stands nearby. Closer to the house a croquet lawn is overlooked by a group of remarkable sweet chestnuts, sprawling and ancient. In late summer drifts of *Cyclamen hederifolium* gleam in the shade, and in the spring more crown imperials do the same. The framework of beautiful old walls, much decorative planting and good individual specimens of trees and other plants make the garden at Doddington a most attractive place. The house, rising above it with superb aplomb, is breathtaking.

The west court at Doddington

Location Doddington, nr Lincoln LN6 4RU, Lincolnshire
OS SK9070 5m W of Lincoln by B1190; signed off
A46 Lincoln bypass **Tel** 01522 694308 **Fax** 01522
685259 **Email** estateoffice@doddingtonhall.free-
online.co.uk **English Heritage Register** Grade II*
Owner Mr and Mrs A. Jarvis **Open** Feb to Apr,
Sun 2–6; May to Sept, Wed, Sun and Bank Hol Mon
2–6 **Area** 12 acres/4.8 hectares

EUSTON HALL

A GRAND LANDSCAPE, DESIGNED BY JOHN
EVELYN AND WILLIAM KENT, AND PRETTY
HIDDEN GARDENS

Euston Hall was built in the 1660s for the
Earl of Arlington and much enlarged for
his grandson, the 2nd Duke of Grafton, by
Matthew Brettingham in the 1750s. A fire in
1902 destroyed much of the house, which was
rebuilt but reduced in size in 1952. So what
may be seen today, with some handsome but
simple 18th-century work left, is much
smaller than the original house.

John Evelyn was a friend of Lord Arlington
whom he advised about tree planting in 1671:
"my Lord was pleas'd to advise with me about
ordering his plantations of firs, elmes, limes,
etc. up his parke, and in all other places and
avenues." In 1677 Evelyn returned and found
things "exceedingly improv'd". In about 1737
William Kent was asked to advise the 2nd
Duke about the house and landscape. His
recommendation that the house be
demolished and something Palladian and much
grander substituted was not accepted –
although Brettingham's later design borrowed
from Kent. A drawing by Kent shows the park
dotted with clumps of trees – an arrangement
criticised by Horace Walpole in 1743: "Clumps
have their beauty; but in a great extent of
country, how trifling to scatter arbours, where
you should spread forests!"

Capability Brown carried out work at
Euston between 1767 and 1769 and was paid
£900 (£53,784 today). It is uncertain what
this work involved but Brown was probably
responsible for the Broad Water, a long and
sinuous lake with an island south-east of the
house, formed by damming the river.

One of the pleasures of the garden today is
that the landscape shows traces of much of
the work of the past. Beautiful 17th-century
gates on elaborate stone piers capped with
urns lead from the pleasure grounds into the
park to the east of the house. Across the park,
to the south-east, William Kent's Palladian
domed temple of 1746 (really a banqueting
house) rises on a slight eminence. South of
the house, Evelyn's woodland rides are visible,
while the walk down to Brown's lake is
delightful – and the walk back, with the
house now seen finely framed in trees, even
more so. In parts of the park, now largely
turned over to arable farming, Kent's clumps

The south lawn at Euston Hall

may still be seen, and there are more, of lime
and beech, remaining in the west park.

Close to the house is a decorative
herbaceous border with a walk of Irish yews
and, on the south side of the house, a
balustraded terrace with urns filled with
annuals. A rose garden is hedged in billowing
rue (*Ruta graveolens*) – a novel use of it and
very effective. One part of the rose garden wa
a golden wedding present to the present
(11th) Duke and Duchess of Grafton from
Queen Elizabeth, the Queen Mother; the
other, celebrating their ruby wedding, was a
gift from estate tenants and staff. In a shady
secret garden a youthful Triton stands in the
middle of a lily pool and beds are filled with
plants with white flowers – clematis, Japanese
anemones, pelargoniums and roses. A
pedimented alcove-seat of Kentian style stand
against a yew hedge.

Location Euston, Thetford IP24 2QP, Suffolk **OS** TL897
3m S of Thetford by A1088 **Tel** 01842 766366 **Fax**
01842 766764 **English Heritage Register** Grade II*
Owner The Duke of Grafton **Open** Jun to Sept, Thur
2.30–5 **Area** 70 acres/28 hectares

THE FAIRHAVEN WOODLAND AND WATER GARDEN

EXQUISITE WOODLAND GARDEN IN THE
MAGICAL SETTING OF THE NORFOLK BROAD

The spirit of the place is so strong at the
Fairhaven Woodland and Water Garden
that it makes gardening seem almost an act o
vandalism. This ancient piece of woodland,
threaded by streams and creeks, is one of the
most beautiful things of its kind that you
could imagine. Henry Broughton, later 2nd
Lord Fairhaven, whose family made the
garden at Anglesey Abbey (*see page 286*),
came here in 1947 and with the greatest tact
unostentatiously animated the place. It was
the Debbage family who did the work, and
George Debbage is still in charge of the
garden.

Exotic plantings – azaleas, berberis, cherries
dogwoods, gaultherias and hydrangeas – were
gently slipped in among the beautiful old
beeches and oaks, and much underplanting

Waterside planting at Fairhaven

now lines the banks of the streams and pools or flows about the feet of shrubs and trees – *Cardiocrinum giganteum*, ferns, irises, lysichitons and sheaves of dazzling Asiatic primulas. The place has a delicious sense of innocent secrecy. Bosky paths suddenly emerge in clearings of dappled light or, most exhilaratingly, open out to give serene views of South Walsham Broad lined with reeds and bulrushes. No garden I know has so many quacks, twitterings, splashes and flutterings of birds. Indeed, there is a bird sanctuary here alongside the garden – an odd idea, for the garden itself seems to provide all the sanctuary that could be desired.

Many gardens give pleasure in a more or less detached way as you wander admiringly in them. Here, a spirit of contentment seems to descend almost as soon as you enter; it would be hard to imagine anyone having a really nasty argument in these surroundings, and if every community had access to such a place, thousands of social workers would become redundant overnight.

Location South Walsham, Norwich NR13 6EA, Norfolk
S TG3613 E of South Walsham village, 9m NE of Norwich by B1140 Tel and Fax 01603 270449
Owner The Fairhaven Garden Trust Open Apr to ct, Tue to Sun (open Bank Hol Mon) 11–5.30 Area
0 acres/69 hectares

FELBRIGG HALL

A MAGNIFICENT WALLED GARDEN WITH FRUIT,
FLOWERS AND ORNAMENTAL TREES

Felbrigg, quite close to the sea at Cromer, stands high on a windy plain – with the spire of Norwich Cathedral visible in one direction and the North Sea in the other. It is a lovely house, charmingly two-faced, with a gabled Jacobean façade and, at right-angles to it and facing west, a chaste Restoration wing of the 1670s. It was built for the Windham family, and the architect of the Jacobean

part was in all likelihood Robert Lyminge who designed Blickling Hall nearby (*see page 290*). The Great Wood to the north of the house, giving protection from coastal winds, was planted in the 17th century and new planting has been made into the 20th century. Humphry Repton, who lived on the edge of the Windham estate, was consulted before 1795 but there is no record of any work by him.

The landscape setting for the house is a splendid one, but on a cold and windy day (not uncommon in these parts) one retreats to the protection of the walled garden, at a little distance from the house, with a sigh of relief – pausing on the way to admire the magnificent sweet chestnut planted in 1680. The kitchen garden, enclosed in 18th-century brick walls, has an enchanting mid 18th-century octagonal dovecote crowned with an elegant lantern built into the centre of the north wall. It forms an eyecatcher at the head of one of the gravel paths which quarter the garden. The box-edged beds are now given over mostly to ornamental purposes, and borders with shrub roses underplanted with lilies and peonies line the walls. Figs, pears, plums and vines are trained against the walls and an orchard is planted with spring bulbs. Many old local cultivars of apples planted here have such splendid names as 'Wyken Pippin' and 'Norfolk Beefing'. Glasshouses contain a 'Black Hamburgh' grapevine (*Vitis vinifera*

The kitchen garden at Felbrigg

'Schiara Grossa') and a collection of tender exotics.

To the south of the walled garden a large collection of crataegus species are planted in grass in regular rows. A National Collection of colchicums held at Felbrigg (over 60 varieties) is a magnificent sight in autumn. They relish the sandy soil and in many places have become naturalised. West of the house an 18th-century conservatory protects camellias and tender ferns; in spring it is suffused with the delicious scent of *Rhododendron* 'Fragrantissimum' in pots. Wide views open out from the conservatory to the south but woodland presses in protectively on the west.

Wyndham Ketton-Cremer left the estate to the National Trust on his death in 1969. He lived alone in the house with no electricity – "not too luxurious", as James Lees-Milne recorded on a visit, "the bathroom and WC were about 300 yards from the bedroom." The house, with its lovely contents and wonderful library, together with the park and rare walled garden, make a perfect gentleman's domain, and much of this character remains today.

Location Felbrigg, Norwich NR11 8PR, Norfolk
OS TG1939 2m SW of Cromer by A148 and B1436
Tel 01263 837444   **Fax** 01263 837032   **Email**
felbrigg@ntrust.org.uk   **English Heritage Register**
Grade II*   **Owner** The National Trust   **Open** Apr to Oct,
Sat to Wed 11–5.30 (walled garden also open Thur and
Fri from mid Jul to end Aug)   **Area** 6½ acres/2.6 hectares

GARDENS OF THE ROSE

ONE OF THE FINEST ROSE COLLECTIONS
IN THE COUNTRY – A MAGNIFICENT
RESOURCE FOR GARDENERS

Roses must be the only genus of garden plants to have whole gardens dedicated to them. As fashionable garden plants they come and go, but among gardeners less interested in rising and falling hemlines they never lose their appeal. It would be hard indeed to think of any distinguished flower garden which has no roses.

The garden of the Royal National Rose Society, which came here in 1960, is one of the best places in the country to study the genus. The collection is enormous, finely

displayed, and covers every type of rose. The emphasis is on modern varieties but there is also an excellent collection of all the chief older strains and of the species. Furthermore, there are trial beds of new varieties so that the

Rosa **'Madame Knorr'**

roses of the future may be scrutinised. Well over 2,000 kinds are displayed, often in attractively contrived settings – on arbours or pergolas for climbing varieties; in beds of different types (sometimes with skilfully chosen companion plants), for the rest. This is meat and drink to the confirmed rosarian but to the non-specialist gardener it provides an excellent opportunity to see roses of every kind put through their horticultural paces. There are other attractions here – mixed borders, a new iris garden and plantings of bulbs – but it is roses that are the overwhelming point of interest.

The Royal National Rose Society is one of the leading specialist plant societies, with a very large membership. It arranges all sorts of events, publishes a valuable journal and gives expert advice to members.

Location Chiswell Green, St Albans AL2 3NR,
Hertfordshire   **OS** TL12 04 2m SW of St Albans by
B4630; Jnct 6 of M1; Jnct 21a of M25   **Tel** 01727
850461   **Fax** 01727 850360   **Email** mail@rnrs.org.uk
Owner The Royal National Rose Society   **Open** end
May to end Sept, Mon to Sat 9–5, Sun and Aug Bank
Hol Mon 10–6   **Area** 26 acres/10 hectares

THE GIBBERD GARDEN

A SUBLIME GARDEN FULL OF
POETRY AND SURPRISES –
IDIOSYNCRATIC AND ORIGINAL

The architect Sir Frederick Gibberd came to live here in 1956, on the edge of Harlow New Town of which he had become the master-planner ten years earlier. Failing to get permission to demolish the undistinguished Edwardian bungalow on the site, he grafted onto it an immense and airy living room with windows facing into the garden. He also inherited some fine garden features, the most striking of which was a lime avenue descending the slope north of the house. The garden was well watered, with the Pincy brook forming its northern boundary and water meadows stretching out on the far bank. Of his garden-making activities Sir Frederick wrote, "I consulted the genius of the place and then exercised some intuition without which no art exists." The garden he made is an amalgam of many different styles; some of the effects he achieved are remarkably beautiful, others are more banal.

A GARDEN OF ORNAMENTS
Terraces and patios, ornamented with sculptures and pots, surround the house, and a narrow lawn and a pool strike northwards, forming strong parallel axes. A concrete octagonal mirador rises at the end of the pool and beyond it the axis is continued with a double hedge of beech, privet and yew. To the west the mirador commands handsome views over a lawn planted with flowering amelanchiers, silver birches and cherries underplanted in spring with swathes of daffodils. On the other side is the lime avenue which continues the axis of the lawn garden deeper into the woods. The limes are planted close together, forming a nave of trunks, and are underplanted with bluebells, wood anemones and wood spurge. A concrete statue of a swan protecting her cygnet (by Mary Gorarra) is glimpsed in an opening, and paths now wind along the banks of a stream that is edged with willows, clumps of petasites, the giant leaves of *Rheum palmatum* and waves of wild garlic.

The garden provides a home for a large collection of sculptures (well over eighty of them), and these vary sharply both in quality and the skill with which they are used in the landscape. A tormented nude figure of a girl by Gerda Rubinstein, for example, is placed as the focal point of a charming walk of coppiced hazels prettily underplanted with silver deadnettle and blue squills. But the statue is both coarse and shrill while the woodland planting with which it is associated is subtle and simple. Alongside it, on the other hand, is an association that works extraordinarily well: a beautiful old sprawling quince spreads its fissured branches over a handsome broad-bellied

The Corinthian columns

stoneware pot (by Monica Young) sitting in a pool of gravel. The contrast of the jagged branches of the tree and the smoothly rounded shape of the pot is very effective. Elsewhere in the garden are other finely judged associations: for example, from the nut walk a path leads through to a secluded lawn enclosed in hedges of mixed purple cotoneaster, hazel, hawthorn and privet where two fonts – one Norman and the other Gothic – placed asymmetrically and apparently casually, give the place a powerful air of drama and mystery. The most memorable use of architectural fragments is in a glade in the extreme north-western corner of the garden where a pair

An old quince at the Gibberd Garden

of soaring fluted stone columns with Corinthian capitals rise from a mossy plinth. A few broken fragments lie in the grass and a row of swagged Coade stone urns perch on stone coping nearby. These were all rescued from the demolition of the old Coutts bank in the Strand in London. Sited among trees in a shady clearing, they have a lovely Arcadian presence.

The Gibberd Garden is like no other and, despite the criticism I have made, has the distinctive charm of an entirely personal approach to garden-making which, at its best, produces effects of great beauty.

Location Marsh Lane, Gilden Way, Harlow CM17 0NA, Essex **OS** TL4913 E of the centre of Harlow, signed off B183 (Gilden Way); Jnct 7 of M11 **Tel** 01279 442112 **Owner** The Gibberd Garden Trust **Open** Apr to Sept, Sat, Sun and Bank Hol Mon 2–6 (Jun to Aug, opens 12.30) **Area** 16 acres/6.4 hectares

GRIMSTHORPE CASTLE

GRAND PERIOD GARDENS – FLOWERS,
FORMALITY AND SUPERB PARKLAND VIEWS

Grimsthorpe, only fairly recently accessible to the public, is an exceptional and exceptionally enjoyable place. The house was first built for Gilbert de Gant in the early 13th century and a remaining tower may still be seen at the south-east corner of the present house. Since the early 16th century the estate has belonged to the Willoughby de Eresby family. It was they who rebuilt the castle later in the 16th century, once again in the late 17th century and, most spectacularly, in the 18th century when Sir John Vanbrugh embarked on a wholescale revision of the house, of which he completed only the north front before his death in 1730.

THE FORMALITY OF THE PAST

The gardens were laid out in around 1680 by George London and engravings by Kip in *Britannia Illustrata* (1707) show the result: the house enclosed on three sides by formal gardens, with parterres in the court to the south overlooked by a central pavilion and on one side of this south court a long tunnel arbour with, on each side, patterns of square beds with a lollipop of topiary at each corner. Beyond the south court an axial ride runs through densely planted woods and is continued by an avenue that runs out across the park. Another Kip engraving in the same book shows the park to the east of the house, with formal expanses of water in the foreground and woods beyond pierced by rides and avenues, three of which are aligned on the house. Some drawings made by William Stukeley in 1736 show a dramatic new garden: the woods beyond the south court have been divided into a bristling star-shaped pattern of rides radiating from a central circular clearing, each ending in a raised bastion on the edge of the wood; and where the avenue had been in the Kip engraving is a long walk raised on bastions. All this is thought to have been designed by Stephen Switzer sometime after 1720. In 1772 Capability Brown produced plans, among which was a design for a 350ft/105m

GLEN CHANTRY

BRILLIANTLY PLANTED GARDEN,
SUPERBLY MAINTAINED BY
PERFECTIONISTS

Although plants rule in this garden, the layout is thoughtfully designed and the best is made of an awkward site. It is awkward in as many ways as a site can be awkward: in terms of the poverty of the soil (slightly acid but stuffed with stone); its exposure on top of a windy hill; lack of water (for this is just about the driest corner of England); and a gawkily sloping terrain. Any one of these problems might have deterred gardeners of less gumption than Wol and Sue Staines but, with the greatest aplomb, they have remedied those defects that are possible to remedy and learned to live with the others – a universal recipe for happiness among gardeners.

Apart from some formal parts of the garden close to the house, the layout they adopted follows the flow of the land, with sweeping expanses of lawn curving about beds. Below the house is a rare feature: a modern rock garden. A naturalistic-looking pool and streams have been created, which provide sites for moisture-loving plants, while trees and shrubs give essential shade to plants such as

Glen Chantry stream garden

hellebores and lilies. There are few gardens I have seen in which ordinary plants look so healthy and more difficult ones seem so remarkably happy. Fritillaries, for example, grow superlatively here – not the everyday crown imperials or snake's head fritillaries with which almost any gardener may have some success, but trickier customers such as *Fritillaria michailovskyi* or *F. pallidiflora*. Species of another exceptionally attractive genus, the peonies, also seem completely at home – such as the tender *Paeonia cambessedesii* from Mallorca, one of the loveliest of them all in leaf and in flower and not at all easy to please. All this is achieved by very hard work – above all by the regular addition of lavish quantities of compost – and the standards of practical gardening are of the highest. It is inspiring to see gardens of this sort but also dispiriting, for when you go home you will find that your own garden seems by comparison horribly neglected.

Location Isham's Chase, Wickham Bishop CM8 3LG, Essex **OS** TL8412 1m W of Wickham Bishop, 8m NW of Chelmsford by A12 **Tel** 01621 891342 **Owner** Wol and Sue Staines **Open** Apr to mid Oct, Fri and Sat 10–4 **Area** 3½ acres/1.4 hectares

g sham bridge across the end of a lake.
is was never made and it is not known if
 of Brown's submissions were accepted.
n the garden today there is a powerful
ling of the past, with many of the
closures shown in the Kip engraving still in
sition. To the east of the house, where Kip
owed a bowling green, there is now a
terre in which the compartments of a
gular pattern of box-edged beds are filled
th a single variety of rose or with lavender.
e parterre is ornamented with fine stone
s, standard variegated holly clipped into
mes, and a lead figure of a warrior. To the
t is a new kitchen garden designed in 1965
 Lady Ancaster. This is a pioneer formal
ager with beautifully clipped cones and
mes of box and an orchard with trees
nted in a pattern of triangular lawns. Old
dlars and quinces have been shaped into
namental domes. The south court, where
p showed a parterre, is still divided into
ee, but now has gravel paths and plain
ns decorated with exactly the urns seen in
e Kip engraving, surmounted with finials
ved to resemble flames. To its south, where
ce there was formal woodland, are two
dens enclosed in yew hedges whose crest is
armingly decorated with topiary – birds,
mb waiters and other fanciful shapes. Inside
ch enclosure are a pool, beds of roses and
unds of box. The woodland beyond is still
rced by a ride where Kip's engraving

showed a ride and avenue.

South-west of the house a long, broad grass
path has herbaceous borders on each side,
backed by yew hedges which are divided in
their length by buttresses of yew. The hedges
swoop down between the buttresses to afford a
clear view of an immense expanse of parkland
and a lake spreading out below. The borders
are planted in repeated bold blocks of a single
variety – pale yellow achillea, golden or rust-
coloured daylilies, white leucanthemums,
Romneya coulteri and sedums.

Immediately to the west of the house a
deep lawn runs the whole width of the house,
with benches overlooking the park. Beyond
the lawn the same swooping yew hedge is
continued, now with a long border of shrub
roses.

The garden at Grimsthorpe stands out
among the less well-known gardens that I
describe in this book, and since house and its
exquisite contents are also outstanding, the
place is all of a piece.

Location Grimsthorpe, nr Bourne PE10 0NB,
Lincolnshire **OS** TF0422 4m W of Bourne on A151
Tel 01778 591205 **Fax** 01778 591259 **Email**
ray@grimsthorpe.co.uk **English Heritage Register**
Grade I **Owner** Grimsthorpe and Drummond Castle
Trust Ltd **Open** Apr to Sept, Sun, Thurs and Bank Hol
Mon (Aug, open Sun to Fri) 11–6 **Area** 3,000
acres/1,214 hectares

The parterre at Grimsthorpe

GUNBY HALL

ATMOSPHERIC WALLED GARDENS
PACKED WITH PLANTS WITH TOUCHES
OF STATELY FORMALITY

Gunby is supposed to be the place referred
to in Tennyson's poem *The Palace of Art*:
"an English home – gray twilight poured/On
dewy pastures, dewy trees,/Softer than sleep –
all things in order stored,/A haunt of ancient
Peace". I had not known that on my first visit
to Gunby and my experience of the place was
certainly memorably peaceful. It was a June
day, no-one else was there, and the house and
garden breathed a private air – I felt almost
like an interloper. There is little of the heritage
industry here, and in this fairly remote corner
(although it is not far from bracing Skegness)
it is unlikely that hordes of visitors would ever
descend on this low-key though unusually
beautiful place.

The brick house, dated 1700 and built for
Sir William Massingberd, is what Pevsner
loftily calls "a mason-bricklayer's rather than an
architect's design". I find it delightful, and the
interior with its panelling and elegant
fireplaces and joinery equally so. The garden is
not the kind of garden anyone exactly
designed; it has more of the air of having
gradually gathered itself about the house in a
comfortable sort of way. Behind the stables,
with an elegant 18th-century clock-cote, is

The walled garden at Gunby Hall

what must have been the original kitchen garden, walled in 18th-century brick. It contains a little domed and columned temple-seat, possibly designed by Mrs Peregrine Massingberd in the early 19th century. It was her husband, a friend of Sir Joseph Banks, who planted many of the fine trees that still ornament the estate. The temple-seat is painted a faded silvery blue and flanked with standard honeysuckles and screens of clipped yew. Apples are trained over arches and underplanted with irises, and on each side an irrepressible jumble of plants presses in, heaving with roses (including standards) and carpeted with catmint, lavender, pulmonaria, rosemary and strawberries among which rises Miss Willmott's ghost (*Eryngium giganteum*). In the middle is a soothing sliver of lawn with a sundial. The walls are covered in clematis and roses, and in late summer there are stupendous sunflowers and a rainbow of dahlias.

A second, much larger, walled garden has beds of fruit and vegetables, old apples, medlars or pear trees growing out of herbaceous borders, and a rose walk. Fruit trees are beautifully espaliered against the south-facing wall. The loudest noise you will hear on a summer's day is the fortissimo but soporific buzz of bees. To one side, behind a yew hedge, a walk of Irish junipers runs along a canal – the former carp pool.

The walled gardens are quite detached from the house, whose setting is much more imposing. On one side are magnificent lawns, grand specimen trees and large rose beds. The entrance to the house has a formal garden of razor-sharp yew hedges, a paved walk with a sundial, and rectangles of catmint. The whole is decorated with sentinel Irish junipers and cubes of clipped golden box capped with spheres. On each side is a cool, simple corridor of yew hedges ending with a bench. If a Savile Row tailor took to gardening, this is the sort of thing he would do – it is the closest that the gardens at Gunby get to showing off. With its gentlemanly and hospitable air, and its unostentatious charm, Gunby is the perfect example of what an English garden is all about.

Location nr Spilsby PE23 5SS, Lincolnshire **OS** TF4666 7m W of Skegness by A158 **Tel** 01909 486411 **Fax** 01909 486377 **English Heritage Register** Grade II **Owner** The National Trust **Open** April to Sept, Wed and Thur 2–6 **Area** 7 acres/2.8 hectares

HATFIELD HOUSE

MAGNIFICENT 20TH-CENTURY GARDENS FOLLOW ANCIENT PATTERNS BELOW A TUDOR PALACE AND A GREAT JACOBEAN HOUSE

Here is a great private estate, maintained in old-fashioned seigneurial splendour, yet throwing its gates open to a public which relishes it. The house was built between 1607 and 1612 to the designs of Robert Lyminge for Robert Cecil, later Lord Salisbury. His descendant, the 6th Marquess of Salisbury (another Robert Cecil) lives here today.

Work on the gardens started at the same time as the building of the house. The Cecils were great gardeners and they employed John Tradescant the Elder, one of the greatest plantsmen of the day (who later became royal gardener to King Charles I). Also involved was the elusive but fascinating Salomon de Caus, the French water engineer and garden designer who was involved in several famous European gardens. In the early 17th century Hatfield was one of the great gardens of its age, but in the 18th century, as was so often the case, the elaborately inventive formal gardens were disposed of and a landscape park running up to the very walls of the house, was

The knot garden at Hatfield

put into place. In the 19th century new formal gardens were made, but it would be fair to say that only in the late 20th century, under the inspiration of the 6th Marchioness of Salisbury, have the gardens resumed the distinction of the past. Lady Salisbury, who as Viscountess Cranborne had revitalised the remarkable gardens at Cranborne Manor (*see page 29*), came to Hatfield in 1972. She was an experienced gardener, a knowledgeable garden historian and plantswoman, and above all she possessed the vitality and imagination needed to give the gardens at Hatfield new focus.

Immediately beside the early Tudor Old Palace, on the site of a 19th-century rose garden, Lady Salisbury created a new four-part knot garden of lively decorative inventiveness. A maze and three "closed knots" are filled with plants of a Tradescantian kind, including those introduced by the Tradescants, father and son, such as goat's beard (*Aruncus dioicus*), Michaelmas daisy (*Aster pilosus* var. *demotus*, formerly *A. tradescantii*) and other plants of their time.

A SPREAD OF GARDENS

The main house's Victorian Privy Garden, enclosed in an 18th-century lime walk, was replanted with sprightly mixed borders, and a Scented Garden with camomile paths is heady with the perfume of honeysuckles, lavender, lilies, Guernsey stock (*Matthiola incana*) and waves of roses. To the south is the Wilderness Garden, a marvellous spread of trees and shrubs with huge quantities of spring-flowering plants in the grass beneath them – cowslips, crocuses, fritillaries, scillas and tulips.

In the East Garden a formal arrangement had been reinstated in the 1840s with an unconvincing "Jacobean" layout of elaborately fussy beds disposed on a large square of lawn overlooked by a terrace and a grand double staircase. The L-shaped beds have gone and in their place are sixteen square box-edged beds of mixed planting which have an avenue of opiary yew shapes down the middle. On either side of the lawn are double rows of clipped mop-headed holm oaks forming shady walks.

The Woodland Garden east of the house, close to the New Pond which dates from Tradescant's time, has been made since 1990.

Here is a spectacular display of snowdrops beneath superb old oaks, and flowering shrubs are being introduced along the paths. In 2002 a completely new garden was underway below the south front of the house, with a sunken parterre, a rose walk and box topiary.

Hatfield is an old-fashioned garden, executed with panache. It is old-fashioned in a particularly modern way, for it is gardened organically throughout; Lady Salisbury was an early member of the HDRA.

Location Hatfield AL9 5NQ, Hertfordshire **OS** TL 2308 In the centre of Hatfield, 20m N of London; Jnct 3 of A1(M) **Tel** 01707 262823 Fax 01707 275719 **English Heritage Register** Grade I **Owner** The Marquess of Salisbury **Open** end Mar to end Sept, Tue to Sun (open Bank Hol Mon; East Garden open only Fri) **Area** 30 acres/12 hectares

HAUGHLEY PARK

A FLOWERY DELL, ANCIENT OAK, GOOD SHRUBS AND A FINE KITCHEN GARDEN

Haughley Park was built in around 1620 for Sir John Sulyard – a fine brick house with crow-stepped gables. Almost exactly two hundred years later the north wing was rebuilt with bow windows and a castellated parapet.

Nothing is known of any early gardening at Haughley and the garden today has been made

The north lawn at Haughley Park

almost entirely since the estate was bought by the present owner's father in 1957. However, one very extraordinary feature of the garden is of great antiquity – an English oak on the edge of the north lawn. This, estimated by Oliver Rackham to be around 1,000 years old, has a girth of 30ft/9m and one giant limb sprawling sideways, propped up on brick piers.

The north lawn is exactly the width of the house, lined with shrubs on each side and with a venerable *Magnolia* × *soulangeana* in the middle. It is open at its northern end and the view is extended along an avenue into parkland. In the wooded dell to the east of the north lawn is a woodland garden with a canopy of old beeches and Scots pines. Here are azaleas, camellias, hydrangeas, mahonias and rhododendrons lavishly underplanted with bluebells, ferns, hellebores, lily of the valley, hostas and rodgersias.

The kitchen garden is especially attractive; its brick walls, partly of the 17th century and partly late Georgian, have a castellated parapet like that of the house, and it is divided into four, with box-edged paths, in the traditional fashion. A long mixed border runs down one wall, and there are arbours of roses and a centrepiece of clipped yew. Although there are occasional eruptions of cornflowers, dahlias and nasturtiums, this is a proper working kitchen garden, with nectarines and peaches trained against the south-facing wall.

On my last visit to Haughley Park in the autumn of 2002 an elderly visitor was making his way methodically about the garden with evident relish. It was a warm afternoon and as I left I made a final visit to the ancient oak where I found the same elderly visitor taking a rest, sitting peacefully on a bench in the dappled shade of the great tree. Haughley has an attractive garden but it is the oak that sticks in the mind.

Location nr Stowmarket IP14 3JY, Suffolk **OS** TM0061 4m NW of Stowmarket, signed off A14 **Tel** 01359 240701 **Owner** Mr and Mrs Robert Williams **Open** May to Sept, Tue 2–5.30 **Area** 8 acres/3.2 hectares

HELMINGHAM HALL

MOATED HOUSE AND FLOWER GARDENS OF DREAMLIKE BEAUTY, RUN BY A PERFECTIONIST

The approach to Helmingham Hall is one of the loveliest of any house in England. The drive curves across an ancient deer park, still with fallow and red deer and studded with remarkable old oaks; it covers an area of 400 acres/162 hectares. The beautiful diapered brick house, started in 1480 for John Tollemache, stands confidently, protected by its moat. South-west of the house is a walled garden, also enclosed by a moat – the kind of garden common in old estates in the Netherlands but a rarity in England. The present garden has 18th-century brick walls but there is evidence that it may even pre-date the house; certainly it is known that before the present walls were built, in1745, the garden was surrounded by a wooden palisade. However, although there are traces of earlier gardens, especially of the 18th century, most of what we see today dates from the 20th century.

The moated garden opens with a burst of decorative exuberance. A box parterre whose compartments are filled with *Santolina chamaecyparissus* and ornamented with stone urns on plinths, is enclosed on three sides by brick walls. Running round the walls are borders edged in lavender and filled with

Hybrid Musk roses underplanted with London pride, *Campanula lactiflora* and *Alstroemeria ligtu* hybrids. The roses, sweetly scented and flowering throughout the summer, rise in ramparts on either side of wrought-iron gates with piers capped with winged horses, which lead into the walled garden.

Here, in the kitchen garden, a central turf path runs the whole length of the garden between narrow herbaceous borders, forming a chasm of flowers. Behind the borders the garden is divided into eight partitions (as it has been since the 16th century), separated by grass paths and by tunnels festooned with sweet peas, ornamental gourds or runner beans. The beds themselves are still used for the traditional cultivation of fruit and vegetables but Lady Tollemache keeps making encroachments for decorative purposes: the end border, facing east, is now full of ornamental plants too big to be accommodated in the long central borders, and against the north-west facing wall a series of beds, separated by buttresses of yew, have all sorts of experimental groupings of plants, many of which come from the excellent Suffolk nursery, Woottens Plants. But fruit and vegetables are still grown here and all in all it is one of the loveliest examples in the country of an ornamental kitchen garden.

A walk running round the outside of the walls, on the grass bank of the moat,

The borders at Helmingham

▷ **The gourd tunnel** at Helmingham Hall

has mounds of clipped yew and narrow flower beds against walls decorated with honeysuckle, roses and espaliered fruit.

A new garden north-east of the house has been made laid out since 1982 by Lady Tollemache. Here is an exceptional eight-part knot of herbs and, beyond it, a four-part pattern of rose beds edged in billowing lavender or hyssop. The roses are all old shrub varieties or species, lavishly underplanted with *Alchemilla mollis*, blue and white *Campanula persicifolia*, geraniums and violas. At the centre of this arrangement a stone figure of Flora, facing back towards the house, rises from a circle of golden thyme which is underplanted with different seasonal bulbs. The whole area, except where it is open to the house, is enclosed in finely detailed yew hedges with beautiful piers and arched openings.

The gardens at Helmingham make reference to the formality of Tudor garden design, and their flowery exuberance is also true to the Tudor spirit. The whole ensemble – park, house and gardens – is remarkably beautiful.

Location nr Stowmarket IP14 6EF, Suffolk **OS** TM1957 9m N of Ipswich by B1077 **Tel** 01473 890363 **Fax** 01473 890776 **English Heritage Register** Grade I **Owner** Lord and Lady Tollemache **Open** May to mid Sept, Sun 2–6 (also groups by appointment, Wed 2–5; individuals may join a Wed group if one has been booked) **Area** 10 acres/4 hectares

HOUGHTON HALL

HISTORIC ESTATE WITH LIVELY NEW ORNAMENTAL GARDENS FOR A GRAND WALLED KITCHEN GARDEN

The first house at Houghton was built in the 17th century but the present one, on a slightly different site, was built in the 1720s for Sir Robert Walpole, almost certainly to the designs of Colen Campbell and James Gibbs. Early in the 18th century there had been an elaborate and fussy formal garden at Houghton but this was changed by Charles Bridgeman who substituted a monumental but much simpler scheme of blocks of planting, rides and avenues. Sir Thomas Robinson saw the plan in 1731, which showed "plumps and avenues to go quite round the Park pale, and to make straight and oblique lines of a mile or two in length, as the situation of the country admits of. This design will be about 12 miles in circumference…at every angle there are to be obelisks, or some other building." One surviving building that served that purpose is the Water House, designed by Henry, Lord Herbert before 1733. This elegant classical building with its first-floor loggia housed a horse-powered pump which provided water for the stables and outhouses. It stands today at the head of a replanted double avenue of horse chestnuts, commanding beautiful views of the house to the south. Only sketchy remains survive of Bridgeman's layout but the atmosphere of sobriety and grandeur, which must greatly have pleased a Whig grandee like Sir Robert Walpole, is wholly present.

A NEW GARDEN

A completely new garden has been made at Houghton in the old brick-walled kitchen garden to one side of the house. Here, largely designed by Julian and Isabel Bannerman, is a sprightly layout of flowers and formality. A pair of herbaceous borders forms the chief axis, running north to south. At the southern end of the axis the Bannermans designed a rustic pavilion of unbarked wood with a grand pediment filled with deers' antlers. Inside is a noble bench, painted chocolate brown

and gold – a William Kent design that echoes his work on the interior of the house. In the south-east corner of the garden, hedged in yew and screened by pleached limes, is a formal orchard of plums planted in straight rows in sixteen rectangles of grass, their edges close mown in strips. The only other ornament is a bench and an urn standing out against the dark yew. The effect is simple, elegant and beautiful.

A rose garden has box-edged beds, each filled with a single variety of rose and with occasional standard roses at the centre. Statues of classical deities stand among the flowery profusion and at the heart of the garden is a sunken pool and fountain, with steps leading down under arches of roses.

On the west side of the garden a walk of flowering cherries runs along beds of *Iris pallida* 'Argentea Variegata'. To one side a raised pool edged in box has a fountain which leaps and falls rhythmically. It is flanked by beds of box and lavender which trace the initials SC – commemorating Sybil Cholmondeley, the present Marquess of Cholmondeley's grandmother. A croquet lawn with a Kentian wooden pavilion is enclosed in yew hedges pierced on one side by openings containing Janus busts which look both ways through the hedge. A garden such as this, full of delight and decoration, is best hidden away from the more sombre and serious landscape that provides the setting for the great house.

The rose garden at Houghton

Location Houghton, King's Lynn PE31 6UE, Norfolk **OS** TF7928 11m NE of King's Lynn by A148 **Tel** 01485 528569 **Fax** 01485 528167 **Email** enquiries@houghtonhall.com **English Heritage Register** Grade I **Owner** The Marquess of Cholmondeley **Open** mid Apr to Sept, Sun, Thur and Bank Hol Mon 1–5.30 **Area** (walled garden) 5 acres/2 hectares

HYDE HALL

THE ROYAL HORTICULTURAL SOCIETY SHOWS WHAT IS POSSIBLE ON TOP OF A WINDY HILL IN THE DRIEST CORNER OF ENGLAND

Mr and Mrs R.H.M. Robinson came to farm at Hyde Hall in 1955. The house is on the top of a hill (by Essex standards a veritable Himalaya) in a windswept part of the country that is also just about the driest place in England. When they came there was no garden, merely a handful of trees eking out an existence in soil that was either hopeless (gravel) or impossible (clay). Not only did they manage to make a garden but they filled it with an astonishing array of plants, including those, such as willows, which should not do in such a dry site. They began opening the garden for the National Gardens Scheme (many visitors must have come to see a garden where gardening was impossible and stayed to marvel at the things that could be persuaded to grow and flourish here) and in 1976 they formed the Hyde Hall Trust which, in 1993, gave the estate to the Royal Horticultural Society.

The RHS has built on the garden that the Robinsons made, which was essentially informal, and has added new formal features. A chunky pergola, clothed in *viticella* clematis and white wisteria, now leads into the garden, and a handsome rose garden, designed by Robin Williams, has two rows of rectangular beds edged in box or yew and a central walk emphasised by tall obelisks of climbing roses. Running parallel to the rose garden, herbaceous borders echo the colours of the roses. At the entrance to the farmhouse an elegant parterre has plants of ornamental foliage, some of them tender – a mimosa (*Acacia*

The Dry Garden at Hyde Hall

...albata) against the wall has already risen to
...e level of the roof. The former farmyard
...nd is now a gently formalised lily pool with
...namental fish and a fine cascade.

...Part of the Robinsons' original garden,
...ermione's Garden, takes advantage of a
...turally boggy site and the shade of an old
... to grow ferns, hellebores, hostas, ligularias
...d rheums. Alongside it is one of the most
...prising areas – the Woodland Garden –
...ere, on the north-east corner of the hill, the
...obinsons managed to establish a windbreak
...d make the naturally neutral soil sufficiently
...d to cultivate rhododendrons. The species
...own here include some of the tender large-
...fed kinds such as *R. macabeanum* and *R.
...ogrande*, commonly seen only in the balmier
...d wetter English gardens. South-east of the
...use the Robinsons laid out a series of island
...ds (often with substantial ornamental trees)
...d borders of winter interest (with grasses
...d heathers). Running along the edge of this
...ea they made a long border of shrub roses
...derplanted with foxtail lilies (*Eremurus
...ustus*).

...One of the newest and most successful
...novations of the RHS is the Dry Garden
...ere rocks rise above gravel and paths wind
...out the undulating site. Here, in a scheme

no doubt inspired by another Essex gardener,
Beth Chatto (*see page 296*), is a very wide
range of plants that thrive in the driest
conditions, many of which will form self-
supporting colonies – cistuses, euphorbias,
lavenders, penstemons, salvias, sedums and
verbenas. Many ornamental grasses, including
some of the larger species of *Cortaderia*, New
Zealand flax (*Phormium* species) and yuccas,
make strong punctuation marks. It is
delightful and very effective – a desert garden
on the top of a hill in Essex.

Location Buckhatch Lane, Rettendon, Chelmsford CM3
8ET, Essex **OS** TQ7798 7m SE of Chelmsford by A130
and minor road **Tel** 01245 400256 **Fax** 01245 402100
Email hydehall@rhs.org.uk **Website** www.rhs.org.uk
Owner The Royal Horticultural Society **Open** mid Mar
to Aug, daily 10–6; Sept to mid Nov, daily 10–5 **Area**
136 acres/55 hectares

ICKWORTH

SPLENDID TOPIARY, HEDGED FORMAL
GARDENS, NOBLE TREES AND WONDERFUL
PARKLAND WALKS

The estate at Ickworth is very ancient –
a licence to impark about 50 acres/20
hectares was granted in the middle of the
13th century. In 1467 it was acquired by the
Hervey family who owned it until it was
transferred to the National Trust in 1956. The
family lived in various houses on the estate
until Ickworth House was built – from 1795,
to the designs of Mario Asprucci for
Frederick, 4th Earl of Bristol but completed
only in 1829. The 4th Earl was also Bishop of
Derry and his Irish estate of Downhill Castle
(*see page 408*) in County Londonderry has a
garden temple very similar in style to the
rotunda at Ickworth.

From the 17th century there was much

18th-century summerhouse at Ickworth

activity in the park, especially of tree planting, and in the 18th century Charles Bridgeman, Thomas Wright and Capability Brown were all consulted about the landscape – though nothing is known of what, if anything, resulted. Brown also advised on a new house – in 1782 William Hervey recorded that "Mr Brown came and brought with him a plan for a house." His plan was rejected but the site he suggested for the new house was chosen for the house that we see today.

18TH-CENTURY WALLED GARDENS
At some distance to the west of the present house the attractive walled gardens that were built in the first years of the 18th century for the old manor house survive, and still have a delightful summerhouse with tall windows and a curved pediment overlooking a formal canal. The water for the canal comes from the river Linnet which flows across the park. Part of the walled garden is now planted as a vineyard.

Gardens were made for the new house in the early 19th century and these, restored by the National Trust, make a fine setting for it. The approach to the house, with its central rotunda and curved wings, is shaded by magnificent cedars of Lebanon, and the north façade overlooks a great circular lawn with a long narrow herbaceous border curving round it in front of the house. South

of the house the garden is laid out with strong lines and bold shapes to suit the powerful architecture. A gravel walk edged with clipped bushes of phillyrea curves all the way about the rotunda, and a slightly broader walk, again with shapes of phillyrea, leads directly away to the edge of the garden where a gently curved terrace walk has views south over parkland. On either side of the broad walk, hidden behind tall box hedges, are enclosed gardens. One has plants of silver foliage and a stumpery – that distinctive Victorian feature of decaying tree stumps in the gloom; the other, gold-variegated plants. Against the house is an orangery planted with camellias and plants with variegated leaves such as fatsias and ivy. Pots of agave and agapanthus stand on the steps and a row of bronze heads by Elizabeth Frink runs along the edge of a lawn.

The parkland at Ickworth is spectacularly attractive and its threaded with walks that reveal its beauties. The Albana Wood Walk

north of the house, planned by the 5th Earl (and 1st Marquis) shortly after the house was finished, encapsulates many of its pleasures. It leads past beautiful old yews and oaks, girdling the deer park (which has a hide from which you may observe the deer). One of the best walks leads to the old walled garden and follows the banks of the river. You may then sweep round the south-western boundary of the park to the Monument, an obelisk built in 1817 and paid for with money raised by the people of Derry. Belts of old woodland often shroud the perimeter of the park and everywhere there are splendid trees – beech, field maple, hornbeam and oak – some of which were already here before the Herveys came in the 15th century. These magnificent trees are by far the most memorable feature of the landscape at Ickworth.

Location Horringer, Bury St Edmunds IP29 5QE, Suffolk
OS TL8161 3m SW of Bury St Edmunds by A143
Tel 01284 735270 **Fax** 01284 735175 **Email** ickworth@ntrust.org.uk **English Heritage Register** Grade II* **Owner** The National Trust **Open** end Mar to beginning Nov, daily 10–5; beginning Nov to 3rd week Dec, Mon to Fri 10–4; 2 Jan to end Mar, daily 10–4; Park open daily 7–7 **Area** (garden) 33 acres/13 hectares; (park) 1,800 acres/729 hectares

The south garden at Ickworth

KNEBWORTH HOUSE

FORMAL FLOWER GARDENS BY EDWIN
LUTYENS, A HERB GARDEN BY GERTRUDE
JEKYLL AND A REVIVED KITCHEN GARDEN

Sir Robert Lytton, a courtier of Henry VII, bought the Knebworth estate in 1490 and built a new house. In 1810 Mrs Elizabeth Bulwer-Lytton destroyed a large part of the house and began Gothicising what remained; this was continued by her son, Sir Edward Bulwer-Lytton, the prolific author of historical romances who wrote under the name Bulwer Lytton (Tennyson called him a "rouged and padded fop"). In Sir Edward Bulwer-Lytton's time the house was given the appearance it has today, with castellations, turrets, quatrefoils and heraldic beasts rising on elaborately carved pillars.

There had been a deer park at Knebworth in the early 14th century and this has remained a feature of the estate to this day. In 1700 Sir Henry Chauncy described the house in his *The Historical Antiquities of Hertfordshire*: "a large pile of brick…in a fair large park, stocked with the best deer in the country, excellent timber and well wooded". An illustration in the book shows the unaltered Tudor house with a walled forecourt and a row of curious trees like a chimney-sweep's brushes. In 1847 Sir Edward Bulwer-Lytton introduced a new

The herb garden at Knebworth

garden extending on a long axis south-west of the house, in (as he wrote in a letter) "the style favoured in the reign of James I, with the stone balustrades, straight walks, statues, and elaborate parterres". By the time *Country Life* illustrated it in 1897 it also had lavish bedding schemes.

The first notable garden designer to work at Knebworth was Sir Edwin Lutyens who had married Emily, the sister of the 2nd Earl of Lytton. In 1909 Lutyens redesigned Sir Edward Bulwer-Lytton's "Jacobean" garden, retaining the same axis but greatly simplifying it. Lutyens's sequence of gardens starts at the house with a sunken lawn flanked by lime walks and a central square pool surrounded by pleached limes. A walk of Irish yews continues the axis, and on each side are rose gardens and rectangular pools. An elaborately shaped screen of clipped yew, with deep niches for statues, has a narrow and enticing central opening. Beyond, is an abrupt change of mood: the small Green Garden is enclosed in yew hedges, and narrow borders on each side of a path are planted with *Alchemilla mollis*, bergenias, epimediums, euphorbias and hart's tongue ferns. The Gold Garden beyond it is a parterre arranged about a fountain pool, with beds filled with yellow-flowered plants or plants with gold variegated leaves. The last garden of the series is the Brick Garden, a

symmetrical pattern of mixed borders planted in blues and silvers. Beyond it, terminating the formal garden, is a pergola of clematis and roses which is slightly raised and has views west along a broad avenue of oaks and horse chestnuts aligned on a distant column and urn – a memorial to Edward Bulwer-Lytton's mother erected in 1866 with the inscription, "Mark, how serene in heaven/The upright column leaves the funeral urn".

Close to the house and hidden behind yew hedges is a herb garden designed by Gertrude Jekyll in 1907 but not put into place until 1982. It seems that Miss Jekyll did not work on the planting schemes for Lutyens's layout here. Her herb garden is an ingenious quincunx of five circular beds filled with culinary herbs, but rather unfortunately edged in industrial bricks which would have made Miss Jekyll quite ill. The walled former kitchen garden was restored in 2001 and planted with herbs and vegetables arranged in a circular pattern, with a tiered fountain and a central lawn of chamomile and thyme. The entrance gate, in simple Chinese Chippendale style, must surely be by Lutyens. On the lawns outside are splendid yews remaining from a 17th-century layout.

There are other attractions in the garden at Knebworth – a replanted Victorian maze, woodland with good specimen trees and, that archetypal English garden feature, a pets' cemetery. This one, however, is unique in having a tomb designed by Lutyens, a miniature of his Whitehall Cenotaph.

Location Knebworth SG3 6PY, Hertfordshire **OS** TL2220
28m N of London; Jnct 7 of A1(M) **Tel** 01438 812661
Fax 01438 811908

A decorative corner at Knebworth

Email info@knebworthhouse.com **Website** www.knebworthhouse.com **English Heritage Register** Grade II* **Owner** Lord Cobbold **Open** frequently end Mar to end Sept (phone for details) **Area** (garden) 25 acres/10 hectares; (park) 250 acres/101 hectares

MANNINGTON HALL

A GRAND COLLECTION OF ROSES IN A WALLED GARDEN, AND A DELIGHTFUL MOATED HOUSE

Mannington is a place of irresistible charm. The moated 15th-century house is faced in silvery flint and tricked out with tall brick chimneys, with the parapet of the house breaking out from time to time in cheerful castellations. The house was bought in the 1720s by Horatio Walpole, brother of Sir Robert Walpole, as a dower house. However, it was not until the 19th century that the Walpoles lived here, preferring the splendours of the much more imposing early 18th-century Wolterton House nearby (*see page 560*). It is perhaps for this reason that Mannington has retained the air of a house intended for the delectation of the family rather than as a setting for grand entertaining.

The moat garden at Mannington

There must have been a moated garden when the house was first built, and lakes to the east and north-east of the house are ancient, possibly medieval fishponds antedating the house. Today, yew hedges and beds of modern roses decorate the garden that surrounds the house within the moat, and the south wall of the house is garlanded with wisteria. Stone busts on plinths gaze back towards the house and waterlilies grow in the moat. Behind the yew hedges a garden of scented herbs is laid out in a pattern of beds cut into the turf, which echoes the dining room ceiling of the house. To one side of an open lawn south of the moat a shrubbery contains horses' graves, marked by a sculpted stone horse's head rising out of long grass. On the other side of the lawn, at the end of a lake, is a little 19th-century Doric temple, presumably placed here when the 4th Earl of Orford came to live at Mannington in 1860.

The Heritage Rose Garden, housed in the walled former kitchen garden at a little distance from the house, contains a very large collection of roses. This was planned in the early 1980s with the help of the famous local rose nurseryman Peter Beales. The roses are grouped historically and arranged in sometimes rather sketchy period designs, giving the visitor a fascinating opportunity to learn about the evolution of roses, from the very beautiful early cultivars which still provide so many fine garden plants, to the modern varieties so often ungainly in habit and violent in colour. Roses do well in this cool part of the country which also has long hours of sunshine. But the true distinction of Mannington comes from the house in its green and watery setting.

Location nr Saxthorpe NR11 7BB, Norfolk **OS** TG1432 18m NW of Norwich by B1149 and minor roads **Tel** 01263 584175 **English Heritage Register** Grade II **Owner** Lord and Lady Walpole **Open** May to Sept, Sun 12–5 (June to Aug, also open Wed to Fri 11–5) **Area** 20 acres/8 hectares

MELFORD HALL

AN OUTSTANDING TUDOR SUMMERHOUSE AND GOOD PLANTS FOR A CHARMING VILLAGE HOUSE

Melford Hall is a village house of unusual beauty, looking serenely over the village green. Before the dissolution of the monasteries the estate belonged to the abbey of Bury St Edmunds; Melford was a country retreat for the abbots. The old house was rebuilt in the middle years of the 16th century for Sir William Cordell, a successful lawyer who became Master of the Rolls. He received Queen Elizabeth at Melford in 1578 in considerable splendour: "200 young gentlemen cladde alle in whyte velvet, and 300 of the graver sort apparrelled in black velvet coates…with 1,500 servyng men all on horsebacke".

Sir William was responsible for the summerhouse which provides the single overwhelming garden reason for coming to Melford. Made of brick with stone dressings and built into the garden wall, it looks both within and without. It is octagonal, of two storeys, with much later sash windows. Each façade rises to a pointed gable crowned with a chimney-like finial at its apex, forming, with a further finial between each gable, a bristling crown of ornament. A room inside is decorated with 18th-century panelling, presumably made at the same time as the sash windows. Gertrude Jekyll came to see it and spotted its

rchitectural distinction in
pite of the fact that it was
hen shrouded in ivy which
he recommended should
e removed.

The garden here, with
orders and specimen trees,
not exciting, although
here are one or two plants
f rare distinction, including
he beautiful Chinese
Xanthoceras sorbifolium with
white hibiscus-like flowers
with maroon centres – "one
f the most beautiful of
mall trees", according to
W.J. Bean – but not often
een in gardens.

The Melford summerhouse

ocation Long Melford, Sudbury CO10 9AH, Suffolk
S TL8646 In Long Melford village, 4m N of Sudbury by
131 **Tel** 01787 880286 **English Heritage Register**
rade II* **Owner** The National Trust **Open** Apr and
ct, Sat, Sun and Bank Hol Mon 2–5.30; May to Sept,
ed to Sun (open Bank Hol Mon) 2–5.30 **Area**
acres/3.6 hectares

THE OLD VICARAGE
GARDEN

SPECTACULAR NEW FORMAL
GARDENS WITH MAGNIFICENT PLANTS
FLAWLESSLY CULTIVATED

n recent years every visit to the Old
Vicarage Garden has revealed new
plendours as Alan Gray and Graham
Robeson pursue their unstoppable ambition
o extend their intricate and opulently planted
arden further into the Norfolk landscape.
They bought the Arts and Crafts vicarage in
973, using it at first for weekends and
olidays; but since 1986 they have lived here
ull-time. There was no garden when they
ame and the garden they have made obeys
he principle of consulting the genius of the
lace. The newly built brick walls and
uildings (they seem to employ a full-time
ricklayer) are sympathetic to the Arts and
Crafts spirit, while carefully focussed vistas
efer to the external landscape by drawing in
hurch towers as eyecatchers. The proximity

of the sea – which is only
1½ miles away – has a
pronounced effect on the
climate, allowing (provided
protection is given from the
wind) the cultivation of
many tender plants. The soil
here is richly fertile loam
which gives their lavish
planting an extra
luxuriance.

The design of the garden,
although generally formal,
is neither geometric nor
symmetrical. A strong
southerly axis extends from
the house: a long grassy
walk of hedges starts with
an avenue of yew pyramids and ends with a
tall-roofed pavilion overlooking the gently
terraced Mediterranean Garden in which
plants like *Beschorneria yuccoides* grow with
abandon. This axis provides a backbone about
which the framework of the garden develops.
Long straight walks, with yew or holm oak
hedges, an avenue of acacias, or rows of apples
underplanted with catmint guide the eye and
the feet to the different parts of the garden,
which vary enormously in character. The
Mediterranean Garden takes advantage of the
drainage afforded by gravelly soil and a slight
downward slope – precious in these flat parts
– to grow a sumptuous array of cistuses,
echiums, lavenders, rosemaries and yuccas. An

Exotic Garden planted in 2000
has sumptuous borders of bananas and palms
underplanted with cannas, dahlias, grasses and
salvias overlooked by a majestic openwork
pavilion of minimalist oriental character. In
high summer the planting looks natural – in
fact much of it has to be bedded out and
some of the more substantial tender plants
require winter protection. A garden inspired
by the Arizona desert resembles a dry river
bed and is planted with drylands species –
agaves, aloes, dasylirions and swathes of self-
sown *Eschscholzia californica*. An open field is
planted simply with daisies and poppies and
any other obliging annuals of the sort that
once decorated cornfields.

Throughout the garden there is evidence
of much skill in planting and cultivation.
There are cool and restrained corners but
overall this is a garden of surprise and drama,
of explosive colour and form – the rumble
of a symphony orchestra rather than the
tootling of a flute.

Location East Ruston, Norwich NR12 9HN, Norfolk
OS TG3528 nr East Ruston church, off A149 signed
Bacton, Happisburgh; left at T junction and ignore
three signs to East Ruston **Tel** 01692 650432
Fax 01692 650233 **Email** erov@btinternet.com
Website www.e-ruston-oldvicaragegardens.co.uk
Owner Alan Gray and Graham Robeson **Open** end
Mar to end Oct, Sat, Sun, Wed, Fri and Bank Hol Mon
2–5.30 **Area** 12 acres/4.8 hectares

The desert garden at the Old Vicarage

OXBURGH HALL

A FRENCH PARTERRE, PRETTY BORDER,
VICTORIAN FORMAL ORCHARD AND A
KITCHEN GARDEN

Oxburgh is a wonderfully romantic moated house with a spectacular 15th-century gatehouse and gabled and crow-stepped walls enclosing a central courtyard. The house was built for Sir Edward Bedingfield after 1482 when he was granted a "licence to crenellate" – and the estate was given to the National Trust by the Dowager Lady Bedingfield in 1952. James Lees-Milne remembered: "I can see Lady Bedingfield enthroned very upright like a benign Byzantine empress in a stiff chair beneath Mary Queen of Scots' needlework."

It is remarkable that such an ancient house should have such a recent garden history – nothing is known of it before the 19th century. The most famous garden feature here is the French-style parterre laid out after 1845 to the east of the house. The design is taken from *La Théorie et la Pratique du Jardinage* by A.J. Dézallier d'Argenville (1709) but the effect is thoroughly Victorian. The design is picked out in dwarf box, rue (*Ruta graveolens* 'Jackman's Blue') and *Santolina chamaecyparissus* and bedded out with bright yellow marigolds (*Tagetes patula*) and bright pink *Ageratum houstonianum*. The effect is jolly but it belongs more happily to a municipal park that to such a sedate and rarefied architectural setting as this.

THE VICTORIAN KITCHEN GARDEN

Beyond the parterre a yew hedge conceals a long turf path running along a handsome mixed border against a wall. Edged in catmint, it is filled with buddleias, daylilies, geraniums, penstemons, peonies and *Perovskia atriplicifolia* – with much repeat planting. Honeysuckle and roses climb on the old brick wall behind it. A Victorian kitchen garden with battlemented walls is planted with a formal orchard of medlars, mulberries, pears, plums and quinces. A long south-west-facing wall is draped with clematis and roses, interspersed with tightly clipped piers of pear. North of the orchard and protected by a wall is a flourishing small kitchen garden of a simple kind, entirely maintained by volunteers – a pretty sight.

Location Oxborough, nr King's Lynn PE33 9PS, Norfolk **OS** TF7401 In the village of Oxborough, 9m E of Downham Market by A1122 and A134 **Tel** 01366 328258 **Fax** 01366 328066 **Email** oxburghhall@ntrust.org.uk **English Heritage Register** Grade II **Owner** The National Trust **Open** Mar, Sat and Sun 11–4; Apr to Jul and Sept to Oct, Sat to Wed 11–5.30; Aug, daily 11–5.30 **Area** 18 acres/7.3 hectares

The parterre at Oxburgh

PECKOVER HOUSE

BUSTLING TOWN GARDEN WITH EXCELLENT
TREES, BORDERS, ROSE ARBOUR AND
GLASSHOUSES

This is a rare opportunity to see a notable town garden. Peckover House is a beautiful early Georgian house built before 1727. The walled garden is as decorative as the house, its variety and charm appearing all the more attractive for its unexpected position in the middle of a busy market town. There are some remarkably large trees – a noble *Gingko biloba*, a *Liriodendron tulipifera* and a splendid *Sophora japonica*.

Close to the house, a 19th-century feature, Alexa's Rose Garden, has been reconstructed from an old photograph. A circle of metal arches support some of the swooniest of all climbing roses – 'Madame Isaac Pereire', 'Climbing Souvenir de la Malmaison', 'Sander's White Rambler', 'Noisette Carnée' and 'Madame Grégoire Staechelin'. At its centre a circular lily pool is surrounded by curved beds cut into the turf and planted with tulips and violets in the spring and cannas and coleus in summer. Nearby a green and white painted summerhouse overlooks an oval lily pool. A pair of topiary peacocks rise above an opening in a yew hedge leading to a gravel

Topiary peacocks at Peckover

The Plantation Garden terrace

path running between borders with mixed plantings of acanthus, buddleias, *Clematis recta*, crocosmia, euphorbias, Japanese anemones and roses. Sections are divided by hedges of *Viburnum opulus* 'Compactum', *Hydrangea arborescens* subsp. *discolor* 'Sterilis' or hibiscus. An arbour of roses spans the path and beyond it a glasshouse contains three large orange trees. A fern house alongside protects tender ferns and orchids and is heavy with the ponderous scent of stephanotis, its narrow passage bringing visitors unusually close to the plants. A range of cold frames and compost bins is hidden behind a hedge of golden privet and against a wall is a swashbuckling Victorian arrangement: a ribbon border in which alternate circles of pale pink and hot cerise busy lizzies are edged with loops of thrift on one side and santolina on the other. Much of the charm of the garden comes from an unemphatic idiosyncrasy which seems to scorn fashion.

Location North Brink, Wisbech PE13 1JR, Cambridgeshire **OS** TF4509 In the centre of Wisbech, well signed in the town **Tel** and **Fax** 01945 583463 **Email** peckover@ntrust.org.uk **English Heritage Register** Grade II **Owner** The National Trust **Open** end Mar to Oct, Sat to Thur 12.30–5 **Area** 2 acres/0.8 hectares

PLANTATION GARDEN

MYSTERIOUS AND HYPNOTIC 19TH-CENTURY
TERRACED GARDENS MADE FROM
ARCHITECTURAL SALVAGE

Oddness alone does not make a good garden but at the Plantation Garden the combination of a powerfully original vision and an unusual site results in a most memorable experience. The Plantation is a mid 19th-century villa on the edge of Norwich, built for Henry Trevor (1819–97). Trevor was a typical Victorian entrepreneur who founded a business in 1842 (with the slogan "Houses Completely Furnished") which provided furniture, upholstery, curtains and complete house interiors. (It survived, latterly as Trevor, Page & Co, until 1983.) From 1846 Trevor made a garden, possibly designed by Edward Boardman, in a former chalk quarry, a wooded ravine behind his house; White's *Norfolk Directory* (1890) described it as "a gem of landscape gardening". After World War II the garden was virtually abandoned, choked with ivy and sycamore saplings, until in 1980 a local group formed the Plantation Garden Preservation Trust and set about restoring it.

Although some fine features had been lost – among them a rustic bridge crossing the ravine and a palm house (probably by Boulton & Paul) – the restoration gradually revealed the essential fabric swamped by undergrowth. At the centre is a circular pool, dated 1857, with a soaring multi-tiered fountain like an openwork steeple, fashioned of Gothic arches, columns and the occasional grotesque mask (including cats sticking out their tongues). The whole is encrusted with ferns, moss and yellow corydalis – an enchanting sight.

AN EXTRAORDINARY TERRACE

The far end of the ravine is finished off with an extraordinary terrace wall scaled by a zigzagging staircase. The wall and staircase are made of flint and brick lavishly larded with enough architectural bits and bobs to stock a reclamation yard. It is a gallimaufry of knapped flint, lumps of limestone, moulded terracotta tiles (several with charming bunches of grapes), fragments of Gothic window cases, balustrades of different kinds and various unidentifiable lumps and knobs, while mosses, hart's tongue ferns and toad flax have colonised the stone. A criss-cross balustrade follows the stairs, with urns of scarlet pelargoniuns on its parapet, and from the top is a splendid view over the garden with its trees and shrubberies, lawn, boisterous bedding schemes and serpentine walks, with the central area spanned by a new rustic bridge. A further wall is encrusted with *objets trouvés* and two curious chimney-like ornaments are fashioned of architectural fragments.

The Plantation Garden would have delighted the artists of the Surrealist movement who loved the poetic results of heterogenous objects intermingled at random. Its rescue by a band of hard-working local enthusiasts is a wholly admirable feat of grass-roots conservation. May it inspire the rescue of other unloved masterpieces.

Location 4 Earlham Road, Norwich, Norfolk **OS** TG2208 On the W edge of Norwich on B1108 close to St John's Roman Catholic cathedral **Tel** 01603 621868 **Fax** 0870 1692343 **Email** chair@plantationgarden.co.uk **Website** www.plantationgarden.co.uk **English Heritage Register** Grade II **Owner** Plantation Garden Preservation Trust **Open** Apr to mid Oct, daily 9–6 **Area** 3 acres/1.2 hectares

SALING HALL

A SPLENDID COLLECTION OF TREES
IN A FINE PARKLAND SETTING, AND
CHARMING WALLED GARDENS

The garden of the amateur – in the true sense of that word – is often of quite special attraction. Hugh Johnson is probably most famous as the man who invented modern wine-writing, but he also loves gardens and plants (especially trees) and has written memorably on both. He and his wife, Judy, came here in 1970 to a delightful 17th-century house with a pretty garden that needed refocussing. An old walled garden, built at the same time as the house, with herring-bone paths of brick and rows of old apple trees clipped into mushroom shapes, makes a fine flower garden – formality blurred by profusion but with firm lines. Bold pyramids of box mark the corners of four central beds filled with roses, daylilies, delphiniums, geraniums, irises and phlomis, and a splendid blowsy lead figure of Flora stands at the centre surrounded by a metal arbour. Mixed beds under the walls are large enough for such ornamental trees as *Koelreuteria paniculata* and *Gleditsia triacanthos* 'Sunburst'.

The walled garden at Saling Hall

These pleasures are an *hors d'oeuvre* for the main course which is the aboretum that lies beyond the walls. Elms and poplars ruled here before the Johnsons came, but now the land has been transformed into a miniature landscape park enriched with marvellous trees woven skilfully into the scene. Eyecatchers – giant stone ball, a pedimented temple, a Japanese arch, a stag on a plinth, a millennium menhir – draw you on but not for long, for you will be sidetracked to savour some tree. Birches, maples, oaks, pines, willows, wingnut and countless others grow as they should – not as exhibits in a museum but as part of a beguiling landscape.

A private garden of this kind has only to honour its surroundings and please its owner and their friends. The garden at Saling Hall is animated by a sense of the pleasure that gardening brings – and this in turn has a palpable effect on the spirit of the place. It is altogether a most rewarding garden.

Location Great Saling, nr Braintree CM7 5DT, Essex **OS** TL7025 6m NW of Braintree by A120 **Tel** 01371 850141 **Fax** 01371 850274 **English Heritage Register** Grade II **Owner** Hugh Johnson **Open** May to Jul, Wed 2–5 **Area** 12 acres/4.8 hectares

SANDRINGHAM HOUSE

STATELY VICTORIAN LAKESIDE PLANTINGS
AND A FINE FORMAL FLOWER GARDEN
FOR A ROYAL HOUSE

The estate at Sandringham goes back to
the 18th century. The old house was
demolished after 1862 (except for a
conservatory, built in 1854 by S.S. Teulon for
the Hon. Charles Spencer Cowper, now a
billiard room) when the estate was bought as
a country retreat for Albert Edward, Prince of
Wales, and the house rebuilt in what Pevsner
calls "frenetic Jacobean". The estate remains in
the possession of the royal family who use it
chiefly for holidays and for shooting.

The gardens, apart from a few old trees, date
from the 1870s onwards. They were designed
by William Broderick Thomas whose nephew,
the architect and garden designer Francis
Inigo Thomas, said of him: "[he] gave up fox-
hunting for laying out the places of country
gentlefolk in the prevailing 'landscape'
manner." Thomas gave the pleasure grounds of
Sandringham the essential character they
possess today. He moved a lake further from
the house to the south-west and made a new
lake to the south. The banks of the upper lake
are shrouded in trees, with a Pulhamite
boathouse/grotto on its north bank and, in a
prominent position on its east bank, the
best, a curious gingerbread pavilion of

rustic stone standing on top of a rock garden.
This, with its pretty panelled interior, was
built in 1915 for Edward's VII's Queen,
Alexandra, and has an inscription, "The
Queen's Nest. A small offering to the blessed
lady from her beloved majesty's devoted old
servant General Probin."

North of the house is a subtle and refined
formal garden designed in 1947 by Sir
Geoffrey Jellicoe. A series of compartments
threaded along a gravel path and enclosed in

The lake garden at Sandringham

high box hedges contain mixed borders of
buddleias, Brompton stocks, echinaceas,
eupatorium, geraniums, irises, rosemary and
roses, with judicious sprinklings of annuals.
Four of the compartments contain nothing at
all except a flawless square lawn. At their
northern end is an 18th-century figure of
winged Father Time. The whole arrangement
is flanked with double pleached lime walks,
one of which culminates in a splendid plump
gilt Buddha guarded by Chinese lions.

The entrance courtyard to the east of the
house has magnificent yew hedges
with finely tailored bays for
benches on either side.

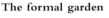

The formal garden

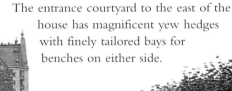

Splendid trees, especially conifers dating from Thomas's time, crowd in all about.

Location Sandringham, King's Lynn PE35 6EN, Norfolk **OS** TF6928 9m NE of King's Lynn by B1440 **Tel** 01553 772675 **Fax** 01485 541571 **English Heritage Register** Grade II* **Owner** HM The Queen **Open** Apr to Oct (closed late Jul and early Aug; phone for details), daily 11–4.45 **Area** 60 acres/24 hectares

SHERINGHAM PARK

A BRILLIANTLY SIMPLE LANDSCAPE PARK
BY HUMPHRY REPTON, MAKING THE MOST
OF A LOVELY SETTING

Sheringham is the last work of Humphry Repton and it gave him special pleasure for it lies in his own home county. His client was a rich young man, Abbot Upcher, who died in 1817 before the work was completed. The site chosen was a lovely combe, close to the coast and with fine sea views – Repton thought that it possessed "more of what my predecessor called *Capabilities*" than any place he had seen in fifty years. Repton was also asked to design a new and grander house to replace the existing farmhouse, which he did in collaboration with his son John. They built a vaguely Italianate villa, tucked away behind rising land to protect it from the fierce coastal winds from the north. Repton also devised a drive that would curl round from the south and reveal the house with its wooded hill behind and the sea and ships

displayed to the east.

Repton's Red Book of proposals for Sheringham shows a domed rotunda on a vantage point to the east of the drive, commanding wide views of the whole estate. This was not built until 1975 when a descendant, Thomas Upcher, commissioned a design from the architect James Fletcher-Watson based on Repton's original.

"MY MOST FAVOURITE WORK"
The route that visitors take through the park today only gradually reveals the character of the place. The path plunges into woodland, with oaks, Scots pines and sycamores most in evidence, but with much underplanting of rhododendrons. Then, after skirting a wood – with views of the house across the valley to the east and cattle grazing in pastures – a path leads across a field, where you may have to dodge the cows, and comes to the temple on a wooded eminence. The view from the temple is extraordinarily beautiful. The house is seen far across the valley, partly enclosed in trees, and behind it the sea is revealed in the distance – a sliver of blue between two sweeps of trees on the horizon.

The Sheringham temple

Repton himself wrote that "This may be considered my most favourite work" and it is indeed a place that is very easy to love. It is visitable on any day of the year, and in any season Sheringham generously yields its charms. Despite its serenity it has a sad history, for Repton, desperately ill with a ngina as it was being made, died in 1818 before its completion.

Location Upper Sheringham, Sheringham NR26 8TB, Norfolk **OS** TG1342 2m SW of Sheringham by A148 **Tel** and **Fax** 01263 823778 **Email** sheringhampark@ntrust.org.uk **English Heritage Register** Grade II* **Owner** The National Trust **Open** daily dawn–dusk **Area** 90 acres/36 hectares

SHRUBLAND GARDENS

SPLENDID 19TH-CENTURY ITALIANATE
GARDENS AND A DELICIOUS WALK OF
SWEET CHESTNUTS

When the Bacon family came to Shrubland in the 17th century the estate had a house going back to the 16th century, a walled garden and a deer park. They built a new house on a different site in the 1770s to the designs of James Paine. A little later, in 1788, the estate was bought by Sir William Middleton who commissioned Humphry Repton to make improvements to the landscape – one of his earliest commissions. Some of Repton's recommendations were carried out but the great event that transformed Shrubland into the garden that may be seen today was the arrival of the architect Charles Barry. In the late 1840s he altered the house and created grandiose Italianate gardens descending in terraces from its western façade. The Descent, a vertiginous flight of stone steps hedged in box, plummets down the hill, interrupted at regular intervals by urns and landings. At the bottom it sweeps round in a broad shallow double staircase, partly embracing a circular lawn with a pool and fountain at its centre. Beyond the pool, but still aligned with the

The Italian Garden at Shrubland

Descent, is an elaborate stone loggia. From here a cross axis runs across at an angle, linking other ornamental episodes – including the curved stone Conservatory or Hot Wall to the south. This was formerly heated with hot water and glazed with glass screens "as a nursery for choice bulbs" to test "the hardiness of Crinums, Amaryllids &c. here". Beyond the Hot Wall is a Swiss garden with a rockery and chalet-style cottage.

The garden at Shrubland is swashbuckling stuff but is it lovable? Sometimes I feel that it needs crowds of elegant ladies swishing past in crinolines and dashing young men sipping champagne to bring it fully to life. It is perhaps more social scenery than sublime landscape.

The most memorable, and undeniably beautiful, area at Shrublands is the Brownslow Terrace north of the house (probably designed by Repton himself) where the walk passes under the limbs of breathtaking old sweet chestnuts and ends with a statue of Diana

An archway at Shrubland

silhouetted against the sky. (In his Red Book Repton describes an intended path here running "along the natural Terrace under the spreading branches of the venerable Chestnut Trees".) The trees were later described in *The Gardeners Chronicle*: "Such boles! Such a world of knots and cracks! Such spiral furrows ploughed in their bark!" The simple terrace and trees were not sweet enough for the Victorian tooth, perhaps, but remain a lovely sight.

Location Coddenham, Ipswich IP6 9QQ, Suffolk
OS TM1252 7m NW of Ipswich **Tel** 01473 830221
Fax 01473 832202 **English Heritage Register** Grade I
Owner Lord de Saumarez **Open** Apr to beginning Sept,
Sun and Bank Hol Mon 2–5 **Area** 40 acres/16 hectares

SOMERLEYTON HALL

GRAND VICTORIAN GARDENS WITH FINE
TREES, WALLED GARDEN, BORDERS,
GLASSHOUSES AND A MAGNIFICENT MAZE

This is one of the most enjoyable and interesting gardens in Suffolk. At a quick glance it seems all of a piece – a lavish Victorian garden to suit a great Victorian mansion. However, there had been a great garden here in the 17th century, as is plainly shown in an estate map in the Suffolk Record Office, dated 1652, when the estate belonged to the Wentworth family. The most spectacular feature shown on this map is a series of four enclosed gardens running northwards from the old house, becoming larger as they extend away from it, and linked by an axial walk. At first the enclosures seem conventionally formal but the last and largest of them is an area of woodland laced with winding paths, described in a survey of 1663 as having a "variety of seats, statues, fish ponds, a house for pleasure newly erected and diverse other rarities". No traces of this garden remain but in the early 18th century a more conventional garden of avenues was laid out, and of this a line of limes running south-east from the house can still be seen.

W.A. NESFIELD'S GARDEN

In 1844 a new house was built for a new owner: Morton Peto. Peto was the archetypal Victorian self-made man who started as a bricklayer, was by his thirties an immensely wealthy building tycoon, and was knighted in 1855. To the Italianate mansion he added gardens, largely designed by W.A. Nesfield. A formal garden west of the house was laid out in 1846 – its original elaborate scheme now much simplified – with urns, rose beds and clipped shapes of golden and common yew. North of the house are lawns and fine trees (oaks, cedars of Lebanon and sweet chestnuts) and a statue of Atalanta gathering the golden apples. A dramatic Wellingtonia with wide-spreading branches stands at the front of the entrance to the walled kitchen garden.

The entrance to the kitchen garden is itself scarcely less dramatic – an arched opening in

The kitchen garden at Somerleyton Hall

a screen of brick and stone with niches carrying urns of flowers, richly carved ornament over wrought-iron gates, and the whole crowned with a pair of bronze agaves in stone troughs. Inside, glasshouses run the whole length of the south-facing wall on each side of the entrance – the original peach houses. Herbaceous borders along the central walk have orchards on either side, underplanted with daffodils, and running across the garden are magnificent ridge and furrow vine houses, probably designed by Sir Joseph Paxton. A cross walk leads under a long pergola with grapevines, roses and an ancient wisteria, to a maze of yew hedges designed by W.A. Nesfield, with a pretty black and white gazebo at its centre.

Any visitor to Somerleyton should also visit the village which Sir Morton Peto rebuilt in picturesque style: a series of thatched, half-timbered cottages *ornés* crowned by high-rising bogus Tudor chimney stacks. Peto went bankrupt in 1866 and the estate was bought by Sir Francis Crossley whose descendant, Lord Somerleyton, still owns it. The garden is finely cared for and very little has changed in it since the 19th century, making it one of the

outstanding survivors of its period in the country.

Location Somerleyton, Lowestoft NR32 5QQ, Suffolk **OS** TM4997 5m NW of Lowestoft by B1074 **Tel** 01502 730224 **Fax** 01502 732143 **Website** www.somerleyton.co.uk **English Heritage Register** Grade II* **Owner** Lord and Lady Somerleyton **Open** Apr to Sept, Thur, Sun and Bank Hol Mon (Jul and Aug also open Tue and Wed) 12.30–5.30; Oct, Sun 12.30–5.30 **Area** 12 acres/4.8 hectares

STOCKWOOD PARK

RECREATED PERIOD GARDENS AND A DELIGHTFUL AND MYSTERIOUS GARDEN BY IAN HAMILTON FINLAY

This place goes under several different names: The Period Gardens at Stockwood Park, and Stockwood Country Park and Mossman Museum are both used o local signposts. Its old name was merely Stockwood Park, where the Crawley family lived in a handsome mid Georgian house which was demolished in 1964. A Georgian stable block and a walled, presumably kitcher

A flock of stones at Stockwood

garden still survive. The estate now belongs to the Luton Borough Council which has opened a museum of rural life (the Mossman Museum) in the stable block, and has created a series of gardens.

The Period Gardens enclosed in the walled garden, of different styles or genres, include a medieval garden, a knot, an Italian garden, a Victorian garden and a cottage garden. They jostle each other cheek by jowl and the effect is hectic and slightly exhausting rather than instructive. Outside the walled enclosure the Dutch garden has a hedge of Leyland cypress, a box parterre whose compartments are filled with different colours of gravel, 18th-century-style urns and bedding plants.

But the overwhelming reason – for some perhaps the only reason – for coming here is to see the Improvement Garden designed by the artist Ian Hamilton Finlay. The core of Finlay's art is poetry, which he has explored in several media, and here he provides a window into 18th-century garden ideas. It is the only substantial work of one of the most original and attractive living garden designers and poets that is open to the public in England. In a relatively small area – part of the original 18th-century park – Finlay richly animates the scene. A brick wall, the Errata of Ovid, is decorated with a series of stone plaques which bear the words: "for DAPHNE read Laurel, for PHILOMELA read NIGHTINGALE, for CYANE read Fountain, for ECHO read ECHO, for ATYS read Pine, for NARCISSUS

read NARCISSUS, for ADONIS read Anemone". Two silver birches grow out of the stone bases of columns mounted on a plinth, with two plaques which read "BETULA PENDULA" and "SILVER BIRCH". Part of an elaborate and giant stone capital erupts from the turf. A flock of roughly shaped flat stones meander across the grass between two runs of ha-ha (excavations of the 18th-century original). An anagramatic inscription reads:

> I HARD POET
> HOT DIP, EAR
> O DIRE PATH

Among a grove of silver birches a now

headless herm is even more enigmatic than Finlay can have intended. Many English 18th-century landscape gardens were rich in classical allusions whose meanings we glimpse only hazily, and here Finlay allows us to take a pleasurable amble and think about the past. At Stockwood the distance from the M1 to Arcadia is surprisingly small.

Location Farley Hill, Luton, Bedfordshire **OS** TL0820
1½m SW of Luton by B4546; signed off Jnct 10a of M1
Tel 01582 546739 **Owner** Luton Borough Council
Open Apr to Oct, daily except Mon (open Bank Hol
Mon) 10–5; Nov to Mar, Sat and Sun 10–4 **Area**
10 acres/4 hectares

THE SWISS GARDEN

ENIGMATIC BUT IRRESISTIBLE GARDEN
OF SHADY WATERSIDE WALKS WITH A
DAZZLING FERN GROTTO

The Swiss Garden is a lively reminder of the astonishing variety of gardens to be found in the British Isles. It is a true original and visitors today may be more than a little puzzled by its Swissness. The garden was made in the early 19th century when Switzerland, and especially alpine climbing, became fashionable. There is a story that the garden was created as a love-nest by the 3rd Lord Ongley for his Swiss mistress; it is also said that

The cottage in the Swiss Garden

The Swiss Garden fernery

Location Old Warden, Biggleswade, Bedfordshire **OS** TL1544 2½m W of Biggleswade by minor roads; signed from A1 and A600 **Tel** 01767 627666 **Fax** 01767 627443 **English Heritage Register** Grade II* **Owner** Bedfordshire County Council **Open** Mar to Sept, daily 1–6 (opens 10 Sun and Bank Hol Mon); Jan, Feb and Oct, Sun and New Year's Day 11–3 **Area** 9 acres/3.6 hectares

WIMPOLE HALL

SUPERB PARKLAND AND RESTORED EARLY 19TH-CENTURY FLOWER GARDENS IN A WONDERFUL SETTING

The garden at Wimpole has just about the busiest history of any garden in England. As Gervase Jackson-Stops wrote: it "provides almost a case-book history of English gardening from 1690 to 1830." The various stages in its evolution, and the numbers of great garden designers involved, fall so thick and fast that it is sometimes hard to keep one's eye on what is remarkable, and enjoyable, about the place.

"EXQUISITE CONTRIVANCES"
The story starts with the building of the first house, for Sir Thomas Chicheley, in the 1640s. Kip's engraving in *Britannia Illustrata* of 1707 shows a formal garden of immense grandeur and complexity. Daniel Defoe, when it was still very new, described it as being filled with "all the most exquisite Contrivances which the best Heads cou'd invent". This garden was possibly the work of George London and Henry Wise and was made even grander in the 1720s when Charles Bridgeman added an elaborate pattern of avenues. Most of this was dismantled later in the 18th century, chiefly by Capability Brown from 1767 onwards, leaving Wimpole Hall by the end of the century enclosed in a naturalistic landscape park with traces of earlier avenues, new billowing belts of trees and serpentine lakes. Brown did, however, leave the spectacular double avenue of elms to the south of the house, which survived until Dutch elm disease destroyed it in the 1970s. Brown also opened out a vista which drew the eye to the Gothic Tower, a ruinous castellated building originally designed by Sanderson

the same Lord Ongley encouraged the women in the village of Old Warden to dress up in tall Swiss hats and red cloaks. At all events, he certainly made the garden here in the 1820s and 1830s, having inherited the estate in 1814.

Ongley was influenced by *Village Architecture* (1830) by P.F. Robinson, who designed Swiss Cottage in London. The wooded grounds are undulating, yet far from alpine, and Robinson's delicious rural cottage sitting on a slope of the greenest grass, with thatch as deep as an eiderdown, is more Regency cottage *orné* than Swiss chalet. The path skirts ponds, swoops over an elegantly arched cast-iron bridge and leads among fine trees – including a magnificent English oak with a tree seat shaded by a deep thatched roof. Curious ornaments and buildings loom up: an Indian kiosk with stained glass windows, a pair of giant stone eagles, and a cast-iron urn with scenes depicting morning and evening (a baby asleep or awake in an angel's arms).

The most astonishing building here is the grotto and fernery which dates from the 1830s. A stained-glass door opens into a mysterious and gloomy passage hung with stalactites, which leads in turn into the brilliant light of the fernery – an elaborate glasshouse with a cast-iron framework (made by the Eagle Foundry of Nottingham), which rises in the centre to a superb dome. The walls are encrusted with tufa and Pulhamite, and cavities are planted with ferns.

The Swiss Garden is enchanting, but is it merely a piece of self-indulgent English whimsy or can it yield some secret meaning? Is it perhaps a celebration of the industrial revolution, using machine-made cast-iron and man-made Pulhamite as the expressive medium for garden ornament? The first metal glazing bars were used on a glasshouse no earlier than 1800, so the elegant fernery dome here shows how quickly a new invention, in the hands of a true craftsman, could be employed with exquisite creativity. These products of the new age are disposed in an Arcadian setting with noble trees, the twittering of birdsong, expanses of water and banks of shrubs rising from shorn turf. Could this be interpreted as the old shaking hands with the new – nature and industry linked together in unexpected harmony?

iller in around 1750 but not put into place ntil 1768. It was not universally praised – "foolish, fantastic mock ruins", Col John Byng called it on his visit to Wimpole in 1790. In 1801 Humphry Repton produced a Red Book for Wimpole but apart from a formal flower garden below the north façade of the house it is not clear to what extent his proposals were put into force.

One of the most attractive features of Wimpole today is the beauty of the house's position – an open site on an airy eminence commanding distant views. To the south, sliding down the hill in front of the house, is a double avenue of limes – a replacement of the ancient elm avenue. Behind the house a mid-18th-century flower parterre (a Victorian nod to the early 18th-century formal gardens on this spot) was replanted in 1994 and tricked out with brilliant bedding plants. This formal garden is enclosed by railings (a suggestion of Repton's), beyond which sheep or cattle graze in parkland studded with trees, with Sanderson Miller's ruin rising in the distance. Repton had the ingenious idea, clearly shown in his Red Book, of framing this view of Brown's park with a pair of gate piers capped with splendid

The flower parterre at Wimpole Hall

early 18th-century urns, and they are still in place. The park, benefiting from much restoration by the National Trust since the 1990s, provides exactly the kind of Arcadian setting for the classical house which the 18th-century landscaper so desired.

Location Arrington, Royston SG8 0BW, Cambridgeshire **OS** TL3351 8m SW of Cambridge by A603 **Tel** 01223 207257 **Fax** 01223 207838 **Email** wimpolehall@ntrust.org.uk **Website** www.wimpole.org **English Heritage Register** Grade I **Owner** The National Trust **Open** mid Mar to Oct, daily except Mon and Fri (open Bank Hol Mon and Good Fri) 1–5 (Jul and Aug, also open Fri 1–5); Nov to Mar, Sat and Sun 10.30–5 **Area** 20 acres/8 hectares

WREST PARK

GRAND EARLY 18TH-CENTURY GARDENS WITH SPLENDID LATE VICTORIAN ADDITIONS

The de Grey family came to live at Silsoe in the 13th century. In the late 17th century Anthony de Grey, 11th Earl of Kent rebuilt the medieval and Tudor house and made grand new formal gardens. Kip's engraving in *Britannia Illustrata* (1707) shows a walled garden south of the house, parterres with circular pools and two mazes of different designs. The central axis of the walled garden is continued beyond gates in the wall by the

The Chinese pavilion at Wrest Park

Long Water – a canal flanked by hedges. Further formal gardens lie to the east of the house and there is a second canal at an angle to the south-east. All this was greatly extended by the 12th Earl (who became the first Duke in 1710). His Great Garden introduced woodland threaded with formal rides on each side of the Long Water, new canals at right-angles to it and, as a magnificent eyecatcher at its southern end, the Pavilion – a beautiful domed building by Thomas Archer, built between 1709 and 1711. Later in the century, between 1758 and 1760, Capability Brown was consulted by Jemima, Marchioness Grey, and his work is commemorated by a tall stone column topped by an acorn, with an inscription that acknowledges "the professional assistance of Lancelot Brown, Esq., 1758" in the beautifying of the gardens. In the 1830s Thomas, Earl de Grey demolished the old house and built in its place (to his own designs) an immense mansion in extravagant French 18th-century style. He also laid out suitably flamboyant parterres on its south side, and these, with swirling patterns of cut turf, curved box-edged beds of annuals and statues of Venus and Adonis and Diana and Endymion, are still in place.

The great charm of Wrest Park comes from the most unlikely mixture of ingredients in which features from the gardens of different periods, and of very different character, live cheek by jowl. Archer's Pavilion is still a dominant ornament in the landscape (Horace Walpole saw it in 1771 and much disliked

The Pavilion and canal at Wrest Park

"the frightful Temple designed by Mr Archer"), rearing up confidently at the far end of a canal, with a fine lead statue of King William III, possibly by Henry Cheere. Here, to the east of the canal, a serpentine stream threads its way through the woods with an elegant Chinese pavilion (a 19th-century reconstruction of an 18th-century original) on its bank. The stream here, spanned by an arched "Chinese" bridge (1876), was a canal in the 1st Duke's garden and was presumably made informal by Capability Brown. The woodland gardens on either side of the Long Water are divided with a curious mixture of straight rides, sometimes leading to Archer's Pavilion, and winding walks. In the north-west corner of the woodland is a bowling green overlooked by a grand pillared building with a pretty interior – built for the 1st Duke and possibly designed by Batty Langley.

One of the oddest surviving buildings at Wrest is a monumental bath house, or hermitage, partly thatched and fashioned of massive blocks of uncut stone. Horace Walpole thought that it was designed by Capability Brown and approved of its "bold good taste". In fact it was built in 1770 and designed by Edward Stevens to resemble a semi-ruined classical building. This lies on the far west side of the garden, behind the handsome Frenchified orangery which, like the house, was designed by Earl de Grey in Louis XVth style, and built under the supervision of James Clephan between 1836 and 1839.

The Wrest Park estate remained in the family until 1917, and after World War II was bought by the Ministry of Public Building and Works, passing in due course to English Heritage. The house, retaining all its splendour, is let out. But the gardens and their beautiful buildings remain, one of the most alluring living anthologies of English garden taste.

Location Silsoe MK45 4HS, Bedfordshire **OS** TL0935 ½m E of Silsoe by A6 **Tel** 01525 860152 **English Heritage Register** Grade I **Owner** English Heritage **Open** Apr to Oct, Sat, Sun and Bank Hol Mon 10–6 **Area** 80 acres/32 hectares

WYKEN HALL GARDEN

SPRIGHTLY GARDEN ROOMS, A SPLENDID ROS
GARDEN AND A CHARMING FARMYARD

Wyken is a busy place, with a vineyard, restaurant and garden. The house is Elizabethan with 17th-century additions, faced with stucco painted a glowing pink-brown. The garden is the creation of the present owners and benefits from existing old flint walls and a background of mature trees.

Facing the entrance to the house is a grou of five circles of box hedging; four of these enclose tiered shapes of clipped yew crowned

ith a pompom and the fifth, at the centre, as a pool and fountain of rich blue ceramic decorated with splotches and squiggles. Behind the house a cluster of formal enclosures, designed by Arabella Lennox-Boyd in 1983, follow the façade of the house. A herb parterre hedged in box and yew has a sundial, standard wisterias and edgings of chives and thyme; another, paved in bricks, has pyramids of yew, mushrooms of cotoneaster, a *Magnolia grandiflora* against the wall and an olive tree in a Tuscan pot; a third enclosure has tall arbours of apples, a pair of weeping mulberries and a bench clasped in

Chickens in the borders at Wyken

yew hedging. Ferns, hellebores, hydrangeas and pulmonarias animate a shady corner.

A former orchard to one side of the house is now a rose garden. Enclosed in hornbeam hedges or walls of brick and flint, it is divided into four by herringbone paths and has a central fountain pool. Here is a large collection of shrub roses underplanted with geraniums, irises, lilies, *Lychnis coronaria* 'Alba', peonies and phlox. A trelliswork pergola running across one end of the garden is draped with honeysuckle, grapevines, roses and wisteria, with ferns and periwinkle in the shade below. A pair of Gothic gates leads to a pool

overlooked by a jetty and seats. From here a path now leads into the wilder and more secluded part of the garden, past a grove of Himalayan birches, under an exquisite old English oak and up a hill to a gazebo smothered in wisteria.

Close to the house is an orchard with a kennel in the form of a miniature church and all sorts of clucking poultry among the trees. Peacocks loll and pose in the formal garden compartments behind the house and chickens strut along a path between borders blazing with hot colours. This cheerful interpenetration of farmyard and garden, and the wonderful oak on the way to the gazebo, are the most memorable things at Wyken Hall.

Location Stanton, nr Bury St Edmunds IP31 2DW, Suffolk **OS** TL9671 9m NE of Bury St Edmunds by A143 and minor road **Tel** 01359 250287 **Fax** 01359 252256 **Owner** Sir Kenneth and Lady Carlisle **Open** Apr to Sept, daily except Sat 2–6 **Area** 4 acres/1.6 hectares

NORTH *of* ENGLAND

ALNWICK CASTLE

SPECTACULAR NEW WATER GARDENS AND
FLOWER GARDENS FOR AN ANCIENT ESTATE

The castle at Alnwick, built close to the river Aln, dates back to the 12th century and since 1309 has been the home of the Percy family, latterly Dukes of Northumberland. By the time the 1st Duke (1750–86) inherited, the castle was in a very poor state and "the grounds unkempt and full of stones", as seen in Canaletto's painting of that time. Both James Paine and Robert Adam worked on new interiors for the 1st Duke but this was largely undone from 1854 when Anthony Salvin carried out alterations costing £250,000 (£10,075,000 today).

The 1st Duke employed Capability Brown to landscape the grounds and the result of his work may be seen in delicious views from the castle, with turf running down to the river and clumps of trees. Several ornamental buildings in the landscape also date from this time. Brizlee Tower, an extraordinary six-floored Gothic tower on rising ground two miles from the castle, was built in 1781 and probably

The cascade at Alnwick

designed by Robert Adam. John Adam's Lion Bridge is of 1773 and Denwick Bridge, probably by Robert Mylne, was built in 1766.

In 1750 a new garden was made close to the castle – an area of 12 acres/4.8 hectares – which in 1777 was enclosed in stone walls. In the 19th century this was a kitchen and flower garden with a central pool and conservatory but by 1950 it was no longer in use and became an estate forestry nursery. It is now spectacularly transformed as the Alnwick Garden, designed by Jacques Wirtz and his son Peter. Work started on the site in the spring of 2000 and by 2002 a large part of the garden had been completed.

The site is a sloping one and the walled space is of irregular shape and divided into two – the larger part at the lower level, with the smaller above it. As you enter the garden the dominating, indeed overwhelming, feature at its heart is a gigantic cascade. It swoops down the slope towards you, outlined in sinuous stone edging, with paths and serpentine tunnels of hornbeam on each side. The flow of water and of the many water jets

that ornament the cascade is controlled by a computer so that no sequence of watery effects is exactly repeated. From time to time – quite unpredictably – immensely high single jets shoot out at angles, soaking passers-by, to the intense delight of the many children who already come here. In spirit and atmosphere this echoes the gardens of the Italian Renaissance which also delighted in the use of water and entertained visitors with *giochi d'acqua*. Behind the hornbeam tunnels, large circular pools are ringed with fastigiate oaks (*Quercus robur* 'Fastigiata'). Each pool has a great water jet, a splendid sight from below, shooting high above the greenery. The detail is beautifully conceived and executed – expertly cut limestone is used to edge the cascade and for paths; the tunnels of hornbeam are finely made and planted.

THE ORNAMENTAL GARDEN

Above the cascade the Ornamental Garden is very different but linked by its use of water. You enter the garden through lovely Italian 16th-century wrought-iron gates bought in the 19th century by the 4th Duke. The shape of this enclosure is very irregular but the Wirtzes have given it harmony by laying out a strongly formal design. At its centre, water from a square raised pool falls into a rill which takes it down the slope into the Cascade Garden. Rills also lead on each side to circular pools at the centre of circular gardens hedged in yew. A pergola with clematis and roses surrounds the square pool and a pattern of square box-hedged beds spread out on either side. Each bed is framed with a screen of crab-apples (*Malus* 'Red Sentinel') expertly pleached high up on a framework of bamboos, leaving the lower part of the trunk bare so that the beds are visible. The beds are planted with ornamental plants, often roses, or with fruit (sometimes intermingled to great effect). The pink rose 'Ballerina' in standard form is underplanted with neat rows of 'Yellow Wonder' strawberries. *Rosa* 'Albertine', again standard trained, is underplanted with different cultivars of blueberry, their exquisite rich blue fruit looking wonderful in September. Deep borders run under the walls of the garden. Here the planting is generous, with large clusters of plants, some familiar (harts' tongue ferns), some much less so (the lovely small-leafed holly, *Ilex aquifolium* 'Myrtifolia'). Substantial ornamental trees – among them *Koelreuteria paniculata, Malus toringo* subsp. *sargentii* or *Ptelea trifoliata* – rise among the mixed planting. Awkward spaces at the edges of the formal beds are resolved by charming triangular beds hedged in dogwood (*Cornus mas*) to chest height, and each filled with a different cultivar of hydrangea.

To one side of the lower garden a serpentine rose garden is filled with David Austin English Roses, including the new cultivar 'Alnwick Castle'. A snaking metal pergola winds among curving rose beds and a superlative 18th-century lead urn from Syon Park (the Percys' great house near London, *see page 546*) forms a marvellous ornament.

Further gardens are to be added – a labyrinth, a Serpent Garden, a Garden of the Senses and a Poison Garden. These, and the already completed parts, are all aspects of a single vision. When finished it will be one of the grandest and most enjoyable gardens in the country.

Location Alnwick NE66 1NQ, Northumberland **OS** NU1813 In Alnwick, 1½m W of A1 **Tel** 01665 510777 **Infoline** 01665 511100 **Fax** 01665 510876 **Email** enquiries@alnwickcastle.com **Owner** The Duke of Northumberland **Open** daily 10–5 (closed 25 Dec) **Area** 12 acres/4.8 hectares

BELSAY HALL

A RARE AND ROMANTIC QUARRY GARDEN AND A FLOWERY TERRACE

The garden at Belsay has various charms, mostly of a minor kind, but one single feature that is so beautiful and unusual as to make it altogether exceptional. Belsay Hall, an austerely beautiful neo-classical house like a Greek temple, was built between 1807 and 1817 to the fastidious designs of its owner, Sir Charles Monck, whose ancestors, the Middletons, had lived here since at least the 13th century. The quarry for the sandstone for the new house was on the estate itself and the resulting workings, a long, deep ravine west of

the house, were transformed by Sir Charles and his descendants into a dramatic picturesque garden of unique splendour – an altogether startlingly romantic contrast to the severe splendours of the Hall.

Outcrops of rock are furred with mosses and liverworts and the cliffs are planted with ferns, yews and rhododendrons. Such distinguished trees as *Cercidiphyllum japonicum* and *Parrotia persica* fringe the path, sometimes forming shady tunnels. The cliffs are occasionally suffused with light and elsewhere cast into the deepest gloom. The passage between them opens out into spacious cathedral-like chambers and from time to time narrows dramatically, forcing you through a slender aperture. When you eventually emerge from the shadowy tunnel you find yourself on the edge of a pasture (note the lovely black poplar on your left), on the far side of which are the beautiful remains of Belsay Castle, the original Middleton dwelling, built between the late 14th century and the early 17th century. If I were an advertising man I would call the ravine the Unique Selling Proposition of the garden at Belsay.

WROUGHT BY A THUNDERBOLT

There are other gardens at Belsay – a winter garden to the west of the house and decorative formal terraces below its south façade, for example – and from the terraces you have tantalising views over the ha-ha of bosomy thickets of rhododendrons pierced by soaring columnar conifers and the occasional billowing old oak. But you cannot enter this area, nor can you visit the remains of the 18th-century park to the north of the old castle. In any case, all that is plainly the work of mortal man, whereas the ravine at Belsay seems to have been wrought by a thunderbolt from the heavens. If Wagner had made gardens he might have done it like this.

Location Belsay, nr Newcastle-upon-Tyne NE20 0DX, Northumberland **OS** NZ0878 14m NW of Newcastle by A696 **Tel** 01661 881636 **Fax** 01661 881043 **English Heritage Register** Grade I **Owner** In the guardianship of English Heritage **Open** Apr to Sept, daily 10–6; Oct, daily 10–5; Nov, daily 10–4 **Area** 50 acres/20 hectares

◁ **The ravine garden** at Belsay Hall

BOWES MUSEUM

THE PERFECT FRENCH PARTERRE
AND WOODED PLEASURE GROUNDS
OF A UNIQUE MUSEUM

Nothing prepares you for the first sight of the Bowes Museum, whether you approach it from the charming old stone streets of the town or from the leafy lanes to the east. You are immediately in France, and the astonishing building rears up like the *hôtel de ville* of some great industrial city. It was built as a museum between 1869 and 1885 to the designs of Jules Pellechet for John Bowes (1811–85), an illegitimate son of the 10th Earl of Strathmore who brought him up as a legitimate son and endowed him with the Bowes estates in County Durham and Yorkshire. Bowes was an ardent francophile who married a Frenchwoman, Joséphine Benoîte, and from 1847 divided his time between France (mainly at the 17th-century Château du Barry at Louveciennes) and England where he lived close to Barnard Castle at Streatlam Castle, the chief English seat of the Bowes family. The museum was seen as an amenity for the people of County Durham, whose coalfields had from the 17th century onwards brought fabulous wealth to the Bowes family. First opened to the public in 1892, it was endowed with the immense collection of decorative arts, chiefly French, which Bowes and his wife had acquired specifically for the museum. Both Bowes and has wife died before the museum was opened. It is today one of the finest decorative arts collections in the country.

AN OVAL PARTERRE

The museum is garnished with a garden to suit. The building, raised on a great terrace, overlooks an oval parterre which, although probably designed by Pellechet, was not put into place until 1982. The compartments of the parterre are raised on a closely mown turf base and the patterns are cut out of turf and filled with gravel of two different colours, or with bedding schemes. Box hedges trace repeated shapes of *fleur de lys* in the centre four compartments, and *coquilles St Jacques* in the four outer ones. Tall cones of clipped yew

The parterre at Bowes Museum

punctuate the whole and a scalloped pool and water jet sparkles at the centre. All the detail is marvellous, as fine an example of a proper French parterre as you will find in England. The arcaded retaining wall of the museum terrace, with a semicircular pool at the centre, forms a noble backdrop. Beds running along the wall have repeated yew cones, and large bushes of holly and *Magnolia grandiflora* underplanted with herbaceous perennials.

An oval carriage drive sweeps about the parterre and leads to higher ground behind the museum. Here, and on each side of the building, is planting of the kind that the French think of as *à l'Anglaise*. Grouped together in mown grass are groups of specimen trees, several of which date from the original 19th-century plantings. Many are the fashionable conifers of the day – the monkey puzzle to the west of the parterre was bought in 1871 for 15 guineas (£682 today). There are also good deciduous trees – limes, maples, oaks, planes and rowans. The most remarkable view in the garden is from the terrace, with the museum behind you and the parterre splendidly spread out below.

Beyond a pair of entrance lodges, with beautiful black and gilt wrought-iron gates, the wonderfully unspoilt rural landscape

seems to go on for ever. You would never get planning permission for the Bowes Museum today and yet, what a triumphant sight it is.

Location Barnard Castle DL12 8NB, County Durham **OS** NZ0516 On the E edge of Barnard Castle **Tel** 01833 690606 **Fax** 01833 637163 **Email** info@bowesmuseum.org.uk **Website** www.bowesmuseum.org.uk **English Heritage Register** Grade II **Owner** The Bowes Musuem Ltd **Open** daily 11–5 (closed 25 and 26 Dec) **Area** 20 acres/8 hectares

BRAMHAM PARK

SUPERB EARLY 18TH-CENTURY
FORMAL LANDSCAPE GARDEN WITH
BEAUTIFUL BUILDINGS

Gardens of this kind – but usually on a more modest scale – were common in England at the beginning of the 18th century but most of them disappeared in the fashion for informal landscaping that became the almost universal craze by the second part of the century. So Bramham is a rare survival; it is also a thoroughly seductive place.

The garden was laid out in the very early 18th century for Robert Benson, 1st Lord Bingley, who in all likelihood designed both his own remarkably attractive house as well the grandiose formal landscape that provides its spectacular setting. Benson had been on the Grand Tour and had seen the latest French gardens; this was the chief influence on his design and he laid out giant patterns of walks lined with beech hedges and animated with ornamental buildings and ornaments. However, unlike a French garden, there is no rigidly geometric frame to the layout: straight vistas, sometimes of vast size, shoot off at unaccountable angles and something surprising – a temple, an obelisk or a distant view back to the house – is suddenly revealed. Furthermore, and again unlike a French garden of this style, a charmingly haphazard dimension is introduced by the rise and fall of the sloping land: a long walk will appear to culminate in a distant stone urn – but you do not realise how far away it is because you are not used to urns

An 18th-century urn

12ft/3.6m high. When you finally arrive at the urn you will discover that the walk continues down the slope beyond it, seemingly without destination but revealing delicious views over the rural landscape.

Fine buildings, all rather later than the garden's original layout, are woven into the landscape. James Paine's summerhouse of around 1760 marks the opening of an immense vista which runs past the garden front of the house, past a noble formal water garden, past a domed Ionic temple (also, possibly by James Paine), to culminate in a soaring obelisk which, in turn, lies at the centre of an explosion of five radiating avenues.

The architect Colen Campbell, seeing Bramham in its heyday, admired the "curious gardens laid out with great judgement"; visitors may easily share his admiration. Bramham nevertheless requires an entirely

different kind of attention from that which you would give to a pretty garden of flowers or a series of neatly harmonious architectural compartments. The only way to appreciate it to the full is to take a long walk and gradually submit to the atmosphere of the place. You will need at least two or three hours to get to grips with the vast landscape, pausing from time to time to relish its beauty from different angles and to think about the sources of its charms. Having seen it once, properly, you will not forget it.

Location nr Wetherby LS23 6ND, West Yorkshire
OS SE4041 5m S of Wetherby by A1 **Tel** 01937 846002
Fax 01937 846001 **English Heritage Register** Grade I
Owner George Lane Fox **Open** Apr to Sept, daily
10.30–5.30 **Area** 66 acres/27 hectares

BRODSWORTH HALL

VICTORIAN FLOWER GARDENS, A TERRACED FERN GARDEN AND A ROSE WALK FOR A FINE HOUSE

The house at Brodsworth is a rare confection – an Italianate mansion designed possibly by an Italian, Cavaliere G.M. Casentini, and built for a Huguenot banking family, the Thelussons, between 1861 and 1863 to replace an 18th-century house. It is cool, neo-classical and resplendent in the palest limestone, quarried on the Brodsworth estate. Fashionable new pleasure grounds were laid out at the same time, and although little of these remained, apart from a backdrop of fine old trees including some magnificent cedars of Lebanon, they have been most handsomely reinstated since English Heritage was left the estate in 1990.

The entrance façade of the house overlooks a deep horseshoe of lawn with a beautiful cedar of Lebanon. A perimeter path is backed by evergreen shrubberies against which there is a solemn parade of white marble statues on plinths. The southern façade of the house overlooks a terrace and turf slope where flights of steps flanked with urns and white marble whippets lead down to a grass walk and a yew hedge with statues in yew niches. In late summer a procession of *Dahlia* 'Bishop of Llandaff' flaunt their

The tree-lined walks at Bramham Park

The Fern Dell at Brodsworth Hall

glowing red flowers against the deep green of the hedge. Beyond the hedge are views of parkland and good trees.

The flower garden to the west of the house beyond the croquet lawn is tricked out with all the decorative splendour of its period. Shaped beds are cut out of immaculate lawns and filled with seasonal bedding plants. Standard fuchsias, plumes of cordylines, fans of Chusan palms and clipped shapes of yew rise among the brilliant colours. At the centre is an elaborate three-tiered stone fountain sculpted, like many of the garden ornaments, by the mysterious Casentini. Rising high above it is a specimen of that archetypal tree of the period, the monkey puzzle.

A GARDEN IN A QUARRY

On the wooded slopes above the flower garden is a columned summerhouse resembling a temple, 18th-century in style but built in the 1860s. It marks the beginning of the Grove, a picturesque garden of walks and ornamental incidents laid out in the quarry from which the stone for the house was taken. Nearby is a raised walk with railings and swagged chains enclosed in neatly clipped ivy; it looks down onto the Fern Dell, a ravine whose sides are rustically terraced with stone. Here is a huge collection of ferns and many small ornamental plants, some of an alpine kind: species irises, *Jeffersonia diphylla*, species lilies and tulips, and

roscoeas. Here, too, is a collection of dwarf conifers, very dwarf at the moment and rather charming – long may they remain so. An artificial "river" of pale gravel flows under a bridge and a tunnel leads to an arcade of roses backed by bamboos and hydrangeas. At the far end of the archery lawn is the Target House, an 18th-century building of the greatest elegance, with a Gothic Palladian window – but thatched and given deeply overhanging eaves in the 1860s to make it conform to the fashion for Swiss buildings. This is the only building from the 18th-century garden to survive. A path leads through a curving metal pergola of grapevines and roses with a series of box-hedged rose beds on each side.

It is unusual to find such a complete example of a late 19th-century garden with so little from other periods. At Brodsworth, the house (with its splendid 19th-century contents) is all of a piece with the garden, forming a most beguiling ensemble.

Location Brodsworth, nr Doncaster DN5 7XJ, South Yorkshire **OS** SE5007 In Brodsworth village, 5½m NW of Doncaster; Jnct 37 of A1(M) **Tel** 01302 722598 **Fax** 01302 337165 **English Heritage Register** Grade II* **Owner** English Heritage **Open** Apr to Oct, daily except Mon 12–6; Nov to Mar, Sat and Sun 11–4 **Area** 15 acres/6 hectares

CASTLE HOWARD

DRAMATIC LANDSCAPE, A BEAUTIFUL WOODLAND GARDEN AND FINE ORNAMENTS FOR A GREAT ESTATE

As you drive to Castle Howard the majestic scale of its setting creeps up on you. The natural surroundings, pretty grand in themselves, merge with a designed landscape covering 1,000 acres/404 hectares. At one moment you are surrounded by wild, austere countryside and the next moment, with no abrupt break, obelisks and temples rise from the moors, with the astonishing castle at the centre of it all. The castle was the first work of Sir John Vanbrugh, helped by Nicholas Hawksmoor, and was built between 1699 and 1726 for Charles Howard, 3rd Earl of Carlisle. Vanbrugh also designed many of the great buildings and ornaments which people the grounds but it is plain that Lord Carlisle himself had a major role in the planning of the landscape.

DRAMATIC APPROACHES

Visitors arrive by driving along an avenue of beech and lime over three miles long. Along the course of the avenue (from south to north) are the Monument designed by F.P. Cockerell (1870); Carrmire Gate designed by Nicholas Hawksmoor after 1726; the Gatehouse designed by Vanbrugh in 1719 with, on either side, his neo-medieval bastioned fortifications (with wings added by William Robinson in 1756 to provide accommodation for sightseers); and the Obelisk by Vanbrugh (1714). Other buildings command attention from the castle itself. To its south is the Pyramid by Hawksmoor (1728) and, closer to the castle, Vanbrugh's Temple of the Four Winds (1724–28). Most remarkable of all, close to the New River south-east of the castle, is Hawksmoor's domed and pillared Mausoleum (1726–29). This was the building that so impressed Horace Walpole that he wrote: "[it] would tempt one to be buried alive."

Although the greater landscape with its dramatic approaches and buildings largely survives, the princely formal gardens close to the castle have radically changed. Ray Wood, a iece of ancient woodland to the east of the ouse, was made in about 1718 into a much dmired semi-formal woodland garden with winding gravel walks and statues. The great ardener of the day, Stephen Switzer, praised it n his *Iconographia Rustica* (1715): "the highest itch that Natural and Polite Gard'ning can ossibly arrive to." Today, although some of the arly 18th-century paths have been reinstated, . is a woodland garden of a completely ifferent kind – a wonderful collection of trees nd shrubs, many exceedingly rare, built up nce 1968 under the supervision of a emarkable plantsman, James Russell, who rought with him as a nucleus a collection of hododendrons from the Sunningdale Nursery vhich he had just sold. It is now one of the nest collections of acid-loving trees and hrubs in the country.

Vanbrugh's formal Wilderness to the south f the castle was redesigned in 1850 by W.A. Nesfield and now sports a grand fountain vith a figure of Atlas supported by Tritons, nclosed in yew hedges. Nearby, the walled ormer kitchen garden has a large collection f roses underplanted with artemisias, hlomis, pinks and santolina. In any other ontext these formal gardens might constitute he chief beauty of the landscape. At Castle Ioward the greater setting of the house is onceived on such a grandiose scale, and

he garden front of Castle Howard

furnished with such sublime monuments, that flower beds and statuary find it hard to engage the attention.

Location nr York YO60 7DA, North Yorkshire
OS SE7170 14m NE of York by A64 **Tel** 01653 648444
Fax 01653 648501 **Email** mec@castlehoward.co.uk
English Heritage Register Grade I **Owner** The Hon. Simon Howard **Open** mid Mar to Oct, daily 10–4.30 (also winter openings; phone for details) **Area** 50 acres/20 hectares

CRAGSIDE HOUSE

A PLUNGING RAVINE FILLED WITH PLANTS, SPLENDID GLASSHOUSES AND A DAHLIA WALK

The very name Cragside gives some idea of what to expect here. Sir William Armstrong commissioned the architect Norman Shaw to transform a modest sporting lodge in wild heathland into a towered and turreted extravaganza suitable for one of the great industrial tycoons of the day. With much chopping and changing, and with saintly patience on behalf of the architect, the work took fifteen years, from 1869 to 1884. The house soars on a stony cliff above the Debdon burn whose water Armstrong harnessed to provide hydraulic power for all sorts of gadgets in

the house (including a lift) and in the garden (in a glasshouse it was used to rotate fruit trees in pots so that the fruit would ripen evenly). By 1900 Armstrong owned almost 30,000 acres/12,145 hectares and had planted 7,000,000 trees; his pleasure gardens covered an area of 1,000 acres/405 hectares, with plantings of rhododendrons on a heroic scale. There is nothing cosy about Cragside.

The most eloquent view of the place is from the banks of the burn below the house where a steel bridge – a wonderfully elegant single span – arches over the water. Among the cascade of rocks that seem to tumble down from the house are wild plantings of rhododendrons and rowans underplanted with small conifers, ferns, heather, saxifrages and sedums. By the banks of the burn a pinetum provides exactly the right note of coniferous gloom. Tree planting started here in the 1860s and many have grown to enormous size, especially North American species like the western hemlock (*Tsuga heterophylla*) and Low's white fir (*Abies concolor* Lowiana Group) – the latter, at over 150ft/45m, the tallest specimen in the country. The soaring shapes of these trees provide the perfect growing counterpoint to the soaring mansion above.

On the far side of the Debdon valley are glasshouses and formal gardens. The fruit-turning platforms in the glasshouses have been restored and a great range of different fruits is cultivated – all superbly clipped and trained;

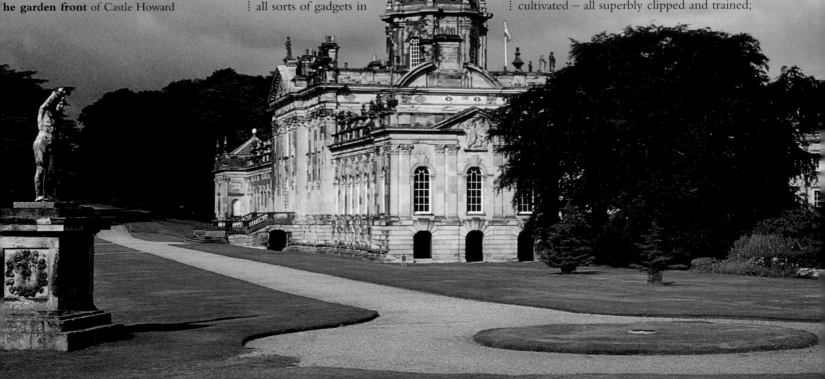

◁ **The ravine garden** at Cragside

in August the smell of ripening exotic fruit is wonderful. To one side, magnificent displays of carpet bedding are spread out on beds angled to display them at their best. There is a fernery in a splendid winding rustic rockery, and glasshouses protect tender plants. On the slopes below is a long terraced dahlia walk with clipped shapes of golden variegated holly. Yet, attractive as these are, they are as the tinkling of piano music after the thunder of the symphony being played in the rocky ravine below.

Location Rothbury, Morpeth NE65 7PX, Northumberland **OS** NU0702 13m SW of Alnwick by B6341 **Tel** 01669 620333/620150 **Fax** 01669 620066 **English Heritage Register** Grade II* **Owner** The National Trust **Open** Apr to Oct, daily except Mon (open Bank Hol Mon) 10.30–7; Nov to mid Dec, Wed to Sun 11–4 **Area** 1,000 acres/405 hectares

DALEMAIN

FLOWER-FILLED FORMAL GARDENS AND A STREAM-SIDE WALK IN A BEAUTIFUL LAKE DISTRICT SETTING

The house at Dalemain was medieval but rebuilt in the mid 18th century, an ancestor of the present owner having acquired the estate in the late 17th century. Built of pale pink-grey stone, it rises serenely on a gentle bluff with beautiful views over perfect rural countryside. There was a landscape park here in the 18th century and, as we shall see, there are other signs of earlier gardening activity. But the planting is essentially 20th century and the garden's attraction comes from its uncontrived charm rather than from any great horticultural ostentation. Dalemain is well equipped to receive visitors but the atmosphere is never institutional (no whiff of potpourri) and you never lose the sense that you are visiting a private domain.

To enter the garden you skirt the south side of the house, which is veiled in roses, *Vitis coignetiae* and variegated ivy and has an ebullient mixed border below. On the other side of the gravel path tall shrub roses rise at the top of a terrace wall, with a field and rural

views below. You walk a little further and are just wondering where the garden is when you see an enormous and beautiful old Grecian fir (*Abies cephalonica*) under whose high spreading branches you pass.

The part of the garden that you now enter, and the adjacent orchard, date from no later than the late 17th century: Sir Edward Hasell's

The Knot Garden at Dalemain

Day Book of 1684 mentions "apricock trees", and that of 1686 refers to the building of an orchard wall. A pretty knot garden with a lily pool and fountain is surrounded in summer by pots of richly scented *Lilium speciosum*. The planting today is all of the 20th century, with box-edged compartments filled with artemisia or rue, sage and santolina, and clouds of white *Viola cornuta*. On one side a tall yew hedge is embroidered with brilliant red *Tropaeolum speciosum*. At the other end a path cuts through dense herbaceous planting – astrantia, eupatorium, fennel, geraniums, phlox and violas – to an orchard partly enclosed in 17th-century walls, with an avenue of hollies clipped into pyramids. A gravel path leads along a mixed border backed by a high south-facing wall, with shrub roses underplanted with geraniums, lamium, pulmonaria and rodgersias. A curtain of clematis veils the far end wall, which has a pretty early 18th-century alcove seat built into it. At its south end a 17th-century summerhouse has a pyramid roof crowned with a sphere.

Passing through a secret-looking gate you find yourself in Lob's Wood, among beech, birch and cherries. A walk skirts the wood on the edge of the Dacre beck whose sparkling waters are seen through branches, with

pastures on its far side. This, with its 18th-century romantic air, encapsulates the spirit of Dalemain. It is a secret garden with nothing trendy, nothing designery. Any child would love it and adults who come to sit on a bench in Lob's Wood and listen to the birdsong may well recover here the innocence of their childhood.

Location nr Penrith CA11 0HB, Cumbria **OS** NY4726 3m SW of Penrith by A66 and A592 **Tel** 017684 86450 **Fax** 017684 86223 **English Heritage Register** Grade II* **Owner** Robert Hasell McCosh **Open** Apr to beginning Oct, Sun to Thur 10.30–5 **Area** 3 acres/1.2 hectares

DUNCOMBE PARK

REMARKABLE 18TH-CENTURY TERRACES AND TEMPLES AND PRETTY VICTORIAN FLOWER PARTERRES

Arthur Young in his *A six months tour through the north of England* (1770) wrote of Duncombe that it was "the place in this country by far the most worth the attention of the curious traveller, [it] cannot be viewed without the most exquisite enjoyment." The house is Baroque and surprisingly grand, with a distinct touch of the Castle Howard about it, and indeed there is a possibility that it was designed with help from Sir John Vanbrugh. At all events, it was begun around 1713 and built by William Wakefield for Thomas Duncombe. It occupies a wonderful site on land high above the rooftops of Helmsley, where the remains of the 13th-century castle provide a ruinous ornament, with the river Rye winding past far below. This view dominates the garden, which is designed specifically to display it to its greatest picturesque effect.

THE GREAT TERRACE

Immediately to the east of the house a plain square of lawn is ornamented with a splendid figure of Father Time stooping over a sundial (early 18th-century and possibly by John Van Nost). Beyond it there opens out one of the grandest garden views in England: a huge, gently curving grassy terrace, half a mile long, running both north and south and overlooking the wooded valley of the Rye whose waters are occasionally glimpsed gleaming through the branches far below. Each end of this East Terrace is marked by a domed and pillared temple of about 1730 – an Ionic Temple to the north (possibly by Vanbrugh) and a Doric Temple to the south (possibly by Sir Thomas Robinson). The Ionic temple is an open rotunda and commands wonderful views to the north and east over Helmsley. The Doric temple at the southern end of the terrace has a surprise: it also marks the beginning of a further South Terrace running due west. From near the western end of this terrace the Broadwalk cuts back north through woodland towards the east façade of the house, ending north-east of the house in a very old yew walk and a monumental serpentine ha-ha, which has been attributed to Vanbrugh, possibly with the involvement of Charles Bridgeman, though there is no archival evidence. Vanbrugh may also have laid out the terraces. At Blenheim Palace he had tried to persuade the Duchess of Marlborough to preserve the ruins of Woodstock Palace as a picturesque landscape ornament; he would certainly have recognised the potential of Helmsley Castle in a similar role. All the work on both house and garden, begun in 1713, was completed by 1730. The terraces, and the evident relish for the picturesque attributes of the landscape, are true pioneers in garden design.

There are other attractive things to see in the garden at Duncombe – Victorian sunken parterres possibly by W.A. Nesfield

flanking the house, and an attractive conservatory (1851, designed by the younger Charles Barry and R.R. Banks) hidden in the woods behind the South Terrace – but it is the unforgettable terraces and their views that command attention. Thomas Duncombe's son, another Thomas, went on to design a similar terrace at Rievaulx, two miles away, in about 1758 (*see page 350*) and a carriage drive was made between the two estates so that visitors could view both terraces.

The terraces at Duncombe and Rievaulx are magnificent. Christopher Hussey in his *English Gardens and Landscapes 1700–1750* (1967) described them as "unique, and perhaps the most spectacularly beautiful among English landscape conceptions of the 18th century". Having seen them in their grand simplicity you may return to your own garden, with its fiddly borders and tedious views, and experience a certain depressing sense of inconsequence.

Location Helmsley YO62 5EB, North Yorkshire
OS SE6082 On the W edge of Helmsley, 12m E of Thirsk
Tel 01439 770213 **Fax** 01439 771114 **Email** sally@duncombepark.com **English Heritage Register** Grade I **Owner** Lord Feversham **Open** Apr to Oct, daily except Fri (Apr and Oct, Sun to Thur) 10.30–6
Area 485 acres/196 hectares

The Doric temple at Duncombe Park

GIBSIDE

AN ARCADIAN 18TH-CENTURY LANDSCAPE OF LONG VIEWS, OUTSTANDING BUILDINGS AND A WOODED VALLEY

Old gardens, surviving only in some battered and truncated form, often have a peculiar beauty. In 1952 Christopher Hussey visited Gibside and described a scene of "tragic desolation…of one of the grandest idylls created in the 18th century". Barbara Jones in her *Follies & Grottoes* (1953) described the house at Gibside as "a tree-filled ruin, and so are its attendant buildings…the Banqueting Hall in Gothic has become an enchanting picturesque ruin." After that was written things got worse until 1965 when the Earl of Strathmore gave a small part of the estate to the National Trust. In 1993 the Trust was able to buy a much greater part and embark on its restoration.

ORNAMENTAL BUILDINGS
This picturesque landscape park was the work of a gentleman landscaper, George Bowes, a coal tycoon who inherited the estate in 1722 and came to live here three years later. The site is very beautiful, with the house on the edge of a wooded valley overlooking the river Derwent. Bowes commissioned the architect James Paine to improve the original Jacobean hall and to build a fine Palladian chapel and mausoleum which, occupying a key position in the landscape, was completed in 1766 six years after Bowes's death. In his lifetime, however, other ornamental buildings were built by the architect Daniel Garrett, including a swashbuckling Gothic Banqueting House and a spectacular Column of British Liberty 140ft/42m high (started in 1750). Capability Brown was consulted about the column in the same year, but there is no evidence that he did any work on the landscape. Between 1746 and 1749 George Bowes planted a great terrace avenue of oaks, half a mile long, the Grand Walk, aligned with the chapel at one end and the Column of British Liberty at the other. To one side of this axis is the Banqueting House, on rising land above an octagonal pool. This, in the separate ownership of the Landmark Trust which rents it out for holidays, is a

The Chapel and Mausoleum at Gibside

wonderfully decorative building with elaborate tracery windows and high rising pointed gables swarming with crockets.

So far the restoration of Gibside has been what the National Trust calls "low key", and indeed one would not like to see a place of such potent character manicured into insipidity. As it is, to saunter along the broad grass Grand Walk flanked by the trees of the avenue, with the great column at one end and the exquisite chapel at the other, is a stirring experience. Scarcely less memorable is the wilder walk along the banks of the river below the ruins of the hall. In this densely populated part of the country Gibside provides an Arcadian retreat of rare beauty and excitement.

Location nr Rowlands Gill, Burnopfield, Newcastle-upon-Tyne NE16 6BG, Tyne and Wear **OS** NZ1858 6m SW of Gateshead by A692 and B6315 **Tel** and **Fax** 01207 542255 **Email** gibside@ntrust.org.uk **English Heritage Register** Grade I **Owner** The National Trust **Open** Apr to Oct, daily except Mon (open Bank Hol Mon) 10–6; Nov to Mar, daily except Mon 10–4 **Area** 354 acres/143 hectares

GRIZEDALE

ANCIENT WOODLAND ON THE GRAND
SCALE, ENLIVENED BY EXCELLENT
MODERN SCULPTURES

This, only a garden by the most elastic of definitions, is a unique piece of landscape animated by modern sculptures and lying at the heart of one of the most beautiful parts of the Lake District, between Coniston and Windermere. This is ancient woodland (Grizedale is Norse for "the valley of the pigs") and its wildness is marvellous to see. The forest is threaded with waymarked paths – over 20 miles of them, suitable for biking or walking. There is also a sculpture trail with over 80 works by such artists as Andy Goldsworthy, Patricia Leighton, Sally Matthews, Kimio Tsuchiya and many others.

A sculpture/seat at Grizedale

The works, by artists of international renown as well as by youthful unknowns, come and go. Some pieces are deliberately ephemeral, made of fallen wood and leaves and destined to decay and to join the humus that feeds the living trees, and some have been consumed by red deer. Others are more permanent, such as Andy Goldsworthy's exquisite Sidewinder, a beautifully fashioned dry-stone crinkle-crankle wall that winds its rhythmic way among trees.

The place is pre-eminently one in which to take a long and rewarding walk. The anticipation of finding a work of art makes you scrutinise the scenery with special attention and you thus find yourself looking at your surroundings – trees, flowers, stones, distant hillsides and, above all, the fluctuating weather – with special care. So the forest becomes a school for looking, with subtle messages about the relationship of art and nature. There are few landscapes described in this book in which the visitor is less visible. There are 9,000 acres/3,644 hectares here, entry free, giving you the opportunity to learn about landscape and to see your own garden with a new eye.

Location Grizedale, nr Hawkshead, Ambleside LA22 0QJ, Cumbria **OS** NY3494 3m S of Hawkshead by B5285 **Tel** 01229 860373 **Owner** The Forestry Commission **Open** daily dawn–dusk **Area** 9,000 acres/3,644 hectares

HACKFALL WOOD

THE DREAMLIKE REMAINS OF AN
18TH-LANDSCAPE GARDEN IN A
ROMANTIC VALLEY SETTING

Hackfall is like a faded Old Master drawing – there is little left but what remains is of lovely quality. There is no visitor centre, no-one to take your money, no-one to bring you a cream tea, and certainly not the slightest whiff of the heritage industry – indeed the very entrance is hard to find. The grassy path leading from the road sparkles with harebells in the summer and as you descend the valley the sound of the river's rushing water lures you on. In wet weather the few paths become very muddy (waterproof shoes or boots are

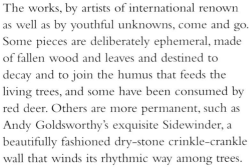

The Rustic Temple at Hackfall Wood

essential and a stick helpful). But persevere, wander at will, and relish the rare atmosphere of the place.

In its 18th-century heyday, Hackfall Wood was much loved: "There is so much to admire, so much to celebrate, that I know not how to proceed in description or speak half the praise due to Hackfall," wrote the indefatigable traveller Colonel John Byng (Lord Torrington) in 1792. Wordsworth urged visitors to the north to make a detour to Hackfall and J.M.W. Turner came here to paint. It remained famous well into the 1930s, when there was a tea room, and on Sunday afternoons charabancs would bring flocks of visitors from Ripon.

A PRECIPITOUS GORGE
The garden was started in 1742 and continued to be developed well into the 1760s, by William Aislabie of nearby Studley Royal (see page 352). It was the ravishing natural landscape that inspired Aislabie to retreat from the splendours of his father's estate and make a garden of his own. A precipitous wooded gorge plummets hundreds of feet down to a lovely loop of the river Ure, by whose banks are curiously sandy beaches. Aislabie animated the scene with ornamental buildings, Gothic in style, of which a few survive in ruinous state: Mowbray Castle and

a Banqueting House at the summit, and Fisher's Hall (bearing the date 1750) below in the woods, while the remains of the Rustic Temple, embraced by the branches of trees, rise out of the mossy ground for all the world like some Mayan relic in the dense Guatemalan jungle. The buildings are dilapidated but the sublime view retains all its power. John Byng had the right idea: "A day…should be devoted to [its] inspection; wine and provisions might be brought in a cart; and then, with music and love to fill the scene, Hackfall would appear an Eden." In many ways it is the purest of gardens – it was not made to adorn a house, for there never was a house here, and it alone creates a sense of place. To enjoy it a special journey had to be made, and its beauties come from a response to its natural surroundings.

The Banqueting House has been acquired by the Landmark Trust, to be let for holidays, and work started on its restoration in 2002.

Location Grewelthorpe, nr Ripon, North Yorkshire **OS** SE2377 ½m NW of Grewelthorpe by the Masham Road; the unmarked entrance is on the right by an old pollarded oak down a cart track **English Heritage Register** Grade I **Owner** Woodland Trust **Open** daily dawn–dusk **Area** 112 acres/45 hectares

HAREWOOD HOUSE

OUTSTANDING VICTORIAN FLOWER TERRACES AND A MAGNIFICENT CAPABILITY BROWN PARK

The house at Harewood was built for Edwin Lascelles, from 1759 onwards, to the designs of John Carr of York, aided by the youthful Robert Adam. Anyone coming to see the garden at Harewood must certainly visit the house which has superlative 18th-century rooms and is all of a piece with its landscape setting. The estate is still owned by the Lascelles family, now Earls of Harewood, and is beautifully kept.

Close to Leeds, in a most populous part of Yorkshire, Harewood is a major tourist attraction. You may catch a whiff of hamburgers but tourist amenities are handled with tact and, as far as possible, do not impinge on the pleasures of house or garden.

The great set piece in the garden is to be experienced on the house's south terrace where Sir Charles Barry (who remodelled the façade of the house between 1844 and 1848 and designed a grand double staircase leading down to the terrace) laid out a great parterre in collaboration with John Fleming. This has recently been restored and gives a vivid impression of a grand Victorian parterre in its confident heyday. At its centre is a scalloped pool with a statue of Orpheus by Astrid Zydower, and on each side are star-shaped pools with elaborate Rococo fountains surmounted by Tritons spouting water. Box-edged beds in swirling arabesques are filled with seasonal bedding schemes for spring and summer, with stone urns and cones of clipped yew rising among them.

CAPABILITY BROWN'S PARK
Below the balustraded southern edge of the terrace the land falls away sharply, with the valley of Gawthorpe beck in the distance. Here is a landscape of the greatest possible contrast to the elaborately decorative garden that lies behind you. It was refashioned by Capability Brown between 1758 and 1774 when he dammed the beck to form a long and sinuous lake and planted clumps and belts of trees on the gentle slopes that rise

yond. Brown did other landscaping work, ¬ishing in 1780 when he was paid £6,800 (¬406,368 today). The banks of the lake ¬e also scattered with trees with, behind ¬em, pastures and grazing cattle or sheep. ¬ is one of Brown's most beautiful, and best ¬eserved, landscapes. Dorothy Stroud, the ¬eat expert on Brown, described it as "one ¬ the most delectable landscapes", and ¬yone wanting to try and understand the ¬ss about Brown could scarcely do better ¬an come to Harewood. The piquant ¬ntrast between Barry's Victorian hijinks ¬d Brown's gently Arcadian scene is an ¬ded attraction.

¬**cation** Harewood, Leeds LS17 9LQ, West Yorkshire ¬**S** SE 3144 7m N of Leeds and 7m S of Harrogate by ¬1 **Tel** 0113 218 1010 **Fax** 0113 218 1002 ¬**nail** business@harewood.org **English Heritage** ¬**gister** Grade I **Owner** The Earl and Countess of ¬**rewood Open** Apr to Oct, daily 10–4.30 **Area** 36 ¬res/15 hectares

¬**he terrace parterre** at Harewood House

HARLOW CARR GARDENS

ROYAL HORTICULTURAL SOCIETY
DISPLAY GARDENS WITH EXCELLENT
TREES AND SHRUBS

Harlow Carr was founded in 1950 as the gardens of the Northern Horticultural Society which in 2001 merged with the Royal Horticultural Society. The merger made every sense, for the purpose of Harlow Carr was, like that of the RHS gardens at Wisley, Rosemoor and Hyde Hall, to display a fine collection of plants in an attractive landscape and show high standards of practical horticulture.

The setting is attractive – a shallow valley through which a stream, the Harlow beck, flows. The place is watery – not only is the rainfall high but drainage is a problem (the word "carr", derived from old Norse, means a fen, pool or boggy ground). The western, and particularly south-western, slopes of the valley are well wooded and the soil (heavy clay) throughout the gardens is acid.

The garden has a rich diversity of sites. Ancient woodland in the south-western corner, formerly part of Knaresborough Forest, with old beech and English oaks, makes an admirable place for camellias, magnolias and rhododendrons. Also found here is a splendid surprise – a solemn row of Doric columns rescued from the Royal Spa Concert Rooms in Harrogate, which was demolished in 1939. Along the stream are drifts of astilbes, ferns, *Gunnera manicata*, hostas, meconopsis and quantities of Himalayan primulas which hybridise freely here. A stream and tarn form part of a garden of limestone rock, with winding walks among conifers and Japanese maples. An arboretum on a higher airy site in the north-west corner of the garden has collections of beech, pines and rowans, and much of the grassland here is left uncut until late in the season to allow the profusion of wildflowers to seed.

Collections of alpine plants, herbs and shrub

The limestone garden at Harlow Carr

roses, and a winter garden, are all of great interest to gardeners. Two National Collections of ferns are held at Harlow Carr (46 species and cultivars of *Dryopteris* and 36 species and cultivars of *Polypodium*). Of special local interest is the National Collection of *Rheum*, including culinary rhubarbs, of which there are 30 species and 115 cultivars. In the 19th century the West Riding of Yorkshire was the national centre of rhubarb growing, with 5,000 tons of forced rhubarb grown every year, and although the number of rhubarb growers has declined, an annual rhubarb festival is still held at Wakefield. Two other collections – of cultivars of the common heather *Calluna* and of the Queluzia section of *Fuchsia* – have yet to be accredited as National Collections.

The RHS will be making many changes to the garden in accordance with the master plan which they have commissioned. Already of great interest to gardeners, Harlow Carr will soon become even more attractive.

Location Crag Lane, Harrogate HG3 1QB, North Yorkshire **OS** SE2854 1½m W of Harrogate by B6162
Tel 01423 565418 **Owner** The Royal Horticultural Society **Open** daily 9.30–6 (or dusk if earlier)
Area 68 acres/28 hectares

HERTERTON HOUSE GARDENS

A RARE PRIVATE GARDEN OF FLOWERY ENCLOSURES, TOPIARY AND MAGICAL ATMOSPHERE

It is fairly easy to categorise most 20th-century gardens – they fall readily into groups sharing common features. Herterton, however, is a precious example of a garden where a pair of expert gardeners have ploughed their own furrow. It is a rare original, although it was inspired by many different influences – the cottage-garden planting of Margery Fish at East Lambrook Manor (*see page 31*), the tidily formal Shakespearean gardens recreated at New Place in Stratford-upon-Avon (*see page 277*) and, surprisingly, *avant-garde* art of the early 20th century.

In 1975 Frank and Marjorie Lawley took a lease on a derelict village house belonging to the National Trust. They rebuilt the stone house and divided the garden with fine stone walls. When they started the garden, what was uppermost in their mind was "considered design and planting, rather than dabbling improvisation". It was to be a garden of compartments, with no repetition of mood but with repetition of such basic structural plants as box, holly and yew.

At the front, along the public lane, are hedges and topiary of box with intervening spaces carpeted with different varieties of dicentra whose filigree foliage is always beautiful. The Lawleys' kitchen window overlooks this Formal Garden and, on the other side of the road, a landscape with a stream (the Hart burn), clumps of trees and rolling pasture that could have been created by Capability Brown. (Brown, as it happens, was born at Kirkharle just up the road from Hartington, and Frank Lawley relishes the thought of his very anti-Brownian Formal Garden confronting the Brownian scene.) A secret Physic Garden, hidden by walls, has at its centre a giant totem of clipped weeping silver pear (*Pyrus salicifolia* 'Pendula'); a pattern of intricately shaped beds edged with red-stemmed London Pride (*Saxifraga* 'Elliott's Variety') spreads out about it, filled with native and medicinal plants; and the whole is overlooked by a former cart shed whose gracefully arched openings have a strong flavour of some stately renaissance loggia.

COLOURS IN A GRID

Behind the house is the largest enclosure, the Flower Garden, in which a maze-like pattern of paths, hedges and topiary of box and yew overflows in high summer with an abundance of herbaceous plants. Underlying this pattern is a firm grid, inspired by the paintings of Piet Mondrian, in which the ingredients are disposed in a modular system with a unit of 3ft/1m. In winter this grid – stripped down to paths, beds and and shapes of gleaming box and yew – is powerfully visible and has austere beauty; in summer it disappears but still exerts an underlying discipline. There is discipline, too, of a wilder kind, in the choice of flower colours. As they extend from the house they change from cool yellows and whites to orange and blue at the centre, and finally to rich reds and purples. The Lawleys think of these colours as symbolic of dawn, a hot midday and a rich summer sunset.

A newly made Fancy Garden is connected to the Flower Garden, sharing its central axis. A high-rising stone gazebo built against the boundary wall rears up at the end of this axis, facing both inwards into the patterned garden and outwards over the pastures and wooded

untryside. The Fancy Garden has a
mmetrical pattern of stone-flagged paths
d box-edged beds with at the centre a
ble stone basin.

Nowhere at Herterton is there the
nd of grand border that is merely an object
distant admiration. Instead, the various
closures of the garden enfold the visitor
in the Flower Garden you are engulfed in
wers – which gives the place a revivifying
timacy. Are gardens good for you? I don't
ow, but I do know that I always arrive at
erterton, as I leave it, with a spring in my
p.

cation Hartington, nr Cambo NE61 6BN,
rthumberland **OS** NZ0288 2m N of Cambo by B6342
01670774278 **Owner** Frank and Marjorie Lawley
en Apr to Sept, daily except Tue and Thur 1.30–5.30
ea 1 acre/0.4 hectares

he Flower Garden at Herterton House

HOLEHIRD GARDENS

AN EXCEPTIONAL RANGE OF GOOD
PLANTS IN A MAGNIFICENT SETTING
OVERLOOKING LAKE WINDERMERE

Few gardens have a site to rival that of
Holehird, on well-wooded slopes above
the eastern shore of Lake Windermere. William
Groves lived here from 1897 and housed his
collection of orchids in a glasshouse designed
by the garden designer Thomas Mawson who
came from these parts. Groves was a subscriber
to the plant-hunting expedition of Reginald
Farrer and William Purdom to China in
1914–15; several plants collected by them are
still to be seen here. After Groves's death the
Lakeland Horticultural Society took over in
1969, restored the gardens, and now look after
them to a very high standard. The plants reflect
the interests of a particularly
knowledgeable amateur garden society

– the kind of organisation that is one of the
essential foundations of the British passion for
gardening. This is, above all, a plant collection
but it takes every advantage of the attractive lie
of the land.

A FEAST OF PLANTS

High rainfall, acid soil, relatively mild winters
and coolish summers dictate the kind of plants
that do well here. In the protection of the
walled garden quite tender plants such as *Acca
sellowiana* (from Brazil) and *Callistemon citrinus*
(from Australia) do well. But it is on the slopes
to the north of the walled garden that
Holehird's characteristic planting is to be
found. Paths wind about beds with collections
of astilbes (a National Collection of over 170
species and cultivars), heathers (with several of
the rarer native species as well as cultivars of
Calluna vulgaris), Polystichum ferns (a National
Collection of over 60 species and cultivars) and
a most remarkable collection of hydrangeas

(over 200 species and cultivars, a National Collection). Throughout the borders are individual plants of note – aquilegias, cyclamen, geraniums, lilies, hepaticas, Himalayan meconopsis, narcissus – all with an emphasis on species rather than cultivars. There are also more substantial trees and shrubs – a beautiful *Davidia involucrata*, dogwoods, witch hazels, magnolias, maples, monkey puzzles, rhododendrons, species roses and much else.

Visiting Holehird is a curiously ambivalent experience. At one moment you are head down in the beds scrutinising something small, rare and wonderful, and the next moment you are gazing beyond the garden to the hills and the lovely waters of Lake Windermere – one of the loveliest views in England. Open all day and every day, Holehird is a rare amenity for gardeners and lovers of plants.

Location Patterdale Road, Windermere LA23 3JA, Cumbria **OS** NY4100 1m N of Windermere by A592 **Tel** 01539 446008 **Owner** The Lakeland Horticultural Society **Open** Daily dawn–dusk **Area** 5 acres/2 hectares

Lake Windermere from the garden at Holehird

HOLKER HALL

FINE TREES AND SHRUBS, PRETTY FORMAL GARDENS AND A WILDFLOWER MEADOW

Holker Hall goes back to the 17th century, with additions in the 18th century and, most splendidly, in the late 19th century when, after a fire, a new east

Sculpted sundial at Holker Hall

wing was built in lively neo-Elizabethan style by the Lancaster architects Paley & Austin. The earliest documented gardens here were formal gardens made for Sir Thomas Lowther in the 1720s, which were embellished with statues brought from London by sea. Sir Thomas married Lady Elizabeth Cavendish, a sister of the 3rd Duke of Devonshire, and the estate subsequently passed to the Cavendishes who still own it. The garden evolved in a piecemeal fashion with landscaping in the late 18th century and adjustments to the formal gardens about the house in the early 20th century by Thomas Mawson, who laid out a formal rose garden with segmental beds and a curving pergola – both of which are still to be seen. This was at the time of Lady Moyra Cavendish who also greatly enriched the plantings of trees and shrubs.

Today, the formal gardens by the house give way gradually to wooded informality. The formal gardens immediately south of the house are attractive, with much finely judged decorative planting, but for me the excitement at Holker starts when you arrive at the 19th-century fountain and pool, with a pebble wall shaded by *Cornus kousa* var. *chinensis*. This wall leads to a flight of steps flanked with cascades like those in an Islamic garden, shaded by large tree rhododendrons and, at the top, a 17th-century Italian statue of Neptune.

If you now turn back towards the house you can walk past a splendid lead figure of Inigo Jones (turning away slightly

he cascade and fountain at Holker Hall

sdainfully) and embark on a looping
ti-clockwise amble through the pleasure
ounds. On the grassy slopes is spread out
marvellous feast of trees and shrubs with a
ckdrop of beautiful old beeches and oaks.
he soil here is acid, the rainfall high, and the
oximity to the sea makes for a benign
icroclimate. A National Collection of 4
nera of the Styracaceae family is kept here
alesia, *Pterostyrax*, *Sinojackia* and *Styrax*).
me of these are of chiefly botanic interest
t others are among the loveliest of garden
ants, such as *Styrax japonicus* with its hanging
ite bell-like flowers, and the graceful
eetly scented *Pterostyrax hispida*. Here are
ny dogwoods, magnolias, rhododendrons,
vans, stewartias and oaks, and tender plants
ch as *Cornus capitata* and *Drimys winteri* seem
tirely at home.

Halfway through your amble you will pass
awson's rose garden and pergola, curiously
lated from the rest of the formal gardens.
est of the garden is a wildflower meadow,
d in a field beyond, a remarkable modern
dial – a concave scoop of slate beautifully
hioned with elaborate gilt calibrations.

ation Cark-in-Cartmel, nr Grange-over-Sands LA11
, Cumbria **OS** SD3577 4m W of Grange-over-Sands
5277 **Tel** 01539 558328 **Fax** 01539 558776

Email publicopening@hooker.co.uk **Website**
www.holker-hall.co.uk **English Heritage Register**
Grade II **Owner** Lord Cavendish of Furness **Open** Apr
to Oct, daily except Sat 10–6 **Area** 24 acres/10 hectares

HOWICK HALL
GARDENS

TERRACED FLOWER GARDENS AND A
HIDDEN WOODLAND GARDEN WITH
EXCEPTIONAL PLANTS

Howick is a deliciously secretive, sleepy
place; on my several visits here I have
seen scarcely more than a handful of visitors,
and more often than not have been alone
except for friendly gardeners. The house, a
grand late Georgian mansion of pale coffee-
coloured stone, was built in 1782 for Sir
Edward Grey to the designs of a local
architect, William Newton of Newcastle. It is
very close to the sea and the garden, sheltered
from the worst winds by old woodland of
beech and oak, has a remarkably mild
microclimate for a place so far north.

The larger setting is that of wooded
parkland, though nothing is known of any
designed landscape here before the 19th
century. In 1808 the architect George Wyatt,
who had been called in to work on the
house, laid out balustraded terraces, with a

pool, on the south side of the house. Urns
decorate the paved area about the pool, sitting
places are clasped in L-shapes of yew, and the
terrace gives way to plantings of waves of late
summer agapanthus, lamb's lugs, rosemary and
roses. Lawns spread far out on each side of the
pool garden, with at each end an *Acer griseum*
and a rarely seen crab-apple, *Malus transitoria*,
forming a handsome wide-spreading crown. A
hedge of lavender runs along the top of the
lower terrace wall, below which are mixed
borders of *Carpenteria californica*, *Choisya ternata*
and roses underplanted with geraniums, irises,
rue and *Galtonia candicans* (the latter rarely
seen doing well in southern English gardens).
From these borders the garden gives way to
informality with a meadow – full of narcissi
in spring – planted with birches and maples,
and a stream running along the boundary,
edged with stands of *Gunnera manicata*.

AN EXCEPTIONAL WOODLAND GARDEN
The soil close to the house is alkaline but in a
hollow to the east of the house it is acid and
here an exceptional small-scale woodland
garden is given special protection by old oaks
and Scots pine. It was planted between the
wars with the essential repertory of camellias,
magnolias and rhododendrons but also
eucryphias, beautiful hoherias, both *Drimys
winteri* and the decorative red-stemmed *Drimys
lanceolata*, and many other trees and shrubs of
distinction and beauty. The underplanting is no
less distinguished – with colchicums, ferns,
waves of meconopsis, peonies, Asiatic primulas,
trilliums and much else. The area of the
woodland garden is less than 3 acres/1.2
hectares, diminutive in comparison with most

The garden front at Howick Hall

gardens of this type, but the quality of planting is of the highest and it packs as much beauty and interest into each square yard as any woodland garden I know.

From the woodland garden a path leads across a high bridge over the road to a wood where the Long Walk follows the Howick burn down to the sea.

Location Howick, nr Alnwick NE66 3LB, Northumberland **OS** NU2417 6m NE of Alnwick by B1340 and minor roads **Tel** and **Fax** 01665 577285 **Email** estateoffice@howickuk.com **English Heritage Register** Grade II **Owner** Howick Trustees Ltd **Open** Apr to Oct, daily 1–6 **Area** 14 acres/5.6 hectares

LEVENS HALL

SPECTACULAR TOPIARY GARDEN OF
WONDERFUL CHARACTER — A GARDEN ICON

Famous gardens can often become overburdened by their renown, sinking self-importantly into a slough of pomposity. Nothing could be less true of the gardens at Levens Hall, which breathe a spirit of entrancing lightheartedness — a suitable setting for one of Mozart's funnier operas: *The Marriage of Figaro*, perhaps. Still privately owned, it is lovingly maintained to the highest standards. Historians treasure it because it is such a rare survival of its time, and garden visitors love it because it is so entertaining.

A MYSTERIOUS FRENCHMAN

The garden was made from 1694 for Colonel James Grahme who commissioned a new design from a fairly mysterious Frenchman, Guillaume Beaumont. As a setting for the house, with its sombre 13th-century pele tower, Beaumont laid out a feast of topiary, chiefly of yew. He also made a dramatic passage of beech hedges which open out half way down into a spacious rondel. Lastly, he made the first ha-ha in England — no laughing matter. All this survives, and age has given topiary and hedges a new and wonderful identity. The topiary has become gigantic and deformed into phantasmagoric shapes of the wildest imaginings: "a peacock here, a huge umbrella-like construction there, an archway, a lion…and a host of other such adornments all

The topiary garden at Levens Hall

shaped out of ductile yew", as *Country Life* put it in 1899. Some of the topiary goes back to the original plantings; some has been renewed, sometimes using the newly fashionable 19th-century gold-leafed cultivar of yew. The trees stand in beds edged in box and in recent times have been underplanted with colourful seasonal schemes — tulips and pansies in spring and verbenas and silver-leafed helichrysum in summer. The beech hedges, too, have become gigantic, so wide that you may inspect the interior, lavishly carpeted with wild garlic in spring. The ha-ha, which allows an unbroken view of grazing sheep and cattle and an avenue of sycamore marching away across the pastures, is mentioned in a letter of April 1695 as "the Ditch behind the Garden" — the earliest known reference in England to a ha-ha.

The present owners have added new borders and a fountain to the gardens and also all the necessary offices of a tourist attraction. But the rare old garden comes first and none of this is allowed to impinge on its irrepressibly delightful character.

Location Kendal LA8 0PD, Cumbria **OS** SD4985 5m S of Kendal by A591 and A6 **Tel** 01539 560321 **Fax** 01539 560669 **Email** levens.hall@farmline.com

English Heritage Register Grade I **Owner** C.H. Bagot **Open** Apr to mid Oct, Sun to Thur 10–5 **Area** 3 acres/1.2 hectares

LINDISFARNE CASTLE

GERTRUDE JEKYLL'S SMALLEST GARDEN IN A
WILD AND BEAUTIFUL ISLAND SETTING

The castle of Lindisfarne is a 16th-century fortress on a dramatic rocky outcrop. It was bought in 1902 in a state of dereliction by Edward Hudson, the editor of *Country Life*, and converted by Sir Edwin Lutyens who loved the existing building and carried out a most sympathetic restoration with a few additions grafted seamlessly on. Essentially a week-end and holiday house for a bachelor, nothing extravagant was needed and the rough moorland of the castle grounds remained largely untouched. Even so, if you were editor of *Country Life* at the beginning of the 20th century and you had a Lutyens house, it went without saying that you should have a Gertrude Jekyll garden. She laid out a little walled enclosure in a rough, stony pasture south of the castle as an ornamental *potager*, with simple paving stones and a sprinkling of ornamentals among the vegetables. It has been restored by the National Trust as a flower

rden, using plants particularly associated with
kyll – aquilegias, irises, Jacob's ladder, lady's
antle, lamb's ears and roses. Its south wall is
wer than the other three so you may peer
er and admire this simple, irrepressibly pretty
anting. To reach it, you must walk across the
sture, dodging the sheep, and there is
mething poignant about this patch of garden
inging to the windswept island.

Although almost certainly her smallest
mmission, Gertrude Jekyll came all the
ay to Holy Island in 1906 to scrutinise
e site. Judith B. Tankard and Martin A.
ood, in their book *Gertrude Jekyll at
unstead Wood* (1996), wrote: "She travelled
Northumberland by train, accompanied
Lutyens; the tide was in, and he never
rgot the sight of Hudson's valet struggling
carry her from the boat."

cation Holy Island, Berwick-upon-Tweed TD15 2SH,
rthumberland **OS** NU1341 11½m SE of Berwick-
on-Tweed by A1 and causeway at low tide; check tide
es, which are also posted at each end of causeway
01289 389244 **English Heritage Register** Grade II
wner The National Trust **Open** Apr to Oct, daily
cept Fri (open Good Fri) 12–3 **Area** 1 acre/0.4 hectare

he walled garden at Lindisfarne

MUNCASTER CASTLE

OUTSTANDING RHODODENDRONS
AND A GRAND TERRACE WALK
OVERLOOKING THE RIVER ESK

Names like Muncaster and Ravenglass
have a wild and romantic ring to them,
and the castle and its setting certainly live up
to expectations. The castle – commanding a
bluff overlooking the Esk valley – is
extraordinarily ancient. A medieval pele tower,
built here on Roman foundations, was later
much expanded and then suavely Victorianised
by Anthony Salvin between 1862 and 1866.
The Penningtons are newcomers; they have
lived here only since the 13th century.

Very little is known of the early garden
history of Muncaster although there was
certainly much tree planting in the 18th
century and the garden today benefits from
precious wind protection to the west. As you
enter, you are immediately aware of one of
the chief interests of the garden: the drive
curves uphill through woods enriched with
splendid mature rhododendrons. It was Sir
John Ramsden, the grandfather of the present
owner, who saw that the acid soil, high

rainfall and mild climate would provide the
perfect place for rhododendrons. Between the
wars he subscribed to the plant-collecting
expeditions of Frank Ludlow, George Sherriff
and Frank Kingdon Ward and enriched the
garden with their new introductions.

On the far side of the castle the land drops
briskly and wonderful views of the Esk estuary
form a spectacular panorama. The wooded
slopes here are densely planted with broad-
leafed trees and dazzle with rhododendrons in
spring and early summer. Running along the
lip of the slope is a remarkable terraced walk
with a broad turf path snaking away from the
castle. Its outer edge is hedged in box, with
regularly spaced piers of golden or common
yew rising higher than the box and echoing
the castellations of the castle. The inner side
of the walk is densely planted with cherries,
magnolias, maples, pieris and rhododendrons.
The view across the valley, with Scafell and the
other lakeland hills rising on the far side, is of
the greatest splendour.

The hedging of the Muncaster terrace is
plainly fairly recent (in any case, golden yew
is unknown before the 19th century), but
this terrace must surely date from the 18th
century when taste dictated gardens from

which, in the words of Stephen Switzer, "the adjacent Country be laid open to View". The terrace is in two parts, separated by a ravine; the part furthest from the house is referred to as the "new" terrace in a drawing of 1810. If you follow the terrace to its end – which you should certainly do – you will pass by a charming little Victorian summerhouse with a high pointed roof of wooden shingles and panels of rustic work. Retracing your steps, new views now present themselves, with the ramparts of the castle suddenly emerging from the woods. There are no flower beds at Muncaster and nothing is on a small scale. The pleasures here come from the castle, with views of its beautiful landscape, and the bold plantings of fine trees and shrubs.

Location Ravenglass CA18 1RQ, Cumbria **OS** SD1096 1m SE of Ravenglass by A595 **Tel** 01229 717614 **Fax** 01229 717010 **Email** info@muncastercastle.co.uk **Website** www.muncastercastle.co.uk **English Heritage Register** Grade II* **Owner** Mrs Phyllida Gordon-Duff-Pennington **Open** daily 10.30–6 (or dusk if earlier) **Area** 77 acres/31 hectares

The Esk valley from Muncaster

NEWBY HALL GARDEN

A GREAT YORKSHIRE GARDEN – FORMALITY, EXCELLENT TREES AND MAGNIFICENT BORDERS

Newby is one of the most attractive and enjoyable gardens in England. Its pleasures are various: it has a strong and harmonious design, excellent and sometimes rare plants and a delightful atmosphere. The house is exceptional – late 17th-century of brick and stone, spectacularly added to by Robert Adam in 1767. There was a notable garden here by the end of the 17th century and Kip's engraving in *Britannia Illustrata* (1707) shows a splendid formal layout with avenues radiating from the west façade of the house. The head gardener at this time was Peter Aram who had formerly worked for London and Wise – they supplied trees for Newby from their Brompton nursery. Of the subsequent history of the garden there are only tantalising glimpses. J.C. Loudon, writing in *The Gardener's Magazine* in 1837 in a bilious mood, did not think much of it: "A mass of flower beds have nothing to recommend them…it is seen at a glance that they have no business where they are." Late in the 19th century the architect William Burges, who built the church in the grounds advised on the garden, restoring some of its formal ingredients. The garden today owes its chief character to two generations of the Compton family – Major Edward Compton, a friend of Lawrence Johnston of Hidcote, and his son Robin Compton, the father of the present owner Richard Compton.

A GARDEN OF COMPARTMENTS

The garden that the Comptons made is divided into compartments but on a much grander scale than Hidcote and spiced with informal interludes. It is firmly connected to the house and arranged about a strong T-shaped axis – a long descending walk south from the house flanked by herbaceous borders, and the handsome Statue Walk (reputedly designed by William Burges) running east and west below the lily pond in front of the house. Formal enclosures find logical positions in relation to these axes –

The great borders at Newby Hall

...via's Garden, the Rose Garden, the ...tumn Garden and others – but are ...erspersed with gardens of woodland ...aracter threaded with winding walks. ...herever you walk there are notable plants to ...mire. A National Collection of dogwoods is ...d here, grouped together to the west of the ...se Garden. It is surprising to see among ...m *Cornus capitata*, a very tender species ...m the Himalayas, looking so vigorous in ...rth Yorkshire. There are other tender ...cies here (*Drimys winteri* is one) and they ...testimony to the Comptons' skill in ...derstanding their site.

...t would be all too easy to embark on lists of ...nts but suffice it to say that you are likely to ...ke many new discoveries here and that ...re are specialist collections of particular ...cies. Richard's brother, James Compton, is a ...tinguished plantsman with a special interest ...among other plants, salvias. (A remarkably ...e collection is deployed in the garden – and, ...in, many are perilously tender.)

...t is a pleasure at Newby to wander in the ...rden, gasp from time to time at the beauty ...the house, plunge into the woodland areas, ...erge into the Autumn Garden (where you ...sit on a bench), fill your notebook with ...new plants you have seen, and go home ...olving to improve your own garden.

...ation nr Ripon HG4 5AE, North Yorkshire **OS** ...467 4m SE of Ripon by B6265 **Tel** 01423 322583

Fax 01423 324452 **Email** info@newbyhall.co.uk **English Heritage Register** Grade II* **Owner** Richard Compton **Open** Apr to Sept, daily except Mon (open Bank Hol Mon) 11–5.30 **Area** 25 acres/10 hectares

NOSTELL PRIORY

CHARMINGLY DISHEVELED
18TH-CENTURY LANDSCAPE AND A
MYSTERIOUS ROSE GARDEN

The priory was an Augustinian foundation established here in the 12th century and the estate was acquired in the 17th century by the Winn family. The house, based on Palladio's Villa Mocenigo, was built for Sir Rowland Winn and possibly designed by Colonel James Moyser in 1730. Certainly the building was supervised by James Paine from 1736 and completed by Robert Adam after 1766. The Winn family remained at Nostell until 1953 when the house and gardens were given to the National Trust. The park, however, remained in private ownership until 2002 when, with the help of the Heritage Lottery Fund, the Trust was able to buy it.

In the early 18th century Stephen Switzer worked here and a drawing by him of *c*.1732 shows "improvements made or to be made". He very probably worked on the most important feature of the landscape – the great serpentine lake west of the house. The pools here go back to the middle ages when they were mentioned in monastic charters but they

received their present form in the 18th century and a dam and causeway separating the Middle Lake from the Lower Lake is shown on Switzer's plan. Separating the Middle Lake from the Upper Lake is a fine bridge designed in 1761 by George Savile, which today carries the A638.

A path over the causeway between the Middle and the Lower Lake runs along the west bank of the Middle Lake, and from here there are views of the house, somewhat masked by tree planting today, across the lake. The house must originally have formed a magnificent ornament from the west bank, and must itself have had unimpeded views from the windows.

The path continues and leads through woods with cedars of Lebanon, English oaks, sweet chestnuts, old yews and the occasional magnolia or rhododendron. Here, in a dell on the site of the quarry from which stone for the house was taken, is a little Gothic battlemented menagerie house designed by Robert Adam before 1776. Shrouded in wisteria and *Vitis coignetiae*, it stands close to a grove of Japanese maples and a magnolia walk with the quarry cliff behind. Here, too, is a terraced turf declivity; a former cockpit, now with a pool, it is the home of smooth and great crested newts. Nearby a recumbent stone dog snoozes in the shade of an old holm oak. A path leads through a stone grotto (probably of the late 18th century), with vaulted interior, niches and pebble floor, to emerge close to George Savile's handsome bridge.

The parkland at Nostell, much of it walled and devoted to arable farming, lies to the

The Menagerie at Nostell Priory

north, beyond Lower Lake and east of the house. At the eastern tip of Lower Lake are a formal pool, boathouse and bridge, all of the 18th century, and at the extreme northern edge of the parkland stands the splendid pyramid-shaped Obelisk Lodge. Open parkland, an avenue and a ha-ha east of the house were all probably laid out in the late 18th century. The National Trust is to restore Obelisk Lodge and the boathouse, replant trees and as far as possible return the parkland to its 18th-century appearance.

Close to the house is a splendid stable block, designed by Robert Adam in the 1770s but with later alterations, almost as grand as the house. Behind it is a curious formal garden of old roses partly enclosed in old brick walls, presumably on the site of an 18th-century kitchen garden. A pattern of shaped beds surrounds a lily pool with at its centre a bronze statue of a naked girl contemplating a shell. At a lower level lawns sweep down, decorated rather oddly with random island beds of roses and with specimen trees dotted about. A further walled garden to one side is derelict.

The house at Nostell Priory is very beautiful and its old parkland setting and wooded pleasure grounds have tremendous character and historic interest. It would be splendid if the National Trust could also turn its attention to the former kitchen garden which has great potential.

Location Doncaster Road, Nostell, nr Wakefield WF4 1QE, West Yorkshire **OS** SE4017 **Tel** 01924 863892 **Fax** 01924 865282 **Email** nostellpriory@ntrust.org **English Heritage Register** Grade II* **Owner** The National Trust **Open** early Mar, Sat and Sun 11–4; end Mar to beginning Nov, Wed to Sun (open Bank Hol Mon) 11–6; Nov to mid Dec, Sat and Sun 12–4 **Area** 346 acres/140 hectares

RIEVAULX TERRACE

AN UNFORGETTABLE TERRACE WALK LINKING TWO TEMPLES, WITH EXQUISITE VIEWS OF RIEVAULX ABBEY

The genius of the place has seldom been consulted with such dazzling results as at Rievaulx Terrace. The idea was that of Thomas Duncombe who in 1758 made the terrace at Rievaulx along the lines of the terraces that his father had already laid out at Duncombe Park (*see page 337*). There was no house at Rievaulx and it is said that he

Rievaulx Abbey from the Terrace

intended linking the terrace at Rievaulx with those at Duncombe – they are two miles apart and would have needed a viaduct across the valley. The idea sounds fanciful but something of the sort may have been started, for a quantity of mysterious masonry was discovered in the valley in recent times.

Rievaulx overlooks one of the most beautiful and romantic scenes in the country: the ravishing ruins of the Cistercian abbey in the Rye valley below and the Hambleton hills beyond. Duncombe made a gently serpentine turf terrace, with mixed woodland and shrubs behind and woodland on the sculpted slopes below. Vistas cut through the woods on the descending slope are each focused on the abbey and each – there are thirteen of them along the terrace – gives a different view. At either end of the terrace is a temple – both probably designed by Sir Thomas Robinson in the late 1750s and concealed from each other by the curve of the terrace. A round Tuscan temple with dome and pillars has an interior with a 13th-century mosaic floor from Rievaulx Abbey, fine plasterwork, and a painted roundel of a winged goddess inside the dome.

The more austere Ionic temple at the other end of the terrace was used as a banqueting house and has an elaborate interior: the coved ceiling is painted with mythological scenes, there is a grand white marble fireplace, and magnificent furniture includes a pair of gilt sofas designed by William Kent in about 1740 for Wilton House. A mahogany table is sumptuously laid as for a feast with Chamberlain Worcester porcelain.

The contrast between the smooth classicism of the temples and their rural setting, with the noble 12th-century abbey lying below and distant views of moorland, forms one of the most beguiling scenes imaginable. Rievaulx Terrace is a single-idea landscape but the idea is so magnificent, and it so completely fulfils the potential of its site, that who could wish for more? Arthur Young wrote in his *A six month tour through the north of England* (1770): "…this is a most bewitching spot."

Location Rievaulx, Helmsley YO62 5LJ, North Yorkshire **OS** SE5784 2½m NW of Helmsley by B1257 **Tel** 01439 798340/748283 **Fax** 01439 748284 **English Heritage Register** Grade I **Owner** The National Trust **Open** Apr to Oct, daily 10.30–6 **Area** 86 acres/35 hectares

SEATON DELAVAL HALL

FINELY DESIGNED FORMAL GARDENS WITH SPLENDID ORNAMENTS FOR AN EXTRAORDINARY HOUSE

The house at Seaton Delaval was designed by Sir John Vanbrugh and built between 1718 and 1729 for Admiral George Delaval. The site could scarcely be more appropriate for a sailor, overlooking Whitley Bay and often shrouded in sea mist – adding even greater drama to Vanbrugh's already thoroughly dramatic house. Of all architects, Vanbrugh was the most vividly aware of the relationship between the houses he designed and the part they played in the landscape. Seaton Delaval is not remotely on the scale of Blenheim Palace or Castle Howard but it rises superbly, facing north across the sea. There is an atmosphere of defiance about challenging all comers. Vanbrugh also designed the garden,

creating a giant raised platform with the house at the centre of the north side and corner bastions of stone which still survive but are masked by later changes. Despite the apparently defensive purpose of the bastions, they were ornamented with fine statues, of which a Diana remains in position; other statues are deployed elsewhere in the garden. More traces of 18th-century landscaping survive, including the remains of an avenue south-west of the house and a soaring obelisk aligned with the south front, but the chief garden interest today is almost entirely 20th century.

JAMES RUSSELL'S LIVELY GARDEN
In 1947 James Russell made a new garden of sprightly formality for the present Lord Hastings. Immediately below the western ramparts of the house he designed a magnificent rose parterre in which an elaborate geometric pattern of box-edged compartments is planted with different cultivars of bedding roses. Vanbrugh would probably have thought this rather frivolous but visitors today may find that it makes an attractively floriferous contrast to the stern, dark grey stone of the house. The extreme western end of the parterre is adorned with a grand marble statue of Samson slaying a philistine. From here, a superb set of early 18th-century wrought-iron gates leads to James Russell's masterly sunken garden with its circular fountain pool at the centre of a rectangular lawn framed by circles of clipped box, each filled with a mound of clipped santolina and an urn on a plinth in the middle

The sunken garden at Seaton Delaval

of each alternate circle. Running along behind the circles of box are rows of "sentry boxes" of clipped yew. The effect is both original and theatrical – in the same spirit as Vanbrugh's house.

Location Seaton Delaval, Whitley Bay NE26 4QR, Northumberland **OS** NZ3276 9m NE of Newcastle-upon-Tyne on the A190 **Tel** 0191 237 3040 **Fax** 0191 237 1493 **English Heritage Register** Grade II* **Owner** The Lord Hastings **Open** May, Bank Hol Sun and Mon 2–6; Jun to Sept, Wed, Sun and Bank Hol Mon 2–6 **Area** 3 acres/1.2 hectares

SIZERGH CASTLE

AN EXCEPTIONAL ROCK GARDEN OF FERNS AND MAPLES, SHRUB ROSES, AND A FINELY PLANTED LAKESIDE WALK

Sizergh is an ancient place, the home of an equally ancient family, the Stricklands, who have lived here since the 13th century. The family, now Hornyold-Strickland, gave the estate to the National Trust in 1950. The castellated house, with its defensive pele tower, dates chiefly from the 14th century and a licence to enclose the park was granted to Sir Walter Strickland in 1332.

The site, sloping attractively but awkwardly to the south and south-east, did not lend itself readily to a formal garden layout but in the 18th century someone had the bright idea of forming a terraced garden running at right-angles south-east of the house, above what had been the castle's moat. The long south-facing terrace wall was used for the cultivation of fruit.

In 1926 the firm of T.R. Hayes & Son of Ambleside was brought in to make major alterations. They built a grand staircase cutting downhill across the terrace and ending in a grand semicircular balustraded platform overlooking a rectangular lake formed out of the former moat. The banks are planted with trees and shrubs – manna ash (*Fraxinus ornus*), several species of willow and, a rarity, the weeping wych elm (*Ulmus glabra* 'Camperdownii') – and from a path encircling the lake the castle is seen handsomely reflected in the water. A second flight of steps runs down the side of the terraced garden and sideways into the Dutch Garden where, between the wars, there had been lavish bedding schemes. Now a path runs down the centre, and lawns on each side, with clipped mounds of variegated box, rise in gentle steps towards a stone summerhouse. Beyond, the rose garden has an avenue of rowans (*Sorbus aucuparia* 'Beissneri', with decorative red new growth), and island beds containing roses of the wilder kind – among them *Rosa sericea* subsp. *omeiensis* f. *pteracantha* with fearsome pink thorns, the Jacobite rose (*R.* × *alba* 'Alba Maxima') and *R. sweginzowii* with spectacular long lacquer-red hips. To the north-east of the castle T.R. Hayes also made a garden that has now become a historic period piece – a rock garden whose chief ingredients are conifers (75 species and cultivars), Japanese maples (mostly *Acer palmatum* cultivars) and an astounding collection of well over 100 hardy ferns. Narrow paths wind between rocks and about an irregular pool whose banks are thick with *Lysichiton americanus*, primulas and rodgersias. Gardens of this sort are desperately

unfashionable but this one is carried off with such devastating aplomb that one's heart warms to it – and many of the plants are absolutely wonderful.

Location Sizergh, nr Kendal LA8 8AE, Cumbria
OS SD4987 3½m S of Kendal by A591
Tel 015395 60070 **Fax** 015395 61621 **Email** ntrust@sizerghcastle.fsnet.co.uk **English Heritage Register** Grade II **Owner** The National Trust **Open** end Mar to Oct, daily Sun to Thur 12.30–5.30 **Area** 14 acres/5.6 hectares

STUDLEY ROYAL

REMARKABLE 18TH-CENTURY VALLEY GARDEN WITH OUTSTANDING WATER GARDENS AND GREAT BUILDINGS, INCLUDING FOUNTAINS ABBEY

In 1744 Philip Yorke wrote: "the natural beauties of the place are superior to anything of the kind I ever saw, and improved in great taste by the late and present owner." Over 250 years later visitors will find it easy to agree with that opinion. Yorke came here just after the death of its creator, John Aislabie, and he saw the first part of the garden in its heyday. Aislabie had been Chancellor of the Exchequer and came a cropper in the South Sea Bubble in 1720, serving time in the Tower before his release in 1723. In 1729 he repaid £2,000,000 (around £165,000,000 today) of illicit South Sea profits before retiring to his Yorkshire estate where he continued to add to the garden which his father, George Aislabie, had begun by 1674.

From 1718 John Aislabie had been at work on a visionary semi-formal water garden incorporating the river Skell in its lovely wooded valley. He laid out a circular Moon Pond (and a crisply pedimented Temple of Piety on its bank) with attendant crescent ponds on each side, all embellished with statues of stone or lead. On the wooded heights above the pools he built a banqueting house (1728–32 by Colen Campbell; it has an exquisite interior with apses, lovely plasterwork and carving) and an octagonal tower (1728, originally built in classical style but lavishly Gothicised ten years later). These

buildings command delicious views over the landscape and also serve as eyecatchers in positions of prominence. Not all the original buildings survive: when Philip Yorke came here in 1744 he saw "terraces interspersed with rock, which makes a Chinese landscape", and a painting of around 1760 (possibly by Balthasar Nebot) shows a Chinese pagoda with typical swooping roof commanding the heights above the valley.

FOUNTAINS ABBEY AS AN EYECATCHER William Aislabie succeeded his father in 1742 and extended the estate further along the valley in 1767, when he acquired Fountains Hall and the ruins of the 12th-century Cistercian Fountains Abbey – which had already been an important part of the borrowed landscape. William Aislabie was responsible for the surprise view of the abbey from Anne Boleyn's seat high in the woods above a curve of the river, and for smoothing the banks of the river Skell as it approached the abbey ruins, so that its shorn turf ran down to the water in characteristic late 18th-century landscape style. After William Aislabie's death the estate passed to his daughter and then to a niece. It remained intact, remarkably little changed, to modern times. The great Palladian house, however, built by John Aislabie between 1728 and 1732 and possibly designed by Colen Campbell, was severely damaged by fire in 1946 and demolished. Only the stable block survives, also possibly by Campbell and now in separate ownership. The Vyners, descendants of the Aislabies, sold the estate to West Riding County Council in 1966 and the National Trust acquired it in 1983.

Visitors today approach the garden by way of the abbey. This is delightfully revealed through the trees as you descend the hill but the pleasure of its sudden, astonishing revelation from the other end of the garden as you pass a bend in the valley is lost. However the whole landscape of Studley Royal is of enchanting beauty and constitutes an altogether painless lesson in garden history from the semi-formal stirrings of the landscape movement in the early years of the 18th century to the full-blown picturesque romanticism of the later years.

The rock garden at Sizergh Castle

The Moon Pond at Studley Royal

Location Fountains, Ripon HG4 3DY, North Yorkshire
OS SE2869 **Tel** 01765 608888 (enquiries and infoline)
Fax 01765 601002 **Website** www.fountainsabbey.org.uk
English Heritage Register Grade I **Owner** The
National Trust **Open** Nov to Jan, daily except Fri (closed
24 and 25 Dec) 10–5; Feb and Oct, daily 10–4; Apr to
Sept, daily 10–6 **Area** 900 acres/364 hectares

SUTTON PARK

FORMAL FLOWER GARDENS, GOOD
TREES AND A SERENE AND SPLENDID
18TH-CENTURY PARK

Sutton Park is a handsome Georgian house built in around 1760, possibly to the designs of Thomas Atkinson. Nothing is known of the garden until the 20th century but the park, to the south of the house, was laid out by Adam Mickle the Elder (who did much work in Yorkshire) at about the same time as the building of the house. As 18th-century parks go it seems remarkably well preserved – a flat site animated by tightly planted clumps of trees.

The garden starts in modern times when Lady Sheffield (or Mrs Sheffield as she then was) sought the advice of Percy Cane in 1962. He laid out the series of terraces below the south façade of the house, with repeated use of soaring cypresses. Immediately below the windows of the house is a border of abutilons, artemisias, cistus, geraniums and santolina, while *Alchemilla mollis*, geraniums and lamb's ears have lavishly sown themselves in the paved terrace beyond. On the terrace below, a pattern of L-shaped and square mixed borders are cut into the turf, with weeping silver pears (*Pyrus salicifolia* 'Pendula') tightly clipped into domes and, at the centre, a beautiful stone wellhead. The lowest terrace, much wider than the upper two, is dominated by a central lily pool and two filigree metal arbours swathed with roses, edged with box and clasped by L-shapes of yew. A grand cedar of Lebanon stands at the east end. The boundary of the lowest terrace, and of the garden, is a beech hedge which dips down to a balustrade in the centre, giving delicious views of Adam Mickle's park and grazing sheep.

West of the house a long open lawn is planted with occasional excellent trees, among them a beautiful old hornbeam (*Carpinus betulus*), a very large Corsican pine (*Pinus nigra* subsp. *laricio*), a big tulip tree (*Liriodendron tulipifera*) and Père David's snakebark maple (*Acer davidii*). The only ornament here is a single 18th-century urn on a plinth close to the widespread branches of the hornbeam, giving just the right arcadian note.

The brick-walled former kitchen garden was built at the same time as the house and has what used to be the village pond at the centre. Today it is largely grassed over and in 2002 an attractive maze was made of close-mown paths through the longer grass. It is now planned to turn it into a wildflower meadow. A part of the kitchen garden remains as an orchard and a new, organic kitchen garden has been made outside the walls.

The entrance façade of Sutton Park is fronted by a courtyard and grand gates to the village street. The house, in true Palladian style, is flanked by a pair of pavilions attached to the house by curved wings. Here, the dominant planting is a pair of splendid cedars of Lebanon, probably dating from the 18th century. With trees as splendid as these, and the delightful architecture of the house, you scarcely need other ornament. It is true of the garden as a whole that the decorative atmosphere of each of its parts seems perfectly harmonious and exactly right: neither too much nor too little.

Location Sutton-on-the-Forest, York YO6 1DP,
North Yorkshire **OS** SE5864 8m N of York by B1363
Tel 01347 810249/811239 **Fax** 01347 811251
Email suttonpark@fsbdial.co.uk **Website**
www.statelyhome.co.uk **Owner** Sir Reginald and
Lady Sheffield **Open** Easter to Sept, daily 11–5
Area 8 acres/3.2 hectares

The terraced garden at Sutton Park

THORP PERROW ARBORETUM

A DELIGHTFUL PRIVATE COLLECTION OF TREES AND SHRUBS OF TREMENDOUS CHARACTER

The house at Thorp Perrow dates from around 1800 but the history of the estate is surprisingly ancient. An area close to the lake seems to have been managed woodland since the middle ages; its name, Spring Wood, often denotes a piece of woodland that is regularly coppiced. Some magnificent old trees survive, such as the beautiful English oak, probably dating from the 17th century, in the Millennium Glade in the northern part of the arboretum. In the 1840s and 1850s a pinetum was made by the then owner, Lady Augusta Milbank, who had seed of the new North American discoveries sent to Yorkshire. The arboretum itself was started in 1931 by Sir Leonard Ropner who added over 2,000 new species and varieties of trees and shrubs. Sir Leonard died in 1977 and his son, the present owner, has developed the collection. The latest printing of the (excellent) catalogue (1999) is well over 100 pages long but new plants are being added all the time and the 2001 addendum includes over 450 additions. All plants are numbered and to identify them you need a copy of this catalogue and its various addenda.

The site is largely flat but it does have the priceless asset of water which forms reflecting surfaces and shimmers of light among the trees. Flowing through the grounds is a stream which at some point, probably when the house was built, was dammed to form a curving lake immediately west of the house, and in the southern part of the arboretum the stream has been given a series of gentle falls and clear pools. Long avenues more or less radiating from the house make it relatively easy to find one's way, and each area is given a reference letter corresponding to the divisions of the catalogue. Trees are grouped by genus – the Cherry Avenue, Maple Glade, Rowan Avenue and so forth. Every major group of hardy trees is represented, and the arboretum has three National Collections of trees: ash (*Fraxinus*, 23 species and cultivars), lime (*Tilia*, 25 species) and walnut (*Juglans*, 10 species). There is also a wide range of shrubs. Roses are for the most part species or cultivars of bolder character – the sort that look best in this kind of setting. Apart from the private gardens between the house and the lake (a lawn decorated with a flock of yew topiary shapes and a lakeside walk with urns of flowers), there are no formal gardens and only the slightest touch of formality.

Thorp Perrow, one of the best privately owned collections of trees and shrubs in the country, is big enough and wild enough to encourage a true sense of exploration. I have been here very early on a spring morning in pouring with rain when the blossom and new growth were lovely, and my last visit, in October 2002, was also early but on a sublime autumn morning of mist giving way to pale sunlight; in any conditions it is an enthralling place to see – big enough to provide an exhilarating walk and rich enough in plants to provide much to admire and learn from.

Location Bedale DL8 2PR, North Yorkshire **OS** SE2585 2m S of Bedale off B6268 **Tel** and **Fax** 01677 425323 **Email** louise@thorpperrow.freeserve.co.uk **Website** www.thorpperrow.com **Owner** Sir John Ropner Bt **Open** daily dawn–dusk **Area** 85 acres/34 hectares

WALLINGTON

IN THE MIDST OF A WOOD, A HIDDEN WALLED GARDEN PACKED WITH PLANTS

Approaching Wallington from the south on the B6342, you cross the river Wansbeck, swooping over a beautiful bridge designed in 1755 by James Paine. Already you sense that you are in a designed landscape. The house is soon revealed on your left, with a curious row of grotesque stone dragon's heads emerging from the turf by the roadside. The house is essentially 17th and 18th century, built for the Blackett family, though it was altered in the 19th century with the advice of John Ruskin for the Trevelyans who gave the estate to the National Trust in 1942.

The chief garden interest lies on the other side of the road from the house where a gate leads into old woodland. It is reputed that Capability Brown (who was born nearby at Kirkharle) laid out a garden here for the Blackett family in the 1760s. If he did, and if it survives, it is remarkably unlike any other of his works. A semi-formal lake lies at the heart of the wood, with the delightful prospect of the mid 18th-century pedimented Portico House rising on the slopes above the lake's north bank; but almost immediately you come to the surprise in the woods – a walled garden, built in 1760 and sloping south and east in a most unusual dog-leg shape.

The planting here is almost entirely the work of the National Trust since 1958.

The lake and yew topiary at Thorp Perrow

The walled garden at Wallington

The garden is packed with plants and incidents — fairly higgledy-piggledy but finely maintained and constrained only by the enclosing walls. A terraced walk running along the north wall provides a good vantage point from which the character of the place is revealed. At the entrance is a surprisingly grand but rustic double staircase, curving back to enclose a pool and fountain. The upper terrace ends in a glasshouse with the elegant Owl House, an 18th-century pavilion, rising behind it. Alongside the glasshouse a new, brilliantly coloured late-summer border bursts with cannas, crocosmias, flamboyant dahlias and kniphofias, soothed by repeated purple-leafed cotinus and the arching fronds of pampas grass. Below it an old brick path runs downhill between yew hedges and under arches of honeysuckle and 'Perle d'Azur' clematis. A hidden paved enclosure has seats, an urn filled with summer bedding and fringed with lambs' lugs, and pots filled with pink mallows and petunias. An orchard-like little arboretum has a large collection of elders (Sambucus, a National Collection), flowering cherries and mountain ash. Against the north-facing lower wall a deep border has campanulas, hostas, hydrangeas, potentillas, pulmonaria and sedums. In the middle of the lawn a sprawling arrangement of conifers and heathers has a decidedly retro flavour.

The unexpectedness of the walled garden in wood, the oddity of the lie of the land, the raised terrace along the top wall and the eccentricity of the garden's shape are what stick in my mind rather than any notable beauty of planting. On more than one occasion I have walked through the noble gloom of the woods to emerge in the brilliant sun and colour of the walled garden — a contrast to relish.

Location Cambo, Morpeth NE61 4AR, Northumberland **OS** NZ0284 12m W of Morpeth by B6343 **Tel** 01670 774283 **Fax** 01670 774420 **English Heritage Register** Grade II* **Owner** The National Trust **Open** Apr to Oct, daily 10–7 (closes 6 in Oct); Nov to Mar, daily 10–4 (or dusk if earlier) **Area** 100 acres/40 hectares

WENTWORTH CASTLE

SUPERB FLOWERING SHRUBS IN AN 18TH-CENTURY SETTING WITH NOTABLE ORNAMENTAL BUILDINGS

In 1789 Horace Walpole wrote: "My favourite of all great seats, such a variety of ground, of wood and water; almost all executed with so much taste." It is sadly unlikely that his opinion would remain unchanged if he saw Wentworth Castle today. The industrial sprawl of Barnsley now lies close by and the traffic of the unlovely M1 thunders relentlessly past in the valley below; where in the early 18th century there was a spectacular parterre of Versailles-like splendour there is now a blank tarmac car park for the staff of Northern College which occupies the palace. Nevertheless, much of beauty and interest remains, and the gardening staff work hard with slender resources to maintain what is left of the garden.

The house was rebuilt for Thomas Wentworth (later 1st Earl of Strafford of the second creation) between 1709 and 1713, when he created a house of palatial splendour from an already handsome house of 1670. His architect was probably a Frenchman, Jean de Bodt, who designed the east range — fifteen bays wide — with an intricately carved

The Gothic eyecatcher at Wentworth

frontispiece. Fifty years later a new south range was added in rather old-fashioned Palladian style, designed by Charles Ross. The result was one of the grandest, and biggest, houses of its date in the country. In the garden Wentworth's ambitions were on the same scale. Below the east front he laid out the parterre I have already mentioned. It is shown in a Kip engraving of 1714, together with more parterres to the south and a formal "wilderness" to the west. But as the century passed, Wentworth became bitten by the landscaping bug and an engraving by Badeslade of 1734 already shows the changes. Crowning the hill behind the house is Stainborough Castle, a Gothic eyecatcher on the grand scale – one of the oldest Gothic garden buildings in the country, of which only a single lonely tower survives, the remainder having collapsed in 1962. Also showing in Badeslade's engraving are two converging avenues: Lady Lucy's Walk and Broad Avenue leading up the slope behind the house. These alignments do survive, converging on an extraordinary obelisk, once crowned by a gilded sun, with the inscription "To the memory of the Rt. Hon. Lady Mary Wortley Montagu who in the year 1720 introduced innoculation of the small pox into England from Turkey". The Broad Avenue leading up to the obelisk is now planted with billowing mounds of rhododendrons, part of the very large collection planted here in the 20th century (a National Collection which now numbers over 300 species). There are also National Collections of magnolias and of cultivars of *Camellia × williamsii*. The underplanting of these shrubs is of high quality and includes several species of meconopsis and waves of Himalayan primulas. Lady Augusta's Walk (also visible in Badeslade's engraving) is now planted with shrubs and such evergreen trees as cedars, pines and yews; a pattern of grass paths radiates out from it.

MELANCHOLY DECAY

In the park, which was laid out in the early and mid 18th century incorporating what was probably a 17th-century deer park, other garden buildings and monuments survive in varying states of dishevelment. A serpentine river is crossed by a bridge, a menagerie house

was altered in the 20th century, a Gothic building of 1759 is ruinous, and a rotunda of 1746 and a monument to the Duke of Argyll (1744) survive. The grounds of Wentworth Castle are a curious mixture of melancholy decay intermingled with the exhilaration that comes from seeing the remaining splendours of the landscape set off by fine plants.

Location Lowe Lane, Stainborough, Barnsley S75 3ET, South Yorkshire **OS** SE3203 4m SW of Barnsley, W of M1 between Jncts 36 and 37 **Tel** 01226 731269 **English Heritage Register** Grade I **Owner** Barnsley Metropolitan Borough Council **Open** mid Apr to June, chiefly by guided tours (phone for details) **Area** 50 acres/20 hectares

The Iris Walk at York Gate

YORK GATE

A BRILLIANTLY DESIGNED AND PLANTED 20TH-CENTURY GARDEN

Y ork Gate was a farmhouse when Frederick and Sybil Spencer bought it in 1951. Their son, Robin, was then seventeen and all three, but especially Robin and his mother, worked on making a new garden on the site of a small orchard. They devised a layout of intimate enclosures in the tradition of Hidcote or Tintinhull, filled with lively and often original planting and the whole animated by a strong decorative sense. Robin Spencer died young in 1982 but his mother continued working in the garden until her death in 1994. Although bristling with ideas beautifully carried out, and an enchanting garden to be in, York Gate has never had the fame it deserves.

The enclosures flow about the house on three sides, harmoniously linked but with no overall dominating pattern. A pair of ethereal white and silver borders are full of *Eryngium giganteum*, white lupins, white phlox, giant *Onopordum acanthium* and *Viola cornuta* Alba Group. At their head, a curious stone sundial (a sphere pierced by an arrow set on top of a tall twisting column) also marks a junction with the Allée, which shoots off at right-angles: a stone path flanked with strips of turf and hedged in beech. The Allée can also be reached by a secret door at the back of a pillared summerhouse whose main façade, in the form of a loggia, stands at the head of the herb garden. This is one of the best parts of the garden, with a central path of gravel edged with granite setts and interrupted in the middle by an old millstone set in the ground. Borders on each side, backed by yew hedges, are filled with herbs and punctuated by tall spirals of clipped box. In high summer the scent of the herbs, intensified by the enclosing hedges, suffuses the loggia and the garden is loud with the buzzing of bees. At the far end of the borders a monumental opening is formed of square columns of yew surmounted by generous yew spheres. A walk of irises leads off at an angle and this too has a beautiful path – a lattice-work pattern of setts laid in gravel – which leads to an open pavilion with a high pitched roof.

Decorative details catch the eye at every turn. *Cedrus atlantica* Glauca Group is deftly espaliered against a dry-stone wall to form long ribbons of colour against the stone; a gap in a hedge looks over a miniature ha-ha to reveal the open countryside – all the more effective in a garden that is otherwise largely inward-looking; a giant cast-iron urn is filled with crocuses, the mass of delicate flowers holding their own in the bold container; a paved area close to the house was made into a bonsai court with some ancient specimens.

In the Spencers' time all sorts of small idiosyncrasies enlivened the place. Ornamental baskets, for example, were distributed in various parts of the garden to receive weeds removed during the owners' perambulations. Some of this detail has inevitably been lost but the strong design of the garden and its delightful atmosphere survive.

Location Back Church Lane, Adel, Leeds LS16 8DW, West Yorkshire **OS** SE2740 4m NW of Leeds, close to Adel church E of the Leeds–Otley road (A660) **Tel** 0113 267 8240 **Website** www.gardeners-grbs.org.uk **Owner** The Gardeners' Royal Benevolent Society **Open** May to Sept, Thur, Sun and Bank Hol Mon 2–5 **Area** 1 acre/0.4 hectares

YORKSHIRE SCULPTURE PARK

MAGNIFICENT MODERN SCULPTURE IN A LOVELY 18TH-CENTURY LANDSCAPE

The Wentworth family came to Bretton in 1407 and the estate descended by inheritance until Wentworth Henry Canning Beaumont, 2nd Viscount Allandale, sold it in 1948. The present Bretton Hall was built in around 1720 to the designs of Sir William Wentworth and Colonel James Moyser. It became a teacher training college in 1949 and later a college of the University of Leeds.

There was probably a deer park here by the 17th century and in the 18th century there was much activity in the parkland. The landscape designer Richard Woods was consulted in 1764 and a neighbour recorded a visit in July 1764: "din'd at Sir Thomas Wentworth's and walked over the Park and view'd his intended improvements." It is likely that the great lake to the south of the house was shaped at this time and the cascade bridge that divides it in two built – but Woods's exact role is not known. Much of the parkland has been turned over to agricultural use in modern times but some old parkland trees survive.

In 1977 the Yorkshire Sculpture Park was founded to organise temporary exhibitions, with sculptures placed throughout the Bretton Hall estate. By far the most memorable part is the area devoted to a large collection of sculptures by Henry Moore (on permanent loan), in wild parkland to the east of Bretton Hall. This is part of Bretton Country Park and is visitable throughout daylight hours. The site, large (96 acres/39 hectares) and very beautiful, is the south-facing slope of a valley, scattered with trees (including some lovely old oaks) and running down to the wooded north bank of the lake. The sculptures are splendidly placed, with plenty of room between them, sometimes rearing up on a slight rise or finely positioned in relation to the trees. Most are of organic shapes which echo the folds of the land or the hummocks of trees but sometimes they rise high like totems, forming markers in the landscape. In a museum many would dominate any but the largest of rooms and in anything smaller would seem horribly cooped up. Here they show their power to animate a very large space without

Henry Moore's Reclining Figure

overpowering it. It is one of the best displays of 20th-century sculpture in any public park in the country.

Elsewhere in the grounds there are opportunities for many other displays. The visitor centre has an exhibition space and there is a further gallery in the walled former kitchen garden adjacent to it. On the wooded slopes that lead down to Bretton Hall there is a group of bronzes by Barbara Hepworth (Family of Man) and several works by Elizabeth Frink. Walks about the lake have sculptures by Antony Gormley, Sol Le Witt and Serge Spitzer. Irritatingly, much of the lakeside is a nature reserve owned by the University of Leeds, with access restricted to students and permit holders only.

Location Bretton Hall, West Bretton, Wakefield WF4 4LG, West Yorkshire **OS** SE2812 1m NW of Jnct 38 of M1 **Tel** 01924 830302 **Fax** 01924 832600 **Website** www.ysp.co.uk **English Heritage Register** Grade II **Owner** Yorkshire Sculpture Park **Open** daily 10–6 (closes 5 in winter) **Area** 500 acres/202 hectares

SCOTLAND

Woodland glade at Achamore

but of glades cleared in the existing woods. The experience of wandering from glade to glade is delightful. This is a big garden and there is much to see, but a useful sketch plan is available and routes of different lengths are waymarked. If you go past the walled garden to the south and climb the gently rising land of Spring Bank you will come to the highest point of the garden with delicious views to the west and northwest of the islands of Islay and Jura.

In 2002, after some uncertainty about the future of the island, Gigha was bought by its inhabitants.

Location Isle of Gigha PA41 7AD, Argyll **OS** NR6348 Off the W coast of Kintyre; ferry from Tayinloan **Tel** 01583 505254 **Fax** 01583 505244 **Website** www.isle-of-gigha.co.uk **Owner** The Isle of Gigha Heritage Trust **Open** daily dawn–dusk **Area** 50 acres/20 hectares

ACHAMORE

AN ISLAND GARDEN WITH EXCEPTIONAL RHODODENDRONS AND OTHER FLOWERING SHRUBS

Visiting Achamore is always exciting – the difficulty of access, slipping across the sound in a boat, increases the excitement. Sir James Horlick came here in 1944 to an existing sporting estate which had the priceless asset of mature trees, chiefly spruce and sycamore, which had been established by his predecessor, Captain William Scarlett (3rd Lord Abinger), to provide protection for game. Although the climate is mild here, strongly influenced by the North Atlantic Drift, westerly gales and salt-laden air make gardening possible only with windbreaks. Sir James wanted to plant rhododendrons and at Achamore, with its mild climate, high rainfall, acid soil and existing protection of trees, he found the perfect site.

In laying out the garden Sir James was helped by Kitty Lloyd Jones and together they built up a marvellous collection of rhododendrons, almost all propagated or bred here at Achamore. These are grouped according to their categories: groups of *R. griersonianum* and *R. thomsonii* hybrids, for example – both of which are among the most

prolific of hybridisers – provide a good opportunity to see the variations. Splendid examples of the great aristocrats of species such as *R. macabeanum* are also grouped together. Although these plants loom large, and certainly provide brilliant spring colour, the garden is also rich in other trees and shrubs – southern beeches (*Nothofagus* species), beautiful examples of *Cercidiphyllum japonicum*, embothriums, eucryphias, rowans, styrax (incuding the rare *S. shiraianum*) and viburnums. The north walled garden houses a collection of conifers, among them such rarities as the Formosan fir (*Abies kawakami*). There is also much herbaceous planting of hostas, lilies, meconopsis, narcissi, Asiatic primulas and much else.

The manner of planting is most attractive. This is, in effect, a garden of compartments, but compartments formed not of the architectural hedges and walls of an Arts and Crafts layout

ARDUAINE GARDEN

IN AN IDYLLIC SETTING BY THE SEA, MARVELLOUS HERBACEOUS PLANTS AMONG TREES AND SHRUBS

The estate at Arduaine was bought in 1897 by James Arthur Campbell, a tea planter and friend of Osgood Mackenzie of Inverewe (*see page 383*). Campbell built a house and started to make a garden at a little distance from the house, choosing as his site an area close to the sea (and thus strongly affected by the North Atlantic Drift, with Asknish Bay to the south and Loch Melfort to the north). For protection from the wind, he planted a shelter belt to the west, chiefly of larch.

James Campbell's collection of species rhododendrons is of outstanding quality. His tea-planting connections provided the seed of a Ceylon rhododendron, *R. arboreum* subsp. *zeylanicum*, which came to Arduaine in a chest of tea; specimens here of this large tree

Meconopsis George Sherriff Group at Arduaine

hododendron are the largest in the British sles. Other species include plants propagated by seed gathered in the wild (such as the late-lowering evergreen *R. auriculatum* from Hupeh, China), species which were among the first to flower in the west at Arduaine (such as *R. protistum* var. *giganteum*), and many other rarities which not only flourish but, on the sloping upper reaches of the garden, look s much at home as in their homeland. Other outstanding flowering trees and shrubs include eucryphias, magnolias and rowans.

Among the many herbaceous plants, especially in the lower garden with its streams and pools, are marvellous spreads of *Cardiocrinum giganteum*, Chatham Island forget-me-not (*Myosotidium hortensia*), meconopsis and Asiatic primulas. Throughout the garden are fine specimens of plants which in any other garden would be regarded as notable. Here, however, the various berberis,

cedars of Lebanon, *Gunnera manicata*, Monterey cypresses and New Zealand flaxes seem positively humdrum alongside the thrilling and beautifully grown rarities that crowd about.

After James Campbell's death in 1929 the estate passed to his son and grandson but in 1964 everything except the garden was sold. The house became the Loch Melfort Hotel and the garden, still owned by the Campbell family, was neglected until 1971 when it was bought by Edmund and Harry Wright, two retired nurserymen who devoted themselves to its revitalisation. Now well cared for in the hands of the National Trust for Scotland, its future seems secure.

Location Arduaine, by Oban PA34 4XQ, Argyll
OS NM7910 20m S of Oban by A4816 **Tel** and **Fax**
01852 200366 **Owner** The National Trust for Scotland
Open daily 9.30–sunset **Area** 20 acres/8 hectares

Himalayan hillside at Arduaine

BENMORE BOTANIC GARDEN

AN OUTSTANDING COLLECTION OF PLANTS IN A WILD AND DRAMATIC SETTING

This garden was until recently known as the Younger Botanic Garden but it has now changed its name. The approach to the garden is very beautiful by whichever route you choose – the ferry from Gourock to Dunoon or the long and lovely drive from the north, from the head of Loch Fyne and along the wooded banks of Loch Eck. The garden itself starts with its own splendid fanfare – a triumphant avenue of Wellingtonias planted in 1863 and now all over 130ft/39m high.

The first plantings of any note here were made by Ross Wilson in 1820, of which some Scots pines still survive. Subsequent owners made their mark, in particular James Duncan who, between 1871 and 1883, afforested 1,622 acres/656 hectares with well over 6,000,000 trees. A photograph taken in around 1870 shows the significance of his work – at that time most of the hillsides were quite bare of trees. Duncan also built grand glasshouses and made formal gardens which no longer survive. Henry Younger bought the estate in 1889 and greatly added to the ornamental planting, as did his son Harry. In 1925 part of the estate was taken over by the Royal Botanic Garden Edinburgh, since when the garden has been spectacularly enriched; it now forms one of the finest plant collections in Britain.

THE INFLUENCE OF CLIMATE

The climate at Benmore, influenced by the North Atlantic Drift, is fairly benign, with mild winters and very high rainfall, which varies between 80in/200cm and 120in/300cm. Wind, whose potential for damage has been mitigated by dense planting over the years, can still have devastating effect – in the winter of 1968 more than 500 trees of over 120ft/36m were blown down. Much of the garden is only just above sea level but much is also hilly, with the land rising steeply towards Benmore Hill to a height of 450ft/136m. The surroundings are very beautiful, and whether you look uphill or down there is always something to admire.

Benmore in its wild setting

The planting throughout the garden is naturalistic with the exception of the Formal Garden in the old walled garden with its collection of around 300 garden cultivars of conifers. Puck's Hut, a pavilion overlooking the walled garden and designed by the architect Sir Robert Lorimer, is panelled with different timbers taken from trees on the estate. The rest of the garden is preeminently a garden for walking in – excellent maps will help you to find your way. Plants are grouped either by habitat (the Chilean Rainforest) or by type of plant (the collection of garden conifers in the Formal Garden). Plants of special interest to the garden – such as rhododendrons and

conifers – are represented by enormous collections (over 650 species and cultivars of rhododendron, for example) and these may be explored by designated walks, though plants will also be found elsewhere in the garden wherever there is a suitable site. Some of the plant collections grouped by habitat have splendid settings – the Bhutanese Glade presents a setting of Himalayan splendour, with the rocky Massan Cliff rearing up beside it and plants such as *Abies densa*, *Betula utilis* and *Sorbus* aff. *thibetica* looking entirely at home.

The garden is also rich in such ornamental

shrubs as cotoneasters, enkianthus, eucryphias, magnolias, osmanthus, pieris and stewartias. Conifers loom large (there are 200 species grown here) but there are many good deciduous trees as well – acers, birches, *Cercidiphyllum japonicum*, nothofagus, rowans and *Styrax japonicus*. Among non-flowering plants are some lovely ferns, native and exotic, and many lichens, liverworts and mosses.

The wild and beautiful setting and the wonderful collection of plants make Benmore exceptional. Other British botanic gardens have notable collections; none has a natural site of such beauty.

Location Benmore, Dunoon PA23 8QU, Argyll **OS** NS1585 7m N of Dunoon by A815 **Tel** 01369 706261 **Fax** 01369 706369 **Owner** Trustees of the Royal Botanic Garden Edinburgh **Open** Mar to Oct, daily 9.30–6 (winter access, weather permitting but no facilities open; phone for information) **Area** 120 acres/48 hectares

BRANKLYN

AN EXQUISITE PLANTSMAN'S GARDEN ON THE EDGE OF A BUSY TOWN

Who would expect to find such an astonishing garden in the couthie suburbs of eastern Perth? Branklyn was the creation of two amateurs of rare gifts, John and Dorothy Renton, who came to live here in 1922. The location itself is sufficiently surprising but the style of garden they chose to make is all the more remarkable.

On a south-facing slope with acid loam, the Rentons created a miniature woodland garden with formal overtones. The rainfall here, at an elevation of just 200ft/60m, is nothing like that of the west coast of Scotland but is still sufficient for a wide range of the sort of plants that interested the Rentons. Dorothy Renton wrote: "There has been no preconceived rule of design about the garden. It has been evolved gradually…it is primarily a home for plants." The garden is nonetheless skilfully and harmoniously arranged. It slopes gently from the north to the south, paths run its length from east to west and occasionally cut across up or down the slope, and more substantial trees and shrubs – a handsome conical spruce

Erythronium tuolumnense at Branklyn

Picea glauca var. *albertiana* 'Conica') or a gracefully spreading Japanese maple – are craftily used to mark the divergence of paths or to form a firm shape among profuse planting. This adds structure to the garden and lures the visitor on. Having said that, it is the plants that are the main meal. Garden visitors to Scotland always find it hard to conceal their envy for the marvellous plants, especially perennials of a Himalayan or Alpine disposition, which seem so effortlessly to flourish in the north and prove so tormentingly difficult in the south. You *can* grow *Cardiocrinum giganteum*, meconopsis, nomocharis and trilliums in England but I have never seen them so lavishly prolific as they appear here and elsewhere in Scotland.

DETAILED INTIMACY OF PLANTING

The Rentons had almost 2 acres/0.8 hectares – a big garden by most people's standards these days – but the number of plants they grew was enormous and they were always conscious of the limitations of space. For this reason the garden is especially rich in smaller shrubs (for example, the smaller kinds of rhododendrons) which makes it of special interest to other gardeners, as does the detailed intimacy of the herbaceous planting. A National Collection of the genus *Cassiope* is held here: 6 species and 19 cultivars of those pretty little ericaceous subshrubs with bell-like flowers.

Although it is packed with rarities, Branklyn looks like a real garden; this is no regimented stamp collection and since John Renton bequeathed the garden to the National Trust for Scotland in 1968, it has been beautifully kept and still has all the character and devoted

attention to detail that are found in the best private gardens made by people who are mad about plants. At Branklyn serious botanising by no means excludes delightful gardening but what sticks in my mind is the memory of individual plants and their settings – tall *Meconopsis regia* with the palest lemon-yellow flowers growing in the shade of a Macedonian pine (*Pinus peuce*); a drift of *Lilium chalcedonicum* with its vermilion Turk's cap flowers on the edge of a little pool; the pale cream flowers faintly suffused with pink of *Fritillaria pallidiflora* among mossy stones. All these lovely exotics look perfectly at home.

Location Dundee Road, Perth PH2 7BB, Perthshire
OS NO1222 On the E edge of Perth by A85
Tel 01738 625535 **Owner** The National Trust for Scotland **Open** Mar to Oct, daily 9.30–sunset
Area 1¾ acres/0.7 hectares

BRODICK CASTLE

ON THE BEAUTIFUL ISLE OF ARRAN,
A FINE WOODLAND GARDEN FOR
A HISTORIC ESTATE

Brodick is a proper castle, a fortified tower of resplendent red sandstone in a superb position facing southwards over Brodick Bay. The castle dates back to the 13th century with many later alterations, including additions by James Gillespie Graham in the mid 19th century. The island was crown property until 1503 when James IV gave it to his cousin, John Hamilton, 1st Earl of Arran. It descended in the Hamilton family (later Dukes of Hamilton) until the 12th Duke failed to produce an heir and his daughter, Mary Louise, married James

The woodland garden at Brodick

Graham, later 6th Duke of Montrose, in 1905. Their descendants gave the estate to the National Trust for Scotland in 1958.

The scenery is very beautiful, with the peak of Goatfell soaring almost 3,000ft/900m above, and spectacular birds to be seen (among them, if you're lucky, golden eagles). The site is a splendid one for a garden – protected from westerly winds and enjoying south-facing slopes which run down to the sea. Furthermore, the effect of the North Atlantic Drift, combined with very high rainfall (around 70in/175cm per annum), allows the cultivation of marvellous woodland plants.

The earliest gardening at Brodick of which there is still evidence was in the fine walled garden south-east of the castle, which bears the date 1710 on an entrance. This, gently terraced, must originally have been the kitchen garden but has now been turned over to ornamental purposes with a cruciform pattern of paths, Victorian style carpet bedding, mixed borders and a fortissimo display of roses filling beds and ramping over arbours, an attractive modern layout.

TENDER RHODODENDRONS

The great distinction of Brodick lies, however, in the woodland garden to the west and south-west. Here, after World War I, the Duchess of Montrose started to plant lavishly, inspired by the quantities of new introductions that were arriving from the expeditions to the Himalayas of George Forrest and Frank Kingdon Ward. Long walks run through the woodland, following the contours of the slopes, and everywhere there are wonderful plants. Such tender rhododendrons as *R. protistum* var. *giganteum* (a Forrest introduction of 1926) and *R. magnificum* (a Kingdon Ward introduction of 1935) – both large, with dramatic leaves – burst magnificently into flower in March. Another Forrest introduction (from Burma in 1925) is the delightful *R. taggianum*, rarely seen growing out of doors in British gardens. More of a shrub than a tree, its flowers in May are white with a pale yellow blotch and deliciously scented. Apart from the very large collection of rhododendrons, there are many other distinguished shrubs here, often tender and often rare – the scented Madeiran lily-of-

the-valley tree (*Clethra arborea*), eucryphias of great splendour, the most dramatic of all buddleias, *B. colvilei*, with lavish panicles of crimson flowers, and magnificent camellias. Everywhere ferns grow with astonishing luxuriance, colonising the undergrowth with their lavish fronds. About the banks of a pool there are waves of Himalayan primulas – including several Forrest introductions – and many other good herbaceous plantings in the woods, including tender Madeiran echiums.

At the southernmost tip of the garden, positioned quite close to the shore of Brodick Bay, is a rare and enchanting garden building

The rose parterre at Broughton House

– the Bavarian summerhouse. This rustic pavilion was built in 1845 to celebrate the marriage of the 10th Duke of Hamilton's son to Princess Marie von Baden. The interior is beautifully fashioned with intricate patterns of pine cones and strips of larch and the exterior swarms with artificial climbers, giving it the appearance of emerging from the undergrowth.

Location Isle of Arran KA27 8HY **OS** NS0136 2m from Brodick ferry **Tel** 01770 302202 **Fax** 01770 302312 **Owner** The National Trust for Scotland **Open** (walled garden) end Mar to end Oct, daily 10–5; (country park) daily 9.30–sunset **Area** (walled garden) 3 acres/1.2 hectares; (country park) 891 acres/360 hectares

BROUGHTON HOUSE AND GARDEN

AN ARTIST'S GARDEN, PACKED WITH PLANTS, FOR AN 18TH-CENTURY TOWN HOUSE

With its harbour on the estuary of the river Dee, Kircudbright is a delightful town with excellent architecture. It became a favoured resort of artists in the 1880s, one of whom, the "Glasgow boy" E.A. Hornel (whose family originally came from Kircudbright), bought Broughton House in 1901. Between 1901 and 1933 he adorned th fine 18th-century house with an enchanting garden. Hornel died in 1933 and the house and garden were passed to a trust until the National Trust for Scotland took over in 1994 and restored it.

The garden, long and narrow, runs down westwards behind the house. Such "rig" gardens are traditional in Scottish town houses growing fruit and vegetables as well as ornamentals and often retaining their original layout. Today, the first part, busy with ornament, is a crowded garden with a Japanese feel – Hornel had made two visits to Japan

d was much taken with its culture. Here are
nifers clipped into shapes, a spreading
anese maple, a clump of bamboo, a bronze
ll, troughs and mysterious shapes of stone –
en a collection of old curling stones takes on
oriental air. Such distinguished trees as *Acer*
seum and *Cornus controversa* 'Variegata' cast
eir shade over moss-covered rocks and a
niature ferny ravine. Paved paths rise and
l, leading to a little pool crossed by stepping
nes and spanned by a scarlet railing doing
ual duty as a Japanese bridge. A bed is filled
th azaleas, epimediums, ferns and shapes of
pped box. *Geranium palmatum* seeds itself all
out. A second pool has a bronze crane, rocks
d lavish leafy planting about its banks, all
erlooked by a cast-iron bench in a bower of
panese anemones and hydrangeas.

A CHANGE OF MOOD

he visit to Japan is brief but memorable – an
tirely different kind of garden now spreads
t. A long narrow paved path edged with box
ns the full length of the garden and on each
le enclosures of different kinds are revealed.
lawn is shaded by a sprawling old magnolia,
th a summerhouse fringed with hellebores
d hydrangeas in its shade. A larger lawn has a
pically Scottish many-sided sundial, a
ectacular old espaliered apple tree – now
untly free-standing – *Cytisus battandieri*,
utilons and eucalyptus. An oval parterre has

a series of oval concentric rings of box
enclosing beds of roses, with a medlar and a
Cercidiphyllum japonicum to one side. A
beautiful glasshouse, originally designed by
John Keppie for Hornel, was destroyed in a
winter gale in 1998 and has been faithfully
reconstructed. It contains such tender exotics
as *Cyathea australis*, *Macrozamia communis* and
old cultivars of pelargonium. An arbour of
gnarled wisteria spans a path and a long mixed
border backed by a wall is brilliant with
eucryphias in late summer. Paths dart off here
and there, old apple trees rise hither and yon,
and the odd soaring tender echium stands in a
corner. You eventually emerge to find yourself
in the shade of a large old cherry tree with an
elevated view over railings of yachts lying
tranquilly at anchor in the harbour below.

Plants crowd in hugger-mugger all around
but never quite take over – a patch of
soothing lawn or a crisp box-edged gravel
path controls the planted profusion. The
garden has changed since Hornel's time but,
judging from old photographs, has retained
much of its former character.

Location 12 High Street, Kircudbright DG6,
Kirkcudbrightshire **OS** NX6055 In the centre of
Kircudbright **Tel** 01557 330437 **Owner** The National
Trust for Scotland **Open** (phone for details; major
restoration of house in 2003/2004) **Area** 2 acres/0.8
hectares

CASTLE KENNEDY

MAGNIFICENT 18TH-CENTURY
LANDSCAPE GARDEN WITH NOTABLE
19TH-CENTURY ADDITIONS

The gardens at Castle Kennedy are
immensely enjoyable to visit and of
fascinating historical importance. There are
two castles here: the atmospheric ruins of the
15th-century Castle Kennedy and, on much
lower ground, at a distance of one mile, the
19th-century Lochinch Castle. The old castle
was built for the Kennedys (later Earls of
Cassilis) and in 1677 the estate was acquired
by Sir John Dalrymple (later 1st Earl of Stair).
However, the castle was destroyed by fire in
1716 and the family moved to a house at
Culhorn, remaining there until Lochinch
Castle was built in the 1860s. Despite the fact
that there was no habitable house here for
almost 150 years, an extraordinary garden was
laid out on the site.

To the north and south of the land – in
effect an isthmus – between the castles are
two lochs, Loch Crindl and the Loch of Inch,
known respectively as the black loch and the
white loch. They act as eyecatchers, glimpsed
through gaps in woods or poised as central
ornaments in the heroic landscape that spreads

Turf terraces at Castle Kennedy

out between them. This was laid out between 1722 and 1750 in the time of the 2nd Earl – designed either by the architect William Adam (who had designed the gardens of the other Dalrymple house at Newliston in West Lothian; *see page 516*) or possibly by William Boutcher. The new landscape hovered between formality and naturalism – "Too form'd for nature – yet too wild for Art", as the poet Samuel Boyse wrote in 1734. The 2nd Earl of Stair had been Ambassador to France and, much impressed by what he had seen at Versailles, wanted something on the grand scale for Castle Kennedy. The magnificent natural setting between the two lochs must have inspired the designer to lay out a bolder and simpler garden than the elaborate pattern of parterres and *allées* that Adam had designed for Newliston. At Castle Kennedy the land was sculpted in giant mounds and terraces about a plain circular pool at the narrowest part of the isthmus – in effect, a pioneer example of "land art" – and the naturally irregular shapes of the lochs were left unchanged. The 2nd Earl was a soldier who had fought with Marlborough and many of the landscape features were named after his campaigns.

THE HEART OF THE LANDSCAPE

The early 18th-century layout was undone at least in part later in the 18th century when more informal notions were fashionable, but deftly reinstated in the 1840s. Today it provides a dramatic heart to a landscape overlaid with later plantings – especially of conifers (including an avenue of monkey puzzles) and of superb stands of rhododendrons. In 1841 J.C. Loudon came to Castle Kennedy and made proposals regarding the gardens around the old castle. It is not known if any of these suggestions were carried out, but there are appropriately boisterous mixed borders in the old castle's walled garden today.

The climate here is strongly influenced by the North Atlantic Drift and the garden is rich in tender species rhododendrons. Exotics are sometimes used with swashbuckling originality – an avenue of embothriums and eucryphias plummets down from the old castle to the banks of the Loch of Inch. There are plenty of

beautiful plants to admire at Castle Kennedy and the grand landscape lying between castles and lochs dramatically animates the scene.

Location Rephad, Stranraer DG9 8BX, Wigtownshire **OS** NX1061 5m E of Stranraer on A75 **Tel** 01776 702024 **Fax** 01776 706248 **Owner** The Earl and Countess of Stair **Open** Apr to Sept, daily 10–5 **Area** 75 acres/30 hectares

CASTLE OF MEY

QUEEN ELIZABETH, THE QUEEN MOTHER'S WALLED GARDEN ON THE WILD COAST OF CAITHNESS.

The castle, originally called Barrogill Castle, was built in the second half of the 16th century for George Sinclair, 4th Earl of Caithness. There were minor alterations by William Burn in the 19th century, and in the 20th century by Hew Lorimer. The estate changed hands more than once before being bought in 1928 by Captain Imbert-Terry who

The walled garden at the Castle of Mey

restored the gardens and planted much-needed shelter belts. During World War II it was a rest home for officers and in 1952 it was bought by Queen Elizabeth, the Queen Mother who used it as a holiday home (especially in August and October) until her death in 2002.

Built of pinkish stone, the Castle of Mey is a characteristic Scottish fortified tower house with towers and castellations. It has a splendid position close to the sea, looking north across the Pentland Firth towards Orkney. Splendid for views, certainly, but less splendid for gardening; violent salt-laden winds off the sea and a very short growing season severely restrict the possibilities. Most of the ornamental gardening here is done in the protection of a walled kitchen garden to the west of the castle, which was probably made in the 17th century – an 18th-century description mentions "plenty of apples, strawberries and cherries prospering within i

...unds despite the harsh climate". The north, ...ward, wall of this garden rises to a height of ...ft/3.6m (it is known as "the Great Wall of ...ey") and gives much protection. Shelter ...lts close to the house are of sycamores – ...uch used close to the sea in these parts and ...parently impervious to salt but even so ...ose at the Castle of Mey are gnarled and ...ttered by the wind. No tree grows well ...re, nor any plant of much size without ...nd protection.

...The space within the walled garden is ...ided into many compartments, with paths ...atly edged with vertical slabs of stone and ...dges made of a charming jumble of plants – ...rberis, black currant, fuchsia, hawthorn, ...neysuckle, privet and sycamore. Throughout ...e growing season these create a shifting ...pestry of intermingled foliage, fruit and ...wers – a delightful effect. A gravel path ...und the perimeter of the garden is lined ...th borders and its inner side is planted with ...nuals and ramparts of sweet peas.

Overlooking a rose garden with oval beds of bedding roses edged in London pride is a glasshouse filled with tender ornamental plants and to one side an area of cold frames. This is still, at least in part, a working kitchen garden and there

are espaliered fruit against the walls, fruit cages and beds of vegetables. In the north-west corner of the garden a gazebo in the form of a castellated tower has windows with rounded arches from which the view is marvellous – over a patchwork of beds and hedges of the walled garden to the castle beyond and its sheltering grove of sycamores swept by the wind into the shape of a smooth bolster.

Close to the castle is a bed named "Windy Corner Rosebed", planted with rugosa roses to celebrate the Queen Mother's 100th birthday. Beyond the castle, a pair of mixed borders, walled on two sides and protected by sycamores, are filled with astilbes, buddleias, fuchsias, potentillas, shrub roses and weigelas. When I was there in late August 2002 immense drifts of *Primula florindae* were just getting into their stride, at least two months later than their flowering time in the south of England and the milder parts of Scotland.

Many visitors will come here because of the Castle of Mey's association with a much loved member of the royal family. But it is a charming place and the garden is a fine example of what may be achieved in a most unpropitious environment. It is also a period piece, containing plants that are beyond fashion, of the sort that the Queen Mother especially enjoyed.

Location Mey, nr Thurso KW14 8XH, Caithness **OS** ND2973 6m W of John O'Groats by A836; 12m E of Thurso by A836 **Tel** 01847 851227 **Website** www.castleofmey.org.uk **Owner** The Queen Elizabeth Castle of Mey Trust **Open** end May to mid Oct (closed 1–14 Aug), Tue to Sat 11–4.30; Sun 2–5 **Area** 100 acres/40 hectares

CAWDOR CASTLE

AN 18TH-CENTURY WALLED FLOWER GARDEN AND INTRIGUING LATE 20TH-CENTURY GARDENS FOR A SPLENDID CASTLE

The castle at Cawdor was built for the Campbell family (later Thanes of Cawdor and later still Earls of Cawdor) in the 14th century and much altered in the 17th and 19th centuries. Together with its handsome crow-stepped outhouses, it makes a deliciously romantic group at the heart of the gardens.

This part of Scotland is famous fruit-growing country and the castle archives show that orchards were cultivated at Cawdor in 1635. A kitchen garden also existed in the first half of the 17th

The Flower Garden at Cawdor Castle

century; later in the century this included such exotics as French sorrel and lamb's lettuce and the first flowering ornamentals (among them a double-flowered hollyhock). The walled Flower Garden was laid out in about 1710 by Sir Archibald Campbell, the brother of the 15th Thane of Cawdor. This garden, hard by the southern façade of the castle, was redesigned in 1850 by the 1st Countess Cawdor who came from a notable gardening family – the Thynnes of Longleat (*see page 93*). Its Victorian character survives today, with a broad turf path running down the centre and deep herbaceous borders on each side backed

Victorian planting at Cawdor

by old apple trees. These borders were painted by George Elgood in 1905 and have retained their ebullient character, with aconitums, astilbes, delphiniums, lilies and monardas enriched with additions of summer bedding plants. Such borders in 19th-century Scottish gardens were often planned to be at their peak in August when the house would have been full of guests for the shooting season. Countess Cawdor also laid out a formal pattern of oval rose beds edged in lavender and with Irish yews, both golden and common, which is still in place. Nearby, enclosed in yew hedges splashed with the scarlet flowers of *Tropaeolum speciosum*, is a box parterre whose compartments are filled with red or yellow

begonias. Most memorable in August is an ethereal bed of white *Galtonia candicans* intermingled with orange tiger lilies.

A gate in the Flower Garden wall leads through to a hidden woodland garden on the slopes running down to the Cawdor burn with its high-arched stone bridge. This part of the garden was developed in the 19th century and further planting was done in the late 20th century. Here are azaleas and rhododendrons, ornamental maples and rowans and some fine old trees from 19th-century plantings, among them a spectacular Wellingtonia.

NEW FORMAL GARDENS

North-east of the castle, in the old walled Lower Garden, some of whose walls go back to the middle ages, the present Dowager Countess Cawdor laid out lively new formal gardens. A holly maze is enclosed on two sides by cloisters of pleached laburnum and by hedges of field maple and yew. A parterre of medicinal and culinary herbs, sweetly scented in high summer, has a central star of low box hedges filled with pinks and chamomile, flanked by elaborately patterned beds of artichokes, herbs and lavender. Cones of yew and lollipops of gooseberries are underplanted with irises and lavender. At the centre of a Paradise Garden, enclosed in a circle of high yew hedges and entered by the narrowest of openings (the eye of the needle?), is a beautiful fountain – a bronze column with a sweeping relief pattern veiled by a film of water which flows over it from the top. It stands at the centre of a circular bed of thyme scattered with bronze cockle shells. The surrounding beds are filled with white-flowered plants – campanulas, feverfew, heathers, hydrangeas, philadelphus and shrub roses.

Cawdor is an admirable example of an easy and harmonious intermingling of ingredients of different periods. There are no dramatic flights of horticultural fancy but everything seems appropriate to the place.

Location Cawdor IV12 5RD, Nairnshire **OS** NH8550 11m N of Inverness by A96 and B9090
Tel 01667 404615 **Fax** 01667 404674 **Email** cawdor.castle@btinternet.com **Owner** The Dowager Countess Cawdor **Open** May to Sept, daily 10–5.30
Area 20 acres/8 hectares

CLUNY HOUSE GARDENS

A PRIVATE GARDEN IN THE PERTHSHIRE HILLS, WITH A WONDERFUL COLLECTION OF PRIMULAS AND OTHER HERBACEOUS PERENNIALS

As naturalistic gardens go, few give the appearance of so little human intervention as Cluny. This is, of course, an illusion, for such convincing wildness only comes as the result of much hard work. The site is paramount here – 600ft/180m up in fine wooded country that slopes down southwards towards the river Tay. The country here has an alpine character and the name Cluny means in Gaelic "meadow place". The soil has patches of deep, natural peat; in some places you could sink to your shins. The rainfall is around 40in/100cm per annum and the woodland provides protection and a perfect environment for marvellous herbaceous plants and shrubs – many of them Himalayan exotics planted by Bobby and Betty Masterton who started the garden in 1950. After the Mastertons' death the garden was taken over by their daughter and son-in-law.

A DISTINGUISHED BACKGROUND

The house at Cluny was built in around 1800 and woodland was developed in the 19th century. Some of the trees are giant specimens among them a vast Wellingtonia whose girth 36ft/11m, the largest girth of any conifer in Britain, and beautiful old fern-leafed beech (*Fagus sylvatica* var. *heterophylla* 'Aspleniifolia'). These provide a distinguished background to many smaller ornamental trees – acers, birches, dogwoods and rowans – intermingled with such shrubs as embothriums, eucryphias, hoherias, magnolias and rhododendrons. But to my eye the greatest splendour of Cluny is the herbaceous planting in the shade of these trees and shrubs. The Mattingleys hold a National Collection of over 100 species of Asiatic primulas and there are few such collections that are displayed in a setting so entirely appropriate. They interbreed freely here (infuriating for the more austere botanist

▷ **Asiatic primulas** at Cluny

but delightful for the gardener), colonising the land with their often decorative rosettes of foliage and graceful stems of flowers – yellow, dusty red, violet, pale orangey-brown, pink and magenta. In May and June they are a marvel to see. The garden is exceptionally rich in bulbous woodland plants – magnificent *Cardiocrinum giganteum*, spring and autumn crocuses, fritillaries, lilies, superb nomocharis and trilliums.

The maintenance of a garden of this sort is arduous. It is gardened organically and all weeding must be done meticulously by hand to preserve precious seedlings. As the plants naturalise they show the gardener the conditions they prefer and in this way the plants themselves gradually enter into the management of the garden. Is the garden at Cluny well-designed – or even designed at all? I cannot answer that question but it is undeniably beautiful and has a powerful sense of place, coming partly from its natural surroundings but chiefly from the rare prospect of so many plants thriving in alien conditions that suit them so perfectly.

Location by Aberfeldy PH15 2JT, Perthshire **OS** NN8953 3½m NE of Aberfeldy; W from Aberfeldy to bridge over Tay and turn R at Weem–Strathtay road **Tel** 01887 820795 **Email** mattingley@dial.pipex.com **Owner** Mr J. and Mrs W. Mattingley **Open** Mar to Oct, daily 10–6 **Area** 6 acres/2.4 hectares

CRARAE GARDEN

A RAVINE GARDEN WITH VIEWS OF LOCH FYNE AND MARVELLOUS FLOWERING SHRUBS

Crarae Garden has a wonderful site in a precipitous wooded glen on the west bank of Loch Fyne. The views over the loch from the upper parts of the garden are very beautiful. A mountain stream, the Crarae burn, cascades down the ravine, occasionally crossed by bridges from which there are also marvellous views. Roy Lancaster said that Crarae reminded him more of a Himalayan valley than any other British garden he knew.

The estate was owned by the Campbell family from 1825. There had been some woodland planting in the early 19th century

The ravine at Crarae

before the Campbells came but the garden was effectively started in 1912 by Grace, the wife of Sir Archibald Campbell (the 5th baronet), whose nephew was the plant collector and pioneer rock-gardener Reginald Farrer. On his return from China in 1914 Farrer came to Crarae, bringing eucalyptus, conifers and rhododendrons for the garden. Lady Campbell had started by laying out flower beds close to the house and a pattern of paths but it was her son, Sir George, the 6th baronet, who from 1925 embarked on the larger landscape which he embellished with fine shrubs and trees from all over the temperate world. His son, Sir Ilay, continued the collection which he passed on to the Crarae Gardens Charitable Trust which increasingly found itself unable to fund the garden. Its future hung perilously in the balance until, after a breakneck public appeal, it was acquired for the National Trust for Scotland in 2002.

RARE PLANTS IN A SUBLIME LANDSCAPE
The garden has a very large collection of rhodendrons (over 400 species and cultivars) but they form only part of much richer and more diverse planting. Among conifers are *Cunninghamia lanceolata* from China; *Picea omorika*, the Serbian spruce from eastern

Europe which forms a tall slender shape; *Saxegothaea conspicua*, a yew-like tree from Chile; and *Tsuga mertensiana*, the mountain hemlock from the Sierra Nevada in California. These, together with other evergreen trees such as eucalyptus and southern beeches (*Nothofagus* species), form a wonderful permanent background to the ephemeral delights of the flowering shrubs which include, apart from the rhododendrons, camellias, drimys, embothriums, eucryphias, magnolias and osmanthus – and also the Japanese *Disanthus cercidifolius* which has unexciting flowers but brilliant autumn colour ("the rich hue of vintage port in candlelight", according to Sir Ilay Campbell). The garden is rich, too, in ornamental deciduous trees, among them acers, cercidiphyllum, cornus, malus, rowans and styrax. All these are naturalistically disposed on the banks of the burn or, splendidly, on the rocky heights above.

Crarae manages to encompass two different things with equal success: it has a rare collection of plants chosen to suit the special microclimate of high rainfall and mild winters; and the planting in this sublime landscape makes wonderful use of the natural topography. The wildness of rocky outcrops, vertiginous slopes and rushing burn form a dramatic natural background to planting of dreamlike beauty.

Location Crarae, by Inveraray PA32 8YA, Argyll **OS** NR9897 10m S of Inveraray by A83 **Tel** and **Fax** 01546 886614 **Owner** The National Trust for Scotland **Open** daily 9.30–sunset **Area** 50 acres/20 hectares

CRATHES CASTLE

WALLED GARDENS WITH ANCIENT YEW HEDGES AND DAZZLING 20TH-CENTURY BORDERS

History can lie heavily on a garden, crushing its spirit in purist authenticity. It can also enrich a garden, giving it extra layers of interest and excitement. The castle at Crathes was built chiefly in the 16th century for the Burnetts of Leys who owned the estate until it was given to the National Trust for Scotland in 1952. The detail of the garden is for the most part of the 20th century but

...uch of their character and charm comes ...om the past.

As early as the mid 17th century Robert ...ordon of Straloch wrote that Thomas ...urnett "has by care and skill subdued the ...enius of the place, for by planting firs and ...her trees of many kinds he has covered the ...rbidding crags…laid it out with gardens and ...othed it with pleasance." A late 18th-century ...tate map shows the walled garden east of the ...stle divided into two spaces, each subdivided ...to four, exactly as it is today. A little later, in ...310, George Roberston referred to "broad ...edges of yew and holly, trimmed with the ...tmost regularity, and exhibiting in some ...aces, the fanciful resemblances of chairs, ...yramids, &c." The marvellous ancient yew ...edges that survive today probably date from ...te early 18th century, and although no chairs ...r pyramids are to be seen, mysterious topiary ...apes like giant snails' shells erupt from time ...o time from the close shaven ramparts.

In the late 19th century there had been ...ectacular borders in the walled garden. They were painted by George Elgood soon after they were planted and his paintings, which were done in October,

show planting of astonishing exuberance. When Gertrude Jekyll visited Crathes in 1895 she wrote: "The brilliancy of colour masses in these gardens is something remarkable." Most modern visitors, especially those used to gardens further south, will have the same response. At the latitude of 57° N Crathes is well north of Moscow and the long hours of summer daylight encourage border perennials to grow with remarkable vigour.

BOLD USE OF COLOUR

The present planting of the garden is dominated, from 1926 onwards, by the influence of Lady (Sybil) Burnett of Leys who had known Lawrence Johnston of Hidcote (*see page 210*) and was influenced by him. The Colour, or Upper Pool, Garden shows the boldness of her ideas. Four right-angles of yew hedges clasp a square pool and the surrounding beds are planted in brilliant reds, oranges and yellows, subdued by occasional sombre notes of purple foliage from berberis, cotinus and fennel. A strong layout, a disciplined if occasionally raucous colour scheme, and much repeat planting (of the roses 'Belle de Crécy' and 'Madame Isaac Pereire', for

example) create an atmosphere of explosive harmony. In the lower part of the walled garden an old clipped Portugal laurel (*Prunus lusitanica*) rises like a beacon among the borders. Lady Burnett's white borders, dating from 1936 and predating the more famous ones made by Vita Sackville-West for Sissinghurst (*see page 177*), are planted with hydrangea, philadelphus and spiraea underplanted with white flowered *Aruncus dioicus*, campanulas, geraniums, lychnis, musk mallow and pulmonaria. However, as Gertrude Jekyll recommended, the whiteness is spiked from time to time with another colour – the purple of orach leaves and the dusky red of *Astrantia* 'Ruby Wedding'. Since the Trust took over, other colour-themed borders have been introduced – purple and red, gold and yellow and blue, purple and silver. All are exceptionally well cared for by an outstanding team of gardeners. The garden is open on every day of the year and is worth visiting in any season. In late summer and autumn, however, the borders in their explosive exuberance offer one of the most memorable pleasures of any garden I know.

The Walled Garden at Crathes

Location nr Banchory AB31 3QJ, Kincardineshire
OS NJ7397 3m E of Banchory and 15m SW of Aberdeen
by A93 **Tel** 01330 844525 **Fax** 01330 844797 **Owner**
The National Trust for Scotland **Open** daily 9–sunset
Area 92 acres/37 hectares

CULROSS PALACE

CHARMING RECONSTRUCTED
17TH-CENTURY TOWN GARDEN
OF FLOWERS, FRUIT AND VEGETABLES

This is the smallest garden owned by the National Trust for Scotland and one of the most unusual. Culross is an ancient and enchanting place, with the remains of a 13th-century Cistercian monastery (now the parish church) and a rare ensemble of houses from the 16th century onwards. Its wealth grew as a result of James VI making it a royal burgh in 1592 and granting it a monopoly for the manufacture of cast-iron griddles.

A TERRACED PERIOD GARDEN

Culross Palace is not a palace at all, but the house of a mine-owner, George Bruce, who had a smart town house built in the late 16th and early 17th centuries. It has been finely restored and behind it, on sloping ground, the Trust had the attractive idea of laying out a terraced period garden to suit, intermingling useful and ornamental plants. The lowermost terrace is a kitchen garden with six raised beds separated by paths of finely crushed seashells. In the beds containing vegetables occasional strips of roughly cut grass are decorated with wild achillea, borage and oxeye daisies. Fruit trees are pleached against a south-facing wall and below this are medicinal and culinary plants such as horehound (*Marrubium vulgare*), southernwood (*Artemisia abrotanum*), valerian (*Valeriana officinalis*) and Welsh onion (*Allium fistulosum*). There is also a tunnel of pleached mulberry and the grapevine 'La Ciotat'. An upper terrace is planted with a long hedge of rosemary and lavender and ornamental native plants such as the oyster plant (*Mertensia maritima*), wallflowers (*Erysimum cheiri*) and beared iris (*I. germanica* var. *florentina*). A vertiginous flight of stone steps leads to an even higher and narrower terrace with a little wattle fence entwined with clematis, honeysuckle and hop and blackberries trained on the wall behind. The view from this point (not for vertigo sufferers) is enchanting – southwards over the garden and the jumbled pantiled rooftops of the village to the waters of the Forth beyond.

Location Culross KY12 8JH, Fife **OS** NS9886 In the centre of Culross, 14m SE of Stirling by A907 and B9037 **Tel** 01383 880359 **Fax** 01383 882675 **Owner** The National Trust for Scotland **Open** Good Fri to Sept, daily 12–5; Oct to Dec, Sat and Sun 12–4 **Area** ¼ acre/0.1 hectares

The garden at Culross

CULZEAN CASTLE

CLIFFTOP GOTHIC PALACE BY
ROBERT ADAM, WITH MARVELLOUS TERRACE
WALLED AND WOODLAND GARDENS

Few houses have so dramatic or romantic setting as Culzean, and Robert Adam designed his Gothic castle to extract every ounce of drama from its cliff-top position facing west across the sea. With his highly developed feeling for landscape, Adam must also have had a vivid notion of the picturesque role in the landscape that his castellated and turreted palace would play. The Kennedy family (later Earls of Cassilis, and later still Marquesses of Ailsa) had lived here since the 14th century, but the present castle was built, incorporating an earlier house, for the 10th Earl from 1777, with final completion in 1792, the year in which both he and Robert Adam died. If you stand on the forecourt you can look across the sea to the jagged silhouette of the Isle of Arran and on a fine day, further south and west to the Mull of Kintyre. At the foot of the cliffs below the castle rocky reefs run into the sea while to the north, in contrast, lies a gentle rural landscape of fields and woodland.

"VERY PRETTY GARDENS"

The castle faces inland over terraced gardens which have their origins in the 17th century - described at the time as "very pretty gardens adorned with terrasses". The top terrace is a simple walk with a castellated wall, from which there are views of ornamental terraces below. A long gravel walk on the first terrace runs along a deep mixed border below the retaining wall, planted with *Acca sellowiana*, callistemons, *Hoheria glabrata*, *Olearia paniculata*, penstemons and drifts of *Galtonia candicans*; the walls above are garlanded with clematis, the beautiful but tender *Mutisia decurrens* and *Vitis coignetiae*, and at the south end of this terrace a fine conservatory of 1850 has passion flowers, plumbago and tubs of *Sparrmannia africana*. In the border against the retaining wall of the terrace below are plenty of bold leaves and bright colours – *Aralia elata* 'Variegata', bananas, crocosmias, *Macleaya* × *kewensis*, *Melianthus major* and huge clumps of rich blue *Salvia guaranitica*

Apart from the pleasure grounds close to the castle, Culzean has hundreds of acres of woodland. This was originally wild moorland, but was planted with trees in the 18th century and again in the 19th century when the 3rd Marquess of Ailsa is reckoned to have planted 5,000,000 trees. Since the National Trust for Scotland took over in 1945, they too have added to the woodland, which has become Scotland's first country park and provides miles of wonderful walks rich in wildlife.

Location Maybole KA19 8LE, Ayrshire **OS** NS2410 4m W of Maybole by B7023 and A719; 12m S of Ayr by A719 **Tel** 01655 884455 **Fax** 01655 884503 **Email** culzean@nts.org.uk **Owner** The National Trust for Scotland **Open** daily 9.30–sunset **Area** 560 acres/226 hectares

DAWYCK BOTANIC GARDENS

ANCIENT ESTATE WITH A
REMARKABLE TREE COLLECTION IN
A PICTURESQUE SETTING

The landscape at Dawyck has a surprisingly long history. From the 13th to the 17th century the estate was owned by the Veitch family and it is known that by the 15th century it was "ringed with trees". In the 17th century the Veitches planted the first horse chestnut grown in Scotland and introduced silver firs (*Abies alba*), some of which still survive. (The Dawyck Veitches were ancestors of the great firm of nurserymen in Exeter and Chelsea, the first of whom, John Veitch of Jedburgh, went to Devon in the late 18th century; the firm remained in business until 1969.)

In 1691 the estate was acquired by James Naesmyth (known as "the Deil [devil] o' Dawick") whose son, Sir James Naesmyth, carried out much planting, including the first European larches (*Larix decidua*) to be planted in Scotland.

n the middle of this terrace is a lawn with a rand scalloped pool and an even grander entral fountain with a Triton balanced on ockle shells and supported by three dolphins pouting water into the basin below. On the far de of the lawn, forming the terrace boundary, slightly raised walk edged with a bed of niphofias runs the whole length of the terrace.

From the castle entrance a lime walk leads puth into the castle policies, past an exquisite amellia house with tall tracery windows, attlements and finials (designed in 1818, robably by James Donaldson, and recently stored); today it is filled with citrus plants in bs. A grand 18th-century walled garden is vided into two parts. The first has a late 9th-century vinery with grape cultivars of the eriod, such as *Vitis vinifera* 'Mrs Pince's Black luscat' and 'Buckland Sweetwater'; a cturesque rockery grotto planted with alpines nd ferns and sporting a grotto-like tunnel vith niches; and a number of good trees, mong them a *Catalpa bignonioides*, a grand edar of Lebanon and magnolias. The second alled garden is divided into four by erbaceous borders meeting in the centre at a

The fountain garden at Culzean

sundial; part of it is a formal orchard and part a nursery, and it is overlooked in one corner by the pretty 18th-century head gardener's house with its own flowery garden.

Deeper into the policies is one of the most attractive and unusual parts of the garden. The 13-acre/5-hectare Swan Pond was made for the 12th Earl of Cassilis before 1823. It is overlooked by a Gothic cottage with ornamental verandah and porch, which originally housed a member of staff and a collection of pheasants and poultry. At the head of an uphill grass ride the Pagoda is a splendid tiered building of vaguely oriental character. Built in 1814, originally incorporating a tea room and a swan house, it fell derelict and was reconstructed in 1997.

The camellia house at Culzean

His grandson, Sir John Murray Naesmyth, rebuilt the house in 1830 to the designs of William Burn, and laid out Italianate terraces with lawns and stone urns in front of the house. In 1897 the estate was bought by Mrs Alexander Balfour whose son, Frederick, continued the tradition of tree planting. In 1978 his son, Alastair, gave the woodland garden, which contains the most important part of the collection, to the Secretary of State for Scotland, from whom it passed to the Royal Botanic Garden Edinburgh. The house and the remainder of the estate are in separate ownership.

NEW CONIFERS FROM AMERICA

The undulating site is densely wooded, with the Scrape burn tumbling down a ravine spanned by a high-arched stone bridge built by a Dutchman in 1830 and known as the Dutch Bridge. The rainfall is not high by west coast standards (around 36in/90cm per annum) but at a height of 700ft/200m winters here are often very cold (the coldest temperature ever recorded was -21°C/-4°F in January 1941). However, the soil is a rich acid loam and with the protection of old shelter belts trees grow well here. In the 19th century many of the new conifers being introduced from the Pacific north-west coast of North America quickly found their way to Dawyck – among them the Douglas fir (*Pseudotsuga menziesii*), the Jeffrey pine (*Pinus jeffreyi*), the noble fir (*Abies procera*), the sugar pine (*Pinus lambertiana*), the western hemlock (*Tsuga heterophylla*) and the Wellingtonia. Many conifers were raised from seed collected in the wild for Sir John Murray Naesmyth by such collectors as David Douglas. The Douglas fir was introduced by David Douglas in 1827 and several specimens at Dawyck survive from the 1835 planting.

A tree of special interest here is the Dawyck beech (*Fagus sylvatica* 'Dawyck'), a very slender fastigiate form of which a natural seedling was found in about 1850 by Sir John Murray Naesmyth. The original survives, planted quite close to the house and widely visible, and is now over 100ft/33m high. Under the Balfours many rhododendrons were planted,

▷ **The burn garden** at Dawyck

in particular those introduced from China by E.H. Wilson. A rhododendron walk they planted in 1900 is being restored with plants propagated from seed gathered in the wild. Many ornamental trees adorn the woodland garden, including birches, cercidiphyllums, cherries, maples and rowans and in spring there is a brilliant display of daffodils – for twenty years Frederick Balfour planted a ton a year (which he had from Tresco Abbey garden). Among those smaller ornamental plants for which Scottish gardens are specially noted are beautiful meconopsis and marvellous trilliums flourishing as they never do in England.

Location Stobo EH45 9JU, Peeblesshire **OS** NT1635 8m SW of Peebles by A72 **Tel** 01721 760254 **Fax** 01721 760 214 **Owner** Royal Botanic Garden Edinburgh **Open** mid Feb to mid Nov, daily 10–6 (Feb and Nov, closes 4) **Area** 60 acres/24 hectares

DRUMMOND CASTLE GARDENS

A GIANT AND BREATHTAKING TERRACED PARTERRE GARDEN FOR A GREAT 17TH-CENTURY HOUSE

After her visit to Drummond Castle in 1842, Queen Victoria wrote in her diary "We walked in the garden which is really very fine, with terraces, like an old French garden" There is indeed a dash of French formality here but it is heavily overlaid with elaborate 19th-century complications, made slightly less elaborate in the 20th century.

The first castle was built here in the 15th century by the 1st Lord Drummond whose family later became Earls of Perth. In the 1630s the 2nd Earl of Perth built a new house in renaissance style, designed by Charles I's master mason, John Mylne, and added elaborate terraced gardens. In around 1675 a gardener called John Reid was employed here; he later wrote the first book on gardening published in Scotland, *The Scots Gard'ner* (1683). In 1807 the Drummond heiress, Sarah, married Peter Burrell who later became the 21st Baron Willoughby de Eresby. In 1818 the garden designer Lewis Kennedy became factor of the Drummond estate and from 1820 supervised a new terraced garden which J.C. Loudon in his *Encyclopaedia of Gardening* (1822) describes: "the grounds extended and highly improved by the present owner, assisted by his ingenious steward Lewis Kennedy." The work was completed by 1838 but the architect Sir Charles Barry did a watercolour in 1828 showing a proposed remodelling of the castle with ornate terraced gardens, and it is possible that he also had a hand in the new garden.

The great parterre at Drummond

PATTERNED AND PRIMPED

The garden that survives today is very much as it was seen by Queen Victoria, though it is now slightly less elaborate. South of the castle a terrace leads to a very grand double descending staircase. The immense formal garden below has the appearance of a giant parterre, dominated by a St Andrews cross of paths. At first sight one reacts with astonishment: it is so large an area – 1,000ft × 300ft/300m × 90m – and so relentlessly patterned and primped. I am not sure that it could be called beautiful but it is undeniably remarkable. A central path runs straight across the garden to a classical arcade with a pool and niches containing a figure of Pan and a boy with a dog, and a grotto wall behind the central arch. This, dating from the 18th century, was originally at Grimsthorpe Castle (see page 304). In the centre of the garden is a multi-faceted sundial designed by John Mylne and dated 1630. Lawns, criss-crossed by further paths, are ornamented with box-edged beds shaped like great fans or triangles and

filled with permanent and seasonal plantings – *Anaphalis triplinervis*, antirrhinums, bedding roses, lambs' lugs, lavender. The whole garden is studded with a profusion of shaped trees and topiary in copper beech, common and gold variegated holly, purple-leafed plum (*Prunus cerasifera* 'Nigra'), juniper and yew (both common and golden), intermingled with statues and urns. The modern planting is, however, very different from the original 19th-century scheme, in which, as we know from photographs and descriptions, most of the large compartments were densely planted with small trees and shrubs, with occasional smaller beds of brilliant annuals.

Laying the garden out must have been a nightmare, for the site is far from even. You are unaware of this until you walk among the parterres when you see that the walks swoop up and down with writhing abandon. To the east, the garden becomes less formal. On the grassy slope below the castle is a scattered group of venerable clipped Portugal laurels, like a herd of exotic creatures, and a fine statue is almost engulfed in a vast spreading mound of clipped yew (apparently a single plant but in fact several, whose

canopies now merge into a vast roof). The waterless gully below is spanned by a magnificent four-arched castellated bridge, with ornamental woodland spreading beyond.

No other British garden has a parterre like that at Drummond. Extraordinary as it is, it does possess a kind of gawkily attractive charm, and there remains a hint of the much more restrained and harmonious renaissance idea of a stately terraced garden spread out below the windows of the house. Something else of renaissance character can be seen as you leave the parterre: a grotto-like niche in the great stairs, decorated with rustication and shells and a mask of Neptune in a keystone.

Location Muthill, nr Crieff PH5 2AA, Perthshire **OS** NN8418 2m S of Crieff by A822 **Tel** 01764 681257 **Fax** 01764 681550 **Email** thegardens@drummondcastle.sol.co.uk **Owner** Grimsthorpe and Drummond Castle Trust Ltd **Open** Easter weekend and May to Oct, daily 2–6 **Area** 15 acres/6 hectares

DUNROBIN CASTLE GARDENS

DELIGHTFUL FORMAL GARDENS FOR A FRENCH-STYLE CHÂTEAU, WITH SPLENDID SEA VIEWS

Hugh de Moravia acquired land in Sutherland at the beginning of the 13th century and his son, William, became the 1st Earl of Sutherland. The daughter of the last (18th) Earl married the 2nd Marquess of Stafford. He subsequently became the Duke of Sutherland, and their descendants still live at Dunrobin.

The first house here was built in the 13th century and is, together with parts of subsequent additions, engulfed in the present extraordinary castle. The idea for its design came from Sir Charles Barry (who had also designed Trentham for the 1st Duke of

The parterre at Dunrobin

containing either white *Potentilla fruticosa* or scarlet dahlias. To the east of the parterre is a summerhouse, built in 1732 for William, Lord Strathnaver (later 17th Earl of Sutherland) and now housing a delightful small museum which contains, among much else, several extraordinary carved Pictish stones.

Dunrobin offers two strikingly different views: from the castle the lively patterns of the parterres are finely displayed, with long views of the sea beyond; from below, as you stand in the parterres surrounded by brilliant colours and the splashing of water, there are wonderful views up to the castle soaring on its cliff above.

Location Golspie KW10 6RR, Sutherland **OS** NC8501 1m N of Golspie by A9 **Tel** 01408 633177 **Fax** 01408 634081 **Website** www.dunrobin.est@btinternet.com **Owner** The Sutherland Trust **Open** Apr to mid Oct, daily 10.30–5.30 (Apr, May and Oct, closes 4.30 and opens 12 on Sun) **Area** 5 acres/2 hectares

EDZELL CASTLE

AN ORNAMENTAL RENAISSANCE WALLED
GARDEN AND 20TH-CENTURY PLANTING
ADORN A MEDIEVAL CASTLE

There are few gardens so small, and so sketchily planted, that have so strong an atmosphere as the walled garden at Edzell. Here are the remains of a 15th-century fortified house which, in the early years of the 17th century, was provided with an ornamental "pleasaunce" by the Lindsay family, Earls of Crawford, who had lived here since 1358.

The roofless tower house, garden walls and fragments of other buildings with crow-step gables present a picturesque scene across a meadow. The garden walls bear a carved stone plaque with the arms of David Lindsay, Lord Edzell, and the date 1604. Three walls are decorated with a series of carved stone panels in relief, showing the Planetary Deities with their symbolic attributes: Mars in full armour carrying a sword, Venus with a flaming heart and a flouncy skirt, Mercury with winged sandals and staff entwined with snakes, and so on. Further panels depict the Liberal Arts (Grammatica, Rhetorica, and so forth) and th

Sutherland; *see page 550*) but it became a collaboration between the Duke himself, Barry, and the architect William Leslie. It is a delightful confection: a jolly château of beautiful pale stone breaking out at every opportunity into round towers crowned with swooping witch's hats, balustrades and machicolations. It rises high on a terrace with rounded bastions, looking confidently out south over the Moray Firth.

The wooded policies at Dunrobin are largely 19th-century, when planned walks were introduced. By far the most notable feature of the landscape, however, is the pair of parterres laid out between the castle and the sea, in part designed by Sir Charles Barry in around 1850. The west parterre has a circular fountain pool surrounded by four circular box-edged beds, each planted with a splendid *Aralia elata*. Further segmental beds are filled with hardy geraniums underplanted

with tulips for the spring and lilies for late summer. Beyond this arrangement four square beds have tall wooden pyramids, one at each corner and one in the middle, trained with *Actinidia kolomikta*, roses, sweet peas and roses. Narrow beds edging the squares are filled with achilleas, bergamot, catmint, daylilies, geraniums and tradescantia, with mop-headed quinces rising at intervals. A second circular pool, with a water jet, is surrounded by segmental beds, each filled in summer with a single variety of antirrhinum and with a conical hornbeam in each corner.

The east parterre is an enormous circular lawn. At its centre a circular pool with a fountain is surrounded by round box-edged beds planted with *Aralia elata*. Outside it, a concentric circle of clipped Irish yews is edged with more box-edged beds, each one

Cardinal Virtues (faith, hope, justice, etc). They are beautifully carved, full of liveliness and humour. The walls also have a pattern of sunken recesses whose purpose is not understood. When I last visited the garden they were planted with alternate blue and white trailing lobelia – very patriotic, but very pedestrian.

At the centre is a sunken garden which was reconstructed just before World War II. Nothing is known in detail about Scots gardens of the early 17th century and the only finding of an archaeological dig was that there had been some sort of central feature. However, a parterre was made here of low box hedges into which Lindsay mottoes are worked from clipped box: *Dum Spiro Spero* ("As long as I breathe I hope") and *Endure Forte* ("Hold firm"). Four angled beds each contain a block of a single cultivar of floribunda rose – scarlet 'Lilli Marlene' and yellow 'Old Gold' – and at the corners triangular beds contain a thistle, rose or fleur-de-lys; a clipped drum of yew at the centre is surrounded

Prudence at Edzell

by mounds of yew. This thoroughly 20th-century arrangement does have something of the lively decorative spirit that characterises the enclosing stone walls.

Built into a corner of the garden walls is a pretty summerhouse of the same date as the garden, with crow-stepped gable, finely carved window surrounds and a niche. In English gardens of this period such garden buildings were often used as banqueting houses in which post-prandial sweetmeats were eaten. Despite its fragmentary state, and sometimes coarse modern planting, Edzell Castle gives much pleasure and the rare decorations of its garden walls, a unique survival of its period, give it unusual distinction.

Location Edzell, nr Brechin DD9 7UE, Angus
OS NO5869 1m W of the village of Edzell, 6m N of Brechin by A90 and B966 **Tel** 01356 648631 **Owner** Historic Scotland **Open** Apr to Sept, daily 9.30–6.30; Oct to Mar, Mon to Sat 9.30–4.30, Sun 2–4.30 **Area** 1 acre/0.4 hectares

Edzell's walled "pleasaunce"

FALKLAND PALACE

FINE FLOWER GARDENS DESIGNED BY PERCY CANE FOR A MAGNIFICENT ROYAL PALACE

The palace and garden at Falkland is one of the oddest ensembles in Britain: an astonishing renaissance palace set in gardens designed by Percy Cane – a pure period piece dating from the late 1940s.

There had been a house here since the early 12th century, which in 1458 was acquired by King James II and turned into a royal palace. In the 16th century, under James IV and James V, it took on its dazzling renaissance character – "a display of early renaissance architecture without parallel in the British Isles", as Mark Girouard described it in *Country Life*. James V was married to Madeleine de Valois, who died young, and subsequently to Marie de Guise. As a result of this connection, the French stone masons Moses Martin and Nicholas Roy came to Falkland and are almost certainly responsible for the lovely detail of the courtyard's east and south ranges with their delightful decoration of roundels, elegant pilasters and tall windows. John Macky, in his *A Journey through Scotland* (1723), described this courtyard as "the beautifullest Piece of Architecture in *Britain*". After James VI became King of England in 1603 the palace was no longer the home of monarchs. In 1887 it was acquired by John Crichton Stuart, 3rd Marquess of Bute, who began a wholesale programme of restoration. In 1947 his grandson, Major Michael Crichton Stuart, commissioned a new garden from Percy Cane.

"SUNDIALS AND PILLARS"

Only scraps of information provide indications of earlier gardens at Falkland: in the 15th century the palace accounts show payments to gardeners and in the 16th century there is known to have been a park and woodland. Charles I laid out a new garden in 1628 "with sundials and pillars". During the Civil War part of the palace was destroyed and in the 18th and 19th centuries the grounds were derelict. Percy Cane was not concerned with history

The mixed border at Falkland

– his response was an aesthetic one to the drama of the architectural setting. To one side of the palace he laid out a giant lawn with island beds about its perimeter, and flower borders between the island beds and the enclosing walls. Where the island beds face each other across the grass they have curved outlines, but straight edges on the other side form formal grass walks along the flower borders – an ingenious arrangement. The planting within the island beds is on a grand scale, with substantial ornamental trees and shrubs at the centre and fringes of herbaceous planting about the edges. One bed, for example, is planted with *Acer palmatum*, *Malus* × *robusta* 'Red Sentinel', *Clerondendrum trichotomum* and *Cornus kousa* var. *chinensis* underplanted with astilbes, catmint, daylilies, geraniums, hostas and trilliums. Many of the trees are now overgrown and their shape distorted where more vigorous neighbours have crowded them out, but the design is effective, especially because of the generous spaces of lawn at the centre. Here you may saunter along what is in effect a very broad grass path with sinuous edges. To the west the palace rises splendidly above the ornamental trees and to the east there are intermittent glimpses of Cane's deep mixed border along the boundary wall (590ft/180m long), with its bold planting and passages of brilliant colour, especially in late summer.

Percy Cane laid out two further areas of the garden. By the north range of the palace a little formal garden has blocks of clipped golden yew backed with cushions of clipped *Brachyglottis* Dunedin Group 'Sunshine' and symmetrical beds planted with blocks of a single variety of rose – blood red 'Frensham' and golden yellow 'Korresia' (the heraldic colours of the Stuarts). At the northern end of the garden, behind a tall yew hedge, is a piece of bold post World War II modernism: a water garden with two rectangular lily pools flanked by processions of fastigiate junipers (*Juniperus communis* 'Hibernica') and prostrate golden juniper (*J.* × *pfitzeriana* 'Pfitzeriana Aurea') – not for the faint-hearted. The conventional response to such a setting as Falkland Palace in the early 21st century would be to create a meticulously researched neo-historical garden, very polite and correct. Percy Cane's was an altogether riskier gamble and the result certainly has a pungent flavour all of its own.

Location Falkland KY7 7BU, Fife **OS** NO2507 In the village of Falkland, 11m N of Kirkcaldy by A912 **Tel** 01337 857397 **Fax** 01337 857980 **Owner** The National Trust for Scotland **Open** Apr to May and Sept to Oct, Mon to Sat 11–5.30, Sun 1.30–5.30; Jun to Aug, Mon to Sat 10–5.30, Sun 1.30–5.30 **Area** 7 acres/2.8 hectares

GLENWHAN GARDEN

PLANTSWOMAN'S LAVISHLY PLANTED
HILL–TOP GARDEN IN A BEAUTIFUL SETTING

Making a garden from scratch always has the potential for an epic saga. In the late 1970s the Knotts came with their young family to Glenwhan to farm. Glenwhan is the Gaelic for "glen of the rushes", which gives the idea of a fairly barren and inhospitable place, and indeed when the Knotts came there was nothing here except gorse and bracken. Furthermore the site, with beautiful views over Luce Bay and the Mull of Galloway, is 300ft/90m above sea level, very close to the sea, and often swept by violent coastal winds. However, the influence of the North Atlantic Drift is strongly felt here, rainfall is around 40in/100cm, and the soil is acid. Tessa Knott knew the gardens at Logan Botanic Gardens nearby (*see page 385*) and those at Tresco Abbey (*see page 66*), both of which gave some idea of the possibilities for her site, with the major difference that hers is not at sea level.

Starting in 1979, Tessa Knott planted shelter belts of conifers and deciduous trees, and broke up the space with thickets of willows, very easily propagated from cuttings. Two pools (or lochans as they called in these parts) were excavated, fed by a rushing stream, and stocked with brown trout and Koi carp. Soon she was ready to plant the kind of ornamentals that attracted her.

DENSE NATURALISTIC PLANTING

Just over twenty years later the garden is densely planted. The lochans are at the heart of the garden, with rising land behind them and flatter ground to their south where the house is. An outer perimeter walk girdles the garden, with subsidiary paths darting off to particular areas. The style of planting is naturalistic and the range of plants is immense. Certain areas are set aside for particular groups of plants – birches, maples, camellias, heathers, hollies, hydrangeas, willows and so on. Otherwise plants of different kinds come thick and fast and the effect is sometimes unsettling. Like some idiosyncratic zoo, exotics are intermingled with perfectly ordinary plants – a soaring eucalyptus, for example, rising

ne lochans at Glenwhan

mong Scots pines, heather and rowans. From
e start of the perimeter walk you come in
ick succession to *Eucryphia milliganii*, a
tus, *Crinodendron hookerianum*, hydrangeas,
cs, *Quercus robur* 'Hungaria' (a very
rrow, columnar form of English oak) and
ododendrons. Trees and shrubs form the
ain meal but there are lovely *hors d'oeuvres*
smaller ornamental plantings – agapanthus,
ythroniums, meconopsis, narcissi, tricyrtis
d trilliums.

On the highest slopes of the garden, north
the lochans, sitting places and viewpoints
erlook the garden to a vast and lovely
norama of the sea. When I was last there, in
e August 2002, the scene was very beautiful:
e dark varnished surface of the waters of the
chans were occasionally ruffled by ducks or
h, and on the banks were swaying fronds of
rtaderia, fringes of rich scarlet crocosmia,
e foliage of bulrushes and irises, and the
ccasional explosive blue of hydrangea. The
esign of the garden is light-handed – it is
sentially a happy home for plants, making
e most of the handsome topography and
e climate.

:cation Dunragit, by Stranraer DG9 8PH, Wigtownshire
S NX1558 7m E of Stranraer by A75 **Tel** and **Fax**
581 400222 **Email** tess@glenwhan.freeserve.co.uk
ebsite www.glenwhan.co.uk **Owner** Tessa and
illiam Knott **Open** Apr to Sept, daily 10–5 **Area** 12
res/4.8 hectares

GREYWALLS

EDWIN LUTYENS'S EXQUISITE GARDEN DESIGN FOR A GOLF-LINKS HOLIDAY HOME

Greywalls (originally called High Walls) was built for the Hon. Alfred Lyttelton in 1901 to the designs of Sir Edwin Lutyens. On the southern edge of Muirfield golf course overlooking the Firth of Forth, it was conceived as a holiday house and a golfing base – there are several other notable courses nearby. It is an enchanting house (Lutyens said it was his favourite) which gave Lutyens every opportunity to display his characteristic charm and ingenuity. He also laid out the garden, intimately related to the house and flowing in a sequence of deftly planned spaces.

The southern entrance façade of the house is concave, sweeping about a turning circle at one corner of a square forecourt of lawns and diagonal gravel paths which run from corner to corner. To one side, immediately south of a wing of the house, is a paved terrace edged with deep beds of lavender and overlooking a walled garden. A broad paved path leads between a symmetrical pattern of beds of acanthus, heuchera, kniphofias, *Lychnis coronaria*, sedums and thalictrum, and there is much repetition of plants (for example, bergenias, campanulas, geraniums, irises, peonies and *Stipa gigantea*) with identical planting in beds on either side of the path. Doors open on each side, one leading to the entrance forecourt and the other to a croquet lawn. The axis opened by the paved path continues southwards along a grass walk edged in stone which runs between rows of rowans rising from box-edged beds filled with periwinkles. On each side of the walk are secret gardens hedged in thornless holly (*Ilex aquifolium* 'J.C. van Tol') and planted with cherry trees in lawns. At the head of the walk, in the boundary wall, a pedimented alcove seat with an opening in its back forms a *claire-voie* giving views out of the garden to the Lothian hills.

On either side of the holly-enclosed beds which flank the central walk are semicircular spaces enclosed in stone walls. Each has paths radiating across lawns to doors in the walls

Greywalls' south garden

whose openings are surrounded by typical Lutyens patterns of terracotta tiles laid edge on. The eastern enclosure is lined with a narrow herbaceous border with a Lutyens se in an arbour of clematis and roses; the weste one has a lawn with a weeping silver pear (*Pyrus salicifolia* 'Pendula') and, along its straight side, a border of purple-leafed *Cotin coggygria* Rubrifolius Group underplanted with lavender and edged in *Lonicera nitida* 'Baggesen's Gold'.

It is said that the original planting at Greywalls was planned by Gertrude Jekyll. Th planting today is quite modern although it often draws on the Jekyll repertory of plants. The beauty of the garden, however, comes from Lutyens's ingeniously deployed spaces. To stay in the hotel, or simply eat a meal and walk in this garden is a wonderful pleasure.

Location Muirfield, Gullane EH31 2EG, East Lothian
OS NT8348 5m W of North Berwick by A198
Tel 01620 842144 **Fax** 01620 842241 **Email**
hotel@greywalls.co.uk **Website** www.greywalls.co.uk
Open to guests of the hotel **Area** 11 acres/4.4 hectare

THE HERMITAGE

A WOODLAND WALK WITH GRAND
TREES, SPECTACULAR CASCADE AND
18TH-CENTURY PAVILION

Any driver hurrying along the busy main road between Perth and Inverness should seize upon the opportunity to stop an visit this bosky and mysterious place – the atmospheric remains of the 2nd Duke of Atholl's 18th-century romantic landscape. Thi originally part of the Dunkeld House estate, was given to the National Trust for Scotland by the 8th Duchess of Atholl in 1943.

An apparently aimless path leads into coniferous woods following the bank of the rushing river Braan. The woods are filled with rare specimens of Douglas fir (*Pseudotsuga menziesii*), some of them of giant size. David Douglas was born nearby at Scone and introduced this fir from the Pacific coast of North America in 1826. Visible from the Hermitage woods, but just over the boundary

◁ **The cascade** at the Hermitage

the Forestry Commission land of Craigvinean Forest, is the fourth tallest specimen in the British Isles, at 194ft/59m – a self-sown seedling dating from around 1887. Progressing in the cool shade of these great trees, you soon see a handsomely arched 18th-century stone bridge and hear a mighty rushing of water. To one side of the bridge is a stone pavilion. Penetrate into the gloom and the roaring of the water becomes even greater. You see light at the far end of the room and emerge onto a viewing platform overlooking a marvellous waterfall in the river below – broad and rocky, with the water cascading down to be trapped in a narrow channel where it rushes below the bridge. In 1805 William Wordsworth and his sister Dorothy visited the pavilion (or Ossian's Hall as it was then called – built in 1785 and later renamed the Hermitage), escorted by the Duke's gardener. Dorothy left a characteristically lively description of what they saw: "the gardener desired us to look at a painting of the figure of Ossian, which…

disappeared, parting in the middle, flying asunder as if by the touch of magic, and lo! we are at the entrance of a splendid room, which was almost dizzy with waterfalls that tumbled in all directions – the great cascade, which was opposite to the window that faced us, being reflected in innumerable mirrors upon the ceiling and against the walls."

The experience is not as impeccably stage-managed today but the waterfall is every bit as dramatic. Nearby, hidden in the woods, is a rustic grotto of the same date: Ossian's Cave. This is all that remains of a garden which in its day was one of the great Scottish beauty spots. Dorothy Wordsworth also describes "quaintly intersected walks" and gardens of "fine flowers among the rocks". All this garden detail has gone but the vivid character and drama of the setting remains.

Location Perthshire **OS** NO0041 1m W of Dunkeld, 16m N of Perth, signed off the A9 **Tel** 01796 473233
Owner The National Trust for Scotland **Open** daily dawn–dusk **Area** 37 acres/15 hectares

HILL OF TARVIT HOUSE

TERRACED GARDENS, BORDERS AND A ROSE GARDEN SURROUND A COUNTRY HOUSE

The 17th-century house at Hill of Tarvit, known in the 18th century as Wemyss House, was originally part of the ancient Scotstarvit estate whose earliest house, the splendid tower house built in 1500, is a notable feature of the landscape in these parts. Hill of Tarvit House was rebuilt by Sir Robert Lorimer in 1906 for a Dundee businessman in the jute trade, Frederick Sharp. At the same time Lorimer also designed a new garden in keeping with the house and its surroundings, and to suit the requirements of his client.

"I ONLY COUNT THE SUNNY HOURS"
The house faces south across a shallow valley with views of pasture and woodland. The façade, of stucco and dressed stone detailing, is decorated with a sundial also designed by Lorimer, with a figure of Ceres surrounded by gambolling putti and a motto, *Horas Non Numero Nisi Serenas* ("I only count the sunny hours") – a suitably buoyant motto for a prosperous Edwardian businessman. Lorimer anchored the house in its setting with a series of terraces linked by a double row of clipped Irish yews. They lead to a grand double staircase, ornamented with crouching lions, which takes you down to the lowest terrace – a long rectangular lawn with a blue Atlas cedar (*Cedrus atlantica* Glauca Group) at each end. On each side of the staircase the terrace wall is embellished with splendidly curved buttresses of clipped yews. On the terrace lawns Mr Sharp and his family and guests played croquet and tennis, and in the fields beyond he had a nine-hole golf course and, in winter, a curling rink.

To one side of the terraces is a rose garden enclosed in yew hedges and entered by a pedimented porch of clipped yew. A symmetrical pattern of beds is arranged about a central raised circular bed, formerly a fountain. Single varieties of bedding roses fill each bed, with occasional standard 'Iceberg'

◁ **The rose garden** at Hill of Tarvit

roses at the centre and, most unforgettably, two magnificent shapes of clipped box 6ft/1.8m high and resembling jellies that did not quite set. The bedding roses are such old cultivars as 'Bloomfield Abundance' and 'Cécile Brunner' but more informal beds about the periphery are lavishly planted with such shrub roses as 'Louise Odier', 'Reine Victoria' and 'Madame Hardy'.

Behind the house a lawn rises, slightly awkwardly, to a long gravel path and a deep mixed border running along a high stone wall. Steps lead up, flanked by giant clumps of New Zealand flax (*Phormium tenax*) – a clever use of a plant that can appear clumsy. Facing you is a further flight of steps, of sweeping semicircles, rising to a fine wrought-iron gate between stone piers with urns, and beyond to a roughly shaped gap in woodland – a fine effect. The borders below the wall are filled with a rather miscellaneous collection of substantial shrubs underplanted with perennials. More memorable than this jumble is the spectacular sight of a whopping eucryphia in the woodland behind, rising high above the wall – a stupendous sight in August and September – and at the far end of the lawn a beautiful old Japanese maple (*Acer palmatum*) curving about a garden bench.

A COMPLETE ESTATE

Hill of Tarvit, however, is not really about plants. Its strength and beauty come from Lorimer's architectural gardens at the front of the house. Frederick Sharp wanted a complete estate – a distinguished house, a garden to match, and woods and productive farmland beyond. In all this Sir Robert Lorimer was intimately involved, inside and out, designing the smallest details down to the knobs on the kitchen cupboard doors. Sharp also filled his house with fine furniture and paintings. What prosperous businessman in the early 21st century would think of devising such a setting for his life and take such an interest in every detail, from curling rink to Old Masters?

Location nr Cupar KY15 5PD, Fife **OS** NO3711 2½m S of Cupar by A916 **Tel** and **Fax** 01334653127 **Owner** The National Trust for Scotland **Open** Apr to Sept, daily 9.30–9; Oct to Mar, daily 9.30–4.30 **Area** 10 acres/4 hectares

HOUSE OF PITMUIES

OUTSTANDING FLOWER GARDENS, PRETTY KITCHEN GARDEN AND RIVERSIDE WALKS

The House of Pitmuies is a handsome 18th-century house with fine contemporary outhouses and walled gardens surrounded by well wooded policies. The distinction of its garden comes chiefly from its present owner, Margaret Ogilvie, who is a skilled and original gardener. The former kitchen garden, retaining a mixture of the ornamental and productive, with beds of fruit and vegetables, lavish garlands of honeysuckle, roses on trelliswork, and cordons of sweetpeas, is delightful but unexceptional. The real excitement comes in the adjacent walled garden which spreads out in front of the house.

Aligned with the gate into the garden is an archway of clipped silver pear (*Pyrus salicifolia* 'Pendula') which frames a view of a long pair of herbaceous borders separated by a narrow turf path running right across the garden. The colour scheme is dominated by purple and pink from such plants as *Geranium psilostemon*, *Silene dioica* 'Flore Pleno', *Stachys byzantina* and *Sidalcea* 'Sussex Beauty', intermingled with plenty of white-flowered and silver-leafed plants. The borders are narrow and the planting rises in floriferous chasms on either side of the grass path. Parallel to these borders

Walled garden borders at Pitmuies

is another pair, aligned with a window of the drawing room, whose ethereal colours of blue, cream, white and yellow are chosen to match the colour scheme of the room within. Both sets of borders are hedged in walls of coppiced *Prunus cerasifera* 'Pissardii' whose fresh pink new foliage in spring becomes increasingly purple and sombre as the season passes, forming in high summer an excellent background to the lively colours of the borders. A cross axis is formed by a distinguished avenue of Tibetan cherry (*Prunus serrula*). There are many other pleasures here – excellent shrub roses, a good collection of *Potentilla fruticosa* cultivars and some remarkable old delphinium cultivars.

The final treat at Pitmuies is a walk in the woods, past a decorative Gothic dovecote and along the banks of the Vinny water. The dovecote is dated 1643 and the Gothic detailing must have been added in the 19th century. There are good trees here, of which the most memorable is a magnificent old *Acer griseum*. Everything seems just right at Pitmuies. Margaret Ogilvie knows her plants and shows a rare sense of atmosphere.

Location Guthrie, by Forfar DD8 2SN, Forfarshire **OS** NO5650 7m E of Forfar by A932 **Tel** 01241 82824 **Owner** Mrs Farquhar Ogilvie **Open** Apr to Oct, daily 10–5 **Area** 25 acres/10 hectares

INVEREWE

When Osgood Mackenzie recalled his memories of coming to Inverewe in 1862 at the age of twenty, he wrote: "I was very young then…and perfectly ignorant of everything connected with forestry and gardening…but I had all my life longed to begin gardening and planting." There had never been a garden at Inverewe, for the coast is lashed by some of the fiercest winds in the British Isles, being only slightly protected from north Atlantic gales by the island of Harris, forty miles to the west. It is on the same latitude as Labrador.

When Mackenzie came here the tallest plant he could see was a scrubby willow

The coastal walk at Inverewe

3ft/1m feet high, and any remotely edible vegetation was instantly consumed by sheep. He fenced off a promontory of land that juts out into the serene waters of Loch Ewe and gradually started to establish evergreen windbreaks of Austrian, Corsican and Scots pine, only later introducing native deciduous trees such as alders, birch and rowans in their lee. It was fifteen years before he was able to begin planting the tender exotics for which the garden became famous. The land was almost destitute of humus; a few pockets of peat survived among the inhospitable rocky outcrops. Fertile soil had to be introduced – a back-breaking job as it had to be brought by sea and then carried in creels on men's backs. The coast, however, benefits from the benign influence of the North Atlantic Drift and enjoys high rainfall of up to 60in/150cm a year.

Once protection from the salt-laden wind was established and the soil improved, an immense range of plants was able to be grown

Crocosmias and rhododendron bark at Inverewe

and Mackenzie built up his collection, drawing on plants from all over the temperate world. Shortly before World War I he was visited by the famous W.J. Bean from Kew – "a proud and happy day", as he wrote in his autobiography. "I had the pleasure of showing him my tricuspidarias, embothriums and eucryphias, my trees of *Abutilon vitifolium*, my palms, loquats, drimys, Sikkim rhododendrons, my giant olearias, senecios, veronicas, leptospermums, my metrosideros, mitrarias, etc." He then goes on, "I have, too, some of the less common varieties" and proceeds to list the real rarities of the collection. Mackenzie died in 1922 and his daughter Mairi (later Mairi Sawyer) took over the running of the garden, which she left to the National Trust for Scotland on her death in 1953.

A MESMERISING JUNGLE

The visitor to Inverewe today will be bewildered and enchanted by the extraordinary plants grown in scenes of jungle-like beauty. Three National Collections of plants are kept here – of brachyglottis (formerly senecio), olearias and *Rhododendron barbatum* – but the whole collection is astonishingly diverse. Among the exotics are many old Scots pines whose bark, like that of giant myrtles, eucalyptus and rhododendrons (especially *R. thomsonii*), is marvellously ornamental; and everywhere there is much strange and beautiful foliage. The mesmerising jungle is laced with paths, sometimes quite narrow and often precipitous, from which from time to time, delicious views of the loch are revealed.

The wild woodland garden of exotics is what has made Inverewe famous but visitors will also relish Osgood Mackenzie's kitchen garden. On terraced slopes near the entrance to the garden below the house, protected by a long curving wall of stone, are beds of vegetables and fruit interspersed with enchanting ornamental planting – all lovingly maintained to impeccable standards, a marvellous sight.

Any latter day gardener, tussling with some minor problem in his or her own garden – an infestation of ground elder, stony soil or a plague of slugs – may like to think of the perseverance and farsightedness of the remarkable Osgood Mackenzie who turned a bare, infertile, gale-swept rock into one of the most remarkable gardens in the world.

Location Poolewe IV22 2LQ, Ross-shire **OS** NG8683 6m NE of Gairloch by A832 **Tel** 01445 781200 **Fax** 01445 781497 **Owner** The National Trust for Scotland **Open** mid Mar to Oct, daily 9.30–9; Nov to mid Mar, daily 9.30–5 **Area** 62 acres/25 hectares

KELLIE CASTLE

INTIMATE WALLED FLOWER GARDEN FOR A HISTORIC ESTATE

The Neuk of Fife is a bight of land jutting out into the North Sea between the estuaries of the Tay and the Forth. Its southern coast is rich in fine old houses and notable gardens which take advantage of protected south-facing slopes and splendid views of the Firth of Forth. Kellie occupies just such a position, rising handsomely in a wooded setting a little distance from the sea. The castle is essentially a fortified tower house of the 16th and 17th centuries, although a house has existed here at least since the 15th century.

A walled garden immediately alongside the castle dates from the 17th and 18th centuries. The Ordnance Survey map of 1855 shows the space to have been divided into six compartments arranged about an axial walk running east and west; nothing is known about the garden before this. The modern garden history of Kellie starts in 1878 when the estate

The walled garden at Kellie Castle

was bought by Professor James Lorimer who restored the castle, by then abandoned. His son Robert became a distinguished architect and garden designer, and as a sixteen-year-old schoolboy in 1880 laid out a delightful walled garden for Kellie Castle. A painting of 1892 by John Henry Lorimer shows great thickets of *Lilium longiflorum* rising below apple trees, and when George Elgood painted the garden in 1899 he showed gravel walks and box-edged beds filled with hollyhocks, poppies and roses. The planting is essentially Victorian in character but Lorimer's design already shows his fondness for what he later described as the essential spirit of 17th-century Scottish gardens – "Great intersecting walks of shaven grass, on either side borders of brightest flowers backed by low espaliers hanging with shining apples."

The walled garden lies hard against the castle walls. A cruciform pattern of paths of gravel and mown grass divides the space with strong and simple axes. Herbaceous borders edged with box flank the vista aligned with the entrance. Lemon-yellow achilleas, violet-blue *Echinops ritro*,

orange heleniums and lavender goat's rue (*Galega officinalis*) are planted in bold drifts, with espaliered pears trained on wires at the back. The vista is closed by bench with an arched back of Arts and Crafts style, designed by Hew Lorimer (Robert Lorimer's nephew). A grass pat forming a cross axis passes between bed of gallica roses and lavender (with great drifts of *Galtonia candicans* in late summer), under an arch of roses to a fir armillary sphere on a plinth. Beds about the walls are largely given over to the cultivation of fruit, vegetables and herbs. Robert Lorimer also designed a delightful little gardener's bothy in one corner, surmounted by a jaunty carved stone bird. It is a delightful and unusual place – a vision of a cottage garden suitable for a castle.

Location nr Pittenweem KY10 2RF, Fife **OS** NO5105 3m NW of Pittenweem by B9171 **Tel** 01333 720271 **Fax** 01333 720326 **Open** daily 9.30–sunset **Area** 1½ acres/0.6 hectares

KINROSS HOUSE

OUTSTANDING 17TH-CENTURY FORMAL GARDENS BY SIR WILLIAM BRUCE FOR HIS OWN HOUSE

The garden at Kinross is a marvellous survival from the late 17th century – on of the grandest and most attractive gardens in Scotland. It was created in the 1680s by Sir William Bruce for his own use, and surviving plans show that the relationship of the garden the house was planned from the start.

Bruce's magnificent classical mansion and its garden are united about a single axis. This started with the old High Street of Kinross which led up to the entrance lodges of Bruce's estate, and although the High Street has now been cut off, the remainder of the axis remains intact. From

The fish gate at Kinross

Herbaceous border at Kinross

lodges it runs straight to the front door of
house, and on the other side it continues in
form of a path to the boundary wall of the
rden where it appears to end at an iron gate
th a magnificently decorated stone surround.
t the visual axis in fact continues for,
ntred on the gate, is the prospect of the ruins
Loch Leven Castle on an island in the
ddle of the loch.

The estate and gardens were restored in the
rly 20th century by the Montgomery family
hose plantings follow the firm structure of
uce's layout. Excellent mixed borders under
e walls, with their beautiful architectural
tailing, are broken from time to time by
ttresses of clipped yew in keeping with the
chitecture of the walls. The path running
om the house towards the loch passes
rough a rose garden ornamented with
lical shapes of clipped yew and then
tween a pair of mixed borders, backed by
dges of clipped purple beech, whose
lours modulate from whites to purples and
ues, to yellows and finally to a triumphant
urish of rich reds. The wrought-iron gate

terminating the path is flanked by tall piers
capped with putti gambolling with dolphins,
and the arch above the gate is topped by a
stone urn filled with fish. (Seven identifiable
species of fish which were found in the loch
in the 17th century.)

Close to the house is a garden hidden
behind yew hedges. Here a summerhouse
with a sweeping ogee-shaped roof overlooks
beds of roses and a fine statue of Atlas
shouldering the universe. Kinross is still
privately owned and both house and garden
are impeccably maintained. Visitors are
welcome in the garden but there is no trace
of the heritage industry; the entrance charge
is by an honesty box and when you are there
you have the impression of being a privileged
guest in a private and splendid domain.

Location Kinross KY13 7ET, Kinross-shire **OS** NO1202
In the centre of the town of Kinross **Owner** Mrs James
Montgomery **Open** May to Sept, daily 10–7
Area 4 acres/1.6 hectares

LOGAN BOTANIC GARDEN

MARVELLOUS PLANTS IN A GARDEN WITH A SUBTROPICAL CLIMATE

Logan Botanic Garden is part of the Royal
Botanic Garden Edinburgh. Because of its
privileged climate (affected by the North
Atlantic Drift but also by the peculiar lie of
the land), it is able to cultivate all kinds of
tender plants, especially those of the southern
hemisphere. The Rhinns of Galloway is a
narrow tongue of land jutting southwards
from Stranraer, with beautiful views of Luce
Bay to the east and the Irish Sea to the west.
The garden lies almost in the middle of this
isthmus and the proximity of the sea on each
side contributes to the mildness of the
microclimate and adds moisture to the air.
Rainfall averages around 38in/95cm per
annum and severe frosts are rare. As in other
coastal gardens, wind is the chief problem,
although that has been at least partly tamed by
the establishment of windbreaks.

The estate was owned by the ancient
McDouall family who had lived here since
the 13th century. Recognising the potential of
the climate, they started making a garden in
the late 19th century, using some of the
tender exotics which were being introduced
to Britain at that time. In 1969 the walled
garden and a further parcel of land alongside
it was given to the Botanic Garden, although
the family continues to live in the house.

SUBTROPICAL EXOTICISM

Logan is first and foremost a plant collection
and its chief attraction to the visitor will be
the prospect of seeing unfamiliar plants
flourishing in the open air. Such plants often
have distinctive character, giving the garden an
atmosphere of subtropical exoticism. The heart
of the garden is formed by an irregular walled
area which provides such traces of formality as
the garden possesses. Wilder passages of
woodland lie outside the walls. The design of
the walled garden is scarcely a chief
consideration but, willy nilly, striking
arrangements of plants are to be seen. A lily
pool is flanked by rows of *Cordyline australis*
underplanted with seasonal bedding and a

border alongside is full of *Gladiolus papilio*, kniphofias and watsonias, with a huge spread of blue and white agapanthus. To one side a magnificent grove of tree ferns is underplanted with different species of herbaceous ferns, a vast spread of the bold *Blechnum chilense* but also much smaller species such as *Doodia media* and *Blechnum gayanum*, with the occasional eruption of *Fascicularia bicolor* – an ornamental grasss with the occasional startling crimson blade among its foliage. Facing south-west, a raised terrace is ornamented with the ruined tower of Castle Balzieland – all that remains of the 15th-century keep of McDouall of Logan. A flight of stone steps curves up to the terrace, freckled with the Mexican daisy *Erigeron karvinskianus*, and the statuesque leaves of the Madeiran *Echium pininana* rise on one side, backed by thickets of ceanothus with electric blue flowers. The walls of the terrace garden are draped with such tender climbers as pale yellow *Jasminum mesnyi*, *Mutisia ilicifolia* with fragile-looking palest pink flowers, and the glowing cerise bell-flowers of *Lapageria rosea*. In the bed below are the Californian white sage (*Salvia apiana*), *Cedronella canariensis* (whose aromatic leaves smell of cedar), a shrubby foxglove from Madeira (*Isoplexis sceptrum*), the Hottentot fig (*Carpobrotus edulis*) and much else that is exotic and tender.

The northern part of the walled garden has lawns and informal plantings of trees and shrubs, with a mixed border against the south-facing wall. Among the shrubs are superb old eucryphias and rhododendrons, and a giant *Magnolia sprengeri* – a noble sight. Outside the walled garden, more trees and shrubs are planted on grassy slopes to the west and south, and there is a woodland pool with a vast swamp of *Gunnera manicata*.

The rows of cabbage palms in the walled garden (an original idea of the McDoualls) make something exotic of a conventional garden feature. Here at Logan they reach their full potential, flowering profusely and producing creamy clouds of blossom whose rich scent pervades the walled garden in summer – in less privileged British gardens they may be hardy but merely limp along. There is something irresistible, too, in the sight of some tricky exotic grown in lavish profusion – waves of the Chatham Island forget-me-not (*Myosotidium hortensia*), for example – rather than in lonely pampered splendour. The range of tender plants grown at Logan is unique in mainland Britain.

Cordyline avenue at Port Logan

Location Port Logan, Stranraer DG9 9ND, Wigtownshi
OS NX0943 12m S of Stranraer by A716 **Tel** 01776 860231 **Fax** 01776 860333 **Owner** Trustees of the Royal Botanic Garden Edinburgh **Open** Mar to Oct, da 10–6.30 **Area** 30 acres/12 hectares

MANDERSTON

GRAND EDWARDIAN FORMAL GARDENS AND AN ATMOSPHERIC WOODLAND GARDEN BY A LAKE

The house was built at the end of the 18th century for General Maitland, remodelled at the end of the 19th century for Sir William Miller, and magnificently transformed into a neo-Adam extravaganza by John Kinross between 1900 and 1905 for Sir James Miller. The estate was inherited by Sir James's nephew, Major Hugh Baillie, who died in 1978, and subsequently inherited by his grandson who owns it today.

The house stands in well wooded policies, with lawns and specimen trees close to it. At a little distance from the house is the walled formal garden, also designed by John Kinross when he was working on the house. Very grand wrought-iron gates and screens, supported on piers capped with putti representing the four seasons, lead into it. A gravel path edged in box runs between borders backed with yew hedges where yellow and pink azaleas are followed by red and pink bedding roses, soothed in late summer by quantities of white *Galtonia candicans*. At the far end of the walk is a pedimented gateway; to one side, at the centre of a sunken garden, a two-tiered fountain is supported on herms; curved beds cut into the turf are filled with summer bedding schemes of pink and red begonias and blue lobelias. A pergola of pink roses introduces a second sunken garden enclosed in rustic walls filled with ferns and aubrieta where a magnificent bronze urn stands on a marble plinth and L-shaped beds have summer bedding. Beyond the walled garden is a range of old glasshouses, one of which preserves splendid tufa-encrusted benches. Visitors to the grand Marble Dairy in the outhouses nearby will pass the beautiful head gardener's house with fine wrought-iron gates through which one may glimpse an impeccable garden.

THE TERRACE AND LAKE

Below the southern façade of the house John Kinross designed a terrace garden with two round pools, beds of red or yellow roses, topiary of silver- or gold-variegated holly and common or golden yew. The terrace is edged with a balustrade and a swashbuckling double staircase leads down. Here the ground falls away to a lawn with views of a lake and woodland.

At the eastern end of the long curving lake, which must date from the 18th-century house, is a stream crossed by a balustraded bridge built in Sir James Miller's time. He also built a boathouse in the form of a Swiss chalet and a rustic bridge spanning the centre of the lake. Planned walks through the woodland on the lake's south bank have excellent flowering shrubs and ornamental trees — acers, azaleas, eucryphias, *Kalmia latifolia*, rhododendrons, rowans and witch hazels — and in summer there are magnificent plants of *Cardiocrinum giganteum*. Where the

The formal garden at Manderston

walks run close to the lake there are splendid views back to the house.

John Kinross's house is, on the whole, severely classical, although its interior occasionally breaks out into fits of remarkable flamboyance — including a staircase made of silver. Edwardian opulence is felt more strongly in the formal garden and the terrace garden; the woodland garden, dating from the late 19th and early 20th century, reflects a quieter mood.

Location Duns TD11 3PP, Berwickshire **OS** NT8154 1½m E of Duns by A6105 **Tel** 01361 883450 **Fax** 01361 882010 **Email** palmer@manderston.co.uk **Website** www.manderston.co.uk **Owner** Lord Palmer **Open** mid May to Sept, Thur, Sun and Bank Hol Mon 2–5 **Area** 56 acres/23 hectares

The south terrace garden at Manderston

MELLERSTAIN

MAGNIFICENT ROSE TERRACES, A GRAND LANDSCAPE AND A SURPRISING COTTAGE GARDEN

In 1642 the estate at Mellerstain was acquired by George Baillie of Jerviswood whose descendants (later Earls of Haddington) have owned it ever since. The present house was designed by William Adam in 1725 to 1726 and by his son, Robert Adam, who between 1770 and 1778 gave it its present gently castellated appearance. William Adam was probably also responsible for laying out the parkland, in particular the two axes which divide the land, meeting north of the house. There had been formal gardens close to the house in the early 18th century but these were removed in the landscaping craze. A version of them, however, was put back in 1909 by Sir Reginald Blomfield, and his grand scheme is the chief landscape ornament today. This was the largest design that Blomfield ever made but, immense as it is, it is simpler than what was originally planned — which would have required, as Blomfield acknowledged at the time, "the resources of Louis XIV".

Blomfield's terraced gardens lie below the south façade of the house where the ground falls away with wonderful views over woodland to the Cheviot hills. A grass terrace below the house, with tall cones of clipped

yew and a mixed border, curves round at each end to provide side views over the lower terraces. From here, a double balustraded staircase leads to a lower terrace with a rose garden planned as a giant parterre. Shaped beds cut into the turf are filled with catmint or with a single variety of white, pink or red bedding roses. Fan shapes or rounded cushions of box topiary are disposed between the beds. A second, even grander, double staircase leads down (embracing a pool of irises and waterlilies) to a simple grass terrace with a classical figure of a man facing back towards the house. At this level Blomfield had originally proposed a gigantic very deep terrace enclosed in raised walks through avenues of trees and supported on bastions.

The lawn slopes southwards, edged with beech hedges, towards a distant pool fringed with trees. As you descend you suddenly find the incline becoming steeper, with the land scooped out in a vast amphitheatre of turf. At the bottom the pool turns out to be the head of a canal, enclosed in a curving balustrade. The canal penetrates the woodland, through which there are walks, and on rising land above the woods, centred on the canal, is a curious eyecatcher – Hundy Mundy – like the west front of a medieval cathedral with two pointed gables and a central arch.

In the wooded policies north of the house is a charming curiosity: a thatched cottage *orné*, part of which is a round tower, formerly a dovecote. It has a garden of a cottagey kind

The terraced gardens at Mellerstain

– swooping beds edged in box, Irish yews, wigwams of runner beans and drifts of irises, pelargoniums, phlox and roses – an unexpected and delightful sight.

Location nr Gordon TD3 6LG, Berwickshire **OS** NT6539 7m NW of Kelso by A6089 **Tel** 01573 410225 **Fax** 01573 410636 **Email** enquiries@mellerstain.com **Owner** The Earl of Haddington **Open** Good Fri to Easter Mon and May to Sept, daily 12.30–5; Oct, Sat and Sun 12.30–5 **Area** 50 acres/20 hectares

MOUNT STUART

AN 18TH-CENTURY WOODED LANDSCAPE GARDEN WITH NOTABLE TREES AND SEASIDE WALKS

The Stuarts (now Crichton-Stuarts and Marquesses of Bute) have lived here sin 1385 when John Stuart, the bastard son of Robert II, was made hereditary sheriff of Bute. The early 18th-century house was largely destroyed by fire in 1877 and the gre new house, a Gothic palace of marvellous splendour which incorporates the wings of the early Georgian house, was designed by Robert Rowand Anderson and completed i the first years of the 20th century. (No visito to the gardens should miss going round the house, with its sumptuous and dramatic interior of marble vaults, painted ceilings, stained glass and magnificent contents.)

The first important developments in the gardens took place in the early 18th century under the 2nd Earl of Bute. At this time the family lived in Rothesay but planting had already begun in the garden before 1722, when work started on the new house. By 1759, in the time of the 3rd Earl, a plan showed a parterre and bowling green close t

Mount Stuart from the great lawn

house, and avenues and rides through
oods dividing the landscape – a pattern
hich survives to this day. The 3rd Earl was
e confidant of George III and of his
other, the Princess Augusta, whose garden at
ew he helped to lay out; he was thus in
fect one of the founders of the Royal
otanic Gardens at Kew (*see page 169*). At
ount Stuart the Earl kept a collection of
hlias long before their hybridisation made
em into a fashionable garden plant.

SPLENDID AMERICAN CONIFERS

he best way to visit the gardens is to start at
e 19th-century pinetum just beyond the
tchen garden at the bottom of the drive.
ere is a splendid collection of conifers,
iefly new introductions from the north-
est coast of America – Wellingtonias
equoiadendron giganteum), Douglas firs
seudotsuga menziesii), western hemlocks
suga heterophylla) and others, all grown to
eat size. Near it is a new arboretum which
rms part of the Royal Botanic Garden
linburgh's International Conifer
onservation Project, and an astonishing
enue of old lime trees. The 18th-century
ttern of rides through the woodland now
comes apparent – six rides converge on a
umphant stone column brought from the
d Earl's English estate of Luton Hoo (*see
ge 506*) and dedicated to Princess Augusta.
om here the pink stone of the astonishing
ouse is seen, gleaming through the trees
ross an enormous lawn.

Behind the house is a pretty rock garden
signed by Thomas Mawson in the 1890s
d, south-west of the house, the Wee
arden, made in 1823 and now giving a
ome to tender exotics from the southern
emisphere. These are attractive but they are
kly chamber music in relation to the
mphonic resonance of the views of the
eam-like pink palace in its formidable
ndscape of lawn and trees.

cation nr Rothesay PA20 9LR, Isle of Bute **OS**
1060 5m S of Rothesay by A844 **Tel** 01700 503877
x 01700 505313 **Email** contactus@mountstuart.com
ebsite www.mountstuart.com **Owner** The Mount
uart Trust **Open** May to mid Sept, daily except Tue
d Thur 10–6 **Area** 300 acres/121 hectares

THE PINEAPPLE

THE LOVELIEST GARDEN PAVILION
EVER MADE, IN AN 18TH-CENTURY
WALLED ORCHARD

The Dunmore Pineapple must surely be one of the most beautiful of all garden buildings. It was built in 1761 as a banqueting house for the 4th Earl of Dunmore who later became Governor of New York. Dunmore Castle fell into disuse, the estate was dismembered and the Pineapple survived only by the skin of its teeth. It was bought by the Earl and Countess of Perth in 1974 and presented to the National Trust for Scotland.

The Pineapple is built into the south-facing wall of a 6-acre/2.4-hectare walled kitchen garden – ornamental buildings are often integrated into walls in Scottish gardens in this way. On the garden side a pedimented portico with a Palladian entrance rises to exactly the height of the garden wall. Above it, forming the base of the Pineapple, is

a circle of seven windows with ogee-shaped frames and finely carved surrounds which burst into flames at each apex. Between each window a pilaster rises into the lower pineapple leaves. The Pineapple itself is magnificently carved in stone and each of the extravagantly curving leaves is drained internally to avoid damage by frost. It was in the past flanked by ranges of glasshouses against the wall.

No-one knows whether pineapples have any particular significance for Dunmore. They were certainly grown in Scottish gardens by the mid 18th century – the earliest date for their cultivation is 1732 when they were grown by James Justice of Midlothian. They may have been grown here at Dunmore – certainly the former glasshouse on either side of the Pineapple were heated, with the flues emerging through ornamental urns which can still be seen running along the crest of the wall.

The Trust has planted a formal orchard in the mown grass that now fills the kitchen garden, but in all

The Dunmore Pineapple

truth the magnificent Pineapple itself is of such consuming interest and beauty that almost any planting would fade into irrelevance. The interior of the Pineapple, by contrast, is relatively restrained and has been finely restored. You may not visit it, but you may rent it as a holiday house through the Landmark Trust.

Location Dunmore, nr Stirling, Stirlingshire **OS** NS8989 On the Dunmore estate (enter by East Lodge) 6m SE of Stirling by A905 **Tel** 01628 825925 **Owner** The National Trust for Scotland **Open** daily 10–sunset **Area** 6 acres/2.4 hectares

PITMEDDEN GARDEN

DELIGHTFUL 20TH-CENTURY FLOWER PARTERRES FOR A SUPERB 17TH-CENTURY WALLED GARDEN

This is the kind of garden that delights visitors and irritates historical purists. At its heart is the Great Garden, a walled enclosure of fine architectural detail. It is one of the very rare dated gardens in Scotland – the entrance bears the date 2 May 1675 and the cipher of its maker, Sir Alexander Seton, together with that of his wife, Dame Margaret Lauder. The old house at Pitmedden was destroyed by fire in 1818, together with all its contents, including the family archives, so there is no documentary evidence to indicate the design of the original garden here. (There is, indeed, precious little archival evidence about any other 17th-century Scottish garden or about principles of garden design of the time; the first book on gardening published in Scotland was John Reid's *The Scots Gard'ner* of 1683, which is almost entirely devoted to practical horticulture rather than aesthetics.)

In 1951 the Pitmedden estate was given to the National Trust for Scotland by Major James Keith. The Trust decided to recreate a formal garden in keeping with the spirit of the period and the architectural character of the walled Great Garden, and they laid out a pattern of four box-edged parterres that were inspired by a mid 17th-century design for the parterres at Holyroodhouse in Edinburgh, shown in a contemporary print. The compartments of the parterres are planted with thousands of bedding plants, disposed in blocks of a single colour, and in one parterre the Seton arms are traced in plants.

The Great Garden is sunken, and on three sides you may look down on it from a walk along the retaining walls. The brilliantly coloured garden that lies below is a thrilling sight with its seductive mixture of patterned formality and lively ornament, and all superlatively maintained. It is disposed about a single axis – a walk of yew pyramids – which runs across the garden from an elegant double staircase to a gate in the opposite wall. An early 19th-century map shows that this axis was continued into the woods beyond the garden wall, in exactly the way that a French garden of this period might have been arranged.

The western wall of the garden, by which you enter, is planted with a series of yew buttresses, clipped into swooping ogee curves and topped with a dashing topknot. At each end of the wall is an elegant pavilion whose roof is also shaped in ogee curves – a common feature of Scottish 17th-century architecture. Excellent herbaceous borders run along the south- and west-facing walls, and on the walls behind are apples superbly trained in espaliers, goblets and fans, looking exactly like illustrations from a French textbook on fruit growing.

OLD SCOTTISH APPLES

Leading up to the Great Garden, new gardens have been added. Yew topiaries march towards the entrance, with a circular pool with two formal enclosures hedged in beech or pleached lime screens and box parterres at the centre. Nearby a tunnel of apples is a showcase for old Scottish varieties with marvellously appetising names – 'Galloway Pippin', 'Lass O'Gowrie' and 'Howgate Wonder'.

Location nr Pitmedden, Ellon AB4 0PD **OS** NJ8828 14m N of Aberdeen by A920 and B999 **Tel** 01651 842352 **Owner** The National Trust for Scotland **Open** May to Sept, daily 10–5.30 **Area** 4½ acres/2 hectares

POLLOK HOUSE

RECONSTRUCTED 17TH-CENTURY FORMAL GARDENS WITH BOX-EDGED PARTERRES AND FINE PAVILIONS

Maxwells first came to live here in the 13th century and in 1911 Sir Herbert Maxwell described the Pollok estate in his book *Scottish Gardens* as "a green oasis round which Glasgow and the neighbouring boroughs have flowed like a dark and rapidly rising tide. Yet…within constant sound of

The Great Garden at Pitmedden

ROYAL BOTANIC GARDEN EDINBURGH

ONE OF THE BEST AND MOST
ATTRACTIVE BOTANIC GARDENS IN THE
WORLD – FABULOUS PLANTS ON A
BEAUTIFUL, HILLY SITE

The citizens of Edinburgh hold the Royal Botanic Garden in high esteem, referring to it affectionately as "The Botanics". It combines, in the most harmonious and attractive way, several attributes: it is a centre of botanical research, an exceptional reference collection of plants, a display garden of horticultural skills, a landscape of great beauty and a wonderful place for a walk.

Its history goes back to 1670 when it was founded as a garden of medicinal plants attached to the university, making it the second oldest botanic garden in the British Isles (only Oxford's is older; *see page 99*). It moved from Leith Walk to its present site in 1820 – high and airy, commanding splendid views northwards across the Firth of Forth to the hills of Fife. The curator and principal gardener at that time was William McNab who devised an ingenious cart to transport mature trees across Edinburgh to the new site

m hooters and whistles, steam hammers and nps, you may see alpine flowers blooming as fusely and with colours as clear as they do the loftiest solitudes of earth." At the time was writing the Pollok estate belonged to Herbert's kinsman, Sir John Stirling-xwell, who was a noted gardener with a cial interest in alpine plants. The Maxwell ily gave the estate to the City of Glasgow 1966, and although Sir John's alpine garden gone (the wall on which part of it was nted is still there) the marvellous house, its tty formal garden and over 350 acres/142 ctares of admirable parkland (almost exactly same extent of ground that it had in the th century) all survive, despite Sir Herbert's xiety about enroaching industrialisation.

The austerely handsome house, enlivened by ved stone garlands on the garden front, was lt in the mid 18th century and was strongly luenced by William Adam. The gardens re transformed by Sir John Stirling-Maxwell iose twenty-first birthday was celebrated in 88 by the planting of an avenue of limes. He devised the delightful 17th-century-style dens which ornament the east and south es of the house. Overlooked by curvaceous ee-roofed garden pavilions of a characteristic ottish 17th-century style are box-edged rterres whose compartments are filled with nmer annuals. A double staircase embracing ountain pool leads to a lower terrace from nich views of parkland open out. To one side the house a path leads to a turf walk tween beds planted with Himalayan birches d waves of hostas backed by rhododendrons another particular interest of Sir John's.

The parterre at Pollok House

A short walk through the woods leads to the remarkable Burrell Collection of decorative arts housed in a restrained building of glass, stainless steel and pink Dumfriesshire stone, which glows among the trees. This fine museum, the work of Barry Gasson Architects, was opened in 1983.

Location 2060 Pollokshaws Road, Glasgow G43 1AT
OS NS5561 3m SW of the city centre by A77 and B762
Tel 0141 616 6410 **Owner** Glasgow City Council (managed by the National Trust for Scotland) **Open** Apr to Oct, daily 10–4; Nov to Mar, daily 11–4 (closed 25–26 Dec and 1–2 Jan) **Area** 361 acres/146 hectares

The rock garden at the Royal Botanic Garden

– creating an instant garden which makes modern attempts at such things seem very feeble. McNab's son James became regius keeper of the garden and in 1870 created the rock garden which the *Gardener's Chronicle* described in 1875 as "the largest and most varied rock garden we have ever seen and the most fascinating…charming beyond the power of expression". James McNab also took great pains over the landscaping of the whole garden, establishing a layout on this undulating site which has made it one of the most attractive of all botanic gardens.

Later in the 19th century, one of the greatest of all plant collectors, George Forrest, came to work in the herbarium here. In 1904 he embarked on the first of six expeditions to China, visiting many places that no westerner had seen before and introducing immense numbers of new plants – over 300 species of rhododendrons, over 150 species of primula, and dozens of buddleias, irises, honeysuckles and lilies. This was the start of the garden's special interest in Chinese plants, of which the Edinburgh herbarium has today the greatest collection outside China. In 1993 the Pringle Chinese Garden was made – a stream and pool overlooked by a scarlet pavilion and a rising bank of Chinese plants disposed in naturalistic profusion, for all the world like a scene from the landscape of Yunnan.

MAGNIFICENT COLLECTIONS

The grassy slopes of the botanic garden are clothed in trees – so many species and such fine specimens. Of the 650 known species of conifer, 450 are grown here, and there are excellent examples of every genus of hardy tree; many non-hardy species are found in one or another of the 11 glasshouses. The collection of rhododendrons is vast, and includes most of the species hardy in a temperate climate. An immense deep herbaceous border, 500ft/150m long, runs below one of the grandest beech hedges you are ever likely to see, and behind it is an admirable demonstration garden. The rock garden presents an enchanting sight, especially in spring, with many difficult plants (erythroniums, fritillaries, trilliums and the exquisite nomocharis lilies) grown to perfection; even trickier alpines are cosseted in the alpine house and its courtyard of troughs and raised beds.

As a place in which to study plants, learn about gardening, push a pram or merely wander in a magical landscape, the Royal Botanic Garden Edinburgh is altogether outstanding. Its only rival in the British Isles is Kew – and there is no admission charge to the cherished "Botanics".

Location Inverleith Row, Edinburgh EH3 5LR
OS NT2475 1m N of the city centre **Tel** 0131 225 9442
Fax 0131 225 0382 **Owner** Trustees of the Royal Botanic Garden Edinburgh **Open** Nov to Jan, daily 9.30–4 (closed 25 Dec and 1 Jan); Feb and Oct, daily 9.30–5; Mar and Sept, daily 9.30–6; Apr to Aug, daily 9.30–7 **Area** 67 acres/27 hectares

SCONE PALACE

BEAUTIFUL PARKLAND AND A
REMARKABLE 19TH-CENTURY PINETUM
FOR A HISTORIC ESTATE

For many non-Scots the first thing to learn about Scone is how to pronounce the place – *scoon*, unlike the delicious baked scone which is invariably best eaten in Scotland. The estate is very ancient; it was a royal residence by 843. In 1604 James VI gave it to Sir David Murray in whose family (later Earls of Mansfield and Viscounts Stormont) it has remained. The great house at Scone dates back to the early 17th century but now has a comprehensively Gothicised appearance – the work of William Atkinson at the beginning of the 19th century.

The park at Scone was landscaped by Thomas White between 1781 and 1786 with unhappy results. In 1804 J.C. Loudon was asked to come and improve on the work, in particular to break up White's many tight clumps of trees into a more naturalistic arrangement. Loudon described Scone in his *Encyclopaedia of Gardening* (1822): "A noble castellated mansion…in one of the finest situations in Scotland, with a lawn in front of great extent, washed by the Tay, and backed by rising grounds covered with wood."

In the middle of the19th century, at the height of the craze for such things, the 4th Earl of Mansfield started to plant a pinetum.

The pinetum at Scone

The interest in conifers had been stimulated by the introduction of new species from the American Pacific coast, and many of these had been discovered by a local man, David Douglas, who was born at Old Scone and became a gardener's boy at Scone Palace. A majestic Douglas fir (*Pseudotsuga menziesii*), propagated from the first seeds brought back by Douglas in 1826, is a wonderful sight. The pinetum includes over 50 species of conifer, some of which go back to the 1848 plantings and has mature specimens of often remarkable trees of great character: the Chinese fir (*Cunninghamia lanceolata*) with glowing cinnamon-coloured bark and gleaming fronds of foliage like demented bottle-brushes; a lovely old western hemlock (*Tsuga heterophylla*) with a deeply gnarled trunk and wide spreading branches, introduced to Scotland in 1852, planted at Scone in 1866 and now one of the largest specimens in Britain; Brewer's spruce (*Picea breweriana*) with wonderfully ornamental and gracefully cascading branches. There is something splendidly solemn about such collections. The subtle seasonal variations of leaf colour, the spectacular eruption of cones and the striking patterns and colours of bark provide things to marvel at in any season. In high summer it is pleasurable to retreat into their shade and relish the cool pine-scented air.

There are sketchy ornamental flower plantings at Scone but it is the old pinetum

...t is the object of exceptional horticultural ...erest. It is also good to see that someone ...s embarked on a reserve pinetum alongside ...e original one. The site is as beautiful as ...udon described it and the parkland on the ...pes below the castle is exceptional.

...cation Scone, Perth PH2 6BD, Perthshire **OS** NO1126 ... NE of Perth on A93 **Tel** 01738 552300 **Fax** 01738 ...2588 **Email** sconepalace@cqm.co.uk **Owner** Trust ...Viscount Stormont **Open** Apr to Oct, daily ...0–5.15 **Area** 100 acres/40 hectares

STIRLING CASTLE

RARE AND DELIGHTFUL
17TH-CENTURY KING'S KNOT GARDEN
FOR A MAGNIFICENT CASTLE

...n 1656 Richard Franck, a Cromwellian ...trooper, was bowled over by the sight of ...irling Castle: "a beautiful and imbellished ...astle, elevated on the precipice of an ...npregnable rock, that commands the vallies ...s well as the town) and all those habitable ...arts about it". The castle, still exactly as Franck describes it, is one of the most unforgettable buildings you will ever see.

It is built on top of a great rock whose western face forms a vertiginous cliff. It must always have seemed a formidable defensive position. There are vague legends of the antiquity of its occupation but the earliest certain date is the beginning of the 12th century when Alexander I built a chapel here, and by 1174 there was enough of a castle for it to be surrendered to Henry II of England under the Treaty of Falaise. The modern appearance of the castle dates from the 15th century in the reign of James IV. The Great Hall was nearing completion in 1503 and a little later one of the most outstanding parts of the castle, the early renaissance palace (probably made by French masons), was completed. Stirling passed in and out of English hands but never lost its importance to the Scottish monarchy until the union of the crowns in 1603 – James VI of Scotland and I of England was the last king to live here.

By the 15th century there were gardens at Stirling on the flat ground below the cliff on the western side of the castle rock. This is an area that has long been known as the King's Park (it had been enclosed under William I – William "the Lion" – in the 12th century) and a new garden was in place for the visit of Charles I in 1633. The English gardener William Watts was working at Stirling in 1625 and the Master of Works accounts show that work was done on the king's garden and orchard between 1628 and 1629. A painting of the castle by Johannes Vorsterman, made around the late 1670s and reproduced in John Harris's *The Artist and the Country House* (1979), shows a great rectangular walled enclosure with a central circle or oval from which paths radiate out directly to each side, and the whole lavishly embellished with tall statues. This, or something like it, is described in the Ordnance Survey *Gazetteer* of 1882: "Near the extreme SW side of the gardens is an octagonal earthen mound with terraces and a depressed centre known as the King's Knot, and probably the place were the old game called The Round Table was played."

If the modern visitor stands on the raised

The King's Knot at Stirling

walk that edges the Bowling Green below the palace at Stirling Castle, an astonishing view opens out. At the foot of the cliff the King's Knot is plainly to be seen, covered in close-mown turf and traced by changes in level. At its centre is an octagonal mound on two levels within a rectangle. This does not precisely correspond with the Vorstermann painting and when exactly it was made is not known – but it is still a wonderful sight. Almost as wonderful is the view to the south, across the Dumbarton road, to the ancient King's Park. It is remarkably unspoilt although, where deer used to graze, golfers now swing their clubs.

Location Castle Wynd, Stirling FK8 1EJ, Stirlingshire **OS** NS7994 In the centre of Stirling **Tel** 01786 450000 **Fax** 01786 464678 **Owner** Historic Scotland **Open** Apr to Sept, daily 9.30–6; Oct to Mar, daily 9.30–5 **Area** 20 acres/8 hectares

Sculptures of Belted Galloways at Threave

THREAVE GARDEN

A WALLED KITCHEN AND ORNAMENTAL GARDEN WITH EXCELLENT PLANTS (ESPECIALLY OLD SHRUB ROSES) IN A LOVELY WOODED LANDSCAPE

Threave House was built in flamboyant Scottish baronial style for William Gordon in 1872 to the designs of the Edinburgh architects J.D. Peddie and C.G.H. Kinnear. The estate was given by Major Alan Gordon to the National Trust for Scotland in 1957 and since 1960 it has been the base of a school of gardening. It is the students who have been largely responsible for creating and maintaining the garden.

The undulating site is well wooded with beeches, conifers and oaks, many of which go back to plantings made shortly after the house was built. A charming sight greets visitors – opposite the car park, grazing in the shade of a fine collection of crab-apples and cherries, is a sculpted group Belted Galloways, a local breed of black cattle with broad white belts about their middles.

WINDING PATHS

There is no strong pattern of design to the garden; areas are linked by winding paths and there is always something interesting or attractive to see. From the entrance a path leads down a slope among beds of mostly shrub roses, which include several varieties of the lovely wild Scottish Burnet rose (*Rosa pimpinellifolia*). Below, the old kitchen garden is enclosed in stone walls and divided into four by a central broad gravel walk flanked by deep herbaceous borders, and a cross walk of beds of 'New Dawn' roses strained on pillars and underplanted with *Salvia × superba*. Each quarter of the garden is under cultivation with fruit or vegetables and a large glasshouse contains tender ornamentals.

Close to the walled garden the path leads to a pool and cascade whose banks are planted with *Gunnera manicata*, hostas, *Iris sibirica*, meconopsis, primulas and rodgersias. The house rises among trees on a slope which in spring is covered in thousands of narcissus bulbs. Bold herbaceous borders run along the path at the foot of the slope and a laburnum arbour leads to a hidden garden with winding walks among shrubs and trees which include several varieties of maple. On lawns nearby are raised rockeries and a large collection of plants of an alpine kind. A shelter here is thatched in heather (a once traditional material) which has now grown a deep eiderdown of moss. From here there are grand views of the lovely rolling wooded landscape. On the slopes above the house is a youthful arboretum and a large collection of heathers laid out in great swathes in the grass like brushstrokes of colour.

Threave is not a place in which to see the latest ideas of garden design in action but it does offer a fine collection of plants excellently grown in a beautiful setting.

Location Stewartry, Castle Douglas DG7 1RX, Kircudbrightshire **OS** NX7560 1m SW of Castle Douglas by A75 **Tel** 01556 502575 **Fax** 01556 502683 **Owner** The National Trust for Scotland **Open** Mar, daily 10–4; Apr to Oct, daily 9.30–5.30; Nov to 23 Dec, daily 10–4 **Area** 65 acres/26 hectares

The kitchen garden at Threave

TOROSAY CASTLE

IDYLLIC ISLAND GARDEN WITH TERRACES,
TENDER PLANTS, SPLENDID STATUARY AND
ROMANTIC SEA VIEWS

The castle is a Scottish baronial mansion (replacing an 18th-century house) built on a superb site in the 1850s for Colonel Campbell to the designs of David Bryce. In the very early years of the 20th century, when the estate was owned by Walter Murray Guthrie, a new terraced garden was built below the south façade of the house. It is rumoured, with no evidence, that this was designed by Robert Lorimer. The uppermost terrace has a circular pond at its centre, narrow borders about its perimeter, and ends with a balustrade and a battlemented fortress-like gazebo in each corner. The enticing terrace ingeniously leads the visitor into the garden which lies beyond and below. But having walked out onto the terrace, you see to one side something far more beautiful than any garden. Beyond the romantic castle on Duart

The lion terrace at Torosay

Point and across the Lynn of Lorne there open out breathtaking views over the water to the mountains of Ben Nevis and Glen Coe on the mainland to the east. The obvious way of using such a rare prospect would have been to have designed the house so that it formed the principle view from its chief rooms, or to have disposed the garden so that it formed the central focus. Suddenly revealed to one side in this way, the combination of surprise and borrowed landscape is unforgettable.

From the terrace, steps lead steeply down to the garden proper, whose ingredients follow no firm axis but are scattered all about. Immediately to one side lies the statue walk, made at the same time as the terrace, displaying a procession of statues emerging from thickets of fuchsia. These, the work of Antonio Bonazzo (1698–1765) were bought from a ruined villa at Padua and, most unusually and attractively, depict estate workers – the gamekeeper, gardener and so forth. The statue walk leads, at an angle, to the lion terrace, overlooked by two recumbent marble lions ("Growler" and "Smiler") gazing down at a sunken lawn. Below the lion terrace is the original 18th-century walled kitchen garden,

now turned over to ornamental purposes. Here are yew hedges and a grand colonnade festooned with clematis, *Vitis coignetiae* and wisteria, and ending in a domed rotunda.

The garden is rich in good plants, among which are some remarkable old western red cedars (*Thuja plicata*) which appear to have been planted at about the time of the building of the house. If this is the case, they are among the oldest specimens in Britain, for the tree was introduced in 1853 by Veitch's nursery. The climate is mild here and a tender *Cornus capitata* by the statue walk has grown to great size and beauty. A woodland garden to the west of the formal gardens is bright with Himalayan poppies and primulas and there is a fine specimen of *Stewartia pseudocamellia* with its dazzling autumn colour. A slightly perfunctory oriental garden on the eastern margin of the garden is an example of exactly what not to do; it serves no purpose here and could scarcely be less appropriate for its beautiful setting, with views eastwards across the sea.

Torosay in itself makes a journey to Mull worthwhile. Its setting in the landscape, the terraced garden, rare statue walk and some excellent plants give great pleasure.

Location Craignure, Isle of Mull PA65 6AY, Argyll **OS** NM7335 1m SE of Craignure by A849 **Tel** 01680 812421 **Fax** 01680 812470 **Owner** Chris James **Open** daily 9–7 (closes dusk in winter) **Area** 11 acres/4.4 hectares

IRELAND

ALTAMONT GARDEN

DISTINGUISHED PLANTING IN AN
ATMOSPHERIC SETTING WITH FORMAL
GARDENS, LAKE AND WOODLAND WALKS

Altamont is an ancient place and the
present house, largely dating from the
mid 18th century, has foundations that go
back at least to the 16th century. In the past it
was known as Rose Hill, and later as Soho,
assuming its present name towards the end of
the 18th century. The garden was started by
Feilding Lecky Watson who rented the house
in 1923; finding it so much to his taste (in
particular the fine acid soil) he bought the
estate. Watson started to build up a collection
of plants, especially of rhododendrons,
with the help (as was the case in many
other Irish gardens) of Sir Frederick
Moore, the director of the National
Botanic Garden at Glasnevin.
Watson died in 1943 and shortly
after World War II his daughter
Corona took charge of the

garden, rescued it from wartime neglect and
started to add much new planting of her own.
She married Gary North in 1966 and after
her death in 1999 the garden passed to
Dúchas, The Heritage Service.

THE BROAD WALK

Such formality as the garden possesses starts
immediately behind the house where three
more or less parallel walks lead down to a
lake. The central Broad Walk forms the chief
axis of the formal garden and is overarched
from time to time by 19th-century Irish yews
trained to meet in the middle. On either side
borders are rich in shrub roses. In Mrs North's
day the lawns that flank the walk, decorated
with many good trees, were also often
ornamented with clucking chickens, giving
the impression of a dashingly aristocratic
farmyard.

The lake is the heart of the garden and was
dug in the 1850s, after the Famine, to provide
labour for the local unemployed. The banks
are lavishly planted with trees and shrubs,
especially rhododendrons added by Mrs

North's father; here too are sitting places and
the occasional grand urn standing among
reeds. Walks about the edge of the lake give
delicious views back towards the house and
lead into woodland on land which slopes
down to the river Slaney. Here are an
arboretum, a bog garden and a most
remarkable Ice Age glen whose air of ancient
wilderness is occasionally contradicted by
some distinguished rhododendron. A flight of
granite steps (100 of them) leads back from
the river towards the house, where paths skirt
a field with exquisite views of the rural
landscape and the Wicklow Hills. The charm
of Altamont lies in the subtle focus of
attention on the natural beauties of the land,
enlivened by distinguished planting.

Location Tullow, County Carlow, Republic of Ireland
9km S of Tullow on the Bunclody road, signed off
N80 and N81 **Tel** (00353) (0)503 59444 **Email**
altamontgarden@eircom.net **Owner** Dúchas, The
Heritage Service **Open** phone for current opening
times **Area** 40 acres/16 hectares

The lake at Altamont

ANNES GROVE

ON THE BANKS OF THE AWBEG RIVER, ONE
OF THE BEST WILD ROBINSONIAN GARDENS
IN IRELAND, AND A PRETTY WALLED
FLOWER GARDEN

Annes Grove preserves a deliciously
secretive and private air, untouched by
the heritage industry. The house is a
gentlemanly 18th-century mansion, known
originally as Ballyhimock when it belonged
to the Grove family; in the late 18th century a
Grove daughter married the Hon. Arthur
Annesley in whose family it has remained.

The site is delightful, with the river Awbeg
forming one of the chief ornaments of the
landscape. The fame of the garden was due to
Richard Grove Annesley who started to
garden here in 1907. Inheriting an essentially
Victorian layout rich in conifers and with an
ornamental flower garden, Annesley
discovered the land running along the Awbeg
valley was of fine acid soil, perfect for the
kind of woodland gardening in which he was
interested. He was in touch with many
notable Irish plantsmen of his time, among
them Hugh Armytage Moore of Rowallane
and John Annan Bryce of Ilnacullin, and like
them took advantage of the marvellous new

The walled garden at Annes Grove

plants being discovered and introduced by
Frank Kingdon Ward and George Forrest.

A long walk winds through woods north of
the house, with the river valley falling away
along its eastern edge. The path is lined with
fine plants – dogwoods, embothriums,
enkianthus, myrtle (*Luma apiculata*), many
rhododendrons, magnolias and much else.
Particularly notable among the dogwoods is
the tender *Cornus capitata* with its pale slightly
acid yellow flowers. An occasional slithery
path or rustic moss-bearded flight of stone
steps leads down past flowering shrubs to the
river, its dark and glassy waters flowing
smoothly and purposefully under alder and
ash. Paths along the river are mown through
long grass, bracken, cow parsley and the
occasional glowing forest of yellow flag iris. A
rocky outcrop juts out from the valley side,
covered in valerian and a grove of white
foxgloves. Above it the largely coniferous trees
which clothe the slope are illuminated in
spring and early summer with bursts of colour
from rhododendrons or the more graceful
flourish of a magnolia. Further downstream
the planting is denser and more exotic:
majestic clumps of *Gunnera manicata* and
lysichiton, or scatterings of Himalayan

primulas spread out below *Cercidiphyllum
japonicum*, cabbage palms (*Cordyline australis*)
and *Drimys winteri*. The occasional rustic
bridge spans the water and at a certain point
you find yourself on the lowest of a series of
formal turf terraces between the back of the
house and the river bank.

Nearer the house a walled garden enclosed
in stone walls and yew hedges, probably an
orchard in the 18th century, today preserves a
decorative 19th-century character. Here a
flagstoned path forming a central axis is
flanked by herbaceous borders backed with
yew hedges, with a pergola of honeysuckles
and roses running off at an angle. A rose
garden has a pattern of symmetrical beds cut
into a lawn. A charming series of beds
containing mounds of multi-coloured lupins
are edged in box forming a looping scrolled
pattern. A path leads up a mound to a
Victorian summerhouse with lattice-work
doors, all but engulfed in escallonia and
fuchsia. More herbaceous borders run under
the walls with the occasional distinguished
shrub such as *Hoheria glabrata*. In the north
part of the garden are beautiful magnolias
with hostas, lilies, pulmonaria and rodgersias
in their shade.

Location Castletownroche, County Cork, Republic of
Ireland 1.6km N of Castletownroche, signed from the
town centre **Tel** and **Fax** (00353) (0)22 26145 **Email**
annesgrove@eircom.net **Owner** Patrick Annesley
Open mid Mar to Sept, daily 10–5 (Sun 1–6) and by
appointment **Area** 40 acres/16 hectares

The magnolia garden at Annes Grove

BALLINLOUGH CASTLE

A ROMANTIC HOUSE IN A SPLENDID PARKLAND SETTING ADORNED WITH NEWLY RESTORED WALLED GARDENS

Ballinlough Castle was built in the 17th century for the O'Reilly family on the site of a medieval tower house and was given its cheerfully castellated air in the late 18th century. Sir Hugh O'Reilly took the name Nugent in 1812. Little is known of the early garden history but Sir Hugh Nugent planted many trees here from 1931 to clothe the undulating land of the demesne and give the castle its present park-like setting. In the mid 19th century a lake divided by an isthmus and a bridge was made below the house, which adds to the impression of an 18th-century landscape park. The water comes from a canal crossed by a rockwork bridge built by Sir Hugh in 1812. Walks about the canal and lake are punctuated by good trees, especially several fine Turkey oaks (*Quercus cerris*), and by views up the hill towards the most castle-like façade of the house.

Since 1994 the garden has been restored by Sir John and Lady Nugent. The very large walled former kitchen garden, with its several compartments, has been thoroughly refashioned, much of it turned to decorative purposes. A pair of herbaceous borders backed

The rose garden at Ballinlough

by beech hedges forms the chief axis of the main enclosed area. Behind the borders lawns are planted with flowering cherries, a magnolia walk and other ornamental shrubs. A former sunken garden, hidden behind beech hedges, has been made into a formal pool shaded by cherries and ornamented with urns of the pink-flowered strawberry (*Fragaria* 'Pink Panda'). A rose garden is divided into four by paths meeting at a central arbour swathed with honeysuckle (*Lonicera etrusca* 'Michael Rosse'), *Clematis viticella* 'Purpurea Plena Elegans' and *Rosa filipes* 'Kiftsgate'. The paths are lined with beds of shrub roses and lavender. Leading off it is a secret garden with mixed borders against three sides and a deep paved area running against a south-facing wall. There are clematises, *Cytisus battandieri*, *Euphorbia mellifera* and roses against the wall, and *Alchemilla mollis*, *Potentilla atrosanguinea*, strawberries and thymes in the cracks between the paving stones. A Gothic bench is half concealed by a billowing bush of yellow tree lupin. A very large formal orchard is planted with espaliered fruit against the walls and free-standing damsons, medlars, mulberries, pears and plums. Nearby is a small vegetable

garden and an ornamental soft-fruit cage.

Between house and walled garden is a decorative old stable yard. Those interested in Irish social history will note the large arched entrance to a tunnel which connects the yard to the kitchen quarters of the house – the only entrance apart from the front door. This arrangement, common in old Irish country houses, permitted servants to go about their often grubby business invisible to the fastidious eyes of the gentry.

Location Clonmellon, County Westmeath, Republic of Ireland 25km W of Navan by N51 and R154; or by Kells and N52 **Tel** (00353) (0)46 33135 **Fax** (0)46 33331 **Owner** Sir John and Lady Nugent **Open** May to Sept, Thur to Sat 12–6; Sun and Bank Hol Mon 2–6 (closed first two weeks Aug) **Area** 40 acres/16 hectares

BALLYMALOE COOKERY SCHOOL GARDENS

FORMAL HERB, FRUIT AND KITCHEN GARDENS EMBELLISHED WITH GRAND HERBACEOUS BORDERS AND AN EXQUISITE SHELLHOUSE

The Allen family is famous for its promotion of delicious traditional Irish food. Myrtle and Ivan Allen, Tim's parents, started the Ballymaloe House Hotel nearby, which many people regard as the best of Ireland's country house hotel/restaurants. More recently, Tim and Darina started the cookery school alongside their own house at Shanagarry in a peacefully rural setting on the edge of a village. On this flat site close to the sea, which is visible across fields, the Allens restored an attractive 19th-century garden and have launched out on ambitious new additions of their own. The garden, which is both ornamental and practical, has a purposeful air which adds to its charm. A wide range of fruit, vegetables and herbs is cultivated to meet the needs of the cookery school and this seems perfectly to suit the rhythm of life at Ballymaloe, where productivity and ornament are woven inextricably together.

Close to the school buildings is a maze-like formal

Ballymaloe shellwork

fruit garden, designed by Jim Reynolds, with apples, apricots, grapes, peaches, pears and pomegranates skilfully deployed. A formal vegetable garden, beautifully kept and gardened organically, is laid out like a parterre, with herring-bone brick paths and hedges of small-leafed box enlivened by lapping waves of nasturtiums, edgings of chives or marigolds and lollipops of clipped bay. It is overlooked by an arbour of golden hop and another of purple beech.

At a distance two 19th-century enclosures are magnificently hedged in beech, with arched openings above which the crest of the hedge rises to echo the opening. Lydia's Garden has lawns, herbaceous borders and a summerhouse with a delightful mosaic floor of broken china artfully disposed and dated 1912. This is linked to a herb garden enclosed in the same superb beech hedges – a herb parterre on the grand scale, with a symmetrical pattern of interlocking intricately shaped beds edged in box, and each bed containing a generous block of a single kind of herb with the occasional angelica, artichoke or giant fennel forming an emphatic plume at its centre. The whole delightful area is overlooked by a wooden viewing platform arrived at by scrambling up a precipitous flight of wooden steps.

To the south of

The herb garden at Ballymaloe

this, a spanking new double herbaceous border, separated by a broad grass path and backed with yew hedges, leads to a dashing summerhouse with a tall pointed roof. The planting is a curious mixture of the coarsely cottagey, with plants such as yellow loosestrife and the fashionable, even trendy, oriental poppy, *Papaver orientale* 'Patty's Plum'. The summerhouse, however, is a rare masterpiece. It has an anonymous air until you enter and its stunning interior bursts upon you – a gleaming extravagance of shellwork exquisitely arranged in endlessly inventive patterns by the grotto artist Blot Kerr-Wilson. Each wall, and the surrounds of the door and

Gothic windows, is encrusted with virtuoso arrangements; each bay is separated by a pilaster formed of alternate vertical stripes of mussels and limpets; the high vaulted ceiling is patterned with stripes of cockles and mussels. It is well up to the best of 18th-century artistry and craftsmanship.

Location Shanagarry, Midleton, County Cork, Republic of Ireland 30km E of Cork by N25 and R632 **Tel** (00353) (0)21 464 6785 **Fax** (0)21 464 6909 **Website** www.cookingisfun.ie **Owner** Tim and Darina Allen **Open** Apr to Sept, daily 11–6 **Area** 10 acres/4 hectares

BANTRY HOUSE

AN 18TH-CENTURY HOUSE IN A WONDERFUL POSITION OVERLOOKING BANTRY BAY, WITH FINE FORMAL GARDENS

Bantry House has a remarkably beautiful position on rising ground above Bantry Bay, looking north-west over Whiddy Island to the Caha Mountains. The early 18th-century house was bought in 1750 by Richard White (later 1st Earl of Bantry) whose family still lives here. The traveller and garden connoisseur Prince Pückler-Muskau came here in 1828 and was especially struck by the tender plants that flourished and by

The terraces at Bantry House

walls "garlanded by ivy and roses antiquely picturesque". Lord Bantry's heir, another Richard, did the Grand Tour, sending all sorts of treasures back to Bantry House between 1820 and 1840. He also developed a taste for Italian gardens and in the 1840s, under their inspiration, created the essential lines of the garden as we see it today. It is one of the outstanding and most attractive formal gardens of its period in the country.

In the early 19th century the new Cork road had been built along the coast below the house. The 2nd Earl of Bantry obscured it by terracing the land above it and forming a wide viewing platform to take advantage of the grand view north over the bay. On the other, south, side of the house he laid out an "Italian parterre" with a central pool. He also built on a new room, the library, whose chief window is exactly aligned on the centre of the parterre and, beyond, on vertiginous flights of stone steps linking terraces on the steep slope above.

RESTORATION UNDER WAY

In recent years the garden has been restored and a further programme of restoration is under way. The terraces overlooking the bay have, once again, their original 19th-century arrangement of fourteen large circular beds, hedged in box and planted alternately with blocks of red hot poker (*Kniphofia* 'Nancy's Red', an old Irish variety) and of *Perovskia atriplicifolia*. This whole area is enclosed in balustrading, now restored, and ornamented with statues and urns. The Italian parterre has been replanted with hedges of common and golden yew, its compartments filled with Brompton stocks and irises. The central pool is enclosed in a circular arbour entwined with wisteria, and the edges of the pool are encrusted with rockwork; at its centre a rockwork mount is decorated with shells and crowned with a pair of fish and a water spout. A balustraded terrace overlooks the parterre on three sides and the flights of steps up the hill are once again ornamented with beautiful basketwork terracotta pots, copied by an Italian pottery from a surviving 19th-century original.

More work needs to be done at Bantry – including the restoration of a magnificent

walled garden at a distance from the house, where a formal orchard has been reinstated. But enough has been done to show how the garden takes such exceptional advantage of its site. The walk up to the top of the steps rewards the climber with one of the loveliest views in Ireland.

Location Bantry, County Cork, Republic of Ireland On the western outskirts of Bantry on the N71 **Tel** (00353) (0)27 50047 **Fax** (0)27 50795 **Owner** Mr and Mrs Egerton Shelswell-White **Open** Mar to Oct, daily 9–6 **Area** 45 acres/18 hectares

BIRR CASTLE DEMESNE

AN OUTSTANDING COLLECTION OF TREES AND SHRUBS, PICTURESQUE RIVERSIDE WALKS AND A MAGNIFICENT WALLED FLOWER GARDEN

The castle at Birr was originally built in the 17th century by the Parsons family (who became the Earls of Rosse), but was heavily Gothicised in the 19th century. The formidable walls and Gothic gatehouse of the castle line one side of the street in the small town of Birr, originally called Parsonstown. The demesne has a marvellous site, with the river Camcor – spanned by an elegant iron suspension bridge – running below the castle

Rose arbour at Birr Castle

and fine trees everywhere, some of which go back to the 18th-century landscaping of the grounds. The 5th Earl subscribed to the plant-hunting expeditions of E.H. Wilson between 1907 and 1911, and a superb collection of magnolias dates from this time. He also terraced the precipitous slope running down to the river close to the castle, making lawns set with ornamental trees and shrubs and picturesque walks along both banks. Below the castle ramparts there is a superb *Magnolia delavayi* planted in 1911 and, on the far side of the river, a vast *M. dawsoniana*, the largest magnolia at Birr.

A FINE FORMAL GARDEN

The 6th Earl, Michael, married Anne Messel who was brought up at Nymans in Sussex, and together they developed the garden. Spending their honeymoon in China in 1935, they started to collect seeds of trees and shrubs with which they immensely increased the range of plants grown at Birr. Today Birr has over 1,000 species of woody plants, making it one of the finest collections in Ireland. Michael and Anne Rosse also transformed a 17th-century pleasure garden north of the house into a fine formal garden. This was well restored in 2000 by their son Brendan, the 7th Earl, and has been renamed The Millennium Gardens. Enclosed by stone walls and hedges of yew, with "cloisters" of pleached hornbeam, it has fine statues and urns of the 17th century. During restoration an infestation of ground elder was removed and many of the beds replanted in the same decorative spirit as the original garden. Here i a fine collection of old shrub roses, a lively border planted in blue, white and yellow, box parterres (incorporating the crossed R's of the Rosse family), and a handsome new gravel path edged with intertwined patterns of box and pyramids of yew. Here too are decorative garden seats with backs formed by a cipher carved in wood – the entwined initials of Michael and Anne Rosse.

To one side of the formal garden is a newly made cruciform canal with masks spouting water. Curious rather than beautiful is the extraordinary tunnel of ancient box nearby, said to date from the 17th century and hailed by the *Guinness Book of Records* as "the tallest

the world", which joins the formal garden
the kitchen garden. A far more remarkable
uriosity is the 3rd Earl's great telescope built
the 1840s; at that time the largest in the
orld, it is housed in a Gothic building to
atch the castle. The 3rd Earl was the first
an to observe, in 1845, the spiral form of
e galaxies. His descendant, the present Earl,
ommemorated the 150th anniversary of this
iscovery by laying out a spiral walk of limes
Tilia cordata).

LAKE, ARBORETUM AND FERNERY
urther west, across a fine meadow, is a
uperlative old English oak planted in the
6th century. Beyond it is a shapely lake, the
rboretum and a fernery. It is the great
ollection of trees and shrubs, and the lie of
e land (especially by the banks of the river
nd lake), that are the most memorable aspects
f the garden at Birr. It is also touched by a
r from disagreeable idiosyncrasy.

ocation Birr, County Offaly, Republic of Ireland On the
dge of the town of Birr, 40km S of Athlone by N52
el (00353) (0)509 20336 Fax (0)509 21583 Owner
he Earl of Rosse Open daily 9–6 or dusk if earlier
rea 120 acres/49 hectares

BUTTERSTREAM GARDEN

A BRILLIANT GARDEN OF MANY
MOODS BEAUTIFULLY EXECUTED BY A
GREAT IRISH GARDENER

Butterstream is one of the most influential
of late 20th-century Irish gardens. It is
not only exceptionally attractive but also
provides a valuable model for gardeners.
Sparked by "the irrational desire to possess a
few roses", Jim Reynolds started his garden at
Butterstream in the early 1970s. The site is
largely flat, with the precious natural feature
of a stream, and winters can be harsh in this
inland part of the country.

The garden is divided into compartments
by hedges of beech, yew and, more daringly,
copper beech. The entrance is unemphatic but
as soon as you arrive in the garden you are
assailed by its distinctive character. From a
formal kitchen garden with bowers of fruit,
neat beds and tall obelisks of clipped bay, an
archway flanked by two giant pots of lilies
leads across the stream further into the
garden. The banks of the stream are overhung
with old ash and sycamore with a rich

The canal garden at Butterstream

underplanting of ferns, ligularia, lysichiton,
petasites and rodgersias, and overlooked on
the garden side by a broad and stately paved
path backed by a beech hedge. An informal,
shady garden is dominated by a noble
Cercidiphyllum japonicum under whose canopy
spread dactylorhizas, ferns, hellebores, hostas
and primulas. A rose garden with narrow
paths and waist-high box hedges is densely
furnished with shrub roses and the occasional
eruption of a giant hogweed. A paved
enclosure has thrilling drifts of orange lilies,
tufts of cinnamon-coloured grass in the cracks
between paving stones, statuesque clumps of
Ligularia dentata and the soothing canopy of
the golden foliage of *Gleditsia triacanthos*
'Sunburst'. Instead of herbaceous borders
you are immersed in giant seas of herbaceous
plants flowing on either side of a broad
grass path.

But the Obelisk Garden contains only
gravel, enveloping yew hedges, a tall obelisk of
clipped yew and rows of box pyramids. In the
Pool Garden, enclosed in box hedges, a
pillared pavilion looks over a rectangular
waterlily pool. Cones, spheres and spirals of

box stand in terracotta pots and in each corner a cube of clipped hornbeam rises on its bare trunk. Nearby a walk of Irish yews leads into an impassive lawn, and from here an opening in a giant wall of copper beech hedging reveals a pair of beautiful pavilions. Each pavilion has a Palladian window overlooking a canal flanked by a row of limes, and a formal cascade from which water tumbles into a square pool.

Throughout the garden the hugger-mugger planting and rapid flow of events is contrasted with the sudden revelation of an empty lawn, a long vista, a well placed ornament or building, or an opening in a hedge. The climax of all this is the pair of pavilions with their attendant canals, cascades and lime avenues – a dash of Versailles in rural County Meath. On a much grander scale than any other part of the garden, these provide a most dazzling surprise – the perfect place in which to sit, enjoy the gentle splashing of water in the cascades, and consider which of the garden's delights you are going to revisit on the way back to the car park.

Location Trim, County Meath, Republic of Ireland On the W outskirts of Trim 40km NW of Dublin by N3 and R154 **Tel** (00353) (0)46 36017 **Fax** (0)46 31702 **Owner** Jim Reynolds **Open** May to Sept, daily 11–6; groups at any time by appointment **Area** 8 acres/3 hectares

CASTLE COOLE

A SUPERB 18TH-CENTURY MANSION SET IN A ROMANTIC LANDSCAPE OF THE PERIOD WITH GOOD TREES

The house at Castle Coole is James Wyatt's masterpiece, built at the end of the 18th century for Armar Lowry-Corry, 1st Earl of Belmore. As cool and as un-cosy as a house can be, it is nevertheless very beautiful. James Lees-Milne thought that "for sheer abstract beauty" it was the best of Wyatt's surviving houses. This was by no means the first house on the estate, on which medieval pottery has been found, and Lord Belmore's grandfather, Colonel John Corry, built a pretty Queen Anne house in 1709 by the banks of Lough Coole. The Queen Anne house, built at the

foot of the hill on which the new house stands, was destroyed by fire as work on the new house was underway. It was approached by an avenue of oaks, some of which still survive, and had a formal garden of parterres, walks, a flower garden and a melon ground. It also had a sunken bowling green whose earthworks are still plainly visible in a field close to the lough. Immediately east of the house there had been a large formal water garden.

EXQUISITE VIEWS

The Wyatt house stands on a grassy eminence surrounded immediately by lawns but with dense plantings of trees to the south. To the north a deep lawn slopes downwards, ending in a ha-ha which, despite its 18th-century appearance, was built in the 1960s. Beyond is pasture land and parkland trees and an exquisite view of Lough Coole whose distant slopes are smoothly planted with belts and groups of trees. This view, well framed by plantings in the pasture, has exactly the atmosphere of a landscape by Capability Brown and it is known that there was much fine tree planting here in the 18th century. When J.C. Loudon described the estate in 1836 he mentioned "magnificent old trees" on the lawn in front of the house – ash, beech, horse chestnuts, English oaks and sweet chestnut, and in particular commented on the

"noble avenue of oaks". Lord Belmore wanted to redesign the landscape in the naturalistic style to provide an appropriate setting for his great new house, but although maps survive showing proposed changes, none exactly corresponds to the present landscape. Nor is there certain knowledge of any designer associated with these proposals, although the name of William King, a landscape designer then working at Florence Court, has been mentioned.

Part of the Castle Coole estate is now a golf course, quite discreetly sited. Much parkland remains, including the site of the early 18th-century deer park made for the Queen Anne house. But the most memorable aspect of the landscape is the perfect Brownian view north of the Wyatt house of woods, pasture and lake. Any visitor to the demesne should also visit the house, if only to admire the best of all views of the lake landscape from the first-floor Bow Room, possibly the only room in the house which, with its touches of Chinoiserie, might be called pretty.

Location Enniskillen BT74 6JY, County Fermanagh, Northern Ireland 1½m SE of Enniskillen by the A4 **Tel** (028) 6632 2690 **Fax** (028) 6632 5665 **Email** castlecoole@ntrust.org.uk **Owner** The National Trust **Open** (Parkland) May to Sept, daily 10–8; Oct to Apr, daily 10–4 **Area** 392 acres/159 hectares

Parkland and lough at Castle Coole

CASTLE WARD

A GRAND HOUSE IN AN ATMOSPHERIC
WOODED DEMESNE ON THE BANKS OF
STRANGFORD LOUGH, WITH FORMAL
TERRACED GARDENS

The position of Castle Ward on undulating
ground at the southern tip of Strangford
Lough looking down a wooded valley towards
the water is memorably beautiful. Mrs Delany
saw it in 1774 when it was recently built and
thought that "it hath every advantage from
Nature that can be desired". The house, built
in around 1763, is delightfully two-faced –
coolly classical on the entrance side and
boisterously Gothic where it looks towards
the lough. The stylistic clash is continued in
the interior, reflecting a difference in taste
between its builder, Bernard Ward, later 1st
Earl of Bangor, and his wife.

By the time Mrs Delany saw Castle Ward
there had already been much planting in the
demesne. A watercolour by her shows the
early 18th-century Palladian garden temple,
possibly designed by Robert Morris, on the
wooded slopes above Temple Water, a formal
canal (today rather informal), which had been
dug in 1724. It is close to the remains of
Audley's Castle, a 15th-century tower house
built to guard the entrance to the lough.
Strikingly visible from the lough side of
Castle Ward, rising above the trees, the tower
is as neatly placed as a purpose-built
picturesque ruin.

Apart from surviving earlier
trees, and traces of 18th-
century parkland the chief
character of the garden is
Victorian. Close to the
house is a walled terraced
garden with much exotic
planting – *Acca sellowiana*,
Beschorneria yuccoides, large
old plants of cabbage palm
(*Cordyline australis*) and
substantial hummocks of
Melianthus major. In high
summer the garden swoons
with the tropical perfume
of the cabbage palms'
flowers. A sunken lawn has
a circular lily pool with a
splendid figure of Neptune

Neptune in the walled garden

Castle Ward from the west

at the centre, brandishing a gold-tipped
trident. Behind a screen of Irish yews a rock
garden with dwarf conifers runs along one
side of a mid 19th-century pinetum with
immense Wellingtonias, a piquant contrast. But
the best things at Castle Ward are the grand
walks in the huge demesne. It is
the larger landscape, with
delicious views of trees and
lough enlivened by the
occasional building – not
least the irresistible house
itself – that constitute the
greatest pleasure.

Location Strangford,
Downpatrick BT30 7LS, County
Down, Northern Ireland 7m NE of
Downpatrick on A25 **Tel** (028)
4488 1204 **Fax** (028) 4488 1729
Email castleward@ntrust.org.uk
Owner The National Trust **Open**
May to Sept, daily 10–8; Oct to
Apr, daily 10–4 **Area** 750
acres/303 hectares

CASTLEWELLAN NATIONAL ARBORETUM

AN EXCEPTIONAL COLLECTION OF TREES
AND SHRUBS AND AN 18TH-CENTURY
WALLED ORNAMENTAL GARDEN

Mrs Delany, that valuable chronicler of Irish houses and gardens in the 18th century, wrote in 1750: "…the Annesleys have walled in and planted with oak, 350 acres of ground for a park…Mr Annesley is going to build a town." The town was Castlewellan and it remains a most attractive example of an 18th-century planned town, planned also to give due prominence to the Annesley demesne.

The castle was not built until the 1850s when the 4th Earl Annesley built the granite castellated house to the designs of William Burn. Beneath its south façade it preserves a terrace walk of distinctly Victorian kind, with a parade of giant mounds of Portugal laurel and spreading shapes of golden yew.

The arboretum was started in the 1870s by the 5th Earl Annesley, incorporating a fine walled garden of 12 acres/5 hectares, now called the Annesley Garden, which had been made in the mid 18th century. This, in conjunction with a further 96 acres/39 hectares of woodland outside the walls, in particular the beautiful land spreading along the north bank of Castlewellan Lake, constitutes the National Arboretum. The whole is set in the context of the Castewellan Forest Park.

The walled Annesley Garden, on a gently south-facing slope, is essentially a garden of trees and shrubs but at its heart is a pair of herbaceous borders backed by yew hedges and interrupted by a splendid fountain. Throughout the garden are notable species, often tender and frequently rare. Here are fine collections of pines, Japanese maples, many different species and cultivars of cypress (including such tender plants as the beautiful *Cupressus cashmeriana*), spruces and many plants from the southern hemisphere (especially New Zealand).

Just outside the Annesley Garden beds of dwarf conifers, not today as fashionable as once they were, now have the character of a period piece. Here too is a spring garden with flowering cherries, crab-apples and attractive planting about a group of pools. In the woods nearby a large collection of rhododendrons is grown among evergreen and deciduous trees. Autumn Wood, on the bank of the lake immediately west of the castle, is a collection of trees and shrubs with especially fine autumn colour – birches, *Cercidiphyllum japonicum*, dogwoods, maples, the American red oak (*Quercus rubra*), thorns and much else.

The fame of Castlewellan lies in its outstanding collection of trees and shrubs (with 34 champion trees of the British Isles and 18 oldest specimens of their species) but the landscape is very beautiful too – the views from the castle terrace southwards over the lake towards the distant Mourne Mountains are lovely. Lastly, and not something remembered with affection by all gardeners, Castlewellan is the birthplace of the gold-leafed form of the Leyland cypress (× *Cupressocyparis leylandii* 'Castlewellan').

Location Castlewellan BT31 9BU, County Down, Northern Ireland On the edge of the town of Castlewellan, 30m S of Belfast by A24 **Tel** (028) 4477 8664 **Fax** (028) 4477 1762 **Owner** Department of Agriculture (Northern Ireland) **Open** daily 10–dusk **Area** 1,136 acres/460 hectares (including the Castlewellan Forest Park)

DERREEN GARDEN

A WILD WOODLAND GARDEN OF
TREMENDOUS CHARACTER, FILLED WITH
GOOD PLANTS AND WITH EXQUISITE VIEWS
OF THE KENMARE ESTUARY

Sir William Petty acquired land at Derreen in the 17th century and by the time of his death owned 270,000 acres/109,311 hectares of Kerry. His daughter, and heiress, married into the Fitzmaurice family (later Marquesses of Lansdowne) and the estate has passed by descent ever since. The present house was built (on older foundations, and with much subsequent rebuilding) in the 1860s. The 5th Marquess of Lansdowne, who inherited in 1866, made it his summer home and started laying out a garden on what had been a site of rocks and scrub oak, planting as windbreak swathes of *Thuja plicata* and *Tsuga heterophylla*, many of which are now giants. The high rainfall and mild climate made it the perfect place in which to grow tender exotics of many kinds. Occupying a promontory of rocky land at the south-eastern end of the creek of Kilmakilloge Harbour, which opens out into the estuary of the Kenmare river, the

The fountain borders at Castlewellan

A grove of tree ferns at Derreen

Knockatee Seat rises even higher and looks out high above quite large rhododendrons towards the peak of Knockatee mountain to the north.

As a piece of naturalistic planting which takes full advantage of its special climate to include many wonderful exotics and which also makes the most of its exceptionally attractive site, Derreen is one of the finest and most attractive gardens of its kind.

Location Lauragh, County Kerry, Republic of Ireland 25km SW of Kenmare by N71 and R571 **Tel** (00353) (0)64 83588 **Owner** The Hon. David Bigham **Open** Apr to Sept, daily 10–6 **Area** 80 acres/32 hectares

THE DILLON GARDEN

A RAVISHING TOWN GARDEN LAID OUT AND BEAUTIFULLY PLANTED BY ONE OF THE GREAT GARDEN MAGICIANS OF THE DAY

Helen Dillon is one of the best gardeners of her day. She defined her ambition as an attempt "to reconcile the collector's instinct with the desire to make a garden that is pleasant to be in", and at 45 Sandford Road you can see how successful she has been since 1972 when she came to this handsome late Georgian house. The garden falls into two parts of very different character – the front garden across which you walk obliquely to approach the front door, and the chief part behind the house, a rectangle enclosed in stone walls.

The front garden is free-flowing, abundant and inviting, with plants straying over onto surfaces of gravel or stone paving. The occasional strong shape emerges – a golden variegated holly clipped into a tall mushroom echoes a silver pear of similar shape on the other side of the garden. There is much yellow – euphorbias, honeysuckle, phlomis, roses, Welsh poppies – which glows in the early morning light, for this is the east side of the house and the first to catch the light. On either side of the steps leading up to the front door are little beds filled with the plant treasures that Helen Dillon loves. Here are arisaemas, celmisias, dactylorhizas, erythoniums, *Onychium japonicum* and other small and often rare exotics, many of which

---

...ting adds much to the beauty of the place. ...he estate belongs today to the 5th ...arquess's great-grandson who in recent years ...s done much work on the garden.

...Derreen is a woodland garden of walks ...anned to take in the beauties of the ...ndscape and to guide the visitor to the many ...otable trees and shrubs that find their home ...re. An excellent leaflet has a map of the ...ths and also indicates especially notable ...ants and vantage points. (The mapless ...anderer, unless possessed of an exceptional ...nse of direction, is quite likely to become ...retrievably lost.)

One walk, the Broad Walk, follows the edge ...the promontory, with delicious shifting ...ews of Kilmakilloge Harbour. Off it, several ...ths lead into the jungly hinterland. One of ...hich, the unforgettably named King's Oozy, ...unges into a flourishing grove of tree ferns ...*Dicksonia antarctica*) of the greatest splendour. ...rst planted at Derreen in around 1900, these ...rns now look completely natural, popping ...o elsewhere in the garden and becoming ...rt of the scenery because the climate suits ...em so well. They show how marvellous ...ch plants are when grown in this way rather ...an struggling for survival, pathetically

---

swaddled in sacking and straw, in gardens whose climate does not remotely suit them.

Soaring above the tree ferns is a huge *Eucalyptus globulus* whose lower trunk is effectively disguised by a coat of moss – the upper part gleaming with cinnamon and silver. Indeed, the planting is often so dense that you must look upwards to identify a tree or shrub. Every walk reveals its beauties, with many excellent rhododendrons, exceptional specimens of such trees as *Cryptomeria japonica* Elegans Group, deodar (*Cedrus deodara*), silver fir (*Abies alba*) and *Styrax japonicus*. There is much recent planting too of camellias and of rarities like *Dacrydium franklinii* with pendulous branches resembling limp pipe-cleaners.

The landscape is punctuated by dramatic outcrops of rocks, usually clothed in moss and often resembling half-submerged prehistoric creatures. Away from the coast the land rises, offering fine prospects of the surrounding landscape. Froude's Seat is a simple bench in an elevated meadow full of buttercups, with a stately 'Loderi' rhododendron close by and a grand view of Kilmakilloge Harbour. The

flawless lawn and nearby one of the very few survivors from the garden the Dillons took over – a splendid old Bramley apple tree with deeply gnarled trunk and limbs, a reminder that the commonplace can be beautiful too. Throughout the garden decorative details emerge amid the profusion – a beautiful metal trellis screen, an armless concrete Venus, a handsome sundial, fine urns, a pair of sphinxes, and pots of rarities in odd corners. The garden is magnificently maintained, the plants bursting with vigour. Once you know it you will want to see it again. You will anticipate the pleasure, always see new things and leave with a spring in your step.

Location 45 Sandford Road, Ranelagh, Dublin 6, Republic of Ireland 2km S of the city centre **Tel** and **Fax** (00353) (0)1 497 1308 **Email** helen@dillongarden.com **Website** www.dillongarden.com **Owner** Val and Helen Dillon **Open** Mar, Jul and Aug, daily 2–6; Apr to Jun, Sun 2–6; also parties by appointment **Area** ¾ acre/ 0.3 hectare

DOWNHILL CASTLE

THE SKETCHY BUT UNFORGETTABLE REMAINS OF AN 18TH-CENTURY LANDSCAPE GARDEN WITH A REMARKABLE CLIFF-TOP TEMPLE

One of the grandest landscapes in the British Isles, with an address of suburban reticence. Downhill was the creation of an obsessive builder, Frederick Augustus Hervey, Bishop of Derry and 3rd Earl of Bristol, who chose as his site rolling land on the north coast of Ireland, and a splendid promontory jutting out high over the Atlantic waves. Although several architects made proposals for the house, an elegant Palladian mansion built in 1775, the supervising architect was Michael Shanahan of Cork who later added various garden buildings which, to put it modestly, enliven the landscape. The house was gutted by fire in 1851 and although rebuilt was subsequently dismantled between the two world wars. What remains today, with sheep and cattle grazing among the ruins, is still a landscape of drama and melancholy beauty.

The most complete surviving building is the Mussenden Temple, circular in plan, and domed and pillared, inspired by Bramante's

need cosseting.

The garden behind the house, usually first seen by visitors through the big windows of the drawing room, is a dazzling revelation. At its centre is a splendid canal, long and narrow and edged in two colours of Kilkenny limestone, grey and very pale grey. The water starts in a circular pool set in cobbles and falls in a gentle cascade into the canal from which, as it gets closer to the house, it descends into two further pools, the last of which is planted with irises and flanked with steps leading down to the paved area immediately behind the house. The canal, a big feature in a small garden, has the paradoxical effect of making the garden seem larger. It took the place, in 2000, of a flawless lawn, so impeccable that it was widely known among garden visitors as the most beautiful lawn they had ever seen (and Irish grass, as we know, is the greenest of all).

Rumours that Helen Dillon was planning to substitute something strange and horrible for the marvellous lawn have been scotched

The canal in the Dillon Garden

by the splendid success of the new canal at the heart of a garden which, though it has formal interludes, is essentially rambling and informal. The canal is flanked by superb mixed borders, predominantly red on one side and blue on the other. Sheaves of the grass *Stipa gigantea* appear on both sides and within each border there is much repeat planting. Behind the borders paths wind among dense planting, with the occasional raised bed to give sharp drainage or to bring some treasure a little closer to the eye. There are touches of formality – for example a sketch of a parterre with crisp hedges and spheres of box – but the compartments are planted informally.

ANTICIPATED PLEASURES

At the end of the canal an arcade of clipped gold variegated ivy provides the opening to a tunnel of clematis, *Akebia quinata*, fruit trees and roses. In a corner there survives another

emple on the Janiculum Hill in Rome and built between 1783 and 1785. The Earl-bishop dedicated it to his cousin Frideswide Mussenden who died at the age of twenty-two before the temple was completed. It stands on the very brink of a cliff, with Magilligan Strand washed by the Atlantic rollers 200ft/60m below. The interior was fitted out as a library, with a crypt underneath. The Earl-bishop wrote at the time, "A luminous idea has just struck me. I might provide a stipend of £10 per year for a priest, and my Roman Catholic workmen could worship in the crypt" – a daringly liberal notion for a Protestant bishop. The Temple, now without its library fittings, may be visited and the views from its windows are spectacular – westwards across the mouth of Lough Foyle to the mountains of Donegal and eastwards towards the town of Portstewart with the Giant's Causeway beyond. On a stormy day the roar of the wind, the cry

of buffeted seagulls and the crashing of waves far below evokes the sublime drama which 18th-century landscapers so relished.

Nearby, the beautiful masonry shell of the house with the remains of a service wing has something of the character of a Piranesi etching, standing serenely on a grassy island enclosed by a ha-ha. On wild moorland in the hinterland a high domed mausoleum rises up – a monument to the Earl-bishop's elder brother, the 2nd Earl and absentee Lord Lieutenant of Ireland to whom the Earl-bishop owed his preferment and wealth. Built between 1779 and 1783 it was badly damaged in the "big wind" of 1839 which toppled the life-size figure which crowned it. The decapitated body lies today forlorn among bushes of escallonia and myrtle at the entrance lodge to the garden.

In more recent times the gardens by the lodge were lovingly tended by

The Mussenden Temple

Miss Jan Eccles who came to live here in 1962, renting the Gothic lodge house from the National Trust. Here she laid out a charming flower garden with hellebores, Himalayan poppies, candelabra primulas, ferns and the fairy-foxglove (*Erinus alpinus*), a native of the Burren, that extraordinary limestone plateau in Miss Eccles's native County Clare. She also enriched the woodland planting along the drive, adding such distinguished trees as *Liquidambar styraciflua*, *Metasequoia glyptostroboides* and *Pterocarya fraxinifolia*. All this serves as an appetising and unexpected overture to the main drama at Downhill – the windswept landscape of grand monuments and giant views.

Location 42 Mussenden Road, Castle Rock, Coleraine BT51 4RP, County Londonderry, Northern Ireland 5m NW of Coleraine on A2 **Tel** and **Fax** (028) 7084 8728 **Email** downhillcastle@ntrust.org.uk **Owner** The National Trust **Open** daily dawn–dusk (Mussenden Temple open Apr, May, Jun and Sept, Sat, Sun and Bank Hol Mon 12–6; Jul and Aug, daily 12–6) **Area** 147 acres/59 hectares

DUNLOE CASTLE GARDENS

CHOICE TREES AND SHRUBS BEAUTIFULLY DISPLAYED IN THE SETTING OF A 13TH-CENTURY CASTLE

The original castle at Dunloe, a fortress guarding the river Laune, was built by the Fitzgeralds in 1215, later passed to the O'Sullivan family and was largely destroyed in the late 16th century. In the 20th century an American, Howard Harrington, came to live in a house near the castle ruins and in the 1920s started a collection of exotic trees. These have been preserved and added to by the current owners who have established a large five-star hotel in the grounds. It is rare that a hotel has a plant collection of such distinction in a setting that is so beautiful – over the river to the south there are views of the Gap of Dunloe and the mountains of Macgillycuddy's Reeks.

The garden is essentially a collection of trees although it does have its moments of attractive design. The Gothic tower of the old castle, for example, is drawn into the garden as

little is known although there are tantalising signs of 18th-century landscaping for the earlier house, and the ruins of a fine gazebo of around 1770 survive in the wood – a triumphant arch crowned by a domed octagonal tower. A large lake, now hidden in dense woodland north-east of the house, also has an 18th-century air. There is a local rumour, but no documentary evidence, that Capability Brown worked here, not visiting the site himself but sending designs from England. Apart from these features most of the existing gardens seem to date from the 19th and 20th centuries.

AVENUES AND RIDES

The first and most striking piece of planting is the avenue of Wellingtonias planted by the 3rd Earl of Portarlington in the 1860s, which runs up to the entrance façade of the house and used, in a great dog-leg, to lead all the way to the Dublin road. To the north and east of the house terraced lawns are planted with rows of Irish yews and ornamented with statues on plinths rising from beds of annuals. The garden becomes more informal as it extends away from the house. A long walk of old beeches leads down to the lake, now rather silted up and with too low a water level but still full of character and with packed woodland of beeches, oaks and limes crowding in. A path skirting the lake has the occasional big old yew on either side and there are patches of ornamental planting – a beautiful *Cornus kousa*, a *Crinodendron hookerianum*, a battered but fine *Cryptomeria japonica* and many rhododendrons.

Aligned with the east front of the house a long ride through woodland is planted with excellent exotics and several exceptional specimens of native trees: very large beeches, a very old sweet chestnut, a fine deodar, a superb common walnut and a Bhutan pine. One of the most remarkable trees here is a perfect old *Acer cappadocicum* whose spreading limbs are dappled with thick moss and with lichen as pale as whitewash. In this setting a perfunctory bed of rugosa roses jokily labelled Route Rugosa strikes a false and feeble note. Apart from this, the walk to the end of this distinguished procession of noble trees is a

an eyecatcher by an enticing walk of decorative trees and shrubs leading up to it. The path is lined with camellias, *Elaeagnus* 'Quicksilver', eucalyptus, *Rhododendron* 'Fragrantissimum' (the climate is very mild here) and golden yews. At the opening of the path is a rarely seen evergreen tree from Japan, *Castanopsis cuspidata*. A few older trees also survive, such as a pair of 17th-century yews of tremendous character – they are male and female, christened Adam and Eve, and plainly planted as a decorative pair. But the tree collection is the main attraction. Some are of specifically Irish interest such as the beautiful example of an unusual hornbeam, *Carpinus henryana*, from western China, discovered by the great Irish plant collector Augustine Henry. The very mild microclimate allows the cultivation of such tender trees as the lovely *Cupressus cashmeriana* and the South American *Lomatia ferruginea* with fern-like evergreen foliage. (W.J. Bean describes the latter as "one of the handsomest trees that have come from S. America.") Another outstanding evergreen is the Chinese swamp cypress (*Glyptostrobus pensilis*) whose falling leaves turn a glowing red. Many good

Old Dunloe Castle

hotels have well-kept gardens but few have such an enticing collection of plants set in scenery so lovely.

Location Dunloe, County Kerry, Republic of Ireland 8km NW of Killarney by R582 **Tel** (00353) (0)64 44111 **Fax** (0)64 44583 **Owner** Hotel Dunloe Castle **Open** May to Sept, daily dawn–dusk **Area** 3 acres/1.2 hectares

EMO COURT GARDEN

AN 18TH-CENTURY HOUSE WITH A LAKE, FORMAL VICTORIAN GARDENS, WOODLAND WALKS AND A FINE DISPLAY OF RARE TREES

The grand domed neo-classical house was built for John Dawson, 1st Earl of Portarlington, starting in 1790 and replacing an earlier house on a different site. In 1930 the estate was sold to the Society of Jesus which sold it in 1969 to C.D. Cholmley-Harrison who restored the house and filled it with fine furniture. It was acquired in 1994 by Dúchas, the Heritage Service.

Of the early garden history at Emo Court

constant pleasure, with many zigzagging detours into the hinterland to scrutinise some more distant enticement – on one occasion a huge Himalayan spruce (*Picea smithiana*). The walk back towards the house, just visible between walls of trees, shows how effective grand planting on this scale is as a suitable setting for a very grand house.

Statuary at Emo Court

Location Emo, County Laois, Republic of Ireland 20km SW of Kildare by N7 **Tel** (00353) (0)502 26573/21459 **Fax** (0)502 26573 **Owner** Dúchas, The Heritage Service **Open** daily 10.30–5.30 **Area** 80 acres/32 hectares

FLORENCE COURT

AN 18TH-CENTURY LANDSCAPE FOR A GREAT HOUSE, WITH 19TH-CENTURY PLEASURE GROUNDS AND A RUSTIC SUMMERHOUSE

The house was built from the mid to the late 18th century for John Cole MP (later 1st Lord Mountflorence) and for his son William (1st Earl of Enniskillen). It has a beautiful position on rising land and is itself the most prominent feature of the landscape – in the words of Mark Bence-Jones "the whole long, grey-gold front has a dream-like Baroque beauty". There had been a simple house here in the earlier 18th century, demolished to make way for the grand new house, set in newly made formal gardens. The Revd William Henry saw it in 1739 and recorded that Sir John Cole twenty years previously had "cut out noble Vistos, laid out gravell Walks, cut down most of ye Woods…and in their stead made regular plantations". In the late 18th century William King worked on a landscape park here, enclosing the whole park with belts of trees threaded with a drive, and dividing the interior parkland with three long belts of trees. The pleasure grounds were laid out by James Fraser (or Frazer) on the slopes beyond the house in the 1840s and have a strong 19th-century character with a beautiful fern-

leafed beech (*Fagus sylvatica* var. *heterophylla* 'Aspleniifolia'), magnolias, monkey puzzles and giant tree rhododendrons.

A charming rustic summerhouse here, with thatched roof and walls patterned with twigs, was restored in 1993; made before 1860, it is shown in a photograph of that date, occupied by a bearded, bowler-hatted gentleman and four ladies of the household. If you sit in one of the pretty rustic chairs today, you may be puzzled by the soft mechanical groaning of a waterwheel powering a sawmill hidden behind trees.

THE ORIGINAL IRISH YEW

At the foot of the slope old meadow land is dazzling in spring and early summer with wild flowers, especially orchids. Beyond it are woodland walks, one of which will take you to a remarkable tree – the original Irish yew (*Taxus baccata* 'Fastigiata'), a chance seedling, one of two discovered in the 19th century by George Willis, a tenant

farmer on the Florence Court estate. He planted one in his own garden, which died in 1865, and gave the other to his landlord. All Irish yews are descended from this single plant, which is female; thus all true Irish yews, whose identity will persist only when propagated by cuttings, are female.

The 18th-century walled kitchen garden at some distance on the far side of the house is a curiosity, more a garden with walls than a walled garden for it is not fully enclosed and some of the walls are freestanding. It has now been turned over to ornamental purposes. One wall is crowned with a pediment and festooned with roses. A very long pergola is covered in clematis, roses and wisteria and underplanted with astrantias, bergenias, hellebores and hostas. A rose garden of Victorian flavour has shaped beds and climbing roses trained on an arbour and on rope swags. Nearby is a grove of flowering cherries.

Location Enniskillen BT92 1DB, County Fermanagh, Northern Ireland 8m SW of Enniskillen by A4 and A32 **Tel** (028) 6634 8249 **Fax** (028) 6634 8873 **Email** florencecourt@ntrust.org.uk **Owner** The National Trust **Open** May to Sept, daily 10–8; Oct to Apr, daily 10–4 **Area** 21 acres/8 hectares

Victorian summerhouse at Florence Court

FOTA ARBORETUM

MAGNIFICENT TREES AND SHRUBS, A 19TH-
CENTURY FERNERY AND A GRAND WALLED
GARDEN NOW UNDER RESTORATION

The estate of Fota Island formed part of the lands granted to Phillip de Barri by Henry II in the late 12th century. The position of the demesne is unusual, and unusually beautiful, occupying an island in the estuary of the river Lee which opens out into the harbour of Cobh. Although it is now linked to the mainland by a causeway it still retains a remote atmosphere. The house at Fota was built first as a hunting box in the early 18th century by the Hon. John Smith-Barry and immensely extended in around 1820 to the designs of Richard Morrison, acquiring a refined Regency character. The chief maker of the garden was James Hugh Smith-Barry who in the first part of the 19th century built formal gardens about the house. The remains of these gardens can be seen: plain, unadorned terraces to the east and south of the house originally had an elaborately patterned parterre of shaped beds. He added large numbers of distinguished plants and also built a Gothic sham castle, designed by the Cork architect John Hargrave, with castellated round towers overlooking the estuary.

After various changes of ownership in the late 20th century the demesne is now in the care of Duchás, the Heritage Service. Much restoration work has been done in recent years and a grand walled garden to the east, the former kitchen garden, had been cleared and was under restoration in 2002. Here venerable thickets of cabbage palm (*Cordyline australis*) have hanging bunches of flowers which perfume the whole garden in high summer, and against a wall is a pretty domed alcove which must date from the early 19th century. A broad gravel walk leads to a handsome vaulted orangery with fine stone urns on the parapet and a collection of oranges and lemons inside. It is flanked by a pair of date palms (*Phoenix dactylifera*) – evidence of how mild the microclimate is here.

A long walk ending in a monumental stone bench links a garden door on the south side of the house to James Smith-Barry's arboretum. That is the most direct route but it is far better to zigzag across impeccable lawns and marvel at the magnificent trees that stand all about. These will range from splendid examples of common trees, like the Durmast oak (*Quercus petraea*) close to the house, to outstanding

The fernery at Fota

examples of less common ones like the Crimean pine (*Pinus nigra* var. *caramanica*) a little further away. Some of the plants at Fota, while perfectly hardy in many parts of southern England, will never attain the size and distinction that they do here. A *Drimys winteri*, for example, here forms a magnificent upright cascade of gleaming foliage. The beautiful evergreen *Hoheria populnea*, with its lavish clusters of white flowers, at Fota assumes the dimensions of a stately tree.

A fernery, in the shade of an old sweet chestnut, dates from the mid 19th century. Its mossy rocks and colonies of mother-of-

A fern-leafed beech at Fota

thousands (*Saxifraga stolonifera*) form a jungly background to a remarkable collection of old tree ferns (*Dicksonia antarctica*). An irregular lake, dappled with waterlilies and fringed with arum lilies and reeds, also has notable trees. Some of these are 19th-century conifers, including some very big Wellingtonias, but others are good examples of less familiar trees. A notable group of *Cornus controversa* is a rarity. Its variegated form was one of the most fashionable trees of the late 20th century but the plainer, and more distinguished, type is seldom seen – at Fota it flowers prodigiously.

Although now in institutional ownership, and an immensely popular place to push prams and take the air, Fota retains the character of a private estate. The magnificent old trees are well cared for and, just as important, much new planting has been done to provide replacements for the future.

Location Fota Island, Carricktwohill, County Cork, Republic of Ireland 15km E of Cork by N25 and R624 **Tel** (00353) (0)21 481 2728 **Website** www.zenith.ie/fota **Owner** Dúchas, The Heritage Service **Open** daily 10–6 **Area** 32 acres/13 hectares

GLENVEAGH CASTLE

AT THE HEART OF A NATIONAL PARK A DRAMATIC 19TH-CENTURY CASTLE WITH EXQUISITE FLOWER GARDENS ON THE BANKS OF A LOUGH

Glenveagh Castle is at the heart of the Glenveagh National Park which consists of 39,881 acres/16,548 hectares of wild, remote and beautiful country. The castle was built between 1870 and 1873 by John Adair who married an American heiress and accumulated an estate of 24,700 acres/10,000 hectares. The granite castle with its keep, turrets and castellations was designed by Adair's cousin, John Townsend Trench. The estate had further American connections, being bought in 1929 after Mrs Adair's death by Professor Kingsley Porter and in 1937 by Henry McIlhenny of the Tabasco Sauce family, who restored the castle and made the gardens. He gave castle, its contents and gardens to the Irish state in 1974.

The site of the castle is very beautiful –

Gothic glasshouse at Glenveagh

facing north-west on a promontory jutting out into Lough Veagh. In Mrs Adair's time the grounds to the east of the castle running down to the banks of the lough were developed as pleasure grounds, and much tree planting established precious windbreaks. Under Henry McIlhenny's ownership there was an immense amount of new planting and planning of new features. In the planting he had the advice of James Russell, the great connoisseur of trees and shrubs, who was responsible for, among much else, the addition of the fine large-leafed species rhododendrons like *R. falconeri* and *R. sinogrande* and the sweetly scented late-flowering *R. maddenii* to the pleasure grounds. This area of the garden, with a long lawn surrounded by dense planting, forms today an outstanding collection of the kinds of trees and shrubs which flourish best in acid soil in a very wet but mild climate – acers, camellias, eucryphias, nothofagus, podocarpus and stewartias. Some plants survive from Mrs Adair's original plantings, including a very large *Griselinia littoralis*, and a canopy of old native trees – silver birch, holly, Scots pine and Durmast oak (*Quercus petraea*) gives much protection to the exotics. Forming the southern boundary of the pleasure grounds the Belgian Walk, named after convalescent Belgian soldiers who stayed here in World War I, is dazzling with flowering shrubs.

Immediately behind the castle, on ground that slopes down towards it, is a walled kitchen garden which has been given an ornamental character. Box hedges divide the compartments, rising in domes at the corners, and flowery borders run across the middle with catmint, dahlias, *Eryngium alpinum*, repeated clumps of *Geranium psilostemon* and loosestrife. Against the castle wall are a long lean-to glasshouse and a high, airy Gothic orangery designed by the artist Philippe Jullian and built in 1958. Throughout the kitchen garden are lead statues, urns and decorative cast-iron benches, which provide a lighthearted atmosphere below the stern castle walls. The little Italian Garden concealed in woods beside the castle is also rich in ornament. Guarded by sphinxes, it is enclosed in hedges of griselinia, above which rise stone statues. Walks up the steep slopes above the castle give astonishing views of the lough and the barren rocky slopes that rise above it.

Location Churchill, Letterkenny, County Donegal, Republic of Ireland 16km NW of Letterkenny by N56 and R255 **Tel** (00353) (0)74 37088 **Infoline** (0)74 37090 **Fax** (0)74 37072 **Owner** Dúchas, The Heritage Service **Open** mid Mar to early Nov, daily 10–6.30 **Area** 28 acres/11 hectares

GLIN CASTLE

PRETTY ORNAMENTAL KITCHEN GARDENS
ADORN A DELIGHTFUL 18TH-CENTURY
GOTHIC CASTLE OVERLOOKING THE
SHANNON RIVER

The castle was built in the 1790s by Colonel John Fitzgerald, 24th Knight of Glin, to replace a 17th-century house on the same site. The Fitzgeralds have lived in these parts since the middle ages and the foundations of the ancient castle remain, beyond the boundary of the present demesne. In the 1820s and 1830s the present house was embellished with a castellated parapet and some turrets, justifying the change of name from Glin House to Glin Castle. This delightful house, a charming ornament rather than an architectural masterpiece, looks north across the broad waters of the Shannon.

At the same time as the house was being given its castle air – in a style which the present owner (the 29th Knight of Glin) describes as "cardboard embattled" – buildings of similar character were being added to the demesne. Two lodges with castellations and Gothic windows survive and, best of all, a lonely bathing pavilion close to the Shannon with two round towers – a dashing landscape ornament. A distinctive eyecatcher, Hamilton's Tower, also close to the river, consists of a square tower and a screen built of rough stone. Nothing is known about any landscaping at Glin but these buildings animate the scene in precisely the way an 18th-century landscaper would have done. Another building in the same tradition, in the woods

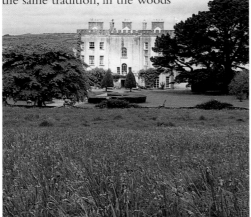

The south front of Glin Castle

Lutyen's oval garden at Heywood

behind the house, is a rough stone hermitage with three Gothic arched openings.

Within the well-wooded demesne close to the house are the pleasure grounds and walled kitchen garden. On a lawn south of the house a noble Monterey pine (*Pinus radiata*) stands, and two large bays clipped into cones open an axial walk leading away from the house between crescents of yew hedging to a billowing *Parrotia persica* at the centre of a long wall with a swooping parapet. Above it an apron of grass, rich in spring with daffodils and bluebells, runs up to woodland.

The 2½ acre/1 hectare kitchen garden slopes at a curious angle and is enclosed in 15ft/4.5m stone walls. Revived in recent years, it now produces an immense range of vegetables and herbs; flowers are also grown for cutting and many fruit trees are espaliered against the walls. The garden is ornamented with an avenue of yews clipped into pyramids, a decorative chicken house with Gothic tracery windows and battlements, a rustic Gothic arbour seat (made in the 1980s) and a curved bench in an exedra of clipped yew. The kitchen garden is a decorative adjunct to the house which also functions as a sublimely elegant bed and breakfast establishment. The interiors, with marvellous furniture, pictures and ornaments, are among the most delightful in Ireland. There are no horticultural fireworks at Glin; its charm comes from the harmony of ingredients – buildings, landscape and gardens intimately interconnected.

Location Glin, County Limerick, Republic of Ireland W of Glin village, 50km W of Limerick by N69 **Tel** (00353) (0)68 34173 **Fax** (0)68 34364 **Email** knight@iol.ie **Owner** The Knight of Glin **Open** by appointment **Area** 5 acres/2 hectares

HEYWOOD

A MASTERPIECE BY SIR EDWIN LUTYENS – A
GIANT OVAL WALLED GARDEN, TERRACES
AND HEDGED FLOWER GARDENS

The house at Heywood was built in 1773 for Michael Trench to his own designs, probably with the help of James Gandon. It i named – surely a unique act of matrimonial piety – after Trench's mother-in-law whose maiden name was Heywood. A lithograph of 1818 shows an 18th-century landscape garde embowered in woods running down to a lak picturesque ornament from this time still enriches the scene: on the drive a Gothic sham castle with castellated round towers stands alongside a sham ruin with splendid tracery windows, but only the ruins of a bridge over the lake survive, and a Temple of the Winds has been demolished.

In the early 20th century the estate passed to Lieutenant Colonel William Hutcheson Poë who, in 1906, commissioned a complete new garden close to the house, designed by Sir Edwin Lutyens with planting by Gertrud Jekyll. This beautiful and ingenious garden survives almost entirely intact, although the planting is sketchy and scarcely very

Jekyllesque. Immediately below the site of the 18th-century house – gutted by fire and later demolished – is a deep terrace, with stone columns finely carved with swags. Below a second, lower terrace, the ground drops away with idyllic views over parkland. At the west end of these terraces Lutyens built a pergola on two levels which both closes off the formal gardens on this side and gives delicious views to the north and west.

At the other end of the upper terrace a broad paved lime walk, backed by a wall ornamented with niches each bearing a bust, leads to one of Lutyens's most dazzling pieces of magic. His Italian Garden is a huge oval walled space with concentric oval terraces descending to an oval pool in the middle of which stands a monumental stone basin supported by a giant plinth. About its edge are hemispheres of stone on which crouch bronze turtles. The whole is overlooked by a steep-roofed pavilion built into the enclosing walls, with a high arched opening and a panel inscribed with lines from Alexander Pope's *Epistle to Lord Burlington* with its injunction, "In all – let nature never be forgot". Lutyens followed this to the letter, for the walls that encircle the top terrace are pierced with oval windows which give glimpses of the rural landscape beyond.

MIXED PLANTINGS

Each terrace has borders along the flagstoned paths: a ring of pink roses on the uppermost terrace and mixed plantings of blocks of bergenias, catmint, hostas, kniphofias or sage on the others. The garden would be improved if this planting were more generous and if the interior walls were also clothed in plants – as indeed they were when the garden was photographed for a *Country Life* article that appeared in 1941.

From the top terrace a beautifully fashioned curving flight of steps penetrates the wall to an upper level where there is a maze of yew-edged enclosures with paved paths and herbaceous borders. From this upper vantage point a grand view opens out, over the oval garden and far into the countryside beyond its walls. The garden at Heywood shows Lutyens at his most irrepressible, deftly making the best of the site at every turn.

Location Ballinakill, County Laois, Republic of Ireland On the edge of Ballinakill village, 8km SE of Abbeyleix **Tel** (00353) (0)502 33563 **Owner** Dúchas, The Heritage Service **Open** daily dawn–dusk **Area** 45 acres/18 hectares

ILNACULLIN

A DREAMLIKE ISLAND GARDEN DESIGNED BY HAROLD PETO AND PLANTED WITH RARE EXOTICS

Making a garden in a place where none had ever existed is a rare challenge. Ilnacullin, "the isle of holly", is an ancient place but the earliest known building is a Martello Tower built in 1805 on the highest point of the island to protect Ireland against possible attack by Napoleon. The island was bought in 1910 by a Belfast-born East India Merchant, John Annan Bryce, who had long enjoyed holidaying in these parts. Between 1911 and 1914 a hundred men worked to make a garden, blasting rock, importing soil from the mainland and planting trees for windbreaks. Bryce commissioned garden buildings from Harold Peto who designed two Italianate buildings close to the western coast of the island: the Casita overlooking a sunken garden with a rectangular pool and, on its far side, an elegant arcaded open pavilion leading to a balustraded viewing platform looking towards the mainland and, in particular, the pointed peaks of the Caha Mountains. The island scenery was gently animated by other architectural features: a dramatic flight of stone steps runs up a slope to an open-columned Greek Temple (also with views to the mainland) and similar steps were made to the Martello Tower dominating the centre of the island. Peto also laid out a large walled garden with a pedimented entrance and a clock tower.

The planting, in contrast to the formality of the architecture, is wild and naturalistic. The very high rainfall – more than 70in/1,800mm per annum is usual – and a site strongly influenced by the Gulf Stream Drift allow the cultivation of a very wide range of plants

The Casita at Ilnacullin

unfamiliar to gardeners from dryer, cooler parts. Rarities from the southern hemisphere are well represented. Here are *Acacia pravissima* from Australia, one of several wattles in the garden; the Kauri pine (*Agathis australis*) from New Zealand, one of many tender conifers; the beautiful tree fern *Cyathea dealbata*, also from New Zealand; *Taiwania cryptomerioides* from south-west China; and many other rare, curious or beautiful trees and shrubs. There is also a very large collection of rhododendrons, the species being particularly well represented. The walled garden has a pair of long borders, the closest that Ilnacullin gets to conventional gardening, and the walls themselves are, naturally, festooned with countless plants.

The charm of Peto's buildings, the heady range of exotic plants and the beauty of the natural scenery make Ilnacullin an exceptional place. Even getting there is special – slipping across the water in a small boat, passing on the way a miniature island on which seals sleepily sprawl as the charms of Ilnacullin come gradually into focus, makes this one of the most memorable journeys to any garden.

Location Garinish Island, Glengarriff, County Cork, Republic of Ireland On an island in Bantry Bay; boats from Glegarriff **Tel** (00353) (0)27 63040 **Fax** (0)27 63149 **Owner** Dúchas, The Heritage Service **Open** Mar and Oct, daily 10–4.30 (Sun 1–5); Apr to May, Sept, daily 10–6.30 (Sun 1–7); Jul to Aug, daily 9.30–6.30 (Sun 11–7) **Area** 37 acres/15 hectares

THE IRISH NATIONAL STUD

A LIVELY JAPANESE GARDEN ALONGSIDE AN OUTSTANDING MODERN GARDEN CELEBRATING THE LIFE OF ST FIACHRA

This is one of the most curious, and beguiling, combinations of different ingredients that I know. Apart from the gardens, the stud itself is one of the world's centres of racehorse breeding and the beautiful horses may be seen grazing in their paddocks or being led from the stables to exercise. Tully also houses the Irish Horse Museum.

The estate of Tully House was bought in

St Fiachra's Garden at the Irish National Stud

The Japanese Garden at the Irish National Stud

1900 by Colonel William Hall-Walker (later 1st and only Lord Wavertree) who founded the stud which in 1915 became the British National Stud. Colonel Hall-Walker was a keen gardener and in 1906 he commissioned a Japanese gardener, Tassa Eida, to make a Japanese garden at Tully. The work took four years and quantities of plants and ornaments were shipped from Japan. Although many of the ingredients are authentic and the effect is delightful, the garden's symbolism is, apparently, unknown in gardens in Japan. Like Pilgrim's Progress it traces an individual's journey from the gate of oblivion to the gateway of eternity, with all sorts of indecisions, torments and temptations at every turn. It has the usual attractive accompaniments of western Japanese gardens – a pool and stream, rocky outcrops, a teahouse, an arched bridge painted scarlet, snow lanterns, flowering cherries and clipped evergreens. All this is attractive but perhaps the most memorable thing is the collection of magnificent bonsai distributed about a flawless lawn close to the bridge. After Eida's time further elements of Japanese inspiration were added: the Garden of Eternity, a dry landscape of rocks and gravel with a splendid *Cercidiphyllum japonicum* at the centre, and a Zen meditation garden.

ST FIACHRA'S GARDEN

An entirely new garden, St Fiachra's garden, was made to celebrate the millennium and completed in 1999 to the designs of Professor Martin Hallinan. St Fiachra was an Irish monk of the 7th century who later lived in France and became the patron saint of gardening. The garden is one of water, woods and rocks. At its heart are two domed monks' cells, beautifully

fashioned of stone, in ground shaped into mysterious mounds and undulations where huge shapes of stone rise up to embrace a path. A very narrow passage leads to an interior with a glowing Waterford crystal "garden" of glass plants and rocks let into the floor and illuminated by fibre optics – a memorable effect. Outside, on an outcrop of rock jutting out into the waters of a lake, is a bronze figure of St Fiachra contemplating a seed clasped in his hand. Water-worn slabs of stone emerge from the lake and paths wind about the banks in the shade of alders and ashes. A second lake, at a lower level, is joined to the first by a spectacular broad but shallow waterfall. In the waters below are 5,000-year-old bog oaks, blackened and preserved by the acidic water, whose jagged shapes rise dramatically from the water. The place has potent character, with drama, mystery and beauty evoked by the simplest of means.

Location Tully, Kildare, County Kildare, Republic of Ireland On the SE side of Kildare town, signed from the centre, 50km W of Dublin by N7 and M7 **Tel** (00353) (0)45 521 617 **Fax** (0)45 522 964 **Email** japanesegardens@eircom.net **Website** www.irish-national-stud.ie **Owner** Irish National Stud **Open** mid Feb to mid Nov, daily 9.30–6 **Area** 5½ acres/2 hectares

JOHNSTOWN CASTLE GARDENS

A GRAND 19TH-CENTURY PERIOD PIECE – A GOTHIC EXTRAVAGANZA OF A HOUSE, WITH A LAKE AND PLANTING TO SUIT

The castle was built in around 1840 for Hamilton Knox Grogan-Morgan to the designs of Daniel Robertson who also laid out the garden. There had been a medieval castle here called Rathlannon, belonging to the Esmonde family, of which the ruined keep, picturesquely shrouded in ivy, survives as an eyecatcher. The new castle, swarming with machicolated towers, stands close to a lake laid out by Robertson, bulging out in two bays on either side of an isthmus where it had been planned to build a bridge. Samuel and Anna Maria Hall's *Ireland: Its Scenery and Character* (1841–43) describes "the noble sheet of artificial water…procured at immense cost"

THE JOHN F. KENNEDY ARBORETUM

A WONDERFUL COLLECTION OF TREES
AND SHRUBS, FINELY LAID OUT IN A
BEAUTIFUL NATURAL LANDSCAPE

The estate whose land forms the heart of the Kennedy Arboretum was called Ballysop. The house was remodelled in 1837 by the Revd W. Gifford and it was probably he who, much later, planted the two monkey puzzles which stand close to the Visitor Centre – the only 19th-century survivals from the old estate. The arboretum, funded from Irish/American sources, was conceived as a joint memorial to President Kennedy and was opened in 1968. Kennedy's ancestors came from Dunganstown 6km away.

It is a magnificent site for a tree collection on high, airy, undulating land. At its highest point of Slievecoilta (889ft/271m) there are stupendous views looking over the arboretum and beyond it to give a *tour d'horizon* of six counties. The collection is enormous, with well over 4,500 species and cultivars of trees and shrubs. They are disposed most ingeniously in two essentially different ways. Spreading out south of the Visitor Centre, on ground that runs down to a stream and lake, groups and belts of trees are deployed in areas of grass, rather in the manner of a landscape park, or strung out along paths. The plants are

and "several turrets of carved stone" on the banks of the lake which is enclosed in bastion-like walls. These still survive; one is a fishing lodge in the form of a castellated tower which emerges from the water of the lake. The Halls noted that throughout the estate "the hand of taste is everywhere apparent."

19th-century photographs show an elaborate formal garden west of the castle, with a Gothic pavilion overlooking a vast parterre, but none of this survives. The planting that visitors see today is all of a piece with the character of the castle; the occasional large rhododendron flaunts its flowers but this is essentially a landscape in which flowers play little part. Bold trees and shrubs, mostly evergreen, including many conifers but also a very fine old holm oak (*Quercus ilex*) and the much less common Californian live oak (*Q. agrifolia*). The lake is the heart of the garden, its sparkling water enlivening the sombre shade of great cedars, cypresses, monkey puzzles, cultivars of Lawson cypresses (including some pretty bilious "gold" forms) and pines. On the far side of the lake from the castle is a formal cascade where a stream flows into the lake, and beyond it, deep in the woods, is the medieval tower of Rathlannon Castle.

The whole ensemble, gigantic Gothic revival castle rising above the dark waters of its lake, and large trees with much of the lugubrious character so congenial to 19th-

The lake at Johnstown Castle

century taste, is one of the best Victorian demesnes surviving in Ireland. It is well cared for by TEAGASC, the Food and Agriculture Authority, which has installed in the castle's outhouses the Irish Agricultural Museum, with excellent exhibits of rural life and crafts, and vernacular furniture.

Location Murrintown, County Wexford, Republic of Ireland 5km S of Wexford by N25 **Tel** (00353) (0)53 42888 **Fax** (0)53 42004 **Owner** TEAGASC, The Food and Agriculture Authority **Open** daily 9–5.30 (closed 25 Dec) **Area** 50 acres/20 hectares

A maple grove at the John F. Kennedy Arboretum

grouped by genus regardless of origin and give the gardener a splendid opportunity to see large numbers of the kinds of woody plants he or she might consider planting – birches, buddleias, chestnuts, dogwoods, escallonias, hollies, magnolias, pines, spiraeas and so on – and on. Behind the Visitor Centre the plants are grouped by regional origin: a grid of plots covers Asia, Australia, Europe, New Zealand, North America and South America. These, of more specialist interest, are nonetheless fascinating, providing a chance to see a full range of the characteristic shrubs and trees of every part of the temperate world.

These are the parts of the arboretum which visitors may enjoy, but much else goes on here. Arboricultural research is conducted on such matters as propagation, the pharmaceutical use of plants and on the insect population of trees; and the Phenological Garden is part of a European cooperative venture in which an identical range of species is studied in each place to record the effect of different climates on tree behaviour.

Location New Ross, County Wexford, Republic of Ireland 12km S of New Ross by R733 **Tel** (00353) (0)51 388 8171 **Fax** (0)51 388 8172 **Owner** Dúchas, The Heritage Service **Open** Apr and Sept, daily 10–6.30; May to Aug, daily 10–8; Oct to Mar, daily 10–5 (closed Good Fri and Christmas Day) **Area** 622 acres/252 hectares

KILFANE GLEN

AN ENCHANTING PICTURESQUE
18TH-CENTURY WOODLAND GARDEN WITH
CASCADE AND COTTAGE ORNÉ, AND MODERN
FORMAL GARDENS WITH SCULPTURES

In 1819 Louisa Beaufort wrote to Sophy Edgeworth, "Mr B, Pa, Ma and I in the inside jaunting car and Richard on horseback all went to Kilfayne, Mr Power's, a very pretty place." In the 1790s Sir John Power had made a picturesque garden in a natural ravine in the demesne of Kilfane. In woodland of beech, larch, pine and sweet chestnut Power had built a cottage *orné* beside a rushing stream

The cottage *orné* at Kilfane

and, opposite it, a spectacular cascade erupting from the cliffside and tumbling into a pool far below.

Susan and Nicholas Mosse knew nothing of this garden when they came to live here; even the ravine was obscured by brambles and fallen trees. Only when they saw some drawings done in 1804 by G.B. Miller from the Dublin Royal Society of Antiquaries did they discover what sort of garden had been here. They managed to locate the site of the cottage, whose foundations survived, and rebuilt it. It stands at the bottom of the valley on a grassy clearing at the edge of the stream where dippers flit. In spring, before the trees canopy is is fully formed, you see it from afar, a most enticing and unexpected prospect as you wind down the precipitous path through the woods. A thickly thatched roof overhangs the walls and a verandah with a floor inlaid with pebbles is supported with rustic columns and furnished with charming rustic furniture.

◁ **The stricken warrior** at Killruddery

From the ground–floor room, now used as a tea room for visitors, there are views through lattice windows to the restored cascade – the view that A. Atkinson, recorded on a visit to "this seat of rural felicity" in 1814: "among the beautiful appendages of the Cottage…[is] that of a Cataract which descends into the valley…in full view of the spectator in the Drawing Room." The ceiling of the upstairs bedroom is painted with a *trompe l'oeil* view of an azure sky fringed with garlands of foliage and flowers and rustic trimmings. Atkinson also described a grotto close to the cataract which "affords from the heat of a vertical sun, a cool and curious asylum"; this, too, the Mosses are restoring. Much clearing of cherry laurel (*Prunus laurocerasus*) and *Rhododendron ponticum* which choked the woodland has allowed anemones, ferns, narcissi and wood anemones to flourish. The Kilfane glen is a perfect piece of historically accurate garden restoration, which gives the visitor the totally convincing and delightful feeling of straying into the picturesque past.

The drama and excitement of the glen should not obscure the Mosses' admirable achievement in making new formal gardens for their house above the glen. Here are a rectangular waterlily pool, a pergola of clematis and roses, a garden of grasses, a pale garden of white flowers and silver or variegated foliage, a formal orchard with circles of crab-apples, and a fernery ending in a mysterious distorting mirror. Here and in the adjacent woodland are several works of art by such artists as William Pye, James Turrell, Bill Woodrow and others. In this upper garden there is, too, a recent restoration of a vista focused on the peak of Slievenamon. So homage is paid to the past but the present is also alive and kicking,

Location nr Thomastown, County Kilkenny, Republic of Ireland 6km N of Thomastown signed on the N9
Tel (00535) (0)56 24558   **Owner** Susan and Nicholas Mosse   **Open** Apr to Sept, Sun 2–6; Jul and Aug, daily 11–6   **Area** 10 acres/4 hectares

KILLRUDDERY

A 17TH-CENTURY ESTATE WITH A RARE EARLY 18TH-CENTURY FORMAL GARDEN AND PRETTY VICTORIAN GARDENS

The Killruddery estate was acquired in 1618 by Sir William Brabazon, later 1st Earl of Meath. The house we see today was built for the 10th Earl to the designs of Richard Morrison in around 1820 in dashing neo-Elizabethan style but incorporating parts that date from the 17th century. In the 1680s, at the time of the 4th Earl, a Frenchman named Bonet laid out a remarkable formal garden which was completed by the early 18th century. A rather naive painting of the Killruddery Hunt with erratic perspective, made in around 1730, shows the garden much as it is today.

Behind the house two parallel canals with a single water jet at the end point towards an avenue which sweeps away up a hill. To one side is a symmetrical pattern of walks hedged in beech, hornbeam and lime and ornamented with statues at meeting points, known as "the Angles" and remarkably similar to the *bosquets* of French 17th-century gardens. Close by is a circular pool with a jet and the remains of formal cascades. On the far side of the canals the Wilderness has the sketchy remains of straight rides through the woodland and a few statues, among them a stricken warrior and a Venus standing high on a plinth.

Closer to the house a pretty *théâtre de verdure* with turf seats is enclosed in hedges of bay. Nearby, a circular space, enclosed with vast beech hedges and lined with a low box hedge, encompasses a huge circular pool with tritons spouting water and a central fountain of birds among reeds. This, now being restored, originally had two concentric circles of beech separated by a walk from which one could see the pool and fountain through windows cut into the inner hedge. A similar but rectangular enclosure has a statue of frolicking putti, and a magnificent conservatory, vaulted and spectacularly domed, built in about 1850, houses a collection of statues. Below the conservatory a Victorian parterre has a four-part arrangement of box-hedged beds filled with bedding roses and lavender, decorated with a central scalloped pool. An ornamental octagonal dairy, with a pretty interior, has stained glass windows with Gothic tracery and a trellis verandah swathed in clematis.

In 1843 the gardens were restored by Daniel Robertson and it is possible that the handsome turf terraces that flank the drive and spread out to one side of the house date from this time. Killruddery successfully ermingles features of different periods with ccess, but the most memorable part of the rden is the bold axis of the two canals nked with their intriguing hedges and rides. his is the only extensive formal garden of its pe and period surviving in Ireland.

cation Bray, County Wicklow, Republic of Ireland km SE of Dublin by N11/M11 **Tel** and **Fax** (00353) 1 286 2777 **Website** www.killruddery.com **Owner** e Earl and Countess of Meath **Open** Apr to Sept, ly 1–5 **Area** 41 acres/17 hectares

KYLEMORE ABBEY

A GREAT WALLED KITCHEN GARDEN, NOW SPLENDIDLY RESTORED, IN A SETTING OF DAZZLING BEAUTY AMONG THE CONNEMARA MOUNTAINS

Kylemore Castle was built from 1864 for a Manchester merchant, Mitchell Henry P, to the designs of James Franklin Fuller – a ldly romantic confection deploying the full cabulary of the Gothic decorated style in

which every parapet has its battlements and no tower is left unmachicolated. Its position on the northern bank of Lough Pollacappul surrounded by the Connemara mountains is wonderfully romantic in itself, and Henry built a causeway across the lough to give visitors a marvellous distant prospect of his house.

Henry was a devoted gardener and he set out to make a garden where no-one had gardened before, draining bogs and clothing the desolate violently windswept hills with many thousands of trees. At some distance from the house, linked by a pinetum, he built a great walled garden on a sloping and irregular site. It was used both as a kitchen garden and as an ornamental garden. Its most spectacular feature was a range of glasshouses on the grandest possible scale – 18 of them, used to cultivate bananas, figs, grapes, melons and much else. Henry died in 1910 and ten years later the estate was bought by the Irish Benedictine Nuns. This order, known as the Irish Dames, had been established in Ypres, Flanders, in the 17th century but was forced to leave in World War I.

The nuns continued to cultivate the walled garden, in particular the kitchen garden, but with reduced labour the ornamental gardens and glasshouses were not maintained. In 1996, with the help of outside funds and a restoration committee, restoration of the walled garden began. Excellent photographs and other documentary evidence, as well as an archaeological dig, has made it possible to reconstruct the garden as it was in its heyday, and it opened to the public in 1999. The immensely expensive rebuilding of the glasshouses is still far from complete but it is plain how impressive they were.

The garden slopes from north to south and a wild stream and trees form a north–south boundary separating the ornamental from the productive garden. The ornamental garden is dominated by two lawns sloping down to meet at a gravel path. Here, elaborate crescent-shaped beds are cut in the turf, brimming with bedding plants, and old plants of cabbage palm (*Cordyline australis*) stand on

Kylemore Abbey kitchen garden

either side. Above, to the north, is the site of the 19th-century glasshouses. At the heart of the glasshouse complex, a circle of metal posts linked by metal arches is decorated with flower baskets hanging from each arch and crowning each post. Within the circle is a bed with segments of turf radiating from its centre, symmetrical patterns of bedding and a mound crowned by a monkey puzzle – these were often used as short-term bedding plants and were moved when they threatened to become too big. Two of the glasshouses have so far been reinstated – a vinery with a curved roof, and a lean-to for general purposes, including the raising of thousands of bedding plants. Close by is the charming head gardener's house which has been restored and furnished, giving a good idea of the status of a head gardener in a great Victorian estate. It commands fine views over the garden.

The kitchen garden is spread out above and below an axial path flanked with herbaceous borders. Beds of vegetables are edged in box and the view of them from the top of the garden is unforgettable. A pattern of productive beds is always a delightful sight but from this vantage point you see over the walls to the countryside beyond – to looming mountains, often shrouded in mist, giving a vivid idea of the desolation of the place before Mitchell Henry came here.

There are other pleasures to sample at Kylemore, not least the astonishing abbey itself. There are fine walks along the banks of the lough, and the nuns, continuing the tree-planting tradition established by Henry, have already planted 10,000 ash and oaks. Kylemore, or Coill Mor, means big wood and this is what the place has become once again.

The *ferme ornée* at Larchill

Location Connemara, County Galway, Republic of Ireland 116km NW of Galway by N59 and R344 **Tel** (00353) (0)95 41146 **Fax** (0)95 41123 **Email** info@kylemoreabbey.ie **Website** www.kylemoreabbey.com **Owner** The Benedictine Order of Nuns **Open** Easter to Oct, daily 10.30–4.30 **Area** (walled garden) 6 acres/2.4 hectares

LARCHILL ARCADIAN GARDEN

A PICTURESQUE LANDSCAPE GARDEN WITH CURIOUS MONUMENTS, WALLED FLOWER GARDEN AND A FERME ORNÉE OF RARE FARMYARD ANIMALS

The house at Larchill is a late Georgian farmhouse of around 1780. The remarkable landscape garden, unique in Ireland and anywhere else as far as I know, is harder to date. Although close in spirit to 18th-century notions of the *ferme ornée*, or ornamental farm, with its intermingling of the Arcadian and the practical, the style of the extraordinary surviving garden buildings suggests a date at the beginning of the 19th century.

South of the house a field slopes away towards a lake where an island has a curious towered and battlemented triangular building like a fort, named Gibraltar. On another island a crude stone temple was in the past connected to the mainland by a causeway and a Chinoiserie bridge. Two gazebos, both with heavy columns, stand on the edge of the field. But the most remarkable building is Fox's Earth, a mound with an underground chamber entered by a Gothic arch and crowned with a domed temple with chubby columns, said to have been built by the then owner, a devoted hunting man, as his last resting place when he expected to be reincarnated as a fox. The present owners have restored the garden meticulously. They have also introduced exotic animals into the field, and the emus, highland cattle and llamas that graze here seem thoroughly in keeping with the spirit of the place.

THE COCKLE HOUSE

Immediately next to the house is a walled former kitchen garden, now finely restored and partly productive and partly ornamental. Built into one corner is the delightful cockle house, a castellated round tower. Its interior on two floors has the remains of beautiful shellwork – cockles, limpets and mussels with a background of intricately worked periwinkles – and the floor is inlaid with pebbles. It has a miniature fireplace and Gothic windows have patterns of stained glass. Stairs lead to the roof from where there are grand views over the battlements towards the landscape garden. Also built into the wall is an arcaded dairy with Gothic windows, with stained glass and tiles depicting military and naval scenes. A fine 18th-century statue of

◁ **The walled garden** at Larchill

imrod (originally in the lake) stands at the
ead of a pool, behind which a pergola of
ses cuts across the garden. A parterre of
aped lawns has an oval centre with radiating
gments forming a rectangle. Herbaceous
orders punctuated by lollipops of lonicera
ne the walls and a formal kitchen garden is
edged with herbs.

In the farmyard outside the walls all kinds
f farm animals are housed in charming
attlemented Gothic-arched buildings – the
oitome of the *ferme ornée* spirit. Here, and in
e fields, is the largest collection of rare
eeds in Ireland.

cation Larchill, Kilcock, County Kildare, Republic of
land 25km W of Dublin by N4 **Tel** (00353) (0)1 628
354 **Fax** (0)1 628 4580 **Email** delascasas@indigo.ie
wner Michael and Louisa de las Casas **Open** May
Aug, daily 12–6; Sept, Sun 12–6 **Area** 63 acres/25
ctares

LISMORE CASTLE

A MAGNIFICENT 17TH-CENTURY TERRACED
GARDEN ENLIVENED BY FINE MODERN
SCULPTURES AND GOOD PLANTING

Lismore is an ancient place; there was a
monastery here in the early 7th century
and the site of Lismore Castle was first built
on by Henry II's son, Prince John, in 1185. In
the late 16th century the estate belonged to
Sir Walter Raleigh from whom Richard
Boyle, 1st Earl of Cork, bought it in 1602. It
passed by marriage to the 4th Duke of
Devonshire in 1753 and has remained in that
family. The present building is a 19th-century
reworking of an essentially 17th-century
house, carried out by William Atkinson from
1811 and Sir Joseph Paxton from 1840. It
stands on a wonderfully romantic site, a
wooded bluff high above the Blackwater river.

The Antony Gormley statue at Lismore

The garden falls into two quite separate
parts. The lower garden, the pleasure grounds,
lies on the slopes below the castle. It is
informally planted with trees and shrubs in
grass – especially notable are the magnolias –
with the occasional eruption of powerful
formality. Immediately below the castle wall is
a circular pool and an avenue of eucryphias
(*E. × intermedia* 'Rostrevor') with at its end a
soaring bronze statue by Eilís O'Conell – a
tall narrow cone of ribbed metal folded about
a mysterious dark opening. Echoing in crisp
outline the baggier shapes of the eucryphias, it
makes a perfect focal point. The same artist
made another beautiful bronze, an abstract
form painted a subtle blue that glows in the
shade of shrubs on the eastern boundary of
the garden. The most memorable plants in the
lower garden are a double procession of

ancient yews believed, "probably inaccurately", in the words of the castle guidebook, "to have been planted in 1707". At the far end of this narrow shady passage a perfectly placed immobile figure – a bronze figure of a man by Antony Gormley – guards the opening of the tunnel, the bronze almost exactly matching the colour of the yews' bark.

"MY ORCHARD AND GARDEN"

The entrance to the upper garden is one of the most attractive and surprising I know. You climb a staircase through the 17th-century outer gatehouse and emerge in a large formal orchard of apple and quince. The terraced upper garden, the original kitchen garden, was laid out after the 1st Earl of Cork came to live here in 1620 and is the earliest surviving garden of its kind in Ireland. His diary of 1626 notes payments "for compassing my orchard and garden at Lismore with a wall two and a half feet thick and fourteen feet high of lyme and stone and two turrets at each corner". A long axial walk descending the terraces is exactly aligned on the slender spire of the Cathedral of St Carthage, and the top terrace, backed by a castellated wall, has a broad grass walk. At the southern end of the terrace are two treats of a completely different kind: marking the end of the walk is a sculpture by Simon Thomas, a cool oval of white Carrara marble with delicately carved convolutions on one side; above it is one of the Earl of Cork's "turrets", a square castellated tower from which there are splendid views over the gardens and over the Blackwater river. A border runs along the top terrace wall, filled with cistus, euphorbia, lilies, *Melianthus major*, mimosa (*Acacia dealbata*) and myrtle (*Luma apiculata*). Mixed borders backed by yew hedges follow the descending axis of the garden, with cross walks and borders catching the eye. There is still a substantial kitchen garden here, with areas of vegetables, soft fruit and espaliered fruit trees as well as the large orchard. On the south-facing wall is a ridge and furrow vinery designed by Paxton and built in 1858. On the high walls outside it are clematis, roses and espaliered fig trees.

Lismore is an attractive garden with a remarkable setting and history but the addition of a number of excellent sculptures has given it a new excitement. In many gardens such things are banged in indiscriminately, used as a sort of all-purpose visual tomato ketchup to impart flavour to an insipid dish, but at Lismore someone has taken much trouble to place them where they both show to advantage and add to the existing character of the place.

Location Lismore, County Waterford, Republic of Ireland In Lismore town, 79km NE of Cork by N8 and N72 **Tel** (00353) (0)58 54424 **Fax** (0)58 54896 **Owner** The Trustees of the Lismore Estate **Open** Apr to Sept, daily 1.45–4.45 (opens 11 in high season) **Area** 7 acres/2.8 hectares

MALAHIDE DEMESNE

THE ANCIENT DEMESNE OF THE TALBOTS WITH SERENE PARKLAND AND A SUPERB COLLECTION OF SOUTHERN-HEMISPHERE EXOTICS

The castle at Malahide is one of the most remarkable buildings in Ireland, owned continuously by the Talbot family from the 12th century until it was sold in 1973. It contains the only surviving medieval great hall in Ireland. Of early gardens here nothing is known. The present park still has some fine trees but much of it has been turned over to a golf course, football pitches, a cricket ground and other games amenities. The park makes a fine place in which to walk but the chief garden interest is the Talbot Botanic Garden which was created by one of the most distinguished of 20th-century plantsmen, the 7th Baron Talbot de Malahide. He inherited the estate in 1948 and gradually built up a worldwide network of sources of plants of th southern hemisphere – in which he was especially interested. He travelled very widely in pursuit of plants, making expeditions to Afghanistan, Australia, Chile, Ethiopia, Kashmir, Mexico and Nepal, and after his retirement in 1958 his collection expanded enormously. The family had also owned an estate in Tasmania, also named Malahide, since the late 18th century, and Lord Talbot finance Dr Curtis's six-volume *Endemic Flora of Tasmania* with illustrations by Margaret Stone one of the epic feats of botanical publication in the 20th century, whose final volumes appeared only after Talbot's death in 1976.

At Malahide the soil is alkaline; it is one of the few Irish gardens bereft of rhododendron Its coastal position brings a mild climate but also wind; however, many of Lord Talbot's plants came from New Zealand or Tasmania and were used to winds more violent than an they would find here. The botanic garden is i two parts: a walled garden to the east of the castle and an informal area of lawns, trees and

The west lawn at Malahide

shrubs about the west lawn. The walled garden, which was built in the 17th century as a kitchen garden, has additional protection from tall hedges of *Griselinia littoralis*. Here are all sorts of distinguished and often unfamiliar shrubs and trees – *Cladastris sinensis* from China, *Pseudopanax ferox* from New Zealand, the very tender *Schinus latifolius* from Chile, the graceful oriental spruce from Turkey (*Picea orientalis*) and many species of olearia of which a National Collection of 48 species and cultivars is kept here. Other Australasian genera represented here are *Athrotaxis*, *Eucalyptus*, *Hebe*, *Ozothamnus* and *Pittosporum*. At the centre of the walled garden is a very pretty restored Victorian glasshouse whose entrance has a high domed roof and a lantern.

The planting on the west lawn is very varied, with paths winding through shrubberies and some excellent old trees. There are many rarities here – the Japanese *Meliosma dilleniifolia*, *Pistacia chinensis* from Kashmir and the bigeneric × *Sycoparrotia semidecidua*. Woody plants form the chief interest but there is also some pretty ornamental planting of snowdrops or cyclamen under trees, and herbaceous underplantings in the shrubbery. There are in all over 5,000 species and cultivars of trees and shrubs, and new plants are constantly being added.

Location Malahide, County Dublin, Republic of Ireland 13km NE of Dublin by R105 and R106 **Tel** (00353) (0)1 846 2184 **Fax** (0)1 846 2537 **Owner** Fingal County Council **Open** (Talbot Botanic Garden) May to Sept, daily 2–5; (Park) daily 10–dusk **Area** (Talbot Botanic Garden) 20 acres/8 hectares; (Park) 250 acres/101 hectares

MOUNT CONGREVE

THE WORK OF A 20TH-CENTURY MASTER GARDENER – A VAST AND EXQUISITE WOODLAND GARDEN PACKED WITH RARITIES

The house at Mount Congreve was built in the early 18th century for the Congreve family and was, like the garden, immensely extended by the present owner, Ambrose Congreve, in the 1960s. There had been a simple terraced garden with woodland of ilexes and sweet chestnuts on the slopes

that lead towards the river Suir. Ambrose Congreve took advantage of the woodland, and its fine site, to make one of the most extraordinary gardens of the 20th century.

This is the garden of a collector, especially of trees and shrubs, and with acid soil, relatively high rainfall and a mild microclimate a wide range of plants can be grown. But Ambrose Congreve's notions of planting are wholly original: despising "dotty" planting and repeat planting, he believes that a single spectacular group best conveys a plant's essence. Paths amble through the woodland, almost invariably curved and usually edged with vast quantities of a single plant – hummocks of Japanese maple or seas of white azaleas fronted perhaps with a deep ribbon of hostas. Quite small herbaceous plants are also used in prodigal quantities – seas of *Omphalodes cappadocica* or epimediums, for example, washing about the trunks of trees. A rare straight path is the 1km long river walk which runs down to the Suir. It is lined with 100 *Magnolia campbellii* on one side and 100 *M. sargentiana* var. *robusta* on the other, with vast numbers of *M.* × *soulangeana* (a small species, you see) in front and hydrangeas in front of them.

Spring at Mount Congreve

It is not only exotics that are treated in this way. Fine native trees, especially oaks and beeches, are used with deliberation and respect. A group of magnificent beeches, for example, stands in a glade on a flawless lawn edged with ramparts of maples and rhododendrons. The trees themselves are frequently used as supports for climbing plants skilfully trained – clematis and roses in quantity but also really large-scale climbers like *Actinidia kolomikta* or *Vitis coignetiae*.

WOODLAND IS THE MAIN ATTRACTION
Although there are one or two pieces of decorative formality – a Chinese pavilion and a pillared temple, for example, and a very large walled garden has finely kept borders and vast ranges of glasshouses – it is the woodland planting that is the main attraction and standards of maintenance are amazingly high. You will search in vain for dead or damaged branches in even the tallest trees.

Mount Congreve has huge collections of all the plants that interest its owner – in some cases they must form the largest collection of their genus in the world. Yet a collection alone can make a fairly boring garden. What is thrilling at Mount Congreve is the brilliantly novel approach to what might be considered a fairly exhausted tradition of woodland planting. Here is a far wider range of plants than you have ever seen in a private garden, deployed in an entirely unfamiliar fashion. Some visitors to Mount Congreve are attracted by the fact that visiting is fairly restricted, but that is irrelevant; the point is, that this is a unique and beautiful garden and well worth the minor inconvenience of the opening arrangements.

Location Kilmeaden, County Waterford, Republic of Ireland 8km W of Waterford by N25 **Tel** (00353) (0)51 384 115 **Fax** (0)51 384 576 **Owner** Ambrose Congreve **Open** by appointment only, Mon to Fri 9–5 (closed Bank Hol) **Area** 180 acres/73 hectares

MOUNT STEWART

A DAZZLING AND IDIOSYNCRATIC GARDEN
WITH FORMALITY, FINE PLANTING AND
DELICIOUS LAKESIDE WALKS

The house, replacing an 18th-century one, was built in the early 19th century for the 1st Marquess of Londonderry and was partly designed by George Dance. The earliest feature of the gardens is a superb building, the Temple of the Winds, built in 1780 to the designs of James "Athenian" Stuart. It stands on rising wooded ground half a mile east of the house with splendid views over Strangford Lough. Here "By day members of the family and their guests would repair…for rest and contemplation, and by night for dessert and post-prandial conversation." In the 19th century it was suggested that the temple be turned into a mausoleum, to which the 3rd Marquess retorted, "I am entirely against the Idea…I have no Taste for Turning a Temple built for Mirth & Jollity into a Sepulchre – The place is solely appropriate for a Junketting Retreat in the Grounds."

The gardens close to the house are the creation from 1921 of Edith, the wife of the 7th Marquess. It was she who discovered the remarkable microclimate enjoyed by Mount

Stewart: warmed by the Gulf Stream Drift, with Strangford Lough acting as a kind of storage heater, and with low rainfall but much humidity in the coastal air. About the house she devised an idiosyncratic series of formal gardens, partly influenced by what she had seen of Italian renaissance gardens but executed with flamboyant panache. The Italian Garden immediately south of the house is in the form of a giant parterre but the beds are edged in startling golden thuja or smouldering purple berberis. The east parterre has an explosion of carmine or yellow crocosmias, scarlet lobelia, purple delphiniums and yellow figwort (*Phygelius aequalis*). Things cool down a little to the west where the planting is blue, lavender and grey, with the occasional jolt of magenta. A series of tall pillars runs along the south side of the garden, each crowned with a monkey made of cement, carrying an urn on his head and sitting on the shoulders of a grotesque figure. A whole

▷ **Monkey column**

The Italian Garden at Mount Stewart

menagerie of cement animals parades on the Dodo Terrace to one side. In the Spanish Garden a summerhouse is flanked by colonnades of clipped Leyland cypress and overlooks an oval pool surrounded by pebbles. Huge trees of *Eucalyptus globulus* loom in the woods behind.

West of the house formality and exuberance continue in a sunken garden. It is surrounded on three sides by a fine pergola with stone pillars, and this is planted with clematis, honeysuckle and roses in which blue, cream or pale yellow predominate. The garden sinks to two lower levels with monumental tree heathers, giant clipped mushrooms of purple sycamore, orange-red azaleas and herbaceous borders. Irish yews flank the entrance to the Shamrock Garden where the Red Hand of Ulster is picked out in red begonias, and there is much yew topiary, including a harp which strikingly resembles the label on a bottle of Guinness. Gertrude Jekyll is said to have had a hand in the planting of the sunken garden which certainly displays the skilful planting and Edwardian character associated with her name. The Shamrock Garden, however, teeters uncertainly on the verge of kitsch.

The entrance façade of the house overlooks a landscape of an entirely different character. Here, the scene is one of serenity, with noble trees planted in greensward that leads gently uphill away from the house. Many of these trees are conifers, among them fine specimens of fashionable 19th-century trees such as holm oak (*Quercus ilex*), mature Wellingtonias, grand Monterey pines (*Pinus radiata*) and Douglas firs (*Pseudotsuga menziesii*).

The revelation of a lake beyond the summit of the slope comes as a surprise, for a lake is usually at the bottom of a declivity, not at its top. This was laid out by the 5th Marquess between 1846 and 1848 and has been finely restored by the National Trust. Lakeside walks pass ornamental trees and glades and occasionally erupt into the sprightly colour schemes of which the 5th Marchioness was so fond. East of the lake blood-red and orange rhododendrons are planted among purple-leafed hazel-nut (*Corylus avellana* 'Fuscorubra') and scarlet maples (*Acer japonicum* cultivars). The banks of the lake are planted with long drifts of arum lily (*Zantedeschia aethiopica*), crocosmias and *Iris laevigata*. Above the north bank of the lake, shrouded in trees and shrubs, are the buildings of Tir Nan Og, the Londonderry family burial ground. Here are many tender shrubs – banksias, callistemons, hakeas and leptospermums – with communities of self-sown echiums.

Mount Stewart is one of the most attractive and stimulating of gardens. Traditional features – the wooded lake, the parterre, the sunken garden – are given a twist and the whole is carried off with exuberance and panache.

Location Newtownards BT22 2AD, County Down, Northern Ireland 15m E of Belfast by A20
Tel (028) 4278 8387 **Fax** (028) 4278 8569 **Email** mountstewart@ntrust.org.uk **Owner** The National Trust **Open** Mar, Sat to Mon 11–6; Apr to Sept, daily 11–6; Oct to Dec, Sat and Sun 11–5 **Area** 78 acres/32 hectares

MOUNT USHER GARDENS

A RARE AND RAVISHING 19TH-CENTURY WOODLAND GARDEN ON THE BANKS OF THE RIVER VARTRY

The estate at Mount Usher has a long history but its origins are vague. It was possibly named after a Wicklow family, the Ushers, of whom there was a notable Archbishop born in 1581. In the early 18th century a family called Tighe who lived at the neighbouring estate of Rosanna annexed the Mount Usher demesne. The Tighes, influenced by fashionable 18th-century English gardens, laid out an ornamental park in the valley of the river Vartry. The garden here was on the itinerary of early 19th-century travellers in Ireland. William Smith noted in his Journal of an *Excursion to the County of Wicklow* (1815) the "awful grandeur" of the Vartry.

The decisive event in the history of the garden was the acquisition of part of the estate – a mill and an acre of land – by Edward Walpole in 1868. He and his three sons acquired more land, including some of the old Tighe demesne of Rosanna, and started to lay out their garden. They had the advice of some of the central plantsmen of the 19th century, among them E.A. Bowles, the great plant collector Augustine Henry, and Sir Frederick Moore of the National Botanic Garden at Glasnevin in Dublin. In 1883 William Robinson described the garden in his *English Flower Garden*: "A quaint creeper-laden mill-house in Ashford, with an acre or two of ground, partly wooded, through which the silvery Vartry River flows." Robinson considered it "a charming example of gardens that might be made in river valleys".

One of the Walpole sons, Thomas, was an engineer and it was he who made the weirs which are such a vital part of the garden. The falls are ornamental in themselves but their crucial role is to provide the calm pools which mirror the plantings of trees and shrubs that crowd about the banks. Thomas Walpole was responsible also for the delightful iron bridges that span the river from time to time.

The visitor to the garden today follows a riverside path leading down into the valley, and it is the serenity of this delicious prospect that strikes first. The grassy banks of the river are richly planted on either side and, as you

The river garden at Mount Usher

get your eye in, you will be amazed by the range of plants – at least 3,000 species – grown here. The climate is mild, the valley gives additional protection and the rainfall is fairly high. There are notable collections of acers, eucalyptus, eucryphias and southern beeches (*Nothofagus* species) – some of these are very early introductions, often propagated by seed direct from the site of origin. Seeds of eucalyptus, of which there are over 60 different kinds, were often sent from Melbourne or Sydney Botanical Gardens. There are countless other notable individual plants, more often than not from the southern hemisphere, such as the Kauri pine (*Agathis australis*) from New Zealand, *Bowkeria citrina* from South Africa, *Telopea truncata* from Tasmania. Although it is the woody plants that command the chief attention there is also much excellent herbaceous planting: here are such orchids as *Dactylorhiza foliosa*, the spectacular giant lily *Cardiocrinum giganteum*, martagon lilies, swathes of Asiatic primulas, and real rarities like the Chilean *Tecophilaea cyanocrocus*, now almost extinct in the wild.

A PLANT-LOVER'S PARADISE

The charm of Mount Usher is that it may be enjoyed in many different ways. It is a plant-lover's paradise but anyone will relish the lovely riverside walks, with brilliant colours and strange shapes reflected in the placid water of the weir pools. The design is of the least obtrusive kind, rather a piece of gently manipulated nature with nothing ostentatious. The Walpoles knew "when to let well alone", which Gertrude Jekyll defined as the essential skill in naturalistic planting. Unlike a botanical garden, where plants are ordered according to genus, the plants at Mount Usher are disposed on the basis of appearance or of appropriateness of site. The devoted plant-spotter, however expert, will see unfamiliar and wonderful plants and will often see them when least expecting it.

Location Ashford, County Wicklow, Republic of Ireland In Ashford village, 50km S of Dublin by N11 **Tel** (00353) (0)404 40116 **Fax** (0)404 40205 **Website** www.mount-usher-gardens.com **Owner** Mrs Madelaine Jay **Open** mid Mar to Oct, daily 10.30–6 **Area** 20 acres/8 hectares

MUCKROSS GARDENS AND ARBORETUM

MIRACULOUS VIEWS OF THE KILLARNEY LANDSCAPE, EXCELLENT TREES AND A WONDERFUL WOODLAND GARDEN

The baronial mansion of Muckross was built for Henry Arthur Herbert to the designs of William Burn and completed in 1843. The Herberts had lived in these parts since the 16th century and there had been an earlier house on the estate. In 1911 William Bowers Bourn bought the estate as a wedding present for his daughter but she died young and her widower gave the estate to the Irish nation in 1932. The estate, of 10,000 acres/4,000 hectares, became the first Irish National Park which, with further land acquired subsequently, now covers an area of 25,000 acres/10,000 hectares. On the eastern banks of the middle lake at Killarney, it looks across the water towards the highest mountain in Ireland, Macgillicuddy's Reeks – one of the most beautiful sites of any garden.

The first known garden at Muckross dates from the time of Colonel Edward Herbert (1693–1770) who reclaimed an area of 140 acres/57 hectares about the house, which involved moving immense quantities of stone Herbert included in his landscaping the picturesque ruins of a 15th-century Franciscan Friary which were admired by Arthur Young and described in his *A Tour of Ireland* (1775). A hermit was installed here to add to the picturesque effect but he took to the bottle and was sacked.

The garden and arboretum that are seen today at Muckross are entirely 19th- and 20th-century. Formal gardens close to the house show a long terrace facing west across the lake (in 1906 there had also been an elaborate parterre here). A huge Monterey pine (*Pinus radiata*) standing at the end of the terrace must be a 19th-century planting. To the east of the house are a sunken garden and a very large rock garden which uses natural spurs of rock. In the well-drained crevices such plants as leptospermums and olearias do well in a part of the world where, although the climate is mild, the annual rainfall can easily go up to 90in/228cm. The rock garden overlooks a magnificent Durmast oak (*Quercus petraea*). Nearby is a finely restored range of glasshouses and, to jollify the terrace of a restaurant, a semicircular parterre with lollipops of bay, box edging and zippy bedding schemes.

To one side of the west lawn, past a stand

The mountainous setting of Muckross

of Monterey pines, a stream garden is thickly planted with arum lilies, *Gunnera manicata*, hostas, *Iris sibirica* and other herbaceous plants enjoying a moist site. Nearby, enclosed in high deer fencing, is the arboretum. Here, on a fine undulating site protected by a canopy of beech (some magnificent), English oaks, Monterey pines and Scots pines, animated in spring and early summer by brilliant rhododendrons, is a very large collection of trees and shrubs. It is one of the most atmospheric parts of the garden. The Old Woodland area gives an impression of jungly informality, with a very large collection of camellias, and another part of the arboretum is used as an extension of the John F. Kennedy Arboretum (*see page 418*) to cultivate trees too tender to survive in a less benign microclimate. Muckross has one of the best and most attractive collections of trees and shrubs in Ireland, deployed in a setting of marvellous beauty.

Location Killarney, County Kerry, Republic of Ireland 4km S of Killarney by N71 **Tel** (00353) (0)64 31440 **Fax** (0)64 33926 **Owner** The Office of Public Works **Open** daily 9–5.30 **Area** 86 acres/35 hectares

NATIONAL BOTANIC GARDENS

SUPERB 19TH-CENTURY GARDENS WITH MAGNIFICENT GLASSHOUSES AND AN EXCEPTIONAL PLANT COLLECTION

The National Botanic Gardens were founded in 1795 when the Dublin Society, under the impetus of Dr Walter Wade, bought land at Glasnevin. In 1838, with the appointment of Dr David Moore as curator of the gardens, their reputation spread far beyond Ireland. David Moore was succeeded in 1879 by his son Frederick (later Sir Frederick) who also had a deep influence on gardening in Ireland, and on the planting of many of the great 19th-century gardens.

Between 1843 and 1869 an extraordinary range of glasshouses was built at Glasnevin, chiefly by the Dublin ironmaster Richard Turner. Called the Curvilinear Range, the glasshouses break out into high vaults and sweeping curves beautifully fashioned of the thinnest glazing bars, giving the buildings an

ethereal lightness despite their great size – they are over 300ft/100m long. The Great Palm House of 1883–84, with its double tiered segmental dome, by Boyds of Paisley, is also a strikingly attractive building.

The earliest map of the garden, dated 1800, shows the layout very much as it is today, with a perimeter walk and paths leading off it. The garden spreads out south from the banks of the Tolka river with part of it, Mill Field, on an island. Much of the garden, particularly the western part, is laid out with walks across grass in which specimen trees are planted. These are grouped by genus and range widely, with notable collections of alders, birch, thorns, hornbeam, maples, oaks and southern beeches. The garden is primarily a botanical institution but it also takes its horticulture seriously. There are around 20,000 species and cultivars grown here, and at the heart of the garden are botanical order beds with plants grouped by family. There are also features of primary interest to gardeners: a display of different kinds of lawn grasses, a rose garden, herbaceous borders and display beds in which annuals can be tested. Several garden cultivars, such as *Solanum crispum* 'Glasnevin', had their origin here. The rock garden, which is in fact full of good things, was not admired by Reginald Farrer: "You take a hundred or a

The curvilinear glasshouses

thousand cartloads of bare square-faced boulders…drop them all about absolutely anyhow…you then plant things amongst them. The chaotic hideousness of the result is something to be remembered with shudders ever after." A further dimension of the garden is that, because entrance is free, it is treated by Dubliners as a public park. There are plenty of sitting places and lavish displays of bedding.

The various glasshouses protect large collections of tender plants. The Palm House has a remarkable collection of cycads and, in one of its wings, a collection of orchids. The latter have been a constant interest of the garden since it was founded. In the 1840s seeds of orchids were germinated here for the first time in any garden. Specialist glasshouses are devoted to alpines, ferns and succulents.

The National Botanic Gardens are among the most attractive of their kind, distinguished for the plants, buildings and atmosphere.

Location Glasnevin, Dublin 9, Republic of Ireland N of the city centre **Tel** (00353) (0)1 837 4388 **Fax** (0)1 836 0080 **Email** nbg@indigo.ie **Owner** Dúchas, The Heritage Service **Open** summer, daily 9–6; winter, daily 10–4.30 (Sun opens 11; closed 25 Dec) **Area** 48 acres/19 hectares

POWERSCOURT GARDENS

A SUPERB IRISH SHOWPIECE – GRAND
TERRACED GARDENS, A LAKE, A JAPANESE
GARDEN AND OUTSTANDING TREES

The house at Powerscourt was built between 1731 and 1741 for Richard Wingfield, later 1st Viscount Powerscourt, to the designs of Richard Castle. The house was gutted by fire in 1974, and all its contents destroyed. Some of the rooms have been re-instated and others are used as a visitor centre. The site, which had been occupied by an earlier house, is magnificent. From the brow of a hill the land swoops down and there are sublime views of the Sugarloaf Mountain in the Wicklow hills. It seems that Castle also laid out the formal gardens in the form of a series of terraces and parterres descending to a large circular pool with its triumphant jet of water. A detailed map of the estate by John Rocque was made in 1760, showing the garden recently completed – a very old-fashioned layout for its date. It clearly shows, to one side

The lake at Powerscourt

Wrought-iron in the terrace garden

of the terraced garden, a large walled enclosure with an intricate pattern of beds, probably a kitchen garden. This survives but is today a pleasure garden with borders, beds of roses, a central fountain and a magnificent late 18th-century wrought-iron gate which came from Bamberg Cathedral in Bavaria.

In 1840 the 6th Viscount asked Daniel Robertson to make new garden plans. He made the formal garden even grander, with a deep top terrace ornamented with fine stonework, urns and statues of Diana, Apollo and the Angels of Fame and Victory. In 1874 the *perron*, in essence a landing, was added to the centre of the grand flight of steps linking the terraces. Designed by Francis Cramner

Penrose, the *perron* has beautiful wrought-iron balustrades and is paved with intricate pebble patterns. The steps are double at this point and embrace at the lower level a Baroque pool with a sundial and a pair of statues spouting water. The great steps end in a flourish where they approach the bottom lake, with a pair of pegasi rearing up – the pegasus is the crest of the Wingfield family. Lawns on either side of the terrace steps have bedding schemes of 19th-century character with clipped mushrooms of Portugal laurel.

The lakeside belongs to a different tradition. At the centre of the circular pool a figure of Triton blows his single jet high into the air, woodland presses in on three sides with the occasional enticing walk opening out, and in the woods, reached by a steep rustic stone stairway, is an open grotto with mossy and fern-shrouded rocks, little cascades and an interior of petrified sphagnum moss. The steps lead down to a further surprise – a delightful sketch of a Japanese garden, laid out for the 8th Viscount in 1908 when such things were all the rage. Here are snow lanterns, a scarlet bridge, Japanese

maples and flowering cherries.

The demesne of Powerscourt is exceptionally well wooded; even the drive crosses parkland studded with magnificent 18th-century beeches. In the 19th century the 6th and 7th Viscounts indulged in a frenzy of tree planting, with an average of 400,000 trees planted each year between 1870 and 1880 in the Ballyreagh plantation. Within the gardens, on the banks and slopes above the lake, the distinctive tree planting is also 19th-century. Reflecting the taste of the time, this is largely coniferous, with splendid specimens of cedar, cryptomeria, Douglas fir (*Pseudotsuga menziesii*), monkey puzzle, spruce, Wellingtonia and others. Among these are distinguished deciduous trees, some of them very rare, like the excrutiatingly slow-growing cutleaf oak (*Quercus robur* 'Pectinata').

Powerscourt is one of the great Irish showpieces and is much visited. Such places are not necessarily agreeable but here, even in high summer, there will always be a fine tree, beautiful stone or wrought-ironwork, a refreshing woodland glade or an exhilarating prospect of the Wicklow countryside to please.

Location Enniskerry, County Wicklow, Republic of Ireland 20km S of Dublin by N11 **Tel** (00353) (0)1 204 6000 **Fax** (0)1 204 6900 **Email** gardens@powerscourt.ie **Website** www.powerscourt.ie **Owner** Powerscourt Estate **Open** daily 9.30–5.30 (dusk in winter; closed 25 and 26 Dec) **Area** 47 acres/19 hectares

ROWALLANE GARDEN

ROMANTIC AND MYSTERIOUS 19TH-CENTURY GARDEN WITH A WONDERFUL WALLED FLOWER GARDEN AND EXCEPTIONAL ROCK GARDEN

The house at Rowallane was built in 1861 for the Revd John Moore. The garden is largely the 20th-century creation of his nephew, Hugh Armytage Moore, who was awarded the Victoria Medal of Honour in 1942. After Moore's death in 1954 the estate was acquired by The National Trust.

The first experience of Rowallane as you proceed down the drive is one of mystery. Lugubrious conifers and old rhododendrons form a dark tunnel and on the edges of the drive mossy rocks erupt from the ground, interspersed from time to time with curious

conical cairns of smooth round stones. This slightly sinister introduction scarcely prepares you for the flower-filled spectacle that is in store.

THE LIVELIEST GARDENING

The walled garden is the scene of the liveliest gardening here. Mixed borders are stuffed with big old shrubs – *Hoheria lyallii*, several venerable magnolias, tree peonies and huge thickets of *Rosa moyesii*. The occasional startling, and rare, rhododendron animates the scene – such as *R. cinnabarinum* Blandfordiiflorum Group with explosive trumpets of red and yellow. Astilbes, hostas, *Kirengeshoma palmata*, meconopsis, primulas, rodgersias and much else form the underplanting. There are touches of formality – cones of clipped yew garlanded in summer with the scarlet flowers of *Tropaeolum speciosum*; a parterre with drums and hedges of clipped box; and a shaped magnolia at the centre of the parterre planted round with a pattern of penstemons. The walled garden has a kind of inner sanctum, a secondary compartment quite different in character from the main part, where a lawn is planted with specimen trees and shrubs, including the cultivar *Viburnum plicatum* f. *tomentosum* 'Rowallane' which

The walled garden at Rowallane

originated here. Steps lead down to a pool flanked by fine stone urns and edged in sheaves of *Iris pseudacorus* and shaded by a *Davidia involucrata*.

Outside the walled gardens a long walk leads across Spring Ground with ramparts of rhododendrons echoing the rolling contours of the land. It leads eventually to a naturalistic rock garden with natural outcrops of rock planted with azaleas, daphnes, olearias and pieris underplanted with beautiful celmisias, meconopsis and primulas. A curiosity, no more, in the wooded pleasure grounds behind the house is a 19th-century bandstand threatened with demolition in Newcastle and rescued by the National Trust which erected it on an existing plinth from which, it is said, the Revd John Moore used to practise his sermons.

Location Saintfield, Ballynahinch BT24 7LH, County Down, Northern Ireland 11m SE of Belfast by A7 **Tel** (028) 9751 0131 **Fax** (028) 9751 1242 **Email** rowallane@ntrust.org.uk **Website** www.ntni.org.uk **Owner** The National Trust **Open** May to Sept, daily 10–8; Oct to Apr, daily 10–4 (closed 24 Dec to 1 Jan) **Area** 51 acres/21 hectares

STROKESTOWN PARK

RESTORED FORMAL GARDEN OF AN
18TH-CENTURY DEMESNE AND A CHARMING
KITCHEN GARDEN WITH OLD VARIETIES
OF FRUIT AND VEGETABLES

The approach to Strokestown Park from the centre of the town is magnificent, the broad tree-lined street leading up to a giant Gothic gatehouse. The house at Strokestown was built for the Mahon family in the 17th century but Palladianized by Richard Castle in about 1730 for Thomas Mahon, when he added two sweeping wings, housing a kitchen and stables. Major Denis Mahon inherited the estate in 1845 and his daughter, Grace, who had married Henry Sandford Packenham, inherited from him. In the late 20th century the estate was bought by a local firm, Westward Garage Ltd, which restored the house and garden and established a Famine Museum in the outhouses. These were opened to the public by 1997.

Very little is known about the early history of the garden, though the walled former kitchen garden has a long history. It is in two parts, with the smaller part running along the southern outer wall of the chief walled garden. In the south-west corner of this outer walled garden is a splendid tall gazebo built in 1740. It has a very pretty upstairs room with decorative plasterwork and fine Palladian windows — it must originally have been used as a modest banqueting house. In the 19th century it was converted into the head gardener's house but has now reverted to its primary, decorative function, and has been finely restored, as have potting sheds and a remarkable range of glasshouses and cold frames. The chief glasshouse is remarkably early, built by James O'Donnell in 1780, and some of the panes go back to that date. Today it houses figs, grapes and peaches. A melon house of 1780, with its 19th-century hot water heating system, is once again in action, with the plants trained on wires and the fruit supported in hessian bags. The kitchen garden beds, gardened organically, are planted with many different cultivars, some dating from the 18th century, of blackcurrants, gooseberries, raspberries, brassicas, potatoes and much else.

THE INNER WALLED GARDEN

The inner walled garden, by far the larger part, is now entirely ornamental and here several contemporary garden designers — Helen Dillon, Luke Dodd and Jim Reynolds — have all had a hand. At the entrance a grass walk lined with Irish yews forms a bold central axis. Interrupted by a scalloped lily pool, it is aligned on a decorative curiosity: what seems to be a gazebo turns out to be an 18th-century Palladian window taken from the house and mounted on a free-standing wall. Beech hedges, with niches clipped into their inner walls, form a cross axis. Two mysterious enclosures of beech lie to one side. One has a lawn with monumental shapes of clipped yew, two triangles, a square and a dumpy column; this is the Sound Garden which will be installed with electronic sensors triggering sounds. A second enclosure has a beech maze of unusual shape with concave mirrors as its goal — self-discovery? A stone and oak pergola of Edwardian character, draped with clematis, honeysuckle, golden hop and jasmine, provides a side entrance linking the kitchen garden. This overlooks a sunken rose parterre with a symmetrical pattern of box-edged beds each filled with a single variety of modern rose. At the centre of each of the larger beds a column supports an old shrub rose, sometimes resulting in an uneasy partnership — the aristocratic rich pink 'Tour de Malakoff', for example, seems struggling to extricate itself from a sea of apricot and yellow 'Glenfiddich'. A very long south-facing herbaceous border, initially planned by Jim Reynolds, runs the whole length of the garden. Subtly colour-graded, with blues, mauves and whites at one end, it warms up as it goes east with the magenta of *Gladiolus communis* subsp. *byzantinus* and *Geranium psilostemon*, and vibrant pink peonies. Very large groups of a single plant, often repeated, give strong shape — *Crocosmia* 'Lucifer', *Euphorbia griffithii*, *Geranium* × *magnificum* and *Macleaya* × *kewensis*.

Anyone visiting Strokestown should certainly also visit the entirely delightful house which has been gently restored but whose décor, contents and arrangement are exactly as they were when Westward took over ownership of the estate. The Famine Museum, which draws on Strokestown estate archives for some of its material, should also certainly be seen. Emerging from it, no doubt in a sombre mood, you may be assailed by appetising smells from the nearby restaurant — a piquant and not entirely happy juxtaposition.

The rose parterre at Strokestown

Location Strokestown, County Roscommon, Republic of Ireland
23km W of Longford by N5
Tel (00353) (0)78 33013
Fax (0)78 33712 **Email** info@strokestownpark.ie
Website www.strokestownpark.ie
Open mid Mar to Oct, daily 11–5.30
Area 6 acres/2.4 hectares

GAZETTEER
of over 1,700
GARDENS

Note: There is access to these places *only* where specifically indicated, with the exception of all public parks, public open spaces and most cemeteries, which are open regularly. For gardens that are regularly open, a telephone number is given from which opening times may be obtained. The English Heritage Register grading, the Cadw/ICOMOS grading and the Scottish Inventory refer only to the *garden or park*. NGS stands for the National Gardens Scheme whose annual publication, *Gardens of England and Wales Open for Charity* (known as The Yellow Book), is an essential reference; SGS stands for Scotland's Garden Scheme which is run in the same way, and its annual publication, *Gardens of Scotland*, is also essential. If a garden has opened for either scheme in recent years, this is stated and a telephone number given where available. Where gardens are owned by the National Trust (for England, Wales and Northern Ireland), the National Trust for Scotland, English Heritage or Cadw, this is indicated (NT, NTS, EH, Cadw respectively).

À La Ronde

Exmouth, Devon OS SY0184
English Heritage Register Grade II
Open regularly (NT) Tel 01395 265514

Rare and enchanting cottage *orné* built in 1796 by Jane and Mary Parminter. Garden today chiefly grass but described in 1811 as "full of bowers, arbours, three obelisks, fountains, glass-houses and rare tropical plants". Late 18th-century landscaping, with ha-ha; the garden was designed to take full advantage of views over the estuary of the river Exe. At a little distance from À La Ronde is The Point-in-View, a nonconformist chapel built by the Parminter Sisters in 1811 with a school and almshouses.

Abbey Dore Garden

see page 188

Abbey Gardens and Precincts

Bury St Edmunds, Suffolk OS TL8564
English Heritage Register Grade II
Open regularly

The site of a great Benedictine house of which only beautiful ruins remain, including the magnificent great gates leading into the precinct. Its grounds have been developed as a public amenity since 1720 when two lime avenues were planted as town promenades – although most of the existing gardens date from the 20th century. A circular garden, enclosed in yew hedges, is laid out with 64 island beds with annual bedding schemes; there is a herb garden, a formal water garden, a garden of old roses and a shrub walk. In the Great Churchyard are winding tree-lined paths. Apart from the beauty of the ruins, there are fine surrounding buildings, including an outstanding 14th-century octagonal dovecote.

Abbey House Gardens

Malmesbury, Wiltshire OS ST9388
Open regularly Tel 01666 822212

Grand mid 16th-century house in the shadow of the beautiful remains of Malmesbury Abbey. Busy modern garden of compartments (with very attractive architectural fragments from the abbey) with borders, parterre, pergola, fountain pool, woodland garden on banks of river and large collection of brilliantly coloured roses.

Abbey Leix

Abbeyleix, County Laois, Republic of Ireland
Open regularly Tel (00353) 502 31683

A Cistercian abbey was founded here in 1188. Late 18th-century house built for Thomas Vesey, 2nd Lord Knapton (and later 1st Viscount de Vesci). In *AZ of Laois* (1837) it is described as "a spacious and handsome mansion, pleasantly situated in a demesne of about 1135 statute acres, embellished with thriving plantations and timber of stately growth". After 1839 a terraced garden was laid out south of the house, modelled, on a more modest scale, on the slightly earlier and very much grander terraced garden at Alupka in the Crimea, belonging to the Voronstov family (probably designed by the English architect William Hunt). (The 3rd Viscount's mother-in-law, wife of the 11th Earl of Pembroke, was a Voronstov.) Watercolours by G.S. Elgood and E.A. Rowe of lavish late Victorian borders are illustrated in Penelope Hobhouse's and Christopher Wood's *Painted Gardens: English Watercolours*

1850–1914 (1988). Ancient oak woodland, chiefly of the durmast oak (*Quercus petraea*), is a notable and very beautiful part of the landscape today, spendidly carpeted with bluebells in spring. An arboretum, chiefly planted in the late 19th century by the 4th Viscount de Vesci, has many notable trees.

Abbey Park

Leicester, Leicestershire OS SK5805 English Heritage Register Grade II Open regularly

Public park laid out in the late 19th century by William Barron & Sons of Elvaston Nurseries, Derbyshire, and opened in 1883; since 1925 it has incorporated the ruins of Leicester Abbey, an Augustinian foundation started in 1143. A tree-lined walk runs along the bank of the river Soar which flows through the park, spanned by a footbridge. Close to the bridge, a 20th-century statue of Cardinal Wolsey, who died in Leicester, was formerly at the Wolsey knitwear factory. On the far side of the river a carriage drive runs round an irregular lake. On its banks are an artificial mound, a bandstand (*c.*1882), a Japanese garden (*c.*1900) with pergola, bridges and pavilion, and refreshment rooms (*c.*1960) with copper-covered roof. On the north banks of the river, a Garden of the Senses opened in 1995.

Abbots Ripton Hall

Abbots Ripton, Cambridgeshire OS TL2477
English Heritage Register Grade II
Open occasionally for charity and by appointment Tel 01487 773555

18th-century house rebuilt by Anthony Salvin in 1856. 19th-century garden transformed by Lord de Ramsey since World War II with the help of garden designers Humphrey Waterfield and Lanning Roper. Lively plantsmanship, elegant vistas and fine ornaments. Decorative garden buildings in the 1970s by Peter Foster: a Gothic summerhouse, Chinese bridge and Chinese fishing pavilion. Grotto by Christopher Thacker (1978).

Abbotsbury Subtropical Gardens

see page 14

Abbotsford

Melrose, Roxburghshire OS NT5134 Scottish Inventory Open regularly Tel 01896 752043

House built 1817–21 for Sir Walter Scott to the designs of William Atkinson, aided by others, including Scott himself who was keenly interested in landscaping and advised many owners of estates – including the Duke of Buccleuch at Bowhill (*see page 448*) and Drumlanrig (*see page 470*). Scott rejected "the tame and pedantic rules of Kent and Browne [*sic*], without affecting the grotesque or fantastic – who shall bring back more ornament into the garden, and introduce a bolder, wilder and more natural character into the park." (*Miscellaneous Prose Works,* Vol XXI, 1827). West of the house, in the Tweed watermeadows, Sir Walter laid out a park with elms, horse chestnuts, Norway maples and sycamores. He also took an interest in the woodland, planting hardwoods (beech, elm, oak and sycamore) among larches and Scots pines. In 1818 he was ordering several species of trees from the nursery of Eagle & Henderson in quantities that ranged from 1,000 to 3,000. In the pleasure grounds about the house today, terraces on the west side give views of the Tweed. An entrance courtyard has the fountain bowl from the Old Mercat Cross in Edinburgh, lawns, geometric flower beds and clipped columns of yew. Another courtyard has raised beds about the walls, a lawn and sundial. The walled kitchen garden, said to be one of Sir Walter's "favourite places of resort", has a Gothic conservatory dating from his time.

Abbotswood

Stow-on-the-Wold, Gloucestershire OS SP1826 English Heritage Register Grade II* Open occasionally for NGS Tel 01451 830173

Fine Cotswold Arts and Crafts garden created by Mark Fenwick with the help, from 1901, of Edwin Lutyens who designed parts of the garden and remodelled the 19th-century house. Lutyens took advantage of the sloping site to design terraces, now with admirable planting, from which there are wide views over parkland. The terraces vary in character: one has lawns and a pattern of shaped beds, another a scalloped pool at the centre and a third a rose garden planted in a maze of box-edged beds. Distinguished woodland planting with stream and exceptional rural views. By the banks of the stream are outcrops of rock put into place by James Pulham. Large heather garden in a pocket of acid soil in the otherwise alkaline ground. Abbotswood intermingles the formal and informal in a most distinguished way, with much fine planting. Mark Fenwick died in 1945 but subsequent owners have cared for it well.

Abercairny

Fowlis Wester, Perthshire OS NT9122
Scottish Inventory

The history of Abercairny goes back to the 13th century and the estate has been owned by the Moray family since the early 14th century. The present house, designed by the Hon. Claud Phillimore, was built after 1960 to replace the early 19th-century Gothic Abercairny Abbey. Park laid out by Thomas White the Elder in 1793, retaining older avenues, one of which, Beech Avenue, remains although it was replanted *c.*1800. White laid out two serpentine lochs and planned drives converging on the house. Some old parkland trees remain and much later planting of good new specimens, particularly beech, oak and lime. Very little remains of a mid 19th-century arboretum of conifers, and Lady Fanny's Walk of silver firs running from the flower garden to the kitchen garden. Flower garden designed by Lewis Kennedy *c.*1812, "distinguished by its simple effectiveness that is far more pleasing than many more elaborate and correspondingly formal arrangements" (as the *Journal of Horticulture & Cottage Gardener* wrote in 1884). It included a central walk of azaleas and rhododendrons with paths leading off, sometimes focused on notable specimens in the arboretum. A bowling green had a terraced flower garden at a higher level. Much of this remains although th bowling green now has specimen trees. The central walk has been decorated with statues from the demolished Abercairny Abbey. Formal gardens by the house with mature cedar of Lebanon and yew topiary shapes. Terraces ornamented with urns, cherubs and a sundial.

Aberdour Castle
Aberdour, Fife OS NT1985
Scottish Inventory Open regularly (HS)
Tel 01383 860519

Castle built in the 14th century for the Douglas family (later Earls of Morton) who have owned it ever since. With many later additions, it was in ruins by 1836. The garden interest here lies in the remarkably early terraces and walled garden. The terraces were built in the late 16th century. In 1687 James Sutherland sent seeds and plants from the physic garden in Edinburgh (later Royal Botanic Garden Edinburgh, *see page 391*), which included almonds, cherries, figs, gooseberries, jasmine, plums, raspberries and tamarisks. The gardener, Charles Liddel, planted three dozen fruit trees in an orchard below the terraces in 1690. A walled garden, with the Douglas arms carved on it, dates from *c.*1632; it was used as a bowling green 1668–1745. Bee boles are built into the wall. Today there are modern herbaceous borders but the beauty and interest of the place is the ancient setting, with its venerable walls and terraces.

Aberglasney Gardens
see page 188

Aberuchill House
nr Comrie, Perthshire OS NN7421
Scottish Inventory

16th-century tower house built for the Campbell family. Old parkland with many mature individual trees and clumps of elm, larch, lime, oak and sycamore – a lime avenue east of the house has trees dating back to *c.*1750. Picturesque late 19th-century valley garden – the Den – made on the banks of the Aberuchill burn, with a waterfall, rustic bridge and a rock garden. 19th-century walled garden with wall-mounted sundial; in the past an ornamental garden (with

notable meconopsis raised from seed brought back from Himalayan expeditions) but now a kitchen garden.

Abney Park Cemetery
Hackney, London OS TQ3386 English Heritage Register Grade II Open regularly

Non-denominational cemetery laid out in the former gardens of Abney House and Fleetwood House by William Hosking and opened in 1840. Handsome main entrance with lodges and gates in the Egyptian style by Hosking, inscribed with hieroglyphs signifying "the Abode of the Mortal Part of Man". Tree plantings by the great Hackney nurseryman George Loddiges – "an arboretum among cemeteries". Winding paths about the perimeter, and towards the centre a Gothic chapel. Cemetery overgrown but with much character and many excellent 19th-century monuments.

Achamore
see page 360

Achnacloich House
nr Connel, Argyll OS NM9534 Scottish Inventory Open regularly Tel 01631 710221

19th-century house designed by John Starforth and built on the site of an earlier house. The site is beautiful, on a headland overlooking Loch Etive. T.E. Nelson inherited the estate in 1917 and was inspired by his uncle, F.R.S. Balfour of Dawyck (*see page 373*), with a love of plants and gardens. A fine woodland garden is the result, with notable acers, halesias, magnolias, rhododendrons – underplanted with bulbs and primulas – all flourishing in the acid soil and mild, wet climate. Terraced gardens south of house with yew hedges and borders of mixed shrubs; Banksian rose, ceanothus and tender clematis festooning the wall.

Acton Burnell Hall
Acton Burnell, Shropshire OS SJ5302 English Heritage Register Grade II

House enlarged by William Baker in mid 18th century for the

Smythe family. Former deer park landscaped in the 18th century. Beehive-like shellwork grotto of *c.*1750 with fanciful designs described by Barbara Jones as like "doodles on a telephone pad". A rare triangular sham castle (known both as Black Dick's Tower and Keeper's Lodge) built 1779–80 on a hillock overlooking a lake. Ruins of 13th-century Acton Burnell Castle south of the hall.

Adare Manor
Adare, County Limerick, Republic of Ireland

The Quin family (later Wyndham-Quin and Earls of Dunraven) came to live here in the 17th century. Present house built in the early 18th century but remodelled more than once in the 19th century to produce an Elizabethan/Gothic hybrid. The early 18th-century garden is shown in a painting of *c.*1740 illustrated in Edward Malins's and The Knight of Glin's *Lost Demesnes* (1976). It shows an entrance forecourt with double avenues of trees and tall topiary cones, and in the background the beautiful remains of a 15th-century Franciscan friary, forming a picturesque eyecatcher in the wooded grounds. In the 18th century there was much tree planting in the demesne, through which the Maigue river flows. The landscape designer James Fraser worked at Adare in the early 19th century. The head gardener at that time, Andrew Coghlan, wrote a remarkably detailed description of the garden for *Gardener's Magazine* in March 1836. He describes fruit trees, a rock garden planted with alpine plants, a water garden, notable trees (including "a grand line of thirty English elm trees, more than 150ft high"), an American border, a greenhouse and "a grapery of exquisite beauty, surrounded by a garden of evergreens". Later in the century the architect Philip Hardwick, who redesigned the south façade of the house, laid out a new formal garden in front of it, with a grand four-part box parterre. The parterre survives today but a golf course has been built in the grounds and the house is a golf club.

Adlestrop House
nr Moreton-in-Marsh, Gloucestershire OS SP2426 English Heritage Register Grade II

17th-century house, formerly the rectory where Jane Austen's uncle, Theophilus Leigh, lived in the 1750s. Garden improved by Humphry Repton when he was working on the adjacent Adlestrop Park (*see below*). Cedars of Lebanon of this period survive, framing views of Repton's landscape at Adlestrop Park.

Adlestrop Park
nr Moreton-in-Marsh, Gloucestershire OS SP2426 English Heritage Register Grade II

Estate of the Leigh family since the mid 16th century. House rebuilt by Sanderson Miller in the 1750s with Gothick south-west front. Gardens partly laid out 1759–63 by Samuel Driver and then redesigned by Humphry Repton from 1799 for James Henry Leigh. Belts and clumps of trees and two pools survive from this time.

Adlington Hall
Adlington, Cheshire OS SJ9080 English Heritage Register Grade II* Open regularly Tel 01625 829206

House of the Legh family, built from 1500, with grand mid 18th-century south façade. Ancient deer park, in which deer were kept until World War I. South of the house, in the centre of the park, is the Wilderness, connected to the house by a lime avenue with late 17th-century gates at its northern end. The grounds are well wooded, with many rhododendrons, winding paths, and the river Dene flowing through it. Fine 18th-century garden buildings punctuate the scene – the Tig House, a Chinoiserie pavilion, a Chinese bridge, a grotto and the Doric Diana's Temple.

Airlie Castle
Airlie, Forfarshire OS NO2952 Scottish Inventory

Castle built in the 15th century with late 18th-century house added. Owned by the Ogilvy family (later Earls of Airlie) since the early 15th century. Late 18th-century walled garden with magnificent yew hedges planted

in the late 19th century and suppposedly representing battle formations at Waterloo. Mixed borders (with old shrub roses) along the yew hedges. Here too are a box parterre and, leading up to the south entrance, a laburnum walk. Part of the garden still used for vegetables. Nearby a wild garden with azaleas, rhododendrons and other flowering shrubs. Picturesque 19th-century woodland – the Den – in the gorges of the river Isla and the Melgam water, with a planned walk along the Isla to a viewing platform.

Albert Park
Abingdon, Oxfordshire OS SU4997 English Heritage Register Grade II Open regularly

Park at the centre of an urban housing scheme of large houses, each with its own garden, laid out in the 1860s; the design, chosen by competition, was won by "Mr Chapman of Dulwich". The park, with open space at its centre and plantings of trees and shrubs threaded with walks forming the perimeter, is enclosed by a circuit road, and the grounds of Abingdon Grammar School lie on one side. A monument to Prince Albert was put up in 1865 to the design of John Gibbs.

Albury Park
see page 118

Aldby Park
Buttercrambe, North Yorkshire OS SE7358 English Heritage Register Grade II*

Early 18th-century house for the Brewster family (later Darley). South-east of the house, remains of a motte and bailey castle which have been incorporated into the garden – part of a layout devised by Thomas Knowlton before 1746. Knowlton's bill of that year to Brewster Darley survives, for "attendance, inspection and direction in making, levelling and forming his gardens and planting the same". Large numbers of trees are listed – 1,000 beech, 500 hornbeams, 2,000 birch and "elmses and privetts". East of the house, a series of grass terraces, also in place in the first half of the 18th century, runs down to the river Derwent. An undated

A

map, probably by Knowlton, shows these lined with trees and shrubs, with paths winding among the earthworks.

Aldenham House
Aldenham, Hertfordshire OS TQ1696
English Heritage Register Grade II

House, built in the late 17th century for the Coghill family, was later owned by the Gibbs family who remodelled it in the late 19th century. Henry Hucks Gibbs (1st Lord Aldenham) and his son Vicary created a remarkable garden in the late Victorian period; it became, in the words of Brent Elliott in *Victorian Gardens* (1986), "the period's most-discussed virtuoso garden". Between 1869 and 1902 a Year Book was kept, describing everything done in the garden. Formal gardens close to the house still show Victorian character – a rose bed in the form of a parterre with a pool, a gravel walk with stone urns, and the remains of a water garden with ornamental rockwork, possibly by James Pulham. By 1918 the arboretum was reported to contain 179 species of oaks, 500 species of thorned plants and much else. Some of these survive in woodland west of the drive, which was formerly arranged in glades. The remains of a double avenue of Turkey oaks survives south-west of the house. The house and a large part of the grounds now belong to the Haberdasher Aske's School.

Aldenham Park
nr Morville, Shropshire OS SO6795
English Heritage Register Grade II

House built on an old site in 1691 for the Acton family and much altered, especially in the 18th and early 19th centuries. There were formal gardens here in the early 17th century. A painting by E. Hotchkiss, done in 1756 and copying "a Plan taken 1625", shows a pretty, formal garden of an unsophisticated kind and an enclosed forecourt with gatehouse, oval beds and a formal grove of trees. Beautiful early 18th-century garden gates, possibly by the Davies brothers of Wrexham (or possibly Robert Bakewell), originally in the forecourt, now form entrance to an avenue on

the Shrewsbury–Bridgnorth road. Chapel incorporating part of an 18th-century garden temple. An elaborate parterre with elegant scroll work and the monogram of the Duchess of Dalberg was made in the 1840s and survived until just before World War II.

Alderley Grange
Alderley, Gloucestershire OS ST7790
English Heritage Register Grade II
Open occasionally for NGS

17th-century house with trees planted in the late 19th century by the botanist B.H. Hodgson (after whom *Rhododendron hodgsonii* is named). New gardens made from 1961 by Alvilde Lees-Milne with some help from Vita Sackville-West, in the style of "gardens of compartments" such as Hidcote, with distinguished planting. Here is a box knot garden of herbs with an astrolabe, a pleached lime allée, a bed of 'Iceberg' roses edged with spheres of box and a 17th-century gazebo.

Aldermaston Court
Aldermaston, Berkshire OS SU5964
English Heritage Register Grade II

The original early 17th-century house, on a much older site, was damaged by fire and demolished. Present house designed by Philip Hardwick and built 1848–51. Remains of 17th-century garden layout, an elaborate 19th-century formal garden and a remarkable 19th-century avenue of yew topiary.

Alexandra Palace
Haringey, London OS TQ2690 English
Heritage Register Grade II Open regularly

A dairy farm, Tottenham Wood Farm, was developed by the Rhodes family as a London Palace of the People, inspired by the Crystal Palace (*see page 465*). After several false starts the site was acquired in 1863 by the Alexandra Park committee. The building of the Great International Exhibition (1862) was moved here, opened in 1873 and was destroyed by fire sixteen days later. A new palace was completed in 1875 and the grounds laid out, in informal landscape style, by Alexander McKenzie. Many other trials and

torments afflicted the enterprise, including changes of ownership and another fire in 1980. Today much of the ground has been given over to sports facilities. A boating lake, one of several pools planned by McKenzie, survives.

Alfriston Clergy House
see page 118

Alnwick Castle
see page 330

Alscot Park
nr Preston-on-Stour, Warwickshire
OS SP2050 English Heritage Register Grade II

An ancient estate on the river Stour, with a manor house since at least the 12th century. In 1747 it was bought by James West, a cloth merchant and MP who lived in London and regarded Alscot as his country retreat – "the comicalist little old house you ever saw", as his wife described it. He rebuilt the house in a delightful Rococo Gothic style in two stages, 1750–52 and 1762–64, but it is not known who the architect was. The grounds were altered in the mid 18th century, possibly with the advice of Sanderson Miller. The 1884 Ordnance Survey map shows a network of planned walks in the pleasure grounds, and an avenue. The avenue was aligned on a mid 18th-century obelisk which does not survive, nor do other buildings of this period: a root house, Chinese seat, a rusticated icehouse and a cascade. The river Stour flows across the park and it was widened at this time to resemble a lake, and existing ponds were modified. Earthworks survive where there was a mid 18th-century Rotunda and a Chinese pavilion. A viewing terrace, similar to that made by Sanderson Miller at nearby Farnborough Hall (*see page 261*), survives.

Altamont Garden
see page 398

Althorp
nr Northampton, Northamptonshire OS
SP6865 English Heritage Register Grade II*
Open regularly Tel 01604 770107

Estate owned by the Spencer family from the 16th century.

Orginally moated, the house was gradually altered, with chief activities in the late 17th century, and given spectacular Palladian additions 1729–33 by Roger Morris. In 1512 John Spencer was granted a licence to impark 440 acres of land, wood and water; the park and pleasure grounds continued to expand and change in subsequent centuries. Tree planting in the park was documented in a remarkable way – a series of stone pedestals bear the dates of tree plantings from 1567 to 1901; John Evelyn praised the system in his *Sylva* (1664). Evelyn visited Althorp again in 1675 and admired the "prospect to Holmby [Holdenby] House (*see page 265*), which being demolished in the late Civil warre, shews like a Roman ruine shaded by the trees about it, one of the most pleasing sights that I ever saw". It is occasionally said, with no evidence, that Le Nôtre designed gardens here. The Kip engraving in *Britannia Illustrata* (1707) – seven years after Le Nôtre's death – shows no pleasure grounds nor any trace of anything especially Lenôtrian: the house sits on its moated island with an enclosed forecourt and walled kitchen gardens to the east; avenues run across the landscape and deer graze in the park. Avenues are still visible in the landscape today, mostly of ash and oak to replace the elm, and with later plantings of lime and London plane. In 1790 Henry Holland (Capability Brown's son-in-law) was working on the house and also produced landscaping proposals which resulted in filling in the moat and taking the park up to the house. W.M. Teulon and W.B. Thomas made new formal gardens west and north of the house 1860–63. In 1966 a "French" garden of hornbeams, beech and limes was made north-east of the house to designs of the 7th Earl Spencer. In 1997 Diana, Princess of Wales, sister of the 8th Earl, was buried on an island in the Oval Pool nearby, in a setting designed by Dan Pearson.

Alton Towers
see page 246

Amesbury Abbey
Amesbury, Wiltshire OS SU1441
English Heritage Register Grade II*

House built 1661 for the 2nd Duke of Somerset to the designs of John Webb, replacing an earlier building. Alterations *c*.1730 by Henry Flitcroft and rebuilt 1834–40 for Sir Edmund Antrobus to the designs of Thomas Hopper. In 1738 Charles Bridgeman made a plan for new gardens for the 3rd Duke of Queensberry – a grand scheme with formal ribbons of trees, bastions, rides through woods, winding paths and informal tree planting. It is not known if anything of this was executed. The park was landscaped in the 18th century. West of the house, a grotto and, built like a bridge over an inlet of the river Avon, a Chinese temple by Sir William Chambers (1772).

Ammerdown House
Kilmersdon, Somerset OS ST7152
English Heritage Register Grade II* Open
occasionally for charity Tel 01791 433709

The house was built 1788–94 for Thomas Jolliffe to the designs of James Wyatt. Wyatt also designed a handsome orangery to the north-east of the house. There was some planting of trees in the park here in the 18th century but anything that survives from that period is eclipsed by the superb garden laid out by Edwin Lutyens in 1902. Its single stroke of genius, fleshed out with much clever detail, is to have devised a link between the house and the orangery, the two great ornaments in the landscape, which are awkwardly related to each other. Lutyens's solution was to make two axes centred on each of the buildings and to link them with the Italian Garden, an elaborate rondel with a circular pool. A parterre of box-edged beds surrounds the pool, with statues standing out against extraordinary ramparts of yew whose inside surfaces are clipped into elaborate scalloped shapes. About this strong but simple plan Lutyens was able to arrange other ornamental schemes, including a fine parterre with clipped Portugal laurels that flanks the path leading to the house. In the park is a rather plain column – like a factory chimney with vaguely decorative ambitions – erected by Colonel Jolliffe in 1853 as a memorial to his father.

Amport House
Amport, Hampshire OS SU2944
English Heritage Register Grade II

House built in 1857 for the 14th Marquess of Winchester to the designs of William Burn. West of the house, probably laid out at the same time, is a parterre with the Winchester coat of arms. Terraced garden south of the house designed by Sir Edwin Lutyens in 1923 with descending rills, an oval pool and fountain, beds of irises and roses, and lily pools. The planting was done by Gertrude Jekyll who also laid out a very elaborate formal rock garden with raised beds.

Ampthill Park
Ampthill, Bedfordshire OS TL0239
English Heritage Register Grade II

Late 17th-century house for Lord Ashburnham on a much older site, enlarged by William Chambers 1769–71. Capability Brown worked on the landscape 1771–72, for which he was paid £2,396 (£143,185 today). In the park south of the house, where in the 16th century there had been a deer park about old Ampthill Castle, are several clumps of trees, some possibly surviving from Brown's work, some of an earlier period. The site of the castle is marked by the Gothic Katherine Cross (1773) in memory of Katherine of Aragon who stayed here – "the mournful refuge of an injured Queen", as Horace Walpole called it. To the east, Russett's Lodge, a 17th-century brick building given a classical façade by William Chambers.

Amwell Grove *and* Amwell Pool
Great Amwell, Hertfordshire OS TL3712
English Heritage Register Grade II

House built 1794–97 by the architect and engineer Robert Mylne for his own use. The house overlooks the New River, part of the system designed to bring water to London (built 1609–13 by Sir Hugh Myddleton). Robert Mylne created the Pool with an island and designed the Coade stone urn (1800) commemorating Myddleton. On a second island, a stone monument to the New River (1818). North of Amwell Lane is Emma's Well (late 18th- or early 19th-century) with a basin fed by the spring from which Amwell takes its name.

An Cala
Ellenabeigh, Isle of Seil, Argyll
OS NM7417 Scottish Inventory
Open occasionally for SGS

Seil is only just an island, separated from the mainland by a narrow strait crossed by a bridge. An Cala is on the west coast, embraced by curving cliffs and looking west towards the south coast of Mull. In the 1930s Colonel and the Hon. Mrs Arthur Murray came to live here and made a garden, building walls and planting shelter belts to give protection from the salt-laden gales. A cascade from the cliffs was diverted to form a stream and pools in the garden where many water-loving plants thrive. The sloping garden was terraced and is now planted with a rose garden, an alpine border and such shrubs as camellias, *Crinodendron hookerianum*, magnolias and rhododendrons.

Anderson Manor
Anderson, Dorset OS SY8897
English Heritage Register Grade II

Brick and Purbeck stone house built in 1622 for John Tregonwell. Original stables and some garden walls, but existing garden largely dates from early 20th century. Mrs Gordon Gratrix bought the estate in 1910 and *Country Life* in April 1915 describes a newly made garden to the east: "a formal walled garden set with knots of box and lavender and small clipped yew and box fantasies… The new lay-out was based upon the traces of the old garden…A garden mound, pleached lime walk and iron gate leading into the orchard were all added at this time." Yew topiary, box-edged beds, sundial and an old summerhouse all possibly early 17th-century. Two lead garden cisterns are dated 1723 and 1764, with the initials F.G.H. and I.W.W. respectively.

Anglesey Abbey
see page 286

Annes Grove
see page 399

Annesley Hall
Annesley, Nottinghamshire OS SK5052
English Heritage Register Grade II*

17th-century house with later additions and probably earlier origins. South-west of the house, 17th-century raised walk with balustrade and central double stair. To the north-west, walled garden with geometric parterre and bedding. Further south-west of house, ornamental woodland and shrubbery with meandering paths. Woodland to the east of the house with motte and bailey at Castle Hill, and remains of an avenue, Byron's Walk, running north–south.

Antony House
see page 14

Antony Woodland Garden and Woods
see page 15

Antrim Castle
Antrim, County Antrim, Northern Ireland
Open regularly Tel (028) 9442 8000

Early 17th-century house built for Sir Hugh Clotworthy (later Viscounts Massereene) and rebuilt in the early 19th century. Destroyed by fire in 1922. Mrs Delany saw the garden in 1758 and wrote that it "was reckoned a fine one forty years ago – high hedges and long narrow walks". The 17th-century Anglo-Dutch style gardens partially survive and have been restored in recent years. They have canals, a cascade, formal pool, hedges of honbeam and lime, a formal wilderness and a large parterre with period plants.

Appleby Castle
Appleby-in-Westmorland, Cumbria OS NY6819 English Heritage Register Grade II*

Castle dating from the 11th century but present building 13th-century with alterations; in a fine position with grounds running down to a curve in the river Eden. Grounds probably laid out by Lady Anne Clifford in the mid to late 17th century. Lady Anne's Bee House north of the castle (it was not used for bees, but was thought to resemble a bee house) has a pyramid-shaped roof. It was either an oratory or quite possibly a garden gazebo, for it has fine views westwards over the river to the far bank. In a map of 1754 it is shown to be in the corner of a formal enclosure, thought to have been a garden. This had two square plots with paths radiating from central circles.

Appuldurcombe House
Appuldurcombe, Isle of Wight OS SZ5479
English Heritage Register Grade II
Open regularly (EH) Tel 01983 852484

House, now a beautiful but partly roofless shell, built in the early 18th century for Sir Robert Worsley on the site of a 16th-century house. In 1779 Sir Richard Worsley consulted Capability Brown who produced a plan but it is uncertain what resulted. The park was certainly landscaped in the 18th century, some of it before Brown was consulted. Parts of an 18th-century park wall survive. North-west of the house the plinth of an obelisk of 1747 commemorating Sir Robert Worsley, struck by lightning in 1831. Parkland now largely turned over to agricultural use but a few mature parkland trees, belts and woodland remain.

Arbigland
Kirkbean, Kirkcudbrightshire Scottish Inventory Open regularly Tel 01387 88288

House built 1755 for William Craik, possibly to his own design; old Arbigland Hall 16th-century on a different site. The gardens almost entirely of the 20th century. House framed in old trees and rhododendrons with, behind it, the Broad Walk which leads through woodland towards the sea. Concealed in the woods are Japan, a bosky water garden, a sunken rose garden of *c.*1920 built on the site of old Arbigland Hall, and woodland glades planted with ornamental trees and shrubs which flourish in this mild coastal position. Acers, camellias, eucryphias, tender species rhododendrons (such as

R. sinograde) and much else grow in lavish profusion.

Arbury Hall
Nuneaton, Warwickshire OS SP3389
English Heritage Register Grade II*
Open regularly Tel 024 7638 2804

House dating back to *c.*1580 but magnificently Gothicised from 1748 by Sir Roger Newdigate with advice from Sanderson Miller. 18th-century landscaped park with interconnected lakes. Mid 18th-century cascade and grotto east of house. Much garden activity in 19th century – an enclosed rose garden with pond north-east of house, and many excellent specimen trees about house. Walled kitchen garden north of stables now houses an arboretum.

Arbuthnott House
Arbuthnott, Kincardineshire OS NO7975
Scottish Inventory Open regularly
Tel 01561 320417

The Arbuthnotts (or Aberbothenoths as they were) have lived here since the 13th century; the present Viscount is the 33rd Laird. The present house is partly a 15th-century tower house transformed into a symmetrical Georgian house 1754–57. Parkland at Arbuthnott goes back at least to the 18th century and surviving limes date from this time. An avenue, Dark Avenue, aligned on the house is shown on a map of 1750; it was replanted with beech in the 19th century and parts of it have been replanted with beech and sycamore in recent times. The landscape designer James Abercrombie did a plan for the grounds in 1792 but it is not known exactly what resulted. A 5-acre/2-hectare terraced garden was laid out 1683–94 for the 3rd Viscount. The garden, enclosed by walls, outhouses and railings, is divided by a pattern of grass paths – three chief paths cutting horizontally across the steep slope, connected by diagonal subsidiary paths. A south-facing wall has espaliered apples, cherries and plums and there is a long range of heated glasshouses. Beds of fruit and vegetables are edged with borders of herbaceous

A

perennials, roses or flowers for cutting. Part of the garden has a large lawn in front of the house and part is an orchard. On a grand scale, this is a type of garden found in many an old Scottish estate.

Archerfield House

nr Dirleton, East Lothian
OS NT5084 Scottish Inventory

House built in the late 17th century for William Nisbet of Dirleton, much altered in the 18th century with, in particular, work by Robert Adam c.1790. It survives, in the words of Colin McWilliam in his "Buildings of Scotland" volume, *Lothian*, as "A forlorn shell, but of the highest value and interest". A beech avenue leading to the house was planted before 1750. In 1778 work on the garden was done by John Hay, a specialist in flower and kitchen gardens and hothouses. The grounds were laid out c.1779 by Robert Robinson. Here, and in his other designs, according to A.A. Tait in *The Landscape Garden in Scotland: 1735–1835* (1980), he "rung all the familiar variations upon lake, clump and belt". Robinson's parkland is now largely arable fields but its structure is still visible. Close to the house, a former shrubbery is now overgrown and a pavilion is now the headquarters of the Edinburgh and Lothian Clay Pigeon Shooting Club.

Ardanaiseig House

nr Kilchrenan, Argyll OS NN0824
Open regularly Tel 01866 833333

House built in splendid Baronial style in 1833 to the designs of William Burn for J.A. Campbell of Inverawe – in a beautiful position overlooking Loch Awe. Notable 19th-century woodland garden – with acers, crinodendrons, enkianthus, eucryphias, hoherias, magnolias, rhododendrons and rowans – goes down to banks of the loch with magnificent views. Terraced gardens east of the house, with beds of herbaceous perennials and annuals; the lowermost terrace, on the lochside, with spring bulbs and wildflowers. The house has been a hotel since 1980.

Ardchattan Priory

nr Connel Bridge, Argyll OS NM9735
Scottish Inventory Open regularly
Tel 01796 481355

13th-century Benedictine priory, part of which, Ardchattan House, was converted into a house before 1600. The abbey church was burnt down by Cromwell's troops in 1654. Beautiful position on the north shore of Loch Etive. Parkland with shelter belts; remaining individual trees include sycamores dating from the 16th century. Woodland garden with good flowering shrubs and trees – acers, embothriums, eucryphias, rowans and stephanandra – and a meadow with spring bulbs and summer wildflowers. By the house, a rose garden with old-fashioned shrub roses and a rock garden for alpines. South of the house, a group of 17th-century sweet chestnuts.

Mary Arden's House

see page 278

Ardgillan Castle

Balbriggan, County Dublin,
Republic of Ireland Open regularly
Tel (00353) 1 8492212

Ancient estate with an early 18th-century house built for the Revd Robert Taylor, with castellations added in the late 18th century. The demesne has 198 acres/80 hectares of woodland, through which walks give views of the sea. Formal gardens west of the house with large collection of roses – species, old shrub roses and modern varieties. Late 19th-century conservatory made by the Edinburgh firm of Mackenzie and Moncur. Walled kitchen garden with rare fruit wall – a free-standing wall with bays to give protection to tender varieties of fruit. Beds of fruit and vegetables and a collection of plants native to Ireland and of exotics introduced by Irish collectors. 19th-century yew walk south of the house.

Ardkinglas

Cairndow, Argyll OS NN1710 Scottish
Inventory Open regularly Tel 01499 600261

Ancient estate of the Campbells with beautiful Arts and Crafts castle designed by Sir Robert Lorimer in 1907 for Sir Andrew

Noble. Lorimer also laid out terraced garden in front of a loggia, giving splendid views over Loch Fyne. The woodland garden is the great thing here, with trees going back to 1750 – such as a silver fir (*Abies alba*) which now has a girth of 31ft/9m. Much tree planting, especially of conifers, in the late 19th century. In more recent times a very large collection of rhododendrons has been built up. Two National Collections of trees are held at Ardkinglas – 33 species of fir (*Abies*) and 24 species of spruce (*Picea*).

Ardnamona

Lough Eske, County Donegal,
Republic of Ireland Open regularly
Tel (00353) 73 22650

House built in the 1830s for the Wray family in a wonderfully attractive setting close to Lough Eske. Samuel Lewis's *The Topographical Dictionary of Ireland* (1837) described Ardnamona as "one of the most picturesque domains in rural Ireland". The Wrays planted a pinetum (which survives) running down to the banks of the lough – 19th-century examples of monkey puzzles, the Nikko fir (*Abies homolepis*), oriental spruce (*Picea orientalis*) and Wellingtonias may be seen. In the late 19th century, in the time of Sir Arthur and Lady Wallace, many rhododendrons and other exotics were planted, some of which have established large communities (like *Crocosmia pottsii*). Very large old rhododendrons survive, both 19th-century cultivars and magnificent species such as *R. sinogrande*. When Kieran and Amabel Clarke came here in 1990 the garden had been neglected for many years and they have done much to restore it.

Ardtornish

Morvern, Argyll OS NM7047 Scottish
Inventory Open regularly Tel 01967 421288

When Sir Walter Scott sailed through the Sound of Mull in 1814 he admired the charms of Loch Aline: "a beautiful salt-water lake, with a narrow outlet to the Sound. It is surrounded by round hills, sweetly fringed with green copse below…There is great promise of beauty in its interior, but we cannot see everything."

Ardtornish House, built in the 1880s on an older site to the designs of Alexander Ross, has a beautiful position at the head of the loch, facing down towards the Sound of Mull. The estate was bought in 1930 by Owen and Emmeline Hugh Smith who greatly added to the existing garden; they were friends of Sir John Stirling Maxwell of Pollok House (*see page 390*), from whom they acquired many species rhododendrons which have now grown to great size. The present owner, their daughter Mrs John Raven, and her late husband also added to the garden. Today, wild and informal, it has a good collection of acid-loving trees and shrubs that relish the high rainfall; among them: acers, davidias, cercidiphyllums, enkianthus, eucryphias, hoherias and hydrangeas. Parts of the house, and cottages on the estate, are let to holidaymakers. Loch Aline remains as beautiful as it was when Sir Walter Scott saw it.

Arduaine Garden

see page 360

Arley Hall

see page 189

Arley House

Upper Arley, Worcestershire OS SO7680
English Heritage Register Grade II

House of c.1965 on the site of earlier houses going back at least to the 16th century. Around the house is a garden made for the house – terraced lawns, flower beds, a rockery and hedges of yew and Leyland cypress. 18th- and 19th-century former kitchen gardens at a little distance north-west of the house are divided into four chief compartments. The walls of a formal water garden of c.1965, the Italian Garden, are planted with camellias with heather at their feet. North of the Italian Garden, a walled garden with glasshouses, and north of that the Magnolia Garden with a curved yew hedge and grass paths running between deep borders of magnolias. South and west of the former kitchen gardens is an arboretum dating back to the early 19th century, much added to when Robert Woodward bought

the estate in 1852. A catalogue, *Hortus Arleyensis*, made in 1907, lists over 300 species of trees. (One of them, still surviving, was thought to be the only known *Sorbus domestica* raised from a wild plant; however, two populations of wild *S. domestica* were found in South Glamorgan between 1983 and 1991.) Park with grassland and mature trees, in particular in the dingle, Naboth's Vineyard, in the south-east, which has a stream with bridges, cascades and pools.

Arlington Court

see page 16

Armley House, *also known as* Gott's Park

Leeds, West Yorkshire OS SE2634
English Heritage Register Grade II

House built in the late 18th century, extended c.1820, reduced again in the 20th century and now accommodating a café and golf course club facilities. The parkland which surrounds the house was possibly designed by Thomas White. In 1810 Humphry Repton produced a Red Book for Benjamin Gott, a cultivated and very successful industrialist whose firm, with almost 1,000 employees, was one of the largest in the country. By Repton's time the site already had thoroughly industrial views and a panoramic view of the city of Leeds. Also visible was Gott's cloth mill, Armley Mill; illuminated by gas lights at night, it delighted Repton and he made it the focus of attention in his new landscape. Repton also concealed the hard lines of a canal and made the wooded banks of the river Ayre more visible; he thought it important to frame specific views "without opening too much the scene, that is too populous to form the principal object of the landscape from the villa". With a golf course in the park, immensely increased urban scenery and dense planting, much of Repton's work has gone, but its principles may st[ill] be studied.

Arniston House

Gorebridge, Midlothian OS NT3259 Scottis[h]
Inventory Open regularly Tel 01875 83051

Magnificent house designed in 1726 by William Adam for Rober[t]

Dundas. Adam also laid out the grounds. His original plan of c.1726 shows an ornate parterre to the south and a formal wilderness to the west, with paths radiating out from a central oval; on two sides of the house avenues lead north and east, each interrupted with circular plantations, with other subsidiary avenues; the northern avenue borrows as an eyecatcher the craggy outline of Arthur's Seat twelve miles away on the edge of Edinburgh. The formal gardens have long disappeared but a stone urn designed by James Adam c.1750 survives among trees at what had been the centre of the wilderness. Traces of some of the avenues survive but much was lost when the grounds were landscaped by Thomas White in 1791. A painting, attributed to Alexander Nasmyth, of c.1800 shows the house framed in billowing clumps of trees and overlooking open parkland, much as it is today. A walled garden was built c.1764 and has remarkable exotic stone gate surrounds formed of architectural salvage from the old Parliament House in Edinburgh, which was demolished in 1808. A grotto is thought to have been built from stone from Old Arniston House (one stone is dated 1644).

Arnos Vale Cemetery
Arnos Vale, Bristol OS ST6071 English Heritage Register Grade II Open regularly

Rare Arcadian cemetery laid out from 1836 with fine quality monuments and architectural embellishments. These range from Charles Underwood's very correct Greek temple lodges of 1837 to the romantic tomb of Rajah Rammohun Roy Bahador (1843) and several monuments by J.T. Tyley & Sons. The design follows Loudonesque principles – main routes curve gently up the slope with serpentine walks leading off on either side.

Arundel Castle
Arundel, West Sussex OS TQ 0107 English Heritage Register Grade II* Open regularly Tel 01903 883136

Castle dating from the 11th century when a motte and two baileys were built by Roger de Montgomery; the present

building is almost entirely of the 19th century – "a great disappointment" say Ian Nairn and Nikolaus Pevsner in their "Buildings of England" volume, Sussex. There had been formal gardens within the castle precinct in the 17th and 18th centuries. Elaborate Victorian parterres had gone by 1914 and nothing came of a proposed flower garden to be designed by Gertrude Jekyll. The garden was substantially remade in the 1990s when a bowling green, known to have been here in the 16th century, was reinstated and enclosed in yew hedges. At the same time an evergreen shrubbery was planted along the lower lawns, a former tennis court. Late 19th-century cricket pitch north-west of the pleasure grounds in the Castle Park. The Great Park (or New Park) to the north was created in the 18th century and is today pasture and woodland. In the south-west part of the park is the curious triangular Hiorne Tower (named after its architect, Francis Hiorne), built in 1796 in chequerwork stone and flint.

Ascot Place
Winkfield, Berkshire OS SU9171 English Heritage Register Grade II*

18th-century house for Daniel Agace. Late 18th-century pleasure grounds north-west of house, with Corinthian temple of late 18th or early 19th century and a Gothic seat of the same date. 18th-century landscape park with, south of the house, a long sinuous lake divided into three compartments. Magnificent Grade I listed grotto by Robert Turnbull, made 1750–70, on the bank of lake with views over it. Three chambers variously ornamented with feldspar stalactites, quartz, flints, tufa, pebblework, pools and seats. Some of the stalactites are very long and pointed, beautifully decorated with zigzags of a brown mineral, like renaissance flamework stitching. Barbara Jones in Follies & Grottoes (1974) describes it as "extremely beautiful, extremely complex, wonderfully preserved".

Ascott
(Buckinghamshire)
see page 70

Ascott Park
Stadhampton, Oxfordshire OS SU6198 English Heritage Register Grade II

The manor of Ascott was acquired in 1518 by Sir Michael Dormer (whose family, now Cottrell-Dormer, later owned Rousham, see page 104). The house became a dower house after the family moved to Rousham but by the early 19th century it had disappeared. In the 16th and 17th centuries the Dormers made an elaborate formal garden of which earthworks, avenues and a few garden buildings survive. 17th-century gate piers stand at the entrance to a grass ride flanked by lime avenues and crossed by the remains of a second avenue of limes. The remains of the garden include a raised terrace, a walled enclosure about a 16th-century farmhouse, rectangular ponds and evidence of other ponds and a canal. Two 16th-century octagonal garden buildings, a 16th-century dovecote and a thatched granary of the 16th and 18th centuries also remain. A 17th-century stone garden pavilion was converted in the 19th and 20th centuries into a cottage.

Ascreavie House
nr Kirkton of Kingoldrum, Angus OS NO3357 Scottish Inventory

House built in the mid 19th century for the Young family to the designs of William Scott of Dundee. In the 1940s the house was owned by the circus Bertram Millses and was bought in 1949 by Major George Sherriff, the great Himalayan plant collector. Sherriff and his wife planted many small alpine plants on the terraces south of the house, both in the ground and in troughs and other containers, but few of these survive. A shelter belt was thinned to form glades in which to plant the acid-loving flowering shrubs he loved, and the garden stretched inexorably up the south-facing slope with rare species rhododendrons, Himalayan birches, eucryphias and the handsome Daphniphyllum himalaense subsp. macropodum. After Sherriff's death in 1967 many plants were given to the Dundee Botanic Garden, but much

remains. British Gardeners: A Biographical Dictionary (1980, Miles Hadfield, Robert Harling and Leonie Highton) refers to Ascreavie as "a renowned garden evocative of the Himalayan scene which [Sherriff] knew so well".

Ashburnham Place
Ashburnham, East Sussex OS TQ6814 English Heritage Register Grade II* Open occasionally for NGS

Ashburnhams came to live here in the 12th century and remained until 1953. House built in 1665, with alterations in 18th and 19th centuries. Formal gardens by house designed by George Dance in 1813, with balustraded terraces and late 20th-century lawns and beds of herbaceous perennials and roses. West of house, orangery designed by Capability Brown overlooking a lawn with a 19th-century design of fan-shapes in dwarf box. Brown did a plan for the grounds in 1767 and much work was carried out: east of the house he extended and animated a chain of lakes, already started by the early 18th century, making walks along their banks and through woods in which he opened glades; a Greek temple, boathouse and grotto date from his time. South of the middle lake, Front Water, walks and rides pass through glades in mixed woodland (shown as the Grove in Brown's plan) enlivened today with rhododendrons and other exotics. North of the house, the park probably dates back to Saxon times. The deer park to the north-east contains areas of semi-natural ancient woodland with scattered ancient oaks. The western part of the park contains belts and clumps which probably date from Brown's time.

Ashby St Ledgers
Ashby St Ledgers, Northamptonshire OS SP5768 English Heritage Register Grade II

Ancient house of the Catesby family, bought by Ivor Guest (later 1st Viscount Wimborne) who from 1904 employed Edwin Lutyens to extend the Elizabethan house and make new gardens. Surviving early 18th-century Statue Lawn south of house, with stone figure of Atlas and statues of the seasons. Lutyens's designs east of house

include a canal garden enclosed in yew hedges, balustraded walks, herbaceous borders, terracing, a lawn with beds of roses; much of the planting was designed by Gertrude Jekyll. Path lined with cherry trees leads to an orchard north of the house, with ancient wellhead, and stone bridge over a canal designed by Lutyens.

Ashdown House
see page 70

Ashridge
Little Gaddesden, Hertfordshire OS SP9912 English Heritage Register Grade II Open regularly Tel 01442 843491; Park and woodland open regularly (NT) Tel 01442 851227

House built on an ancient, formerly monastic site to the designs of James Wyatt 1808–13 for the 7th Earl of Bridgwater. South of the house, terrace and parterre with yew hedges. To the east, a sunken Italian Garden with a central stone pool surrounded by a circle of yews and lawns with geometric beds – overlooked to the north by Jeffry Wyatville's orangery. A path leads round to the south garden with an arboretum, rhododendron walk and avenue of Wellingtonias. South-west of the house, a brick fernery with ferns planted in rockwork. To its south-east, set in an amphitheatre, a grotto containing a monument to a favourite horse (d.1857) and the entrance to a flint-lined subterranean tunnel leading to the Duchess's Private Garden, a lawn with island beds and shrubs. Nearby, hedged in yew, a circular rose garden, the Rosary, with a stone fountain pool at the centre. To its west, the Monk's Garden, a sunken parterre with box plants clipped into heraldic devices; in its centre, the Holie Well (1820, by Jeffry Wyatville), a Gothic conduit head and octagonal moat. Humphry Repton advised the 7th Earl of Bridgwater in 1813 and produced a Red Book; the pleasure grounds of the house largely correspond to his suggestions, though the western garden is much less elaborate than that proposed. Park laid out in the 1760s, taking in the 16th- and 17th-century deer park. Capability

Brown worked here 1759–68 but the results are not known. At the extreme north-west of the park, at the end of the Prince's Riding, the Bridgwater Monument (1831–32 by Jeffry Wyatville). Today there is a golf course in part of the park.

Ashstead Park
Ashstead, Surrey OS TQ1958
English Heritage Register Grade II

House built 1790 for Richard Howard to the designs of Joseph Bonomi, replacing a 17th-century house. Celia Fiennes visited Ashstead c.1703 and admired "severall gardens walled in". J.C. Loudon wrote about Ashstead in the *Gardeners Magazine* in 1829, describing a geometric garden and gravel walk. The chief interest today is the formal garden north of the house made by Poantia Ralli c.1900. Below a terrace a semicircular balustrade encloses a lawn with common and golden yew clipped into topiary shapes. At the centre, smaller pieces of topiary and bedding schemes are enclosed in an elaborate stone surround. The house today is a school.

Ashton Court
Long Ashton, Somerset OS ST5571
English Heritage Register Grade II*

The house at Ashton Court has a long history; parts of it date from the 15th century, but there was much rebuilding in the mid 16th and 17th centuries after the estate was bought by the Smyth family who sold it in 1960. 16th-century deer park and ancient oak pollards of remarkable beauty in Clerkencombe Wood. 18th-century landscaping includes a ha-ha. Early 19th-century well-wooded landscape by Sir Hugh Smyth with advice from Humphry Repton.

Ashton Memorial Gardens *and* Williamson Park
Lancaster, Lancashire OS SD4961 English Heritage Register Grade II Open regularly

Public park designed by J. Maclean and given to the people of Lancaster in 1881. Named after an industrialist and philanthropist, James Williamson, who was

created Baron Ashton. A memorial to him by Sir John Belcher, erected 1907–9 and costing more than £87,000 (£4,479340 today), dominates the park and, from its elevated site, the city of Lancaster too. Nikolaus Pevsner, in his volume on *North Lancashire* in the "Buildings of England" series, calls it "the grandest monument in England". It is a domed Baroque extravaganza, the interior a single chamber with mosaics. Next to it is a conservatory (a former palm house, now used for butterflies) designed by Belcher and Joass c.1909. To the north and south are the landscaped former quarries, now well wooded with sinuous paths. South of the memorial, a lake with rocky cliffs on three sides is traversed by a stone balustraded footbridge. The southern quarry has dramatic hollows and eminences.

Ashwell Bury
Ashwell, Hertfordshire OS TL2639
English Heritage Register Grade II

Early 19th-century house remodelled 1922–23 by Sir Edwin Lutyens. Gertrude Jekyll made plans for the garden in 1907–8 but there have been several alterations. West and south-west of the house, a terrace and lawn; a yew hedge with recesses cut into it was intended by Miss Jekyll to enclose small flower borders. North of the lawn, a rose garden with a grass mound enclosed in a box hedge. Kitchen garden enclosed by yew hedge, probably as planned by Miss Jekyll.

Aske Hall
Aske, North Yorkshire OS NZ1703
English Heritage Register Grade II*
Open regularly Tel 01748 822000

Neo-Georgian front on old and complicated house, going back at least to the 15th century. Pleasure grounds with terraced walks down towards a lake. North of terrace walk, a temple-like Gothick summerhouse c.1770, possibly by Capability Brown. In the park, a lake with a late 18th-century temple on a promontory. Oliver's Ducket south-east of the hall beyond the park is a castellated building, part of Richmond Castle given new life as an eyecatcher.

Astley Hall
Chorley, Lancashire OS SD5718
English Heritage Register Grade II
Open regularly Tel 01257 515555

16th-century house with 17th- and 18th-century alterations. A painting of c.1710 by an unidentified artist in John Harris's *The Artist and the Country House* (1979) shows Astley Hall standing in one corner of a walled garden which is laid out in rectangular lawns with walks and statues. In the south-east, overlooked by a pavilion built into the garden wall, is a lake. This in essence remains today. Parkland east of the house is now playing fields.

Aston Hall
Birmingham, West Midlands OS SP0889
English Heritage Register Grade II
Open regularly Tel 0121 327 0062

Magnificent Jacobean house built for Sir Thomas Holte, possibly designed by John Thorpe. The estate remained in the Holte family until the 19th century when much land was sold off for development. In 1850 attempts were made to turn the grounds into a public park but bad management and the accidental death of Mrs Powell, "the female Blondin", during a high-wire act, led to the grounds being closed. House and grounds were acquired by the City of Birmingham in 1864. The house is now handsomely restored with period furnishings and the grounds are now a public park. Traces of the 17th-century pleasure grounds are still visible close to the house where modern formal gardens have been made. In the park, some 20th-century avenues follow 17th-century alignments. Sports facilities and a playground have been provided in recent times.

Athelhampton House Gardens
see page 16

Attingham Park
nr Shrewsbury, Shropshire OS SJ5409
English Heritage Register Grade II*
Open regularly (NT) Tel 01743 708162

Early 18th-century house (known as Tern Hall) remodelled by George Steuart 1783–85 for Noel

Hill, later 1st Lord Berwick. Very beautiful old parkland. Thomas Leggett carried out landscaping work 1769–72. Humphry Repton was consulted (Red Book, 1798). As a result, the Tern was made into a smooth curving river south-east of the house, with the water-level maintained by a weir. This survives in essence, together with some of Repton's planting, including a superb grove of cedars of Lebanon north of the house by the banks of the river. Repton increased the length of the drive to make the park seem bigger, but his suggestion that a spire should be added to the tower of Wrotoxeter Church, two miles away, to make a more effective eyecatcher was not adopted.

Auchincruive House
nr Ayr, Ayrshire OS NS3823 Scottish Inventory Open occasionally for SGS

Early 18th-century house, with later additions, on a fine site in a loop of the river Ayr. A formal landscape was laid out by William Boutcher for the Hon. Colonel Charles Cathcart from 1723. 18th-century parkland running up to the river, with a few original trees and a splendid building – the Tea Pavilion or Oswald's Temple (the Oswalds bought the estate in 1764) – designed by Robert Adam in 1778. It is a round castellated building with blind arches and rises from protective walls decorated with round towers. In the woodland some of Boutcher's *bosquets* survive. Since 1927 the estate has been the premises of the West of Scotland Agricultural College.

Auckland Castle Park
Bishop Auckland, County Durham OS NZ2130 English Heritage Register Grade II* Open regularly Tel 01388 601627

Auckland Castle, the residence of Bishops of Durham, was started in the 11th century with much enlargement in the 17th and 18th centuries. A terraced walk encloses the garden, with a sunken lawn to the east (a former bowling green), and views over the walls to parkland to the east and north. There had been a deer park here in the middle ages and there were deer in the 18th century. In the

park, the river Gaunless winds from south to north through its wooded valley. Close to its western bank is a large deer shelter built in 1760 with Gothic detailing. In the northern part of the park the Coundon burn, a tributary of the Gaunless, flows through wooded areas with paths, and is traversed by three 18th-century stone bridges. In the centre of the park is the Bishop Auckland golf course.

Audley End House
see page 286

David Austin Roses
see page 246

Avenham Park
Preston, Lancashire OS SD5328 English Heritage Register Grade II Open regularly

Public park designed by Ernest Milner in 1861, incorporating an existing walk along the river Ribble. In the centre of the park, open grassland slopes south-east towards the river. Belts of trees protect the park on three sides with open views to the south. In the northern part of the park a Boer war memorial in the form of an obelisk. South of it, the Japanese Garden with a pond, ornamental trees and a ravine with rockwork. To the south-east, a 20th-century open air theatre. In the south-east part of the park, an arcaded shelter, the Belvedere, of 1865.

Avenham Walk
Preston, Lancashire OS SD5328 English Heritage Register Grade II Open regularly

Remarkable public promenade bought by the town of Preston in 1697. It lies on a spur of land overlooking the river Ribble and consists of a narrow rectangular gravel walk lined on each side by lime trees. The original trees were felled in 1738 and those seen today range from the 18th to the 20th century. Samuel and Nathaniel Buck's engraved panorama of Preston (1728) show the walk jutting out towards the river, with promenaders plainly visible among the trees. Then it was on the edge of the town; today it is surrounded by buildings.

A

Avington Park

Avington, Hampshire OS SU5332
English Heritage Register Grade II*
Open regularly Tel 01962 77920

16th-century house with major alterations in the early 18th century, possibly by John James. Deer park made from 1765 and, at the same time, a landscape park made for the 3rd Duke of Chandos in the style of Capability Brown with serpentine lake, cascade and clumps and belts of trees. Lime avenues in the park seem, at least in part, to date from an earlier period. 19th-century conservatory in the style of Sir Joseph Paxton.

Avondale

Rathdrum, County Wicklow,
Republic of Ireland
Open regularly Tel (00353) 0404 46111

House built in 1779 for Samuel Hayes, possibly to his own design. Hayes was also an expert dendrologist and wrote A Practical Treatise on Planting and Management of Woods and Coppices (1794). Anne Plumptre in her Narrative of a Residence in Ireland (1817) (quoted in Edward Malins's and The Knight of Glin's Lost Demesnes (1976)) described the demesne: "The sides of the river [Avon] are sometimes fringed with close thickets of wood, sometimes with fine lawns having majestic forest-trees scattered about; in parts the dell is quite inclosed, having only majestic rocks covered in ivy and rock-plants on each side." In the 19th century Charles Stewart Parnell lived at Avondale and the house is now a museum devoted to him. In 1904 the Avondale demesne was bought by the state as a forestry school, with trees planted in one-acre plots to form a Forest Garden along continental lines. The plant collector Augustine Henry advised on the planting from 1913. Some trees survive from Samuel Hayes's time and there is an excellent range of conifers dating from the early 20th century.

Aynho Park

Aynho, Northamptonshire OS SP5133
English Heritage Register Grade II

17th-century house for Richard Cartwright, remodelled in the early 18th century by Thomas Archer for Thomas Cartwright and again by John Soane for William Cartwright after 1800. A formal garden had been here in the early part of the 18th century but in 1760 Capability Brown submitted a plan, for which he was paid £263 1s 3d (£19,027 today), and between 1761 and 1763 was paid £1,080 (£77,986 today). Almost all the formal gardens south of the house were removed and Brown made a long sloping lawn ending in a ha-ha at the boundary of the park where an elm walk may have been broken into clumps and other informal groups of trees planted. William Cartwright consulted Humphry Repton, who came to Aynho in 1796, but the outcome is not known; it is possible that the formal rose garden west of the house was made at this time.

Ayscoughfee Hall

see page 288

Babington House

Babington, Somerset OS ST7051
English Heritage Register Grade II

Plain but distinguished early 18th-century house built for Henry Mompesson whose niece built the church of St Margaret which now stands so decoratively nearby – "lovably placed on a lawn in front of the house", as Pevsner charmingly puts it. Victorian shrubberies, 18th-century icehouse and 19th-century fernery. Lakes and woodland suggest modest landscaping in the 18th century; in the 1740s the remains of the village were obliterated to enable this. The house is now a smart hotel, restaurant and club.

Babworth Hall

Babworth, Nottinghamshire OS SK6880
English Heritage Register Grade II

18th-century house altered in 1790 for John Bridgeman Simpson by Humphry Repton. In 1792 Repton also produced a Red Book for the grounds, in which he includes a painting of his youthful clients sitting under an ancient oak making music (with possibly Repton himself playing the flute behind) in an idyllic landscape of rolling pasture and dense planting; this is contrasted with "despotic fashion" which shows shorn parkland, young trees and his clients struggling in a blast of wind. However, it is not known what changes Repton made. Present parkland has a drained lake and is planted with trees.

The Backs

(Cambridge)
see page 294

Baddesley Clinton

see page 247

Badger Dingle

Badger, Shropshire OS SO7699
English Heritage Register Grade II

House built in 18th century, remodelled by James Wyatt 1779–83 for Isaac Hawkins Browne, demolished 1952. In the 1780s William Emes, in association with John Webb, laid out the Dingle, a wooded ravine with American plants, a stream, cascades, pools with caves, seats and boathouses. Part of this scheme, a pillared rotunda, possibly by James Wyatt, survives, and at the other end of the ravine are the remains of James Wyatt's Pigeon House, based on the Tower of the Winds in Athens. The site today is much overgrown.

Badminton House

Badminton, Gloucestershire OS ST8028
English Heritage Register Grade I
Open occasionally for charity

Remarkable landscape on which many of the greatest garden designers worked from the 17th to the 20th century. Since the early 17th century, the estate of the Somerset family (later Dukes of Beaufort). Late 17th-century house with 18th-century alterations by Francis Smith of Warwick, James Gibbs and William Kent. In the late 17th and early 18th century, George London and Henry Wise, followed by Charles Bridgeman, designed formal gardens. The 1st Duchess of Beaufort was a great plant collector and commissioned a Florilegium in 1703 from the Dutch botanical artist Everard Kickius, which survives at Badminton and shows the immense range of exotics grown both at Badminton and at the Somersets' house in Chelsea (Beaufort House, where Beaufort Street is today). A Kip engraving (1700–10) shows grandiose formal gardens of great complexity east of the house, linked to the greater landscape setting by a series of giant avenues quartering the land (some of these survive in part). Celia Fiennes stood on the roof of the house in 1699 and described "the rows of trees on all sides… you may stand on the leads and look 12 ways down to the parishes and grounds beyond all thro' glides or vistos of trees; the Gardens are very fine and Water works." The architect and garden designer Thomas Wright worked at Badminton in the mid 18th century and designed several buildings on the estate; the Hermitage is one of the very few surviving 18th-century root houses. He also designed Ragged Castle (a rustic stone crenellated building), lodges and a fortress-like barn with towers for dovecotes. Wright's buildings are charming and mysterious but the grandest garden building at Badminton – and one of the grandest anywhere – is William Kent's Worcester Lodge of c.1746. Centred on the house, it has a magnificent position on the crest of an escarpment at a great distance to the north. Domed and pedimented, flanked by a pair of pyramid roofed rooms, it has an open archway providing a park entrance with, above it, a banqueting room with huge arched windows and triumphant views down across the park to the house three miles away. William Kent also did drawings for other landscape schemes at Badminton but these seem not to have been executed. Capability Brown was consulted in the 1760s but it is not known what, if anything, he did here. In modern times, a formal garden of box and yew hedges on the east front is by Russell Page – the last commission before his death in 1985 – in which box-edged compartments are filled with roses or knots of sage and santolina. West of the house is a new ornamental kitchen garden. In recent times there has been much planting in the park of new avenues of limes and chestnuts.

Balcarres

nr Colinsburgh, Fife OS NO4704
Open regularly Tel 01333 340206

16th-century tower house of the Lindsay family (Earls of Crawford and Balcarres), remodelled in the 19th century by William Burn and David Bryce. Terraces to the south side of the house were built in the 1840s. A photograph in H. Inigo Triggs's Formal Gardens of England and Scotland (1902) shows the lowest terrace overlooking magnificent formal gardens with parterres de broderie, crisply clipped topiary, an octagonal pool, a superb zigzag boundary yew hedge and arcadian views of parkland. Triggs wrote that "the old garden…deservedly ranks amongst the finest in Scotland." The terraces remain, still very ornamental but not in quite the state illustrated by Triggs. The parkland is very beautiful and there are woodland walks.

Balcaskie

nr Pittenweem, Fife OS NT5203
Scottish Inventory

The house was built 1668–74, the first house designed by the greatest Scottish architect of the day, Sir William Bruce, who built it for himself. Bruce lived here only briefly; by the end of the 17th century it had been sold to Sir Robert Anstruther, in whose family it has remained. Bruce also laid out a terraced garden south of the house where the ground slopes down towards the Firth of Forth. He centred the axis of the garden on the house, and was to do the same at Kinross House (see page 384). Bruce chose a spectacular eyecatcher as the focal point of the axis at Balcaskie – the Bass Rock, a pointed lump of rock that rears out of the Firth of Forth thirteen miles away to the south. W.S. Gilpin advised on the garden in the 1820s and part of his work involved restoring the terraces. Sir Walter Scott saw the garden in 1827 and wrote that it was "in good old style with its terraces and yew hedges. The beastly fashion of bringing a bare ill-sheared park up to your very door seems going down." The wall of the top terrace was rebuilt at this time, with Roman busts placed on the tops

B

of buttresses, and Gilpin planted evergreens – cedars, holm oaks and pines – at either end of the terraces to frame sea views. In the 1840s W.A. Nesfield designed a parterre for the top terrace, which no longer survives. The garden is still cared for and the beautiful terraces now provide a background to plantings of tender cistus, hoherias, myrtles and sophoras.

Balgone House

nr North Berwick, East Lothian OS NT5682
Scottish Inventory

Early 18th-century house for the Grant-Suttie family, incorporating older parts. By 1739 there were formal gardens here, with an avenue leading to a cliff edge where there was a semicircle of trees. D. Croal, in *Sketches of East Lothian* (1885), describes formal flower gardens north of the house with a "broad avenue [which]… leads to the edge of a wooded precipice". The flower gardens have been succeeded by beech hedges and grass walks, but the picturesque "wooded precipice" survives. Balgone Heughs is a natural stone outcrop covered with deciduous planting: beech, birch, oak, Scots pine, sycamore and yew. Croal wrote of it: "As a piece of landscape gardening, we…could conceive of nothing finer."

Ballinlough Castle

see page 400

Ballyfin

Mountrath, County Laois,
Republic of Ireland

18th-century house rebuilt in magnificent neo-Classical style 1821–26 for Sir Charles Coote to the designs of Sir Richard Morrison and his son William Vitruvius Morrison. The demesne had been landscaped in the 18th century, with the house looking down across a wood-fringed lawn to a great lake. The demesne is notable for two outstanding garden buildings. On rising ground behind the house is a great tower in Norman style, probably designed by the Morrisons as an observatory for Sir Charles, a keen astronomer. James Howley, in *The Follies and Garden Buildings of*

Ireland (1993), describes it as "the finest of all folly towers to have been built in Ireland". The Morrisons were probably also responsible for a multi-chambered rustic grotto by the lake. With a curious portico supported on rustic stone columns, its interior is decorated with fossils. The house today is a school.

Ballymaloe Cookery School Gardens

see page 400

Ballywalter Park

Newtownards, County Down, Northern Ireland Open regularly Tel (028) 4275 8264

Estate created by the merging of the demesnes of Ballyatwood House and Spring Vale House, with a spectacular 1840s Italianate palazzo built for Andrew Mulholland (later Lords Dunleath), owner of the largest linen mill in Northern Ireland and Mayor of Belfast, to the designs of Sir Charles Lanyon. In 1847–48 Mulholland clothed the landscape in 90,000 trees, including many exotics. Large collection of rhododendrons started in the late 19th century. 1863 conservatory built onto the garden front of house. Under restoration in 2002.

Balmanno Castle

Dron, Perthshire OS NO1415
Scottish Inventory

Castle built in the late 16th century for George Auchinleck, restored in the early 20th century by Sir Robert Lorimer. Lorimer also designed garden walls, an ogee-roofed garden house and a gatehouse – all in 17th-century style – and laid out the grounds. An orchard and kitchen garden south of the house were removed to create new parkland so that "cows could be seen to graze beneath the windows". Lorimer's new walled garden south-west of the castle has a 17th-century style summerhouse, and a central grass path is edged with shrub borders backed by espaliered fruit trees. Flower beds were designed in shapes of stars and circles. By the gatehouse an enclosed garden has a central obelisk-shaped sundial surrounded by four lawns.

Balmoral Castle

Crathie, Aberdeenshire OS NO2595 Scottish Inventory Open regularly Tel 013397 42334

The Balmoral estate goes back to the 15th century when it was known as Bouchmorale and owned by the Gordons, who built the first castle here. However, its early history is eclipsed by its illustrious 19th-century fame when it was bought by Queen Victoria and Prince Albert in 1852 for £32,000 (£1,631,040 today). A new house was built 1853–56 to the designs of William Smith of Aberdeen with the help of Prince Albert (of Saxe-Coburg-Gotha). Prince Albert loved the Scottish landscape – "very German-looking", he said – and thought that Loch Tay was "very like Thüringen". Formal gardens by the castle were designed by John Thomas. The *Gardeners' Chronicle* described the garden to the west in 1876: "In the centre of each [bed] is a full-sized bronze wild boar, placed, as it were, sitting on its haunches, with its head and shoulders visible above the foliage…a strange but telling effect." The boars have gone (one to another part of the garden) and today beds of alpines, ferns, lavender and roses are ornamented with a statue of a chamois. The east formal garden had, according to the *Gardeners' Chronicle*, "a very pretty design of flower garden in scroll-work, edged with Box, with a very handsome fountain at its centre". Today there is a lawn and mixed borders. There was no kitchen garden at Balmoral in the 19th century – all produce was sent up from Frogmore. Today there is a walled garden with a long range of glasshouses, and beds of vegetables and ornamentals.

Balnagown Castle

Kilmuir Easter, Ross-shire OS NH7675
Scottish Inventory

Ancient estate of the Ross family. The castle was started in the early 14th century for Hugh, 5th Earl of Ross who was the brother-in-law of King Robert the Bruce; it was much modified in the 16th century, with several later alterations. The last Ross to live here died in 1942. 18th-century parkland with a herd of red deer and surviving parkland trees –

beech, horse chestnut, lime and oak. South-east of the castle, in the valley of the Balnagown river, an Italian Garden was laid out in 1847 under the direction of Lady Mary Fitzgerald Ross. Flights of stone steps link the terraces, with an Italian wellhead and a fountain pool (now dry and planted as a flower bed). Monkey puzzles and rows of Irish yews ornament the terraces and in the river below there is a cascade and walks below the sandstone cliffs. The estate belongs today to the Al Fayed family, of Harrods fame.

Bantry House

see page 401

Bargany House

nr Dailly, Ayrshire OS NS2400 Scottish Inventory Open regularly Tel 01465 871249

Late 17th-century house for the 2nd Lord Bargany (of the Hamilton family) in a fine position on the south bank of the Water of Girvan. Parkland was laid out in the 18th century by William Adam and George Robertson, and much altered by W.S. Gilpin c.1826. From Gilpin's time are clumps along the river, individual parkland specimens of beech, chestnut, lime and sycamore and an avenue of limes along the old main road. Rock garden, or Hermit's Garden, west of the drive was laid out c.1927 on either side of the Laughlan burn with azaleas, *Cercidiphyllum japonicum*, Japanese maples, rhododendrons and viburnums, with primulas and many rock plants.

Barlborough Hall

Bolsover, Derbyshire OS SK4778
English Heritage Register Grade II
Open by appointment Tel 01246 435138

Late 16th-century house, possibly by Robert Smythson, for Francis Rodes, much altered in 19th and 20th centuries. House surrounded by walled gardens of various dates, some going back to the late 16th century. In a walled garden to the south of the house, a gabled gazebo dated 1582 or 1587, with an elaborate 16th-century fireplace. There is evidence that Francis Rodes made a park when his house was built. Today there is scattered planting; some of the

park has been turned over to arable farming and the west side was taken for the M1 motorway.

Barncluith

nr Hamilton, Lanarkshire OS NS7254
Scottish Inventory

Quite close to the Hamilton Palace estate (*see Chatelherault page 457*), Barncluith came into the Hamilton family when William Hamilton married the heiress in 1507. William's grandson inherited in 1583 and some time in the following century built a remarkable terraced garden in the valley of the river Avon. John Macky, in his *A Journey Through Scotland* (1732), described it: "a very romantick garden called Baron cleuh, which consists of seven hanging terras-walks, down to a river side. In some of those walks are banquetting-houses, with walks and grottos, and all of them filled with large evergreens, in the shapes of beasts and birds." H. Inigo Triggs in *Formal Gardens of England and Scotland* (1902), wrote, "It would be difficult to find a more romantic or picturesque site for a garden than this"; he shows a detailed plan and elevation of the terraces and a photograph showing them, and a banqueting house, looking distinctly disheveled. The dishevelment has continued to the present time – a remarkable early Scottish formal garden which no-one seems to want to save.

Barningham Hall

Barningham, Norfolk OS TG1435
English Heritage Register Grade II

House built in 1612 for Sir Edward Paston. Nothing is known of the garden before the early 19th century when, in 1807, John Thurston Mott consulted Humphry Repton. Not all Repton's advice was taken, and another of Repton's clients, Abbot Upcher of the neighbouring Sheringham Park (*see page 320*), reported, "Repton hurt at seeing his oaks cut down in the park and his plans which he had given to Mott so entirely departed from." However, Repton did remodel the front of the house in collaboration with his son, John Adey Repton, 1805–07, and it is possible that a serpentine lake eas of the house was made as a result of Repton's advice.

Barnsley House
see page 190

Barnsley Park
Barnsley, Gloucestershire OS SP0805
English Heritage Register Grade II*

Early 18th-century grand Baroque house for Brereton Bourchier, set in 18th-century parkland. Late 18th-century dovecote. Pillared orangery of stone and cast-iron by John Nash (1807). Formal gardens close to house laid out for the present owner, Lord Faringdon, c.1960. Woodland south-west of the house, planted with radiating avenues, laid out in the 1970s.

Barnwell All Saints' Manor
Barnwell, Northamptonshire OS TL0484
English Heritage Register Grade II

Manor of the Montagu family, demolished some time after 1716. Precious vestiges of an early garden – a rectangular pond, a raised walk, terraces (where there had been "garden knotts") and other earthworks. The garden was probably created in the late 16th or early 17th century.

Barnwell St Andrew's Manor
Barnwell, Northamptonshire OS TL0585
English Heritage Register Grade II

Barnwell Castle was built in the 13th century and given to Peterborough Abbey. After the dissolution of the monasteries it passed to the Montagus who built a new house in the 16th century, much altered in the late 19th and early 20th centuries. Gardens of the 20th century take advantage of the ancient and picturesque setting of the remains of the castle and its enclosures.

Baronscourt
Newtownstewart, County Tyrone, Northern Ireland Open occasionally for Ulster Gardens Scheme Tel (028) 8166 1683

Great house built for the 8th Earl of Abercorn 1779–81 to the designs of George Steuart, remodelled in 1791 by Sir John Soane. Terraced garden south of

house with herbaceous borders, rose garden and *potager*. Lakes in the grounds, one of which has a rhododendron walk.

Barrington Court
see page 17

Barrington Park
Greater Barrington, Gloucestershire
OS SP2013 English Heritage Grade II

Palladian villa built in the 1730s for Earl Talbot, possibly to the designs of William Smith of Warwick. 18th-century park with traces of avenues surviving from an earlier formal garden. Garden buildings survive from the late 18th century – a Gothic seat, a Gothic temple and a domed dovecote with an Ionic portico. The river Windrush flows through the grounds, diverted in the 18th century to form a lake.

Barrow Court
Barrow Gurney, Somerset OS ST5368
English Heritage Register Grade II
Open occasionally for NGS

Jacobean house on the site of a Benedictine nunnery. Garden designed by Francis Inigo Thomas for Henry Martin Gibbs 1892–96. An open exedra of iron railings overlooks the rural landscape, with twelve piers capped with stone busts carved by Thomas Drury, showing the progressively ageing face of a woman. The exedra forms one end of a terraced tennis lawn, with a double flight of steps to the upper level and ramparts of clipped yew in front of the house. At the far end of the tennis lawn an avenue of limes leads to a stone embrasure with a statue, and to one side is a courtyard with a stone table for *al fresco* meals. The quality of masonry is of the highest, and the simplicity and strength of the layout masterly.

Barwick Park
Barwick, Somerset OS ST5614
English Heritage Register Grade II*

The estate was bought by John Newman of Yeovil in 1758; he probably built the house which was heavily refashioned in the 19th century to give it an even older air. The grounds are notable

for curious buildings, probably dating from the end of the 18th century and marking the boundaries on the four compass points. The Cone is 70ft/20m high, like a slender ice-cream cone upside down and capped with a ball finial; Jack the Treacle Eater is a rough and monumental stone arch crowned with a tower with a conical roof and a figure of Hermes at its peak; the Fish Tower resembles a chimney stack; and the Obelisk is a comparatively sober – well – obelisk. In woodland near a lake is a grotto which Barbara Jones in *Follies & Grottoes* (1974) describes as "the most blood-chilling of all grottoes…a circular cave of rough rocks". To reach it you have to pass through "a jagged stone arch, like a set of jumbled false teeth, with sharp rocks set inwards". Will you ever get out?

Basildon Park
Basildon, Berkshire OS SU8178
English Heritage Register Grade II
Open regularly (NT) Tel 0118 984 3040

Estate going back to the 16th century but present house designed by John Carr from 1776 for Sir Francis Sykes. Capability Brown designed a kitchen garden and possibly advised on the park in 1778. The present park surrounds the house and contains many good mature trees planted as specimens or in clumps – beech, horse chestnut, limes, oaks and sweet chestnut. The kitchen garden, now largely grassed over, has an orangery designed by J.B. Papworth of c.1843, now converted into a house. Nothing is known of what Brown did here. Formal gardens by the house were partly designed by David Brandon c.1843, with advice from W.A. Nesfield and Edward Kemp – a lawn and balustraded terrace walk. North of the lawn, a croquet lawn edged with borders. North of the house, a grass platform with thatched umbrello (1990s) at centre of mid 19th-century rose garden.

Basing House
see page 71

Bateman's
see page 119

Bath Botanical Gardens
see page 18

Batsford Arboretum
see page 191

Battersea Park
see page 120

Battle Abbey
Battle, East Sussex OS TQ7415
English Heritage Register Grade II

Remains of a Benedictine abbey founded c.1070 on the site of the battle of Hastings. The estate was owned by the Duke and Duchess of Cleveland 1857–1901, when the Duchess carried out much planting, making among many other things a Robinsonian wild garden and an orchard of mulberries and figs. Little trace of what she did survives. The garden is composed of lawns, terraces and the abbey buildings, or traces of buildings. North of the site of the high altar, where King Harold was killed, is a lawn with a walk of camellias and yews against the precinct wall. In the park, old ponds, possibly monastic stew ponds. Much new planting of trees to replace those lost in the 1987 storm.

Bawdsey Manor
Bawdsey, Suffolk OS TM3337
English Heritage Register Grade II

Late 19th- and early 20th-century house built for the Quilter family. The ruins of a Martello tower (blown up by Sir Cuthbert Quilter) were used to build underground grottoes. A tunnel led to an artificial cliff or rockery made of cement studded with Pulhamite stone, intended as a home for alpine plants. A pergola with rough stone columns led to a walk running along the top of the cliff. Bawdsey Manor became a research station for the RAF (specialising in radar), and on Quilter's artificial cliff alpine plants were replaced by gun emplacements.

Bayfordbury
Bayford, Hertfordshire OS TL3110
English Heritage Register Grade II

Mid 18th-century house altered in early 19th century for the Baker

family. Lawn south-east of house flanked with groves of mature cedars, Chinese lace bark pine (*Pinus bungeana*), Wellingtonias and yews. South-west of the house, the remains of a rock garden built by James Pulham 1845–46 – part of it now a car park. South-west of the house, a lake made in 1772 with several mature specimen trees – incense cedar (*Calocedrus decurrens*), *Liquidambar styraciflua* and swamp cypress. In the park north-east of the house, a pinetum started in 1837 (quite early as such things go) with advice from J.C. Loudon, with many later plantings. In the valley of the Bayford brook is a fine collection of *Abies*, *Larix*, *Picea* and *Pinus* species, many now grown to great size. South of the pinetum, on the eastern boundary of the park, Sailor's Grove with mature cedars of Lebanon and a monumental Doric column commemorating members of the Baker family. Early 19th-century octagonal brick-walled kitchen garden. At its centre, a pond and basin probably by James Pulham.

Bayham Abbey
nr Lamberhurst, East Sussex OS TQ6436
English Heritage Register Grade II
Open regularly (EH) Tel 01892 890381

13th-century abbey buildings now in ruins. In addition to the 18th-century Dower House, a house was built in the grounds, also called Bayham Abbey, 1870–72, for Marquess Camden, to the designs of David Brandon. In 1800 Humphry Repton produced a Red Book, as a result of which a lake was made by damming the river Teise, with weirs and cascades, and the beautiful abbey ruins became the focal point of the landscape. The Victorian house has fine plantings of trees, a maze and terraced gardens with balustrades and urns.

Beaminster Manor
Beaminster, Dorset ST4801
English Heritage Register Grade II

Early 19th-century house with garden gateway built up of architectural salvage of distinguished local provenance – from Alderman Beckford's Fonthill Splendens (*see page 476*) and the Horseys' Clifton Maybank, also in

Dorset. Surprisingly rural garden for a village house, with parkland, lake, stream with a cascade, and bridge with tufa castellations.

Bearwood College, *also known as* Bear Wood

Sindlesham, Berkshire OS SU7768
English Heritage Register Grade II*

1822 house built for John Walter, chief proprietor of *The Times*, rebuilt 1865–74 on a palatial scale by Robert Kerr for John Walter III at a cost of £150,000 (£5,072,400 today). William Sawrey Gilpin worked on the garden *c*.1819, when he was art master at the nearby Royal Military College of Sandhurst, but there was already a garden in place, which J.C. Loudon visited in 1818, heartily recommending it to "the young gardener…[who] will there see a practical illustration of the principles of massing, grouping, and of every kind of planting." Today the pleasure grounds lie to the west and south of the house, with formal terraces leading to lawns and a rock garden in a former claypit. This was made by James Pulham 1879–85, with a stream, pools, naturalistic artificial rockwork and mature trees and shrubs. Entrance drive north of house runs through 225yds/250m of Wellingtonias. Large and complicated lake in park south-west of house which is now a school.

Beaumont Park

Kirklees, Huddersfield, West Yorkshire
English Heritage Register Grade II
Open regularly

The first public park in Huddersfield, laid out 1882 by R.S. Rugdale on land given to the city by H.F. Beaumont. The long and narrow curving site is dominated by the Main Walk which runs its whole length, originally flanked by flower beds but these have been grassed over; a rockery to the north of the walk survives. Formal gardens in the southern part of the park have suffered: a bandstand in the form of a Chinese pagoda has gone, a lake has been filled in, a pavilion has been demolished. Two terraces have flower beds now planted

with roses. The wilder northern part of the park has winding walks but the castellated refreshment rooms, The Castle, were demolished in the 1960s.

Beckford's Ride

Lansdown, Bath, Somerset OS ST7367
English Heritage Register Grade II

William Beckford of Fonthill came to live in Bath in 1822. Behind his house at 19–20 Lansdown Crescent he made a 4-acre/1.6-hectare terraced orchard with a battlemented gateway leading to the upper slopes. A path, with stone benches from which to face the views south and west over Bath, led among wild plantings to a grotto tunnel and ultimately to Beckford's Tower on Lansdown Hill high above. The tower, in what Pevsner describes as "funereally Graeco-Egyptian style", was designed 1825–26 by Henry Edmund Goodridge. After Beckford's death the tower was converted to a chapel (in 1848) and a graveyard made surrounding it. It is now a museum and visitors may see this last vestige of Beckford's Bath garden.

Beckley Park

Beckley, Oxfordshire OS SP5711
English Heritage Register Grade II*

Tudor house, remarkably unchanged, possibly a hunting lodge, built for Lord Williams of Thame between the moats of a much earlier castle. In the 9th century the estate belonged to King Alfred. The park was enclosed in a stone wall in the 1190s. The present, remarkable garden is the creation of Percy Fielding who bought the estate in 1919. Fielding, an architect who had worked with Sir Reginald Blomfield, made garden enclosures in which clipped box and yew are the chief (sometimes unique) ingredients: one is enclosed by very tall hedges of yew concealing two parallel rows of yew topiaries of different designs – dumb waiters, helixes, animals and various geometric shapes; one is a knot of box, with pyramids of clipped box; one has a lawn hedged in yew with topiary ornaments running along its crest.

Beddington House

Beddington, Surrey OS TQ3265
Open regularly Tel 020 8770 4781

House built *c*.1530 for Sir Nicholas Carew on an earlier site, with many later alterations. Francis Carew (later Sir Francis) inherited in 1539. Carew travelled in Europe as a young man and developed an interest in orange trees which he successfully grew at Beddington. Baron Waldstein described "a most lovely garden" on his visit in 1600. He saw remarkable water gardens with, among other things, "a figure of a Hydra out of whose many heads the water gushes". This elaborate garden became famous in its day and Elizabeth I visited it thirteen times. John Evelyn visited Beddington in 1658: "a fine old hall, but a scambling house, famous for the first Orange gardens in England…planted in the ground, and secur'd in winter with a wooden tabernacle and stoves." He also noted, "The pomegranads beare here." Loudon's *Encyclopaedia of Gardening* (1822) describes "The orange trees of Beddington… introduced from Italy by a knight of the noble family of the Carews". He says they survived into the early 18th century, rising to 14ft/4m high, but were "entirely killed by the great frost of 1739–40." The house (now Beddington Place) still survives and Ian Nairn's and Nikolaus Pevsner's *Surrey* volume in the "Buildings of England" series reads, "In the garden outside the Hall an early C18 orangery wall, nearly 200 ft[60m] long."

Bedford Square

Camden, London OS TQ2981
English Heritage Register Grade II*

Bedford Square is the only complete Georgian Square remaining in Bloomsbury. Part of the Bedford Estate, the houses were built 1775–80, and until 1893 the whole square was sealed off with gates. The square gardens are enclosed in the original late 18th-century cast-iron railings, with gates and overthrows on the north and south sides. The planting is informal, with mature trees, especially London planes, and shrubberies of holly, laurel and privet giving a Victorian character to the garden.

Bedgebury Pinetum

see page 120

Belcombe Court, *also known as* Belcomb Brook Villa

Bradford-on-Avon, Wiltshire OS ST8160
English Heritage Register Grade II*

House of 16th-century origins, remodelled in 1734 for Francis Yerbury by John Wood the Elder. West of the house, a lake with on its far bank a domed rotunda. At the northern end of the lake, a grotto, and in the open parkland west of the lake, an 18th-century cottage. Tim Mowl and Brian Earnshaw, in their *John Wood: Architect of Obsession* (1988) write : "[this] enclosed garden of artificial events destroyed the natural view across the Avon which Wood had intended the house to command."

Belgrave Square

City of Westminster, London OS TQ2879
English Heritage Register Grade II

Belgrave Square, developed by Thomas Cubitt and designed by George Basevi, was completed *c*.1827. The gardens are enclosed in railings and have a perimeter belt of shrubs, and a path from which lesser paths lead to a central lawn with a raised mount and roses. Lesser clumps of shrubs about the central area and varied mature trees and shrubs throughout. A memorial to Simon Bolivar (1874) on the eastern corner and, nearby to the north, the Leonardo da Vinci Memorial (1982).

Belhaven House

Westbarns, East Lothian OS NT6678
Scottish Inventory

Early 20th-century house with lodge designed by Sir Robert Lorimer. From 1970 until his death in 1993 this was the home of Sir George Taylor, a former director of the Royal Botanic Gardens Kew. Sir George built up a remarkable collection of plants, many rare and many tender, taking advantage of the mild climate of the site which is a quarter of a mile from the sea. Here are troughs of rare alpines, a spinney with a profusion of spring bulbs, glasshouses full of tender orchids, a collection of ancient cultivars of

pinks and such extreme rarities as *Salix* 'Boydii', collected at Lochnagar and never since seen.

Belhus

nr Aveley, Essex OS TQ5781
English Heritage Register Grade II

Early Tudor house, remodelled in 18th century and demolished in 1956. 17th-century enclosed formal garden overlaid when Capability Brown landscaped the grounds from 1753 for Lord Dacre, who was relieved to find that "he has not grown too great to Despise my little Business." Brown made repeated visits and he and Lord Dacre remained friends throughout Brown's life. In the 1770s Richard Woods did minor work on the park. The park today has a golf course and the M25 motorway runs across Brown's much discussed lake north-east of the house. In 1759 Lord Dacre had written, "I have had Brown down with me at Belhouse and am going to make a Pool…it will be a very great ornament to that side of the Park and quite change the Face of it." A curving strip of woodland planned by Brown, the Shrubbery, survives to the west of the site of the house.

Belle Isle

Lisbellaw, County Fermanagh, Northern Ireland

17th-century demesne of the Gore family, with house rebuilt in manorial style for the Porter family *c*.1890 to the designs of Morley Horder. The demesne has a remarkable topography – occupying eight islands at the northern end of the beautiful Upper Lough Erne. The picturesque possibilities of the landscape here were appreciated in the late 18th century: an aquatint made by J. Fisher in 1794 and reproduced in *Lost Demesnes* by Edward Malins and The Knight of Glin (1976) shows sheep grazing to the water's edge, a thatched hermitage and splendid views of the other islands. J.C. Loudon described the island on which the house is situated in his *Encyclopaedia of Gardening* (1822): "charmingly diversified by hills, dales, and gentle declivities, which are richly clothed in old timber,

B

rough which gravel walks are conducted, and a temple erected, from which a panoramic view is obtained, not only of this, but of the other wooded islands of the ...ch. One of them is exclusively ...ed as a deer park." This ...scription is very close to that ...ven by Arthur Young in his *A ...ur of Ireland* (1775), indeed so ...ose that it might be thought that ...udon had borrowed Young's ...ords. The estate still exists – parts ...it now offer self-catering ...commodation.

...elle Isle
...ndermere, Cumbria OS SD3996
...glish Heritage Register Grade II*

...ouse built 1774 on an island in ...indermere for Thomas English ...d designed by John Plaw. ...ikolaus Pevsner, in the ...uildings of England" volume, *...umberland and Westmorland* ...967), says that "it was the first ...ansion in the Lake District ...cided upon for picturesque ...asons." Grounds laid out by ...homas White in the early 1780s. ...chs from the house lead to a ...ckly wooded perimeter walk ...out the island, which gives ...ews of the house and lakeside ...enery. Between 1783 and 1786 ...hite was paid £2,355 ...140,735 today).

...elmont Park
...page 121

...elsay Hall
...page 331

...elton House
...page 288

...elvedere
...llingar, County Westmeath, ...public of Ireland
...en regularly Tel (00353) 44 42820

...ladian villa built *c.*1740 to the ...signs of Richard Castle for ...obert Rochfort, Lord Bellfield ...d later 1st Earl of Belvedere) ...a lovely site overlooking Lough ...nell. Arthur Young, in his *A ...ur of Ireland* (1775) admired ...beautiful lawn of undulating ...ound margined with wood… ...ke Ennel…flows beneath the ...ndows. It is spotted with islets; a ...omontory of rock, fringed with

trees, shoots into it, and the whole is bounded by distant hills." Robert Rochfort's younger brother George built a house nearby, also designed by Richard Castle. The brothers quarrelled and as a result, in 1760, Robert Rochfort built the Jealous Wall to obliterate views of his brother's demesne. By an unknown architect, it is a giant sham ruin (the largest in Ireland) in the form of an irregular façade, with Gothic windows and ragged roofline. It survives in apparently excellent condition – but it is hard to know if it has become more ruinous since it was built. Of about the same date is a Gothic arch, whose design is taken from Thomas Wright's *Universal Architecture* (two parts: 1755 and 1758), a grotesque sham ruin built of rustic stonework. A third building, surviving only in a very decrepit state, is an octagonal Gothic gazebo built on rising ground to take advantage of views of the lake. Magnificent balustraded terraces south of the house, also with fine views. The demesne has recently been restored with help from the Great Gardens of Ireland restoration programme.

Belvoir Castle
nr Grantham, Leicestershire OS SK8233
English Heritage Register Grade II
Open regularly Tel 01476 870262

Castle first built in the 11th century for Robert de Todeni. The 1st Earl of Rutland (previously Sir Thomas Manners) rebuilt the ruinous castle in the early 16th century and many alterations followed; the Manners family (now Dukes of Rutland) owns it today. The castle sits dramatically on top of a hill. A painting of 1731, attributed to Thomas Badeslade and illustrated in John Harris's *The Artist and the Country House* (1979), shows an astonishing garden in which a helical drive curves about the hill with below it a labyrinthine formal garden. By the mid 18th century this garden had been dismembered. All that is left are six statues of *c.*1680 by Caius Gabriel Cibber – there were originally seven and they are plainly visible in the Badeslade painting winding up the hill. Capability Brown came here in

1779 and produced landscape plans but nothing came of them (the bill was £496 (£29,760 today)). Early 19th-century landscaping south of castle with a curious dry-stone grotto crowned with a rustic octagonal summerhouse. Early 19th-century Gothick dairy. Neo-Norman mausoleum built 1826–28 by B.D. and P. Wyatt, now at the end of an avenue of cherry trees.

Bemersyde
Mertoun, Berwickshire OS NT5933
Scottish Inventory Open occasionally for SGS

Open occasionally for SGS 16th-century tower house, with alterations in the 18th, 19th and 20th centuries. In 1831 J.M.W. Turner drew here to illustrate Sir Walter Scott's poems. Woodland established in the late 18th century has magnificent beeches and oaks from original plantings. On a cliffside, a favourite view of Sir Walter Scott's, are famous hanging oaks and other trees clinging to the cliff. In the pleasure grounds south of the house is a venerable sweet chestnut thought to be at least 500 years old, with a 17th-century sundial nearby. Also south of the house are old yews from a Victorian parterre. From 1921 Bemersyde was the home of Field Marshal Earl Haig. Inspired by a postcard of Hampton Court Palace gardens (*see page 146*), he laid out a sunken garden with crazy-paving paths quartering it. Around the walls and paths are masses of arabis, armerias, auriculas, potentillas, strawberries and violas. A walled kitchen garden built *c.*1790 is in the curious shape of a half octagon; still used for fruit and vegetables, it also contains a tennis court.

Benham Park
Speen, Berkshire OS SU4367
English Heritage Register Grade II

House built for the 6th Lord Craven in the 1770s to the designs of Henry Holland. Brown extended the park sloping away from the house down towards a lake with the river Kennet beyond. *The Beauties of Berkshire* by E.W. Brayley and J. Britton (1801) praised its "simplicity and beauty" and noted a "small wooden bridge

of three arches, built after a Chinese design" – which is no longer to be seen. North of house, formal gardens possibly partly designed by W.A. Nesfield, with a sunken parterre. A grandiose double staircase climbs the slope to a terrace overlooking the parterre. Further to the north there had been a temple and in the late 18th century an outdoor theatre, of which remains may be seen.

Beningbrough Hall
nr Newton upon Ouse, North Yorkshire
OS SE5158 English Heritage Register Grade II
Open regularly (NT) Tel 01904 470666

Beautiful early 18th-century house built for John Bourchier. An 18th-century map shows avenues in the park but there are no signs of them today. W.S. Gilpin made proposals *c.*1827; some of the cedars, poplars and thorns in the south part of the park could be part of his planting scheme. An American Garden of trees and shrubs to the east of the house dates from the 1840s. New gardens close to the house date almost entirely from the estate's acquisition by the National Trust in 1957, with borders, a lily pool, a garden of box-hedged compartments filled with roses and a tunnel of pleached pears.

Benington Lordship
see page 289

Benmore Botanic Garden
see page 361

Bentley Priory
Harrow, Greater London OS TQ1593
English Heritage Register Grade II

An Augustinian priory was founded here in the early 13th century. A new house was built in 1775 and acquired in 1788 by the Hon. John James Hamilton (later 9th Earl and 1st Marquess of Abercorn). W.S. Gilpin advised on the grounds in the early 19th century and in 1852 the estate was sold to Sir John Kelk, treasurer of the Royal Horticultrural Society 1865–66 and builder of the Albert Memorial, who had great glasshouses and bedding schemes at Bentley. In the 20th century the

estate was dismembered, the house became a girls' school and in 1936 it was acquired by the RAF. Only traces of the old landscape survive, including a remarkable earthwork, possibly the remains of a medieval deer park boundary.

Benvarden
Dervock, County Antrim Open regularly
Tel (028) 2074 1331

18th-century house for the Macnaghten family on a site dating from the 17th century; enlarged at the beginning of the 19th century; bought in 1798 by Hugh Montgomery whose descendants still own it. Splendid 2-acre/0.8-hectare walled garden made before 1788 and gardened continuously ever since, with vinery and melon pit. Ornamental gardens with box and lavender parterre, a rose parterre with fountain and mixed borders. Romantic pleasure grounds by the river Rush which is crossed by an iron bridge of 1878.

Berkeley Castle
Berkeley, Gloucestershire OS ST6899
English Heritage Register Grade II*
Open regularly Tel 01453 810332

Castle started in the 11th century but with few changes since the 14th century when it was already owned by the Berkeley family who still live here. A Kip engraving shows formal gardens here in the early 18th century but nothing remains. Terraced gardens on south side of the castle, where in the late 19th century Georgina, Lady Fitzhardinge planted "the best hardy plants and shrubby things" (as Gertrude Jekyll wrote) – the gardens at this time were painted by such artists as George Elgood and Ernest Rowe. Major Robert Berkeley, who inherited in 1942, was a nephew of Ellen Willmott and a friend of both Gertrude Jekyll and Vita Sackville-West (who described the castle as "rose red and grey…the colour of old brocade"). The present garden reflects Robert Berkeley's interests: old fig trees trained against the castle walls, buttresses of *Magnolia grandiflora* and such tender shrubs as *Carpenteria californica*, *Cytisus battandieri* and pomegranate. In the castle grounds are Park House

B

(castellated kennels and stables, also serving as an eyecatcher) and Park Lodge in similar style (possibly a hunting stand).

Berkeley Square

City of Westminster, London OS TQ2880
English Heritage Register Grade II

Berkeley Square was built up from 1745 and the present layout of the gardens dates from the late 1760s, as do the existing railings and entrances on each of the four sides. The central area is turfed, with a broad gravel path forming an oval about the perimeter. Secondary paths lead from the perimeter to the centre where there is a pumphouse of 1800 with four stone baskets. There are many fine old London planes of an especially upright habit, supposedly planted in the late 1780s by Edward Bouverie who lived in the square. A statue of a girl pouring water ("a pathetic little fountain", says Pevsner) by Alexander Munro, donated before 1867 by the 3rd Marquess of Lansdowne, stands at the southern end of the garden; it replaced an equestrian statue of George II, removed in 1827.

Berrington Hall

nr Eye, Herefordshire OS SO5063
English Heritage Register Grade II*
Open regularly (NT) Tel 01568 615721

House built 1778–81 for Thomas Harley to the designs of Henry Holland. North of the house is a shrubbery walk, and leading from the entrance lodge to the house an avenue of clipped mounds of golden yew. An 18th-century brick-walled former kitchen garden has a pair of mixed borders flanking the central path and a collection of historic apple varieties, especially Herefordshire ones. Capability Brown (Henry Holland's father-in-law and frequent collaborator) was consulted about the park from 1778. Brown's park – a notably complete example of a Brown design – lies substantially south of the house. Its irregular lake (with an island) was planned, when seen from the house, to resemble a loop in a river. Most of the park is grassland with many mature trees.

Bettisfield Hall

Clwyd, OS SJ4636
Cadw/ICOMOS Register Grade II

The site of Sir Thomas Hanmer's famous 17th-century garden, one of the earliest formal gardens in Wales and in its day containing a remarkable collection of plants. Hanmer's *Garden Book*, written by 1659, describes the range of plants he grew: anemones, arbutus, auriculas, colchicums, fritillaries, hyacinths, jasmine, narcissi, roses, tulips and much else. He also makes a very early mention of the cedar of Lebanon: "we have of late had some few plants raised from seed, which are yet very small, so that it is rare in England, as well as the rest of Europe." The seed had first arrived in England 1638–39.

Bicton College of Agriculture

see page 19

Bicton Park Gardens

see page 20

Biddulph Grange Garden

see page 248

Biel

nr Stenton, East Lothian OS NT6376
Scottish Inventory Open by appointment
Tel 01620 860335

Ancient estate of the Dunbar family, going back to the 12th century. 16th-century tower house with 18th- and 19th-century alterations. Elaborate early 19th-century Gothic extravaganzas by William Atkinson were removed in 1952, and some of the prettier fragments used to decorate a terrace wall. Terraced garden dating from the 17th century is now planted with bedding plants and roses and climbing plants on the retaining walls; informal plantings of trees and shrubs with winding walks in the lower terraces. From the terraced garden steps lead down to the banks of the Biel water where woodland was planted by 1700; with much subsequent planting, it is now established as a wild woodland garden. Arboretum with conifers and some good deciduous trees, including an outstanding old London plane.

Bilton Grange

nr Dunchurch, Warwickshire OS SP4971
English Heritage Register Grade II

18th-century farmhouse with, as a separate building adjacent to it, a new house built 1841–46 to the designs of A.W.N. Pugin for Captain J. Washington Hibbert. In the pleasure grounds east of the house, a terrace enclosed by a "noble open-work stone terrace wall…[with] the date of the house [1846] beautifully and quaintly cut in Old Letter". Formal gardens of the mid 19th century, now rather simplified. A long avenue of monkey puzzles alternating with yews, a walk of copper beech, an avenue of deodars (*Cedrus deodara*) and good specimen trees date from this time. The park has a lime avenue and scattered specimen trees. The house is today a school.

Bingham's Melcombe

Melcombe Horsey, Dorset OS ST7702
English Heritage Register Grade II

Picturesque, irregular and delightful house of the Bingham family, built over several periods from the 15th century. The gardens were restored by Sir Geoffrey Jellicoe who described them as "probably unique in showing three periods of indigenous English landscape design unaffected by foreign influence. Two walled gardens are typical of the enclosed gardens of the Middle Ages." An astonishing ancient yew hedge of great height runs along a former bowling green west of the house; *Country Life* in June 1902 described "a stupendous yew hedge…planted about the time of Henry VIII" – it was then 14ft/4.4m high and 18ft/5.5m deep. Late 17th-century dovecote with conical roof and a semicircular brick summerhouse in an 18th-century garden wall.

Birkenhead Park

Birkenhead, Merseyside OS SJ3089 English Heritage Register Grade I Open regularly

Public park, the first to be established at public expense, designed by Sir Joseph Paxton and opened in 1847. The land here was marshy, which Paxton ingeniously drained by digging lakes, using the spoil to make hillocks to animate the site. Paxton devised a system of traffic segregation to divide the park into areas of different character. The outer carriage drive, Park Drive, was for pleasure traffic only, with a footpath along its outer edge. Clumps and belts of trees were established along Park Drive and are largely intact. Two irregular lakes, both with islands and both with mounds and undulations, lie in the north-western and north-eastern parts of the park. The latter has a boathouse on its western bank, with a pavilion superstructure designed to be used as a bandstand. The island is wooded and has a decorative covered bridge, the Swiss Bridge. Bowling greens, playing fields and cricket pitch, with pavilion, nearby. Close to the north-western lake is a rugby ground and stand. The great American landscape designer, Frederick Law Olmsted, visited Birkenhead Park in 1850 and was influenced by it in his design for New York's Central Park which opened in 1858.

Birmingham Botanic Gardens

see page 249

Birr Castle Demesne

see page 402

Bishop's Palace

Wells, Somerset OS ST5545
English Heritage Register Grade II
Open regularly Tel 01749 786691

It is the marvellous buildings, the moated setting and the occasional distinguished tree that give the Bishop's Palace garden its charms. Pevsner seems positively excited when he writes: "the most memorable of all bishop's palaces in England…exquisite beauty of setting". Mid 14th-century crenellated walls decorated with the occasional tower rise above the moat and enclose the palace. The present palace dates partly from the early 13th century to the mid 19th century. Also surviving are the splendid remains of Bishop Burnell's Hall, built in the 13th century and now with all the aplomb of a carefully placed sham ruin in an 18th-century landscape park. In front of it, on the edge of an impeccable lawn (the home lawn of the most exclusive Palace Croquet Club) stands a lovely American walnut (*juglans nigra*). There are other good trees and also some rather perfunctory flower planting. Celia Fiennes was crisply dismissive after visiting Wells in 1698: "the Bishop's Palace is in a park moated round, nothing worth notice in it." She could scarcely have been more wrong. An attractive turf walk leads between moat and wall (which is planted with climbing roses) to a cascade and springs, which first gave the place its name. If you walk south of the palace and its moat and across Palace Field (often with cattle grazing) you may turn back and see one of the most remarkable views in England – the cathedral and palace set in an unspoilt rural landscape.

Blagdon Hall

Blagdon, Northumberland OS NZ2177
English Heritage Register Grade II

The architectural history of Blagdon Hall is uncertain. John Harris's *The Artist and the Country House* (1979) has a painting attributed to Thomas Smith (which he dates *c*.1700–10), showing a fine upright mansion with sophisticated formal gardens and a remarkable pavilion/island in a canal. Pevsner says the house was begun around 1735. At all events, the chief surviving garden features before the 20th century date from the later 18th century – a boathouse on a serpentine lake with a Gothic ruin on its north bank and a circular temple of 178 at the east end of the lake. Both Sir Edwin Lutyens and Gertrude Jekyll worked on the garden (Lutyens's daughter Ursula had married Lord Ridley). In 1929 Miss Jekyll designed a quarry garden with suitably naturalistic planting (drifts of snake's head fritillaries and autumn crocuses) and borders along a yew walk. Lutyens, completing the work in 1938, designed a *rond-point* with a Coade stone urn, terraces and a canal. The canal, running away from the façade of the house, was one of Lutyens's last works. The landscape is flat, and as there was nothing to serve as an eyecatcher Lutyens designed the canal to become narrower as it extended away from the house, ending it with a large circular pool, 50ft/15m across, with a 12ft-/3.6m-high bronze statue of Milo by John Graham Lough. All this survives but there is little trace of Jekyll's work today.

Blair Adam House

Cleish, Kinross-shire OS NT1295
Scottish Inventory

House built in 1733 to the designs of William Adam for his own use. Adam laid out formal grounds with a series of avenues radiating out from the house; some of the original beeches survive but much was destroyed when the parkland was made informal after 1748. Adam's grandson, the Rt Hon. William Adam, planted clumps and individual parkland trees after 1792. Fine 18th- and 19th-century trees remain and there has been some 20th-century planting. In the 19th century all the paths in the 4-acre/1.6-hectare walled garden (built 1755–61) were edged with flower borders – a total of 1,054yds/948m noted in 1842. William Adam's son John established woodlands from 1748 and J.C. Loudon's *Encyclopaedia of Gardening* (1822) found Blair Adam "remarkable for the extent of the plantations on a barren-like peat soil". By 1842 the *Gardeners' Magazine* was able to describe "nearly 1000 acres of thriving plantation". The woodlands were sold to a timber merchant in 1925 and replanted after 1937 when the Forestry Commission acquired them and smothered the land with relentless plantings of conifers. The house became a hotel in 1925, was used by the Polish army in World War II and came back to the family in 1971. In 1966 the M90 motorway was built through the western edge of the policies.

Blair Castle

Blair Atholl, Perthshire Open regularly
01796 481207

The Murray family (later Earls and Dukes of Atholl) have lived at Blair Castle since the 13th century. The existing castle is partly 13th-century but largely 18th- and 19th-century. The castle has a fine position on wooded

slopes but it seems that there were no gardens here of note before the 18th century. The 2nd Duke made formal gardens in the 1740s and 50s, of which a plan in Georges-Louis Le Rouge's *Jardin Anglo-Chinois* (1766) shows a simple six-part formal garden in front of the castle and a pattern of avenues radiating from it. The Whim, a Gothic screen serving as an eyecatcher, was built in 1762 on rising land north of the castle. The Hercules Garden, a large irregularly shaped walled garden built by the 2nd Duke in 1744 and named after a statue on a hill east of the castle, had a square formal pool which later on was given a western extension. After some years of neglect, and use as a nursery for Christmas trees, the walled garden has been restored in recent years and has a grand double herbaceous border, yew hedges and topiary. North of the castle, Diana's Grove is a formal wilderness also laid out under the 2nd Duke, with rides through woodland converging on a statue of Diana. Much of the woodland today consists of conifers planted in the 19th century but the old pattern of rides seems to survive.

Blairquhan Castle

Maybole, Ayrshire OS NS3605 Scottish
Inventory Open regularly Tel 01655 770239

Castle built 1820–24 to the designs of William Burn for Sir David Hunter Blair, replacing the old castle, a 14th-century tower house. Sir David was an epic tree planter, planting half a million trees between 1803 and 1814. He made a loch in the parkland and most of the surviving trees were planted by him; a few date from the mid 18th century, including a lime avenue. Remarkable old woodland dates from the 17th century. Arboretum established by Sir Edward Hunter Blair in 1858, with many later additions. A lugubrious sight is the "Dool" tree, an old sycamore east of the castle used for hangings after trials by the laird. Walled garden, first laid out in 1816, with good recent ornamental planting – a rose walk, laburnum walk and herbaceous borders. An 1820 glasshouse remains, with cellars underneath probably used for mushroom growing.

Blaise Castle *and* Blaise Village

see page 21

Blenheim Palace

see page 72

Blickling Hall

see page 290

Bloomsbury Square

Camden, London OS TQ3082
English Heritage Register Grade II

Bloomsbury Square was developed by Lord Southampton from 1662. Two rows of houses facing each other across a greensward formed the approach to Southampton House whose walled courtyard formed the northern boundary of the square. John Evelyn dined with Lord Southampton in 1665 and wrote in his diary that "he was building a noble square or Piazza." An engraving by Sutton Nicholls of 1731 shows the fenced central area divided by paths like a union jack. Southampton's daughter married William Russell, 5th Earl of Bedford, thus joining the Southampton and Bedford estates. In c.1807 the 6th Duke of Bedford consulted Humphry Repton about the design of the Bloomsbury Square gardens. Repton had already designed the Russell Square gardens but his proposals for Bloomsbury Square were rejected; it is not know who designed the present layout with its shrubberies lining the railings, paths round central lawns and scattered mature trees. The statue of Charles James Fox by Sir Richard Westmacott on the northern boundary was erected in 1836. The southern part of the gardens was redesigned in the mid 20th century with geometric paths and slightly raised beds for flowers and shrubs; it was modified by David Lee c.1969 with a paved area and curved shrubberies.

Boconnoc

Lostwithiel, Cornwall OS SX1460
English Heritage Register Grade II*
Open occasionally for NGS

17th- and 18th-century house. The ancient estate (owned by the Carminows in the 14th century,

who first made a deer park here) was bought in 1717 by Thomas Pitt, Governor of Madras. His grandson, another Thomas Pitt who became 1st Lord Camelford, was a friend of Horace Walpole and of Sir Richard Lyttelton, his wife's uncle, to whom in 1771 he erected an obelisk "to perpetuate that peculiar character of benevolence which rendered him the delight of his own age and worthy of veneration of posterity". The obelisk is framed by a pair of classical shrines of the same date. Lord Camelford was also responsible for much work in the park, possibly influenced by his landscaping brother, the Earl of Chatham. G.S. Gilbert's *Historical Survey of Cornwall* (1820) describes the house set "in a delightful lawn of nearly one hundred acres, which is neatly varied by new plantations and straggling trees. The surrounding dells and ravines are watered by the river Lerran, over which the wooded hills rise in beautiful succession." A pinetum was established in the 1840s – the great period for such things – and conifers continued to be planted late in the 19th century. It is illustrated in an aerial photograph in Christopher Taylor's *Parks and Gardens of Britain: A Landscape History from the Air* (1998).

Bodnant Garden

see page 192

Bodysgallen

nr Llandudno, Conwy OS SH7979
Cadw/ICOMOS Register Grade I Open to
customers of the hotel Tel 01492 584466

House built on an older site c.1620, with many later alterations. The site is steeply sloping and was terraced to the south and east, probably when the present house was built. By the end of the 18th century there was a terrace walk, designed to display views of the Conwy valley, its estuary, and the peaks of Snowdonia – it is mentioned in Thomas Pennant's *A Tour in Wales* (1782), who describes the peaks being visible "over the tops of trees". The terrace walk survives, although there is no sign of the covered seat "formed out of an old bed of Oak, inlaid…with the

date of 1581", seen by Fenton and described in his *Tours in Wales* (1804–13). The terrace gardens today present a delightful array of formal gardens – a rose garden, topiary (of box, juniper and yew), urns, stately walks and a dazzling parterre with radiating box-edged beds full of herbs. Some of these features are plainly recent, and the garden has been most attractively restored since it became a hotel in 1980. The antiquarian Sir Richard Colt Hoare came here in 1806 and described the house being "enlivened by a gay parterre"; this would have been too early for the later 19th-century revival in such formal features, nor were such things commonly made in 18th-century gardens, so it could well have dated from the 17th century. But no-one knows exactly where in the garden it was.

Bolfracks Garden

nr Aberfeldy, Perthshire OS NN8248 Scottish
Inventory Open regularly Tel 01887 820344

18th-century house for the Menzies family, Gothicised in the early 19th century, in a wonderful position overlooking the Tay valley. A walled former kitchen garden, probably dating from the time of the original house, is now an ornamental garden with borders, trees and shrubs. Behind the house, peat beds are used to cultivate choice acid-loving plants. Nearby is a water garden on the banks of the Bolfracks burn, with ornamental shrubs (especially azaleas and rhododendrons), meconopsis and primulas.

Bolsover Castle

Bolsover, Derbyshire OS SK4770
English Heritage Register Grade I
Open regularly (EH) Tel 01246 822844

Castle keep (or Little Castle) built in the early 17th century on 12th-century foundations by Sir Charles Cavendish, the son of Bess of Hardwick (*see* Hardwick Hall *page 263*). Part of the new keep has been attributed to Robert Smythson and part to John Smythson. The family ceased to use the house in the early 18th century, after which it was tenanted. The 7th Duke of Portland gave it in its ruinous state to the nation in 1945. Today, cared

B

B

for by English Heritage, it is uninhabited but the interiors of some of the rooms have been finely reinstated and the ensemble of buildings remains very beautiful. A Kip engraving in *Britannia Illustrata* (1707) shows the castle rising up in a largely agricultural landscape, with no sign of a garden; however, there had been a garden in the early 17th century and it partly survives in the form of the Fountain Court. Here is a very rare early 17th-century garden fountain (the fountain of Venus), an elaborate castellated structure carved with lions' masks and cherubs and surmounted by a vaguely draped figure of Venus emerging from her bath. It is possible that it was made for the visit of Charles I and his queen, Henrietta Maria, in 1634. After a banquet in their honour, the Fountain Court was the setting for a performance of Ben Jonson's masque *Love's Welcome to Bolsover*, of which Roy Strong wrote in *The Renaissance Garden in England* (1979): "The theme of the entertainment, as D.J. Gordon has observed, is mutual love and its nature, finding its perfect exemplars in the King and Queen."

Borde Hill Garden
see page 122

Boscobel House
Shropshire OS SJ8308
English Heritage Register Grade II
Open regularly (EH) Tel 01902 850244

16th-century farmhouse remodelled in early 17th century as a retreat for John Giffard, a Catholic. Famous as the hiding place of Charles II after his defeat at the Battle of Worcester in 1651. The Royal Oak, a descendant of the tree in whose branches the king supposedly hid, may still be seen. An engraving by Wenceslas Hollar of c.1660 shows the house in its well wooded surroundings with a formal garden of compartments and a mount with an arbour on top. A similar garden exists today, made in the 19th century probably with deliberate reference to Hollar's engraving; the mount survives.

Bosvigo House
see page 21

Boughton Hall
Boughton, Northamptonshire OS SP7565
English Heritage Register Grade II

Present house built to the designs of William Burn in 1844 for Sir George Howard who had married the Wentworth heiress to the estate. In the 18th century William Wentworth, the 2nd Earl of Strafford (of the 2nd creation), a friend of Horace Walpole and bitten by the Gothicising bug, had animated the landscape with several remarkable buildings – an obelisk (1764), the Hawking Tower (c.1755) which serves as an entrance lodge, the castellated Bunker's Hill Farm (1776), and the Spectacles (1770), a park eyecatcher with a tall Gothic arch flanked by slender castellated towers.

Boughton House Park
see page 250

Bourton House Garden
see page 194

Bowes Museum
see page 332

Bowhill House
nr Selkirk, Selkirkshire OS NT4227 Scottish Inventory Open regularly Tel 01750 22204

Ancient estate of the Douglas family – the "very pretty little estate" bought by the 2nd Duke of Buccleuch c.1745 for his younger son. A spectacular new house was designed by William Atkinson and built 1812–19 to replace an early 18th-century house. In the early 19th century W.S. Gilpin worked on the grounds, creating and planting two lochs, and making picturesque walks about the policies. Woodland with much 19th-century planting, particularly of conifers. Terraced gardens made for the new house, the uppermost a modern parterre with two crescents and a star, part of the Scott arms (the family name is Montagu-Douglas-Scott). West of the house, a heather garden and a parterre with clipped yews.

Bowood
see page 73

Bradenham Hall
see page 291

Bradenham Manor
Bradenham, Buckinghamshire OS SU8297
English Heritage Register Grade II

Late 17th-century house rebuilt for Sir Edmund Pye. In the 19th century it belonged to Isaac D'Israeli, the father of Benjamin Disraeli (who abandoned the apostrophe). Benjamin Disraeli wrote some of his novels here, and in *Endymion* (1880) describes the garden: "glade-like terraces of yew trees, which give an air of dignity to a neglected scene". Lawns and terraces surround the house today, with a terraced formal Wilderness of woodland and grass paths.

Bradgate Park
Newton Linford, Leicestershire OS SK5310
English Heritage Register Grade II
Open regularly Tel 0116 2362713

15th-century house abandoned in the 18th century; the ruins of the house stand in the south-eastern part of what is now a public park. A pattern of wall foundations confirms the formal garden shown in a Kip engraving (for what he calls Broadgate House). In *Britannia Illustrata* (1707) Kip shows a plain but substantial terraced garden. East of the house is an enclosure of c.1500, called the Tiltyard, with raised walks about its sides; it was possibly used as a practice ground for jousting. A deer park was enclosed here in 1241. In the 18th century the whole park of 803 acres/325 hectares was enclosed in a 7ft/2m high stone wall. Earthworks visible in an aerial photograph in Christopher Taylor's *Parks and Gardens of Britain: A Landscape History from the Air* (1998) corroborate Kip's engraving.

Bradley Court
Bradley Green, Gloucestershire OS ST7493
English Heritage Register Grade II

16th-century house for the Berkeley family, with later alterations. A Kip engraving of 1712 shows a pretty, formal garden, and a (surviving) brick gazebo with ogee roof, cleverly placed on a west wall to give views both back to the house and out over countryside. Present

garden made largely since 1970, with lively plantsmanship. Modern grotto with pool among trees, a parterre of herbs, a grass walk to a statue of Diana and much else.

Bramdean House
Bramdean, Hampshire OS SU6128
English Heritage Register Grade II
Open occasionally for NGS and private groups by appointment Tel 01962 771214

Early 18th-century house. On the slope rising behind the house is a sequence of three enclosed gardens disposed about an axis aligned with the centre of the house. At the lowest level, with a circular pool set in paving, a grass path leads between deep herbaceous borders, behind which are lawns with shrubs and trees. A wrought-iron gate, with urns on piers, leads to the second garden in which a kitchen garden is combined with ornamental planting. The final enclosure is an orchard with flowering cherries and a walk of Irish yews, with much underplanting of daffodils. At the back, aligned with the central walk, is an attractive 18th-century summerhouse crowned with a belfry and also serving as an eyecatcher.

Bramham Park
see page 332

Brampton Bryan Park
Brampton Bryan, Herefordshire OS SO3772
English Heritage Register Grade II

Bramptons lived here at least from the 12th century, though the name died out in 1309 when Margaret, daughter of the last Brampton, married a Sir Robert Harley. The present house is 18th-century but the gatehouse of the medieval castle is in the grounds. George London worked on the garden here c.1690. The park is grassland with areas of woodland, clumps and other groups of trees. In the centre of the park is a deer park, now enclosed with iron railings, dating from the late 15th or early 16th century; deer were last kept here in the early 20th century. South of the deer park, a 666yd/600m line of sweet chestnuts, probably dating from the late 17th century. A second,

shorter, line joins it at its south-westerly end.

Bramshill Park
nr Hartley Wintney, Hampshire OS SU7559
English Heritage Register Grade II*

Great Jacobean house on an older site, built 1605–12 for Lord Zouche. Deer park east of the house by 1347. Terraced walled gardens with octagonal turrets on main walls and bowling green with loggia and Jacobean seats. Double avenue of oaks leading from main front. Rides through woodland to lake with island, and site of a maze.

Branklyn
see page 362

Braxted Park,
formerly known as
Braxted Lodge
Great Braxted, Essex OS TL8515
English Heritage Register Grade II*

17th-century house rebuilt for Peter Du Cane I to the designs of Sir Robert Taylor, with alterations in 19th century. Deer park here since the mid 13th century. A formal garden made before the mid 18th century, with a triple lime avenue south of the house. Three further avenues were laid out in the 1750s, radiating from a circular forecourt south of the house. In the early 19th century Peter Du Cane II enlarged existing pools to make a lake, with a bridge running across its eastern end. At the west end of the lake, an elaborate icehouse of the late 18th or early 19th century. The park was enlarged by Peter Du Cane III 1825–31, which involved demolishing some of the village houses near the church. Exotics were planted in the 19th century, of which many survive – among them cedar of Lebanon, cork oak (*Quercus suber*), swamp cypress, tulip tree and Wellingtonia.

Breamore House
Breamore, Hampshire OS SU1519
English Heritage Register Grade II
Open regularly Tel 01725 512233

House built in the 1580s, on an older site, for William Dodington. In 1748 the estate was bought by Sir Edward Hulse whose

...escendants still own it. Deer park ...om 1239 but the present park ...as landscaped in the 1820s. Partly ...alled kitchen garden now has ...e 20th-century formal gardens ...ith yew hedges and statuary. ...reamore Wood, part of which ...as the deer park, now has an ...boretum.

Brechin Castle

...echin, Angus OS NO5959 Scottish ...ventory Open regularly Tel 01356 624566

...he history of Brechin Castle goes ...ck to the early 14th century but ...e present castle is an early 18th-...entury remodelling of an earlier ...d simpler house by James Baine ...nd Alexander Edward for the 4th ...arl of Panmure. The most notable ...arden feature at Brechin is the ...markable 14-acre/5.6-hectare ...8th-century walled garden, which ...as added to after 1868. Apart ...om its enormous area, it is ...otable for having walls which ...reak out into large curved lobes ...eltering various features of the ...arden: buildings such as ...asshouses or cold frames, or ...anted features such as a ...ollection of rhododendrons. The ...anting is generally informal, with ...enty of room for substantial ...namental trees such as a pair of ...dars of Lebanon dating back to ...e mid 18th century. A circular ...y pond is surrounded by box-...dged flower beds and nearby is an ...utumn Garden with maples for ...utumn colour and a large ...ollection of rowans.

Brentry House, *now* Brentry Hospital

...estbury-on-Trym, Bristol OS ST5778 ...glish Heritage Register Grade II

...ouse designed in 1802 in Greek ...vival style by Humphry Repton ...nd his son, John Adey Repton, ...r William Payne, a Bristol ...erchant. Humphry Repton also ...esigned the landscape on the ...opes of Brentry Hill so as to ...ake the most of the westerly ...ews of the Severn estuary and ...e distant hills of south Wales. ...his is a rare example of a single ...hole estate being designed by ...epton, who was much taken ...ith Brentry Hill and its "pleasing ...d extensive view" of other ...otable country houses such as

Kingsweston (*see page* 498) and Blaise Castle (*see page* 21) and "the picturesque assemblage of gardens and villas in Henbury and Westbury". Little except the house (now the hospital administration block) and the position, with mutilated views, survives.

Bretby Hall

Bretby, Derbyshire OS SK3022
English Heritage Register Grade II

Present house built from 1813 to the designs of Jeffry Wyatville. Earlier house built in early 17th century for Philip Stanhope, 1st Earl of Chesterfield and rebuilt by his son after 1660 – shown as a U-shape about a courtyard in a Kip engraving in *Britannia Illustrata* (1707), surrounded by complex and beautiful formal gardens. Particularly striking were the elaborate water gardens. These have been attributed to the Frenchman Grillet who also made the cascade at Chatsworth (*see page 255*). One of the waterworks, a water clock, played "Lillibullero", the song of the 1688 Revolution which brought William III to the throne. Traces of this garden may still be seen, among them terracing to the west of the house, some pools, and one or two sweet chestnuts dating from the 17th century. In the park there are scattered trees, a few surviving from the avenues seen in the Kip engraving. The house became a hospital before World War II but closed in the late 1990s and plans were made to convert it into flats.

Brickwall

Northiam, East Sussex OS TQ8324
English Heritage Register Grade II*
Open occasionally for NGS

Early 17th-century house incorporating earlier house, with alterations in the late 17th and 19th centuries. South of the house, walled garden with gravel walk flanked by shapes of yew topiary, planted by 1729 with crisp pyramid shapes; those visible today are baggy and misshapen. Lawns on either side and a rectangular pool to the east. Beeches have been tightly clipped against the western wall. South of this, a second walled enclosure, the former kitchen garden, with more

old clipped yews, and a modern chessboard garden with pieces of clipped golden or common yew, made in 1980–82.

Bridge End Gardens

Saffron Walden, Essex TL5338
English Heritage Register Grade II*
Open regularly Tel 01799 510444

Gardens laid out *c*.1794 for Atkinson Francis Gibson near his house at the corner of High St and Castle St. William Chater developed the garden from 1839 for Francis Gibson, A.F. Gibson's son. The family opened the garden to the public from the late 19th century and it was acquired by the town council in 1918. In *Gardens for Small Country Houses* (1912) Gertrude Jekyll and Lawrence Weaver give a plan and photographs of the Dutch Garden at Bridge End, showing an elaborate parterre with scrollwork, topiary and a central fountain and lily pond. By the 1980s the topiary had become large and misshapen; it has since been restored. A yew maze was laid out *c*.1840 and was replanted with yew in 1991, following the original pattern. A circular rose garden has also been restored.

Bridwell

nr Uffculme, Devon OS ST0512
English Heritage Register Grade II

House built 1774–79 for Richard Hall Clarke. Late 18th-century landscaped park with lake and islands on land sloping down towards the river Culm. The Museum, now derelict, was built in 1809 using medieval architectural fragments from Plymouth, with volcanic lumps and Gothic windows. Two curious ornaments animate the scene – a bunch of stalagmites rising from a base of knucklebones and a pyramid of stalagmites incorporating a piscina.

Brightling Park, *formerly* Rose Hill

Brightling, East Sussex OS TQ6821
English Heritage Register Grade II

House built *c*.1700, with alterations late in the 18th century, for the Fullers, who were Wealden ironfounders. Park laid out as a

deer park *c*.1745–50, with improvements continuing into the 19th century. South-east of the house, a chain of lakes was formed in the mid 18th century. Ornamental buildings designed by Robert Smirke were introduced into the landscape by Jack Fuller in the early 19th century, most of them outside the park: a domed rotunda on a knoll south-west of the house; the Hermit's Tower east of the park wall; the Observatory to the west of it; Brightling Needle (or the Obelisk) to the north; and the Pillar to the south. Almost the entire park, of 524 acres/212 hectares, was enclosed in a stone wall *c*.1825, at a cost of £10,000 (£346,600 today). In 1806 Humphry Repton was consulted and produced a Red Book but little was done as a result, apart from a walk by the house linking planted compartments.

Broadlands

nr Romsey, Hampshire OS SU3520
English Heritage Register Grade II*
Open regularly Tel 01794 505010

The house dates from the 16th century but was remodelled for the 2nd Viscount Palmerston by Capability Brown in the 1760s and by Henry Holland in 1788. When Celia Fiennes saw Broadlands *c*.1696, she wrote: "The Gardens are walled in, some with brest walls some higher with flower pots on them, severall places with open grates to look through with stone balls or figures on the pillars…the Gardens are not finish'd but will be very fine." In the late 19th century W.A. Nesfield made additions to the house (later removed) and laid out a parterre south of the house, of which only hedges, topiary and a fountain pool survive. The 1st Viscount Palmerston, who bought the estate in 1736, removed the earlier formal gardens but seems to have used Brown's advice only in architectural matters: to enlarge a handsome orangery, built *c*.1736; to provide a new Gothic façade for Spursholt Farm to act as an eyecatcher; and to Gothicise a dairy. The river Test flows magnificently through the grounds, with lawns running down to it from the house, and

riverside walks. An arboretum is laid out on the banks of a tributary to the river and everywhere there are fine trees.

Broadleas Gardens

see page 74

Broadmoor Hospital

Crowthorne, Berkshire OS SU8564
English Heritage Register Grade II

Hospital for the criminally insane, designed by Joshua Jebb and opened in 1863. Grounds laid out, in particular to the south, to give patients long views of the countryside. Immediately south of the main buildings is a series of lawns originally used by the inmates for bowls and croquet. Terraces and further lawns with mature trees, among them cedars of Lebanon. A 14-acre/6-hectare kitchen garden laid out in ten sections, but now partly given over to sports grounds, was fully productive in the 1870s. Some inmates worked in it, and it produced 50lb of rhubarb for each patient annually; purgatives were thought to have therapeutic value for the mentally ill.

Brockenhurst Park

Brockenhurst, Hampshire OS SU3001
English Heritage Register Grade II

Old estate bought in 1769 by Edward Morant who improved both house and grounds. His son may have consulted William Emes about the park in the late 18th century. Old house demolished in 1960 and modern style country house (by Harry Graham) built soon after. Remarkable formal gardens laid out by John Morant in the late 19th century on the site of a former kitchen garden. The centrepiece is a canal fringed with *Cotoneaster horizontalis*; lawns on either side have rows of yew topiary shapes backed by hedges of bay (*Laurus nobilis*). Fine old evergreen trees – *Quercus* × *hispanica* 'Lucombeana', Scots pines and Californian redwoods (*Sequoia sempervirens*) – rise behind the hedges. At the end of the canal a double staircase leads to a fountain pool at the centre of a grass terrace with arches of clipped holm oak. It was this part of the garden that Gertrude Jekyll must have been thinking of when she wrote of Brockenhurst in *Some English Gardens* (1904): "the spirit of the pure Italian gardens…it is none the less beautiful because it is a garden almost without flowers, so important are its permanent forms of living green walls." The park is well wooded with ancient oaks and many exotics from 18th- and 19th-century plantings.

Brocket Hall

nr Welwyn Garden City, Hertfordshire OS TL2113 English Heritage Register Grade II

House designed by James Paine and built from 1760, at first for Matthew Lamb and after 1768 for his son, Sir Pennistone Lamb (later Viscount Melbourne). Pleasure grounds were formerly part of a park in the early 18th century but were remodelled as a pleasure circuit with walks by a lake (the Broadwater, formed by damming the river Lead) by Richard Woods in the 1770s. The lake, spanned by a weir with a bridge by James Paine (1772–74). Lawns and mature cedars of Lebanon by the house and west of it. The Temple (James Paine, mid to late 18th century), with a marble basin said to have been used for taking syllabub. Richard Woods's park now dominated by two golf courses and traces only remain of 18th-century planting. Early 20th-century avenue south-west of house.

Brockhampton Park

Brockhampton, Worcestershire OS SO6855 English Heritage Register Grade II

18th-century house for Bartholomew Richard Barneby, designed by Thomas Farnolls Pritchard. Garden by the house has an elaborate parterre designed by Alexander Roos in 1865 and reinstated in 1996. East of kitchen garden, a grotto-like rockery of tufa with a niche and rustic seat. Park with many mature trees. To the east, a lake and planned walks in woodland. Thomas Leggett produced a design for the park in 1769 but this was not used. Elliptical walled kitchen garden, probably of the 1770s, now with a private house within.

Brockhole

South Lakeland, Cumbria OS NY3901 English Heritage Register Grade II Open regularly Tel 015394 46601

House built 1899–1902 for William Gaddum to the designs of Dan Gibson, then a partner of the garden designer Thomas Mawson. A paved terrace runs across the south-west façade of the house, linking formal spaces about the house. A rectangular garden with a lawn and borders in front of an orangery. West of the house, a paved garden with L-shaped box-edged beds. The terrace ends with a viewing platform from which there are views of the lake and Langdale Pikes. South-west of the house, a line of Irish yews and a monkey puzzle that is probably part of the original planting. Stone terraces south of the house and sloping lawns with large boulders. North of the house, woodland with many conifers was part of Gibson's scheme, as are a group of pines and hollies west of the house. More terraces here, overlooking a croquet lawn from which paths lead to the lakeside.

Brockhurst

East Grinstead, West Sussex OS TQ4037 English Heritage Register Grade II*

Arts and Crafts house bought in 1908 by Frederick Hanbury, a cousin of Sir Thomas Hanbury of La Mortola on the Italian Riviera. Hanbury discovered a natural outcrop of Tunbridge Wells sandstone which he used to form a ravine and rock garden; for this he took advice from E.A. Bowles and Reginald Farrer. It covered an area of almost 4 acres/1.6 hectares and was irrigated by a spring-fed stream and ornamented with decorative cascades. The estate was broken up in 1954 but Hanbury's rock garden survives in the garden of Barton Pines, a house built in the 1950s, and has been well restored by new owners.

Brocklesby Park

Brocklesby, Lincolnshire OS TA1210 English Heritage Register Grade I Mausoleum open by appointment Tel 01469 560214

House built in 1603 for Sir William Pelham and much altered,

especially after a fire in 1898. Landscaping by Capability Brown for Charles Anderson Pelham (later 1st Baron Yarborough) from 1771 – Brown was paid £2,800 (£165,200 today) on account in 1778. His "Plan for for the Intended Alteration" shows the park encircled by a continuous belt of trees threaded with a winding walk, and clumps, and once a circle, of trees in open parkland; now much obscured by later planting. South of the house, a woodland ride with late 18th-century buildings: Mary Carter Temple; a grotto; a Hermitage or roothouse; and Arabella Aufrere's Temple. The walk eventually arrives at Mausoleum Woods, 240 acres/97 hectares of woodland containing the Pelham mausoleum by James Wyatt (completed in 1792) with, among other monuments, a beautiful figure of Sophia Aufrere, a Pelham wife who died young, by Joseph Nollekens. Humphry Repton was consulted after 1791 (Red Book) but it is not known what, if anything, was done on his advice. Formal gardens close to the house, with yew hedges and topiary designed by Sir Reginald Blomfield, who also worked on the house after the 1898 fire.

Brodick Castle

see page 363

Brodsworth Hall

see page 333

Brogdale Horticultural Trust

see page 122

Brompton Cemetery

Kensington and Chelsea, London OS TQ2577 English Heritage Register Grade II* Open regularly

Cemetery laid out by Benjamin B. Baud, with planting advice by J.C. Loudon, opened in 1840. Long rectangular site with a central avenue with a "great circle" of arcades and catacombs and a chapel – now densely populated with monuments. Many trees, in particular mature limes along the avenue, and scattered specimen trees.

Brook Cottage

see page 75

Brookwood Cemetery

Brookwood, Surrey OS SU9556 English Heritage Register Grade II Open regularly

Cemetery opened in 1854, designed by Henry Abraham, with detailed planting, in particular of evergreens, by Robert Donald, an associate of J.C. Loudon. Designed to take the pressure off the inner-London cemeteries and to cater for the burial of Londoners of all denominations and religions, it still has a Parsee chapel and a Muslim area. It was one of the last to be privately financed by a joint stock company. Bodies were brought by a special train from a platform built for that purpose at Waterloo station. In the 1920s part of it became a military cemetery, divided into national zones, and continued to be used for this purpose until after World War II. The American section, with a long lawn bordered by evergreens leading to the mausoleum, was designed by Egerton Swarthout of New York in 1929; the Canadian war memorial building was designed by Edward Maufe and built 1945–46. The northern part of the cemetery has tree-lined paths, glades of evergreens and shrubs.

Broughton Castle

see page 76

Broughton Hall

Broughton, North Yorkshire OS SD9450 English Heritage Register Grade II Open regularly Tel 01756 799608

16th-century house for the Tempest family, with many later alterations. 18th-century landscaping in the park. Formal gardens by W.A. Nesfield, 1855–57 – one of the best surviving examples of his work. On the north side of the house, a walled garden with an Italianate gazebo has an ornate scrolled parterre; a similar parterre to the south of the house. Fountain against the south wall of the house, flanked by balustraded steps. A conservatory projects into the gardens from the south side of the house.

Broughton House and Garden

see page 364

Broxmouth Park

nr Dunbar, East Lothian OS NT6977 Scottish Inventory

Late 18th-century house on an older site, probably designed by James Nisbet. J. Macky, in *A Journey Through Scotland* (1724), described "another delicious seat of the Duke of Roxburgh…with a good avenue…and a spacious parterre in the middle of a fine park, prodigiously planted with the trees in great thickets between it and the sea." This was the garden of the 1st Duke of Roxburgh, who knew such French gardens as Fontainebleau, Sceaux and Marly. He made a new garden at Broxmouth 1709–12, with a walled deer park north-west of the house and a formal wilderness and water garden to the east. It was possibly designed by William Adam who had worked for the Duke at Floors Castle (*see page 476*). Fragments survive – the deer park, the wilderness, with moderr planting but some original paths, and the canalised Brox burn with formal cascades.

Broxwood Court

Pembridge, Herefordshire OS SO3654 English Heritage Register Grade II

House built after 1955 when an earlier and larger Victorian house was demolished. Garden and walk were designed by W.A. Nesfield c.1860. South-east of the house, a yew walk has a broad grass path running between yew hedges decorated with regular bays clipped in the hedges. An iron gate opens into a formal garden with an avenue of Irish yews leading to a bench backed by a hedge of *Cupressus macrocarpa*. West of the house is an avenue of conifers – deodars (*Cedrus deodara*), Wellingtonias (*Sequoiadendron giganteum*) and Scots pines (*Pinus sylvestris*). The avenue passes through an arboretum with many mature trees, before leading to the park. Planned walks lead from the house through the arboretum.

B

Brunswick Park

Sandwell, West Midlands OS SO9995
English Heritage Register Grade II
Open regularly

Public park designed by William Barron & Son and laid out in the late 1880s. At the heart of the park there had been a mining pit mound which was retained, with paths leading to its summit, but this was levelled in the 1930s. North of this is an open lawn surrounded by plantings with winding paths. Barron's original pool is now a paddling pool and various sports facilities – bowling greens, putting green and tennis courts – are later additions.

Bryan's Ground Gardens

nr Presteigne, Herefordshire OS SO3366
Open occasionally for NGS
Tel 01544 260001

Bryan's Ground is an attractive Arts and Crafts house built for the Misses Holt immediately before World War I, to the designs of Groome and Bettington of Hereford. Since 1993, it has been the home of David Wheeler and Simon Dorrell, and the office of the admirable gardening journal *Hortus* which they founded in 1987. When Wheeler and Dorrell came to Bryan's Ground the only part of the garden to survive was the Sunk Garden below the terrace to the south of the house. They set about restoring this and making a new garden of sprightly formal character. The new garden includes a snaking path through a dazzling grid of thirty different varieties of apple underplanted with sheaves of *Iris sibirica*; a parterre of Portugal laurels and a formal herb garden of lozenge-shaped beds; a garden of roses trained on obelisks; a walk of pleached limes; a lawn hedged in yew and planted with rows of *Pyrus calleryana* 'Chanticleer'. The Sunk Garden now has a circular pool, mounds of box, pots of lilies, Irish yews and lavish drifts of catmint and fennel. To the south, concealed behind trees and dense plantings of shrubs, a grassy walk runs along old park railings to a rustic bastion-like belvedere in the shade of trees, from which

there are beautiful views over pastureland to rising hills.

Brympton d'Evercy House

Brympton d'Evercy, Somerset OS ST5215
English Heritage Register Grade II*

The house goes back to the 15th century when the estate belonged to John Sydenham. In the early 17th century there was a garden of note here. Thomas Gerard's *The Particular Description of the County of Somerset* (1633) describes the house as "daintily seated and furnished with all manner of conveniences as gardens, orchards, groves, &c." A spectacular new south range was added towards the end of the 17th century and a Kip engraving in *Britannia Illustrata* (1707) shows a busy formal garden of that date – long avenues, a bowling green, regular groves, a terrace walk, pool and formal wilderness. The house survives in fine state and the boundaries of these gardens are for the most part still visible today.

Buckhurst Park

Withyham, East Sussex OS TQ5035
English Heritage Register Grade II*

Estate created by amalgamating Buckhurst with Stoneland. House built 1690 and altered in the 18th, 19th and 20th centuries. Formal gardens south-west of the house designed by Edwin Lutyens in 1903 when he was also working on the house. Terraces below the house, with a sunken garden, oblong lily pond, grass walks and mixed borders. Gertrude Jekyll had done the original planting but present planting dates from the 1990s. South-west of the house, two buttressed terrace walls with planting between the buttresses have staircases at each end linking the various terraces to a lawn below. North-west of the sunken garden terrace, a series of hedged compartments. A broad grass path runs between beech hedges towards a lake and glades of rhododendrons and mature oaks. A bridge runs across the weir at the northern end of the lake where Lewis Kennedy in 1819 designed walks. Humphry Repton produced a Red Book in 1805 but it is not known what resulted. The

park was laid out in the 18th century and has clumps and scattered individual trees.

Buckingham Palace, *formerly known as* Buckingham House *and the* Queen's House

City of Westminster, London OS TQ2879
English Heritage Register Grade II*
Open regularly Tel 020 7321 2233

Early 18th-century house, rebuilt by John Nash 1826–30 and completed in 1837 by Edward Blore. There are 40 acres/16 hectares of walled gardens, the largest area of private gardens in London. The earliest garden activity dates back to the early 17th century when James I, who had become obsessed with encouraging the silk trade, planted a garden of (the wrong kind of) mulberry trees. In the early 18th century, when the Duke of Buckingham owned the estate, there were formal gardens with terraces, pools and parterres. New, informal gardens, were laid out by Nash when he was working on the house, with the planting advice of William T. Aiton of Kew Gardens. At their heart is a serpentine lake with an island. The privacy of the gardens was ensured by much perimeter planting along the walls, some of which date back to the 18th century. Winding paths thread the perimeter plantings. A very large lawn separates the west terrace of the house from the lake. The 18th-century Admiralty Temple, or Summerhouse, attributed to William Kent, stands in the north-west part of the garden, with the Waterloo Vase (1812) to its south and rose gardens between the two. The lake provides a sanctuary for water birds (among them pink flamingoes) and its banks are planted with many moisture-loving plants.

Buckland Abbey

Yelverton, Devon OS SX4866
Open regularly (NT) Tel 01822 853607

13th-century Cistercian abbey which became the home of the Grenville family after the dissolution of the monasteries and was much altered at that time. Sir Francis Drake lived here later in

the 16th century. Formal but slightly wambly box-hedged herb garden designed by Vita Sackville-West after 1953. New Elizabethan Garden with gravel walks, box-edged beds and a central raised circular pool made in 2001.

Buckland Park

Buckland, Oxfordshire OS SU3498
English Heritage Register Grade II*

Estate belonging to the Throckmorton family in the 17th century. In the mid 1750s Sir Robert Throckmorton commissioned a new house from John Wood, father and son, of Bath. The park was landscaped a little later by Richard Woods (he was paid £6-6-0 (£453 today) on account in 1759. As Fiona Cowell, who single-handed rescued Woods from oblivion, wrote in *Garden History* (1986): "The elegantly laid-out park does not look like the work of a beginner, and the irregularly-shaped ponds linked by bridges and cascades and backed by ornamental plantations are all typical of Woods's mature style." It seems likely that Richard Woods also designed the garden buildings that ornament the landscape – an Ionic rotunda, a rusticated icehouse and an exedra.

Bulstrode

Gerrards Cross, Buckinghamshire OS SU9888 English Heritage Register Grade II*

House built 1861–70 for the 12th Duke of Somerset to the designs of Benjamin Ferrey – but a park had existed here since the early middle ages and a house, built in the late 17th century, had been bought in 1706 by Hans Willem Bentinck, 1st Earl of Portland who laid out formal gardens, possibly with the help of Henry Wise and Claude Desgots. An engraving by T. Willson of *c*.1720, illustrated in John Harris's *The Artist and the Country House* (1979), shows the garden with an enclosed pattern of parterres and an oval pool with eight avenues radiating from it. The 2nd Duchess of Portland, who lived here from 1734 to 1785, was a distinguished plantswoman, introducing many new plants to the garden. From 1793 Humphry Repton landscaped the grounds for the 3rd Duke, correcting "the

geometric taste in gardening"; nevertheless, as John Harris wrote, "the ghost of the formal gardens remains impressed upon the Reptonian parkscape." In the 20th century the estate was owned by Sir John Ramsden who planted many rhododendrons.

Burford House Gardens

see page 195

Burghley House

see page 292

Burley House

Burley on the Hill, Rutland OS SK8810
English Heritage Register Grade II

House built 1696–1700 for Daniel Finch, 2nd Earl of Nottingham (later 7th Earl of Winchelsea), replacing an earlier house destroyed in the Civil War. John Evelyn described the earlier house in 1654: "among the noblest seates in England, situate on the brow of an hill…neere a Park Waled in, & a fine Wood at the descent." This house had been built for the 1st Duke of Buckingham, for whom John Tradescant the Elder was working by 1622; he would have been responsible for planting the garden. London and Wise are mentioned in 1701 in connection with a new garden which consisted of three terraces below the south front of the house, ending in a vast semicircular apron with a parterre. This arrangement was changed to something much simpler by Humphry Repton who made a Red Book for the 9th Earl of Winchelsea after visiting in 1795. There had been a park here in Norman times, roughly the size of the present park. The Duke of Buckingham had laid out a pattern of rides and avenues, much of which may be seen today. The south avenue, becoming a ride as it approaches the house, is shown in Peter Tilleman's painting of *c*.1729 in John Harris's *The Artist and the Country House* (1979).

Burslem Park

Stoke-on-Trent, Staffordshire OS SJ8735
English Heritage Register Grade II
Open regularly

Public park designed by Thomas Mawson and opened to the public

B

in 1894. Late 19th-century Elizabethan-style pavilion overlooking a terraced formal flower garden with a bandstand nearby. Pulhamite rockery with cascade and pool and an aviary nearby. There are also tennis courts, bowling greens and a children's playground.

Burton Constable Hall

Burton Constable, East Yorkshire OS TA1836 English Heritage Register Grade II* Open regularly Tel 01964 562400

The Constable family came to live here in the 12th century and still live here. The present house was built in the 16th century, with alterations made chiefly in the 17th and 18th centuries. There was a park here by the 14th century. In the late 17th century a pattern of avenues aligned on the house was laid out and parts of them survive – in particular the south avenue. Capability Brown was consulted in 1767 and made regular visits until 1782. Thomas White was consulted in 1768. Brown worked on the house as well as on the park – which is most probably the result of a collaboration between William Constable, Brown and White. South-west of the house is a long thin lake with, at its northern end, the Menagerie (c.1757–60), and the lake is spanned by Brown's bridge with a dam. The northern part of the park is largely arable farmland. Clumps and individual trees from the 18th century are still visible. South-west of the house are lawns and trees, probably part of Brown's plan, and an orangery remodelled in the 1780s. To the north is a formal garden with a pattern of rectangular lawns, enclosed by a semicircular ha-ha by Brown. The lawns are ornamented with a pattern of yew trees and statues. North of the hall is the site of the great flower garden made in the 1750s and 1760s by William Constable, a learned plantsman.

Burton Park

Barlavington, West Sussex OS SU9617 English Heritage Register Grade II

Ancient site with new neo-Grecian house built in 1831 for John Biddulph to the designs of Henry Bassett. Terraced garden east of the house, with geometric rose garden and formal lily pools connected by a rill. Beyond it are lawns with specimens and clumps of conifers dating from a mid 19th-century layout. South of the house, lawns down to a lake, Chingford Pond, with a coppiced nut walk leading to a landing stage. Park probably established in the 16th century; now mostly arable land with intermittent woodland.

Burton Pynsent

Curry Rivel, Somerset OS ST3724 English Heritage Register Grade II

The estate was given by Sir Robert Pynsent to William Pitt (later Earl of Chatham) in 1765. There had been an Elizabethan house when William Pitt came here but he added a new wing, which is today all that survives of the house. Pitt was an enthusiastic landscaper and clothed the slopes about the house with trees. His gardener, worried by the quantities of trees needed, said to him, "Bless me, my Lord, all the nurseries in the county would not furnish the hundredth part", and Pitt replied "No matter, send for them from London." Macaulay records that relays of labourers worked even by torchlight planting the large numbers of cedars sent from London. The finest part of the landscape is the south-facing slope looking towards the Somerset levels and the site of the Battle of Sedgemoor. On the far side of the valley, to the south-west of the house on Troy Hill, is a column designed by Capability Brown and erected in 1766 at a cost of £2,000 (£131,000 today) to the memory of Sir William Pynsent and in gratitude to him.

Burwarton House

Burwarton, Shropshire OS SO6185 English Heritage Register Grade II

19th-century house by Anthony Salvin for the Hon. G.F. Hamilton, reduced and altered in the 1950s by Philip Skeicher & Partners. 19th-century formal gardens extended by Brenda Colvin in the 1920s, one of her earliest commissions. Rose garden with yew hedges also by Brenda Colvin.

Bury Court

see page 76

Busbridge Lakes

Busbridge, Surrey OS SU9742 English Heritage Register Grade II*

House formed from the stables of the 17th- and 18th-century house demolished c.1906. A natural setting of wooded valley and rocky cliffs forms the basis of romantic pleasure grounds. A string of ponds runs along the valley, with a rockwork bridge and sham bridge over a weir. A hermit's cave has an iron grille and a vaulted chamber from which a tunnel leads to a circular chamber probably of 1756. Rockwork grotto of late 18th or early 19th century. 18th-century Doric Temple, rustic pavilions, sham ruins and two mock Roman altars. The Ghost Walk is a rising path through a cleft in the cliff with alcoves and niches and fanged entrance arches. Barbara Jones, in *Follies & Grottoes* (1974), describes it as "An enchanting romantic garden…bathed in a golden glow of contentment, though at least one folly was surely intended for a shiver."

Buscot Park

see page 77

Bushy Park

Richmond, Greater London OS TQ1569 English Heritage Register Grade I Open regularly

The first land to be enclosed here, 400 acres/162 hectares, was enclosed in 1491 by Sir Giles d'Aubeny. It became part of Cardinal Wolsey's Hampton Court estate in 1514 and Henry VIII's deer park after 1529. Further acquisitions of land were made until it had an area of 1,099 acres/450 hectares, the second largest royal park in London after Richmond Park. In 1638–39, under Charles I, water was brought to Bushy Park and to Hampton Court Palace by creating a canal, the Longford river, 12 miles long, to bring water from the river Colne. It was planned by Nicholas Lane and cost £4,000 (£330,080 today) and still forms the western boundary of the park. George London planted avenues 1689–99; the chestnut avenue, planted with two rows of chestnuts on each side and a further four rows of limes flanking them, still runs south straight across the park from the Teddington Gate. Towards the southern end of the avenue is a circular pool (c.1699) with in its centre the Diana Fountain. Erected in 1713, this shows Arethusa (not Diana) on top of an elaborate rusticated column with putti and sea monsters. The statue, possibly by Francesco Fanelli, was previously in the Privy Garden at Hampton Court Palace but was originally commissioned for Charles I's queen, Henrietta Maria, at Somerset House. A lime avenue, also part of London's scheme, runs west from the Diana Fountain, and a fragment continues east of it. North-east of the fountain is a chain of pools and west of it the Waterhouse Woodland Gardens, laid out since 1949 by J.M. Fisher. From 1986 lime avenues were replanted, following London's plan. Throughout the park are excellent trees, and in parts of it red and fallow deer graze.

Butterstream Garden

see page 403

Buxted Park

Buxted, East Sussex OS TQ4923 English Heritage Register Grade II*

Early 18th-century house on an ancient site, with later alterations. Formal gardens about the house date from the 19th century, with many 20th-century changes. Parkland surrounds the house, with a few old parkland trees and, in its north-eastern corner, the remains of a lime avenue planted in the late 17th century, which probably formed the entrance avenue for the earlier house. The house is now a hotel.

Cabbages and Kings

see page 124

Cadhay

Ottery St Mary, Devon OS SY0896 English Heritage Register Grade II Open regularly Tel 01404 812432

16th- and 17th-century house built for the Haydon family about a paved courtyard, decoratively faced with sandstone and flint laid in chequerboard pattern. Early 20th-century garden, handsome yew hedges and a walk of Irish yews south of the house. Old, possibly medieval fishponds and adjacent parkland with ha-ha.

Cadland House

Fawley, Hampshire OS SU4699 English Heritage Register Grade II*

House built in the 1770s for the banker Robert Drummond to the designs of Henry Holland in collaboration with Capability Brown (Holland's father-in-law; they were both customers of Drummond's Bank), with pleasure grounds also designed by Brown. At the same time a fishing lodge was built three miles from the house, also with designed pleasure grounds. All was finished by 1780. William Gilpin saw the estate ten years later and wrote of the main house: "it is one of the most elegant and seems to me one of the most comfortable houses in the country…The clumps he has managed with great judgement." The main house, requisitioned during World War II, was demolished in 1953; the fishing lodge was burnt down, rebuilt, then again damaged by fire and rebuilt and enlarged in the 20th century. Brown encircled the house with plantings of trees and shrubs, and since the 1980s there has been much restoration, using plants recommended by Brown. Brown also planned walks to take advantage of the beautiful setting overlooking the Solent. One walk leads from a lawn close to the house, through a shrubbery, round to the south where it becomes a terraced walk cut into a bank above the beach, and thence through woodland, with glimpses of the sea, before curving back towards the house.

Caerhays Castle

see page 22

Calke Abbey

see page 251

Cally

nr Gatehouse of Fleet, Kircudbrightshire OS NX6055 Scottish Inventory Cally Garden Nursery open regularly Tel 01557 815029

Cally Palace was built c.1763–65 to the designs of Robert Mylne for James Murray. Mid 18th-century park, of which a few original trees (beech and oak) survive near the house, and some 19th-century conifers. Woodland planted in the 18th and 19th centuries. In 1939 the estate with a total area of 600 acres/242 hectares was sold to the Forestry Commission which has planted up over 500 acres/202 hectares of the total, thus destroying most of the old planned landscape. The 18th-century walled garden, 2.7 acres/1 hectare in area, has been used in recent years as the premises of an outstanding nursery, Cally Gardens, run by Michael Wickenden. Specialising in herbaceous perennials, many them rare, it has a stock of around 3,500 different varieties. The house is now Cally Palace Country House Hotel, which owns the only other remaining part of the old policies.

Calverley Park *and* Calverley Gardens
Tunbridge Wells, Kent OS TQ5839
English Heritage Register Grade II
Open regularly

Urban development by Decimus Burton, laid out in 1828 with detached villas and terraces about the declivity of Mount Pleasant. The original landscape scheme, integral to the development, is now much simplified, with mown grass and many fine mature trees. Leafy and green, it is a prototype of the Garden City. In a valley south of the grounds of Calverley Hotel, an area known as Calverley Gardens was developed in the early 19th century as a public park, with winding paths and lawns. Herbaceous borders flank a bowling green with sunken rose gardens nearby, and herbaceous border is laid out beside a bandstand. Mature trees and shrubs about the perimeter.

Cambridge College Gardens
see page 293 and see names of individual colleges

Cambridge University Botanic Garden
see page 296

Cammo
Edinburgh OS NT1775
Scottish Inventory Open regularly

Estate going back to the 15th century, bought in 1710 by Sir John Clerk of Penicuik (*see page 522*). The house was rebuilt at this time, with later alterations by William Adam; it is today a ruin. Between 1711 and 1719 Sir John laid out a pattern of axial paths, avenues, vistas and roundels centred on the house and its formal gardens; this scheme, and some of its plantings, substantially survives. It was gently made less formal when landscaping took place after 1778, when the formal gardens by the house were removed, a ha-ha was built and scattered parkland trees were planted. The estate was bequeathed to the National Trust for Scotland in 1975 and is now public open space.

Camperdown House
nr Dundee, Forfarshire OS NO3533
Scottish Inventory Open regularly

Estate going back to the 17th century, when it was bought by Alexander Duncan (later Viscounts Camperdown). The 2nd Viscount (later Earl) built the present house 1821–28 to the designs of William Burn. Parkland, surrounded by walled woodland, was planted in the 19th century. A lime avenue of *c.*1860 survives, and many individual 19th-century parkland trees. Dundee Corporation acquired the estate in 1946, and much of the land (now designated a Country Park) is now a golf course, a caravan park, pony grazing and public recreation grounds. The weeping form of wych elm (*Ulmus glabra* 'Camperdownii') first appeared as a chance seedling here in the first half of the 19th century, and a specimen may still be seen. In 2003 Dundee Corporation was raising money to transform the house into "a historic country house museum and gallery".

Campsea Ash Park
Campsea Ash, Suffolk OS TM3355
English Heritage Register Grade II

The house here, High House, was built for the Hon. W. Lowther

from 1883 by Anthony Salvin, who rebuilt the 17th-century house in Victorian Tudor style. The house was demolished in 1955 but the gardens remain. Especially remarkable are the parts of a 17th-century formal garden, probably laid out by John Sheppard. There are two canals, one 380ft/175m long, flanked to the east by a venerable yew hedge. A parallel canal, separated by a group of very old cedars planted in grass, is divided in two. A circular bowling green is enclosed in old yews. The remains of a complex pattern of avenues survive in the park. An avenue of limes which lead up to the north façade of the house survives but this seems to be a 19th-century replanting. In Penelope Hobhouse's and Christopher Woods's *Painted Gardens: English Watercolours 1850–1914* (1988), paintings done in the early 20th century by G.S. Elgood and E.A. Rowe show flowery borders, substantial yew topiary and a canal below the walls of the house, edged on its far side by a monumental yew hedge with busts on plinths set into niches.

Cannizaro Park
Wimbledon, Greater London OS TQ2370
English Heritage Register Grade II*
Open regularly

18th-century house named after Francis Platemone, Duke of Cannizaro, who lived here in the early 19th century. The house was much altered after a fire *c.*1900 and is now a hotel. The site, on the edge of Wimbledon Common, had parkland laid out in the 18th century for Henry Dundas, Viscount Melville, but the present garden is largely the work of E.K. Wilson who owned Cannizaro 1920–47. Ornamental woodland has good mature trees and flowering shrubs, in particular a spectacular azalea dell and a splendid heather bank. Lady Jane's Wood (named after Viscountess Melville) has some of the oldest trees, including 18th-century beeches, and there are good cedars of Lebanon, sweet chestnuts, limes and oaks. A charming Gothic aviary is modelled on Pisa cathedral, the former kitchen garden has been made into an

ornamental garden, and there is a walled rose garden. The estate, with 34 acres/14 hectares of land, was bought by Merton Borough Council in 1958 and is now a public park.

Cannon Hall
Cawthorne, South Yorkshire OS SE2708
English Heritage Register Grade II
Open regularly Tel 01226 790270

Late 17th-century house on an ancient site, remodelled in the late 18th century by John Carr of York for John Spencer. Richard Woods laid out pleasure grounds and park in the 1760s. Pleasure grounds surround the hall, with a terrace on the south side commanding views over parkland and lakes. To the east, a formal garden, with lawns and geometric beds, between the kitchen garden and a ha-ha, is overlooked by a Camellia House, or Orangery. Above a pool south-east of the formal garden are fragments of a 16th-century archway and tracery window. A path leads through woods and shrubs to more fragments of windows, which mark the division between pleasure grounds and park. The remainder of the pleasure grounds are wooded: beech, oaks, pine and sweet chestnut are underplanted with shrubs, including many rhododendrons. A series of lakes run across the park south of the house, with cascades and bridges, all disposed according to Woods's design. Planting was arranged so that the lakes were visible from the house and views of the house from the lakeside were framed by trees. An aerial photograph of it is illustrated in Christopher Taylor's *Parks and Gardens of Britain: A Landscape History from the Air* (1998).

Cannons, *also known as* Canons Park
Edgware, Greater London OS TQ1791
Open regularly

Of all the gardens described in J.C. Loudon's *Encyclopaedia of Gardening* (1822), Cannons seems particularly to hold his interest. When Loudon knew the house the garden had disappeared – all there was to see was "A dull flat of rich pasture, intersected by rows of elms, and surrounded by a brick wall". But

this had been one of the grandest houses and gardens of the early 18th century, and had been made by a self-made man, as Loudon notes: "The place is remarkable in having been the site of the improvements of the celebrated Duke of Chandos, who rose from the rank of a private gentleman, James Bridges, Esq. Married into the family of Lake, then proprietors of Canons. Having made his fortune as a paymaster in the German war, and acquired his title, he built the magnificent mansion at Canons in 1712." The garden was the last design of George London, the royal gardener, who died in 1714. It had a 10-acre/4-hectare parterre, an 8-acre/3.2-hectare formal wilderness of over 1 acre/2.4 hectares, a 7-acre/2.8-hectare pool and an 11-acre/4.4-hectare kitchen garden. Alexander Pope considered it the summit of vulgarity, and was thought to have ridiculed it (as "Timon's Villa") in his *An Epistle to Lord Burlington* (1731): "At *Timon's Villa* let us pass a Day,/Where all cry out, 'What sums are thrown away!'" After Chandos's death the house was demolished and the land returned to agriculture. Today, the last surviving part of the old park, owned by Harrow Borough Council and now called Canons Park, is a public park with recreational facilities and allotments.

Canons Ashby House
see page 252

Capel Manor
see page 125

Capheaton Hall
Capheaton, Northumberland OS NZ0380
English Heritage Register Grade II
Open by written appointment only

Fine house designed in 1668 by Robert Trollope for Sir John Swinburne. A painting by Peter Hartover of 1674, illustrated in John Harris's *The Artist and the Country House* (1979), shows a garden newly made for the house. A walled forecourt is flanked by identical four-part enclosed gardens with a central pool and tiered fountains, tall pieces of topiary, and narrow flower borders running along the walls. There had also been formal gardens beyond the walls, with avenues dividing the landscape, but these, and the walled gardens by the house, were lost when landscaping took place in the second half of the 18th century. The handsome gate piers visible in Hartover's painting were saved and now stand at the village entrance to the park. West of the house is a sham ruined chapel which was surely made as part of the 18th-century landscaping, but Barbara Jones's *Follies & Grottoes* (1974) dates it to the early 19th century.

Carberry Tower
nr Musselburgh, East Lothian OS NT3669

Ancient estate with 16th-century tower house which has seen many later alterations and changes of ownership – from John de Crebarrie in the 13th century to the Church of Scotland in 1961 (it is now a residential conference centre). A large arboretum and shrubbery were planted by the 15th Lord Elphinstone after 1861; in 1985 the dendrologist Alan Mitchell measured 100 particularly interesting trees. Italianate garden (1910) to south of house, originally with bedding schemes but now planted with roses, has a 17th-century multi-faceted sundial.

Carclew
Perran-ar-worthal, Cornwall OS SW7838
English Heritage Register Grade II
Open occasionally for NGS

House substantially remodelled in 1749 by Thomas Edwards for William Lemon and gutted by fire in 1934; ruins remain but a new house was built at some distance in 1963. Landscaping of the parkland in the second half of the 18th century. Much ornamental planting 1824–68 by Sir Charles Lemon who was a sponsor of J.D. Hooker's Himalayan expedition of 1848–51. The head gardener at this time was William Beattie Booth who had worked at the Royal Horticultural Society's garden at Chiswick under John Lindley and was an authority on camellias. (Lemon's gamekeeper was Joseph Lobb, the father of William and Thomas who became notable plant collectors for Veitch of Exeter.) The garden still contains a remarkable collection of plants,

some of them particularly fine specimens of their species, with a distinguished horticultural pedigree.

Cardiff Castle *and* Bute Park
Cardiff OS ST1876 Cadw/ICOMOS Register Grade I Open regularly Tel 029 2087 8100

There was a Roman fort (whose remains are still visible) close to the site of Cardiff Castle; in 1085, William I ordered the building of a new castle. In the 15th century, when the Beauchamp family lived here, there was a flower garden, or "plaisance" before the great hall. From the late 16th century the Herberts made a new garden. In the 18th century Lord Mount Stuart (later 4th Earl of Bute) commissioned Capability Brown to work on the grounds. He laid out a new drive and lawns, and planted groups of trees on the ramparts and about the keep. In the 19th century the castle was transformed by the architect William Burges for the 3rd Marquess of Bute. Burges included an extraordinary sunken roof garden – a marble-lined court surrounded by covered walks, mosaics and bronze columns. From the garden are panoramic views, with Castell Coch visible on the edge of Cardiff – another medieval castle which Burges transformed into an extraordinary fanciful decorated retreat for the Marquess. In 1871 part of the grounds of Cardiff Castle were laid out for the Marquess as a public park, Bute Park, designed by Andrew Pettigrew; *The Journal of Horticulture and Cottage Gardener* described it in 1877: "The grounds are extensive; many trees have been planted in them lately, and groups and long borders of various kinds of choice shrubs formed, lawns laid down, and narrow and broad walks made." This is very much the character that Bute Park has today, with the addition of a sports ground at its northern end.

Carnell, *formerly* Cairnhill
nr Hurlford, Ayrshire Open occasionally for SGS

The Carnell estate is an old one and the present house dates back

to the 16th century with 18th- and 19th-century alterations. The distinction of the garden starts with the Findlay family in the 20th century. In the old walled kitchen garden they laid out a series of flower gardens with a superb herbaceous border (with a canal running parallel to it) and a border of shrubs underplanted with phlox. By the house there is a battlemented yew walk and more herbaceous borders. Facing the house across a lawn are two squares of old lime trees which commemorate the square formations of Scottish troops at the Battle of Dettingen (1743).

Carrigglas Manor
Longford, County Longford, Republic of Ireland
Open regularly Tel (00353) 043 45165

17th-century estate with beautiful stable block of *c*.1790 by James Gandon. House rebuilt 1837–40 in Gothico-Tudor style for the Lefroy family to the designs of Daniel Robertson. Wild woodland garden and stream with waterside planting and pools. Formal garden with roses and *potager*.

Carshalton House, *now* St Philomena's School
Sutton, Greater London TQ2764
English Heritage Register Grade II

Early 18th-century house for Edward Carleton who went bankrupt in 1713. Alterations after 1716 for Sir John Fellowes who also went bankrupt, in 1720, having just had time to ask Charles Bridgeman to work on the garden. East of the house is a late 18th-century lake, possibly informalised from a formal pool of Bridgeman's time. On its eastern shore is a remarkable building, the Water House, probably designed (*c*.1719) by Henry Joynes who had been Comptroller of Works at Blenheim Palace. It has a decidely Vanbrughian air, its tower bristling with finials and battlements rising above an arcaded façade; part of it was an orangery and part a bath house. At the southern tip of the lake (which today is usually dry), a grotto or hermitage of before 1721. This, and the Water House, have an unexpectedly picturesque

character in a landscape of Bridgeman's time.

Carton
Maynooth, County Kildare, Republic of Ireland

Ancient estate of the FitzGerald family (Earls of Kildare and later Dukes of Leinster) from the 12th century who leased the estate to the Talbots (of Malahide *see page 424*). The Talbots built the present house but, after the FitzGeralds returned in 1739, it was transformed for the 19th Earl of Kildare by the architect Richard Castle. The FitzGeralds lived here until 1949, since when it has changed hands more than once. A painting by Johann van der Hagen of *c*.1730, reproduced in Edward Malins's and The Knight of Glin's *Lost Demesnes* (1976), shows the house set in spectacular formal gardens with a semicircular forecourt from which avenues radiate into the landscape. Behind the house is a walled garden with a four-part arrangement of lawns and topiary and formal rides cut through woodland. When the 20th Earl (and later 1st Duke of Leinster) married Lady Emilia Lennox, daughter of the 2nd Duke of Richmond (of Goodwood, *see page 481*) in 1747, she gradually removed almost all of the old formal layout and laid out 50 acres/20 hectares of walled pleasure grounds by the house. The Duchess turned an old thatched cottage into a shellhouse with Gothic tracery windows and an interior ornamented with elaborate patterns of shellwork, mirrors and panels of twigs; in 1849 it was enlarged into a cottage *orné* and set in a flower garden. She also supervised plantings of formal wildernesses and increasingly informal groups of trees, and landscaped the Rye water that flows through the demesne, writing to her husband (busy in London): "New river is beautiful. One turn of it is a masterpiece in the art of laying out, and I defy Kent, Brown or Mr Hamilton to excel it." A painting by George Barret of *c*.1764 (reproduced in *Lost Demesnes*) shows the landscape clothed in trees, with lawns running down to the curving

river bank. It is said, by Horace Walpole, that Capability Brown was invited to design the landscape at Carton and decline[d] saying, "I have not finished England yet." In around 1815 [the] house was enlarged by Richard Morrison for the 3rd Duke who had the river widened again and added an Italianate garden agains[t] the south front of the house. Thi[s] still exists, with four parterres about a scalloped pool, and the wooded demesne is still extraordinarily beautiful. Carton House is today the home of a g[olf] club, with two full-length course[s] laid out in 2002 and 2003.

Cassiobury Park
Watford, Hertfordshire OS TQ0897
English Heritage Register Grade II

The manor of Cassiobury belonged to St Alban's Abbey in the middle ages and was acquire[d] by Sir Richard Morrison in 154[0] and by marriage to the Capel family (later Earls of Essex). A ne[w] house was built 1674–83 to the designs of Hugh May; this was succeeded by a house designed b[y] James Wyatt (1800–13), which w[as] demolished in 1927. An engravin[g] by Kip in *Britannia Illustrata* (170[?]) shows parterres, pools and topiar[y] on two sides of the house, with the surrounding landscape patterned with tree-lined rides through woodland and formal groves of trees. This was probably the work of Moses Cook *c*.1672 for the 1st Earl of Essex, of whom John Evelyn wrote "no man is more industrious in planting wit[h] walks, ponds and rural elegances about his seat." George London, with whom Cook collaborated, worked on the garden *c*.1697; Charles Bridgeman in the 1720s; Thomas Wright in 1739; and Humphry Repton 1801–2. In 1795 the Grand Union Canal wa[s] built across the park from north t[o] south. The estate began to fall apart when the Earl of Essex sol[d] 185 acres/75 hectares for development in 1908. Watford Borough Council acquired most of the remaining land, using som[e] of it for a golf course and some for public open space, which retains some old parkland trees. The West Hertfordshire Golf Course has the remains of two

17th- or 18th-century lime avenues.

The Castle

Castle Eden, County Durham OS NZ4238
English Heritage Register Grade II

House built *c*.1765, on an older site, to designs by William Newton for Rowland Burdon. Pleasure grounds to the north and north-west of the house take advantage of the picturesque scenery of the Castle Eden dene through which a burn flows out into the sea north-east of the castle. Paths wind through woods to the burn which is animated by bridges, weirs and cascades. Part of the dene was planted as an arboretum in the late 19th or early 20th century. Castle Eden dene became a well known beauty spot which J.R. Boyle's *The County of Durham its Castles, Churches and Manor Houses* (1892) described as "an unbroken scene of secluded sylvan beauty… Beetling crags, crystal waterfalls, the kings and lords of the forest, wild flowers in endless variety…a veritable paradise." The Garden of Eden is a gamekeeper's cottage, rebuilt in 1881, enclosed in an orchard. There is a golf course in the southern part of the park.

Castle Ashby Gardens
see page 252

Castle Bromwich Hall Gardens
see page 253

Castle Coole
see page 404

Castle Drogo
see page 23

Castle Hill
Filleigh, Devon OS SS6728
English Heritage Register Grade I

The Fortescue family had owned this estate since the 15th century but until the late 17th century their chief residence was at Weare Giffard, also in Devon. The house dates from the 16th century but was rebuilt in the late 17th century and much altered from 1728 for Hugh Fortescue, 1st Earl Clinton by Roger Morris with advice from Lord Burlington;

alterations 1796–1802 by Sir John Soane; severely damaged by fire in 1934, with much loss of contents. The making of the garden dates, essentially, from two periods – Hugh Fortescue's work in the early 18th century and his half-brother and heir, Matthew Fortescue's, landscaping activities after 1751. The first garden was in the French style, on a grandiose scale but with distinctive English characteristics. Two paintings by J. Lange of 1741 (destroyed in the 1934 fire) show the garden. In one the south front of the newly Palladianised house is seen overlooking a series of dizzying scalloped turf terraces with curved palissades of trees on each side, a pair of obelisks on bastions and a huge formal pool at the bottom of the slope. The second painting shows the view from behind the house and depicts, south of the pool, a long wide walk, lined with palissades of trees, piercing the woodland and rising uphill to the horizon, with an eyecatcher of a triumphal arch (which survives today). Charles Bridgeman's name has been mentioned as a possible designer of the garden but there is no evidence. Matthew Fortescue overlaid this landscape with a late 18th-century park; a plan of *c*.1763 shows the sculpted terraces gone and the formal pool turned in a long narrow lake with a cascade at each end. A painting of 1785, done from the south, shows the house in a thoroughly naturalistic setting of rolling hills, billowing woodland, and cattle grazing in meadows with clumps of trees. Throughout the 18th century garden buildings and ornaments were added: a Hermitage, the Indian House, the Bowling House, Vulcan's Temple, the Satyr's Temple, Holwell Temple, a Menagerie, a Chinese Temple, a Gothick Castle (from which the estate took its name) – some of which survive. The later landscaping has not completely obliterated the earlier garden – for example the southerly vista from the house, down to the water and up to the triumphal arch on the horizon is still to be seen. The two gardens merge into each other, creating a savoury amalgamation. In the 1930s Christopher Hussey described the

panorama of the garden at Castle Hill: "a prodigious string of golden-hued buildings, crowned here and there by little domes… against a background of lofty trees."

Castle Hill
Torquay, Devon OS SX9363 English Heritage Register Grade II Open by appointment Tel 01803 214801

Garden of extravagantly mannerist Arts and Crafts style in the sedate environs of Torquay, designed by Fred Harrild (who had been articled to Sir Edwin Lutyens) *c*.1928–34 for Horace Pickersgill. Precipitous terraces with bold masonry, pool with statuary, yew topiary, a gatehouse with portcullis and a fountain pool with dragon gargoyles. Fine views over Lyme and Tor Bays.

Castle Howard
see page 334

Castle Kennedy
see page 365

Castle Menzies
Weem, Perthshire OS NN8349
Scottish Inventory

Ancient estate of the Menzies family which owned the estate until 1910. 16th-century castle altered by William Burn 1839–40. Notable woodland planting throughout the 19th century; Sir Robert Menzies is said to have planted two million trees, deciduous and coniferous, 1844–1903 – chiefly beech, larch, oak and Scots pine but also some of the newer introductions of conifers such as Corsican pine (*Pinus nigra* subsp. *laricio*) Douglas fir (*Pseudotsuga menziesii*) and western hemlock (*Tsuga heterophylla*). Sir Robert also planted an arboretum; rich in conifers, which included deciduous trees such as the Californian *Arbutus menziesii*, of which there cannot be many specimens in Perthshire. Little survives of the arboretum today.

Castle of Mey
see page 366

Castle Ward
see page 405

Castletown House
Celbridge, County Kildare,
Republic of Ireland
Open regularly Tel (00353) 1 628 8252

Great Palladian house built from 1722 to the designs of Alessandro Galilei for the Rt Hon. William Conolly, Speaker of the Irish House of Commons. Mrs Pendarves saw it in 1732: "[the] situation was very fine, and the country extremely pleasant – some wood and pretty winding rivers." By 1739, when an estate plan was drawn, a pattern of avenues radiated out from the house, some of which partly survive. In 1739 Conolly's Folly was built (possibly designed by Richard Castle) to close the western vista – an elaborate multiple arcade crowned at its centre with a soaring obelisk with an overall height of 140ft/40m. It cost £400 (£33,008 today) and was a famine relief project, paid for at a rate of a halfpenny a day (so it is the product of 96,000 man/days of labour). In 1743 another extraordinary building was erected: the Wonderful Barn, acting as an eyecatcher at the end of a vista east of the house, is a giant inverted cone, 70ft/20m high, with a spiral staircase built about its outside wall, a door at each storey and surmounted by a battlemented viewing platform. On each side is a much smaller dovecote, similarly cone-shaped but without an external staircase. All this survives in good condition. In 1748 William Conolly's son Tom married Lady Louisa Lennox. the sister of Emily, Duchess of Leinster (*see* Carton, *page 454*). Like her sister, she was infected by the landscaping bug, enhancing the banks of the river Liffey which flows through the demesne: "I found some very pretty rocks that the sods would never stay on in time of flood and therefore have left them bare which has good effect coming out of grass, and will afford some pretty romantic seats close to the water-edge, where I am going to plant some willows." Lady Louisa continued to embellish her estate and, in the words of Edward Malins's and The Knight of Glin's *Lost Demesnes* (1976), "She died in 1821, seated in a tent on the lawn in order that

she might look at the landscape she loved." The estate was owned by Conolly descendants until 1965 when it was auctioned and bought by developers who secured permission to build a housing estate by the drive. In 1967 the house, with 120 acres/48 hectares, was bought by Desmond Guinness and it became the headquarters of the Irish Georgian Society.

Castlewellan National Arboretum
see page 406

Catchfrench
St Germans, Cornwall OS SX3059
English Heritage Register Grade II

Ancient house, altered in the late 18th century for the Glanville family. Francis Glanville consulted Humphry Repton in 1792 and a Red Book was produced in the same year. Repton enthused (as he did): "the romantic situation of the house…the delightful scenery with which it is everywhere surrounded, leave little else to be done, but to give the whole place an air of extent and importance, by removing the appearance of a road so near its boundary." Repton altered the approaches, opened out views and was probably responsible for the "terrace and shrubbery, tastefully laid out, with abundance of plants and flowers" which G.S. Gilbert noted in his *Historical Survey of Cornwall* (1820).

Catton Hall
Old Catton, Norfolk OS TG2312
English Heritage Register Grade II*

Late 18th-century house, with fine views southwards to the city of Norwich, built for Jeremiah Ives, a silk merchant and twice mayor of Norwich. Ives consulted Humphry Repton in 1788, which resulted in Repton's first commission but no Red Book. Stephen Daniels, in his *Humphry Repton* (1999), describes such early work as essentially in the style of Capability Brown but Repton "was to create a more sociable-looking landscape, in views out across the surrounding landscape, of cottage and cathedral". Much of Repton's plantings survive. A domed camellia house was added to the south-west façade of the house *c*.1860.

C

Caversham Court
Caversham, Berkshire OS SU7074
English Heritage Register Grade II

Public park on the river Thames, opened in 1934 in the grounds of the former rectory of St Peter's Church (the rectory was demolished in 1933). Terraced walk running east–west divides the park which contains a mid 17th-century brick gazebo and parts of 17th-century garden walls. Terraced lawn with specimen trees running down to river. North of the terraced walk, demonstration allotments.

Caversham Park
Caversham, Berkshire OS SU7276
English Heritage Register Grade II

Ancient estate on the river Thames, passing through the hands of Lord Craven in the 17th century, Lord Cadogan in the 18th century, Major Marsack after 1784, and William Crawshay in 1838. The house burnt down (for the second time) in 1850 and was rebuilt. The Crawshays sold the house in 1920 when it became a school and then, during World War II, the office of the BBC's Monitoring Service, which it remains. In 1718 Lord Cadogan commissioned Stephen Switzer to make canals, fishponds, terraces and a great parterre – at a total cost of £1,394 (£109,805 today). These gardens were laid out on the slopes running down towards the river south of the house. There were two canals, each 233yds/200m long, of which one appears to survive, and there is still terracing to be seen. In the 1760s Capability Brown was called in. He thinned out the woodland south of the house and simplified Switzer's scheme, removing the parterre but leaving a terrace and two canals. The estate is today ringed with housing and most of what is left of the park is now Reading Crematorium, allotment gardens and playing fields.

Cawdor Castle
see page 367

Cefn Bryntalch
Abermule, Powys OS SO1796
Cadw/ICOMOS Register Grade II*

House built c.1870 to the designs of G.F. Bodley and Philip Webb

and bought by the composer Peter Warlock c.1896. Terraced gardens were laid out on a south-west slope, probably designed by Bodley or Webb. A series of formal enclosures are connected by paths and steps with, south of the house, a sunken lawn and oval flower beds. An amphitheatre has a grass bank and a curved stone terrace backed by a row of Lawson cypresses – Warlock liked to come here to compose.

Central Parks
Southampton, Hampshire OS SU4112
English Heritage Register Grade II
Open regularly

Remarkable chain of 52 acres/21 hectares of public open space whose shape is unchanged since the middle ages. In the past this was "lammas land" – land which was private property from 1st January until lammas day (1st August) but thereafter became common land for the rest of the year. The land at Southampton was held on this basis until the 19th century when the last of the private owners was bought out by the town in order to provide public space. The design was influenced by J.C. Loudon, with an axial walk linking the parks. The parks have many monuments: a cenotaph by Sir Edwin Lutyens (1919); a memorial to the *Titanic* engineers (1914 – the *Titanic* sailed from Southampton on her maiden voyage); a statue of Lord Palmerston (1869 – he lived near Southampton), and many others. There are sports facilities, including a famous cricket pitch where an All England XI has played a Hampshire XI every year since 1867.

Centre for Alternative Technology
see page 195

Chantmarle
Frome St Quintin, Dorset OS ST5802
English Heritage Register Grade II*

Early 17th-century Ham stone house for John Strode of the notable Dorset and Somerset family. Exquisite new garden of architectural character added from 1910, to the designs of Francis Inigo Thomas who took full

ornamental advantage of a former moat which he elaborated into a canal backed by a wall ornamented with obelisks and niches with shell carving. This runs across the entrance forecourt and forms the backbone of his design. Balustraded fountain pool in south garden and terrace walk above a croquet lawn. Not as exuberant as his work at Athelhampton (*see page 16*) but exquisitely subtle and refined.

The Chantry
Chantry, Somerset OS ST7246
English Heritage Grade II*

Late Georgian house for James Fussell of famous local family of ironfounders and tool makers. Picturesque landscape on slopes down to the river Frome, with lakes, one of which was used to provide power for the Fussell works below. In the park below the house is an elaborate grotto – massive stones arranged higgledy-piggledy with a view of a lake – and an icehouse. The early Victorian church of the Holy Trinity beside the house is decorated with angels holding edge-tools. In recent times this was the home of the writer Anthony Powell.

Charborough Park
Charborough, Dorset OS SY92 97
English Heritage Register Grade II*

House built for Sir Walter Erle before 1661. Celia Fiennes came here in 1685: "a pretty seate of Mr Earle's my relation [Thomas Erle was her first cousin]…on the brow of a hill, whence you have large prospects of 20 mile round…a good wood behind the house, good gardens wall'd with plenty of fruit." A painting of c.1740 of the house from the north-west shows a formal garden with statues, urns and an elaborate four-part parterre with a swirling pattern. Late 18th-century park by unknown landscaper. South-west of the house, linked by a path flanked with massive statueless plinths, a great octagonal Gothic tower, over 100ft/30m high, built in 1790. It was struck by lightning in 1838 but rebuilt even higher. A grotto of c.1840 close to the house. Park enlarged in the 1840s, with new

wall built along the Wimborne to Dorchester turnpike and imposing new classical entrances – still a prominent feature of that road.

Charlecote Park
see page 254

Charleston
see page 126

Charleston Manor
West Dean, East Sussex OS TV5200
English Heritage Register Grade II*

House started in 12th century, with later alterations. Garden made in the 1930s, designed by Walter Godfrey for Sir Oswald Birley. Godfrey wanted to create an atmosphere of privacy and variety with the garden's areas "self-contained, sheltered and generally unapproached save by well planned paths and archways". East of the house, a lawn enclosed in yew hedges has a border with grey and silver plants under the south-facing wall of a tithe barn clothed in climbing plants. East of the lawn, an avenue of topiaried yew. To the south, the ground is terraced with the highest terrace forming a walk leading west to a medieval dovecote. To the west of the house, a garden house has its own little walled formal garden with four rectangular beds of herbaceous planting and a pool edged in stone. To its west, an orchard and a walled kitchen garden.

Charleville Forest,
also known as
Charleville Castle
Tullamore, County Offaly,
Republic of Ireland
Open regularly Tel (00353) 506 21279

Magnificent Gothic revival house built 1800–12 to the designs of Francis Johnston for Charles William Bury, 1st Earl of Charleville. Sir Charles Coote, in his *Statistical Survey of the King's County* [the old name of County Offaly] (1801) described its "1500 acres delightfully wooded… Clodiagh river runs with rapidity through the demesne, which is well supplied with several mountain streams, and with several rustic bridges, which with cascades have altogether the most charming effect. The grotto, which

commands a principal fall, is finished in true rustic style, the tumbling rocks, the hermit's bed. are most happily situated, and the incrustations and petrifactions give it all the venerable appearance of antiquity." The naturalistic grotto, built in the side of a hill, is made of unworked lumps of stone and has two chambers. James Howley, in his *The Follies and Garden Buildings of Ireland* (1993), writes of it: "As with all good grottoes.. one experiences a sense of trepidation before being drawn into the darkness of the interior." Another notable ornamental building in the demesne is Campden Tower, a three-storey triangular tower with a castellated parapet. William Ashford's three views of the demesne, painted in 1801 and illustrated in Edward Malins's and The Knight of Glin's *Lost Demesnes* (1976), show a wonderfully picturesque landscape of riverside walks, a broad torrential cascade and an elegant Gothic dairy overlooking a lake. In 1811 J.C. Loudon laid out an arboretum at Charleville. Much earlier than this, however, is the beautiful oak described in Thomas Pakenham's *Meetings with Remarkable Trees* (1996). At least 400 years old, it has a girth of 26ft/7.8m and immensely wide-spreading limbs. Pakenham writes that "In May 1963 a thunderbolt splintered the main trunk from top to bottom. The tree survived, but the head of the family, Colonel Charles Howard-Bury, dropped dead a few weeks later."

Chartwell
nr Westerham, Kent OS TQ4551 English Heritage Register II* Open regularly (NT) Tel 01732 866368

House in a beautiful position, dating back to the 17th century but radically remodelled and enlarged in 1923 by Philip Tilden for Sir Winston Churchill who lived here until his death in 1965. Tilden also laid out terraces and garden walls. East of the house, a chain of pools in a valley with a rockery and ornamental plantings. It was this valley prospect that caused Sir Winston to say, "I bought Chartwell for that view." North of the house, walled four-part rose garden with free-standing wisteria at the centre. Steps lead to a lawn with a herbaceous border on the western side. To the east, a long terrace with a pergola and pavilion. The former kitchen garden contains the beech-hedged Golden Rose Garden with a pair of parallel borders of yellow roses of different varieties underplanted with catmint and lambs' lugs. Other parts of the kitchen garden were planted with shrubs, specimen trees and climbers after 1966 under the direction of Lanning Roper. Chartwell is not an exciting garden but, because of its association with Sir Winston, it possesses a powerful sense of place. In parts of the garden, especially where his outdoor studio stands, one has the feeling, despite the crush of other visitors, of being an interloper in a private world.

Chastleton House
see page 78

Chatelherault
nr Hamilton, Lanarkshire OS NS7353
Scottish Inventory Open regularly
Tel 01698 426213

Chatelherault was built as an ornamental landscape building for the grounds of Hamilton Palace. The late 16th-century palace was rebuilt in the late 17th century for the 3rd Duke of Hamilton with advice from Sir William Bruce and Sir Christopher Wren, although James Smith seems to have executed the design. It was the largest new house in Scotland for the richest family in the country. It was demolished in 1927. Chatelherault, part banqueting house, part kennels, but of gigantic size – at least as wide as the chief façade of the palace – was built to the designs of William Adam in 1732. It was placed on rising land at the end of a broad double avenue one mile long, facing the front of the palace. On the far side of Chatelherault, as A.A. Tait points out in *The Landscape Garden in Scotland: 1735–1835* (1980), "was an entirely different landscape, as wild and enclosed as the other was formal and expansive. Chatelherault stood here on the brink of a steep ravine and looked over a tumbling river and the park stocked with wild white cattle to the ruined castle of Cadzow...

here, cheek by jowl, were the two attitudes to gardening, each expressed in the most extreme manner." When the building was completed, a terrace walk gave views of the ravine, and a parterre and bowling green were laid out alongside it. The front part of the building formed the banqueting house and at the back, in a walled enclosure, were the kennels. The two giant pairs of two-storey pavilions linked by a single-storey screen, bristling with pediments and urns, have been beautifully restored by Historic Scotland, and the parterre reinstated in the walled garden behind. The source of the French name is uncertain although it is said that one of the Hamilton titles was Duc de Châtelhérault. The M74 motorway now divides its great park and sand extraction has altered the land, but surviving in the grounds, on the banks of the river Avon, are the ruins of the 13th-century royal palace of Cadzow Castle. Nearby are some extraordinary old oaks – ring-dating has given a date of 1444 – and the ancient breed of white cattle has been reintroduced. The Hamilton family mausoleum also remains, an austere but spectacular domed building, built 1842–58 by David Hamilton, David Bryce and Alexander Richie at a cost of £130,000 (£5,460,000 today). Chatelherault Country Park, as it is now called, preserves an area of 494 acres/200 hectares of the original Hamilton Palace park which the Scottish Inventory describes as "the largest formal designed landscape in Scotland". Of the rest, the Strathclyde Country Park has 1,100 acres/445 hectares devoted to a theme park and sports facilities of every kind. The remainder has disappeared beneath buildings and roads.

Chatsworth
see page 255

Beth Chatto Gardens
see page 296

Chawton House
Chawton, Hampshire OS SU7036
English Heritage Register Grade II

16th-century house for the Knight family, with 17th-century alterations. 13th-century deer park

landscaped in the 18th century. 20th-century formal gardens with topiary hedges, herbaceous borders, terracing and sundial. Jane Austen's brother Edward was heir to the Knights' estate, changing his name to Knight when he inherited in 1812. Jane Austen lived in a cottage in Chawton and often visited. But Chawton was a busy village with much coach traffic in the early 18th century, and she loved to observe it from the windows of her house: "a countless number of Postchaises full of boys pass yesterday morng – full of future Heroes, Legislators, fools and Villains."

Cheadle Royal Hospital
Stockport, Greater Manchester OS SJ8586
English Heritage Register Grade II

The former Manchester Royal Hospital for the Insane was opened in 1849. It was part of the philosophy of 19th-century lunatic asylums that they should have "spacious grounds for husbandry, and gardening, and exercise". Here there were originally 30 acres/12 hectares of meadow, 11 acres/4.5 hectares of arable land, 2½ acres/1 hectare of kitchen garden and 5 acres/2 hectares of flower garden. A model dairy farm provided milk for the asylum. Today the site has been reduced to 22 acres/9 hectares and has lawns, a flower garden, a bowling green and the original cricket pitch ("large enough for any county match") with its pavilion protected by a belt of trees.

Chelsea Physic Garden
see page 127

Chelwood Vachery, *formerly called* Trimmer's Pond
Wych Cross, East Sussex OS TQ4330

Late medieval hall house, rebuilt. Arts and Crafts garden laid out by L. Rome Guthrie 1906–7 for the banker and MP Stuart Montagu Samuel. On the wooded slopes below the house, Guthrie laid out refined terraced gardens with semicircular steps, retaining walls with bastions (with Jekyllesque planting in the stonework), shaped

lily ponds, lawns and a grand Italian wellhead. He also laid out an elaborate kitchen garden with a pergola enclosing a fruit store. The house is now a Management Training Centre.

Chenies Manor
see page 79

Chenies Place
Chenies, Buckinghamshire OS TQ0198
English Heritage Register Grade II*

House dating from the 1890s, designed by C.E. Kempe and now divided; the other half is called Woodside. The garden was designed for Adeline, 10th Duchess of Bedford from 1893 by Edwin Lutyens and Gertrude Jekyll, the first garden on which they collaborated. Already it shows the distinctive approach – a harmoniously related sequence of spaces deftly connected. The river Chess flows across the northern part of the garden whose chief axis runs south to north. This follows a stepped path flanked with borders backed with yew hedges to the Pond Court (the pond no longer exists) which has low walls, paving and a central pillared arbour, and continues over a bridge spanning the river, to a rose garden and a lawn.

Chequers
Ellesborough, Buckinghamshire OS SU8405
English Heritage Register Grade II

Ancient estate associated with the Hawtrey family who owned land here from the 13th century. 16th-century house built for William Hawtrey, with 18th- and 19th-century alterations. The estate was given to the nation in 1917 by Sir Arthur Lee (later Lord Lee of Fareham) and is used as the country seat of prime ministers. Gardens designed 1892–1909 by Reginald Blomfield and by H. Avray Tipping 1911–12. Tipping made formal gardens close to the house – a broad, flagged path to the north and an entrance courtyard with a central lawn to the east. To the south, below Blomfield's terrace, he laid out a sunken walled rose garden with box-edged beds and a central sundial. Large park to the west and north-west, with pasture,

woodland and occasional individual trees or clumps. Many bushes of native box plants growing beneath trees, causing it to be listed as a Site of Special Scientific Interest.

Chevening Park
Chevening, Kent OS TQ4857
English Heritage Register Grade II*
Open occasionally for NGS

Early 17th-century house for Richard Lennard, 13th Lord Dacre, reputedly by Inigo Jones but radically remodelled in the 18th century. An engraving by Kip of 1719 shows complex formal gardens south of the house. In 1776 a formal canal, forming the central axis of the old formal gardens was made into a naturalistic lake by Charles, 2nd Earl Stanhope. An urn of 1780 by John Bacon commemorating Lady Chatham was placed on the west bank and a collection of Roman tombstones was arranged on the south-west bank. In 1820, on the site of the earlier formal gardens south and west of the house, the 4th Earl Stanhope laid out Italianate parterres and planted a maze. A hexagonal walled garden of *c.*1775 has a gardener's cottage of the same date and a beehouse of 1850. In 1967, on the death of the 7th Earl Stanhope, the estate passed to a trust, under the terms of which the house was to be used as the official residence of a nominee of the Prime Minister. Since 1980 the gardens have been revitalised under the supervision of Elizabeth Banks Associates.

Chicheley Hall
Chicheley, Buckinghamshire OS SU9045
English Heritage Register Grade II*
Open by appointment Tel 01234 391252

Present house built 1719–24 for Sir John Chester. Francis Smith of Warwick was involved in the design. Sir John started to make a new garden in 1700, consulting George London. The result of London's contribution is not known, but a U-shaped canal, still extant below the east front of the house, dates from this time. Charles Bridgeman was consulted in 1726 but nothing resulted. A terrace running along the east front of the house gives views over the canal garden – the canal encloses a lawn on three sides and is surrounded by a raised walk. To the north, a formal Wilderness, a grove of trees, with the remains of an 18th-century pavilion. A row of fishponds runs parallel outside the eastern arm of the canal, their banks planted with trees and shrubs. North of the house, a recently planted lime alley and laburnum walk. In the park, an avenue flanks the drive and an 18th-century dovecote stands close to the remains of an old lime avenue.

Chicksands Priory
Chicksands, Bedfordshire OS TL1139
English Heritage Register Grade II

House of *c*.1813 for the Osborne family by James Wyatt; its core is the remains of a 12th-century Gilbertine priory. North of the east front, a Gothic orangery of *c*.1800, possibly by Wyatt, was an important event in the planned circuit walk of the pleasure grounds (now largely lost). To the south-west, an obelisk of 1816 celebrating Waterloo. Two obelisks in the woodland mark the ends of the Long Drive – that at the north possibly by Wyatt; the southern one built in 1889. The park has two lakes, separated by a curved cascade, formed by damming the river Flit. 18th-century walled kitchen garden with a range of glasshouses.

Chiddingstone Castle, *formerly* High Street House
Chiddingstone, Kent OS TQ4945
English Heritage Register Grade II
Open regularly Tel 01892 870347

A 17th-century house, enlarged in the 18th century and Gothicised in the early 19th century by William Atkinson. There was an elaborate formal garden here, made for Sir Henry Streatfeild in the early 18th century, but this was obliterated by early 19th-century landscaping. East of the castle is a lake with a stone sham bridge concealing a dam. On its eastern bank, a series of caves cut into natural rock. An octagonal wellhouse, a summerhouse and the remains of an orangery are linked together by a castellated

wall – all probably designed by Atkinson.

Chiefswood House
nr Melrose, Roxburghshire OS NT5333
Scottish Inventory

House built 1820–21 for John and Thomas Smith, friends of Sir Walter Scott. Woodland on the banks of the Huntly burn, with planting going back to *c*.1800 and much late 20th-century ornamental planting. Bog garden on the banks of the burn with ferns and other waterside plantings. Nearby, a shrubbery with acers and flowering shrubs. Rose garden by the house and a bed of pinks. Walled garden with fruit trees, a sundial, and cutting garden with box-edged beds.

Chiffchaffs
see page 24

Childerley Hall
nr Cambridge, Cambridgeshire OS TL3561
English Heritage Register Grade II* Open occasionally for NGS

Elizabethan house, rebuilt 1850. Garden probably contemporary with the Elizabethan house, moated and banked on three sides. Raised circular prospect mounds on two outer angles of garden. Gardens today with lawns and modern collection of shrubs. There had been a deer park here in the 16th century; when it was enlarged by Sir John Cutt in the second quarter of the 17th century, the inhabitants of the village of Great Childerley were moved. The park is now agricultural land.

Chilham Castle
Chilham, Kent OS TQ0653
English Heritage Register Grade II*

Only parts of the 12th-century castle survive (a keep and a curtain wall), and this incorporated parts of an even more ancient building. In the early 17th century Sir Dudley Digges built a new castle, altered in the 18th, 19th and 20th centuries. John Tradescant the Elder is traditionally associated with the design of terraces south-east of the house; there is no documentary evidence to support this but in 1618 Sir Dudley Digges did lead a diplomatic

mission to Russia, of which Tradescant was a member. Only the lowest terrace survives, supporting a bowling green; there are 19th-century replacements of the others. There was a medieval deer park here, and 17th-century planting in the park – of which parts of an avenue of sweet chestnuts and limes south of the castle survive. In 1777 Capability Brown produced plans for "alterations of the place" but this seems to have concerned the architecture of outhouses only. The estate has recently changed hands and the garden may once again open to the public.

Chillingham Castle
Chillingham, Northumberland OS NU0625
English Heritage Register Grade II
Open regularly Tel 01668 215359

The castle dates back to the mid 14th century, with many subsequent alterations, and has been for centuries the home of the Earls Grey and their relations. The park, of 6,000 acres/2,429 hectares, was made in the 13th century and is famous for its unique herd of white cattle. Pevsner notes that the park "retains the character of a medieval landscape, apparently uncultivated since that time." In the early 19th century Jeffry Wyatville laid out formal gardens close to the castle. The Italian Garden, enclosed by battlemented walls on two sides, with a turf terrace, is a parterre with box-edged beds – some with *broderie* patterns – and bedding plants. Woodland garden planted with rhododendrons has a stream and weir.

Chillington Hall
Brewood, Staffordshire OS SJ8606
English Heritage Register Grade II*
Open regularly Tel 01902 850236

18th-century house probably by Francis Smith of Warwick for the Giffard family who have lived here since the 12th century. The park at Chillington was almost certainly landscaped *c*.1761 by Capability Brown, although there is no certain documentary evidence. The architect James Paine, who designed a bridge here, wrote in his *Plans of Noblemen's and Gentlemen's Houses* (1767): "At

another neck of this beautiful water is erected another bridge, concealing the other extreme of water, built by Lancelot Brown, Esq., who designed and conducted the execution of the improvements of this justly admired park." The "beautiful water" is an immense irregular lake across the park south-west of the house. Near James Paine's bridge at the south-east end of the lake is a ruinous Gothic temple of *c*.1772, and by the southern tip of the lake an Ionic temple, perhaps by John Soane, of the 1780s. Woodland west and south-west of the house contains fine old oaks and Scot pines, possibly surviving from Brown's plantings. An unwelcome new ingredient of the park is the M54 motorway, built in the 1970s and passing within 100yds/90m of the Ionic temple. South of the house is an attractive formal garden laid out by H. Inigo Triggs in 1911 with a geometric arrangememnt of rose beds and a hedge of *Cupressus macrocarpa*.

Chilston Park, *also known as* Sandway Place
Boughton Malherbe, Kent OS TQ8950
English Heritage Register Grade II

A house has been here since the 13th century. The present house, partly 15th-century, was much altered in the 18th century, with subsequent alterations. Formal gardens in the 17th century, of which a double lime avenue east of the house remains. John Evelyn visited the estate in 1666. Formal pools of this time were naturalised in the mid 18th century by Thomas Best. Much tree planting in the 19th century, of which mature specimens of cedars of Lebanon, Scots pines and tulip tree survive.

Chilton Hall
Chilton, Suffolk OS TL8942
English Heritage Register Grade II

The remains of a moated early Tudor house built on the site of a medieval house. Built for the Crane family whose memorials, going back to the 15th century, may be seen in the village church. Park created in the 16th century – disparked before 1751. There

survives a rare 16th-century garden walled in brick, with arched recesses and ornamental castellated capping.

Chippenham Park
Chippenham, Cambridgeshire OS TL6669
English Heritage Register Grade II
Open occasionally for NGS

17th-century house, rebuilt by John Tharp after 1791 and again in 1886. Park landscaped, with a new lake, in 1795 by William Emes, with later work by Samuel Lapidge. Over 1,000,000 trees were planted in this period. In Ash Wood to west of lake, two canals, probably remains of an early 18th-century formal garden. Two lines of limes, on each side of the park, said to represent the positions of the British and French fleets at the battle of La Hogue. John Tharp had a glasshouse 440ft/132m long, of which no trace survives.

Chirk Castle
see page 196

Chiswick House
see page 127

Cholmondeley Castle
Malpas, Cheshire OS SJ5351
English Heritage Register Grade II
Open regularly Tel 01829 720383

The Cholmondeley family (later Earls and Marquesses of Cholmondeley) have lived here since the 12th century. The present, wonderfully romantic, castle was built 1801–4 and 1817–19 to the designs of the 4th Earl Cholmondeley and William Turner, replacing a 16th-century house remodelled by Sir John Vanbrugh in 1712. In the late 17th century there were grand formal gardens here, designed by French gardener, Lecocke, and by George London. John Macky, in *A Journey through England* (1724), described them as "not inferior to any in England". Statues by John Van Nost and ironwork by Jean Tijou were supplied. Only a canal, north of the castle, survives of this layout. Today the gardens are largely of the 20th century but with good details from the past. South-east of the castle, specimen trees date back to the 18th century, with much planting after 1960 when James Russell advised. The Temple Garden south of the castle is laid out about an irregular pool in a dell. A wrought-iron gate is probably by Tijou, from the old formal gardens. A late 19th-century rotunda stands on a hillock west of the pool and another temple (*c*.1830) is placed on an island. A second pool to the west is surrounded by a wild garden. To the north-west, a rose garden with cruciform paths and a sundial was laid out in the 1950s. William Emes was asked to landscape the park in 1777 (his fee was £500 (£29,880 today)) and parkland trees and shelter belts survive from this time.

Christ Church
(Oxford)
see page 100

Christ's College

Cambridge, Cambridgeshire OS TL 4558
English Heritage Register Grade II
Open regularly Tel 01223 334900

The college was founded in 1442 and refounded in 1505 when the earliest surviving buildings were built. A garden was made shortly after the refounding of the college but there is no detailed information about it. In the Fellows' Garden is a mulberry reputedly planted by John Milton in 1628 but almost certainly one of the 300 planted in 1608 and recorded in the college accounts: "Item for 300 mulberrye plants, xviii.s". Also in the Fellows' Garden, a bathing pool first referred to in 1748 and a summerhouse with a loggia (all originally set in a formal wilderness). 18th-century busts on plinths of Ralph Cudworth, John Milton (who spent seven years at Christ's) and Nicholas Sanderson, and a memorial urn to Joseph Mede. In 1825 the Fellows' Garden was laid out in "gardenesque" style, with winding paths, beds like islands or promontories, and plants arranged to display the "individual beauty of trees, shrubs and plants in a state of nature" as recommended by J.C. Loudon who possibly laid out the garden himself. The courts of Christ's are well planted in modern times with a range of

ornamental trees, flowering shrubs and a fine collection of irises.

Christchurch Mansion

Ipswich, Suffolk OS TM1644
English Heritage Register Grade II
Open regularly 01473 433554

16th-century house for Paul Withipoll on the site of an Augustinian Priory founded in the 12th century. The house is now a museum and since 1895 the gardens have been a public park. The grounds are well wooded with some fine old trees making a distinguished backdrop to the paraphernalia of public park life – a bandstand, bowling greens, drinking fountains and tennis courts.

Churchtown Botanic Gardens

Southport, Merseyside OS SD3618 English
Heritage Register Grade II Open regularly

Opened in 1875, funded by entrance fees, the botanic gardens were acquired by Southport Corporation and became a public park in 1937. Close to the main entrance in the south-west, a museum designed by Mellor & Sutton *c*.1876. To its north, a fernery of *c*.1876 with an interior of rustic stone grottoes, rockwork and mirrors. In front of the fernery, a terrace with beds for summer bedding schemes and steps down to a long serpentine lake, running north–south, a dominant feature of the park. Two ornamental cast-iron bridges cross the serpentine lake and lead to winding walks along the bank. On the eastern bank, rockwork and rustic tunnels, and further east, banks from the spoil of the lake planted with trees. Beyond the trees, a lawn and a bandstand. To the north, recreational facilities – bowling greens, children's playground, "crazy golf".

Chyknell

nr Bridgnorth, Shropshire OS SO7793
Open occasionally for NGS

Victorian house with outstanding garden designed in 1951 by Russell Page with yew hedges, a lawn framed in pleached limes and

beech hedges, a lilac walk, a formal rose garden and a rectangular lily pool. A virtuoso display of garden-making with simple ingredients, and a rare surviving example of a layout by one of the best 20th-century garden designers.

Chyverton

Zelah, Cornwall OS SW7951
English Heritage Register Grade II
Open by appointment Tel 01872 540648

18th-century house with landscaped park dating from the 1770s when the estate was owned by John Thomas. Thomas planted 94 acres/38 hectares of woodland and created a new carriage drive leading through woodland and across a bridge over a lake. The great distinction of Chyverton as a plant collection began with the sale of the estate in 1924 to Treve Holman. With the advice of George Johnstone of Trewithen (*see page 67*) and Harold Hillier (*see page 87*), Holman enriched the planting with outstanding shrubs and trees. He also subscribed to some of Frank Kingdon Ward's Himalayan expeditions. His son, Nigel, the present owner, has maintained the tradition of plantsmanship and the garden is full of distinguished plants. These include a vast collection of magnolias, among which are new cultivars bred at Chyverton (such as *Magnolia dawsoniana* 'Chyverton Red') and tender species (such as the rare evergreen *M. nitida*) which require the mild southern Cornish climate to flourish.

Cirencester Park
see page 197

City of London Cemetery

Newham, London OS TQ4186 English
Heritage Register Grade II Open regularly

Cemetery laid out by William Haywood (who also designed the buildings) opened in 1855. The land, acquired from Lord Wellesley, had previously been farmland on the edge of Epping Forest. Two chapels by Haywood – Church of England and Nonconformist. The layout combines long straight vistas and winding paths with lavish planting of trees and shrubs,

especially evergreens. The Victorian fondness for weeping and evergreen trees is displayed (the weeping holly, for example, combining the notions of both sorrow and eternity). Lavish plantings of spring bulbs and in the late 20th century well planned use of ornamental grasses. Many excellent 19th-century monuments.

Civic Square

Plymouth, Devon OS SX4754 English
Heritage Register Grade II Open regularly

Urban square laid out by Sir Geoffrey Jellicoe in 1957 as part of the civic layout of Plymouth during its post-war development. Between the Guildhall and the Civic Centre, it has an L-shaped pool, a lawn with mature chestnuts and limes, and more recently planted wych elms. Irregularly shaped raised beds are planted with trees and shrubs or with bedding schemes. Much attention was paid to paving materials, with alternating limestone and slate, or pebbles set in concrete, to give different effects in different weathers. Jellicoe said that he wanted an effect of "dignity and frivolity…a civic amenity to be enjoyed by townspeople at all times".

Clandon Park
see page 128

Clare College
(Cambridge)
see page 294

Claremont Landscape Garden
see page 129

Claverton Manor
see page 25

Claydon

Middle Claydon, Buckinghamshire
OS SP7125 English Heritage Register Grade II
Open regularly (NT) Tel 01494 755561

Late 18th-century house built for Ralph, 2nd Earl Verney, incorporating an earlier house. Beautiful Rococo interiors by Luke Lightfoot. Formal gardens with terraces, lawns and mature trees about the house. Mid 18th-century Gothic fernery in south

garden. Park, landscaped by James Sanderson of Reading 1763–76, surrounds the house, with long curved lake to the west, which Sanderson formed by damming a stream. The southern end of the lake marked by Sanderson's brick and stone arch. To the west, a double avenue and old oaks.

Clearwell Castle

Clearwell, Gloucestershire OS SO5707
English Heritage Register Grade II

Gothick house on an older site, designed by Roger Morris and built *c*.1728 for Thomas Wyndham. A formal garden was laid out before 1712, but little evidence of it survives except a terraced outline. Two 18th-century statues, of Hercules and a child on a sphinx, face the house across a circular forecourt. There had been a 17th-century park for the earlier house, and scattered parkland trees remain.

Cleeve Prior Manor

Cleeve Prior, Worcestershire OS SP0849

C

Late 16th-century brick house built on land formerly owned by Evesham Abbey which had been acquired by Worcester Cathedral at the dissolution of the monasteries; it passed later into the hands of the Ecclesiastical Commission which still owned it in the 20th century. An article in *Country Life* in 1903 has detailed photographs of a remarkable garden of yew topiary, in particular a series of mushroom shapes called the Twelve Apostles and the Four Evangelists, lining the entrance path to the house. The article makes the interesting suggestion that the topiary at Cleeve Prior Manor could have been the inspiration for the better known Sermon on the Mount topiary at Packwood House (*see page 273*), just over the border in Warwickshire. The garden is also illustrated in paintings made in 1901 by G.S. Elgood for Gertrude Jekyll's *Some English Gardens* (1904). Gertrude Jekyll noted "narrow grass paths bordered with old-fashioned flowers…how grandly the flowers grow in these old manor and farm gardens." The paintings are also illustrated, and the garden described, in Penelope

Hobhouse's and Christopher Woods's *Painted Gardens: English Watercolours 1850–1914* (1988). In 1988, when Penelope Hobhouse saw the garden, the yews, though misshapen, were still in place but "the rest of the garden is a wilderness".

Clevedon Court

Clevedon, Somerset OS ST4271
English Heritage Register Grade II*
Open regularly (NT) Tel 01275 872257

Remarkable and delightful 14th-century house built for Sir John de Clevedon, with alterations in late 16th and late 19th century. The estate was owned by the Elton family from 1709 until it was given to the National Trust by Sir Arthur Elton in 1961. Behind the house, the steep slope was splendidly terraced in about 1700 – "one of noblest ranges of terrace walks in England" as Gertrude Jekyll wrote in her *Wall and Water Gardens* (1901), though she strongly disapproved of the bedding schemes then in place. Today the planting is much more informal, with good shrubs – the tender *Buddleja colvilei*, *Magnolia grandiflora* and *Mahonia lomariifolia* – and pretty underplanting of agapanthus, crinums and other bulbous plants. An ornamental octagonal summerhouse of 1720 looks out along the middle terrace, with a Gothic loggia of the early 19th century at its far, eastern, end. The surroundings of house are densely planted with fine old holm oaks dating from the early 19th century, and a mulberry, described in 1822 as being ancient, is still flourishing. The only ugly thing here is the terrifying proximity of the M5.

Clifton Park

Rotherham, South Yorkshire OS SK4392
English Heritage Register Grade II
Open regularly

A public park based on an estate which had in the 18th century belonged to Joshua Walker of the Walker Iron & Steel Works. Walker built a house designed by John Carr of York 1783–84. House and much of the park were bought for £25,000 (£1,171,000 today) by Rotherham Council in 1891. Mature specimen trees and

avenues gave great character to the place, although much has been lost by elm disease. A large rock garden with cascade, pools and rills, and planted with Japanese maples and junipers, was completed in 1951 – although in recent times it has been without water. There are also war memorials, a bandstand, an ornamental lake with fountains and various playgrounds and sports facilities. By the house, which is now a museum, is a maze built in the 1990s and a rose garden.

Clipsham Hall

Clipsham, Rutland OS SK9716

House built in the late 16th century, with late Victorian east front added for J.W.H. Davenport-Handley. In the 1870s an existing avenue of yew hedges, probably planted *c*.1800, was clipped into topiary by the estate forester, Amos Alexander. Some of the shapes were geometric, others represented creatures (a camel, a deer, an elephant), and some local notables. In recent years more topiary has been made to celebrate the first moon landing, the coronation of Queen Elizabeth II and Amos Alexander himself.

Clissold Park, *formerly* Newington Park House

Hackney, London OS TQ3286 English Heritage Register Grade II Open regularly

House built *c*.1790 for Jonathan Hoare and renamed Clissold House in the 19th century. Estate became a public park in 1889 and is now enclosed in railings with intermittent perimeter planting. The villa-like house overlooks a curve of the New river in the eastern part of the park, and a 19th-century cast-iron bridge crosses the river south of the house. The grounds were landscaped in the late 18th century. Two lakes in the northern part of the park were probably made from disused clay pits. Good mature trees throughout the park, with horse chestnuts used to line paths. A zoo was formed west of the house in the 19th century; further to the west, a bowling green is flanked by bedding schemes and a rose garden has a central drinking fountain. Several

games and recreational facilities – cricket pitch, children's playground, football pitch, tennis courts and paddling pool.

Clitheroe Castle

Clitheroe, Lancashire OS SD9204
English Heritage Register Grade II

The castle is a 12th-century roofless keep and part of its grounds were developed as a public park in the 1920s. South-east of the castle, terraces and a war memorial surrounded by gardens. Southern slopes of castle mound are laid out with ornamental gardens, and a formal rose garden to the west has at its centre a pinnacle from the Houses of Parliament, brought here in 1937. Games facilities – bowling greens, putting green and tennis courts; recreation ground with tree-lined walks in south-west part of park.

The Dorothy Clive Garden

see page 198

Cliveden

see page 79

Clumber Park

see page 257

Cluny House Gardens

see page 368

Clyne Gardens

see page 199

The Coach House

Bettiscombe, Dorset OS ST4000
Open occasionally for charity

Gardens designed by notable garden designers are especially interesting. Penelope Hobhouse has been one of the most successful English garden designers of the late 20th and early 21st century. Inspired by Italian renaissance gardens and the English tradition of flower gardening, she has designed for clients in Europe and America. She came to live in the Coach House in 1993 and made a new garden with only herself to please. A walled flower garden overlooked by the house has strong bones of box and yew. Here are the foliage plants she loves and a profusion of

distinguished flowering plants, many of which are allowed to self-sow. The second part of the garden has hornbeam hedges, yew topiary and exquisite views over the Dorset countryside. A meadow has spring bulbs, raised beds are full of vegetables, a canal is edged in stainless steel.

Cobham Hall

Cobham, Kent OS TQ6868
English Heritage Register Grade II*
Open regularly Tel 01474 823371

House started in 1580 for William, 10th Lord Cobham, incorporating earlier buildings, with alterations in 17th, 18th and 19th centuries. Only sketchy knowledge of early garden activity. Terraces to north of house possibly date from formal gardens of the 17th or 18th century. Remains of 17th-century avenues focused on house; the only substantial one, to the south-west, of limes, 330yds/300m long. In 1790 Lord Darnley asked Humphry Repton to advise on the grounds and a Red Book was produced. Repton wrote, "The Park is extensive, the trees large and the verdure beautiful, but there are no walks, no shrubberies, no agremens, nor any object of interest to ladies. We must give it time." Repton's work at Cobham went on for twenty-five years. Among much else, a new drive was made, an "irregular modern flower-garden" laid out to the north-east, and a small formal garden embraced by the wings of the house was designed. A *porte cochère* added to the north of the house served also as a "bridge" to the 18th-century terrace on the north side, which ended in a bastion made in 1812 to overlook parkland to the west. All this in essence remains today. 583yds/500m to the south-east of the house is James Wyatt's magnificent mausoleum, designed in 1783 for the 3rd Earl of Darnley.

Cockenzie House

Cockenzie and Port Seton, East Lothian
OS NT4075 Scottish Inventory

The house was built in the late 17th century for the harbourmaster of the Winton estate's harbour, with a three-part

walled garden and ornamental garden buildings. The central garden compartment has two circular mid 18th-century gazebos. In the same compartment is a (probably) 19th-century clinker- or lava-built grotto with a curious pinnacled roof and its entrance framed by the jawbones of a whale. The interior has seats and decorative shellwork. Another garden compartment has a lawn with fruit trees which include apples and damsons as well as ornamental cherries.

Cokenach

nr Barkway, Hertfordshire OS TL3936
English Heritage Register Grade II

House built *c*.1716 on an ancient site. Late 17th-century and early 18th-century formal garden with canals still surviving. In the 1820s and 1830s General Sir William Clinton planted many exotic trees from William Cobbett's nursery at Kensington. An order in December 1828 included several North American trees – hickory (*Carya* species), honey locust (*Gleditsia triacanthos*), North American persimmon (*Diospyros virginiana*) and tulip tree (*Liriodendron tulipifera*). The park today is pasture and arable land with clumps and individual trees and areas of woodland. The southern part is crossed by the remains of a late 18th- or early 19th-century avenue. In the mid 18th-century avenues and rides in the northern part of the park were aligned on the canals. Walled kitchen garden, present in 1700, is divided into three compartments – a kitchen garden, ornamental garden with a pergola, and a swimming pool garden.

Colchester Castle Park

Colchester, Essex OS TL9925 English Heritage Register Grade II Open regularly

Castle built on the site of a Roman Temple of Claudius of *c*.AD54. The Roman town wall forms the boundary between the upper and lower parks, and fragments of other Roman structures remain. In the mid 18th century the bank of the castle bailey was landscaped by Charles Gray to form a walk, with a Dori summerhouse at the north-west corner and a rotunda, now ruined, at the south-east end. The park was opened to the public in 1892 when a lime avenue, the Mayors' Walk, was planted north of the castle, running east–west. Another lime avenue was planted in the late 19th century north of the bailey walk, with a cast-iron bandstand of the same period. The northern part of the park has a pond, serpentine paths, bowling greens, putting greens and a children's playground.

Coleby Hall

Coleby, Lincolnshire OS SK9760
English Heritage Register Grade II

Early 17th-century house built for William Lister, with many alterations. 18th-century park with a pool. The estate was owned in the late 18th century by Thomas Scrope who was an amateur architect, friend and fellow Grand Tourist of Sir William Chambers; in 1762 Chambers designed for him a domed Temple of Romulus and Remus, with domed apses, as an eyecatcher terminating an avenue. Scrope himself embellished his grounds with designs of his own – a Temple to Pitt (c.1770) and a "ruined" Roman arch as a gateway (c.1780).

Coleorton Hall

Coleorton, Leicestershire OS SK3917
English Heritage Register Grade II*

House built 1804–8 for Sir George Beaumont to the design of George Dance. Beaumont was an artist, connoisseur and friend of artists and writers – Sir Walter Scott started *Ivanhoe* while staying here, and Constable drew in the grounds. Uvedale Price and William and Dorothy Wordsworth helped to lay out the grounds. North-east of the house, under a yew, is a large boulder known as the Pondering Stone, carved with the words "Brought here in 1818". To the north, steps with Coade stone busts (1817) of Milton and Shakespeare lead via a walk to Beaumont's Memorial. An avenue of limes planted in 1811 runs east–west in the woodland, with at the west end a memorial to Sir Joshua Reynolds, and at the eastern end Coade stone busts

of Michelangelo and Raphael. To the north is the Grove, ornamental woodland with walks designed with the advice of Uvedale Price. East of the house, the Upper Lawn has a terrace walk along its eastern side, with viewing bastions. Many specimen trees planted to the east, some with slates recording their planting, largely in the 1830s. At the southern end, the terrace turns west to give views over the Winter Garden. This was made after 1806, with the advice of William Wordsworth, and includes steps, rockwork and a grotto with shellwork by Dorothy Wordsworth in front of which is a fountain pool. To one side, Scott's Seat, a stone alcove, and on the western edge of the garden, a pedimented monument with a verse by Wordsworth composed in 1808. There had been a park here by 1303; part of it was lost to coal mining and part still bears the scars of mining – the source of Beaumont's wealth.

Coleton Fishacre Garden

see page 26

Combe Abbey

nr Coventry, Warwickshire OS SP4079
English Heritage Register Grade II*

Cistercian Abbey founded in 1150, with many alterations. There were formal gardens in the 17th century but these were destroyed when Capability Brown was called in by the 6th Baron Craven. Between 1771 and 1774 Brown received £7,150 (£427,284 today). His chief work was the creation of a lake, formed by damming the Smite brook and enlarging earlier fishponds. He may also have been responsible for some of the tree-planting about the house. In the 1860s, to the south of the house, W.A. Nesfield made terraces, a moat and an Italian parterre enclosed in yew hedges. An arm of the moat was extended to connect with Brown's lake. A double avenue of chestnuts and limes was planted c.1900 along the southern approach drive. The head gardener at this time, William Miller, also laid out a knot garden and carried out much tree planting, including a grove of *Sequoia sempervirens*.

Combe Bank

Sundridge, Kent OS TQ4855
English Heritage Register Grade II*

Early 18th-century Palladian house, replacing an older one, designed by Roger Morris for Colonel John Campbell who became the 4th Duke of Argyll in 1761. 18th-century urns about the house were previously arranged in two rows on the east lawn, flanked by shrubberies. Two summerhouses ornamented the lawn at this time, of which one survives in a modified state. Terraces to the south of the house. Caves cut into a rocky ridge in the early 19th century or possibly earlier, with an icehouse. Lake to the north, with a boathouse whose façade has a rockwork arch. The house is now a school. The M25 cuts through Combebank Wood.

Combe House

Gittisham, Devon OS SY1497
English Heritage Register Grade II

Medieval house remodelled in the late 16th century for Henry Beaumont, with subsequent alterations, particularly in the late 17th century for the Putt family. There was a deer park here in the 16th century and north and east of the house fine garden walls survive from the late 17th century or earlier. An apple cultivar, 'Tom Putt', is named after an early 18th-century Thomas Putt who lived here. The house is now a hotel.

Combermere Abbey

Marbury cum Quoisley, Cheshire OS SJ5844
English Heritage Register Grade II
Open by appointment Tel 01948 662880

Tudor house for the Cotton family, with later alterations especially in the late 18th century. In the 1790s Sir Robert Salusbury Cotton landscaped the park, possibly with the help of John Webb. At its heart is the natural lake, the Comber Mere, overlooked by the house on its southern bank. West of the lake is Brankelow Cottage, or Folly, a keeper's cottage with arrow slits and pinnacles. When built in 1797 it had a dairy and a summer sitting room decorated by the family's daughters. North of it is an obelisk of 1865 commemorating Field Marshal Viscount Combermere.

Some of the park is now arable land but some pasture remains and many trees, in particular beeches and sweet chestnuts.

Commonwealth Institute

Kensington and Chelsea, London
OS TQ2579 English Heritage Register Grade II
Open regularly

The Commonwealth Institute was built 1960–62 to the designs of Robert Matthew, Johnson-Marshall & Partners. The gardens were laid out from 1960 by Dame Sylvia Crowe. In front of the building she designed an elaborate water feature – a channel, fountains and jets – and a secluded area with a lime avenue and seats. A mirror pond is designed to reflect the façade of the building.

Compton Acres

see page 26

Compton End

Compton, Hampshire OS SU4625
English Heritage Register Grade II*

Farmhouse with small garden laid out by G.H. Hitchin 1895–c.1914). South and east of the house, formal compartments hedged in yew and box. Brick path running eastwards from the house, between borders backed by yew hedges, to a sundial. South of this walk, beds cut into turf surrounding a square pool. South of the house, a box parterre for bedding schemes, with steps down to the Rockery Garden, a dell with a winding path, small pools and an ivy bower. Beyond it, rose beds, a croquet lawn, and steps past a summerhouse to a kitchen garden and orchard.

Compton Place

Eastbourne, East Sussex OS TV6098
English Heritage Register Grade II

Elizabethan house remodelled by Colen Campbell 1726–31 for Spencer Compton. Charles Bridgeman worked at Compton Place 1728–38 and was paid £1,360 (£112,227 today) in all, but nothing is known of what he did; Capability Brown's name is mentioned in 1766 but his work, if any, is not known; Humphry Repton produced a Red Book in

1803 but his proposals were rejected. Seldom have so many famous names been linked to a garden with so little to show for it. The gardens today are largely 19th and 20th century. A turf terrace runs along the south façade of the house, with rose beds. South and west of the house, lawns and scattered trees. To the east of the terrace, a path lined with stone plinths leads to a grove of beech, chestnut and holm oak, with a circular lawn and a mound with a metal rose arbour. To the west, at some distance across what is now a golf course, a pedimented ornamental flint building, possibly dating from 1740.

Compton Verney

nr Kineton, Warwickshire OS SP3152
English Heritage Register Grade II*

House built 1714 in Vanbrughian style for George Verney, 12th Lord Willoughby de Broke, enlarged in the 1760s by Robert Adam and altered in the 19th century. Formal gardens contemporary with the 1714 house were removed when Capability Brown worked here 1768–74, for which he was paid £3,830 (£228,880 today). In the park he united five pools to make a single serpentine lake: Compton Pools. The noble three-arched bridge which carries the drive was part of Brown's scheme but possibly designed by Robert Adam. Parkland surrounds the house, with woodland on most boundaries – an avenue of Wellingtonias on the eastern boundary. The estate has been restored over recent years and the house is now an art gallery.

Compton Wynyates

Tysoe, Warwickshire OS SP3444

House built in the early 16th century for Sir William Compton (later Marquesses of Northampton) and still owned by the family. Capability Brown did some work on the grounds in the 1760s but it is uncertain what (Brown designed the park for another Compton estate, Castle Ashby, *see page 252*). The most famous feature of the garden here was an extraordinary collection of topiary in the Best Garden. These, despite their antique air, dated only from the

C

late 19th century and are illustrated in Gertrude Jekyll's *Some English Gardens* (1904) with a painting by G.S. Elgood showing monumental blocks of yew crowned with topiary birds among flowery borders. In 1980, to the consternation of many people, the topiary garden was obliterated. The garden is discussed in Penelope Hobhouse's and Christopher Wood's *Painted Gardens: English Watercolours 1850–1914* (1988) which reproduces the Elgood painting and one of a slightly later date by E.A. Rowe. Penelope Hobhouse writes: "Although the Best Garden had little real historical justification many today find the empty lawns and tarmacadam driveway unsympathetic."

Condover Hall

Condover, Shropshire OS SJ4905
English Heritage Register Grade II

Magnificent late Elizabethan house built for Thomas Owen. Grand Victorian formal gardens on three sides of the house, with drive along an avenue of mounds of clipped yew, box-edged squares with pillars or cones of yews, a parade of Irish yews and terraces with topiary below the south façade. All this is visible in a poignant aerial photograph taken in 1953 and illustrated in Marcus Binney's and Ann Hills's *Elysian Gardens* (1979). The house today belongs to the Royal Institute for the Blind and the gardens have been radically simplified.

Conock Manor

Chirton, Wiltshire OS SU0657
English Heritage Register Grade II
Open occasionally for NGS

Built *c.*1700 to replace an earlier house, with later additions. East of the house, a lawn with topiary hedges, sundial and specimen trees. Along the north wall, an early 19th-century picturesque thatched dairy with rustic porch. To the east, beyond a stable block, a garden with hexagonal pool and distinguished flowering trees and shrubs, among them cherries, dogwoods and magnolias. To the south, beech hedges and clipped box with a shrub walk of the 1930s with good trees. A pleached

lime walk links gardens on both sides of the stable.

Constable Burton Hall

Constable Burton, North Yorkshire OS SE1691 English Heritage Register Grade II
Open regularly Tel 01677 450428

House built 1762–68 for Sir Marmaduke Wyvil to the designs of John Carr of York. There had been an even grander Elizabethan house here; Kip's engraving in *Britannia Illustrata* (1707) shows the old house standing in the midst of formal gardens: a forecourt with four circular pools, a sunken bowling green, an enclosed garden with patterns of ovals and triangles, and a formal garden of rows of trees. Beyond the garden walls, a curious pattern of canals and a pool. The existing garden east of the house seems to follow the pattern of the old garden – and some old yews and the remains of an avenue possibly survive from that date. Park with lake and 18th-century deer shelter; to the north-east, a farm has a castellated south façade planned as an eyecatcher from the park.

Cooke's House

West Burton, West Sussex OS TQ0013
English Heritage Register Grade II
Open occasionally for NGS; private visits welcome Tel 01798 831353/831371

Late 16th-century house built for the Cooke family. The present garden was laid out in the 1920s by Wilfred Holland in a series of intimate enclosures with stone walls, flagstone paths and yew hedges. A formal rose garden has box-edged beds and a sundial. The Green Garden Room has a lawn and topiary of yew. The Border Walk is a turf walk with herbaceous borders and yew hedges with towers at each end. A formal herb garden has a geometric pattern of pebbles and stones, and a kitchen garden is hedged in beech.

Copped Hall, *also known as* Copt Hall

Epping, Essex OS TL4301 English Heritage Register Grade II* Open by appointment Tel 020 72671679

House built from 1753 on a site going back to at least the 16th

century. House gutted by fire in 1971; the shell now under restoration (see below). A notable earlier house, built in the 16th century for Sir Thomas Heneage, had elaborate gardens and a deer park, both of which were overlaid by 18th-century landscaping. Capability Brown advised here, possibly in the mid 1740s, and an undated bill for £31 15s (£2,620 today) was paid for "My journeys and trouble and Mr Griffin's Demeasurement of the ground round the House". Brown probably planted the tree belt to the west of the park and landscaped the view of the lake to the east. In the 1890s C.E. Kempe, who also worked on the house at that time, laid out a great Italianate garden west of the house. This magnificent place, with topiary, balustraded terraces, broad walks, fountains and pavilions, was illustrated in two articles in *Country Life* in 1910. Its overgrown and derelict remains were poignantly displayed in more recent photographs in Marcus Binney's and Ann Hills's *Elysian Gardens* (1979). In the 1980s the M25 was built across the southern part of the park. The Corporation of London bought the surviving parkland in 1992, and in 1995 the Copped Hall Trust managed to buy the mansion and gardens. Their aim is "to permanently protect the site, to carefully restore Copped Hall and its garden for educational and community benefit".

Corby Castle

Wetheral, Cumbria OS NY4754
English Heritage Register Grade I

Medieval tower house, with 17th- and 19th-century alterations, in a beautiful position on the east bank of the river Eden. Pleasure grounds laid out by Thomas Howard 1709–39. Howard made the connection between his own Eden and that of Milton as described in *Paradise Lost*: "There Eden's lofty banks/Now nearer crown with their inclosures green,/As with a rural mound, the champaign head/Of steep wilderness; whose hairy sides/With thickets overgrown, grotesque and wild." Howard animated a dramatic wooded riverside walk south of the castle.

It starts with a statue of Polyphemus near a cascade spouting from a mask; a temple stands at the top of the cascade which has a grotto cut into the rock beneath it; from Water Gate, a stone arch, a stepped cascade leads down to the river where, in Howard's time, masques were performed, including one he wrote himself, *Sensuality Subdued*, a version of Milton's *Comus* "adapted to the scene of the cascade at Corby"; in the cliffs north of the cascade is a series of grottoes, and a grass walk leading south from the cascade along the river bank has more grottoes; further along the bank was the finishing flourish of the early 18th-century garden – the Tempietto, an early 18th-century Tuscan temple. Sir John Clerk of Penicuik (*see page 522*) visited in 1734 and wrote, "This place is by nature exceeding charming & indeed so full of natural beauties that I think no place of my acquiantance in Britain is equal to it…as Corby Castle stands on a Rock it affords a very agreeable winding walk down to the River where there are some artificial grotos…on the River side is a large walk…beautified all along with grotoes & Statues of the Rural deities." In the mid 19th century Philip Howard continued the walk, ornamenting it with a statue of St Constantine and a stone shelter with a seat.

Cornbury Park

nr Charlbury, Oxfordshire OS SP3418
English Heritage Register Grade II*
Open regularly Tel 01608 811276

Cornbury has an ancient history connected with the royal forest of Wychwood and the nearby royal palace of Woodstock (*see page 560*). The present house is an early 17th-century remodelling for Henry Danvers, Earl of Danby, the founder of Oxford Botanic Garden (*see page 99*). Nicholas Stone, who made the grand entrance gates for the botanic garden, also worked on the new house at Cornbury. John Evelyn was a friend of Danvers and went to Cornbury in 1664 "to assist him in the planting of the park". He describes the house as being "in the middle of a sweete park,

wall'd with a dry wall". A deer park, formerly part of Wychwood forest, is now pasture with park trees and the remains of several 17th-century avenues and rides radiating from the house. The avenue, called Tower Light, of lime and beech, borrows the tower of Charlbury church as an eyecatcher to the north. A lake south of the house is formed of ancient fishponds. To the south of the park is an octagonal stone-walled kitchen garden.

Cornwell Manor

Cornwell, Oxfordshire OS SP2727
English Heritage Register Grade II

Earlier house with mid-Georgian façade; the estate is mentioned in the Domesday book. 18th-century parkland. Informal woodland garden running into formal flower garden with a terraced lawn and mixed borders edged with box. Beyond a ha-ha, a series of lakes the south-east. Triangular pool garden made in the 1930s by Clough Williams-Ellis who also worked on the house. The pool is on a grass terrrace with steps down to a pool house, protected on two sides by yew hedges.

Corpus Christi College

Oxford, Oxfordshire OS SP5106
English Heritage Register Grade II*
Open regularly Tel 01865 276700

College founded by Bishop Foxe in 1517 but the earliest building, of the 15th century, predates the foundation. Bishop Foxe wrote: "We…have founded…a certain bee garden, which we have name the College of Corpus Christi, wherein scholars, like ingenious bees, are by day and night to make wax to the honour of God and honey dropping sweetness to the profit of themselves and of a Christians." Bees were reputed to swarm in the President's Garden in the 17th century. In the front quad is a 17th-century sundial with a perpetual calendar mounted on a 16th-century pilla and crowned by a modern pelican, the college crest. The 1726 *Oxford Almanack* shows the quad with topiary echoing the shape of the sundial. The college adjoins the old city wall where there is a raised terrace walk dating from the early 17th century, which had a mount at its west end (of which traces remain) with a summerhouse.

Corsham Court
see page 81

Cortachy Castle
nr Kirriemuir, Perthshire OS NO4059
Scottish Inventory Open occasionally for SGS

16th-century castle bought by the Ogilvys (later Earls of Airlie) in 1625 and enlarged in 1872 to the designs of David Bryce for the 10th Earl of Airlie whose descendants still live here. His wife, Blanche, was a knowledgeable gardener who established a wild garden, damming a burn to form a pool with an island, and planting azaleas and rhododendrons underplanted with hostas and primulas in an old beech wood. From 1848 she built up an arboretum, or American garden, with many conifers, and in a walled garden laid out a double yew walk and borders with topiary.

Cotehele
see page 27

Cothay Manor
see page 28

Cothelstone Manor
Cothelstone, Somerset OSST1832
English Heritage Register Grade II

In the foothills of the Quantocks, a picturesque house of mid 16th-century origins, built for the Stawell family and much altered in the 17th and 19th centuries. Sir John Stawell had a deer park here by 1583. There had been a formal garden north of the house, where a 17th-century banqueting house remains. The Stawells finally sold Cothelstone in 1789 to the Esdaile family who built a new neo-classical house on the wooded slopes high above the old manor. This was demolished in recent times although fragments survive. On the slopes between the houses is very beautiful parkland – the most notable part of the landscape today – presumably part of the Stawells' old deer park.

Coton Manor Gardens
see page 258

Cottesbrooke Hall
see page 259

Coughton Court
see page 259

Court of Hill
nr Nash, Shropshire OS SO6072
English Heritage Register Grade II

Ancient house, rebuilt in late 17th century. Octagonal dovecote with a weathervane dated 1767. Entrance to kitchen garden by 18th-century pavilion, with pediment and Doric columns modelled on St Paul's, Covent Garden, which reveals axial view over kitchen garden and giant views of Teme valley and the south Wales hills. Small 18th-century park.

Courteenhall Hall
Courteenhall, Northamptonshire OS SP7653
English Heritage Register Grade II

House built in the 1790s on an old site for Sir William Wake to the designs of Samuel Saxon. Humphry Repton was consulted about the siting of the new house in 1791 and produced a Red Book of suggestions. He chose an elevated site for the house, linked to the stables by a shrubbery and trees, with a lawn to the south and east of the house. He also proposed a "parterre for flowers in small beds", a *corbeille* (a round flower bed dressed to seem like a basket) and a *reposoir* (sitting place) which may not have been made. His proposal for ponds in the park and a rustic temple was rejected.

The Courts
see page 82

Cowdray Park
Easebourne, West Sussex OS SU8921
English Heritage Register Grade II*
Open occasionally for NGS

Cowdray House was started by Sir David Owen, who inherited the estate in 1492, and completed by 1542. It was almost completely destroyed by fire in 1793 but its ruins survive as the chief focus of the designed landscape

surrounding the Victorian house, Cowdray Park, which lies one mile to the east. Traces of the Tudor privy garden and later formal gardens survive about the ruins. Cowdray Park has extensive pleasure grounds dating from the early 19th century onwards. Here are lawns, terracing, a fountain pool, a laburnum tunnel and borders. To the west, lawns run down to a wooded valley with lakes and much planting of flowering shrubs, especially rhododendrons. Capability Brown made improvements 1768–74, probably making a ha-ha to separate the pleasure grounds from the park.

Cowley Manor
Cowley, Gloucestershire OS SO9614
English Heritage Register Grade II*

17th-century house, rebuilt in the 1850s by George Somers Clarke for James Hutchinson; enlarged 1892–1902 for Sir James Horlick of Malted Milk Company fame. The site is very fine, overlooking the wooded slopes of the Chum valley where the river has been formed into a series of pools. Close to the house are the remains of a remarkable neo-Baroque water garden which must date from Horlick's time. A great stone pilastered wall is punctuated by a series of lions' masks which spout water into a canal below. The water now flows down a formal cascade into a circular pool guarded by crouching lions. In the 1990s the gardens were enriched with borders and plantings of herbaceous perennials in the fashionable German naturalistic style by Noel Kingsbury. Recently a nursing home, the house has now being converted into a hotel.

Cragside House
see page 335

Craighall Rattray
Rattray, Perthshire OS NO1748
Scottish Inventory

The Rattrays are said to have first come to these parts in the 11th century and they still live here. An ancient keep was altered in the early 16th century and again in the 19th century when it was give its present Baronial air. It has a

spectacular position on the brink of a cliff plummeting into Ericht Gorge. Sir Walter Scott came here in 1793 and the Baron of Bradwardine's castle, Tully-Veolan, in *Waverley* was possibly modelled on Craighall Rattray. Parkland still grazed, and planted with beech, horse chestnut and limes dating from the 19th century. Ancient deciduous woodland in the gorge – a Site of Special Scientific Interest for plants and insects.

Craigiehall
nr Dalmeny, Edinburgh OS NT1675
Scottish Inventory

House designed c.1695–99 by Sir William Bruce for the 3rd Earl of Annandale (later 1st Marquess of Annandale), with additions in the 19th century by William Burn and David Bryce. In the early 18th century the estate passed by marriage to the Hope family (of Hopetoun, *see page 492*). A walled garden was built in 1708, which was leased in 1716 to a local gardener who had to "keep the garden, with the parterre flower garden and bowling green in as good condition as they were at his entry". In 1753 the Hon. Charles Hope (who changed his name to Hope Weir and then Hope Vere) went on the Grand Tour with the young Robert Adam. He returned in 1755 and started to embellish the grounds of Craigiehall. He created a deer park on the far side of the river Almond, reached by crossing a rustic stone bridge with a two-storey rustic grotto alongside it. On high ground in the deer park he built a circular temple with grand views; its top floor, considered a hazard to low-flying aircraft (Edinburgh airport is nearby), was removed in 1975. The house now belongs to the Ministry of Defence and is the headquarters of Scottish Command.

Craigmillar Castle
Edinburgh OS NT2870 Scottish Inventory
Open regularly Tel 0131 661 4445

The castle has a splendid position in hilly ground on the south-eastern edge of Edinburgh, close to the park of Holyrood House (*see page 492*). It was built in the 15th century for the Preston

family who had been here since the 14th century. Today it is a ruin, but a very complete one, and splendidly situated on a rise partly shrouded in trees. There were gardens here in the 16th century, of which much evidence remains: square, terraced compartments; South Field, walled in stone with the remains of two viewing towers and a large P-shaped pond; a viewing terrace on the south side of the castle, overlooking South Field; and East Garden, a walled enclosure in front of the chapel. Woodland contains the remains of the 19th-century Laird's Walk, with berberis, box, rhododendrons and roses underplanted with leopard's bane (*Doronicum pardalianches*), snowdrops and violets. There was a deer park in the middle ages, now planted with ash, holly, oak, rowan and sycamore.

Cranborne Manor Gardens
see page 29

Cranbury Park
nr Hursley, Hampshire OS SU4423
English Heritage Register Grade II*
Open occasionally for NGS

House built c.1790 for Lady Dance-Holland whose brother-in-law, the architect George Dance the Younger, probably designed the house. Formal gardens by the house include a circular fountain pool with Irish yews and urns, a circular rose garden and an oval one. Plantings of specimen trees lead to a wall topped with urns above a ha-ha. To the north, a circular pool and a ride lead to a grotto over a spring with a plaque bearing some lines written by William Wordsworth on a visit here. A second ride leads to a summerhouse with Tuscan columns, also probably designed by Dance. A curiosity in the pleasure grounds is a sundial made in 1720, supposedly to a design of Sir Isaac Newton. In the wooded park is the Castle, an eyecatcher in the form of a sham ruin, built in 1770 from fragments of the 13th-century Cistercian Netley Abbey.

Crarae Garden
see page 370

Crathes Castle

see page 370

Creagh

Skibereen, County Cork, Republic of Ireland

Attractive early 19th-century house in exquisite position on the east bank of Baltimore Bay. Peter Harold-Barry came here in 1945 and made a wild garden of jungly charm, enlivened by fine camellias, rhododendrons and occasional tender rare plants such as *Lomatia ferruginea* and *Telopea mongaensis*. A meandering former mill pool is edged in bold waterside planting and the derelict mill assumes the character of a picturesque eyecatcher. A large walled kitchen garden has been restored in recent years. Best of all are the walks on lawns along the banks of the bay.

Creech Grange

Steeple, Dorset OS SY90 82
English Heritage Register Grade II*

Tudor house rebuilt 1738–41 and much changed in mid 19th century in neo-Tudor style. The remains of a remarkable early Georgian garden survive: three rectangular pools originally part of a grand formal scheme. The estate at this time belonged to the Bond family; Sir Thomas Bond was one of the speculators who in the late 17th century developed new land in London round about Albemarle St, giving his name to Bond St. The Grange Arch, castellated and enriched with stumpy obelisks, stands south of the house on the brow of Creech Hill, and was built before 1746.

Crewe Hall

Crewe Green, Cheshire OS SJ7354
English Heritage Register Grade II

Early 17th-century house for Sir Randulph Crewe, with later alterations. A painting of c.1710 by an unknown artist, illustrated in John Harris's *The Artist and the Country House* (1979), shows an entrance forecourt with corner pavilions and, to the east, a fine compartmented garden with statues. W.A. Nesfield designed new formal gardens c.1860, chiefly to the north of the house. A visitor in 1863 saw "curves of variegated gravel and its thick box

edging, its broad terraced walks and flights of steps guarded by quaintly carved balustrades and strange heraldic monsters". A muted version of this survives. In the park which surrounds the house, a lake was formed in the 18th century. Today there is much commercial woodland in the park. Capability Brown, William Emes and John Webb are said to have worked here but there is no evidence. Humphry Repton advised John Crewe c.1791 about an ornamental lake and new approaches, but the result is not known. Close to the kitchen garden is the Apple House, an octagonal brick building of c.1636.

Crichel House

Moor Crichel, Dorset OS ST9908
English Heritage Register Grade II

A painting of around 1700 shows a neat house of Jacobean style with a pretty, formal garden in an enclosed forecourt. House rebuilt for Humphry Sturt from 1743, after a fire; at some point in the 18th century the park was landscaped by an unknown designer, during which the village of Moor Crichel was moved to accommodate a lake. In about 1907 Harold Peto designed a new formal garden for Lord Alington in front of the south façade of the house. This was illustrated in *Country Life* in January 1908 and shows a restrained formal garden, with topiary, Irish yews and bedding schemes spread out below the loggia of the house, with views over the lake which is overlooked by a rotunda and fringed with cedars of Lebanon. *Country Life* described it as "an ample and dignified Italian garden with broad and simple lines in harmony with both house and site". This beautiful and skilfully designed garden was destroyed c.1960.

Cricket House

Cricket St Thomas, Somerset OS ST3708
English Heritage Register Grade II*

There had been an Elizabethan house here before a new house, designed by Sir John Soane, was built 1801–4 for Admiral Hood (the Hoods later became Viscounts Bridport). There are formal

gardens close to the house but the most memorable aspect of the place is the position of the house in a very wide well wooded valley which must have been landscaped in the 18th century although no designer has been identified. In the early 19th century the small village close to the house was removed and a series of lakes created in the valley below the house. The park was extended in the 1830s until it occupied virtually the whole of the parish. On the north side of the valley a covered seat, the Admiral's Seat, made supposedly for Lord Nelson from fragments of the Elizabethan house, was built to allow views of the sea at Lyme Bay. The house has in recent years become a hotel, and a wildlife park is also based here.

Croft Castle

Croft, Herefordshire OS SO4465
English Heritage Register Grade II
Open regularly (NT) Tel 01568 780246

Late 14th- or early 15th-century castle of the Croft family, remodelled in the 18th century. North of castle, walled garden with several compartments, beech or yew hedging and terraces, and paths of patterned brick and cobbles. Most of the castle gardens were designed by Graham Stuart Thomas after 1957. South of the castle, two terraces and axial path with a pool – probably the remains of a formal garden made before the mid 18th century. West of the terraces, earthworks associated with ponds, presumably also part of the early formal garden. Park created c.1500, with signs of ridge and furrow fields showing early cultivation. Remarkable avenues of sweet chestnuts radiating north and west from the castle survived the 18th-century landscaping of the park and probably date from between 1620 and 1680. Fishpool Valley in the eastern part of the park was probably part of an 18th-century picturesque landscape scheme. At its northern end, a grotto-like seat facing down the valley and halfway down a Gothick pumphouse. In the north of the park, a few oak pollards survive, estimated to be 500 to 600 years old.

Crom Estate

Newtownbutler, County Fermanagh,
Northern Ireland Open regularly (NT)
Tel (028) 6773 8118

Old Crom Castle was built in 1611, destroyed by fire in 1764 and replaced by the present castellated mansion, built 1834–36 for the Earl of Erne to the designs of Edward Blore. William Sawrey Gilpin, the prophet of the picturesque, was asked to improve the landscape. The estate today, 1,900 acres/769 hectares of it, with the largest oak forest in Northern Ireland, is regarded as a nature reserve but it does retain some attractive buildings associated with the landscape. The Tower on Gad Island is a castellated keep, built c.1847 – a famine relief project. Crom Church, built in 1840, stands on a peninsula in the lough and looks very much like a deliberate eyecatcher. Estate buildings such as The Cottage and Inishkerk Lodge are in the cottage *orné* picturesque style.

Croome Court

Croome D'Abitot, Worcestershire OS
SO8844 English Heritage Register Grade I
Open regularly (NT) Tel 01905 371006

The Coventry family (later Earls of Coventry) have lived in Worcestershire since the 16th century. The 6th Earl transformed the estate, commissioning a new house and landscape park from Capability Brown (his first major independent commission). The house was built 1751–52, with advice from Sanderson Miller. The great problem at Croome was drainage, particularly affecting the site of the house itself; Brown solved this by building an elaborate system of culverts which directed the water into a new lake, to form one of the chief ornaments of the landscape. The drainage system at Croome was widely admired and copied. According to Catherine Gordon, in *The Coventrys of Croome* (1999), "The whole project is thought to have cost an amazing £400,000 – around £28m in today's terms." Throughout the 19th century there was little new work in the park and in the 20th century it decayed or was turned over to other uses – an airfield, a sewage works, a cricket ground

and for agriculture. In 1996 the National Trust bought 669 acres/271 hectares of the parkland (the house and pleasure grounds remaining in separate ownership), of which the chief ornament is Croome river, a very long and narrow curving lake to the west and south of the house. On the north bank of the lake is a monument to Brown, erected by the 6th Earl in 1797 (long after Brown's death), with an inscription celebrating Brown's "inimitable and creative genius" which "formed this garden scene out of a morass". The lake is ornamented with a grotto (1765–67 by Brown and containing the nymph Sabrina), two iron bridges of the 1790s, an urn on a pedestal by James Wyatt (1800), a Coade stone druid on a plinth (1794, by James Wyatt), an Island Temple on the lake by Robert Adam (1776) and, on the north-east bank, a Temple Greenhouse also by Adam (c.1760). Many other buildings and ornaments ornament the park, chiefly the work of Adam, Brown and Wyatt, they form one of the most outstanding groups in any 18th-century park. Even the church of St Mary Magdalene, on the park boundary north of the house, was designed by Brown, with an interior by Adam, as an eyecatcher. The park is particularly well documented and it seems that every 18th-century ornament except for some statues and a possibly pasteboard obelisk, has survived. The National Trust took on an immense task in acquiring the park and embarking on the restoration of this great monument to 18th-century taste. Part of the Croome Court estate, Pirton Park, is in separate ownership (*see page 523*).

Crossing House

see page 297

Crowcombe Court

Crowcombe, Somerset OS ST1436
English Heritage Reghister Grade II

Grand house built 1725–34 by Nathaniel Ireson for Thomas Carew MP. In a valley behind the house (the Glen), an 18th-century sham ruin made in part from fragments of the destroyed medieval chapel of Halsway nearby. It is possible that this ruin was put in place by Thomas Carew – a painting of 1725 with newly planted trees clothing the slopes shows a building in this position. If this is so, it is one of the earliest uses of architectural fragments in this way. A stream flows down the valley and there are pools and a rustic bridge. Dorothy Wordsworth, who lived not far away at Alfoxton, came here in 1798 and scoffed at these picturesque embellishments but admired the great beauty of the landscape.

Crowe Hall

Widcombe, Bath, Somerset OS ST7663
English Heritage Register Grade II Open occasionally for NGS Tel 01225 310322

In a wonderful position on the northern slopes of Bath, with views to the Arcadia of Prior Park (see page 58). The well wooded grounds retain the character of a country estate although it lies within the boundaries of the city of Bath. The house was built in the late 18th century for Brigadier Crowe and much altered in the early 19th century for the Tugwell family who terraced the slopes and created the essential framework of the garden as it is today; later work in the 20th century by the Barratt family. Italianate terraces, with excellent Japanese maples, lie close to the house. One of them, a sunken garden, has a stone balustrade and urns, with a scalloped pool and fountain at the centre. Other enclosed gardens decorate the slopes below, with walks descending through woods enlivened by a 19th-century grotto. Excellent trees and shrubs and splendid spring bulbs ornament the garden.

Crown Point

nr Trowse Newton, Norfolk OS TG2206
English Heritage Register Grade II

New house built from 1865 (replacing an 18th-century house) for a banker, Sir Robert Harvey, to the designs of H.E. Coe at a cost of £20,000 (£912,200 today). The gardens were laid out from 1868 by William Broderick Thomas with formal lawns, balustraded walls with bastions, a sunken garden with yew topiary, a cherry

walk, a rock garden and an azalea garden. Harvey reduced Trowse Newton Old Hall, a 15th-century ruin, to a picturesque tower with medieval tracery, to serve as an eyecatcher at the end of a new double lime avenue. It all proved too expensive, and Harvey, whose bank was not doing well, committed suicide in 1870. In recent times the house was a hospital (Whitlingham Hospital) and since 2000 has been divided into flats.

Croxdale Hall

Croxdale, County Durham OAS NZ2737
English Heritage Register Grade II*
Open by appointment Tel 0191 3780911

18th-century remodelling for William Salvin of a Tudor house. South-east of the house, garden enclosed on three sides by 18th-century walls. Orangery of c.1765 at the centre of a south-facing wall with embrasures for protecting fruit. To the south of the garden, two lakes. To the west of the house, picturesque walks by the banks of the Croxdale beck which flows, with occasional cascades, through a steep wooded ravine. The northern part of the park is well wooded in parts, with a chain of pools at the centre. In the southern park is a canal which was in the past flanked with the trees of an avenue.

Croxteth Hall

nr West Derby, Merseyside OS SJ4094
English Heritage Register Grade II
Open regularly Tel 0151 2285311

An ancient site dating to pre-Conquest times and part of the royal forest of Toxteth by the early 13th century. In the mid 15th century the park was acquired by Sir Richard Molyneux whose family, later Earls of Sefton, remained here until the 20th century. The house was built in the 16th century, with many subsequent alterations. Pleasure grounds of lawns scattered with trees and shrubs lie largely to the west of house and correspond to the 18th-century layout. Two formal canals in this part of the garden. North of the house, the site of an 18th-century wilderness, is ornamental woodland. Park lies chiefly to east and south-west of

house. Substantial tree clumps, rides, and a stream which flows into the river Alt. 18th-century walled former kitchen garden north of the house.

Croxton Park

Croxton, Cambridgeshire OS TL2559
English Heritage Register Grade II*

House built for Edward Leeds 1760–61, replacing a medieval manor house which had been rebuilt in the 16th century. In the park are surviving earthworks of a rare circular moated garden with a raised walk and canal; these gardens date from the late 16th century and were abandoned when the park was made in 1761. There had been a deer park here by the 16th century. In 1825 Samuel Newton bought the estate and increased the park by clearing away what remained of the old Croxton village. The pattern of village streets, old hedge enclosures and medieval ridge and furrow field systems is still visible. Christopher Taylor illustrates Croxton Park in his Parks and Gardens of Britain: a Landscape History from the Air (1998) and describes it as "one of the best preserved medieval landscapes in East Anglia".

Crystal Palace Park

Bromley, London OS TQ3470 English Heritage Register Grade II* Open regularly

The Crystal Palace, designed by Sir Joseph Paxton for the Great Exhibition of 1851 in Hyde Park, was moved here in an enlarged version 1852–54. It was set in grounds laid out by Paxton, and although the Palace was destroyed by fire in 1936, much of Paxton's layout survives in what is now a public park: two parallel terraces 550yards/500m long, running north–south; the outline of an east–west axis planted with plane trees; the Intermediate Lake and the Lower Lake, with islands. On the islands are 27 lifesize bronze statues of prehistoric monsters made in 1854 by B.W. Hawkins; Baedeker's London (1900) described these as "full-sized models of antediluvian animals, – the Megalosaurus, Ichthyosaurus, Pterodactyl, Palaeatherium, Megatherium, and the Irish Elk (found in the Isle of Man) –

together with the contemporaneous geological formations". The whole area is today a public park with many sports facilities, some of them very ugly. Much work was carried out on the park in 2002 (including the restoration of the "antediluvian animals") but it remains a pale and rather depressing shadow of its 19th-century magnificence.

Culford Park

Culford, Suffolk OS TL8370
English Heritage Register Grade II
Open regularly Tel 01284 729318

Now a school, the house was built in 1790 for the 1st Marquess of Cornwallis and was greatly enlarged by Earl Cadogan at the beginning of the 19th century. Thomas Wright did a plan for new gardens in 1742 but it is not known if this was executed. Humphry Repton advised in 1791 and produced a Red Book; he made a serpentine lake from a river and spanned it with a balustraded bridge flanked with urns. He was also much concerned with the need for plenty of planted cover for game shooting. An aerial photograph of Culford in 1953 in Elysian Gardens (1979) by Marcus Binney and Ann Hills shows guilloche patterns of beds flanking a path and a remarkable grass terrace with rounded corner bastions.

Cullen House

Cullen, Banffshire OS NJ5066
Scottish Inventory

17th-century house of the Ogilvies (later Earls of Findlater and Earls of Seafield) with later additions by William Adam, Robert Adam, James Playfair and David Bryce. Wild garden where the 7th Earl of Findlater in 1780 asked his gardener to "plant American oak, chestnut, walnuts etc". By 1782 there were "all kinds of trees and shrubs, through which serpentine gravel walks have been made". In 1847, the Highland and Agricultural Society of Scotland recorded that "31,686,482 trees had been planted in 8,223 acres." Only traces of these great works, including some fine trees, remain. The house and 17 acres/7 hectares was bought in 1983 by the

architect Kit Martin and converted into separate dwellings.

Culross Abbey House

Culross, Fife OS NS9886 Scottish Inventory
Open occasionally for SGS

House built 1608 for Sir Edward Bruce (later 1st Lord Kinloss) and enlarged later in the 17th century. Remarkable terraced gardens built before 1693, when they were shown in a drawing by Slezer. The Gardeners' Magazine in 1842 described "a number of lower terraces, slopes and platforms, of great antiquity, some with stone steps, balustrades and vases and among them some very old fruit trees". After 1952, when the house belonged Lord and Lady Elgin, a splendid collection of shrub roses was planted on the terraces; it included every cultivar of Rosa rugosa and every hybrid musk. A summerhouse dated 1674 is built into a vaulted recess in the terrace wall.

Culross Palace

see page 372

Culzean Castle

see page 372

Cumberland Lodge

Old Windsor/New Windsor, Berkshire/Surrey
OS SU9671 English Heritage Register Grade I

The house, the largest building in Windsor Great Park, was built in the mid 17th century but has 19th-century alterations. The estate, in the middle of the park, was acquired when Crown land was sold to private individuals during the Commonwealth; when the land reverted to the Crown at the Restoration in 1660, it became the home of the Ranger of the Great Park. From 1672 to 1702 it was occupied by Hans Willem Bentinck, 1st Earl of Portland, and during this time Henry Wise made a garden, probably designed by Bentinck himself; Wise's A Generall Plann of Windsor Great Park (c.1712) shows Cumberland Lodge with formal gardens standing at the point where two avenues intersect. After Bentinck, the house was occupied by the Duke and Duchess of Marlborough who found it "a thousand times more agreeable than Blenheim". (The

C

Duchess had become Joint Ranger of the Great Park). By the mid 18th century the formal gardens had been succeeded by a lawn with a wilderness divided by rides and serpentine walks. In the park, Great Meadow Pond was the scene of landscaping activities at the time of the Duke of Cumberland, George III's, brother who succeeded the Duchess as Ranger in 1744. Overlooking the pond there was a temple by Henry Flitcroft, who also designed a Chinoiserie bridge and a classical boathouse; none of these buildings remains.

Curraghmore

Portlaw, County Wexford, Republic of Ireland Open regularly Tel (00353) 051 387 101

Ancient house of medieval origins transformed in the mid 18th century into a Baroque palace by a Waterford architect, John Roberts, for the 1st Earl of Tyrone of the second creation (the senior branch of the family, the de la Poer Beresfords, later became Marquesses of Waterford). Mark Bence-Jones, in *Burke's Guide to Country Houses: Ireland* (1978), writes: "The demesne at Curraghmore is unsurpassed in Ireland in its size, its romantic scenery and its splendid woods, which are part of a primeval forest." In 1752–54 Lady Tyrone made a grotto decorated with minerals and shells and containing a portait statue of herself by John Van Nost the Younger; the statue carries a scroll in one hand bearing the words, "In two hundred & sixty one days these shells were put up by the proper hands of the Rt. Hon. Cathⁱᵉ Countess of Tyrone 1754." A notable eyecatcher and memorial, the Le Poer Tower, was erected in 1785 as a memorial to the Earl of Tyrone's son, niece and a friend. It stands high on a wooded hill, with grand views from its top. In the middle of the 19th century the garden designer James Fraser designed an oval flower garden to surround the shell grotto. He also designed parterres, not all of which were successful; one was too close to the lake and filled with water. In 1863 the Marquess of Waterford bought a cast-iron

fountain at the Great Exhibition in Paris for the parterre at Curraghmore: it cost £3,000 (£136,830 today). Curraghmore is famous, too, because it was here as gardener's boy that William Robinson started his horticultural education.

Cusworth Park

Cusworth, South Yorkshire OS SE5403 English Heritage Register Grade II Open regularly to the public Tel 01302 737411

Mid 18th-century house for William Wrightson, remodelled by James Paine later in the century. In the 1760s Richard Woods landscaped the park, taking advantage of the stream below the house to form a chain of ponds. Between the highest pond and the next one down, Woods built a boat-house/grotto which, seen from the upper water, appears to be its culmination; the third pond, beyond a dam, thus comes as a surprise. Woods made no pleasure grounds, but a connecting path from a lawn by the house to the lakes below has a grove of beech, chestnut, elm, larch and tulip trees on one side and, on the other, a flowery shrubbery of evergreens interspersed with honeysuckle, jasmine and roses. Since 1961 the estate has been owned by the local authority: the house is a museum and the grounds a country park. Much of the park is now arable land and the Doncaster bypass cuts across its west side.

Dalemain

see page 337

Dalhousie Castle

nr Dalkeith, Midlothian OS NT3263

The Ramsays of Dalhousie built a tower house in the mid 15th century on a fine site overlooking the South Esk river, and additions were made in the 18th and 19th centuries. J.C. Loudon's *Encyclopaedia of Gardening* (1822) describes "extensive and romantic pleasure-grounds. The river Esk washes the base of the castle; and its lofty wooded banks afford delightful summer walks." A little later Loudon, in his *Arboretum et Fruticetum Britannicum* (1838), refers to an "extensive collection of trees and shrubs, more or less

remarkable" at Dalhousie. Nothing much of this remains; in 1972 the castle was turned into a hotel, with a spa, and in 1982 the Scottish Inventory noted that "The designed landscape is substantially derelict."

Dalkeith House, *also known as* Dalkeith Palace

Dalkeith, Midlothian OS NT3367 Scottish Inventory Open regularly (Dalkeith Country Park) Tel 0131 663 5684

Ancient estate of the Douglases of Dalkeith, from whom it passed by descent to the Duke of Buccleuch. The present house, incorporating an old castle, was built 1702–11 to the designs of James Smith, for the widow of the 1st Duke of Buccleuch (formerly Duke of Monmouth) who was beheaded in 1685 for leading the rebellion against his uncle, King James II. There had been a deer park at Dalkeith by 1637 but the parkland had increased, so that J.C. Loudon, in his *Encyclopaedia of Gardening* (1822), could describe "upwards of 800 acres, surrounded by a stone wall 9ft high. It is magnificently wooded and watered by two streams, the North Esk and the South Esk which pass by the house." Although some of this is now under arable cultivation, parts of it retain a parkland character and the remains of old avenues are visible. In 1792 a magnificent bridge, designed by Robert Adam, was built to take the west drive over the North Esk river. W.S. Gilpin designed a parterre *c*.1832 in the form of two circles – "curved forms in a Garden are always more agreeable to the eye than *squares & angles* & they will not do in this case" – but one of the reasons they would not do is because the site was above the banks of the river South Esk which curves at this point. As the centrepiece to the parterre William Burn designed a remarkable conservatory – twelve-sided with columns crowned with elaborate finials. The conservatory survives, without its glazing, but the parterre has gone. A little later, in 1838, Charles M'Intosh, one of the great professional gardeners of the day, became head gardener and laid out a new kitchen garden.

Dallam Tower

Beetham, Cumbria OS SD4881 English Heritage Register Grade II Open occasionally for NGS

Early 18th-century house for Daniel Wilson. Terraced gardens by the house probably date from the 17th century; they are shown in a map of 1733. Early 19th-century conservatory, attributed to George Webster of Kendal, with curved roof and cast-iron glazing bars. South-east of the house, the Japanese Garden with rockwork, a stream-fed pool, dwarf conifers and Japanese maples. Park with scattered mature trees and a herd of fallow deer; it had been a deer park in the 18th century.

Dalmahoy

Ratho, Midlothian OS NT1468 Scottish Inventory

Estate on the edge of the Pentland hills, which belonged to the Dalmahoy family in the 13th century and later passed to the Dalrymples (Earls of Stair) and to the Douglases (Earls of Morton). The present house was built for George Dalrymple to the designs of William Adam and completed in 1725. Parkland, with a deer park, was established in the 18th century, with an avenue laid out in 1725, but became increasingly informal later in the century, with a man-made loch with ornamental trees about its banks. Pleasure grounds by the house still show the remains of 18th-century ornamental plantings of yew and sweet chestnut. Two golf courses were laid out in the park in 1927 and since 1990 the house has been the Marriott Dalmahoy Hotel and Country Club.

Dalmeny House

Dalmeny, Edinburgh OS NT1678 Open regularly Tel 0131 331 1888

The Primrose family (later Earls of Rosebery) acquired the Dalmeny estate in 1662. The old house, Barnbougle Castle, dates from the 15th century and remains; a little further from the coast, a delightful Tudor Gothic mansion was built 1814–17 to the designs of William Wilkins. Woodland was established by the end of the 18th century and a park was laid out when the

new house was built. After 1868, the 5th Earl, who married Hannah de Rothschild, planted an arboretum west of the house, with, latterly, species rhododendrons, many of which came from the Rothschild garden at Exbury (*see page 82*), among the trees.

Dalton Hall

South Dalton, East Yorkshire OS SE9545 English Heritage Register Grade II*

House built 1771–76 on an older site for Sir Charles Hotham, probably designed by Thomas Atkinson. Pleasure grounds were laid out 1723–37, possibly with the advice of the 3rd Earl of Burlington and his head gardener, Thomas Knowlton. West of the house, a terrace lawn with shaped beds designed by William Broderick Thomas in the 1870s. Beyond this, on the far side of an oval lawn, a yew-lined walk leads to a garden pavilion, by Colen Campbell or Roger Morris 1733–34, built at a cost of £294 (£24,261 today). On the south side of the oval lawn, a serpentine path leads west. Parkland, largely laid out in the 19th century, probably with the help of W.B. Thomas, surrounds the house.

Danbury Place, *also known as* Danbury Park

Danbury, Essex OS TL7604 English Heritage Register Grade II Open regularly

House built 1832 for John Round to the designs of Thomas Hopper on or near the site of a 16th-century house. 19th-century formal gardens east of the house, with terrace, lawn and hedges. Park dates from the 16th century. A plan of 1758 shows woodland and pools as they are today but also such formal landscape features as rides and avenues which have since disappeared. The park is now a Country Park.

Dane John Gardens

Canterbury, Kent OS TR1457 English Heritage Register Grade II Open regularly

Ancient gardens, now public gardens, within the old city wall of Canterbury – probably the oldest public garden in the country. A terrace walk against th ty wall leads to a central feature, e mount, which is one of a oup of Romano-British burial ounds of the 1st or 2nd century D. This became a Norman stle, disused by the 12th century en all citizens of the city had e access to the land. By the th century all the land occupied the modern gardens was ned by the Mayor and ommonalty. The gardens were ndscaped in the early 1800s and rious monuments and buildings ded later in the century.

anesfield
edmenham, Buckinghamshire OS SU8184

ectacular castellated neo-Tudor use built 1899–1901 for Robert udson, the son of a soap tycoon, the designs of W.H. Romaine-alker. It has a beautiful position the Chiltern Hills with views er the river Thames. This view is e focal point of terraces on the pes below the house, where omaine-Walker laid out a gnificent parterre with a grand ntral tiered fountain pool, box-ged compartments and yew piary of spirals and bumpy apes. Beyond it, lawns slope wn to woods which lead down the river. In 1991 the house came a hotel.

angan Castle
m, County Meath, Republic of Ireland

ouse of the Wesley family (later ellesley, Lords of Mornington, rls of Mornington and Dukes Wellington), built in the early th century. Mary Pendarves saw e grounds in 1732: "…there is a -grove dedicated to Vesta, in the idst of which is her statue…a ound covered with evergreens, which is placed a temple with e statues of Apollo, Neptune, oserpine." In 1744 a traveller, ac Butler, saw canals on which ock naval battles were fought, a rt with cannons, and twenty-five elisks. By 1747, when Mrs elany came, the canals had come an informal lough, with ands and a wooded terrace with alks and sitting places: "The ounds as far as you can see ery way is waving in hills, and les, and every remarkable point s either a tuft of trees, a statue, a

seat, an obelisk, or a pillar" (*The Autobiography and Correspondence of Mary Granville, Mrs Delany* (1861)). James Howley, in his *The Follies and Garden Buildings of Ireland* (1993), mentions an engraving of the estate done by W.H. Bartlett in 1845: "[it] shows the devastated estate with a sole obelisk outlined on a hill behind the shell of the house." Howley also suggests that Dangan may have been the inspiration for the landscape at nearby Larchill (*see page 422*) which also has a lake with a fort.

Danson Park
Bexleyheath, London OS TQ4775
English Heritage Register Grade II

House built from *c*.1760 for John Boyd to the designs of Sir Robert Taylor. Park possibly designed by Capability Brown; although there is no definite evidence, Dorothy Stroud in her *Capability Brown* (1975) says: "The management of the rather flat terrain and fine lake has…Brown-ish qualities." However, Nathaniel Richmond has also been suggested as the designer. Since 1925 the remaining part of the park (an area of 183 acres/74 hectares) has been a public park, with boating on the lake, a café, bowling green, tennis courts and sports fields. The walled former kitchen garden has been made into ornamental gardens with a pergola, rose beds, paved paths and a pool.

Dartington Hall
see page 30

Davenport House
Worfield, Shropshire OS SO7595
English Heritage Register Grade II*

House built 1726 by Francis Smith of Warwick for Henry Davenport. Landscape park of the mid 18th century when Sharington (also known as Sherrington) Davenport had visits from his friend William Shenstone of The Leasowes (*see page 501*). Surviving paintings by Thomas Robins show a garden of Rococo enchantment, with a pattern of avenues on either side of the house, one of which borrows the church of St Peter, Worfield, as an eyecatcher. Robins's painting

showed several garden buildings, some of which have been destroyed in recent times and only one of which, a ruinous grotto, survives.

Dawyck Botanic Gardens
see page 373

Daylesford House
Daylesford, Gloucestershire OS SP2526
English Heritage Register Grade II*
Open occasionally for NGS

House built 1788–93 on an old site for Warren Hastings to the designs of Samuel Pepys Cockerell. Park landscaped at this time by John Davenport. Gothic orangery of *c*.1780 designed by John Davenport. Edward Kemp did much planting in the garden in 1855, using the repertory of chiefly acid-loving shrubs he was to make so fashionable – *Aucuba japonica*, azaleas, berberis, cotoneaster, heathers, Portugal laurel and "mixed dwarf Evergreens". Lanning Roper designed an American Walk here in the 1960s, with an avenue of tulip trees. Rose garden and splendid late 18th-century walled kitchen garden with ornamental planting finely replanted by Lady Mary Keen in 1989.

Dean Cemetery
Edinburgh OS NT2374
Scottish Inventory Open regularly

Cemetery laid out from 1845 in the former pleasure grounds of the 17th-century Dean House in its picturesque setting. The ground slopes south to the river, the Water of Leith, and the layout, taking advantage of the wooded banks of the river, was initially conceived as informal and flowery, with herbaceous borders and brilliant bedding schemes. Parts to the north were laid out later in a more formal fashion, with a grid of paths. The planting is a mixture of evergreens – particularly holly and yew (common, gold and Irish) – and weeping forms of ash, cherry and oak. There is an outstanding collection of distinguished 19th-century monuments, some by the architect William Playfair, including his own tomb.

The Deanery
Wells, Somerset OS ST5545
English Heritage Register Grade II

The former deanery of Wells is 15th century, very attractive, overlooking the cathedral green and resembling a miniature collegiate building in Oxford or Cambridge. It is now used as diocesan offices, and new houses for cathedral canons were built within the Liberty on part of its grounds in the 1960s. The existing garden is nondescript but there remains a fine medieval wall and the place is sacred to the memory of William Turner, Dean of Wells 1551–54 and 1561–68, who has been called the father of English botany; he was the author of the first herbal in English (*A New Herball*, published in three parts 1551–68). There is no evidence that he gardened at Wells, though he surely must have done so, and nothing is known of the early appearance of the garden. Turner is commemorated in a plaque fixed to the deanery wall, installed at the instigation of John Harvey and unveiled by him.

Deanery Garden
Sonning, Berkshire OS SU7575
English Heritage Register Grade II*

House and garden by Edwin Lutyens (with Gertrude Jekyll) for Edward Hudson, completed in 1901. One of the most admired of Lutyens's houses – "a dream house" as Gavin Stamp called it – designed in conjunction with the garden so that the two are inseparable. The site is a walled orchard of irregular shape surrounded by village houses. Formal gardens lie behind and on each side of the house. A rill, planted with irises, runs between two lawns, each with a border on its far side, linking pools. To its east is a square lawn planted with quinces. On each side of the centre of the rill are flights of steps, leading south to the orchard and north to a long yew-hedged bowling green. The rill garden is raised on a terrace so that its south side overlooks the semi-formal orchard which opens out from a *patte d'oie* of paths, each starting with a circular flight of steps.

Deene Park
Deene, Northamptonshire OS SP9592
English Heritage Register Grade II
Open regularly Tel 01780 450278

The Brudenell family came here in 1514. The present house, with its castellations and towers, is chiefly a mixture of Tudor and 18th-century architecture. There had been a formal garden here in the early 17th century, with a large quartered parterre and a rectangular pool with an island. In the early 18th century the Duke of Montagu's gardener at Boughton House (*see page 250*), van Meulen, supplied hundreds of fruit trees and probably made suggestions about the planting. Further formal gardens were made in the 18th century, and at that time avenues ran across the park. The gardens as they are today are essentially 20th century, with mixed borders with many shrub roses, good mature trees and a parterre designed by David Hicks.

The Deepdene
nr Dorking, Surrey OS TQ1749
English Heritage Register Grade II

In the 17th century the Hon. Charles Howard bought a farmhouse here, above a steep-sided valley, or dene, and laid out gardens on levelled ground at the bottom of the amphitheatre formed by the dene. A new house was built on a slightly different site, from 1767, by the Hon. Charles Howard (later 10th Duke of Norfolk) but this was demolished in 1969 and replaced by an office block. The 17th-century garden was planted with a wide range of plants: John Aubrey described "cherry trees, myrtles etc. …a great many orange trees and syringas…21 sorts of thyme… it is stored full of rare flowers, and choice plants." Howard also made a cave in the valley side and laid out narrow walks; Aubrey describes a tunnel piercing the hill "through which as through a tube you have a vista over all the south part of Surrey and Sussex to the sea." In the 19th century The Deepdene was owned by Thomas Hope who planted many exotic trees in the dene. Some of the paths survive (some barred by World War II "dragons' teeth") but

D

the garden, battered by the 1987 storm, presents a sorry sight.

The Dell

Doncaster, South Yorkshire OS SK5502
English Heritage Register Grade II
Open regularly

An ancient quarry at Hexthorpe, in use as early as 1568, was turned into a garden as part of the Hexthorpe Flatts public park, 1928–29. The sides of the quarry are densely planted with ornamental shrubs and there is a pool and rockery. A water channel takes water to a moated island with the remains of a bandstand. Specimen trees and shrubs still ornament the garden but the fabric is tired.

Denham Place

Denham, Buckinghamshire OS TQ0487
English Heritage Register Grade II

Ancient, formerly monastic estate, bought by Sir Roger Hill in the late 17th century when the old house was rebuilt. A painting of c.1705, possibly by John Drapentier and illustrated in John Harris's *The Artist and the Country House* (1979), shows an elaborate and delightful garden with sculpture gardens, parterres, much topiary, an ornate pavilion in a canal and a formal wilderness. This was almost entirely removed in the 1770s except for the walled garden to the south and parts of garden walls, gate piers and some sculptures. It is suggested that Capability Brown was involved in landscaping but there is no evidence. The canal seen in the Drapentier painting was turned into a lake. The house is now offices.

Denmans

see page 130

Derby Arboretum

Derby, Derbyshire OS SK3535 English Heritage Register Grade II* Open regularly

Public park, designed by J.C. Loudon and opened in 1840, on the site of the private pleasure grounds and kitchen garden of Jedediah Strutt, a Derby industrialist, who commissioned the work. Loudon laid out a pattern of serpentine walks (gravel in his time; tarmac today), often

edged with mounds on which he planted specimen trees. This characteristic style of planting survives, which had the advantage of both enlivening a flat site and displaying the trees well. He drew on a wide range of sources for the plants (mistletoe was supplied by Mr Godsall of Hereford). The essential layout of the park also remains, though much of the detailing has gone. At the centre of the park, a fountain pool with tufa and ferns was added post Loudon, but a limestone rock garden to the west and an early 19th-century cottage to the north were here in Loudon's time, when the latter was adorned with flower gardens.

Derreen Garden

see page 406

Derrymore House

Bessbrook, County Armagh,
Northern Ireland Open regularly (NT)
Tel (028) 3083 8361

Lovely and surprisingly early grand cottage *orné* with thatched roof and quatrefoil openings, built 1776 for Isaac Cory MP. The demesne was laid out by John Sutherland and admired in 1803 by Sir Charles Coote: "The very fine improvements at Derrymoore… show the correct and elegant taste of Mr Sutherland, who planned them and supervised their execution. The young plantations already display a fine appearance of wood, the approaches are extremely well planned and the cottage, which is as yet the only residence is without exception the most elegant summer lodge I have ever seen."

Derwent Gardens

Matlock Bath, Derbyshire OS SK2958
English Heritage Register Grade II
Open regularly

Public park laid out late 19th century on the banks of the river Derwent. Late 20th-century layout incorporating earlier features. Gravel paths, lawns and beds. To the west, a wooded bank of tufa and a grotto – one of several tufa features which in the 19th century were fed with thermal springs. Views to the east across the river to Lovers' Walk among the wooded slopes and limestone cliffs.

Dewstow House

nr Caldicot, Gwent OS ST4688
Cadw/ICOMOS Register Grade II*

House built before 1804 and bought by Henry Oakley, a horticulturist, in 1890. He specialised in ferns for which he constructed a series of remarkable underground chambers lit by skylights, which partly survive. These were lined with rockwork, like grottoes, with pools and rills (originally with goldfish), stalactites, and niches to accommodate the ferns. Above ground, rockwork and pools ornament the garden, which has lawns and specimen trees, but the real excitement was going on underground.

The Dillon Garden

see page 407

Dingestow Court

Dingestow, Gwent OS SO4509
Cadw/ICOMOS Register Grade II*

Ancient site for an Elizabethan farmhouse, much altered in the 18th and 19th centuries, with many changes of ownership. A formal garden was laid out in the 18th century, which was altered by Edward Milner from 1883 with a gravel terrace, a rustic summerhouse, turf banks, winding walks and a balloon-shaped hedged kitchen garden. A landscape park was laid out in the 1760s; surviving parkland trees date chiefly from the 19th century: mainly beeches, horse chestnuts, limes and oaks.

Dirleton Castle

Dirleton, East Lothian OS NT5184 Scottish
Inventory Open regularly Tel 01620 850330

The castle dates back to the 12th century but the present fabric is largely 13th- to 16th-century. Three families have been associated with the estate: the de Vaux, the Halyburtons and the Ruthvens (Earls of Gowrie). In the 17th century a new house was built on the neighbouring Archerfield estate (*see page 438*); Dirleton Castle was abandoned and its garden became the flower garden to the Archerfield estate. This was kept up well into the 19th century: *The Journal of Horticulture and Cottage Gardener*

described it in 1865 as having "some of the best examples of modern flower gardening, together with others of a style some two centuries old". At this time, informal flower beds were linked by gravel walks and the perimeter wall was planted with magnolias, myrtles, roses and wisteria, some of which remain. A splendid 20th-century double herbaceous border, said to be the longest in the world, is the chief ornament of the garden today. A sunken bowling green west of the castle is surrounded by yew trees.

Ditchingham Hall

Ditchingham, Norfolk OS TM3292
English Heritage Register Grade II

House built c.1715 for the Revd John Bedingfield, remodelled in the early 20th century. In the 18th century a stream in the park, the Broome beck, was dammed to form a serpentine lake with two islands. Woodland to north-east of lake and boundary plantings substantially enclose the park. Fine mature parkland trees. Capability Brown's name has been mentioned in connection with the park but there is no evidence.

Ditchley Park

nr Charlbury, Oxfordshire OS SP3921
English Heritage Register Grade II*
Open by appointment Tel 01608 677346

House by James Gibbs, started in 1722 for George Lee, 2nd Earl of Litchfield. Gibbs introduced a giant terrace below the north façade of the house and a *patte d'oie* of three avenues radiating southwards across the park. In 1777 the 3rd Earl of Litchfield called in Capability Brown to dam a stream north of the house and form a lake. A rotunda, by Stiff Leadbetter c.1761, stands to the west, and an early 18th-century grotto is built into the lake's south bank. Many American trees planted in the old quarry area below the lake – 143 species have been listed. J.C. Loudon laid out the pleasure grounds 1805–10. The estate was bought in 1933 by Ronald and Lady Nancy Tree: "There was virtually no garden when we first went to Ditchley, only a few flower beds set higgledy-piggledy on a grass lawn unkempt and uncared

for," as Ronald Tree wrote in his autobiography, *When the Moon was High* (1975). They commissioned Geoffrey Jellicoe to design a new garden – his first commission. He reinstated Gibbs's terrace (lost during 18th-century landscaping) and created grand Italianate gardens with a magnificent parterre and water garden (with veils of water-spouts) to the south-west; this survives in simplified form. The estate belongs today to the Ditchley Foundation and is well cared for.

Ditton Park

Datchet, Berkshire OS TQ0077
English Heritage Register Grade II

New house built 1813–17 by William Atkinson for the Montagu family. The moated site goes back to the 14th century when Sir John Moleyns had a licence to impark. Pleasure grounds on the moated enclosure, with a lawn and walks in woods. 18th-century walled garden and brick summerhouse. Park has survivals of an early 18th-century avenue, and there was a formal wilderness of this date.

Docwra's Manor

see page 298

Doddington Hall

Doddington, Cheshire OS SJ7046
English Heritage Register Grade II

Ancient site, with a house designed by Samuel Wyatt in 1777 for Sir Thomas Broughton. Capability Brown also submitted plans for the new house; these were rejected but part of his garden proposals may have been adopted. Large lake, Doddington Pool, east of the house, with a three-arched stone boathouse of the late 18th century. The lake's southern bank may have been serpentined by Brown, and some oak clumps from his time survive.

Doddington Hall (Lincolnshire)

see page 299

Doddington Place

Doddington, Kent OS TQ9457
English Heritage Register Grade II
Open occasionally Tel 01795 886101

House built 1860s for Sir John Croft to the designs of Charles

Trollope. Gardens laid out by Markham Nesfield from 1874 – a terrace with a lawn, a sundial against the south façade, and a gravel walk leading east to the gardens. Low brick walls surround a lily pool enclosed by grass walks and borders. To the south, a rock garden with pools, and beyond it the park. North of the house, beyond yew hedges, an informal woodland garden. Many trees in the park were lost in the 1987 storm, but a line of old horse chestnuts, possibly earlier than the house, survives.

Dodington House

Dodington, Gloucestershire OS ST7579
English Heritage Register Grade II*

The estate belonged to the Codrington family from the 16th century until 1984. A new house was built to the designs of James Wyatt and completed in the 1820s. Alexander Pope visited in 1728: "pretty enough, the situation romantic, covered with woody hills stumbling upon one another confusedly, and the garden makes a valley betwixt them with some mounts and waterfalls." Capability Brown landscaped the park 1764–67, bringing pasture up to the walls of the house, making two lakes by damming the river Frome, and clothing the slopes above the house in beech woods. The lakes were linked by a serpentine aqueduct and cascade, with a Gothic tower above it. For all this work Brown charged £1,368 (£89,604 today). William Emes and John Webb modified the landscape later in the century. The Codringtons used to open the house and park but after 1984 new owners allowed no access; in 2003 the estate was sold to the vacuum-cleaner inventor James Dyson, so visitors may be admitted in the future.

Dogmersfield Park and King John's Hunting Lodge

Dogmersfield, Hampshire OS SU7751
English Heritage Register Grade II

18th-century Dogmersfield Park was built for Ellis St John whose son, Paulet St John, laid out a Rococo park in the mid 18th century, with a canal and belvedere at the centre of radiating walks. John Harris's *The Artist and the Country House* (1979) shows two views of Dogmersfield – one of c.1747 and one of the 1750s; the latter shows the belvedere, like a lighthouse, on the top of a mound from which ramps lead down to the radiating walks. Park landscaped later in the 18th century by William Emes. King John's Hunting Lodge (owned by the National Trust and tenanted) was built as an eyecatcher on the edge of the park in 1770 – a delightful little brick building with Gothic windows and three soaring gables crowned with urns. From 1947 its tenant was the interior decorator John Fowler who laid out a dazzling small formal garden of hornbeam hedges, topiary, borders and hornbeam "hedges on stilts" (*palissade à l'Italienne*).

Donnington Grove

Shaw-cum-Donnington, Berkshire
OS SU4568 English Heritage Register Grade II

Ancient site, with a delightful Gothic house built before 1772 for James Pettit Andrews and designed by John Chute of The Vyne (*see page 554*), a friend of Horace Walpole. Pleasure grounds with woodland to north-west and east. A path runs south-west, crossing a lake by a wooden bridge, to a Gothic pavilion on a peninsula. Nearby, 18th-century Gothic fishing lodge on the river. In the eastern part of the pleasure grounds, a late 18th-century orangery or garden house. Golf course and trout farm in the south park; some old parkland trees surviving but the western edge of the park now overrun by the A34 Newbury bypass. In woods north of the house, the ruins of the 14th-century Donnington Castle (a Cavalier stronghold in the Civil War) and another golf course in the western part of the north park.

Down Hall

nr Hatfield Broad Oak, Essex OS TL5213
English Heritage Register Grade II

House built 1871–73, to the designs of F.P. Cockerell, to replace a 17th-century house where the poet Matthew Prior lived briefly at the end of his life, 1719–1721. In 1720 Prior commissioned James Gibbs to design a new house for him, and Charles Bridgeman (whom Prior called *virtuoso grand jardinier*) to plan a garden. (A rare example of a poet making sufficient money substantially to create a fine estate; Prior's collected verse, in a grand folio volume, had made a profit of 4,000 guineas (£330,834 today) and he also had financial support from his friend Robert Harley, 1st Earl of Oxford). Work on the garden proceeded, and in 1720 he wrote: "We have laid out squares, rounds and diagonals, and planted quincunxes at Down," and later, "I am glad Bridgeman has begun so well." Prior loved Down – "more than Tully did his Tusculum, or Horace his Sabine field" – but he died before the garden was completed, and Gibbs's house was never built. An avenue of hornbeam survives from Bridgeman and Prior's garden, as well as a temple, possibly by James Gibbs. In the late 19th century a formal garden was laid out west of the house, of which a pool set in a lawn survives.

Down House

see page 131

Downe Hall

Bridport, Dorset OS SY46 93
English Heritage Register Grade II

House built late 18th century for William Downe, with fine views southwards over the town of Bridport. 18th-century pleasure grounds and miniature park with terraced gardens on sloping ground below south façade. Well treed grounds. House divided into flats and new houses built in pleasure grounds in the 1990s after a protracted campaign by the Dorset Gardens Trust to preserve the garden.

The Downes

Trelissick Road, Hayle, Cornwall OS SW5537
English Heritage Register Grade II

Arts and Crafts house and garden designed 1867–68 by Edmund Sedding for W.J. Rawlings. The garden, illustrated in Edmund Sedding's brother J.D. Sedding's *Garden-Craft Old and New* (1891), shows a central axis passing between parterres with topiary and arcaded yew hedging and ending in a domed pavilion. The garden was executed essentially in this form although details were altered; colour-themed planting schemes used hardy plants. One of Sedding's assistants, John Paul Cooper, described the garden in an article in *Architectural Review*: "The garden holds the house in a quiet embrace, and its levels fall by a series of steps and terraces till the garden melts away into the woods below. The house is linked with the site, wedded to its scenery, blended with nature." The house is now a convent of the Daughters of the Cross of Liège and the garden's layout survives in essence although the parterres have been turned to lawn.

Downhill Castle

see page 408

Downton Castle

Downton-on-the-Rock, Shropshire OS SO4474 English Heritage Register Grade II*

For devotees of the picturesque landscape garden, Downton Castle is sacred ground: the home of the garden philosopher and picturesque polemicist Richard Payne Knight who inherited the estate in 1770. The house was built 1772–78, to Knight's own designs, as castle-like and castellated as you could wish, with picturesque towers and turrets. It looks out over the valley of the river Teme, a readymade picturesque landscape which Payne Knight seized upon and animated by contriving paths, building rustic bridges and making such appropriate ornaments as a hermit's cave (with, as Barbara Jones, in her *Follies & Grottoes* (1974) notes, "a round rock room of terrifying earthiness"), a bath house and a grotto. It is worth noting that Payne Knight's grandfather, a pioneer industrialist, had come here drawn not by the beauties of the landscape but by the source of water power. Payne Knight commissioned the artist Thomas Hearne to paint views of the garden; done 1784–86, they give a vivid idea of the garden in its heyday.

Drayton House

nr Lowick, Northamptonshire OS SP9680
English Heritage Register Grade I

Simon de Drayton was given a licence to crenellate his house and to impark in 1328. The house preserves its castle air, but has had many subsequent additions. Garden established in the late 16th century, with two banqueting houses built 1650. A grand formal garden was made east of the house c.1700, when a parterre was laid out by Tilleman Bobart with statues supplied by John Van Nost. Henry Wise supervised plantings of limes in the garden and the park. John Morton's *Natural History of Northamptonshire* (1712) describes "a very fine wilderness with flowering shrubs" and later in the century Horace Walpole admired "pyramidal yews, treillages, and square cradle walks with windows clipped in them". W.A. Nesfield made a new parterre in 1846 but this was removed 100 years later and the garden returned to its early 18th-century appearance. In the park, avenues of lime and oak, planted in the early 18th century, retain some of the original trees. A double avenue of elms (Pall Mall) was replanted in 1977 with limes, walnuts and London planes. At the head of this avenue are splendid early 18th-century wrought-iron gates and a screen, probably by Jean Tijou.

Dropmore House

Dropmore, Buckinghamshire OS SU9285
English Heritage Register Grade II

House started in 1792 for Lord Grenville and almost entirely destroyed by fire in 1990, since when the garden has been vandalised and structures stolen. Lord Grenville started to landscape his grounds as soon as the house was finished, planting many trees – some of which came from his brother, Lord Buckingham, at nearby Stowe (*see page 107*). In the 1820s he planted a pinetum of 62 acres/25 hectares around a lake west of the house. Lawn south of the house with rhododendrons. Formal gardens west of the house with long pergola punctuated by elaborate 19th-century wire aviary with Chinese tiles. To the east,

D

19th-century grotto of concrete blocks (possibly from London Bridge) and a 19th-century sarcophagus containing the remains of Lord Grenville's dog Tippo. Parallel with the south garden, the Italian garden has yew hedges, a damaged stone balustrade, a small pool, a loggia and a gate leading to the pinetum. Here many trees survive and there is a stone alcove from old London Bridge, placed by the lake c.1839.

The Drum, *formerly* Somerville House
Gilmerton, Edinburgh OS NT3068
Scottish Inventory

Handsome Palladian house built 1726–34 for Lord Somerville to the designs of William Adam. According to A.A. Tait, in *The Landscape Garden in Scotland: 1735–1835* (1980), William Adam probably also laid out formal gardens at The Drum, with an old dovecote borrowed as an eyecatcher for the western avenue and "three Gothic arches" to the east. The Edinburgh Mercat Cross stood at the south end of the main avenue from 1756 to 1866. The focal ornaments do not all survive but the vistas remain open. Old parkland, now used for pasture, still has fine old trees, including an avenue of beeches, some of which go back to 1730. Cedars of Lebanon planted here were said to be among the first planted in Scotland. Adam designed a look-out tower commanding views over the deer park and the skyline of Edinburgh, but this was a casualty of 19th-century mining on the site.

Drumlanrig Castle
nr Thornhill, Dumfriesshire OS NX8599
Open regularly Tel 01848 330248

There was a Roman fort at Drumlanrig. In the 14th century the estate was owned by the Douglas family, from whom it has passed by descent to its present owner, the Duke of Buccleuch and Queensberry. The present house was built in the 1680s to the designs of Robert Mylne (and probably with the advice of Sir William Bruce) for the 3rd Earl of Queensberry; the result is extraordinarily exotic. James Macaulay, in *The Classical Country House in Scotland 1660–1800* (1987), describes it as "like a pink marble palace in the steaming heat of the Indian subcontinent". When it was completed it was set in a bleak landscape; Daniel Defoe describes it in his *A Tour thro' the whole Island of Great Britain* (1724) as being "like a fine picture in a dirty grotto, or like an equestrian statue set up in a barn". However, the hills were soon clothed in trees, an immense formal garden was laid out, and a giant pattern of radiating avenues linked by cross avenues continued into the landscape to the south. A map of the estate by John Rocque (before 1739) shows the castle at the centre of these gardens, which were still in existence at the end of the 18th century when William Gilpin, the pioneer of the picturesque, saw and hated them. By the early 19th century the estate had been neglected by the profligate 4th (and last) Duke of Queensberry. His successor, the 3rd Duke of Buccleuch and Queensberry, took the estate in hand and he and his son, the 4th Duke, restored the gardens, reinstating the formal gardens close to the house, probably under the direction of the head gardener (and notable garden writer) Charles (M'Intosh who started a fashion by using heathers instead of bedding plants for parterres). These gardens were in turn grassed over and have been partly reinstated in recent times; but the planting today has a jolly Victorian flavour. An aerial photograph in Christopher Taylor's *Parks and Gardens of Britain: A Landscape History from the Air* (1998) shows the earthworks and cropmarks of the early Victorian restoration.

Drummond Castle Gardens
see page 374

Duddingston House
Duddingston, Edinburgh OS NT2972
Scottish Inventory

Suave and beautiful mansion designed by Sir William Chambers for the 8th Earl of Abercorn and built in 1763; the brief was to "build a modest but elegant house suitable for a confirmed bachelor". J.C. Loudon's *Encyclopaedia of Gardening* (1822) says that the grounds were laid out by James Robertson and quotes from *Beauties of Scotland*: "[the grounds] show all that money or art can do to adorn a nearly flat surface, through which a small stream of water naturally runs; clumps, groves, canals, lakes, isles, cascades, temples, shrubbery, serpentine walks and spreading lawns." The burn is still there and traces of cascades remain. Good parkland trees survive, in particular beech and oak, some of which date from the 18th century. Much of the original grounds has been lost to coal mining and (since 1894) a golf course.

Dudmaston Hall
nr Quatt, Shropshire OS SO7488
English Heritage Register Grade II
Open regularly (NT) Tel 01746 780866

The house was built towards the end of the 17th century, possibly to the designs of Francis Smith of Warwick, for Sir Thomas Wolryche. In 1777, two years after William Whitmore had inherited the estate, William Emes made proposals for landscaping. This was not carried out but very shortly afterwards William Whitmore's wife, Frances, in conjunction with the gardener, Walter "Planter" Wood, made paths, seats and cascades in the Dingle – enhancing an already picturesque valley to make it even more picturesque. In an account of her mother's gardening activities, Frances Whitmore's daughter says, "the Dingle was a pet of our dear mother's." She also describes "Planter" Wood's friendship with William Shenstone and said that he had "imbibed his notions of taste at Shenstone's Leasowes" (*see page 501*). The Dingle, recently restored by the National Trust, is now probably the most complete surviving Shenstonian garden.

Duff House
nr Banff, Banffshire OS NJ6963 Scottish Inventory Open regularly Tel 01261 818181

Palatial house built from 1735 for William Duff (Baron Braco and later Viscount Macduff and Earl Fife). In the 18th century there was much landscaping activity. By 1767 William Reid reported that he had "near finished the planting with clumps and belts…the riverside walk was formed from the Bridge of Banff to the Bridge of Alva." There was much planting in the park – "fifteen miles in circumference, chiefly laid out by the late Mr White", according to J.C. Loudon in 1804. William Adam built a Temple of Venus on Doune Hill and an Island Temple (or fishing pavilion) on the river. Both these survive, as does a Gothic mausoleum of 1790, but since 1906 the estate has been dismembered, the house neglected and a golf course built in the park.

Dullingham House
Dullingham, Cambridgeshire OS TL6258
English Heritage Register Grade II
Open occasionally for NGS

Early 18th-century house with later alterations. In 1799 Humphry Repton advised Colonel Christopher Jefferson on the grounds and a Red Book was produced. To the north of the house, a bowling green and *claire-voie* with a vista of parkland with scattered trees. Repton laid out a sloping lawn with trees south of the house, a hedge to conceal the road, and views over parkland.

Dulwich Park
Southwark, London OS TQ3373
English Heritage Register Grade II

Public park opened in 1890 on land given by Dulwich College. Much of the park is well wooded, with tree planting along the boundaries and enclosing central lawns. A peripheral drive girdles the park, with paths linking its various parts. In the south-west part of the park, a lake with a wooded island. To its west, a sculpture by Barbara Hepworth, *Two Forms (Divided Circle)* (1970), and to its east an aviary. In the centre of the park, a bowling green, bedding schemes, herbaceous borders, a pavilion and children's playground.

Dunchurch Lodge
Dunchurch, Warwickshire OS SP4871
English Heritage Register Grade II

House built on an older site 1906–7 to the designs of Gilbert Fraser for John Lancaster. Garden designed by Thomas Mawson in 1908. Mawson laid out balustraded terraces south and west of the house, with a flagged walk and flower beds below the house. A rose garden hedged in box leads to a circular Sun Dial Court enclosed in Japanese maples and box hedges, with a "helio-chronometer" on a stone column. At the lower level is a tennis court from which steps, flanked with golden conifers, lead to informal pleasure grounds. Here are lawns, specimen trees and flowering shrubs, a lake and a summerhouse. West of the house, Mawson laid out a group of enclosed gardens designed to provide "snugness in all weathers"; these survive in a simplified form. Mawson also designed a kitchen garden, walled in a purple-brown brick whose colour was thought to harmonise with the foliage and blossom of fruit trees. The house today is a management college.

Duncombe Park
see page 337

Dundas Castle
nr South Queensferry, Edinburgh OS NT1177 Open to groups by appointment Tel 0131 319 2039

Castle built c.1424 for the Dundas family (who had lived here since c.1120), to which was added in 1818 a Tudor Gothic mansion by William Burn. There were renaissance gardens but little survives except for a magnificent tiered fountain and sundial with an inscription saying that it was made for Sir Walter Dundas in 1623; today it stands east of the castle. In the first half of the 18th century George Dundas planted many trees, built walls, and planted a "twist walk" of yews (some of which appear to survive). In 1735 he laid out a bowling green, with four staircases leading to it, a summerhouse in each corner, and ornamented with statues. The pleasure grounds today have mown lawns with some good trees – oak, sweet chestnut, sycamore and wych elm – some of which survive from 18th-century plantings.

Dundonnell House

nr Dundonnell, Ross-shire
OS NH0988 Scottish Inventory
Open occasionally for SGS

Delightful house built in 1767 for Kenneth Mackenzie of Dundonnell. The estate was bought in 1956 by three brothers – Alan, Alastair and Neil Roger. Together they made an excellent new garden. A mid 19th-century walled garden, with its original grid pattern of paths, was divided into compartments with yew and box hedging. A venerable yew, said to be the second oldest in Scotland, is a superb ornament. On another lawn are several specimen trees and, more unusually, specimen bamboos, of which many were planted in the garden. The Rogers brothers loved bonsai, of which they built up a remarkable collection, some of them planted in exquisite containers by Hans Coper or Lucie Rie. Mixed borders full of good plants and edged with box line the walls which are planted with fruit or climbing ornamentals. A Victorian glasshouse is planted with tender climbers such as *Berberidopsis corallina* and *Lapageria rosea* and shrubs. Alan Roger, the last of the brothers, died recently and the estate has been bought by the musical librettist Sir Tim Rice.

Dunglass House

Dunglass, East Lothian OS NT NT7671
Scottish Inventory

House, built on an older site in 1807 to the designs of Richard Crichton for Sir James Hall, gutted by fire in 1947 and demolished. Colin McWilliam, in his *Lothian* volume in "Buildings of Scotland", described the house as "a masterpiece of picturesque classicism". In the pleasure grounds, a hexagonal gazebo of 1718 which used to overlook a bowling green now obliterated by forestry. Formal grounds used to surround the house but these were lost after its demolition. The 15th-century Dunglass Collegiate Church in the grounds was woven into the picturesque landscape planned here 1776–32. Four ornamental bridges cross the Dunglass burn, of which the oldest dates from the 17th century. Woodland formed an

important part of the landscape but very little remains.

Dunham Massey

see page 199

Dunkeld House

nr Dunkeld, Perthshire OS NO0142
Scottish Inventory

The estate, on the banks of the river Tay, was acquired by the Earls of Atholl (later Dukes) in the 17th century, and a house designed by Sir William Bruce was built 1676–84; the present house, on a new site overlooking the river, was built in 1900. Stanley Hill, near the site of the original house, was made c.1754 as a six-tiered terrace. A 19th-century pamphlet, *The Duke of Atholl's Grounds*, describes it as "a beautiful wooded knoll, mounded and terraced in the formal style… there is a battery of small cannon on it for firing salutes." The hill remains, but is derelict. Woodland has very early specimens of larch (*Larix decidua*) planted in 1750; the first at Dunkeld were planted in 1738 – among the earliest in the country. Two 18th-century grottoes by the river: East Grotto, a domed chamber in the river bank, and West Grotto of rustic stone with Gothic arches. 18th-century planned walks on Craig a Barns Hill lead to the 18th-century Lady Charlotte's Cave, said to be a birthday surprise for the wife of the 3rd Duke. An American Garden dating from the mid 19th century in old woodland of beech and oak is planted with azaleas, rhododendrons and kalmia and later plantings of conifers. The Hermitage (*see page 380*) was originally part of the Dunkeld House estate. The house is now the Hilton Dunkeld House Hotel.

Dunloe Castle Gardens

see page 409

Dunrobin Castle Gardens

see page 375

Duns Castle

Duns, Berwickshire OS NT7754
Scottish Inventory Open by appointment
Tel 01361 883211

14th-century house, transformed into a baronial extravaganza by

James Gillespie Graham 1820–23. The Hay family has lived at Duns since the 17th century. Parkland, with a great lime avenue planted 1690–1710 badly damaged in a gale c.1880; trees that were blown down were winched back into position and survive to this day. A few other old trees survive but most of the present planting dates from the late 19th century. William Hay designed a new walled kitchen garden 1802–07, surrounded by shrubberies. Thomas White Junior did a plan for the parkland in 1812 but his work was amended by William Hay who planted clumps and copses of beeches to frame views of the castle.

Dunster Castle

see page 31

Dunvegan Castle

Dunvegan, Isle of Skye OS NG2449
Open regularly Tel 01470 521206

The MacLeods of Dunvegan have been here since the 13th century and part of the defences of the present castle date back to that time. The castle was much altered in around 1500, for Alasdair Crotach ("Hunchbacked Alastair") MacLeod, and since then there have been many further alterations; externally it is now largely 19th-century but still looks every inch a castle, and has a splendid position overlooking Loch Dunvegan. There was much tree planting in the late 19th century – and very many losses in a storm in 1921 – and more coniferous and deciduous planting has been added since. The policies are watered by a stream and there are two spectacular natural cascades. Ornamental planting is almost entirely of the late 20th century. In the water garden there is much excellent planting of *Cardiocrinum giganteum*, ferns, lysichiton, meconopsis, *Rheum palmatum* and rodgersias. The unusual Californian *Clintonia andrewsiana* is also seen here. An old walled garden, probably originally for fruit and vegetables, with a 16th-century sundial, has recently been turned over to ornamental purposes.

Durlston Park

Swanage, Dorset OS SZ 0378
Open regularly

Public park made by George Burt in the 1880s as the setting for Durlston Castle, built c.1890 as a restaurant, taking advantage of its cliff-top position. Below the restaurant Burt built a gigantic Portland stone globe surrounded by massive stone benches inscribed with the points of the compass. Stone plaques of an educational kind give information about geography, time differences, hours of sunshine in different parts of the world and so on. Burt's intentions were not exclusively educational; he erected other plaques which form a kind of running commentary on the beauties of the scene, such as "An iron coast and angry waves/You seem to hear them rise and fall/And roar rock thwarted in their bellowing caves/Above sea 149 ft." The *Sole Official Guide to Swanage* (1919) says Durlston "presents much scenic beauty and, thanks to the late Mr George Burt, it offers also opportunities for literary and moral culture." Below the great globe, at the foot of stone steps, a viewing terrace gives views north-east to Studland promontory and south-west to a lighthouse and the Tilly Whim Caves (now closed because of rock falls), which mark the end of Burt's park. Now in the care of the Swanage Urban District Council, the park is promoted for bird and flower spotting, rather than for Burt's loftier notions of the sublime. Burt also made a rare garden for himself at Purbeck House (*see page 526*)

Dyffryn Gardens

see page 201

Dyrham Park

see page 201

Earlshall

Leuchars, Fife OS NO4621
Open occasionally for SGS

16th-century tower house (oddly renamed Earlshall Castle in very recent times) built for the Bruce family and restored in the 1890s for Robert Mackenzie by Robert Lorimer, who also made the enchanting garden of Arts and

Crafts character. The site – a field of potatoes when Lorimer came – is a rectangle enclosed by 16th- and 17th-century stone walls. Lorimer divided the space into ornamental enclosures: a Pleasance of magnificent old yew topiaries (mature specimens transplanted from a garden in Edinburgh) arranged in a pattern of St Andrews crosses; a croquet lawn and rose terrace; and a four-part kitchen garden and orchard intermingled with ornamental planting. A stone garden house has a gable above a window decorated with stone monkeys and another bears the inscription "Here ye shall see no enemy but winter and rough weather". The garden is Lorimer's masterpiece and one of the best of its kind in the country.

East Lambrook Manor

see page 31

Eastbury

Tarrant Gunville, Dorset OS ST9312
English Heritage Register Grade II*

The remains of Sir John Vanbrugh's largest country house apart from Blenheim and Castle Howard, started in 1718 for George Dodington and continued for his nephew, George Bubb Dodington (later Lord Melcombe). House and gardens were said to have cost £140,000 (£11,480,000 today). Grand formal gardens about the house and in the surrounding parkland by Charles Bridgeman before 1725; the evidence for them survives in mounds and banks on the ground – first noticed by aerial photographers searching for bronze age barrows and later confirmed by archaeologists on the ground (an aerial photograph is shown in Christopher Taylor's *Parks and Gardens of Britain: A Landscape History from the Air* (1998)). Climax of the chief vista was a rectangular amphitheatre with an immense pedimented pillared temple whose ground plan was 50ft by 30ft/15m by 9m. In 1762 the estate passed to the 2nd Lord Temple of Stowe who, failing to sell it or let it, blew it up in 1775, leaving only part of the original entrance courtyard, which is now used as a private house. No

E

garden buildings survive but the archaeological evidence of the site was still in place until the 1960s when a large part of it was destroyed by ploughing.

Eastgrove Cottage Garden
see page 202

Eastnor Castle
see page 203

Easton Lodge
Little Easton, Essex OS TL5924
English Heritage Register Grade II
Open regularly Tel 01371 876979

Ancient estate, originally an Elizabethan hunting lodge, owned by the Maynards since the 16th century. The estate was inherited in 1865 by Frances Evelyn Maynard (when she was three) who in 1881 married Lord Brooke (later 5th Earl of Warwick). In 1902 the Countess of Warwick (known as Daisy) commissioned Harold Peto to design a new garden. It was on a very grand scale; a magnificent domed trellis pergola (one of two flanking a croquet lawn) is illustrated in Ann Hills's and Marcus Binney's *Elysian Gardens* (1979). Articles and spectacular photographs appeared in *Country Life* in 1918 and 1921; it was one of the most talked about gardens of its day. In World War II the house was requisitioned and after the war it was demolished and the estate dismembered. Since 1993 the enterprising owners of part of the old estate, Brian and Diana Creasey, have restored parts of the Peto garden. In 2002 Stansted Airport announced its plan to build a new runway one mile from Easton Lodge.

Easton Neston
Easton Neston, Northamptonshire
OS SP7049 English Heritage Register
Grade II* Open occasionally for NGS

Very beautiful house begun in late 17th century for Sir William Fermor, with possible advice from Christopher Wren, and remodelled in the first years of the 18th century by Nicholas Hawksmoor. Wren made suggestions for the garden as well as the house, commenting on the appropriate height of walls to allow a view of Towcester, and on the design of greenhouses. Sir William Fermor bought the famous collection of classical antiquities, the Arundel Marbles, and distributed them about the garden. They remained here until 1755 when they were given to the University of Oxford and are now in the Ashmolean Museum. In the park are remains of early 18th-century avenues, with some original limes surviving. 20th-century formal gardens on three sides of the house, with large bow-ended pool east of the house. Some of the statues here come from the Stowe sale of 1921. North of the basin, a 17th-century garden building dated 1641.

Easton Park
Easton, Lincolnshire OS SK9327
English Heritage Register Grade II

The house, Easton Hall, first built in the middle ages, was demolished *c.*1948. Photographs in *Country Life* of 1902 show a superb 19th-century formal garden – a sunken garden, terraces, balustrades, urns, ornate bedding schemes and in the distance a magnificent double hump-backed yew hedge continuing the axis to an avenue running away across parkland. The terraces descended to the banks of the river Witham. In Marcus Binney's and Ann Hill's *Elysian Gardens* (1979) one of these photographs is juxtaposed with a desolate picture taken in the late 1970s, after many years of neglect, clearly showing the layout with its beautiful walls and the gazebos built into them, and the shaggy remains of the double yew hedges.

Eaton Hall
Eaton, Cheshire OS SJ4160
English Heritage Register Grade II*

Eaton has been owned by the Grosvenors (now Dukes of Westminster) since the 12th century. The present house is a 19th-century reworking of a 17th-century house and is chiefly the work of Alfred Waterhouse, 1870–72. Badeslade's plan of the estate in 1738 shows the house set at the heart of extensive formal gardens, with avenues extending across the park. But the park was landscaped in the mid 18th century, with much planting south of the house, and the formal gardens removed to reveal vistas framed by the park planting; a tithe map of 1839 shows no traces of avenues or of formal gardens. Serpentine and other pools east of the house were laid out by John Webb 1804–06. In the mid 19th century W.A. Nesfield recreated formal gardens about the house and these, in one form or another, have continued in recent times. A long Broad Walk has at one end Alfred Waterhouse's Parrot House (an Ionic Temple with a domed roof), and at the other his loggia flanked by Roman columns – both of the 1880s. The Italian Garden was redesigned by Edwin Lutyens 1896–98, and again by Detmar Blow in 1911. In the late 20th-century, designs by the Duchess of Westminster and Arabella Lennox–Boyd incorporated statues of 1852 by Raymond Smith and early 19th-century stone and cast-iron balustrading.

Ebberston Hall
Ebberston, North Yorkshire OS SE8983
English Heritage Register Grade II*

A delightful Palladian pavilion designed by Colen Campbell in 1718 for William Thompson. The pavilion was originally linked by a curved wall on each side to smaller pavilions, of which only one remains. The Thompsons' main house was 30 miles away, near Beverley, and Ebberston was thought of as a rural retreat. Behind the main pavilion a great canal was made, flanked by walks and topiary. This was (and is) overlooked by a three-bay loggia at the first-floor level. The canal is stepped, with water flowing over formal cascades, and it fits neatly into a narrow, steep-sided wooded valley. It is not known who the designer was, but the name of Stephen Switzer has been mentioned. Christopher Hussey, in *English Gardens and Landscapes 1700–1750* (1967), considers the garden "to be ranked among the outstanding, and among the first, formal landscape gardens of the 18th century".

Eccleston Square
City of Westminster, London OS TQ2878
English Heritage Register Grade II
Open occasionally for NGS

Eccleston Square was developed by Thomas Cubitt and laid out in 1835. The square is long and rectangular, enclosed in railings backed by mature plantings of trees and shrubs. Since the 1980s an especially active gardens committee has enriched the planting and laid out many small gardens devoted to particular groups of plants, among them camellias, ferns, irises and roses. The garden holds a National Collection of ceanothus of more than 70 species and cultivars.

The Eden Project
see page 32

Edmondsham House
see page 33

Ednaston Manor
Brailsford, Derbyshire OS SK2342
English Heritage Register Grade II

House and garden were designed for W.G. Player by Edwin Lutyens from 1912; interrupted by World War II, they were completed in 1919. Courtyard to the west, with curved brick wall and climbing plants; three openings are centred on avenues of horse chestnuts, the central one being the entrance drive. Herringbone brick terrace to south of house, with a pavilion at each end linked to the house by a brick wall, thus forming an enclosed space with beds of roses and shrubs edged in stone. To the east, a balustraded terrace with steps leading to a lower terrace, with lawns and a yew hedge. Steps lead down to what used to be an orchard, now with specimen trees and shrubs.

Edwardes Square
Kensington and Chelsea, London OS
TQ2489 English Heritage Register Grade II

Developed from 1811 by Louis Léon Changeur, with a large communal garden of 5 acres/2 hectares laid out by Agostino Aglio 1814–20. Garden enclosed by railings, with a peripheral path winding through belt planting of trees and shrubs and secondary paths leading to a central lawn. Excellent mature trees – *Ailanthus altissima*, *Catalpa bignonioides*, cherries, horse chestnuts and sycamores. Greek-style lodge, or "Temple" built in southern part of garden *c.*1820.

Edzell Castle
see page 376

Eglinton Castle
nr Kilwinning, Ayrshire OS NS3242
Scottish Inventory Open regularly

There is not much garden left here but the history of the place is so remarkable that it is a wonderful place to visit and in which to think of the past. The Elintouns, later Eglintons and Earls of Eglinton, first lived here in the 11th century. Disasters struck the family – the castle was burnt down in 1526 and the 4th Earl was murdered in 1586. A new castle was built, which Thomas Pent's survey of 1608 describes as "well planted and beautified with gardens, orchards and parks". Another new house was built in the late 18th century to the designs of John Patterson, who had to sue the 12th Earl for non-payment of his bill. J.C. Loudon's *Encyclopaedia of Gardening* (1822) notes "the trees of the park are large, of picturesque form and much admired. The kitchen garden is one of the best in the country." In 1839 the estate achieved its apotheosis when the 13th Earl staged a Tournament – a revival of a medieval tournament; it cost £40,000 (£1,130,000 today). A 4-acre/1.6-hectare jousting area was laid out on the far side of the Lugton river (a bridge had to be built) and many thousands of visitors – estimates range from 80,000–200,000 – came from all over Britain and the Continent, among them Prince Louis Bonaparte. Two 250ft/75m long temporary saloons – for banqueting and balls – were built and visitors wore costume of the 14th and 15th centuries. It rained unremittingly for the first two days. The family fortunes finally collapsed in 1927. The Eglintons removed the castle roof to avoid paying rates and during World War II the house was used by the arm for gun practice; by the end of the war it was a ruin. In 1978 the remains of the estate were given to Irvine Development Corporation for use as a "public recreational resource". The castle ruins remain, the Tournament Bridge has lost its Gothic parapet, gazebos are derelict, the stable block is a factory and the remains of the formal gardens have been vandalised. Only the old parkland, with good surviving trees, evokes the splendours of the past.

Eltham Palace
see page 132

Elton Hall
Elton, Cambridgeshire OS TL0892
English Heritage Register Grade II*
Open regularly Tel 01832 280468

House of several periods, going back to the late 15th century but of largely 18th- and 19th-century appearance. Terraced gardens and pleasure grounds laid out in the 1890s by Edward Milner with hedges, topiary and knot gardens. Bowling green, terrace, rose garden and fountain pool designed by A.H. Hallam Murray, possibly on the site of the Elizabethan garden. The garden has been well restored in recent years and a Gothic orangery added. Park with the river Nene as its western boundary, with trees planted as perimeter belts and as parkland specimens.

Elvaston Castle Country Park
see page 260

Elvetham Hall
Elvetham, Hampshire OS SU7856
English Heritage Register Grade II

House built c.1859, on the site of a 16th-century house, for the 4th Lord Calthorpe to the designs of S.S. Teulon. Pleasure grounds with balustraded terraces and linking steps. Lawns divided into quadrants, borders and shrubs. There was a deer park by 1350 and an 18th-century landscaped park (the New Park), now partly a golf course, has a lake formed by damming a stream, an avenue and races of intersecting avenues. In 1591 Elvetham was the site of an "entertainment" arranged for Elizabeth I by Lord Hertford after the triumphant defeat of the Armada, vividly described in Roy Strong's *The Renaissance Garden in England* (1979). An emblematic garden was made for the occasion in the park (its site is still visible in aerial photographs), with Elizabeth as "the moon goddess…who rules over the watery empire". A crescent-shaped lake with islands was made; one of the islands had trees like ships' masts, a second had a fort built by Neptune to defend England, and the third a mount 20ft/6m high with spirals of privet symbolising Spain – "Yon ugly monster creeping from the South,/To spoyle these blessed fields of Albion". This dramatic celebration of Elizabeth's great victory ended in "a great firework display in which Neptune's fort vanquished the wicked monster mount".

Elvingstone House
nr Gladsmuir, East Lothian OS NT4674
Scottish Inventory

Neo-Jacobean house built 1837 on an older site to the designs of John Tait. Parkland was planted with good trees after the house was built – chiefly deciduous but later with a few conifers. Sir David Low bought the house in 1944 and bred narcissi, concentrating on pale yellow forms. He also developed 22 acres/9 hectares of plum orchards, underplanting the trees with narcissi. G. Allan Little's *Scotland's Gardens* (1981) describes "One of East Lothian's loveliest sights… the near-naked boughs hung with pure white blossom and the ground beneath carpeted with pale yellow blooms nodding in the April wind." Sir David also added to the parkland trees and used the old walled garden as a narcissus nursery, growing many different fruit trees against the walls. Today it has box hedges and a herbaceous border forming its chief axis. In the 1990s a science park was built on the estate; an 18th-century dovecote survives.

Emmanuel College (Cambridge)
see page 295

Embley Park
East Wellow, Hampshire OS SU3220
English Heritage Register Grade II

Late 19th-century neo-Elizabethan house on an older site (in the 19th century the home of Florence Nightingale's family), now a school. Plantings of trees and shrubs close to the house date from the late 18th and early 19th centuries, with streams, pools and glades. Early 20th-century rock and water garden. Woodland walk to Southampton Water and the New Forest. American Garden and grotto (later incorporated into a cottage) now in separate ownership.

Emmetts Garden
see page 134

Emo Court Garden
see page 410

Encombe
Corfe Castle, Dorset OS SY94 78
English Heritage Register Grade II*
Open occasionally for charity

The Purbeck stone house was started in about 1734 for John Pitt, who possibly designed it himself. John Scott bought the estate in 1808 and his descendants lived here until 2002. Landscaped in the mid 18th century, with lakes made or reshaped from earlier pools at this time. South of the house, at the end of a lake, a Brobdingnagian arch of huge rocks, built before 1780, from which there were originally views down to the sea. Half a mile above the house to the north, an obelisk erected in 1835 in honour of Lord Stowell.

Endsleigh House
see page 34

Englefield House
Englefield, Berkshire OS SU6271
English Heritage Register Grade II
Open regularly Tel 01189 302221

Englefields lived here from the 9th century but were dispossessed by Queen Elizabeth c.1560. The Paulet family (Marquesses of Winchester) acquired it in 1635 and it passed by marriage to the Benyon family in the 18th century, who still live here. The present house is 16th-century with 19th-century alterations. Formal terraced gardens on each side of the house, dating from the 1850s and probably designed by Richard Armstrong. Park surrounding house, part of which was a deer park in c.1600 and still contains deer. To its east, a long irregular lake with several islands; a series of formal canals in the mid 18th century, linked to the house by an avenue, this was made informal, probably in the 1770s. The landscape designer Richard Woods had been employed at about this time but it seems that no designs of his were carried out.

Enville Hall
Enville, Staffordshire OS SO8286
English Heritage Register Grade II*

Late 18th-century house, incorporating much older parts, built for the Grey family (Earls of Warrington). Mid 16th-century deer park, developed in the mid 18th century as a landscape park with the help of William Shenstone, survives in a fairly disheveled state. South-west of the house, on high grazing land, is the Gothick mid 18th-century Shepherd's Lodge; now ruinous, it had in its heyday a lounging room and an observatory and commanded fine views over the hilly and varied terrain. Closer to the house, and attributed to Shenstone, is a series of pools connected by cascades. Running north from a twelve-sided brick bastion is a hornbeam tunnel leading to a ruinous 18th-century grotto. A grove of yews conceals Shenstone's Chapel, built before Shenstone's death in 1763. South of the house, Temple Pool had in 1747 a remarkably early Chinoiserie temple but it was demolished in 1777. There are many other buildings – for example, a pagoda, a hermitage, a Gothic boathouse, a spectacular mid 19th-century fountain pool – all in more or less ruinous or vestigial condition. In its heyday this must have been an enchanting place. It certainly became very popular with visitors, so that by the 1770s a carriage drive was laid out to accommodate them. Essex Wood, south-west of the house, has signs of earlier rides and avenues and some fine mature trees.

Enys
Mylor Bridge, Cornwall OS SW7936
English Heritage Register Grade II

The Enys estate belonged to the Enys family from the middle ages until the death of Miss Elizabeth Enys in the late 20th century. The garden was the first in Cornwall to be referred to in print – in the 1709 edition of Camden's *Magna Britannia*. An engraving in Borlase's *Natural History of Cornwall* (1758) shows the house flanked by groves of trees, with alignments of trees running across the land and formal gardens with a pair of ogee-roofed pavilions extending to one side of the house. This looks like an old-fashioned garden of its date, of the sort that a Cornish squire might prefer. In the 19th century J.D. Enys introduced many new plants, including those collected on his travels in Patagonia and New Zealand. Among these was the Chatham Island forget-me-not (*Myosotidium hortensia*), introduced to England in 1859. By the time J.D. Enys published his *Trees and Shrubs and Plants growing at Enys* in 1909, the garden had a notable plant collection with over 1,000 species and cultivars.

Erddig
see page 204

Eridge Park
Frant, East Sussex OS TQ5635
English Heritage Register Grade II*

House built 1938–39 to the designs of John Denman. Ancient park mentioned in the Domesday Book and confiscated by William the Conqueror; in 1344 it was described as a "chase containing 600 acres"; by 1400 it was stocked with deer. In the mid to late 16th century the Eridge estate, owned by the Nevill family (which still owns it), became a centre of the Wealden iron industry. South of the house, a terrace with an avenue of tulip trees dates from the early 18th century. In the late 18th century the 2nd Earl of Abergavenny made Eridge his home, built a new house (which no longer exists) and laid out a landscape park after 1792 as a

E

setting for the house. The park is the most important feature. Its southern part, the Old Park, was once the medieval deer park and there are scattered oaks from that time. The essential planting of the late 18th-century New Park – belts, copses and woodland in pasture – survives, and across the middle of the park there are a series of lakes and ponds in a valley. A stream flows south to north, linking ponds, some of which were associated with 16th-century iron founding. A horse chestnut walk, planted *c.*1870 to link the house with the picturesque Eldridge Rocks, survives. In Saxonbury Wood, in the southernmost part of the park, the five-storey Saxonbury Tower was built in 1828 as part of Lord Abergavenny's picturesque landscape. Some of the farm buildings were Gothicised to add to the picturesque scene.

Eton College
Eton, Berkshire OS SU9677
English Heritage Register Grade II

School founded in 1440, with several buildings from the 15th century surviving. Illustrations in Loggan's *Cantabrigia Illustrata* (1690) show that there were gardens at Eton before the end of the 17th century. The Fellows' Garden existed in the 17th century, much smaller than it is today. The Headmaster's Garden may at that time have been at least partly a kitchen garden – for it had a dovecote and Loggan shows only part of it laid out ornamentally, in a geometric pattern. By the late 19th century the Fellows' Garden had assumed its present appearance, with scattered plantings of trees and a perimeter walk. Loggan shows the Provost's Garden laid out in a cruciform pattern; today it has a lawn with borders about its edge, and at the centre formal beds enclosed in paving edged with box surround a central sundial. Among trees and shrubs is a large holm oak. King Prajadhipok of Siam's Garden next to it was laid out in 1929 with raised borders about two lawns and a statue of Perseus in an alcove. Luxmoore's Garden on an island in the Thames was laid out

by a housemaster, H.E. Luxmoore, in the late 19th century in Robinsonian style with winding paths and informal groups of trees and shrubs.

Euston Hall
see page 300

Exbury Gardens
see page 82

University of Exeter
see page 35

Exton Hall
Exton, Rutland OS SK9211
English Heritage Register Grade II

19th-century remodelling of an earlier house, with the ruins of the early 17th-century old hall remaining to the south. South of the house, a terrace and formal lawns which in the 19th century had parterres. To the east, a balustraded wall overlooks the pool garden; south-east of this, more pools adapted from formal 17th-century canals lie among a shrubbery and specimen trees. To the west of the house, an octagonal 18th-century dovecote with an ogee roof, serving as an eyecatcher. In the park to the east, a Y-shaped lake overlooked at the north by Fort Henry House, converted from three Gothick cottages. Fort Henry itself is a very decorative summerhouse designed by William Legg with crenellated parapet and Gothick details (1785–88). To the west, in woodland, the surviving part of an arcaded Bark Temple (1846). There had been a deer park at Exton by 1185, possibly on the site of the existing Tunneley Wood to the west of the lake.

Eythrope Park
Waddesdon, Buckinghamshire OS SP7613
English Heritage Register Grade II

Estate, going back to the 15th century, adjacent to Waddesdon Manor (*see page 110*), acquired by Alice de Rothschild in 1875 shortly before her brother Ferdinand bought Waddesdon. An 18th-century house had been demolished in 1810 and Miss Alice built The Pavilion, designed by George Devey and much enlarged in 1935 by James de

Rothschild. House surrounded by pleasure grounds – a parterre, a pond, and box-edged beds for seasonal bedding – with open views eastwards across a lawn with trees to the lake. A walk leads south to the river and towards the lake where there is a mid 18th-century grotto of tufa with quartz ornament and artificial stalactites. At the head of the lake, a late 19th-century cascade. Miss Alice had a garden of 60 acres/24 hectares with an Italian Garden, a Dutch Garden, a Mexican Garden of succulents and a Rose Garden with over 300 varieties. The framework of lawn, specimen trees, belts of trees and shrubs remains, although the detailing is now of a simpler kind. Fine kitchen garden with 19th-century glasshouses.

Fairfield
Stogursey, Somerset OS ST1843
English Heritage Register Grade II
Open occasionally for NGS

Ancient house dating from the 12th century but now essentially late 16th century, in a fine position close to the Quantocks. Late 18th-century park for which Sir John Acland had the road diverted, building two lodges on the new road. A garden wall survives from this period, dated 1784. In the early 18th century there had been a formal canal in front of the house but an engraving of 1791 shows the results of Sir John Acland's activities – the house set in parkland, with no sign of formal gardens, and wooded hills sweeping up behind it. A 20th-century woodland garden is rich in bulbs and shrubs.

The Fairhaven Woodland and Water Garden
see page 301

Fairmile Hospital
nr Cholsey, Oxfordshire OS SU5985
English Heritage Register Grade II

Psychiatric hospital, later known as Moulsford Hospital and now Fairmile Hospital, designed by C.H. Howell, with building starting in 1868. In the following year a nurseryman, Joseph Harding of Wallingford, was

commissioned to plant hedges and trees on the boundary, and in 1871 Robert Marnock was commissioned to lay out the grounds for which he was paid £30 (£13,000 today); the following year, the Annual Report noted "the planting of trees and shrubs in the grounds in front of the Asylum, in continuation of Mr Marnock's plan". Gardening, and working on the asylum's farm, were encouraged among the patients, fifty of whom were thus employed in 1871. Today much of the 19th-century planting is mature and a modern flower garden is used as a therapeutic garden. A 19th-century kitchen garden is now a sports field.

Falinge Park
Rochdale, Greater Manchester OS SD8914
English Heritage Register Grade II
Open regularly

Public park based on a private estate and designed by Thomas Mawson, opened to the public 1906. In the southern part of the park, large expanse of lawn and new bandstand (2000). At the centre of the park, the ruins of 18th-century Falinge Hall with, to its east, Mawson's sunken Sun Garden enclosed in brick walls and with lawns and beds for seasonal bedding schemes. To the north of the park, a small lake and a stream connecting it to a rock garden. Informal plantings of trees and shrubs.

Falkland Palace
see page 377

Fanhams Hall
nr Ware, Hertfordshire OS TL3715
English Heritage Register Grade II

Early 18th-century house rebuilt in Jacobean style 1898–1901 by W. Wood Bethell who also designed formal gardens to the south-west and north-west of the house: a lawn, a trapezoidal sunken garden with yew hedges, a terrace with a geometric pattern of borders, a parterre and a croquet lawn and putting green. North-west of the parterre, past lawns with specimen trees, a Japanese garden laid out *c.*1901–5 by Professor Suzuki to the designs of Mr Inaka. A curving wisteria-

draped pergola leads to a rock-strewn lawn and a pool crossed by bridges. A Japanese house overlooks the northern end of the pool, close to a point where a second pool begins. This is crossed by a zigzag bridge of grey granite and overlooked by another building, a Shinto shrine. West of the Japanese house, a lake with a wooden green bridge, and on the northern side, an Austrian house among mature trees. The pools are richly planted with many mature Japanese maples.

Farnham Park
Farnham, Surrey OS SU8448
English Heritage Register Grade II
Open regularly (EH) Tel 01252 713393

Farnham Castle was begun in 1138 for Bishop Henry de Blois, a grandson of William the Conqueror. Partly demolished in the Civil War, it was restored from 1662 by Bishop Thorold. The see of Farnham was transferred to Guildford in 1927 and the castle now belongs to the Church Commissioners. In the 19th century Bishop Sumner made ornamental walks about the ramparts, edged with exotic flowers and climbers, and the outer moat was planted with trees. The 14th-century deer park was laid out as a landscape park under Bishop North in the late 18th and early 19th centuries. An avenue of elms focused on the castle was planted by 1762 and was replaced with limes and beeches in the mid 20th century. Today there is a golf course in the park but roe deer still graze here.

Farnborough Hall
see page 261

Faulkbourne Hall
Faulkbourne, Essex OS TL8016
English Heritage Register Grade II

15th-century brick house for Sir John Montgomery, incorporating parts of an earlier house. Traces of an early garden remain, including part of a 16th-century garden wall. At the end of the 19th century Christopher Parker made new gardens. Lawns and path on north and east side of house are flanked by the moat, and related pools are treated as water gardens

mixed borders by the north wall of house, and a lawn overlooked by a grass terrace. Walled garden to the north, with central borders backed by fruit and vegetables.

Fawley Court *and* Temple Island

Fawley, Buckinghamshire OS SU7684
English Heritage Register Grade II*
Open regularly Tel 01491 57491

Late 17th-century house, for Sir William Freeman, on an older site, with the Thames flowing through the grounds. In 1707 his nephew, John Freeman, succeeded, and in the 1730s created pleasure grounds, possibly with the advice of Edmund Waller (of Hall Barn, *see page 484*) and John Aislabie (Waller's stepfather, of Studley Royal, *see page 352*). South-east of the house, the wooded pleasure grounds survive from John Freeman's garden. A flint temple, with Gothic façade and grotto behind, decorated with pebbles and knucklebones, had been built before 1732 to house some of the Arundel marbles which Freeman had bought jointly with Waller in 1720. This is one of the earliest Gothic garden buildings. John Freeman's son, Sambrooke, succeeded in 1752 and continued to develop the garden, calling in Capability Brown before 1771 when Mrs Lybbe Powys described the grounds as "laid out by Mr. Brown with his usual taste", and containing a menagerie and a "most elegant dairy". East of the Gothic temple a covered bridge of flint and stucco dates from *c.*1731. Of the same date, north-west of the house, a flint-faced dairy with Norman doorway. In the woodland to the south, mid 18th-century ornaments – an urn, a pedestal with lions' heads and a sundial. In the park, some fine old London planes, some of which date from the 18th century. 300yds/300m north-east of the house, a fishing temple with pale stucco on Temple Island in the Thames was designed by James Wyatt in 1771 to serve as an eyecatcher from the house. The interior, with an 18th-century statue of a Bacchante, has the earliest known Etruscan decorative theme in England, inspired by Wedgwood's Etruscan Ware.

Fawsley Hall

Fawsley, Northamptonshire OS SP5656
English Heritage Register Grade II*

Early 16th-century house for Richard Knightley, with many later alterations; abandoned after 1913, it became a warehouse and, after restoration, a hotel in 1998. Ancient park, going back to the 13th century, still preserves its 18th-century appearance. Two triangular lakes, and other ponds, and the remains of 18th-century avenues and rides with mature parkland trees. Mid 18th-century kitchen garden with original brick walls. Horace Walpole came here in 1763 and noted "the ground Brown is laying out and making a large piece of water". If Capability Brown did work here, nothing is known of the results and no plan is known to survive.

Felbrigg Hall

see page 301

Fenton House

see page 134

Ferney Hall

nr Onibury, Shropshire OS SO4377
English Heritage Register Grade II

18th-century house rebuilt in 1875, after a fire, by S. Pountney Smith. 18th-century parkland. Samuel Peckham Phipps consulted Humphry Repton (Red Book, 1789), and, since Ferney Hall is very close to Richard Payne Knight's Downton Castle (*see page 469*), in similarly picturesque countryside, Repton felt he ought to visit Payne Knight "who has given such consummate proof of good taste in the improvement of his own place…one of the most beautiful and romantic valleys that the imagination can conceive." Payne Knight met Repton and scrutinised his plans for Ferney, which he much disliked. Payne Knight had little time for professional landscape improvers and saw that Phipps "only employed an improver, to be like the rest of the world, and have his grounds laid out in the newest fashion". Phipps, however, died in 1790 and it seems unlikely that work by Repton was carried out, though the English Heritage Register suggests that "It is probable that Repton was responsible for creating or enlarging the series of ponds along Ferney Hall Dingle, and suggesting woodland walks in this region."

Fernhill Gardens

Sandyford, County Dublin,
Republic of Ireland Open regularly
Tel (00353) 1 295 6000

In a marvellous position, with views over Dublin Bay, Fernhill is a garden of special charm and interest. The house dates from the 18th century but the garden is largely the creation of the Darley family from 1860 onwards. Mr Justice Darley laid out the Broad Walk, a gravel path which opens with a beautiful sweet chestnut and is shaded by a progression of Wellingtonias which pierce old woodland of beech and oak. A curious old feature is the "laurel lawn", a great expanse of low-growing clipped cherry laurel (*Prunus laurocerasus*) which forms a sheet of glistening green among old beeches. The woods have good ferns and many flowering shrubs, among them outstanding species rhododendrons. On the far side of the house are a rockery and stream garden; here, too, is the original 18th-century garden, with fruit and vegetables growing alongside ornamental plants. The estate was bought in 1934 by Joseph Walker and the Walker family have maintained and enriched the garden. Susan Walker, the present owner, has built up a splendid collection of primulas.

Ffynone

nr Boncath, Pembrokeshire
Cadw/ICOMOS Register Grade I

A house, on an old estate, was built in the 1790s for John Colby to the designs of John Nash, and altered 1902–7 for J.V. Colby by Francis Inigo Thomas. Inigo Thomas also designed an extraordinarily elaborate Italianate terraced garden; his beautiful drawing for it is illustrated in David Ottewill's *The Edwardian Garden* (1989). In the event, only the upper terrace was completed, with a five-bay belvedere, balustrading and a semicircular exedra at each end – one with a lily pool and stepping stones, the other with a bronze bust of Lloyd George (by Kathleen Scott, *c.*1930). The entrance drive passes through woodland and is flanked with plantings of rhododendrons and other flowering shrubs. Some very old yews survive in the woods. There had been much tree planting in the late 18th century; in 1796 60,000 trees were sent from a Norwich nurseryman, John Mackie, including "Larch Fir, Beech, English Elms and Scotch Fir".

Fillingham Castle

Fillingham, Lincolnshire OS SK9586
English Heritage Register Grade II

Gothic castle built for Sir Christopher Wray *c.*1760–*c.*1770, possibly designed by John Carr of York. 18th-century landscape park and various Gothic or Gothicised buildings on the boundaries – Ermine Lodge, at the end of an avenue, with crenellated walls running along the road, and other gateways.

Fingask Castle

nr Rait, Perthshire OS NO2227 Scottish
Inventory Open occasionally for SGS

Castle built *c.*1592, much altered *c.*1674, with 19th-century additions. Owned since 1642 by the Threipland family who still live here. A splendid site on the edge of the ravine of the Craig burn and with views of the river Tay and the Sidlaw hills. Remarkable grass terraces by the castle probably date from 1672–89. Topiary garden laid out 1850–82 with corkscrews, dumb waiters and obelisks of box, holly and yew surviving but misshaped. Mid 19th-century statuary with such figures as "Tam O'Shanter" and "Willie brewed a Peck o' Maut". Bank leading down to the burn with yews of the 17th century or earlier. 17th-century woodland with much planting in late 18th century, of which many deciduous trees remain. A sundial in the garden, dated 1562, came from Holyrood Palace (*see page 492*) and is one of the oldest in Europe.

Finlaystone House

Langbank, Renfrewshire OS NS3673
Scottish Inventory Open regularly
Tel 01475 540505

The estate, close to the banks of the river Clyde, goes back to the 14th century when it was owned by Sir John de Canyelstoun. It passed by descent (sometimes through the female line) until it was sold in 1882 to George Kidston, from whom it descended to the Macmillan family who own it today. The present house is in part 14th-century but was altered in the 18th century and comprehensively rebuilt in 1900 for George Kidston to the designs of Sir George Burnet, a Glasgow architect. The garden history at Finlaystone starts in the 18th century when rides were laid out through woodland – a lime avenue survives from this time. Apart from that, the gardens are largely 20th-century. Formal terraced gardens, with views of the Clyde, were laid out when the new house was built. A rose garden has a battlemented yew hedge and a herbaceous border was laid out in 1939 by Marion Macmillan. 140 acres/56 hectares of woodland and areas of informal garden, including a bog garden, take advantage of the waters of the Finlaystone burn.

Finsbury Circus

City of London, London OS TQ3281 English
Heritage Register Grade II Open regularly

Laid out 1815 by William Montague, following an earlier plan, of 1802, of George Dance. None of the original houses remains (they have been succeeded by largely 20th-century office blocks) but the oval garden at the centre preserves its perimeter walk, serpentine paths, lawns, some of its 19th-century plane trees, and beds of shrubs. There is a bowling green at the centre of the garden and a drinking fountain housed in an ornamental pavilion with witch's hat roof and Gothic detailing (1902, John Whitehead & Son).

Finsbury Park

Haringey, London OS TQ3187 English
Heritage Register Grade II Open regularly

Public park designed by Alexander McKenzie and opened

F

1869. Enclosed in a perimeter belt of trees and shrubs, the main body of the park is open grass with scattered mature trees. At its centre the banks of a boating lake are planted with alder and willows. The New River curves across the north-east part. Much of the original detail has gone, in particular the Hornsey Wood Tea House which stood at the highest point of the park. Of the American Garden, little survives except for a few rhododendrons.

Firle Place

West Firle, East Sussex OS TQ4707
English Heritage Register Grade II
Open regularly Tel 01273 858307

Tudor house for Sir John Gage, much altered in the 18th century. Formal terraces along the north-west and north-east sides of the house; on the north-west side they rise through four levels to link house to park. South-east of house, a lawn and balustraded wall with a flight of steps to an early 18th-century thatched summerhouse. Further to the south-east, turf terraces, shown on a map of 1775 but probably much earlier. Much new planting in the park in the 1990s after storm damage and Dutch elm disease. Tree belts on western and northern boundaries. In the centre of the park to the north, a series of ponds linked by weirs, largely dating from no later than the mid 18th century.

Fishbourne Roman Palace Garden

see page 135

Flaxley Abbey

Flaxley, Gloucestershire OS SO6915
English Heritage Register Grade II

Remains of a 12th-century Cistercian abbey, with alterations in 16th, 17th and 18th centuries. There was a deer park here in the middle ages. A Kip engraving of 1712 shows walled gardens and a parterre. Late 18th- to early 19th-century park designed to open views to the parish church of St Mary. New formal garden by Oliver Messel in the 1960s.

Flete

Holbeton, Devon OS SX6251
English Heritage Grade II Open regularly
Tel 01752 830308

16th-century house built for the Hele family, radically transformed by Norman Shaw 1878–85 for Henry Bingham Mildmay of Baring's Bank. Water garden designed in 1925 by Russell Page, to which he refers in his *Education of a Gardener* (1962): "At this time I was also working in Devonshire at a great house which lay at the head of an estuary thrusting down between hanging oakwoods to the sea…My problem here was rather special. I had to make a rocky stream and a garden which would come into flower only in autumn. This limited my choice…but the hunt for plants was fascinating." Garden of architectural character laid out for Lady Mildmay in the 1930s. Many excellent trees and shrubs – including several tender species.

Flintham Hall

Flintham, Nottinghamshire OS SK7346
English Heritage Register Grade II

House of medieval origins, rebuilt in 1798 and with 19th-century alterations. Remarkable conservatory built in 1853 to the designs of T.C. Hine for T.B. Thoroton Hildyard; built of stone, it has a cast-iron roof 30ft/9m high in the form of a barrel vault and is connected with the house by a door which opens onto a balcony. Spring Garden, to the south-west of the house, with fine trees underplanted with spring bulbs. 18th-century landscape park with a lake and islands. 18th-century walled garden with fruit trees, ornamental shrubs and excellent borders.

Flitwick Manor

Flitwick, Bedfordshire OS TL0234
English Heritage Register Grade II

17th-century house, altered in the 18th century for the Brooks family. South-west of the house is an 18th-century grotto/bridge ("a nice wide grass bridge crossing nothing", as Barbara Jones described it in *Follies & Grottoes* (1974), built of clinker and brick with a pebble-decorated interior.

18th-century lime avenue approach drive. Area north of the present estate, now built over, had in the early 19th century walks with rustic seats, and buildings with a *ferme ornée* at the centre. Late 18th-century park, and arboretum of 1819 planted by John Thomas Brooks. The house is now a hotel.

Floors Castle

nr Kelso, Roxburghshire OS NT7134 Scottish
Inventory Open regularly Tel 01573 223333

Ancient estate of the Ker family (later Earls and Dukes of Roxburghe). House designed by William Adam and begun in 1721 for the 1st Duke but transformed 1837–43 by William Henry Playfair into a gigantic neo-Jacobean mansion. It has a very beautiful position, in flat country but with lovely views across parkland to the winding river Tweed (in exactly the position that Capability Brown would have chosen had he designed the landscape). In the 18th century this parkland was divided into fields and is now sparsely planted, with clumps of trees framing the house. In the early 18th century a pattern of avenues, in which William Adam must have had a hand, was focused on the house, and parts of the alignments of oaks and sweet chestnuts of this period remain. A 4-acre/1.6-hectare walled kitchen garden was built 1857–60 – fine 19th-century glasshouses remain (built by R. and A. Stirling of Galashiels), and there are beds of fruit and vegetables, and grand modern herbaceous borders. In the outer walled garden, a new parterre was laid out to celebrate the Millennium.

Florence Court

see page 411

Folly Farm

see page 83

Fonthill

Fonthill Gifford, Wiltshire OS ST9131
English Heritage Register Grade II*

Ancient estate bought by Alderman William Beckford c.1736, who modified the existing house, which was destroyed by fire in 1755 and replaced by a new

mansion, Fonthill Splendens. None of this now remains. From 1796, Alderman Beckford's son, William Beckford, started building a new house, which became Fonthill Abbey, at a little distance from Fonthill Splendens, to the designs of James Wyatt. Its main tower collapsed in 1825 and most of the rest of the building was demolished. A further house, also called Fonthill Abbey, on a different site, was built 1846–52 for the Marquess of Westminster to the designs of William Burn, but demolished in 1955. Alderman Beckford started landscaping his grounds c.1740, enlarging fishponds into a lake with a boathouse (which still exists) and building a bridge reached via a causeway with two large stone vases. He also built Trinity Church at Fonthill Gifford in 1748 (now replaced), to form part of his landscape. From c.1793 the younger William Beckford took over the landscape, and was probably responsible for building caves and grottoes on the banks of the lake. These grottoes, ornamented by Josiah Lane c.1794, still stand, in the words of Christopher Thacker, "battered, stupendous and superb". Starting in 1793, Beckford walled in 1,976 acres/800 hectares of land – only parts of the wall remain. He also planted "above a million of Trees" in 1796, and made an "American Plantation" north-east of the lake with some of the newly introduced North American trees. Trees survive in this area but virtually all are post-Beckford. Of his glasshouses, rosarium, thornery and herb garden nothing remains at all.

Foots Cray Place

Bexley, London OS TQ4772
English Heritage Register Grade II

A complicated site consisting of two mid 18th-century landscape parks which were linked together in a single estate in the early 19th century, than redivided in the 1890s. In 1822 Nicholas Vansittart bought the estate with a house called Foots Cray Place, modelled on Palladio's Villa Rotonda and built c.1756 for Bourchier Cleeve, possibly to the designs of Isaac Ware. Eleven years later, he bought

the adjoining estate of North Cray Place with its Capability Brown park. North Cray Place had been owned at the end of the 18th century by Thomas Coventry, and in 1781 Brown was paid £1,300 (£77,688 today) to advise. He had widened the river Cray to form a long thin lake across the middle of the park, with a dam, weir and five-arched bridge at its northern end. Some parkland trees survive in the surrounding meadows and may date from this time. In the late 1890s the two estates were divided once again. In 1912 Samuel Waring (of the firm Waring & Gillow) bought Foots Cray Place and most of the land, and consulted Thomas Mawson about the gardens. However, the designs were never fully implemented and only a flight of terraces to the south-east of the site of the house survives. In 1946 Foots Cray Place became a museum but was destroyed by fire in 1950; and the house at North Cray Place was demolished in 1962.

The Forbury Garden

Reading, Berkshire OS SU7173 English
Heritage Register Grade II Open regularly

19th-century public garden on the site of the former precincts of Reading Abbey. The abbey was founded in 1121 but the site has been in use at least since 870 when a Viking encampment was here. The garden was formed of two parts, the first (designed by George Clacy) opening in 1856 and the second, separated by a wall, in 1861; they were united in 1873. The eastern part is dominated by Forbury Hill, planted with trees and surmounted by a flat platform from which there are views over the garden. A 19th-century rose garden survives east of the hill. A main walk, flanked with lawns and bedding schemes, encircles a fountain pool and ends, at the north-east corner of the park, with an alcove incorporating fragments of the 12th-century abbey. The western part of the park is chiefly lawn, with beds for bedding schemes and a cast-iron bandstand of 1896. A memorial to the Battle of Maiwand (1880), designed by George Simmonds and erected in 1886, has a giant cast-iron lion on a tall stone plinth. Barbara Jones

Follies & Grottoes (1974) calls it "a fine big snarling lion with tail at half-lash".

Forcett Hall

Forcett, North Yorkshire OS NZ1712
English Heritage Register Grade II

House designed by Daniel Garrett and built *c.*1740, a remodelling of a Jacobean house. A painting of *c.*1770 in John Harris's *The Artist and the Country House* (1979) shows a lake south-west of the house with a grotto, behind which is a mount capped with a rotunda. All this survives, except the rotunda, and it is possible that the grotto was designed by Thomas Wright. Wright may also have designed the park, whose boundary is marked by tree belts and which contains the earthworks of an Iron Age *oppidum* – an ancient feature that would have appealed to Wright.

Forde Abbey

see page 35

Forty Hall

Enfield, London OS TQ3398 English Heritage Register Grade II Open regularly

This was the site of Elsynge Palace, an older house acquired in 1492 by Sir Thomas Lovell; it became a royal palace *c.*1540 and Henry VIII's children were brought up here. Adjacent to Royal Enfield Chase, a further 375 acres/152 hectares were imparked at this time. The palace was surrounded by "Court yardes Gardens Orchards and Courtyard with the field adjoining called the Walks". Forty Hall was built in 1629 for Sir Nicholas Rainton and the palace demolished after 1656, with the old gardens probably destroyed at the same time. Pleasure grounds include features from the 18th century: an irregular pool (described in a 1773 sale catalogue as "a fine sheet of water"), a mound formed of the lake's spoil, and a splendid cedar of Lebanon, also mentioned in the sale catalogue. The park dates back to the early 16th century and has various earthworks, possibly the remains of the palace's water gardens. The estate was bought from the last private owner, Derek Parker Bowles, by Enfield Urban District Council in 1951; Forty Hall is now a museum and the grounds a public park.

Fota Arboretum

see page 412

Foxley

Yazor, Herefordshire OS SO4146
English Heritage Register Grade II

18th-century house, demolished in 1948. The home of the picturesque landscapist and theorist Sir Uvedale Price who put his ideas into practice here after 1757. Wanting a landscape of picturesque character, he removed formal gardens about the house and turned his attention to the woodland in the park. Here he made rides and wooded walks "diversified with different prospects". The woods – of ash, beech, sweet chestnuts and larches – were planted for beauty and also for profit. Some of the trees survive, as do the routes of walks and rides. The Ragged Castle, built *c.*1743, is a castellated stone building in the south-east of the park.

Frampton Court

Frampton-on-Severn, Gloucestershire OS SO7507 English Heritage Register Grade I Open by appointment Tel 01452 740267

House built in the 1730s for Richard Clutterbuck who married Mary Clifford, the heiress of the estate; Cliffords live here still. Formal water garden made shortly after the house was built, with, at the head of a canal, one of the most beautiful of all garden buildings – a Rococo Gothic orangery, designed by William Halfpenny in the 1740s with two protruding bays, ogee curves to the windows, crockets wherever possible, elaborate tracery glazing bars and the whole crowned by an octagonal lantern, all worked in golden Bath stone. There are pretty flower borders at Frampton, and good trees, but the orangery is in a class of its own.

Franks Hall

Horton Kirby, Kent OS TQ5567
English Heritage Register Grade II

House built on an older site in 1591 for Lancelot Bathurst. 19th-century gardens reflecting the 16th- and 17th-century layout. Four brick gateways, now free-standing, survive from the old garden, but the original walls have gone. North-west of the house, a square lawn with specimen trees bounded on three sides by a raised walk. A pair of ornamental brick piers mark the start of a 19th-century lime avenue. To its west, a paddock with specimen trees and woodland walk. Further west, a small garden with Italian cypresses. A stone niche with rockwork formerly contained a statue. Knot garden of box to south-west of house.

Friar Park

Henley-on-Thames, Oxfordshire SU7582
English Heritage Register Grade II

The estate of Frank Crisp who built a mansion here in the late 1880s and made an elaborate garden, possibly with advice from H.E. Milner. The house became a convent in the 1950s but is now once again a private house. Crisp was famous for an extraordinary rock garden, built from 1896 by James Backhouse using 23,000 tons of rock and including a (fairly) small version of the Matterhorn. It contained about 4,000 alpine plants (Reginald Farrer, a serious Alpinist was scornful: "the very rich are out to purchase the glories of the Alps at so much a yard") and, according to Lady Ottoline Morrell who visited it in about 1905, had "elaborate caves and underground lakes, lit up with electricity and festooned with artificial grapes, spiders, and other monsters". The rock garden, probably the largest ever made in England, survives, as do a topiary garden modelled on the maze at Versailles, an Elizabethan herb garden, a Japanese garden and lakes.

Friarwood Valley Gardens

Pontefract, West Yorkshire OS SE4521
English Heritage Register Grade II
Open regularly

Mid 20th-century public park designed by R.W. Grubb on land on or near the site of the garden of a 13th-century Dominican friary. The land had in recent times been used for private gardens and an orchard but is today an informal park, designed chiefly for walking and sitting rather than playing games – although there is a bowling green. Old fruit trees have been retained from its past, and many other flowering trees and shrubs added.

Frogmore Gardens

Windsor, Berkshire OS SU9776
English Heritage Register Grade I
Open occasionally Tel 020 73212233

Estate within Windsor Home Park, owned by the Crown since *c.*1550 and subsequently tenanted, at first to private individuals and latterly to members of the royal family. Frogmore House was built for Thomas May in 1684 to the designs of his uncle, Hugh May, the royal architect, and remodelled for Queen Charlotte by James Wyatt after 1792. Queen Charlotte first consulted Mr Alderson, a clergyman, "a Yorkshire gentleman" and friend of the poet and gardener William Mason. Plants began to flow in – in January 1792, 200 birch, 100 laburnums and 600 sweet chestnuts – and 1791–1815 the Queen spent £24,000 (£783,444 today) on the gardens. Major William Price, brother of the picturesque landscaper Uvedale Price, was chiefly responsible for laying out the grounds, and he turned a formal canal into a serpentine stream to resemble a lake, with an island. Several ornamental buildings were put up – a Gothic ruin by James Wyatt (1797), an octagonal temple (1793) and a rustic thatched hermitage (1793). Princess Elizabeth painted the ceiling of the octagonal temple and was involved in the planning of many garden buildings. She also worked with James Wyatt in planning the ornaments for many of the *fêtes* of which the queen was so fond; an aquatint of the Jubilee *fête* held in October 1809 shows the scene on the lake – floating chariots, rowing boats with pennants, and mermaids in boats made to resemble floating bushes. Throughout the 19th century additions were made to the gardens: a pretty Indian kiosk of white stone in the 1850s, and a rustic tea room by S.S. Teulon in 1867; and of greater moment, the two mausolea designed by Professor Ludwig Gruner and A.J. Humbert of Dresden – one for the Duchess of Kent, completed in 1862, and a second, the Royal Mausoleum, built 1862–71, where Prince Albert and Queen Victoria are buried. In recent times many trees have been planted, often gifts to the present Queen.

Fulham Palace Garden *and* Bishop's Park

Hammersmith and Fulham, London OS TQ2476 English Heritage Register Grade II* Open regularly Tel 020 7736 5821

Fulham Palace was built in the early 16th century for Richard Fitzjames, Bishop of London, on a site dating back to pre-Norman times (the Bishops of London have held the manor since 704). It was rebuilt in the 1760s by Stiff Leadbetter, with alterations in the 19th century. Walled kitchen garden south-east of the palace, built in the 16th century, but only the Fitzjames gate is of this date; the remainder is 18th-century. Bishop Grindal in the 16th century was a keen plant collector and his 17th-century successor, Henry Compton, Bishop of London from 1673 until his death in 1713, was one of the most distinguished plant connoisseurs of the day. Stephen Switzer, in his *Ichnographia Rustica* (1718), says that Compton had "a thousand species of exotick plants in his stoves and gardens, in which last place he had endizoned a great many that have been formerly thought too tender for this cold climate." Compton was also Head of the Church for the American Colonies and took a special interest in American plants; he was among the first to grow many new introductions, among them the box elder (*Acer negundo*), *Magnolia virginiana* and *Gillenia trifoliata*. The gardens today are largely 19th- and 20th-century in character, with lawns, shrubberies and many mature trees. A knot garden of herbs has recently been added. Various sports and recreational facilities in the Bishop's Park – bowling green, children's playground and tennis courts. The Bishop's Walk is a splendid 980ft/300m avenue of mature London planes.

F

Gamlingay

nr Sandy, Cambridgeshire OS TL2251
English Heritage Register Grade II

The estate was bought after 1660 by Sir George Dowing I. On his return from the Grand Tour, his grandson, Sir George Downing III, built a new house 1712–13 and made an elaborate garden of which earthworks only survive, the estate having been abandoned in 1776. Shapes of walled enclosures and a long terraced walk and traces of old paths are visible. Most remarkable is the outline of a large trapezoidal lake, now dry, dammed on one side, from which water flowed into a series of pools. A walk along the top of the dam gave views of the pools. To the north of the lake were rides through woods. All this is illustrated and excellently descibed in Christopher Taylor's *Parks and Gardens of Britain: A Landscape History from the Air* (1998).

The Garden House
(Devon)

see page 36

The Garden House

Cottered, Hertfordshire OS TL3129
English Heritage Register Grade II*

Garden in Japanese style, started in 1905 in three flat fields on the edge of Cottered by Herbert Goode, the glass and china merchant. At the centre, a chain of connected pools sunk between hillocks, with a network of paths and bridges. The hillocks are decorated with ornamental buildings and planting. The whole garden is enclosed by a finely made Japanese fence and mature trees, among them several pines. It was not until 1924 that Goode built a house on the site, Cheynes House. The estate was later divided and a new house, The Garden House, built adjacent to the garden in 1966.

Gardens of the Rose

see page 302

Garendon Park

Loughborough, Leicestershire OS SK5019
English Heritage Register Grade II

There had been a Cistercian abbey here from 1113. In the 1730s Ambrose Phillips, a member of the Society of Dilettanti, embarked on a magnificent new house on his return from the Grand Tour. (The house, remodelled in the 19th century, was demolished in 1964.) South and south-east of the house, the remains of canals laid out by Ambrose Phillips. The park, now largely agricultural land, still preserves ornamental buildings designed by Phillips: south-west of the site of the house and raised on a mound, an Ionic Temple of Venus (whose statue of Venus was destroyed during Luddite riots in 1811); west of this, a Corinthian Triumphal Arch, based on the Arch of Titus in Rome; to the east, an obelisk of brick. There had been a well wooded park at Gardendon by 1640; Phillips made rides through the woods and planted avenues to link the house and ornamental buildings. A herd of deer survived until World War II when they were shot and the park ploughed.

Garnons

Mansell Gamage, Herefordshire OS SO3943
English Heritage Register Grade II*

18th-century house rebuilt 1815–22 by William Atkinson in picturesque style for John Geers Cotterell, at the suggestion of Humphry Repton. Repton produced a Red Book in 1791 in which he suggested filling in a formal canal, planting groups of trees to conceal unwelcome views and emphasise others, creating a lake to look like a stretch of the river Wye, and creating grass carriage drives leading to the chief beauties of the grounds. All these proposals were carried out and most of it remains.

Garrick's Villa, *formerly* Hampton House

Richmond, Greater London OS TQ1469
English Heritage Register Grade II Temple
open occasionally Tel 020 88920221

House built in the 17th century and altered in 1775 by Robert Adam for David Garrick who bought the estate in 1754. On the river side of Hampton Court Road, Garrick had built Shakespeare's Temple on the banks of the Thames – an octagonal building designed to house Roubiliac's portrait bust of Shakespeare, now in the British Museum. In the 1750s Capability Brown advised how to connect the temple with the house and its gardens on the far side of the road, recommending an underground tunnel ending in a grotto at the house's side. When Dr Johnson heard of this he said, "David, David, what can't be over-done, may be under-done." Garrick was inspired by this experience of landscaping to introduce into his play *Lethe, or Aesop in the Shades* (1740) a passage about the landscaping of the Elysian Fields; in it, he admires the place's "capabilities" and recommends that the Styx be made into a serpentine. In Garrick's play *The Clandestine Marriage* (1766) a character says "Ay, here's none of your strait lines here – but all taste – zig-zag – crinkum-crankum – in and out – right and left – twisting and turning like a worm, my Lord."

Garsington Manor

Garsington, Oxfordshire OS SP5801
English Heritage Register Grade II*
Open occasionally for NGS

16th-century gabled house of great charm, the home, 1915–24, of Lady Ottoline Morrell. Italianate garden made by Lady Ottoline, with yew hedges, terraces, statues and a flower garden of twenty-four box-edged beds, each with a seasonal bedding scheme, punctuated by rows of Irish yews. In her journal for June 1915, she wrote: "It is already much more beautiful, we have made one terrace and walk around the pond, and in the autumn we are arranging to plant yew hedges that will grow like a tall, dark wall round the water. It is more Italian than any other place in England that I have ever known."

Gatley Park

Aymestry, Herefordshire SO4449
English Heritage Register Grade II

House rebuilt in the 1630s, with alterations in the late 19th and early 20th centuries. Gardens near the house of Arts and Crafts character, with possible influence of Gertrude Jekyll. Dry-stone walls support raised beds and on the west side of the entrance court there are a pair of parallel yew hedges with bold crenellations. The steep slope south of the house has been terraced with dry-stone walls; stone steps link the terraces which have lawns and flower beds. On the top terrace are some terracotta urns with Gertrude Jekyll's seal. West of the house, yew hedges about a paved yard and a kitchen garden. Park goes back to the early 14th century. South-west of the house, many good specimen trees planted in the 1960s with the advice of James Russell.

Gawsworth Hall

Gawsworth, Cheshire OS SJ8969
English Heritage Register Grade II*
Open regularly Tel 01260 223456

Extravagantly timbered late Elizabethan house, with later alterations, built for the Fitton family. In front, lawns with specimen trees run down to a pool. Beyond the forecourt, late 20th-century garden of rose beds, hedges of holly and yew and a fountain pool. Behind the house, Tudor brick walls enclose a great space, the site of ancient gardens, with a raised walk, a pattern of terraces and the site of a canal plainly visible. These early gardens are undocumented but it seems probable that they were made in the 17th century.

Gawthorpe Hall

Padiham, Lancashire OS SD8034
English Heritage Register Grade II
Open regularly (NT) Tel 01282 771004

House built c.1605 for the Revd Lawrence Shuttleworth, whose ancestors had lived here in the 14th century, possibly designed by Robert Smythson. Sir Charles Barry made alterations to house and garden 1849–51. Gardens today substantially as designed by Barry in swashbuckling neo-Jacobean style. A balustraded terrace in front of the hall sweeps round to enclose a semicircular parterre. A balustraded terrace walk runs on each side, ending in an ornamental seat. Stone steps lead up from the garden on each side of the house, with stone urns decorated with encaustic tiles designed by A.W.N. Pugin. To the east of the house, a rose parterre, a simplified verson of Barry's desig[n]. On the south side of the house, Barry had laid out an elaborate parterre which is now a lawn flanked by steps and balustraded terraces. Formal gardens largely surrounded by woodland.

Gayhurst Court

Gayhurst, Buckinghamshire OS SP8446
English Heritage Register Grade II

Ancient site where there had bee[n] a medieval deer park. Present house largely 16th-century, altere[d] in the 18th and 19th centuries, t[he] last time by William Burges. Capability Brown is said to have worked on the grounds before 1763 but what he did, if anythin[g] remains uncertain. Before 1793 Humphry Repton was consulted his work involved the strip of pleasure grounds running north from the house, called Digby's Walk; the path passes underneath the B526 via a vaulted tunnel which is fronted with a Gothic façade designed by Repton. On the far side of the road, Gayhurst Spinney and parkland, with a sto[ne] bath house dated 1751, possibly designed by Brown and embellished by Repton. From he[re] there are views, probably designe[d] borrowing the landscape of the neighbouring Tyringham House (*see page 552*) to the east, where Repton also worked. William Burges was involved in Digby's Walk in the 1860s, designing a p[air] of carved stone pedestals in nich[es] in a yew hedge and two parterre[s] of box north-east of the house.

The Georgian Garden

see page 38

The Gibberd Garden

see page 302

Gibside

see page 338

Gilling Castle

Gilling East, North Yorkshire OS SE6076
English Heritage Register Grade II

A 14th-century tower house wit[h] Elizabethan and 18th-century alterations. Grassed viewing platforms and terraces close to castle possibly dating from the early 18th century. Ancient park with 18th-century entrance avenue (replanted in late 20th century) and ancient earthworks; part of it is now a golf course.

Glamis Castle
Glamis, Forfarshire OS NO3848 Scottish Inventory Open regularly Tel 01307 840393

Fairytale pink castle, with battlements and witches' hat towers, dating from the 10th or 11th century, with many alterations, especially in the 19th century. Originally a royal hunting lodge, it was given to John Lyon in 1372 (the Lyons became Lords of Glamis and later Earls of Strathmore and Kinghorne). The 9th Earl married an heiress, Mary Bowes, in 1755 and the family named became Bowes-Lyon. A map of 1735 shows "all the Parks, and Meadows and Plantations, Courts and Gardens as presently laid out", with a formal garden north of the castle running up to the Dean water. These gardens were lost when the policies were redesigned in informal fashion by James Abercrombie from 1768. A great entrance avenue went at the same time. The poet Thomas Gray had seen it in 1765: "You descend to the Castle…through a double and triple avenue of Scotch Firs, 60 or 70 feet high, under three gateways. This approach is full a mile long." Gray also described outhouses and enclosures surrounding the castle, "bordered with three or four ranks of sycamore, ashes, and white poplars of the noblest height, and from 70 to 100 years old", and many alleys lined with other trees "of great nature and size", which included black cherry trees, laburnums". This spectacular layout was made in the time of Patrick Lyon, the 3rd Earl, who succeeded in 1646. A replacement avenue was planted in the 19th century and remains. Parkland laid out in the 18th century has surviving original ash, beech, lime and oak. A late 18th-century shrubbery was turned into a pinetum in the mid 19th century – which Alan Mitchell surveyed in 1981, listing 130 notable trees. An early 20th-century Autumn, or Italian, garden was designed "on the lines of the old French gardens" by Cecilia, wife of the 14th Earl and

mother of Queen Elizabeth, The Queen Mother. Enclosed in yew hedges, it has a fan-shaped parterre (originally planted in rainbow colours), beech alleys, a fountain and two gazebos. A wrought-iron gate, made by a local smith, George Sturrock, was erected to celebrate the Queen Mother's 80th birthday.

Glasgow Botanic Gardens
Great Western Road, Glasgow OS NS5667 Scottish Inventory Open regularly Tel 0141 334 2422

The Glasgow Botanic Gardens had their origin as a physic garden, founded in 1707 for the University of Glasgow. In 1817 it moved to a larger site at Sandyford where, from 1821, W.J. Hooker (later Director of Kew) had a great influence on its development. In 1839, needing more room and better conditions, it moved to its present site. It now belongs to the Glasgow Corporation but maintains its role as the university's botanic institution as well as being a public park. It has a collection of 12,000 taxa, many of them tender plants cultivated in a magnificent range of glasshouses. The best known of these is the Kibble Palace, a circular glasshouse 150ft/45m in diameter, designed by James Boucher and James Cousland and built by James Boyd & Sons of Paisley. It houses a large collection of Australasian tree ferns (some of which were planted in 1881) and much else. Also under glass, in eleven further houses, are fine collections of species begonias (one of the largest in the world), orchids (especially *Dendrobium* and *Paphiopedilum*), succulents, economic plants, aquatic plants and tropical flowers. An arboretum was founded in 1977 with a collection of trees introduced by David Douglas who had been a student in the garden. The gardens, with fine lawns, winding paths and sitting places, make an attractive public park.

Gledstone Hall
Gledstone, North Yorkshire OS SD8851 English Heritage Register Grade II

House designed by Sir Edwin Lutyens and built 1925–27,

replacing an 18th-century house by John Carr of York. The result, according to Gavin Stamp's *Edwin Lutyens: Country Houses* (2001), is "very correct…but somehow cold and unloveable". Lutyens also designed a new garden – a remarkable sunken garden aligned with the pedimented centre of the south façade of the house. A long narrow canal runs between the retaining walls, overlooked on either side by terraced walks and ending with a raised circular mirror pool. The far southern end of each of these walks culminates in a dazzling L-shaped pergola from which there are magnificent views over the moors. Gertrude Jekyll carried out planting plans.

Glemham Hall
Little Glemham, Suffolk OS TM3459 English Heritage Register Grade II

House built in the early years of the 18th century for the North family on the site of a grand Elizabethan house. There had been a park here in Tudor times. The Norths made a formal garden near the house at the time it was built but this had been removed by the end of the 18th century. An avenue north of the house still existed when Humphry Repton came to give advice to Dudley Long North in the 1790s, but Repton thought it acted as a tunnel, focusing blasts of cold north wind onto the house, and proposed removing it. Another, to the south, survives – part of what Repton called a "strait-mall" in his Red Book of proposals (dated 1791). He was worried that the hall, a very large red-brick building with little ornament, too closely resembled a work house, and proposed adding pediments to the façades and painting the bricks to look like stone. He wanted to open up views of the countryside (passing traffic on the boundary road would add to its "cheerfulness", he said), pointing out that trees close to the house were essential, as were distant views of woodland, but that it was not essential to own the distant woodland – boundaries could be concealed, with a ha-ha, to give the appearance of uninterrupted and extensive land. In this way,

one could avoid "the appearance of a new place without ancestry, or of an old one fallen to decay". Many of Repton's ideas were carried out and the park at Glemham, handsomely visible from the A12 as you hurry past, is remarkably beautiful.

Glen Chantry
see page 304

Glen House
nr Innerleithen, Peeblesshire OS NT2933 Scottish Inventory

An old estate, with records back to the 13th century, but the present house built in fortissimo Scots baronial style after 1852 for a Glasgow businessman, Charles Tennant (later 1st Lord Glenconner), to the designs of David Bryce. Sir Robert Lorimer made alterations to house and garden 1905–07. Parkland, laid out in the early 19th century, protected by shelter belts and with beeches, elms, lime and oaks as well as conifers. *The Gardeners' Chronicle* in 1899 described the Glen as "a sylvan retreat of endless variety and inexhaustible beauty". A walled flower garden had in the early 20th century magnificent displays, with herbaceous borders and elaborately patterned bedding schemes. Glen House is now available as "serviced rental accommodation".

Glenarn
Rhu, Dunbartonshire OS NS2684 Scottish Inventory Open regularly Tel 01436 820493

House built in the 1830s for the MacGeorge family. W.J. Hooker, Professor of Botany at Glasgow University and later Director of Kew, was a family friend from whom the MacGeorges had seeds. From 1927 the estate was owned by the Gibson family who had many friends in the gardening world – such as Sir John Stirling Maxwell (of Pollok House, *see page 390*) and Mairi Sawyer (of Inverewe, *see page 383*). The Gibsons also had seed from the Ludlow and Sherriff and Kingdon Ward expeditions; after World War II the collection grew rapidly. The estate was bought in 1983 by the present owners, Michael and Sue Thornley, who have restored the

garden. This now has an outstanding collection of rhododendrons and also crinodendrons, embothriums, eucryphias, and magnolias. Several species of Himalayan primulas are established in woodland clearings. The site is attractive, with a burn flowing through a glen, and natural outcrops of whinstone, which formed the basis for a rock garden. The garden is notably well documented – the Gibsons kept records of all acquisitions from 1927, and the Thornleys have continued them.

Glenbervie House
Glenbervie, Kincardineshire OS NO7680 Scottish Inventory Open occasionally for SGS

Ancient site; old house remodelled *c.*1700 and in the 19th century. Walled garden on a slope by the banks of a burn, with a grand 19th-century conservatory, yew hedges, herbaceous borders, serpentine box hedges, beds of vegetables and fruit and a summerhouse – a decorative feast of flowers and vegetables in the old Scottish style. 19th-century woodland garden, also on the burn, with good trees and shrubs and a water garden with moisture-loving plants.

Glendoick
nr Perth, Perthshire OS NO2023 Scottish Inventory Garden open occasionally for SGS; nursery open regularly Tel 01738 860205

Mid 18th-century house on a much older site, built for Robert Craigie. Estate bought in 1900 by Alfred W. Cox, the first of four generations of the Cox family who were all mad about plants and gardens. Alfred's son E.H.M. Cox wrote the pioneer *A History of Gardening in Scotland* (1935) and explored the Himalayas with Reginald Farrer in 1919. The juniper *Juniperus recurva* var. *coxii* was named after him. E.H.M. Cox's son Peter has also hunted plants; he went to China with Roy Lancaster in 1981, and has been to China repeatedly since. Among his introductions are *Rhododendron dendrocharis*, *R. sinofalconeri*, *R. ochraceum*, *R. platypodum*,

R. denudatum, R. miniatum and *R. huanum*. Together with his father, he built up a remarkable collection at Glendoick. The woodland garden is full of these plants and has lovely underplantings of meconopsis and primulas. By the house are scree gardens for smaller ericaceous shrubs and for alpines. Peter's son Kenneth now runs the family nursery on the estate, specialising in ericaceous plants.

Glendurgan Garden
see page 38

Glenveagh Castle
see page 413

Glenwhan Garden
see page 378

Glin Castle
see page 414

Gloddaeth
Llandudno, Conwy OS SH8080
Cadw/ICOMOS Register Grade I

The Mostyn family acquired Gloddaeth in 1460, but the oldest part of the present house is 16th-century, with many later alterations. The woods were planted by Sir Roger Mostyn in the early 18th century and laid out with walks and rides – some of these are still visible although obscured by the great size of the old trees and by later planting. The trees are beech, chestnut, lime, oak and yew and the walks, straight or zigzagging, are lined with trees. Thomas Pennant's *A Tour in Wales* (1782) describes "straight walks, intersecting each other, or radiating from a center, distinguished by a statue". A large lead statue of Hercules by John Van Nost, on a stone plinth, remains; from it, radiating walks are still visible. Terraced gardens in front of the house, with a canal at the bottom, probably date from an earlier period than the woods and were certainly here by the end of the 18th century. Behind the house is a "Druidical" stone circle, a Victorian whimsy, probably put here by Lady Augusta Mostyn. The house is today a school, St David's College.

Glynde Place
Glynde, East Sussex OS TQ4509
English Heritage Register Grade II*
Open regularly Tel 01273 858224

House built 1568–69 for William Morley, with alterations in the mid 18th century. Terracing by the house, with a lime avenue extending east into the park. Terracing existed here by 1717 but was less extensive, and most of the detailing – yew hedges, a pool, mixed borders – is 20th century. Park probably dating from mid 19th century. Brick-walled mid 18th-century kitchen garden.

Glynllifon
Llandwrog, Gwynedd OS SH4555
Cadw/ICOMOS Register Grade I

House built 1836–48 to the designs of Edward Haycock for the Wynn family (later Lords Newborough) on a much older site. The pleasure grounds are animated by various oramental buildings and crossed by the valley of the Afon Llifon (on whose banks are the remains of a notable collection of bamboos). The hermitage (after 1825) is an octagonal rustic Gothic building, originally equipped with a hermit who was sacked for drinking. It was later used as the chapel for a pets' cemetery nearby, which was established in the late 18th century. A grotto, known as Mill Folly, was built in the late 19th century to resemble a ruined mill, with an underground chamber possibly originally used as a fernery. An 18th-century icehouse was converted into a nymphaeum, eerily lit with blue glass let into the roof. The park was probably laid out in the middle of the 18th century and was entirely walled by the early 19th century. An extraordinary castellated fort equipped with cannons in the centre of the park, Fort Williamsburg, was built in 1761. In 1954 the house and park were sold to Caernarvonshire County Council and the house is now a college.

The Gnoll Estate
see page 205

Gnome Reserve
see page 39

Gobions, *also known as* Gubbins
North Mymms, Hertfordshire OS TL2503
English Heritage Register Grade II
Open regularly

Ancient estate of the More family from at least the 14th century. Sir Thomas More probably wrote *Utopia* here, and the family remained here until 1693. In 1836 the estate was merged with the neighbouring Brookmans Park, and Gobions House was demolished *c*.1838. In 1708 Gobions had been bought by Sir Jeremy Sambrooke who made a new garden of which George Bickam the Younger wrote in 1750, "the famous garden of Sir *Jeremy Sambrook*, at *Gubbins*… deserves a Traveller's Admiration", adding that he would see there "a sensible Resemblance in Miniature of *Stow*". He described a "Forest of Oaks through which have been cut an infinite Number of Alleys", a grotto, orange trees, statues and a summerhouse. All this was the work of Charles Bridgeman in the 1730s. Only vestigial fragments of this remain – two canals, a mound where a statue stood and the ruins of a temple by James Gibbs. Gibbs's Gothic arch, a very early Gothic garden building, of the 1730s, survives on the edge of a housing estate to the south-east of the park. The site of the pleasure grounds and part of the park of Gobions is now a public open space.

Godinton House
see page 136

Godmersham Park
Godmersham, Kent OS TR0651
English Heritage Register Grade II*
Open occasionally for NGS

House built on an older site in 1732 for Thomas Brodnax. Close to the house, garden of the late 1930s. By the south front, a paved terrace and lawn, and to the west of the house, an Italian Garden with a rectangular pool and balustraded walls. Walled garden to east of house, with 17th- and 18th-century walls. Flower gardens planted after 1935 with advice from Norah Lindsay. Loggia overlooking a swimming pool with a late 17th-century statue of

Neptune. East of the stables, enclosed in yew hedges, a topiary garden with a central 18th-century fountain. Jane Austen was a frequent visitor to Godmersham; her brother Edward Austen-Leigh owned the estate 1797–1852.

Godolphin House
Godolphin Cross, Cornwall OS SW6031
English Heritage Register Grade II*
Open regularly Tel 01736 763194

The Godolphins built the house here in the early years of the 16th century and were knighted in the mid century. A ghost of a garden, whose exact nature remains in doubt. Pevsner's "Buildings of England" volume *Cornwall* (1st edition of 1951) sets the tone – "remains of quite an ambitious garden can still be seen in the solitude which surrounds present day Godolphin." Borlase's *The Natural History of Cornwall* (1758) describes the house as "situated in a large and well-wooded park" and has an illustration showing the castellated house with a loggia overlooking a forecourt (exactly as it is today) and pyramid-roofed pavilions in the outer corners. It also shows lines and groves of trees but is otherwise uninformative about the garden. An estate map of 1786 shows formal gardens with a central walk, and in 1985 Mary Schofield, the wife of the owner, wrote: "the garden at Godolphin was non-existent when my husband came in 1937. I have no very rare specimens but there are early avenues of trees and an old Box hedge of about 20ft high." However, a new owner Mrs L.M.P. Schofield, has been restoring the house with funding from English Heritage and perhaps more will be discovered about the garden.

Goldings
Bengeo, Hertfordshire OS TL3114
English Heritage Register Grade II

House built 1871–77 for Robert Smith to the designs of George Devey, on an older site. Grassed terraces and lawns by the house and specimen trees such as cedars and Wellingtonias. The park, now partly playing fields and agricultural land, has clumps, belts and individual trees and, to the south-east, Goldings Canal, a

serpentine stretch of running water. Two walled kitchen gardens, largely 19th-century, with surviving gardeners' bothies and a cottage.

Goldney House
Clifton, Bristol OS ST5772 English Heritage Register Grade II* Open occasionally for charity Tel 0117 903 4873

Rare town garden made by the Goldney family who bought the Clifton estate in 1694. Thomas Goldney II rebuilt the house from 1720 and set about improving the garden. The Goldneys were Quakers and Thomas Goldney was a partner in the Coalbrookdale iron-founding works run by his friend Abraham Darby, another Bristol Quaker. Cast-iron gates and railings – the first to be used in a garden? – were part of early 18th-century improvements to the garden at Goldney. But Thomas Goldney III, who inherited in 1731, had the greatest influence on the garden. A visitor described it in 1735: "to Thos. Goldneys at Clifton, went thro his Gardens &c which are very fine with Walks, Greens [i.e. evergreens], Waterworks, Summerhouses &c there were many Lemons and Orange Trees with fruit on them." An extraordinary grotto approached by a subterranean passage was begun in 1737 and completed in 1764. It has three chambers, one of which is pillared and vaulted, a cascade and pool and a sea god, the whole dazzlingly decorated with exotic seashells, fossils and decorative stones, among them Bristol Stone or "diamonds" (clusters of small quartz crystals). John Wesley thought it was "the largest and most beautiful of its kind that I ever saw". The garden also contains an orangery of *c*.1730; a mid 18th-century canal; a Gothic castellated prospect tower (1764), built both as a belvedere and to house a beam engine which pumped water for the grotto cascade; and, below the belvedere, a terrace and bastion which Goldney built to command view of Bristol harbour and, no doubt, his own merchant ships.

Goodnestone Park
see page 137

Goodwood House
Westhampnett, West Sussex OS SU8808
English Heritage Register Grade I
Open regularly Tel 01243 755048

Ancient estate, bought in 1697 by Charles Lennox, 1st Duke of Richmond. A Jacobean house was altered in the 18th century by Matthew Brettingham and, comprehensively, by James Wyatt. Much planting of exotic trees in the 18th century in High Wood north of the house, including American species supplied by Peter Collinson. Patterns of avenues, some replanted in modern times, follow 18th-century aligments. South-east of the house, a cricket pitch, lawns and many trees, among them several magnificent cedars of Lebanon, some of which date from the mid 18th century (1,000 four-year-old plants were planted in 1761). In the park, to the north of the pleasure grounds on a raised site with beautiful south-westerly views towards Chichester, is Carné's Seat, a stone belvedere flanked by sphinxes, designed in 1743 by Roger Morris. North of it is an exquisite shellhouse, recently restored, decorated in dazzling patterns of shellwork by the 2nd Duchess and her daughters.

Gorhambury
St Michael, Hertfordshire OS TL1107
English Heritage Register Grade II
Open regularly Tel 01727 854051

16th-century estate of the Bacon family. Present house built 1774–84 for the 3rd Viscount Grimston to the designs of Sir Robert Taylor. Historically, Gorhambury is most notable for its association with Sir Francis Bacon who inherited the estate in 1601 and in 1608 resolved to "give directions of a plott to be made to turn ye pond yard into a place of pleasure." Inspired by his cousin, Robert Cecil of Hatfield House (*see page 306*) who also recently made a notable water garden, he transformed the pond yard and built near it a supplementary house to be used in summer, Verulam House. John Aubrey visited the pond yard garden in 1656, when it was in decay, and described a 4-acre/1.6-ectare garden in which pools were decorated under the water

with coloured pebbles and where, on an island in the central pool, there was "a curious banquetting-house of Roman architecture, paved with black and white marble". He did a sketch of the garden, showing four L-shaped pools clasping the corners of a central square pool with a square island in the middle. Verulam House was demolished in the 1660s but the pond yard, without the banqueting house, survived. In 1934 Violet, 4th Countess of Verulam, who loved the place and used to camp there with her sons, had the dry ponds dug out, revealing some of the coloured pebbles that Bacon had used to line them. Today the ponds are overgrown and completely dry. In 1825 pleasure grounds about the house were laid out by William Sawrey Gilpin. A 16th-century brick-walled kitchen garden is now used as a paddock.

Gosford House,
formerly **Wemyss House**
nr Longniddry, East Lothian OS NT4578
Scottish Inventory Open regularly
Tel 01875 870201

House built on an older site to the designs of Robert Adam 1790–1800 for the 7th Earl of Wemyss; since knocked about, enlarged in the late 19th century, partly destroyed by fire in 1940 and much of the roof lost in an attack of dry rot in 1948 – but the Wemyss family still lives here. The site is a fine one on the south shore of the Firth of Forth, with views south to the Pentland Hills and north to the Sidlaw Hills of Fife. The pleasure grounds, and probably the parkland, were laid out by James Ramsay when the house was being built. A plan of the park in 1799 shows clumps of trees, some of which form a crescent facing Gosford Bay. Ramsay laid out a group of pools about the pleasure grounds, with trees and grass paths on their banks. A mausoleum, built for the 7th Earl, forms the focal point of a vista. The original design is blurred but still visible. Late 19th-century terraced formal garden west of the house originally had sunken beds with patterns of box hedges and low-growing plants. Most of the planting removed in the 1930s and

now partly grassed over and partly with roses.

Graigueconna
Bray, County Wicklow, Republic of Ireland
Open regularly by appointment
Tel (00353) 1 282 2273

Early 20th-century garden made by L.B. Meredith, an alpine specialist who wrote *Rock Gardens* (1908). Meredith also planted notable trees – a large *Eucalyptus globulus* survives from his time and a beautiful Himalayan dogwood, *Cornus capitata*. Although Meredith's rockeries survive, only a few alpine plants remain and Graigueconna now has a wide range of good planting. The tender evergreen maidenhair fern, *Adiantum venustum*, is established here and there is a good collection of choice forms of the lenten hellebores (*Helleborus* × *hybridus*). The garden has fine views of the Little Sugar Loaf Mountain and enticing paths through rocky passages and ornamental planting. In the lower part of the garden a long mixed border has many shrub roses.

The Grange
nr Northington, Hampshire OS SU5636
English Heritage Register Grade II*

17th-century house rebuilt in Greek revival style 1804–9 for Henry Drummond to the designs of William Wilkins. Traces survive of a 17th-century garden – terraces, now grassed over, and gate piers. Wooded parkland with a chain of serpentine lakes and a cascade date from early 19th-century landscaping of the park.

Grantully Castle
Logierait, Perthshire OS NN8951
Scottish Inventory

Castle built in the early 15th century for Alexander Steuart, with alterations in the 16th and 17th centuries. The Steuarts remained here until 1890. A remarkable walled garden was laid out in 1626 for Sir William Steuart. Parts of the original walls survive and two huge yews could date back to the early 17th century. Converted into an Italian Garden c.1890, it was later neglected and grassed over, but

since 1964 replanted. North of the castle, splendid remains of a lime avenue planted in 1626. The original entrance drive went down the avenue; in 1896 a new entrance gate was designed by Sir Robert Lorimer, set in the wall of the barmkin (the Scots word for the courtyard of a tower house).

Gravetye Manor
see page 138

Graylingwell Hospital
Chichester, West Sussex OS SU8606
English Heritage Register Grade II

Psychiatric hospital opened in 1897 with grounds laid out by R. Lloyd, the Surrey Asylum head gardener at Brookwood, who was an experienced designer of asylum landscapes. The designs were in accordance with the recommendations of the Commissioners in Lunacy's Suggestions and Instructions (1856 with subsequent revisions) which said that the gardens "should be of ample extent so as to afford proper means for healthful exercise. They should all be planted and cultivated, and any trees existing within them should be preserved for shade." It was also thought important that they should have "an uninterrupted and beautiful view of the country". The gardens are chiefly composed of six "airing courts", into which the wards open directly. They are lawned, with occasional specimen trees, and planted around their perimeters with flowering shrubs and trees. Each originally had a wooden shelter, of which a few survive; in addition, there were fountain pools in the centre of each court. A farm and kitchen garden were also made – work in both were regarded as an important element of therapy for male patients.

Gray's Inn
Camden, London OS TQ3081 English
Heritage Register Grade II* Open regularly

This was the site of the manor of Purpoole in Holborn, and the London house of Sir Reginald le Grey who died in 1308. It has been an Inn of Court since the mid 16th century; the Hall was built in 1556 and destroyed during

World War II bombing, but parts of it were saved and it was reconstructed. Shakespeare's *Comedy of Errors* was first performed here in 1594. From 1597 the Gardens, or Walks, were laid out to the north-west of Gray's Inn Hall. These are shown in an engraving in Stow's *Survey of London* (1720): tree-lined walks descending towards the east with, at the centre of the topmost terrace, a mount with a pavilion. Tradition has associated the design of these gardens with Francis Bacon. He became a Bencher of Gray's Inn in 1586 and it is known that he was a member of a small committee established to look into the building of the Walks; his chambers were on the west side of Coney Court (now Gray's Inn Square), overlooking the field in which the Walks were to be made. Bills survive from the late 16th century for large numbers of trees, in particular elms which were presumably used to line the chief walks, but also for such flowering ornamentals as cherries, eglantine, pinks, primroses, standard roses, violets and woodbines. A gardener, Richard Brooks, was paid £12 (£1,485 today) per annum from 1600. The Walks were increasingly simplified, with plans in 1761 and 1769 prepared by a "Mr Brown" – quite possibly Capability Brown; Harwood's map of 1799 shows a much reduced layout: the mount and pavilion have gone and there are five well-spaced rows of trees. In 1803 Verulam Buildings and in 1825 Raymond Buildings were built on part of the Walks. Today, fine 19th-century London planes are the chief ornament of what remains. A catalpa, which legend says was planted by Francis Bacon in the 16th century, is more likely to remain from the plantings of the 1760s.

Great Barr Hall
Great Barr, West Midlands OS SP0495
English Heritage Register Grade II

18th-century house, built on an older site in 1777 for Joseph Reilly. In the early 18th century there were pleasure gardens which included a Great Meadow, shrubbery and summerhouse. Mid 18th-century landscape park with stream, cascade and flower garden

G

laid out possibly with the help of William Shenstone, a family friend (see The Leasowes, page 501). Late in the 18th century and early in the 19th century Humphry Repton and John Nash laid out new approaches, made the Upper Pool and cut walks through the woodland.

Great Comp
see page 139

Great Chalfield Manor
Great Chalfield, Wiltshire OS ST8663
English Heritage Register Grade II
Open regularly (NT) Tel 01225 782239

House built in the 15th century for Thomas Tropenell. New gardens made 1905–12 when the house was restored by Sir Harold Brakspear. Brakspear himself designed some of the architectural features (a gazebo and stone-edged lily pond), and Alfred Parsons was involved in the garden design. East of the house, a "pleasaunce" with flagged path, formal rose garden and monumental topiary yew shapes. Steps lead down from a paved terrace to a flagged path running below the house, with orchard and lower moat beyond. South-west of the house, a walled fruit garden and more yew topiary.

Great Dixter
see page 140

Great Fosters
see page 140

Great Harrowden Hall
Great Harrowden, Northamptonshire OS SP8870 English Heritage Register Grade II*

Early 18th-century house for Thomas Watson, with older origins. Formal gardens laid out at the same time as the rebuilding of the house: a series of enclosures with brick walls and iron screens. In the east parterre, three early 18th-century lead statues of men wrestling by John Van Nost (there had been a fourth but it was said to have been melted down to repair the roof in the 19th century; its plinth survives). To the north and south of the east parterre, 18th-century walled kitchen gardens, one of which was an orchard. In other enclosures there are a rectangular pond and an early 18th-century octagonal gazebo. 18th-century park protected by shelter belt planting; in the 18th century a ride across the park linked it visually with the axis of the garden. Today the house is a golf clubhouse and an 18-hole course has been made in the park.

Great Maytham
Rolvenden, Kent OS TQ8627
English Heritage Register Grade II
Open regularly Tel 01580 241346

House built 1909–10, incorporating parts of an 18th-century house, for H.M. Tennant to the designs of Edwin Lutyens in his grandest Wrenaissance style. Gardens by Lutyens, possibly with help from Gertrude Jekyll, south-west of the house. Steps lead down at the centre and at each end of a terrace to a lawn with a flagged path, walled on the north-west side. Behind the wall, three partly walled enclosures with a pergola, a brick gazebo, a square pool, flower beds and climbers on the walls. Part of this area has private gardens for the residents of the house, which is now divided into flats for the Country Houses Association. The walled garden, which belonged to the 18th-century house, was the origin of Frances Hodgson Burnett's The Secret Garden.

Great Rissington Manor
Great Rissington, Gloucestershire OS SP1917 English Heritage Register Grade II

17th-century house on an ancient site, restored and altered by Falconer, Baker & Campbell 1924–25. John Campbell designed the terraced garden of Arts and Crafts flavour, with a pergola, thatched gazebo and dovecote. Changes in the post-war period include the planting of a small arboretum.

Great Tangley Manor
nr Guildford, Surrey OS TQ0246

Late Elizabethan gabled and timbered manor house. Gertrude Jekyll as a child knew and loved the garden when it, and the house, were derelict. In 1884 the estate was bought by Mr and Mrs Wickham Flower who restored the house and made a new garden. The garden, when still young, was illustrated in Country Life (1891) which described it as "a triumph of art, and a very notable example of garden construction. It should appeal to Englishmen [!] by its truly English picturesqueness and beauty." The photographs show an elaborate alpine garden, a border of irises, a pergola, a rock garden, and a covered way crossing the moat and leading to a walk of yew topiary. This new garden was described by Gertrude Jekyll in Some English Gardens (1904) ("a paradise for flower-lovers") and illustrated by G.S. Elgood. It is evocatively described in Penelope Hobhouse's and Christopher Wood's Painted Gardens: English Watercolours 1850–1914 (1988), illustrated with splendid paintings by Thomas Hunn, which show the garden at its zenith, its borders heavy with irises, larkspurs and Japanese anemones and the moat dappled with water lilies. Penelope Hobhouse writes that the garden has "today vanished inside urban sprawl".

Great Tew Park
Great Tew, Oxfordshire OS SP3929
English Heritage Register Grade II

Large and complicated estate with an enclosed park dating back to the 16th century. Early 17th-century house owned by Lord Falkland who entertained Abraham Cowley, Ben Jonson and Edmund Waller here. Three contemporary walled gardens survive. This house was demolished in the early 19th century and after 1815 a new house, incorporating an 18th-century dower house, was built on a site nearby. Humphry Repton had been consulted in 1803 and a Red Book was produced but it is not known which of Repton's landscaping ideas, if any, were carried out. J.C. Loudon leased much of the farmland 1808–11, had new roads built, and possibly laid out part of the estate – at Cow Hill – making a lake by widening a stream, as Repton had proposed.

Greathed Manor, formerly Ford Manor
nr Lingfield, Surrey OS TQ4142
English Heritage Register Grade II

House built 1868 for Joseph Spender Clay to the designs of Robert Kerr. West of house, oval formal garden of the early 20th century, possibly by Harold Peto. A balustraded wall encloses stepped terraces and flower beds surrounding an oval pool. Deep terrace beneath south façade of house with views of park and woodland.

Green Park
City of Westminster, London OS TQ2879
English Heritage Register Grade II
Open regularly

Green Park, like St James's Park (see page 172), was part of the monastic estate that Henry VIII took over in 1532 and made into a deer park, building the Palace of St James alongside it. Charles II improved the park – known at that time as Upper St James's Park – 1660–62 and opened it to the public. He built "a snow-house and an ice-house, as the mode in some parts of France and Italy, and other hot countries for the cool wines and other drinks for the summer season". The king's habit of taking his "constitutional" walks here is said to have been the origin of Constitution Hill, which forms the southern boundary of the park. In the 18th century it became a popular place for walks, and George II's queen, Caroline, took a particular interest in the park. The Queen's Walk, forming the eastern boundary of the park, was probably laid out by Charles Bridgeman c.1730, and became a fashionable promenade in its time. In 1749, to celebrate the treaty of Aix-la-Chapelle (which ended the war of the Austrian succession), a firework display was organised to take place at the same time as the first performance of Handel's Music for the Royal Fireworks. 11,000 fireworks, arranged on a great framework 410ft/123m long by 114ft/34m high, were to be fired, and an Italian firework maestro and an English army officer were in command; but a conflict of orders resulted in an explosion and onlookers were killed in the ensuing chaos. The park today is largely grass with many groups of trees and scattered specimens. Axial paths lead across the park, among them an avenue of London planes, the Broad Walk, a 20th-century addition, which runs south-east from the northern boundary, and is aligned on the Queen Victoria Memorial on the east side of Buckingham Palace.

Greenbank Garden
Clarkston, Glasgow, Renfrewshire OS NS5656 Open regularly (NTS)
Tel 0141 639 3281

The house, built in 1764 for Robert Allason, a Glasgow merchant, is very pretty – stone and stucco with a dashing pediment crowned with urns. A walled kitchen garden of the same date as the house is divided into compartments with, at its heart, a rondel of clipped yew. Old espaliered apple trees rise out of mixed borders (with many shrub roses) and beds are still devoted to fruit and vegetables. The charm of the place comes from the fact that this is a country house, with a country house garden of old-fashioned character that defies the surrounding suburbia.

Greencombe
see page 39

Greenwich Park
see page 142

Greys Court
see page 84

Greywalls
see page 379

Grimsthorpe Castle
see page 304

Grizedale
see page 339

Groombridge Place
see page 143

Grosvenor Square
City of Westminster, London OS TQ2880
English Heritage Register Grade II

The Daily Journal of 12th July 1725 recorded: "There is now

building a square called Grosvenor Square which for its largeness and beauty will far exceed any yet made in or about London." The garden, one of the largest London Square gardens of its day, was planned as an essential ornament of the speculative development. A drawing of *c.*1725 by the surveyor John Alston shows the oval garden with a central rectangle from which eight paths radiate to the boundary, the resulting segments filled with planting. By 1729 the garden had cost £2,871 (£236,915 today) and Alston was charged with maintaining it at a salary of £40 (£3,300 today) per annum. The planting was very elaborate – Todd Longstaffe-Gowan's *The London Town Garden* (2001) says that it "had more planting material than most of the great London squares combined". A gilded equestrian statue of George I was placed at the centre in 1726. In the early 19th century the grand formal scheme was replaced by an informal layout of winding paths, shrubberies and trees, and the statue of George I was replaced by an octagonal shelter. In 1948 a statue of President Roosevelt (by Sir William Reid Dick) was erected close to the northern boundary.

Grove House, *formerly* Rosehempton Great House
Wandsworth, London OS TQ2174
English Heritage Register Grade II

The first house on the site was built *c.*1630 for Sir Richard Weston (later Earl of Portland), Charles I's Lord Treasurer. The present house was built after 1777 for Sir Joshua Vanneck to the designs of James Wyatt, and there have been later alterations. It now belongs to the Froebel Educational Institute. The garden north of the house was laid out in the mid 19th century with a balustraded terrace with steps down to gravel walks and grass flats, the whole area enclosed by low stone walls ornamented with urns. At the northern end, the wall curves about in a bow with a circular fountain pool. A path runs east from the terrace towards a lone urn on a pedestal with

wooded grounds beyond. Here is a stone mausoleum, designed by William Burn and built 1863–65 for Mrs Lyne-Stephens, the ballerina Pauline Duvernay. To the north, a late 18th-century lake with a sham bridge probably by Wyatt and Rooks. A grotto of the 1890s by T.B. Harpham was originally part of a more elaborate scheme which included a cascade.

Grovelands, *formerly called* Southgate Grove
Enfield, London OS TQ3094
English Heritage Register Grade II*

House, now in separate ownership from the chief part of the grounds, built *c.*1797 for Walker Gray to the designs of John Nash. The grounds today are a public park. Humphry Repton advised in 1797 and although no Red Book is known, it was probably Repton who made the artificial lake with islands that forms the chief ornament of the park today, as well as the ha-ha enclosing the pleasure grounds from the north-east to the south-west. Woodland and scattered trees survive in the park, part of which has been made into a golf course. Thomas Mawson, in his role as landscape architect to Southgate Council, advised on alterations when it became a public park. There are bowling greens, a children's playground and tennis courts. A polygonal walled kitchen garden of *c.*1800 survives.

Gunby Hall
see page 305

Gunnersbury Park
Hounslow, London OS TQ1979
English Heritage Register Grade II
Open regularly Tel 020 8992 1612

The house, built in 1801 on an earlier site, was remodelled in 1835 for Nathan Mayer Rothschild, the founder of the great London merchant bank. (A secondary house, the Small Mansion, was built 1803–10.) In the 1740s William Kent removed a patchwork of formal gardens south of the house and made much more informal pleasure grounds. A round pond north-west of the house survives from

this time, as well as the outline of a crescent-shaped pool south-east of the house. In the latter part of the 18th century the house was used as a summer residence by Princess Amelia, George III's aunt. A Doric Temple north of the Round Pond is of this date. An orangery by Sydney Smirke dates from *c.*1836 and sham Gothic ruins are of the same period. Near the stables are the remains of a Japanese garden, made by the Rothschilds, who also created the lake – the Potomac – from a former claypit, with a Gothic boathouse on its bank. The grounds are ornamented throughout with many good mature trees.

Gunton Park
Gunton, Norfolk OS TG2234
English Heritage Register Grade II*

House built on an older site for William Harbord (later Sir William) after he inherited the estate in 1742, to the designs of Matthew Brettingham, with additions by Robert Adam (who also designed the parish church) from 1767 and Samuel Wyatt from 1780. Gutted by fire in 1882 and restored from 1982 when it was converted into flats. Charles Bridgeman is thought to have worked at Gunton *c.*1730. The Grove north of the house, with a mount and walks, survives in outline. Bridgeman is also said to have laid out an amphitheatre at Gunton. An avenue extending south of the house was in position by 1784 and it was extended in the 19th century; it survives in outline. Humphry Repton was consulted by the 2nd Baron Suffield *c.*1810 and a charming drawing by Repton and his son, John Adey Repton, dated 1816, for an orangery set in its own flower garden survives. The orangery was never built, and it is not known if any of Repton's suggestions were carried out. In 1812, however, Gunton was described as being "more remarkable for the extensive plantations of the park in which it stands than for the size or architecture of the mansion". W.S. Gilpin planted clumps of trees in the eastern parkland by 1835. Early 19th-century formal

gardens with walls and terraces south of the house are now much simplified. To the west of the house, a late 19th-century arboretum.

Gwydir Castle
Llanrwst, Conwy OS SH7961
Cadw/ICOMOS Register Grade I
Open regularly Tel 01492 641687

Delightful early 16th-century house on an older site, for the Wynn family. A second house, for the summer, Gwydir Uchaf, was built on a crag above the main house, with fine views over the Conwy valley. Walls and gateways survive of the early 16th-century gardens, and a modern parterre represents a Tudor rose. On a sloping lawn, a long avenue of yews leads to a massive stone seat. An octagonal pool, now with Victorian rockwork, is possibly of the 16th or 17th century. In the Royal and Statesmen's Gardens are trees planted by visiting notables from the end of the 19th century but there are much older trees, including a sweet chestnut, from the first years of the 18th century. A zigzag walk behind Gwydir Castle, known as Lady Mary's Walk (referred to in the 16th century as "a low melancholy walk"), leads up to Gwydir Uchaf. Here are traces of the 17th-century garden – a viewing platform, ancient yews, a viewing mount with a spiral path and, nearby, the bowling green.

Hackfall Wood
see page 339

Hackthorn Hall, *also known as* Hackthorn Park
Hackthorn, Lincolnshire OS SK9982
English Heritage Register Grade II

The Cracroft family came here in the early 17th century. The site had been inhabited since the middle ages but the present house was built in the late 18th century to the design of James Lewis. Walled landscape park with curving lake. Christopher Taylor, in his *Parks and Gardens of Britain: A Landscape History from the Air* (1998), writes of Hackthorn: "of

no artistic merit and had no designer. Yet parks such as this dot the English landscape and give it much of its character."

Hackwood Park
nr Basingstoke, Hampshire OS SU6449
English Heritage Register Grade I

Formerly a hunting lodge on the Basing estate (there was a deer park here in 1280), the present house was built in the 1680s for the 1st Duke of Bolton (formerly Marquis of Winchester, whose Basing House, *see page 71*, had been destroyed in the Civil War), and remodelled 1800–13 by Lewis Wyatt for the 1st and 2nd Lords Bolton. Beautiful early 18th-century formal gardens probably laid out by the architect James Gibbs, with buildings designed by him, of which only one, the Menagerie Temple, survives complete. Eight avenues radiating from a *rond-point*; an oval pool with equestrian statue of George I; fragments of a pillared rotunda by Gibbs; terrace with two pavilions; and an amphitheatre. In 1691 Celia Fiennes commented on the "good house and fine Parke" at "Hacket".

Haddo House
nr Methlick, Aberdeenshire OS NJ8634
Scottish Inventory Open regularly (NTS)
Tel 01651 851440

Gordons (later Earls, and Marquesses, of Aberdeen) came here in the 13th century and still live here. New house designed in 1731 for the 2nd Earl. 17th-century deer park where fallow deer grazed until the end of the 19th century. Adam designed parterres by the house; their shapes are retained but now have modern herbaceous borders. Landscaped in the mid 19th century by James Giles who dug two lakes, laid out paths and planted the pleasure grounds with exotic trees. Giles also planted woodland on the crests of hills to emphasise their size.

Haddon Hall
see page 262

Hadspen Gardens
see page 40

H

Hafod

Cardiganshire OS SN7673
Cadw/ICOMOS Register Grade I
Open regularly Tel 01974 282568

In its day one of the most famous late 18th-century picturesque landscape parks. Thomas Johnes of Croft Castle (see page 464) inherited the estate, and from 1783 created a garden influenced by the ideas of his cousin, Richard Payne Knight (see Downton Castle page 469). His essential plan was to animate the natural beauties of the Ystwyth valley with bridges, a cavern over a waterfall, the planting of immense numbers of trees, paths and viewing points from which to admire the landscape. John "Warwick" Smith's paintings of 1792 show water gushing through a narrow rocky passage, an arched stone bridge above the rapids, and paths winding along the river banks. Johnes was anxious to prove, in his work on the landscape, "that by beautifying it I have neither shorn nor tormented it." So well known did it become that Johnes built a hotel, the Hafod Arms, to accommodate visitors. In 1994 the Hafod Trust (Ymddiriedolaeth yr Hafod) was established in partnership with Forest Enterprise with the aim of restoring the landscape in accordance with Johnes's concept of "a working, wooded parkland, in the Picturesque style". The trust received a Heritage Lottery Fund award of £330,000 in 1998. Paths have been opened and there has been much clearing of woodland, so that Johnes's ideas may gradually be seen displayed – the natural setting is very beautiful.

Hagley Hall

Hagley, Worcestershire SO9180
English Heritage Register Grade I
Open regularly Tel 01562 882408

House built for Sir George Lyttelton (later 1st Lord Lyttelton) 1754–60, to the designs of Sanderson Miller. The park goes back to the middle ages but is most notable for its 18th-century ornamental buildings. The layout, with drives to beauty spots, was probably devised by Lyttelton himself. Horace Walpole was enraptured by it: "such lawns, such woods, rills, cascades, and a thickness of verdure quite to the summit of the hill". Most of the park lies east of the house where a spur of land rises between two valleys. On the top of the spur open grass land, Castle Lawn, slopes up to Miller's Gothick ruined castle of 1747–48, which Horace Walpole described as having "the true rust of the Baron's wars". In the woods on the northern slope of the spur are Pope's Seat and Pope's Urn (1744). Across the valley is the Ionic Rotunda (1747) designed by John Pitt. West of the Rotunda, the Prince's Pillar (c.1752, possibly by Henry Keene), a Corinthian column surmounted by a statue of Frederick, Prince of Wales. To the north-east the Doric Temple of Theseus (1758) by James "Athenian" Stuart.

The Haining

nr Selkirk, Selkirkshire OS NT4627
Scottish Inventory

House started in 1794, replacing an early 18th-century one, for Mark Pringle. Parkland dating from the late 18th or early 19th century, now partly farmed and with a few old trees left. A loch predates the park, having been here by 1660. There had been a herd of fallow deer until 1939 – the deer park is now grazed by sheep. Woodland of the 18th or early 19th century with some very old trees (especially "the Laird's Oak"). In the 19th century there was a collection of wild animals here, which visitors from Selkirk came to see. The estate suffered much during World War II when it was under military occupation.

Hainton Hall

Hainton, Lincolnshire OS TF1784
English Heritage Register Grade II

17th-century house built for the Heneage family with many later alterations, including those of the late 20th century. Park landscaped by Capability Brown. A drawing of c.1780, possibly made by Brown, survives at Hainton, showing a belt of trees planted about the park, looking much as it does today. Early 19th-century icehouse in the grounds.

Hale Park

Hale, Hampshire OS SU1818
English Heritage Register Grade II*

House built on an older site in around 1715 by the architect Thomas Archer for himself, and remodelled in the 1890s by Henry Holland. Parkland of the late 17th and 18th centuries with lime avenue and chestnut avenues. Ha-ha south of the house separating park and pleasure grounds – in which there is a circular pool surrounded by yew hedges and topiary shapes.

The Hall

Bradford-on-Avon, Wiltshire OS ST8260
English Heritage Register Grade II

House built c.1620 for John Hall, a clothier, restored in the mid 19th century. The garden layout is essentially 19th-century, made when the house was under restoration. South-west of the house, a steep slope with terrace and retaining walls. Originally lavishly planted, this has now been simplified to lawns and gravel paths. A row of 19th-century yews runs parallel to the terrace. Steps lead down from the terrace to the main lawn with a 15th-century dovecote and pergola. South-east of house, a mill-stream, boathouse and the river Avon. Tuscan summerhouse and wild rock gardens. North-west of the house, an archery lawn, rose border and 19th-century Doric summerhouse.

Hall Barn

Beaconsfield, Buckinghamshire OS SU9489
English Heritage Register Grade II*
Open for NGS by written application only to The Hon. Mrs Farncombe

Late 17th-century house, on an older site, built for the poet and statesman Edmund Waller. Waller started the gardens here after his return from exile in 1651 but the garden is chiefly the work of his grandson, Edmund Waller III, in the 1720s and 1730s. Edmund Waller III was much influenced by his stepfather, John Aislabie of Studley Royal (see page 352), who lived at Hall Barn 1711–20. A canal on the south-west side of the house has a high yew hedge with, at its northern end, Colen Campbell's Great Room of 1724 (badly damaged by fire in 1840) and at the south, the Fishing Temple of the same period, also probably by Campbell. To the west, a castellated Gothic pavilion of c.1740, overlooking a bowling green with a statue of Aesculapius (100 BC) in the south-east corner. In the centre of the park, south and south-west of the house, is the Grove, woodland with a patte d'oie of rides at the centre of which is a Temple of Venus of the early 18th century, probably by Colen Campbell. Rides lead to eyecatchers – the figure of Aesculapius and the canal to the north-east; an obelisk with trophies of gardening tools (early 18th-century probably by Campbell) on a bastion projecting into the park to the north-west. The Grove suffered in the storms of 1987 and 1990 but new planting has been made. The northern part of the park, north of the house, is scarred by the M40 motorway where once there was a medieval hunting park.

Hall Place
(Bromley, Kent)

see page 144

Hall Place

Leigh, Kent OS TQ5446
English Heritage Register Grade II*
Open occasionally for NGS

House built on an old site for Samuel Morley, 1871–72, to the designs of George Devey who also laid out the garden. Terraces on three sides of the house. North-west terrace with views across a lawn to a lake with mature trees on each side and a shrubbery further west. Rustic summerhouse by lake and bridges over three inlets. North-east terrace overlooks enclosed gardens with yew hedges and yew topiary drums and spheres with a central fountain. To the south-east, 19th-century rose garden and L-shaped pergola with climbing roses and a summerhouse in the angle. Ornamental woodland to the south-east with maples and flowering shrubs planted with the advice of Lanning Roper. Many excellent trees through the garden, some of them unusual, such as Arbutus menziesii, Fraxinus excelsior f. diversifolia, Quercus palustris and Sorbus torminalis.

Hall's Croft

see page 277

Halswell Park

Goathurst, Somerset OS ST2533
English Heritage Register Grade II

16th-century house built for Nicholas Halswell, with a much grander mansion grafted onto it in 1689 by Sir Halswell Tynte. His grandson, Sir Charles Kemeys Tynte, was a friend of Henry Hoare II of Stourhead (see page 106) and of Coplestone Warre Bampfylde of Hestercombe (see page 43) – a trio of 18th-century gentleman landscapers, all of whom made remarkable gardens. Halswell survives (more or less) in multiple ownership. A painting of it by John Inigo Richards, done in 1764, shows the estate in its heyday – the house overlooking a lake, with wooded banks, and a rotunda, "Mrs Busby's Temple", rising on an eminence. Sir Charles animated his landscape with a number of buildings, almost all of which survive in varying degrees of dishevelment – a very decorative Bath stone bridge with rustication and much ornament attributed to Thomas Wright (1755); a rockwork screen built of massive stone slabs, possibly by Thomas Wright (c.1755); The Temple of Harmony by Thomas Prowse, with an interior by Robert Adam (1764), now finely restored; Robin Hood's Hut, a Gothic pavilion with ogee arched loggia, probably designed by Henry Keene (1765) and well restored as a house; and Patcombe Farm, originally the Temple of Pan, designed by John Johnson (1771), now restored as a private house. An old photograph survives of the Druid's Temple, a thatched rustic building remarkably similar to one shown in a Thomas Wright engraving of 1755. What remains of the landscape is very impressive – "perhaps the finest 'undiscovered' garden of its period in England", as Gervase Jackson-Stops wrote.

Halton House

Halton, Buckinghamshire OS SP8810
English Heritage Register Grade II

House built in the 1880s for Alfred de Rothschild, designed by W.R. Rogers. Balustraded terraces by the house, with a circular fountain pool. A lawn and cypresses now occupy the site of circular beds which the Rothschilds planted with bedding plants in three dimensions. North-west of the house, an oval Italian Garden with a lawn and the remains of a mosaic path with a ruinous gazebo. To the north, an informal pond and (dry) cascade. Owned by the RAF since 1919, it is hard to imagine a Rothschild garden ever looking like this.

Ham House
see page 145

Hamerton
Cambridgeshire OS TL1379
English Heritage Register Grade II

In the village of Hamerton, north-west of Huntingdon, are the earthworks of a 16th- or 17th-century garden behind the former manor house, now the rectory. Sale particulars of the house, dated between 1669 and 1683, describe "several yardes behind it, and ponds of water, with a great garden and other lesser gardens and faire orchards well planted with good fruit, consisting of abut ten acres". Still visible are a canal with a raised walk, and outlines of walks and beds.

Hammerwood Park
Forest Row, East Sussex OS TQ4339
English Heritage Register Grade II
Open regularly Tel 01342 850594

House built c.1793, designed by Benjamin Latrobe, with many alterations in the 19th century. Terraces in front of south façade of house, with yew hedging. Further from the house, informal plantings of trees and shrubs. East of the house, an Italian Garden with central fountain pool, urns, seats and statuary. To the east, a valley with rhododendrons and water gardens, possibly planted by Oswald Augustus Smith, a cousin of Augustus Smith of Tresco Abbey (see page 66). It is possible that Latrobe was involved in laying out the park. It has the appearance of being designed as a whole and planned to make the best of views of the landscape. South of the house, pasture and restored tree clumps and a serpentine lake.

Hampton Court
(Herefordshire)
see page 206

Hampton Court House
Richmond, London OS TQ1569 English Heritage Register Grade II*

House built in 1757 on the edge of Bushy Park for Anne Maria Donaldson, the mistress of the 2nd Earl of Halifax. Gardens laid out 1757–69 and attributed to Thomas Wright who may also have designed the house. Pond west of the house; to its south-west, a magnificent grotto built into a mound, restored 1983–86 by Diana Reynell and Simon Verity. Between the grotto and the house, an octagonal Gothic hut raised on a mound, probably by Wright. North-west of the house, a semicircular rose walk and 19th-century iron arbour backed by a yew hedge; formal rose beds south-west of the house.

Hampton Court Palace (London)
see page 146

Hamstead Marshall Park
Hamstead Marshall, Berkshire OS SU4166
English Heritage Grade II

A complicated and fascinating site, with the last traces of a palatial manor house designed c.1660 by Sir Balthasar Gerbier and completed by William Winde, for the Earl of Craven. It was destroyed by fire in 1718 and Kip's engraving in Britannia Illustrata (1707) is virtually the only evidence of its appearance – a giant courtyard house, open to the west, set in elaborate walled gardens with parterres and avenues running across the park. Virtually all that survives today, close to Hamstead Marshall church, are six of the original gate piers, still in their original positions, some of them marooned, wall-less, in a field. Also surviving is part of the walled enclosure south-west of the house, which seems in the Kip engraving to have been used as a formal orchard. North-west of the former house, a dovecote and granary, visible in Kip's engraving,

are now a private residence, Ivy House. However, the site is much more ancient than the mid 17th century, having been held in the 13th century by the Marshals of England – there was a deer park and fishponds by this time, and a substantial house. The fishponds, various 13th-century mounds and the remains of a medieval park pale survive.

Hanbury Hall
see page 207

Handsworth Park, *formerly* Victoria Park
Handsworth, West Midlands OS SP0590
English Heritage Register Grade II
Open regularly

Public park, opened 1888 and laid out by R.H. Vertegans of Chad Valley Nurseries, Edgbaston. Lake to the west, formed by damming the Grove brook. Sunken garden now grassed over, with beds of shrubs to one side. Late 19th-century cast-iron bandstand and cast-iron *umbrello* and drinking fountain of the same date. Other original buildings have gone or are mutilated. Late 20th-century sports centre screened by ornamental trees and shrubs. To the east, late 19th-century boating pond laid out by Edwin Kenworthy (who also designed a boathouse which does not survive). Shrubbery with rhododendrons, and lawns with geometric beds for summer bedding.

Hangingshaw House
Hangingshaw, Selkirkshire OS NT3930
Scottish Inventory

Here, in the heart of Ettrick Forest, there had been a 15th-century tower house. The present house was built in 1846 but the Hangingshaw Terraces to the south of the house are thought to survive from the 16th century. A colonnaded summerhouse, latterly a pigsty, stands at one end of the top terrace. Some old trees of holly and yew could date from the 16th century. The parkland predates the present house, with a beech avenue and a single magnificent oak dating from c.1750.

Hanley Park
Stoke-on-Trent, Staffordshire OS SJ8846
English Heritage Register Grade II
Open regularly

Public park designed by Thomas Mawson and opened 1897. In two parts: the Cauldon Grounds and Hanley Park proper. The first has a terrace with two fountains and steps leading down. At the entrance on the west side, a terracotta fountain at the centre of an oval marked by paths. Perimeter walk through shrubbery to the south. The second was planned about a central pavilion with ground falling away in terraces; the second terrace is a flower garden. A canal cuts across the site, crossed by a bridge. There are such amusements as a boating lake, bandstand, oval bowling green and tennis courts.

Happisburgh Manor
Happisburgh, Norfolk OS TG3830
English Heritage Register Grade II

House built in the vernacular style in 1900 for Albemarle Cator to the designs of Detmar Blow. The site is close to the coast and Detmar Blow laid out a series of enclosures with lawns and borders, and with flint walls to give protection from the wind. The slightly sloping ground allowed the building of terraces, one of which is curved, laid with herring-bone patterned bricks; these give views to the sea. A thatched summerhouse is illustrated approvingly in Gertrude Jekyll's and Lawrence Weaver's *Gardens for Small Country Houses* (1912).

Harburn House
nr West Calder, Midlothian OS NT0460
Scottish Inventory

House built in 1804 for Alexander Young, replacing an older house on a different site. Wooded pleasure grounds with planned walks through early 19th-century beech woods; ponds; and ornamental bridges over a burn. A late 19th-century summerhouse is "finicky and delectable" according to Colin McWilliam in his volume *Lothian* (1978) in the "Buildings of Scotland" series. Parkland partly designed in 1815

by Thomas White the Younger, with a large lake fed by Bents burn and clumps and belts of trees such as copper beech, common beech, lime, oak, sweet chestnut and sycamore. The house is now a hotel.

Harcourt Arboretum
see page 85

Hardwick Hall
see page 263

Hardwick Park
Sedgefield, County Durham OS NZ3429
English Heritage Register Grade II*

House built 1634 and altered in the 18th century for John Burdon. Burdon commissioned the architect James Paine to design several buildings for his pleasure grounds. He also planned a palatial house, for which a design by Paine survives, but ran out of money before it could be built. South of the house, a long thin lake curves round through woodland, open to the west. East of the lake there was a banqueting house by Paine, enclosed by an amphitheatre of trees, but no trace of it survives. A Gothic gatehouse by Paine, built as a ruin and incorporating medieval fragments of Guisborough Priory, overlooks the lake from the east. Paine's bridge crosses the lake, and just to the north of the western tip of the lake are the ruins of his Temple of Minerva on a hillock. It had a lavishly decorated interior, with plasterwork and paintings, and the exterior had busts of notable authors, from Homer to Pope, in niches. Between the temple and the house there had been a lake; this was drained in the 19th century and the land given over to farming. In the woods to the west of the former lake are the ruins of Paine's Gothick summerhouse, Bono Retiro, at the head of a rectangular pool originally connected to the lake by a cascade. Paine's bath house, of which no trace survives, stood to the north. All in all, this amounts to one of the most pitiful sights imaginable.

Harewood House
see page 340

H

Harlaxton Manor

Harlaxton, Lincolnshire OS SK8832
English Heritage Register Grade II*
Open regularly Tel 01476 403000

"It floats like a vision at the end of its avenue; it rises mysteriously out of the snows or ebullient from the late summer cornfields; it changes from season to season, and light to light. It is a work of genius." So wrote Mark Girouard of Harlaxton in *The Victorian Country House* (1979). Harlaxton was built 1831–42 for Gregory Gregory, a mysterious scholarly connoisseur, to the designs of Anthony Salvin and William Burn. Burn also designed parts of the garden in a consciously neo-Jacobean style to suit the house – Baroque terraces to the east and a huge five-roomed conservatory on the southern corner of the house. To the far side of the west terrace lawn is the south garden, with balustraded steps and statuary leading to the south pond against a background of wooded parkland.

Harleyford Manor

Great Marlow, Buckinghamshire OS SU8284
English Heritage Register Grade II

Thames-side villa designed by Sir Robert Taylor and completed in 1755 for William Clayton. North-west of the house, the Grove is terraced and was probably an 18th-century pleasure ground, with a late 18th-century Gothic dairy possibly built as an eyecatcher. In the south-west corner of the Grove, a shell grotto with the river just visible. The slope between the dairy and grotto is planted with 19th-century specimen trees and evergreens – box, holly, Portugal laurel and yew. A statue of Sir Robert Clayton (1714) in the Grove. Capability Brown is reputed to have worked here but there is no evidence; it is possible he shaped the islands in the river. In the north of the park, mixed woodland and an 18th-century domed temple facing north over what is now a golf course.

Harlow Carr Gardens

see page 341

Harrington

Harrington, Northamptonshire OS SP7280
English Heritage Register Grade II*

Medieval manor which had belonged to the Order of St John of Jerusalem, later belonging to the Stanhope family. House demolished in 1745. Surviving earthworks are evidence of an elaborate formal garden, known as The Falls, of the late 17th or early 18th century when the 3rd Earl of Dysart owned the estate. The Earl of Dysart also owned Ham House (*see page 145*) where there was a notable late 17th-century garden. The humps and bumps at Harrington trace a symmetrical layout with terraces, paths, canals and pools. They are vividly shown in an aerial photograph in Christopher Taylor's *Parks and Gardens of Britain : A Landscape History from the Air* (1998).

Harrington Hall

Harrington, Lincolnshire OS TF3671
English Heritage Register Grade II
Open occasionally for NGS

Elizabethan house built for the Copledyke family, with many later changes. Rare 17th-century terrace with gazebos forming one side of a croquet lawn with borders. The terrace, now with a brick path edged with aromatic herbs, may have been designed to look down onto a knot garden – there was a 19th-century formal garden here. Early 18th-century kitchen garden. In the 19th century Rose Baring, beloved of Alfred Tennyson, lived at Harrington Hall and was the subject of his poem *Maud*, and thus of the song "Come into the garden, Maud".

Hartlebury Castle

Hatlebury, Worcestershire OS SO8371
English Heritage Register Grade II
Open regularly Tel 01299 250416

Medieval castle of the Bishops of Worcester; the present building dates from the 14th century, with much remodelling in the 17th and 18th centuries. Moat to the west of the castle. Entrance forecourt with flower beds running about the exterior walls, just as they did in the late 18th century. Pleasure grounds south of the castle, with sunken garden with lawn, trees

and shrubs and raised walks about three sides. The essential garden layout dates from the time of Bishop Hough who was elected in 1717. There was a deer park here from 1339 and deer remained here until at least the 1660s. Park close to castle, with grassland and three avenues – of beech, horse chestnut and lime. To the east and north, much of the park is now arable farming.

Hartsholme Park

Boultham, Lincolnshire OS SK9469 English
Heritage Register Grade II Open regularly

The Victorian house, Hartsholme Hall, was demolished in 1952. The grounds, partly laid out by Edward Milner in 1862, survive as a 240-acre/97-hectare public park. A lake has a Gothic boathouse and a rustic bridge. A column beside the lake, put in place in 1902, bears the memorably unmemorable inscription, "To commemorate the establishment of the Lincoln water-works 1846". The lake is, in fact, a reservoir for drinking water.

Hartwell House

Hartwell, Buckinghamshire OS SP7912
English Heritage Register Grade II*

House built some time between late 16th and early 17th centuries for Sir Alexander Hampden, with later alterations. The garden is well known from a set of eight beautiful paintings by Balthasar Nebot, made in 1738. These are in Buckinghamshire County Museum in Aylesbury and are illustrated in John Harris's *The Artist and the Country House* (1979). They show a beguiling garden of topiary, palissades, water and statues. It is not known whether these pictures are an accurate depiction of the garden as made, or a visualisation of some proposed plan that was not executed exactly as shown. It is known that James Gibbs designed "several ornamental buildings", some of which are seen in Nebot's paintings and survive in the garden today, but not all in the same positions. The garden now is chiefly lawn. Of Gibbs's chief surviving buildings (all of them *c*.1730), the Doric Column is east of the house, the Gothic Tower north-west of the house in what had been the Wilderness, and the

Ionic Temple, with four flanking terms, to the south-east where the canal shown by Nebot had been. The park dates from the mid 18th century or later and was probably laid out by Richard Woods; he worked at Hartwell 1759–60 and is known to have supplied many trees and shrubs in this period. The house is now a splendid hotel and the grounds are well cared for.

Haslam Park

Preston, Lancashire OS SD5130 English
Heritage Register Grade II Open regularly

Public park opened in 1910, with later additions by Thomas Mawson. A stream, the Savick brook, flows from east to west across the park, running into a lake to the east. The Lancaster canal forms the north-eastern boundary, flowing over the brook on an aqueduct built in 1797. Water from the canal is chanelled over a cascade. To the east, a broad walk with limes along its western side. To the west, bowling greens and a pair of pavilions.

Hatch House

Newtown, Wiltshire OS ST9028
English Heritage Register Grade II

House of 16th- or 17th-century origins, remodelled in 1770 and again, by Detmar Blow, in 1908. Walled garden to west of house, with terrace and borders. A central axis from the centre of the house runs through gates to a lawn with a sundial and up steps to a loggia, dated 1658 but altered by Blow. The terrace wall, dividing the walled garden into two parts, has busts of Roman emperors originally from nearby Stockton House. North of the house, steps rise up to yew hedges which lead to an enclosed bowling green.

Hatchlands Park

see page 146

Hatfield House

see page 306

Hatfield Priory

Hatfield Peverel, Essex OS TL7910
English Heritage Register Grade II

House built 1768–70 for John Wright, possibly by John Phillips. Grounds laid out by Richard

Woods in 1765 with linked ponds, belts or plantations on the north, west and east boundaries and a ha-ha running across southern parkland. Gardens restored since 1979, modifying Woods's plan to suit the house which was built after his plan was made. A cascade was made at this time below the lower pool and a Gothic temple built as an eyecatcher on the boundary to the south of the house.

Anne Hathaway's Cottage

see page 278

Hatherop Castle

Hatherop, Gloucestershire OS SP1505
English Heritage Register Grade II

16th-century house, much altered, after damage by fire in the mid 19th century, by Henry Clutton for Lord de Mauley. Park landscaped after 1778 by Richard Woods in conjunction with the neighbouring Williamstrip Park. Italianate garden west of house made before World War I to the designs of Walter Frederick Cave.

Hatley Park, *formerly* Hatley St George

Hatley St George, Cambridgeshire
OS TL2750 English Heritage Register Grade II

17th-century house, with much later alteration. An engraving by Kip in *Britannia Illustrata* (1707) shows the house, then called Hatley St George, with an avenue leading up to an entrance forecourt and fine regular gardens behind the house. It was at that time owned by the antiquarian Sir Robert Cotton. Today there are formal gardens to the south of the house, with a lawn and fountain enclosed by a stone balustrade. There are long rectangular ornamental ponds and garden ornaments from the 17th to the 19th century. An avenue runs south from the house in the position shown by Kip. Landscape park largely 19th-century.

Hatton Grange

nr Ryton, Shropshire OS SJ7604
English Heritage Register Grade II
Open occasionally for NGS

18th-century house designed by Thomas Farnolls Pritchard for Plowden Slaney. 18th-century par by an unknown designer. South of the house, a ravine garden with chain of pools, possibly medieval fishponds in origin. In the late 18th or early 19th century a carriage drive was made to the pools, with planned walks along their banks. Woodland of beech and oak enriched in the 1930s by Major R.O.R. Kenyon-Slaney with flowering shrubs – especially magnolias and rhododendrons. Octagonal temple designed by Clough Williams-Ellis c.1960.

Hatton House
nr East Calder, Midlothian OS NT1268
Scottish Inventory

House built about a 15th-century core in the late 17th century for Charles Maitland, Lord Hatton (later Earl, and Duke, of Lauderdale) who also owned Ham House (see page 145). Hatton House was destroyed by fire in 1952. In 1683 Sir Robert Sibbald, in Scotia Illustrata, described "the noble dwelling of Haltoune where are fine gardens and a large park with a high wall about it". There was much later garden activity but in the 19th century the estate changed hands several times and by 1875, according to J.R. Findlay in Hatton House, the "deer parks were sadly curtailed, the finest timber felled, the artificial cascades and ponds except one all drained." Today, only lovely fragments survive: the south terrace with ogee-roofed two-storey gazebos, a bath house, gate piers with the Lauderdale arms and a summerhouse dated 1704.

Haughley Park
see page 307

Haverfordwest Priory
Haverfordwest, Pembrokeshire OS SM9515
Cadw/ICOMOS Register Grade I

The Augustinian priory was founded in the 13th century. The site of a cloister garden survives from this period and has been excavated. A stone-paved path ran round the garden, probably edged with a hedge, and an octagonal shape at the centre was probably the site of a plinth for a central ornament such as a cistern. Excavation of the subsoil suggests that trees or small shrubs were

planted in the garden. East of the priory is a grid of ten raised beds, rectangular or square, supported on low stone walls and originally separated by paved paths. Some evidence suggests that one of the beds was originally the base of a turf seat, and post holes could have contained supports for trelliswork. At all events, this is an exceptionally rare garden layout to survive from the 15th century.

Hawarden Castle
Hawarden, Clwyd OS SJ3265
Cadw/ICOMOS Register Grade I
Open occasionally for NGS

There are two Hawarden Castles on the estate – old and new. The old is the ruins of an early medieval castle and the new is a romantic castellated house, the reworking of an earlier house called Broadlane Hall and built 1809–10 for Sir Stephen Glynne to the designs of Thomas Cundy. Terraced formal gardens south of the new castle were laid out when it was built. To the west, a picturesque landscape, with the ruined towers and ramparts of the old castle forming a splendid ornament on the skyline. An open vista linking the two castles is flanked with banks of shrubs (especially rhododendrons) and trees. The castle mound has grass walks and a row of lime trees planted in the 1730s. One of Sir Stephen Glynne's daughters married W.E. Gladstone (through whom the estate descended), who is remembered in Gladstone's Walk laid out in 1853. This links various ornamental features – an icehouse, a curious 18th-century turf amphitheatre, a pool and a stone column. W.S. Gilpin advised on the picturesque landscape in the early 19th century and there was much tree planting in the latter part of the century.

Hawkstone Park
see page 208

Hayne Manor,
also called **Haine** *or* **Haine Castle**
Stowford, Devon OS SX4286
English Heritage Register Grade II

The Harris family lived here from the 16th to the 19th century.

Remains of late 18th-century and early 19th-century Gothic house, possibly by Jeffry Wyatville. Surviving but disheveled parkland of the same date as the house; woodland area, known as the Wilderness, with a mid 18th-century grotto with a shell-lined interior.

Hazelbury Manor
Box, Wiltshire OS ST8368 English Heritage Register Grade II Open occasionally for NGS and by appointment Tel 01225 812952

Medieval house, altered in 16th and 17th centuries and restored in early 20th century by Harold Brakspear. On three sides of the house, walled enclosures date from the 17th century, now with 20th-century gardens – a rockery, lawns, yew hedges, topiary, borders and an ornamental orchard with pools, fountains, statues and seats. North of the house, a late 20th-century pinetum. Of the same date, in the field to the south-west, a series of rides, a replica (not full size) of Stonehenge in clipped yew and, to the north-west, two earth mounts.

The Hazells
Sandy, Bedfordshire OS TL1950
English Heritage Register Grade II

Formerly a grange of Chicksands Priory, rebuilt in the late 17th century and altered in the 18th century for the Kingsley family. Park of the 1760s by Nathaniel Richmond for Francis and Elizabeth Pym (*née* Kingsley). Francis Pym consulted Humphry Repton in 1791 and a Red Book was produced. Repton much admired the 1720s grass terrace: "an object of such comfort and convenience that it would be unpardonable to destroy it entirely." He made designs, with Gothic and classical facades, to improve the existing pavilion at the south end of the terrace and laid out the park which has fine old sweet chestnuts. He also planted trees to conceal boringly flat country to the east: "an attempt to let in distant flat country is never picturesque." Yew walk, summerhouse, terrace and other formal gardens by house.

Headland
see page 41

Heale Garden
see page 86

Heaselands
nr Haywards Heath, West Sussex OS TQ3122
English Heritage Register Grade II

Ernest Kleinwort came to live here in 1932, rebuilt the existing house and designed new gardens. Formal gardens lie to the south, with a terrace, a sunken garden with rose borders and a central lily pool from which a lawn descends, ornamented with specimen trees, to a valley and stream. East of the sunken garden, a walled garden with conifers and rhododendrons and other formal flower gardens. In the valley, water gardens with pools and cascades, the banks lavishly planted with trees, shrubs and moisture-loving herbaceous plants. South of the valley, oak and pine woods planted with rhododendrons.

Heathcote
Ilkley, West Yorkshire OS SE1047
English Heritage Register Grade II

House designed in 1906 by Edwin Lutyens for J.T. Hemingway; the grandly intricate suburban villa, hidden chastely behind walls, must be the most exciting house in the street. The garden, also designed by Lutyens, is all of a piece with the house. An oval courtyard to the north provides entrances to garage and outhouses as well as to the house. A paved terrace runs across behind the house, from which there are views of Ilkley Moor. Grand steps lead down at each end of the terrace, with rectangular pools and parterres of roses and lavender. Beyond is a great terraced oval lawn with a path running about its circumference.

Heathfield Park
Heathfield, East Sussex OS TQ5820
English Heritage Register Grade II

Late 17th-century house, rebuilt in 1766 by Sir Robert Taylor, and in 1896–97 by Sir Reginald Blomfield. By the house, gravel walks, terraces, lawns and borders. South-west of the terraces, a walk through exotic conifers and glades of shrubs. The park is largely wooded, with a string of spring-fed pools in its southern part, probably made in the early 18th century by

the Fuller family as pen ponds for iron founding. On the north-western boundary, Gibraltar Tower of c.1792 commemorates General Elliott and the siege of Gibraltar. In 1794 Humphry Repton produced a Red Book, making proposals for the setting of the house and of Gibraltar Tower, but it is not known if they were carried out. His serpentine walk along the north-eastern boundary of the park was put into place and has been the scene of much recent replanting.

Heaton Park
Prestwich, Greater Manchester OS SD8304
English Heritage Register Grade II
Open regularly Tel 0161 234 1456

House built 1772–89 for Sir Thomas Egerton to the designs of James Wyatt. 20th-century terraced garden on south front of house, with geometric beds and bowling greens to the south-east below the terrace. North of the house, classical temple by Samuel Wyatt built 1795–1802, commanding spectacular views to the Pennines. Since 1902 the estate has belonged to Manchester Corporation and the grounds used as a public park. West of the house, between the stables and the home farm, a garden with lawns and geometric beds. South of the home farm, a grotto set into a slope. To the west, the Dell, a wood with winding paths to a lake overlooked by a 20th-century bandstand. The park was landscaped by William Emes 1770–72, with further work by John Webb 1808–09. The northern and north-eastern part was a deer park until at least 1844. There is now a golf course here. Much of the park is open grassland with scattered trees, some 20th-century avenues, and surviving parts of 18th-century perimeter belt planting. To the south, a 20th-century boating lake with, to its south, the façade of the former town hall of Manchester (1822–24, designed by Frances Goodwin).

Hedsor House,
formerly known as **Hedsor Lodge**
Hedsor, Buckinghamshire OS SU9086
English Heritage Register Grade II

House built 1865–68 to the designs of James Knowles, but

H

there had been houses here as early as the 16th century; in 1778 Sir William Chambers had designed a new house (on a site to the west of the present house) for the 2nd Lord Boston, and the grounds were probably remodelled at this time. Pleasure gardens about the house date from the early 20th century, with yew hedges, a lily pool, the Dutch Garden and a sunken garden. Chambers may have been responsible for Lord Boston's Folly on a prominent position north of the house. This is a large Gothic building with two castellated towers which has in recent times been converted into a private house known as Hedsor Towers. In the park, traces of an 18th-century lime avenue survive, including a few of the trees, surrounded by ancient oak woodlands. The avenue had in the early 18th century extended from the neighbouring Cliveden estate (see page 79) to the south.

Heights of Abraham

Matlock Bath, Derbyshire OS SK2958
English Heritage Register Grade II*
Open regularly

Late 18th-century pleasure ground created to display the picturesque beauties of the Derwent valley. Started by the Simpson family in 1787, with a zigzag path on the south-facing slopes of Masson Hill. At the top is the Victoria Prospect Tower (1844) with spiral staircase leading to viewing platform. The entrances to two caverns, Great Masson Cavern and Rutland Cavern, are concealed by 20th-century café entrances. The Gothic Upper Tower House (1830) with round crenellated towers was built as the home of the manager of the gardens and to provide refreshment for visitors.

Heligan

see page 42

Helmingham Hall

see page 308

The Hendre

Hendre, Gwent OS SO4514
Cadw/ICOMOS Register Grade II*

House built on an older site c.1830 for the Rolls family, who had lived here at least since the 17th century, and Gothicised late in the century by Sir Aston Webb. The Rollses became Lords Llangattock; the son of the 1st Lord, Charles Rolls, founded the firm of Rolls Royce in 1906. 19th-century pleasure grounds with terraced lawns, balustrading, a sunken garden with a fountain and yew topiary. An arboretum has a good collection of conifers. Park probably dating from the 17th century, landscaped in the 19th century by Lord Llangattock and H.E. Milner, with a new drive planted with trees and shrubs, rockwork ornaments and vistas cut through woods.

Henham Hall

Henham, Suffolk OS TM4578
English Heritage Register Grade II

The Tudor house here was rebuilt 1793–97, after a fire, by James Wyatt for Sir John Rous, later Earl of Stradbrooke. The house was demolished in 1953 but fragments remain – walled gardens with crinkle-crankle walls, a castellated dairy, an octagonal dovecote, and stables crowned with a cupola. Humphry Repton was consulted in 1790 and produced a Red Book. Much of Repton's work survives, in particular the various new drives he planned and some of the plantings in the park.

Henley Hall

nr Middleton, Shropshire OS SO5476
English Heritage Register Grade II

Much altered Elizabethan house. Early 18th-century landscaping, and 18th-century orangery and walled kitchen garden of similar date. Wrought-iron gates and screen probably by Robert Bakewell before 1725. Pulhamite rock garden of c.1910 and other signs of ornamental gardening in late 19th and early 20th centuries, such as a paved rose garden with sundial.

Barbara Hepworth Museum and Sculpture Garden

see page 43

Hergest Croft Gardens

see page 209

The Hermitage

see page 380

Herriard Park

Herriard, Hampshire OS SU6646
English Heritage Register Grade II

House built on an older site in 1704, designed by John James but probably with the advice of William Talman; demolished in 1966 and a new house built. Earthworks survive from early formal garden – George London had worked here in 1699 and in 1730 an avenue was laid out connecting Herriard with the neighbouring estate of Hackwood Park (see page 483). Octagonal walled garden built 1796–97 with surrounding shrubbery walk with exotic plantings. Humphry Repton advised George Purefoy Jervoise in 1793 (discussed in Repton's Sketches and Hints on Landscape Gardening (1794)).

Herterton House Gardens

see page 342

Hestercombe

see page 43

Herstmonceux Castle

Herstmonceux, East Sussex OS TQ6410
English Heritage Register Grade II*
Open regularly Tel 01323 833816

Castle built from 1441, with remodelling in late 18th century and alterations in 20th century. Walled garden to north of castle was probably laid out shortly after the castle was built, and in the 18th century was a kitchen garden. Today it is divided into three compartments and its design is largely 20th-century, chiefly by W.H. Godfrey 1933–35. A central axis links the compartments, starting with a flagged path flanked by yew, with rectangular lawns and herbaceous borders to each side. Steps lead to a second compartment, with a circular rose garden and lawns on each side. A loggia links it to the third compartment, with a box parterre flanked by a tennis court and a rose garden. The park was probably in existence by the 12th century and there was a deer park by the early 15th century. Today there are lakes and patches of woodland in the eastern part but the park is largely turned over to arable farming.

Hesketh Park

Southport, Merseyside OS SD3418 English Heritage Register Grade II Open regularly

Public park designed by Edward Kemp, possibly with the help of Sir Joseph Paxton, and opened 1868. Wooded and undulating site with a large irregular lake just south-west of the centre. On the southern edge of the lake, a large conservatory, moved in 1877 from the grounds of a house in Southport. Nearby, a rockwork arch and two aviaries flanking a path. In the northern park, a sunken rose garden, and to the east, a garden for the blind. On an elevated site north-east of the centre, the Fernley Observatory, opened in 1901.

Hesleyside

nr Bellingham, Northumberland OS NY8183
English Heritage Register Grade II

17th- and 18th-century house of the Charlton family, built round a 14th-century pele tower. An unsigned survey of the estate in 1776 has been attributed to Capability Brown but Dorothy Stroud's Capability Brown (1975) says it "bears little resemblance to his usual designs", although noting the presence today of "fine timber and a small cascade on the Hesleyside burn". Signs of an earlier, probably 17th-century, formal landscape with radial avenues across parkland.

Hethersett

Littleworth Cross, Surrey OS SU8945
English Heritage Register Grade II
Open occasionally for NGS

House built in 1872 for Harry A. Mangles to the designs of Norman Shaw. Harry Mangles's brother, James, was a pioneer collector and breeder of rhododendrons, whose collection was moved to Hethersett on his death in 1884. South of the house, a meadow surrounded by woodland of birch, Douglas fir and Scots pine underplanted with rhododendrons, with some of the original Mangles hybrids surviving. Pigeon house and donkey shelter designed by Edwin Lutyens.

Heveningham Hall

Heveningham, Suffolk OS TM3573
English Heritage Register Grade II*

Magnificent house by Sir Robert Taylor, completed by James Wyatt, built 1778–80 for Sir Gerald Vanneck. Orangery of before 1784 by James Wyatt, who also probably designed the temple south-east of the house. Capability Brown consulted in 1781 but it seems that most of his work consisted of adjusting existing features rather than making major changes. There was already a landscaped park in place, made by Sir Gerald's father, which included a very Brownian lake in a key position below the house. Brown deformalised rides in woodland, created new turf rides wide enough to take a carriage, and carefully arranged views. He also designed a new walled kitchen garden with a crinkle-crankle wall. Magnificent curved grass terraces forming an amphitheatre behind the house are designed by Kim Wilkie and were begun in 1999.

Hever Castle

see page 147

Hewell Grange

Tardebigge, Worcestershire OS SP0069
English Heritage Register Grade II*

Medieval estate acquired by the Windsor family (later Earls of Plymouth) at the dissolution of the monasteries, before 1558. The present house was built 1884–91 by Bodley and Garner for the 1st Earl of Plymouth. Since 1946 the house has been a Borstal. South-east of the house, the French Garden – a rectangular lawn divided into four compartments edged with beech hedges and with a Coade stone statue of a draped female figure, in an arbour of yew at the centre of each. A Country Life photograph of 1902 shows the French Garden with parterres of ornate bedding schemes and countless rose-twined arches. West of the house and south of the French Garden, woodland with many specimen trees and planned walks. East of the house, steps down to a sunken rock garden with ferns. There had been a deer park here from 1561. Large lake east and north-east of house. Humphry Repton, who produced a Red Book in 1812, was very critical: he thought that the designer of the park had "never seen the Spot, but on a map". He thought the house was too low and had poor views, the lake lacked interest, the park was bleak, clumps of trees were "like huge warts" and the park enclosed by unrelieved belts of trees. Much work was done following Repton's suggestions.

Hexton Manor

Hexton, Hertfordshire OS TL1030
English Heritage Register Grade II

17th-century house with early 20th-century alterations. East of the house, lawns and two fountain pools. From the east lawn a flight of stone steps leads down to the bank of a lake. To the south, lawns, shrubs and specimen trees. To the north-east, walks about the lake and through woodland at the Rookery where a stream flows over cascades and weirs. Park, with pasture and arable land and scattered mature trees and belts.

Heydon Hall

Heydon, Norfolk OS TG1127
English Heritage Register Grade II*

16th-century house for Henry Dynne, with subsequent remodelling. *Patte d'oie* of avenues to the south probably dates from early 18th century but trees were replanted in mid 19th century. Curved lake in park. 18th-century walled kitchen garden. Icehouse and obelisk in Icehouse Plantation. Formal rose garden, arboretum and shrubbery.

Heythrop Park

Heythrop, Oxfordshire OS SP3626
English Heritage Register Grade II*

Mansion designed by Thomas Archer for Charles Talbot, 12th Earl and 1st Duke of Shrewsbury, and built 1706–11. Gutted by fire in 1831; restored and altered in 1923. Early 18th-century formal garden possibly by Henry Wise. The 2½m-long Grand Avenue and Wilderness (which now has a

19th-century rockery) were made before 1713. 18th-century alcove bower close to the Wilderness. Lakes, cascades and woodland walks made in mid to late 18th century. A Gothic moss house of *c.*1780 stands close to a cascade. An aerial photograph of the house in its setting, showing the Grand Avenue and the Wilderness, is illustrated in Christopher Taylor's *Parks and Gardens of Britain: A Landscape History from the Air* (1998).

Heywood
see page 414

Hickleton Hall

Hickleton, South Yorkshire OS SE4805
English Heritage Register Grade II
Open by appointment Tel 01709 892070

House built from 1745 for Geoffrey Wentworth to the designs of James Paine. Formal gardens round house, laid out in the early 20th century with terraces, an oval pond with statue, concrete obelisks, box parterre with 18th-century urn and a bowling green. 19th-century park with summerhouse in a quarry and statues on pedestals.

Hidcote Manor Garden
see page 210

The High Beeches
see page 148

High Glanau

Lydart, Gwent OS SO4907
Cadw/ICOMOS Register Grade II*

House built in the Arts and Crafts style 1922–23 to the designs of Eric Francis for H. Avray Tipping, the garden designer and writer. The site is beautiful, on a high plateau, with the Wye valley to the west. Avray Tipping laid out a series of stone terraces leading to an octagonal pool from which paths lead downhill through a wild setting to a dell with a stream. For his own garden, he put into practice the ideas he had recommended at an RHS conference in 1928: "Let there be some formalism about the house to carry the geometric lines and enclosed feeling of architecture, but let us step shortly from that into wood and wild garden."

High Tor

Matlock Bath, Derbyshire OS SK2958
English Heritage Register Grade II*

19th-century pleasure grounds on the east bank of the river Derwent. A path leads to the top of High Tor with dramatic cliff-top viewpoints from a path, Giddy Edge, which runs along the crest of the cliff. Two caves, Fern Cave and Roman Cave, are no longer accessible to visitors. High Tor Hotel, on the western bank of the river and outside the area of the pleasure grounds, is built in early 19th-century cottage *orné* style, thoroughly in keeping with the picturesque setting.

High Wall

Headington, Oxford, Oxfordshire OS SP5306
English Heritage Register Grade II

Early 20th-century house designed by Walter Cave for Miss Katherine Fielden. Garden designed by Harold Peto *c.*1912 with magnificent pergola with classical stone columns and an octagonal gazebo at its centre overlooking a croquet lawn. Peto also made terracing, an octagonal pool and an oval rose garden, but this part of the garden was sold for redevelopment in the 1970s. Percy Cane also worked on the garden in the 1920s but it is not known what he did.

Highbury Hall

Birmingham, West Midlands OS SP0682
English Heritage Register Grade II

Venetian Gothic house built 1878 to the designs of John Henry Chamberlain for Joseph Chamberlain (no relation), the radical politician (father of Nevill Chamberlain) and later first Chancellor of Birmingham University, who had made a fortune from the manufacture of screws. Immensely elaborate garden designed by Edward Milner and his son Henry from 1879. A semicircular lawn in front of the house had clipped shapes of box and holly, sinuous paths and flowery parterres. A lake had two islands and rustic bridges. Countless rhododendrons were planted – and replanted when they languished. An "Elizabethan" rose garden was enclosed in yew hedges; a formal

"Dutch" garden of bulbs was laid out; there was a rock garden by James Pulham; an "Italian" garden had a fountain, terracotta pots full of sunflowers, gates from Siena, and dwarf cypresses at the corners of flower beds; a hothouse contained a great collection of tender orchids – one of the best of its time – and thirteen other glasshouses housed azaleas, begonias, cyclamen, ferns, primulas and roses. A model farm with Jersey cows, pigs, poultry and sheep was also part of this urban estate. The house survives, used by the City of Birmingham for civic functions, and much of the original garden layout may be seen.

Highclere Castle

Highclere, Hampshire OS SU4458
English Heritage Register Grade I
Open regularly Tel 01635 253210

Ancient estate with medieval deer park. 18th-century house of the Herbert family, rebuilt for 3rd Earl of Carnarvon by Sir Charles Barry 1839–42, when it became the largest house in Hampshire. Park landscaped from 1770 by Capability Brown for Henry Herbert (later 1st Earl of Carnarvon), much altered by later landscaping. 18th-century temple (Jackdaws Castle) with Corinthian columns, east of castle. Fishing pavilion on lake designed by Barry but with interior in the style of William Kent (possibly from 18th-century house at Highclere). 18th-century walled kitchen garden on site proposed by Brown. The rhododendron *R.* × *altaclerense* was bred at Highclere in 1831 by J.R. Gowen. The hybrid holly *Ilex* × *altaclerensis* also had its origins here.

Highdown
see page 149

Highgate Cemetery

Camden, London OS TQ2877 English
Heritage Register Grade II* Open regularly

Cemetery laid out by David Ramsay and opened 1839, on the site of the garden of Sir William Ashurst who had been Lord Mayor of London in 1693; some details of the 17th-century garden – a terrace, a fine old cedar of Lebanon – survive. Highgate Cemetery soon became fashionable: "In such a place the aspect of death is

softened," wrote *The Lady's Newspaper* in 1850. It expanded to 37 acres/15 hectares in 1855 and by 1888 around 100,000 burials had taken place here. The architect Stephen Geary designed the entrance: a Gothic gatehouse linked to two chapels (Anglican and Nonconformist). Paths wind about the sloping site among mature trees and much elaborate funerary architecture. An extraordinary sight is a passage called Egyptian Avenue whose entrance is flanked by pairs of plump Egyptian columns, possibly designed by J.B. Bunning. It is lined with memorials and leads to the Circle of Lebanon, a circle of tombs about an old cedar of Lebanon. Throughout the cemetery are many fine, curious or flamboyant monuments. After much neglect and vandalism the Friends of Highgate Cemetery was formed in 1975 to protect it. It is one of the few cemeteries to charge for entrance, which does nothing to deter the countless visitors who come to admire Karl Marx's tomb with its famous inscription – WORKERS OF THE WORLD UNITE.

Highgrove

nr Tetbury, Gloucestershire Open to selected groups by written appointment

Garden made by the Prince of Wales from 1980, which Timothy Mowl, in his *Historic Gardens of Gloucestershire* (2002), describes as "the first hands-on, genuinely personal royal garden in this country since Prince Frederick Louis's Kew of the 1740s". In his garden-making the Prince had advice from some of the notable gardeners of the day – among them, Miriam Rothschild, the Marchioness of Salisbury, Sir Roy Strong and Rosemary Verey. The garden has a wildflower meadow, a walk of golden yew topiary underplanted with thyme, an arboretum, a sundial garden (with only black and white flowers), a cottage garden, a walled kitchen garden and a woodland garden. It is is rich in ornaments which range from a bronze gladiator to a spiky metal gilt heron perched in a nest of leaves (designed by Isabel and Julian Bannerman) on top of a cast-iron column rescued from Victoria Station in London.

H

Decorative buildings include a vernacular dovecote (by David Blisset), a chickenhouse like a church (by Richard Craven), a charming fairytale treehouse for the young princes (by William Bertram) and the millennium Sanctuary (designed by Keith Critchlow with walls of clay and straw). The Bannermans have contributed many notable effects – a Wall of Gifts made of stone fragments given to the Prince, a wonderful stumpery with ferns and hellebores, a pair of green oak temples with pediments filled with driftwood, and a path of ammonites. Last, and not least, the whole garden is maintained organically.

Highnam Court
Highnam, Gloucestershire OS SO7919
English Heritage Register Grade II*
Open occasionally for NGS

17th-century house on an ancient site, with later alterations, especially 1840–55, by Lewis Vulliamy for Thomas Gambier-Parry. Medieval deer park later developed as a landscape park. A map of 1757 shows a Great Pool and several ponds, the remains of medieval fish ponds, and a formal garden. The pools were made into a single lake in the 19th century. Gambier-Parry laid out a garden, in the words of *Country Life* in 1899, of "light and shade and finely constructed colours", and Vulliamy designed an Italianate terrace with balustrade, urns and bedding schemes. Gambier-Parry also consulted James Pulham, who made an elaborate rock and water garden with pools linked by a stream. The planting was lavish, as *Country Life* recorded: "Ferns and rock plants in luxuriant masses clothe the stone while lofty and well positioned conifers of noble kinds rise like sentinels above." He also made, of Pulhamite, two grottoes and a cave. The house is now a music school but the garden survives.

The Hill, *also known as* Inverforth House
Camden, London OS TQ2686
English Heritage Register Grade II*
Open regularly Tel 020 8455 5183

Early 19th-century house radically remodelled in the late 19th and early 20th centuries for W.H. Lever (later Lord Leverhulme). Gardens designed from 1906 by Thomas Mawson, who built terraces (using the spoil from the excavation of the Hampstead Tube) to take advantage of the fine views over Hampstead Heath. South of the first terrace, past a lily pool, an immense and complicated pergola embraces two sides of the garden at rectangles. An extension of it continues south, leading over a bridge and through a temple to a belvedere overlooking the heath. Built of oak mounted on pale Portland stone columns, the whole stands on arcaded brick ramparts. Ends and corners are marked by trelliswork domes or sweeping roofs. It was built over a long period as Lever acquired more land in a piecemeal fashion – and was completed in 1920. Since 1990 the pergola has been finely restored.

Hill Close Gardens
Warwick, Warwickshire OS SP2764 English Heritage Register Grade II* Open regularly Email info@hillclosegardens.warwick.uk.com

A group of 19th-century hedged gardens originally laid out on the edge of the town to provide gardens for urban dwellers. They were not merely allotments, for they had lawns, flower beds, beds of vegetables and fruit and summerhouses. Furthermore, they had the privacy of enclosure. They were derelict by 1998 and only saved from being built on at the last moment. Restored by a group of volunteers, with four of the charming original summerhouses surviving, they open a window on a most attractive aspect of garden history.

Hill Court
Walford-on-Wye, Herefordshire OS SO5721 English Heritage Register Grade II

Beautiful late 17th-century house built for Richard Clarke. Formal garden to north of house, with marble fountain, lawns with shrubs and a Gothic summerhouse. South of the house, a late 17th-century walled kitchen garden with early 18th-century wrought-iron gates is now a flower garden; it is crossed by a path leading to a second set of grand gates. South-

east of house, mid 20th-century water garden with a Chinese pavilion. South of the walled garden, a walk with yew topiary. This is part of a scheme planned in the early 19th century to reveal views of the 13th-century Goodrich Castle to the south – originally framed by the gates in the kitchen garden. The house, formerly the home of an antique dealer and full of beautiful things, is now the premises of a German firm of plastics manufacturers.

Hill Hall
Theydon Mount, Essex OS TQ4899
English Heritage Register Grade II

House built from 1557 for Sir Thomas Smith on a site going back to the 12th century. Pevsner's *Essex* (1965) in the "Buildings of England" series describes it as "one of the most important earlier Elizabethan houses in the country" but, alas, shortly after that was written, the house was gutted by fire. Smith was a very cultivated and much travelled man. He made a garden south of the house with ponds on three sides, which survive. Parts of a 17th-century garden – a terrace with steps down to a lawn, with a canal east of the house and some trees along the drive, may date from the 17th century. In 1791 Humphry Repton advised R. Vernon-Harcourt and a Red Book was produced. Perimeter planting on the northern boundary of the park probably dates from this time. In the 1980s the M25 motorway was built across the park south of the house.

Hill of Tarvit House
see page 381

Hill Top
nr Sawtrey, Cumbria OS SD3795
Open regularly (NT) Tel 01539 436269)

This very pretty 17th-century house in lovely country between Coniston and Windermere was the home of the children's books author and artist Beatrix Potter. She was a keen supporter of conservation and a friend of Canon Hardwick Rawnsley, the co-founder of the National Trust, and on her death in 1953 left this house and 4,000 acres/1,619

hectares of wild Lakeland countryside to the National Trust. As a shrine to a famous and much-loved person it is full of atmosphere – the contents remaining as they were at her death. The cottage garden, restored by the Trust, with its orchard, roses, herbs and vegetables is a convincing evocation of the sort of garden known to Peter Rabbit. The repertory of plants – feverfew, geraniums, hollyhocks, honeysuckle, lupins and snapdragons – and the jolly jumble style of their arrangement are delightful. Beatrix Potter's potent imaginary world of cottage gardens and country life seen through animals' eyes has influenced generations of gardeners, and Mrs Rabbit's exhortation to her son Peter – "Don't go into Mr McGregor's garden: your father had an accident there; he was put into a pie by Mrs McGregor" – must have filled many a child with a fearful desire to enter such tempting forbidden territory.

The Sir Harold Hillier Gardens and Arboretum
see page 87

Hillsborough Castle
Hillsborough, County Down, Northern Ireland Open regularly Tel (028) 9052 0700

House built in the late 18th century for Wills Hill, 1st Marquess of Downshire, to the designs of R.F. Brettingham, and much enlarged in the early 19th century. The castle became the residence of the Governor of Northern Ireland in 1924 and was badly damaged by fire in 1934. It is now the residence of the royal family when in Northern Ireland, and is used by the Secretary of State for Northern Ireland and Ministers for official receptions. The demesne is well wooded and parkland has mature trees. The grounds have some good ornamental buildings, among them Cromlyn's Chapel, a sham ruin dating from the late 18th or early 19th century, roughly built of monumental slabs of stone. Almost certainly of the same period is an icehouse whose entrance is given

the appearance of a grotto. A most curious domed and pillared Ionic temple, Lady Alice's Temple, made of cast-iron, was put up in 1880. Standing on the bank of a lake, it is aligned with a descending walk of Irish yews on the far bank. Now outside the demesne but visible from it, is an extraordinary eyecatcher, a giant fluted column crowned with a statue of the 3rd Marquess, erected in 1848.

Hilton Maze
Hilton, Cambridgeshire OS TL2966
English Heritage Register Grade II

Remarkable 17th-century turf maze on the village green, made by William Sparrow in 1660. At the centre, a stone obelisk surmounted with a sphere. An inscription on the obelisk records the death of William Sparrow in 1729 at the age of eighty-eight and records that "hos gyros formavit anno 1660". The design of the maze is circular, 45ft/14m in diameter, with a four-part almost symmetrical arrangement of paths.

Hilton Park
Clones, County Monaghan, Republic of Ireland Open regularly Tel (00353) 47 56033

17th-century estate of the MacMahon family bought in 1734 by Dr Samuel Madden. New house built for the Madden family in the late 18th century and rebuilt in the early 19th century after a fire. Mrs Delany saw the demesne in 1748: "The place is pretty, a very fine wood of all sorts of forest trees planted by Dr Madden just by the house surrounded by a fine river." Splendid views over wooded lawn to lake. Canal between lakes possibly survives from a 17th-century formal garden. Good 19th-century conifers, rhododendrons and other flowering shrubs. The estate is still owned by the Madden family who have restored the gardens.

Himley Hall
Himley, Staffordshire OS SO8891
English Heritage Register Grade II

Ancient site with new house built in the 18th century for the

6th Baron Dudley (created Viscount Dudley and Ward in 1763). The 2nd Viscount called in Capability Brown who produced a plan in 1779; in 1780–81 he was paid a total of £1,200 (£71,712 today). North of the house, pleasure grounds were laid out with paths and views over the north park. To increase the park south of the house, Brown recommended destroying a hamlet and rerouting the road, which was done. Brown planted tree belts along the western and northern boundaries of the park. The northern part of the park has been mostly ploughed up but Brown's recommendations here were for only sparse plantings of trees. East of the house, a golf course made in the 1970s.

Hinton Ampner Garden

see page 87

Hinton House

Hinton St George, Somerset OS ST4112
English Heritage Register Grade II

Complicated house of the Poulett family, started in the late 15th century but now essentially of early 18th-century appearance. Pevsner, on a melancholy note, apologises for his perfunctory description, "as Earl Poulett would not allow me to see inside." John Leland's *Itinerary in or about the years 1535–1543* refers to Sir Hugh Poulett's deer park at Hinton. Great formal garden in the 17th century visited by Cosimo de' Medici in 1669. He noted "gardens both for utility and pleasure. On the one hand they contain all those sorts of plants and fruits which the climate will allow, and on the other a parterre, very different from the common usage of gardens in England. For, where these have sanded walks perfectly levelled… and flat spaces covered with very green turf and without ornament, this…is a meadow with different beds having borders of bricks on end, filled with flowers." Late 18th-century landscape park with lakes. Statue of Diana on a plinth, enclosed in double circle of limes shown on the map. The Pouletts remained at Hinton until well after World

War II when the estate was dismembered, the house being turned into flats.

Hinton Manor

Hinton Waldrist, Oxfordshire OS SU3799
English Heritage Register Grade II

Early 18th-century house incorporating Tudor house. Formal gardens and pleasure grounds perhaps made in the mid 17th century, incorporating earthworks of the Norman Hinton Castle and its former moat. The Norman motte was converted into a mount, probably during the 17th century, with a spiral path; it is now thickly planted with shrubs. 20th-century formal garden of box hedges and topiary against east front of house, with an early 18th-century circular fountain pool.

Hinwick Hall

Podington, Bedfordshire OS SP9362
English Heritage Register Grade II

Mid 16th-century house for the Tyringham family, with several changes of owner and alterations, especially in the 18th century. Early 20th-century formal gardens. Sunken garden south of the house surrounded by low stone walls and hedging. Square pool flanked by lawns. In the park west of the house, a lime avenue 333yd/300m long replanted in late 20th century on mid 18th-century alignment.

Hinwick House

Podington, Bedfordshire OS SP9362
English Heritage Register Grade II

Early 18th-century house for the Orlebar family who remained here until 1994. A garden was made at about the same time, handsomely shown in the painting attributed to William van der Hagen by John Harris in *The Artist and the Country House* (1979). This shows the garden to the east of the house with sweeping shapes cut out of a huge oval (of lawn?), edged with lines of trees and with a statue on a stepped plinth at the centre. Crescents of old limes, possibly the early 18th-century originals, survive in this position.

The Hirsel

nr Coldstream, Berwickshire OS NT8240
Scottish Inventory Open regularly
Tel 01573 224144

Site going back to Neolithic times. The estate was bought by the 1st Earl of Home (and 6th Baron) in 1611, and has belonged to the family since. Present house built to the designs of William Adam 1739–41 but engulfed by William Atkinson's work of 1813–15. Terraced gardens about the house lead down towards the river Leet. Here are the remains of a Victorian rosery, mixed borders and an alpine garden. 18th-century walled kitchen garden with a tulip tree reputedly planted in 1742. Parkland about the banks of the Leet water, dating from before 1750, transformed by 1841 into a picturesque landscape with summerhouses at viewpoints along planned walks. Very old oaks and sweet chestnuts close to the house but most of the park trees date from the 19th century. Woodland dating back to before 1750, with deciduous trees and conifers underplanted with azaleas and rhododendrons dating from the late 19th century and now of huge size.

Hodges Barn

see page 211

Hodnet Hall

see page 213

Hoghton Tower

Hoghton, Lancashire OS SD6226
English Heritage Register Grade II
Open regularly Tel 01254 852986

House built c.1560 for Thomas de Hoghton, with alterations in the 17th and 19th centuries. A painting by Arthur Devis of c.1734 in John Harris's *The Artist and the Country House* (1979) shows the house standing in a walled enclosure on the top of a bald hill with an entrance avenue rolling "down the hill like a carpet", as Harris puts it. The hill is today no longer bald, but well wooded on all but the south-west side. The forecourt, the Tilting Yard, remains as shown in the Devis painting, but now grassed over. South of the house, a walled rose garden and rampart garden. On this side of

the house, a series of terraces run down the slope.

Holdenby House Gardens

see page 265

Holehird Gardens

see page 343

Holker Hall

see page 344

Holkham Hall

Holkham, Norfolk OS TS8842
English Heritage Register Grade I
Open regularly Tel 01328 710227

Great house started in 1722 for Thomas Coke (later Lord Leicester) on the site of an Elizabethan house. Coke probably designed the house himself, in collaboration with Lord Burlington and William Kent, and with Matthew Brettingham as a draughtsman. Coke took an equal interest in the landscape setting, on which work started before the house, and in this Kent was at first the chief designer. The southern approach to the house is marked by Kent's Triumphal Arch (designed 1739 but not completed until 1752) south of the lodges. An avenue runs dead south, interrupted by an obelisk (William Kent, 1729–30) standing at the highest point of the estate (which, being Norfolk, is not at all high). To the west, a temple also by Kent (of 1729–31). The drive continues over a slight hill, revealing the house in the dip below, and then curves between a serpentine lake to the west and the house to the east. On the north lawn of the house Kent planted his favourite semi-formal clumps which Horace Walpole so disliked ("I know no clumps I would give sixpence to see, but those in Grosvenor Square"). In 1762 Capability Brown came to continue the work in the park, adding many trees and naturalising the park's appearance. In 1780 superb new walled kitchen gardens, covering 6 acres/2.4 hectares, were built at a cost of £10,000 (£587,600 today) west of the lake – they are now a commercial nursery. Humphry Repton produced a Red Book in 1789 for Thomas Coke (later 1st Earl of Leicester) who had

inherited in 1776. Repton recognised the magnificence of the park (at 2,000 acres/810 hectares, the largest in Norfolk) and concentrated his attentions on the more intimate areas of the woods about the lake where he planned walks and picturesque buildings. It is uncertain if any of this was done. W.A. Nesfield and William Burn made new formal gardens close to the house 1849–57, with a great parterre to the north overlooking the park. An aerial photograph of the landscape is illustrated in Christopher Taylor's *Parks and Gardens of Britain: A Landscape History from the Air* (1998).

Holland Park

see page 150

Hollycombe House

Liphook, West Sussex OS SU8529
English Heritage Register Grade II*
Open regularly Tel 01428 724900

House first built in 1803 as a cottage *orné* for C.W. Taylor to the designs of John Nash, and much altered in 1892 for Sir John Hawkshaw. New gardens were made at this time: west of the house, walled gardens; below the south front of the house, a balustraded terrace and then turf terraces with a series of pools descending the slope; an arboretum, with much additional planting in the late 20th century of specimen trees and shrubs in lawns (a clearing in the arboretum has a fine collection of Waterer's hybrids of *Rhododendron molle* subsp. *japonicum*). The estate today is known as the home of the Hollycombe Steam Collection.

Holme Lacy House

Holme Lacy, Herefordshire OS SO5535
English Heritage Register Grade II*

Late 17th-century house on an ancient site, built for the 2nd Viscount Scudamore probably to the designs of Hugh May. The house has been a hotel since 1995. West of the house, an orangery probably of the late 17th century, with formal gardens of wide axial walks and yew hedges to the south and west. The formal gardens were probably laid out in the early years of the 18th century, before 1720.

H

South of house, the Battle Garden, a sunken lawn running down to a fish pond. Double terraces run round on three sides, and in the southern half of the garden they slope downwards and curve out on each side to form an amphitheatre-like space overlooking the pond. West of the Battle Garden, compartments hedged in yew; the chief compartment, the Flower Garden, has flower beds, yew topiary and domes of clipped golden yew. South of the Flower Garden, the Green Walk, with yew hedges and a view eastwards over the Battle Garden to the countryside beyond. West of the house, a raised walk gives views over the garden and south into the deer park – there had been a deer park here by 1577. Present park, chiefly pasture with specimen trees and some old parkland oaks and sweet chestnuts.

Holme Pierrepoint Hall

Holme Pierrepoint, Nottinghamshire
OS SK6238 English Heritage Register
Grade II Open regularly Tel 0115 933 2371

House originally of the 16th century for the Pierrepoint family, with subsequent alterations and partly rebuilt in the 1870s. A parterre laid out in a courtyard c.1875, finely reinstated by present owners: an intricate symmetrical three-part arrangement of irregular shapes edged in box and planted with spring bulbs, irises and roses, with a sundial at the centre. East of house, yew trees interplanted with box and beech and an informal shrub border. Behind the house, a Site of Special Scientific Interest where *Tulipa sylvestris* and *Ornithogalum nutans* grow wild.

Holwood Park

Bromley, London OS TQ4263
English Heritage Register Grade II

House built 1823–26 for John Ward to the designs of Decimus Burton, replacing an 18th-century house, partly by Sir John Soane, which had been owned by William Pitt the Younger. In c.1791 William Pitt consulted Humphry Repton, but no Red Book was produced and it is

uncertain what came of the meeting. In the later 18th century there had been ornamental pleasure grounds but these were largely removed when Pitt opened up views from the house – such as are revealed to the south today. In the park, areas of dense woodland and a string of pools. North of the house, "Caesar's Camp", an Ancient Monument.

Holyroodhouse Palace

Edinburgh OS NT2774 Scottish Inventory
Open regularly Tel 0131 556 5100

The palace was started for James IV in 1501 but its appearance today is largely the result of the rebuilding, 1671–79, to the designs of Sir William Bruce and Robert Mylne. The site is magnificent, with the Royal Mile leading up through the heart of old Edinburgh on one side and the wild, hilly landscape of Holyrood Park on the other, crowned by the crag of Arthur's Seat. A drawing of c.1647 by John Gordon of Rothiemay – one of the earliest surviving depictions of a known Scottish garden – shows elaborate but jumbled formal gardens with parterres. In 1670 a physic garden was founded in St Anne's Yard north of the palace – the origin of the Royal Botanic Garden Edinburgh (*see page 391*). The palace garden today has a 19th-century air, with ornamental trees, shrubberies, lawns and walks about the beautiful and picturesque ruins of Holyrood Abbey (from c.1195). A grand Scottish sundial, dated 1633, stands on the northern edge of the garden. In relation to the splendours of the palace and of the landscape of the park the gardens are, to put it mildly, distinctly *sotto voce*.

Homewood

Knebworth, Hertfordshire OS TL2319
English Heritage Register Grade II

House built c.1901–2 for the Dowager Countess of Lytton to the designs of Edwin Lutyens, her son-in-law. Lutyens also designed the gardens. A paved terrace under the south-east façade has yew hedges at each end; these continue down, with niches cut in them, to a parallel gravel terrace at a lower

level. Box-edged beds on either side of central steps lead down to a further walk, with a lawn and trees and a kitchen garden. South-west of the house, a croquet lawn.

Honing House

Honing, Norfolk OS TG3229
English Heritage Register Grade II*

House built 1748 and altered c.1788–92 by Sir John Soane and by Humphry Repton in 1792, for Mrs Cubitt. Repton also advised Thomas Cubitt on the grounds, producing a Red Book in 1792; he was paid only £5-5-0 (£284 today) so little seems to have come of his advice. The park today is enclosed in belts and plantings of trees, with mainly open parkland south of the house. This, as it happens, would have been in line with Repton's ideas – he abhorred the sight of arable land in a park.

Honington Hall

Honington, Warwickshire OS SP2642
English Heritage Register Grade II*
Open regularly Tel 01608 661434

Beautiful house, built in 1682 for Sir Henry Parker. An engraving by Buck shows formal gardens to the west of the house running down to the river Stour. These were destroyed when the grounds were landscaped in the Rococo style in 1749 by Joseph Townsend with advice from Sanderson Miller. Several pretty buildings, including a grotto by Sanderson Miller, can be seen in a painting of 1759 by Thomas Robins the Elder, but none survives. 19th-century parterre before south front of house and, to the south-west, a formal garden of c.1930 with rectangular parterres and a circular bed.

The Hoo

nr Kimpton, Hertfordshire OS TL1819
English Heritage Register Grade II

Ancient estate, from the 13th century, of the Hoo family. 17th-century house rebuilt in the 1760s by Sir William Chambers and demolished in 1958. Capability Brown is said to have worked on the park in the 1760s (a drawing by him for a bridge exists but it was never built) and is reputedly responsible for damming the river

Mimram to form a lake north-east of the house; the lake largely filled in in the 20th century and obscured with planting. To its west, an 18th-century icehouse. Park mostly pasture with some arable farming and scattered areas of woodland about the perimeter. Kitchen garden enclosed in 17th-century brick walls, now largely grassed over.

The Hoo

Willingdon, East Sussex OS TQ5802
English Heritage Register Grade II*

House built in 1902 by Edwin Lutyens for Alexander Wedderburn. Lutyens laid out three terraces below the south front of the house. The upper terrace has flagstones, lawns and a border running along the top of the retaining wall and against the house. Three semicircular flights of steps lead down to a rectangular lawn with borders at each end and a rose border along its southern edge, with a gap in the centre where a wrought-iron balcony pierces the parapet wall and overlooks the terrace below. The lower terrace is reached by steps at each end, each flight with a square gazebo to one side. The lower terrace has a gravel walk, with bands of lawn and mixed borders below the lower storey of each gazebo. Beneath the balcony set into the retaining wall is a circular lily pool. Trees and a hedge run along the south side of the terrace, with a further iron balustrade at the centre. The house is now flats.

Hope End

Colwall, Herefordshire OS SO7241
English Heritage Register Grade II
Open occasionally for NGS

House built in 1750s and later converted to stables; new house, built nearby in 1815 and probably designed by J.C. Loudon in startling Moorish style, demolished in 1873; the present house is the old stables converted back into a house c.1976 and now a hotel. The gardens were designed by J.C. Loudon before 1822, when he referred to them in his *Encyclopaedia of Gardening*: "The house and grounds recently improved from our designs; the latter highly romantic by nature,

and well wooded." A picturesque valley east of the house survives from Loudon's work. South of the house, the valley was cut back to form a limestone cliff and open up views; north of the house, a serpentine pool with islands was created by damming the Cradley brook. Loudon planned walks along the valley and some of these may still be followed. In about 1990 a Gothick grotto was built by the pool and a Gothic ruin on an island. In the 1980s and 1990s various ornamental buildings were added – two ruined temples, a seat and a belvedere. A deer park was made in the mid 18th century and the park is now pasture with scattered trees.

Hopetoun House

nr South Queensferry, West Lothian
OS NT0879 Scottish Inventory
Open regularly Tel 0131 331 2451

Spectacular and palatial house started in 1699 to the designs of Sir William Bruce for Charles Hope (later 1st Earl of Hopetoun) and completed by 1756 to the designs of William Adam, John Adam and Robert Adam. Sir William Bruce is thought to have laid out a garden but nothing is known of it. William Adam designed the formal landscape from 1720 but only vestiges survive – a pool, a bowling green with urns and a Little Garden. West of the house, a lime avenue leads to woodland where a diagonal ride corresponds to Adam's plan and leads to Adam's Wilderness which has sweet chestnuts and yews surviving from the original planting. A pinetum was established here in the 19th century. It is disappointing that such a splendid house is set in such a modest landscape.

Horniman Gardens

Lewisham, London OS TQ3473
English Heritage Register Grade II
Open regularly Tel 020 8699 1872

The Horniman Museum was built 1897–1901 to the designs of Harrison Townsend for J.F. Horniman, a tea merchant whose own collection formed the nucleus of the museum. An avenue of horse chestnuts leads from the museum entrance to the gardens west of the museum, which were laid out when the building was completed. Parallel to the avenue, a rose garden, sunken garden with bedding schemes and a semicircular pergola. Sweeping lawns at the centre are planted with specimen trees and the boundaries are screened with belts of trees. In the north, a bandstand, menagerie and clipped laurel hedges. A Coade stone group of a pelican with figures was made in 1797, designed by Lady Diana Beauclerk for the Pelican Life Insurance Company of Lombard St.

Horsted Place

Little Horsted, East Sussex OS TQ4618
English Heritage Register Grade II

House built 1850–52 with alterations in the 20th century. Balustraded terraces under east and south fronts are contemporary with the house, and gardens were designed by Sir Geoffrey Jellicoe in 1966. To the east, a rectangular lawn with corner beds of annuals. To the north, a path with an orangery, a high wall and a shrub border. From the south terrace, a walk of pleached limes extends. A path running across the northern side of the lawn passes through rose-covered arches, across a serpentine shrub border and into a woodland shrubbery. A secondary path from the lawn runs through a tunnel of apples and winds south through glades to the woodland shrubbery; a parallel path passes through a laburnum tunnel. A golf course occupies much of the former park, and in the remaining part only a few parkland trees survive, with a shelter belt to the west.

Horton Court

Chipping Sodbury, Gloucestershire
7785 Open regularly (NT)
01249 730141

House built in 1521 for William Knight, a courtier to Henry VII and Henry VIII (whose divorce from Catherine of Aragon he helped to arrange). Remarkable detached "ambulatory", or loggia, with arches and slender columns of striking renaissance character – no doubt inspired by what Knight had seen in Italy (he had studied at Ferrara University). Below the ambulatory, terraces are linked by grass steps to medieval stewponds.

Horton Hall

Hackleton, Northamptonshire OS SP8154
English Heritage Register Grade II

House demolished in 1936; only lodges and stables remaining. The estate of the Parr family in the 17th century and later of the Montagus (Earls of Manchester and Earls of Halifax). 18th-century landscape park with two serpentine lakes (Horace Walpole called them "a fine piece of water" in 1763) separated by a dam concealed by a rusticated bridge which, it is presumed, originally carried the drive to the Menagerie (*see page 270*). In a spinney nearby, a mid 18th-century icehouse and, on the bank of the lake, an 18th-century brick boathouse. On the north-eastern boundary of the park, two other 18th-century buildings: the Arches is a three part triumphal arch and the Temple, with an Ionic portico, now a private house. The architect Daniel Garrett was at Horton in 1750, designing "Gothic Bridges etc".

Horton Park

Bradford, West Yorkshire OS SE1431 English Heritage Register Grade II Open regularly

Public park opened in 1878. Laid out with broad straight promenade and winding peripheral carriage drive, the two linked by winding narrow paths. A cast-iron bridge spans an irregular lake at the centre of the park. A stream from the lake follows the promenade in a culvert with occasional cascades. A now waterless pond with a fine stone and polished granite fountain is today outlined with rose beds and grass. Three bowling greens with pavilions are enclosed in hedges and shrubs and there is a children's play area.

Houghton Hall (Norfolk)

see page 310

Houghton Hall

Sancton, East Yorkshire OS SE8839
English Heritage Register Grade II

Fine house, built *c*.1765 for Philip Langdale to the designs of Thomas Atkinson, on a site going back to the early 14th century. Park laid out by Thomas White in 1768. South of the house, two lakes connected by a cascade. This, together with clumps of trees and perimeter planting, closely follow White's plan. Nikolaus Pevsner and David Neave's "The Buildings of England" volume on *Yorkshire: York and the East Riding* (1997) describes the estate as "The perfect Georgian country house in a beautiful parkland setting".

Houghton Lodge

Houghton, Hampshire OS SU3433
English Heritage Register Grade II*
Open regularly Tel 01264 810502

Exquisite cottage *orné* built *c*.1800 in the style of John Nash, possibly as a fishing lodge, in a beautiful raised position overlooking the river Test. Open lawns with trees and shrubs. Curious entrance lodge of flint in the form of a grotto. Kitchen garden with cob walls, which now houses the Hampshire Hydroponicum – "the garden of the future" – in which flowers, fruit and herbs are grown without soil.

Houndwood House

nr Reston, Berwickshire OS NT8562
Scottish Inventory

A hunting lodge was built here for the priors of Coldingham *c*.1170. The present house is a tower house, built before 1550 but altered in the 19th and 20th centuries. Wild Garden north of the house has a burn with old rhododendrons planted along its banks (an article in *Scottish Field* in 1918 admired the "myriad hue…riot of colour"). A Japanese garden was laid out here *c*.1920, of which fragments remain.

House of the Binns
also known as The Binns

nr Linlithgow, West Lothian OS NT0578
Scottish Inventory Open regularly (NTS)
Tel 01506 834255

The Binns has probably been inhabited since prehistoric times; Binns Hill is thought to have been the site of a Pictish fort. There was a house here in the 15th century belonging to Archibald Meldrum, and in 1621 the estate was bought by Thomas Dalyell, in whose family it remained until 1944 when it was ("with pictures, plenishings and an endowment") given to the National Trust for Scotland. The present house is essentially 17th-century, with castellations added in the early 19th century. Fine parkland with a round and battlemented eyecatcher tower on the high point of Binns Hill, built in 1826 to the design of Alexander Allan. Formal gardens south of the house, with terraces built in the 1820s; now with a lawn, shrubs and herbaceous borders.

House of Dun

nr Montrose, Angus OS NO6759
Open regularly (NTS) Tel 01674 810264

Grand villa designed in 1730 by William Adam for David Erskine, Lord Dun in a beautiful position on land sloping down to Montrose Basin. The Erskines remained here until the estate was given to the National Trust for Scotland in 1980. Lady Augusta's Walk (named after Lady Augusta Kennedy-Erskine, the daughter of William IV and Mrs Jordan) follows a tumbling burn through woodland and the remains of a 19th-century rock garden, and preserves an air of agreeable melancholy. Long gravel walk in front of house runs along a wall on which are trained old varieties of apple and pear, many of them local varieties. Walled garden at end of walk has formal rose garden and plants dating from the 1880s.

House of Pitmuies

see page 382

How Caple Court Gardens

nr Ross-on-Wye, Herefordshire OS SO6030
Open regularly Tel 01989 740626

House of Arts and Crafts character in a beautiful position looking south over the Wye valley towards the Brecon Beacons. The garden is also in the Arts and Crafts style, with terraces, Italianate statues, a pool, Irish yews, shrub roses and a pergola. For some years this potentially very attractive garden looked promising but in recent times seems to have declined.

Howard Park

Glossop, Derbyshire OS SK0395
English Heritage Register Grade II
Open regularly

Public park designed by H.E. Milner and opened in 1888 in association with public baths and hospital – a rare example of such a comprehensive development. Hospital and bath house were designed by a Manchester architect, Mr Murgatroyd. The bath house has ornamental presence at the entrance to the park – an Italianate building with arched windows and a 100ft/30m campanile-like tower designed to remove vapours from the bath house boiler. In the centre of the park, a stream with a series of rockworks, cascades and pools. In the south-east corner, close to the south entrance, a lake. The entrance path leads to the Wood Memorial Fountain (1889). The park is well planted with bold groups of trees and shrubs to contrast with open expanses of grass.

Howard Park and Gardens

Letchworth, Hertfordshire OS TL2232
English Heritage Register Grade II
Open regularly

Public park, named after Ebenezer Howard, the pioneer town planner, and laid out 1904–11 as part of Letchworth Garden City. The park contains Letchworth's first public building, the Arts and Crafts Memorial Hall (Barry Parker and Raymond Unwin, 1905–6) in the northern end of the park. From it a swathe of trees runs to a serpentine paddling pool and, to its east, a stone plaque commemorating Ebenezer Howard. In the southern part of the park, bowling and putting greens. The C.F. Ball Memorial Garden of *c*.1936 is a sunken rose garden. On the western boundary, the First Garden City Heritage Museum (originally Parker and Unwin's office). Built 1907 as a medieval hall house, it has a thatched roof and was extended in 1937.

Howick Hall Gardens

see page 345

H

Howsham Hall

Howsham, North Yorkshire OS SE7363
English Heritage Register Grade II

Jacobean house built for Sir William Bamburgh on a beautiful site by the river Derwent. Formal gardens east of the house made in the early 18th century, of which a terrace remains. Park landscaped in the late 18th century when the estate belonged to Nathaniel Cholmley and when most of the earlier formal gardens were destroyed. It is said that Capability Brown advised here, in particular suggesting the destruction of the village green and all the houses on the west side of the high street in order to incorporate the land into the park. The house is now a school.

Howth Castle

Howth, County Dublin, Republic of Ireland

In a beautiful position on the north side of Dublin Bay, Howth Castle was built in the 15th century, on an older site, with additions made in the 18th and 19th centuries. The St Lawrence family has lived here for over 800 years. John Rocque's map of County Dublin (1757) shows formal gardens about the castle and a pattern of rides through woodland. These were probably laid out in the 1730s when work was also being done on the house. The formal gardens are shown in great detail in a painting of c.1740, illustrated in John Harris's *The Artist and the Country House* (1975). Enormous surviving beech hedges may well date from the early 18th century and could be the remains of the formal rides. On the steep wooded hill above the castle is a remarkable collection of rhododendrons, started in the late 19th century. Edwin Lutyens worked on the house in 1910 and laid out a pretty box parterre with stone flagged paths.

Hughenden Manor

Hughenden, Buckinghamshire OS SU8695
English Heritage Register Grade II
Open regularly (NT) Tel 01494 755565

Early 19th-century house on an ancient site. Bought in 1847 by Benjamin Disraeli, who wrote in 1863, "we have restored the house to what it was before the Civil Wars, and we have made a garden of terraces, in which cavaliers might roam, and saunter, with their ladye-loves!" Terrace on south side of house, with statues and vases and a rectangular parterre. Restored bedding schemes of the 1880s and a tiered fountain. Park of pasture and trees with a lake. Woodland north-west of the house includes Disraeli's German Forest, planted c.1861, with paths devised by Disraeli's wife, Mary-Anne, cutting through the existing beech woods. One mile south-west of the house, on rising land, a tall Bath stone pillar designed by E.B. Lamb and erected in 1862 by Mary-Anne Disraeli to celebrate the life of her father-in-law, Isaac d'Israeli.

Hunger Hill Gardens, Stonepit Coppice Gardens *and* Gorseyclose Gardens

Nottingham, Nottinghamshire OS SK5841
English Heritage Register Grade II*

In the late 18th and early 19th centuries it became the practice to set aside land for small rented gardens on the edge of rapidly expanding towns. These, typically of between an eighth and a sixth of an acre (a twentieth or a fourteenth of a hectare), were enclosed by hedges and used to cultivate ornamental and productive plants. They sometimes had ornamental summerhouses (often used as occasional residences) and glasshouses. This Nottingham group of detached town gardens, now largely used as allotments and engulfed by urban development, is the largest surviving group in England.

Hunstanton Hall

Hunstanton, Norfolk OS TF6941
English Heritage Register Grade II

The romantically moated house belonged to the L'Estrange (later Le Strange) family and goes back to the 15th century, with substantial Jacobean and Victorian remodellings. It suffered two fires and was converted into flats in 1948 when the estate was dismembered and the garden and park divided. Formal garden within the moat laid out in the 19th century with yew hedges, lawn and bedding schemes. Early 18th-century walled garden to the west, with mid 19th-century herbaceous borders restored in the 1980s. In the park, south of the house, is an octagonal pool and an octagonal island with a pavilion, the Octagon, built in 1655 for Sir Hamon Le Strange. P.G. Wodehouse was a frequent visitor to Hunstanton Hall. In *Very Good, Jeeves* (1926) there is a memorable scene in which a cabinet minister, the Right Hon. A.B. Filmer, is trapped in the Octagon on the island by an aggressive swan. Bertie Wooster came to the rescue: "I located the Right Hon. He was in the middle of the Octagon, seated on the roof and spouting water like a public fountain."

Huntercombe

Burnham, Buckinghamshire OS SU9380
English Heritage Register Grade II

The core of the house is a 14th-century timber-framed hall, with alterations made in the 17th, 18th and 19th centuries; its present appearance largely 19th-century. George Evelyn bought the estate in 1656 and was succeeded by his son, another George, whose cousin, John Evelyn, described the gardens in 1679 as "sweet gardens, exquisitely kept, though large". Estate bought in 1871 by the Revd Richard Cavendish Boyle whose wife, Eleanor Vere Boyle, a friend of Queen Victoria, developed Evelyn's garden and wrote children's books and books on gardening. L-shaped walled garden with 16th-century brick walls, ornamental gate piers, a lawn and herbaceous borders. East lawn, with clipped yews, and further east, large trees and shrubs planted informally. The house is now a children's hospital.

Hurstbourne Park

Hurstbourne Priors, Hampshire OS SU4448
English Heritage Register Grade II

Estate of the Wallop family (Earls of Portsmouth). Late 18th-century house by James Wyatt, burnt down in 1870. But two paintings, done in 1748 by John Griffier II and illustrated in John Harris's *The Artist and the Country House* (1979), show that there had been another house here – a plain early 18th-century house but with extravagant Baroque wings (Thomas Archer is rumoured to have worked for John Wallop, 1st Earl of Portsmouth). The paintings show the house overlooking a long canal with, at its far end, an astonishing arcaded cascade with a castellated pavilion in the style of Vanbrugh on the hill behind it. This second house was rebuilt in 1894 and demolished in 1965. The pavilion survives, now called Andover Lodge. Also surviving is a grotto-like domed building of flint with a statue of a Roman emperor inside – probably of the early 18th century.

Hutton-in-the-Forest

Skelton, Cumbria OS NY4635
English Heritage Register Grade II
Open regularly Tel 01768 484449

Medieval pele tower with 17th-, 18th- and 19th-century additions. A Kip engraving in *Britannia Illustrata* (1707) shows grand formal gardens with a double avenue leading to the entrance forecourt and a circular fountain pool; another circular pool is shown in the woods beyond the house, and to the north, a garden divided into six squares outlined by rows of plants and with a single tree at the centre of each square. Traces of this arrangement are still visible, and some gate piers are probably original. North of the house, walled garden with borders, yew hedges and topiary, the walls dating from the early 18th century. North-east of the house, late 17th- or early 18th-century dovecote and woodland with paths. William Sawrey Gilpin advised on the park in the early 19th century, resulting in the park close to the house being connected with the deer park.

Hyde Hall

see page 310

Hyde Park

see page 151

Hylands Park, *formerly* Hylands

Widford, Essex OS TL6804
English Heritage Register Grade II*
Open regularly

House built c.1728 for Sir John Comyns and remodelled c.1800 by Humphry Repton, possibly in collaboration with his son, John Adey Repton. Humphry Repton also advised on the park, and probably constructed the lake on the north-east boundary and carried out the tree planting associated with it. Areas of woodland in the park, with scattered mature trees and shelter belts. The park has been a public park since 1966.

Ickwell Bury

Northill, Bedfordshire OS TL1445
English Heritage Register Grade II

Ancient site, once the property of the Priory of St John of Jerusalem. The old house became a school but was destroyed by fire in 1937 and a new house was built in 1940. Garden, with red brick walls possibly of 17th century, originally a series of kitchen gardens but today with a modern planting of flower and vegetable beds. Limestone obelisk of c.1803. West of the house, irregular lake probably dating from the mid 19th century. East of lake, walled garden with octagonal brick dovecote of c.1680. In the park north of house, fishponds and moat and, north-west of house, a long double avenue of horse chestnuts.

Ickworth

see page 311

Iford Manor

see page 88

Ightham Court

Ightham, Kent OS TQ5957
English Heritage Register Grade II

House built 1575 for the Willoughby family. Late 17th- and early 18th-century formal gardens, of which grass terraces and walls to east and north of the house survive. Walled gardens to the south-east of the house are of the same date. North of the house, the Wilderness, where an old lime avenue centred on the house was badly damaged in the 1987 storm. In the Wilderness, fish ponds and two moated mounds, one of which has the remains of an icehouse and the other, formerly, had a summerhouse. These may be of an earlier date than the gardens.

Ightham Mote
see page 152

Ilnacullin
see page 415

The Image Garden
Crosby Ravensworth, Cumbria OS NY6117 English Heritage Register Grade II

19th-century walled terraced garden made by Thomas Bland (1799–1865), a self-taught composer, painter and sculptor. He ornamented the garden with many of his own sculptures and paintings. Around seventy sculptures can still be seen, distributed about the walls, some standing on plinths; several of them are portraits of writers – Burns, Scott and Shakespeare. Paintings or bas-reliefs showing scenes from the writers' works used to be set in niches in the walls, but have not survived.

Ince Blundell Hall
Ince Blundell, Merseyside OS SD3302 English Heritage Register Grade II* Open by appointment Tel 0151 9292596

House built 1720–50 for Robert Blundell whose family had held land here since the 12th century. Robert's son, Henry, inherited in 1761 and, falling under the influence of his neighbour, the connoisseur Charles Towneley, started to collect antique sculpture which he housed in buildings erected for the purpose; one, an art gallery (1802–10), was modelled on the Pantheon. A terrace on the south front of the house runs across the Pantheon, with steps down to a sunken oval space with a mound and an early 19th-century Tuscan column supporting an eagle. South and west of the house, lawns and trees where there had been formal gardens in 1760. To the west, a neo-classical temple (1775) planned as a sculpture gallery. South of the house, a lake, in place by 1786, with ornamental woodland and paths to its west. 18th-century walled park with grassland and scattered mature trees.

Inkpen House, *formerly* Inkpen Rectory
Inkpen, Berkshire OS SU3764 English Heritage Register Grade II* Open occasionally for NGS

House built in the late 17th and early 18th centuries for the Brickenden family. Dr Colwell Brickenden, who died in 1714, probably laid out the garden, apparently following advice from a design in John James's *The Theory and Practice of Gardening* (1712). The garden survives in essence today, with a grass terrace south of the house and a lime walk to the east. A *patte d'oie* of alleys of yew, holly and beech, cut into the slope, run south, south-east and south-west. Two alleys frame views of Inkpen Hill and one a mount within the garden. As James wrote in the introduction to his book: "I esteem nothing more diverting and agreeable in a Garden, than a fine View." The whole site is 3½ acres/1.4 hectares and the garden is one of the most complete small gardens of its date and character to survive.

Innes House
nr Elgin, Elginshire OS NJ2764 Scottish Inventory

House started in 1640 for Robert Innes to the designs of William Ayton, with alterations in the 18th century. Walled formal garden south of house made in 1916 for the Tennants (who bought the estate in 1910) with yew hedges, herbaceous borders and a rose garden. East of the house, an azalea walk and spring garden. Arboretum made by the Tennants, with excellent trees. The house today is a venue for corporate functions, weddings and the like.

Intwood Hall
Intwood, Norfolk OS TG1904 English Heritage Register Grade II*

A house was built here in 1560 for Sir Thomas Gresham; the present house is neo-Tudor, incorporating some old fabric, built in 1807 to the designs of Arthur Browne for Joseph Salusbury Muskett. To the north and north-east of the house, 16th-century walled gardens survive. From the house, an axial path leads to the north between golden yews and lawns to a battlemented wall with a central gateway and a further walled garden beyond. This second area is crossed by an axial path and a third enclosed garden has an octagonal summerhouse in one corner. East of the house, another summerhouse, dating from the mid 16th century. A painting by an unidentified artist, of *c*.1680, illustrated in John Harris's *The Artist and the Country House* (1979), shows a garden to the front of the house enclosed in elaborate white painted railings.

Inveraray Castle
Inveraray, Strathclyde OS NN0908 Open regularly Tel 01499 302203

House built for the 3rd Duke of Argyll from 1745 to the designs of Roger Morris and William Adam, followed by Adam's son John. Further work by William Mylne and his brother Robert. The result is a Georgian Gothic fantasy in a beautiful position at the head of Loch Fyne. An estate plan of 1756 shows a beguiling mixture of informal and formal ingredients – the river Aray winding through the park and patterns of avenues and rides cutting across the landscape. The landscape was ornamented with several notable buildings – Roger Morris's columnar dovecote (1747–48), a hexagonal fishing pavilion designed by Alexander Nasmyth (1802–3), Bealach an Fhuarain Grotto, possibly by William Adam (1747), and a noble garden bridge by John Adam (1758). Despite the survival of all these and other buildings, the garden today has little of its old character, although the natural setting remains exceptionally beautiful.

Inveresk Lodge Garden
nr Musselburgh, East Lothian Scottish Inventory OS NT3472 Open regularly (NTS) Tel 0131 555 6363

Late 17th-century house with later additions, in a walled garden. In 1959 Mrs Helen Brunton gave the estate to the National Trust for Scotland, which has planned the garden so as to provide a layout which would inspire gardeners with ideas for their own gardens.

Graham Stuart Thomas laid out a rose border (with many old shrub roses) with good companion planting; good use is made of smaller flowering trees; a raised alpine bed if full of ericaceous plants; and the garden is generally a model of appropriate, varied and floriferous planting in a small space.

Inverewe
see page 383

The Irish National Stud
see page 417

Island Gardens
Tower Hamlets, London OS TQ3878 English Heritage Register Grade II Open regularly

Public park opened "amid great enthusiasm" in 1895. The site, on the riverside looking across to Greenwich Hospital, is very fine and was, *c*.1680, chosen by Sir Christopher Wren as the best position from which to view the beauties of Greenwich. The southern boundary of the park is a riverside walk with views up and down the river as well as across it. A shrubbery on the northern boundary encloses a winding walk with, to the south, a lawn and mature London planes and such flowering trees as almonds and cherries. Rose bedding to the east and, on the western side, the entrance to the Greenwich Footway Tunnel.

The Japanese Garden
Bitchet Wood, Kent OS TQ5654 English Heritage Register Grade II*

Garden laid out 1919–21 for Hugh Micklem, probably designed by Raymond Berrow. It follows closely a garden illustrated in Joseph Conder's *Landscape Gardening in Japan* (1893). The garden is enclosed in perimeter planting of trees and shrubs and the site is animated by several artificial hillocks, some high enough to give views out of the garden. A lake disposed among the hillocks has a rocky cascade, bridges and a teahouse, and winding paths, sometimes in the form of stepping stones set in sand, about its banks. Stone lanterns and ornamental stones

with plantings of such trees as Japanese maples and yews. To the west of the lake, a bog garden with irises and other waterside plants.

The Jellicoe Roof Garden
Guildford, Surrey OS SU9949 English Heritage Register Grade II Open regularly

Harvey's Department Store was designed 1956–57 by Geoffrey Jellicoe & Partners. Jellicoe also designed a roof garden which he dscribed as "primarily a sky garden and the underlying idea is to unite heaven and earth; the sensation is one of being poised between the two." Its chief components are a large lily pool with fountains and a series of biomorphic (that is, naturally shaped) flower beds and paved viewing platforms. After a period of disuse, the garden was restored by 2003, once again with its café, thus giving shoppers a rare opportunity to sip their coffee in a Jellicoe garden.

Jesmond Dene, Armstrong *and* Heaton Parks
Newcastle-upon-Tyne, Northumberland OS NZ2567 English Heritage Register Grade II Open regularly

Public park running along the wooded valley (or "dene") of the Ouse burn. By the late 19th century the grounds of Heaton Hall, laid out in the 18th century, possibly by Richard Woods, for the Ridley family of Blagdon (*see page 487*), belonged to Lord Armstrong and were acquired by the city in 1879. Jesmond Dene and Armstrong Park originally formed Sir William Armstrong's own garden, laid out in the mid 19th century at a cost of £6,000 (£279,000 today). The whole became a public park in 1884 and in 1894 the *Gardener's Chronicle* described "the beautiful valley, so richly ornamented with trees and shrubs". Cascades and bridges enliven the riverine scene and there are many good trees. The remains of a 12th-century tower house (King John's Palace, also known as Adam of Jesmond's Camera) survive in the old Heaton Hall grounds, as do traces of the 18th-century landscaping.

J

In Armstrong Park are the ruins of the medieval St Mary's Chapel and the roofless remains of Sir William Armstrong's banqueting hall.

Johnstown Castle Gardens

see page 417

Julians

Rushden, Hertfordshire OS TL3032
English Heritage Register Grade II

Early 17th-century house, remodelled c.1715 for Adolphus Metekerke. North of the house, formal gardens designed by Colonel Reginald Cooper. Semicircular steps lead from a paved terrace to a lawn enclosed in brick walls. The lawn is terraced into two compartments linked by semicircular steps. Both compartments have borders flanking the lawn and the southern lawn has a central pool. Park with scattered ornamental trees. Brick walled kitchen garden, dated 1823, now with lawn and shrubs.

Kailzie House

nr Peebles, Peeblesshire OS NT2738 Scottish Inventory Open regularly Tel 01721 720007

Kailzie House was built on an older site in 1803 for John Nutter Campbell and demolished in 1962. The estate had many changes of owner: from 1638 to present times, at least nine families have owned it. In 1811 a walled garden and head gardener's house were built; in 1965 the owner took over the house, and the garden, long neglected, was restored. A sundial, of the same date as the walled garden, stands at the centre, and there is also an early 19th-century glasshouse. Hedges of copper beech divide spaces and there are grand double herbaceous borders, a laburnum walk and a rose garden. A wild garden runs along the banks of the Kailzie burn where trees were planted in the early 19th century. The Burnside Walk has a *Gingko biloba*, azaleas and rhododendrons and massed plantings of Himalayan primulas. The Major's Walk has flowering shrubs underplanted with meconopsis, polyanthus and primulas. A cypress walk leads to the Duck Pond, originally made

for curling and skating but now a wildfowl sanctuary.

Keats House

Hampstead, London OS TQ2785
English Heritage Register Grade II
Open regularly Tel 0207 435 2062

House built 1815–16, where the poet John Keats lived 1818–20 and wrote "Ode to a Nightingale", inspired by a nightingale's song in the garden. The garden was replanted in the late 1970s, with advice from Peter Goodchild, based on what was known about gardens in Keats's time. Trees and flowering shrubs are the chief ornaments, with a mixed border along the eastern boundary and island beds at the north-east and south-east corners of the house, planted with flowering shrubs. Part of the house is now a Keats library and museum.

Kedleston Hall

see page 265

Keele Hall

Keele, Staffordshire OS SJ8144
English Heritage Register Grade II

House rebuilt for Ralph Sneyd 1855–60 to the designs of Anthony Salvin, 300 years after another Ralph Sneyd had built the first house here. In 1950 it became the campus of the University College of North Staffordshire (which became the University of Keele in 1962). William Emes landscaped the park c.1768, enlarging existing ponds and planting trees to conceal working farms within the park. Emes also laid out pleasure grounds around the hall, with flowering shrubs under the drawing room window and a ha-ha to separate them from the park. W.S. Gilpin carried out further planting in the park, especially around the lakes, turned a quarry north-west of the house into a fernery approached by a dog-legged tunnel, and constructed an artificial stone crag. Immediately south-west of the house, W.A. Nesfield designed a parterre c.1845, destroyed in World War II but reinstated in a simplified form in 1985. Nesfield also made a terrace on the south-east side of the house, with urns and stone seats.

Keillour Castle

Fowlis-Wester, Perthshire OS NN9725
Scottish Inventory

Ancient and beautiful site on a ridge between two gorges. The present house was built c.1877 for William Thomson to the designs of Andrew Heiton. In 1938 the estate was bought by Major and Mrs George Knox Finlay – both distinguished gardeners and both winners of the RHS Veitch Gold Medal; Mrs Knox Finlay also won the RHS Victoria Medal of Honour. 19th-century woodland garden transformed by the Knox Finlays. West of the house, the Den, in the gorge of the Horn burn, is full of acers, magnolias, rhododendrons and rowans grown under the woodland canopy. East of the house, the Snib has precipitous banks down to another burn with flowering shrubs on the slope and waterside planting along the burn, especially rare primulas such as *P. nana*, *P. gracilipes*, *P. griffithii* and *P. sonchifolia*. Water is pumped by a hydraulic ram to a watery woodland garden by the drive, where eucryphias, magnolias and rhododendrons are planted about a pond, with swathes or gentians, irises, meconopsis, primulas and trilliums. Throughout the garden are great rarities, especially species lilies and such members of the lily family as *Nomocharis* and *Notholirion*.

Keir House

nr Dunblane, Perthshire OS NN7798
Scottish Inventory

The Stirling family came here in 1448 and still own the estate. The house is 18th-century, with 19th-century alterations. 18th-century parkland with many parkland trees – beech, lime and oak – probably dating from the period 1790–1810. Woodland dating back to the 17th century, with 19th-century buildings, among them a ruinous cascade and grotto, and a bathing house designed by Sir Robert Rowand Anderson. A woodland garden and pinetum was established c.1850 by Sir William Stirling Maxwell. Conifers with underplantings of exotic shrubs; a curved wall with statues and elaborate gates forms the focal point of an avenue of conifers

planted c.1860. An arboretum planted 1820–40 suffered terribly in the gales of 1955 and 1968 and has been replanted. Many of the trees introduced to Scotland from 1850 have come to Keir. Of the 94 notable trees measured by Alan Mitchell in 1970, several conifers were some of the first introductions to Scotland. Mid 19th-century and later formal gardens with terraces, steps, fountains, topiary, yew hedges, herbaceous borders and a formal rose garden.

Kellie Castle

see page 384

Kelmscott Manor

see page 90

Kelston Park

Kelston, Bath. Somerset OS ST7066
English Heritage Register Grade II

House built 1760 by John Wood the Younger for Sir Caesar Hawkins on the site of the summerhouse of an Elizabethan house. Lying to the west of Bath, it commanded fine southerly views over the valley of the river Avon. The garden has a unique nine-sided irregular walled garden of the 18th century. Park landscaped by Capability Brown 1767–68, for which he was paid £500 (£30,000 today). Brown, contrary to all that is said about his destruction of earlier landscapes, was careful to retain sight lines and avenues from an older garden.

Kemeys House

nr Newport, Gwent OS ST3892
Cadw/ICOMOS Register Grade II

House built in the 16th century for the Kemeys family. A barn is of the same date, as is a terraced walled garden – a remarkably complete miniature estate of the period. It is now separated from the winding river Usk by the dual carriageway of the A449 immediately alongside the house.

Kemp Town Gardens

Brighton, East Sussex OS TQ3303
English Heritage Register Grade II

Kemp Town, on the eastern edge of Brighton, was developed from

1823 by Thomas Kemp MP, with the architects Amon Wilds and Charles Busby. The development was a disaster; Kemp lost £500,000 (£23,420,000 today) and died in comparative poverty in Paris in 1844. The houses were built about a rectangle and semicircle of open ground, facing south towards the sea. The gardens, in the open ground overlooked by the houses, were to be maintained by a charge on the residents. They were designed in 1828 by Henry Phillips in a naturalistic style with trees and shrubs; this, with perimeter walks and open lawns for games, is essentially the character of the gardens today. In the 1830s an underground passage was made under Marine Parade to provide residents with their own private seaside esplanade. The esplanade, possibly designed by Sir Joseph Paxton, has walks leading down to the steeply sloping and well planted ground above the beach.

Kenilworth Castle

Kenilworth, Warwickshire OS SP2772
Open regularly (EH) Tel 01926 852078

Castle built in the early 12th century, with much subsequent alteration to the end of the 16th century. In the early 13th century a small lake was transformed into an immense mere, on the edge of which, in 1417, a royal garden, the Pleasance, was made for Henry V. Its earthworks survive, showing a rectangle enclosed in a double moat (illustrated in an aerial photograph in Christopher Taylor's *Parks and Gardens of Britain: A Landscape History from the Air* (1998)); there was a wooden banqueting house here until the 16th century. Kenilworth's great claim to garden fame comes from the garden made 1565–75 by Queen Elizabeth's favourite, Robert Dudley, Earl of Leicester. A letter by Robert Laneham, written in 1575, describes the garden: "Beautified with many delectabl fresh, and umbragioous bowerz, arberz, seatz, and walks, that with great art, cost, and diligens wear very pleasantlie appointed." Queen Elizabeth visited twice, and on one occasion George Gasgoigne's masque in her hono as performed. Sir Walter Scott's [no]vel *Kenilworth* describes one of [th]e Queen's visits. There have [be]en attempts to reinstate the [Tu]dor garden but none very [sa]tisfactory – the present version [is] based on a plan of 1656; [ne]vertheless, the castle itself, in [ru]ins since after the Civil War, [re]serves potent atmosphere.

The John F. Kennedy [A]rboretum
[se]e page 418

[K]ennington Park
[La]mbeth, London OS TQ3177 English [He]ritage Register Grade II Open regularly

[Pu]blic park designed by James [Pe]nnethorne and opened 1854. [Bo]undaries sheltered with trees [an]d shrubs and in the park mature [tr]ees, some dating from the [or]iginal plantings – ash, holm oak, [ho]rse chestnut and *Robinia* [ps]eudoacacia. On the west [bo]undary, two semi-detached [co]ttages, designed by Henry [Ro]berts in 1851 and displayed in [th]e Great Exhibition at the request [of] Prince Albert as an example of [hi]gh quality working man's [dw]ellings. Nearby, rose beds and [pa]ths leading to a bandstand and [te]nnis courts. In the south-east, an [en]closed formal garden with a [pe]rgola, a symmetrical pattern of [flo]wer beds, and recreational and [ga]mes facilities.

[K]ensal Green [C]emetery, *or* [A]ll Souls Cemetery
[Ke]nsington and Chelsea, London [OS] TQ2382 English Heritage Register [Gr]ade II* Open regularly

[C]emetery opened 1833, with [bu]ildings by J.W. Griffin who may [al]so have laid out the cemetery; a [M]r Liddell, a pupil of John Nash, [is] another possible claimant. [A]nglican and Nonconformist [ch]apels and catacombs along [no]rthern boundary wall. A central [a]venue runs east–west, with [cu]rving paths leading off and the [A]nglican Chapel as a centrepiece. [R]ich in good monuments and in [pl]aces romantically overcrowded. [M]ature trees along the avenue, [an]d many individual trees, [es]pecially evergreens, among [th]e tombs.

Kensington Gardens
see page 152

Kentchurch Court
Kentchurch, Herefordshire OS SO4125
English Heritage Register Grade II

14th-century castle, rebuilt before 1807 by John Nash for John Scudamore whose family had lived here since the 15th century. Gardens by the house probably made when it was rebuilt: grass terraces by the entrance forecourt, ornamental woodland and stream to the north of the house. Park already established by *c.*1500; in the 19th century there was a herd of *c.*130 fallow deer. Today it is pasture with specimen trees.

Kentwell Hall
Long Melford, Suffolk OS TL8647
English Heritage Register Grade II*
Open regularly Tel 01787 310207

Moated mid 16th-century brick house of romantic splendour, built by the cloth-trading family of Clopton. (John Clopton was associated with the building of the exquisite parish church of Long Melford.) The approach from the village is by a gatehouse and a grand lime avenue, 1 mile long, said to have been planted in 1678. Walled gardens to the north of the house follow the original Elizabethan layout, with espaliered fruit trees and flower gardens. To the east of the house, on the island, a lawn and very old cedars of Lebanon. Beyond the moated areas, a shrubbery and walk of yews said to date from the 17th century. Humphry Repton was consulted by the then owner, Richard Moore, after 1797, but it is not known if anything came of it. In the entrance courtyard, a modern maze of different colours of paving brick, depicting a Tudor rose, designed by Minotaur designs and made in 1985.

Kenwood House
see page 154

Key Hill Cemetery
Birmingham, West Midlands OS SP0588
English Heritage Register Grade II
Open regularly

The earliest cemetery in Birmingham, designed by the

architect Charles Edge and opened 1836. *A Pictorial Guide to Birmingham* (1852) described it as "tastefully laid out in walks, interspersed with lawns and shrubberies". The layout chiefly follows a grid pattern, and memorials of many notable 19th-century Birmingham figures are to be found.

Kidbrooke Park
Forest Row, East Sussex OS TQ4134
English Heritage Register Grade II

Early 18th-century house for William Nevill, 16th Lord Abergavenny, with 19th-century alterations. Humphry Repton advised on the grounds *c.*1803 but no Red Book is known. South of a wooded shrubbery (Valley Field), to the south of the house, Repton made a water garden. The Kid stream is lined with dressed stone, has stepping stones and a cascade, and its upper reaches ornamented with pools and islands. The stream flows northwards through a tunnel, passes to the east of the house, and flows into the long, narrow Lower Lake north-east of the house. At the south end of Valley Field, Repton made vistas from the house to the parkland, and features of the landscape were framed although they are now partly obscured. West of the house, formal gardens designed by W.H. Godfrey in 1924 – a paved terrace, flower beds and urns with steps to a circular pergola with stone columns. Park now largely rough grass with a few clumps and individual trees.

Kiddington Hall
Kiddington, Oxfordshire OS SP4122
English Heritage Register Grade II
Open occasionally for NGS

17th-century house, rebuilt by Charles Barry *c.*1850. Barry also made a conservatory against the west façade of the house, which now, without its glass, forms a loggia. Sir Charles Browne commissioned Capability Brown to landscape his grounds in 1740, making it one of Brown's earliest works – he was only twenty-four at the time – but it is possible that the work was not completed until the 1760s. Brown dammed the river Glyme to form a lake with a

tree-covered island; beyond the lake the land rises and, as Dorothy Stroud points out in her *Capability Brown* (1975), "is planted with groups of trees, many of which are of considerable age." Formal gardens by Barry to west and south of house, with terrace and balustrading. Octagonal mid 19th-century boat house on lake.

Kiftsgate Court
see page 213

Kildonan Lodge
Kildonan, Sutherland OS NC9022
Scottish Inventory

A shooting lodge in wild country, built in 1896 for the Duke of Sutherland. A painting by G.S. Elgood, done in 1914, is illustrated in Penelope Hobhouse's and Christophere Wood's *Painted Gardens: English Watercolours 1850–1914* (1988). It shows a windswept but exuberant border of delphiniums, foxgloves and sweet williams. The garden today is more restrained, with terraces, bedding plants, a rose garden and a rock garden.

Kildrummy Castle Gardens
nr Alford, Aberdeenshire OS NJ4516
Open regularly Tel 019755 71203

The original castle at Kildrummy was a royal house built in the 13th century; its ruins ornament the landscape today. The estate was bought in 1898 by Colonel James Ogston, a soap tycoon who built a new castle (now the Kildrummy Castle Hotel, which overlooks the gardens) and planted up the valley of the Backden burn, which he dammed in places to form pools. He also built a great bridge spanning the valley, modelled on the famous 14th-century Brig o'Balgownie in Aberdeen. The garden is in the tradition of Robinsonian wild gardens, with a very wide range of trees and shrubs (including a large collection of hybrid and species rhododendrons). A rock garden laid out by the firm of James Backhouse & Co was made in the quarry from which the stone for the old castle was taken. It is planted with an excellent range of alpine plants.

Kilfane Glen
see page 419

Kilkerran
Dailly, Ayrshire OS NS3002
Scottish Inventory

Ancient estate of the Fergussons who came here in the 14th century and have remained, except when the estate was confiscated by Cromwell in 1650 (it was returned shortly after). Early 18th-century house, replacing a medieval tower house, designed successively by James Smith and William Adam with additions in the 19th century by Gillespie Graham and David Bryce. The site is the valley of the Water of Girvan, with moorland hills rising to 1,000ft/300m. The hills have been planted with trees since 1715 when James Fergusson started experimental plantings. Today there is a mixture of deciduous and coniferous trees and some ornamental plantings of azaleas and rhododendrons. Lady Glen is a steep ravine planted with silver firs in the mid 18th century. A carriage drive up the glen, Sir Adam's Walk, was made in the late 18th century to take visitors to a notable waterfall. 18th-century parkland with an old lime avenue and the later use of exotic conifers as parkland trees.

Killerton
see page 45

Killruddery
see page 420

Kilmokea
Campile, County Wexford, Republic of Ireland
Open regularly Tel (00353) 051 388109

The house, formerly a rectory, was built in 1794. The gardens are 20th-century and fall into two distinct parts. That close to the house, with borders and lawns, is attractive but not exciting. A quite separate garden lies across a lane and through a door in a wall; here is a small woodland garden of enchanting character, with old trees and rich in excellent plants, especially such shrubs as camellias, eucryphias, hoherias, magnolias and rhododendrons. Herbaceous plants include Asiatic primulas, *Gunnera manicata* and (in this very

K

mild area) self-sown *Echium pininana*.

Kimberley Hall
Kimberley, Norfolk OS TG0904
English Heritage Register Grade II*

The Wodehouse family came here in the 1380s but the present house was built after 1700 for Sir John Wodehouse to the designs of William Talman, altered in the later 18th century and again in the 19th and 20th centuries. In 1762 Sir Armine Wodehouse consulted Capability Brown who produced a plan the following year. Brown worked here for five years and was paid £3,000 (£197,955 today). He enlarged a lake to an area of 28 acres/11.3 hectares and also supplied designs for "alterations near the house" and for a greenhouse. The banks of the lake on the south-west side were densely planted with trees, leaving largely open ground between the house on its eminence and the lake. 19th-century formal gardens by house, with yew topiary and bedding schemes possibly by Anthony Salvin *c*.1835 when he was working on the house.

King Edward VII Hospital
nr Midhurst, West Sussex OS SU8824
English Heritage Register Grade II

Tuberculosis sanatorium opened in 1906. Formal gardens designed by the architect Percy Adams with planting schemes by Gertrude Jekyll. The site chosen was high and airy with fine views of the South Downs. The gardens, which substantially survive, are laid out south of the hospital, overlooked by the wards. The ground is terraced, leading down to a lawn, and the whole is enclosed in woodland. The sandy soil was suitable for the Mediterranean plants, which Gertrude Jekyll especially liked, and she used cistus, lavender and santolina. She also saw the retaining walls of the terracing as an ideal site for her characteristic "wall gardening" and these she planted with aubrieta, campanulas, *Cerastium tomentosum*, pinks, stonecrops and thrift. Fresh air and the sort of exercise provided by light gardening were regarded as therapeutic for tuberculosis patients, who were encouraged to work in the gardens.

King's College
Cambridge, Cambridgeshire OS TL4458
English Heritage Register Grade II*
Open regularly Tel 01223 331212

College founded 1441 by Henry VI. An engraving of *c*.1744 by James Essex shows King's adorned with a spectacular new garden laid out below the western façade of the Gibbs Building and extending across the Backs. This may have been designed by Charles Bridgeman or by Essex himself, and it is not known if it was ever laid out. It shows two parallel rectangular pools between the Gibbs Building (or Fellows' Building, built 1723–29 to the designs of James Gibbs) and the river Cam; on the far side of the river is an enormous shaped pool overlooked at its far end by a temple – the whole surrounded by formal walks on both sides of the river. The account of the garden in *Cantabrigia Depicta* (1763), however, describes something quite different: "There are several gardens and Orchards belonging to this College; and, besides the River that runs thro' them, there are some Moats and Canals, with thick shady Groves of Elms, which render the Avenues to the College exceeding pleasant; and no pleace is capabale of greater Improvement, by cutting Vistas through the Grove." The lawns between the Gibbs Building and the river were levelled in 1771 and a serpentine river walk was made in 1818. Today, the view of King's from the Backs shows a fringe of trees and fairly wild pasture west of the river, and beyond it, smooth lawns running up to the Gibbs Building – one of the simplest and best views in Cambridge.

King's Gardens *and* South Marine Gardens
Southport, Merseyside OS SD3317 English Heritage Register Grade II Open regularly

South Marine Gardens opened as a public park and lake in 1887 and was later linked by King's Gardens which were opened in 1913 – all part of the seaside development of Southport. Lake crossed by a bridge and with a perimeter path and with such recreational facilities as bowling greens, a model village, miniature railway and "crazy golf". To the south, a circular fountain pool with curved flower beds set in grass.

Kingston Lacy
see page 45

Kingston Maurward Gardens
see page 46

Kingsweston House
Shirehampton, Bristol OS ST5477
English Heritage Register Grade II

Part of the site, from which much of the landscape is visible, is public open space. A Kip engraving of 1712 shows the old house at Kingsweston, a gabled Tudor house overlooking fine formal gardens in which two enclosures of parterres lay threaded on an axis joining the house to a garden pavilion. The house belonged to Sir Edward Southwell, a Bristol merchant, and in the background of Kip's engraving you can see ships in Bristol harbour. Sir Edward commissioned a new house from Sir John Vanbrugh, which was built 1710–25, but the layout of the garden remained essentially unchanged although Vanbrugh designed various new garden buildings for it – a banqueting house (The Echo, because it echoed the entrance on the east front of the house), a loggia, brew-house and Penpole Lodge with an arched rusticated entrance. All these survive except the last which was demolished in 1950. Later in the 18th century, with advice from Norborne Berkeley (of Stoke Park, Bristol, *see page 542*) and Thomas Wright (who designed the park at Stoke Park), landscaping started. A little later Capability Brown was consulted about "Alterations about the House and Terras", and a fee of £84 paid (£6,048 today), so the work could not have been very extensive. Today, in multiple ownership, the estate presents a forlorn aspect; nevertheless, the house and garden buildings survive, fragments of old lime avenues may be seen, and the old layout of the garden is plainly displayed.

Kinnaird Castle
nr Brechin, Angus OS NO6357 Scottish Inventory Open occasionally for SGS

Castle built in 1790 to the designs of James Playfair for Sir David Carnegie and remodelled 1854–62 by David Bryce. The Carnegies (later Earls of Southesk) have lived here since 1401. The site is a fine one, with the river South Esk flowing through the policies. The *Ordnance Survey Gazetteer* for 1885 described "an ancient French chateau with many lofty steep-roofed towers and turrets…The park…with four hundred fallow deer, comprises between 1300 and 1400 acres…most of the trees were planted towards the close of last century, but there are several 170–400 years old." The deer park was established by the end of the 17th century and is still there, enclosed in high walls; fallow deer have now been joined by Soay sheep. Terraced garden with yew hedges south-west of the castle was laid out in 1862, probably by David Bryce, with balustrading and cast-iron gates, approached from the house by a grand stairway. In woodland, an octagonal summerhouse designed by Agnes, Lady Carnegie *c*.1800, with lattice windows and fir cone ceiling.

Kinross House
see page 384

Kirby Hall
see page 266

Kirtlington Park
Kirtlington, Oxfordshire OS SP5019
English Heritage Register Grade II

House built 1742–46 for Sir James Dashwood to the designs of William Smith and John Sanderson, influenced by an earlier proposal by James Gibbs. Plans for laying out the grounds were supplied by Thomas Greening, the royal gardener, in the mid 1740s. No sooner had some of this work been done than Sir James commissioned Capability Brown to design the grounds, which undid Greening's work (by 1752 Brown had been paid £100 (£8,252)). Brown replaced Greening's formal wilderness with dense plantings on each side of the house and open lawns in front of the two chief façades, adorned with specimen trees. A ha-ha almost entirely enclosed the pleasure grounds about the house. Brown's work survives in essence today.

Kirkby Fleetham
North Yorkshire OS SE2894

By the river Swale a Palladian house was built for the Aislabies (*see* Studley Royal, *page 352* and Hackfall Wood, *page 339*) by the 1750s with, by 1771, a landscape park. Arthur Young went there and described it in *A Six Month Tour of the North of England* (1771): "Kirkby one of the seats of *William Aislabie* Esq; of *Studley*, and the grounds greatly ornamented by him." The house was connected to the village by a mile-long viewing terrace which Young described: "the edge of it planted, and temples, etc., built at those points which command the best views: At the bottom a stream winds in a beautiful manner and forms several cascades: The principle prospect is from a temple about the middle of the plantation; from which you look down upon the river very picturesquely, and command a very noble prospect over a fine country, beautifully variegated with woods, villages, scattered houses, inclosures, etc." No trace of the garden is visible today but in the parish church of St Mary there is a fine monument by Flaxman of the last Aislabie heir.

Kirkharle Hall, *renamed* Kirkharle Farmhouse
Kirkharle, Northumberland OS NZ0182
English Heritage Register Grade II

The house today is the remains of an early 18th-century house belonging to the Loraine family. Its importance comes from its association with Capability Brown. Brown was born in a farmhouse at Kirkharle and was employed as an estate worker by Sir William Loraine in 1732 at the age of sixteen. Sir William was a great improver; he planted 24,000 forest trees, 488,000 quicksets and 580 fruit trees, 1694–1738, and it is possible that Brown made landscape suggestions at this time. Brown certainly returned to Kirkharle Hall, and a plan of *c.*1770, probably in his hand, shows new proposals for the landscape; however, it is not known if this scheme was executed, and nothing survives today. John Hodgson's *A History of Northumberland* (1820–58) discerns at Kirkharle "The magic hand of Capability Brown" which "contrived to throw the sweetest charms into the fields of his nativity and to convert the landscape around the mansion of their lord into 'a woody theatre of stateliest view'."

Knebworth House

see page 313

Knepp Castle

Shipley, West Sussex OS TQ1521
English Heritage Register Grade II

Site inhabited since at least the 11th century. The new castle, Gothic and castellated, was designed by John Nash for Sir Charles Merrick Burrell and built 1806–13. The pleasure grounds were planted in the 19th century with oaks and sweet chestnuts, and an arboretum was made by Ethelred Burrell of the famous gardening Loder family. The park had been agricultural land before being developed, possibly with Nash's advice, when the new castle was built. A serpentine lake east of the house was made from a 16th-century hammer pond. Hillhouse Lawn to its east is a rectangular space of open ground, a "forest lawn" of the sort recommended by William Gilpin in his *Remarks on Forest Scenery* (1791). The ruins of the old castle, some distance south of Hillhouse Lawn, were planted with trees to act as an eyecatcher.

Knightshayes Court

see page 47

Knole

nr Sevenoaks, Kent OS TQ5454
English Heritage Register Grade I
Open regularly (NT) Tel 01732 450608

Great 15th-century house for Thomas Bourchier, Archbishop of Canterbury. Estate acquired by Sir Thomas Sackville in 1556 and house remodelled in the early 17th century. Kip's engraving in *Britannia Illustrata* (1707) shows an extensive but austere formal garden, much of whose layout is

extant today. The walled gardens cover an area of 27 acres/11 hectares, and much of the Kentish ragstone walls date from the 16th century – a beautiful sight. Deer park established in the middle ages. Knole was the childhood home, and obsession, of Vita Sackville-West of Sissinghurst (*see page 177*).

Knoll Gardens and Nursery

see page 48

Knowsley Park

Knowsley, Merseyside OS SJ4493
English Heritage Register Grade II

Estate owned by the Stanley family (later Earls of Derby) since 1385. There had been a building here in the 14th century but the present house dates from the 15th century, with many subsequent alterations and additions. South of the house, terraced lawns descend to Home Pond. To the east of the house, another stretch of water, Octagon Pond, with, on its far bank, the Octagon – a mid 18th-century classical buildings attributed to William Kent. North of the pool, a castellated building, Bridge Lodge, designed by William Burn *c.*1840. North of the house, an American Garden. In the park, a double lime avenue, planted in the early 20th century, runs from the west façade of the house to the western park boundary. North-east of the house, lake and White Man's Dam, with a boathouse designed by William Burn in 1837. Capability Brown was consulted 1775–76; "a new kitchen garden" and "alterations of the Grounds round the house" are mentioned. It is possible but uncertain that he was responsible for White Man's Dam and the planting of belts and tree clumps in the park. In the south-east part of the park is Riding Hill which is shown in a painting by Peter Tillemans of before 1729, illustrated in John Harris's *The Artist and the Country House* (1979). It is seen crowned with a summerhouse, the top of the hill sculpted into a series of concentric hedged terraces. There was at this time a racecourse in the park and Riding Hill would have offered a fine prospect of it. North of house,

a brick-walled kitchen garden – was this designed by Brown?

Kylemore Abbey

see page 421

Kyre Park

see page 214

Lacock Abbey

see page 91

Ladbroke Square Gardens

Kensington and Chelsea, London OS TQ2480 English Heritage Register Grade II

Ladbroke Square was developed by Thomas Allom from 1842, partly on the site of the Hippodrome Racecourse (1837). Garden enclosed in railings with a perimeter planting of trees and shrubs. A walk along northern side, with subsidiary winding paths about central lawn. Many mature trees and decorative underplanting of flowering shrubs. Gardener's cottage in north-east corner.

Lady Herbert's Garden

Coventry, West Midlands OS SP3379 English Heritage Register Grade II Open regularly

Public garden laid out 1930–38, the creation of a Coventry industrialist, Sir Alfred Herbert, in memory of his second wife, Florence, who had died in 1930; Herbert wanted to make "a haven of peace and floral beauty". Sir Alfred asked his cousin, the architect Albert Herbert, to design the garden and, at the heart of it a group of almshouses, Lady Herbert's Homes. Part of the 14th-century city wall runs across the garden and its lowest point is planted as a rockery. On the sloping site there are flagstoned walks, lawns, borders and ornamental trees.

Lainston House

Lainston, Hampshire OS SU4431
English Heritage Register Grade II*

17th-century house, rebuilt in 1700. Earthworks of terraces – the remains of a 17th- or early 18th-century formal garden – descend from east side of house to a pond. On the axis of the terraces is an avenue of limes, now obscured by woodland. Walled forecourt with loggia, balustraded terrace and

small topiary garden. A hexagonal walled kitchen garden is now a car park. Gertrude Jekyll worked at Lainston in 1922 but it is not known what she did.

Lake House

Wilsford, Wiltshire OS SU1338
English Heritage Register Grade II

16th-century house, restored in 1898 by Detmar Blow, gutted by fire 1912 and restored by Blow. Until 1922, gardens consisted of walled kitchen garden, bowling green with old yew hedge and a lawn running down to a side stream of the Avon, east of the house. Since then a water garden has been made between the side stream and the Avon. East of the house, a formal rose garden enclosed in flint walls and yew hedges. Shrub borders south of the house and another beside bowling green. To the south, the main lawn leads to woodland, with a pleached lime alley to one side.

Lakemount

Glanmire, County Cork, Republic of Ireland
Open regularly Tel (00353) 21 4821052

Perfectionist garden made from the 1970s onwards by Mrs Margaret Cross and her son, Brian. On a south-sloping but windy site high above the river Lee, the Crosses made an intricate garden full of excellent plants finely grown. Mrs Cross established the framework of hedges, essential here to give wind protection. Among much decorative planting, a *Cornus controversa* 'Variegata' is underplanted with waves of white *Camassia leichtlinii*, and a white-stemmed Himalayan birch (*Betula utilis*) rises from a plum-coloured mound of Japanese maple – all set off by flawless lawns. Brian Cross continues to add new plants and in a relatively small area (*c.*2 acres/0.8 hectares) has built up a remarkable collection.

Lambay Castle

Lambay Island, County Dublin, Republic of Ireland

Lambay Island, just off the coast north of Dublin, has a history going back to the Vikings. There was an early fort here and old fortifications survive. The island was

bought in 1904 for £5,250 (£284,340 today) by the Hon. Cecil Baring (later 3rd Lord Revelstoke). From 1905, Edwin Lutyens built a new house incorporating the 16th-century fort, enclosing the castle, outhouses and gardens in a circular rampart wall built of the local stone – a crystal-flecked blue-green porphyry – 700ft/210m in diameter. The island is swept by strong winds and gardens were laid out in courtyards enclosed by the castle and its ancillary buildings, for which Gertrude Jekyll did planting plans. Jane Brown, in *Gardens of a Golden Afternoon* (1982), wrote: "Lambay Castle has for years been the private retreat of Lord Revelstoke and a private nature reserve, but the planting of the courtyards was sacrificed years ago."

Lambeth Palace

Lambeth, London OS TQ3079
English Heritage Register Grade II*
Open occasionally for NGS

Archbishops of Canterbury have owned this site since the 12th century and the present ensemble, from the 13th century onwards, is one of the largest groups of medieval buildings in London. There has been a garden here since at least the 14th century when details of the vegetable seeds bought by Roger the gardener are known. There was at this time both a Great Garden and a flower garden, as well as a 9-acre/3.6-hectare park. A Kip engraving of 1714 shows formal gardens and a raised terrace walk. The present gardens are largely 20th-century, with lawns, rose beds, mixed borders and bedding schemes. In the 1980s woodland was thinned, an Elizabethan-style herb and physic garden planted by Lollards Tower, and a Palladian temple built on the mound. Since the 19th century, part of the garden (known as the Archbishop's Park), to the east of the private garden, has been set aside as a public park, with lawns and sports field.

Lambton Castle

nr Chester-le-Street, County Durham OS NZ2952 English Heritage Register Grade II

The estate has belonged to the Lambton family since the 12th

L

L

century. Only the early 19th-century part of the house, by Ignatius Bonomi, survives; this had been an addition to an 18th-century house. The chief natural ornament of the grounds is the river Wear which flows east–west across the centre of the site, with the house on its northern bank; the pleasure grounds consist chiefly of walks to display the beauties of the setting. Few of the garden details of the 19th century – a flower garden, a conservatory, a suspension bridge – survive. In the park, a little woodland and a few trees remain, but much has been turned over to arable farming.

Lamellen
St Tudy, Cornwall OS SX0577
English Heritage Register Grade II

16th-century house, much altered in 19th century. The house lies in a wooded valley with a stream and pools. Planting started in earnest in the mid 19th century, especially of conifers, at the time of John Magor who had married the heiress to the estate. His grandson, E.J.P. Magor, introduced rhododendrons from E.H. Wilson's expeditions to China of 1899 and 1902, and from the later collections of George Forrest and Frank Kingdon Ward, and carried out some hybridising. His son, Major E.W.M. Magor, continued to enrich the planting, adding groups of camellias, eucryphias, nothofagus and podocarpus. His daughter, Mrs J.D. Peter-Hoblyn, now lives at Lamellen.

Lamorbey Park
Bexley, London OS TQ4673
English Heritage Register Grade II

Mid 18th-century house built for William Steele on an earlier site, with alterations in the late 18th and early 19th centuries. Mid 18th-century park. Terraced lawns by the house date from the mid 19th century. Golf course in the northern part of the park, which still retains some of its parkland character. Two lakes formed by damming a tributary of the river Shuttle, and two icehouses (of 1790 and c.1840). A single wall of the 18th-century kitchen garden survives. The house is now Rose Bruford College.

Lamport Hall
Lamport, Northamptonshire OS SP7674
English Heritage Register Grade II
Open regularly Tel 01604 686272

The Isham family came here in 1560; the present house is largely 17th-century, designed by John Webb, with additions in the early 18th century by Francis and William Smith of Warwick. John Isham, who rebuilt an earlier house in the 1560s, "aplyed himself to plantinge, buildnge, making of pooles", and there was a formal garden under the west front in the early 18th century. William Burn designed a new terrace and balustrading in 1861 (the gap in the balustrading was made, accidentally, by a tank during World War II). In 1847 Sir Charles Isham made a pioneer rock garden here, one of the earliest alpine gardens in England (by the 1890s, it was populated with garden gnomes; Sir Charles was a keen spiritualist and believed in fairies as the spirits of nature). In 1857 he also made, south of the hall, the Italian Garden – a box parterre with central pool. Park laid out by John Webb in the 1820s, incorporating a late 17th-century avenue of walnuts, replanted in 1929 with horse chestnuts.

Langdon Court
Wembury, Devon, OS SX5149
English Heritage Register Grade II

Medieval house, rebuilt in 1577 for Vincent Calmady and altered in the early 18th century for Josiah Calmady. An early 18th-century painting shows a formal garden of rare charm. On sloping ground to the south of the house is an axial arrangement of terraced walled gardens, with statues in the first garden and, at the lower boundary wall, a gateway and stairs running down to a wooded area. Further enclosures extend westwards, with more statues, two corner pavilions and a tall tower. The layout of the garden survives, although the tower is no longer there. The house is now a hotel.

Langley Park
Langley, Norfolk OS TG3500
English Heritage Register Grade II

House built in the 1740s with some involvment of Matthew Brettingham. Sir Thomas Proctor Beauchamp consulted Capability Brown who supplied plans for the park in 1765; existing belts and plantations are in his style. North of the house, a 19th-century formal garden with terrace and steps down to a lawn and narrow lake. East of the house, a 19th-century arboretum with excellent mature trees. Since 1946 the house has been a school.

Langley Park
Wexham, Buckinghamshire OS TQ0181
English Heritage Register Grade II

House built in mid 18th century to the designs of Stiff Leadbetter as a hunting lodge for the 3rd Duke of Marlborough. Capability Brown was commissioned to lay out the grounds, sending a plan to the Duke in 1763, who replied, "I like it very well." Work began in 1764 and lasted ten years, costing £21,500 (£1,418,677 today). South and west of the house is a curving lake, probably made by Brown. The park is pasture with belts, clumps and individual specimen trees. In the north-east corner of the park there had been pleasure grounds, with a Palladian temple by Roger Morris (c.1740) and a 100ft/30m memorial column in oriental style by F.P. Cockerell (1864) – both of which were demolished. There remains a rhododendron garden, with mature oaks, which is bounded to the south by a semicircular ha-ha of c.1743.

Langleys
Great Waltham, Essex OS TL6913
English Heritage Register Grade II

Early 17th-century house, rebuilt c.1710–19 for Samuel Tufnell to the designs of William Tufnell (no relation, so far as is known). In 1719 Samuel Tufnell paid Charles Bridgman £156 7s 2d (£12,342 today) for "Works & plants in ye Gardens". Bridgman possibly made the semicircular ha-ha on two sides of the garden to the east of the house, but this has also been attributed to Humphry Repton who came to advise in 1803. On the east front of the house, a terrace leading to a formal Dutch Garden with box hedges, a statue and low terrace beyond, and an avenue of cypresses running east for 700ft/200m between shrubs. 18th-century park with scattered mature trees.

Lanhydrock
see page 49

Larchill Arcadian Garden
see page 422

Larmer Tree Gardens
see page 92

Lartington Hall
Lartington, County Durham OS NZ0217
English Heritage Register Grade II

Late 17th-century house, with 18th- and 19th-century alterations. Formal garden by the house has buttressed wall with gate piers surmounted by statues of Bacchus and Hercules, each of the buttresses capped with a statue or an urn. Terraced gardens, with statues (some of them cement) of many different kinds, thought to have been laid out by Joseph Hansom who made alterations to the house in the early 1860s. Park with a stream with cascades, Scur beck, flowing through it and a fishpond at the southern boundary. Some specimen trees of a characteristically 19th-century type – cedars, monkey puzzles and Wellingtonias.

The Laskett
Much Birch, Herefordshire OS SO5030
Open very occasionally to small groups

In 1973 Sir Roy Strong and his wife, Dr Julia Trevelyan Oman, moved to The Laskett and started to make a garden. In The Roy Strong Diaries 1967–1987 (1997), Sir Roy described it as "the garden we created over twenty years, a paradise into which I could escape the dolours of public life. All our cats are buried here." Within two months of moving, Sir Roy wrote to a friend, "I have really become a passionate gardener. Reclamation began with the kitchen garden… We began creating our herb nursery near the garage and last week I planted no less than 80 sorts of cabbage." The garden is formal: a series of walks, vistas, allées, knots and avenues decorated with all kinds of decorative buildings and ornaments. Sir Roy calls it an "autobiographical garden" and this is certainly the case; among many autobiographical interludes are a pale blue and ochre urn commemorating Sir Roy's winning of the Shakespeare Prize in 1980; a pillared temple celebrating his directorship of the Victoria and Albert Museum (1974–87); and the Ashton Arbour in memory of Sir Frederick Ashton, two of whose ballets were designed by Julia Trevelyan Oman. There is a highly productive vegetable garden and a large collection of fruit trees, in particular crab-apples and quinces. Stylistically, the spirit of the garden is firmly in the past, particularly the Renaissance. However, when Sir Roy takes visitors round the garden his commentary adds an entirely novel dimension – if there were music as well, it would become an Arcadian Gesamtkunstwerk.

Latimer Park
Latimer, Buckinghamshire OS SU9998
English Heritage Register Grade II

Early 19th-century house on an old estate owned by the Cavendish family in the early 17th century; Cavendishes remained here until 1951. Loudon's Encyclopaedia of Gardening (1822) describes it as "A small place of no great note but here introduced, because referred to by G. Mason as having been laid out by Brown"; but there is no other evidence for this. South and west of the house there is a long slender lake formed in the 1750s by damming the river Chess. The river has a series of weirs and cascades, and once had ornamental buildings and a "Dutch yacht" to decorate the waters of the lake. The park has been largely turned to arable farming and few trees remain. The house is now the National Defence College.

Lauriston Castle
Edinburgh OS NT2076 Scottish Inventory
Open regularly Tel 0131 336 2060

Late 16th-century tower house for Sir Archibald Napier, much altered in the 1820s. Formal garden north of the house, with croquet lawn edged with yew trees and a 19th-century rose garden with box-edged beds and 17th-century Italian wrought-iron gates. Pond garden in a quarry, with an island planted with rhododendrons and decorated with a statue of Diana, the whole surrounded with lawns and shrubs.

Laverstoke Park
Laverstoke, Hampshire OS SU4949
English Heritage Register Grade II

Henri Portal, a Huguenot papermaker, founded a papermill in Laverstoke in 1719 and bought the manor house. In 1798, his grandson, Henry, built a new Palladian house on a different site, designed by Joseph Bonomi; the old manor house was demolished in 1852. The park and pleasure grounds date from the early 19th century. Lawns and shrubberies close to the house, with a terrace to the west leading to a rockery. Parkland planted with many specimen trees, mostly in the 20th century. Flowing through the park, the river Test was dammed to provide water power for the papermill – now called Mill Pond.

Lavington Park
East Lavington, West Sussex OS SU9416
English Heritage Register Grade II

18th-century house on a much older site, enlarged by Detmar Blow in 1903. South and south-west of house, walled gardens with terracing, some of which may date from the original Elizabethan house. Built into the garden wall in the south-east corner is a brick building which may date from the 16th century. To the west of the house, a swimming pool probably designed by Edwin Lutyens (whose daughter, Mrs Wallace, lived here). 18th-century park north of the house, with trees surviving from 19th-century plantings.

Layer Marney Tower
Layer Marney, Essex OS TL9217
English Heritage Register Grade II
Open regularly Tel 01206 330784

Spectacular eight-storeyed brick gatehouse of c.1650, built for the 1st Lord Marney; the proposed courtyard house was never completed. The gardens are largely

of the 20th century. Rose gardens enclosed in yew hedges beside north-west corner of house, with a central statue. South of the gatehouse, a broad path flanked by mixed borders. In 1904 the new owner, Walter de Zoete, imported urns and statues from Italy, which he used to embellish the gardens. There had been a deer park here by the 13th century and traces of medieval parkland remain.

The Leasowes
Halesowen, West Midlands OS SO9784
English Heritage Register Grade I
Open regularly Tel 01384 815538

The garden at The Leasowes was the creation of William Shenstone who inherited the estate in 1735 and began to lay out the grounds in around 1743. He was a farmer, and conceived his estate as a *ferme ornée*, an ornamented farm, in which the agriculture would be carried on in a sublime landscape. In Shenstone's "Unconnected Thoughts on Gardening" (1764) he wrote that gardening "consists in pleasing the imagination by scenes of grandeur, beauty, or variety". At The Leasowes, two wooded valleys with pools were animated with planned walks which took the visitor to inscriptions evoking the memory of friends and making allusions to literature; to monuments referring to classical antiquity; to seats, ornamental buildings, cascades and contrived vistas. Nature was only gently shaped and was embellished in order to stimulate the workings of the imagination. Unlike most 18th-century landscapers, Shenstone was not a rich man but a modest farmer whose annual income was around £300 (£24,756 today). Many of his embellishments were for this reason made on the cheap, fashioned of wood rather than stone, and therefore shortlived. In Shenstone's lifetime The Leasowes became famous and much visited; it was here that Samuel Johnson gave his opinion that landscape gardening was "innocent amusement". After Shenstone's death, the estate changed hands many times and decayed, but some of his more permanent buildings survived to recent times – his Gothic Ruined Priory (which

incorporated medieval fragments of nearby Halesowen Abbey) was inhabited until 1917 and demolished only in 1965. In 1906 Halesowen Golf Club bought the estate; Shenstone's house is now the clubhouse and part of the grounds a golf course. In 1997 the local authority, Dudley Metropolitan Borough Council, received £1.3 million from the Heritage Lottery Fund to restore the landscape but only a little work seems to have been carried out and the project was suspended by the HLF in 2000.

Leazes Park
Newcastle-upon-Tyne, Tyne and Wear
OS NZ2464 English Heritage Register Grade II
Open regularly

The first purpose-built public park in Newcastle, designed by John Laing and opened in 1873. Laing laid out a lake with an island and a pavilion and facilities for skating, bowls and croquet. The park was to be enclosed with a belt of trees with winding walks. The park survives today largely as planned, although a bandstand and the pavilion (burnt down in the 1990s) have gone.

Ledston Hall
Ledston, West Yorkshire OS SE4328
English Heritage Register Grade II*
Open regularly Tel 01423 523423

17th-century mansion on a much older site. Paintings by John Setterington of 1728, illustrated in John Harris's *The Artist and the Country House* (1979), show a very elaborate garden with much formal water, topiary and avenues. This garden was possibly designed by Charles Bridgeman and there survive plans attributed to him. Traces of the garden remain, including a brick pavilion visible in the Setterington paintings. To the east of the house an intricate pattern of alleys, groves and serpentine walks of beech were planted in 1967 to recreate one of Bridgeman's designs. An estate map of 1802 suggests that a simplified and informalised version of this scheme existed at that time.

Leeds Castle
see page 155

Lees Court
Sheldwich Lees, Kent OS TR0156
English Heritage Register Grade II

House built c.1652 for Sir George Sondes on an older site. Pevsner describes the lavishly pilastered south front as "one of the marvels of English C17 architecture". In the early 18th century there had been complex formal gardens. In 1908 Thomas Mawson laid out new formal gardens on the same site, south-east of the house. He designed a flagstoned terrace with a sunken rose garden and a fountain, and seats sheltered by blocks of clipped yew. To the south-west, a yew-hedged tennis court and a smaller sunken garden and lily pool. In the park, the remains of early 18th-century avenues. The house has been divided into flats.

Leeswood Hall
Leeswood, Clwyd OS SJ2561
Cadw/ICOMOS Register Grade I

House built c.1724–26 for George Wynne, the owner of a lead mine, probably to the designs of Francis Smith of Warwick. Pleasure grounds were laid out at the same time. They are described in J.C. Loudon's *Encyclopaedia of Gardening* (1822): "the grounds occupy a fine slope, and were laid out by Switzer above a century ago, whose magnificent iron gateway, through which the forecourt of the house is entered, still remains." It is known that Wynne made payments to Switzer and it seems certain that the pleasure grounds were designed by him. Switzer was an important figure in the transition between formal and informal landscaping. At Leeswood he laid out lawns close to the house; blocks of woodland through which vistas were opened; a circular mount; a turf amphitheatre; and pools. All this in essence survives, as does Loudon's "magnificent iron gateway", the great White Gates, which were probably made by either Robert Davies or Robert Bakewell as a *claire-voie* for Switzer's scheme. Wynne's house and garden are said to have cost £40,000 (£3,200,000 today); by the 1740s his lead mine was exhausted and Wynne died destitute in London in 1756.

Leigh Court
Abbot's Leigh, Bristol OS ST5474
English Heritage Register Grade II

House built near the site of a Tudor house c.1810 for Philip John Miles a banker, to the designs of Thomas Hopper. In 1814 Humphry Repton was consulted and he produced a Red Book although, as was often the case, only some of his proposals were carried out. He regretted that he had not been consulted on the siting of the new house ("dreadfully exposed…[to] the torrent of wind proceeding from the Atlantic"). The garden was described in 1829: "Immediately around the house is a thriving plantation of evergreens, intermingled with trees of great size and beauty, some of which overhang a narrow romantic glen which separates the pleasure grounds and lawn from the Park, to which deer are confined by an iron fence scarcely perceptible." The estate is now in multiple ownership. In Paradise Bottom (part of Leigh Woods owned by the Forestry Commission) excellent trees survive, and hints of Repton's landscaping include an avenue of Irish yews leading to a knoll where the Red Book proposed to build a temple. Repton's landscape has been partly restored and it may be visited.

Leigh Park
Havant, Hampshire OS SU7109 English Heritage Register Grade II* Open regularly

Now a public park to a large housing estate, Leigh Park was originally laid out from 1829 onwards as a park and pleasure grounds for Sir George Staunton. Staunton was a diplomat attached to Macartney's embassy in China and became a learned scholar of Chinese; the grounds at Leigh Park were in part modelled on those of the Chinese Imperial Park at Jehol. A lake had a boat house, bridge and summerhouse in Chinese style, and and plants were brought back from China. Staunton commissioned Lewis Vulliamy to build a detached library to house his collection of Chinese writings – an octagonal Gothic building which still survives, although the house has

L

long gone. Also surviving is the domed Rotunda with Doric columns and the Staunton Memorial, a hexagonal garden house. Some exotic trees and shrubs are still to be seen.

Leighton Bromswold Castle
Leighton Bromswold, Cambridgeshire OS TL1175 English Heritage Register Grade II

Earthworks of the early 17th-century garden of a 15th-century prebendal manor house. A new house was projected before 1608 by Sir Gervase Clifton, possibly to the designs of John Thorpe who did a drawing for it, but only the gatehouse was built. The garden was south-east of the house, bounded on three sides by a bank forming a raised walk, and with four shallow ponds, one at each corner of the garden. An avenue, probably dating from the 17th century, leads from the gatehouse to the church.

Leighton Hall
Leighton, Powys OS SJ2404 Cadw/ICOMOS Register Grade I

House built c.1850–56 for the Liverpool banker and industrialist John Naylor to the designs of W.H. Gee. House and garden cost £275,000 (£11,000,000 today). Edward Kemp laid out the pleasure grounds with terraces by the house; winding walks through a shrubbery to an octagonal pool; a geometric rose garden; a terrace and bastions overlooking the park; lawns with specimen trees and shrubs; a serpentine lake with a formal cascade and ornamental planting. A 19th-century pinetum has several mature conifers of that period. It was here in 1888 that the Leyland cypress (× *Cupressocyparis leylandii*) had its origin, a chance bigeneric hybrid between *Cupressus macrocarpa* and *Chamaecyparis nootkatensis*. The original tree was lost in a storm in 1954; its parents still survive.

Leith Hall
nr Huntly, Aberdeenshire OS NJ5429 Open regularly (NTS) Tel 01464 831216

The Leith family lived here from the middle ages; the Hon. Mrs Leith-Hay gave the estate to the National Trust for Scotland in 1945. The present house is 17th century but with much later alteration. The garden, although it preserves traces of an 18th-century layout (when there was much work done on the house), is essentially 20th-century, made by Charles and Henrietta Leith-Hay before World War I. The West Garden has a long double herbaceous border climbing a slope and a rose border. Nearby is a rock garden dating from the 1920s, with dwarf conifers, heathers and a collection of primulas.

Lennoxlove
nr Haddington, East Lothian OS NT5172 Scottish Inventory Open regularly Tel 01620 823720

Estate, formerly known as Lethington, going back to the 14th century when the Maitlands (later Earls of Lauderdale) built a tower house. This remains, with additions in the 17th and 19th centuries, and in 1912 it was restored by Sir Robert Lorimer. On a site formerly occupied by a bowling green east of the house, Lorimer also laid out a sunken garden with Italian wrought-iron gates; a sundial, dated 1679 with an octagonal dial and seventeen faces, stands on a lawn, with herbaceous borders to the south. To the north and south are yew hedges clipped into battlements. In 1674 the 1st (and only) Duke of Lauderdale, who also owned Ham House (*see page 145*), enclosed the park in 12ft/3.6m walls – it is reputedly the earliest enclosed park in Scotland. Once well planted with trees, it is now given over to grazing.

Leonardslee Gardens
see page 156

Leuchie House
nr Northberwick, East Lothian OS NT5783 Scottish Inventory

Ancient estate, with a house built 1779–85 for Sir Hew Dalrymple. Formal landscape contemporary with an earlier house was replaced c.1800 by a more informal landscape, possibly designed by J.C. Loudon. Parkland remains, with fewer trees but the vestigial remains of an avenue. Walled kitchen garden dated 1807, divided in two by a wall – originally with an orchard in the southern part and ornamental gardens in the northern; today the garden is partly cultivated for fruit and vegetables and partly ornamental, with borders, a rose garden and a lawn with specimen trees.

Levens Hall
see page 346

Lever Park
Rivington, Lancashire OS SD6314 English Heritage Register Grade II

16th-century house, Rivington Hall, with 18th-century additions. The house is enclosed in gardens, with lawns and mature trees. Country park commissioned by Lord Leverhulme from Thomas Mawson, 1910–11, on the eastern bank of a reservoir. Its most striking ornament is a reconstruction of the ruin of Liverpool Castle, with three avenues radiating from it across the park. The park is a mixture of open ground, woodland and avenues.

Lexham Hall
East Lexham, Norfolk OS TF8617 English Heritage Register Grade II Open occasionally for NGS

Early 17th-century house, rebuilt in early 18th century for Edmund Wodehouse and altered in 19th century by Sir Jeffry Wyatville for Colonel F.W. Keppel. 18th- and early 19th-century landscaping with a sinuous lake. 20th-century formal garden south of the house. 19th-century octagonal dairy and probably 18th-century crinkle-crankle wall in kitchen garden.

Lord Leycester's Hospital
see page 268

Lichfield Cathedral Close *and* Linear Park
Lichfield, Staffordshire OSSK1109 English Heritage Register Grade II Open regularly

The cathedral close had a walk of lime trees laid out in the 17th century, known by the 18th century as the Dean's Walk. In 1776 some of the trees were removed, at the suggestion of Humphry Repton, to open up views of the cathedral from Stowe Pool to the north-east. Repton also made suggestions for the garden of his friend Anna Seward who lived in the Cathedral School (formerly the Bishop's Palace) overlooking the close; the foundations of her summerhouse flanked by yews survive, as does another summerhouse. South of the cathedral is Minster Pool with a walk laid out in 1772 under the inspiration of Anna Seward, who also, having much admired the Serpentine in Hyde Park, suggested curving the north bank of the pool. At the western end of the pool is the New Free Library and Museum, with decorative Museum Gardens laid out in 1859. The gardens are continued westwards, beyond a rockery and pool, as Beacon Park, well treed and with playing fields. There is a good aerial photograph of this rare urban landscape in Christopher Taylor's *Parks and Gardens of Britain: A Landscape History from the Air* (1998).

Lilleshall Hall
Lilleshall, Shropshire OS SJ7414 English Heritage Register Grade II

Neo-Tudor house built in 1829 to the designs of Sir Jeffry Wyatville for Lord Gower (later the Duke of Sutherland). Wyatville also designed balustraded terracing to south and west of house. This included a circular parterre with concentric beds, a four-part water garden with fountain, and an extraordinary 570ft/170m-long tunnel-arbour covered with apples leading to a rose garden. A long, broad grass walk, at first with rectangular beds, led to an arcaded pavilion in the distance. Much use was made of bedding on a grand scale, as an article in *Country Life* in 1898 explained: "the blaze of colour is attained by boldly contrasting various hues to secure rich effect, dark colours are opposed to light; zonal pelargoniums, calceolarias, and tuberous begonias being amongst the most important plants used."

Lincoln Arboretum
Lincoln, Lincolnshire OS SK9871 English Heritage Register Grade II Open regularly

Arboretum designed by Edward Milner and opened to the public in 1872. 19th-century bandstand, cast-iron shelter, pool, and good remaining trees. A conservatory, also by Milner, has gone. In its heyday the arboretum was the setting for annual Temperance Galas when brass bands would play to as many as 20,000 visitors.

Lincoln's Inn Fields
Camden, London OS TQ3081 English Heritage Register Grade II* Open regularly

Building of private houses here started in the mid 17th century, the site originally being two fields, Cup Field and Purse Field. By 1682 diagonal walks crossed the area and in 1735 a formal layout of grass and gravel paths was authorised. The present layout is essentially 19th-century, with a cruciform pattern of paths meeting at a central octagonal bandstand (1880, by James Wild, curator of the Sir John Soane's Museum). The outer boundary is planted with shrubberies and mature trees, with gaps to allow views. Lawns with many good specimen trees. Drinking fountains of c.1880 in north-west and south-east corners.

Lindisfarne Castle
see page 346

Lindsey House
Kensington and Chelsea, London OS TQ2677 English Heritage Register Grade II Open by written appointment only (NT); phone 01494 528051 for details

House built c.1674 for Robert Bertie, 3rd Earl of Lindsey, incorporating earlier material, with much subsequent alteration. The house is now divided and the garden belongs to Number 100 Cheyne Walk. Walled garden laid out in 1909 to the ingenious designs of Edwin Lutyens and Gertrude Jekyll for Sir Hugh Lane: three strips of lawn separated by paved paths, originally with a central circular pool. Alcoves in the rear wall, aligned with paths, and a mixed border along north-east wall. Trees and shrubs, some surprisingly large for a small space, give shade and seclusion.

Linley Hall
nr More, Shropshire OS SO3492
English Heritage Register Grade II

The More family came to live here in 1580 but the present house was built in the 1740s for Robert More who was a friend of Linnaeus and a knowledgeable botanist. The avenue, of beech and oak, felled 1916 and replanted 1937, may have survived from a 17th-century alignment for an earlier house. 18th-century parkland, with temple of the same date on the banks of a lake, concealing an earlier icehouse.

Linton Park
Linton, Kent OS TQ7549
English Heritage Register Grade II

Early 18th-century house for Robert Mann on an earlier site, altered in the early 19th century. It stands on a fine site with southerly views – in Horace Walpole's words it stands "like the citadel of Kent, the whole county its garden". J.C. Loudon was consulted about the grounds in 1825, and as a result a lake was made in the southern part of the park, terraces and walks laid out south and east of the house, and an avenue of beech and lime planted beside the north drive. Loudon recommended the planting of "rare and elegant exotic trees…such as Cedars, Pines, Evergreen Oak, American Oaks, Magnolia"; many good specimen trees remain. It was probably his suggestion, too, to have the avenue of Wellingtonias planted between the house and the church.

Lismore Castle
see page 423

Lismore House
Cross Street, Helston, Cornwall OS SW6527
English Heritage Register Grade II

House built 1835 for Glynn Grylls. Surviving walled gardens of the same date as the house, with some attractive picturesque details – a rustic summerhouse, a grotto-like arch and a cast-iron garden pump dated 1844 – in a setting of lawns, flowering shrubs and trees. A rare example of an early 19th-

century town garden full of the atmosphere of its period.

Lisselan
Colnakilty, County Cork, Republic of Ireland
Open regularly Tel (00353) 023 33249

Picturesque towered house built in the 1850s for William Bence-Jones to the designs of Lewis Vulliamy. The house has a splendid position facing down to the banks of the river Argideen. The garden is a period piece in Robinsonian style, taking advantage of the valley setting. The microclimate is very benign and eucalyptus, hoherias, mimosas and myrtles flourish here, as well as hardier azaleas, magnolias, maples and rhododendrons. There are herbaceous borders, a water garden and a rockery. Mature trees, some dating from the 19th century, form a distinguished background.

Lister Park
Bradford, West Yorkshire OS SE1535 English
Heritage Register Grade II Open regularly

Public park laid out 1870–1904 on an ancient site. The Cartwright Memorial Hall, designed by Simpson & Allen, was named after the inventor of the power loom, the Revd Dr Edmund Cartwright; built 1899, it houses a museum. Today, a parterre in front of the hall has a dazzling display of carpet bedding, continuing a tradition that goes back to the early 20th century. The Botanical Garden, originally planned to show every family of plants in the British flora, has specimen trees and shrubs. A stream flows along its edge and into a serpentine lake with four islands, on the north-east side of the park. Three bowling greens preserve their original pavilion. By 2003, with the help of Heritage Lottery funding, the lake had been splendidly restored, with a handsome boating pavilion, and an entirely new garden, the Mughal Garden, had been laid out with pools, rills and fountains.

Little Boarhunt
Liphook, Hampshire OS SU8330
English Heritage Register Grade II

Ancient farmhouse, rebuilt in Arts and Crafts style by the architect

and garden designer Harry Inigo Triggs as a home for himself in 1910. H.I. Triggs also laid out a new garden with a sunken garden and rill surrounded by dry-stone walls and a pergola with ogee-roofed gazebos in each corner. Little Boarhunt is described in Gertrude Jekyll's and Lawrence Weaver's *Gardens for Small Country Houses* (1912). Only half-an-acre/0.2 hectares in area, "It shows how the qualities that make the beauty of the historic formal gardens may be reproduced in little for houses of moderate size."

Little Moreton Hall
see page 215

Little Onn Hall
Church Eaton, Staffordshire OS SJ8517
Open occasionally for NGS and by
appointment Tel 01785 840154

An ancient site, with a medieval moat, but the present house dates from the 1850s for the Ashton family. Garden designed by Thomas Mawson in the 1890s and described in his book *The Art and Craft of Garden Making* (1900). His clients, the Misses Ashton, found they did not have enough money to complete the garden as planned, but enough was finished to make an excellent garden of its period. Mawson designed terraces on two sides of the house, a circular paved rose garden from which there are views over parkland, and a rustic summerhouse overlooking the moat. A waterlily canal, ending at either end in an octagonal pool, looks like Mawson's work but probably dates from the 1920s.

Little Sparta, *formerly* Stonypath
Dunsyre, Lanarkshire OS NT0748
Has been open regularly in recent years

Ian Hamilton Finlay (b.1925) made this garden, which is as complete an expression of an artist's ideas as could be imagined. Finlay is a poet, designer and publisher whose work has ranged widely. His Wild Hawthorn Press, founded in 1961 with Jessie McGuffie, published works of "concrete poetry" (involving typographical and graphic expressiveness) although its first

publication was Finlay's own *Glasgow Beasts, an a Burd*, which is delightful but incomprehensible to readers unfamiliar with Glasgow *patois*. The journal *Poor. Old. Tired. Horse.*, which ran from 1962 to 1968, published similar material. In 1966 Finlay and his wife, Sue, came to Stonypath (as Little Sparta was originally known), a stone croft in the wild and austere moorland of the Pentland Hills. Finlay had already been experimenting with the use of inscribed objects in the landscape, and here he was able to develop the idea to its full. The key to his garden is his belief in the interaction between sculptures, inscriptions and objects and the landscape in which they are set – one is not merely the setting for the other. It is a poetic garden, and like much poetry requires an effort from the reader and a submission to its mood. In a marshy part of the garden, among irises, a stone slab is inscribed with the words See POUSSIN Hear LORRAIN; in a carpet of deadnettle, Pan's pipes bear the words When the wind blows/Venerate the sound; a tombstone-like slab by the trunk of a silver birch has the slogan BRING BACK THE BIRCH; in a grove of trees, a bright red cut-out figure of Apollo chases a green Daphne. There are more worrying ideas in the garden – a pair of gate piers have finials in the form of grenades; a sequence of stones by a lochan has a quotation from French revolutionary St Just: THE PRESENT ORDER IS THE DISORDER OF THE FUTURE. Little Sparta is an Arcadia in which real life makes its appearance, sometimes painfully. Although it draws on ideas of the past, it is wholly modern. It is too personal a work to inspire imitators but its effect is to renew one's faith in the possibility of gardening as an art.

Little Thakeham
Thakeham, West Sussex OS TQ1015
English Heritage Register Grade II

House designed by Edwin Lutyens in 1902 for Ernest Blackburn. This was one of Lutyens's favourite houses – "the best of the bunch", he called it. Lutyens also designed the garden layout, with Blackburn

himself devising the planting. It is simple and unostentatious – a sequence of interconnected spaces with stone-flagged paths, yew hedging, plain terracing, a lily pool and water garden and a long pergola providing the climax of the chief, southern axis. The pergola ends in a characteristic Lutyens flourish – a platform from which stone steps lead east and west to a lawn and an orchard. J.C. Shepherd and G.A. Jellicoe in their *Gardens and Design* (1913) say of Little Thakeham that "it settles into its surroundings as though it had been there always." The house is now an admirable hotel.

Littlecote
nr Chilton Foliat, Wiltshire OS SU3070
English Heritage Register Grade II

House of medieval origin, rebuilt in the 16th centuryand with subsequent alterations. A painting by an unidentified artist of c.1705–10, illustrated in John Harris's *The Artist and the Country House* (1979), shows three walled enclosures to the south, east and west of the house, with topiary, espaliers and regular beds, and avenues crossing the landscape to the west. These walls remain and have been extended. In the western enclosure a lawn rises to a rectangular terrace. North of the house, a later walled garden was developed in the late 19th century with a terraced lawn, mature yews and a circular pool. A yew hedge runs across at the back and beyond it is a canal with cascades whose water comes from the river Kennet. Running along the northern wall is a long herbaceous border first laid out in the early 20th century. An early 19th-century gazebo stands to the north-west, and fine gates with lion and unicorn finials pierce the northern wall on the house's central axis. The house is now a hotel.

Llanerch Hall
St Asaph, Clwyd OS SJ0572
Cadw/ICOMOS Register Grade II

Garden famous because of the beautiful painting of 1662 by an unknown artist now in the Yale Center for British Art. The painting shows an elaborate formal terraced garden of Italianate character descending the slopes between a tall gabled house and a circular pool with a figure of Neptune. It is known that these gardens were made in about 1660 by Mutton Davies on his return from a visit to Italy. J.C. Loudon's *Encyclopaedia of Gardening* (1822) describes "formal walks, clipt trees and hydraulic statues. Among the images and water tricks was a sundial, which, on the spectator's approach, spouted in his face… The whole place is now modernised, and the fine old house too much so." John Harris, in *The Artist and the Country House* (1979), writes: "This is a magical garden revealing what could be laid out even by the squirearchy in remote places; and what has been lost to us." Only faint traces of the garden survive today.

Llanfihangel Court
Llanfihangel Crucorney, Gwent OS SO3220
Cadw /ICOMOS Register Grade I

Early Tudor house on a medieval site, which has passed through a bewildering succession of owners. The gardens and park were laid out in the late 17th century when John Arnold lived here. Surviving terraces north of the house, leading down to a square walled enclosure, are shown in a painting of the 1680s. There were also formal gardens east of the house, of which, a stone two-storey pavilion survives. The 1680s painting shows the park with formal groves and radial avenues, of which traces remain. The south avenue survives, but the ancient sweet chestnuts appear to be at the end of their life.

Lochryan House
Cairnryan, Wigtownshire OS NX6806
Scottish Inventory

Delightful house built 1701 for Colonel Agnew whose family had owned the land since the early 15th century. Early 18th-century walled garden east of house, with a walk of clipped bay trees leading to the garden door of the house. The garden is divided in four, with twin summerhouses in two corners. Victorian glasshouses are used to cultivate figs, nectarines, peaches and tender ornamentals.

The axis of the bay tree walk is extended eastwards outside the walled garden by a grass path with specimen trees and rhododendrons on either side. The eastern part of the garden is rich in good trees and shrubs – *Drimys winteri*, eucalyptus, hoherias, magnolias, myrtles and rowans.

Locke Park
Barnsley, South Yorkshire OS SK3405
English Heritage Register Grade II
Open regularly

Public park, opened in 1877 as an extension of Barnsley Park (the "People's Park"). Named after Joseph Locke, an apprentice of George Stephenson, who became engineer to the Grand Junction Railway and whose widow gave the land to the city. Serpentine walk, iron arches, ornamental fountain pool (now dry and planted with bedding), statue of Joseph Locke and much mature planting of holly, laburnum, lilac and rhododendrons along former quarry walls. Above the quarry, a row of columns taken from a Barnsley bank, an ornamental drinking fountain and views of the city. Locke Park Tower, a pleasure observatory and belvedere dated 1877. Decaying bandstand in southern part of park, with views of Drax power station.

Locko Park
Dale Abbey, Derbyshire OS SK4038
English Heritage Register Grade II
Open occasionally for NGS

House probably of late 17th century, with many subsequent alterations, especially in the mid 19th century by Henry Stevens of Derby, who also laid out the gardens about the house. To south and west, lawns and informal beds with views south over park to lake. Terraced gardens on north-west side of house, the top terrace with triangular beds radiating from circular beds. Terrace backed by kitchen garden wall with entrance flanked by piers with winged lions. Winding path through pleasure grounds with trees and shrubs, glades and informal beds. Park laid out by William Emes who did a plan in 1792 – largely open pasture with scattered trees and clumps. East of house, Gothic

19th-century icehouse. Lake south-west of house planted with trees to frame views of house.

Lodge Park
Sherborne, Gloucestershire OS SP1412
English Heritage Register Grade I
Open regularly (NT) Tel 01451 844130

Early 17th-century house, of charming and rare early classical character, built as a deer-coursing stand for John Dutton who lived nearby at Sherborne House. It overlooked a walled deer park made for that purpose at the same time. A new deer park was laid out in the 1720s by Charles Bridgeman; he was paid £70 (£5,740 today) in 1729 "for his journeys to Shireborn and making a plan for [Sir John's] New Park." A plan dated 1725 and attributed to Bridgeman survives. From that date an immense amount of tree planting took place, including a "Great Avenue"; a canal-like pool was also made, as well as a garden behind the house which was encircled with a ha-ha to separate it from the park. The house was backed by woodland in which there were winding serpentine walks. Many of the larger features of Bridgeman's design may still be seen, making it one of the most complete surviving examples of his work.

Logan Botanic Garden
see page 385

Logan House
Kirkmaiden, Wigtownshire OS NX0942
Scottish Inventory Open regularly
Tel 01776 860231

The McDouall family were granted land in the Rhinns of Galloway in 1295. The present house was built 1702. Woodland garden established from 1869; part of it is now part of Logan Botanic Garden (*see page 385*), as is the walled garden where the most vulnerable plants were cultivated. Many species rhododendrons were propagated from seed from George Forrest's and Reginald Farrer's expeditions, also embothriums, eucalyptus and, in a scree garden, olearias. Although much of the original garden has been separated off, what remains is fascinating and

shows how the McDouall family in the 19th century saw the potential of the rare climate of this narrow peninsula.

Londesborough Park
Londesborough, East Yorkshire OS SE8745
English Heritage Register Grade II*

House built 1839 on an ancient site, with later alterations – to the north-west of the site of a former house and its 17th-century gardens. In 1643 the estate was owned by Richard Boyle, 1st Earl of Cork (later 1st Earl of Burlington) who laid out gardens 1660–80 and reintroduced deer into the park. A Kip engraving in *Britannia Illustrata* (1707) show the 1st Earl's garden: an avenue leading to an outer entrance court, and an inner court with a path flanked by lawns and intricate beds. Behind the house, a lawn with statues flanked by topiary walks and ending in circular pool and curved viewing platform. All this was probably designed by the architect Robert Hooke who was working on the house at the time. Traces of this garden remain – an arched retaining wall south of the house, the viewing platform, and a pair of 17th-century gate piers. The 3rd Earl, who lived chiefly at Chiswick House (*see page 127*), spent £1,600 (£132,032 today) on garden works 1728–32, retaining much of the 1st Earl's garden but adding, with the advice of his gardener Thomas Knowlton, avenues of Turkey oak and walnuts radiating from the house – of which traces remain. South-west of the house, Burlington replaced a bowling green with a pool and a walk through trees and shrubs to a circular clearing from which winding paths lead. In the park, a series of lakes linked by cascades, scattered mature trees and shelter belts. Burlington died in 1753 and the estate passed to his son-in-law, William Cavendish (later 4th Duke of Devonshire).

London Road Cemetery
Coventry, West Midlands OS SP3477 English Heritage Register Grade II* Open regularly

Cemetery designed in 1845 by Joseph Paxton, incorporating quarry workings whose hillocks

and hollows, with mature elm trees, ornamented the landscape. A contemporary description said that it had "more the air of a gentleman's park than a city of the dead". It was planned for Anglicans and Nonconformists, with a Jewish burial ground added in 1863. The hilly site is richly planted with largely coniferous trees and shrubs, and has winding and looping walks. A terrace walk forms a barrier – visual and auditory – along the London Road, with views west over the cemetery. The northern part of the cemetery, designed as a pleasure ground, has no graves and contains a monument to Paxton designed by Joseph Goddard.

London Wetland Centre
Barnes, London OS TQ2277
Open regularly Tel 020 8409 4400

The Wildfowl and Wetlands Trust was established in 1946 by Peter Scott to preserve the habitats of wildfowl. The London Wetland Centre is an offshoot which opened in 2000 on a 100-acre/40-hectare site at Barn Elms – formerly reservoirs of Thames Water. To emphasise that ecology begins at the home, the Wetland Centre commissioned a series of sustainable gardens from notable garden designers of the day. Arne Maynard's turfed walls are supported by split oak which will gradually decay and provide habitats for ferns and fungi; groves of silver birch are underplanted with bluebells, primroses and other native woodland plants; Isabelle van Groeningen and Gabriella Pape's planting of swathes of herbaceous perennials was designed to attract insect and bird life; Cleve West's garden shows how to conserve water and use drought-tolerant plants.

Long Barn
Weald, Kent OS TQ5250 English Heritage Register Grade II* Open occasionally for NG

The 14th-century house, with later alterations and possibly the birthplace of William Caxton, was bought by Harold Nicolson and Vita Sackville-West in 1915. Garden designed by them with brick terrace, lawn with a line of

L

Irish yews clipped into drums, and terraces to the south with lawns and box hedges. A grass terrace with yews clipped into cones overlooks the Delphic Grove with grass, woodland and a swimming pool. The Dutch Garden was made from 1925 with help from Sir Edwin Lutyens: six L-shaped beds, with edges of raised bricks and filled with mixed planting; a sundial at the centre; and a thorn hedge along one side. Harold Nicolson and Vita Sackville-West lived here until 1930 when they bought Sissinghurst Castle (*see page 177*). Contemporary photographs of the garden at Long Barn show profusely exuberant planting verging on occasional chaos. Vita Sackville-West wrote her poem *The Land* (published 1926) at Long Barn, in which she avowed, "The country habit has me by the heart."

The Long Walk

Knaresborough, North Yorkshire OS SE3456
English Heritage Register Grade II
Open regularly

Knaresborough became known as a spa town as early as the late 16th century. Most famous was the Dropping Well on the banks of the river Nidd, described by Leland in 1538 as "a welle of wonderful nature…For out of the great rokkes by it distillith water continually into." Close to the well is a cave called Mother Shipton's Cave, supposedly the birthplace of a 15th-century soothsayer. In around 1739 The Long Walk was improved by the landowner, Sir Henry Slingsby, who planted trees along the river bank. It runs along the west bank of the river and was planned both as an access route to the Dropping Well and Mother Shipton's Cave (both of which survive) but also as a promenade from which to relish views of the town and its 14th-century castle rising on the east bank of the river. In 1697 Celia Fiennes came to "the Spaw at Knarsborough" and visited a garden by the castle where was all manner of Curiosityes of Flowers and Greens, great variety, there is also a Cherry garden with green walkes for the Company to walk in, and a Great seate in a high tree that gives a pleasant prospect."

Longford Castle

nr Salisbury, Wiltshire OS TU1726
English Heritage Register Grade II*

House completed in 1591 for Sir Thomas Gorges; altered in the 19th century by James Wyatt and Anthony Salvin. Robert Thacker's engraving of *c*.1680 shows gardens with a balustraded terrace, parterres, topiary, a fountain and rows of narrow flower beds. This was the garden seen *c*.1695 by Celia Fiennes who describes "the gardens one below another with low walls to give the view all at once; here was fine flowers and greens dwarfe trees and oring and lemon trees in rows with fruite and flowers at once, and some ripe, they are the first oring trees I ever saw." Four-columned *tempietto* built in 1769, with statue of Flora by John Cheere. Capability Brown visited in 1777 and 1778. The formal gardens were removed, though the *tempietto* survived, and Brown is thought to have been responsible for the boundary plantings of trees and scattered clumps in the parkland. Formal gardens were restored south of the castle in 1832, possibly to the designs of W.A. Nesfield. Originally with carpet bedding, herbaceous perennials were introduced after World War II but the layout was preserved.

Longleat

see page 93

Longner Hall

nr Atcham, Shropshire OS SJ5211
English Heritage Register Grade II

House designed by John Nash for Robert Burton and built *c*.1805, replacing an earlier house. Nash also built a Gothic conservatory. Humphry Repton was consulted (Red Book, 1804) but it is not known what, if anything, resulted. At all events, someone had the skill to lay out the idyllic 19th-century parkland on the banks of the river Severn.

Longstock Water Gardens

see page 94

Longstowe Hall

Longstowe, Cambridgeshire OS TL3055
English Heritage Register Grade II*

16th-century house, remodelled in the late 19th and early 20th centuries. Neo-classical formal gardens of Edwardian character with parterre of box-edged rose beds, rose pergola, brick walls and stone balustrading with finials and urns. Grass walk forming an axis on the garden front leads between herbaceous borders and yew hedges to a lake with a flight of steps descending between balustraded brick walls. Lawns and specimen trees on each side. Irregular lakes formed from old fishponds and linked by a stone bridge and cascades. Avenue on north-west axis of house. Deer park made after 1571 and landscaped after enclosure in 1799.

Loseley Park

see page 157

Lotherton Hall

nr Aberford, West Yorkshire OS SE4535
English Heritage Register Grade II
Open regularly Tel 0113 2813259

18th-century villa, enlarged in the late 19th and early 20th centuries for Colonel Frederick Trench-Gascoigne. Gardens of Edwardian character designed for Mrs Laura Gascoigne, probably with advice from her friend Ellen Willmott. Yew hedges and a path between borders lead to a summerhouse made from a former entrance to the house. Parallel to this, two gravel paths run between lawns with clipped yews. To the south-east, winding paths run through a shrubbery to the Dell, a rock garden which in the past had a fernery and Japanese garden. North-east of the hall, the paved William and Mary Garden has a rectangular pool and is divided into box-edged beds with spiral box topiary. A modern lime avenue leads to a stone temple which was originally a portico from Parlington Hall, another Gascoigne house.

Lovers' Walks

Matlock Bath, Derbyshire OS SK2958 English Heritage Register Grade II* Open regularly

Walks on the east bank of the river Derwent, associated with the mid 18th-century development of the spa. Two paths, one running along the river and one roughly parallel running along the cliff top, are linked by paths climbing the wooded slope. Promenade called Jubilee Grounds added in 1887 at the northern end of the river walk, with a bandstand and rockeries. South of it, on the river walk, a tufa grotto. Near it, a path climbing the slope, Birdcage Walk, one of the walks attributed to William Emes. At the southern end of walk, view of cascade. On the slopes, paths lead to viewing platforms at various points but some of the views are now obscured by overgrown planting.

Lower Gatton Park, also known as Gatton Park

Gatton, Surrey OS TQ2752
English Heritage Register Grade II

Older house rebuilt in 1936 for Sir Jeremiah Colman after a fire. Ian Nairn's and Nikolaus Pevsner's *Surrey* (1971) volume in "The Buildings of England" series describes it as "poor quality Classical Revival, like an Officers' Mess". Capability Brown worked in the park here 1762–68, making a serpentine lake with islands and a temple on its banks; he also supplied plans for a "great water menagerie". The total cost of his work was £3,055 (£200,102 today). Early 19th-century formal gardens by the house have been removed, but a rockery with pools and cascades made by James Pulham, using Pulhamite stone, survives. In its heyday, as the *Journal of Horticulture and Home Farmer* (1913) reported, it was "adapted for heaths, alpines, and bog plants and aquatics". The house today is a school.

Lowesby Park

Lowesby, Leicestershire OS SK7207
English Heritage Register Grade II

Early 18th-century house, extended in 1910 by Edwin Lutyens who also remodelled the garden, chiefly south of the house. This is a typical Lutyens design, with deft architectural details – walls, terraces and steps – and characteristic lawns, pools, yew hedges and enclosures. But much

of his work is so perfectly in harmony with earlier features that it is hard to tell what is by Lutyens and what is much earlier. South of the house, for example, is a pedimented summerhouse listed as possibly *c*.1912 – but it appears on early 19th-century maps and probably dates from the mid 18th century. In the park, an avenue running north-east from the house, already present in 1815, partly replanted in the 1990s. Another avenue to the north-west, where there had been a drive in 1815.

Lowther Castle

Lowther, Cumbria OS NY5223
English Heritage Register Grade II

The Lowther family owned the estate here from the 12th century until the mid 20th century. The present castle was built 1807–14 to the designs of Robert Smirke. It was no longer inhabited after 1935 and was later stripped of its roof; the walls still stand. The park was used for army training in World War II. A Kip engraving in *Britannia Illustrata* (1707) shows the house on an immense axis, continued into the landscape with an avenue, and with exceedingly grand gardens. Only the faintest traces of this survive, among them an alignment of trees north of the house. Capability Brown advised on the park in 1763 and 1771, and although plans were produced nothing was carried out. John Webb also prepared a design which may have been partly executed. Thomas Wilkinson laid out paths along the river Lowther which flows through the north-west part of the park. Traces of avenues survive and there are many areas of woodland and scattered plantings.

Ludstone Hall

nr Claverley, Shropshire OS SO8094
English Heritage Register Grade II

Jacobean house built for John Whitmore, surrounded by a possibly earlier moat. Gardens made after 1870 when the estate was bought by J.R. Cartwright. Boisterous sunken four-part knot garden, with hedges and topiary of clipped box – mounds, spirals and playing card suits. Mixed borders, a

L

pergola and a late 20th-century woodland garden.

Luffness
nr Aberlady, East Lothian OS NT4780
Scottish Inventory

16th-century house, with Norse foundations, built for Sir Patrick Hepburn and bought by the Hope family in 1739, who remodelled it in 1822 to the designs of William Burn. Of the once extensive 19th-century formal gardens there remains a sunken parterre with radiating beds like the spokes of a wheel, once with bedding schemes now with roses. The surrounding lawns are ornamented with clipped yews. Walled garden west of the house, built 1822, square in plan but with an internal diamond-shaped enclosure where tender fruit such as figs, greengages, peaches and nectarines were cultivated; the first apricots grown out-of-doors in Scotland were cultivated here. Walks through woodland lead to the remains of a 13th-century Carmelite monastery.

Lulworth Castle
East Lulworth, Dorset OS SY8582
English Heritage Register Grade II
Open regularly (EH) Tel 01929 400352

Purbeck stone castle (although a "lodge", ie a secondary house) built c.1608 for Thomas Howard, 3rd Viscount Bindon. 600-acre/243-hectare deer park made shortly after building of house. An engraving of 1721 by Mrs Humphry Weld (the wife of the then owner) shows the castle set in extraordinarily elaborate formal gardens, with avenues, parterres, statues, pools, topiary and a long axial vista running up the hill behind the house to an arcaded pavilion. The landscape gardener Richard Woods was consulted in 1769 but it is uncertain what he did apart from an icehouse of c.1770, of which his design survives. Basire's engraving of 1773 and Theodore de Bruyn's painting of 1781 suggest that landscaping had by then all but obliterated the formal gardens, although a fragment is said to have remained until c.1960. Lake created in mid 19th century. The castle was gutted by fire in 1929 but the exterior

has been restored by English Heritage.

Lumley Castle
Little Lumley, County Durham OS NZ2851
English Heritage Register Grade II

Sir Ralph de Lumley was given a licence to crenellate in 1389; the castle was altered in the 16th century and again in the late 17th century by Sir John Vanbrugh. Three drawings of c.1721, attributed to Charles Bridgeman, show a double avenue widening out as it extends away from the façade of the house to embrace an oval lake formed by damming the river Wear, and serpentine walks and formal groves in the woods. Vanbrugh also designed gardens, and in 1729 Stephen Switzer stayed at Lumley and he would surely have discussed the garden. The name of Thomas Wright is also associated with the garden, and a design by Thomas White for the park survives. Yet in the park and gardens there is no evidence of the work of any of these designers. The park is crossed from the south-east to the north-west by Park burn which flows through a steep wooded valley, with the castle on its western bank. The river Wear forms the western boundary of the estate. A few old trees, especially limes, survive in the park, as do earthworks connected, presumably, with 18th-century landscaping. Some of the park has been turned over to agricultural use and in the south there is a golf course. The estate is still owned by the Lumley family but the castle is a hotel.

Lupton Park
Brixham, Devon OS9055
English Heritage Register Grade II*

18th-century house for Charles Hayne, which suffered a series of alterations and accidents, ending in a fire in 1926, after which the house was reconstructed in smaller form. Formal gardens dating from the 1840s, when the house was altered by George Wightwick, with balustraded enclosure, box-edged beds, fountain pool and Irish yews. John Swete, the travelling vicar, painted the house in the late 18th century, showing a

fine Palladian mansion with turf running up to the walls, undulating wooded landscape and delicious views of the sea. Today the house is a school.

Luscombe Castle
Dawlish, Devon OS SX9476
English Heritage Register Grade I

The castle was built 1800–4 to the designs of John Nash for the banker Charles Hoare. The garden was designed by Humphry Repton who produced a Red Book in 1799. Between 1799 and 1800, Repton was paid £52-10s (£1,575 today), a very modest amount. Formal gardens remain west of the house with a circular rose garden and pattern of box-edged beds about a sundial. Repton's Red Book recommendations suggested dense woodland plantings to the north and north-east of the house, and a curved belt of woods to the south, leaving open views down the valley towards the sea. The appearance of the park today corresponds to these proposals. J.C. Loudon visited Luscombe in 1842 and commented, "The grounds are said to have been laid out by the late Mr John Veitch"; it is perfectly possible that Veitch's nursery in Exeter had been involved in the making of the garden. Loudon saw "a number of large magnolias and other choice trees and shrubs" and noted substantial olive trees in the kitchen garden as well as lemons, citrons and limes.

Luton Hoo
Hyde, Bedfordshire OS TL1018
English Heritage Register Grade II*

17th-century house, rebuilt by Robert Adam for the 3rd Earl of Bute after 1762. The house was gutted by fire in 1843 and, after rebuilding, bought by Sir Julius Wernher in 1903. Capability Brown laid out a park 1764–74 for which he received a total of £10,420 (£687,563 today). In the valley of the river Lea to the east of the house, Brown created a series of undulating lawns running down to two serpentine lakes. The traveller Arthur Young saw this in 1770, admiring the "fine beeches" and "the finest water I have ever

seen". He noted three pleasure boats on the lake, one of which had ornamental sails and flying colours. Brown's park survives without major change. In the early 20th century Sir Julius Wernher made admirable formal gardens south of the house, designed by the architect Charles Mewès (who worked on the house) and built by William Romaine-Walker. The gardens are terraced, with urns, balustrades, a circular lily pool, box-edged rose beds with box topiary and a pair of domed temples – all of which survive.

Luttrellstown Castle
Clonsilla, County Dublin, Republic of Ireland

Ancient estate of the Luttrell family (Earls of Carhampton). House rebuilt in the 18th century and Gothicised in the early 19th century by a new owner, Luke White. The estate changed hands several times and since 1988 has been owned by the Luttrellstown Golf and Country Club. The river Liffey flows through the demesne which is well wooded. In the 18th century it was a famous picturesque landscape, with streams flowing through the woods and decorated with rustic cascades. A remarkable late 18th-century Gothic building in the form of a rustic stone screen bridges a valley, with arches over path and stream. Of the same period is a pedimented Doric temple and cold bath finely placed on the wooded banks of a lake. In the early 19th century Luke White continued the tradition of planting trees at Luttrellstown.

Lydiard Park
Lydiard Tregoze, Wiltshire OS SU1084
English Heritage Register Grade II
Open regularly Tel 01793 770401

House of medieval origins, rebuilt in the 1740s for the 2nd Viscount St John, probably to the designs of Roger Morris. By 1766 earlier formal gardens had been destroyed when the grounds were landscaped. Remains of three early 18th-century avenues survive. A lake which was part of the 18th-century landscaping was drained in the early 20th century, a few pools remaining. Parkland has scattered mature trees.

Lyme Park
see page 215

Lynford Hall
Lynford, Norfolk OS TL8294
English Heritage Register Grade II

On an old site, the present Lynford Hall was built 1856–61 to the designs of William Burn for Mr Lyne-Stephens and his wife ("a French ex-ballet-dancer and noted beauty", as Pevsner scrupulously notes). A canal-like part of a stream, Long Water, possibly dates from the 18th century. Formal gardens by William Burn, with balustraded terracing and parterres about house with urns and statuary. Doric Temple of Mercury by William Burn of c.1862. Late 19th-century arboretum and woodland administered by the Forestry Commission.

Lyppiatt Park
Lyppiatt, Gloucestershire OS SO8805
English Heritage Register Grade II*

Early 16th-century house, with remains of 14th-century house, enlarged by Sir Jeffry Wyatville in 1809. A Kip engraving of 1712 shows a formal garden of which tantalising traces survive today. Late 19th-century lawns planted with specimen trees, and Victorian pinetum north of house. The Great Terrace, supported on bastions, is planted with shrubs and specimen trees.

Lytes Cary Manor
see page 49

Lytham Hall
Lytham, Lancashire OS SD3528
English Heritage Register Grade II

House on an ancient site, built 1757–64 for Thomas Clifton to the designs of John Carr. A screen wall, attached to the south-west wing of the house, known as Monks' Walk and probably 17th- or 18th-century, has stepped and triangular buttresses and is attached to an 18th-century cottage and a privy. In the past, this wall may have extended as far as a high earthen mound in the woods south of the hall. An 18th-century dovecote in the woods north-west of the house. Park surrounding the house is pasture th occasional clumps of trees d, to the west, a golf course.

yveden New ield

page 268

Madingley Hall

dingley, Cambridgeshire OS TL3960
glish Heritage Register Grade II
en occasionally for NGS

th-century house for Sir Francis ynde, with alterations in 18th d 20th centuries. A Kip graving in *Britannia Illustra* 707), at the time the estate was ned by Sir John Cotton, shows ple formal gardens on two es of the house, with an axial le leading through woodland to ircular courtyard followed by a r-part walled entrance recourt. These formal gardens d been laid out partly on the e of a 16th-century hunting rk. Nothing of these gardens mains. In 1756 Sir John Hynde otton consulted Capability own. A new lawn with a gravel lk was made north of the use, a coach road made, and a nal and other formal pieces of ter filled in, except for one nich was to be part of a lake. For is, completed the following year, own received £500 (£38,683 day) but Sir John provided rses, carts, wheelbarrows and all cessary plants. New formal rdens made before World War I, th a balustraded terrace and rden; those north of the house rtly overlaying Brown's lawn and lk. In the park, serpentine lake d sham bridge, and some old dars of Lebanon possibly planted Brown.

Madresfield Court

adresfield, Worcestershire OS SO8047
glish Heritage Register Grade II*
en regularly Tel 01684 573614

ne Lygon family (later Earls eauchamp) has lived here since e early 15th century. The house s rebuilt in the late 16th ntury, remodelled in the late 8th century and given its present sential character by Philip ardwick 1863–88. East of the use, a series of enclosures, ssibly designed by Thomas awson in 1903. North of this

garden, Caesars' Lawn with busts of the twelve caesars in niches cut into a yew hedge. North and west of the house, 19th-century pleasure grounds, well planted with specimen trees, divided by three avenues – of cedars, oaks and poplars. A Tuscan temple seat stands beyond the west end of the poplar avenue. North-west of the house, the Sundial Garden, a curved enclosure with holly hedges, a gravel path flanked with borders and an armillary sphere at the centre. To one side, a yew maze. East of this, the Rocks is a Pulhamite rock garden originally planted with ferns, and to its west, a Wild Garden of the 1880s with native deciduous trees and long grass with wildflowers. There was a park here by the 17th century when avenues were planted; this was landscaped in the 18th century and remodelled in the late 19th century.

Maer Hall

Maer, Staffordshire OS SJ7938
English Heritage Register Grade II

Late 17th-century house, enlarged in 19th century but restored to 17th-century extent in the 1960s. There had been formal gardens at Maer by the end of the 17th century, of which only traces are visible today. Lawns and specimen trees are the chief ornaments of the gardens close to the house. North-west of the house is the site of an 18th-century Wilderness with, on the hillside above, walks disposed in a diagonal pattern with mature yew trees, possibly the remains of old hedging. Above it, a terrace has a semicircular bastion ringed with mature yews. Park to west of house landscaped for Josiah Wedgwood II (the son of the master potter) in the early 19th century under the supervision of John Webb. From the pleasure grounds steps lead down to walks round the wooded banks of a lake, Maer Pool. Further woods and open grassland to the west. The former gravel quarry on the Maer Hall estate is now part of the Dorothy Clive Garden (*see page 198*)

Magdalen College (Oxford)

see page 100

Malahide Demesne

see page 424

Malleny House Garden

Balerno, nr Edinburgh, Midlothian
OS NT1666 Scottish Inventory
Open regularly (NTS) Tel 0131 449 2283

Malleny House, preserving a country house atmosphere despite spreading suburbia all about, has a surprisingly long history, going back at least to the 15th century. The present, very attractive house was built c.1635 for James Murray of Kilbaberton, with a late-Georgian extension. A walled garden, entered by splendid Arts and Crafts style wrought-iron gates, has at its centre four giant yew trees clipped into pointed mushrooms. Roses are everywhere in the garden, which has a National Collection of 19th-century shrub roses (90 species and cultivars). There is also a collection of Bonsai arranged by the Scottish Bonsai Society. Sir Herbert Maxwell, in his book *Scottish Gardens* (1911), remarks how attractively old-fashioned Malleny was to have the garden placed so close to the house: "…you step from the ivy-grown house direct among the borders, and all the fleeting phases of the season may be enjoyed from the windows."

Mamhead

Kenton, Devon OS SX9381
English Heritage Register Grade II*

Dr Richard Pococke came here in 1750 and noted, "a fine situation on the side of a hill, with beautiful plantations of most sorts of fir and cedar of Lebanon, with walks through it; the most beautiful part is a terrace up the side of the hill behind the house, and a winding walk around the hill." The estate has a superb site on the slopes west of the river Exe with views down to its estuary. The original house at Mamhead was built in the late 17th century for Sir Peter Ball, altered in c.1770 by Robert Adam for the Vaughns, Earls of Lisburne, and finally, after a fire, was transmuted 1828–38 into a Gothic-Tudor palace by Anthony Salvin for R. W. Newman, a

Dartmouth merchant who became an MP. In the mid 18th century Thomas Ball planted North American exotics. In 1772 Lord Lisburne wrote to Capability Brown to say that he wanted "to make some alterations at this place to render it more commodious and aggreeable…I should be glad to make what improvements the scene is capable of under the Direction of a Genius whose Taste is so superior and unrivalled." Brown did give advice but it seems likely that only his less complicated recommendations were implemented. Salvin's new house was the occasion of new gardens by the house. An aerial photograph of 1952 in Marcus Binney's and Ann Hills's *Elysian Gardens* (1979) shows these still in place, with a four-part parterre and pool below the southern façade of the house, and a semicircular garden with fan-shaped beds to one side. They are still there, but with simplified planting.

Manchester Square

City of Westminster, London OS TQ2881
English Heritage Register Grade II

Manchester Square was developed in the 1770s, when the 4th Duke of Manchester's new house was built on the north side of the square (the Duke was attracted by the good duck shooting nearby). The name Manchester House was changed in 1797 to Hertford House when it was bought by the 2nd Marquess of Hertford; it now houses the magnificent Wallace Collection. The remainder of the square had been completed by the late 1780s and a central garden was laid out probably by 1784. It is roughly circular and enclosed in railings, with a perimeter planting of mixed shrubs and trees and a central lawn with a bed of roses. Some fine mature limes and London planes.

Manderston

see page 386

Mannington Hall

see page 314

The Manor House (Upton Grey)

see page 95

Manor House Gardens

Lewisham, London OS TQ3975
English Heritage Register Grade II

House built 1771–72 for Thomas Lucas, probably designed by Richard Jupp. Since 1902 the house has been Lee Public Library and the gardens a public park. The grounds retain much of their old character, with a winding path through trees about the boundary and a central lawn with pond and island. The banks of the pool are planted with mature beech, horse chestnuts, London planes and *Robinia pseudoacacia*. A late 18th-century icehouse survives on the western boundary. To the east of house, bedding schemes and a lime avenue, and south of the house, a 1980s design of raised beds with scented herbs.

Mapperton House Gardens

see page 50

Marble Hill

Richmond, Greater London OS TQ1773
English Heritage Register Grade II*
Open regularly Tel 020 88925115

Delightful Thames-side Palladian house built 1724–c.1729 for Henrietta Howard (the mistress of George II; later Countess of Suffolk) to the designs of Roger Morris. Both Alexander Pope and Charles Bridgeman advised on the gardens; a plan attributed to Bridgeman shows a very ornate garden. An engraving after a painting by Augustin Heckel, done in 1749, shows the grounds descending in shallow turf terraces to the river, with formal groves of trees on each side framing a view of the house. The turf terraces are still in place, the formal groves have become informal, and the grounds, which are now a public park, are informally planted with shrubberies and trees (including a superb black walnut dating from the early 18th century).

Marchmont

Polwarth, Berwickshire OS NT7448
Scottish Inventory

House on an old estate, built in 1754 to the designs of Thomas Gibson for Hugh Hume, 3rd Earl

M

of Marchmont. Parkland with good trees, some of which go back to the late 18th century. The Great Avenue, described in 1827 by Robert Chambers as "the most imposing thing of the kind I ever saw", suffered in the great storms of 1881 but was replanted with beech and once again has great presence in the landscape. Formal gardens west of the house were laid out c.1726 with a pool, Italian statues and urns – now much simplified. A lawn runs south to the park, with banks of flowering shrubs framing views of the Cheviot Hills. Specimen trees are planted about the periphery of the pleasure grounds.

Margam Park

see page 217

Marino

Clontarf, County Dublin, Republic of Ireland
Open regularly

18th-century house bought in 1755 by James Caulfield, 1st Lord Charlemont, who commissioned Sir William Chambers to enlarge it. He also commissioned from Chambers a garden pavilion, the Casino, which was built 1758–65 in the neo-Classical style, an exquisite building in all its details, both inside and out. From the balustraded roof of the Casino there are views over Dublin Bay and the Wicklow Hills. In laying out his demesne, Charlemont commissioned other ornamental buildings, among them a Hermitage in the form of a thatched roothouse, a Gothic alcove seat and a Gothic temple known as Rosamund's Bower on the wooded banks of a lake. The house was demolished in 1921 and the other garden buildings have long since gone but the Casino, magnificently restored, remains, defiantly confronting creeping suburbia all about.

Markyate Cell, or Markyatecell

Markyate, Hertfordshire OS TL0157
English Heritage Register Grade II

House built from 1539 for Humphry Bourchier, on a site going back to a 12th-century nunnery, and rebuilt c.1825 for Daniel Goodson Adey to the

designs of Robert Lugar. Formal gardens by the house date from the early 20th century with terracing, borders, lawns, a rose garden, a pergola and ornamental woodland. Park probably landscaped at the same that the house was rebuilt in the early 19th century. The river Ver flows intermittently to fill a lake. The park is largely pasture with mature parkland trees, including many limes and sycamores. The parish church stands just outside the southern boundary of the park, with a lime avenue running up towards its south-east front.

Marlay Demesne

Rathfarnham, County Dublin,
Republic of Ireland
Open regularly Tel (00353) 01 493 7372

The first house here, known as the Grange, was built in the early 18th century and sold c.1760 to David La Touche who renamed it Marlay after his wife's family. Parkland, woods and lakes suggest the work of an 18th-century landscaper. In the early 19th century there was a picturesque garden with a thatched cottage orné and rustic bridges over streams. At a little distance from the house is a magnificent three-part walled kitchen garden, presumably dating from the 18th century; in recent years this has been restored with help from the Great Gardens of Ireland restoration programme. An ornamental garden has an early 19th-century orangery overlooking a fountain pool, and borders have plants of the period. A working kitchen garden has vegetable and fruit cultivars of the early 19th century.

Marlborough College

Marlborough, Wiltshire OS SU1868
English Heritage Register Grade II

The school was founded in 1843; with, as its nucleus, a late 17th-century house, Marlborough Castle, built for the 6th Duke of Somerset. Gardens were laid out in the late 17th or early 18th century with parterres and shaped lawns. The mound of the Norman castle west of the house had a banqueting house on top, a cascade and a grotto. Celia Fiennes came here c.1702 and described

"the Mount…that you ascend from the left hand by an easye ascent bounded by quick set hedges cut low…you have a prospect of the town and country round." She added: "in the midst of the top of the mount was a house built and pool, but that's fallen down." The mount remains, with a spiral path and vestiges of the grotto.

Marsh Court

King's Somborne, Hampshire OS SU3533
English Heritage Register Grade II*

House by Edwin Lutyens, designed in 1901 for Herbert Johnson ("adventurer, stockjobber and sportsman", as Christopher Hussey called him) built in Tudor style, of white clunch (in effect, chalk), with tall barley-sugar twist chimney stacks. Lutyens also designed an exceptionally complicated garden. A "piazza" at the entrance has lawns, a sundial and elaborately patterned paving. The sunken garden has a flight of convex steps leading down to a narrow pool with lilies, edged on each side by flights of steps and square planters. At the top level are borders against walls crowned with balustrades. A walk between yew hedges leads to a pergola with oak beams and piers made of tiles. A water garden of pools is set back within the pergola; there are shapely niches in the flanking brick walls. The architect H. Goodhart-Rendel thought that it was "one of those complicated gardens full of architecture and water which photograph very well but do not perhaps add very greatly to the pleasure of life" (quoted in Gavin Stamp's *Edwin Lutyens: Country Houses* (2001)).

Marston Hall

Marston, Lincolnshire OS SK8943
English Heritage Register Grade II
Open regularly Tel 01400 250225

17th-century house, with many later alterations, of the Thorold family, who had lived here long before that. Informal planting of shrubs and trees, with some notable old specimens, among them an ancient wych elm, said to have been planted in the 16th century, a laburnum of similar age, and old walnuts. The garden was

partly planned in the 1960s and 1970s by John Codrington. Rose garden with yew hedges and a sundial. Close to a walled kitchen garden, an 18th-century pavilion with a Gothic façade and detailing added by John Partridge in 1962 and an interior of the same date by the doyenne of grottologists, Barbara Jones, painted with exotic birds, tropical scenes and an English landscape park.

Marston House

Marston Bigot, Somerset OS ST7545
English Heritage Register Grade II

Jacobean house, rebuilt in the early 18th century for the Earl of Cork and Orrery and subsequently much changed. Its great claim to garden fame is that Stephen Switzer laid out the grounds here in 1729, and a print of 1739 by R. Parr shows exactly what he did. In front of the house are circular pools in an oval forecourt; on one side, an orchard area contains a curious criss-cross pattern of walls on which espaliers were trained; behind the house is a great walled rectangle with winding walks through groves of trees and bastion-like towers in each of the far corners with ladders for access. The gardens were completed in 1733, shortly after Lord Orrery wrote to a friend: "We are hard at work both within and without doors, but in the gardens are out-doing Hannibal, and working thro' rocks more obdurate than the alps." These formal gardens were destroyed by the 7th Earl of Cork and Orrery in about 1776.

Marwood Hill Gardens

see page 51

Mathern Palace

Mathern, Gwent OS ST5290
Cadw/ICOMOS Register Grade II*

Medieval palace of the Bishops of Llandaff, bought in a ruinous state in 1894 by H. Avray Tipping, the garden designer and writer. He transformed "the sordid untidiness of a hopelessly ill-contrived and unrepaired farmstead" into an Arts and Crafts garden of stone-walled terraces, yew hedges crowned with elaborate topiary, borders, a sunken rose garden and pergola. Avray

Tipping lived here only briefly, leaving in 1912 when he inherited a family estate. Mathern was latterly owned by the British Steel Corporation, and its layout and some detailing survives.

Mavisbank

Loanhead, Midlothian OS NT2865
Scottish Inventory

House built for Sir John Clerk of Penicuik (*see page 522*) from 1723, designed by William Adam and Sir John Clerk, in a splendid setting by the Esk valley. Clerk laid out a courtyard parterre between the pavilions that flanked the house and a *patte d'oie* of avenues radiating from it. He created a Wilderness, with inscriptions on pedestals, and a circular kitchen garden surrounded by a river. He incorporated the ancient tumulus above the house into the garden design and, in the words of his friend Roger Gale in 1739, "made a winding ascent up to it, with hedges planted from the bottome to the top." Gale wrote of the garden, "You would there think yourself rather in a valley near Tivoli than Edenborough." In the late 19th century Mavisbank became a lunatic asylum under the forbidding name of New Slaughton House. It was gutted by fire in 1973. Only the shell of this beautiful house remains, and that only because the Secretary of State for Scotland refused permission to demolish it in 1987.

The Maze

Saffron Walden, Essex OS TL5438 English Heritage Register Grade II Open regularly

Turf maze of circular pattern but with four equally spaced, slightly raised bastions bulging out from the circumference; it is 138ft/40m across at the widest point. Although claimed to be of medieval origin, the first mention of the maze is 1699 when it was recut; it has been recut several times since, with the addition of a brick underlay in 1911.

Megginch Castle

Errol, Perthshire OS NO2424 Scottish Inventory Open regularly Tel 01821 64222

Castle built about a 15th-century tower house, with alterations in

16th and again in the 18th century when Robert Adam worked on the interiors. The Drummonds acquired the estate 1664 and their descendants still here. Long before the building of the castle there had been a monastery at Megginch; surviving enormous and ancient yews are said to date from the th century. Parkland planted in e early 18th century – oaks uth of the castle date from 09. Several remarkable old enues – of oaks (1726), of beech 750), of limes (1760) and of ore oaks (1827). Woodland rden with ancient chapel stroyed by John Knox but built – with a holly avenue ding to it, which probably dates m 1600. Pinetum of exotic nifers started in 1840. Terrace rden west of the castle (where e ancient yews are) laid out by dy Charlotte Drummond 830 with gold- and silver-riegated holly, extravagant iary figures, a crown of gold d common yew planted for een Victoria's golden jubilee in 87, and parterres planted with ips and forget-me-nots in ring, and with summer bedding. double red camellia sent from ina in 1794 still flowers. Rose rden north of the castle, started the 18th century. Top walled chen garden dates from 1575 e date on a sundial on the ll), partly used as a herb and ysic garden. Kitchen garden tension made in 1796, with hot lls for growing tender fruit – ricots, peaches and nectarines still grown. North of the chen garden, an old orchard h many old cultivars – the ole still very productive (two s of Victoria plums are sold ry year). Megginch is a most markable and attractive place.

elbourne Hall
page 270

elbury House
bury Sampford, Dorset OS ST57 05
lish Heritage Register Grade II*

e house at Melbury was ashioned for Sir Giles angways in about 1530 and atly enlarged from 1692 by Sir omas Strangways. The Fox-

Strangways, later Earls of Ilchester, were a great gardening family who also owned Abbotsbury nearby, where a garden was started by the 1st Countess Ilchester in the late 18th century (it is now known as Abbotsbury Subtropical Garden, *see page 14*). At Melbury there had been formal gardens in the 17th century, of which traces of radial avenues survive. There was landscaping in the 18th century but no designer's name has been attached to it. In the late 20th century some attractive modern planting was done about the house with the advice of Penelope Hobhouse. The greatest glory of Melbury today is the surviving ancient parkland with magnificent old oaks.

Melford Hall
see page 314

Mellerstain
see page 387

Mellor's Gardens
Rainow, Cheshire OS SJ9476
English Heritage Register Grade II Open for groups by appointment Tel 01625 573251

A garden made in the 19th century by James Mellor, a Methodist and follower of Swedenborg who believed that the natural world was an allegory of the spiritual world. The garden layout follows the spiritual journey of Christian in John Bunyan's *Pilgrim's Progress* (1698) from when he passes through the Wicket Gate after his flight from the City of Destruction, until his triumphant arrival at the Celestial City – with the Slough of Despond, Giant Despair, the Valley of Humiliation and all the other obstacles on the way to salvation. Mellor also carved Biblical quotations on stones, and many of these are still in the garden which is well cared for by the present owners. The garden was originally planted only with plants mentioned in the Bible, but few of these survive. In its day, Mellor's garden was much visited; every Sunday a wagonette from Manchester would bring visitors to be shown round by James Mellor, who would preach to them when they arrived at the Celestial City.

Mells Manor House
Mells, Somerset OSST7249
English Heritage Register Grade I

Early 16th-century house, much altered in 1900, in a fine position in the centre of the village close to the church. Before the Reformation it had been a palace of the Abbot of Glastonbury, who had a deer park here. An ancient enclosure survives close to the house, a square space enclosed by medieval walls supported by rounded buttresses – was this the abbot's privy garden? An estate map of 1680 shows this area simply marked as "The Garden". The Horner family acquired the estate at the dissolution of the monasteries. In the 17th century there was an enclosed forecourt on the west side of the house, with two pavilions and gardens. Edwin Lutyens came here in 1900 to make modifications to the house and to advise on the garden; planting suggestions came from Norah Lindsay. In her autobiography, *Time Remembered* (1933), Frances Horner vividly evokes the old garden, recalling "a vision of constant garden life…of long days and moonlit evenings when we sat out, and strolled among the scented borders, or slept out in the loggia and watched the stars till darkness brought sleep and silence to us at last."

Mells Park
Mells, Somerset OS ST7148
English Heritage Register Grade II

The former estate of the Horner family; a house was built for them in the mid 18th century, altered by Sir John Sloane in the early 19th century, and gutted in a fire in 1917. A new house was built in 1923 for Reginald McKenna, designed by Sir Edwin Lutyens. Park landscaped in the 18th century by unknown designer. Formal gardens close to the house by Lutyens but later destroyed. Small formal garden by Russell Page in the 1960s, completed by François Goffinet in 1970s.

Melsetter House
Island of Hoy, Orkney OS NO2789
Open by appointment Tel 01856 791352

There was a house here in the 16th century, built for William

Moodie of Snelsetter, which was added to in the 18th century. In 1898 the island was bought by Thomas Middlemore who commissioned the Arts and Crafts architect W.R. Lethaby to extend the house. Melsetter became a favourite place for followers of Arts and Crafts ideas, including Duncan Grant and May Morris who described it as "A sort of fairy palace on the edge of the northern seas…a very lovable place". A walled garden, with a teahouse and dovecote, is thought to date from 1738. The steading and outbuildings were designed by Lethaby who also raised the walls of the walled garden. Gates and other decorative iron work are in Arts and Crafts style. A shrub garden, protected by hawthorn and sycamore, has fuchsias, olearias and laburnum. A walled lawn is planted with snowdrops, daffodils and bluebells and, east of the house, a lawn has specimen trees with mixed borders lining the walls. A photograph of 1942 in David Ottewill's *The Edwardian Garden* (1989) shows the east parterre with small rectilinear beds cut into grass and filled with tulips.

Melton Constable Hall
Melton Constable, Norfolk OS TG0331
English Heritage Register Grade II*

The Astley family first lived here in 1236. A new house was built 1664–c.1670 by Sir Jacob Astley, which was altered in the 19th and 20th centuries. A Kip engraving in *Britannia Illustrata* (1707) shows a very grand garden: a double avenue leads up to the entrance forecourt and continues beyond the house; and a great canal behind the house is flanked by four elaborate parterres on each side. Capability Brown was consulted by Sir Edward Astley in 1764 and supplied drawings for a temple, aviary and Gothic summerhouse for which he was paid £2,500 (£164,962 today). West of the house, a bath house, seen in Kip's engraving, still stands, but it was Gothicised and enlarged in the 1760s, possibly by Brown. The park, which had is origins in a 13th-century deer park, was landscaped in the 18th century but

Brown's contribution is not known; he may have created the lake south of the house with an 18th-century teahouse on its west bank. In the 1840s, formal balustraded terraces with urns, steps and geometric bedding schemes were laid out against the south and west façades of the house.

Melville Castle
nr Dalkeith, Midlothian OS NT3167
Scottish Inventory

Ancient estate with a house built for Henry Dundas (later Viscount Melville) 1786–91 to the designs of James Playfair. Woodlands famous in their day (Sir Walter Scott celebrated "Melville's beechy groves" in "Grey Brother") and the 1st Viscount planted every native British tree (not a large undertaking; there are only 33 species). Much planting, especially of conifers, in the late 19th century. After a period of uncertainty, after becoming a hotel and then closing, the castle, with three golf courses in the grounds, reopened as a hotel in 2003.

M

Memorial Garden
Walsall, West Midlands OS SP0198 English
Heritage Register Grade II Open regularly

Public garden opened in 1952, designed by Geoffrey Jellicoe as a memorial to the dead of the two World Wars. On a raised site on Church Hill, the Memorial Garden is enclosed in high brick walls. A chapel in the form of a pavilion has a roof shaped like two stubby pyramids; nearby is a fountain with a single jet of water. Narrow lawns run down each side of the garden, with paths and beds of shrubs and silver birches. A viewing terrace along the outside north-west wall of the garden gives views over Walsall towards Wolverhampton. At its head is a Modern Movement former gardener's house. To the east, St Matthew's Close, also designed by Jellicoe, has shrubs and trees.

Menabilly
nr Fowey, Cornwall OS SX1051
English Heritage Register Grade II

The Rashleigh family came to Menabilly in 1596 and their

descendants still live here. The house was built at about that time but rebuilt in the early 18th century and altered again in the early 19th. Borlase's *The Natural History of Cornwall* (1738) describes a flourishing garden in the early 18th century: "Every thing that belongs to the flower garden and grows in any part of England, will thrive and flourish here." In the late 18th century Philip Rashleigh, a gentleman geologist and author of *Specimens of British Minerals* (1797), built a grotto in which to deploy some of his collection of minerals. C.S. Gilbert's *Historical Survey of Cornwall* (1820) describes it as octagonal, built of enormous sea pebbles, with eight pediments and a conical roof. Inside was a table made of thirty-two specimens of polished Cornish granite, and "The walls of this splendid fabric are adorned with shells of almost every description, minerals and a great number of stones of great brilliancy." The grotto survives in a ruinous state. In the 19th century there was much serious planting of exotics and part of a valley was named Hooker's Grove in honour of J.D. Hooker. It has nothing to do with gardens but is possibly relevant to the atmosphere of the place that Daphne Du Maurier was a tenant of the house for many years, and is said to have based Manderley in her novel *Rebecca* on Menabilly.

The Menagerie

see page 270

Mentmore House,
also known as
Mentmore Towers

Mentmore, Buckinghamshire OS SP9019
English Heritage Register Grade II*

House designed by Joseph Paxton and his son-in-law, G.H. Stokes, for Baron Mayer de Rothschild and built 1850–55. Paxton was also responsible for laying out the grounds. The drive from Cheddington, south-east of the house, is lined with an avenue of Wellingtonias. Gardens about the house have terraces, gravel paths, parterres and some fine trees, notably cedars of Lebanon. East of the formal gardens, the pleasure grounds had in the 1870s a fernery, maze and rose garden, all of which

have gone though an aviary remains. Miriam Rothschild's *The Rothschild Gardens* (1996) has a photograph of the spectacular parterres that existed before World War II. A 19th-century arboretum still contains fine trees.

Merevale Hall

Merevale, Wawickshire OS SP2997
English Heritage Register Grade II*

House dating from 17th century but rebuilt *c*.1840 for William Stratford Dugdale to the designs of Edward Blore. In the mid 19th century W.E. Nesfield designed double terraces south-east of the house, with formal bedding and clipped yews. Central steps lead down, opening at an axis which runs across lawns and is continued in a path into the Wilderness beyond. Landscape park enclosed in walls 1836. Lake south-east of house and woodland to its north and east.

Mereworth Castle

Mereworth, Kent OS TQ6653
English Heritage Register Grade II*

Splendid house, built 1722–25, based on Palladio's Villa Rotonda and designed by Colen Campbell for John Fane (later Earl of Westmorland). 18th-century landscape park which, according to Horace Walpole in 1752, had a scheme of formal pools and hedges to the south of the house. The house was originally moated but the moat was filled in *c*.1860 and balustraded terraces with formal beds were built about the house; this arrangement remains today. East of the house, an avenue leads to further formal gardens with a lawn enclosed in hedges, an enclosure of bedding, a sunken garden with herbaceous borders, and an octagonal kiosk surrounded by an intricate pattern of beds of roses and shrubs. An 18th-century triumphal arch, designed as an eyecatcher at the head of the valley south of the house, is now hidden by woodland planting.

Merrow Grange

Guildford, Surrey OS TQ0250
English Heritage Register Grade II

House built 1868, later enlarged. Serpentine paths lead to rockwork

garden made by James Pulham for Francis Baring-Gould *c*.1907, with a pond planted with bamboos and Chusan palms, a glazed fernery or grotto with brick, tufa and stone walls, and a trellis causeway, the whole set in a landscape of pools, miniature cliffs and glades. Artificial mound capped with Pulhamite seat and rocky overhang. Long Walk edged in Pulhamite, with scattered use of Pulhamite ornamentation. Several specimen trees, chiefly evergreens.

Merton College

Oxford, Oxfordshire OS SO5106
English Heritage Register Grade II
Open regularly 01865 276310

College founded by Walter de Merton in 1264. The earliest surviving buildings date from the 13th century and Mob Quad, completed in 1373, is the earliest complete college quad in Oxford. Loggan's *Oxonia Illustrata* (1675) shows the garden at Merton with a tunnel arbour, a summerhouse and a parterre. The gardens overlook Merton Field and Christ Church Meadow. The Fellows' Garden, which backs onto the old city wall, has a raised walk dating from the late 17th century and an early 18th-century summerhouse. Some good trees remain, including an early 18th-century lime avenue, horse chestnuts and sycamores. Merton Grove, with a lawn, serpentine path and mature trees, forms the western college boundary.

Mertoun

nr St Boswells, Roxburghshire OS NT6131
Scottish Inventory Open regularly
Tel 01835 823236

House started in 1703 to the designs of Sir William Bruce for Sir William Scott, with alterations in the 1840s (by William Burn) and in the early 20th century (these later alterations removed in the 1950s). The river Tweed flows splendidly through the grounds, dividing the parkland which was laid out from 1750. Parkland trees such as lime, oak and sycamore appear to date from the late 18th century. Woodland developed in the 19th century but trees felled after World War II and replanted with conifers. Old formal gardens

by the house were replaced from 1912 by lawns and specimen trees, with a herbaceous border on a new terrace. Walled garden built from 1750 round Old Mertoun House (now the head gardener's house). Fruit and vegetables are still grown, with espaliered fruit trees on the walls and lining a central path.

Mesnes Park

Wigan, Greater Manchester OS SD5706
English Heritage Register Grade II
Open regularly

Public park laid out by John McClean and opened in 1878. A carriage drive leads from the main entrance in the south-eastern corner towards the focal point of the park, the Pavilion (1880, designed by W.H. Fletcher); on raised ground, it commands wide views over park and town. A long narrow lake with three islands runs along the south-west boundary of the park, with rockwork and a cascade by James Pulham. To its south, a rose garden, the Padgett Memorial Garden. North of the lake, an 1890 bandstand with, to its west, a garden for the blind. Bowling greens, tennis courts and a putting green along the western boundary.

Methven Castle

Methven, Perthshire OS NO0426
Scottish Inventory

Estate going back to before the 14th century. Present castle built 1664 for Patrick Smythe to the designs of John Mylne. Pinetum established in 1830 – according to J.C. Loudon, the first in Scotland. An avenue of deodars (*Cedrus deodara*) was planted in 1868 by the Dowager Lady Elgin from seed brought back from India where her son was Viceroy. In 1955 Alan Mitchell listed 37 outstanding trees here – in the nick of time; most were felled in 1960.

Middleton Park

Middleton Stoney, Oxfordshire OS SP5223
English Heritage Register Grade II

The estate at Middleton Park was bought by William Villiers, 3rd Earl of Jersey, in 1737. The 18th-century house was demolished in

1934, to be succeeded by a new house designed by Sir Edwin Lutyens in collaboration with his son Robert for the 8th Earl of Jersey. Jennifer Sherwood's and Nikolaus Pevsner's *Oxfordshire* (1974) describes Middleton as "probably the last great country house to be built in England". Park of the second half of the 18th century, now chiefly arable land but a few cedars of Lebanon, belts of woodland and clumps of trees survive. In the early 19th century the 5th Earl of Jersey added to his park on the east side, which involved demolishing the old manor house and adjacent cottages; these were replaced by new picturesque cottages outside the park. All this seems to have been part of the improvements proposed by Lewis Kennedy from 1811.

Miller Park

Preston, Lancashire OS SD5328 English Heritage Register Grade II Open regularly

Public park, incorporating earlier riverside walks, designed by Edward Milner in 1864 and named after Alderman Miller who acquired the land for the park. It lies immediately to the west of Avenham Park (*see page 440*) separated by a railway embankment. In the north of the park, three terraces of which the central one has a broad path with urns on plinths and a statue of the 14th Earl of Derby (1873, by Matthew Noble); a double staircase leads to the lower terrace below which are lawns with a circular fountain pool (*c*.1865) and a bandstand (late 20th-century), and formal beds surrounded by beech hedges. North of the Derby monument, on steeply sloping ground, an area of rockwork with, to its east, formal beds about a spiral path, with a sundial at the centre.

Millichope Park

Millichope, Shropshire OS SO5288
English Heritage Register Grade II*
Open occasionally for NGS

House built 1835–40 for the Revd Norgrave Pemberton, designed by Edward Haycock. 18th-century landscaping, possib by William Emes. Rotunda by George Steuart built 1770 on a rocky cliff above a lake. Cliff and lake are later than the rotunda and possibly the site of a quarry which provided stone for the new house. A drive cuts through the hill on which the rotunda stands, and curves round the lake. 19th-century landscaping with much tree planting, especially of new North American conifers.

Milton Abbey
Milton Abbas, Dorset OS ST7901
English Heritage Register Grade II*
Open regularly Tel 01258 880489

After the demolition of all the monastic buildings except the abbey church and abbots' hall, a new, gently Gothic house was built around the hall from 1771 for Joseph Damer, Lord Milton (and later 1st Earl of Dorchester) under the supervision of Sir William Chambers. Chambers may not have designed it, although he said of it, "I have three or four years past been building a cursed Gothick House for this unmannerly imperious Lord." Today the house is a school. Capability Brown came to advise in 1763 and worked for Lord Milton until 1770. He came back in 1774 and designed a new estate village; the original substantial village was in the way of his lordship's landscaping schemes, and when some of the villagers proved unwlling to move, Lord Milton forced them out by undamming a stream. One of the intended purposes of this removal was to allow the creation of a lake in the valley below the house; this, ironically, proved impossible and the lake was eventually built some distance from the house. A Gothic sham ruin was built in about 1790. High above the abbey church is the Norman St Catherine's Chapel, approached by an extraordinary turf stairway.

Milton Hall
Peterborough, Cambridgeshire OS
TL1499 English Heritage Register Grade II*

Late 16th-century house with later alterations, including those by Henry Flitcroft in the 1740s and Sir William Chambers in 1773. In 1791 the 4th Earl Fitzwilliam consulted Humphry Repton and a Red Book was produced, though

not all Repton's proposals were accepted. Orangery of 1791, possibly by Chambers. The pleasure grounds today have fine speciment trees and there is a flower garden below the main front of the house. An avenue of yews leads to a lake. Most of the park has perimeter tree belts, copses, clumps and individual trees. In the deer park, remains of an avenue with ancient oaks. Kitchen garden with 18th-century walls. An Italianate garden with fine 18th-century wrought-iron gates opening towards the lake, and a mulberry tree described as "very ancient" in 1891. Kennels of 1767 in the form of a ruined medieval gateway.

Milton Lodge
see page 52

Minley Manor
Minley, Hampshire OS SU8258
English Heritage Register Grade II

Extravagantly grandiose French-style house built in the mid 19th century for Raikes Currie to the designs of Henry Clutton; Mark Girouard, in his *The Victorian Country House* (1979), describes the style as "aggressive anarchy". James H. Veitch of the firm of nurserymen Veitch & Sons laid out gardens in the late 19th century. West of the house, the sunken Dutch garden and the site of a parterre, now radically simplified. The original parterre was a wonder of its time, as Brent Elliott in *Victorian Gardens* (1986) relates: "laid out in the form of a family crest, but employing for the purpose a mass of miniature conifers. Retinosporas (juvenile cypresses) were arranged in a scroll pattern against a groundwork composed of 80,000 seedling yews; panels of dwarf hollies in different colours were added to provide a nocturnal effect, their foliage shining under electic light." Close to the Dutch garden an orangery and the remains of yew-hedged enclosures. Beyond this, to the west and south, the Plain, where large beds in turf used to be filled with herbaceous perennials and shrubs. A broad grass walk leads through plantings of specimen trees and rhododendrons in grass.

South-east of the house, a lake with islands reached by a bridge, and with a boathouse.

Minterne
see page 52

Misarden Park
see page 217

Missenden Abbey
Great Missenden. Buckinghamshire
OS SP8901 English Heritage Register Grade II

17th-century house on the site of a 12th-century Augustinian abbey but much altered. East of the house, a stream from the river Misbourne had been diverted to the garden to flow out beneath a Gothic flint and brick summerhouse of c.1800 and under two flint bridges. It curves round to the park south of the house, where it used to feed a lake (but is usually dry). West of the house, an evergreen shrubbery walk with box, holly, Portugal laurel and yew. The park, scarred by the Great Missenden bypass, remains pasture and retains many parkland trees, among them chestnut, lime, oak and sycamore. The park was probably laid out after the estate was sold in 1787 to James Oldham, "an opulent ironmonger of Holborn". The house is now an adult education centre.

Moccas Court
Moccas, Herefordshire OS SO3543
English Heritage Register Grade II*
Open regularly Tel 01981 500381

House built for Sir George Cornewall 1775–81, designed by Robert Adam. The greatest natural ornament of the landscape is the river Wye which flows across the park, passing close to the house. In the northern part of the park, a walk or ride called Monnington Walk, lined with mature pines and yews, is said to have been laid out in the late 17th century. Capability Brown did a plan for landscaping the grounds in 1778 and some of his proposals were carried out. The estate gardener and forester, Mr J. Webster, reputedly planted 300,000 oaks between the mid 1790s and 1836; many oaks of this period survive, as well as sweet chestnuts. In the Upper Park are several veteran trees – sweet

chestnuts possibly of the 17th century, and oaks and limes of the 18th and 19th centuries. There had been a deer park here at least by the 16th century.

Moggerhanger Park, *also known as* Mogerhanger
Moggerhanger, Bedfordshire OS TL1348
English Heritage Register Grade II
Open occasionally for NGS

House built from 1791 by John Soane for the Thornton family. Godfrey Thornton consulted Humphry Repton in 1792. Repton laid out pleasure grounds about the house, and paid special attention to the woodland to the west, which he particularly admired, cutting walks through it to carefully chosen views. In the park, Repton planted trees to hide a boundary to the north, and in the woods to the west, cut a sweeping ride. Repton's work is largely intact.

Monreith House
Monreith, Wigtownshire OS NX5642
Scottish Inventory

The Maxwell family came to Monreith in the 15th century and still live here. The present house was built in the late 18th century, with additions by Sir Robert Smirke in 1821. The ruins of the earlier Maxwell house, Myrton Castle – 17th-century with a 16th-century tower – remain on high ground above White Loch. 18th-century parkland now reduced in extent but with old tree clumps remaining; the White Loch and castle ruins are notable landscape features. In 1877 the 7th Baronet, Sir Herbert Maxwell, inherited the estate. He was the author of *Scottish Gardens* (1908) and a knowledgeable gardener. In his book he describes a piece of needlework made in the 18th century by the wife of the 3rd Baronet, depicting flowers growing at Monreith – among them, anemones, auriculas, carnations, convolvulus, Guelder rose, hyacinths, lupins, scarlet lychnis, Madonna lilies, mulleins, scabious, sunflowers and sweet williams. Sir Herbert made a woodland garden with species rhododendrons and many trees, the whole carpeted in

narcissi (a special love) – now disheveled. Sir Herbert also made a terraced garden south of the house, which was described by his grandson, the author Gavin Maxwell: "sloping, haphazardly planned, and surmounted by a half-circular terrace on whose gravel surface a short cut growth of box or privet spelt the Latin words of the 102nd psalm: 'the days of man are but as grass, for he flourisheth as a flower of the field'."

Montacute House
see page 53

Monteviot House
nr Jedburgh, Roxburghshire OS NT6424
Open regularly Tel 01835 830380

Early 18th-century house, with later alterations for the Kerr family (Earls of Ancram and Marquesses of Lothian). The position of the house is very beautiful, overlooking the wooded valley of the river Teviot. There were formal gardens here in the 19th century and a woodland garden has many good trees, mostly dating from the late 19th century. In the 1960s Percy Cane redesigned parts of the garden to make a river garden south-west of the house. Here, a great sloping lawn with mixed borders, backed by a curving brick wall with a central pavilion, flows down the slope towards two grand flights of steps which lead to the river's edge. Behind the river garden, the rose terrace is a walk along a high buttressed wall clothed with climbing roses, with beds of roses on the other edge of the path. Below the south façade of the house, a herb garden with box-edged beds and a central sundial also has views of the valley.

Moor Park
Farnham, Surrey OS SU8646
English Heritage Register Grade II

Jacobean house bought in around 1680 by the diplomat Sir William Temple, whose *Upon the Gardens of Epicurus* (1692) was very influential, especially on the development of the English landscape garden. Sir William's garden at Moor Park is shown in a drawing attributed to Kip and

M

dated c.1696–1700, illustrated in John Harris's *The Artist and the Country House* (1979). It shows a sequence of ornate formal gardens, with parterres, overlooked by an imposing banqueting house. Beyond the formal gardens and screened by a "hedge on stilts" (*palissade à l'Italienne*) are curious serpentine walks through woodland – very *avant garde* for the date and perhaps this is an example of the "sharawadgi" ("irregularity") that Sir William said was characteristic of Chinese gardens. In 1971, according to Ian Nairn's and Nikolaus Pevsner's *Surrey* in the "Buildings of England" series, the garden was "a wilderness of weeds and blocked up lakes". Of Temple's work, they found a loggia and "fragments of a brick Baroque summerhouse" which could be the banqueting house seen in the Kip drawing.

Moor Park
Preston, Lancashire OS SD5431 English Heritage Register Grade II Open regularly

Public park laid out 1833–35, with alterations by Edward Milner in the 1860s. The park is enclosed in perimeter plantings with a serpentine walk leading through. Open ground at the centre of the park, with a 20th-century pavilion and a 17th-century stone known as the "starting-chair", said to have been a marker post for the 17th-century racecourse on this site. To the north-west, an area designed by Edward Milner with paths through a rockery on undulating ground. Nearby is an early 20th-century observatory. Bowling greens and pavilions to the south-west. In the north-east part of the park, a school with, to its west, a serpentine lake.

Moor Park
Rickmansworth, Hertfordshire OS TQ0793 English Heritage Register Grade II*

Ancient site, with 17th-century house rebuilt 1720–28 for Benjamin Styles by Sir James Thornhill and altered by Robert Adam in the later 18th century. Lucy Harington, Countess of Bedford, made a great garden 1617–27, "with very great care, excellent contrivance and much cost". It included a "grotto

embellished with figures of shell-work, fountains and water works" which Sir Roy Strong in his *The Renaissance Garden in England* (1979) attributes to Isaac de Caus. The estate was occupied 1627–30 by the Earl and Countess of Pembroke (of Wilton House, *see page 558*, where de Caus also worked) who added to the garden. In 1685 Sir William Temple, recalling what he had seen thirty years earlier when he spent his honeymoon here, described the garden as the "perfectest figure of a garden"; he was so taken with the place that he called his own estate in Surrey, Moor Park (*see page 511*). On one side of the house there were four parterres with statues and fountains, a grotto, cloistered walks, summerhouses, walks with trees and a terrace. On the far side of the house was a Wilderness with rockwork and fountains. In the 1720s Charles Bridgeman made plans for a new garden but there is no evidence of his work and it is not known how much, if anything, was carried out. In the 1750s Capability Brown remodelled the pleasure grounds and the park. In the 1830s Italianate gardens were designed by Robert Cundy II and c.1910 Thomas Mawson worked here. In the mid 20th century, golf courses were made in the park and the house became the clubhouse. Nothing of Lucy Harington's garden remains. Brown's work survives in the informal pleasure grounds to the south-east of the house, and in the park many parkland trees remain. Much of the 1830s garden survives.

The Moot
Downton, Wiltshire OS SU1821 English Heritage Register Grade II*

The Moot is the remains of an 11th-century castle of motte-and-bailey type, formerly part of the same estate as that of the early 18th-century Moot House but separated since c.1964. Garden development of The Moot dates from the early 18th century. Central area, wooded and crossed by many paths, most of which follow the curving lines of ditches and ramparts. Lime avenue runs east and west, with yew circles to

the east and the remains of a temple or arbour – a floor of cobbles and knucklebones. North and south of avenue, elevated walks; the northern walk has two viewing points, with yew trees at summit. Southern walk climbs to the site of an 18th-century hexagonal Temple of Mercury, only the floor of pebbles and knucklebones remaining. To the west, a theatre; curved tiers cut into the grass slope descending to an oval orchestra and three-lobed pond. Remains of a 19th-century curving loggia. Deep outer ditch of site partially overlooked by elevated rampart, raised higher in the 18th century, with remains of clipped yew hedging.

Morden Hall
Merton, London OS TQ2668 English Heritage Register Grade II Open regularly (NT) Tel 020 8545 6850

House built c.1768 on a moated site which before the dissolution of the monasteries had been part of Morden Hall Park, belonging to the Abbey of Westminster. In 1941 the house and park were acquired by the National Trust. The park has an area of 125 acres/50 hectares, through which the river Wandle wanders. In the 18th century it had provided power for a snuff mill which remained in business until 1923. Rustic bridges cross the river and in 1920 the last private owner, G.E. Hatfeild, laid out a splendid rose garden which survives. Also on the banks of the river are 18th-century statues of Venus and Cupid, and of Neptune.

Moreby Hall
nr Stillingfleet, North Yorkshire OS SE5943 English Heritage Register Grade II

House built 1828–33 for Henry Preston to the designs of Anthony Salvin, at a cost of £40,000 (£1,646,666 today). Formal gardens were made for the house, of which sunken compartments survive to the west, screened with mature yews – there was originally a formal rosery here. A walk past an arrangement of urns leads to steps and a serpentine pool surrounded by shrubs with, to the south, a Gothic pavilion of c.1832 which probably incorporates part of the 14th-century windows of

York Minster, salvaged from the fire of 1829. South of the house, a paved terrace and balustrade with early 19th-century urns on pedestals and views over a bowling green enclosed by clipped yews and parkland.

Morrab Gardens
Penzance, Cornwall OS SW4730 English Heritage Register Grade II Open regularly

Public park, originally the private garden of Morrab House, built 1865–66 for a brewer, Samuel Pidwell, and now a public library. In 1889 the estate was bought by the city of Penzance and the garden redesigned by Reginald Upcher for its new function as a municipal park. He devised a Loudonesque scheme of winding paths. *The Garden* in 1895 described "some fine clumps of Bambusa Metake, and good plants of Cordyline australis, Agaves, &c., but isolated too much instead of being planted in bold clumps", so it sounds as if Upcher had also followed Loudon's method of displaying individual plants to show their characteristic features. The Cornish garden historian Douglas Pett in *The Parks and Gardens of Cornwall* (1998) described the state of the garden: "The recent obligatory 'privatisation' of horticultural maintenance by local authorities, has destroyed the individuality, and much of the quality, of these once famous gardens."

Moseley Old Hall
see page 271

Mote Park
Maidstone, Kent OS TQ7854 English Heritage Register Grade II Open regularly

Ancient estate where a deer park was established in the 14th century, one of the first in the county. The present house was built c.1793 for the 3rd Baron of Romney (later 1st Earl). Pleasure grounds developed in woodland from 1839, where a network of paths edged with ornamental trees and shrubs linked glades planted with specimen trees. The deer park was landscaped in the late 18th and early 19th centuries. A lake was formed from the river Len, a

Doric temple was built to overlook the lake and house, and boathouses were built for the lake. The earthworks of an early 18th-century formal garden are visible. Today the park is a public amenity.

Mottisfont Abbey Garden
see page 96

Moundsmere Manor
Preston Candover, Hampshire OS SU6243 English Heritage Register Grade II* Open occasionally for NGS

House designed 1908–9 by Sir Reginald Blomfield in Hampton Court style for Wilfred Buckley. Garden, also designed by Blomfield, partly survives – yew hedges, formal rose gardens (with a wellhead and garden house), a sunken canal garden, herbaceous borders and a yew walk. Excellent pinetum planted in the 1930s, with several rarities. Walled kitchen garden with curved vinery.

Mount Congreve
see page 425

Mount Edgcumbe
see page 54

Mount Ephraim
Hernhill, Kent OS TR0655 English Heritage Register Grade II Open regularly Tel 01227 751496

House built 1878 for Sir Edwyn Dawes on the site of a 17th-century house. Terraced gardens, laid out in the early 20th century, descending a gentle slope north of the house towards a 19th-century lake; the lowest terrace has two pavilions built into the retaining wall. On the far bank of the lake, woodland garden with rhododendrons. West of the terraces, a rock garden. East of the house, beyond a circular fountain pool, an 18th-century ha-ha separates the garden from the park.

The Mount House
Alderley, Gloucestershire OS ST7790 English Heritage Register Grade II

Late 17th-century house, altered in 18th century. The traveller and botanical artist Marianne North spent her last years here and made a garden from 1886. Lawns, a border, circular pool and ornamental trees and shrubs. A sundial above the terrace commemorates Marianne North's pet opossum mouse, Sir Henry. A great collection of her paintings is housed in a specially made building in the Royal Botanic Gardens Kew (*see page 169*).

Mount Merrion House
Mount Merrion, County Dublin, Republic of Ireland

Estate of the Fitzwilliam family from the 14th century, with a new house built 1711 for the 5th Viscount Fitzwilliam in a lofty position with views over Dublin Bay. F.E. Ball's *History of the County of Dublin* (1902) says that it "can compare in the beauty of its demesne with many of the great places in England, and has few rivals in Ireland". Drawings by William Ashford, commissioned in 1805 and illustrated in Edward Malins's and the Knight of Glin's *Lost Demesnes* (1976), show a charming picturesque landscape garden. A classical pedimented temple has views down wooded slopes to the bay. A thatched rustic summerhouse stands on the edge of a clearing and a Gothic pavilion looks over a deer park with ancient trees. The estate was dismembered *c.*1925, by which time it was engulfed in suburban development.

Mount Stewart
see page 426

Mount Stuart
see page 388

Mount Usher Gardens
see page 427

Mounton House
Mounton, Gwent OS ST5193
Cadw/ICOMOS Register Grade II*

Arts and Crafts house built 1911–12, designed for his own use by H. Avray Tipping in conjunction with Eric Francis. South and south-east of the house, Avray Tipping laid out a terrace descending to a bowling

green; a great pergola clothed in rambler roses and wisteria built about a lily pool; an enclosed rose garden; and a parterre of peonies overlooking a lawn. Beyond the formal gardens, he made a wild garden with paths, planted rockeries and made a naturalistic water garden in a gorge. The house is today a special school.

Mowbray Park, *formerly known as* People's Park
Sunderland, Tyne and Wear OS NZ3956
English Heritage Register Grade II
Open regularly

Public park laid out by Mr Lawson (gardener to Lord Londonderry) and Joseph Smith (who had worked for the Duke of Devonshire at Chatsworth) and opened to the public in 1857. Serpentine lake with islands, bowling green, tennis courts, winding walks and many monuments. The park is divided by a railway cutting spanned by a cast-iron bridge.

Muckross Gardens and Arboretum
see page 428

Mulgrave Castle
nr Whitby, North Yorkshire OS NZ8412
English Heritage Register Grade II*

Ancient estate going back to before the Norman Conquest. The ruinous remains of the 12th-century and later castle survive; half a mile to the north-east is the new castle built before 1735 for the Duchess of Buckingham, with additions by John Soane in the 1780s. The site is beautiful, on high ground among wooded valleys close to the coast. In 1792 Lord Mulgrave consulted Humphry Repton who made one of his rare excursions to the north of England and set out his proposals in a Red Book. Repton was much taken with the site, writing that of all the places he knew, it was, with the one exception of Mount Edgcumbe (*see page 54*), "altogether the most magnificent, the most beautiful, the most romantic and abounded in the greatest variety of pleasing and interesting objects". As usual,

he paid attention to the approaches to the house which should "display the beauties of the place and excite admiration, without terror, by leading the road along an easy ascent and protecting it from every appearance of danger." Repton suggested disposing of arable l and and planting more trees close to the house to connect it visually to the wooded valleys below, and that views eastwards, taking Whitby Abbey as an eyecatcher, should not be entirely cut off. The landscape remains substantially as Repton planned it.

Muncaster Castle
see page 347

Munstead Wood
nr Godalming, Surrey OS SU9842
English Heritage Register Grade I
Open occasionally for NGS

House built 1896–97 for Gertrude Jekyll to the designs of Edwin Lutyens. Gertrude Jekyll lived here until her death in 1932 and throughout this period Munstead Wood was the scene of her garden experiments and the most complete expression of her garden ideas. The site today is about 10 acres/4 hectares but in her time covered some 15 acres/6 hectares; parts of the estate were sold off after her death: The Hut (designed for her by Edwin Lutyens, now called Munstead Wood Hut), and its "hidden garden"; a gardener's cottage, Munstead Orchard, and its belvedere, the Thunder House (both by Lutyens); and the Quadrangle, where the stables had been. The remaining garden is largely a woodland garden with many oaks, Scots pines, silver birches and sweet chestnuts. South of the house, a lawn spreads out from which the Broad Walk and subsidiary paths lead into the woodland. Here Miss Jekyll planted many rhododendrons, drifts of narcissi, a fern walk, a lily walk (with plantings of *Cardiocrinum giganteum*), an azalea clearing and a heath garden, in which some of the native bracken and whortleberry was left to provide

a background to many different heathers. North-west of the house, Miss Jekyll had gardens of a more formal character: a nut walk, a spring garden flanked with borders of tree peonies, and a shrub walk. In recent years the present owner has carried out much restoration.

The Murrel
Aberdour, Fife OS NT1886
Scottish Inventory

Very attractive house designed in 1908 in Arts and Crafts style by Frank Deas for his own use. Large walled garden with bold buttresses and with tiles on the top of the wall matching those of the house. Planned for different uses, with an area of fruit and vegetables, a rose garden and ornamental gardens divided by yew or box. A burn flows through the garden, in part canalised and made into a water garden. The new garden was described and photographed in Gertrude Jekyll's and Lawrence Weaver's *Gardens for Small Country Houses* (1912). The authors point out the importance of the high walls "in a country of wide spaces and low wind-swept hills".

Murthly Castle
Little Dunkeld, Perthshire OS NO0740
Scottish Inventory Occasionally open for SGS

15th-century castle for the Abercrombie family, altered in the 17th century for Sir George Steuart, with more alterations in the 18th and 19th centuries. Remarkable old parkland dating from the 17th century, with remains of original planting. An avenue of limes interspersed with yews is said to date from *c.*1711 and there are 19th-century avenues of oaks and beeches. Many remarkable conifers, 150 of which were measured by Alan Mitchell in 1983, including exceptional Douglas firs (*Pseudotsuga menziesii*), western hemlocks (*Tsuga heterophylla*) and an avenue of *Thuja plicata* over 100ft/30m high. Walled formal garden with 1669 summerhouse, redesigned in the 1970s to include a vegetable garden enclosed by old box and yew hedges, a rose garden, topiary and herbaceous borders.

Museum Gardens
York, North Yorkshire OS SE5952
English Heritage Register Grade II
Open regularly Tel 01904 551805

St Mary's Abbey was founded by Benedictine monks who came here in 1086. The abbey was dissolved in 1539 and the ruins of the church that survive today date chiefly from the 13th century. Walls, a gatehouse and the *hospitium* (guest house) also survive and there are many carved fragments in the museum. When the Yorkshire Philosophical Society acquired the site for the museum in 1827, one of the conditions was that it should establish "scientific gardens", and in 1844 Sir John Murray Naesmyth was asked to make an appropriate plan. A botanic garden with order beds (now grassed over) was established south of the *hospitium*. The garden is now chiefly lawns with specimen trees and winding circuit walks. At the centre is an octagonal observatory built by Thomas Cooke 1832–33, which at that time contained the largest refracting telescope in the world. The chief beauty of the place today is the remarkable setting of the monastic buildings.

Museum of Garden History
see page 157

Myatt's Field
Lambeth, London OS TQ3176 English Heritage Register Grade II Open regularly

Public park given to London County Council in 1889 by William Monet whose family had owned it since 1770. Its name comes from a person who had rented the land 1818–69 as a market garden. Enclosed in iron railings, with serpentine paths and central lawns. Bedding schemes and rose beds in the north-eastern part, and a heather garden to the south. Especially attractive late 19th-century bandstand in the north-western park. Two avenues of London planes and many good mature trees. Bowling green, children's playground and tennis courts.

M

Myddelton House Gardens

see page 158

Naboth's Vineyard

Dublin, County Dublin, Republic of Ireland

A garden made by Jonathan Swift from 1721 on a piece of land he leased when Dean of St Patrick's. At a little distance from the Deanery (where he also had a garden), it was a walled garden of around 1½ acres/0.6 hectares, in part of which he grew fruit and ornamental plants. Nothing is known of its layout. The only surviving plan dates from 1749, after Swift's death, showing its area, orientation and position but nothing else (it is illustrated in Edward Malins's and the Knight of Glin's *Lost Demesnes* (1976) which describes all that is known of the garden). We know that Swift liked roses, for he wrote a poem about entertaining the Vicereine Lady Carteret in the garden; instead of receiving her in grand rooms, he "Thought it more courtly and discreet,/To scatter Roses at her Feet;/Roses of richest Dye, that shone/With native Lustre, like her own". The site of the garden has long since been built over.

Nannau

nr Dolgellau, Gwynedd OS SH7420
Cadw/ICOMOS Register Grade II*

Thomas Pennant, in his *A Tour in Wales* (1784), described Nannau as having "perhaps the highest situation of any gentleman's house in Great Britain". It lies at over 750ft/230m on the side of Poel Offrwn mountain in the wild and lovely scenery of Snowdonia. It is an ancient place, belonging in the 15th century to Howel Sele, a cousin of Owain Glyn Dwr. Sele was murdered in murky circumstances and his romantic story thrilled 18th-century visitors to Nannau. Thomas Roscoe, in *Wanderings and Excursions in North Wales* (1838), said that "the chief attraction of the spot lies in the beauty and romantic traditions of the park". The deer park was originally medieval and its transformation into a designed

landscape dates from the 18th century. The terrain is rocky and uneven, part parkland and part woodland, including some ancient woodland. Precipice Walk is a circuit walk planned to take in the chief beauties of the landscape, such as the views over the Mawddach valley to the mountains and sea beyond – but almost any view in these parts is beautiful. Occasional ornamental buildings adorn the scene: a 19th-century Gothic circular building with turrets, a Tudor gateway with turrets in the deer park wall and a square watch tower. Two arches commemorate the coronation of George IV in 1820, one of which is placed to frame a view of Cader Idris.

Narford Hall

Narford, Norfolk OS TF7613
English Heritage Register Grade II

House started c.1700 for Sir Andrew Fountaine and altered in the 18th and 19th centuries. A plan in Colen Campbell's *Vitruvius Britannicus* (1725) and drawings of c.1727 by Edmund Prideaux show an elaborate formal garden of which only slight but seductive traces survive. North of the house, beyond a lake (possibly an informalised canal from the formal garden), is a classical temple of the early 18th century.

Nashdom

Burnham, Buckinghamshire OS SU9284
English Heritage Register Grade II

House by Edwin Lutyens for Princess Alexis Dolgorouki, built 1906–8 – "a whitewashed brick palace for parties on the Thames", as Gavin Stamp called it in *Edwin Lutyens: Country Houses* (2001). Garden also by Lutyens: a circular rose garden with a circular pergola and York stone paving (both gone), balustraded terrace with York paving (gone) along the top of a massive bastion-like wall from which a double flight of grand staircases leads to what had been a lawn (now a car park). To the south, woodland with surviving trees and rhododendrons. The house is now converted into flats.

National Botanic Garden of Wales

see page 218

National Botanic Gardens (Republic of Ireland)

see page 429

The National Forest

Derbyshire, Leicestershire and Staffordshire

A remarkable landscape regeneration project in the Midlands, started in 1995 by the National Forest Company. By 2002 it had planted 4 million trees and established 7,660 acres/3,100 hectares of new woodland; 2,198 acres/890 hectares of this area had formerly been disused mines or otherwise derelict land. 1,812 acres/734 hectares of the area is dedicated to nature conservation. The whole project should be completed 2017–22, with 30 million trees planted.

The Necropolis

Cathedral Square, Glasgow OS NS6065
Scottish Inventory Open regularly

The first planned cemetery in Glasgow, started in 1828 – before this date everyone except lunatics or the unbaptised had to be buried in a churchyard. A public competition was set up to choose a design for the Necropolis. In the end, the proposals of several submissions were amalgamated and executed by a landscape designer, David Mylne, who became the first superintendent. The cemetery was non-denominational. The dramatic hilltop setting was terraced and laid with a simple pattern of paths and planted with evergreens. The greatest ornament is the very large number of distinguished monuments, some by outstanding architects such as Alexander "Greek" Thomson (the A.O. Beattie monument). Only one monument was added after 1900 (to the Blackie publishing family) so the Necropolis constitutes a great memorial to the great and the good in a flourishing period of Glaswegian history.

Ness Botanic Gardens

see page 219

Nether Lyppiatt Manor

Thrupp, Gloucestershire OS SO8703
English Heritage Register Grade II

Early 18th-century house built for Charles Coxe. Garden chiefly walled, with much replanting since 1980 (when the house was bought by Prince Michael of Kent), with advice from Rosemary Verey who designed a raised horseshoe-shaped flower bed. There are also a rose maze, two knots of herbs, a secret garden with white or black flowers and woodland walks edged with scented shrubs. South of the house, in the woods, an obelisk raised in memory of the horse Wag who died in 1721.

Netherbyres

nr Ayton, Berwickshire OS NT9463
Scottish Inventory Open occasionally for SGS

House built c.1834, on a much older site, for Captain Sir Samuel Brown, probably to the designs of George Angus. In the early 18th century the owner of Netherbyres was William Crow, a knowledgeable gardener. He wrote to a friend giving information about his gardening activities: "I deal only in the hardy flowering shrubs and yet they have suffered by the long intensive frost…and the best of all flowering shrubs, my peaches (of which I have a wall 300ft long) have lost the greatest part of their small wood." An unusual elliptical garden, probably built by Crow, survives at Netherbyres; with an area of 1½ acres/0.6 hectares, it is built of stone lined with brick, against which espaliered fruit trees are still grown. Today, ornamental planting is mixed with fruit and vegetables, with beds of roses and flowering shrubs and fine collections of meconopsis and primulas. Some time after 1860 glasshouses were added. Parkland has ash, elm, oak and holly which date from c.1800 or possibly earlier. The policies are edged with woodland where there was once a canal. Formal gardens by the house used to have an elliptical shape, echoing the walled garden, but now consist of a lawn with trees and a herb garden with box-edged beds.

Nettlecombe Court

Nettlecombe, Somerset OS ST0537
English Heritage Register Grade II

Tudor house of the Trevelyan family, with 18th-century alterations. Deer park first recorded in 1532. Formal garden made in late 17th century, which included a water garden: "altering the Green Court front with iron gates and palisades opposite to which is a new canal-pond, and a new cascade of five falls or breaks about 26 feet perpendicular falling in the middle of said canal." New park made in the 1730s by Sir John Trevelyan, with many oaks surviving from this time; 150 different epiphytic lichens have been identified growing on the oaks. Grounds landscaped by John Veitch of Exeter from 1792, with ha-ha. J.C. Loudon admired the kitchen gardens on his visit in 1842: "an admirable kitchen garden here, with the walls covered with the very best kinds of peaches, nectarines and pears, all in fine order, while the fig ripens as a standard. We observed a very excellent kind of cabbage…which is called the Nettlecombe cabbage."

Nevill Holt Hall

Nevill Holt, Leicestershire OS SP8193
English Heritage Register Grade II

14th-century house with several subsequent alterations. The estate was owned by the Nevill family from the 15th to the 19th century. Garden to the north-west of the house, walled to the north and west with kitchen garden wall to the east. Lawn divided by remains of a raised avenue, and trees and shrubs to the west. To the north of the garden, steps lead up to a raised bank with a platform from which there are views of the parkland; on a 17th-century map this is called The Stand and may have been used for hawking or for viewing deer coursing. There is an early 18th-century sundial on The Stand. The 17th-century plan shows the garden as a formal orchard with walnut and cherry trees. Three walled kitchen gardens to the east date from the 17th century. One of these now has a private house; the second has a vegetable garden with box- or terracotta-edged beds and glasshouses; the third is a flower garden with a temple of *c*.1905 against a wall.

New College (Oxford)

see page 102

New Hall

Boreham, Essex OS TL7310
English Heritage Register Grade II

Ancient estate with history going back to 11th century, when it was owned by Waltham Abbey. Henry VIII acquired the estate in 1517 and rebuilt the earlier house; alterations later in the 16th century and subsequently. George Villiers, Duke of Buckingham, lived here in the early 17th century, when John Evelyn visited New Hall in 1656 and wrote: "Garden a faire plot, & the whole seate well accommodated with water; but above all the Sweete & faire avenue planted with stately Lime-trees in 4 rowes for neere a mile in length." In Buckingham's time 1,500 oaks and 2,000 walnut trees were planted, probably under the supervision of John Tradescant who had worked for Buckingham since at least 1624. The landscaper Richard Woods was paid £250 – £16,496 today) in 1767 by the then owner, Lord Waltham, and it seems probable that he was responsible for the lake. This was described in 1768 as "a noble sheet of water" by a visitor who also reported that Lord Waltham was "laying out the gardens and park with such taste, as to render the situation delightful". The walled kitchen garden dates from the 16th century and was the oirginal Great Garden. The approach avenue admired by Evelyn has been replanted.

New Park

Petersham, Surrey OS TQ1774

Spectacular Thames-side estate of the Earl of Rochester, with a house built 1692–96 by Matthew Banckes. The house was burnt down in 1710 but it existed long enough for a Kip engraving to appear in *Britannia Illustrata* (1707), showing a magnificent garden of immense complexity with parterres, groves, a huge mound, monumental terracing, elaborate

patterns of rides cut through woodland and a giant axial vista centred on the house. A painting of the house *c*.1700, attributed to Adrian van Diest, is illustrated in *The Artist and the Country House* (1979) by John Harris. Harris suggests the garden was possibly by George London. The great mound in the garden had been part of the royal hunting grounds of Richmond and was built as a hunting stand by Henry VIII. It is the only feature of Rochester's garden to survive, in the north-west corner of what is now Richmond Park (*see page 529*).

New Place *and* Nash's House (Stratford-upon-Avon)

see page 277

New Place

Haslemere, Surrey OS SU9134

Fine Arts and Crafts house built 1897–1901 for the publisher Sir Algernon Methuen to the designs of C.F.A. Voysey, who also designed the garden. The site is a sloping one, which Voysey terraced and divided into compartments walled in stone and with fine wrought-iron gates designed by him. A four-part rose garden was designed by Gertrude Jekyll in 1902 and she also advised Lady Methuen on planting in other parts of the garden. At the foot of the slope, in a wilder setting, a Japanese garden was laid out by Japanese gardeners.

New Walk

Leicester, Leicestershire OS SK5904 English Heritage Register Grade II Open regularly

A public walk, originally to be called Queen's Walk, established in 1785 and leading from the fashionable 18th-century quarter of Leicester to the racecourse, now Victoria Park. The city paid for the labour but the cost of trees and shrubs, which lined the walk (£250 – £14,240 today) was raised by public subscription. When opened it ran through countryside with fine views of the unenclosed landscape. Gradually, from 1824, buildings were put up on each side and eventually it was entirely built up. It is now a traffic-free conservation area lined with trees.

Newark Castle Gardens

Newark, Nottinghamshire OS SK7954
English Heritage Register Grade II
Open regularly

Early 12th-century castle built for Alexander, Bishop of Lincoln and largely destroyed in the Civil War. Restored by Anthony Salvin 1845–48 and bought by Newark Corporation 1889. Grounds laid out as a public park with lawns, a terrace walk, winding paths and beds of shrubs. Some good mature specimen trees, planted on raised mounds, probably date from the mid 19th century.

Newark Park

Ozleworth, Gloucestershire OS ST7893
English Heritage Register Grade II
Open regularly (NT) Tel 01453 842644

16th-century house, built as a hunting lodge for Sir Nicholas Poyntz, with subsequent alterations. There was a deer park here, contemporary with the house, but a new walled deer park was made in the late 18th century. Pool south-west of the house, with the Monkey House, a Gothic brick summerhouse of the late 18th century. 19th-century rockery and new formal garden east of the house since 1970.

Newbattle Abbey

Newbattle, Midlothian OS NT3366 Scottish Inventory Open occasionally for SGS

The abbey was a 12th-century Cistercian foundation of which the buildings have been almost completely destroyed. After the Reformation the estate passed to the Kerrs (Earls, and later Marquesses, of Lothian) who remained here until 1930 when the building became an education college. The present house dates from the 17th and 18th centuries, with 19th-century remodelling by William Burn and David Bryce. J. Macky's *A Journey Through Scotland* (1724) describes the gardens: "on each side of the gate there is a large stone Pavilion; and through four square green courts you come to the Palace, each of the first three courts having rows of statues on each side, as big as life, and in the fourth court the biggest holley trees I ever saw."

Today a mid 19th-century garden has a splendid parterre laid out by Constance, Marchioness of Lothian and completed in 1872. Divided by broad paved paths, it has shaped beds cut out of turf and edged in box, scalloped stone planters and mounds of clipped box. The site of the abbey church is traced in gravel with circular beds of roses indicating the positions of pillars.

Newbold College, *formerly known as* Moor Close

Binfield, Berkshire OS SU8470
English Heritage Register Grade II*

Late 19th-century house built for Charles Birch Crisp who commissioned a formal garden from the architect Oliver Hill 1910–11 (Hill's first commission). Hill created an extravagantly exuberant design of rectangular enclosures and subtle changes of level. At the centre of the garden is a pair of pavilions linked by a pergola, with a sweeping double staircase curving down to a lower level. Above the pergola is a fountain pool and below it a plain narrow lawn edged in paving which leads to a sunken lily pool at one end and an elaborately patterned terrace at the other. His original planting included pots of agapanthus, hollies, hydrangeas and yews, and narrow beds of hostas, irises, lilies and lupins.

Newburgh Priory

nr Coxwold, North Yorkshire OS SE5476
English Heritage Register Grade II
Open regularly Tel 01347 868435

An Augustinian priory was founded here in the 12th century. At the dissolution of the monasteries the estate passed to Anthony Bellasis whose descendants became the Viscounts and then Earls of Fauconberg. The house as it is today is partly 17th- and largely 18th-century work. In John Harris's *The Artist and the Country House* (1979) two remarkable paintings of Newburgh Priory are shown, depicting the garden as it was in the late 17th century. One shows a enclosure separated by an ornate fence, with a series of square or rectangular beds in one half and a dazzling

array of circular beds and much more fanciful shapes, with mop-headed plants rising above, in the other. Harris describes this as "a fine late Elizabethan garden". A map of 1722 shows that these gardens still survived in outline, but a map of 1744 shows new schemes. Estate accounts show that £3,000 (£247,560 today) was spent on the garden in the period 1734–38 but it is not known exactly what was done. Today a lake survives north of the house, with the ruins of an ornamental building. The figure of a horse is cut into the hillside beyond. South of the house, where once there was such an ornate garden, there are lawns, flower beds and topiary.

Newby Hall Gardens

see page 348

Newcastle General Cemetery, *also known as* Jesmond Old Cemetery

Newcastle-upon-Tyne, Tyne and Wear OS NZ2565 English Heritage Register Grade II Open regularly

Cemetery laid out by the architect John Dobson in 1836, who also designed some striking buildings for it – among them a neo-Greek entrance lodge and some of the memorials (including a huge Gothic tower of 1843 in memory of Archibald Reed, six times Mayor of Newcastle). Many people notable in Newcastle history are buried here – Pevsner calls it "a sort of Tyneside Père Lachaise". The site is 10 acres/4 hectares in area, with many good mature trees; Dobson's original plan had shown perimeter planting and planted mounds. Parts of the cemetery were destroyed in the 1970s for a proposed road scheme which was never built.

Newhailes, *formerly* Whitehill

nr Musselburgh, East Lothian OS NT3272
Scottish Inventory Open regularly (NTS)
Tel 0131 665 0253

House built 1686 close to the Firth of Forth to the designs of the architect James Smith for his own use. In 1709 the estate was bought by Sir David Dalrymple and the

N

N

family remained here until the estate was given to the National Trust for Scotland in 1997. From 1721 Sir James Dalrymple laid out Rococo pleasure grounds, forming waterfalls and pools in a stream with "a variety of grottoes and walks upon its banks". He also erected an obelisk (1746) in memory of his cousin, the 2nd Earl of Stair (of Newliston, *see page 516*) who fought at the battle of Dettingen. Joseph Spence visited Newhailes during his Scottish tour of 1758–60 and described "woods coming down…towards the shore…for tis a very pleasing place; (and only wants a few openings to catch the sea oftener in ye walks & in intermix light among the shades) & a few scattered clumps & little touches in the more modern way." In the pleasure grounds today Sir James's Rococo garden survives in essence, with a grotto (*c.*1774–81), originally with "shells, Corals and other things of the kind", sent from Canton by William Dalrymple. Nearby is a ruinous classical teahouse which probably dates from *c.*1700 (probably moved from another site). Trees of lime and yew on the banks of the burn date from the 18th century. An early 18th-century semicircular walled flower garden (now without flowers) also survives. The kitchen garden, with 18th-century walls, is now a commercial nursery.

Newhall

nr Penicuik, Midlothian OS NT1756
Scottish Inventory

House built in 1703 for Sir David Forbes, replacing a 17th-century house that had belonged to the Pennycuicks. Sir David was the brother-in-law of Sir John Clerk of Penicuik (*see page 522*). The site, overlooking the wooded ravine of Newhall Glen with its burn, is very beautiful. In the early 18th century a series of circuit walks were laid out to take advantage of its scenes, in particular of a cascade, the Fairies Linn, and the wooded banks of the burn. All the sites on the walk, with names such as Peggy's Poool, Craggy Bield and Mary's Bower, may still be identified. The poet Allan Ramsay, a friend of Sir David's son John and a frequent

visitor to Newhall, was inspired by the scenery of the glen in his pastoral comedy *The Gentle Shepherd* (1725).

Newick Park

Newick, Lewes, East Sussex OS TQ4219
English Heritage Register Grade II

16th-century house, remodelled in mid 18th century. West of the house, the Dell, a stream in a steep cutting, possibly the result of 16th-century iron workings. By the early 18th century it had been laid out with winding paths, and a brick summerhouse survives from this time. James Henry Sclater, a founder member of the Royal Horticultural Society, and his sons, planted many exotics here 1840–60 – the result much praised by William Robinson in *The English Flower Garden* (1883), especially "boldly grouped" ferns. There was possibly a medieval deer park here but the present park is essentially 18th-century, with a serpentine lake. In the late 18th there was a star-shaped pattern of rides radiating out from a central point, from which a few trees survive.

Newliston

nr Kirkliston, West Lothian OS NT1173
Scottish Inventory Open regularly
Tel 0131 333 3231

The Dundas family came to live at Newliston in the early 15th century. A new house was designed by Robert Adam in 1789 for Thomas Hog whose father had bought the estate in 1747. In 1665 Elizabeth Dundas married Sir John Dalrymple, later 1st Earl of Stair, of Castle Kennedy (*see page 365*). Their son, the 2nd Earl, served as Ambassador to Versailles 1715–20, and was much influenced by the gardens he saw. Gardens at Newliston were laid out for him 1720–40 by William Adam; Adam's design of *c.*1725 shows a square walled enclosure, with round bastions at each corner, containing an immensely elaborate array of formal gardens, cut in half by a canal (fed by the river Almond), and crossed by diagonal avenues with *rond-points*. In the south-east corner is the Hercules Garden, laid out on the pattern of the union jack, supposedly to commemorate

the battle of Dettingen (1743) in which Lord Stair fought as a Field Marshal. This survives, originally planted in lime trees, now in birch. Other fragments of the detail and much of the pattern of this great layout are also visible.

Newnham College

Cambridge, Cambridgeshire OS TL4458
Open regularly Tel 01223 335700

One of the first women's colleges, founded in 1871 with splendid brick buildings of the 1870s designed by Basil Champneys in elaborate gabled Dutch style. Pevsner's *Cambridgeshire* volume in "The Buildings of England" notes "a certain feminine daintiness, and an atmosphere almost of Pieter de Hooch". The first Principal, Anne Jemima Clough, determined that gardens were important to the atmosphere of the college and (as Jane Brown wrote in *The Making of the Gardens: Newnham College, Cambridge* (1989)) "supervised the arrangement of the garden in a mid-Victorian style that was familiar to her, with serpentine paths through the shrubberies and orchard trees." Further work was done on the gardens by James Backhouse in the 1890s, by the architect A.H. Powell in Arts and Crafts taste from 1906, by Gertrude Jekyll in 1911 and by the architect W.C. Watson in 1912. The gardens today have spacious lawns, groves of trees and individual specimens, borders, yew hedges and a rectilinear pattern of paths linking the college buildings. In front of Sidgwick Hall is a sunken garden with circular pool and shaped rose beds in each corner. Ronald Gray, discussing the planting in his *Cambridge Gardens* (1984), claims that "No college is so well provided for all seasons." He describes the very wide range of shrubs (some unfamiliar, such as *Celastrus orbiculatus*), bulbs, herbaceous perennials and trees (including one of the largest specimens of *Sorbus latifolia* in the country).

Newnham Paddox

Monks Kirby, Warwickshire OS SP4783
English Heritage Register Grade II

18th-century house demolished in 1952; only splendid 18th-century

wrought-iron gates and gate piers survive. Capability Brown advised the 5th and 6th Earls of Denbigh 1745–54, partly on architectural matters but also about altering "ye great canal" and creating a "serpentine water" from earlier fishponds north and east of the house. Only part of the lake remains; much of it was obliterated when new formal gardens were made in the 1870s, whose outlines survive today. 19th-century pinetum in north-western woodland.

Newsham Park

Liverpool, Merseyside OS SJ3791 English
Heritage Register Grade II Open regularly

Public park laid out by Edward Kemp from 1865 and based on the estate of the Molyneux family, which was bought, with its 18th-century house, by Liverpool Corporation in 1845. The house is in the north-western part of the park and the whole of the northern part is enclosed in a carriage drive. To the east, an irregular lake crossed by a bridge; the eastern bank has winding paths among trees planted on a raised bank. South of the lake, the round pond enclosed in trees, and west of it, two tennis courts. Open area to north-west largely turf with sports pitches. In the southern part of the park, bowling greens with a pavilion and a late 19th-century octagonal bandstand.

Newstead Abbey

see page 272

Newton Don

nr Kelso, Roxburghshire OS NT7137
Scottish Inventory

House built on an older site 1817–20 for Sir Alexander Don to the designs of Sir Charles Smirke. Early 19th-century deciduous woodland, with later plantings of conifers and rhododendrons, and a late 19th-century rustic summerhouse with decorative panels of bamboo and wood. Parkland of the same date, with an oak avenue of *c.*1900. In the late 19th century the walled garden had ribbon bedding schemes, colour-themed borders and a notable collection of Malmaison carnations; these were introduced

by Lady Nina Balfour (wife of Charles Balfour who had inherited the estate in 1872), who had a great influence on the garden in this period.

Newton House

Newton, Midlothian OS NT3369
Scottish Inventory

Late 17th-century house on an older site. Walled gardens date from the 17th and 18th centuries. A fruit wall divides part of it into an orchard, with espaliers against the wall, box-edged borders running along the enclosing walls, and fruit trees in the centre. The other part is divided into yew-hedged compartments arranged about an axial walk centred on the house. Here are borders, a rose garden with box-edged beds, a yew garden with topiary of peacocks and finials, and a central sundial garden. About the perimeter are informal plantings of rhododendrons and substantial trees with a winding perimeter walk.

Newton Park

Newton St Loe, Somerset OS ST6964
English Heritage Register Grade II

House built 1761, designed by Stiff Leadbetter for William Gore Langton. Capability Brown worked here *c.*1760, creating a series of lakes separated by weirs, now largely silted up. Ruins of medieval St Loe castle overlook the lakes. Humphry Repton was consulted in 1796 and produced a Red Book. His work involved a subtle reworking of Brown's landscape, creating a new entrance drive to replace an existing avenue, and altering the level of the lakes. Repton also built an arcaded temple on the far side of the lake (now demolished), and a battlemented gateway (designed by John Nash) was erected to emphasise views of the ruined castle. The house today is a Further Education College and the landscape, though disheveled, is very beautiful.

Newton Surmaville

nr Yeovil, Somerset OS ST5615
English Heritage Register Grade II

Jacobean house for the Harbin family, descended from Joan de

Surmaville who died in 1307. A pool south-east of the house is the lone survivor of five medieval fish ponds. Octagonal summerhouse built by Swayne Harbin in the 1740s, now a cottage, with elegant keystones and tall sash windows. Harbin's neighbours and friends, Mr Phelips of Montacute (see page 53) and Mr Goodford of Chilton Cantelo also had summerhouses and each was visible from the others. According to Country Life (September 1952), if "a flag was flown from one the owners of the other two would gallop over for a convivial evening". George Harbin added a grand conservatory in the late 1840s.

Nieuport House
Almeley, Herefordshire OS SO3152
English Heritage Register Grade II

Early 18th-century house. The newly built house was given formal gardens and, south of the house, traces of these remain; a very large sweet chestnut also survives, possibly of that time. The formal gardens were removed c.1767 but W.A. Nesfield reinstated a formal scheme c.1870, of which a surviving tazza (vase) is probably a part. In the park, a lake south-east of the house linked to another lake further to the south-east by a wooded dingle. A deer park was made in the early 18th century, and avenues were planted, radiating from the house into the park.

Nonsuch Palace
Surrey OS TQ2462

One of Henry VIII's many palaces, left to ruin in the late 17th century. It was built for the King 1538–46 as a hunting lodge in Hampton Court Chase – but a very grand hunting lodge, hence its name. The village of Cuddington (between Cheam and Ewell) was destroyed to make way for it. It was set in a Little Park of 671 acres/272 hectares and a Great Park of 1,000 acres/405 hectares. In 1556 it was sold by Mary I to Henry Fitzalan, 12th Earl of Arundel who, dying in 1579 without an heir, left the estate to his son-in-law, John, Lord Lumley. By 1591 Lumley had transformed the garden, inspired by what he had

seen of Italian gardens in 1566. It was, according to Sir Roy Strong in The Renaissance Garden in England (1979), "the first large-scale symbolic garden in the Italian Mannerist style to have been attempted in England". Baron Waldstein saw it in 1600 and marvelled at its splendours: "the garden which is the finest in the whole of England, and exceedingly delightful". He saw "numerous marble obelisks" and the Grove of Diana in which "a gentle flow of water bathed Diana and her two nymphs; Actaeon had approached; he was leaning against a nearby tree to hide himself and gazing lecherously at Diana." Elizabeth I was seen as Diana ("Queen and huntress, chaste and fair", as Ben Jonson wrote). In 1603, once again in royal ownership, Nonsuch was given by James I to his queen, Anne of Denmark. Edward Somerset, 4th Earl of Worcester (of Raglan Castle, see page 528) became Ranger of the Great Park and had a garden designed c.1609 for his house, Worcester Lodge, by Robert Smythson – a square enclosure with raised walks planted with fruit trees overlooking quatrefoil-shaped flower-beds. In 1682 it was sold to Lord Berkeley, under whom the palace became a ruin. Nothing of it remains above ground, but an archaeological excavation by Professor Martin Biddle 1959–60 revealed much evidence about the palace and its garden.

Norbury Park
Norbury, Surrey OS TQ1553
English Heritage Register Grade II

Early 19th-century house now separated from the site described here. Picturesque pleasure grounds laid out here in the late 18th century by William Lock, with a network of walks on the steeply sloping hillside and fine views over the Mole Valley to Box Hill. The slopes were already well wooded when Lock came, with oaks, beech and ancient yews, the latter forming a group called the Druid's Grove. W.S. Gilpin admired Lock's work, describing the result as "a good Alpine picture". Lock's paths survive although the site is now overgrown.

Norfolk Park
Sheffield, South Yorkshire OS SK3685
English Heritage Register Grade II
Open regularly

In the middle ages the land here was part of the deer park of Sheffield Manor, which by the early 17th century covered well over 2,000 acres/810 hectares. In the 17th century it passed by marriage to the Howard family, Dukes of Norfolk. The Howards made a public park for "the operative class" here from 1841, and opened it to the public in 1848 with, as the Duke's factor reported in 1855, "walks, carriage drives, plantations of Trees and Shrubs and a large space of open ground". Enclosed in wooded belts, the park retains much of its original character, with the later addition of sports facilities and a children's playground. Fine mature trees survive from original plantings, including a double avenue of Turkey oaks (Quercus cerris) and a lime avenue. From 1999, after winning a Heritage Lottery Fund grant, much restoration has been done. The lodges have ben restored, a multi-purpose building, the Centre in the Park, has been put up, the historic landscape restored and more sports facilities added.

Norris Castle
East Cowes, Isle of Wight OS SZ5196
English Heritage Register Grade II

Castle built in 1799 for Lord Henry Seymour to the designs of James Wyatt. Humphry Repton was consulted in 1805 but no Red Book is known. To the north-east of house, sloping lawn with copses on either side running towards the sea. A designed promenade along the shore has been destroyed since the 1940s. Scattered mature trees in the park: cedar of Lebanon, deodar (Cedrus deodara) and Wellingtonia.

The North Canonry
Salisbury, Wiltshire OS SU1429
English Heritage Register Grade II

House of medieval origins, rebuilt in 16th and 17th centuries and restored by Sir George Gilbert Scott in the 19th century. Long garden behind the house, walled

on each side and running down to the river Nadder on whose banks there is an early 18th-century gazebo. At its western end is the wall of the cathedral close, with a central opening. Another wall, with central wrought-iron gates, crosses the garden a third of the way down; beyond this, a double herbaceous border runs all the way down to the close wall. The axial layout probably dates from the 18th century. Gertrude Jekyll, in Wood and Garden (1899), called it "one of the most beautiful gardens I have ever seen".

North and South Marine Parks
South Shields, Tyne and Wear OS NZ3767
English Heritage Register Grade II
Open regularly

From 1869 a public park was made on the southern banks of the Tyne estuary, incorporating the existing dunes and beach of Bents Park. By the early 20th century a chain of marine parks had been created, an area of well over 100 acres/40 hectares. Today the parks, with some good late 20th-century additions, display a wide range of ornaments and amenities: bowling greens, a braille garden, a rock garden, terraces, lawns, plantings of shrubs and trees, and seaside walks. In the North Marine Park are two early 19th-century navigational beacons.

Northbourne Court
Northbourne, Kent OS TR3352
English Heritage Register Grade II*

House built 1616 for Sir Edwin Sandys, largely demolished in 1750. New house built c.1780 on a slightly different site. Remarkable surviving early 17th-century walled garden with spectacular triple terrace at the south-western end, which originally faced the old house standing at the far end of the enclosure. Planting entirely 20th-century, with a long herbaceous border, lily pond and Mediterranean-style planting on the terraces taking advantage of the sharp drainage – agapanthus, helianthemums, lavender, Mexican daisy and rosemary. Further walled enclosure to the south, with glasshouse, vegetable beds and more borders.

Northfield House
Balerno, Edinburgh OS NT1566
Scottish Inventory

House and garden designed in 1910 by W.C. Watson for his own use. The garden is compartmented in Arts and Crafts style, with a central yew roundel enclosing a circular bed of roses and grey foliage plants; a pleached lime walk; an orchard divided by yew hedges, with ornamental plantings of rhododendrons and roses; and a kitchen garden. The only informal part is the Herbarium, a woodland garden of azaleas and rhododendrons with winding walks.

Norton Conyers
Wath, North Yorkshire OS SE3176
English Heritage Register Grade II
Open regularly Tel 01765 640333

Ancient house, remodelled in the 16th and 17th centuries and acquired in the 17th century by the Graham family who still live here. Possibly 17th-century bowling green with, to one side, stone plinths once occupied by early 18th-century statues and urns. North of the hall a mound, possibly 16th-century, and a water garden. 18th-century kitchen garden with contemporary orangery, now planted with herbaceous borders.

Nostell Priory
see page 349

Nottingham Arboretum
Nottingham, Nottinghamshire OS SK5640
English Heritage Register Grade II
Open regularly

Arboretum and public park designed by Samuel Curtis and opened 1852. Curtis laid out serpentine paths, lawns, a lake, borders, shrubs and trees planted in groups or as specimens. Refreshment rooms designed by H. Moses Wood were modified by Sir Joseph Paxton and are now the Arboretum Hotel. Among several monuments, the Chinese Bell is a curious combination of a bell brought from Canton in 1857 and Russian cannons brought back from Sebastopol. A collection of roses, very large dahlia border,

N

rockery and carpet bedding. The arboretum has been restored with a grant from the Heritage Lottery Fund.

Nun Appleton Hall
nr Cawood, North Yorkshire OS SE5540
English Heritage Register Grade II

There had been a Cistercian priory here in the 12th century. House of late 17th-century origins, much changed in 19th and 20th centuries. Park of 17th century or earlier, with shelter belts and views over Ings (meadowland). Possibly medieval fishpond in woods east of house. General Lord Fairfax (who defeated Charles I at the Battle of Naseby in 1645) owned Nun Appleton in the 17th century and the poet Andrew Marvell tutored his daughter, Mary. Marvell lived at Nun Appleton for some years and wrote his garden and pastoral poems here; *Upon Appleton House* describes "fragrant Gardens, shady Woods,/Deep Meadows, and transparent Floods".

Nuneham Park
Nuneham Courtenay, Oxfordshire OS SU5498 English Heritage Register Grade I

House built for the 1st Earl Harcourt from 1756, designed by Stiff Leadbetter, with later alterations. On a wooded knoll overlooking the Thames, it commanded a panorama of the spires, towers and domes of Oxford – an English version of views of Rome from the *campagna*. In the 1760s the village and the old church along the river were destroyed to clear the ground for Lord Harcourt's landscaping schemes. A new model village was built a mile away on the turnpike, and in collaboration with James "Athenian" Stuart, a new church of classical inspiration was built in 1764 – a domed temple conceived as an appropriate ornament in the landscape (the rector was aghast and said of Stuart that "he has done everything to me except cutting my throat"). The destruction of the village inspired Oliver Goldsmith's poem *The Deserted Village* (1770) with its mournful line "The country blooms – a garden and a grave". Lord Harcourt himself laid out the

early landscape – opening out vistas and making a walk to connect house and church. In 1777 the 2nd Earl, a disciple of Jean-Jacques Rousseau, invited William Mason to lay out a picturesque flower garden north of the house. Capability Brown was asked in 1778 to landscape the park south of the house. Horace Walpole had not liked the garden at Nuneham Park when he visited in 1773 – "rough as a bear", he had called it – but in 1782, after the changes of Mason and Brown, he thought it "one of the most beautiful landscapes in the world". In the 1830s a picturesque arboretum was laid out by W.S. Gilpin on a new site by the Oxford road. Today, the Nuneham Courtenay estate is owned by the University of Oxford and the Gilpin arboretum is part of a 55-acre/22-hectare piece of land used by the Oxford Botanic Garden as an arboretum (*see page 99*).

Nunhead Cemetery
Southwark, London OS TQ3575 English Heritage Register Grade II* Open regularly

Cemetery laid out by J.B. Bunning and opened in 1840. A hilly site for which Bunning, influenced by J.C. Loudon, devised a layout of gently curving paths which give great variety of viewpoint. Many mature trees survive from 19th-century plantings, among them *Ginkgo biloba*, holm oaks, limes and London planes. In the 1970s the cemetery was taken over by the London Borough of Southwark, which has retained part of it as a cemetery and converted the remainder into public open space.

Nunnington Hall
Nunnington, North Yorkshire OS SE6779 English Heritage Register Grade II Open regularly (NT) Tel 01439 748283

Older house, remodelled in the late 17th century for Richard Graham, 1st Viscount Preston. The site by the river Rye is very attractive. The gardens are terraced and enclosed in 17th-century walls with rusticated gate piers and arches of the same date. The mysterious garden designer Mr Beaumont of Levens Hall (*see page 346*) visited in 1702 but the result, if any, is not known. The estate

was bequeathed to the National Trust in 1952 and the present plantings reflect their work. Here is an orchard of old local apple cultivars, a spring meadow, beds of catmint and roses, and an iris garden.

Nunwell
nr Brading, Isle of Wight OS SZ5987 English Heritage Register Grade II Open regularly Tel 01983 407240

Early 17th-century house on an older site for Sir John Oglander, remodelled in the 18th century and with later alterations. There was garden activity here in the 17th century, with much planting of fruit trees and flowers, but nothing is known of the layout. 19th-century formal garden to east of house, with central steps leading down from a terrace to a symmetrical layout with central circular fountain pool, urns on pedestals and clipped box hedges surrounded by a lawn. Views of parkland to the east, over curved balustraded wall. A grotto below northern end of balustrade, and steps lead down to a lily pool. Arboretum laid out *c.*1963 by Vernon Russell-Smith, west of house.

Nunwick
nr Simonburn, Northumberland OS NY8874 English Heritage Register Grade II

Mid 18th-century house designed by Daniell Garrett for Lancelot Allgood. Park landscaped in the 1760s. Remarkable castellated Gothic kennels dated 1768 and centred on the entrance front of house. By the path to the kennels, a spiral column – "looks part of something Jacobean", says Barbara Jones in *Follies & Grottoes* (1974). In 1766 part of the medieval Simonburn Castle was rebuilt as a Gothic eyecatcher for the entrance avenue at Nunwick, but it collapsed in the 1940s.

Nymans Garden
see page 159

Nynehead Court
Nynehead. Somerset OS ST1322 English Heritage Register Grade II*

17th-century house with earlier origins. 18th-century landscape

park by unknown designer, crossed by river Tone with weir. South of the house is a delightful surviving Victorian parterre: from a central circular box-edged bed, curving and triangular beds radiate outwards, filled with purple sage, santolina or golden *Lonicera nitida*. The whole is enclosed on three sides by bold *guilloche* patterns of box, and at each corner a terracotta urn rises high on a plinth of brick. An avenue of conical yews, planted in 2000 to celebrate the millennium, extends the formality into the park-like garden beyond. Here are superb trees, especially old sweet chestnuts, oaks (including a beautiful Lucombe oak), beeches and in the far south-east corner, a marvellous oriental plane. To the east, a large walled garden with the remains of an orchard and more mature trees. There had been a pinery here in the early 19th century – Dodds of Salisbury supplied 15 pineapple plants in 1837 at 5 shillings (£31 today) each. The parish church of All Saints overlooks the garden, to which it is linked by a superb old tunnel of yews.

Oakes Park
Norton, South Yorkshire OS SK3682 English Heritage Register Grade II

18th-century house for the Morewood family, remodelled in the early 18th century for Richard Bagshawe. A map of 1753 shows formal gardens to the south of the house where today there is a flagged terrace, lawns and specimen trees. North of the house, a canal may have been part of the 18th-century formal gardens and a single row of trees corresponds to the 1753 map. The park dates from the early 19th century, with much 19th-century tree planting surviving.

Oakly Park, *also known as* Oakley
nr Bromfield, Shropshire OS SO4876 English Heritage Register Grade II*

The name is derived from the ancient oaks that grow here close to the banks of the river Teme. 18th-century house, much altered, in particular by C.R. Cockerell for the Hon R.H. Clive 1819–36. The

1st Lord Clive had consulted Capability Brown in 1772 but any plans were cut short by Clive's suicide in 1774 (at another Clive estate, Claremont (*see page 129*), where Brown had also been working). William Emes came here shortly afterwards; although it is not known precisely what Emes did, landscaping was certainly carried out in the late 18th century. Cockerell built a conservatory in 1824 (demolished in the 1930s) which was the centrepiece of a formal garden of box-edged beds, bedding schemes and a fountain; a watercolour of 1850 by Harriet Clive shows boisterous planting with towering yuccas. Late 19th-century maze.

Oare House
Oare, Wiltshire OS SU1563 English Heritage Register Grade II Open occasionally for NGS

House built in 1740 for Henry Deacon, a London wine merchant. 20th-century additions for Sir Geoffrey Fry by Sir Clough Williams-Ellis. 18th-century lodge with lime avenue leading to east front of house. Outline of west terrace, and lawn, probably 18th-century, but present garden largely 20th-century. Library garden, south of the house, designed by Peter Coats in the 1980s with clipped yew hedges, pergola with wisteria and lily pool. Paved terrace to west front of house; large lawn with railings and *claire-voie* on the western side, with rectangular pool beyond and vista cut through woods. The lawn is flanked by mixed borders. 18th-century walled kitchen garden.

Oatlands
nr Weybridge, Surrey OS TQ0865 English Heritage Register Grade II

The medieval palace of Oatlands, rebuilt by Henry VIII from 1538, was close to the centre of Weybridge where a fragment of a Tudor wall survives in a housing estate. The present house, built in 1794 for the Duke of York to the designs of Henry Holland, is on the site of Oatlands hunting lodge replacing an earlier house on the same site. The 9th Earl of Lincoln (later 2nd Duke of Newcastle-under-Lyme) inherited the estate in 1730, when it had an intricate formal garden of immense complexity, as seen in John Rocque's map of 1737. From the 1740s this was developed in the new landscape style with the help of William Kent, Joseph Spence and possibly Philip Southcote. By the 1770s a long narrow lake, Broadwater, was overlooked by terraces to the south, with two Doric temples; the Temple of Vesta; a menagerie designed by Kent; a gateway by Inigo Jones (from the old Oatlands Palace); a bowling green; and a grotto by the Lanes of Tisbury. The grotto was large and elaborate, with two storeys and many different chambers – Barbara Jones in *Follies & Grottoes* (1974) calls it the Lanes' "masterpiece" and says it cost around £40,000 (£3,080,000 today). It was destroyed, amid howls of outrage, in 1948. Some of the garden buildings, including Jones's gateway and the temples by Kent, were broken up to provide the stone for a rockery. One Doric temple survives, some pre-1770 gate piers, and Broadwater itself.

The Officers' Terrace
Chatham Dockyard, Kent OS TQ7569
English Heritage Register Grade II

A terrace of twelve houses built for naval officers 1720–31. Behind each house, separated by a lane running the whole length of the terrace, are rectangular walled gardens, laid out on slightly rising land and terraced. A 1774 model of the street survives in the National Maritime Museum, showing the intricate geometric layout of each garden, no two quite identical. Each had its own entrance, with steps leading up to the first terrace; the steps were covered by arched wooden roofs with partly glazed sides and could therefore be used as small greenhouses or garden rooms. Two of these covered steps survive, as does the essential layout of all the gardens, giving rare insight into the design of small urban gardens in the early 18th century.

Olantigh Towers
nr Wye, Kent OS TR0548 English Heritage Register Grade II Open occasionally for NGS

House of complicated history going back to 1508 when Sir

Thomas Kempe built a new house on an older site. Present house, the truncated remains of a house built in 1903 for John Sawbridge Erle-Drax. 19th-century pleasure grounds. Under south-east façade of the house, a terrace with large fountain and an elaborate underground room whose front is possibly of the 18th century. North-east of the house, 19th-century parterres around a fountain. North of the house, a lake dating from 1850 formed by widening an earlier formal canal. The lake was partly filled in when a water garden was made in the 1920s with a rockery nearby. South-west of the water garden, an American garden. Mid 18th-century circular walled kitchen garden on eastern boundary. In the storm of 1987, 80 percent of the trees in the pleasure grounds and park were lost, and there has since been much replanting.

Old Alresford House
Old Alresford, Hampshire OS SU5833
English Heritage Register Grade II

House built 1749–51 for Admiral Lord Rodney by William Jones. Pleasure grounds with modern rose garden separated from park by ha-ha. The park was landscaped from 1764 by Richard Woods, incorporating a pond made in the 12th century by Godfrey de Lucy, Bishop of Winchester, who constructed the Great Weir, a dam across the river Alre. Woods also extended the existing kitchen garden.

Old Durham Gardens
Old Durham, County Durham OS NZ2842
English Heritage Register Grade II
Open regularly Tel 0191 3866111

There was a medieval manor house here but it was demolished c.1720. The garden has three walled enclosures. The south-eastern enclosure has an early 17th-century gazebo and modern planting (1990s) of lawn and shrubs; the north-eastern enclosure is grassed; the western garden has a terraced walk with a flower bed and views of the east end of Durham cathedral. The gazebo in the neighbouring enclosure rises above the garden wall at the centre of the walk.

The Old Rectory
(Burghfield)
see page 97

The Old Vicarage Garden (East Ruston)
see page 315

Oldbury Court
Fishponds, Bristol OS ST6376
English Heritage Register Grade II

Early 17th-century house overlooking the valley of the river Frome, built for the Kemeys family and eventually demolished in 1960. Humphry Repton was consulted in 1799. Picturesque wooded valley with walks described by Shiercliff's *Guide to Bristol and Hotwells* (1789) as "elegant rural walks…carved through the wood and precipices which border the Frome, which is seen flowing below." This is now a public park and retains much atmosphere despite the "unsympathetic and chaotic modern planting" noted in some areas by the Avon Gardens Trust.

Oldway House
Paignton, Devon OS SX8861
English Heritage Register Grade II
Open regularly Tel 01803 201201

Mansion built 1873 for the sewing-machine tycoon Isaac Singer, designed by G.S. Bridgman. Much altered 1904–7. The garden is of rare interest: a layout by the great French neo-classical designer Achille Duchêne, famous in England for his work on Blenheim Palace (*see page 72*). Here are both informal (lakes, a waterfall, grotto, rock garden) and formal features (an Italianate garden) blended artfully together.

Orchardleigh Park
Orchardleigh, Somerset OS ST7751
English Heritage Register Grade II*

Ancient estate of the Champneys family. The character of the very beautiful wooded grounds survives, with a 13th-century church on an island; a boathouse and a rotunda of 1760 are survivals of the Champneys's 18th-century landscaping activities. New house built for the (publishing) Duckworth family 1855–58, designed by Thomas

Henry Wyatt. The Duckworths made a great mid Victorian garden here, of which only traces survive. *Country Life* in December 1901 published photographs of the South Terrace with ornate balustrade, putti bearing vases, a deep lawn with scalloped beds and bedding schemes, clipped umbrellas of Portugal laurel, aloes in pots and "floral triumphs in choice vases". The poet Sir Henry Newbolt married a Duckworth and was a frequent visitor to Orchardleigh, on which he based "Gardenleigh" in his novel *The Old Country* (1906); he is buried in the churchyard. Arthur Duckworth died in 1986 and since then the estate has changed hands several times and parts sold off hither and thither. The chairman of one of the owners of the estate became the largest personal bankrupt in English history. A golf course has been built on part of the site.

Orchards
nr Godalming, Surrey OS SU9943
English Heritage Register Grade II*

House built 1897–1900 for William and Julia Chance to the designs of Edwin Lutyens. When the Chances were planning to built a house here, they saw Lutyens at work on the nearly completed Munstead Wood (*see page 513*) ("a revelation of unimagined beauty"), introduced themselves and "as a result of this meeting we became the owners of a Lutyens house with a Jekyll garden." The garden is to the east of the house, taking advantage of beautiful views over the Thorncombe valley. Steps from a terrace with a loggia lead down to a sunken Dutch garden with a symmetrical pattern of semicircular stone seats set in arches of yew and flanked by tiled pillars capped with urns. A central path leads between circular beds with topiary, lavender, rosemary and white china roses to a water tank with spouting lion's mask. A path between yew hedges ornamented with topiary leads between borders to a formal kitchen garden with a central octagonal dipping pool surrounded by roses trained on hoops and chains.

Orleton Hall
Orleton, Shropshire OS SJ6311
English Heritage Register Grade II

18th-century remodelling of an older house for the Cludde family. Remains of a moat, possibly medieval, which encircled the house until 1728. Timber-framed late 16th-century gatehouse. Early 18th-century dovecote. 18th-century walled garden with octagonal gazebo. Magnificent Chinoiserie octagonal two-storey summerhouse with ogee roof and first-floor balustrade.

Osborne House
see page 98

Osterley Park
Isleworth, London OS TQ1478
English Heritage Register Grade II*
Open regularly (NT) Tel 020 8232 5050

The house at Osterley was built c.1575 for Sir Thomas Gresham, a financier and diplomat. John Norden described it in his *Speculum Britanniae* (1596): "a fair and stately building of brick…It standeth in a parke by him also impaled, well wooded, and garnished with manie faire ponds." The house was altered in the 18th century (for the banking Child family) by Sir William Chambers and Robert Adam. The estate was given by the 9th Earl of Jersey to the National Trust in 1949. Little remains of the earlier landscape except the pools which were here in Tudor times; one south of the house is now a serpentine in 18th-century style, and others lie north of the M4 motorway. An 18th-century Menagerie (attributed by some to Sir William Chambers) survives nearby; Horace Walpole saw it in 1773 and described it as "a menagerie full of birds that come from a thousand islands". (It stands in Windmill Lane and is marked The Aviary in the *London A–Z*.) There was a pattern of avenues, probably dating from the late 17th century, which are still visible in Rocque's map of 1745. Some good specimen trees remain, especially cedars of Lebanon but also catalpas, holm oaks, limes, oaks and swamp cypress. In recent years the National Trust has done much tree planting and has introduced a pretty Regency flower garden.

O

Despite the intermittent pleasures of the landscape, the splendours of the house's interior and the charm of its architecture, there is something gloomy about the atmosphere of Osterley and its flat site. It is not helped by the fact that the grounds are bisected by the M4 motorway, which cuts across the pools admired by John Norden, and are horribly close to a Heathrow flight path – all in all, probably the nastiest position of any great house in England.

Oulton Hall
Rothwell, West Yorkshire OS SE3527
English Heritage Register Grade II

18th-century farmhouse with much 19th-century alteration. John Blayds consulted Humphry Repton in 1809 and a Red Book was produced the following year. Blayds, the son of a wholesale grocer, became a merchant banker and changed his name from Calverly, borrowing that of a fellow director with its coat of arms. The site at Oulton was so unprepossessing, close to burgeoning Leeds and overlooking a common and many buildings, that Repton could see no redeeming features: "The leading feature of the landscape was a mean row of tenements"; he recognized that it was not a question of "Improvement…it is rather the creation of a new place." Repton's suggestions included making two lakes close together, to seem like a noble river in the valley to the east, and covering their banks with a dense planting of trees to obliterate all sight of the "tenements". A temple would be built on the far bank of the northern lake, on whose distant wooded slopes rose the acceptably elegant great house of Temple Newsam with its Capability Brown park (*see page 547*). Repton hated the job and it brought out the disdainfully snobbish side of his character. He dismissed his work at Oulton in *Fragments on the Theory and Practice of Landscape Gardening* (1816) as a "nameless specimen of improvement in the north of England". Much of the essence of what Repton proposed, including some original trees, may still be seen. On the south side of the house are formal gardens, a

20th-century version of what W.A. Nesfield did here 1851–52. The house is now a hotel and a golf course has been made in the park.

Overbecks Garden
see page 55

Overbury House
Overbury, Worcestershire OS SO9537
English Heritage Register Grade II*

18th-century house, altered by Richard Norman Shaw 1897–1900, altered again in the 20th century. Formal 19th-century gardens south of the house, much altered in the 20th century by Geoffrey Jellicoe, Guy Dauber and Aubrey Waterfield, and simplified by Russell Page in 1968. The south garden has rows of pear-shaped Irish yews between a swimming pool and a sunken croquet lawn. To the west, the Kemerton Walk runs between wide borders dominated by shrub roses. The 18th-century park is now partly grassland, with signs of medieval ridge and furrow fields and specimen trees, and partly arable land. The park had deer in the late 18th century.

Owlpen Manor
Owlpen, Gloucestershire OS ST8098
English Heritage Register Grade II
Open regularly Tel 01453 860261

Irresistibly seductive late medieval house on an ancient site, with Tudor and later additions. Terraced gardens on steeply sloping ground south of the house, with ancient yew topiary, date from the late 17th or early 18th century. 17th-century gazebo (Court House). There are modern plantings and a pool, but it is the character of the terraces below the splendid house, and its setting in the unspoilt rural landscape, that give the place its beauty.

Oxburgh Hall
see page 316

Oxenfoord Castle
nr Dalkeith, Midlothian OS NT3865
Scottish Inventory

Tower house, built for the MacGill family in the 16th century, enlarged by Robert Adam in 1780 for Sir John Dalrymple (later Earl

of Stair), and remodelled in the 1840s by William Burn. Terraced formal gardens by the house (supposedly modelled on those at another Dalrymple estate, Castle Kennedy, *see page 365*), laid out in the mid 19th century for the 8th Earl. Dutch garden east of house enclosed in castellated yew hedges with mixed planting in square beds cut into a lawn. Woodland garden, with sequoia avenue planted c.1863 along the Broad Walk to celebrate the marriage of Edward VII. The castle was a school from 1931–93 and is now being developed as "an exclusive hotel and adult adventure centre".

Oxford Botanic Garden
see page 99

Oxford College Gardens
see page 100 and see names of individual colleges

Oxton House
Kenton, Devon OS SX9282
English Heritage Register Grade II

House built in the 16th century for the Martyn family and rebuilt and greatly enlarged in the 18th century by a Martyn relative, the Revd John Swete, a prebendary of Exeter Cathedral and an indefatigable traveller, diarist and watercolour artist. The surviving volumes of Swete's manuscript diary, with over 600 watercolours, are kept in the Devon Record Office (Exeter) and are a valuable source of information about Devon 1789–1801. He died in 1821 at the age of sixty-nine. He was given the Oxton estate by a Swete cousin on condition that he changed his name from Tripe – a happy suggestion. After rebuilding the house, from 1781, he applied a highly developed taste for the picturesque, creating a new garden embellished with a thatched Gothic two-storey summerhouse, a monumental ruined gateway (rebuilt twice to achieve the full ruinous effect), a cast-iron bridge of Doric character, and the cliff of a 40ft-/11m-high quarry, in the planting of which he took great delight. Although the estate is now in divided ownership, some of Swete's garden buildings survive.

Packington Hall
Great Packington, Warwickshire OS SP2283
English Heritage Register Grade II
Open occasionally for NGS

Packington Hall was built in 1693 for Sir Clement Fisher and enlarged in the 1760s for the 3rd earl of Aylesford to the designs of Matthew Brettingham. Also on the estate is Packington Old Hall, to the north-east, built from 1679 for another Sir Clement Fisher, the uncle of the above. Both houses had formal gardens with avenues and canals, of which no traces remain. Capability Brown was consulted c.1749 – his earliest known surviving landscape drawing is a proposed plan of this date for the park at Packington. He also designed buildings, of which a grotto survives south-east of the house, and created two lakes in the park south of the house.

Packwood House
see page 273

Painshill Landscape Garden
see page 160

Painswick Rococo Garden
see page 220

Palm House
Botanic Gardens, Belfast, County Down, Northern Ireland Open regularly
Tel (028) 90 324 902

Magnificent curvilinear glasshouse with cast-iron frame designed by Richard Turner of Dublin, completed in 1840. A graceful domed centre is flanked by wings – the cool wing containing ornamentals, and the warm (or "stove") wing with temperate and tropical plants and a collection of economic plants.

Pampisford Hall
Pampisford, Cambridgeshire OS TL5048
English Heritage Register Grade II*

Older house, remodelled in late 19th-century by G. Goldie. Gardens and pleasure grounds largely designed by Robert Marnock with terraces, lawns and walks close to the house and a sunken Italian garden. Vista through cedar avenue from south-

east front of house. Very large collection of conifers, over 400 species and cultivars with substantial groups of individual genera – 100 junipers and 50 cypresses, for example.

Panshanger
nr Hertford, Hertfordshire OS TL2812
English Heritage Register Grade II*

Early 19th-century house on a older site, demolished in 1953–54. Capability Brown worked here intermittently 1755–64 and was paid a total of £618 (£44,294 today) but it is not known what h[e] did. In 1799 Humphry Repton advised the 5th Earl Cowper and produced a Red Book. Cowper added the Cole Green estate to Panshanger and Repton thought that the estate should be given "a degree of extent and consequence which it could not boast exclusive of the others, while each possesses its independent privacy and seclusion, their united lawns will, by extending thro' the whole valle[y] enrich the general face of the country." The park is now owned by a gravel extraction company. The remains of formal gardens survive by the site of the house. The park is dominated by Repton[']s Broad Water, formed by damming the river Mimram. The mid 18th-century Riverside Cottage standin[g] in the valley bottom is possibly pa[rt] of Brown's work but it was made more picturesque, possibly as a result of Repton's work, in the early 19th century. Much woodland in the southern park and, in the south-west, the remains of an oak avenue. Early 18th-century octagonal brick-walled kitchen garden now grassed over.

Papplewick Hall
Papplewick, Nottinghamshire OS SK5451
English Heritage Register Grade II*
Open by appointment Tel 0115 9633491

House built 1781–87 for the Hon[.] Frederick Montagu who was a friend of the poets Thomas Gray and William Mason. Mason wrote part of his poem *The English Garden* at Papplewick; in it Mason encourages the gardener to be inspired by "Poet's feeling and Painter's eye". Montague improve[d] his garden, no doubt under Mason's influence. The house looks west over the valley of the river Leen which forms the park's boundary. A dilapidated temple stands on the far bank, with a monument to Mason nearby and, on the east bank, another to Thomas Gray, both of *c*.1799.

Parham House
see page 161

Park Place *and* Temple Combe
Wargrave, Berkshire OS SU7782
English Heritage Register Grade II*

The present estate has two houses. Park Place, an early 18th-century Palladian mansion built for Lord Archibald Hamilton, passed through the hands of several owners and was rebuilt *c*.1871 after damage by fire. Temple Combe was built in the late 18th century and demolished in the 20th century; a new house (Happy Valley) was built 1963–64, designed by Hadley & Partners. At Park Place, terracing on the west side was in place by the mid 18th century. South-east of the house, several specimen trees including 18th-century cedars of Lebanon, and entrances into a network of 18th-century grottoes cut into the chalk. A tunnel leads 570ft/170m south to the Happy Valley hillside, emerging in a grotto flanked by ruinous brick and flint buildings built as Grecian ruins. South of the grotto, Conway Bridge (1763) framing a view of the Thames beyond. North-west of Happy Valley, an 18th-century flint alcove and a Chinoiserie summerhouse. South of Happy Valley, the grounds of the former Temple Combe, and to the south-west, the Druidic Temple (1787), a henge of 45 granite megaliths with lintels. The 18th-century parkland has two golf courses. To the north-east, an obelisk raised in 1837 to celebrate Queen Victoria's accession; it was part of the spire of St Bride's, London, designed by Sir Christopher Wren.

Park Town
Oxford, Oxfordshire OS SP5107
English Heritage Register Grade II

Communal garden east of the Banbury Road, laid out after 1853 by Samuel Lipscombe Seckham and William Baxter Sr. Part of the development of north Oxford, in this case with handsome villas, Park Villas, designed at the same time probably also by Seckham. Parts of a pinetum – mature Bhutan pine, Scots pine and monkey puzzle – survive. Other good trees remain and the layout, although slightly altered, is in essence as planned – worth studying by modern urban planners and anyone who enjoys well designed townscape.

Parnham
Beaminster, Dorset OS ST47 00
English Heritage Register Grade II*

The house at Parnham was built for Robert Strode in the 16th century, modified in the 17th century and comprehensively changed by John Nash 1807–11 for Sir William Oglander. Formal garden of architectural character and great beauty made 1911–14 by the south façade of the house. A deep balustraded terrace has fanciful stone gazebos in each corner (resembling those at Montacute (*see page 53*)) and below, an immense lawn with narrow rills flowing away from the house, and parallel rows of superb giant cones of clipped yew. With no evidence at all, this layout has been attributed to Francis Inigo Thomas who worked at two other gardens in Dorset, Athelhampton (*see page 16*) and Chantmarle (*see page 456*). Photographs in *Country Life* in August 1908 show a deep terrace running along the south façade of the house, with a low wall and urns, and, below, a sunken garden with yew topiary. So whoever designed the garden in 1911 followed an existing pattern. Beyond the lawn is a pool at a lower level, and on all three sides dense woodland with some magnificent old cedars of Lebanon. This was restored under the ownership of the furniture maker John Makepeace who lived here until 2000.

Pashley Manor
see page 162

Patshull Hall
Patshull, Shropshire OS SJ 8000
English Heritage Register Grade II

The Astley family came here in the mid 15th century and the present house was rebuilt 1750–54 by James Gibbs for Sir John Astley. Celia Fiennes visited Patshull in 1698, in particular to see the "Gardens which are talk'd off as the finest and best kept". In one of the longest descriptions in her *Journals*, she describes an extraordinary formal garden: "in this outward Court you may see the house and Court full of Statues in grass-plotts with a broad paved path to the house; in the middle on the one side are flower gardens and the parke, the other side other grounds with rows of trees…and then in the front this large opening to this garden where there is a fountaine allwayes playing, very high the water, the gravel walkes and fine flowers and greens of all sorts in potts and on the borders…the grove I mentioned is the finest I ever saw, there are six walks thro' it and just in the middle you look twelve wayes which discovers as many severall prospects either to the house or entrance or fountaines or gardens or fields." Capability Brown was consulted in the 18th century but it is not known what, if anything, resulted. In 1958 the estate was surrendered in lieu of death duties. The house was a hospital 1966–88, an 18th-century temple became a bar (later part of a hotel) and a golf course was laid out in the park. Of the great garden described by Celia Fiennes not a trace remains.

Pavilion Gardens
Buxton, Derbyshire OS SK0573 English Heritage Register Grade II* Open regularly

Public park laid out by Edward Milner in 1871, probably originating as the private gardens of Buxton Hall in the 17th century and including an earlier layout by Joseph Paxton. To the west, serpentine walks along the banks of the river Wye which flows over several cascades. Some of the planting along the river banks goes back to the 18th century when the 5th Duke of Devonshire wanted to add to the charms of Buxton spa. By 1838, the part of the park associated with Paxton was described by W. Adam, in *Gem of the Peak*, as "admirably laid out and enriched with shrubs and luxurious plantations". The Pavilion, built 1870 but rebuilt 1984 after a fire, is the chief building of the park and houses a café and shops. Below it is a terrace on the bank of the river, with paths to a late 20th-century bandstand, a copy of an earlier one. Milner's ornate footbridge crosses the river, and from it his cascade can be seen. In the southern part of the park, a string of lakes, probably fishponds for Buxton Hall, naturalised by Paxton.

Paxton House
nr Berwick-upon-Tweed, Berwickshire OS NT9443 Scottish Inventory
Open regularly Tel 01289 386291

Palladian villa built 1758–66 for Patrick Home, probably to the designs of John and James Adam, with interiors by Robert Adam. Parkland with ha-has laid out in the 1760s, probably by Robert Robinson, and elm, oak and sycamore survive from the original planting. 18th-century woodland with naturalised beech and sycamore still has walks (including those along Paxton Glen) which were laid out by Robinson. Formal gardens south and west of the house were laid out in the late 19th century, with changes after World War II. Lily pool south-west of the house, backed by yew hedges and with beds of shrubs and specimen trees and shrubs in lawns. The gardens have undergone much restoration in recent times.

Pearson Park
Hull, Humberside OS TA0830 English Heritage Register Grade II Open regularly

Public park designed by J.C. Niven and opened 1861. Open lawns to the north and in the centre, with a small serpentine lake in the south-west. North of lake, stone cupola from Hull town hall moved here in 1912. Central walk from main entrance to the east has good trees, among them a Lucombe oak. To the north, a statue of Prince Albert (1868); east of the lake, one of Queen Victoria (1860) (both by Thomas Earle). Flower beds, specimen hollies and ornamental trees. Bowling greens and a children's playground.

Peasholm Park
Scarborough, North Yorkshire OS TA0389
English Heritage Register Grade II
Open Regularly

Public park laid out in 1912 close to the beach at North Sands. Lake formed by damming Peasholm beck, and, throughout the park, buildings and ornaments of Japanese character. A "willow pattern" bridge, guarded by stone lions, runs across to an island on the lake, on which there is a Japanese garden with a pavilion. Peasholm beck flows down a glen, planted with bamboos and shrubs, with cascades and rustic bridges.

Peckham Rye Park
Southwark, London OS TQ3474 English Heritage Register Grade II Open regularly

Public park laid out on what had been farmland and opened 1894. Enclosed by belts of trees on each side except to the north. Lake with island and woodland walk along its banks; an arboretum; rock and water gardens, an American garden with rhododendrons; a Japanese garden; massed bedding schemes on an oval lawn; and an Old English garden with paved paths and an axial pergola. Among sports and recreation facilities are a bowling green, children's playground, cricket pitch, football ground, open air theatre and tennis courts.

Peckover House
see page 317

Peel Park
Bradford, West Yorkshire OS SE1734 English Heritage Register Grade II Open regularly

The first public park in Bradford, opened in the early 1850s. A raised walk/terrace runs east and west across the park, with a viewing platform at its western end giving a prospect of Manningham valley and the heights of Heaton. In the southern part of the park, paths wind among trees, following the original plan, and there are later tennis courts and bowling greens. North of the terrace, paths lead down into a valley past a lead figure of Robert Peel flanked by statues of Autumn and Spring. In the north-east part of the park is an ornate drinking fountain. In

P

the north-west corner, a large lake with, to its south, an ornate early 18th-century doorway from the old Bradford Hall. The banks of the lake are planted with trees and shrubs.

Pell Wall

nr Market Drayton, Shropshire OS SJ6733
English Heritage Register Grade II

House built by Sir John Soane (the last of his country houses) 1822–28 for Purney Sillitoe. Extraordinary lodge for the north drive, triangular in plan and deftly combining classical and Gothic ingredients. Soane also designed the kitchen garden with the head gardener's house. Formal gardens surviving from the early 19th century, and a rustic summerhouse. Italian garden made in 1909 by a new owner, J. Munroe Walker; later walled in and converted into a swimming pool, it was triumphantly restored in the 1990s by the Udall family.

Pencarrow House

see page 55

Penheale Manor

Egloskerry, Cornwall OS SX2687
English Heritage Register Grade II

Remains of a medieval house incorporated in a later Tudor house, enlarged in the 17th century for Sir John Specott. Additions by Sir Edwin Lutyens in 1921. 17th-century terracing to east and west of house suggests possible early garden activity. Lake's *Parochial History of the County of Cornwall* (1867) described Penheale as "one of the finest and best preserved specimens of ancient manorial residences in the country…gardens and fishponds are in good keeping with the mansion…the main entrance is through an avenue of fine lime trees [which still exists], whose growth is only excelled by the magnificent chestnuts and oaks of the surrounding groves." Lutyens designed a new sunken garden with nine box-edged beds and borders running along the walls. Gertrude Jekyll executed planting plans for this and other parts of the garden. A terraced parterre with monumental yew hedges also dates from this period.

Penicuik House

Penicuik, Midlothian OS NT2159
Scottish Inventory. Open occasionally for SGS

Estate of the Clerk family from 1646; new house built for Sir James Clerk to his own design, starting in 1761; 19th-century alterations; the house was gutted by fire in 1899 and today the family lives in the converted 18th-century stable block. Sir John Clerk had started to modify the old formal gardens even before he had inherited the estate in 1722, planting over 300,000 trees, many of them arranged in avenues. He also made Hurley Cave, an artificial tunnel with a grotto which carries the inscription *Tenebrosa occultaque cave* ("Beware of dark and hidden things"); a machicolated circular watch tower high on Knight's Law; and a walled garden. Clerk paid much attention to his planting – part of the park, for example, he described as being "planted with oaks, firs, walnuts ashes plums Elms of all kinds & and other sorts of Trees. The border of this circular ground near the walk is planted with sweet Bryer Laurel Rose bushes & a great variety of shruibs and flowers." Clerk was aware of the agricultural aspects of his estate, taking great delight in grazing livestock, ponds for carp and perch, and planting many trees for timber.

Penjerrick

see page 56

Penns in the Rocks

Withyham, East Sussex OS TQ5234
English Heritage Register Grade II* Open occasionally for NGS Tel 01892 864244

17th-century farmhouse, rebuilt *c*.1700, with later alterations. The great feature of the garden is a series of natural outcrops of toffee-coloured Wealden sandstone south-west of the house. In 1938 Lady Dorothy Wellesley had a Temple of Friendship built on an eminence facing back towards the house to celebrate "the poets who loved Penns"; their names, including that of W.B. Yeats, are inscribed on the floor. East of the house, Lady Dorothy turned a 19th-century former walled kitchen garden into an ornamental

garden (later replanned by Lanning Roper). Here, an avenue of 'Conference' pears is flanked by three beds on each side, each of which contains three pear trees underplanted with the rose 'Frau Dagmar Hastrup'. The intervening spaces have pairs of rectangular box-edged beds, with domed shapes of box surrounded by lavender or santolina. Mixed borders run round the walls and ornamental trees are planted in grass. South of the walled garden, an avenue of mulberries and a circular stone seat. Parkland with a few clumps and individual trees and areas of woodland. South of the house, a lake, probably once a hammer pond, with a classical temple of the 1960s.

Penrhyn Castle

see page 221

Penshurst Place

see page 163

People's Park

Halifax, West Yorkshire OS SE0823 English Heritage Register Grade II* Open regularly

Public park given to the town by the carpet manufacturer and philanthropist Sir Francis Crossley, designed by Joseph Paxton with the help of Edward Milner and opened to the public in 1857. The chief building of the park is the Crossley Pavilion designed by G.H. Stokes, Paxton's son-in-law. Designed like a loggia, it contains a statue of Sir Francis and has an inscription: "The rich and poor meet together – the Lord is maker of them all". A terrace runs along the western edge of the park, with seven classical statues by Francesco Bienaime. In the centre of the park, a bandstand and fountain, and to the east, a serpentine pond with island and cascade. There are good trees, especially to the south, some of which (ash, beech and horse chestnut) are part of the original plantings.

Peover Hall

Peover Superior, Cheshire OS SJ7773
English Heritage Register Grade II
Open regularly Tel 01565 632358

The Mainwarings were here by the 13th century and remained until 1919. The present house was

built in the late 16th century, with many subsequent alterations. Formal gardens about the house, with yew topiary dating from the late 19th century and late 20th-century additions. South of the house, yew-hedged enclosures contain a pink garden, a white garden and a lily pond garden with an aviary. North of the lily pool garden, a rose garden, herb garden and an Elizabethan style knot garden laid out *c*.1980. North-west of the house, a lawn with pleached lime avenues leading to the Theatre garden enclosed in yew hedges, and a temple made in 1996 using an 18th-century doorcase. An opening in the hedge in the Theatre garden leads to a shrubbery with a rockery and azalea dell. The park was landscaped in the late 18th century, possibly by William Emes.

Petworth House

see page 164

Philipps House, *also known as* Dinton Park

Dinton, Wiltshire OS SU0031
English Heritage Register Grade II
Open regularly (NT) Tel 01985 843600

Magnificent house, incorporating earlier fabric, built *c*.1820 for William Wyndham to the designs of Sir Jeffry Wyatville. The house is surrounded by handsome rolling parkland which must have been laid out before the present house. It has shelter belts and fine mature parkland trees (including a sweet chestnut dating from before 1700) and slopes decoratively down towards the Nadder valley.

Pickenham Hall

Pickenham, Norfolk OS TF8503
English Heritage Register Grade II

House built 1902–05 by Robert Weir Schultz for G.W. Taylor. 18th- and 19th-century parkland with the river Wissey winding across. Schultz also laid out gardens of Arts and Crafts style: a terrace with views to a lake, herbaceous borders and a sunken rose garden enclosed in yew hedges, a dovecote and a gazebo. A Chinese garden with a teahouse is close to a bridge over the river.

Piercefield Park

see page 221

Pinbury Park

Duntisbourne Rouse, Gloucestershire OS SO9504 English Heritage Register Grade II

16th-century house belonging to the Poole family and, late in the 17th century, to Sir Robert Atkyns, the Gloucestershire local historian. Altered in 1894 by Ernest Barnsley who lived here with his brother, the furniture maker Sidney, and with Ernest Gimson. Beautiful views over the beech woods of the Frome valley. Early 20th-century terraced gardens and, north-west of the house, the Nun's Walk, an avenue of old yews.

Pine Lodge Gardens

see page 57

The Pineapple

see page 389

Pinkie House

Musselburgh, East Lothian OS NT3572
Scottish Inventory

The house was begun in the 16th century for the Bishop of Dunfermline, from whom it was acquired by Sir Alexander Seton (later 1st Earl of Dunfermline) in 1597. Many alterations were made to the house in the 17th century for Sir Alexander, who also built a walled garden east of the house, with renaissance gateways, an elaborate semi-octagonal summerhouse and a multi-faceted sundial. In the walled garden is an inscription (in Latin) which says: "Here there is nothing that savours of enmity, not even for defence against enemies; no ditch, no rampart; but for the gracious welcome and hospitable entertainment of guests a fountain of pure water, lawns, ponds and aviaries". Overlooking the garden is a gallery in the house dating from Seton's time and decorated with all sorts of mottoes and moral exhortations; one reads: "Oft in palaces there is labour and grief, while peace and joy abide in the cottage". West of the house he built a remarkable fountain which bears the inscription: "From this fountain unsurpassed for coolness and purity, there flows water benign alike for head and limbs". The house is now a boarding house for Loretto School.

Pirton Park
Pirton, Worcestershire OS SO8746
English Heritage Register Grade II

Formerly part of Lord Coventry's Croome Court estate (see page 464), Pirton was a deer park at least by the 17th century – the Fallow Deer Park, to distinguish it from the Red Deer Park which was also on the Croome estate. It was landscaped by Capability Brown in the 1760s as part of the work he was doing on the chief part of the Croome estate. A long ridge runs from the south-west to the north-east, with a lake, Pirton Pool, in the north-eastern corner. On the ridge south-west of the pool, cedars of Lebanon and limes probably date from the 1760s. A ride to the south-east leads to Pirton Tower, a wall and circular tower designed by James Wyatt in 1797 at the highest point of the park.

Pishiobury
Sawbridgeworth, Hertfordshire OS TL4813
English Heritage Register Grade II

Late 16th-century house, rebuilt 1782–84 by James Wyatt. An engraving by John Drapentier of c.1698 in Chauncy's Historical Antiquities of Hertfordshire (1700) shows the "very neat and fair pile of building for the Manor House" and the garden "with a fair bowling green…enclosed with a brick wall topped with stone balls upon it and 2 fair walks planted with trees." A deer park and fanciful pavilion are also visible. The pleasure grounds today have lawns, shrubs and recently planted trees. The park, where Capability Brown possibly advised on reshaping the lake, retains remains of avenues. The 18th-century brick-walled kitchen garden contains a 16th-century brick summerhouse with pyramidal roof – possibly the one seen in Drapentier's engraving. The southern compartment is open on one side to overlook a canal, with further canals beyond woodland. An 18th-century gardener's house is set into the north wall.

Pitchford Hall
Pitchford, Shropshire OS SJ5204
English Heritage Register Grade II

Splendidly picturesque Elizabethan black-and-white house built for Adam Otley. Its fame as a garden is wholly dependent on an exquisite treehouse which dates from the late 17th century and was recorded by 1714. Held aloft in the limbs of a lime tree, it has a mid 18th-century interior in ornate Gothick style, with a coved cornice of arches and ribbons and in the ceiling a sunburst with the mask of a woman's face at the centre. It is the only Grade I listed treehouse in the country.

Pitmedden Garden
see page 390

Pitshill and The Manor of Dean
Tillington, West Sussex OS SU9422
English Heritage Register Grade II

Two houses on the same estate. Pitshill, a 17th-century house on a fine elevated site, altered in the 18th century for William Mitford. The gardens date largely from the late 19th century, with lawns and trees (including some fine holm oaks) by the house. West of the house, among holm oaks and yews, is an early 19th-century circular shellhouse with coloured glass windows, said to have been created by the three Mitford sisters. The Manor of Dean also dates from the 17th century and has a series of courtyard gardens: a rose garden with a sundial (from Pitshill); a rectangular lawn with urns (also from Pitshill); and a rock garden. Grass Walks is a woodland garden planted in the mid to late 19th century with mature trees, flowering shrubs and bulbs.

Pittville Park
Cheltenham, Gloucestershire OS SO9524
English Heritage Register Grade II

Pittville was developed from the early 1820s by Joseph Pitt, a developer who by 1812 was making £20,000 (£525,200 today) a year. A pump room was built 1825–30 to the designs of John Forbes, who also laid out the park south of the Pump Room – planned as an integral part of the new estate of terraced houses and villas. In the park, lawns, a lake with its banks planted with trees and shrubs, and two bridges designed by Forbes. To the south, lawns, serpentine paths and an arboretum. To the west of the lake, playing fields and a pitch-and-putt golf course.

The Plantation Garden
see page 317

Plas Brondanw Gardens
see page 222

Plas Dinefwr
nr Llandeilo, Carmarthenshire OS SN6122
Cadw/ICOMOS Register Grade I

The old castle was built in the 12th century, high above a loop in the river Towy. A new house, called Newton, was built nearby in the 15th century and changed its name to Plas Dinefwr in 1782. Paintings by an unknown artist of c.1670, illustrated in John Harris's The Artist and the Country House (1979), depict both houses: the old castle, ruinous after the Civil War, rising on its wooded eminence; and the new house (rebuilt at about this time) overlooking ornate formal gardens with much topiary. In the 18th century, when the estate was owned by George Rice, a landscape park was made, almost entirely walled by 1774. Capability Brown visited Dinefwr in 1775 and submitted plans; it is not known precisely what the outcome was but clumps of beech (which are not native to Wales) survive exactly as shown in his plan and the walk to the old castle is still known as Brown's Walk. (Even this is uncertain – Brown was not alone in planting clumps, and the walk already existed in the 17th century, although he may have planted it up.) The park today has areas of woodland and specimens and clumps of parkland trees, with some 19th-century plantings of exotic conifers. Part of the park, a deer park by the 17th century, has a herd of white cattle.

Plas Newydd (Anglesey)
see page 223

Plas Newydd
Llangollen, Clwyd OS SJ2141
Cadw/ICOMOS Register Grade II*

Cottage made famous by the "ladies of Llangollen", Eleanor Butler and Sarah Ponsonby, who came to live here in 1780 to pursue a life of rustic and decorative simplicity. There was no garden here when they arrived and they proceeded to create a picturesque landscape strongly influenced by the romantic writings of their time. Winding walks led through a shrubbery and wooden boards attached to trees had suitably romantic quotations. A walk called the "Home Circuit" took in, in the manner of a ferme ornée, the shrubbery, dairy, fowl yard and drying green, and a Gothic arch led to enclosures of fruit, vegetables and flowers. The whole was adorned with rustic embellishments: a bower overlooking the valley, rustic bridges, a birdcote and seats. Only traces of this charming garden survive today.

Plas-yn-Rhiw
see page 224

The Pleasaunce
Overstrand, Norfolk
OS TG2440 English Heritage Register Grade II*

Two late 19th-century seaside villas converted by Edwin Lutyens 1897–99 for Cyril Flower, 1st Lord Battersea. Lutyens also designed the garden. To the north is a terrace with steps down to a lawn and sea views. At the west end, an open octagonal pavilion with steps down to a sunken rose garden. From the pavilion, a covered walk runs south, parallel to the house. Between walk and house, a paved pool garden, and lawn, shrubbery and mature trees to south. Paintings by Beatrice Parsons, showing the garden in its early 20th-century heyday, with spectacular borders, are illustrated in Penelope Hobhouse's and Christopher Wood's Painted Gardens: English Watercolours 1850–1914 (1988). The house is now a Christian Endeavour Holiday Home.

Plumpton Place
Plumpton, East Sussex OS TQ3613
English Heritage Register Grade II*

16th-century moated house with many alterations and remodelled from 1928 by Sir Edwin Lutyens for Edward Hudson, the founder of Country Life. Lutyens also designed the garden, with the help of Gertrude Jekyll, little of whose original planting survives. From the entrance in a gatehouse, an axial path runs across a garden flanked by the gatehouse wings and across the moat to the west forecourt of the house (the bridge is a 1986 replacement of the original). The forecourt is divided into two squares of grass with standard Portugal laurels and with shrubs and climbing plants against the wall of the house. North-east of the house, two pools are separated by grass banks; irises are planted about the moat and bulrushes on the banks of the pools. A path leads through down the east side of the pools, among ornamental trees underplanted with bulbs. West of the upper pond, a garden of shrub roses hedged in beech – all this added in 1993–94. West of it, an orchard and arbour for climbing plants. Gavin Stamp, in Edwin Lutyens: Country Houses (2001), calls Plumpton "a dream of loveliness in a beautiful garden".

Plumpton Rocks
Plumpton, nr Harrogate, North Yorkshire
OS SE3653 English Heritage Register Grade II* Open regularly Tel 01423 863950

Daniel Lascelles bought the estate in 1755, started to build a mansion designed by John Carr of York, changed his mind and bought the adjoining estate of Goldsborough Hall. But he nevertheless created an extraordinary landscape here, working around giant outcrops of stone, partly natural and partly the result of ancient quarrying. Lascelles started planting in 1755 – a bill from Mr Telford, a York nurseryman, for 2,000 trees came to £17 8s 2d (£1,434 today). He also built a dam, flanked by giant ball finials, and transformed a series of pools into a magnificent stretch of water, overlooked on its northern side by the most dramatic of the rocky outcrops. A

P

rocky boathouse was built, and throughout the park are curious caverns, natural or man-made. By 1798, when E. Hargrove's *The History of the Castle Town and Forest of Knaresborough* was published, Plumpton Rocks had become a notable tourist attraction. Hargrove wrote that it was "much resorted to during the summer months, on account of its beautiful pleasure ground, which for its singularity of situation and diversity of pleasing objects, has not its equal in Great Britain." It was painted by Turner in 1798 and survives today with some of its original planting, especially hollies, yews and pines.

Pluscarden Abbey
nr Elgin, Morayshire OS NJ1457 Scottish Inventory Open regularly Tel 01343 890257

Priory of the Valliscaulian Order, founded in 1230 and dissolved *c*.1586. In 1943 it was offered by the owner, Lord Colum Crichton-Stuart, to the Benedictine monks of Prinknash Abbey in Gloucestershire, who restored the buildings and founded a new community in 1948. Little of the old abbey buildings survives but the whole precinct, 10 acres/4 acres in area, is enclosed in a massive rubble wall – of which the Scottish Inventory says, "this could be the oldest garden in Scotland." In early monastic times herbs and vegetables were grown here and in 1540 a French gardener, Guillaume Lubias, cultivated the gardens and planted fruit trees. The monks today cultivate barley and potatoes in rotation, vegetables and fruit, and bee skeps are productively installed in the ancient boles in the walls. East of the abbey are some old trees – copper beech, cypress, lime, holm oak and two ancient yews.

Plympton House
Plympton, Devon OS SX5455
English Heritage Register Grade II

Early 18th-century house built for the Treby family. Walled gardens of the same date, one of which is dominated by a mount from whose summit are views of the village and the ruins of Plympton

Castle. Kitchen garden has recessed arcading for espaliered fruit trees. The house became a lunatic asylum in 1835 and is now St Peter's Convent, a care home.

Poles Park
Thundridge, Hertfordshire OS TL3516
English Heritage Register Grade II

House built in 1890s for Edmund Hanbury to the designs of Ernest George, replacing an earlier 19th-century house. South-east of the house, steps lead down a terrace bank to a sunken parterre, now a lawn. This was designed in the 1840s by Robert Glendinning, when it had an elaborate scalloped fountain pool at the centre of shaped beds radiating outwards and filled with bedding plants and standard roses. West of the house, an arboretum with specimen trees in informal lawns, an orchard, and a rose garden enclosed in yew hedges. The park is dominated by the A10 dual carriageway running across it, and a golf course to the north.

Polesden Lacey
see page 165

Pollok House
see page 390

Pontypool Park
Pontypool, Gwent OS SO2800
Cadw/ICOMOS Register Grade II*

The Hanbury family of ironmasters came to Pontypool *c*.1576. The first house on this site was built *c*.1694 by Major John Hanbury and was altered in the 18th and 19th centuries. Old formal gardens, with terraces, a bowling green and canal, were swept away when the park was brought up to the house by Capel Hanbury Leigh shortly after 1800. He dammed the Nant y Gollen stream to form two lakes, and in the 1850s an American garden was planted – a large arboretum with newly introduced trees from the American continent such as coastal redwoods (*Sequoia sempervirens*), monkey puzzles and Wellingtonias. A hermitage was built in the park in the 1830s, a rustic stone building with a conical roof and a splendid vaulted

interior of beautiful patterns of shells and minerals, and furnished with rustic chairs – an outstanding example of its kind. Since 1920 the grounds have become a public park with a bandstand, sports facilities and play area. The house is a school.

Pope's Garden
Richmond, London OS TQ1672 English Heritage Register Grade II

The remains of a grotto is the last surviving part of the garden made by the poet and garden theorist Alexander Pope from 1719. The garden was separated from the house on the river by the road from London to Hampton Court, and Pope built a tunnel underneath it, made to look like a grotto, with flanking rooms decorated with minerals, shells and stalactites, most of which have now been lost; Samuel Johnson wrote that Pope had "extracted an ornament from an inconvenience, and vanity provided a grotto where necessity enforced a passage." Pope's elegant and gentlemanly riverside villa, where he lived for twenty-five years, with its lawn running down to the water, is shown in a painting of *c*.1730, *The Thames at Twickenham*, by Peter Tillemans. The garden behind the house was, without being precisely symmetrical, strongly formal in character, with regular groves of trees, a shell temple, mounts, an orangery, a bowling green and an obelisk in memory of his mother. Walks were generally straight, but one or two followed a serpentine route. Pope influenced garden theory of his time, and his own garden, of essentially formal character, anticipated aspects of landscaping principles of the later part of the 18th century – for example, in his use of contrast between light and shade. Horace Walpole, referring to the memorial obelisk, noted that "the passing through the gloom from the grotto to the opening day, the retiring and again assembling shades, the dusky groves, the larger lawn, and the solemnity of the termination at the cypresses that lead up to his mother's tomb, are managed with exquisite judgement."

Port Eliot
St Germans, Cornwall OS SX3557
English Heritage Register Grade I

The Eliot family came here in 1553 and remain, now with the title Earl of St Germans. There was an Augustinian priory here; part of the 13th-century building survives in what is an early 19th-century house designed by Sir John Soane and built 1804–6. In the mid 18th century, Edward Eliot (later the 1st Lord Eliot) carried out some landscaping, draining an inlet from the river Tiddy and building an embankment to allow access to old parkland north of the house. A grotto and rockwork in Craggs Wood also dates from this time. Eliot also made a lake with, a little later, an ornamental dairy, possibly designed by Soane. Humphry Repton produced a Red Book for Port Eliot in 1792 and, acknowledging Lord Eliot's own landscaping activities, wrote in his slightly oleaginous way, "Like the conquered magician I break my wand in the presence of superior skill." Despite his broken wand, some of his suggestions for planting were accepted. G.S. Gilbert in his *Historical Survey of Cornwall* (1820) wrote: "The gardens are extremely fine. They produce in abundance all the vegetables which adorn the tables of the nobility. Among these are many rare fruits, the natives of milder climates, and which can only be raised in England by botanical knowledge and peculiar care. The lawns and glen which surround the mansion display a brilliant and never-failing verdure." In the 19th century there was much planting of shrubs, especially rhododendrons, and in the 20th century the 8th Earl of St Germans added summerhouses and temples and an enclosed formal garden north of the house. The present Earl had a maze laid out in 1975.

Port Lympne Gardens
see page 166

Portman Square
City of Westminster, London OS TQ2881
English Heritage Register Grade II

Portman Square was developed 1764–84 and the garden was laid

out by 1780. The original garden had been a formal 18th-century Wilderness and a Turkish kiosk (no longer extant) was placed in it in the early 19th century. The present layout is largely 19th-century, and 19th-century railings, removed for the war effort in World War II, were replaced in 1972. Path from the entrance winds across a central lawn, to the south of which is dense planting of shrubs and trees.

Portmeirion
see page 225

Portrack House
Holywood, Dumfriesshire OS NS9382
Open occasionally for SGS

18th-century house with 19th-century additions, latterly owned by the Keswick family. Its garden fame is due to the work of the late Maggie Keswick and her husband, Charles Jencks, who, since 1990, made the extraordinary "Garden of Cosmic Speculation" here. Maggie Keswick was a notable scholar of Chinese gardens; her book, *The Chinese Garden* (1978), is the best modern book on the subject. She was influenced in the making of the Portrack garden, where immense curved lakes were excavated and the spoil built up in beautifully striated turf terraces, by Chinese notions of geomancy and of *feng shui*. Charles Jencks is an author, designer and architectural theoretician whose book *The Language of Post-Modern Architecture* (1977) has been very influential. Their garden, with its esoteric symbolism and original landforms, owes little to any European tradition of garden making. Where in an 18th-century landscape garden the symbolic references would have been devoted to classical culture, at Portrack they refer to science: a model of the double helix in a herb garden; Lagrange's equations of mechanics forming the gable of a glasshouse; metal models of the universe mounted ornamentally as the caps of piers; and a wrought-iron gate formed of Soliton waves (pulses of energy). In his book *The Architecture of the Jumping Universe* (1997), Jencks wrote that "the universe…is much more creative, self-organizing and unpredictable than anyone had thought twenty years ago…the universe is, in fact, cosmogenic, meaning that it jumps all of the time to new levels of organization." To reflect this, the garden at Portrack will be an evolving landscape. In Britain, where almost all gardens (and much else) are of a traditional kind, this dazzling new impetus is wonderfully refreshing.

Pound Hill Garden
see page 104

Poundisford Park
Pitminster, Somerset OS ST2220
English heritage Register Grade II

Mid 16th-century house for William Hill, with alterations in the 17th and 18th centuries. The site is much more ancient, for it was part of the 13th-century deer park of the Bishops of Winchester who owned the Manor of Taunton. West of the house, brick summerhouse with a grand broken pediment, steeply pitched roof and dashing weather vane, built in Sir Roger Hill's time, in the first years of 18th century. 18th-century landscaped park.

Powderham Castle
nr Exeter, Devon OS SX9683
English Heritage Register Grade II*
Open regularly Tel 01626 890243

Large and complicated house of several periods, the home since the late 14th century of the Courtenay family (later Earls of Devon). Enlarged in the 16th century, much altered throughout the 18th century (James Wyatt, 1794–98), and again from 1837, with major works by Charles Fowler. It has a fine position, looking eastwards down the slopes to the estuary of the river Exe. A medieval deer park was landscaped in the 18th century, when there was much planting of trees, especially of splendid cork oaks and Lucombe oaks which are particularly associated with Devon gardens. A triangular belvedere of 1773 in a prominent position. Formal terraced gardens to the east of the castle contemporary with Charles Fowler's work, survive in a more modest form, with Irish yews, mixed borders, a sundial, and jaunty yew topiary of dolphins.

Powerscourt Gardens
see page 430

Powis Castle
see page 226

Pradhoe
Shropshire OS SJ3524
English Heritage Register Grade II

House built in 1785, incorporating an older building, for the Revd David Pritchard who never lived in the house. The estate was sold to the Kenyon family in 1803 and it remains in their hands. Grounds laid out by John Webb, and his landscaping largely survives: the park is known as the Lawn, a corruption of the Welsh *lawnt*; flower gardens close to the house; a rockery known as the Alps; a rose garden; and a conservatory. The remains of the Museum with knucklebone floor.

Preston Manor *and* Preston Park
Brighton, East Sussex OS TQ3006
English Heritage Register Grade II
Manor open regularly Tel 01273 292770

Preston Park is a public park, opened in 1884 and designed by James Shrives and Philip Lockwood on part of the Preston Manor estate. The medieval Preston Manor was altered in the 17th century and rebuilt in 1783, with later alterations. Formal gardens existed here by 1617 but the present layout is essentially early 20th-century. To the north and north-west of the manor, lawns, shrubberies and mature trees. A lawn to the south of the house, with steps to the west leading down to a walled garden with a rose garden, shrubbery, herbaceous border, laburnum tunnel and lawn. The park lies to the south, with playing fields at the centre overlooked by a clock tower (1882) on a ridge to the east. At the extreme west of the park, on the other side of Preston Road, a large rockery with cascades and a pool, trees, shrubs and rock plants. At the southern end, bowling greens with two pavilions and tennis courts. Shrubberies about the pavilions and a dahlia walk between the tennis courts. To the south, the Rotunda café and a garden of modern roses.

Prestonfield House
Newington, Edinburgh OS NT2772
Scottish Inventory

House built in 1689, possibly to the designs of Sir William Bruce, for Sir James Dick, Lord Provost of Edinburgh, whose previous house had been destroyed by fire in an anti-Catholic riot by students in 1681 (Sir James was in fact an Episcopalian). In 1748 the estate was inherited by Sir Alexander Dick, President of the Royal College of Physicians and friendly with many of the great Edinburgh figures of the day. He was also a keen gardener, planting many trees and laying out grassed walks planted with crocuses, daffodils and snowdrops. In 1774 he was awarded a Gold Medal from the Royal Society of Arts for the cultivation of a cultivar of rhubarb (reputedly from the Great Wall of China) for medicinal purposes. He cultivated tender fruit, and Lord Cockburn's *Memorials of our Time* (1856) records: "Between the loch and the house was a sort of Dutch garden admirably kept. Beside the bowling green, it had several long smooth lanes of turf, anciently called bowling alleys, parterres and lawn interspersed, fountains, carved stone seats, dials, statues and trimmed evergreen hedges. How we used to make the fountains spout!…A very curious place." The Dutch garden was removed in the first half of the 19th century but some of its ornaments, all dated 1687, survive: stone benches, a Bacchus fountain and a sphinx. There is now a golf course in the park and Duddingston Loch, formerly part of the estate, has been a bird sanctuary since 1928. The house has been a hotel for over forty years.

Prestonhall
nr Dalkeith, Midlothian OS NT3966 Scottish Inventory Open occasionally for SGS

House built 1791on the site of an earlier house to the designs of Robert Mitchell for Alexander Callander. 18th-century parkland, with many trees planted in the early 19th century including an avenue of limes which survives – as do good specimens of cedar, sweet chestnut and sycamore. Large numbers of bulbs – aconites,

crocuses, narcissi and scillas – naturalised in recent times. Wild garden on the banks of the river Tyne established in the late 19th century by Cecilia Burn-Callander, a noted plantswoman, with azaleas, conifers and rhododendrons from Sikkim. The estate is still owned by the Callander family and much new planting has been done recently.

Prestwold Hall
Prestwold, Leicestershire OS SK5721
English Heritage Register Grade II

Estate owned from *c.*1653 by the Packe family. 17th-century house with many alterations, especially from 1842 when it was comprehensively remodelled by William Burn. Formal gardens south of the house by Burn, with balustraded terraces, lawns, pools and beds. West of the house, woodland with laurels and rhododendrons. East of the house, a row of cedars, already in 1780 said to be of "notable size", and further east, a woodland garden. Parkland surrounds the house, probably laid out in the 1760s when the house was being rebuilt. J. Nichols's *History and Antiquities of Leicester* (1795–1811) described the house shortly after this time, "boosomed in calm serenity". Today the southern part of the park is largely farmland, with shelter belts to the south. North of the house, pasture and such parkland trees as beech and horse chestnut.

Prideaux Place
Padstow, Cornwall OS SW9175
English Heritage Register Grade II
Open regularly Tel 01841 532411

The Prideaux family came here in the 16th century and still live here. Carew's *The Survey of Cornwall* (1602) describes "a new and stately house" but the present house is largely the result of remodelling in the 18th century, with further alterations in the 19th century. The position, high up above the town of Padstow, with views of the Camel estuary and the moors beyond, is lovely. There had been a garden here in the 16th century, to the east of the house, and traces of its walls may still be seen; it became part of a

deer park in the 18th century, which remains in place to this day. Edmund Prideaux made many alterations to the garden after he inherited it in 1728. Leaving some of the 16th-century terracing (which survives), he added a pillared temple in 1739 (which also survives) and an obelisk (which has gone). Also surviving is a stone seat (1740) on the terrace, decorated with Roman architectural fragments which Prideaux brought back from Italy. In the 19th century further features were added: a dairy turned into a grotto, a shellhouse along the Green Walk in the woodland, and a sunken garden of late Victorian character which was restored in 1992.

Primrose Hill
Lucan, County Dublin, Republic of Ireland
Open regularly Tel (00353) 1 628 0373

Elegant Regency villa, possibly designed by James Gandon. Late 20th-century garden made since 1950 by Mrs Cicely Hall and her son, Robin, with a rare collection of fastidiously chosen plants which range from cottage garden delights such as the double-flowered buttercup (*Ranunculus acris* 'Flore Pleno') to real aristocrats like *Paeonia rockii*. An outstanding collection of snowdrop cultivars is of special interest among a spectacular spring display of crocuses, cyclamen, erythroniums and hellebores. Throughout the year there is something of distinction to be seen, and since plants are more important than convenience, the paths are described as "too narrow for perambulators".

Primrose Hill
City of Westminster, London OS TQ2882
English Heritage Register Grade II
Open regularly

Primrose Hill is a north-westerly extension of Regent's Park and both formed part of the land appropriated as a great royal chase by Henry VIII. Primrose Hill later became the property of Eton College, from which it was bought in 1841 as a public amenity. It is a high, undulating site 206ft/63m above sea level, with superlative views over

P

London. especially to the south-east and south. A network of paths covers the open grassland of the hill, and below the summit, which is kept open to preserve the views (and for flying kites), are many specimen trees and clumps. A wildflower meadow has recently been laid out and primroses (of course) re-established; the area had apparently taken its name from the prolific quantities of these flowers in the 16th century. There are many games facilities, among them an outdoor gymnasium and multi-purpose sports pitch. The view from the top of the hill over the largely mediocre and anonymous architecture of the City to the south-east is deeply upsetting.

Prince of Wales Park

Bingley, West Yorkshire OS SE1140
English Heritage Register Grade II
Open regularly

Public park opened to the public in 1865. The management committee established in 1869 that "drinking, gambling, and Sunday games, together with the public discussion of politics and religion were not to be allowed." The park is enclosed in woodland, with open heathland in the north-east part of it. In the south-west corner, a drinking fountain presented in 1866 by the Total Abstainers of Bingley. A circuit path runs about the park and there are many good mature trees; 15,000 were planted when the park was opened, among them fifty sent by the Prince of Wales from Sandringham.

Prince's Park

Liverpool, Merseyside OS SJ3688
English Heritage Register Grade II
Open regularly

Park designed by Sir Joseph Paxton in 1842 in association with a housing development, also designed by Paxton. The park was planned for the private use of residents but was taken over by the Liverpool Corporation in 1918. South-east of the main entrance, an obelisk memorial (1885) to Richard Vaughan Yates, the owner of the land. Irregular lake with island curved into the

north-east corner of the park. Most of the park is open grassland with groups of trees and specimens. Bowling greens and tennis courts to the west.

Prior Park Landscape Garden

see page 58

Priorwood Garden

Melrose, Roxburghshire OS HT5434
Scottish Inventory Open regularly (NTS)
Tel 01896 822493

The garden is immediately adjacent to the grounds of Melrose abbey. Its walls date from the 18th century and in one corner is an early 19th-century gardener's cottage. The present garden was started in 1976 with financial help from Bettina, Lady Thomson. A hedge of rugosa roses divides the space into an orchard and a garden of flowers for drying ("everlasting flowers"). A collection of apple cultivars shows the evolution of the fruit from those introduced by the Romans to those of the 20th century – a fascinating sight. A hut used for drying the flowers is open to the public. The garden now grows around 200 varieties of flowers of different types suitable for drying, and is the only one in Britain devoted to the subject – an unusual and charming place.

The Priory Gardens (Gloucestershire)

see page 227

Priory Gardens

Orpington, London OS TQ4666 English
Heritage Register Grade II Open regularly

13th-century monastic estate. The present house has parts dating from that time but is largely of the 15th and 17th centuries. In 1919 it was bought by Cecil Hughes who made an Arts and Crafts inspired parterre garden with herbaceous perennials. Sir Geoffrey Jellicoe, a family friend, designed a new Theatre garden c.1927, with a raised grass platform and stone steps as seats, a "box office" enclosed in yew hedges, and a rose garden and pergola. Since 1962 the gardens have been a public park, with a public library and museum.

Promenade Gardens

Lytham St Anne's, Lancashire OS SD3228
English Heritage Register Grade II
Open regularly

Municipal seaside promenade made in the late 19th and early 20th century. The promenade faces south-west over a miniature golf course and a boating lake to the sea and St Anne's pier beyond. It is enlivened with a sequence of buildings and monuments – among them a cast-iron bandstand (c.1900), a statue of a lifeboatman (c.1890 by W.B. Rhind) and an octagonal pavilion (c.1900). Planting includes banks with shrubs, and lawns with beds for seasonal bedding.

Purbeck House

Swanage, Dorset OS SZ0378

Purbeck House was built in about 1875 by the builder George Burt, a partner in the firm of John Mowlem & Co. Burt recycled building materials to make his house and embellished the garden with architectural fragments and statuary, almost all of which come from London sites on which he had worked; they were brought by sea as ballast after delivering stone from the Purbeck quarries. The house – rising prominently in Swanage High Street – became a convent after Burt's death and, more recently, was converted into a hotel. The garden preserves many of the features that Burt introduced – the rusticated stone arch (1844) which had been an entrance to Green Park; three 17th-century stone statues from the Royal Exchange (destroyed by fire, for a second time, in 1838); and iron columns from old Billingsgate Market (rebuilt in 1874). Also surviving is a "Chinese" pavilion with very occidental Doric stone columns, floored with Pugin and Barry tiles from the Houses of Parliament, removed in 1880 when Mowlem carried out renovations. At the far end of the garden is a circular stone summerhouse with a stone tiled roof on top of a grass mount. Fine old Irish yews survive, as does a magnificent old weeping ash whose sprawling limbs are supported by rustic stone columns. Although much has

gone, and the garden has a disheveled air, it still has great character. Burt also made Durlston Park (see page 471)

Purley Hall

Purley, Berkshire OS SU6475
English Heritage Register Grade II*

House built in early 17th century for Francis Hyde with many subsequent alterations. Under the ownership of Francis Hawes, Charles Bridgeman was commissioned to lay out a garden c.1720. Hawes lost money in the South Sea Bubble and only part of the scheme was carried out; what was, only partly survives. West of the house and aligned with it, a canal surrounded by a terraced lawn. The westerly axis has as an eyecatcher in a shrubbery: a flint Rustic Seat, pedimented and rusticated, dated 1746. South of the house, a lawn and terracing surrounded by mature trees, including some 18th-century limes.

Pusey House

Pusey, Oxfordshire OS SU3596
English Heritage Register Grade II

Puseys lived here from the 13th century; John Allen Pusey built the present house1746–48. 18th-century landscaping includes a serpentine lake south of the house, with a Chinoiserie bridge (a mid 18th-century design). Mid 18th century stone bridge over stream to the west, and Mrs Brotherton's Temple (c.1759). South of the house, a terrace designed by Geoffrey Jellicoe after 1935 for Mr and Mrs Michael Hornby. The Hornbys did much excellent planting throughout the garden and around the lake, and made grand borders in the walled kitchen garden. In the 1960s and 1970s the garden, regularly open to the public, was widely admired. The estate has since changed hands twice and there have been many changes in the grounds.

Putney Vale Cemetery

Wandsworth, London OS TQ2272 English
Heritage Register Grade II Open regularly

Cemetery laid out by J.C. Radford and opened in 1891. Designed on

a grid plan, with later extensions following a radial layout. Mixed conifers and deciduous trees. Garden of Remembrance of 1935–8 by the Kingston Road entrance; originally a rose garden, now with bedding schemes enclosed in box hedges and a lavender walk.

Putteridge Bury, also known as Putteridge Park

Offley, Hertfordshire OS TL1124
English Heritage Register Grade II*

Early 19th-century house, rebuilt in early 20th century for Thomas Clutterbuck. Garden by Edwin Lutyens and Gertrude Jekyll to south, east and south-west of house, incorporating older pattern of paths. Pond lawn with rectangular reflecting pool and yew hedges. A lawn leads south between yew hedges to a circular lawn. To the east, rose garden with symmetrical pattern of shaped rose beds edged in *Stachys byzantina* and divided by patterns of lavender. The roses were originally carefully colour selected; magenta and pink plants were never adjacent to yellow or salmon. The rose garden was restored in the 1990s.

Pylewell Park

nr Lymington, Hampshire OS SZ3595
English Heritage Register Grade II*
Open occasionally for NGS

Early 18th-century house on an older site, with later alterations. There were formal gardens here in the 17th century when Sir James Worsley lived here. Formal gardens close to the house today are 20th-century with lawns, a parterre of roses with Chinese urns, and a balustraded terraced lawn overlooking parkland. Excellent woodland garden with the Broad Walk leading through and mown paths winding between trees and shrubs of many varieties. Lake with Japanese bridge, beyond which is a large collection of rhododendrons dating back to the early 20th century. Former kitchen garden now planted with ornamentals, in particular camellias, including tender species against the wall.

Pyrford Court

Pyrford, Surrey OS TQ0358
English Heritage Register Grade II

House built from c.1907 for Lord Iveagh to the designs of Clyde Young. South-facing orangeries flank the house which has a balustraded terrace. A large lawn is edged with trees and flowering shrubs – cherries, lilacs and magnolias. Brick walls enclose the lawn on two sides, with a wisteria-clad loggia against the north wall and a pergola to the south and east. An enclosed paved garden has a lily pool, fountains, topiary and borders of peonies. There is a rose garden, kitchen garden and rock garden in pine woods.

Quarry Park *and* Dingle Gardens

Shrewsbury, Shropshire OS SO4812 English Heritage Register Grade II Open regularly

19th-century public park built from 1877 on the banks of the river Severn, with a bandstand, summerhouse and obelisk. At the heart of the park is the Dingle, a quarry now planted with trees and shrubs, with a rock garden and alpine plants and superb bedding schemes. The whole is enlivened by several monuments – a Gothic entrance, a statue of Sabrina in a grotto, and the gateway of the Shoemaker's Arbour, "originally erected on Kingsland in 1679 and removed to the present site in 1877"; it is ornamented with figures of Crispin and Crispian, the patron saints of shoemakers.

Queens' College

Cambridge, Cambridgeshire OS TL4458 English Heritage Register Grade II Open regularly Tel 01223 335511

College founded in 1446, re-founded in 1448 by Henry VI's queen, Margaret of Anjou ("to laude and honneure of sexe feminine"), and again in 1465 by Edward IV's queen, Elizabeth Woodville (hence Queens' rather than Queen's). Beautiful buildings of the 15th-century survive, including Old Court in which there is a splendid sundial of 1642. The college accounts contain an item: "For stone and worke about chappell diall £1. 14s. 0d"). The college overlooks the Cam and is intimately connected to it. Erasmus was Professor of Divinity and a fellow of Queens' 1511–14 and relished the river view; part of the west bank is today known as Erasmus's Walk. Celia Fiennes visited in 1697 but made no comment on gardens: "Queens' College is old but a stately and lofty building." The Fellows' Garden on the west bank of the river was lost when the new Cripps Court was built in 1975; only an ancient mulberry survives. The wooded Grove, with spring bulbs, is also on this side of the river. A new Fellows' Garden has been made on the east bank.

Queen's Park

Blackburn, Lancashire OS SD6927 English Heritage Register Grade II Open regularly

Public park designed by J.B. MaCallum and opened in 1887. At the heart of the park is an irregular lake in two parts, separated by a channel. Ornamental boathouse at south-east end of lake, built 1888–92 and on the northern bank a brick shelter. Curving paths link different areas south of the lake, passing through groves of trees. North of the lake, bowling greens planted about with shrubs and trees, and tennis courts. The amphitheatre garden (early 20th century) is enclosed in golden privet but the bandstand that stood at its centre has gone. Water tumbles over rocks and formerly flowed into pools before the amphitheatre garden was built.

Queen's Park

Bolton, Greater Manchester OS SD7009 English Heritage Register Grade II Open regularly

Public park designed by William Henderson and opened in 1866. The park is laid out with the chief formal ingredients at the centre and less formal areas of grass, water and woodland about the perimeter. A terraced walk is backed with beds and a shrubbery. Within the beds, three statues on tall plinths of Benjamin Disraeli, James Dorrian and J.T. Fielding. A walk leads southwards to a circular flower bed. To the west, winding walks among trees and a lake with the remains of a cascade. In the eastern park, tennis courts and a bowling green.

Queen's Park

Brighton, East Sussex OS TQ3303 English Heritage Register Grade II Open regularly

Park originally laid out for private housing but since 1892 a public park, designed by George Ward and Francis May. A stream with cascades flows down the middle of the park to a serpentine lake. To the west, a café, terrace and children's play area. North of the lake, a drinking fountain of 1893. To the east of the park, bowling green and tennis courts. At the southern end of the park, the façade of the 1830 Royal Spa, "an elegant Pump Room intended for the supply of the celebrated Mineral Waters of Germany", now part of a nursery school.

Queen's Park

Chesterfield, Derbyshire OS SK3770 English Heritage Register Grade II Open regularly

Public park designed by William Barron & Sons, opened to the public in 1893. The park is divided into three roughly circular areas, each with a perimeter walk. To the south-east, a cricket ground. To the north, an irregular lake with islands. To the south-west, a bandstand, a conservatory moved here from Chatsworth (*see page 255*) c.1920, and a sports centre. The cricket ground is partly enclosed by plantings of mature trees and has an ornamental 19th-century pavilion with a cupola. The islands in the lake are planted with trees and a miniature railway runs round it, passing between trees and shrubs. Much ornamental planting in the south-west: rose beds about the bandstand, a formal rose garden north of the sports centre behind a hedge of conifers, beds for seasonal planting schemes and a serpentine herbaceous border.

Queen's Park

Crewe, Cheshire OS SJ6855 English Heritage Register Grade II Open regularly

Public park designed by Edward Kemp and F.W. Webb, opened in 1887 to celebrate Queen Victoria's diamond jubilee. The park is a perfect oval, with a belt of trees and shrubs about the perimeter and an axial walk crossing it from east to west. The entrance from the north leads down Central Avenue, flanked with many flower beds, rows of silver birches, sycamores and clipped yews, to a Boer War memorial at the centre of the park. At the west end of the axial walk, a bandstand with a copper cupola. To the south, a lake crossed by a bridge. In the north-west corner, a shallow valley planted with trees and shrubs, and an aviary. A scented garden and Gulf War memorial nearby. In the north-east, various games facilities: a bowling green, crazy golf and a children's playground.

Queen's Park

Hendham Hall, Greater Manchester OS SD8500 English Heritage Register Grade II Open regularly

Public park designed by Joshua Major and opened in 1846. At the centre of the park is the Museum and Art Gallery, from which a network of winding walks opens out. East of the museum, formal gardens with a rose garden. Many ornaments in this area have been lost. West of the museum, land slopes steeply down with open lawns and specimen trees. To the north of the park, an arboretum laid out in 1973.

Queen's Park

Heywood, Greater Manchester OS SD8511 English Heritage Register Grade II Open regularly

Public park laid out by Major Cartwright and opened in 1879. The chief axis of the park runs north and south with, at its centre, a late 19th-century pool, now filled in and planted with roses. South-west of it, a sunken garden with flower beds and a late 19th-century statue of Bacchus. To its south, a polychrome brick and tile refreshment room. Open grassland with specimen trees to the south-west. In the north-western corner, various recreational facilities: an aviary, bowling green, pet area and tennis courts. An obelisk (1920s) in the north-east corner commemorates Albert Lee who drowned in the river Roch, which flows past the park boundary at this point, while trying to rescue a friend. A mid 20th-century open air theatre overlooks an open area. In the south-eastern park, a large boating lake and an artificial mound which had a series of rockeries and grottoes.

Queen's Park

Longton, Staffordshire OS SJ9042 English Heritage Register Grade II Open regularly

Public park opened in 1888, the first public pleasure ground in the potteries. It was laid out by John H. Garrett, land agent to the Duke of Sutherland, who had given the land. In the western part of the park, a network of curving tree-lined carriage drives and paths between shrubberies and lawns with bedding schemes. Close to the centre of this part of the park, a cast-iron octagonal bandstand made by Dean & Lowe. To the west, two lakes with islands, and to the east, an elaborate clock tower. The eastern park is more open, with a central drive lined with common and copper beech. Among recreational facilities are bowling greens, a children's playground and tennis courts. When the park opened it was managed by a uniformed superintendent, who lived in the half-timbered lodge at the entrance, an assistant and six labourers. The area of the park is 45 acres/18 hectares.

Quenby Hall

nr Hungarton, Leicestershire OS SK7006 English Heritage Register Grade II Open regularly Tel 0116 2595224

The Ashby family came to Quenby in the 13th century and remained here until 1904. The present house was built from c.1620 for George Ashby. In the early 20th century Harold Peto was consulted about the garden but little is known about his work here. A sunken garden survives from this period and the 18th-century walled kitchen garden has been converted into a flower garden with box-edged beds. The park dates from the late 17th or early 18th century, now pasture with mature scattered trees. An avenue linking house and church survives from the original laying out of the park.

Q

Quendon Hall

Quendon, Essex OS TL5131
English Heritage Register Grade II

House started in 16th century for
Thomas Newman, remodelled in
late 17th century and with later
alterations. Forecourt walls and
gate piers, farm buildings and
dovecote are all of the 17th
century. Remains of a late 17th-
century formal garden – a moat,
or canal, to east of house and a
long lime avenue north of the
house aligned on Newport
church. Another avenue,
continuing the axis, south
of the house.

Raby Castle

Raby with Keverstone, County Durham OS
NZ1221 English Heritage Register Grade II*
Open regularly Tel 01833 660207

14th-century castle altered in the
17th, 18th and 19th centuries but
retaining a splendid medieval
character. The castle stands at the
centre of its park, with two lakes to
its south connected by a cascade –
possibly the work of Thomas
Wright in the 1740s. Many trees
planted 1727–46 and the park wall
was built at that time. West of the
castle, the Terrace Walk leads to the
Temple, a Gothick pavilion of mid
to late 18th century, probably by
Daniel Garrett, commanding views
of lake, park and castle. Outside the
park, on elevated land to the
north-west, is James Paine's
Gothick Home Farm, with great
presence in the landscape. West of
the lake, on the north side of Bath
Wood, the Bath House of 1752 by
Sir Thomas Robinson, and a rustic
18th-century cottage. In the
north-west corner of the park, an
eyecatcher by John Carr of York,
built in 1780 – an archway flanked
with towers and with a Gothic
window above. Thomas White
produced a design for the park in
1771 and was paid £1,400
(£83,664 today). His plan, which
included new serpentine lakes, was
only partly executed. Kitchen
garden north of the castle, largely
20th-century garden but
incorporating earlier features
including a central pool and yew
hedges. There are now geometric
beds, 18th-century urns, lawns,
borders and glasshouses (including
a 19th-century fig house).

Radway Grange

Radway, Warwickshire OS SP3647
English Heritage Register Grade II*

Elizabethan house Gothicised
c.1745 by Sanderson Miller whose
father (also Sanderson Miller) had
bought the estate in 1712. 18th-
century landscaped park with
scattered trees and buildings by the
younger Sanderson Miller. In its
southern corner, Edgehill Tower of
c.1746 (also known as the Castle),
a Gothic crenellated tower and
gateway. Nearby is the Cottage of
1744, Gothic and asymmetrical. In
the garden, a statue of Caractacus
in chains, made for the Edgehill
Tower but found to be too large
for its niche. Gardens from c.1925
by house, with lawns, herbaceous
borders, an enclosed rose garden
and a yew topiary garden.

Raglan Castle

Raglan, Gwent OS SO4108
Cadw/ICOMOS Register Grade I
Open regularly (Cadw) Tel 01291 690228

The present castle was given its
appearance in the early 15th
century by Sir William Ap Thomas
whose granddaughter, Elizabeth,
married Sir Charles Somerset
(later 1st Earl of Worcester; the
family later became Marquesses of
Worcester and Dukes of Beaufort)
in 1492. The 3rd Earl, a cultivated
courtier, inherited in 1549 and
made a new garden, laying out a
series of giant terraces on two
sides of the castle, with a lake, the
"greate Poole" at the foot of the
north-western terraces. The poet
Thomas Churchyard described it
in The Worthines of Wales (1587):
"The curious knots, wrought all
with edged toole,/The stately
Tower, that looks ore Pond and
Poole:/the fountain trim, that runs
both day and night,/Doth yield in
show a rare and noble sight". The
4th Earl inherited in 1589 and
added to the garden – a moat
walk (with fifteen brick and
shellwork niches containing busts
of Roman emperors) and a water
parterre at the head of the lake.
The Earl, who later lived at
Nonsuch (see page 517), was in
touch with the latest garden ideas.
Today the terraces are plainly
visible, the moat walk with its
niches remain (without Roman
emperors) and the outline of the
water parterre is visible. In the
Civil War the castle was taken by
Commonwealth troops. The
Somersets moved to Badminton in
Gloucestershire (see page 441) in
the 1670s, and never lived at
Raglan again, but the estate still
belongs to the family, although it
is in the care of Cadw.

Ragley Hall

Alcester, Warwickshire OS SP0755
English Heritage Register II*
Open regularly Tel 01789 762090

House built 1680–c.1690 for the
1st Earl of Conway to the designs
of Robert Hooke; interior
completed by James Gibbs in the
1750s. A Kip engraving in
Britannia Illustrata (1707) shows a
magnificent formal garden
symmetrically disposed about the
house, with avenues radiating
across the land. Shortly before
1758, Capability Brown
landscaped the grounds for the 1st
Marquess of Hertford. Horace
Walpole wrote to George
Montague in 1758, "Browne has
improved both the grounds and
the water though not quite to
perfection." The 18th-century
parkland is largely intact; the lake,
south of the house, is thought to
date from the 17th century but
was enlarged by Brown. In 1874
formal gardens were made west of
the house, with two parterres and
a circle of formal bedding
500ft/150m in diameter. Hedges
enclose the outer half of this circle
which forms a curved terrace
overlooking the park.

Rainthorpe Hall

nr Tasburgh, Norfolk OS TM2097
English Heritage Register Grade II
Open occasionally for NGS and by
appointment Tel 01508 470618

16th-century house, with
alterations in the 19th century.
Gardens south of the house, with
17th-century wall to north and
east and a knot garden of box
below the south-east façade of the
house. A lawn runs down to the
river Tas and another is enclosed
by yew hedges and a ha-ha. South
of the house, a rectangular lily
pool, probably originally a
fishpond. A hazel nuttery beyond,
and several mature trees in the
grounds.

Ramsbury Manor

Ramsbury, Wiltshire OS SU2570
English Heritage Register Grade II

House replacing an earlier
building, built c.1681–83 for Sir
William Jones, almost certainly to
the designs of Robert Hooke. Park
probably developed c.1775, with
an arm of the river Kennet
widened to form a lake which is
crossed by an 18th-century bridge
east of the house. Open parkland
with scattered mature trees and
some woodland, with belts of trees
on most boundaries. An orangery
of 1770, probably designed by
Robert Mitchell, south-east of the
house. Late 17th-century walled
kitchen garden. 18th-century bath
house by pool nearby.

Ranelagh Gardens

Kensington and Chelsea, London OS
TQ2878 English Heritage Register Grade II

In the grounds of Ranelagh
House, immediately east of the
Royal Hospital at Chelsea,
Richard Jones, 1st Earl of
Ranelagh, laid out public pleasure
gardens in the 1690s. Its
centrepiece was a Rotunda,
150ft/45m in diameter, in which
music was played and food and
drink could be consumed. There is
a delightful painting by Canaletto
of the Rotunda in the National
Gallery, London. The gardens had
a canal, pool, lime avenue, Chinese
bridge and temples. Edward
Gibbon considered Ranelagh
Gardens "the most convenient
place for courtship of every kind –
the best market we have in
England." It was closed in 1803,
the house and Rotunda
demolished shortly afterwards, and
the grounds added to those of the
Royal Hospital. Today, the old
Ranelagh gardens (as visitors to
the Chelsea Flower Show may
discover) are more mysterious:
jungly and intimate, with paths
meandering through dense
plantings of shrubs and mature
trees.

Raveningham Hall

Raveningham, Norfolk OS TM3996
English Heritage Register Grade II*
Open occasionally for NGS

House built in the late 18th
century for Sir Edmund Bacon.

Largely 20th-century gardens,
with a notable herbaceous borde
running along the outside south-
facing wall of the kitchen garden
Borders on each side of a terrace
against the south façade of the
house. To the east, shrub roses an
yew hedges with a shrubbery
beyond. Fine mature trees. A lim
avenue runs south from the hou
across a lawn and 18th-century
parkland.

Raynham Hall

nr Fakenham, Norfolk OS TF8825
English Heritage Register Grade II

Beautiful house on an older sit
built for Sir Roger Townshend
from 1619 in collaboration wit
the master mason William Edge
There were formal gardens her
by 1661 and drawings of c.172
by Edmund Prideaux, show law
and walks east of the house, a
formal layout to the west, a
topiary walk to the river
Wensum, and a lake (the lake
been dug in 1724–26). This lay
largely survives, with an avenu
instead of the topiary walk. By
1667 a park of 800 acres/324
hectares was enclosed and had
500 deer.

Rayne Thatch

Long Ashton, Bristol OS ST5573
English Heritage Register Grade II

The house at Rayne Thatch,
in 1907, was originally the es
office for the Wills family esta
at Bracken Hill nearby.
Extraordinary rock and water
gardens were laid out 1908–1
James Pulham, who also mad
rock gardens next door at
Bracken Hill. One of the roc
Rayne Thatch bears the
inscription "FH 1910" – Fre
Hitchins was Pulham's forem
The garden runs along the
contour of a steep north-faci
slope, well wooded with ash,
cherries, hollies, oaks and pin
There are several linked poo
Gothic pump house, a grotto
sitting places and cascades. T
occasional Japanese maple gi
an oriental air. In its heyday
garden was illuminated by
coloured electric bulbs suspe
from the trees.

Red House

Bexley, Greater London OS TQ5074
Open regularly (NT) Tel 01892 890651

House built for William Morris in 1859 to the designs of Philip Webb. Herman Muthesius described it as "the first private house of the new artistic culture, the first house to be conceived as a whole inside and out". The house was built in an old orchard and the garden was conceived at the same time as the house. Philip Webb marked existing orchard trees on his plans; according to *The Gardens of William Morris* (Jill Duchess of Hamilton, Penny Hart and John Simmons (1998)) "so close were some trees to the house that, it is said, ripe apples would occasionally bounce through the open windows on warm autumn evenings." J.W. Mackail, in his *The Life of William Morris* (1899), wrote: "Red House garden, with its long walks, its mid-summer lilies and autumn sunflowers, its wattle rose-trellises enclosing richly-flowered square garden plots, was then as unique as the house it surrounded." In 2003, when the National Trust bought the estate, its head curator, Tim Knox, said "The key to success will be to make the four-acre garden into the pre-eminent Pre-Raphaelite garden, filled with plants Morris used for his textile design."

Redleaf

nr Penshurst, Kent OS TQ5245
English Heritage Register Grade II

Grounds laid out from *c.*1800 by Mr Wells and admired by J.C. Loudon. The house was demolished in the mid 20th century and several houses built on the land. Rocky Lawn has exposed rocks in turf, which are sometimes used to edge raised beds, with rustic steps or paved paths between them. To the east, the Fernery, a sloping bank with large stones. The Dutch garden was enclosed in a screen of American shrubs and is laid out with a pattern of diamond-shaped beds divided by brick paths, now overlooked by a new house, The Orangery; originally there was a thatched conservatory here. To the west of the site of the original

house, a park in a valley with the river Eden forming its western boundary. In the northern part of the park, a dramatic outcrop of red sandstone. Wells created a circuit walk about the estate, with rustic seats and resting places; two rustic huts survive.

Redlynch Park

nr Bruton, Somerset OS ST7033
English Heritage Register Grade II

House of 1670 for Sir Stephen Fox, much altered in 1740s. Handsome orangery of *c.*1670 in walled garden. The traveller Dr Richard Pococke wrote in 1754: "the ground of the park is very fine, and there is a large piece of water before the house." New wing by Edwin Lutyens in 1901, burnt down in a suffragette demonstration in 1914 and rebuilt. East of house, terrace, steps and summerhouse by Lutyens. Terraced walks overlook parkland, to the south, with scattered trees.

Regent's Park

see page 167

Reigate Priory

Reigate, Surrey OS TQ2549
English Heritage Register Grade II

Priory founded 1235, converted into a house 1541, largely rebuilt in the 1770s, with later alterations. Formal walled gardens overlooking park to south and west. Hedged enclosure with central pool. Wooded pleasure grounds north and east of house, with Monks' Walk between borders. Garden wall probably of 18th century. South of the house, a small open park with some woodland, probably enclosed in 16th century or earlier. Grounds are now a school and playing fields.

Renishaw Hall

see page 274

Revesby Abbey

Revesby, Lincolnshire OS TF3162
English Heritage Register Grade II

House designed in 1844 by William Burn for James Banks Stanhope. An earlier house here, destroyed by fire, had been the home of the botanist and explorer

Sir Joseph Banks until his death in 1820. There had been a deer park in the middle ages and there are signs of 18th-century landscaping. Remains of formal gardens close to the house. A collection of 18th-century German statues were formerly displayed in the garden but these have now gone.

Rhinefield, *also known as* Rhinefield Lodge

Brockenhurst, Hampshire OS SU2603
English Heritage Register Grade II

Neo-Elizabethan house (with a "Moorish smoking room" copied from a room at the Alhambra) built 1888–90, on a much older site, for Lionel Walker Munro to the designs of W.H. Romaine-Walker and A.W. Tanner, who also laid out formal gardens. On the axis of the window of the Great Hall a long canal, flanked by a series of parterres, leads to a grille and wrought-iron gates which give onto the New Forest. Nearby is a turf amphitheatre, made in the 1980s when there was much restoration of the garden with advice from the Hampshire Gardens Trust. To the east of it, a series of grass terraces. In 1859 an arboretum, rich in North American conifers, was laid out by John E. Nelson, enclosing the house and garden and creating a splendid backdrop for them. Rhinefield is now a hotel and conference centre.

Ribston Hall

Little Ribston, North Yorkshire OS SE3953
English Heritage Register Grade II

House built on an old site in 1674 for Sir Henry Goodricke and remodelled in the 18th century, probably by John Carr of York. The Kip engraving in *Britannia Illustrata* (1707) shows the garden that must have been made for the new house: house and garden are enclosed in rampart-like walls with bastions and stand on banked up ground; the garden is divided into many enclosures with topiary, fruit-trees pleached against a wall, parterres and pavilions, and the river Nidd looping round to one side. A west-facing terrace with views over the river is one of the few traces of this to survive. In the 19th century a pinetum was

planted near the 18th-century kitchen garden where, in the 18th century, the Ribston Pippin apple was raised; the original tree was still here when *Herefordshire Pomona* was published 1880, and was said to have been raised from seed brought from Normandy in 1709. A Gothic pavilion of the same date as the pinetum stands north-west of the house.

Richings Park, *also known as* Riskins

nr Slough, Berkshire (formerly in Buckinghamshire) OS TQ0279

All that remains of Richings Park is the name, now attached to an eastern suburb of Slough, caught in the angle of the M25 and the M4. In the early 18th century the estate was owned by the Apsley family. The Tory statesman Allen, 1st Earl Bathurst (of Cirencester Park, *see page 197*), married the heiress Catherine Apsley in 1704 and thus inherited Richings, living here when parliament was sitting. It was the meeting place of many notable writers and garden connoisseurs, among them Joseph Addison, Henry Bolingbroke, William Congreve, John Gay, Alexander Pope, Lawrence Sterne and Jonathan Swift. Pope lived nearby at Twickenham (*see Pope's Garden page 524*) and helped Bathurst lay out the garden. When the estate was sold in 1739, it had a canal 1600ft/487m long, a greenhouse with oleanders and oranges, woods with winding paths, a cave overhung with periwinkle, arbours of laurel, lilac, philadelphus and woodbine, and a bench inscribed with verses written by Bathurst's literary friends.

Richmond Palace

Richmond, Greater London OS TQ1877

Great Gothic palace built on the banks of the Thames at Richmond for Henry VII on the site of Edward III's Shene (or Sheen) Palace, destroyed by fire in 1499. The new palace completed, and gardens at least partly made, by 1501 when Henry's son, Prince Arthur, married Catherine of Aragon; at the wedding, guests passed "through his goodly gardeyns, lately rehersid, unto his galery upon the walls." The

garden was on the site of present-day Old Deer Park, north of Richmond Green (where the Tudor gatehouse bearing Henry VII's arms may still be seen) and south-west of the Royal Botanic Gardens at Kew. Drawings by Anthonis van Wyngaerde show it in 1562, and Wenceslaus Hollar's engravings in 1638. New gardens were constructed 1610–12 in the reign of James I, on which both Salomon de Caus and Constantino de'Servi worked. The palace was almost entirely destroyed during the Commonwealth.

Richmond Park

Richmond, Greater London OS TQ2073
English Heritage Register
Grade I Open regularly

Richmond Park covers an area of 2,500 acres/1,012 hectares and has royal connections going back to the 13th century when it was called the Manor of Sheen. Under Henry VII the name was changed to Richmond, after the King's Yorkshire title of Earl of Richmond. Henry VIII hunted here and his hunting "stand", or mound, may still be seen in the north-western corner of the park close to Pembroke Lodge. From the top is a famous view of St Paul's Cathedral, 12 miles away. The park was developed from 1630 when a royal warrant from Charles I requested "a bill for His Majesty's signature for payment of an imprest to Edward Manning for railing in coppices, making ponds, cutting lawns in the New Park at Richmond, and bringing a river to run through the grounds". In 1637 this New Park (as opposed to the Old Deer Park on the banks of the Thames to the west, where Richmond Palace was, *see above*) was enclosed in a wall 8 miles long. Many English oaks still survive from before that time. The site is undulating and well watered, with the Beverley brook flowing through it and a large lake, Pen Ponds, at the centre. There are several notable buildings. Pembroke Lodge to the north-west was originally a mole-catcher's cottage and was rebuilt in 1788 by Sir John Soane for the Countess of Pembroke. White Lodge, to the east of Pen Ponds, was built as a hunting lodge for

R

George I to the designs of Roger Morris c.1727–29, with later additions; it has been the Royal Ballet School since 1955. Thatched House Lodge, in the south-west corner of the park, was built for Sir Robert Walpole (who was Ranger of the park) c.1727, possibly to the designs of William Kent; in 1805 Humphry Repton laid out the pleasure grounds there for Viscount Sidmouth. The Queen's Ride, an avenue of oaks and sweet chestnuts which runs from White Lodge to the north-west, and the long hornbeam walk to the south of Pembroke Lodge, were laid out in the mid 18th century. Isabella Plantation, an area of 84 acres/34 hectares, was planted by Lord Sidmouth from 1831 – most of the beech, oaks and sweet chestnuts date from that time. It was developed as woodland and water garden from 1950, first by J.M. Fisher and latterly by George Thomson, and now has a splendid collection of azaleas and camellias, a beautiful glade of Japanese maples, a bog garden and heather garden. Since the early 20th century Richmond Park has been a public park, and now has two golf courses, rugby and football pitches and a polo field.

Richmond Terrace Walk
Richmond, Greater London OS TQ1874
English Heritage Register Grade II*
Open regularly

Public promenade laid out on the top of Richmond Hill c.1700, with a double row of pleached trees, to provide a prospect of this romantic stretch of the river Thames. It quickly became a fashionable place to visit; Joseph Addison wrote about it before 1712, and a beautiful painting by Leonard Knyff (c.1720) survives. The poet James Thomson wrote about the view from Richmond Hill in *The Seasons* (1727): "Heavens! What a goodly Prospect spreads around,/Of Hills and Dales, and Woods, and Lawns,/and Spires,/And glittering Towns,/and gilded streams, till all/The stretching Landskip into smoke decays!" In 1782 Carl Moritz described it as "one of the finest prospects in the world…

Whatever is charming in nature, or pleasing in art, is to be seen here." In 1902 an act was passed to preserve the view, the first example of the legal protection of a landscape view. Today the walk it is a public open space and the original trees have been replanted with American oaks and limes.

Rievaulx Terrace
see page 350

Riffhams
nr Danbury, Essex OS TL7706
English Heritage Register Grade II

House built 1815–17 for J.R. Spencer Phillips. Humphry Repton was consulted in 1815 and made a plan for the grounds but no Red Book is known. Boundary plantings in the park and two pools south of the house, created by damming the stream, resulted from his advice. To the south of the house, a 19th-century balustraded terrace overlooking a lawn, with a fine cedar of Lebanon to the south-east.

Ripley Castle
Ripley, North Yorkshire OS SE2860
English Heritage Register Grade II
Open regularly Tel 01423 770152

The Ingilby family came here in the 14th century, although the present castle is chiefly late 18th-century. Terraced walk about castle, with views over lakes and parkland. Walled kitchen garden now partly turned over to ornamental purposes, with an orangery in the north wall overlooking a lawn and borders. An early 19th-century garden temple is aligned with a path that leads north through trees. The park has venerable oaks and sweet chestnuts; Capability Brown is rumoured to have worked here, but there is no evidence.

Risby Hall
Rowley, East Yorkshire OS TA0035
English Heritage Register Grade II

Foundations only of a late 17th-century house built for James Bradshaw and demolished after a fire. The remains of a late 17th-century garden are visible: a raised terrace, an elongated pond, a pyramidal earthwork. In woodland

to the east, aligned with the terrace, a canal with yew trees along one side. A pool is overlooked by a late 18th-century Gothick building.

River Gardens
Belper, Derbyshire OS SJ3448 English Heritage Register Grade II Open regularly

Public gardens laid out on the banks of the river Derwent 1905–6. In the north of the park, a boathouse partly screened by Pulhamite rockwork. To the east, impeccable lawns and flower beds and a Pulhamite rockwork fountain. North-east of the boathouse, a twelve-sided bandstand with an ogee copper roof, made by Messrs Wheeldon of Belper when the garden was laid out. Lawns are planted with shrubs and largely coniferous specimen trees. North-east of the bandstand, a teahouse in Swiss chalet style, also built by Wheeldon; originally thatched with heather, it now has a tiled roof. Close to the teahouse, a pool with Pulhamite rockwork.

Riverhill House
Sevenoaks, Kent OS TQ5452
English Heritage Register Grade II
Open regularly Tel 01732 458802

Early 18th-century house, replacing a Tudor farmhouse, altered in 19th century by John Rogers, a botanist and scientist. Rogers laid out the gardens, planting many of the newly introduced plants of Robert Fortune and J.D. Hooker. Garden terraced to south of house, with a wooden summerhouse on the top terrace. West of the house, pleasure grounds with a rockery. North-east of house, walled gardens, ornamental shrubbery and rose walk. Much damage in 1987 storm and extensive replanting.

Rivington Gardens
Rivington, Lancashire OS SD6314
English Heritage Register Grade II

Gardens and pleasure grounds designed by Thomas Mawson for the 1st Viscount Leverhulme who built a prefabricated wooden house which was burnt down by a suffragette in 1913. Its successor,

a bungalow, was demolished in 1947. The grounds are now a public garden. They lie on steeply sloping land, divided down the middle by Roynton Lane. The land west of the lane is planted with trees; that to the east, where the house stood, is more formal. Throughout the garden, giving it architectural unity, are terraced flagstone paths, stone steps and garden buildings of dressed rubble. Close to the site of the house, the Pigeon House, built in French-Gothic style (1910, by R. Atkinson). To the south-east, two stone staircases lead down from a square lawn to two stone archways with steps down to a boating lake – an area called the Italian Garden. Rockwork cliffs and a cascade to the west of the lake. Nearby, the Great Lawn has a pavilion with Tuscan columns, with a further lawn and pavilion to the south. Japanese garden south-west of the site of the house, with a lake and waterfall. Wild woodland garden west of Roynton Lane, with a steep gorge crossed by bridges to the south.

Roath Park
Cardiff OS ST1879 Cadw/ICOMOS Register Grade I Open regularly

Public park designed by William Harpur and opened to the public in 1896 at a total cost of c.£55,000 (£3,286,800 today). Over half the site is occupied by an enormous rectangular lake with a bathing platform, landing stage and boat house. At the northern end are five lakes which the head gardener, William Pettigrew, described as "five artistically constructed islands, destined to become the homes of water fowl". Fishing was also permitted and the waters were stocked with trout. The *Gardeners' Chronicle* in 1911 mentioned the problem of otters and great crested grebes eating all the trout. The layout of the grounds is largely informal, with winding paths, lawns and specimen trees and shrubs, many of which survive from original plantings. North of the lake, the Wild Garden has woodland of beech, holm oaks, oaks, pines and sycamores, with the Roath brook

winding through it. South of the lake is the Scott Memorial, a tapering clocktower in the shape of a lighthouse, erected in 1910 to celebrate the departure from Cardiff of Captain Scott's *Terra Nova* for the Antarctic.

Roberts Park, *formerly known as* Saltaire, *or* Salts Park
Saltaire, West Yorkshire OS SE1338 English Heritage Register Grade II Open regularly

Park designed by William Gay for the wool manufacturer and benefactor Sir Titus Salt for the recreation of the inhabitants of his model industrial village of Saltaire. (The village, designed by Lockwood & Mawson, was begun in 1853 and by 1871 had a population of 4,300.) The park was opened to the public in 1871 and Salt's Mill was closed so that workers could attend the opening ceremony. A terraced walk runs across the park from east to west; a tea room built into it has a roof designed to give views of the cricket ground to the south, and over the town. The platform has a statue of Sir Titus Salt by F. Derwent Wood (erected 1903). North of the terrace are gardens with widening paths occasionally edged with rocks. A bandstand was demolished during World War II. A pamphlet published in 1903 said that the park was "very tastefully laid out…It may be safely said that this Park is one of the most beautiful in the world."

Rockbeare Manor, *also referred to as* Rockbeare House
Rockbeare, Devon OS SY0394
English Heritage Register Grade II

18th-century house owned in the late 18th century by Sir John Duntze at which time Richard Polwhele's *History of Devonshire* (1793–1806) described it as "a mansion house pleasantly situated in excellent walled gardens". Twin pavilions, originally a billiard room and an orangery. Symmetrically laid out model farmyard. Early 20th-century walled garden with central fountain pool and borders, possibly designed by P. Morley Horder who restored the house in the 1920s.

Rockingham Castle
Rockingham, Northamptonshire OS SP8691
English Heritage Register Grade II*
Open regularly Tel 01536 770240

11th-century castle, converted from the 16th century into a private house by Edward Watson and his descendants. It occupies a fine site on a promontory overlooking the valley of the river Welland. An old double yew hedge, the Elephant Walk, on the western side of the castle, is said to date from the 1670s. But the gardens mostly date from the 19th century and later. A circular rose garden hedged in yew probably dates from the early 19th century; in a valley south-west of the castle, the Grove was planted with exotic trees and shrubs by Richard Watson in the 1840s. In the park are the remains of 17th-century avenues of elm and lime, and there was much additional planting in the early 19th century.

Rode Hall
Odd Rode, Cheshire OS SJ8157
English Heritage Register Grade II
Open regularly Tel 01270 873237

House built c.1700 for Randle Wilbraham on an older site, with much subsequent alteration. Terraced gardens to west of house designed 1861 by W.A. Nesfield, with a circular rose garden with clipped golden yews on either side and a summerhouse. Nesfield's flower beds have been filled in. Wild garden west of the house, with mature conifers and a grotto whose interior is decorated with shell and pebble work. To the north, a rockery and stream. This area was probably laid out by John Webb 1803–12. The park is dominated by Rode Pool, a long narrow lake running along the north-west boundary. Humphry Repton advised in 1790 and was scornful of the landscape – "much more consistent with the view from a Cottage or Farm house than from the Portico of a Gentleman's Seat." He suggested making the lake, and probably planting blocks of woodland. John Webb was responsible for executing the work.

Rodmarton Manor
see page 227

Rokeby Park
Rokeby, County Durham OS NZ0814
English Heritage Register Grade II*
Open regularly Tel 01833 690100

House built 1725–31 by Sir Thomas Robinson. By the house, lawns, a line of 18th-century urns, and various ornamental antiquities such as a Roman milestone and several Roman altars. East of the house, paths lead down to the river Greta which flows along the eastern boundary of the grounds. An artificial cave, Scott's Cave, is cut into the limestone cliffs; it is named after Sir Walter Scott who wrote an epic poem, *Rokeby* (1813), celebrating the dramatic scenery and the history of the Rokeby family. Nearby, an 18th-century rustic bridge spans the river. Parkland surrounds the house, enclosed in walls built in 1725, and planted in the 1730s.

Roker Park
Sunderland, Tyne and Wear OS NZ4059
English Heritage Register Grade II
Open regularly

Public park opened 1880 and based on Roker dene, a natural wooded ravine close to the sea. There are bowling greens and tennis courts, and a bandstand of 1880 survives. A metal footbridge leads down to the beach at Roker Rocks and a seafront promenade.

The Roof Gardens
see page 168

The Rookery, *formerly* Well House *or* Streatham Well
Lambeth, London OS TQ3070
Open regularly

Mineral springs were discovered in Streatham in 1659, and in the early 18th century the Well House was built to accommodate visitors to the spa. The house was demolished and the grounds became a public park in 1913. The former kitchen garden now has formal gardens with paved paths, a rose pergola and a central pool close to the site of the original well. In the north-west part of the park, a terrace with displays of bedding and lawns with mature cedars of Lebanon. A rock garden to the north, with a stream and

plantings of heather and rhododendrons.

Rosemoor Garden
see page 58

Roslin Glen *and* Hawthornden Castle
Roslin, Midlothian OS NT2863
Scottish Inventory Open regularly

The glen is a precipitous wooded gorge through which the North Esk river flows. From the early 17th century it was laid out with riverside walks leading to the remarkable 15th-century Roslin Chapel (with extraordinary carvings), the 15th-century Roslin Castle and the partly 15th-century Hawthornden Castle. In the 18th century it became a popular destination for travellers in search of picturesque scenery. Dorothy and William Wordsworth visited it in 1803 and Dorothy wrote in her *Journal*, "I never passed through a more delicious dell than the glen of Roslin." Hawthornden Castle was inherited in 1610 by the writer William Drummond, a friend of Ben Jonson (who once walked from London to visit Drummond and on arrival found his friend sitting under a tree). Drummond loved the scenery of the glen: "Deare wood, and you, sweet solitary place,/Where from the vulgar I estranged to live". A warren of caves in the cliffs below Hawthornden Castle was relished by 18th-century visitors. Much of the site is today Roslin Country Park, managed by Midlothian Council.

Rossie Priory
Inchture, Perthshire OS NO2830 Scottish Inventory Open occasionally for SGS

An ancient site with nothing monastic about it. The present house, in elegant Regency Gothic style, was built c.1807 to the designs of William Atkinson, mostly demolished and rebuilt in 1949 to the designs of Sir Basil Spence. The estate has been owned by the Kinnaird family since the 14th century. The largely 19th-century garden was much improved by Lady Kinnaird in the late 20th century. A Victorian water garden with a fountain pool is now a sea of distinguished

planting – astilbes, ligularias, meconopsis, primulas and rodgersias. The Terrace Garden south of the house is planted with roses, shrubs and herbaceous perennials. 18th-century wrought-iron gates lead into the terraced walled garden where fruit and vegetables are still grown, beds are cultivated for cutting flowers and tender plants are grown in a glasshouse. Near the walled garden is a terraced Victorian topiary garden.

Rotherfield Hall
Rotherfield, East Sussex OS TQ5429
English Heritage Register Grade II*

House built 1535, with 17th-century and late 19th-century additions; Francis Inigo Thomas was responsible for those of 1897 and he also designed the gardens to the east and west of the house. To the east of the house, walled forecourt with grass turning circle and central sundial. At the eastern side, steps flanking a pool lead up to grassed terraces with, pointing away, a long narrow bowling green cut into the slope, with groves of trees on each side and an arched niche with a statue of the water-bearer. West of the house a walled garden with a terrace, balustraded walls, steps, arcade, summerhouses and gazebos. A parterre at a lower level, with a pool and box hedges, and, beyond it at the foot of a grass bank, a lawn with garden houses surmounted by dovecotes at each end. South of the house, a Tuscan arcade and a rose garden. In the park west of the garden, a stream linking a series of hammer ponds. Inigo Thomas built four stone bridges spanning the stream, with a boathouse in the form of a square tower with a Roman arch leading to the landing stage.

Rotherfield Park
East Tisted, Hampshire OS SU6932
English Heritage Register Grade II*
Open occasionally for NGS

Tudor house rebuilt for James Scott 1815–21 to the designs of J.T. Parkinson. The romantic castellated house was given further Gothic, and Elizabethan, character later in the century. There was a deer park here in the 16th century. In the pleasure grounds, a

balustraded terraced lawn overlooking parkland (with remains of an early 18th-century lime avenue), old-fashioned shrub rose garden with central pool, double yew hedges with golden yew buttresses. Planting advice from Norah Lindsay in 1928. Walled kitchen garden with herbaceous borders. Woodland divided by closely planted avenues.

Roundhay Park
Leeds, West Yorkshire OS SE3338
English Heritage Register Grade II

House built 1826 for Thomas Nicholson to the design of John Clark. Park laid out at the same time with two lakes, Upper Lake and Waterloo Lake. Today, much woodland survives to their north, with golf courses beyond. A stream running through Great Head Wood, immediately north of Waterloo Lake, passes through the Gorge which in the 19th century had naturalistic rockworks and cascades. To the west of an area of open grassland, the Castle, a sham ruin with two round towers. On the western bank of Waterloo Lake, an early 20th-century boathouse has been converted into a tea room. The house, now a hotel, looks eastwards over parkland and the lakes. Close to the house is a 300ft-/90m-long canal overlooked by a summerhouse. The grounds are a public open space.

Rous Lench Court
Rous Lench, Worcestershire OS SP0153
English Heritage Register Grade II*

16th-century house, much altered c.1840. Remarkable and splendid topiary garden on west-facing terraces above the house – probably the creation of the Revd W.K.W. Chafy 1876–1916 but incorporating a much earlier garden. To the north of the house's forecourt, an opening pierces a high yew hedge clipped into towers and buttresses and leads to the Italian Garden where a lawn, divided into four by herring-bone brick paths, has a circular pool with a figure of Mercury at the centre. The east-west axis of the Italian Garden continues eastwards up the terraced gardens above the house, where a gravel path leads

R

through the Lower Yew Avenue, 120yards/110m long. From here, steps lead east to the Lower Pleasance, enclosed on three sides by elaborately topiaried yew hedges and on the fourth by a gravel walk, and with a central circular yew arbour. The axial path continues eastwards through a yew tunnel with an entrance in the form of a clipped cottage, and ends in a trellis arbour and seat. Broad walks flanked with yew hedges run down either side of these main compartments, and openings leads across to the central compartments. Other enclosures are found, such as the Secret Garden (a rock garden with pools, a rill, monoliths and curved paths) to the east of the Lower Yew Avenue. To the north, a pinetum with mature conifers. It seems possible that the layout of the terraced gardens was established in the 17th century. But what is of that period and what is the work of the Revd Chafy is impossible to unravel on the basis of present evidence. At all events, it is a rare and enchanting place.

Rousdon
Combpyne Rousdon, Devon OS SY2990
English Heritage Register Grade II

Giant mansion built 1874–78 for Sir Henry Peek (of Peek Frean biscuits) by Ernest George in a dramatic position on the very edge of cliffs and landslips above Humble Point, to the west of Lyme Regis. Terrace along south front of house. Ornamental lake, ha-ha and parkland. Walled kitchen garden, glasshouses, gazebos with sea views. In recent years Rousdon has been occupied by Allhallows School but it has since been sold and the estate divided.

Rousham House
see page 104

Rowallane Garden
see page 431

Rowntree Park
York, North Yorkshire OS SE6050 English Heritage Register Grade II Open regularly

The first municipal park laid out in York, made for the Rowntrees

(Quakers, chocolate manufactureres and philanthropists), completed in 1921. Designed by Frederick Rowntree, W.J. Swain and P.W. Woods (the head gardener at the York Cocoa Works), it was also thought of as a memorial to the employees of Rowntree & Co killed in the Great War. Trees and shrubs were supplied by James Backhouse Nurseries of York and roses by Walker & Son of Scarborough. It stands on the banks of the river Ouse. The entrance from Terry Avenue has magnificent early 18th-century wrought-iron gates by Jean Tijou (supposedly from Richings Park in Buckinghamshire, see page 529). A beck was dammed to make a serpentine lake with a bridge over it; a bandstand, tea room, rockery (with cascade) and a pergola were made, and there was much planting of trees and shrubs. Bandstand, pergola and other features have gone.

Royal Botanic Garden Edinburgh
see page 391

Royal Botanic Gardens Kew
see page 169

Royal Hospital, Chelsea
Kensington and Chelsea, London OS TQ2878 English Heritage Register Grade II

Royal Hospital founded in 1682 by Charles II and built 1682–1702 to the designs of Sir Christopher Wren, with additions by Sir John Soane 1814–17 and other alterations; Thomas Carlyle (who lived nearby) called it "Quiet and dignified and the work of a gentleman". The grounds were laid out 1687–92 by George London and Henry Wise. The Great Court to the north-west (now Burton Court) had a geometric layout of paths, lawns and avenues, the central avenue extending out of the gardens as far as Royal Avenue to the north (which originally was intended as part of an avenue running all the way to Kensington Palace). Today, Burton Court has an avenue of planes and Royal Avenue is planted with limes. South-east of

the hospital, formal gardens went down to the river, with a central avenue flanked with L-shaped canals. Railings ran along the river bank, with a pavilion at each end. When Ranelagh Gardens (see page 528) were closed, the land they occupied became part of the Royal Hospital grounds. In the 19th century the grounds were remodelled; canals and pools were filled in but the avenue south-east of the hospital, with lawns on either side, was left in position. In 1849 an obelisk was placed in the middle of the avenue, and railings erected at its southern end on Chelsea Embankment. The hospital grounds have various sports and recreational facilities.

The Royal Hospital, Haslar
Gosport, Hampshire OS SZ6198
English Heritage Register Grade II

Hospital for the Royal Navy, opened in 1753. Its grounds of c.62 acres/c.25 hectares were laid out informally, resembling parkland. An "airing court" (built by 1775) was a circular walled enclosure, 1 mile in circumference, with views of the Solent. The Officers' Terrace, a series of houses built in the mid 1790s, has private walled gardens for each house, laid out when the houses were built, along the lines of those at Chatham Dockyard (see The Officers' Terrace, page 518).

Royal Lodge
Old Windsor, Berkshire OS SU9672
English Heritage Register Grade I

The house is the remains of a grand cottage orné (170ft/68m long; the largest cottage ever built?) designed for George IV by Sir Jeffry Wyatville in the 1820s and 1830s. John Nash and W.T. Aiton may have designed the original garden. Lying within Windsor Great Park, the house is enclosed in woodland dating back to the 18th century. The western face of the house overlooks a terrace, designed in the mid 1930s by Geoffrey Jellicoe, which runs round the south side of the house to overlook a sunken garden with roses and herbaceous planting, hedged in beech. The woodland is planted with camellias and

rhododendrons and includes a recreated 1951 Chelsea Gold Medal garden designed by Sir Eric Savill and T.H. Findlay.

The Royal Pavilion
see page 171

Royal Victoria Park
see page 59

Rudding Park House
Follifoot, North Yorkshire OS SE3353
English Heritage Register Grade II

House built for the Hon. William Gordon from 1805, on an older site. Humphry Repton was consulted in 1790, when Lord Loughborough was the owner, and a Red Book was produced, but it is not known if his proposals were accepted. South of the house, a parterre designed by James Russell in the 1950s was destroyed when a caravan park was made. West of the house, James Russell also helped lay out a series of paths radiating through the woods from a mid 19th-century marble vase, said to have come from Crystal Palace Park and possibly designed by Joseph Paxton. The house is now a conference centre.

Rufford Abbey
nr Wellow, Nottinghamshire OS SK6464
Open regularly (EH) Tel 01623 822944

A Cistercian abbey was founded here in 1146 and the estate passed to George Talbot, 4th Earl of Shrewsbury in 1537 after the dissolution of the monasteries. Ruins of the abbey remain, together with additions made in the 17th and 19th centuries. John Byng thought it "very melancholy" on his visit in 1789. There were formal gardens here in the 17th century. An early 18th-century Tuscan bath house was converted in 1889 into a conservatory for tender exotics. The existing gardens are almost entirely late 20th century. The Queen Mother's Walk has pleached limes and urns, and a series of compartmented gardens are decorated with modern sculpture. There are borders, a herb garden, a pergola and an

arboretum of species of birch and oak.

Runnymede
Egham, Surrey OS SU9972 Open regularly (part NT) Tel 01784 432891

Runnymede is famous for the sealing of the Magna Carta by King John in 1215. It is a charming place among trees and water meadows on the banks of the Thames. A pair of lodges by S Edwin Lutyens, rather ponderous, with pyramidal roofs, guards the entrance. The Magna Carta Memorial, erected by the American Bar Association, ornaments the landscape – a columned temple-like building with the inscription, "To commemorate Magna Carta, symbol of freedom under law". Here, too, is the John F. Kennedy Memorial, a noble vertical stone slab with the inscription, "This acre of ground was given to the United States of America by the people of Britain in memory of John F. Kennedy"; it stands in a glade landscaped by Jellicoe & Coleridge. On the far bank of the river is a piece of land, Ankerwycke, acquired by the National Trust in 1998 – the grounds of the 11th-century St Mary's priory, of which the ruins may still be seen. There is a magnificent old yew here, reputedly 2,000 years old.

Rushmore Park
Tollard Royal, Wiltshire OS ST9518
English Heritage Register Grade II

In 1714 the rights of the ancient forest of Cranborne Chase passed to George Pitt and the house was rebuilt by his grandson, another George, in 1817. In 1880, on the death of the 6th Lord Rivers, the estate was inherited by Lt. Genera Augustus Henry Lane Fox who added the names Pitt Rivers to his name. Pitt Rivers developed the public pleasure gardens, now calle the Larmer Tree Gardens (see page 92), and collected exotic animals, which were kept at Rushmore in The Railes, a former deer park going back to 1618. Two beech avenues were planted: the General's Avenue and Chase Avenue. The house is now a school.

R

Russell Square
Camden, London OS TQ3081
English Heritage Register Grade II
Open regularly

Built from 1800, part of the Bedford estate. After 1802 the 6th Duke of Bedford asked Humphry Repton to lay out the square garden on the already prepared site ("this insipid shape", wrote Repton). A statue of the 5th Duke of Bedford (by Sir Richard Westmacott) was erected on the southern edge of the garden looking southwards along Bedford Street to Bloomsbury Square, and Repton advised that trees and shrubs nearby should be pruned so that the statue stood out against the sky. Avenues of limes were to converge on the statue, and a regular pattern of curved and straight paths ran under trees and shrubs. Repton wrote that he wanted to avoid "a bigoted adherence to forms and lines, whether straight, or crooked, or serpentine". Today the gardens, enclosed in their railings, are luxuriantly leafy and still preserve a pattern of paths close to the early 19th-century arrangement. In 1959 a paved central area had three fountains surrounded with bedding and roses. By 2002 this had been simplified, with a central open space with benches and new fountains.

Rydal Hall
Rydal, Cumbria OS NY3606
Engish Heritage Register Grade II*

The Fleming family were here by at least the 16th century and still own the Rydal estate though not the house. House built in the 16th century, added to in the 17th century and remodelled in the early 19th century. North-east of the house, a 17th-century bridge crosses the Rydal beck at the point where a waterfall descends into a plunge pool and on into a gorge. By the water's edge is what Sir Daniel Fleming called "my Grott-House", which he built 1668–69 – a stone building with a window overlooking the cascade, pool and bridge which was originally panelled within. This became a famous beauty spot in the 18th century, admired by Thomas Gray and William Gilpin,

described by Wordsworth ("The eye reposes on a secret bridge/Half grey, half shagged with ivy to its ridge") and painted by Joseph Wright of Derby. South of the house, terraced gardens by Thomas Mawson of c.1909, with a double staircase of stone, a circular lily pool and a lawn with shaped beds edged in box. A lower double staircase descends on each side of a columned recess crowned with a miniature Tuscan temple.

Rydal Mount
Rydal, Cumbria OS NY3606
English Heritage Register Grade II
Open regularly Tel 01539 433002

16th-century house, extended in the 17th and 18th centuries and rented by the poet William Wordsworth from 1813 to his death in 1850. In the garden is a mount, of uncertain origin but possibly medieval, now shrouded in planting, from the top of which are fine views. The slopes of the garden are terraced with dry-stone walls, in one of which is a stone summerhouse built in Wordsworth's time. Lavish planting of trees and shrubs. Dora's Field was planted with daffodils in memory of Wordsworth's daughter.

Ryton Organic Gardens
see page 275

St Aelhaiarn Churchyard
Guilsfield, Powys OS SJ2111
Cadw/ICOMOS Register Grade II*
Open regularly

The 14th-century church (with later alterations and much restored by G.E. Street 1877–79) stands at the centre of a roughly circular churchyard whose layout is essentially medieval. About its perimeter is a series of old yew trees, clearly planted to ornament the landscape. Underneath one of them is a headstone which reads, "Here lyeth ye body of Richard Jones/of Moysgwin, gent.,/who was interred December ye 10th 1707/aged 90/Under this yew tree/Buried would he bee/For his father and hee/Planted this yew tree". No-one knows when the

yews were planted but this tree, not the largest in the churchyard, must, according to the epitaph, date from the 17th century.

St Ann's Court
nr Chertsey, Surrey OS TQ0267
English Heritage Register Grade II*

International-style house lying in part of the 18th-century landscape of St Ann's Hill (see below), designed 1938 by Raymond McGrath for the garden designer Christopher Tunnard. Tunnard designed his own garden, leaving the 18th-century landscape relatively untouched. He made a simple but strongly architectural courtyard garden with paving, a rectangular and circular pool, planters, and beds for planting let into the paving – all closely related to the curves and straight lines of the house. A viewing terrace was built to frame an Arcadian view into the landscape of turf and woodland, at the centre of which is a splendid old cedar of Lebanon.

St Ann's Hill
nr Chertsey, Surrey OS TQ0267 English Heritage Register Grade II Open regularly

Ancient wooded site going back to the Bronze Age. In the 18th century it was part of an estate owned by Elizabeth Armistead, the mistress, and later wife, of Charles James Fox MP. The Foxes landscaped their grounds and built a gazebo in 1794; W. Keane's *Beauties of Surrey* (1849) describes the site, where "vases and tablets of poetry are to be seen along the shady walks of that very retired and lovely country". Paths lead to the top of the hill from which are fine views of the river Thames. Here are the ruins of the 14th-century St Ann's Chapel and an octagonal summerhouse with a mosaic depicting St Ann. On the south-west side of the hill is the Dingle, a clearing with specimen trees and rhododendrons. The grounds have been a public recreation ground since 1927. Parts of the estate are now St Ann's Court (see above).

St Catherine's College (Oxford)
see page 102

St Catherine's Court
St Catherine's, Bath, Somerset OS ST7771
English Heritage Register Grade II*

The site at St Catherine's is an ancient one: a grange belonging to Bath Abbey had been here in the middle ages and the monks' fishponds can still be seen. The present, very decorative house is early 17th-century, rebuilt in parts in the 19th century. The gardens, terraced to accommodate the slope, have followed the same pattern: the layout is 17th century, and some of the stonework, but with much reworking in the late 19th century. Paved terraces, balustrades, urns and stairs animate the slope, with Irish yews forming emphatic punctuation marks. All this was much admired by H. Inigo Triggs who described and illustrated the gardens in *Formal Gardens in England and Scotland* (1902).

St Donat's Castle
St Donat's, Glamorgan OS SS9368
Cadw/ICOMOS Register Grade I

Castle, started in the 12th century for the de Hawey family, on a splendid site at the head of a valley, looking down to the Bristol Channel. The castle has had many alterations, including those associated with the ownership of the American newspaper tycoon William Randolph Hearst from 1925 to 1951, but it retains its medieval character. Terraced gardens south of the castle date from the 16th century and are reached through a Tudor doorway – a very rare survival of a Tudor garden layout. From the broad top terrace there are fine views of the Bristol Channel. The terraces are laid out with lawns and flower beds, and the third terrace has a formal rose garden with twenty Tudor-style "king's beasts" – tall squatting heraldic creatures on plinths, rather Hollywoodian and dating from Hearst's time. An Italianate pavilion with a Gothic window is set into the terrace wall overlooking the rose garden. The planting of the terraces, such as it is, is wholly 20th-century and perfunctory; they would provide an admirable setting for bold modern planting, such as the

National Trust has done at Powis Castle (see page 226). By the 1530s there were two deer parks here, one for fallow deer and one for red deer. The castle is used today as a United World College (Atlantic College).

St Fagans Castle
see page 228

St Giles House
Wimborne St Giles, Dorset OS SU0311

17th-century house built for Sir Anthony Ashley Cooper, 1st Earl of Shaftesbury, and extended by Henry Flitcroft 1740–44. Landscaping in the mid 18th century, which included a sinuous lake south of the house and a magnificent mid 18th-century shell-lined grotto "finished by Mr Castles of Marylebone" and possibly helped by the famous grotto maker Josiah Lane of Tisbury.

St George's Gardens
Camden, London OS TQ3082
English Heritage Register Grade II*
Open regularly

Public garden laid out in the late 1880s on the site of an 18th-century burial ground for St George's, Bloomsbury and St George the Martyr. Many 18th-century monuments survive, several of fine quality. Paths wander among lawns and mature specimen trees – among them catalpa, oak, plane and weeping ash. There are rose beds and bedding schemes.

St James's Park
see page 172

St James's Square
City of Westminster, London OS TQ2980
English Heritage Register Grade II

St James's Square was developed by Henry Jermyn, 1st Earl of St Albans, from 1662. Nothing was done about a central garden until the 18th century; in 1726 it was recorded that it "hath lain, and does lie, in a filthy condition and as a common Dung hill". In the same year a survey by Thomas Ackres was made, and in the following year Charles Bridgeman was asked to lay out a garden. He

S

designed an octagonal garden with iron railings enclosing it, a central circular pool 150ft/45m in diameter, with a fountain and surrounded by a gravel walk and the entire area outside paved in Portland stone; it was completed in 1728. James Ralph, in *A Critical Review of the Publick Buildings, Statues and Ornaments in and about London and Westminster* (1734), wrote, "St. James's-Square has an appearance of grandeur superior to any other plan in town." Bridgeman was paid £5,630 (£464,587 today) for the work. In the early 19th century, a statue of George III (by John Bacon the Younger) was placed in the centre of the pool, which was filled in in 1854. John Nash redesigned the garden 1817–18 with curving walks and a shrubbery about the pool. The gardens were replanted in the 20th century, railings replaced in 1987, and new planting designed by John Brookes in 1974. The layout today has perimeter planting of shrubs and trees within the railings, and a cruciform pattern of paths meeting at the statue of George III which is surrounded by four obelisks – these had ornamented the railings in Bridgeman's layout.

St John's College
(Cambridge)
see page 295

St John's College
(Oxford)
see page 103

St Leonards Gardens
St Leonards, East Sussex OS TQ7908 English Heritage Register Grade II Open regularly

Private gardens laid out in association with the development of several villas in 1829 by James Burton (the father of Decimus Burton), later acquired by Hastings Corporation and opened as public gardens. The villas, in varied architectural style (some probably designed by Decimus Burton), still overlook the gardens. The garden today has winding paths, lawns, a pool and shrubberies. In the eastern part of the park, a raised shrubbery was planted in 1939 as a border for the blind, with aromatic plants.

St Luke's Gardens
Kensington and Chelsea, London OS TQ2778 English Heritage Register Grade II Open regularly

The churchyard of St Luke's, built 1820–24 to the designs of James Savage, was turned into a public garden and opened in 1887; it was designed by the Borough Surveyor, Mr Strachan, and planted by Veitch's nursery in Chelsea. Paths follow the boundaries of the rectangular space, with lawn and seats in the centre; there are circular rose beds to the north and south, and smaller circular beds for bedding schemes to east and west. Mature trees along the boundaries, and as specimens in the lawn.

St Mary
Painswick, Gloucestershire OS SO8610 English Heritage Register Grade II Open regularly

The 15th-century parish church of Painswick has a superlative churchyard. The tombstones, from the 17th century onwards, are of memorable quality, and the churchyard is ornamented with an astonishing collection of clipped yews – ninety-nine of them, planted *c.*1792. Packed closely together, most are standards clipped into upright and rounded shapes – an unforgettable sight.

St Mary's Pleasance,
also known as
Haddington Garden
Haddington, East Lothian OS NT5173 Scottish Inventory Open regularly

This was the orchard of the delightful 17th-century Haddington House (now divided into flats), which lies immediately adjacent to the site. It dates from the 17th or early 18th century and, in a derelict state by 1972, it was given by the Duke of Hamilton to the Haddington Garden Trust to "preserve the garden at Haddington House as an open public precinct and to develop it as an old Scottish garden." Built into the north garden wall is a 17th- or early 18th-century apple house. New gardens include a knot garden with 17th-century plants, a cottage garden with shrub roses, a pleached alley of laburnums, a meadow garden, an orchard of old cultivars of fruit and a 17th-century style viewing mount with a spiral path.

St Michael's Convent,
formerly Park Hill
Lambeth, London OS TQ3171 English Heritage Register Grade II

House built *c.*1835 for William Leaf to the designs of J.B. Papworth. Garden designed in the late 19th century by Robert Marnock, with a terrace west of the house ornamented with urns and sculpture and a garden house closing its north end. Small lake in south-west part of grounds and fragmentary remains of a James Pulham rock garden north of the house.

St Michael's Mount
Cornwall OS SW5129 English Heritage Register Grade II Open regularly (NT) Tel 01736 710507

The tidal island of St Michael's has been inhabited from pre-Christian times and there was said to have been a Celtic monastery here before the Benedictines came in the 11th century. After the Reformation it became royal property, passing eventually to the St Aubyn family in the 17th century and to the National Trust in 1954. The present house is a marvellously picturesque ensemble of monastic buildings and later domestic additions, including some very pretty Gothick work of the mid 18th century. Gardening here is a matter of conquering the wind but the microclimate is benign. Monterey pines and evergreen oaks have been planted to subdue the wind, with thickets of such wind-and salt-tolerant shrubs as euonymus and griselinia. As a result, all sorts of tender exotics flourish among the rocks – aeoniums, aloes, mesembryanthemums and much else, including substantial tender shrubs such as brugmansias. Such planting takes advantage of all sorts of nooks and crannies and the effect is delightful, but more a kind of enlivened natural landscape than a designed garden.

St Nicholas
Richmond, North Yorkshire OS NZ1700 English Heritage Register Grade II

17th-century house, with 18th-century additions, on the site of a Benedictine hospital founded in the 12th century. The garden became famous under the Hon. Robert James (1873–1960) who laid out a garden 1905–25, roughly contemporary with that of Lawrence Johnston (whom he knew) at Hidcote (*see page 210*), and in a similar tradition. On a south-facing slope, with acid soil, James created a compartmented garden of Arts and Crafts flavour, with much use of local stone and of hedges, and brilliantly ornamented with a very wide range of plants. James was one of the pioneers in the rediscovery of old shrub and species roses, and these loom large (the multiflora rambler 'Bobbie James', bred by Sunningdale Nurseries in 1961, is named after him). The Old Orchard, enclosed in yew hedges and stone walls, is planted with fruit trees underplanted with spring-flowering bulbs. A yew hedge with topiary has an opening with a grass path from which there are views of the ruins of Easby Abbey. Borders erupt with unfamiliar, finely used plants. James got seed of rhododendrons from the expeditions of Frank Kingdon Ward and George Forrest to add to the large collection of flowering shrubs.

St Osyth Priory
St Osyth, Essex OS TM1215 English Heritage Register Grade II

Augustinian priory founded in the early 12th century, with a beautiful late 15th-century castellated gatehouse. The present building, largely 16th century with 19th-century alterations. 18th-century landscaped park with tree belts to east, north and south-western boundaries. Several avenues of mature trees cross the park, which is partly a deer park and partly used for agriculture. In Nun's Wood a group of pools, and to the south of it, the remains of an 18th-century shell grotto in Grotto Wood. Mid 20th-century formal gardens north-east of gatehouse, with rose garden, parterre and topiary garden and a very large yew hedge.

St Pancras Gardens
Camden, London OS TQ2983 English Heritage Register Grade II Open regularly

The old church at St Pancras dated from pre-Norman times (St Pancras was a Roman saint and a 7th-century altar was discovered here). The present building, although it incorporates earlier fabric, was built 1847–48 to the designs of Roumieu & Gough. The churchyard, together with the burial ground for St-Giles-in-the-Fields, was made into a public park in 1877. It retains many monuments, including an outstanding one to the architect Sir John Soane and his wife. The layout of the garden is geometric, with paths aligned on the church or on prominent monuments and linked to peripheral paths. Surrounding areas of lawn are planted with mature trees and there are small areas of bedding.

St Paul's Waldenbury
St Paul's Walden, Hertfordshire OS TL1821 English Heritage Register Grade 1 Open occasionally for NGS Tel 01438 871218/871229

House built in the early 18th century, with additions by James Paine in the 1760s and Arthur Castings in the late 19th century. The gardens were laid out in the early 18th century and, remarkably, preserve the essential and delightful character of this time. North of the house, a lawn flanked by pleached lime walks, each with a statue at the far end: Samson and the two Philistines and Hercules and Antaeus. From this point, a slender *patte d'oie* of allées lined with beech hedges sweeps northwards through woodland; the ground is very uneven, and the allées dramatically swoop down and up again. Each has an eyecatcher; two are statues within the garden and the third, to the north-east, is the spire of St Paul's Walden parish church. Two parallel walks cut across the allées, the northern one crossing a turf theatre with an 18th-century rotunda and pool, and a bronze figure of a warrior (known here as "the Running Footman"). An avenue forms the eastern boundary of the garden, interrupted by a statue of Venus and Adonis by Scheemakers and culminating in an octagonal brick pavilion dated 1735. South of the house is a herb garden designed in 1992 by Sir Geoffrey Jellicoe who in the 1930s had helped to restore the garden.

St Peter's Square

Hammersmith and Fulham, London OS TQ2278 English Heritage Register Grade II
Open regularly

Developed from c.1825 and possibly designed by J.C. Loudon. The rectangular square garden is enclosed by railings, with trees and shrubs planted about the perimeter and a lawn at the centre. At the centre, a bronze statue, "The Greek Runner" (1926), by Sir William Richmond. Many good mature trees. Since 1915, most unusually for a private garden of this kind, the square gardens have been open to the public.

St Pierre Park

Mathern, Gwent OS ST5190
Cadw/ICOMOS Register Grade II

The Lewis family came here in the 13th century and remained until the end of the 19th century. The present house is Tudor, with later alterations. There had been a medieval deer park here and fallow deer were kept until the 20th century. Pools in the park dating from the middle ages were developed in the 16th and 17th centuries for ornamental purposes. The park was landscaped in the late 18th century but some of the parkland trees – oaks, planes and sweet chestnuts – are very ancient and probably pre-date the 18th-century landscaping. There was much tree planting also in the 19th century. Today there are two golf courses in the park and the house is a golf and country club.

Saling Grove

Great Saling, Essex OS TL7025
English Heritage Register Grade II

Mid 18th-century house altered in 19th century. In 1790 John Veldham consulted Humphry Repton; it is not known if a Red

Book was produced but the work he did remains largely intact today. A pool was made west of the house and belts of trees planted along the west and north-west boundary road. In woods west of the house, paths wander among mature trees in a Reptonian way. South of the house, an axial path runs between borders to a circular hedged enclosure with a sundial.

Saling Hall

see page 318

Saltoun Hall

nr East Saltoun, East Lothian OS NT4668
Scottish Inventory

Estate going back to the 12th century, with Gothic house built from 1819 to the designs of William Burn for the Fletcher family (Lords Milton). Parkland retains fine old trees from the late 18th and early 19th centuries. In the early 19th century there were grand formal gardens with parterres, each with a central fountain. The compartments had themes: the evergreen, or winter garden; the fruit, or harvest garden; the physic, or spring garden; and the flower, or summer garden. These delightful-sounding gardens had gone by 1846. The house is now divided into flats.

Saltram House

see page 60

Saltwell Park

Gateshead, Tyne and Wear OS NZ2561
English Heritage Register Grade II
Open regularly

Public park laid out in 1876 by Edward Kemp but incorporating the gardens of Saltwell Towers, made from 1853 onwards for a stained glass manufacturer, William Wailes. The ruinous house, with polychrome tiles, stands at the centre of the park, with its walled garden and a modern formal rose garden in the former kitchen garden. There is an octagonal bowling green designed by Kemp, and a pair of late 19th-century cast-iron aviaries nearby. With lawns, a late 20th-century bandstand, a lake laid out by Kemp, the whole park is enclosed in perimeter planting of trees and shrubs.

The Salutation

Sandwich, Kent OS TR3358
English Heritage Register Grade II

House designed in 1911 by Edwin Lutyens for Gaspard and Henry Farrer. Lutyens also designed the garden, probably without Gertrude Jekyll's help. Gardens to south-east and south-west of house, with yew-hedged lawns, flagged paths, a formal rose garden and a grass walk on the axis of the house flanked by herbaceous borders and roses trained on columns. Lawns lie behind the borders on each side of the walk, the southerly one with drums of clipped holm oak. Additional gardens since c.1977, with a small lake and informal water gardens, and mixed borders flanking a brick path running along northern boundary wall.

Sandbeck Park *and* Roche Abbey

nr Maltby, South Yorkshire OS SK5690
English Heritage Register Grade II*

A Cistercian monastery was founded in the 12th century; after the dissolution of the monsteries it was acquired by the Saunderson family (Viscounts Castleton) and the estate passed in 1723 to a cousin, Sir Thomas Lumley (later 3rd Earl of Scarbrough). House built from c.1765–68 to the designs of James Paine for the 4th Earl of Scarbrough. Pleasure grounds with lawns to east and west, made probably under the supervision of the older Adam Mickle 1771–72. The great interest at Sandbeck lies in the park, and especially in the work of Capability Brown who also worked on the setting of the ruins of Roche Abbey, one mile to the west of the house. Brown first came here in 1766 but there was no contract until 1774 when he was asked "to finish all the Valley of Roach Abbey in all its parts, according to the Ideas fixed on with Lord Scarbrough (With Poet's feeling and with Painter's Eye)." Brown was at first involved with the creation of lakes east of the house, and a little later worked on the western part of the park, from which views of Roche Abbey open out. Brown's work on the ruins consisted of grassing over the horizontal remains and leaving the vertical buildings rising from close-

mown turf – like "a neat bowling green", as William Gilpin wrote critically, after his visit in 1776. Gilpin thought that ruins were not Brown's thing: "Many a modern Palace he has adorned…but a ruin presented a new idea: which I doubt whether he has suffciently considered."

Sandford Park

Sandford St Martin, Oxfordshire OS SP4126
English Heritage Register Grade II

Early 18th-century house for the Croker family. 17th- or early 18th-century spiral mount. 18th-century park with series of lakes and cascades formed from the river Dorn. A seven-arched bridge of the same period spans the river, with an elaborate Chinoiserie pavilion on its banks. 18th-century walled kitchen garden.

Sandleford Priory

Greenham, Berkshire OS SU4764
English Heritage Register Grade II

The priory was an Augustinian foundation of c.1200. In the late 15th century the priory was closed and the estate privately tenanted. A new Gothic house, incorporating part of the priory, was built 1780–1 to the designs of James Wyatt for Mrs Montague, who asked Capability Brown in 1781 to make a survey. She got on very well with Brown and shortly after wrote to her sister-in-law, "He has made a plan to make my grounds, in prospect of the house and new rooms, very pleasing." She later wrote describing the transformation of the grounds into "a lovely pastoral – a sweet arcadian scene". Brown died in 1783 but the work was completed posthumously under Samuel Lapidge. Brown's work seems chiefly to have been involved with the valley east of the house, where he created or enlarged the serpentine Brown's Pond. Today the house is a school and there is a caravan park in the grounds.

Sandling Park

nr Hythe, Kent OS TR1436
English Heritage Register Grade II
Open occasionally for NGS

House built c.1950 to replace late 18th-century house by Joseph

Bonomi, destroyed by bombing in 1942. Woodland garden planted from 1846 in acid greensand, a rarity in the predominantly chalky soil of east Kent. 19th-century trees, enriched with much planting in the 20th century of camellias, magnolias, maples and rhododendrons and lavish spring underplanting of bluebells and lily-of-the-valley. The 18th-century walled kitchen garden of the old house remains.

Sandon Park

Sandon, Staffordshire OS SJ9528
English Heritage Register Grade II
Open regularly Tel 01889 508004

House built 1852 to the designs of William Burn after the 18th-century house had been destroyed by fire. South of the house, grass terraces with beds and urns. To the east, pleasure grounds with lawns, shrubberies, specimen trees and winding walks with a rose garden at the centre. To its south, a yew-hedged circular enclosure, now grassed over, with a Coade stone group and a small alcove seat. William Emes, John Webb and W.A. Nesfield all worked on the garden and pleasure grounds 1778–c.1850 but little of their work survives. Landscape park, largely the work of William Emes from 1778, who did much tree planting, removed fences and hedges and created the parkland sward. Several monuments in the park: Perceval's Shrine (c.1815) a Gothic seat commemorating the assassinated Prime Minister Spencer Perceval; to the east, Trentham Tower (c.1840), part of Sir Charles Barry's demolished Trentham Hall (*see page 550*), moved here c.1911; in the extreme south-eastern corner of the park, Pitt's Column (1806), commemorating Pitt the Younger. 18th-century walled former kitchen garden west of house.

Sandringham House

see page 319

Sarsden House

Sarsden, Oxfordshire OS SP2823
English Heritage Register Grade II*

House rebuilt for the Walter family after a fire in 1689. Estate bought in 1792 by James Haughton

S

Langston whose son, John, consulted Humphry Repton in 1795. A Red Book was produced the following year. Balustraded terrace with parterre and pools at west front of house, approached from Humphry Repton's son George Repton's loggia of *c*.1825. A lake, probably created by Humphry Repton from former fishponds. Path leads over a rusticated bridge designed by Repton (*c*.1796), past the site of an 18th-century rotunda overlooking the lake, to a boathouse designed by Repton *c*.1796, built of stone in the form of a rusticated temple. The neighbouring Sarsden Grove, built for unmarried Langston sisters, was remodelled in 1825 by George Repton as a cottage *orné*. Humphry Repton also redesigned the park, of which mature clumps of lime trees survive. 18th-century wrought-iron gates from earlier formal gardens survive in various parts of the garden.

Saunton Court
Braunton, Devon OS SS4537
English Heritage Register Grade II

Medieval house, owned successively by the Chichester and the Luttrell families, and altered by Sir Edwin Lutyens for G. Rankin in 1932. Lutyens designed a new garden to the east and north-east of the house, skilfully deploying some of his favourite ingredients – a rill, a flight of concave-convex steps, a niche and lily pond, and finely detailed stonework including herring-bone laid walls of Devonian character.

Savill and Valley Gardens
see page 173

Sawston Hall
Sawston, Cambridgeshire OS TL4849
English Heritage Register Grade II

15th-century house, remodelled in the 16th century for the Huddleston family; house burnt down and rebuilt after a visit by Mary Tudor in 1553. Remains of moat on two sides, with climbing plants on the balustrades of retaining wall. Enclosures hedged in yew, and a garden of roses and lavender. Small landscaped park of early 19th century.

Sayes Court
Deptford, London TQ3777

The manor house of Sayes Court was given to John Evelyn and his wife, Mary, on their marriage by his father-in-law, Sir Richard Browne. Evelyn had left England during the Civil War, returning to live at Sayes Court with his wife in 1652. In 1653 he wrote in his journal: "I began to set out the ovall garden at Sayes Court, which was before a rude orchard…This was the beginning of all the succeeding gardens, walks, groves, enclosures, and plantations here." His plan from this time survives in the British Library, showing the oval garden. In the great winter of 1683–84, when the Thames froze, Evelyn's garden suffered: "…many of the greenes and rare plantes utterly destroied. The oranges and mirtills very sick, the rosemary and laurels dead." In 1698 the Czar of Russia, Peter the Great, rented Sayes Court (while Evelyn stayed with his brother George at Wotton House, *see page 561*) when he came to England to study shipbuilding at the Royal Naval Dockyard, but vandalised the garden (by, among other things, having himself trundled through hedges in a wheelbarrow), and did much damage to the house. According to Evelyn's journal, Sir Christopher Wren and George London (the royal gardener) estimated the damage to house and garden at £150 (£11,775 today). Both house and garden have long since disappeared, but the name survives, given to a grim public park just off the High Street in Deptford.

Scampston Hall
Rillington, North Yorkshire OS SE8675
English Heritage Register Grade II*
Open regularly Tel 01944 758224

Late 17th-century house for William Hustler, on the site of a medieval house, with alterations in the 18th and early 19th centuries. An elaborate early 18th-century plan, possibly by Charles Bridgeman, was thought to have been Scampston but in the revised edition of *Charles Bridgeman and the English landscape Garden* (2001) Peter Willis says that it is not. 18th-century landscape park. Capability

Brown visited in 1772 and by March of the following year Sir William St Quintin was writing to thank him for a plan for a cascade, "which I like very much", and listing the works that he had carried out: making a ha-ha (to conceal the road, now the A64, from the park), altering the lake and forming an island. He ends, "I beg your acceptance of some Hams." There are three lakes in the park, with a serpentine separated from another by Brown's cascade (which collapsed in the mid 20th century but has been reinstated). In the south-east corner of the park, Deer Park Lodge of *c*.1767, possibly by John Carr of York, has a castellated Gothic façade. The park today is very much as Brown left it.

Scarisbrick Hall
Scarisbrick, Lancashire OS SD3912
English Heritage Register Grade II

House dramatically remodelled 1837–45 for Charles Scarisbrick by A.W. Pugin and later altered by Pugin's son, Edward. Little remains of the 19th-century gardens – lawns, shrubberies, specimen trees and a rose garden. A park surrounds the house, with streams and a lake in the flat marshy land. West of the house, a woodland garden with rhododendrons and a long belt of woodland along the southern boundary. The park was probably laid out for the earlier house in the 1790s, but Humphry Repton produced a Red Book in 1803 and the lake may have been a result of his suggestions.

Scone Palace
see page 392

Scotney Castle Garden
see page 174

Scott Park
Burnley, Lancashire OS SD8233 English Heritage Register Grade II Open regularly

Public park designed by Robert Murray and opened 1895. The park is divided by a stream flowing from the south to the north-west, with paths following and crossing it. A serpentine path encircles the whole site. From the main entrance in the north-east, one path leads south-west into the

stream's wooded valley and another south-east, flanked with rose gardens, to a monument to J.H. Scott (a Burnley businessman, Alderman and Mayor). To the west, a 19th-century octagonal bandstand. There are bowling greens and tennis courts.

Scott's Grotto
Ware, Hertfordshire OS TL3513
English Heritage Register Grade II*
Open regularly Tel 01920 464131

Scott's Grotto was originally in the grounds of Amwell House but is now engulfed in housing. John Scott, a Quaker, built the grotto, the largest in England. He had finished the first part by 1764 when he wrote to a friend, "I have finish'd my Shell Temple, both the Inner Room or Grotto and the Portico, and now begun another Cavern or Subterraneous Grot." There are five subterranean chambers, most of which retain their 18th-century decoration of flint, shells and minerals. Two other garden buildings survive near the Grotto: a restored flint-covered rustic summerhouse (*c*.1766) and an octagonal Gothick gazebo (*c*.1768). Barbara Jones, in *Follies & Grottoes* (1974), finds Scott morbid and says he "was a most industrious mole, and his grotto suggests a shell-decorated coal mine." But Samuel Johnson thought that the grotto was a "Fairy Hall; none but a poet could have made such a garden." The Grotto is now owned by the local authority and has been restored.

Scottish National Gallery of Modern Art
Belford Road, Edinburgh Open regularly
Tel 0131 624 6200

The gallery is housed in a splendid building like a Greek temple, formerly John Watson's School. Built in 1825 to the designs of William Burn, it was intended for "the fatherless children of the professional classes". It was converted 1981–84 into the gallery which had previously occupied Inverleith House in the centre of the Royal Botanic Garden Edinburgh (*see page 391*). In 2002 a remarkable and beautiful piece of landscaping was completed to the

designs of Charles Jencks – a great sinuous turfed and terraced bank and three echoing curved pools. From the terraces of the bank, which rises to a height of 21ft/6.3m, there are fine views of the garden and the Edinburgh skyline. It is named the Landform Ueda, after a theory of natural shapes formed in weather systems. It was Jencks's intention that "the landform will create a gateway to the area and identify the gallery from the road as a special place – the locus of contemporary art in Scotland." This is the only public work in Britain of one of the most interesting of modern designers (but see Jencks's own garden at Portrack, *page 524*). The grounds of the gallery are also embellished with works by such artists as Ian Hamilton Finlay, Dan Graham, Barbara Hepworth, Henry Moore and Rachel Whiteread.

Sculpture at Goodwood
see page 175

Seaforde Gardens
Seaforde, Counry Down, Northern Ireland
Open regularly (028) 44811 225

House built for the Forde family (who have lived here since the 17th century) in the early 19th century. Splendid 5-acre/2-hectare walled garden divided in two: one part is a commercial nursery specialising in shrubs and trees; the other an ornamental garden (restored in the 1970s) with a hornbeam maze, Victorian urns and an arbour of *Rosa mulliganii* at the centre. Here are two avenues of eucryphias (a National Collection, of which 21 species and cultivars is held here). Outside the walled garden, the Pheasantry housed a collection of pheasants in the 18th century. It is now pleasure grounds with grand 19th-century conifers, some of enormous size, azaleas, magnolias and rhododendrons.

Seaton Delaval Hall
see page 351

Sedgwick Park
Nuthurst, West Sussex OS TQ1826
English Heritage Register Grade II

Ancient site with 17th-century house remodelled in the 18th

century and rebuilt 1886 for Mrs Emma Henderson by Ernest George and Harold Peto. George and Peto also designed a new formal garden south of the house. Descending from a deep paved terrace, steps lead to a semicircular terrace with curved yew hedges from which a walk, hedged in yew, runs across a lawn. At the end, steps lead down to a water garden with buttresses of yew flanking a long rectangular pool. Other formal gardens to the east of the house include a croquet lawn, pergola and rose garden. In the park to the north of the house, a very long canal (432ft/130m), a survival from some earlier, undated landscape scheme.

Sefton Park

Liverpool, Merseyside OS SJ3787 English Heritage Register Grade II* Open regularly

Public park designed by Edouard André and Lewis Hornblower, opened in 1872. The first public park in England to be influenced by new French ideas of park design, with paths disposed in bold circles and ellipses, and planting and mounding concealing paths from each other. The park is divided into many enclosed spaces of varying size to accommodate different activities. From the main entrance in the north-west corner, an avenue with cast-iron lampstands passes an obelisk with drinking fountains (1906, commemorating Samuel Smith). The avenue ends at the meeting point of several paths, marked by a fountain; to the north, a curved aviary with rustic rockwork arches. Two streams run across the park: that from the east flows through a series of cascades and rockwork pools, called the Dell, past a beautiful octagonal palm house (1896, designed by Mackenzie & Moncur and magnificently restored in 2001), and into a long serpentine lake running south to the bottom of the park. From the north, a second stream also joins the lake at this point, after passing through a run of cascades and pools; at its northern end is a rustic rockwork grotto, and it is adorned with a statue of Peter Pan (1928, by Sir George Frampton) and a

bandstand (19th century) on an island. The park's rockwork was designed by a French craftsman, Monsieur Combaz.

Sennowe Hall

nr Gateley, Norfolk TF9825
English Heritage Register Grade II

18th-century house, enlarged 1855–56 by Decimus Burton, and again in the early 20th century. In the early 20th century Edward Skipper laid out formal gardens in the Italian style by the house. A shallow terrace against the south façade has steps down to two grassed terraces enclosed by balustrades. Massive steps link these terraces at each end, with domed open pavilions beside each flight of steps. Open parkland, with a lake and boathouse to the south, and on rising ground beyond the river Wensum, a lion on a pedestal (1909).

Seton House

Seton, East Lothian OS NT4175
Scottish Inventory

The house, built in 1790 for Alexander Mackenzie on the site of Seton Palace, was designed in Robert Adam's splendid castle style – with towers, machicolations and arrow slits, but also with elegant Georgian windows. The Seton family came here in the 12th century but the date of the palace is not known, though it was extensively restored after a fire in 1544. Nor, although fine 16th-century garden walls with circular vantage points remain, is it known how the old garden was laid out. Burns flow through the policies, and north of the house the Dell, in a ravine, is planted with acers, magnolias and rhododendrons down to the banks of the burn.

Sezincote

nr Moreton-in-Marsh, Gloucestershire
OS SP1731 English Heritage Register Grade I
Open regularly

The house is a charming oddity, built from 1805 onwards for an East India Company nabob, Charles Cockerell, to the designs of his brother, Samuel Pepys Cockerell. He was helped by the artists Thomas and William Daniell, who had studied and

painted Indian architecture. It is crowned with a voluptuous onion-shaped copper dome, and pretty domed minarets embellish the roofline. Curving out from the south side of the house is a conservatory with large scalloped Moghul windows, which ends in a lavishly decorated octagonal pavilion topped with onion-shaped finials and a central copper dome echoing that of the house. This irresistible piece of orientalism is set in as English a setting as you could find, with fine trees to be seen everywhere. Thomas Daniell was responsible for the delightful bridge, decorated with cast-iron brahmin bulls, which spans the stream to the north of the house. Below it is a pool with a curious fountain in the form of a snake entwining a tree trunk; candelabra primulas flourish about its banks. Upstream from the bridge, the Temple Pool has a Coade stone figure of Souriya in an elaborate stone shrine. The banks of the pool are planted with cherries, crab-apples and more rarified shrubs such as the angelica tree (*Aralia elata* 'Variegata'). The banks of the stream are also well planted, with daylilies, hostas, *Iris sibirica*, lysichitons and rodgersias, and with ornamental trees and shrubs planted in the surrounding grass – cercidiphyllum, dogwoods, maples and others. Humphry Repton is said to have had a hand in the landscape at Sezincote but the only documentary evidence is a "before and after" painting showing the tidying away of some outhouses which draw the eye from the conservatory. South of the house is a formal Mughal garden designed in the 1960s by Graham Stuart Thomas. Here, overlooked by the domed house, is an octagonal pool with two slender canals stretching away and flanked by Irish yews.

Shakespeare's Birthplace

see page 276

Shardeloes

Amersham, Buckinghamshire OS SU9397
English Heritage Register Grade II*

Mid 18th-century house on an earlier site for William Drake,

designed by Stiff Leadbetter and with later work by Robert Adam and James Wyatt. In 1726 Montague Garrard Drake paid Charles Bridgeman £50 (£4,000 today) for work on the grounds. An engraving in *Vitruvius Britannicus* (1739) shows a canal north of the house and an immense geometric layout, chiefly at some distance from the house at the end of an avenue. By 1761 the canal had been made into an informal lake, although parts of the formal gardens remained, but when Nathaniel Richmond was employed to landscape the grounds 1763–70, the formal layout was lost. Richmond and his foreman, Henshaw, were paid £2,300 (£151,765 today) for the work. In 1794 Humphry Repton produced a Red Book and recommended a drive through the beech woods to the north of the house, from which views of the house would be carefully revealed. Traces of the drive remain, with individual horse chestnuts and limes surviving from the late 18th century. A clump of trees suggested by Repton survives, as does the planting at the east of the lake to conceal a dam. J.C. Loudon's *Encyclopaedia of Gardening* (1822) describes Shardeloes as "situated on the brow of a hill, overlooking a broad sheet of water, planned by Bridgeman. The park is much varied in surface, and richly clothed in beechwoods." The estate is now in divided ownership and the house has been divided into flats since c.1960. It is illustrated in an aerial photograph in Christopher Taylor's *Parks and Gardens of Britain: A Landscape History from the Air* (1998); Taylor notes that "Shardeloes remains a particularly well preserved late-eighteenth-century landscape".

Sharpham House

Ashprington, Devon OS SX8257
English Heritage Register Grade II*

Older house rebuilt by Sir Robert Taylor c.1770 for Captain Philemon Pownall in a fine position on a promontory overlooking the river Dart; an octagonal gazebo of c.1720 overlooks the river. 18th-century landscape park with ha-ha,

remaining in largely unaltered state and described by Dorothy Stroud in her *Capability Brown* (1975) as "traditionally ascribed" to Brown, but no evidence is cited. J.C. Loudon visited Sharpham in 1842 but found it "in a state of sad neglect" and he noted the absence of recent planting: "An old place, with nothing but old trees, leaves the mind without hope. There is nothing to look forward to but their decay."

Shaw House

Shaw, Berkshire OS SU4768
English Heritage Register Grade II

Grand late 16th-century house, replacing an older house and built for Thomas Dolman, a rich clothier. The house was owned by Humphry Dolman 1618–66 and he may have laid out the Great Garden with a raised walk. The site of the Great Garden is today partly covered by school buildings and a tennis court but an early 17th-century (or possibly late 16th-century) raised walk survives on three sides, planted with old clipped yews.

Sheffield Botanical Gardens

Sheffield, South Yorkshire OS SK3386
English Heritage Register Grade II
Open regularly

The Sheffield Botanical and Horticultural Society was formed in 1833 to make a botanical garden. A competition to lay out the new gardens was won by Robert Marnock and the completed gardens were open to members of the society in 1836; the public were admitted on four days a year. Today the gardens are maintained as a public park by Sheffield Parks Department and have more of the character of a public park than that of a botanical garden. They contain a long range of conservatories built 1836–38 to the designs of Benjamin Taylor – among the earliest curvilinear glasshouses in the country and finely restored in 2002. Winding paths follow Marnock's original scheme, a rose garden is enclosed in yew hedges, areas of woodland have good specimen trees in clearings, a rock

S

S

garden has a cascade and pool, and a Crimean war memorial (brought here in 1960) terminates a vista. The gardens received a Heritage Lottery Fund award of £5,000,000 which, together with other fund raising, has financed a restoration due for completion in 2004.

Sheffield General Cemetery

Sheffield, South Yorkshire OS SK3485
English Heritage Register Grade II
Open regularly

Nonconformist cemetery, designed in 1836 by the architect Samuel Worth, who was also responsible for an Egyptian-style entrance (from Cemetery Road), a chapel with a dash of Doric mixed with Egyptian, and a classical gateway flanked by lodges at the head of Cemetery Avenue. Curving paths link different parts of the cemetery and there is much planting of trees, in particular weeping forms of ash and holly. A Church of England extension on the east side is thought to have been laid out by Robert Marnock; originally separated by a wall called Dissenters' Wall, but today linked by an axial walk. In the 1980s the Church of England part was largely cleared of headstones and has become a public park.

Sheffield Park Garden

see page 176

Sheldon Manor

nr Chippenham, Wiltshire OS ST8814
English Heritage Register Grade II

House dating from the 13th century, with much later alteration, especially in 17th and 18th centuries. There were two gardens and two orchards here in the 13th century but apart from that nothing is known of gardens before the 20th century, with most of the planting after World War II. Stone walls, yew hedging and paved paths provide the framework for lavish planting, especially of shrub roses. A formal water garden has lead urns and statues.

Sherborne Castle

Sherborne, Dorset OS ST6416
English Heritage Register Grade II*
Open regularly Tel 01935 813182

The now ruinous old castle was first built in the 11th century for Bishop Roger of Salisbury. In the 16th century it was leased by Sir Walter Raleigh who abandoned attempts to live there and in the last years of the 16th century built a new castle a quarter of a mile away. In 1617 this was given to Sir John Digby, whose descendants live there today. Capability Brown was consulted in 1756 and 1775–79; nothing appears to have been done as a result of the first consultation but landscaping work in the 1770s (including a serpentine lake between the two castles with a Gothic dairy nearby) was charged at £1,250 (£75,000 today). The ornamental Pinford Bridge was built in about 1790; a drawing in the castle museum shows that it was designed by Robert Adam and the Hon. Captain Digby. Today, the ruins of the old castle form a picturesque ornament in the landscape – splendidly visible from the Exeter –Waterloo railway.

Sherborne House

Sherborne, Gloucestershire OS SP1614
English Heritage Register Grade II
Park open regularly (NT)

House built in the mid 16th century for Thomas Dutton, subsequently much changed, and rebuilt 1829–34 by Lewis Wyatt. The beautiful park (which is owned by the National Trust and has waymarked paths) was probably originally a deer park contemporary with the Tudor house. Modern, post 1960, formal gardens by the house.

Sheriff Hutton Park

Sheriff Hutton, North Yorkshire OS SE6655
English Heritage Register Grade II*

Early 17th-century house for Sir Arthur Ingram, with alterations in the 18th and 19th centuries. A plan and survey of 1624 shows an oval deer park "well stored with fallow deer and set with near 4,000 decayed or decaying oaks… a fair new lodge…garden enclosed with a brick wall with mount

walks and fair ornaments". Sir Arthur planted shrubs, roses and fruit trees bought in London. On one occasion he sent some rose bushes with instructions to "set them at every corner of the knots and cut the privet into beasts and set the court walls with honeysuckle." In 1637 twenty heraldic beasts were carved in stone by Thomas Ventris, a York sculptor, as garden ornaments. In the 18th century a landscape park was made, incorporating many of the old oaks. In the park immediately south-east of the hall, a statue by John Ashbie of a Roman soldier on a plinth, made in 1638. Terraces and walls survive from the early 17th-century garden.

Sheringham Park

see page 320

Shibden Hall

Calderdale, West Yorkshire OS SE1025
English Heritage Register Grade II
Open regularly Tel 01422 352246

Early 15th-century house built for William Otes, a cloth merchant, with subsequent alterations. Terraced gardens to the east, south and west of the house, laid out in 1836 by William Gray for Anne Lister. In 1855 Joshua Major and Son designed a "shawl" garden for the south terrace – inspired by the colourful swirling patterns of Paisley shawls. This does not survive, although an aerial photograph of 1930 shows it in place. South of the west terrace, a valley garden with cascade and flowering shrubs. In the park north-east of the house, a boating lake formed in the 1830s by damming the Red beck. The grounds today are a public park.

Shipton Court

Shipton-under-Wychwood, Oxfordshire
OS SP2717 English Heritage Register Grade II

Jacobean mansion built c.1603 for the Lacey family. The estate changed hands many times until it was bought by W.F. Pepper in 1900. He commissioned the architects Perkins & Bulmer to redo the interior (destroying every trace of Jacobean work) and to lay out a formal garden – a water garden with a lily pool in the

form of a canal, with a dovecote and summerhouse. Ground between house and water garden terraced with dry-stone walls, the upper terrace originally turfed for croquet and tennis. Wild garden with stream, cascades ("the Lifts"), ponds and woodland.

Shirburn Castle

Shirburn, Oxfordshire OS SU6996
English Heritage Register Grade II

14th-century castle for the de Lisle family; a park was first enclosed at the same time. Estate bought in 1716 by Thomas Parker, later Baron Macclesfield, who made many alterations. A bowling green was in place by 1718 and a water garden ("Upper Duckery" – now a serpentine lake) by 1720, and avenues laid out. Early 19th-century orangery in formerly walled flower garden, first laid out in the 18th century. Stone rotunda built 1741 to the design of Westby Gill among trees close to the flower garden. West of flower garden, woodland with avenues (Clare Walk). Path through trees to part of the old water garden ("Lower Duckery") to domed stone orangery built 1720–40. 18th-century walled kitchen garden. Pevsner, as he noted in the "Buildings of England" volume *Oxfordshire* (1974), was not allowed to inspect Shirburn Castle. He points out that the 18th-century traveller Lord Torrington was twice refused admission, after which he wrote in 1785, "a very ugly place in a very ugly country…melancholy and tasteless" (sour grapes?).

Shirenewton Hall

Shirenewton, Gwent OS ST4793
Cadw/ICOMOS Register Grade II*

Early 19th-century house built for William Hollis on an older site. In 1900 the estate was bought by Charles Liddell, a merchant in the Far Eastern trade. In a field south-west of the house he laid out a Japanese garden with a series of ponds, cascades, bridges and winding paths, with bonsai maples and pines. There are stone lanterns, a pagoda, tea pavilion and red painted archways. It is so well done that it is likely that he had the help of Japanese gardeners.

Terraced gardens about the house also have oriental features: a Chinese bronze fountain and bowls; a platform with green and yellow tiles supporting a pavilion housing an enormous bronze bell and a smaller pavilion crowned with a dragon.

Shireoaks Hall

Shireoaks, Nottinghamshire OS SK5580
English Heritage Register Grade II*

Early 17th-century house for the Hewett family, possibly designed by Robert Smythson, with much later alteration. South-west of the house, a long canal with many cascades and oval and circular pools was already derelict when a visitor saw it in 1825: "the glittering cascade…gone to ruin." The canal had been the central line of a three-part *patte d'oie* flanked by avenues of beech and centred on the house. This, and various other ornamental features now disappeared, dates from the early 17th century. North-east of the house are the remains of a 17th-century terrace leading to walled kitchen gardens.

Shobdon Court

Shobdon, Herefordshire OS SO4062
English Heritage Register Grade II

Remains of early 18th-century house, the bulk of which was demolished in 1933. Parts of the layout of an early 18th-century formal garden survive. An arcaded terrace south of the house is probably 18th-century. It overlooks a gravel walk, terraces and lawns with many specimen trees. Sunken garden within 6ft-/1.8m-high remaining walls of old house. To the north and east, shrubbery with specimen trees, some of which may date from the 18th century. The original early 18th-century formal gardens, probably by Thomas Greening, were largely done away with when the landscape park was remodelled c.1750, but new formal gardens were put in place in the 19th century, possibly following the old design. North of the house, a grass walk lined with mature oaks leads to the Arches, a mid 18th-century eyecatcher incorporating Romanesque parts of Shobdon church, removed when it was rebuilt. East of the house, on a hillock, an 18th-century Ionic temple and old sweet chestnuts.

Shobrooke Park

Shobrooke, Devon OS SS8501
English Heritage Register Grade II
Open regularly Tel 01363 775153

19th-century house for John Henry Hippisley, gutted by fire in 1945 and demolished in 1947. Mid 19th-century lodges by T.L. Donaldson survive, with gate piers and gates. Park, with the river Creedy flowing through it, partly made in mid 19th century but probably incorporating earlier work, with lakes (one of which is crossed by a bridge), and fine trees. Remains of 19th-century gardens with terraces, fountain, ornamental seat and sundial.

Shortgrove Park

Newport, Essex OS TL5235
English Heritage Register Grade II

17th-century house, with later alterations, destroyed by fire in 1966, the shell only remaining. Capability Brown advised the Earl of Thomond on the design of the grounds in 1758. Peter Muilman's *History of Essex* (1770) reported recent improvements to the estate and noted a "lawn…encompassed by fine plantations" and, spanning the river Cam which flows through the grounds, an "elegant stone bridge over three arches" (designed by Matthew Brettingham the Elder 1758–62). Brown widened the river and was probably responsible for planting the surviving perimeter tree belts. The widened river was narrowed again to accommodate the M1 motorway which runs along the western boundary of the park. 18th-century dovecote north of site of the house, with a pool to the east probably by Brown.

Shotover House

nr Oxford, Oxfordshire OS SP5806
English Heritage Register Grade I
Open occasionally for NGS and by appointment Tel 01865 874095

Part of the royal forest of Shotover in the middle ages. In 1613 Timothy Tyrrell became ranger of the forest and built a house (before 1666 when the estate was disafforested). James Tyrrell inherited in 1701, starting a new house (from 1715, probably designed by the Oxford builder William Townesend) and laying out formal gardens. Neither was complete when he died in 1718 and they were finished by his son, General James Tyrrell. The formal gardens are an outstanding early 18th-century survival – extending east and west along strong axes on either side of the house. The east façade, with its loggia, overlooks a lawn with a circular pool and fountain with grass terraces. Beyond it are the fishpond and the Long Canal (1,000ft/300m long) pointing away from the house. The vista ends in a remarkably early castellated and pinnacled Gothic temple (*c*.1718) resembling Oxford collegiate architecture of the kind associated with William Townesend at the time. West of the house are the pleasure grounds for which General Tyrrell was responsible. He commissioned two garden buildings from William Kent *c*.1730: an obelisk and a domed and rusticated octagonal temple which faces down three rides and towards the obelisk to the north; this part of the garden originally had serpentine walks through the woods. The layout survives substantially intact and is remarkably beautiful.

Shrubland Gardens

see page 321

Shugborough

see page 276

Shute House

see page 60

Sissinghurst Castle Garden

see page 177

Sissinghurst Court

Sissinghurst, Kent OS TQ7837
English Heritage Register Grade II

House partly of the 17th century, remodelled and extended in the 1920s. South and south-east of the house, garden of compartments laid out from 1930 with yew hedges, outstanding herbaceous borders, and a pergola with clematis and roses. A rectangular sunken pool garden is enclosed in yew hedges.

North of the pool, a lawn with a summerhouse and rectangular rose beds on three sides.

Sizergh Castle

see page 351

Skibo Castle

nr Dornoch, Sutherland OS NH7389
Scottish Inventory

Skibo is a Norse name and the site probably has its origins as a Viking settlement. In the 12th century the estate belonged to Gilbert, Archdeacon of Moray, later Bishop of Caithness and Sutherland, and the grounds at Skibo were first laid out by monks from the Bishop's Palace at Dornoch. After many changes of ownership it was bought by the great philanthropist Andrew Carnegie who commissioned a gigantic new castellated castle designed by Ross and Macbeth, built 1900–5. At the same time an older terraced garden was remodelled by Thomas Mawson with a balustraded staircase. Today there are herbaceous borders and, at its foot, a formal rose garden with a pool. A late 19th-century walled garden has a range of glasshouses used for cultivating tender fruit – apricots, figs, grapes and peaches – and beds of fruit and vegetables. Woodland has some trees going back to the 18th century and a collection of specimen trees with azaleas and rhododendrons. In recent years the castle has become the Carnegie Club – "A private residential golf and sporting club, with an international membership limited by invitation". The policies are finely maintained.

Slane Castle

Slane, County Meath, Republic of Ireland

Ancient estate of the Conyngham family. The present house, designed in battlemented Gothic style by James Wyatt, was started in 1785 for the 2nd Lord Conyngham. The grounds were laid out by John Sutherland, with much tree planting, in the late 18th century. The work was criticised by Sutherland's younger rival, James Fraser ("exhibits many of the beauties and defects of his style") but J.C. Loudon, in his *Encyclopaedia of Gardening* (1822),

described Slane as "A splendid mansion…and the grounds, through which flows the Boyne, planting and being otherwise improved." The demesne today is finely wooded and covers an area of 1,500 acres/607 hectares. Castle badly damaged by fire in 1991 but now restored. Home of legendary rock concerts and such amusements as Medieval Festivals.

Slaugham Place

Slaugham, West Sussex OS TQ2627
English Heritage Register Grade II

A grand late 16th-century house was built here for Sir Walter Covert to a design by John Thorpe, of which only the ruins survive – which include a pair of octagonal brick towers. A new house was built in 1901 to the south. Garden walls to the north of the old house date from the late 16th century to the early 17th century. A raised turf walk, supported on a dry-stone wall, is crowned with an old yew hedge clipped into bastions. There are lawns, many bulbs and rock plants and herbs planted in the walls.

Sledmere House

Sledmere, East Yorkshire OS SE9364
English Heritage Register Grade I
Open regularly Tel 01377 236637

House built 1751–53 for Richard Sykes and much added to by Sir Christopher Sykes from 1783, probably to his own designs. Thomas White and Capability Brown were both consulted about the landscape, in 1776 and 1778 respectively, and Sir Christopher adopted some of their suggestions. Terrace south of house, with a lawn terraced down to a rectangular grassed platform. Views to the Castle (1778, by John Carr), an ornamental farmhouse, and to the south to a pedimented deer house (1792, probably by Sir Christopher Sykes). West of the house, lawns and a late 20th-century knot garden with an 18th-century fountain. Parkland enclosed in shelter belts. South-east of house, remains of a pre-1755 avenue which Brown wanted partly to retain. West and south-west of the house, farms (Marramatte and Life Hill), probably designed by Sir

Christopher and conceived as landscape ornaments visible from house, now obscured by mature planting. In *The Beauties of England* (1812), John Bigland writes of Sledmere: "The circumadjacent hills are adorned with elegant farmhouses covered with blue slate, and resembling villas erected for the purpose of rural retirement."

The Slopes

Buxton, Derbyshire OS SK0573
English Heritage Register Grade II
Open regularly

Pleasure grounds, laid out *c*.1818, probably by Jeffry Wyatville, for the 6th Duke of Devonshire, to form a setting for the Crescent and buildings relating to the Spa. The land slopes up steeply from the Crescent, grassed and planted with scattered trees, with terraces and paths forming a series of ellipses ascending the slope. Fine 18th-century urns on plinths from Londesborough Hall, another Devonshire estate (*see page 504*), ornament the terraces. *The Butterly Directory* described the Slopes in 1835: "opposite the Crescent, a fine rising lawn has been laid out with very great taste, where the company promenade."

Smithills Hall

Bolton, Greater Manchester OS SD6911
English Heritage Register Grade II
Open regularly Tel 01204 332377

Former private estate, now a country park, the house a museum. House dating from the 14th century, with many alterations, especially by George Devey in the late 19th century. Formal terraced gardens under south and east fronts of house. Parterre reconstructed in 1998–99. Grass mound with sundial to south-west of house. East of the house, viewing platform, with access from terrace walk, overlooking wooded valley with cascade and rustic bridge north of house. Trees in the valley underplanted with rhododendrons. The house is surrounded by parkland with some shelter belts, especially to the west. Raveden Clough, a densely wooded valley, runs along the eastern boundary.

S

Snowshill Manor

see page 229

Somerhill,
formerly **Sumerhill**

nr Tonbridge, Kent TQ5337 English Heritage
Register Grade II Open by appointment
Tel 01732 352124

House built 1610–13 for the 4th
Earl of Clanricarde, probably to the
designs of John Thorpe. Alterations
in the 19th century by Anthony
Salvin and in the 20th century by
Sir Herbert Baker. Celia Fiennes
visited Somerhill in 1697 and
described the house standing on a
hill "in a good large parke…with
visto's of walks cut through and
across, a great many which delights
the rider or walker being so shady
with lofty trees." She also noted a
bowling green. Apart from that,
nothing is known of early garden
activity at Somerhill. A painting
(1810–11) by J.M.W. Turner in the
National Gallery of Scotland shows
the house standing at the top of a
wooded hill looking westwards
down through woods to the lake
and to cattle grazing in meadows.
Formal gardens laid out in the
19th century, with lawns and a
geometric pattern of paths. Yew
hedges and bedding by south and
east fronts, with a terrace and
pergola to the east.

Somerleyton Hall

see page 321

South Hill Park

Bracknell, Berkshire OS SU8766
English Heritage Register Grade II

House built 1760 for William
Watts, rebuilt in late 19th century
by Sir Arthur Divett Hayter (later
Lord Haversham). Formal terraces
to the south and east, flanked by
wooded pleasure grounds. Rose
garden with yew hedges and a
walk of Irish yews. Parterre with
knot garden. In the park, lakes to
north and south and several fine
cedars of Lebanon.

Southill Park

Southill, Bedfordshire OS TL1441
English Heritage Register Grade II*
Open occasionally for NGS

Early 18th-century house owned
by Admiral of the Fleet George
Byng (later 1st Viscount

Torrington). Early 18th-century
formal gardens removed when
Capability Brown landscaped the
grounds in 1777, though the
Round Basin immediately to the
north-west of the house, remains.
The house is surrounded by
parkland on three sides; on the
north-eastern boundary, Brown
made a lake which has a bridge of
c.1800 by Henry Holland. By the
north bank of the lake, Holland
also designed a Tuscan fishing
temple to be seen across the water
from the house. The park survives
largely intact.

Southwark Park

Southwark, London OS TQ3579
English Heritage Register Grade II
Open regularly

Public park designed by A.
Mackenzie and opened 1869. At
the centre of the park, a lake and
island with, to the north, a
semicircular formal garden with a
pergola and rose beds. Sports and
recreation facilities: all-weather
athletics pitch, bowling green,
swimming pool. An extension on
land acquired in the 1980s, King's
Stair Gardens, has an undulating
lawn with ornamental trees and
fine riverside views.

Spa Gardens,
formerly **Jephson Gardens**

Leamington Spa, Warwickshire OS SP3165
English Heritage Register Grade II
Open regularly

Public gardens laid out by J.G.
Jackson 1846–48. Slightly
serpentine paths and good
specimen trees in lawns. Lake with
island to south-west. Carpet
bedding still maintained. Several
ornamental buildings – an aviary,
circular temple commemorating
Dr Jephson (1848, by D.G.
Squirhill), an obelisk (1875, by
John Cundall) and a fountain of
1868, also by John Cundall.

Spains Hall

nr Finchingfield, Essex OS TL6734
English Heritage Register Grade II*
Open occasionally for NGS

House built c.1585 for William
Kempe, incorporating an early
15th-century moated house. Part
of the moat survives as a dry

ditch, but in the 17th century
some of it was incorporated in a
series of pools south of the house.
Garden walls date from 16th and
17th centuries but little is known
of early gardening activity. In
1807 Thomas Ruggles consulted
Humphry Repton but no Red
Book was produced. Repton
reshaped one of the old fishponds
into a lake and was probably
responsible for the plantings on
either side of it. A walled garden
contains rose hoops, possibly from
Repton's time. Formal flower
gardens south-east of the house,
laid out in the mid 19th century
with terraces and a view of the
lake.

Spetchley Park

see page 230

Spring Hill House

nr Chipping Camden, Gloucestershire
OS SP1234 English Heritage Register
Grade II

House built in the 1760s for the
6th Earl of Coventry, to the
designs of Capability Brown,
subsequently much altered. House
planned for the Earl as a retreat,
within the park, also designed by
Brown, of Croome Court (*see page
464*). Some of Brown's landscape
survives, though subsequent 19th-
century tree planting by General
Lygon, said to represent the
disposition of troops at Waterloo,
has obscured it.

Springfield Park

Hackney, London OS TQ3487
English Heritage Register Grade II
Open regularly

Public park, opened 1905 on the
site of three gardens of which one,
White Lodge (also known as
Springfield House), an early 19th-
century villa, survives. The site is a
fine one, with views over the Lea
Valley and across Walthamstow
marshes; the river Lea forms the
north-eastern boundary. Much
perimeter planting, with paths and
further winding walks linking the
entrances and chief features. Small
lake with wooded island and
several mature specimen trees on
lawns. Bedding schemes close to
White Lodge. Bowling green and
tennis courts.

Squerryes Court

Westerham, Kent OS TQ4453
English Heritage Register Grade II
Open regularly Tel 01959 562345

Ancient site, occupied since at least
the 13th century. Present house
built 1680–86 for Sir Nicholas
Crisp. Badeslade's print (1719) of
Squerryes Court in John Harris's
History of Kent shows a pretty,
formal garden with several walled
enclosures, parterres flanking the
house and a sunken bowling green
behind the house. Grounds
landscaped in the 18th century
when a lime avenue was
refashioned into a clump and
formal pools west of the house
were turned into a naturalistic lake.
West of the lake, a Palladian temple
of 1735. East of the house, formal
gardens remain; a 19th-century
scheme immediately by the house
has rectangles of lawn, standard
rhododendrons and clipped drums
of Irish yews on the flanks. Mature
specimen trees on lawn to south-
east. To the south, path rises to
horizon viewpoint with Cenotaph
to General Wolfe of c.1760. North-
east of the house, a topiary garden
made since 1964.

Stackpole Court

Stackpole, Pembrokeshire OS SR9796
Cadw/ICOMOS Register Grade I

Ancient estate of the de
Stackpoles; Sir Leonard de
Stackpole was a notable crusader.
They were succeeded by the
Vernons of Haddon Hall (*see page
262*) and the Campbells of
Cawdor (*see page 367*). The house,
built in the middle ages and
rebuilt in the 18th century, does
not survive. Between 1780 and
1840 the Campbells made 80
acres/32 hectares of lakes. There
are many structures associated
with these lakes: a fine eight-
arched bridge, a boathouse, a
hidden bridge (with a path passing
over a cascade) and various sluices
and weirs to control the flow.
Some of the pools were stocked
with fish, others were planted with
lilies (which thrive today). An
article by A.P. Rowler in the
Gardener's Chronicle in 1909
records: "The mansion overhangs a
beautiful artificial lake…and
commands a view of a most
delightful landscape, including

woodland, lake and park." Rowler
describes a wide terrace on the
south front of the house and
writes, "the tender plants that
thrive…particularly on this
terrace, betoken the mild character
of the climate," and goes on to
describe a very wide range of
plants, among them *Agapanthus
africanus*, *Escallonia × exoniensis* and
Pittosporum tobira. He describes
"charming woodland" entered
from the terrace with "many large
evergreen Oaks, magnificent
gnarled Limes…nine gigantic
Beech trees, forming a circle, their
heads a dome, and constituting a
natural temple". He also describes
many exotic conifers and "grand
specimens" of deciduous trees such
as oriental planes and tulip trees.
The terrace survives today, as do
many of the plants he noted.

Stamford Park

Altrincham, Greater Manchester OS SJ7787
English Heritage Register Grade II
Open regularly

Public recreation ground designed
by John Shaw Snr, opened 1880. It
was originally designed to provide
cricket and football pitches
(cricket pitch designed so that it
could be flooded and frozen to
provide skating in winter), bathing
pool, tennis courts, croquet lawns
and an area for quoits – combined
with ornamental gardens. The park
today has the cricket pitch at its
centre with other facilities round
about it, the largest of which is the
football pitch to the east. North-
east of the cricket pitch, two
ponds, one the original bathing
pool. East of cricket pitch, an
island bed, a circular rose garden
and a circular bed enclosed in a
low evergreen hedge. This
corresponds to the original layout
which had, however, much more
elaborate planting. Bowling greens
to south of cricket pitch. Much
planting of trees and shrubs,
especially evergreens, throughout
the park, with several hollies
clipped into cylindrical shapes.

Stamford Park

Stalybridge, Greater Manchester
OS SD9899 English Heritage Register
Grade II Open regularly

Public park designed by Gregory
Hill, opened 1873. The park, long

and narrow, is divided in the middle by Darnton Road running east and west. Formal gardens lie to the south, dominated by a large boating lake. The perimeter of the southern park is wooded, with paths leading to the open centre. At the meeting of paths, various objects of interest: granolithic boulders, monuments to people of note, an 18th-century market cross, and so on. Large conservatory (1907) in the centre, with an aviary to one side. To the north, bowling greens, tennis courts, children's playground and putting green. To the west, the Cock brook flows through the Valley, or Dingle, well wooded and underplanted with rhododendrons and laurels; ornamental rockwork along the path and viewing points from time to time. In the northern park, late 19th- or early 20th-century kiosk, and boathouse of the same period on the western bank of the lake. The steeply sloping banks of the lake are wooded and a separate fishing lake lies to the north.

Stanage Park, also known as Stanedge
nr Knighton, Powys OS SO3372
Cadw/ICOMOS Register Grade I

An old estate for which Charles Rogers commissioned a new house from 1803 to the designs of Humphry Repton. Repton also laid out the grounds, and at this stage in his career, strongly influenced by picturesque ideas, he was much taken with "The wild and shaggy Genius of Stanedge". The site, on high ground between two hills and overlooking a park with two streams, presented all sorts of opportunities for landscaping. The woods, streams, deer park and ponds gave Repton a head start. He adjusted the drive so that the house was revealed only when visitors had penetrated the park, and made more pools. After 1807, 65,000 trees were planted – horse chestnut, larch, oak and sweet chestnut. It is not known what Repton did in the pleasure grounds but a splendid surviving cedar of Lebanon dates from his time. Charles Rogers started an arboretum in around 1840, with trees from the Himalayas – some of them very

recent introductions, such as the deodar (*Cedrus deodara*), Himalayan fir (*Abies spectabilis*) and Bhutan cypress (*Cupressus torulosa*).

Stancombe Park
nr Dursley, Gloucestershire OS ST7397
English Heritage Register Grade I
Open by appointment Tel 01453 542815

House built *c*.1825, and rebuilt after a fire in 1886, reproducing the original Regency style. It lies below Stinchcombe Hill, at the head of a valley, with splendid views of parkland. Formal gardens to the south of the house include colour-themed double borders enclosed in patterns of box. At the bottom of the valley, hidden away, is a lake with an island connected with a Chinoiserie bridge. Overlooking the lake is a Bath stone Tuscan temple. This part of the garden contains the romantic garden created by the Revd David Edwards in around 1840, with mysterious tunnels and rich in exotic buildings of vernacular, Egyptian or classical inspiration.

Stanford Hall
Stanford, Northamptonshire/Leicestershire
OS SP5879 English Heritage Register Grade II
Open regularly Tel 01788 860250

Late 17th-century house, built on the banks of the river Avon for Sir Roger Cave, remodelled in the 1740s by William Smith of Warwick. Serpentine lake west of the house; east of it, the Avon was dammed in the mid 18th century to form another lake with a cascade and bridge at its southern end. A pattern of avenues, probably planted when the house was built, is still visible. The longest, a double avenue of oaks one mile long, runs north-east of the house.

Stanley Park
Blackpool, Lancashire OS SD3235 English
Heritage Register Grade II* Open regularly

Public park designed by Thomas Mawson and opened in 1926. At the heart of the park, strongly designed formal areas with an irregular boating lake to the east and a golf course occupying the chief part of the northern park. Except for the north, the whole park is enclosed in perimeter planting. At the centre, a circular

Italian garden from which paths radiate outwards. The circular space is enclosed by a pergola supported on Tuscan columns. At its centre, a marble fountain surrounded by geometric beds. To the south, tennis courts and athletics ground. On the south shore of the lake, a bandstand in the form of a circular classical temple. Bowling greens to the north-west of the lake and a sunken rose garden with lily ponds.

Stanley Park
Liverpool, Merseyside OS SJ3693 English
Heritage Register Grade II Open regularly

Public park designed by Edward Kemp and opened 1870 – it cost a total of £154,398 (£6,690,065 today). In the western part of the park, a southern boundary is formed by a screen wall with blank arcading, a central pavilion and an octagonal pavilion at each end, designed in Gothic style by E.R. Robson, the city architect. The wall has blocked doors which used to give access to the park from private gardens. It overlooks a terrace with geometric flower beds, and beyond this a second terrace with three bowling greens overlooked by a cast-iron viewing pavilion designed by Robson. In the south-west corner of the park, a large conservatory (1899, by Mackenzie & Moncur) and a cast-iron bandstand; a children's playground and tennis courts nearby. To the north, a lake crossed by an ornamental stone bridge with a Gothic-style pavilion at its southern end, from which there are walks among trees and mounds on the banks of the lake. Park to the east, open grassland, playing fields and a sports centre.

Stanmer Park
Stanmer, East Sussex OS TQ3309
English Heritage Register Grade II
Parkland open regularly

House built 1722–27 for Henry Pelham to the designs of Nicholas Dubois. Dubois seems to have laid out gardens – bowling green, kitchen gardens and pools; and Charles Bridgeman was consulted in 1726, probably to supervise tree planting. The Pelham family, later Earls of Chichester, continued to

develop the grounds into the early 20th century. The pleasure grounds about the house are close to the late 18th-century arrangement, with lawns and excellent trees, some of which date back to 18th-century plantings. South of the house, a Coade stone monument (1775) commemorating Thomas Pelham II's father-in-law, Frederick Meinhart Frankland. In the park, the largely 18th-century village of Stanmer is a notable feature. The park has diverse uses today – as playing fields and arable farmland. Great Wood, to the south-west, provides shelter and retains its 18th-century pattern of paths; it was the site in the 18th century of a menagerie. Kitchen gardens walled in flint and brick, to west of the house, laid out by Dubois in the 1720s, now containing a commercial nursery.

Stanstead Bury
Stanstead Abbots, Hertfordshire OS TL3911
English Heritage Register Grade II

Late 15th-century house, with many alterations. West of house, 16th-century earthworks of three terraces. East of the house, ground also terraced, with an 18th-century ha-ha as its eastern boundary. Park, enclosed in 1577, now largely arable land with belts of trees. To the south-east of the house, walled kitchen garden whose brick walls date from the 16th to the 18th century.

Stansted Park
Stoughton, West Sussex OS SU7610
English Heritage Register Grade II*
Open regularly Tel 023 92412265

Ancient house, originally a royal hunting lodge, rebuilt 1686 for Richard Lumley, 1st Earl of Scarborough by Robert Hooke or William Talman, rebuilt in 1786 by James Wyatt, burnt out in 1900, and a new house built immediately afterwards by Arthur Blomfield. A Kip engraving in *Britannia Illustra* (1707) shows a magnificent garden disposed about a double avenue running east and west, with the house at its centre. All this has disappeared, although replanted avenues have followed old aligments, and 19th-century and early 20th-century gardens by the house echo the earlier formality.

Stanway House
see page 231

Stapleford Park
Freeby, Leicestershire OS SK8118
English Heritage Register Grade II

16th-century house for the Sherard family, altered in 17th and 19th centuries. Little is known of any early garden but archaeological evidence suggests parterres, possibly early 18th-century, east of the house. The park goes back to the early 16th century, when enclosure took place, and there was a deer park by 1640. Capability Brown was consulted in 1775 and the serpentine lake emerging from woodland to the east of the house is characteristic of his work; some tree clumps date from this time, as well as individual trees, in particular oaks. Late 19th-century plantings of beech, horse chestnut, limes and Turkey oaks.

Staunton Harold Hall
Staunton Harold, Leicestershire OS SK3821
English Heritage Register Grade II*

The Shirley family came here in 1423 when Ralph Shirley married the heiress Margaret de Staunton, whose family had held the manor since the 12th century. The Shirleys remained until 1940 when the house was requisitioned by the army. House started in 1763, incorporating a Jacobean and earlier house. Close to the house, standing in parkland with a view of the lake, is the chapel of Holy Trinity, built during the Commonwealth by Sir Robert Shirley whose famous, and very moving, inscription may be seen in it: "In the yeare 1653 when all things sacred were throughout ye nation Either demollisht or profaned Sr Robert Shirley Barronet founded this church whose singular praise is to have done the best things in ye worst times and hoped them in the most callamitous". The chapel is now owned by the National Trust and is open regularly (Tel 01332 863822). There was a deer park here by 1324. A Kip engraving in *Britannia Illustra* (1707) shows the house looking out over a series of enclosed and terraced gardens with pools, fountains and

S

topiary, and on one side an orangery overlooking lawns and an ornate fountain. These were the gardens laid out by the 1st Baron Ferrers, Sir Robert Shirley's second son. By the time Thomas Smith painted the house, c.1764–67, this had been superseded by a suave Brownian scheme, the formal water changed to a serpentine lake. This was the scene until quite recently, and since the estate was broken up in 1954 much clearing of trees has taken place; although little of the historic gardening past remains, the view is very beautiful.

Stepleton House

Iwerne Stepleton, Dorset OS ST8611
English Heritage Register Grade II

Early 17th-century house acquired in 1654 by the Fownes family and in 1745 by Julines Beckford who thoroughly Georgianised it. The grounds were landscaped in the mid 18th century, with a lake formed by damming the river Iwerne. Peter Beckford's kennels (he was a devoted hunting man who wrote a classic on the subject, *Thoughts upon Hare and Fox Hunting* (1781)) were built in the 1770s and survive as cottages. Peter Beckford was a first cousin of William Beckford of Fonthill (*see page 496*). 18th-century kitchen gardens laid out in Queen Anne style in the early 1990s.

Stevenson House

nr Haddington, East Lothian OS NT5474
Scottish Inventory

Courtyard house, on a site dating from the 13th century, built in the 17th century for the Sinclair family. Parkland, with the Tyne river flowing through it, dates from the early 19th century. The entrance drive was an avenue by the mid 18th century and has been replanted in recent times with cultivars of sycamore. Pleasure grounds by house with formal rose garden, colour-themed borders and a rock garden. Walled garden dating from the early 19th century, with a weeping ash as a centrepiece. Double herbaceous borders backed by espaliered apples. Lawns with specimen trees and some beds for fruit and vegetables.

Sticky Wicket

see page 62

Stiffkey Old Hall

Stiffkey, Norfolk OS TF9742
English Heritage Register Grade II

House built for Nathaniel Bacon 1576–81, partly demolished in mid 17th century. Gatehouse dated 1604. Garden walls and terrace east of the house, with remains of a gazebo, are 16th-century. Today there are lawns, herbaceous borders and a rose garden along the terrace. Parkland to the west includes site of another part of the 16th-century garden, with remains of a water channel. The gardens were planned radially about the house and in careful proportion to it.

Stirling Castle

see page 393

Stobhall

nr Perth, Perthshire OS NO1334 Scottish
Inventory Open regularly Tel 01821 640332

House (the Dowery House) built in the late 17th century for the 2nd Earl of Perth on the site of a medieval castle which was destroyed in the Civil War. A 14th-century chapel (with splendid paintings of c.1630 showing the mounted kings and emperors of European and African countries) and various outbuildings form a picturesque group. The Drummond family (later Earls of Perth) had lived here since the 14th century and (after much dynastic toing and froing) the Drummonds once again own the estate. Walled garden by the house dates from the 17th century and has a four-faced sundial raised on a column, dated 1643. In the first half of the 19th century, Clementina Drummond is said to have planned the garden, though it is not known what this involved. By the early 20th century the house was uninhabited. In *Scottish Gardens* (1908) Sir Herbert Maxwell apologises for including "among Scottish gardens a place where a garden was, but is not. Our excuse is that Stobhall remains in its desolation one of the most fascinating places in the realm." It is curious that only six years earlier H. Inigo Triggs had

described the Stobhall walled garden in *Formal Gardens in England and Scotland* (1902), giving no suggestion that it was derelict – "Nothing could be more simple; and yet there is a quaint charm about the garden, with its bright flowers and sentinel like trees." In 1953, when the estate returned to the Drummonds, under the ownership of the 17th Earl of Perth, the gardens were restored. The walled flower garden, still with its sundial, is divided into four box-edged beds filled with mixed plantings and roses and adorned with columns of topiary. A bridge crosses a burn into a woodland garden in the valley, with rhododendrons and ornamental trees. A path leads down to the banks of the Tay and to Campsie Inn where the river rushes over a great cascade – the scene of Conaghar's death in Sir Walter Scott's *Fair Maid of Perth*.

Stobo Castle

nr Peebles, Peeblesshire OS NT1736
Scottish Inventory Water garden open
occasionally for SGS

Splendidly castellated castle, built 1805–11 for Sir James Montgomery to the designs of Archibald and James Elliot in the policies of Weston House. Parkland goes back to the 18th century and some of the original oaks and limes survive, some of the latter from avenues. An article in *Transactions of the Highland & Agricultural Society* (1880–81) on "Old and Remarkable Trees of Scotland" describes four trees at Stobo – an ash, a beech, an oak and a sycamore. John Hay designed attractive formal gardens in 1872 – a "Rosery, Flower Garden and Shrubbery" – but it is not known if they were put into place. Terraced gardens were laid out south of the castle 1909–12, when the estate was owned by Hylton Philipson. At about the same time, Philipson made a fine water garden which was also a hydroelectric scheme. Three lakes are linked by a burn which flows over a great cascade and along rills and small pools. Where it runs through a narrow wooded gorge a garden of Japanese character was made, with stepping stones, a hump-backed bridge and a

summerhouse. Trees planted include *Acer cappadocium*, *Cercidiphyllum japonicum*, *Kalopanax septemlobus* var. *maximowiczii* and *Sciadopitys verticillata*. Since 1975 Stobo Castle has been a health spa.

Stobshiel House

Humbie, East Lothian OS NT4663
Open occasionally for SGS

The estate goes back to the 17th century; part of the house is of that date, but is largely of the 18th and 19th centuries. A walled garden was made in the 19th century, divided by a castellated yew hedge and used for cultivating fruit and vegetables as well as ornamentals. In World War I Miss C.Nisbet started to introduce all kinds of interesting plants. After a period of neglect it was bought in 1984 by Mr and Mrs Peter Ferguson-Smyth who impeccably restored it. A long central gravel path, edged in box, links a series of lavishly planted and delightful box-edged mixed beds – a dazzling patchwork of colour.

Stockwood Park

see page 322

Stoke Edith Park

Stoke Edith, Herefordshire OS SO6040
English Heritage Register Grade II

House destroyed by fire in 1927. The estate was bought in 1670 by Thomas Foley, head of the greatest iron-founding family in the West Midlands, who was attracted by the woods for charcoal production. George London visited Stoke Edith in 1692 and laid out the formal gardens which are probably those depicted in the famous Stoke Edith needlework hangings now at Montacute House in Somerset (*see page 53*) and at the Victoria and Albert Museum. In 1792 Humphry Repton was consulted and produced a Red Book later that year. He proposed major alterations – rerouting the main road, demolishing part of the village and rebuilding it elsewhere, and removing the church spire and the parsonage (both of which competed with the house in the landscape). In the event, the road was moved, the formal gardens disposed of and the park modified

with coppices and groups of trees planted to frame views from the house. It was at Stoke Edith that Repton met his future associate, the architect John Nash. According to Repton, the Foley of the day said of them: "If you two, whom I consider to be the cleverest men in England, could agree to *act together* you might carry the whole world before you." A formal garden was reinstated after 1854 with a parterre designed by W.A. Nesfield and part of this scheme survives.

Stoke Park

Stoke Gifford, Bristol OS ST6277
English Heritage Register Grade II*

The house at Stoke Park was built in the mid 16th century and remodelled 1749–52, and again, 1760–64, by Thomas Wright for Norborne Berkeley (later Lord Botetourt). The garden is the most complete surviving landscape by one of the most enigmatic of 18th-century landscapers, Thomas Wright. The site, on an escarpment, is very beautiful, looking east over the Frome valley and south to the city of Bristol. Wright planted woods with serpentine walks linking viewpoints, garden buildings and ornaments. Clearings in the woods were treated as outdoor rooms, given seats and decorated with flowering shrubs. Bishop Pococke in his *Travells* (1764) described Stoke as "justly reckon'd among the finest places in England". Little of Wright's garden buildings and monuments survives. The footings of Wright's rotunda have been rediscovered, and the remains of an obelisk, but the most complete building is the now restored Beaufort Monument (1756). Its restoration by the Avon Gardens Trust led the way in the revaluation and conservation of Stoke Park. After Lord Botetourt's death in 1770, Stoke became a dower house for Badminton House (*see page 441*) but it was well cared for into the early 20th century. In 1908 it became a home for the mentally handicapped and passed in due course to the National Health Service, whose attempt to cover the park in houses was thwarted by a campaign of local residents. The house has been vandalised and is now empty and its future uncertain – a pitiful sight and a dismal history. Despite the immediate proximity of the M32, the park at Stoke retains a glimmer of its Arcadian charms.

Stoke Park
Stoke Bruerne, Northamptonshire OS SP7448 English Heritage Register Grade II Open occasionally for NGS

Beautiful house of Palladian inspiration, built for Sir Francis Crane 1629–35 and attributed by Colen Campbell to Inigo Jones. A central building was connected by two colonnades to pavilions (originally a chapel and a library). The central part was destroyed by fire in 1886, leaving only the pavilions. Formal gardens by the pavilions, with a grass terrace and balustrade separating them, and a lily pool and fountain. Magnolias along the terrace wall and many shrub roses.

Stoke Park
Stoke Poges, Buckinghamshire OS SP9682 English Heritage Register Grade II

House, on a much older site, designed by Robert Naismith in 1789 and completed by James Wyatt in the 1790s for John Penn. The remains of the Elizabethan manor house stand to the north-east of the present mansion. In c.1750 Capability Brown laid out the park – one of his earliest commissions – forming the serpentine lake east and south-east of the house. Nathaniel Richmond was employed in the 1760s to work on the park but what he did is not known. Humphry Repton produced a Red Book in 1792, in which he recommended a "highly polished garden scene" in pleasure grounds to the west of the house separated from the park by a ha-ha. This was put into place c.1808 and John Penn was also influenced by William Mason's poem The English Garden (1772–81); traces of his garden, including some stone seats, survive. In the park, old oaks, and to the north, a Roman Doric column by James Wyatt (1800) commemorating Edward Coke who owned the estate in the early 17th century. To the south, a memorial to Thomas Gray erected

in 1799 and planned as an eyecatcher to be seen from the park – a giant sarcophagus on a pedestal, with verses from Gray's Elegy in a Country Churchyard. (The poem is said to be inspired by Stoke Poges, where Gray's mother lived.) The house is now a hotel, surrounded by a golf course, with housing in parts of the park.

Stoke Poges Gardens
Stoke Poges, Buckinghamshire OS SP9682 English Heritage Register Grade II

On the east side of Stoke Park and south of the church. Land given for a garden in 1928 by Sir Noel Mobbs, where he and his wife Helen have a memorial. Laid out by Milner, Son and White in the early 1930s. Yew-hedged enclosures off a central walk provide intimate spaces for memorials. Ornamental gardens include parterres, an elaborate sunken water garden surrounded by a pergola, rock gardens, a rose garden, and lawned areas with trees and shrubs.

Stoke Rochford Hall
Stoke Rochford, Lincolnshire OS SK9128 English Heritage Register Grade II

A remarkably ancient site with a continuous history of habitation from at least Roman times. The present house was built 1841–43 to the designs of William Burn for Christopher Turnor (at a cost of £60,000 (£2,532,199 today)). 18th-century landscaping. The Cringle brook flows through the park, linking pools of possibly medieval origin, some of which were made into a lake in the 18th century, spanned by an early 19th-century bridge. Formal gardens designed by Burn, with terraces and balustrading but now lacking the statues that animated them. In 1847 Burn also designed a 60ft/18m obelisk in memory of Sir Isaac Newton (a Lincolnshire man, born not far away at Woolsthorpe, see page 561).

Stokesay Court
nr Onibury, Shropshire OS SO4478 English Heritage Register Grade II

Grand neo-Elizabethan mansion built 1889 to the designs of Thomas Harris for J.D. Allcroft.

Harris also designed outhouses and kitchen gardens. The garden was designed by Henry Ernest Milner with, south of house, a balustraded terrace, sloping lawn, shrubbery with trees and a formal pool with fountain and urns. Elaborate rockery and a rustic octagonal summerhouse with thatched roof. Country Life in 1901 wrote of the garden: "thousands of Alpine plants grow in perfection. Ingenious hands and excellent taste have worked here."

Ston Easton Park
Ston Easton, Somerset OS ST6254 English Heritage Register Grade II Open occasionally

Fine Palladian house built c.1750 for the Hippisley family on the site of an earlier house. In 1792 Humphry Repton produced for Henry Hippisley Coxe a Red Book of recommendations. As a result, a stream north and east of the house was dammed to make a more imposing river, with two weirs and a bridge. Early 19th-century gardens by Lady Hippisley. In the late 20th century, restoration of the gardens was carried out under the supervision of Penelope Hobhouse. The house is now a smart hotel/restaurant.

Stonefield Castle Hotel
South Knapdale, Argyll OS NR8671 Scottish Inventory

Castle built 1837 to the designs of William Playfair for John Campbell on the west bank of Loch Fyne. Campbell's cousin and friend, Dr A. Campbell of Oronsay, went to India and collected seed in Darjeeling. He also had seed from Sikkim of the rhododendrons discovered by J.D. Hooker and described in his book, The Rhododendrons of Sikkim-Himalaya (1849–51) – probably the most influential rhododendron book ever published. Seeds of many of these came to Stonefield and over 21 specimens of Hooker rhododendrons survive in the garden. Examples in the Wild Garden include R. arboreum (the white form), R. falconeri subsp. eximium, R. falconeri and R. niveum. There are other good

shrubs and some outstanding exotic conifers at Stonefield but it is these magnificent early Hooker rhododendrons that are the great treasures.

Stone House Cottage
see page 232

Stone Lane Gardens
see page 62

Stonehurst
West Hoathly, West Sussex OS TQ3431 English Heritage Register Grade II

House built for John Stewart c.1910 to the design of Norman Searle, on an earlier site. Garden by Thomas Mawson from 1907. North of the house, a series of brick-walled gardens: a croquet lawn, pergola and swimming-pool garden (formerly a rose garden). The pergola links an observatory to a loggia and dressing rooms. To the east of the house, a terrace with tea chalets at each end and a large rock garden.

Stoneleigh Abbey
Stoneleigh, Warwickshire OS SP3371 English Heritage Register Grade II* Open regularly Tel 01926 858585

Cistercian abbey founded in the 12th century and transformed into a grand Georgian house, chiefly by Francis Smith of Warwick, 1714–26. The house stands at the centre of parkland across which the river Avon flows, joined by the river Sowe. In 1808 Thomas Leigh consulted Humphry Repton and a Red Book was produced. Repton suggested broadening the Avon to bring it close to the house, and enlivening the banks of the river by means of "those graceful and picturesque combinations we admire in the works of the best painters such as Gaspard Poussin and Claude Lorraine, and in the garden scenery of the graceful Watteau". The Red Book shows an intensely picturesque scheme, with wild planting on the banks, an ornamental bridge, an urn rising among plants and seats at the river's edge – all of which was done. Later in the 19th century, existing terraces west and south of the house were given balustrades, steps and urns, with formal

plantings of box, yew and bedding schemes – possibly the work of W.A. Nesfield. Another formal garden was made at this time between the kitchen garden and the Avon. Both these schemes were modified, and simplified, by Percy Cane in the 1930s.

Stonewall Park
Chiddingstone Hoath, Kent OS TQ5042 English Heritage Register Grade II Open occasionally for NGS

Early 19th-century house for John Woodgate, replacing a 16th-century house on a different site. Deep valley to north of house planted as pleasure grounds, with ornamental shrubs under a canopy of beech and oak. Outcrops of rock, and a stream flowing down the valley, with falls and pools filling a large pool just to the north of the house. Early 19th-century park south of the house separated by a brick ha-ha.

Stoney Road Allotments
Coventry, West Midlands OS SP3276 English Heritage Register Grade II*

A remarkably ancient site outside the medieval city walls of Coventry, dating back to the 12th century when it was owned by the Earl of Chester. After passing through the hands of many notable owners, including members of the royal family, it was bought in 1819 by the Marquess of Hertford who divided it into small gardens and paddocks for renting out. By 1870 there were many such small plots, "all well cultivated, and much sought after in consequence of their easy distance and pleasant situation". After several changes of ownership, the site (of c.12 acres/4.8 hectares) now belongs to Coventry City Council and still contains allotments cultivated by tenant gardeners. The plots are typically enclosed in hedges of box, hawthorn, holly or privet and are used for both ornamental and productive gardening. One plot retains exactly the layout which it had in 1887, with an avenue of apple trees running up to a summerhouse; several other old summerhouses, often with lively detailing, survive.

S

Stonor

Stonor, Oxfordshire OS SU7489

English Heritage Register Grade II*

Open regularly Tel 01491 638587

An ancient estate in the Chiltern hills; the Stonor family, which still lives here, has owned it since at least the 12th century. The present house incorporates medieval work and was substantially remodelled in the early 17th century and again in the following century. A painting of the late 17th century, in John Harris's *The Artist and the Country House* (1979), shows an enclosed entrance forecourt with an ornate gateway and, to one side of the house, a large walled garden divided into twelve square beds with plants trained against the walls. The forecourt and its gateway have gone but the walled garden survives, now a kitchen garden with glasshouses and a frame yard (for cold frames). House and garden are surrounded by a park grazed by fallow deer, with many substantial old trees. To the north and south-east are wooded areas crossed by rides.

Stonyhurst College

nr Hurst Green, Lancashire OS SD6939

English Heritage Register Grade II*

Open regularly Tel 01254 826345

16th-century house on a much older site, with many subsequent additions, in particular those connected with its conversion into a school in the late 18th century. To the west, the Avenue leads between two canals to a walled forecourt – all, in essence, dating from the late 17th or early 18th century. In a walled garden south of the school house, two ogee-roofed pavilions of *c*.1700 and a circular lily pool of the same date. An octagonal stone observatory dates from 1838. Path from lily pond leads east to neighbouring garden with 20th-century parterre and a sunken circular lawn, called the Bowling Green, enclosed in yew. To the east, a terrace and the Dark Walk of yews. The poet Gerard Manley Hopkins taught here in the 1870s and wrote of "a garden with a bowling green, walled in by massive yew hedges, a bowered yew walk with two real Queen Anne summerhouses". Parkland north and west of the school, with some mature trees and clumps and various playing fields.

Stourhead

see page 106

Stover Park

Teigngrace, Devon OS SX8374

English Heritage Register Grade II

House built 1776–80 for James Templer and probably also designed by him. Landscaping of the same period and a terrace surrounding the house. In 1850 the house was described as standing "on a pleasant eminence in a finely wooded park". In the 19th century Veitch's nursery of Exeter advised on the planting and introduced rhododendrons. Pedimented and pillared Ionic temple and a bizarre grotto with windows cut into the stone. 18th-century 20-acre/8-hectare lake now part of the separate Stover Country Park. Stover House is now a school.

Stowe Garden

see page 107

Stradbally Hall

Stradbally, County Laois, Republic of Ireland

Late 17th-century house for the Cosby family, with alterations in the 18th and 19th centuries. In John Harris's *The Artist and the Country House* (1975) a painting of Stradbally of *c*.1740 shows a very elaborate, bizarrely attractive but slightly chaotic formal garden laid out chiefly on the slopes above the house. According to Edward Malins and The Knight of Glin in *Lost Demesnes* (1976), very little of the garden survives.

Stradsett Hall

Stradsett, Norfolk OS TF6605

English Heritage Register Grade II

Elizabethan house. Thomas Philip Bagge developed the park after he inherited in 1807, work already started by his father from 1791. He consulted Humphry Repton in 1808 but nothing came of that. In 1810 John Claudius Loudon was appointed to remodel the park, which was then chiefly fields and hedges. His work involved much moving of earth, drainage (into an ornamental lake) and the planting of clumps and individual trees. Loudon built a curious cast-iron bridge over a ha-ha, with a cattle-gate, and was also responsible for laying out and building new kitchen gardens and planting fruit trees. Loudon's estimate had been £4,000 (£115,520 today) but it rose on completion, by 1813, to £7,000 (£178,430 today).

Stratfield Saye House

Stratfield Saye, nr Basingstoke, Hampshire OS SU6961 English Heritage Register Grade II Open regularly Tel 01256 882882

House built in mid 17th century for the statesman Sir William Pitt (Pitt the Elder). Estate bought for the Duke of Wellington in 1817 and the house rebuilt to the designs of Benjamin Wyatt. Park, dating from the 13th century, landscaped from 1745 by George Pitt, 1st Lord Rivers, who also planted an arboretum. River Loddon dammed to form a lake. Much tree planting in the 19th century including, inevitably, an avenue of Wellingtonias. Splendid monument to Wellington on the public road in front of the east lodges – a great column with a statue of the Duke on the top – by Baron Marochetti in 1863 at a cost of £3,000 (£138,930 today).

Stratford-upon-Avon gardens

see page 276

Stratton Park

East Stratton, Hampshire OS SU5440

English Heritage Register Grade II

House built on an earlier site by George Dance the Younger in 1803, of which only the noble Tuscan portico survives; a new house behind it was built in the 1960s, designed by Stephen Gardiner & Christopher Knight. There was a deer park and formal gardens here in the 1660s when the estate was owned by Sir William Russell. The western boundary of the park is the site of a Roman road; an estate map of the 1730s shows formal gardens incorporating the Roman road as a "love walk". Humphry Repton was consulted by Sir Francis Baring in 1803 and the present parkland with perimeter plantings and clumps of trees is probably the result.

Strawberry Hill

Richmond, Greater London OS TQ1572

English Heritage Register Grade II

Open regularly Tel 020 82404224

Strawberry Hill, then "a little plaything house", was comprehensively remodelled from *c*.1749 in the Gothic style for Horace Walpole, who started making the garden as soon as he bought the house. He made several garden buildings – a sham bridge, a shell bench, a rustic cottage and the Chapel in the Wood. Only the last, with blue and gold fan vaulting, designed by John Chute in 1772, survives, to the south-west of the house. The original stained glass, and the 13th-century shrine Walpole brought from Rome are no longer there. The layout of the grounds today, a lawn and trees, scarcely has the full Walpolean ring to it.

Strawberry House

Hounslow, London OS TQ2178

English Heritage Register Grade II

18th-century house, incorporating parts of an earlier house. The original layout of the walled garden may be 18th-century but the garden today is largely of the 20th century. Paved courtyard behind house, and steps to a circular pool with a sculpture of the Goose Girl and a fountain. A long lawn extends northwards, with a mixed border against the east-facing wall and shrubs and trees at the northern end. A brick path runs along the axis of the lawn, passing through a pergola planted with clematis, roses and a wisteria. Two rectangular pools and paved paths in the eastern part of the lawn.

Strokestown Park

see page 432

Strone

Cairndow, Argyll OS NN1810

Scottish Inventory Open regularly

Originally part of the Ardkinglas esate (*see page 438*), Strone has magnificent 18th-century woodland, marvellous wild scenery on the banks of the Kinglas river and an outstanding collection of conifers. Among them are a Douglas fir (*Pseudotsuga menziesii*) 170ft/50m high, a grand fir (*Abies grandis*) 202ft/60m high (the tallest in Britain), a sawara cypress (*Chamaecyparis pisifera*) 81ft/24m (equal second tallest in Britain; the tallest, at Killerton (*see page 45*), is 3½ft/1m taller) and a western hemlock (*Tsuga heterophylla*) 164ft/49m high.

Studley Royal

see page 352

Sudbury Hall

Sudbury, Derbyshire OS SK1532

English Heritage Register Grade II

Open regularly (NT) Tel 01283 585305

Very beautiful late 17th-century house for the Vernon family who have lived in these parts since the 16th century. A painting of the house by John Griffier of *c*.1700, illustrated in John Harris's *The Artist and the Country House* (1979), shows the south front overlooking a walled garden with pools, statues, topiary and a pattern of shaped lawns. More gardens, probably an orchard and a kitchen garden, lie on each side of the forecourt. Today, grass terraces descend the slope on the south-west side of the house, with a lily pool on the middle terrace. The terraces have yew topiary and flower beds, all of late 20th-century origin. This area was originally laid out by W.S. Gilpin in the 1830s. To the south-west of the house, a lake; water is shown here in the Griffier painting. The park to the north of the house has a mid 18th-century deercote in the form of a battlemented gatehouse with turrets and a curtain wall. Parts of 18th-century tree belts and other woodland survive.

Sudeley Castle

see page 233

Sufton Court

Mordiford, Herefordshire OS SO5737

English Heritage Register Grade II*

Open regularly Tel 01432 870268

The Hereford family came to live here in the 12th century. In the 1780s James Hereford built the present house, possibly designed by Anthony Keck, and commissioned a landscape park. Humphry Repton produced a Red Book in 1795 whose chief recommendations were to remove clutter and open out views in the existing park, to make the best of the position overlooking the Vale of Hereford, and to lay out beds of fragrant flowers close to the house. Present-day views from the house are close to Repton's panoramic view in the Red Book.

Sulgrave Manor
see page 280

Sundridge Park
Bromley, London OS TQ4170
English Heritage Register Grade II

House, on an older site, built from 1799 for Mr (later Sir) Claude Scott to the designs of John Nash in association with Humphry Repton. Repton had advised the previous owner of the estate, E.G. Linde, in 1793, and a Red Book was produced. When Claude Scott bought the estate in 1796, Repton recommended excavating a great terrace on the hillside for the new house, giving fine views to the south. He also made a lake south-west of the house, with a pavilion on its west bank. The terrace in front of the new house was given a formal layout but this was much simplified in the late 20th century. Much of the park is today taken over by golf courses, and the house is used as offices.

Sunnyhurst Woods
Darwen, Lancashire OS SD6722
English Heritage Register Grade II
Open regularly

19th-century woodland later developed as a public park and opened in 1903. The site is long and narrow, with the Sunny Hurst brook running its length accompanied by loosely parallel walks, and woodland, especially along the northern boundary. The stream is dammed to form a paddling pool, to the east of which is a canal with the Kiosk (1911–12) and the 18th-century Sunnyhurst Cottage, now a visitor centre. Nearby is an oak planted

in 1913 to commemorate a visit by George V and Queen Mary.

Sutton Courtenay Manor House
Sutton Courtenay, Oxfordshire OS SU5094
English Heritage Register Grade II
Open occasionally for NGS

House of the 13th century onwards but nothing much remains that is older than the 17th century. Garden made by Norah Lindsay after she came to live here in 1895. The Long Garden, photographed in its prime for *Country Life* in 1930, shows a dreamlike profusion of tall topiary shapes rising above a sea of herbaceous planting kept moderately in check by box hedging and gravel paths. Christopher Hussey wrote in *Country Life* in 1931: "Colonel and Mrs Lindsay have created something exquisite, in which colour and atmosphere and romance blur the lines of objective truth." The Long Garden survives only in part today. The Persian Garden has a square pergola and a modern knot of berberis and box. An alley of beech and hornbeam with yew portals leads to a kitchen garden. A wilderness garden has shrubs and trees underplanted with spring bulbs, and walks lead across meadows by the river. Jane Brown, in *Eminent Gardeners* (1990), quotes Norah Lindsay's niece, Lady Diana Manners (later Lady Diana Cooper), who described her aunt in the garden at Sutton Courtenay, "dressed mostly in tinsel and leopard-skins and baroque pearls and emeralds". The garden was "simplified" in sweeping modernistical style by Brenda Colvin in 1959 for the Hon. David Astor.

Sutton Park
Sutton Coldfield, West Midlands OS SP1097
English Heritage Register Grade II
Open regularly

Public park with remarkably diverse ancient origins, going back at least as far as a 12th-century royal deer park. In the 16th century it was given to the people of Sutton in perpetuity, for grazing and woodland. In the 18th century pools were made for industrial

work in the mills. In 1879 a railway line was built through the park, which had become a place of recreation – with shelters, gates and a park keeper's house, mostly built in rustic style with heather-thatched roofs. This huge area of almost 2,500 acres/1,012 hectares still shows traces of its medieval and earlier origins, and of the subsequent uses to which it was put. It has much woodland (some of medieval origin), bronze age mounds, golf courses, a Victorian boathouse, a former dance-hall (now a café), remains of an 18th-century spade and sheet-metal mill and a button mill, the remains of a Roman road (Icknield Street), and much else.

Sutton Park
(Sutton-on-the-Forest, North Yorkshire)
see page 353

Sutton Place
nr Guildford, Surrey OS TQ0153
English Heritage Register Grade II*

House built *c.*1520–*c.*1530 for Sir Richard Weston. By 1700 it had a series of walled gardens and a double avenue of trees running north from the gatehouse. In 1902, when the estate belonged to Lord Northcliffe, Gertrude Jekyll advised and produced planting plans. In 1980 it was bought by Stanley J. Seeger who commissioned Sir Geoffrey Jellicoe to make new gardens. He designed a canal with stepping stones leading to the Paradise Garden, with serpentine paths between lawns and borders. The Plane Tree Garden has a lawn edged with borders, a single plane tree and two *claire-voies* which give views out of the garden. In the Surreal Garden a false perspective is created by a narrowing path with, alongside it, a series of splendid stone urns (from Mentmore House, *see page 510*) which increase in size as they recede. In the Nicholson Garden an enormous white marble relief by Ben Nicholson overlooks a pool. All these varied and inventive ingredients are held firmly in a framework of crisply defined enclosures. In the park, Jellicoe laid out a serpentine lake with crescent-shaped islands.

Swainston
Calbourne, Isle of Wight OS SZ4487
English Heritage Register Grade II

House partly 12th- and 13th-century and partly late 18th-century – now a hotel. Late 18th-century landscape park partly turned over to agriculture but with scattered trees, some shelter belts and the fading glory of its Arcadian past. In its southern part, the shell of a late 18th-century Doric temple with pediment and columns.

Swallowfield Park
Swallowfield, Berkshire OS SU7365
English Heritage Register Grade II
Open regularly Tel 0118 9883815

The park at Swallowfield was enclosed by Edward III in 1354 and the estate remained in the royal family until the late 16th century. In the 17th century it was owned by the Hyde family (Earls of Clarendon); in the 18th century at first by the Pitts and later the Russells who remained until 1965. The present house is late 17th-century, by William Talman and others. A formal landscape of rides, still present in the 1760s, had gone by the 1790s when the park was wholly landscaped, as had a *patte d'oie* of avenues in the pleasure grounds which radiated from the south front of the house. The present pleasure grounds are terraced, with woods, walks and mature trees. A pets' cemetery has the grave of Bumble, a dog belonging to Charles Dickens. The park, with the Blackwater river flowing across it, is chiefly pasture with many specimen park trees. The house is now divided into flats for "active retired people".

Swarkestone Old Hall
Swarkestone, Derbyshire OS SK3728
English Heritage Register Grade II*

The remains of the 17th-century house of the Harpur family. A fine if enigmatic garden building survives – a three-storey pavilion with two ogee-roofed towers and a loggia, now finely restored by the Landmark Trust and available for holiday lets. It overlooks a rectangular walled enclosure but no-one knows the purpose of the building – was it purely

ornamental, for banqueting; a grandstand from which to view sports; or a "bowle alley house"? West of the site of the old hall, an enclosure with rubble walls where ploughing revealed a pattern of formal gravel paths. No more than that is known abut the garden.

Swerford Park
Swerford, Oxfordshire OS SP3631
English Heritage Register Grade II

A hunting lodge owned by the Duke of Buccleuch in the late 18th century. The estate was bought in 1810 by J. Smith Barry who probably made the lake in the valley below the house and the Waterloo Bridge carrying the drive which runs over the dam at the east end of the lake. In this he possibly had the advice of J.C. Loudon who was living and working at Great Tew nearby. The river Swere runs through the pleasure grounds, passing through woodland and tumbling over cascades.

The Swiss garden
see page 323

Swinton Castle
Swinton, North Yorkshire OS SE2079
English Heritage Register Grade II*

Late 17th-century house, on an old site, for Sir Abstrupus Danby. Garden east of the castle, laid out by George London in 1699 with a walled court with a pattern of paths and beds or lawns ornamented with topiary, urns and statues. By the early 19th century this part of the garden had lawns and a shrubbery; the formal garden was probably destroyed when landscaping was carried out in the 1760s. West of the castle, a rustic bridge at the end of Boat House Pond (one of several lakes) and a ruined boathouse nearby. Further west, a miniature henge of standing stones and two stone coffins, probably Roman. Further west, the banks of Lake Superior have massive rocky promontories and a large grotto on the north bank. The lakes date from the 1760s when they were formed under the supervision of Mr Jones. The picturesque additions of grottoes, rockwork, rustic bridges and so on were supervised by

Adam Mickle after 1796. His client, Sir William Danby, was a Grand Tourist, collector of paintings by Claude, Poussin and Salvator Rosa and highly susceptible to picturesque notions.

Sydney Gardens
Bathwick, Bath, Somerset OS ST7565
English Heritage Register Grade II
Open regularly

18th-century pleasure grounds developed by Charles Harcourt Masters at a time when Bath was at its height as a fashionable spa; it opened to the public in 1795. Amusements included "Horns and Clarionets every Wednesday evening", two bowling greens and swings (but swinging was banned on Sundays) and a maze. At the centre of the maze was Mr Merlin's swing from which a subterranean passage led to a shell-lined grotto. Jane Austen, who lived for a time at 4 Sydney Place, wrote to her sister Cassandra: "It would be pleasant to be near Sydney gardens. We could go into the Labyrinth every day." There were occasional gala evenings of fireworks and music. A hotel was opened in 1796 (now the Holburne of Menstrie Museum), neatly placed to form an eyecatcher at the end of Great Pultney Street. The gardens were later mutilated by the building of the Kennet and Avon Canal and the railway line. Today, with some fine trees but shorn of their exotic delights, they form an agreeable sylvan setting for the museum.

Syon Park
Isleworth, London OS TQ 1776
English Heritage Register Grade I
Open regularly Tel 020 8560 0882

There was an abbey of Bridgettine nuns here in 1431, and the estate was acquired by the Duke of Somerset in 1547. He built the present house, which was comprehensively remodelled by Robert Adam 1762–69 for the 1st Duke of Northumberland, whose family still owns the estate. The site is a very beautiful one, close to the river Thames with Richmond (and, today, Kew Gardens) on the other side. It is known that the nuns cultivated 30 acres/12 hectares of walled gardens and orchards in the 15th century. The

Duke of Somerset imparked the estate and made formal terraced gardens by the house – the modern rose gardens south-west of the house today stand on that site. From 1547 the Duke's physician was William Turner – one of the great plantsmen of the day and later, 1550–53 and 1558–64, Dean of Wells (*see page 467*) whose book, *The Names of Herbes* (1548) (one of the first books in English to describe plants), was dedicated to the Duke of Somerset and must in part have been written at Syon. He helped the Duke establish a botanic garden here. In around 1760, the 1st Duke of Northumberland consulted Capability Brown (who also worked for the Duke on the landscape of Alnwick Castle, *see page 330*). Dorothy Stroud, in her *Capability Brown* (1975), says that Brown moved walls of the old formal gardens east of the house, made a ha-ha and gravel walks, and sloped the ground between the house and the river so that views of Richmond, and up and down the river, might be revealed. Brown also created two lakes, with a woodland garden and botanical garden about the northern lake. The 3rd Duke commissioned a superb domed Great Conservatory 1827–30, designed by Charles Fowler; formal flower gardens and a pool to the south of the conservatory were made at the same time. The gardens were first opened to the public in 1837 and they remain a fascinating and beautiful place to visit.

Tabley House
Tabley Inferior, Cheshire OS SJ7277
English Heritage Register Grade II
Open regularly Tel 01565 750151

The de Leycester family came to Tabley in the middle ages and Sir Peter Byrne Leycester employed John Carr of York to build a grand new Palladian house on a new site, 1761–69. East of the house, there are remains of an elaborate Victorian parterre with clipped yews. North of the house, a shrubbery with winding walks and specimen trees. Pool with dog's graveyard on an island. 18th-century landscape park with a large irregular lake, Tabley Mere, to the south, with an island on which

there is a castellated Folly Tower of c.1780. Shelter belts about much of the park's perimeter, with walks through them, especially south and west of Tabley Mere. John Webb worked on the park from 1803.

Tackley Water Garden
Tackley, Oxfordshire OS SP4820
English Heritage Register Grade II*

Rare, possibly unique, water garden made c.1620 by John Harborne, with triangular and square pools each with a peninsula. Illustrated in Gervase Markham's *Cheape and Good Husbandry* (1623 edition). The house has disappeared, but pools and ornamental gates may still be seen. An early 17th-century dovecote and stables, both associated with Harborne's house, also survive. Most poignant of all is the aerial photograph in Christopher Taylor's *Parks and Gardens of Britain: A Landscape History from the Air* (1998). Taylor points out, noticing the distance from the house to the garden, "Although obviously a garden, Tackley was also designed to cater for Harborne's two great loves, fishing and wildfowling."

Tapeley Park
see page 63

Taplow Court
Taplow, Buckinghamshire OS SU9086
English Heritage Register Grade II
Open regularly Tel 01628 591209

Site going back to the early 7th century when a burial mound for a Saxon lord, Taeppa, was made. Present house designed by William Burn in 1855 for Charles Pascoe Grenfell. Formal gardens with terraces close to the house with topiary, urns, a rectangular rose garden and pergola. To the west, across a lawn, a churchyard (church demolished in 1828) with 17th-century walls, a few surviving memorials and Taeppa's burial mound (the various precious objects buried with Taeppa are now in the British Museum). South of churchyard, panoramic westerly views over the Thames valley with Windsor Castle and Eton College chapel. Pleasure grounds to the west, with cedar walk (some of the cedars of Lebanon date from 18th

century), and escarpment dropping to the Thames. The walk was probably planned in the 18th century by the 1st Lord Orkney, who bought the estate c.1700; there are further walks through woodland on the slopes. Before World War I, under Willie Grenfell (later 1st Lord Desborough) and his wife, Ettie, Taplow became a centre of social life and one of the chief meeting places of the Souls – a more serious-minded, and socially much grander, prototype of the Bloomsbury group. Jane Abdy and Charlotte Gere in *The Souls* (1984) point out how convenient Taplow was, only twenty minutes by train from Paddington: "The platform at Taplow was, by strange coincidence, the longest in England, perfectly suiting the huge number of Lady Desborough's guests."

Tatton Park
see page 235

Taymouth Castle
Kenmore, Perthshire OS NN7846
Scottish Inventory

15th-century fortified house of the Campbells on the banks of the river Tay, with additions by William Adam c.1733 and many subsequent changes which resulted in the present Gothic mansion. The Campbells (latterly Earls and Marquesses of Breadalbane) remained here until the 1920s when the house became a hotel and a golf course was laid out in the park. The parkland was designed by William Adam c.1720, and the estate, caught in a loop of the Tay, is shown in a painting attributed to John Norie and John Griffier II (possibly painted 1733–39), illustrated in John Harris's *The Artist and the Country House* (1979). The painting also shows a great walled formal garden to one side. The park was made informal 1754–60, and the new picturesque landscape, including a sham ruined tower, was admired by Richard Pococke in his *Tours in Scotland* (1760). J.C. Loudon in his *Encyclopaedia of Gardening* (1822) described Taymouth as "the most magnificent residence in the county…the mountain, lawn, and banks of the waters, are richly

clothed with wood, through which are led magnificent walks. Of trees, the lime and larches have attained to a great size, and there is an avenue of the former 450 yards in length, scarcely equalled anywhere." All this has given way to golf and there is little left of the splendours of the landscape.

The Temple
City of London, London OS TQ3180
English Heritage Register Grade II
Open regularly

The gardens of the Inner and Middle Temple may have their origins in the establishment of the Knights Templar in around the middle of the 12th century. By the 14th century they were used by law students, and in 1608 were granted to Benchers of the Inner and Middle Temple in perpetuity. The southern part of the gardens was lost in 1870 when the Victoria Embankment along the river Thames was made. The terrace running along the north side of the Inner Temple, known in the 16th century as the Great Garden, preserves an 18th-century sundial by Edward Strong Senior. In Fountain Court the fountain and basin of 1681 is reputedly the first permanent fountain in London. At the south end of Middle Temple Garden is a sundial of 1719. The planting is all of recent times. Throughout the area are lawns and specimen trees; the Inner Temple Garden, which also has a lawn and pool, has examples of *Ailanthus altissima*, *Catalpa bignonioides*, *Ginkgo biloba*, magnolia and sorbus.

Temple Dinsley
Preston, Hertfordshire OS TL1824
English Heritage Register Grade II

House built 1714 and remodelled by Edwin Lutyens 1908–9. Lutyens also designed a series of intricate garden spaces to the west and north of the house, with planting by Gertrude Jekyll c.1909. The chief ingredients are a rose parterre with a loggia flanked by two garden pavilions; the Diamond Garden with a lawn and a path leading between rose borders; a herbaceous garden, pergola garden (with a belvedere) and rose garden. The park, first lai out in the 18th century, has woodland and pasture with scattered specimen trees and the remains of an avenue. Lutyens designed the Piggery (c.1908) with its steep pyramidal roof as an eyecatcher in the park.

Temple Grounds
Richmond, North Yorkshire OS NZ1600
English Heritage Register Grade II

The grounds of a 17th-century mansion, Yorke House, which was demolished in the 1820s. The site, now chiefly parkland, is bounded to the west by the river Swale. Two fine buildings survive: Culloden Tower, an octagonal banqueting hall of 1746 with a beautiful interior, possibly designed by Daniel Garrett and now belonging to the Landmark Trust; and the Menagerie of 1769, with Gothic detailing, which has been converted into a house known as Temple Lodge. Yorke House was to the south of the site, on sloping ground close to the river, and traces of its terraced gardens may still be seen. Lady Oxford visited Richmond in 1745 and reported that Mr Yorke had "a good house there with hanging gardens on the side of the hill". Many mature trees survive in the park, some of which can be identified as those shown in a 1729 map.

Temple Newsam
Leeds, West Yorkshire OS SE3532
English Heritage Register Grade II
Open regularly Tel 0113 2647321

Ancient site, owned by Ilbert de Lacy in the 11th century and passing through several hands until it was acquired by the Ingram family (later Viscounts Irwin) in 1622. The Ingrams Jacobeanised the existing early Tudor house, giving it the form it has today. Since 1922 the estate has belonged to Leeds City Council and the house has become a museum with a superb decorative arts collection. Leonard Knyff painted the house in 1699 (and was paid £10 (£755 today) by Lord Irwin). Kip's subsequent print, in Britannia Illustrata (1707), shows a garden of parterres, pools, courts and avenues disposed about a central axis aligned on the house, and a large

kitchen garden and orchard to the west. This is the garden that had been designed by Peter Monjoye for Sir Arthur Ingram shortly after 1622. The whole was set in a wild landscape – now, suburban Leeds. Traces of the formal garden survive, including a terrace on the southern side of the house and patterns of enclosures to the west, where modern formal gardens have been made. In the 1760s Capability Brown worked on the park, and was paid £2,500 (£183,400 today) for the period 1765–70. Brown sloped the ground away from the house, with lawns planted with trees leading down to two lakes. His plans included sham bridges, a menagerie, a rotunda and a dairy – none of which survives. An anonymous poem of 1767 describes the park at Temple Newsam: "Sweet waving hills, with wood and verdure crown'd,/ And winding vales, where murmuring streams resound:/Slopes fring'd with Oaks which gradually die away,/And all around romantic scenes display". Today it is a much used public park.

Tendring Hall Park
Stoke-by-Nayland, Suffolk OS TL9935
English Heritage Register Grade II

A Tudor house here was replaced by a house by Sir John Soane (completed by 1786) for Admiral (later Sir) Joshua Rowley. After military occupation in World War II, the house was demolished in 1955. An earlier, mid 18th-century, fishing lodge survives, overlooking the lake, and an 18th-century dovecote. Humphry Repton was consulted and produced a Red Book in 1791. He created the lake by deformalising a much earlier canal, opened up views of anything he regarded as ornamental in the landscape (such as the tall tower of the parish church of St Mary), extending sight lines more deeply into the park, and planting to conceal what he disapproved of.

Terling Place
Terling, Essex OS TL7714
English Heritage Register Grade II

House built 1772–73 for John Strutt to the designs of John

Johnson. South-east of the house, a semicircular ha-ha enclosing a mid 19th-century geometric layout of box-edged beds and paths. Of the same period, three avenues radiating out from the north-west front of house. Park developed in 18th and 19th centuries, now with woodland, pasture and arable land. The house stands on the northern side of the valley of the river Ter which flows through the park.

Tewin Water
nr Welwyn Garden City, Hertfordshire
OS TL2614 English Heritage Register Grade II

House rebuilt after 1797 for Henry Cowper. In 1799 the 5th Earl Cowper consulted Humphry Repton, who produced a Red Book of proposals. West of the house, Repton suggested an informal lawn separated from the river by a serpentine walk. The kitchen garden to the north should be hidden behind a belt of trees and the eastern end of the lawn should overlook the park south of the river. This was done, and late in the 19th century a parterre was laid out below the west façade and the lawn extended from the south façade to the river. The park is divided by the river Mimram which runs close to the house, flowing into a lake to the south-east; it was the view of the house from this point that Repton thought "the best of all possible aspects". The park is largely enclosed in belts of trees, with mature specimen trees south and west of the house.

Thame Park
Thame, Oxfordshire OS SP7103
English Heritage Register Grade II*

A Cistercian abbey was built at Thame c.1140. The present house incorporates the Tudor abbot's lodgings but was otherwise largely built in the 1740s for the 6th Viscount Wenman. The pleasure grounds lie to the north and south of the house. The south lawn, with fine old cedars of Lebanon, is protected from the west by trees and shrubs. A fishpond on the lawn has a wooden boathouse at its southern tip. The park, of possibly medieval origins, has two partly surviving 18th-century avenues.

Theobalds
nr Cheshunt, Hertfordshire OS TL 3201

Garden laid out by Robert Cecil, Lord Burghley, 1575–85. It was visited in its heyday, in 1600, by Baron Waldstein who describes many features of the garden: "an overhanging rock or crag (here they call it a 'grotto') made of different kinds of semi-transparent stone, and roofed over with pieces of coral, crystal, and all kinds of metallic ore. It is thatched with green grass, and inside can be seen a man and a woman dressed like wild men of the woods…In the garden you see lilies and other flowers growing among the shrubs; the garden also contains some alabaster busts of the Caesars." Sir Roy Strong describes it in The Renaissance Garden in England (1979) as "the most influential Elizabethan garden". It was very large and elaborate: the Great Garden alone was 7 acres/ 2.8 hectares in area, and contained nine knots, each 70ft/20m square, with a white marble fountain in the central knot. In Lord Burghley's day the garden was managed by John Gerard, the great herbalist. Under James I Theobalds was exchanged by Robert Cecil for Hatfield Palace. James I enlarged the park and in 1620 enclosed the estate in a brick wall nine and a half miles long; parts of it may still be seen. During the Commonwealth Theobalds was all but destroyed; only a few fragments survive, and part of the grounds are now a public park (the Cedars).

Thirlestane Castle
nr Lauder, Berwickshire OS NT5347 Scottish Inventory Open regularly Tel 01578 722430

Magnificent castle, dating from 1590 but much altered in 1673 by Sir William Bruce for the 1st (and only) Duke of Lauderdale, with further alterations in the 19th century. Little is known of early garden history; formal gardens were made when Bruce worked on the house, but nothing remains. 19th-century parkland of mixed deciduous trees is still maintained, with regular new planting, and woodland of the same period is mixed deciduous and coniferous. East of the house,

a formal rose garden in lawns on an upper terrace with a sundial. Nearby, a curved herbaceous border about a tennis court.

Thompson Park
Burnley, Lancashire OS SD8433 English Heritage Register Grade II Open regularly

Public park, opened 1930. The river Brun flows through the middle of the park, with an irregular boating lake to its east, spanned by a Venetian bridge of concrete. South-east of the lake, a semicircular rose garden with the Mackenzie Memorial (1931 by F. Roslyn) erected in memory of the heart specialist, Sir James Mackenzie. North-west of the lake, the sunken Italian Garden, with formal beds in grass surrounded by raised paths with a loggia on a raised terrace at each end, and a pergola. To the south-west, a circular garden enclosed in beech hedges, with a herbaceous border about an inner circular path. Much planting of mature trees and shrubs about the perimeter of the park and on the banks of the stream and lake.

Thoresby Hall
nr Ollerton, Nottinghamshire OS SK6371
English Heritage Register Grade I

Park enclosed out of Sherwood Forest in 1683 by William Pierrepoint, 4th Earl of Kingston. The 17th-century house (largely by William Talman) was destroyed by fire, its 18th-century successor (by John Carr) demolished in 1868, and a new house built in the 1860s by Anthony Salvin. A painting by Leonard Knyff of c.1705, illustrated in John Harris's The Artist and the Country House (1979), shows an elaborate water garden in front and to one side of the house. To the west of the house was a formal lake which fed a cascade in the formal gardens. In the late 18th century the park was landscaped, probably by Francis Richardson and possibly with Capability Brown's help. In 1791 Humphry Repton was consulted by Charles Pierrepoint and a Red Book was produced. Repton was chiefly concerned with naturalising the canal and cascade, in which, as Anna Seward told him, "the sullen waters take their

T

measured leaps...surely they might be allowed to strike the eye with transient sublimity, and roar down the mountain over craggy fragments, and flash through intercepting bushes." Repton also made new walks and a bridge, but the naturalistic cascade, with immense quantities of rock brought in, cost almost a third of the total cost of £1,700 (£71,876 today). In the 1860s new formal gardens were made about the house, with advice by W.A. Nesfield although Anthony Salvin was in charge. This layout is still substantially in place and may be seen in an aerial photograph illustrated in Christopher Taylor's *Parks and Gardens of Britain: A Landscape History from the Air* (1998).

Thornbridge Hall
Ashford-in-the-Water, Derbyshire
OS SK1970 English Heritage Register Grade II

House built after 1870 for Frederick Craven to the designs of J.B. Mitchell-Withers, with a walled entrance forecourt with urns and statues. Formal gardens to south and east of house. Paved terrace below east front leading down to terrace with urns and Dutch garden with clipped evergreens, urns and statues. To the south of the formal gardens, a summerhouse, rose garden and croquet lawn. Lawn below east terrace runs down to a pool and rock garden with a cascade. An alpine walk is flanked by rhododendrons. Above it, the Beech Walk with Greek herms of the Four Seasons. Further up, urns and fruit trees, with a classical temple (from Clumber Park, *see page 257*) behind.

Thornbury Castle
Thornbury, Gloucestershire OS ST6390,
English Heritage Register Grade II

Castle built for Edward Stafford, 3rd Duke of Buckingham from *c.*1511. The garden at Thornbury is one of the earliest English gardens of which a description survives. A contemporary description says that Stafford employed a gardener "diligent in making knots" and gave details of the garden: "On the south side...is a proper garden,

and about the same a goodly gallery...On the east side of the castle...is a large and goodly garden to walk in, closed with high walls imbattled...a large and goodly orchard [is] full of newly grafted fruit trees well laden with fruit, many roses and other pleasures; and in the same orchard...are other goodly alleys." The castle is now a hotel and restaurant but there is no trace of the original garden.

Thorndon Hall, *now* Thorndon Park
nr Little Warley, Hertfordshire OS TQ6191
English Heritage Register Grade II*

House on an ancient site, built 1764–70 for the 9th Lord Petre to the designs of James Paine. The 8th Lord Petre (1713–43) had been a remarkable plantsman and garden maker. A plan of *c.*1740 shows an immense layout combining the formality of giant avenues with the informality of paths winding in woodland. Daniel Defoe visited it in 1738 and wrote: "the whole Plan is the most extensive and beautiful of any yet executed in this Kingdom." Lord Petre, equally concerned with the planting, used an immense range of plants, paying particular attention to leaf colour. His nurseries at Thorndon held a huge number of plants, many of them newly introduced, including an especially rich collection of American species. When the 8th Lord Petre died, at the age of only thirty, his friend the Quaker plant introducer Peter Collinson wrote to Linnaeus that it was "the greatest loss that botany or gardening ever felt in this island". Capability Brown landscaped the grounds 1766–72, obliterating the earlier gardens, for which he was paid £5,059 (£333,818 today). Brown's lake survives but little of his other work. There is now a golf course in the grounds and the remainder is a Country Park owned by Essex County Council. Gutted by fire in 1878, the house is now flats.

Thornton Manor
Thornton Hough, Merseyside OS SJ2981
English Heritage Register Grade II*

Early Victorian house bought in 1888 by W.H. Lever (later 1st

Viscount Leverhulme), soap manufacturer, philanthropist and founder of Port Sunlight. The house was transformed into a neo-Elizabethan mansion (chiefly by Douglas & Fordham) and a garden was designed by Thomas Mawson in conjunction with Lord Leverhulme and laid out from 1905. South of the house, a terrace with geometric beds and, at each end, a lime walk extending beyond the house. Columned pergola (the Forum) enclosing a lawn north of the western lime walk. To the north, a kitchen garden and a loggia with a balustraded roof walk giving views over the kitchen garden, gardens and park. To the west, geometric beds and a sunken rose garden where a path leads west to woods with ornamental pools. Parkland to south of house, with trees as specimens or in clumps. To the west, a lake with islands and a canal aligned with the house; dense plantings of trees about the banks. Ornamental kitchen garden, originally with urns, a fountain and arched pergolas, now stripped of ornament.

Thorp Perrow Arboretum
see page 354

Thorpe Hall
nr Peterborough, Cambridgeshire OS
TL1798 English Heritage Register Grade II*
Open regularly Tel 01733 330060

House built for Oliver St John in the mid 17th century on an ancient site. The builder was Peter Mills, who was later associated with Hugh May, Roger Pratt and Christopher Wren in the rebuilding of London after the Great Fire of 1666. Walled garden of the same date, with stone urns at each corner, ornate gateways and 18th-century iron grilles. The Best Garden to the east of the house has an 1850 parterre and raised walks on two sides. 18th-century stone summerhouse to south-east of house. South-west of the house, on the site of a Victorian children's garden, a rose garden with an oval pool and a brick summerhouse. Small park, with traces of 17th-century avenues and medieval fishponds

associated with the old manor house (on a different site).

Thorpe Hall, *now* The Lady Nelson Home
Southchurch, Essex OS TM1821
English Heritage Register Grade II

17th-century house, rebuilt in the 1820s, enlarged in 1926. Garden laid out from 1913 by Countess Byng with much planting of trees and shrubs. Loggia south of the house overlooking lawns. From the upper lawn, steps down to a sunken rose garden. To the west, a chain of pools and lakes whose banks are planted with moisture-loving plants. The largest lake has a cascade and rock garden at its western end, with mature specimen trees and rhododendrons around its banks. Since 1960 Thorpe Hall has been a Lady Nelson home.

Threave Garden
see page 394

Tillmouth Park, *now* Tillmouth Park Hotel
Twizel, Northumberland OS NT8842
English Heritage Register Grade II

Neo-Elizabethan house, built 1882 to the design of Charles Barry Jnr, replacing an 18th-century house built for Sir Francis Blake. Wooded grounds bordered by the river Till, with formal alignment of paths. Walks along river, with viewing terrace overlooking park. Pleasure grounds on either side of the Deanburn. North of the river, on an eminence, is the ruined Twizel Castle, built in about 1770 and designed by James Nisbet for Sir Francis Blake but never completed. It looks too large ever to have been a sham ruin but it makes a grand picturesque ornament on its wooded height.

Tillypronie
nr Tarland, Aberdeenshire OS NJ4308
Scottish Inventory Open occasionally for SGS

Ancient estate, with new house built in 1867. Bought in 1951 by the Astor family who still own it. They built up an arboretum, planted many trees and shrubs on the lawns of the ornamental garden (including 130 varieties of dwarf conifer) and made a water

garden about a lochan and stream, with advice from Vernon Russell-Smith. Terraced garden south of the house, with herbaceous border and shrub roses.

Tintinhull House
see page 63

Tirley Garth
Willington, Cheshire OS SJ5466
Open occasionally Tel 01829 732301

House built 1906–12 in austere Tudor style to the designs of C.E. Mallows, initially for Bryan Leesmith (of the chemical firm Brunner Mond, which became ICI) and completed for a textile manufacturer, R.H. Prestwich. Splendid gardens firmly related to the house were laid out by Thomas Mawson and Mallows, making use of a gentle descent for terraced compartments with tennis lawns, a semicircular sloping rose garden with radial and concentric paths, and a long vista ending in a spectacular circular kitchen garden. At the bottom of the slope is a Robinsonian dell garden.

Titsey Place
Titsey, Surrey OS TQ4055
English Heritage Register Grade II
Open regularly Tel 01273 407056

Estate acquired by Sir John Gresham in 1534 and still in the family's ownership. New house built in 1775, much altered in 1832. Gardens laid out by William Gresham Leveson-Gower in the mid 19th century. Grounds terraced, with winding walks passing through plantings of ornamental trees and shrubs. A rose garden and herbaceous borders are mid 20th-century additions by Thomas Leveson-Gower, who also added to the planting about the two lakes south of the house. In the park (the site of the village demolished in 1775 to make room for it), remains of a Roman villa. Scattered parkland trees in the park, the southern part of which is cut off by the M25.

Toddington Manor
Toddington, Gloucestershire OS SP0333
English Heritage Register Grade II

House built 1820–35 for Charles Hanbury-Tracy to his own design

– it cost more than £150,000 (£6,000,000 today). Formal gardens for an earlier house here, illustrated in a Kip engraving of 1715, had very elaborate parterres on either side. Versions of them were recreated in the 19th century and their remains (the layout is intact) are shown in an aerial photograph of 1949 in Marcus Binney's and Ann Hills's *Elysian Gardens* (1979). There remain balustrades with Gothic detailing, a Gothic fountain and statues. The park was laid out in the 19th century, with a serpentine lake formed by damming the river Isbourne.

Tollymore Forest Park

nr Newcastle, County Down, Northern Ireland Open regularly

The Tollymore estate on the edge of the Mourne mountains goes back to the early 17th century when it was owned by the Maginnes family; in the 18th century it was owned by the Hamiltons (Lords of Limerick and later Earls of Clanbrassill). 18th-century house for James Hamilton, Lord Limerick (possibly by Thomas Wright of Durham), with 19th century additions demolished in 1952. The 1st Earl (as he was by 1768) was one of the first estate owners in Ireland to plant an arboretum. Thomas Wright may also have been responsible for the notable 18th-century garden buildings that ornament the demesne: a rustic hermitage, a Gothic bridge with castellations and quatrefoil apertures, a barbican gate of similar design and a barn masquerading as a Gothic chapel. In 1955 the Tollymore estate became the first state forest in Northern Ireland: 1,556 acres/630 hectares of splendidly wooded grounds with waymarked trails. The 18th-century buildings survive and there are many fine trees to admire, especially conifers. The entrance has a fine avenue of deodars (*Cedrus deodara*).

Tong Castle

Tong, Shropshire, OS SJ8007

The castle was designed by Capability Brown in 1765 for George Durant, a successful

Havana merchant. Calvert's *Picturesque Views of Staffordshire and Shropshire* (1830) described it as "fancifully composed, partly of Moorish, and partly of Gothic architecture, and produces a grand effect from the numerous and widely extended minarets and pinnacles, and the stately crown given to the whole by two lofty and magnificent Turkish domes." Durant's son filled the grounds with curious ornaments and buildings: a cast-iron weeping willow which wept through pipes, a hermitage (with a hermit called Carolus), the jaw bones of a whale, Aeolian harps which made music in the wind, and much else. The house was demolished in 1954 and in the 1970s the M54 motorway was built across the grounds. Two buildings survive: a pyramidal hen house of brick and stone (at Vauxhall farm) and Tong (or Knoll) Tower close to the Weston Park estate (*see page 238*) for which it serves as an eyecatcher.

Tongue House

nr Tongue, Sutherland OS NC5958
Scottish Inventory

Late 17th-century house with additions in the 18th and 19th centuries, on a splendid site on the eastern shore of the Kyle of Tongue, a long narrow sea loch. A walled garden east of the house was made in the mid 18th century and is a characteristic example of an old Scottish garden, intermingling ornamental and productive plants. Divided into four by cotoneaster hedges, it has a pair of mixed borders running north and south, with a sundial (dated 1714) as a focal point. One corner of the garden is for vegetables, another is an orchard. All this lies below the west-facing windows of the house and presents a delightful scene. It is not great art but it is the kind of garden that most people love.

Torosay Castle

see page 395

Tortworth Park

Tortworth, Gloucestershire OS ST6992
English Heritage Register Grade II

The Tudor manor at Tortworth (Tortworth Court) was near the

parish church and a Kip engraving (c.1710, when the estate was owned by Matthew Ducy Morton) shows that it had ambitious formal gardens of a slightly jumbly kind. In the garden, the famous Tortworth sweet chestnut still survives – one of the very few trees so special that it is marked on the Ordnance Survey map; John Evelyn saw it in 1664 and said that it had been a boundary tree in the 12th century. In the 19th century a new house, Tortworth House, was designed by S.S. Teulon for the 2nd Earl of Ducie and built 1849–52 on the site of a 15th-century deer park, at some distance south-west of the old manor. Terraces on the south side of the house were also designed by Teulon. A lake and an arboretum (with advice from William Holford at Westonbirt, *see page 239*) were made in the 1840s. Notable trees survive in the arboretum, in particular American oaks and hickories. The estate was sold to HM Prisons and has since had a complicated history, with the house being gutted by fire in 1990 – but the landscape remains intact.

Tottenham Park

nr Marlborough, Wiltshire OS SU2463
English Heritage Register Grade II*
Open by appointment Tel 01672 512161

17th-century house remodelled for Charles, Lord Bruce (later 1st Marquess of Ailesbury) by Richard Boyle, 3rd Earl of Burlington, from 1721, and rebuilt 1826 for the 4th Marquess of Ailesbury to the designs of Thomas Cundy. The estate lies in the Savernake Forest, a royal forest since the Conquest, much of it imparked by the Seymours from the 15th to the 17th century. From the 1660s beech avenues were planted in the park; three of these are aligned on the house, and Grand Avenue is 3 miles long. Lord Burlington designed a banqueting house (demolished in 1824) and an octagonal summerhouse which survives in the deer park south-west of the house. Capability Brown was consulted by Lord Bruce, probably from 1763. Lord Bruce's father-in-law was Henry Hoare of Stourhead (*see page 106*) and it seems likely that he too was

involved in planning the landscape. Rectangular pools by the house were removed, trees near the house were thinned, a serpentine walk made about the garden, a new walled kitchen garden and flower garden were built. Rides through the forest were left intact. In 1781 an Ionic column was erected on the axis of the house, 1½ miles to the west-north-west. The house is now a school.

Towneley Hall

Burnley, Lancashire OS SD8530
English Heritage Register Grade II
Open regularly Tel 01282 424213

House built in the 15th century, with alterations in the 18th and 19th centuries; now a museum. The Towneley family have owned land in these parts since at least c.1200. South-east of the house, a lawn with a rectangular pool with absidal ends, dating from before 1735, and a (probably) early 20th-century Italian garden with a parterre of shaped beds; to its east, a lime walk already here in 1834. North-west of the house, wooded pleasure grounds and, south-west of the house, a ride cut through the woods to the medieval Foldys Cross – a feature present by c.1777. Charles Towneley, the great connoisseur and collector of classical sculpture, inherited in 1758 and planted many trees and shrubs in the pleasure grounds 1798–1803. Parkland to north and north-east of house, with double avenue crossing the park from the north-east façade and mature scattered trees and shelter belts still in place; 8,000 trees were planted 1812–13. Playing fields and a golf course in the park.

Townhill Park

Southampton, Hampshire OS SU4515
English Heritage Register II

18th-century house, rebuilt after 1910 for Sir Samuel Montagu (later 2nd Lord Swaythling) by Leonard Rome Guthrie, who also laid out formal gardens with terracing on the sloping ground to the west. The terraced garden led to a sunken garden with a pergola; the planting was by Gertrude Jekyll who also laid out a herb garden nearby. Between the wars,

the 3rd Lord Swaythling and his head gardener, F. Rose, hybridised rhododendrons, receiving 13 Awards of Merit from the RHS 1932–46. During World War II the house became a convalescent home for wounded soldiers and in 1994 the house and garden were sold to the Gregg and St Winifred's School Trust. Since 1997 the Friends of Townhill Park Gardens, with help from the Hampshire Gardens Trust, have been restoring the gardens, which are very well described in David Ottewill's *The Edwardian Garden* (1989).

Trafalgar House, *formerly* Standlynch House

nr Charlton-All-Saints, Wiltshire OS SU1823
English Heritage Register Grade II

House built 1731–34 for Sir Peter Vandeput to the designs of John James, with later alterations. Suggestions that Charles Bridgeman designed the garden here now seem without foundation. 18th-century landscape park with the river Avon forming the western boundary. Scattered mature trees, open parkland (some of it now turned over to agriculture), and dense woodland along the Avon. Terraced formal gardens added to the house by William Butterfield in 1859.

Traquair House

nr Innerleithen, Selkirkshire OS NT3335
Scottish Inventory Open regularly
Tel 01896 830323

A wonderfully romantic house, dating from the 15th century and altered by James Smith 1695–1705. The estate was formerly part of Ettrick Forest and there was a house here by the early 12th century. It was a royal estate until the late 15th century and from 1491 belonged to the Stuarts (Earls of Buchan); the Maxwell Stuarts still own it. In the park, a mid 18th-century avenue was replanted with sycamores 1827–61. 18th-century woodland has some trees from c.1745 remaining. A woodland walk following the Quair Water, with a rustic bridge, has ornamental trees planted in the 19th century;

measured by Alan Mitchell in 1982, they include good specimens of *Abies alba*, *Abies procera*, *Picea orientalis* and *Pseudotsuga menziesii*. Formal gardens laid out in the early 18th century have surviving double terraces (originally with twin gazebos) now with modern mixed planting including shrub roses. East of the house, a modern beech maze and, on the site of an orchard nearby, herbaceous borders, rose beds, croquet lawn and an 1834 heather-thatched summerhouse. In the policies, a magnificent pair of wrought-iron gates, the Bear Gates, dating from the 1730s and kept shut since *c*.1747 as a gesture of support for the Jacobite cause, on the order of the 5th Earl on his return from imprisonment in the Tower of London.

Trebah
see page 64

Treberfydd
Llangasty Tal-y-Llyn, Powys OS SO1225
Cadw/ICOMOS Register Grade II*
Open occasionally for NGS

Fine neo-Tudor castellated house, replacing an 18th-century one, built 1848–52 to the designs of J.L. Pearson for the Raikes family, ardent Tractarians. W.A. Nesfield laid out gardens in 1850 with three elaborate parterres: a circular one with twelve box-edged beds about a fountain; an intricately fashioned box-hedged design with the initials R and F (for Robert and Frances Raikes); and a lawn with a central deodar (*Cedrus deodara*) surrounded by triangular flower beds. Nesfield's layout survives today, with some original planting. A cottage *orné* of 1857 was also designed by Pearson.

Tredegar House
see page 236

Tregothnan
St Michael Penkevil, Cornwall OS SW8541
English Heritage Register Grade II*
Open occasionally Tel 01872 520325

Boscawens (later Viscounts Falmouth) have lived at Tregothnan since the 14th century. The present house is 17th-century but was rebuilt to the designs of

---

William Wilkins 1816–18. There had been formal gardens here in the 17th century, which were described by Celia Fiennes (who was a cousin of Hugh Boscawen) on her visit in 1698: "his house stands on a high hill in the middle of a parke with severall rows of trees with woods beyond it…the garden…has gravel walks round and across, but the squares are full of goosebery and shrub-trees and looks more like a kitchen garden…out of which is another garden and orchard which is something like a grove, green walks with rows of fruit trees." In the early 19th century the grounds were landscaped with the advice of Humphry Repton, who produced a Red Book in 1809. He planted a shelter belt to the south-west which provides, in words of Viscount Falmouth in 1968, "an attractive walk to the kitchen garden flanked by a double line of very old *Camellia japonica*." Some time in the early 19th century a *parterre de broderie* of box was laid out on a terrace by the house. Later in the century there was much new planting, especially of rhododendrons. The garden today is very well maintained with a continuing tradition of discerning plantsmanship. A recent experiment has been the cultivation of *Camellia sinensis*, the source of tea.

Tregrehan
St Blazey Gate, Cornwall OS SX0553
English Heritage Register Grade II*
Open regularly in the spring
Tel 01726 814389

The Carlyon family has been at Tregrehan since 1565 although the present house dates from the early 19th century. There has been garden activity here since the early 18th century. Unusually early pinetum started in 1830 by William Carlyon. Thurston's *British and Foreign Trees and Shrubs in Cornwall* (1930) describes it as "a special feature of the grounds…one of the choicest collections of rare trees and shrubs in the County". W.A. Nesfield designed an ornate parterre on a terrace in 1843 – it is now a swimming pool. After World War II, Miss G. Carlyon bred many new cultivars of camellias and

---

enriched the planting of the garden.

Trelissick
see page 65

Trelowarren
Mawgab-in-Meneage, Cornwall
OS SW7223 English Heritage Register
Grade II Open regularly Tel 01326 221366

The Vyvyans came here in the 15th century; the family still lives here. The existing house dates partly from that time but was remodelled in the 17th and mid 18th centuries. Little is know about the early history of the garden. *Gardeners' Magazine* (1830) published an "Account of the Botanic Flower-Garden now forming at Trelowarren for the culture of hardy plants"; Thurston's *British and Foreign Trees and Shrubs in Cornwall* (1930) describes "beautiful and ancient woods containing fine beeches, Spanish chestnuts, limes, etc. Present owner Sir Courtenay Vyvyan has greatly developed the shrub garden"; David Hunt's and Douglas Pett's *Historic Gardens in Cornwall* (1991) comment: "This, certainly the first, and probably the only systematic botanic garden in Cornwall has disappeared without trace."

Trengwainton Garden
see page 66

Trent Park
Enfield, London OS TQ2997
English Heritage Register Grade II
Park open regularly

The estate was formed in 1777 when part of the royal hunting park of Enfield Chase was sold to Dr Richard Jebb (later Sir Richard), physician to George III. House altered by Sir William Chambers after 1777 and in the 19th century; much remodelling in the 20th century, in particular in 1926 for Philip Sassoon, by Charles Holder. Today the estate is in divided ownership: the house and formal gardens are in institutional use, and the remainder is a Country Park owned by Enfield Borough Council. The park, which still has trees remaining from Enfield Chase, was landscaped for Dr Jebb; Humphry Repton's name, though

---

with no evidence, has been mentioned. Pools and a lake in the park probably date from this time and there was much replanting of oaks in the mid 19th century. Gardens developed between the wars with advice from Norah Lindsay: a long terrace north of the house overlooking a lawn with views to the lake, a formal paved swimming pool with an orangery beyond it, and exuberant borders east of the orangery. The pool and orangery survive, with a yew-hedged enclosure and stone-edged pools on each side. In 1934 sculptures were brought here from Wrest Park (*see page 325*), including an obelisk and column at the end of the east–west approach avenue. Another obelisk from Wrest Park was erected north-west of the house, seen through a vista cut in the woodland.

Trentham Gardens, *formerly* Trentham Park
Trentham, Staffordshire OS SJ8640
English Heritage Register Grade II*
Open regularly Tel 01782 657341

There was an Augustinian priory here in the middle ages and the estate was acquired by James Leveson, a wool stapler, in 1540. The Levesons, later Leveson-Gower, by an exceedingly complicated process of marriage and inheritance, became Dukes of Sutherland. From 1833 the 2nd Duke commissioned Sir Charles Barry to transform the old house into an Italianate palace of astonishing splendour, with a garden to match; by 1841 the work had cost £123,000 (£4,736,730 today). By the beginning of the 20th century the pollution of the river Trent, which flows through the grounds, had became so great as to make the house uninhabitable and it was demolished 1910–12. The earlier house had formal gardens in the 17th century but these were destroyed when Capability Brown landscaped the grounds from 1759. Brown enlarged an existing lake south of the house, which took its water from the Trent. By 1791 the traveller John Byng was able to write, "my old friend L. Brown is to be traced at every turn: he certainly was a grand

---

planner and leveller of ground – and a judicious former of water; the lake, here, is very fine." In the southern part of the park, crowning Tittensor Hill and forming an eyecatcher beyond the southern tip of the lake, is a stone column with a colossal bronze statue of the 1st Duke (1836, by Sir Francis Chantery). Sir Charles Barry's garden, known as "the Versailles of the Midlands", between the house and the lake, with its balustraded terraces, parterres, golden yews, statues, pavilions and pools, was the epitome of the grandest 19th-century neo-classical garden design. Park and garden survive as a jolly public park and certainly not in the pristine state that the Dukes of Sutherland would have demanded. There is an aerial photograph of it in Christopher Taylor's *Parks and Gardens of Britain: A Landscape History from the Air* (1998).

Trerice
nr Newquay, Cornwall OS SW8458
Open regularly (NT) Tel 01637 875404

Beautiful pale grey granite Elizabethan manor house of the Arundell family in lovely country. Gardens largely made since the National Trust acquired the estate in 1953. Terraced forecourt with Irish yews and borders, a lawn (the Bowling Green) flanked by borders and ending in a seat, a formal orchard of old varieties of fruit trees behind the house and many tender plants taking advantage of sunny walls. A barn houses a collection of old lawn mowers. The garden is not exciting but it is delightful and th National Trust has happily preserved its low-key charm.

Tresco Abbey Gardens
see page 66

Tretower Court and Castle
see page 237

Trewarthenick
Tregony, Cornwall OS SW9044
English Heritage Register Grade II

Late 17th-century house, altered in the late 18th century and earl

19th century. A drawing by Edward Prideaux of 1727 shows the south front of the house, with a curved forecourt containing some planting, overlooking a fairly naked landscape with an avenue extending away from the house. In 1792 Humphry Repton was consulted by Francis Gregor and produced a Red Book in the same year. The effect of his work can be seen in an engraving of 1831 showing exactly the same view as Prideaux's drawing: open ground in front of the house remains but the forecourt has gone, the slopes are clothed with trees and the line of the avenue has been deformalised. Repton developed the habit of leaving avenues in position but removing some of the trees to open out cross vistas. Repton also laid out a (surviving) picturesque garden, with a pool, to the north of the house.

Trewithen
see page 67

Tring Park,
formerly **Trengues**
Tring, Hertfordshire OS SP9210
English Heritage Register Grade II

The park at Trengues is mentioned in the Domesday Book; it belonged to Earl Eustace whose daughter Mathilde married King Stephen. The present house, originally called Tring Manor, was built c.1682, probably by Sir Christopher Wren, and remodelled in 1872. Charles Bridgeman laid out new gardens in the 1720s and they are shown in an engraving in *Vitruvius Britannicus* (1739) – an immensely elaborate scheme surrounding the house, which included a 1,100ft × 100ft/330m × 33m canal south of the house, of which no trace remains. In 1786 the estate was sold to Drummond Smith who landscaped the park and removed the most elaborate formal gardens east of the house. The estate changed hands several times before 1872, when it was acquired by Baron Lionel de Rothschild who gave the estate (with 4,000 acres) to his son Nathaniel, as a wedding persent. Nathaniel and his son Walter cherished the estate and did much planting. In 1974 a motorway (the A41(M)) was built

across the park, the southern part of which is now owned by the local authority and has public access. A lime avenue follows the western border of the southern park, and the eastern part, Park Wood has a pattern of early 18th-century rides, some flanked by yew avenues, focused on Nell Gwynn's Monument (early 18th-century, probably by James Gibbs), an obelisk visible from the house. From the obelisk a ride leads north-east to a Temple (early 18th-century, probably by James Gibbs). The northern part of the park is largely pasture with clumps and individual trees. The former kitchen garden, with 18th-century brick walls, contains a supermarket in one part and is filled with houses at the other.

Trinity College
Cambridge, Cambridgeshire OS TL4458
English Heritage Register Grade II
Open regularly Tel 01223 338400

Trinity was founded in 1546 and its magnificent Great Court laid out 1597–1605 by Thomas Nevile. The college is illustrated in Loggan's *Cantabrigia Illustrata* (1690): on either side of its great early Tudor gatehouse, in what is today Trinity Street, were trees and formal gardens – one to the right of the gatehouse was reputedly used by Isaac Newton when he was a fellow of the college. To the right of the gatehouse today is an apple tree, said to be propagated from the tree at Newton's childhood home of Woolsthorpe Manor in Lincolnshire (*see page 561*) which inspired his theory of gravity. More gardens lay behind the Chapel (four elaborate knot gardens are shown in Hamond's 1592 map of Cambridge) and the land beyond the river was divided into two pastures with grazing cattle, edged in double avenues and with a central walk leading to a gatehouse. Only Great Court remains today virtually identical to its 17th-century appearance, divided by paths into six plats and with a magnificently ornate, canopied, late Elizabethan fountain at the centre. Henry James loved Great Court and in *English Hours* (1905) says that "the buildings that surround it, with

their long, rich fronts of time-deepened gray, are the stateliest in the world." In the 19th century a Fellows' Garden was made west of Queen's Road, laid out in 1873 by William Broderick Thomas who was working on the new garden at Sandringham (*see page 319*) in the 1870s. Among the shrubs, trees and lawns is a splendid meadow garden with fritillaries, lilies and many wild plants of meadowland. A perimeter walk about the garden is known as the Roundabout, a name often extended to the garden itself. Ronald Gray, in his book *Cambridge Gardens* (1984), says that certain paths were laid out by the philosopher Ludwig Wittgenstein "in accordance with mysterious mathematical principles". The great botanist John Ray was an undergraduate at Trinity and became a fellow. He studied the flora of the Cambridge area and published the results as *Catalogus plantarum circa Cantabrigiam nascentium* (1660).

Trinity College
(Oxford)
see page 103

Trinity Hall
Cambridge, Cambridgeshire OS TL 4458
English Heritage Register Grade II
Open regularly Tel 01223 332500

Trinity Hall was founded in 1350. 14th-century buildings survive but were refaced in the 18th century. Henry James wrote in *English Hours* (1905): "If I were called upon to mention the prettiest corner of the world, I should draw a thoughtful sigh and point the way to the gardens of Trinity Hall." The garden history of the college is patchy. It had its own vineyard within a few years of its founding. The Fellows' Garden, on the east bank of the river, is enclosed in 17th-century walls with an 18th-century gate. It has an excellent modern herbaceous border, and a group of horse chestnuts which probably date from the early 18th century (Henry James, mysteriously, thought them "one of the most heart-shaking features of the garden"). The college is tucked away between Trinity College to the north and Clare College to

the south, and its chief garden interest today is in the ground that runs down to the east bank of the Cam, with lawns and specimens and groves of trees – a surprisingly open and Arcadian space for such an enclosed setting.

Tudor House Garden
see page 108

Tullynally Castle
Castlepollard, County Westmeath,
Republic of Ireland Open regularly
Tel (00353) 44 61159

17th-century house of the Pakenham family, rebuilt in the early 18th century and subtly Gothicised, and immensely enlarged for the 2nd Earl of Longford by Francis Johnston in the early 19th century, with towers and castellations. In the 18th century there was a formal water garden but this does not survive. Nor does the American garden admired by Maria Edgeworth in 1834: "I never saw in England or Ireland such beautiful gardens as she [2nd Countess of Longford] has made. In a place where there was formerly only a swamp and an osiery she has made the most beautiful American garden." Walled garden with central avenue of 200-year-old yews and modern mixed borders. Modern Chinese garden with pagoda and Tibetan water garden. Old trees and shrubs in woodland walk to lake (the river Sham – a lake masquerading as a river) with many modern additions by Thomas Pakenham (the present owner) who has also planted an arboretum.

Tylney Hall Hotel
see page 109

Tyninghame House
nr East Linton, East Lothian OS NT6279
Scottish Inventory Occasionally open for SGS

Pink sandstone Scottish baronial mansion, incorporating parts of an older house, designed by William Burn in 1839 for the 9th Earl of Haddington whose family had lived here since the early 17th century. John Macky's *A Journey through Scotland* (1732) says that in about 1702 the Earl of Haddington "hath planted many millions of trees in a sandy down

or links and they thrive mightily. He hath also laid out several avenues through his park, which, when fully grown, will be as noble as any in Britain." E.H.M. Cox's *A History of Gardening in Scotland* (1935) also describes remarkable holly hedges planted at Tyninghame in about 1705, which by 1835 were 2,952yd/2,699m long. An 18th-century walled former kitchen garden was in the 20th century turned into an ornamental garden; there is a splendid castellated yew walk ornamented with statues and with a central fountain pool dividing it. On each side of the yew walk are walks of apples or roses, a formal kitchen garden and many good trees and shrubs. From the 1950s the wife of the 12th Earl of Haddington had a great influence on the garden. West of the house, a parterre was laid out at the time of William Burn's work; originally filled with bedding plants it is now planted with shrub roses in box-edged beds decorated with stone urns. Lady Haddington also made a secret garden on the site of old tennis courts; at its centre is a trelliswork pavilion shrounded in clematis and roses, and box-edged paths snake through beds filled with old shrub roses and herbaceous perennials. Tyninghame House was sold in 1986 and divided into multiple ownership. The walled garden is in separate ownership from the main garden.

Tyntesfield
Wraxall, Somerset OS ST5071
English Heritage Register Grade II*
Open regularly (NT) Tel 0870 458 4500

Anthony Gibbs was a guano tycoon from Exeter who founded the firm of Anthony Gibbs & Sons. In 1843 his son William inherited the firm and bought an old house, Tyntes Place, near Bristol. Over the next 20 years he was taking at least 50%, sometimes 100%, of the firm's profits, which gave him an annual income of between £45,000 (£2,025,000 today) and £90,000 (£4,050,000 today). In the 1860s he spent some of this money radically remodelling the house, renaming it Tyntesfield. The Bristol architect John Norton did the work and created an extravaganza of Gothic inventiveness. A devout Christian, Gibbs also paid for the building of several churches, among them Butterfield's chapel for Keble College, Oxford and a private chapel at Tyntesfield where a resident chaplain lived in a house in the rose garden. The garden had terraced walks and topiary, a walled rose garden and a Gothic seat. A park and arboretum were made, containing a remarkable collection of trees. The last member of the family to live at Tyntesfield died in 2000, and after a national appeal and help from the Heritage Lottery Fund, the estate was bought in 2002 by the National Trust for £24,000,000.

Tyringham House
Tyringham, Buckinghamshire OS SP8546
English Heritage Register Grade II*

Estate of the Tyringham family going back to the middle ages and beyond. Present house built 1793–97 for William Praed to the designs of Sir John Soane. Humphry Repton is said to have been commissioned c.1793, but no documentary evidence is known. The estate was sold c.1903 to F.A. Konig who commissioned gardens from Charles F. Rees c.1911 and, more spectacularly, from Sir Edwin Lutyens 1924 –28. Rees's formal gardens close to the house have a grand rose garden to the south-west and a sunken lawn surrounded by yew hedges with an absidal end. North of the rose garden, a yew-hedged enclosure with conifers. On the north-east corner of the house Rees made a sunken pool garden with a loggia and pergola. Lutyens's garden lies below the north-west façade of the house. A swimming pool in the form of a canal forms the central axis, flanked by lawns and flower beds enclosed in walls of yew. The far end of the pool is flanked by a pair of domed pavilions – the Bathing Pavilion and the Temple of Music – with a circular pool with columns beyond. The axis to the north-west had been continued with a further pool running down a double avenue of elms but this has gone. The house and gardens have been a health clinic since 1967.

Ugbrooke Park
Chudleigh, Devon OS SX8778
English Heritage Register Grade II*
Open regularly Tel 01626 852179

The original house was medieval but it owes its present appearance to a reworking 1763–66 by Robert Adam for the 4th Lord Clifford. Capability Brown was consulted in 1761 and three lakes were made, two of them linked by a cascade, but the grounds are unadorned with ornamental buildings of any kind. In Dorothy Stroud's words, "Brown's landscape relied for its effect on the water and plantations by which he emphasised the natural contours" (*Capability Brown*, 1975). Dryden's Seat is a grassy hillock where the poet John Dryden is thought to have composed "The Hind and the Panther" (1686–87). Lord Clifford's chaplain, Father Joseph Reeve, who died in 1820, wrote "A poem on Ugbrooke" in which he sings the praises of the scene composed by Brown: "To shade the hill, to scoop and swell the green/To break with wild diversities the scene/To model with the Genius of the place/Each artless feature, each artless grace".

Undercliffe Cemetery
Bradford, West Yorkshire OS SE1734 English Heritage Register Grade II Open regularly

Cemetery designed by William Gay and opened in 1854. Central promenade, lined with grand monuments, dividing the site in two. Part of the cemetery is reserved for Nonconformist burials and part of that for Quakers only. Throughout the cemetery are the graves of many notable 19th-century Bradford figures. The cemetery directors were conscious of the beauty of the site: "The situation…is one of great beauty", and the public were welcomed "to avail themselves thereof, either as a place of relaxation or for contemplative retirement".

Uppark
Harting, West Sussex OS SU7717
English Heritage Register Grade II*
Open regularly (NT) Tel 01730 825415

House, on a beautiful airy site on the South Downs, by William

Talman c.1690 for Ford Grey, later Earl of Tankerville. Upper two floors almost completely destroyed by fire in 1989, now beautifully restored by the National Trust – an epic feat of craftmanship. A Kip engraving in *Britannia Illustrata* (1707) shows formal gardens, possibly by George London; by c.1730 they had gone, as Peter Tillemans's painting of the house of that date shows. North of the house, an oval walled garden survives, designed by Capability Brown. Humphry Repton was consulted and produced a Red Book in 1810; an illustration shows the house facing downhill over open land, with dense plantings of trees behind and to each side. Repton's recommendations consisted chiefly of thinning trees to open views; it is possible that he was also consulted earlier about approaches to the house. In recent years the National Trust has restored the garden "in the early 19th-century 'picturesque style'", which sounds Reptonian.

Upton House
see page 280

The Vale
Edgbaston, Birmingham, West Midlands OS SP0584 English Heritage Register Grade II

Gardens associated with student halls of residence, part of the University of Birmingham campus. The 40-acre/16-hectare site was landscaped in the mid 20th century by Mary Mitchell as part of the whole development scheme of the architects Casson and Conder. A bowl of ground overlooked by the halls of residence has sweeps of lawn running down to an elliptical lake, with groups of specimen trees. Plantings of trees and shrubs about the banks are planned to frame vistas. An attractive example of the kind of idealistic college landscaping still thought desirable in the 1950s but very rare today.

Valentines Park
Redbridge, London OS TQ4387 English Heritage Register Grade II Open regularly

Late 17th-century house for James Chadwick, with 19th-century alterations. Part of the grounds

were made into a public park in 1899, and the house, and further land, was acquired by 1907. The original 18th-century entrance gates survive on a new site south of the house. North-east of the house, a canal, probably of the 18th century, with an 18th-century grotto at one end. Another pond south-east of the canal. In the south-west part of the park, a lake with ornamental woodland. Lawns and mature trees throughout the park. Several sports and recreational facilities – bowling greens, cricket pitch, football pitch, swimming pool and tennis courts.

Valley Gardens
Harrogate, North Yorkshire OS SE2955
English Heritage Register Grade II
Open regularly

The chalybeate and sulphurous springs of Harrogate became so established that by the late 17th century there were twenty bathing houses here. Celia Fiennes in 1697 found the smell of the water "strong and offensive". To give public access to some of the wells, the site of the Valley Gardens, formerly called Bog Fields, was designated by an Act of Parliament of 1770 as a piece of land that could never be enclosed. In 1841 a footpath was made and stone wellheads installed over the most important of the thirty-six wells here. Today, with the springs sealed off, it has become a public park with lawns, rose beds, stream (with cascades and pools), a bandstand, function room and pavilions. A children's playground, miniature golf course, bowling green and tennis courts provide for more, or less, active pursuits.

Valley Gardens, *formerly* The People's Park *and* South Cliff Gardens
Scarborough, North Yorkshire OS TA0427
English Heritage Register Grade II
Open regularly

Public gardens on the cliffs – the result of the discovery of a mineral spring at South Cliffs in 1626, which formed the basis of a spa. A spa promenade was made in 1839 and gardens along the

cliff were laid out by George Knowles. In 1856 Joseph Paxton added a Grand Hall to the promenade and built a bandstand and Italianate gardens with formal flower beds and stone staircases to give access to the cliffs. A Swiss chalet was built near the entrance in 1860 and a summerhouse in 1862. North of this site, the People's Park (now Valley Gardens) was developed from 1862. From 1880 the South Cliff gardens expanded to the south, the Belvedere Rosary was made from 1883, and the gardens continued to grow, with various appropriate seaside amusements provided. Despite disasters – the Paxton Grand Hall was consumed by fire in 1876, and the Holbeck Hotel at the southern end fell into the sea in 1993, taking a large chunk of the gardens with it – it remains a much loved public park.

Valleyfield
Culross, Fife OS NT0087 Scottish Inventory

The house, abandoned in 1918 and subsequently demolished, had been an 18th-century mansion overlooking the Firth of Forth, owned at the end of the 18th century by Sir Robert Preston. Humphry Repton produced a Red Book of recommendations for laying out the grounds c.1801 –Valleyfield became his only Scottish landscape; he never visited the site but sent his sons to survey it. Repton himself became extremely unpopular in Scotland by tactlessly claiming, in his *Observations on the Theory and Practice of Landscape Gardening* (1803), how much Scotland had need of his services, describing the art of landscape design there as undeveloped and influenced "only by those imitators of Brown's manner, who had travelled to the north". Repton made a walled formal flower garden laid out in terraces on a south-facing slope north of the house, with a ha-ha enclosing it outside the walls. A canal at the southern end of the garden was planned to have a smooth reflecting surface and be stocked with fish. Repton also made alterations to the wooded valley of the Bluther burn which flows through the policies: "by taking advantage of the romantic glen and wooded banks of the river, an approach has been made which for variety, interest, and picturesque scenery may vie with anything of the kind in England." (J.C. Loudon thought that in doing this Repton had ruined "a dell of the most exquisite kind".) In 1918 the estate was taken over by the East of Fife Coal Company which mined at Valleyfield. In 1932 the Forestry Commission bought 70 acres/28 hectares of the High Valleyfield woodland and felled Repton's plantings. So, although the site of the walled flower garden remains and some rustic bridges across the burn, Scotland has had its revenge on Repton.

Vann

nr Hambledon, Surrey OS SU9837
English Heritage Register Grade II
Open occasionally for NGS and by
appointment Tel 01428 683413

House built in the 16th century, with later alterations. Garden made from 1910 by the Caroe family with advice from Gertrude Jekyll. A yew arch leads into the old garden, partly enclosed by house and barn. Brick paths, strips of lawn and rectangular mixed borders with cones of clipped yew. Lawn to south of house, with pergola flanked by herbaceous borders. Old Field Pond overhung with oaks and planted with waterlilies. A yew walk encloses a stone-lined watercourse whose margins are planted with moisture-loving plants. Old Japanese maples with a statue and seat at the end of the walk. Gertrude Jekyll particularly advised on the woodland garden, where four pools are crossed by stone bridges. Here, ash, birch and oak are underplanted with bluebells, celandines, cow parsley and snake's head fritillaries; exotic ferns, rodgersias and hostas on the edges of the pools.

Vauxhall Gardens, formerly New Spring Gardens

London Borough of Lambeth,
London OS TQ3078

Pleasure gardens founded c.1660 on the south bank of the Thames,

close to what is today the junction of Vauxhall Bridge and the Albert Embankment; the site is now obliterated by buildings. The gardens quickly became a popular and fashionable attraction. John Evelyn and Samuel Pepys both frequented them and the latter wrote in 1667: "It is very cheap going thither, for a man may go to spend what he will, or nothing, all is one – but to hear the nightingales and other birds, and here fiddles and there a harp, and here a jews trump, and here laughing, and there fine people walking, is mighty divertising". The gardens were at first quite simple but in their heyday in the mid 18th century they were filled with ornamental buildings. J.S. Muller's engravings after Samuel Wales's paintings, made after 1751, show walks between rows of trees (illuminated at night by lanterns) passing under grand archways, "Chinese Pavilions" (elaborately arcaded buildings with "supper boxes"), a Gothic/Moorish bandstand, a Rotunda and a magnificent statue of Handel by Roubiliac (today in The Victoria and Albert Museum). In 1786 61,000 people came to a fancy dress extravaganza attended by the Prince of Wales. In 1816 the Prince Regent welcomed the opening of the first Vauxhall Bridge which provided readier access to his favourite playground. By the mid 19th century (when they were described by Thackeray and Dickens) the fortunes of the gardens were fluctuating and they finally closed in 1859.

Ven House

Milborne Port, Somerset OS ST6818
English Heritage Register Grade II

Fine brick and stone house built for James Medlycott in c.1720, designed by Nathaniel Ireson. Formal gardens, designed by Richard Grange, contemporary with the house – a grand entrance forecourt, wrought-iron gates, pools and two avenues of topiary. On the south garden front, a pair of parterres with topiary in narrow beds. Traces of these gardens may still be seen, and the remains of early avenues and an 18th-century landscape park. Grand conservatory by Decimus

Burton added to west end of house in 1836, overlooking formal south terrace gardens (a Victorian revival of the early 18th-century formal garden). The surviving terrace and sunken garden was in its late Victorian heyday decorated with urns, pots of aloes, a walk of clipped Portugal laurels and, as described in Country Life in October 1898, "standard roses planted in little round beds and surfaced with white tufted pansies".

Vernon Park

Stockport, Greater Manchester OS SJ9090
English Heritage Register Grade II
Open regularly

Public park, opened in 1858. Stockport Museum, masked by a shrubbery, dominates the southern part of the park, with two bowling greens and shelter to the west. A sunken garden to the east, on the site of a former lake. To its east, a steep bank with terraced walks leading down to the eastern boundary of the park, with views over the river Goyt which has a weir at this point. North of the museum, the ground descends towards a circular pool surrounded by winding paths and, beyond it, a circular garden enclosed in a holly hedge.

Victoria Embankment Gardens

City of Westminster, London OS TQ3079
English Heritage Register Grade II*
Open regularly

Gardens laid out 1864–70, after the embankment of the Thames, by Sir Joseph Bazalgette (who also constructed London's first drainage system). Starting just north of Westminster Bridge, they follow the curve of the Thames to end below the Savoy Hotel, immediately to the west of Waterloo Bridge. The gardens have lawns, specimen trees and seasonal bedding schemes. Throughout, there are monuments and memorials – among them, to Robert Burns, Lord Cheylesmore (by Sir Edwin Lutyens), General Gordon, Lord Portal, Robert Raikes and Sir Arthur Sullivan. In the southernmost section, close to the Ministry of Defence, are

Queen Mary's Steps, a fragment of the Tudor Palace of Whitehall discovered in 1939.

Victoria Park

Hackney, London OS TQ3583 English Heritage Register Grade II* Open regularly

Public park designed by James Pennethorne and opened 1845. The site had previously been brick fields, market gardens and farmland. It covers an area of 215 acres/87 hectares and was the first and largest of the 19th-century public parks in London. Much perimeter planting and a winding peripheral carriage drive. Throughout the park, many mature trees. In the western part, a large irregular lake formed from an old gravel pit, with two islands, and alders and willows on its banks. Formal bedding schemes in this part of the park, and a deer park and menagerie. Further, smaller lakes in the eastern park, east of Grove Road. Close to the eastern boundary, two alcoves removed from the parapet of old London Bridge and brought here c.1860. Extravagant drinking fountain with putti and dolphins given by Mrs Burdett-Coutts in 1861 and designed by Henry Darbishire. Revived 19th-century formal garden nearby, with yew hedges, pergola, mixed borders, bedding schemes and rose beds. Many sports and recreational facilities throughout the park – among them a bowling green, pitches for cricket and football, running track and tennis courts.

Victoria Park

Leicester, Leicestershire OS SK5903
English Heritage Register Grade II
Open regularly

Public park, on the site of an 18th-century racecourse, opened in 1883. Lodges at the main entrance to the north, at the end of New Walk (see page 515), designed by Sir Edwin Lutyens. Tree belts enclose the park, which is open grassland in the centre, used for sports. Lutyens also designed the war memorial (1923) – a monumental square arch with a shallow dome, standing on the western side of the park – and its approach – a tree-lined walk with bedding and shrubs.

Victoria Park

Tipton, West Midlands OS SO9295
English Heritage Register Grade II
Open regularly

Public park on the site of a derelict colliery, designed in 1898 by William Barron & Sons. It opened in 1901 and cost £6,500 (£363,350 today). On a site of over 30 acres/12 hectares Barron laid out winding paths, lawns, a large lake and a cricket ground. A late 19th-century cast-iron umbrello (designed in 1860 by Walter Macfarlane & Co of Glasgow) survives close to the entrance. The cricket ground remains, with later tennis courts. Islands on the lake are planted with willows and conifers. An early 20th-century bowling green is secluded behind a shrubbery.

Victoria Tower Gardens

City of Westminster, London OS TQ3079
English Heritage Register Grade II
Open regularly

A triangular site immediately south of the Houses of Parliament, with the Thames to the east. Laid out as public gardens in the late 19th century and extended c.1914. A central lawn is ornamented with one of the finest public monuments in London – Rodin's Burghers of Calais (1895). Paths run around the perimeter of the garden, shaded by mature London planes. The Buxton Memorial, a Gothic fountain by S.S. Teulon (1866) on the south-east lawn, formerly stood in Parliament Square. In the north-west corner of the garden, a statue of the suffragette Emmeline Pankhurst by A.G. Walker (1930).

Virginia Water

Egham, Surrey OS SU9669
English Heritage Register Grade I
Open regularly

The Virginia brook had formed the southern boundary of Windsor Great Park, north of which there was a moated manor house, Manor Lodge, built in the 13th century. Fom 1749 the Duke of Cumberland, Ranger of Windsor Great Park, employed Henry Flitcroft to dam the brook to form Virginia Water, an immense

V

irregular stretch of water with long fingers running west, north and east. Flitcroft also built a belvedere (which survives, now called Fort Belvedere) on the southern bank, and a Palladian bridge (since replaced) across the western finger. At the end of that finger a Chinese teahouse was erected on China Island, connected to the mainland by a Chinoiserie bridge and with a Chinese junk floating in the water; none of these survives. The Greening family probably laid out the walks and beautiful woodland plantings about the lake with fine beeches and sweet chestnuts. In the 1780s George III enlarged the lake and had Paul Sandby design a rockwork cascade (inaugurated 1797) at the base of the eastern finger, which is still in place. From 1826 George IV added, on the bank of the lake, the picturesque ruins – columns, capitals, walls and plinths – of the Temple of Augustus, taken from the Roman city of Leptis Magna; they remain in position, a sight of melancholy splendour. North-east of the cascade is another building dating from the Duke of Cumberland's time – the Clockcase Tower, a Gothick tower attached to a later lodge on a hill. At the south-western base of the northern finger of the lake is a moated island, the site of the 13th-century Manor Lodge. It was also the site of an enchanting Chinoiserie fishing house designed by Jeffry Wyatville and Frederick Crace, built 1825–27 at a cost of £8730 (£317,976 today); rebuilt 1867–68, it was demolished by Edward VIII who thought it spoilt the view from Fort Belvedere. At the northern end of the eastern finger of the lake is a splendid Canadian totem pole presented to Elizabeth II in 1958 to celebrate the centenary of British Columbia. The landscape today has a delightful Arcadian character, with good walks about the banks of the lake, and is plainly much loved by local residents.

Voewood, *also known as* Home Place

nr Holt, Norfolk OS TG0939
English Heritage Register Grade II*

House designed by Edward S. Prior and built 1903–5 for the

Revd Percy Lloyd on a site which previously had been turnip fields. Prior also laid out the garden, disposed about a strong north–south axis. South of the house, a terrace with a pergola leads down to a sunken garden, with a croquet lawn on each side, a raised circular pool, and flower parterres divided by diagonal paths. Behind the house is a kitchen garden with elaborate formal orchards. A plan and photograph of this fine garden are illustrated in David Ottewill's *The Edwardian Garden* (1989).

The Vyne

Sherborne St John, nr Basingstoke, Hampshire OS SU6356 English Heritage Register Grade II Open regularly (NT)
Tel 01256 883858

Called the Vyne possibly because the first grapevines were planted here AD 276–282 under the Emperor Probus. Medieval house, rebuilt in the early 16th century for the 1st Lord Sandys (Lord Chamberlain to Henry VIII) whose family had been here since 1386. (There was a deer park here from 1270.) Alterations in the mid 17th century by John Webb, and again in the 18th century. From 1653 the estate belonged to the Chute family; Sir Charles Chute bequeathed the estate to the National Trust in 1956. John Webb designed two domed garden pavilions, of which one survives north-east of the house (with the "Hundred Guinea" oak behind it, said to date from the 14th century). An 18th-century portrait of a dog ("Chalons") at the house shows in the background a parterre and a bowling green. Another painting at the house, by J.H. Müntz in 1755, shows the house overlooking a lawn and a lake, much as it is today except that in the 18th century the trees on either side were arranged in formal groves. A Chinoiserie bridge crossed the lake in the 18th century but this was replaced by an elegant metal one in 1860. A Robinsonian wild garden was laid out before World War I with spring bulbs naturalised in grass. Good herbaceous border and yew hedges planted since acquisition by National Trust.

Waddesdon Manor

see page 110

Wadham College (Oxford)

see page 103

Wadhurst Castle

Wadhurst, East Sussex OS TQ6331
English Heritage Register Grade II

House built *c.*1818–20, on an ancient site, for James Louis West. The grounds were designed to form an appropriately picturesque setting for the castellated villa. Terrace walk south-east of the house was described in the early 19th century as being "adorned by little thousands of American and flowering shrubs". To its south, a rectangular lawn and a paved rose garden with a sundial laid out 1909–25. In a former quarry south-west of the pleasure grounds, a sunken garden among rhododendrons and ornamental trees. In the park, a deep winding ravine runs north–south. Ravine Wood has a stream and pools, the northernmost one of which is designed to be seen from the castle. Parallel to the west side of the ravine, deciduous woodland in Long Wood divides the park and frames views southwards.

Wakehurst Place

see page 179

Walcot Hall

nr Lydbury North, Shropshire OS SO3484
English Heritage Register Grade II
Open occasionally for NGS

House built for the 1st Lord Clive (Clive of India) by Sir William Chambers 1764–67, a remodelling of an earlier house. Very large kitchen garden in the early 18th century (700,000 bricks were used to build the walls). Landscape park from 1774 by William Emes who possibly connected a series of pools into the great curving lake, with islands and bridges, shown on an estate survey of 1827; it is still a feature of the landscape today. Hermitage – a thatched "Indian temple" – built in 1802–3 but destroyed by fire in the 20th century.

Waldershare Park

Waldershare, Kent OS TR2848
English Heritage Register Grade II

House built 1705–12 for Sir Henry Furnese, possibly to the designs of William Talman. An engraving by Thomas Badeslade of 1719 shows a very elaborate garden in the style of George London. Traces of this garden survive. The formal wilderness south of the house has been replanted but the original rides are still in place and some sweet chestnuts and oaks may be original plantings. Early 18th-century wrought-iron gates lead into the wilderness. At the southern end of the west ride is a brick belvedere with views over the park. This, built in 1725, was possibly designed by Lord Burlington. Much of the park is now arable land; trees suffered badly in the 1987 storm but there has been replanting. There is an 18th-century walled kitchen garden. The house has now been divided into flats.

The Walks

King's Lynn, Norfolk OS TF6219 English Heritage Register Grade II Open regularly

The New Walk, or Mall, was laid out *c.*1713, lined with lime trees, between the castellated town walls and the commercial and residential part of the town. Later in the century it was extended eastwards beyond the town wall and across the marshes, and in the 19th century this extension was gravelled and planted up. The Town Walk, running north and south, was established in the early 19th century.

Wall Hall

Aldenham, Hertfordshire OS TQ1399
English Heritage Register Grade II

18th-century house, with later alterations. In 1802 Humphry Repton advised George Woodford Thellusson on the grounds and produced a Red Book. Lawns, trees and woodland now form the pleasure grounds. South-east of the house, a Gothic sham ruin of *c.*1800, among trees. Further to the south-east, a second Gothic ruin of the same date and a path to an icehouse (*c.*1800) in woods. East of the house, an Italian garden was

made between the wars – now a lawn enclosed in yew hedges and the remains of a pergola. In recent years the estate has been part of the University of Hertfordshire which has put up buildings in the grounds. The park is dominated by a golf course.

Wallington

see page 354

Walmer Castle

see page 180

Walpole Park, *formerly known as* Pitzhanger *or* Pitshanger

Ealing, London OS TQ1780
English Heritage Register Grade II
Open regularly Tel 020 85671227

House built in the 18th century; enlarged by George Dance *c.*1768; bought by Sir John Soane in 1800, who demolished all except part of Dance's work and rebuilt the house. Since 1902 it has been a public library and the grounds a public park. The grounds were laid out by John Haverfield of Kew who designed a serpentine lake west of the house, later turned into a sunken garden. Soane designed a bridge for it, which survives, and also erected classical ruins north of the house, which do not. Present gardens largely 20th-century, with mature trees surviving from the 19th century. The sunken garden has a pond, fountain and stream, and paved paths, and is planted with dwarf conifers. An open-air theatre to the west, and beyond it a formal pool with fountain and two islands. Fine bedding displays by the house. 18th-century walled kitchen garden, now a rose garden with a pergola. Modern axial avenues in the park.

Wanstead Park

Redbridge, London OS TQ4187
English Heritage Register Grade II*

Wanstead House (previously Wanstead Hall) built in the 16th century, and a great new house built 1714–20 for Sir Richard Child (later 1st Earl of Tylney) to the designs of Colen Campbell (Campbell's first great Palladian house), demolished 1823–24. In the late 17th and early 18th centuries an immense formal garden, partly designed by George London, was made for a newly rich banker, Sir Josiah Child. John Evelyn's journal describes a visit in 1683 "to see Sir Josiah Child's prodigious cost in planting walnut trees about his seate, and making fish-ponds, many miles in circuit, in Epping Forest, in a barren spot, as oftentimes these suddenly monied men for the most part seate themselves." The garden was extended after Campbell's new house was completed. Parts of it survive today: an octagonal pool west of the house's site and a canal connected to a later lake in the eastern part of the grounds. On the southern boundary, a group of ponds and an 18th-century temple. Since 1882 the grounds have been a public park and in the western part are a cricket ground and golf course.

Warbrook House
Eversley, Hampshire OS SU7761
English Heritage register Grade II*

House built 1724 by John James for himself; James (1672-1746) was an architect, Clerk of the Works at Greenwich under Hawksmoor, Vanbrugh and Wren. His claim to garden fame is that he translated Antoine Joseph Dézallier d'Argenville's *La Théorie et la Pratique du Jardinage* (1709) as *The Theory and Practice of Gardening* (1712), which popularised the ideas of André Le Nôtre and described for the first time in print in English the ha-ha (or "ah, ah" as James called it). James designed his own formal gardens, of which various ingredients survive: a splendid canal lined with trees extending away from the pedimented entrance of the house; yew trees, possibly the remains of a hedge of James's time; and a sundial, the only surviving ornament from the garden. There is now a modern sunken garden with octagonal pool to the south of the house. In the landscape to the east and south of the house are the remains of an avenue and signs of old formal tree planting.

Wardour Castle
Wardour, Wiltshire OS ST9226
English Heritage Register Grade II*

The first castle at Wardour, Old Wardour Castle, was built in the 14th century and destroyed during the Civil War 1643–44. The new castle was built on a different site 1770–76 for the 8th Lord Arundell to the designs of James Paine. The old castle had had a modest formal garden but, in advance of the building of the new castle, the grounds were landscaped 1764–70 by Richard Woods, with the ruins of the old castle assuming a picturesque role in the landscape. Woods enlarged the pool to the west of the old castle and started making a series of new pools, never completed, in front of the new one. He also cleared the grounds to open out views from the new castle, and built a terrace running from the old castle to the Lady Grove north of it. Woods also designed several garden buildings: a greenhouse (now called the camellia house); a pinery with heated walls; an icehouse; a cold bath; and a Gothic temple (demolished 1985). In 1773 Lord Arundell consulted Capability Brown, and although there is no evidence, the banqueting house may have been designed by him and he may have had a hand in the planning of the garden about the new house. In 1792 Josiah Lane built a grotto close to the old castle, "rising twenty feet into the air", in the words of Christopher Thacker's *Masters of the Grotto: Joseph & Josiah Lane* (1976), "a jagged array of tufa knobs and spikes like the boney excrescences on the back of a stegosaurus". The great house, in recent times a girls' school, has now been divided into flats.

Wardown Park
Luton, Bedfordshire OS TL0822
English Heritage Register Grade II

Late 19th-century house designed by T.C. Sorby for F.C. Scargill. Bought by Luton Corporation in 1904, and the grounds converted to public pleasure gardens. The house, at the centre of the gardens, is today a museum and picture gallery. South of the house, a lawn with formal beds for summer bedding schemes. To the east, an informal lawn planted with mature specimen trees and an octagonal rustic summerhouse of c.1880. Sports facilities in the northern part of the park. In the southern part of the park, a long serpentine lake with mature trees and an island. Two bridges, one of which is an ornamental iron suspension bridge of 1908. Early 20th-century boathouse. Lawns surround the lake, with many trees, some of them dating from the late 19th century.

Warley Park
Warley Woods, Birmingham, West Midlands OS SP0186 English Heritage Register Grade II Open regularly

Public open space – now entirely engulfed by urban development – owned by the City of Birmingham, with the remains of a Humphry Repton landscape. Repton was commissioned by Samuel Galton in the 1790s to design the setting for a house which Galton was about to build; Repton's surviving Red Book is dated 1795. Fragments of his landscape survive: clumps of trees and specimen trees, and the Great Copse, a piece of old woodland which Repton shaped and embellished with a temple (which does not survive).

Warley Place
Great Warley, Essex OS TQ5890
English Heritage Register Grade II

17th-century house, with much later alteration, demolished in 1939. John Evelyn owned the estate 1649–66 but no details of gardening activity are known. The estate is mentioned only once in his journals when, in May 1649, he wrote, "I purchaesd the manor of Warley Magna in Essex." The garden fame of Warley Place comes from a much later notable gardener, Ellen Willmott (1858–1934), who inherited it from her parents in 1888. In her heyday she employed eighty-five gardeners and grew 100,000 different plants – making it into one of the greatest plant collections in the world. As Dr W.T. Stearn wrote, "For certain genera, such as *Epimedium*, *Hedera*, *Iris*, *Narcissus* and *Rosa*, she acquired almost every variety that cash or persuasion could obtain." In 1880 she inherited a fortune of £140,000 (£6,385,400 today) from her godmother, Helen Tasker, most of which she spent on gardening. Her annual expenditure 1890–1900 with just one nurseryman, Louis R. Russell, was as high as £1,500 (£82,545 today). She also had two gardens abroad: Tresserve in the French Alps and Boccanegra on the Italian Riviera. Since 1977 the site of the garden at Warley Place, which had become derelict, has been leased to the Essex Naturalists Trust which has been working on its restoration. Some of Miss Willmott's plantings survive and some sweet chestnuts and quantities of naturalised *Crocus vernus* subsp. *albiflorus* are even said to date from Evelyn's time.

Warmley House
Siston, Kingswood, Bristol OS ST6672
English Heritage Register Grade II
Open regularly

Palladian house built in the mid 18th century for William Champion, a Quaker copper smelter. Champion made Warmley into the largest industrial site of its time in the world, with 76 acres/30 hectares of mills, presses, assembly shops and workers' cottages. In his garden, a lake used water recycled by a steam pump from the mill, and a giant figure of Neptune was placed at the centre of the lake and a castellated summerhouse on its bank. Another, Gothic summerhouse was built of slag. The passage, vaults and chambers of a grotto of the 1760s are lined with clinker, the byproduct of copper smelting; originally there was a stream and cascades within the grotto. Champion went bankrupt in 1769 but his house remains, now an old people's home, and features of his garden survive – an industrial pioneer's Arcadia of rare if rather disheveled interest. The gardens are now a public open space, some of which is shared by a caravan park.

Warnham Court
Warnham, West Sussex OS TQ7549
English Heritage Register Grade II

House built c.1828 for Henry Tredcroft, with much alteration in 1866 by A.W. Blomfield. Gardens laid out 1864 by Edward Milner, with later alterations by his son Henry. Three grass terraces descend the slope in front of the south façade. North of the house, a pinetum laid out in 1880 "under the personal supervision of Harry J. Veitch" who was then owner of the great Veitch nurseries. Conifers survive from the original plantings, with bulbs planted in grass and island shrubberies.

Warwick Castle
see page 281

Watcombe Park, *also known as* Brunel Park
Torquay, Devon OS SX9167
English Heritage Register Grade II

This had been the estate of the engineer Isambard Kingdom Brunel, who bought it in 1847 and started building a house – it was unfinished at his death in 1859. A new house was built in about 1870 for J.R. Crompton to the design of J. Watson. While his house was being built, Brunel had laid out a garden with advice from William Nesfield, and with help in the water garden from William Simpson of Pimlico; with his head gardener, Alexander Forsyth, Brunel planted an arboretum with many evergreens (*Cupressus macrocarpa*, *Pinus wallichiana*, Wellingtonias, monkey puzzles and holm oaks), many of which survive and are fine specimens. The estate is now in divided ownership and the house (Brunel Manor) is a Christian Conference Centre.

The Water Gardens
Harlow, Essex OS TL4409
English Heritage Register Grade II*
Open regularly

Water Gardens built 1960, designed by Sir Frederick Gibberd and included as part of his master plan of 1947 for the building of Harlow New Town. The 2.5 acre/1 hectare site is rectangular and lies between the Town Hall and the Technical College. It is terraced, using varied paving materials, with steps and ramps on each side connecting it with the town centre. The upper terrace has a canal 250ft/75m long, enlivened by seven fountains. Further fountains spout water from lion's head masks set in the canal's

W

retaining wall into a second, parallel canal. Rose beds run along the southern edge of the terrace. Steps from a central brick pump house lead down to a third terrace with a geometric pattern of beds and square pools and gardens enclosed by clipped yew bays. Statues, including Rodin's "Eve", ornament the gardens.

Waterlow Park
Camden, London OS TQ2887 English Heritage Register Grade II* Open regularly

Public park, opened in 1891 on the site of the gardens of Lauderdale House and a neighbouring house since demolished. The land was given by Sir Sydney Waterlow who wanted to provide "a garden for the gardenless". Lauderdale House was built in the late 16th century and had many subsequent alterations. A fine sloping site with belts of shrubs and trees along most boundaries. A series of pools west and south of the house are surrounded by shrubberies and trees. Brick terraces south-west and south-east of the house have walls of the late 17th or early 18th century. Good herbaceous border at foot of south-west terrace. Many good specimen trees throughout the park. Tennis courts, putting green and open-air theatre.

Waterperry Gardens
see page 111

Waterston Manor
Puddletown, Dorset OS SY7395
English Heritage Register Grade II

Exceedingly ornamental 17th-century house with enriched gables, niches and much stone carving. Nothing is known of any early garden here but a new garden of Arts and Crafts style was made bordering the river Piddle east and north-east of the house just before World War I; this was probably designed by P. Morley Horder, the architect in charge of restoring the house for the new owner, Captain Gerald Carter, who had bought the estate from the Earl of Ilchester. An article in *Country Life* in February 1916 shows a garden below the east front of the house, with a narrow rill edged with stone, a scalloped pool at the centre, and on each side low stone

walls and a newly planted yew hedge. All this lay below the dining room window and was aligned with a grand flight of stone steps rising into the woodland to the east. It has been simplified but stately formality survives – a canal, a walk of pollarded limes and good trees. The house is thought to be the model of Bathsheba's Weatherbury Farm in Thomas Hardy's *Far from the Madding Crowd*.

Wayford Manor
Wayford, Somerset OS ST4006
English Heritage Register Grade II
Open occasionally for NGS and groups by appointment Tel 01460 73253

Early 17th-century house built for Giles Daubeney and restored by Sir Ernest George in about 1902 for Ingham Baker. Outstanding Arts and Crafts garden by Harold Peto, made from 1902 onwards, incorporating the Jacobean upper terrace and taking full advantage of ground sloping southwards. Peto created a series of terraces and enclosures, walled in stone or hedged in yew, running down to a wild garden with immense magnolias. At the east end of the upper terrace, with its long turf walk, he built a loggia whose arched opening looks west along the terrace and south over the garden. All this is harmoniously fitted into the existing irregular pattern of the old house and its outhouses. West of the house, now in separate ownership, is Wayford Woods, a woodland garden made between the wars by the Baker family. Rich in fine flowering shrubs, especially camellias and rhododendrons, and with drifts of snowdrops and bluebells, it has a wild and charming character. It is open every day, payments to an honesty box.

Weald and Downland Open Air Museum
see page 181

Weald Park
South Weald, Essex OS TQ5794 English Heritage Register Grade II Open regularly

17th-century house, with many alterations, demolished c.1950. A painting attributed to William van der Hagen of c.1720, illustrated in John Harris's *The Artist and the*

Country House (1979), shows a fine Tudor house with walled gardens and an ornate little parterre. There is no trace of these today. In the former park are the remains of two avenues radiating out from the Belvedere Mount where, in the 18th century, there had been an ornamental tower. A chain of lakes, probably enlarged c.1738 from former fishponds, runs across the park. Since 1953 Weald Park has been a Country Park owned by Essex County Council.

Wedderburn Castle
nr Duns, Berwickshire OS NT8052
Scottish Inventory

Castle built 1770–78, incorporating a 17th-century tower house, to the designs of Robert and James Adam for Patrick Home. Parkland dating from at least the 18th century, with ash, beech, lime, sycamore and yew of that date. Scattered woodland for shelter and game cover dates from the 18th century. Fragmentary remains of probably 19th-century terraces about the house.

Welbeck Abbey
Welbeck, Nottinghamshire OS SK5674
English Heritage Register Grade II

The abbey of Welbeck dates from the 12th century and its remains were incorporated in the early 17th-century house which was designed for Sir Charles Cavendish by Robert Smythson; alterations in 18th, 19th and early 20th centuries. Of the 17th-century gardens no trace remains. A walled kitchen garden, which survives, was laid out by Francis Richardson in 1744 and he also landscaped the grounds east of the house in the mid 18th century. The park at Welbeck was already notable for its trees, especially oaks, which were described in Hayman Rooke's *Descriptive Sketches of Some Remarkable Oaks in the Park at Welbeck* (1790). Many of these were at the end of their life and an immense programme of tree planting was undertaken. In twenty-five years 2,000 acres were planted with beech, birch, larch, oaks, sweet chestnuts and tulip trees, supervised by the head gardener, William Speechly. In

1789 the 3rd Duke of Portland consulted Humphry Repton and a Red Book was produced. Among Repton's proposed alterations, earth was to be removed to make the house more prominent, the lake enlarged, and ornamental walks made in the woods about it, with openings to reveal the beauties of the scene, including especially notable ancient trees. In 1793 a second Red Book was commissioned. This dealt with the whole character of the estate, suggesting among much else that all estate buildings be built in the Gothic style to match the house. Through lack of money, very little was implemented. The Duke of Portland's son, the Marquess of Tichfield, commissioned a third Red Book in 1803, which proposed a new classical house on a knoll in the deer park – which was never built. In the later 19th century new gardens were made close to the house but these have been removed. Today the house is leased to the Ministry of Defence.

Well Hall
Greenwich, London OS TQ4275
English Heritage Register Grade II

In the early 16th century the house here had belonged to Sir Thomas More's daughter, Margaret Roper. It was demolished in 1733 but a Tudor brick outhouse survives, with the date 1568 (which was possibly added later). The house was moated and had enclosed gardens; a walled garden, probably of the 16th century, remains, and a bridge of the same date crosses the eastern part of the moat. All the planting is 20th-century, with mature specimen trees on a lawn to the east of the site and bedding schemes to the south-east. A rose garden with a central fountain has been laid out in the walled garden, and, to the south, a 1930s formal garden with a pergola and sunken circular rose garden. The outhouse is now an art gallery and restaurant.

Well Hall, *also known as* Well Vale House
Well, Lincolnshire OS TF4473
English Heritage Register Grade II

18th-century house for James Bateman. In 1727 Bateman

commissioned Thomas Richardson of York to make a formal garden with a canal and cascade, parterres and a wilderness – similar to the surviving garden. It has been suggested that Charles Bridgeman may have been involved. A series of lakes to the east and west of the house suggests later 18th-century landscaping but there are also signs of earlier formal terracing on the slopes above.

Wentworth Castle
see page 355

Wentworth Woodhouse
Wentworth, South Yorkshire OS SK3997
English Heritage Register Grade II*

Palatial 18th-century house incorporating the 17th-century house of the Wentworth family who became Marquesses of Rockingham. The estate passed to the Fitzwilliam family in the late 18th century. Humphry Repton was consulted by Lord Fitzwilliam in 1790 and produced a Red Book. Repton softened the contours of the land, involving immense earth-moving, and planted trees so that vistas of the house, and of existing garden buildings, were maintained. Much of Repton's park was destroyed when opencast mining between the house and the mausoleum to the east took place 1956–61. Emmanuel Shinwell, Minister of Power and Fuel after coalmining was nationalised in 1946, told Lord Fitzwilliam, "I'm going to mine right up to your bloody front door"; 370,000 tons of coal were removed, and although trees were replanted, vistas were not accurately preserved and the levels were never the same. The park is ornamented with several notable monuments: Henry Flitcroft's Hoober Stand (1748), a curious narrow pyramid erected to celebrate victory at Culloden; the Keppel Monument by John Carr (1773), a Tuscan column; the Mausoleum by John Carr (1785) surrounded by obelisks (the whole "not to entertain the eye, but to instruct the mind"); and the Needle's Eye (1780), an archway surmounted with an urn and with curiously Moorish arches. The pattern of rides and walks within the park dates in part from the 18th century and was devised to display the house and the various park ornaments. Today the estate is in divided ownership.

Werrington Park

nr Launceston, Cornwall OS SX3387
English Heritage Register Grade II

The estate at Werrington had belonged to Sir Francis Drake and was bought from his nephew by William Morice in 1650. The house was much altered for the Morice family in the 18th century, with more changes after 1775 when the estate was sold to the Duke of Northumberland. In 1882 the estate was sold to the Williams family of Caerhays (*see page 22*). Much landscaping activity in the 18th century. Richard Pococke, in his *Travels Through England* (1750) describes the estate as "beautifully improved in wood and lawn" and goes on to list various monuments built by Sir William Morice: a ruinous castle; a temple of the sun; a triumphal arch; a hermitage; the tomb of Horatii; and others. He concludes: "This park is to be looked on as one of the most beautiful in England." The "tomb of Horatii" survives, a curious, very unclassical building of three rough cones of rubble set on an arched plinth. None of the others survives; Barbara Jones in her *Follies & Grottoes* (1974) says of one that "The present owner's father blew it up in the 1880s or 1890s because it wasn't real, so it was probably a sham ruin." There have been vague suggestions, by Pevsner and others, that William Kent may have had something to do with the house and garden buildings; this is partly on stylistic grounds (for example, the hermitage here resembled Kent's hermitage in Richmond Park) and partly because Nicholas Morice in the early 18th century married Catherine Herbert, daughter of the Earl of Pembroke who moved in Kentian circles. But no solid evidence has come to light. J.C. Williams made an arboretum at Werrington from 1908 onwards to accommodate the overflow of rare plants from Caerhays.

West Dean Gardens

see page 182

West Green House Garden

see page 112

West Park

Macclesfield, Cheshire OS SJ9174 English Heritage Register Grade II Open regularly

The first public park in Macclesfield, designed by William Barron and opened in 1854. Mature planted belts enclose the park. In the eastern part, a very large bowling green with surviving formal flower beds on each corner. The western part of the park has winding paths and a central area for cricket and other sports. Steep valley with stream and pool. Some of Barron's characteristic style of planting, including the use of several different varieties of yew, remain, and some of the specimen trees are part of the original scheme. Most of the original ornaments and buildings of the park have gone.

West Park

Wolverhampton, West Midlands
OS SO9099 English Heritage Register
Grade II Open regularly

Public park, opened in 1881 and designed by R.H.Vertegans, and surviving much as he planned it. At the north end, a large figure-of-eight boating lake has its original wooden shelter and cast-iron bridge. North of the lake, a splendid 1896 conservatory (designed by Dan Gibson, Thomas Mawson's architect partner) forms part of a group of glasshouses. A pattern of concentric paths has at its centre formal flower beds and bedding schemes, with a belt of mature trees and shrubs screening it from the rest of the park. The former archery lawn and bowling greens have been converted into tennis courts.

West Wycombe Park

see page 113

Westbourne Road Town Gardens, *formerly* Westbourne Road Leisure Gardens

Birmingham, West Midlands OS SP4048
English Heritage Register Grade II

A rare surviving group of rented town gardens dating from the mid 19th century. 18th-century Birmingham was surrounded by such gardens, in separate blocks quite detached from any houses and available for rent. As the town expanded, these gardens were lost and very few survive. J.C. Loudon noted in 1831 that there were over 2,000 such gardens let out at annual rents of between 17s 6d and 30s (£33–£57 today). At Westbourne Road the surviving gardens are used as allotments to grow fruit and vegetables, and for ornamental plants. Only one original brick summerhouse survives. There are a few mature fruit trees, and a handsome stand of Corsican pines (*Pinus nigra* subsp. *laricio*), planted in the 1880s to conceal the railway line which was widened at that time.

Westbury Court

see page 237

Weston Park
(Shropshire)

see page 238

Weston Park

nr Sheffield, South Yorkshire OS SK3487
English Heritage Register Grade II
Open regularly

A public park which includes the buildings of the Weston Park Art Gallery and the Sheffield City Museum. The house, Weston Park, had been a private house whose mid 19th-century garden was remodelled by Robert Marnock before it was opened to the public in 1875. Marnock's layout, with specimen trees in close-mown grass, curving paths and seats and shelters, substantially survives. Marnock's bandstand also survives. Several ornaments remain: an obelisk designed by James Gamble and erected in 1875; a 1854 statue of Ebenezer Elliott (a mill-owner who had opposed the Bread Tax), moved here from Sheffield Market Place; a monument to the Yorkshire and Lancashire Regiment (1922); and a Boer War Memorial moved from Sheffield Cathedral forecourt in 1957.

Westonbirt Arboretum

see page 239

Westonbirt School Gardens

see page 240

Westover

Calbourne, Isle of Wight OS SZ4286
English Heritage Register Grade II

18th-century house, rebuilt in the early 19th century. Late 18th-century landscape park with a lake near the northern lodge, and the drive carried over a late 18th-century bridge. South of the house, a lawn with fine mature trees and flowering shrubs and a late 18th- or early 19th-century icehouse. Walled kitchen garden with swimming pool and ornamental trees and shrubs.

Westwood Park

Boycott, Worcestershire OS SO8763
English Heritage Register Grade II

House originally part of the estate of a 12th-century nunnery (which later became a private house, Westwood House, now in separate ownership). Westwood Park was built in 1598 as a hunting lodge and greatly extended after 1660. A Kip engraving in *Britannia Illustrata* (1707) shows an extraordinary house at the centre of a pattern of rides cut through woods. The park was probably created in 1539, and in the 17th century there were two deer parks, one for fallow deer, the other for red deer. Most of the park today is arable land and a few old pools survive.

Whatton House

Long Whatton, Leicestershire OS SK4924
English Heritage Register Grade II Open occasionally for NGS Tel 01509 842268

Late 19th-century house, replacing an 18th-century house destroyed by fire. Largely 19th-century gardens by house. Lawn to north-east of house, with flower beds flanking a statue of an elephant. Terraced garden south of house, with axial walk and Irish yews. Rose garden south of kitchen garden, laid out in 1898 in a cruciform pattern with terracotta statues at each corner. The Broad Walk leads west to the Bogey Hole, a former icehouse converted into a grotto from 1831. This is the site of a late 19th-century Chinese Garden, with rock-lined paths and a bark summerhouse originally made as the setting for oriental statues. Arboretum south-west of house, with many mature specimen trees. Park laid out *c*.1802–3, now arable farmland.

Whinfell Quarry Garden

Sheffield, South Yorkshire OS SK3182
English Heritage Register Grade II
Open regularly

Public park since 1968, based on the former estate of Whinfell House which was destroyed by fire in 1971. The quarry had been planted with about 10,000 trees after 1898, drastically thinned ten years later. Shortly after, paths, steps and a series of rock pools were laid out by James Backhouse & Co of York. In 1915 the plant hunter and nurseryman Clarence Elliot was asked to design a garden in Little Quarry. Many good trees survive today – in particular cherries, conifers and maples. Elliott's garden, which had consisted of detailed planting of alpines among shrubs and trees, has lost its focus.

Whitchester

nr Duns, Berwickshire OS NT7158
Scottish Inventory

Farmhouse enlarged and made grander in the 19th century. Bought in 1878 by an Edinburgh brewer, Andrew Smith. Woodland garden established by Smith but largely planted since 1957 with an outstanding collection of over 400 kinds of rhododendrons, cultivars and species. Also distinguished trees and shrubs such as *Cercidiphyllum japonicum*, *Embothrium coccineum* and eucryphias. The house is now a Christian guesthouse and retreat.

Gilbert White's House

see page 115

Whitehall Palace, *formerly* York Place

London OS TQ3079

A former residence of the Archbishop of York, Thomas Wolsey, and appropriated as a royal palace by Henry VIII in 1529. Extensive building work transformed it into the largest

W

palace in Europe. The Great Garden, laid out in the 1540s, was described by a visitor, Leopold von Wedel, in 1584: "…the queen's garden, in which there are thirty-four high columns, carved with various fine paintings; also different animals carved in wood, with their horns gilt, are set on top of the columns…In the middle of the garden is a nice fountain with a remarkable sundial, showing the time in thirty different ways." The garden is seen in detail in the background of a painting of Henry VIII and his family by an unknown artist, painted in the 1540s – one of the earliest surviving detailed paintings of an English garden (illustrated and discussed in Roy Strong's *The Artist and the Garden* (2000)). Whitehall Palace was destroyed by fire in 1698; only Inigo Jones's Banqueting House and a fragment of Tudor brickwork survived.

Whitehall Park

Darwen, Lancashire OS SD6920
English Heritage Register Grade II
Open regularly

Public park opened in 1879. Long narrow site with entrance to the north-east from which a path climbs a gentle slope between shrubberies with, as it curves south, the Catlow Drinking Fountain (c.1901), of wrought iron with a canopy, erected to commemorate the coronation of Edward VII. A stream flows across the park, broken into cascades and pools, in the largest of which is the cast-iron Lightbown Fountain (1886). Paths wind through the wooded valley to levelled grass terraces from which there are views of the fells at Longride and of the Pennines.

Whitfield

nr Kingstone, Herefordshire OS SO4233
English Heritage Register Grade II
Open occasionally for NGS and to groups by appointment Tel 01981 570727

18th-century house, much altered in the 19th and 20th centuries. Late 19th-century terraced gardens south of house, with yew topiary and fine octagonal fountain pool probably of c.1768 and brought from Copped Hall

(*see page 462*) in 1968. East of the house, late 19th-century curved terraces. North of house, a vista down a series of ponds made in the 1960s. A woodland garden to the east of the Goldfish Pool and woods flanking the canal. Park laid out in the 18th century, especially after 1775 by Lady Catherine Stanhope who made the Beech Walk and walks through Big Wood. West of the house, Beech Walk leads to a mid 19th-century pinetum with outstanding specimens at the northern end of Big Wood – a sweep of woodland running along the western boundary of the park. More woodland to the east, but the central part of the park is open farmland with occasional mature specimen trees.

Whittingehame

East Lothian OS NT6073
Scottish Inventory

Estate now in divided ownership: Whittingehame Tower (the 13th-century keep of the Douglas family) and Whittingehame House (early 19th-century, designed by Sir Robert Smirke for James Balfour). The two buildings are on opposite sides of the steep wooded glen of Whittingehame water. In 1819 W.S. Gilpin was asked to lay out the grounds of Balfour's new house, making walks along the river bank and exploiting views of the picturesque Tower. North of Whittingehame Tower, an arboretum dating from the early 19th century with cedars, eucalyptus, eucryphias, monkey puzzles and nothofagus. Here too is the Whittingehame Yew, thought to be about 700 years old, whose widespreading braches cover a vast span. In the 19th century a double avenue of limes was planted along the north entrance drive to Whittingehame House.

Whittington Castle

Whittington, nr Oswestry, Shropshire
OS SJ3331 Open regularly

Ancient site going back at least to the reign of King Offa (d.AD 796). A castle was built for Sir Foulke Fitz Warin in the reign of Henry III (13th century) of

which parts survive, including grand towers, parts of the walls and two pools of the original moat. The Fitz Warins had connections with the royal family, and lived here until the 15th century. In 1998 the local community set up the Whittington Castle Preservation Trust, taking a 99-year lease on the castle and its 12 acres/4.8 hectares of land. A geophysical survey of part of the site has revealed signs of a medieval garden. A mound, previously thought to have been defensive, with a wooden bailey on top, is now considered to have been a prospect mound for the garden. It rose out of the moat, linked by a causeway, and was probably surmounted with a pavilion. The flower garden was surrounded by canals.

Wicksteed Park

Kettering, Northamptonshire OS SP8777
English Heritage Register Grade II
Open regularly

Public park made by the industrialist and philanthropist Charles Wicksteed and opened in 1921, with a lake, water chute, bandstand, sports facilities, a theatre and pavilion. A formal rose garden, now given over to bedding schemes, was added in 1924. To the north-east are the remains of Humphry Repton's park (1793) for Barton Seagrave Hall.

Widcombe Manor

Widcombe, Bath, Somerset OS ST7563
English Heritage Register Grade II

Delightful house of Baroque character, built c.1727 for Philip Bennet; its ornate pedimented south façade with pairs of pilasters overlooks a forecourt with a pool and a fine 16th-century Venetian tiered fountain with gambolling putti. Early 18th-century garden with some surviving details – formal pool and cascade, terrace, classical summerhouse and miniature park. Garden of Arts and Crafts style added in the early 20th century, with new terracing; Harold Peto's name has been mentioned in connection with this work but there is no evidence.

Wightwick Manor

see page 283

Wilbraham Temple

Great Wilbraham, Cambridgeshire OS TL5557 English Heritage Register Grade II

16th-century house with later alterations, originally a residence of Knights Templar. North-east of house, pleasure grounds with a wilderness, stream and ornamental woodland. Park with hints of 18th-century character, some perimeter belts and clumps of trees, and much new planting; 1,000 trees planted 1981–84: beech, field maple, limes, oaks and Scots pines.

Wilbury House

nr Newton Toney, Wiltshire OS SU2241
English Heritage Register Grade II

House built in 1710 for William Benson to his own designs, with later alterations. North of the house, an early 18th-century formal layout survives. A beech avenue runs north from the house towards a Doric column dedicated to Queen Victoria and dated 1877. At its southern end the avenue is flanked by urns on pedestals commemorating Admirals Nelson and Cornwallis. At the northern end of the avenue a further beech avenue runs eastwards to an early 18th-century octagonal temple. The temple stands on a mound under which is a grotto (this had been a boathouse for the adjacent lake which is now dry). Another grotto, of c.1710, south-west of the house. To the south of the house, a formal garden of the 1950s: a lawn slopes down to a parterre with a central pool.

Willersley Castle

Matlock Bath, Derbyshire OS SK2957
English Heritage Register Grade II

Old estate, of complicated ownership, going back to the 16th century when it was owned by the Talbot family. In 1782 it was sold to the pioneer mill-owner Richard Arkwright, who built a new house (a picturesque castle), designed by William Thomas. The gardens are largely 19th- and 20th-century. West of the house, a rock garden with steps leading to alpine beds; evergreen shrubberies press in on two sides. A path leads

through woodland to the west of Cat Tor. The walk is edged with rocks, and yews above are planted so that the picturesque roots are visible. The walk continues to the bank of the river, with a view of a cascade, and then on to a weir built to provide water for Arkwright's mill. North-east of the house, a long terrace walk with evergreen shrubs and trees on each side. The walk ends at a cliff planted with yew and turns north-west, snaking through an area of box and yew, with rock faces on one side, scattered groups of rocks, and dramatic views down the river valley. The house today is a holiday centre.

E.H. Wilson Memorial Garden

see page 241

Wilton House

Wilton, Salisbury, Wiltshire SU0930
English Heritage Register Grade I
Open regularly Tel 01722 746720

Wilton House is built on the site of a medieval nunnery, founded by King Alfred. The present house was built from 1543 for William Herbert who became 1st Earl of Pembroke in 1551. Alterations by Isaac de Caus in 1636, with advice from Inigo Jones who also advised John Webb on remodelling the interior, 1648–50. Isaac de Caus also designed a great garden south of the house. A drawing of the late 1630s, attributed to him, is illustrated in John Harris's *The Artist and the Country House* (1979); it shows an ornate arrangement of formal ingredients symmetrically disposed about a central walk. The walk ended with a magnificent renaissance grotto which was lavishly decorated and equipped with water spouts. Celia Fiennes saw it c.1685 and described "figures at each corner of the roome that can weep water on the beholders". She also heard "the melody of Nightingerlls and all sorts of birds" counterfeited by water flowing through pipes. Fragments of this great grotto survive on a different site, built into an outhouse – the only surviving trace of one the finest renaissance gardens in England. Its layout was finally destroyed when a Palladian bridge, designed by the 9th Earl of Pembroke and Roger Morris, was built in 1737 to span the river Nadder south of the house. This was part of a new landscape scheme which also involved widening the Nadder to form a lake. In the late 1750s a *casino* on a hill to the south was built by Sir William Chambers. In 1779 Capability Brown produced a survey at a cost of 8d (£2 today) per acre, but it is not known what, if anything, resulted. West of the house, an Italian garden was laid out in the 1820s to the designs of Sir Richard Westmacott with low walls, statuary, central fountain, a loggia and an orangery. In 1971 David Vicary designed a new garden in the forecourt to the north of the house, with pleached limes and a box parterre.

Wimbledon Park

Merton, London OS TQ2472
English Heritage Register Grade II*
Open regularly

Wimbledon Park is the remaining part of the estate of the Tudor Wimbledon Palace which was begun in 1588 for Sir Thomas Cecil, later Earl of Exeter. Charles I's Queen, Henrietta Maria, lived here in the 1640s, when the house was remodelled by Inigo Jones and Nicholas Stone. In the early 18th century this house was demolished, as were two subsequent houses. Sir Thomas Cecil's magnificent house had a great garden, of which a plan by Robert Smythson dated 1609 survives; it is well described in Roy Strong's *The Renaissance Garden in England* (1979). In 1642 André Mollet redesigned the gardens for Henrietta Maria. John Evelyn visited in 1662 and wrote, 'It is a delicious place for prospect"; he was helping at the time "to contrive the garden after the modern". In 1731 a new garden was designed by Charles Bridgeman for the Duchess of Marlborough; the results are seen in Rocque's map of 1746 in *An Exact Survey of the City's of London, Westminster…and the Country Near Ten Miles Round*. In 1764 Capability Brown made a plan for the landscape for Viscount (later 1st Earl) Spencer, for which he was paid £1,760 (£127,090

today). Of Brown's work, his spectacular lake and some tree planting survives. In the 1840s Sir Joseph Paxton designed new formal gardens beside Lord Spencer's house. The park today is chiefly taken up with various sports and recreational facilities, not least the All England Tennis Club.

Wimborne Road Cemetery

Bournemouth, Dorset OS SZ09 92
English Heritage Register Grade II*
Open regularly

In 1859 Christopher Crabbe Creeke, a founder of the Architectural Association, became Surveyor to the Town Commissioners of Bournemouth and remained in the job until 1879. Among much other work, he laid out the Wimborne Road Cemetery from 1876 onwards. It covers an area of over 20 acres/8 hectares and is planned so that winding walks radiate out from the cemetery chapel, also designed by Creeke. Much planting of evergreens, and a magnificently varied range of memorial monuments.

Wimpole Hall

see page 324

Windsor Castle and Home Park

Windsor, Berkshire OS SU9777
English Heritage Register Grade I

Windsor Castle was first built in the late 11th century by William the Conqueror, not far from the Saxon royal hunting lodge at Old Windsor. In the 12th century parts of Windsor forest were enclosed as a deer park. In the early middle ages there were gardens for growing herbal plants within the castle's curtain walls. Gardens outside the walls were established later, and by the time Kip's engraving of the castle was published (*c.*1708), they were highly developed – an elaborate formal design enclosed in walls. Henry Wise, the royal gardener, did much work on the north (the Maastricht Garden), east and south sides of the castle from 1690 onwards, and when Celia Fiennes visited Windsor in 1698,

she saw "a garden cut in squares and figures, with all sorts of flowers and greens which has at its end a cut hedge and leads to a sort of orchard with dwarfe trees". From the 1820s Jeffry Wyatville built the East Terrace Garden (replacing the 17th-century King's Garden), with planting by W.T. Aiton, the Director of the Royal Gardens. Aiton's bedding schemes were replaced with rose gardens in the 1950s, but clipped domes of golden yew and statues on plinths preserve a sedate early 19th-century flavour. During all this time, Home Park was gradually extended, as far as the river Thames to the north and spreading out east and south of the castle where it runs about the garden of Frogmore (*see page 477*).

Windsor Great Park

Old Windsor and New Windsor, Berkshire and Surrey OS SU9672
English Heritage Register Grade I
Much of the park open regularly

Windsor Great Park was a royal hunting park in Windsor Forest from the 11th century. It covers an area of *c.*2,500 acres/1,012 hectares, and runs from Home Park (*see above*) to the north, to Virginia Water (*see page 553*) to the south, and includes the Savill and Valley Gardens (*see page 173*). It is linked to the castle by the 3-mile Long Walk which is aligned with the castle's south front and runs at first along the western boundary of Home Park. The avenue is planted with double rows of horse chestnuts and planes – a 1940s replanting of the original 17th-century elm avenue. There are several notable buildings in the park: Cumberland Lodge (*see page 465*), Fort Belvedere at Virginia Water (*see page 553*), Cranbourne Tower (a remnant of the early 17th-century Cranbourne Lodge on the park's western boundary, the home of the Windsor Forest Ranger) and, also on the western boundary, the late 18th-century Forest Lodge. Cranbourne Tower stands at the centre of a pattern of rides probably dating from the early 18th century when Henry Wise laid out parterres and terraces about the house for its occupant,

Lord Ranelagh. At Forest Lodge, Humphry Repton was consulted in the 1790s about the house and its setting; it is thought that he laid out a flower garden and serpentine paths. The most memorable ornament of the Great Park is probably the remarkable collection of ancient oaks, some of which are a thousand years old.

Winkworth Arboretum

see page 183

Winter Garden

Sheffield, West Yorkshire OS SK3587
Open regularly Tel 0114 221 1900

The Winter Garden is a splendid giant glasshouse added to Sheffield Town Hall and opened to the public in 2002 at a cost of £7,000,000. It was designed by the architects Pringle Richards Sharratt as part of the regeneration of Sheffield's city centre. With a great vault of wooden arches made of larch, it houses a collection of over 150 species of temperate exotics which have the space to grow to their full size. Among them are substantial eucalyptus and such trees as the Norfolk Island pine (*Araucaria heterophylla*) which will grow to a height of 150ft/45m. The landscaping was designed by Waddle Landscape Design. The adjacent Peace Garden has modern fountains – a pattern of vertical jets – balustrades, fine stonework and beds of tender exotics.

Winton House

nr Pencaitland, East Lothian OS NT4369
Scottish Inventory Open occasionally for SGS

Estate going back to the 12th century when it was owned by the De Quincey family. The present house was built in the early 17th century but is much obscured by alterations made 1797–1805 by John Paterson. 18th-century woodland with much later replanting. In the late 19th century there was "a large and finely wooded park". Few old trees survive, but there has been some replanting and there is a modern avenue of Canadian maples. Terraced gardens south of the

house, laid out 1846–85 with beds of shrubs. At the foot of the terraces, a beech hedge and beyond, the banks of the Tyne water.

Wisley Garden

see page 184

Witley Court

see page 242

Wivenhoe House

Wivenhoe, Essex OS TM0324
English Heritage Register Grade II

House built 1758–61 to the designs of Thomas Reynolds. The old deer park was landscaped 1776–80 by Richard Woods for Colonel Rebow; and the results can be seen in John Constable's idyllic painting of 1816 (in the National Gallery of Art, Washington, DC) which shows the house veiled in trees on the far side of Woods's pond, with clumps, belts and individual trees and cattle peacefully grazing. In the 1840s W.A. Nesfield designed gardens for the house and planting in the park, but no details are known. The estate today belongs to the University of Essex.

Woburn Abbey

Woburn, Bedfordshire OS SP9632
English Heritage Register Grade I
Open regularly Tel 01525 290666

The abbey was a Cistercian foundation, and begun in 1145. In 1547 it was acquired by Sir John Russell whose descendants (later Earls and Dukes of Bedford) still live here. The house, on the site of the abbey, is today largely of the 17th and 18th centuries, with work by Sir William Chambers, Henry Flitcroft and Henry Holland. The earliest surviving room in the house is a remarkable renaissance grotto designed by Isaac de Caus and made before 1627 for Lucy Harington, Countess of Bedford: the vaulted chamber (which must originally have been open onto the garden; modern French windows now fill the arched openings) is encrusted with shells and ornamental rockwork, and niches have figures of Neptune, Cupid, mermaids,

W

dolphins and reclining female figures. In the early 18th century George London laid out formal gardens west of the house. In 1788 Henry Holland built a pretty polygonal Chinese Dairy which, according to Dorothy Stroud's *Henry Holland* (1966), had fine porcelain vessels for ladies to make butter. Holland also laid out pleasure grounds as a setting for the dairy. In 1804 the 6th Duke consulted Humphry Repton; the opening words of his Red Book read, "I must condemn what Mr Holland has done at Woburn, as a Landscape Gardener." Repton proposed new pleasure grounds, which Stephen Daniels, in his *Humphry Repton* (1999), says included "hothouses, flue walls and a series of terraced winter gardens…an American garden, an arboretum, a Chinese garden surrounding the Dairy, a rosary, a taxonomic botanic garden and a menagerie". These were made over the next few years, but little of them remains today. The dairy survives, and another Chinese building, a pavilion designed by Sir William Chambers in 1757 but not built until 1833, stands at the centre of a maze. The pleasure grounds today are chiefly mature woodland and lawns. Repton also worked on the park which is today partly occupied by a Safari Park. Herds of deer are still kept in the park, and Repton's summerhouse, the Thornery, survives. Woburn Abbey was a pioneer in opening to the public and providing appropriate family amusements; as early as 1965 there were over 400,000 visitors.

Woburn Farm
Chertsey, Surrey OS TQ0565
English Heritage Register Grade II

House built *c*.1748, with later alterations. Philip Southcote laid out an Arcadian ornamented farm, a *ferme ornée*, from 1735, which was described in Thomas Whately's very influential *Observations on Modern Gardening* (1770). Its essential idea, in Whately's words, was to bring "every rural circumstance within the verge of a garden". A planned walk was laid out to encircle pasture land and run through the

arable. In places it was ornamented with a hedgerow "enriched with woodbine, jessamine, and every odoriferous plant, whose tendrils will entwine with the thicket"; in places it passed by clumps of evergreens or thickets of shrubs; at times a view of an octagon (probably designed by William Kent), a ruin or "a neat Gothic building" was revealed. The sounds of the farmyard were an integral part of the experience, "even the clucking of poultry". Today some 18th-century planting remains, probably parts of the pathside hedgerows and shrubberies, as well as the foundations of the octagon.

Wollaton Hall
Wollaton, Nottinghamshire OS SK5339
Open regularly Tel 0115 915 3900

Wollaton Hall was designed by Robert Smythson for the mayor of Nottingham, Sir Francis Willoughby, and built 1580–88. It cost £8,000 (£1,270,880 today) and was paid for from profits taken from coal mined on the Willoughby estate. The original garden, which no longer exists, was of great historical importance; Wollaton is the earliest known example of an English house and garden conceived simultaneously, as the great renaissance villa gardens of Italy had been. It had another feature in common with Italian renaissance gardens: house and garden were disposed about the same axis. Robert Smythson's plan is built up of nine squares, arranged three by three, with the house at the centre. It is illustrated and discussed in both John Harris's *The Artist and the Country House* (1979) and Roy Strong's *The Artist and the Garden* (2000). There was a deer park here in the 16th century, and although it was landscaped in the 18th century, traces remain of earlier formal avenues radiating from the house. Humphry Repton was consulted by the 6th Baron Middleton after 1816 but nothing is known of the result. In the 19th century a parterre was made, on the site of the 17th-century garden, extending south-west towards the Great Pond in the park. There is a cast-iron octagonal camellia

house, or orangery, designed by Sir Jeffry Wyatville *c*.1824, with carpet bedding and herbaceous borders. Wollaton Hall is now a natural history museum and is set in a park of 200 acres/81 hectares.

Wollerton Old Hall
see page 243

Wolterton Hall
Norfolk OS TG1631 English Heritage
Register Grade II* Park open regularly
Tel 01263 584175

The house was built on an older site in the 1730s for Horatio Walpole and is still owned by the Walpole family. Charles Bridgeman is said to have been consulted in the 1720s and plans attributed to him for an elaborate formal garden exist, although it is not known if the garden was ever made; a lake south of the house roughly corresponds to a pool in the plans. W.S. Gilpin is also said to have worked here in the 1830s. All that remains for visitors to see is a melancholy but compelling landscape of parkland, old trees, a lake and glimpses of the house shrouded in trees. Apart from that, the only notable built ornament in the landscape is the ghostly tower of the derelict St Margaret's Church — all that remains of the village that once stood here.

Wood House,
also known as **Wood**
South Tawton, Devon OS SX6596
English Heritage Register Grade I

House designed by Daniel Gibson and gardens by Thomas Mawson for William Lethbridge, completed *c*.1905. On a sloping site, Mawson laid out a bold pattern of formal gardens: a square tennis lawn and bowling green to the west, separated by a pergola, and, on the south-facing slope, arranged on an axis with the house, a rectangular croquet lawn enclosed in yew hedges, a circular lily pond flanked with gazebos, and a circular sundial court enclosed in dry-stone walls. To the east, a large kitchen garden with frame yard and glasshouses. Having become a hotel and now back in private hands, the garden substantially survives and has been undergoing restoration.

Woodchester Park
nr Woodchester, Gloucestershire
OS SO8021 English Heritage Register
Grade II Park open regularly (NT)
Tel 01452 814213

House first built *c*.1600, followed by a long and complicated architectural history until A.W.N. Pugin produced drawings for a new house for William Leigh in 1845. Pugin dropped out of the commission and the building was started under the supervision of C.F. Hansom and B.J. Bucknall. The result, in the words of *Gloucestershire* (by David Verey and Alan Brooks) in Pevsner's "Buildings of England" series, is "one of the most remarkable Victorian country houses in England". But the house was never completed — all work ceased in about 1870, with the builders' scaffolding still in place. Almost nothing is known of gardens for the earlier house here: there is a rumour that Capability Brown was consulted, but no evidence, and it is known that Humphry Repton was in touch in 1809 with the then owner, Lord Ducie, but nothing is known of what became of it. There is a chain of lakes in the wooded valley and the unfinished, deserted mansion makes a wonderfully romantic and powerful ornament in the landscape.

Woodstock Gardens
Inistioge, County Kilkenny,
Republic of Ireland Open regularly
Tel (00353) 056 52699

Beautiful house, built for the Fownes family in 1745 to the designs of Francis Bindon. After the marriage of a Fowne heiress to William Tighe, the estate passed to the Tighes who owned it until recent times. Sir Joseph Paxton visited Woodstock in 1844 and much admired the garden: "…it is the best kept place in Ireland, the lady [Lady Louisa Tighe] being rich and personally fond of gardening." Edward Malins and Patrick Bowe in *Irish Gardens and Demesnes from 1830* (1980) describe Woodstock as "one of the great gardens of the day", and reproduce photographs taken *c*.1895 of a parterre and a terrace garden. The parterre was laid out

by the head gardener, Charles Macdonald, who had previously worked at two notable 19th-century gardens, both belonging to the Duke of Sutherland and both with fine parterres – Dunrobin Castle (*see page 375*) and Trentham Hall (*see page 550*). The parterre at Woodstock lay at the foot of a series of grass terraces and had four great panels edged in mounded turf and low hedging, with arabesques of hedging, patterns of coloured gravel, topiary shapes and urns. The terrace garden was a gravel path with a central pattern of circles of box-edged beds filled with bedding plants or coloured gravel. The focal point was a beautiful domed glasshouse designed by Richard Turner. In the 20th century the garden decayed and in 1922 the house was destroyed by fire; now only the shell remains. Since 1999, under the Great Gardens of Ireland restoration programme, much work has been done to restore the gardens; Lady Louisa's walk, the bath house, the terraced flower garden and the walled garden had all been restored by 2003. There has been much clearing of woodland and cataloguing of trees. Some good 19th-century trees survive – including a spectacular walk of noble firs (*Abies procera*) and of monkey puzzles.

Woodstock Manor
or **Palace**
Oxfordshire OS SP4416

On what is now the Blenheim Palace estate, the ruins of Woodstock Manor remained here until the early 18th century (*see* Blenheim Palace page 72). It was built for Henry I who also (*c*.1100) enclosed a park and provided it with a menagerie of exotic wild animals (which included a porcupine sent from Montpellier). Rosamond's Bower was made at Woodstock under Henry II – a maze where the king is supposed to have made love to his mistress, Rosamond Clifford. Here, too, was Rosamond's Well, also known as Everswell. The architectural historian Sir Howard Colvin wrote: "one of the most agreeable features of Everswell must have been the Queen's garden, which was laid out round one of the pools." He also suggested that the idea for the water garden may have come from Sicily, with which Henry II's court had close connections. Rosamond's Well still survives on the Blenheim estate – the 9th Duke of Marlborough had the water piped all the way to the Blenheim Palace kitchen (although, despite its legendary provenance, it was not thought superior to the town water).

Woolsington Park
Woolsington, Tyne and Wear OS NZ1970
English Heritage Register Grade II

17th-century house, with later alterations. There had been a formal garden here in the early 18th century. Pleasure grounds with late 18th-century orangery separated from park by a ha-ha. Paved garden with box parterre and rose arbour. Belts and clumps of trees in the park, and lake formed by damming the Ouse burn. The site is alarmingly close to Newcastle airport, a juxtaposition to bring on fits of nostalgia.

Woolsthorpe Manor
Woolsthorpe-by-Colsterworth, Lincolnshire OS SK9224 Open regularly (NT) Tel 01476 860338

Early 17th-century stone house, on an earlier site, built for the parents of Sir Isaac Newton who was born here in 1642. In an orchard in front of the house is an old apple tree, said to have been grafted from the tree from which an apple fell to inspire Newton with his theory of gravity. The present tree has been identified as a cultivar called 'Flower of Kent'. The simple garden is a charming place, and although the falling apple is almost certainly a myth, the garden will forever be associated with the great scientist.

Worcester College
Oxford, Oxfordshire OS SP5006
English Heritage Register Grade II*
Open occasionally Tel 01865 278300

College refounded in 1714 in buildings taken over from

Gloucester Hall which, in turn, had been refounded in 1560 after the original Gloucester College (founded in the 1280s) had been dissolved under Henry VIII. The Provost's Lodgings were designed in the 1770s by Henry Keene, and in the early 19th century the swampy ground in front of the Lodgings was landscaped, with a lake and picturesque plantings of trees and shrubs. A 16th-century stone gateway was moved to the banks of the lake as part of the landscaping. With its Palladian front and now overlooking the wooded banks of the lake, the Lodgings resembles a country house. Mavis Batey's *Oxford Gardens* (1982) describes Worcester's garden as "the only true landscaped garden in Oxford, having its own designed piece of water". Part of the Provost's Garden was laid out in 1903 in flowery Arts and Crafts style by Alfred Parsons who was a cousin of the wife of the Provost of the day, Revd Dr C.H. Daniel.

Worden Hall
Leyland, Lancashire OS SD5320
English Heritage Register Grade II

House demolished in 1960, leaving some outhouses and an 18th-century service wing. Mid 19th-century formal gardens, possibly designed by W.A. Nesfield, south of the site of the house. A sunken lawn enclosed by a balustrade with ironwork gates is aligned with the former house front. Geometric paths and patterned beds, probably of the late 20th century. A 19th-century conservatory, formerly attached to south-west corner of house, remains. West of it, a beech maze, late 20th-century but on the site of a maze designed in 1888. South of formal gardens, rolling grassland and trees with walks along the wooded banks of the Shaw brook. Late 19th-century icehouse in the wood. South-east of the house site, a probably early 19th-century ruined arch crosses the brook close to a cascade; it is attached to a turret on one bank and another arch on the other. Park with open grassland and trees. Part of the park has sports fields and a miniature railway.

Workington Hall
Workington, Cumbria OS NY0028
English Heritage Register Grade II
Open regularly Tel 01900 326408

Mid 14th-century fortified house, the ancient home of the Curwen family, rebuilt in late 18th century by John Carr of York and now "a controlled ruin". Park landscaped by Thomas White in the 1780s. Perimeter belts of trees survive, and a ride which followed the circumference of the park. In the Upper Park, White removed old field boundaries and did much tree planting; today it is farmed and only tree belts remain. In the park is Schoose, a model farm with a castellated gatehouse, built at the turn of the 18th to 19th century.

Wormleybury
Wormley, Hertfordshire OS TL3505
English Heritage Register Grade II

House built on an older site 1767–69 for Sir Abraham Hume to the designs of Robert Mylne, with later interiors by Robert Adam. In the garden, the remains of mid 18th-century formal terracing, with a crescent-shaped lake reworked from a formal canal and pool, and a yew walk with a stone urn (*c.*1770, probably by Robert Mylne). In his *Encyclopaedia of Gardening* (1822), J.C. Loudon describes Worleybury as "A good house and pleasant grounds, but chiefly remarkable for its horticultural productions, Sir Abraham having introduced various new plants from China and India". Park landscaped in the 18th century, with stream and lake. The Wormley bypass now cuts across its eastern part.

Wortley Hall
Wortley, South Yorkshire OS SK3199
English Heritage Register Grade II
Open regularly Tel 0114 288100

Wortleys first lived here in the 12th century. In the early 16th century a park was made, and late in the 17th century the old house was rebuilt by Sir Richard Wortley. In the 18th century it was rebuilt by Giacomo Leoni, with additions by Matthew Brettingham and John Carr of York. During the first half of the

19th century garden terraces below the south front of the house were created. The advice of W.S. Gilpin was possibly sought but the results are unclear. There was a famous head gardener in this period, Joseph Harrison, who was probably at least partly responsible for laying out the gardens. Today they present a sequence of grass terraces linked by steps. One lawn has a circular pool and clipped golden yews. A stone alcove seat stands on the west side. South of the terraces, a fishpond and icehouse in a wooded area. The estate is now in multiple ownership. The house became an educational centre for the Trade Union and Labour Movement in 1950.

Wotton House
Wotton, Surrey TQ1246
English Heritage Register Grade II*

House of the Evelyn family, built from the 16th century but now largely 19th-century in character. John Evelyn, writer, garden maker, diarist and tree-lover, was born here in 1620 and made a garden from 1643 in collaboration with his brother George. Inspired by the Italian Renaissance, Evelyn laid out terraces with statues, a temple, a fountain, a mount – all intact today. A curious Tortoise House with pilasters and pediment dates from *c.*1825. East of the house, a late 19th-century grotto where the Evelyn of the time used to go to sulk. The house today is a conference centre.

Wotton House
Wotton Underwood, Buckinghamshire OS SP6816 English Heritage Register Grade II*

House built 1704–14 for Richard Grenville and rebuilt by Sir John Soane in the 1820s after a fire. In the gardens and pleasure grounds, the remains of an early 18th-century formal garden, possibly designed by George London – a rectangular pond to the north of the house and a rectangular walled garden to the south. The latter is connected to the house by an arcaded terrace and double staircase. An orangery is set into the west side of the terrace and a

pavilion is built into the south garden wall. Pleasure grounds west of the house, with ornamental planting in woodland, possibly designed by Capability Brown in the 1750s, following the ideas of William Pitt, 1st Earl of Chatham. Lake to the north, with islands, on one of which is a brick and flint grotto of the 1750s. Lake narrows and is crossed by a wooden Palladian bridge, a late 20th-century reconstruction, to conceal a dam. Water flows into the semi-formal lake, the Warrells, with a pair of Tuscan pavilions (1750s) to the east and a long vista up towards the house. Many other 18th- and 19th-century features in the pleasure grounds.

Wrest Park
see page 325

Wrotham Park
Potters Bar, Hertfordshire OS TQ2499
English Heritage Register Grade II

House built in 1754 for Admiral John Byng to the designs of Isaac Ware. West of the house, pleasure grounds with collections of exotic trees and shrubs, sunken flower gardens, pools, a serpentine lake and a network of paths. Domed mausoleum (1880) north-west of house. A survey of the grounds was made in 1765 by Samuel Lapidge, Capability Brown's associate; Brown himself visited Wrotham, but it is not known what resulted. There was much work on the park in the late 18th century and in the 19th century. Today the perimeter is largely enclosed by trees and here are individual trees and clumps within the park, which is chiefly pasture.

Wroxall Abbey
Wroxall, Warwickshire OS SP2270
English Heritage Register Grade II

The abbey was a Benedictine nunnery founded in 1135, of which fragments only survive, together with the much altered church. There was an Elizabethan house here, belonging to the Burgoyne family, which was bought by Sir Christopher Wren in 1713. Wrens lived here until 1861 when the estate was bought by the Dugdales who replaced the

W

16th-century house with a Tudor-Gothic mansion. A balustraded Victorian garden has bedding schemes and topiary of box and yew. Close to the church are yew hedges and a remarkable wall with lobe-shaped alcoves designed to shelter fruit trees – probably designed by Wren. Gate piers, of the same date, have wrought-iron gates designed by Clough Williams-Ellis. The park has notable remains of 17th-century avenues. The house has been a school since 1934.

Wroxton Abbey

Wroxton, Oxfordshire OS SP4141
English Heritage Register Grade II*
Open regularly Tel 01295 730551

The abbey was an Augustinian foundation dating from the early 13th century. Some medieval buildings are incorporated into the existing house, which was built in the early 17th century for Sir William Pope (later 1st Earl of Downe), with later alterations. Later in the same century the estate passed to the North family. Early in the 18th century Francis North consulted Henry Wise about new gardens, which were made by Tilleman Bobart, the son of Jacob Bobart, the first director of the Oxford Botanic Garden (see page 99). Terraces, a canal and other formal gardens were made east of the house. These lasted only a short time, for after 1737 Francis North filled in the canal and grassed over the formal gardens, leaving only the terraces which are visible today. Sanderson Miller was then called in to lay out new gardens. He built a castellated Gothic dovecote south-west of the house, and, east of the Great Pond, as part of a Rococo scheme, a huge formal cascade, a serpentine stream, a smaller cascade and several Chinoiserie buildings, of which one only, a stone bridge, survives. In 1739 an obelisk was built to commemorate a visit from Frederick, Prince of Wales. Although the flimsier Chinese buildings have disappeared – and thus much of the Rococo spirit – the obelisk, dovecote, a Doric temple and icehouse may be seen, and the great cascade has been restored, along with the

serpentine stream flowing below it.

Wych Cross Place

Forest Row, East Sussex OS TQ4131
English Heritage Register Grade II*

House designed for Douglas Freshfield in 1904 by Edmund Fisher. Gardens designed by Thomas Mawson to the south and west of house. Balustraded terrace below south façade of house forms chief east–west axis. Steps lead from top terrace to the main terrace, with views across the valley. At its centre, a lily pool with a fountain and statue of boy and dolphin. Wrought-iron gates at each end of the terrace, and another at the head of a flight of steps which leads down from the centre of the terrace, becoming increasingly informal as it extends from house. At the lower level, a cross walk leads down rough stone steps through a rockery bank to informal pleasure grounds. From the west end of top terrace, steps down to a bowling green surrounded by a yew hedge. A balustraded terrace west of house, with steps down to a rose garden with stone summerhouse. A gate leads to a lawn with a fountain and shrub border. The top terrace leads east to a kitchen garden which was also carefully designed by Mawson with fine detailing and an axial layout.

Wycombe Abbey, formerly Loakes Manor

High Wycombe, Buckinghamshire
OS SU8692 English Heritage Register
Grade II

House built in the 17th century, with 18th- and 19th-century additions. The estate was sold in 1896 to found a school. Park possibly laid out by Capability Brown in around 1762 for Lord Shelburne. In the east park a narrow lake, the Dyke, survives from this time, with a cascade marking the juncture of the lake and a stream. The park retains some of its 18th-century character and much pasture remains, with some trees still in place.

Wyken Hall

see page 326

Wynnstay

Ruabon, Clwyd OS SJ3042
Cadw/ICOMOS Register Grade I

Estate of the immensely rich Williams-Wynn family, which they acquired in the 17th century when Sir John Wynn married the Eyton heiress. House designed by Benjamin Ferrey and built 1858–65 after the earlier house was gutted by fire. From 1768 there were major works in the grounds. In 1769 Lord Verulam described the house in his *Northern Tour* as "situated in a well-wooded park which has all the advantages that the genius of Mr. Brown, who is coming down here to superintend his works, can call for". Brown laid out pleasure grounds and redesigned the park, making a lake in the valley north-west of the house. There was much planting of deciduous trees, clumps and belts. A great avenue, planted before 1740, was left in the park and still remains, a mixture of horse chestnuts, limes, sweet chestnuts and sycamores. The grounds are rich in notable buildings and monuments, among them a dairy designed like a Doric temple (1782–83 by Capability Brown); a bath house (c.1784); a Doric column commemorating the 4th baronet (1789 by James Wyatt); and Waterloo Tower celebrating the great victory (after 1815). Brown's pleasure grounds, enclosed by a ha-ha, has a lawn with scattered specimen trees – cedars of Lebanon, fern-leafed beech, hollies, oaks and tulip trees; planting after Brown's time includes monkey puzzles and Wellingtonias. The A483 trunk road runs from north to south across the park, dividing it precisely down the middle.

Wynyard Park

nr Stockton-on-Tees, Cleveland OS NZ4225
English Heritage Register Grade II*

18th-century house, remodelled in the 19th-century – by Philip Wyatt in the 1820s and by Ignatius Bonomi in the 1840s for the 3rd Marquess of Londonderry. Early 19th-century walled kitchen garden, and Italian gardens north-west of house. Grounds supposedly laid out by

W.S. Gilpin in the 1820s but no details are available. Large Y-shaped lake in park overlooked from the balustraded terrace on the south front of house. North-east arm of lake traversed by the late 18th-century Lion Bridge with Coade stone ornaments. Woodland and open parkland with scattered trees in the park. In the park south-east of the hall, the Wellington Obelisk of 1827, made to celebrate the Duke's visit. North-west of the house, in wooded ground, two early 19th-century temples, Greek and Roman.

Wythenshawe Park

Wythenshawe, Greater Manchester
OS SJ8189 English Heritage Register
Grade II

Estate of the Tatton family who owned land in the area from the 13th century although there is no known house before the 16th century. The present house, extended c.1830, incorporates early 16th-century work. The estate was bought from the Tatton family in 1926 and given to the City of Manchester. The house is now an art gallery and museum and the grounds a public park. Gardens by the house have a pond, lawns with specimen trees and woodland to the north. The park, surrounding the house on three sides, has open grassland with clumps and belts of trees much as shown in an 1830 estate map. An avenue of chestnuts, planted c.1934, runs eastwards from the house across the park. A statue of Oliver Cromwell (1857, by Matthew Noble), formerly in Manchester city centre but brought here in 1967, stands east of the house in line with the avenue.

Yalding Organic Gardens

see page 185

Yarnton Manor

Yarnton, Oxfordshire OS SP4711
English Heritage Register Grade II

House, on an old site, built in the early 17th century by Sir Thomas Spencer. Walled gardens restored in the late 19th century, following the pattern of the 17th-century

gardens, by the architect Thomas Garner who was restoring the house at the time. Here are a stone gazebo built into a boundary wall, a pleached lime walk, a lawn surrounded by a terraced walk, and a sunken flower garden enclosed in yew hedges. A wrought-iron gate links the gardens to an avenue of poplars.

Yester House

Gifford, East Lothian OS NT5467
Scottish Inventory

13th-century castle superseded, on a different site, by the house built 1699–1728 for John Gray, 2nd Marquess of Tweeddale, to the design of James Smith and Alexander MacGill. Minor alterations in the 18th century by William Adam and Robert Adam. Park enclosed in 1676. Paintings of the garden, c.1685, illustrated in John Harris's *The Artist and the Country House* (1979), show one of the most elaborate formal Scottish gardens of its date – a great enclosed layout about an axis linking the entrance gate to the castle, with parterres, pools, a maze, an ornate water pavilion and cascade, statues and topiary. All this had gone by 1752 when James Bowie advised on landscaping the garden. Today the house is set in wooded parkland with traces of avenue alignments surviving. Kiosk south of the house is an intriguing modern oddity – a glazed clocktower from the Caledonian Railway Station in Edinburgh, placed here in 1970.

York Gate

see page 356

York House

Twickenham, Greater London OS TQ1673
English Heritage Register Grade II

There had been a house here in the 16th century, Yorke Farm, when this was part of the royal manor of Twickenham. The present distinguished 17th-century Thames-side house has had numerous owners, among them the 1st Earl of Clarendon in the 17th century and the Comte de Paris in the 19th century. The last private owner was the Indian merchant Sir Ratan J. Tata who bought the house in 1906. He installed in the riverside garden a splendid fountain, pool and cascade, and flamboyant late 19th-century marble statuary, probably by a Roman sculptor, Orazio Andreoni. The house is today the offices of the London Borough of Richmond upon Thames.

Yorkshire Sculpture Park
see page 357

Youlston Park
Shirwell, Devon OS SS5837
English Heritage Register Grade II

An estate of the Raleigh family and then of the Chichesters. Hugh Chichester built a new house in the early 16th century and the family remained here until 1920. House much altered, especially in the 18th century. The site is a fine one, in a valley sloping to the west. Park landscaped, probably in the mid

18th century, for Sir John Chichester, with mature parkland trees and woodland with mature trees and rhododendrons. A noble avenue of sweet chestnuts approaches the house from the south.

Youngsbury
nr Ware, Hertfordshire OS TL3617
English Heritage Register Grade II*

House built 1745 for David Poole, with 19th-century

alterations. Capability Brown produced a plan for the grounds, undated but probably of the 1760s, which has the inscription "Plan proposed by Lancelot Brown for the Improvement of Youngsbury remarking that Nature had do[ne] so much that little was wanting, but enlarging the river". The river Rib flows across the park, widened at Brown's suggestion into a serpentine, the Broad Water, due south of the house. Brown's

planting proposals of copses, clumps and individual trees were carried out. Many mature trees here, including some plane trees probably of the 18th century. On the southern boundary of the park, the remains of the 16th-century moated manor house.

INDEX BY COUNTY

This index is divided into four: England, Wales, Scotland and Ireland. Gardens with illustrated entries are in *italic*.

INDEX OF PEOPLE

READING LIST

General

Bibliography of British Gardens by Ray Desmond (1988) is an immensely valuable list of bibliographical references to 5,500 gardens in the British Isles.

The following contain detailed descriptions of, and sources of further information for, thousands of gardens and designed landscapes in Britain. Individual volumes may be bought from the addresses shown. The English Register and Scottish Inventory are in the process of revision; the Welsh Register was completed in 2002.

Register of Parks and Gardens of Special Historic Interest in England (Individual volumes for every county in England, 1985 onwards. Available from English Heritage, National Monuments Record Centre, Great Western Village, Kemble Drive, Swindon SN2 2GZ)

An Inventory of Gardens and Designed Landscapes in Scotland (5 volumes, 1987 onwards; supplementary volumes from 2000. Available from Historic Scotland, Longmore House, Salisbury Place, Edinburgh EH9 1SH)

Register of Landscapes, Parks and Gardens of Special Historic Interest in Wales (6 volumes, 1994 onwards. Available from Cadw, Crown Building, Cathays Park, Cardiff CF10 3NQ)

General History

The Genius of Gardening by Christopher Thacker (1994) is an excellent historical survey covering Britain and Ireland.

Gardening in Britain by Miles Hadfield (1960), covering Britain but not Ireland, is attractively written and still valuable.

Lost Demesnes: Irish Landscape Gardening 1660–1845 by Edward Malins and the Knight of Glin (1976) is the most valuable book on Irish gardens, with excellent illustrations.

Irish Gardens and Demesnes from 1830 by Edward Malins and Patrick Bowe (1980) covers the period 1830–c.1970, with good illustrations.

A History of Gardening in Ireland by Keith Lamb and Patrick Bowe (1995) is a useful general survey with a few illustrations.

The Landscape Garden in Scotland 1735–1835 by A.A. Tait (1980) is scholarly and detailed, packed with rather small illustrations, and with excellent sources.

A History of Gardening in Scotland by E.H.M. Cox (1935) was a pioneer book which is still valuable, despite only vague references; only a few, but good, illustrations.

The Historic Gardens of Wales: An Introduction to Parks and gardens in the History of Wales by Elisabeth Whittle (1992) is short but packed with information and with good illustrations.

Books on particular periods

Mediaeval Gardens by John Harvey (1981) covers the whole of Europe, with Britain well covered, with good illustrations and references.

The Renaissance Garden in England by Roy Strong (1979) covers the period from the end of the 15th century to the mid 17th century. An excellent text, with many valuable illustrations and references.

English Gardens and Landscapes 1700–1750 by Christopher Hussey (1967) is an excellent pioneering account of a key period, with many good illustrations.

Georgian Gardens: The Reign of Nature by David Jacques (1983) covers the period 1730–1830. A good history of the English landscape garden with some useful illustrations (especially plans) and references.

The Flowering of the Landscape Garden: English Pleasure Grounds 1720–1800 by Mark Laird (1999) is a highly original account of flower gardens in the period of the landscape garden, with excellent illustrations and sources.

Victorian Gardens by Brent Elliott (1986) is original and scholarly, with good pictures and excellent sources.

The Edwardian Garden by David Ottewill (1989) covers the period immediately before World War II. An excellent text, with many good illustrations (including valuable plans) and excellent references.

The English Garden through the 20th Century by Jane Brown (1999) is particularly useful for Modern Movement gardens and the period after World War II, with many good illustrations.

Local Books

Avon

(The county no longer exists; its northern part has reverted to Gloucestershire; its southern to Somerset and various unitary authorities)

Parks and Gardens of Avon by Stewart Harding and David Lambert (1994) Excellent text with much local detail and good pictures.

Cambridge

The Historic Gardens of Oxford and Cambridge by Mavis Batey (1989) Much valuable information, many pictures, not so good on Cambridge as on Oxford.

Cambridge Gardens by Ronald Gray (1984) Good text, with much information on planting, and colour photographs.

Cornwall

The Parks and Gardens of Cornwall by Douglas Ellory Pett (1998) An excellent and wider-ranging book with good historical illustrations and valuable sources.

Devon

The Garden History of Devon: An illustrated guide to sources by Todd Gray (1995) Austere but valuable guide to sources with some excellent quotations and a few good pictures.

Devon Gardens: An Historical Survey edited by Stephen Pugsley (1994) is a collection of essays with some excellent material.

Gloucestershire

Historic Gardens of Gloucestershire by Timothy Mowl (2002) Lively, opinionated and well written with good pictures and sources.

Kent

Garden of England: Evolution of Historic Gardens in Kent by Elisabeth Hall (undated) Thin but useful with some excellent illustrations

London

The Glorious History of London's Parks and Gardens edited by Mireille Galinou (1990) A collection of valuable essays, with excellent illustrations and sources.

The London Town Garden by Todd Longstaffe-Gowan (2001) Invaluable history with many excellent illustrations and excellent sources.

Oxford

Oxford Gardens by Mavis Batey (1982) Invaluable fact-filled book by the doyenne of garden historians with good illustrations.

Shropshire

Historic Parks and Gardens of Shropshire by Paul Stamper (1996) Much out of the way information and good pictures.

Somerset

Somerset Parks and Gardens: A Landscape History by James Bond (1998) Good text, very well illustrated.

Suffolk

Suffolk's Gardens and Parks: Designed Landscapes from the Tudors to the Victorians by Tom Williamson (2000) Outstandingly good text, very good pictures and sources.

Worcestershire

A Survey of Historic Parks and Gardens in Worcestershire by Richard Lockett (1997) Comprehensive survey with a few good pictures.

Books on Garden Designers

Charles Bridgeman

Charles Bridgeman and the English Landscape Garden by Peter Willis (1977: revised edition 2002) is profusely illustrated and the only book on Bridgeman.

Capability Brown

Capability Brown by Dorothy Stroud (1950: revised edition 1975) despite its age remains the most valuable single book on Brown.

Gertrude Jekyll

The Gardens of Gertude Jekyll by Richard Bisgrove (1992) has a good text and much practical detail with planting plans. Lovely photographs, not always of Jekyll gardens.

Gertrude Jekyll: Essays on the life of a working amateur edited by Michael Tooley and Primrose Arnander (1995) has valuable essays by various hands with excellent historical illustrations.

Gertrude Jekyll at Munstead Wood by Judith B. Tankard and Martin A. Wood (1996) is outstandingly good, with a complete list of her garden commissions.

Edwin Lutyens and Gertrude Jekyll

Gardens of a Golden Afternoon by Jane Brown (1982) is attractively written, with good illustrations and sources.

Humphry Repton

Humphry Repton by Dorothy Stroud (1962) is a pioneer book on Repton and still valuable.

Humphry Repton: Landscape Gardener 1752–1818 by George Carter, Patrick Goode and Kedrun Laurie (1982) is the catalogue of an influential exhibition and remains an excellent source on Repton.

Humphry Repton: Landscape Gardening and the Geography of Georgian England by Stephen Daniels (1999) is the best book on Repton, packed with valuable information, excellent illustrations and references.

Architecture

The evolution of gardens often goes hand-in-hand with that of houses, so the architectural history often has a bearing on landscape history. Nikolaus Pevsner's 'Buildings of England' series, started in 1951, with volumes devoted to every county, is an invaluable guide. 'Buildings of Scotland' is nearing completion; 'Buildings of Wales' has published three volumes (*Clwyd*, *Glamorgan* and *Powys*); and 'Buildings of Ireland' has published two (*North Leinster* and *North West Ulster*).

Another essential reference is Howard Colvin's magisterial *Biographical Dictionary of British Architects 1600–1840* (revised edition 1995). For the later period Mark Girouard's *The Victorian Country House* (1979) is excellent, with splendid illustrations. Burke's *Guide to Country Houses: Ireland* (1978) by Mark Bence-

Jones and James Howley's *The Follies and Garden Buildings of Ireland* (1993) are excellent Irish sources.

Illustrations

Britannia Illustrata by Leonard Knyff and Jan Kip (1707; a good, cheap reprint was issued by the National Trust in 1984) A superb collection of very detailed bird's eye views of notable houses and gardens in an important period of garden history.

The Artist and the Country House by John Harris (1979) is a very valuable history of 420 paintings of country houses and gardens in Britain and Ireland in the period 1540–1870, profusely illustrated.

The Artist and the Country House: from the Fifteenth Century to the Present Day by John Harris (1995) is a well illustrated catalogue of an exhibition at Sotheby's of 144 country houses and their settings, none of which were included in Harris's earlier book.

The Artist & the Garden by Roy Strong (2000) Admirable, original text, superb illustrations and sources. Covers the period from the 1540s to the early 19th century.

Painted Gardens: English Watercolours 1850–1914 by Penelope Hobhouse and Christopher Wood (1988) Covers English and Scottish gardens, charming paintings, valuable text.

ACKNOWLEDGEMENTS

I am, above all, grateful to the owners of gardens who kindly allowed me to scrutinise and photograph their gardens. Sarah Rutherford at English Heritage; Elisabeth Whittle at Cadw; and Krystyna Campbell and Samantha Hadwin of Historic Scotland were all extremely helpful. I thank them for permission to draw on information from, respectively, the *Register of Parks and Gardens of Special Historic Interest in England*; the *Cadw/ICOMOS Register of Parks and Gardens of Special Historic Interest in Wales*; and the *Scottish Natural Heritage/Historic Scotland*

Inventory of Gardens and Designed Landscapes in Scotland. Alyson Rogers at the National Monuments Record Centre was very helpful and I am most grateful to her. In Ireland Jim Reynolds provided helpful inspiration and I am much indebted to the excellent and pioneering publications of Mark Bence-Jones, Patrick Bowe, James Howley, The Knight of Glin and the Edward Malins. The staff of the Lindley Library were, as always, wonderful.

Everyone at Dorling Kindersley associated with this book has been friendly, helpful and very efficient; in alphabetical order: Murdo

Culver, Helen Fewster, Lee Griffiths, Anna Kruger, David Lamb and Peter Luff. I am, once again, deeply grateful to my wife, Caroline, who edited this book with her usual meticulous skill. She was also immensely helpful in planning it.

Patrick Taylor

Dorling Kindersley would like to thank Robin Pridy, Jane Simmonds and Letitia Luff for editorial assistance, and Steve Josland and Rachael Smith for design assistance.